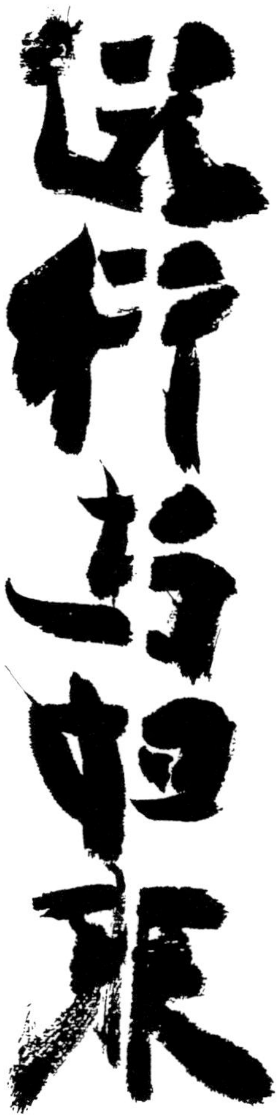

Cai Guo-Qiang

# Odyssey and Homecoming

远行与归来

Edited by Simon Schama

DelMonico Books • D.A.P.
New York

# Contents

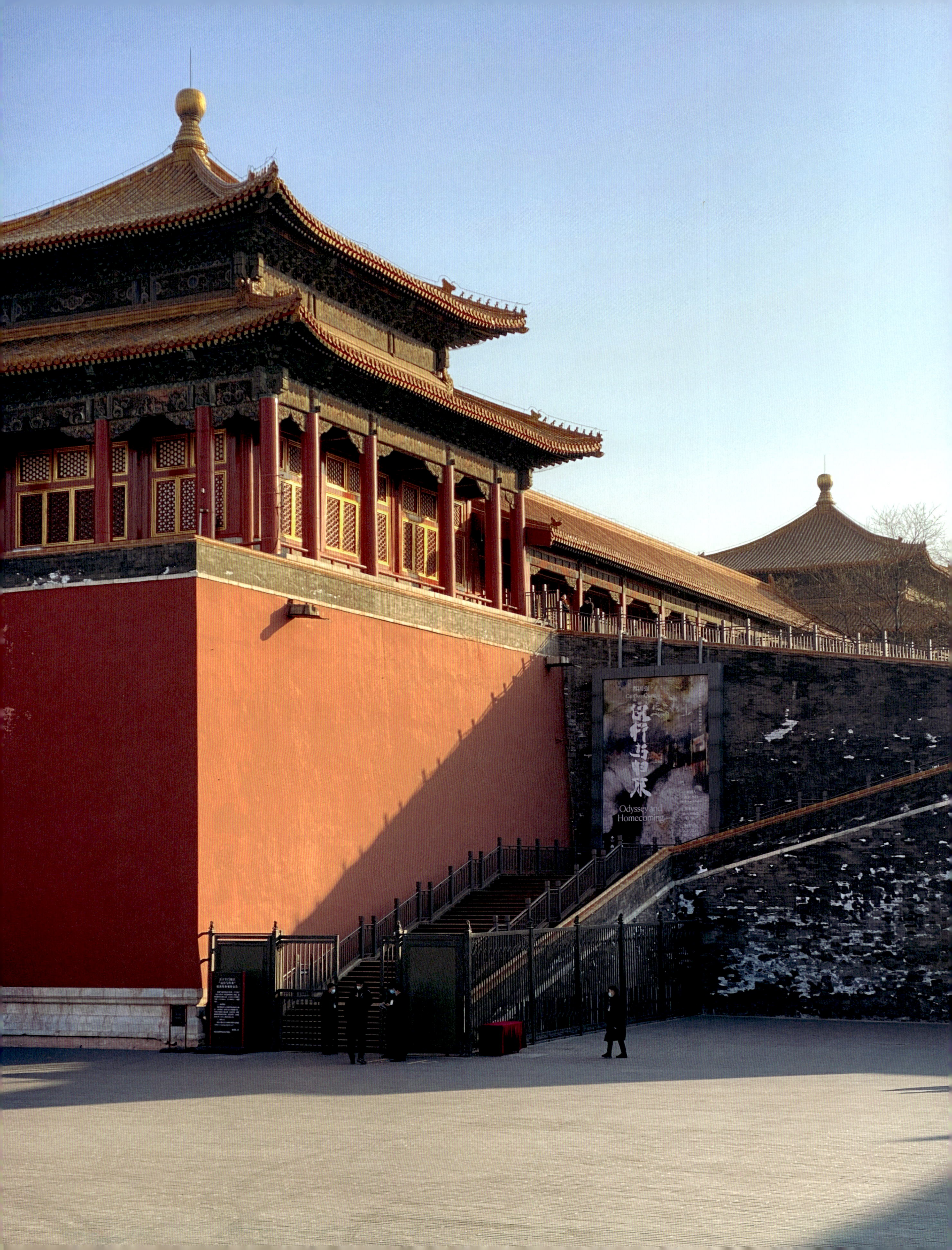
Odyssey and
Homecoming

# Foreword

This stupendous, blazing, and profound exhibition of the art, thought, and vision of Cai-Guo-Qiang opens a few days before the return of light: winter solstice in the northern hemisphere. The timing could hardly be more auspicious. The connectedness of the world has been broken by the ravages of the pandemic. We have all been separated and immobilized, fearfully walled off, with the companionship of work and friendship shrunk into safe space. But, as its title implies, *Odyssey and Homecoming* is a liberating invitation to emerge from our physical and psychological confinement to accompany Cai in his cross-cultural epic, minds and eyes wide open to the possibility of transforming discoveries, attentive dialogues.

Cai's prolific career has been about breaking barriers, those separating two-dimensional painting from multi-dimensional live events. He has painted with fire and smoke, the fugitive moment of an explosion fixed in imprinted marks and strokes. Spectacularly documented here, it has also been a refutation of the assumption that voyaging purposefully presupposes an abandonment of origins. There is no zero-sum game here between home and away. Chinese roots, Japanese flowering, Western burgeoning are all part of the same organic growth, perennially ramifying. In a world turning inwards, agitated by chauvinist suspicion, Cai's art faces outward. These galleries are flooded with the illuminations that have come from the artist's engagement with classicism (consumed in fiery ruin and by the attrition of time); the numinous flow of Gothic Christian light; the play between color and darkness at the heart of Spanish art; and the botanical humanism of Renaissance cultivation. His master-hero, El Greco, personifies the vitality of a transplant, an irrepressible engrafting whose distinctiveness owed much to his origins in the world of shimmering, almost iridescent, icons set down amidst the formal austerities of Spanish Catholicism. For Cai, movement is kinetic, and his own sensibility moves observantly between the physical and the metaphysical universes, between a fixed site and illimitable cosmic space. To reflect for a moment on the improbability of any contemporary Western artist returning the favor, of undertaking an odyssey through Asian art (as Vincent van Gogh did with Japanese woodblock prints), is to appreciate that perhaps only Cai could have had the ambition, integrity, and concentrated stamina to have accomplished this ecumenical communion across time and space.

In some quarters, minimalism still attracts reverence—hard-edged art immunized against easy optical comfort, impervious to reading, oblivious to history, soberly self-contained, armored in objectivity. But this is not the place in which scrambling, beleaguered humanity currently finds itself. Right now, cerebral essentialism is the coldest of comforts. It's a great joy, then, to be enfolded in Cai's unapologetic maximalism, in explosions of eye-popping spectacle and philosophical ignitions that burst and drift; to surrender to his exhilarating profusions of paint, to luscious saturations of his color, to the bounding wildness of his galloping lines; to be swept along in his passages from material to immaterial worlds; to move through shadow fields and theatres of crumbling stone toward some immanently glowing horizon.

There is a word usually missing from even the most appreciative commentaries of Cai's art, a quality which has never been so apparent as in this majestic exhibition: generosity. His work is the least self-regarding contemporary art I know, the most democratically invitational, expansive, and infinitely exploratory. It is not, in the end, the property of the "art world," but a precious possession given to all of us, to reaffirm our connected humanity.

Simon Schama
November 2020

*Odyssey and Homecoming* exhibition poster at the Meridian Gate, Palace Museum, Beijing, 2020. Photo by Cai Guo-Qiang

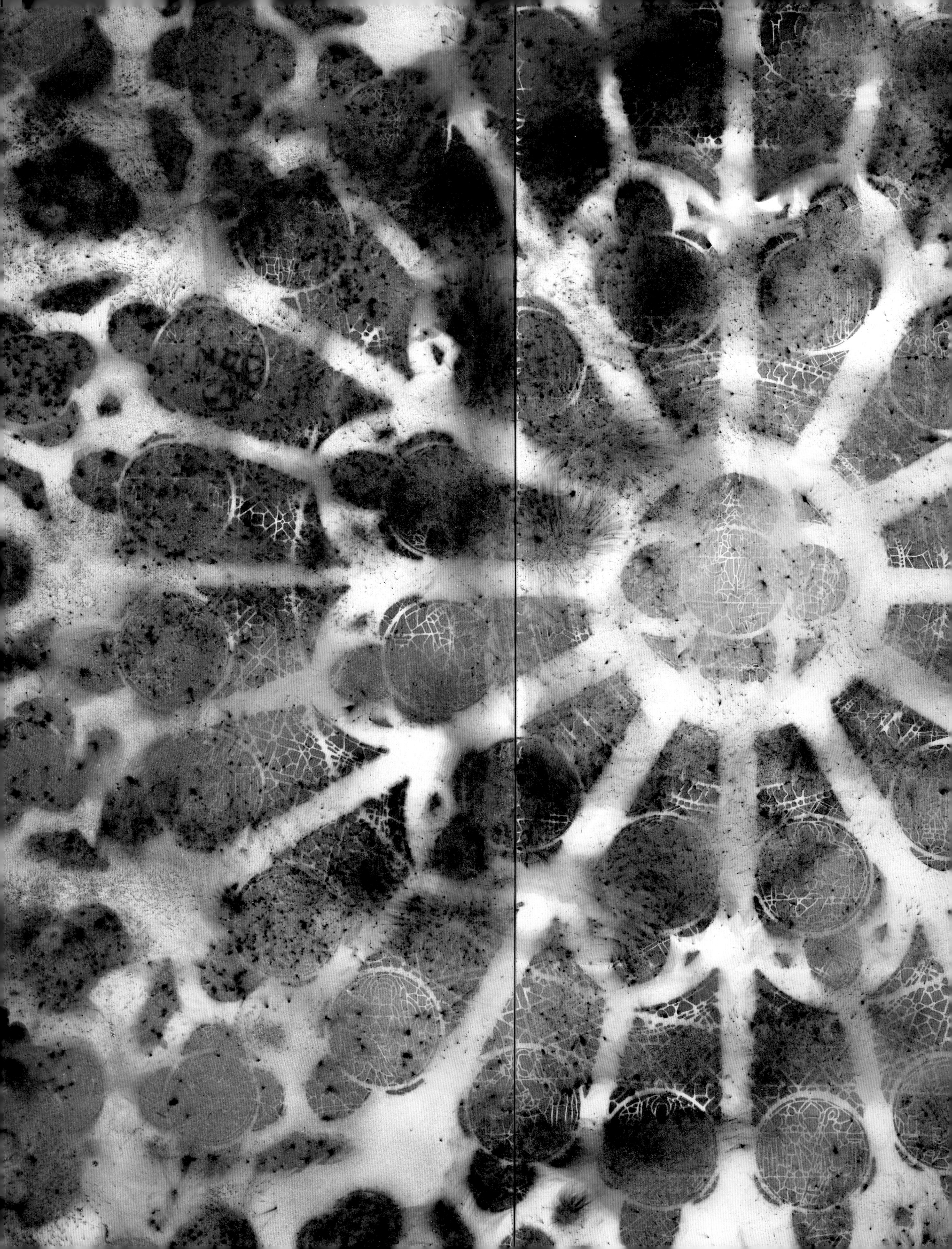

# The Long Line of Fire

## *Explosive Epiphanies in Cai Guo-Qiang's Odyssey Through Western Art History*

Simon Schama

It was so unexpected to see the bats hanging on Cai's studio wall that at first I couldn't read them properly—the vespertilian forms fluttering on the canvas, or ominously suspended, the ink marks translating into silky skeins and leathery wings, while all about them crimson stains bloomed amidst a granular spray of sooty particulates (no. 7.2). But then it was mid-February. Only in China had the virus gone viral. Here we were in breezy Manhattan, albeit with our minds on China, not as the crucible of pandemic, but as the site of this majestic exhibition. As always in my experience Cai was exuberantly merry, buzzing with creativity. All the same, I shouldn't have needed to be told that the bats were Cai's response, his *Apocalypse Now* gesture, not just to our own fateful moment of pestilence, but to the last stage of a journey through art history he had been living for three years. He had traveled from the Pompeiian cataclysm through the Renaissance, communed with El Greco, meditated with Cézanne at Mont Sainte-Victoire, and flowed with the river of time from the Bolshevik Revolution to China's upheavals and thus back to whence he came. But the Christian Middle Ages lay in wait, like a bat in the rafters.

Now that time had come to haunt him and all of us, along with the vocabulary of medieval self-examination. Plague, apocalypse, mortality had returned. Modernity, it turns out, may be medieval. The previous spring, April 2019, had sent an early signal: the burning of Notre-Dame, caused moreover by an accident of Cai-like historical irony. Electrical wiring on the roof, designed to scare pigeons, had shorted and the sparks did their explosive work, the birds not themselves charred like Cai's ceramic murmuration of ten thousand black starlings but singed nonetheless in the conflagration (no. 9.1). Cai and I had spoken about the theology of light which Abbot Suger and his 12th-century builders had realized in stone and glass at Saint-Denis. Romanesque basilicas constructed with massy blocks and piers as citadel sanctuaries were replaced by the Gothic architecture of verticality, solid walls pierced by radiant windows so that, thanks to flying buttresses, they seemed nothing more than containing skins or membranes for the bowls of light flooding the interior. At Notre-Dame, destroyed and rebuilt many times, the survivor of previous fires and assaults by Protestant iconoclasts and French revolutionaries, only a few of the great windows retained their medieval glass. But who better than Cai to understand, both instinctively and conceptually, those repeated cycles of destruction and resurrection, the paradoxical coupling of seemingly opposed impulses to make the organically breathing, perpetually renewing whole? In effect, he didn't need to go searching like a medieval pilgrim (though in so many ways he shares their devotional temper) for the essence of medievalism. It had come to him and the numinous record of that communion is the startlingly beautiful *Black Light No. 1* (opposite; no. 7.4). The painstaking re-creation in stencil of a great Gothic rose window, similar to those at Notre-Dame, Saint-Denis, or Chartres, along with the lancet windows beneath was itself a worshipful act of complex devotional care. But then of course the analogy of a window, with its radial spoke armature, to the structure of blooming botany is yet another instance of the unforced connection between Cai's sensibilities and the mystical edge of *Western* spirituality. The gunpowder painting returns to the majestic simplicity of some of Cai's earliest explosion work. *Black Light* is both immediate history and cosmic detonation, an instantaneous slice of time as the explosion shears away the window from its structure. As with other recent works—*Heaven Complex No. 3* for

Detail of *Black Light No. 1* (no. 7.4)

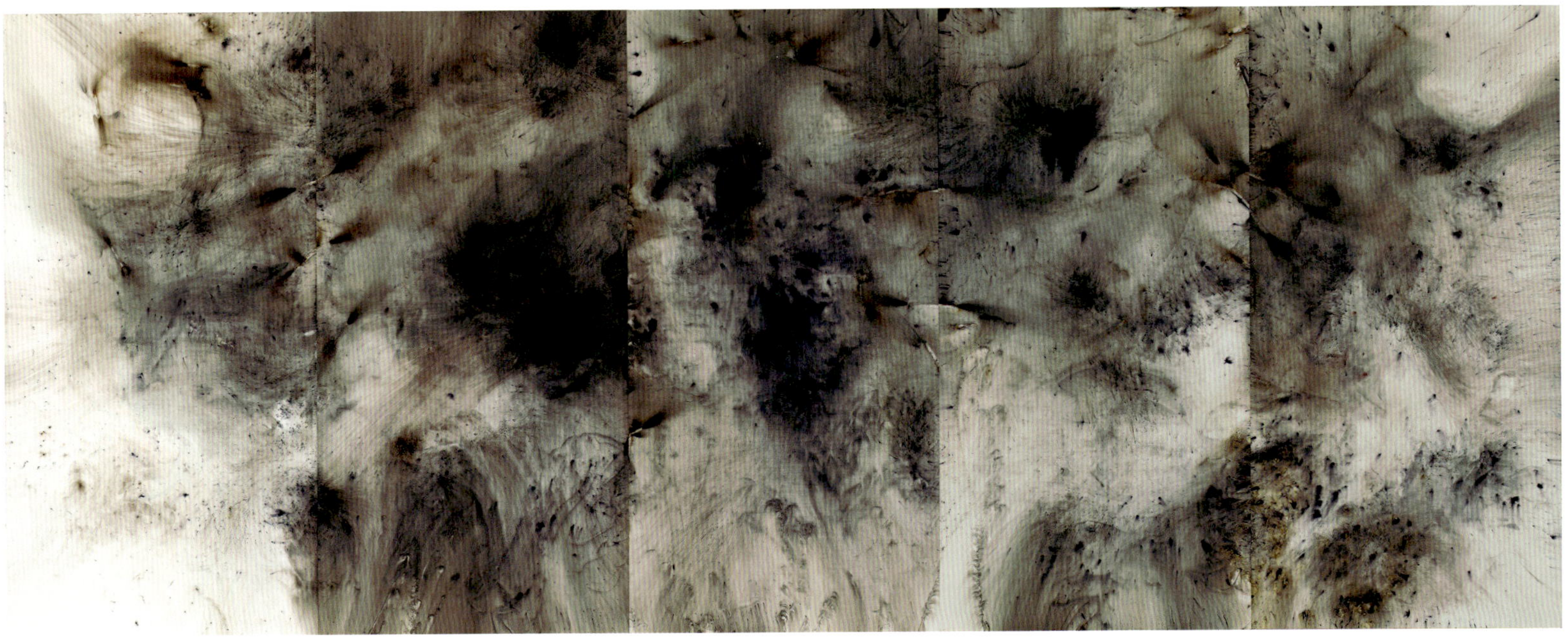

Figure 1. Cai Guo-Qiang, *Heaven Complex No. 3*, 2017. Gunpowder on canvas, 300 × 750 cm. Photo by Yvonne Zhao

instance (figure 1)—the black flare at the periphery even in passages where it eats away the webbed armature acts as a foil, intensifying the hot radiance of the light. As such, it seems to me to be, like so much of Cai's work, a vision of luminous re-creation; lit with hope rather than shrouded in fatalistic despair.

In a way, Cai Guo-Qiang has always been a history painter, not in the literal and laborious sense that he has wanted his work to document events of his own lifetime and others but rather in a deeper involuntary sense in which his visual and tactile reflections on human and natural life amidst the flow of time, even cosmically measured, has been triggered by the course of fateful shatterings: nuclear annihilations, ancient eruptions, modern revolutions (that last a word which originally signified the rotation of fortune's cycle, a *return* to where we began). So we should not be surprised that through the timing of *Odyssey and Homecoming*, along with its site in the Palace Museum in Beijing, Cai, always visionary, has become prophetic. His vision is the correction to complacency, to the shallow, self-deceiving assumption that life trots on pretty much as it has been, and that the future is just the present only more so. Cai's certainty is uncertainty, including the ways in which his own work might turn out, the exhilaration of the unanticipated, and deep creativity conditional on the relinquishing of rigid control over the process of image-making. There never has been anything "ready-made," either about him or his work. For Cai, instability is the condition of energy; the universe began with a mighty bang and Kabbalah's earthly materialization dependent on shattered vessels and the cooling of fiery shards of light. Cai's profundity is magmatic, the recognition that the appearance of stability is a willed cultural and political convenience. But it is helpless before natural reality, the assumption of surface stasis violently torn open by the inexorable shifting of tectonic plates, volcanic eruptions, oncoming tsunamis, and fracturing geology. Elemental power (the universe in which Cai's seeing mind is immersed) will always defeat political power and expose its pretensions as trivial and deluded. A surging force field can make microbial events titanic, so that invisibly minute organisms can alter the world more decisively than all the utterances of grandstanding autocrats. Equally, though, all these sunderings and combustions are—as they anciently have been in geological time—reshapers of the future. Eucalypts require the intensity of forest fire heat to split open the pods by which a fresh cycle of forestation may be seeded. So it is with Cai's visual philosophy of history (articulated as "The Spirit of Painting"), and who, right now, could possibly argue with that?

There is another respect in which this exhibition is both timely and providential in its site. One of the world's gravest conflicts, as much psychological as political, is that dividing internationalists from nationalists. On the one side there are those who wish only to live with neighbors who speak, look, pray, and cook exactly like themselves and for whom words like "foreigner" or "immigrant" are synonymous with "alien" and "enemy." On the other side are those millions in metropolitan conurbations who are content with, and celebrate, lives spent in mixed company, be it a city, a village, or a whole country. This is the division between defensiveness and expansiveness, openness and xenophobic paranoia, and it is getting more bitter and irreconcilable every day. The pandemic has only aggravated that polarization, its Asian beginnings offering unscrupulous politicians an opportunity to cast the disaster as some sort of alien invasion from the East.

It could hardly be more auspicious, then, for Cai Guo-Qiang, rooted in China, whose long "return" has been via Japan, Spain, Italy, and France, but whose "domicile" is in the United States, to have a spectacular show which not only transcends those crude polarities but actually makes universalist transcendence the organizing principle of a lifetime's work. What better moment than a time of universal sickness to work with a medium, gunpowder, the lethal power of which was discovered inadvertently on a search for an elixir of immortality, and which has long been invested with powers of healing as well as killing? As for his primary place of belonging, Cai has redefined the idea nomadically, making it clear that "home" for him is as much El Greco's Spain or Cézanne's Provence, as his birthplace of Quanzhou. Cai's kind of home is infinitely portable, elastically open,

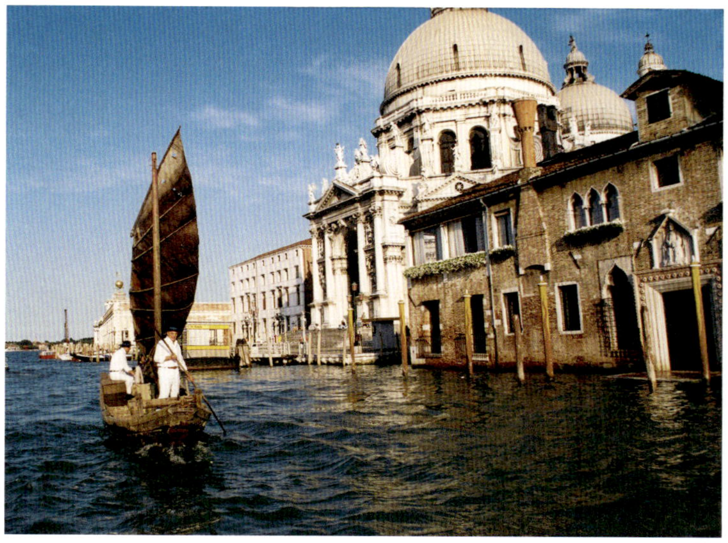

Figure 2. Cai Guo-Qiang sailing the wooden fishing boat brought from Quanzhou, China, in the Grand Canal, as part of *Bringing to Venice What Marco Polo Forgot*, at the 46th Venice Biennale in 1995. Photo by Yamamoto Tadasu

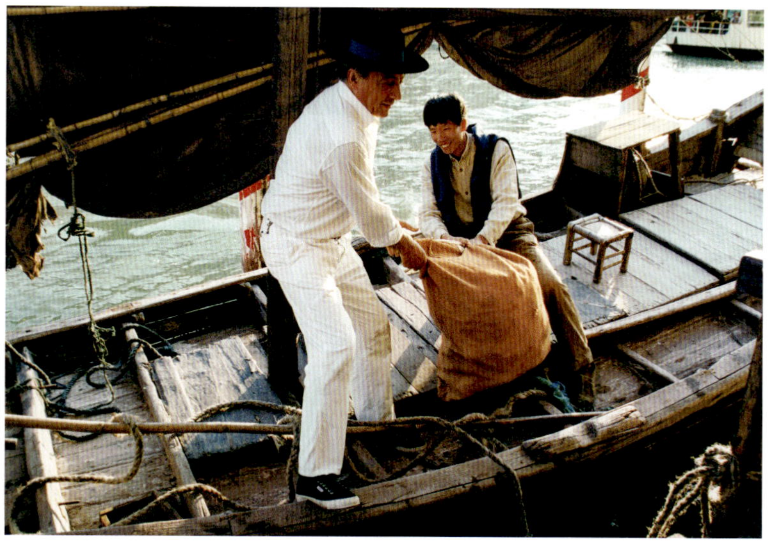

Figure 3. Cai Guo-Qiang unloading a bag of Chinese herbs and ginseng (100 kg), as part of *Bringing to Venice What Marco Polo Forgot*. Photo by Yamamoto Tadasu

constantly receptive. It's this resistance to the empty commonplaces which equate home with territory or with language that makes his work and his life so heroic.

From the start, he was, like Quanzhou itself, outward-facing. The brilliant conceit made for the Venice Biennale of 1995, *Bringing to Venice What Marco Polo Forgot*, in the shape of a junk made from his hometown timbers and loaded with a cargo of Chinese herbal medicines (figures 2 and 3), was itself a winning reversal of the assumed directional flow of cultural influence, and owed something to the instinctive theatricality that has been part of his repertoire since working at the Quanzhou Gaojia Opera Troupe in the late 1970s. Apprenticeship in painting was never a zero-sum game for Cai. Cherishing his father Cai Ruiqin's passion for calligraphy and classical Chinese literature didn't mean that he wasn't also open to the exhilarating experimentalism of 19th- and 20th-century European painting, for example, revealed in *Exhibition of French Rural Landscape Paintings from the 19th Century*, shown in Shanghai in 1978 (figure 4). Try-out painting became second nature to Cai so that in the early works of the late 1970s onward

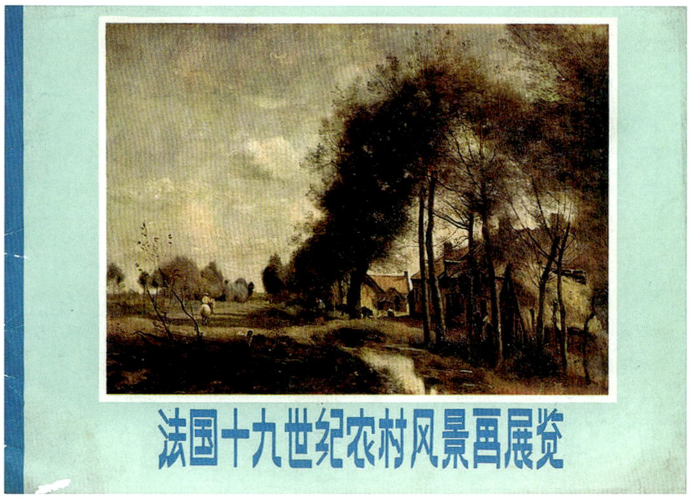


Figure 4. *Exhibition of French Rural Landscape Paintings from the 19th Century*, 1978 (catalogue cover). Cover image: Jean Baptiste Camille Corot, *The Sin le Noble Road near Douai* (1873). © National Art Museum of China

there were conceptual and stylistic visits with Van Gogh, Monet, Bonnard, and the Nabis (no. 8.1 and figure 5), and strong nonlocal paint tonalities in the manner of the Fauves and Die Brücke.

Perhaps it's not a coincidence that many of those modernists, above all Van Gogh and Monet, were themselves not just enthusiasts but collectors of the Japanese woodblock prints which swept the world of Western art in the last third of the 19th century. Even at this early stage of his development there was something of a feedback loop between East and West. But when Cai moved to Japan and began to explore an art fashioning what would be uniquely his, it would not be the woodblocks themselves which would fire his experiments but the volcanoes which are obsessively present in Hokusai's series, Mt. Fuji in particular. One may speculate whether or not it's the twin quality, the *yin-yang* of volcano imagery—the ineffable serenity of their dormancy, never free from the unpredictability of their reawakening—which made them so magnetic in Cai's creative imagination. This is in striking contrast to how they appear in the work of Romantic artists like the catastrophist John Martin (1789–1854) who depicted the Vesuvian eruption many times. The impulses for his earliest gunpowder works, including the *Projects for Extraterrestrials* series, have been identified canonically with the kind of happenings staged much earlier in Japan by the Fluxus group or with the occasional slash-and-burn gestures of Miró in his late turn to dark passion and with other such self-conscious assaults on art's pretensions to be defined by its posterity. Even though Cai has made a point of talking about his combustible restlessness with academic and conventional norms, it seems to me that the gunpowder work has never been vulgarly polemical. The aim of the explosions has been as much creative as destructive, indeed to make the point of the inseparability of apparently opposite phenomena; in other words to *make something*, even if just from smoke, soot, color, flame, and light. In this sense he seems closer to the great wood sculptor David Nash (b. 1945) whose spiritually charged sacrificial charrings and burnings enact a whole carbon lifecycle. Nor does the ostensible brevity of the experience compromise its endurance. In fact, foreknowledge

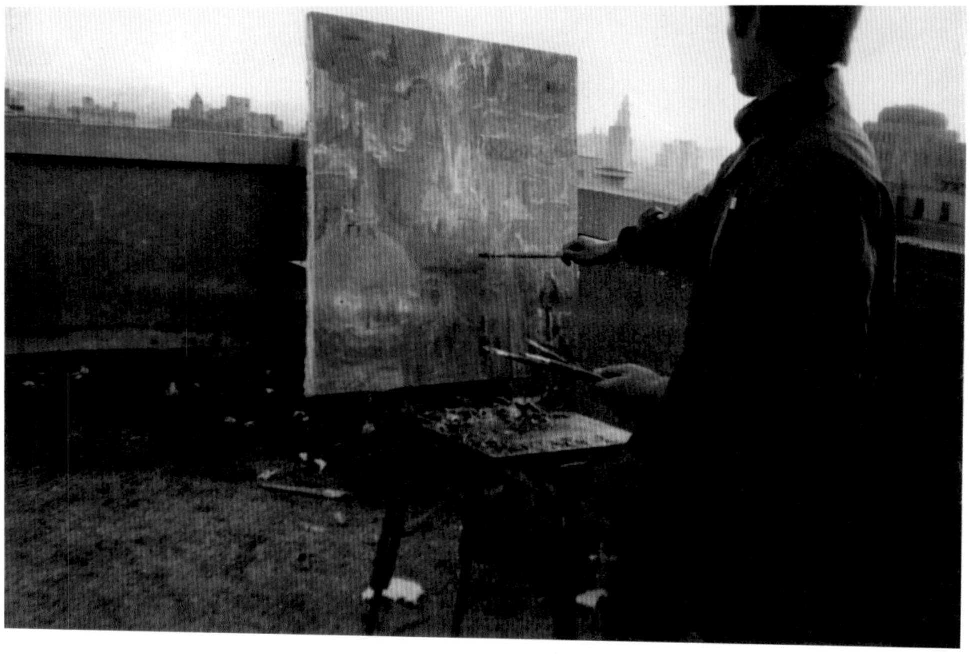

Figure 5. Cai Guo-Qiang experimenting with modernist painting styles in Shanghai in 1982

of that brief temporality may actually intensify concentrated receptiveness so that the detonation and day or night fireworks actually leave trace marks deeply imprinted on our memory.

Cai's work in stage design, his instinct for the transformational possibilities of drama, have served him well. Like Gian Lorenzo Bernini who was also a set designer, impresario, composer, and dramaturge as well as sculptor, designing engulfing stage effects like the flood which at one point seemed to threatened to flow over the edge of the stage and into the audience, Cai uses what he tellingly calls the "acts" of his daytime fireworks to pace the emotional and sensory impact of his work. Throughout, the art impact is consciously designed as an open-ended collaboration between the offering of the artist—including the public performance of the almost ritualized acts of stencil laying, powder drawing and scattering, ignition, and uncovering—and the shared response of the public audience. Nothing could be further from the forgettable one-hit-wit moments common in contemporary art, in which gestures of self-congratulatory cleverness are bestowed on the viewer as a benison of cool.

But then for millennia, "cool" has been the preferred medium of classicism, and classicism has been the thread binding together long-separated generations in a common assumption about the definition of beauty, in particular its realization in the human nude. The art history through which Cai has traveled has, of course, featured moments of dissent and resistance, all the way from Christian Gothic to Rembrandt's etchings of the half-undressed; to Manet's *Olympia*, Cézanne's *Bathers*, Picasso's *Demoiselles d'Avignon*, Duchamp's *Nude Descending a Staircase*, and Jenny Saville's *Prop*. By and large, though, the line from the classical Venus to Velázquez's *Rokeby Venus* to Ingres's *Grande Odalisque* holds fast, presupposing as it does an unchallengeable eternity of line and form bloodlessly trapped in cold marble, or in Ingres's case, paint made to mimic the texture of stone or unmeltably frigid ice cream.

This is not the line of beauty which engages Cai. There is an alternative tradition, hot rather than cold, explosively temporary rather than embalmed and eternal, Dionysiac and sensually combustible rather than Apollonian, the line first suggested by Nietzsche and sustained and deepened by Aby Warburg's readings of Botticelli. Cai has himself (and not crudely) made the analogy between the eruption of Vesuvius and sexual climax, and implied that Pompeii's heavily eroticized art and culture is somehow of a piece, at least in our memory, with its fatal consummation in the killing streams of molten lava. The 18th-century antiquarian archaeologist Richard Payne Knight was persuaded enough by the phallic bronzes and carved stones found in the original excavation of Pompeii that they were evidence of a formal devotional cult to publish his extended essay *Discourse on the Worship of Priapus* in 1772. Which is not to say that the mega-explosion in the amphitheater of Pompeii was designed, primarily, to be a gunpowder *Satyricon*; rather that it represented another stage in Cai's ongoing negotiation between the physical and the metaphysical, matters sensual and matters spiritual. But a number of the gunpowder paintings are jubilant translations of Pompeiian couplings rendered somehow simultaneously abstract and arousing, dissolving bodies of color, licked by fire.

Enter (and exit, pursued by lava) the illustrious Pliny the Elder, the studious and weighty writer with whom "Western" art history truly begins. As described by his nephew, Pliny the Younger, the uncle—exemplary Roman soldier, lawyer, procurator, and scholar—died while attempting to rescue friends from the fumes and flames of Vesuvius. He left behind him an immense mountain of research into the physical world: geological, geographical, mineralogical, medical, and the rest, which the dutiful and admiring younger Pliny then collated and edited to make the multi-volume *Natural History* which is still one of the literary marvels of the ancient world. It is also the very first sketch of the lives, careers, and techniques of the sculptors and painters of Greek antiquity and is in fact compulsively readable in those chapters. Almost every kind of painterly challenge is broached: choice of palette (ultrasimple for the greatest of the masters, Apelles of Kos); illusionistic effects (the birds that flew down to try

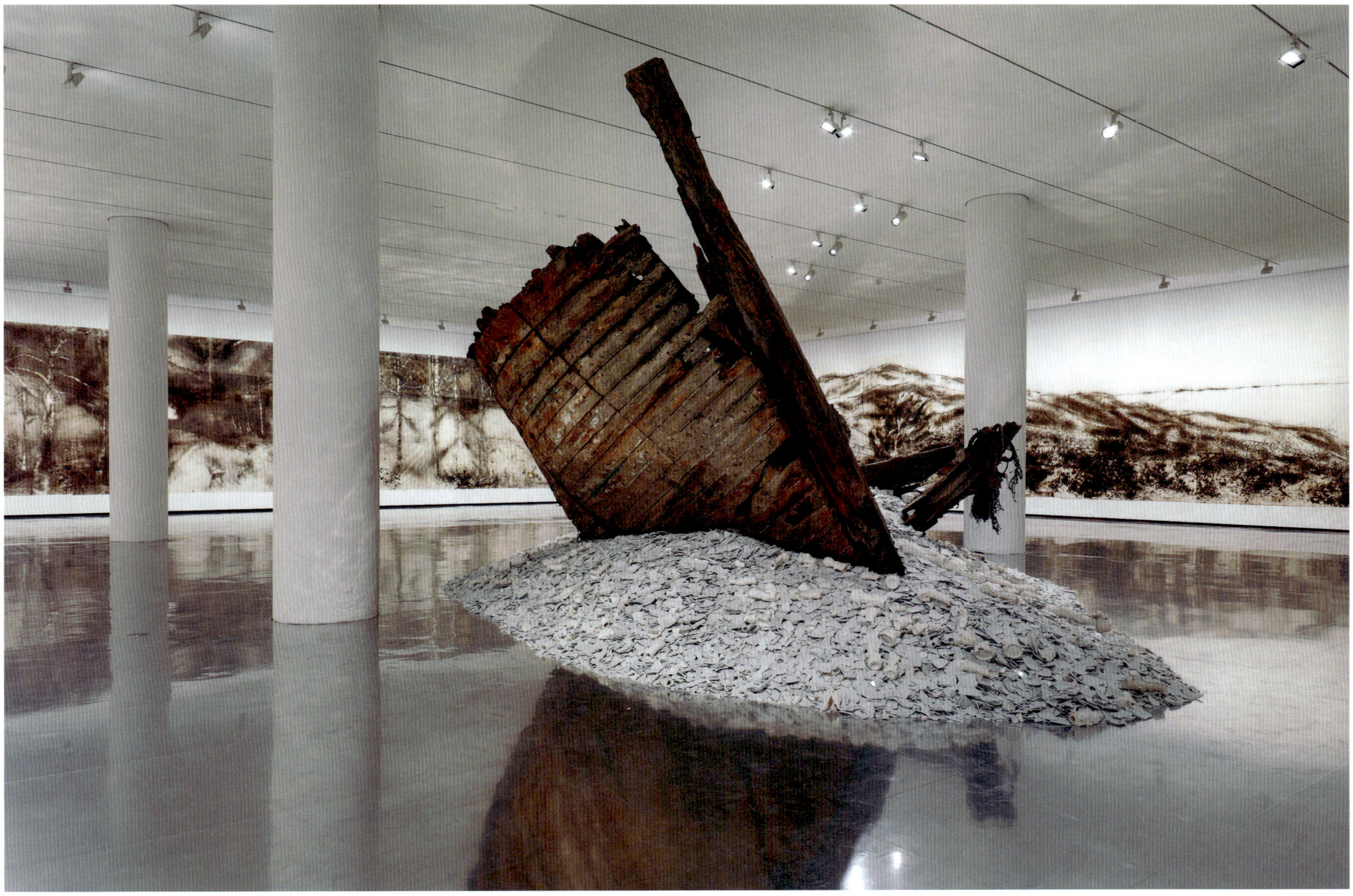

Figure 6. Cai Guo-Qiang, *Reflection—A Gift from Iwaki*, 2004. Excavated wooden boat and porcelain figurines, boat: 500 × 500 × 1500 cm. Photo by Anders Sune Berg, courtesy Faurschou Foundation

to eat Zeuxis's painted grapes); selectivity in combining the best features from many different models to make the ideal nude; even the role of accidental impression (Protogenes, despairing of painting the foam on a dog's muzzle throwing his sponge at the canvas and ... *eureka*). Aside from the irrepressible human animation of the minibiographies, what links Pliny to the Pompeian matrix and thus to Cai's reenactment of its consuming fire, is that in the morphological organization of the ancient texts, art does not come into being, self-armed like Athena from the brain of Zeus, but arises naturally from physical substance: painting from pigment, pigment from vegetable and mineral matter, supports fashioned in ways that retain and expose the material reality of their fabric. Art is not immune from natural processes which can decompose as well as compose. Lurid polychrome paint can disappear over the ages to give the mistaken impression that classical sculpture was always meant to be undecorated. Greenish-brownish skies which seem to be a candid representation of northern European climate are in fact the result of the fugitive tendency of inexpensive smalt blue. The history of art, then, is indeed a *natural* history, inescapably suspended between resolution and dissolution and affirmed in some of Cai's most affecting work like *Reflection—A Gift from Iwaki* (2004) where porcelain figurines of the Avalokitesvara Bodhisattva (Guanyin) are both cargo and shoal on which the carting vessel is beached (figure 6). The fate of art, like that of ourselves, is contingent, not secure, much less embalmed.

Hence the scorch on a cast *Farnese Hercules* (no. 3.2). Cai's intention to remove several casts of classical figures from the frozen security zone of museum display and deliver them instead into the fire of creative destruction was dramatically intensified by the magnitude of the powder explosion which seems to have been more overwhelming than expected. This outcome was deliberate. Cai writes about abandoning the "meticulously curated" explosion process he had used for his *City of Flowers in the Sky* (figures 2.9–10), and reverting instead to manual patterning of gunpowder and manual ignition. As Cai wrote of his Pompeii project in 2019, "This time there was an inferno that couldn't be subdued with mere fire extinguishers in the howling wind. But this was precisely the animalism and lack of control that I wanted. It wasn't only explosion art, but also fire art, wind art." To display the exploded figures, the flame-roasted *Hercules*, the *Plum Venus* (no. 3.1), beside their pristine originals was to liberate them from museum frigidity, to restore the heat of their moment of creation. In the case of the multiple *Pseudo-Senecas* set beside the marble heads (no. 3.12; figure 3.15), the burnt versions almost seemed like a reproach against Stoicism, of which the philosopher-tragedian was the enduring personification. Likewise the enormous bolt of canvas serving as a wrapping for the cast figures became itself a spectacular print of the life of the explosion. As such, it too acted as a repudiation of classicism's abhorrence of the display of process, the residual marks of the uncertainties of making. Only the strongest and most

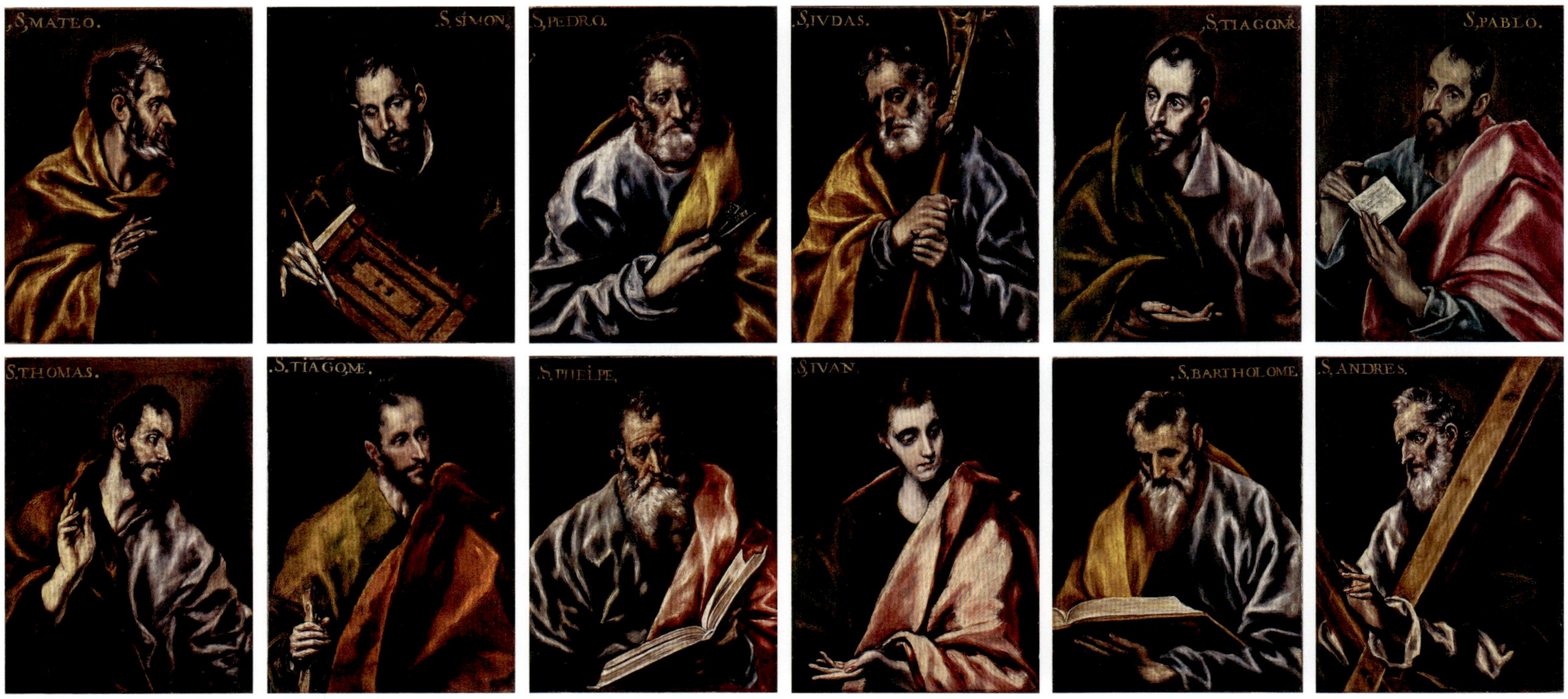


Figure 7. El Greco, *Apostolados*, 1610–14. Oil on canvas, 12 panels, 70 × 53 cm each. Collection of the National Sculpture Museum, Valladolid, Spain

confidently revolutionary makers of art—Rembrandt above all others—not only rejoiced in the conscious display of such marks (on etchings and drawings in particular) as tracers of creativity's restless self-alterations, but actually reconceived them as integral to the artwork itself. Such confessions of uncertainty, of creative restlessness, open the work to two exhilarating variables: the intervention of the materials themselves, either in resistance to, or acceleration of, the prepared line and form (Rembrandt well understood the differential absorption of distinct kinds of paper, especially Japanese, and manipulated that knowledge to brilliant effect); but also the variable of the beholder's liberty to interpret. That kind of art is open-ended, flattering to those who make its completion through their own imaginative immersion. And such is Cai's art.

An *Individual's Journey Through Western Art History* might presuppose some sort of canonical narrative through which the exploring traveler would make his way, stopping off at all the recognized stages: Classical, Romanesque, Gothic, Renaissance, Modern, and so on. Needless to say, that has not been Cai's plan at all. Points of engagement were supplied by invitations from great museums like the Prado and the Uffizi to mount shows, including explosion events, featuring responses, in his own idiom, to masterworks in their collections. Pieties of intercultural dialogue have colored the project. But Cai's approach has never been programmatically dutiful. Instead he has proceeded like a rogue pilgrim, moving from site to site, seeking fellow outriders, privileging those, like himself, who worked against academic conventions and often did so in visionary, rather than naturalistic, language, artists who have conceived their work as cosmic drama.

No one more so than El Greco, with whom Cai passionately identifies, as his *Selfie* (2017) (no. 1.6) homage to the Cretan master's *Saint Sebastian* makes dramatically plain. El Greco's nomadism—from Candia to Venice, on to Madrid, ending up in Toledo—seems not just to anticipate Cai's own restive travels, but also to make the case that all the stopping places fed into the development of a vocation and image-making manner that was independent from each of them and definitely more than the sum of an itinerary. El Greco's standing as a free spirit, a stylistic maverick, consciously thumbing his nose at academic classicism, committed to the primacy of color, yet radically defying what was thought to be seemly combinations of hue and tone: all this must have beckoned to Cai as an intimation from afar of much of what he was seeking. And not least, there is (at least to my mind) a fuliginous atmospheric burning through so many of El Greco's most powerful pictures that goes well beyond a touch of *sfumato* here or there. Instead, it's a tenebrous darkling shade, a mantling of blackness, against which saturated brilliance, be it of Christ's blood-red robe in *El Espolio* or in the operatic lead-tin yellows and blues of his *Apostolados* (figure 7) transforms sacred histories and saintly icons into mystical apparitions, cloaked in smoke and drenched in acid; visions not at all of this world. Dusky Toledo itself seems to bob on the crest of its hill, poised between celestial ascent and abysmal plunge.

Despite our modern embrace of El Greco's incommensurable peculiarity, his holy wildness, these startling qualities did not arrive all by themselves, fresh off the boat from Crete. Doménikos Theotokópoulos's Candia was Venetian, and like pre-expulsion Toledo, strongly marked by a kabbalistically inclined Jewish presence. So even though it's said that he learned much from Titian (I'm not actually sure what that might be), it's more likely that his true mentor, in spirit if not in person, was Titian's notoriously prickly and alienated sometime-apprentice of but a few days: Tintoretto (figure 8). El Greco would have arrived in Venice in the late 1560s when Tintoretto was reaching his feverish prime. Pitchy, tenebrous grounds and backgrounds; an addiction to madder and carmine; the liberation of color from local description, the balletic arrangement of forms and figures so that they deploy in pictorial, not naturalistic space; expressive rather than

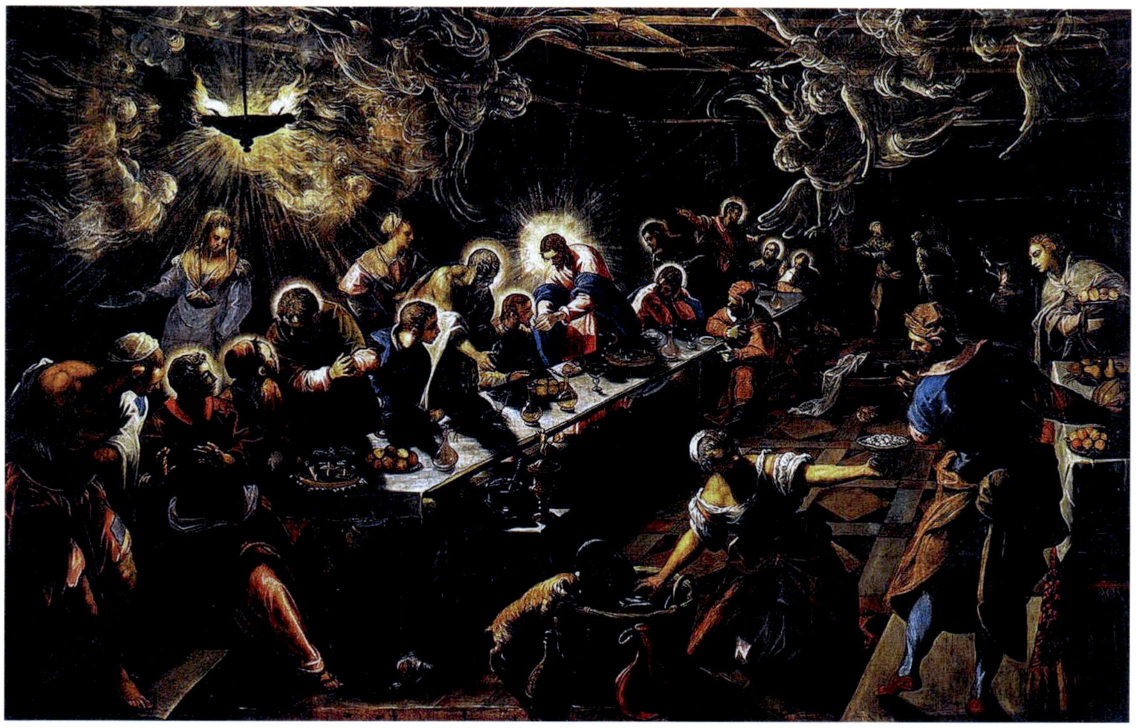

Figure 8. Jacopo Tintoretto, *The Last Supper*, 1592–94. Oil on canvas, 365 × 568 cm. Collection of the Church of San Giorgio Maggiore, Venice

classical anatomy; above all, the orchestration of every element to make up a physically felt sacred drama—all those (anti-Titianesque) characteristics appear over and over in Tintoretto and they reappear even more spectacularly in El Greco.

It could not have been fortuitous that Cai's artist residence and the paintings that resulted took place in the Salón de Reinos, the Hall of Realms, since the entire history of that building was marked by the representation of military violence and its counterpart, the ostensible escape to peace and renewal. In origin, as part of the Casón del Buen Retiro it was designed by the Count-Duke Olivares, King Philip IV's first minister, strategist, and cultural majordomo to display the classical virtues of the monarchy: invincibility in war (when the reality was anything but), Christian nobility, and courtly magnanimity. Diego Velázquez, who played a major role in the planning and execution of the space and the installation of a processional series of large canvases, hung his own *Surrender of Breda* (now in the Prado), which was unique in its humane ambiguity about the laurels of victory (figure 9). Ostensibly it represents the presentation of the keys of Breda by the defeated Dutch commander Justinus of Nassau to the victorious general the Marques Spinola who has gallantly dismounted from his horse in a gesture of compassionate peer-recognition. In historical reality Spinola did indeed permit the march out of the Dutch troops with their colors. But in a move of breathtaking unorthodoxy, Velázquez has, at least, equalized the representation of the soldiery. Jubilant Spanish officers, trim and knightly, crowd the picture space behind Spinola while the defeated are represented as earthier more commonplace types. One of them with what seem to be blood-like traces on his white costume, the two hues surely not fortuitous, stares unforgettably out at us with an expression of dismayed resignation. To know anything about Velázquez is to know that his personification of the defeated as men of the people, in contrast to the victorious grandees, was the opposite of the social condescension you might expect in a court commission. Rather the opposite in fact; as with *Las Meninas*, *Vulcan's Forge*, and *Los Borrachos* (*The Triumph of Bacchus*), it's the street casting who get to be the stars.

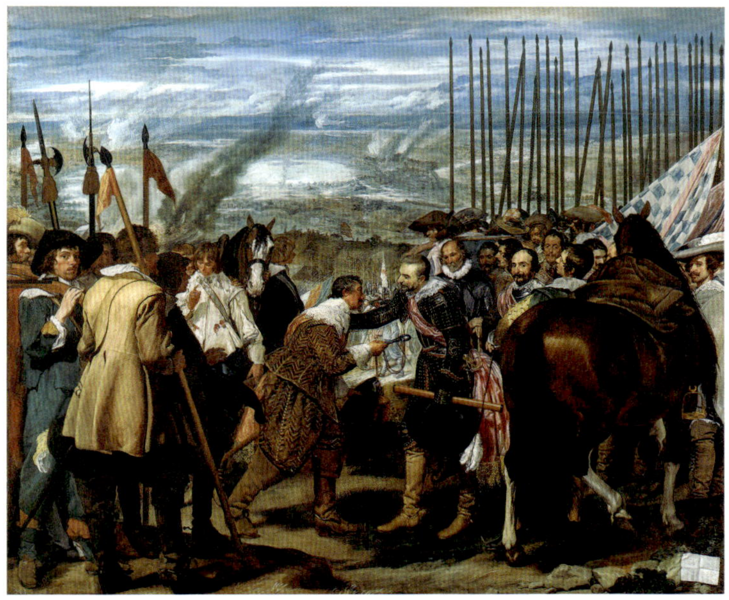

Figure 9. Diego Velázquez, *The Surrender of Breda*, 1634–35. Oil on canvas, 307 × 367 cm. Collection of the Prado Museum, Madrid

The daring implication (as audacious as monarchy reduced to a small framed mirror image on the back wall in *Las Meninas*) is that victory isn't all it's cracked up to be; *victor ludorum*, only up to a point. That point was never more movingly and savagely represented as when *Guernica* returned to Spain once the Falange regime was no more, and was installed in the first instance in the former army museum, the Hall of Realms.

There is, of course, another immortal Prado masterpiece which embodies, all at the same time, (and in a way Picasso was quite conscious of, an anticipation of the nocturnal bombing of

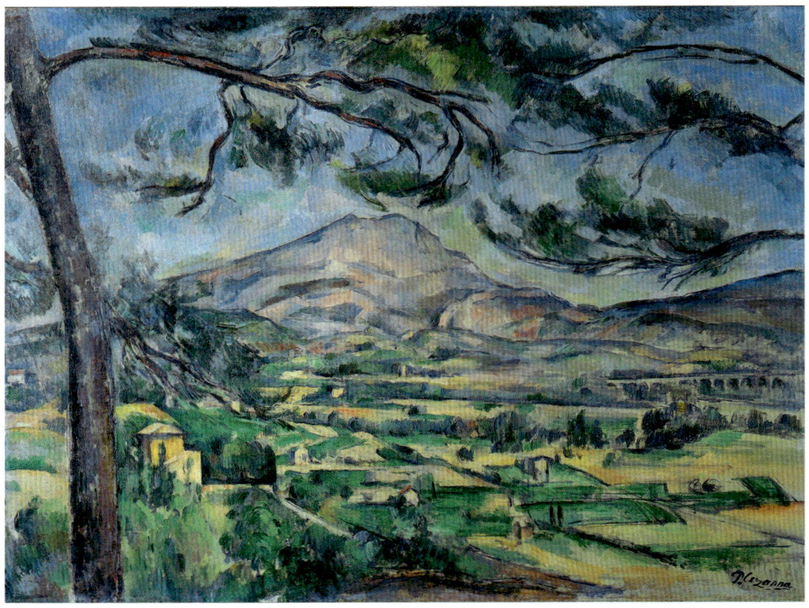

Figure 10. Paul Cézanne, *Montagne Sainte-Victoire with Large Pine*, c. 1887. Oil on canvas, 67 × 92 cm. Collection of the Samuel Courtauld Trust, The Courtauld Gallery, London

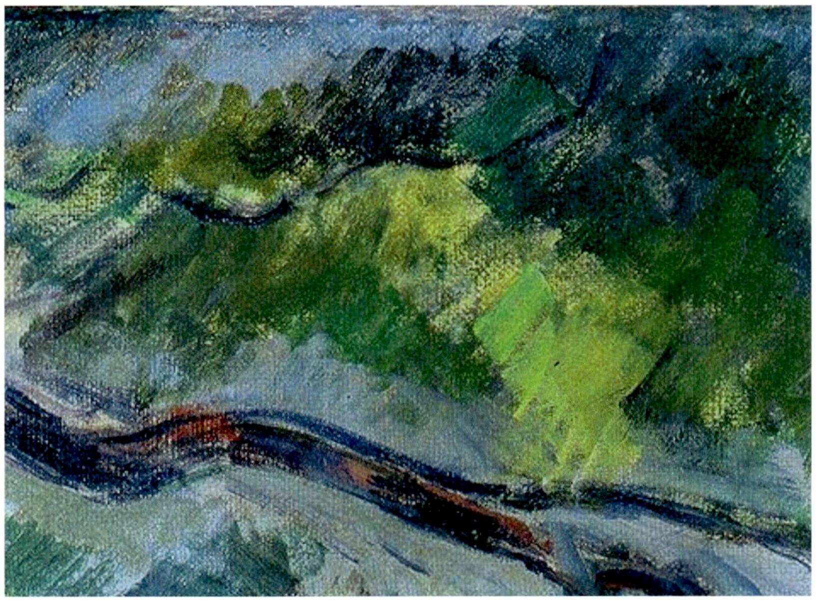

Figure 11. Brushwork detail of foliage on pine tree in figure 10

his epic) the pitiless destructiveness of military carnage, the translation of butchery into sacred martyrdom, and the draining of exactly that sacred light which for the medieval Christian mind *was* the emanation of God: Goya's *The Third of May 1808* (figure 1.10). This is the painting of Goya's with which Cai chose to engage most deeply, and no wonder. All the academic rules of painting have been blown away. Light has been reduced to the lantern which affords just enough of a gleam to enable serial murder. The human head and face have been turned into a mush of blood and tissue; the executed prisoner, simultaneously maddened, terrified, and defiant, takes up the attitude of the crucified Savior, complete with the stigmata appearing on his palms. It is, then, a study in brute power and though more despairingly nihilistic than anything in Cai's emotional and philosophical makeup, it is, like his work, a moment of transfiguration: the prisoner morphed into redeemer; blood and bullets; fire and death-light made the agency of resurrection. In Cai's sympathetically echoing response, the firing squad seems eaten up by its own choking smoke while the martyred prisoner is radiantly backlit at the moment of his immortalization.

*The Spirit of Painting* (no. 1.27), the immense epic canvas filling what, in Velázquez's day, had been nearly an entire wall of the Salón, recapitulates and synthesizes all these mortal extinctions and obstinate re-awakenings and burgeonings: a flash of Toledo lightning, a blooming pond of crimson, half tissue, half blossom, a rising hill above which sport the celestial carnival of Rubens's Ovidian frolics and metamorphoses; a descent into blotting obscurity; all the comings and goings of earthly and unearthly life.

The sense in which the Spirit of Painting can, or perhaps must, accommodate both dramatic agitation and philosophical meditation is present in another of Cai's longtime fixations: Paul Cézanne's serial landscapes of Mont Sainte-Victoire in Provence. There is, of course, a whole Chinese tradition behind this. Unless one counts the decoration of Roman and Pompeiian villas with decorative pastoral scenes (and lovely as some of them are I'm not sure we should) landscape painting begins in earnest in the 10th century with the artists of Northern Song dynasty (960–1127). Immense peaks through and around which the spirit of *qi* circulates, embody the potent authority of the Song emperor following a prolonged period of catastrophic anarchy and civil war. It was in the century that followed that the first Chinese art academies were founded, prescriptive teachings were written and circulated, and painting became the norm for the mandarin scholar class, almost as indispensable as the obligation to master elegant calligraphy. But what is striking about the greatest masterpieces of that era is that, while many of them incorporate scenes from the animated human realm, they also consciously mediate between the human and the spiritual universe. Pavilions located halfway up the rock face mark portals from the quotidian to the eternal world, disembodied, self-effacing, and in the Daoist way, ultimately profound. As the hand of the painter and the eye of the beholder ascend so the painterly marks themselves become more suggestively airy, as if solid forms were dissolving into celestial illumination.

The play between solid form and dancing light is rehearsed over and over in Cézanne's Mont Sainte-Victoire works, all sixty of them in oils, drawings, and watercolors, executed over nearly thirty years. Going back to them, as he often did, right up to the years before his death in 1906, seeking different viewpoints, they have a claim to be, among all his series, the one which most faithfully represents Cézanne's own evolving understanding of the "spirit of painting," a key concept for Cai's recent development. They also represented his own "homecoming," since unlike painters like Van Gogh, Matisse, and Picasso, Cézanne was a born Provençal. Though he exhibited for a time with the Impressionists, like Matisse and Van Gogh, it was only when he escaped Paris that he also became liberated from the optical imperative that the subject of painting was light itself, especially in its mercurially flickering indeterminacy.

Cézanne was not impervious to painting light. Crucial to the hypnotic effect exerted by pictures like *Montagne Sainte-Victoire with Large Pine* at the Courtauld Institute of Art (figure 10), is the dialogue between rock and the pine-scented heat-tremble of light. The indistinctness with which Cézanne has represented the needle clusters hanging on the branches suggests a faint breeze-pushed motion. The whole top half of the painting is composed contrapuntally, the lines of the foreground branches made to rhyme with the contour of the mountain so that whether our line of vision ascends or descends, it does so in a continuing, musical loop, as if caught in a color-drenched fugue.

Cézanne has changed the subject of painting from light to paint itself. The drama is on the surface of the canvas: the paint laid on in dabs with a square-ended hog bristle or palette knife, sometimes loosely and thinly as with the mid-ground ochres and greens that describe the valley in the Courtauld painting and its little cottages (figure 11), sometimes more densely in the needle foliage and the hot blue sky. The effect is tessellated, as if patches of paint were creating a new kind of mosaic or sewn quilt of color (figure 12). It's a commonplace of the art historical literature that Cézanne's genuine interest in geology (one of his collegiate friends from Aix-en-Provence with whom he still walked in the countryside was in fact a geologist) led him, especially in the pictures of the Bibémus rock quarry, to construct heaps and blocks with their own independent massing (figure 13). It was this heavy faceting which would inspire the Cubist fixation on the geometric engineering of things, as well as their urge to disassemble the logic of coherent form. That may well be true, but it became routine for Braque and Picasso to work in monochromes or a tightly reduced palette, even though one of the colors habitually used was very like Cézanne's duns and tawny ochres. For Cézanne, on the other hand, the building blocks of painterly construction were tight slabs of intensely saturated color—so that he became a lodestar for Matisse as much as Picasso. Paint began to lead a compositional existence independent from what it was ostensibly describing. *Disegno* was *colore*.

For a while now, Cai's response to Cézanne's exercises in harmony and equipoise seems to have been explosively disruptive. Around thirty years ago, he proposed staging an explosion event on the face of Mont Sainte-Victoire (for the benefit of extraterrestrials as well as the rest of us) which would take the form of an ascending dragon, its fire fusing together Eastern and Western traditions and perceptions (no. 6.1). The project was never realized, but Cai's recent work about the mountain has been at least as meaningfully spectacular. In the most epic of his Mont Sainte-Victoire gunpowder paintings, Cézanne's shimmering light and the adamantine line of the mountain have been sprayed with a freckled scrim of particulate debris, as if they were fragmentary shards from quarry detonations (no. 6.10). (And Cézanne was of course much obsessed with that abandoned rock quarry of Bibémus not far from Sainte-Victoire and Aix-en-Provence.) It's also as if Cai wanted to reenact the birth pangs of the mountain, born as it must have been from primordial volcanic upheaval.

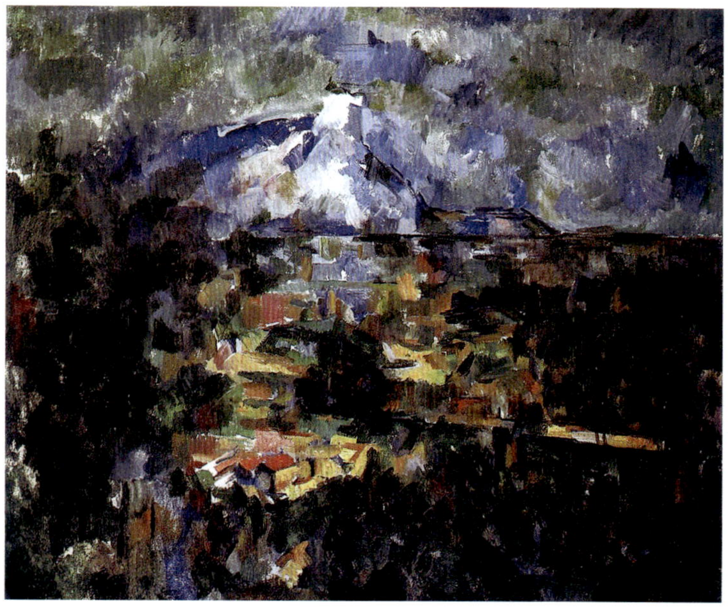

Figure 12. Paul Cézanne, *Mont Sainte-Victoire Seen from Les Lauves*, 1904–6. Oil on canvas, 59.9 × 72.2 cm. Collection of Fine Arts Museum of Basel

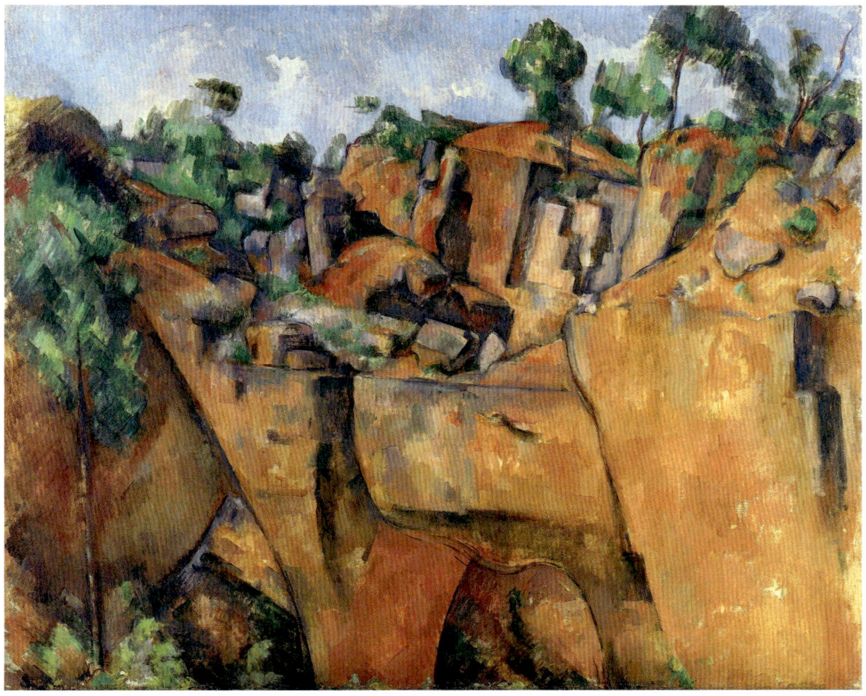

Figure 13. Paul Cézanne, *Bibémus Quarry*, c. 1900. Oil on canvas, 65 × 81 cm. Collection of Folkwang Museum, Essen, Germany

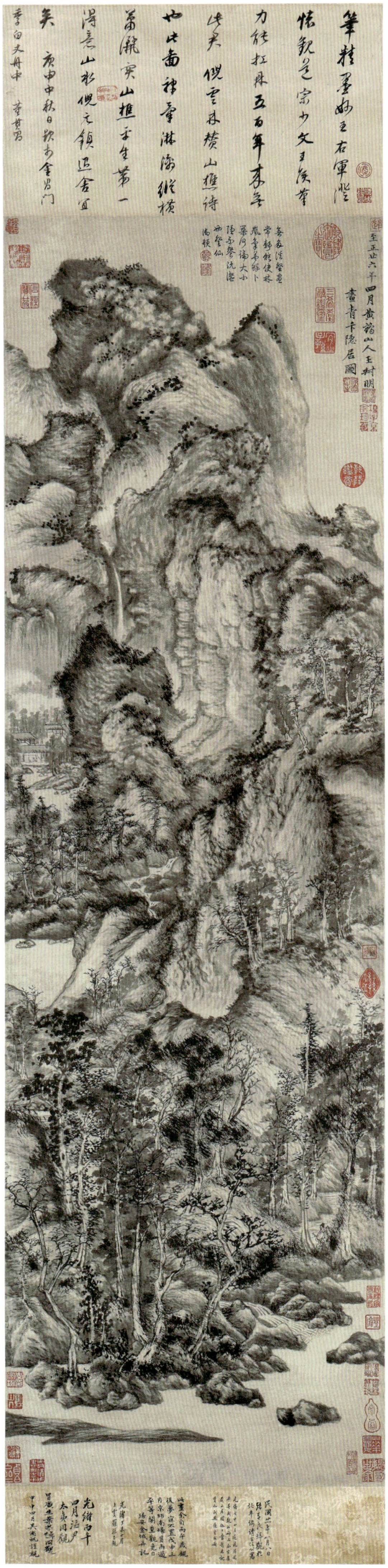

Figure 14. Wang Meng, *Dwelling in Seclusion in Qingbian Mountains*, 1366. Ink on paper, 141 × 42.2 cm. Collection of the Shanghai Museum

Cai's default mode, after all, both before and after ignition is meditative, an attentiveness to the stirring and settling of creation amidst the havoc of destruction. So is it with these epic pictures: the product of a double-homecoming, both to Cézanne's Aix-en-Provence and also to the tradition of Chinese mountain painting (*shanshui*). In the tremulous, writhing-dragon vision of the 14th-century artist Wang Meng, for instance, painting in a frenzy of agitated stabs (figure 14), could embody not the adamantine authority of Northern Song landscapes, but rather a crisis of disintegration and uncertain outcomes (apt in Wang Meng's case since he died in prison at the hands of his enemies in the government of Ming Emperor Taizu). Some of Cai's variations on this dialectic between primordial energy and settled grace revert to inky monochrome, or a two-color choice, using indigo pigmented gunpowder, a darkened version of the intensity of Cézanne's skies, for the freckling of the rock. In other images he elegantly marries up memories of the claw-shaped overhanging pines that frame many Chinese classical landscapes with the comparable framing forms used by Cézanne (no. 6.11). My hunch is that, on seeing these paintings, visitors to the exhibition will intuitively feel the unforced confluence of Eastern and Western traditions which is at the heart of Cai's constant vocation.

Although in the West there was a long tradition of mountain monasteries and hermitages, it was not until Romantic writers, poets, and painters made horror and terror sensations to be sought after that rocky landscapes were treated with anything except fear and loathing. Dragons were monsters; mountain caves the lair of demons; Daoism would have been mystifying. No one scaled the summits for therapeutic disembodiment, only to get down the other side as fast and as safely as possible. But although Dante and his guide Virgil painfully plod up Mount Purgatory, stopping on seven terraces populated by those groaning under the weight of atonement for whichever sin they had specialized in, eventually there was a passage through a wall of flame and admission to the Earthly Paradise.

If not exactly a picnic, the Terrestrial Paradise did at least offer an inkling of what the Heavenly version might portend. So it may be with a strong sense of the Renaissance as a cultural flowering that Cai made paradise gardening the leitmotif of his dialogue with the Italian Quattrocento. Floralia shaped the six-act daytime firework drama in the Piazzale Michelangelo, which, as the filmed recording reveals, was, even by Cai's standards, a spectacle of astounding beauty: shoots and forests of intense color rising magically as if accelerated by some celestial fertilizer to curtain the city and its dumbstruck viewers. And it blossomed again in many of the gunpowder paintings shown in the Uffizi Galleries exhibition *Flora Commedia*, many of which had had actual plants and flowers strewn amidst the stencils before ignition. The engineering of destruction and the burgeoning of nature lived alongside each other in the Renaissance. It's sometimes forgotten that Leonardo da Vinci (whose drawings supplied Cai with templates for variations) was, at one and the same time, an exacting observer of natural phenomena, especially in the plant world, and an inexhaustible inventor of weaponry, fortifications, and ever more ingenious machinery of death for his Sforza patrons in Milan.

The terrestrial paradise had a long tradition in medieval Christian iconography, often depicted as a garden fenced or

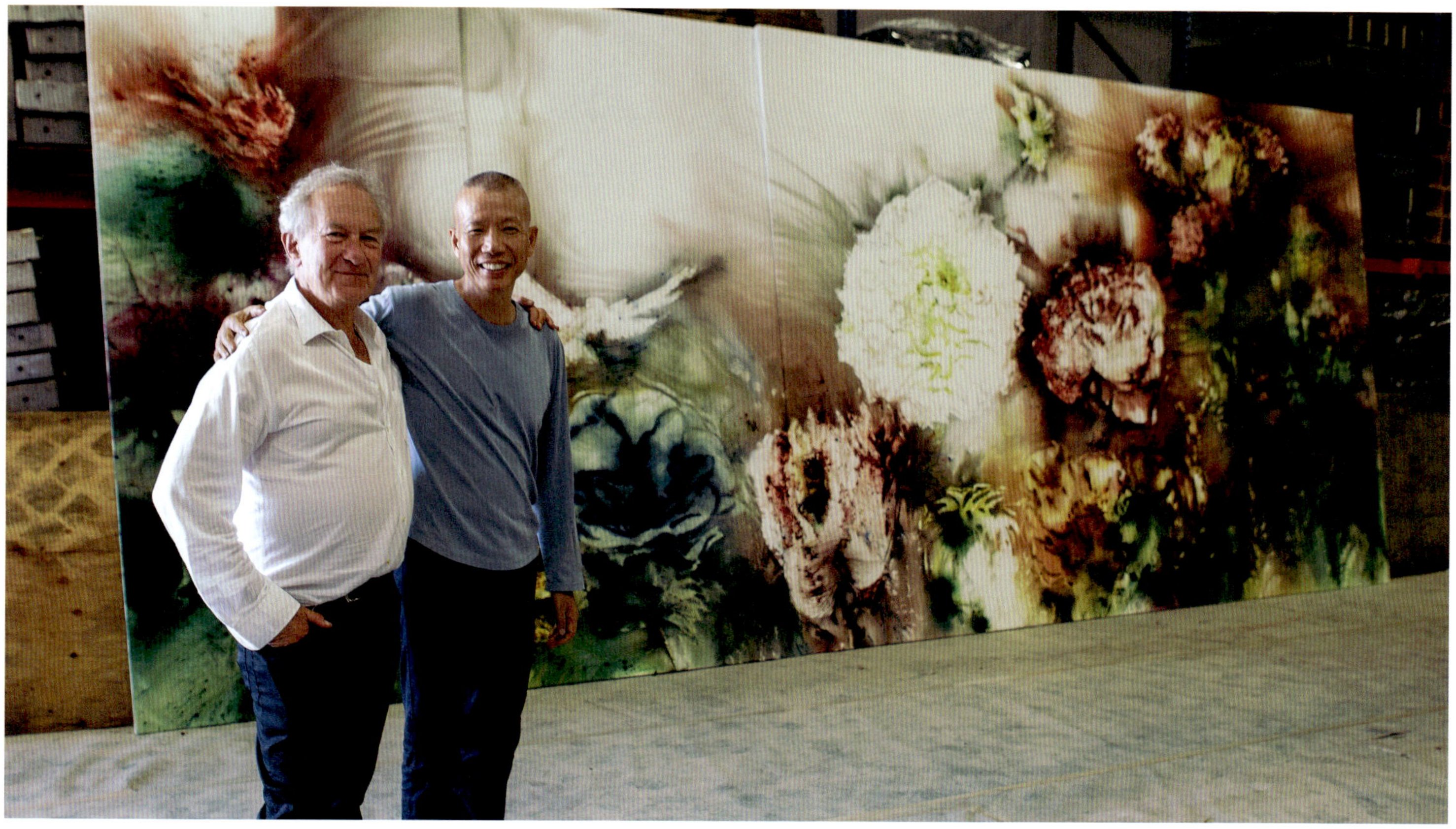

Figure 15. Simon Schama and Cai Guo-Qiang in front of Cai's work *Heaven Complex No. 1* in 2017. Photo by Wen-You Cai

walled against heathens, demons, wild beasts, and other sundry evildoers. But a dramatic shift in meaning took place when the walls came down and Renaissance explorers and navigators encountered worlds, east and west, wholly innocent (as their skimpy dress or nudity proclaimed) of the psycho-drama of sinful shame, sacrifice, and redemption. An actual search for the Garden of Eden obsessed some of the learned explorers like Columbus and Sir Walter Raleigh, both of whom wasted years and pains on the futile quest, though since Columbus was convinced that Eden would be located as the nipple surmounting a breast-like island, his fixation is sweetly understandable.

But if the explorers failed to bring back the precise coordinates of Eden, many of them returned with something more precious and certainly more substantive: flora from Asia, Africa, America, and the Caribbean which suddenly extended the range of botanical knowledge beyond any anticipation. When learned horticulturalists laid out their botanical gardens, they did so not just with divisions of utility in mind—medical, edible, and the like—but according to an enthralled conviction that if they got the morphology just right they would be privy to a cosmic revelation. Their Aristotelian side drove them towards encyclopedic compendiousness: the entire world in its infinite variety seeded, cultivated, and ordered. But their Neo-Platonist side offered something more ecstatic: that if the known species were gathered and perfectly ordered, perhaps according to some mystically disclosed pattern, there would come a moment of revelation when the new garden would yield up the esoteric principles governing creation itself. The way to this sublime knowledge lay down the garden path.

If only. I write all this, not with Botticelli's Flora and her fluttering drapery echoed in Cai's renditions (no. 2.5) delivering a definition of painted beauty but amidst *una primavera avvelenata*, a poisoned spring in which lilac blooms alongside invisible, fatal contagion. "It's as if nature is laughing at us," one of my friends observed. But we are not laughing back. I don't know anyone who hasn't felt that, with the retreat of polluted air and ambient light, the stars and moon have shone down with radiance the like of which we have never before seen; and with the drone of traffic muffled, the birdsong (and in our neck of the woods the frog song) has sounded out more musically. Within the shadowland of fear, our receptiveness to the burgeoning of nature has ever been more acute. And the same may be said of the life-sustaining elixir of art for which, there is every sign the public are avidly thirsty.

Above all, I believe that art which engages with the great, serious matters of our condition, and that of the earth we inhabit, is more needed than ever before. If, among the winnowings brought about by the pandemic, there is a discarding of the cheaply fashionable, the gaudily meretricious to make space for profound reflectiveness, then that is all to the good. And among the work that will endure and not just beyond our present plight, will be that of Cai Guo-Qiang. His "odyssey and homecoming" is, of course, a triumphant conquest over cultural defensiveness; but when we experience his art, we travel somewhere further still: into the cosmic space where crass matter perishes and transforming creativity is born.

---

*Sir Simon Schama is an internationally renowned historian, art historian, and Professor of Art History and History at Columbia University. He has composed and hosted multiple acclaimed documentary series for the BBC, including* Simon Schama's Power of Art *and* The Romantics and Us with Simon Schama. *When he worked on episodes of* Civilisations *which covered great art from the Stone Age to contemporary times, he presented Cai Guo-Qiang's art creation in its final episode. He is the curator of the exhibition* Odyssey and Homecoming *and editor-in-chief of this volume.*

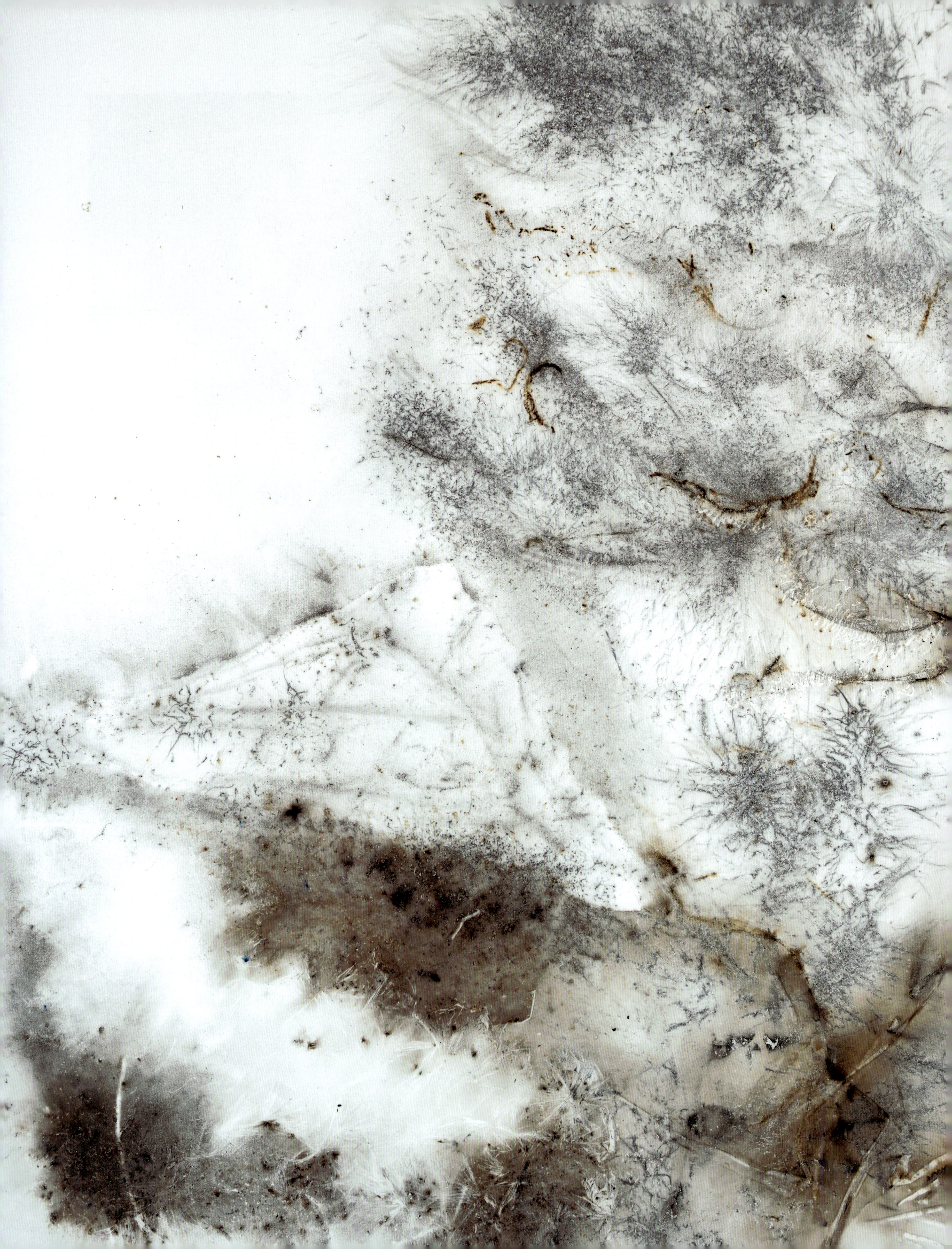

# Homecoming, Ongoing

Cai Guo-Qiang

## Preface: The Palace Museum and the Bicycle

Using this exhibition as an opportunity to talk about my personal connection with the Palace Museum seems somewhat sentimental, but having this opportunity and *not* talking about it would be unfeeling. I would also like to take this opportunity to express my endless thanks and gratitude to the members of the Palace Museum for their support in the past and present.

Once upon a time, I was on a long-distance bus back to Quanzhou from Fuzhou, where I had gone to buy a plaster bust. A tire burst and all the passengers got off the bus. Some went to help change the tire, some stood smoking along the road, and I went for a stroll in the nearby field. I only saw one other person in the field. After getting back on the bus, I discovered that this person was sitting directly across the aisle from me. He had apparently noticed me from our earlier stroll and, noting the plaster bust I was holding, asked me, "Are you a painter?" He told me the man seated to his other side was Feng Xianming, the resident authority on ceramics at the Palace Museum. He himself was a graduate student of Mr. Feng's. The two were on their way to Dehua to inspect an excavated kiln. *His* name was Li Yihua, and we have been friends ever since (figure 1). We grew closer when I later went to study in Shanghai and would visit him whenever I went to see exhibitions in Beijing. I will never forget bicycling inside the Forbidden City as the glow of dusk settled around me ...

He later became the head of the Forbidden City Publishing House at the Palace Museum. After completing college, I looked into studying abroad. He said, "Go to Japan, the Palace Museum has more connections there, we can help!" He found me a financial guarantor in Japan, as well as a contact at the airline to help me and my accompanying 100 kilograms of artworks aboard the flight. Mr. Yang Xin, the new Deputy Director of the Palace Museum, wrote me a letter of reference. When I met with day-to-day difficulties upon first arriving in Japan (figure 2), Li Yansheng, the traditional Chinese painting and calligraphy expert who had worked at the Palace Museum and was then already well established in Japan, offered his support. Li Yihua also introduced me to the owner of Nigensha, a publisher known for its facsimile reproductions of classical paintings, as well as the painter Higashiyama Kaii and the calligrapher Aoyama San'u. He would tell people, "This young man will 'explode' when he comes to Japan!"

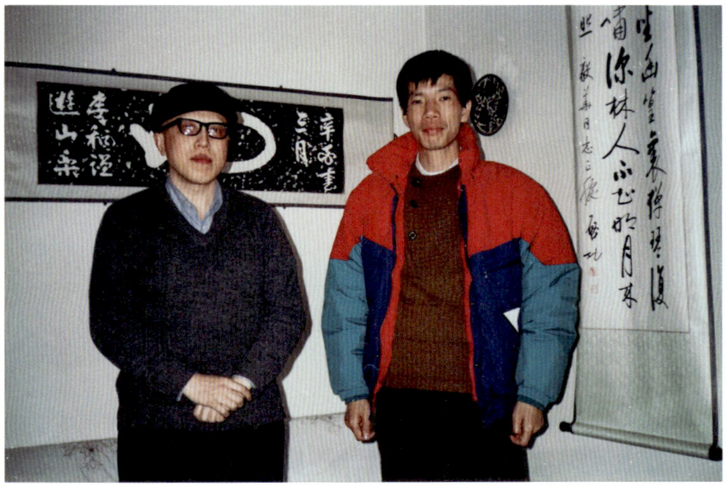

Figure 1. Cai Guo-Qiang with friend Li Yihua around 1986–90

Detail of *Cypress of Mont Sainte-Victoire* (no. 6.11)

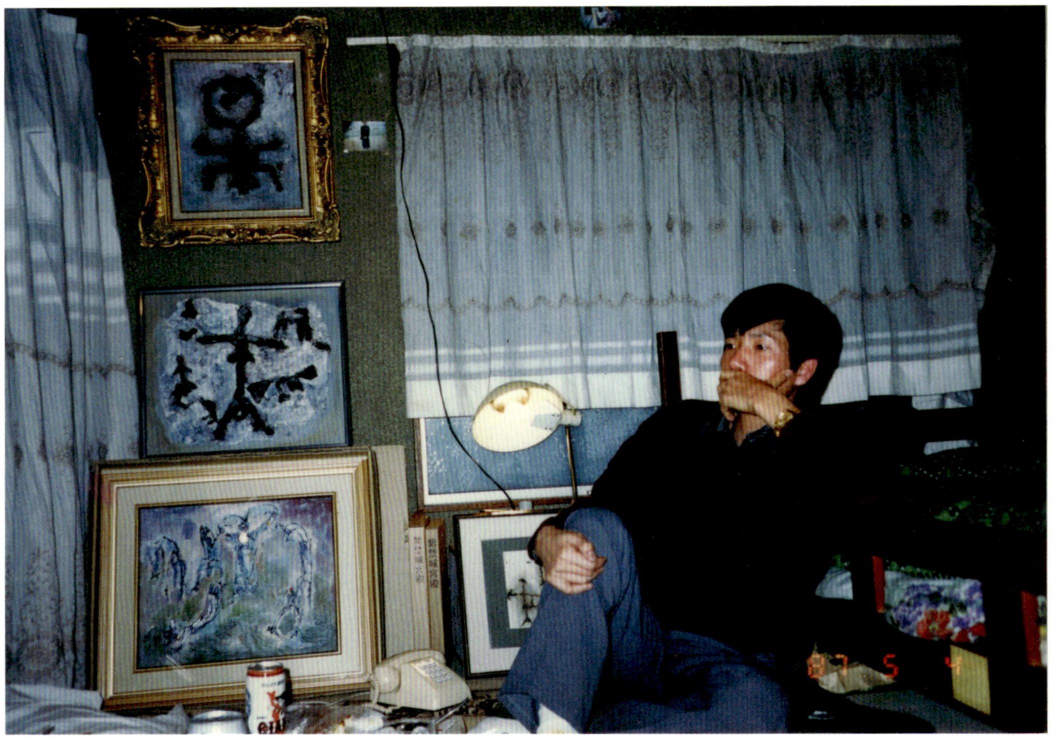

Figure 2. Cai Guo-Qiang at home in Japan in 1987. Photo by Hong Hong Wu

Compared to the art world, these "guardians of tradition" at the Palace Museum were quicker to appreciate my work; they believed that this was the way to create history. As a boy from Quanzhou—where "the skies are high and the emperor is far"—I found their encouragement indescribably heartening.

Much of my work has engaged in dialogue with history and art history, using them as subjects. Although my artworks have toyed with conceptualism and made use of explosions, my childhood dream of becoming an artist was actually of becoming a painter, rather than someone who traipses around the world doing big projects. These days, art has sunk into a listless state. I want to return to art history, revisiting those artists who inspired my admiration or curiosity in my adolescence. In 2009, I traveled with my daughter through Greece, Italy, and Spain, retracing the life trajectory of El Greco, whom I have revered since my teenage years. This journey seemed to foreshadow another journey that was to come ...

In 2017, I launched the project *Individual's Journey Through Western Art History*. Through a series of exhibitions at institutions including the Prado Museum, Pushkin Museum, Uffizi Galleries, Pompeii ruins, and National Archaeological Museum of Naples (figures 3 and 4), I have held up Eastern culture and spirit as a mirror to reflect and start dialogues with the periods of Western art history represented by these collections as I strive to seek new possibilities in contemporary painting.

"Odyssey" and "Homecoming"—today, I have returned to the Palace Museum, the very place that once sent me abroad (figure 5). This exhibition is a showcase of my journey through art

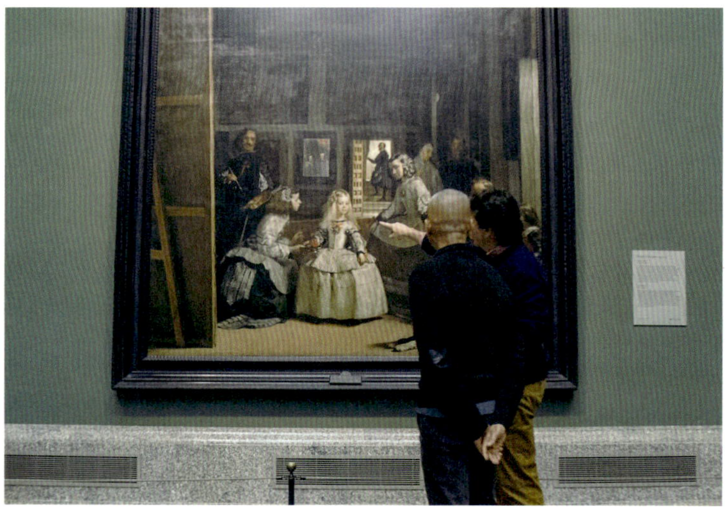

Figure 3. Cai Guo-Qiang and Alejandro Vergara, co-curator of his Prado exhibition, before Velázquez's *Las Meninas* in Madrid in 2017. Photo courtesy the Prado Museum

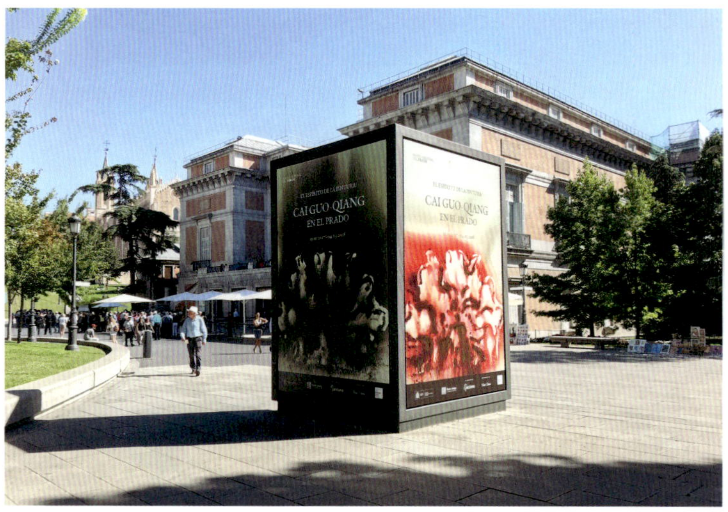


Figure 4. A poster kiosk for Cai Guo-Qiang's solo exhibition outside the Prado Museum, Madrid in 2017. Photo by Anqi Xu

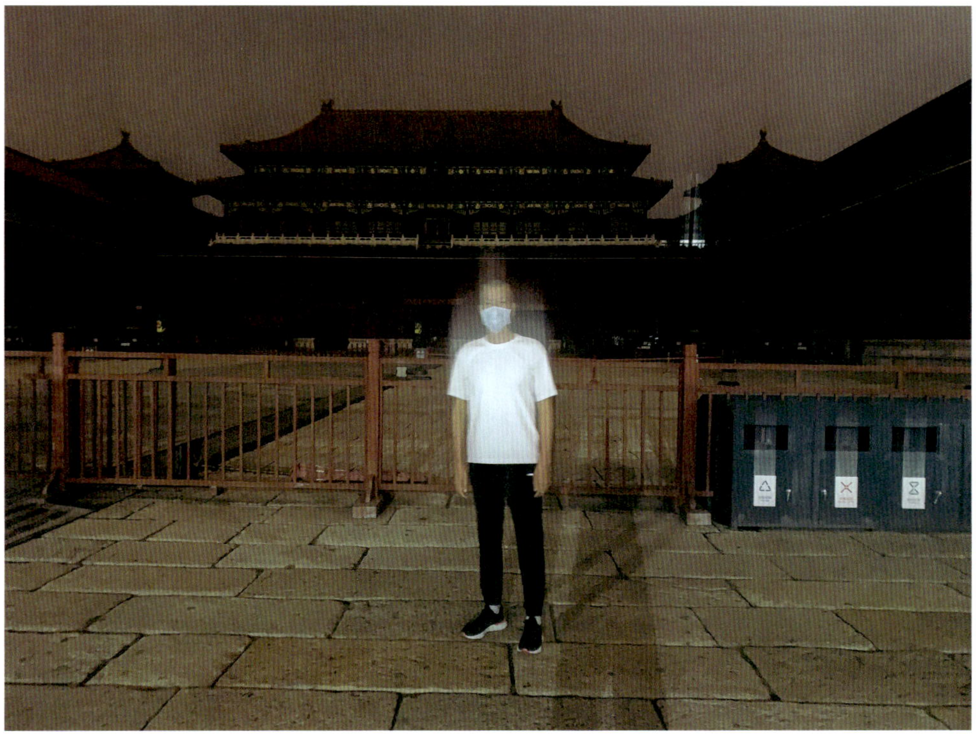

Figure 5. Cai Guo-Qiang in front of the Meridian Gate of the Palace Museum, Beijing in 2020. Photo by Cai Canhuang

history, but it is also an artist's political stance: to regard himself as the heir to all human cultural heritage and to treat cross-cultural masters as his own predecessors. I hope visitors will see how the fusion of and dialogue between the past and present, East and West, can all coexist in an artist from China. Showing this may have some special significance in a world that is currently deglobalizing to a state of mutual isolation.

A recurring question has faced the palaces of Western art through which I have journeyed: how can these institutions act as cultural guardians of the past, while also becoming agents of cultural ignition for new eras, sparking boundless creativity in today's artists? This question persists here in the Palace Museum, which symbolizes the glory of Chinese civilization. When we tell the world about the five thousand years of cultural heritage housed here, the unasked question on the audience's minds may be, "And then? What about now?" Cultural confidence is not only derived from inheriting immense cultural wealth, but also from the creation of new wealth. That is what forms the confidence of the now.

My odyssey was never a departure, and my homecoming is still under way. The odyssey is not only westward, and the homecoming is not strictly eastbound; it is not as simple as that. My homecoming is a return to the spirit of Chinese culture, and it is also a return to my original aspirations surrounding my love of painting—a deep affection that I hold for my predecessors in art history and the act of painting that has never diminished over the years. The odyssey brings me closer to myself. It is an encounter with my interior self. As I walk farther away, I walk deeper within. The odyssey is also a search for a greater hometown. I seek to encounter more artists from the past and present, from China and abroad, and through them to discover a shared "far-off land," a cosmic and eternal hometown. In the end, this is an act of self-nourishment from different cultures, spaces, and times.

I have toiled away at catalogue essays for almost each exhibition on my *Journey* to document my creative processes and thoughts in each moment. I will not repeat them here.

The sudden onslaught of the novel coronavirus forced all these cultural meccas I had just left to shut down all at once. People are panicking and debating over how the world will change post-pandemic, how humankind will never again be the same. Perhaps our predecessor artists are chatting and chuckling right now inside those exhibition galleries newly emptied of crowds: "Hey, didn't we create these things on the walls during all those catastrophes? Including the Black Death?" Much as my *Journey* strives to find constancy in an everchanging world, I still wish to explore some fundamental questions, no matter where the pandemic takes us: What are our relationships with other people, with nature, and with the cosmos? And: Why do we love to paint? These are some of the considerations behind my works exhibited at the Palace Museum, considerations that have remained unchanged throughout my artistic pursuit across the decades.

## Sightseeing Through History

*1*

I began browsing through a tome of *Shiji* (*Records of the Grand Historian*) on my father's bookshelf soon after I learned to read. This was my first "odyssey" as a young boy. I could not have truly understood the text back then, but I was unwittingly captivated by the magnificent and turbulent history within the book, the monumental events that took place from generation to generation over this immense period of time in this vast, vast land, as well as the very fact of knowing that there were people who documented something called "history." I am extremely grateful to my father, who loved history and art history and was a manager of

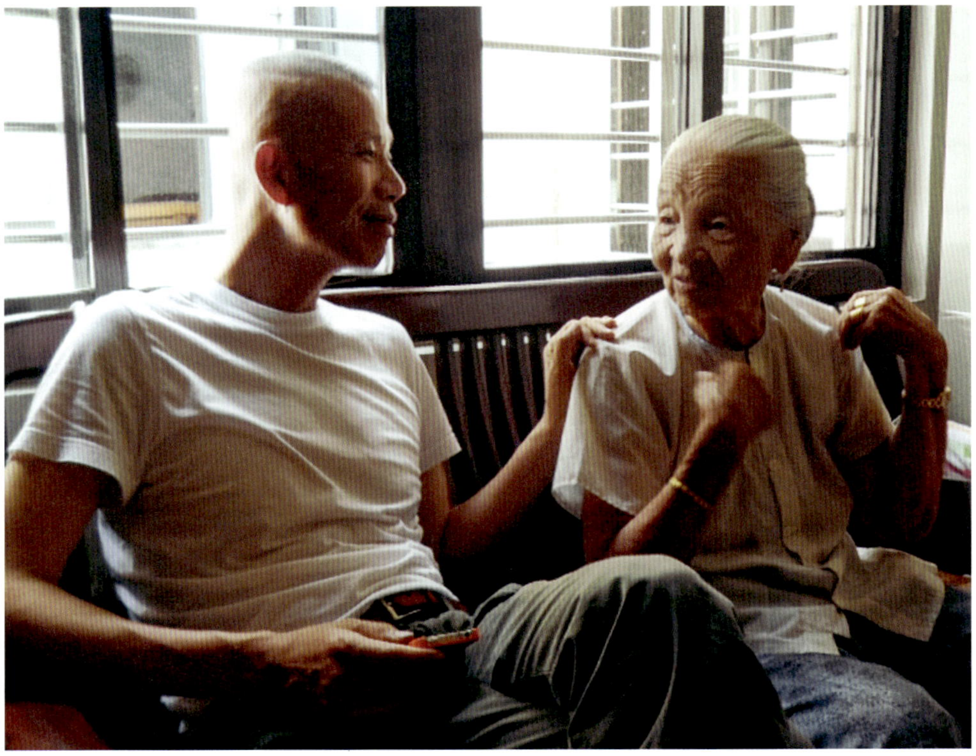

Figure 6. Cai Guo-Qiang and his grandmother in Quanzhou in 2011. Photo by Hong Hong Wu

"internal-use books" at the Xinhua Bookstore. During the Cultural Revolution, there was a bookstore in every city that provided internal-use books for perusal by local high-level officials, books whose contents and forms provided subjects of criticism. My father handled works including Absurdist literature of "American Imperialism," as well as "Soviet Revisionist" novels like *And Quiet Flows the Don* by Mikhail Sholokhov and books by the latest Nobel Prize laureates. He always brought these books home in secret and demanded that I read them in one day. This was my sightseeing odyssey through the modern cultures abroad.

Sociopolitical diversity and international complexity were the realities that accompanied my upbringing. At school, I was a Tri-Merit Student who excelled in scholarship, morality, and health. At the same time, I was the boy who secretly tuned into "enemy stations" at night, clutching my radio under the blankets. I grew up on these parallel trajectories. The distant, foreign land across the strait was also the land of my dreams.

*2*

It is my belief that, willingly or not, we bear the marks of our ancestors. My heart ached when I first ventured abroad and realized how behind we were back home, but it was clear to me that *we* were the unworthy ones—*we* had let down our ancestors, not the other way around. Likewise, we have inherited the creations of all of humankind's exceptional predecessors as part of our wealth. If art today is unexceptional, then we are the ones letting down our predecessors.

I have always believed that, were we able to open up the deepest crevices of life, allowing a connection and interflow with the energy of the primordial cosmos, we would then be on the right path to the ultimate truth. Our forerunners' self-cultivation and nurturing made them who they were. My greatest takeaway from dialoguing with art history is the feeling that humans are capable of carrying a cosmos within themselves. Like the ancient saying made famous by the recent pandemic, "in different lands, we share the same moon." Back in all those eras when transportation and communication were difficult, people from different times and places looked up at the same moon and, independently, opened their inner eyes.

## Homeland and *Jianghu* (江湖)

*1*

My cultural values and methodologies include the concepts of *yin* and *yang* from the *Yijing* (*I Ching*), the idea that anything pushed to an extreme will inevitably be reversed, the dialectical relationship between construction and destruction, and a spirit of neutrality, harmony, and tolerance. In both life and art, I care about *feng shui* and momentum. I believe in the unseen world, from every tree and blade of grass to the lives and deaths of people and our imaginings of heaven ... I want to believe that my ancestors, including my grandmother who left us at a hundred years old, have souls (figure 6). I want to believe that these souls linger in the undetectable dark energy that composes ninety-five percent of the universe.

I grew up in an alternative, a very *jianghu* (江湖), way. Weathering political chaos and cultural destruction, Chinese society at the time was closed off from information, but it longed to break

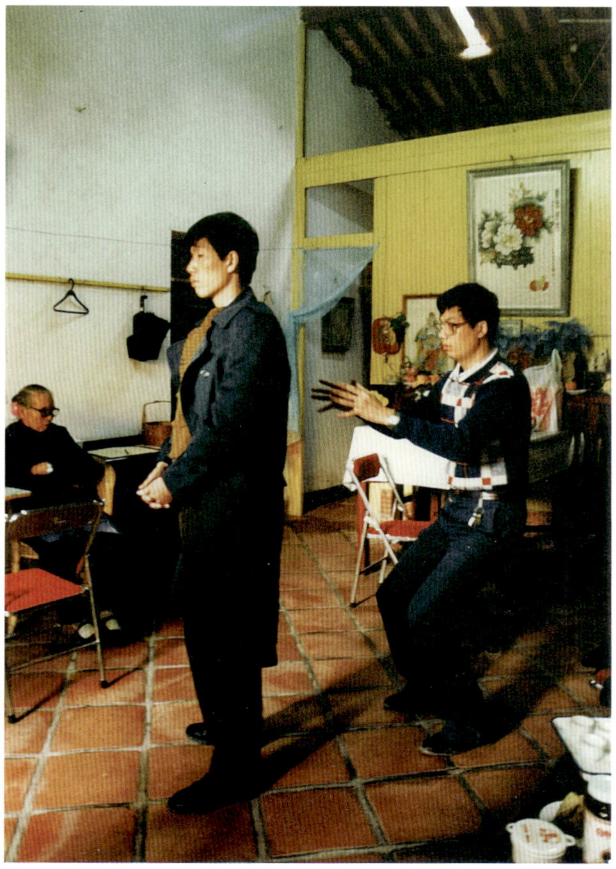

Figure 7. Cai Guo-Qiang with Yang Shiying, a *qigong* master, in Quanzhou in 1993. Photo by Tatsumi Masatoshi

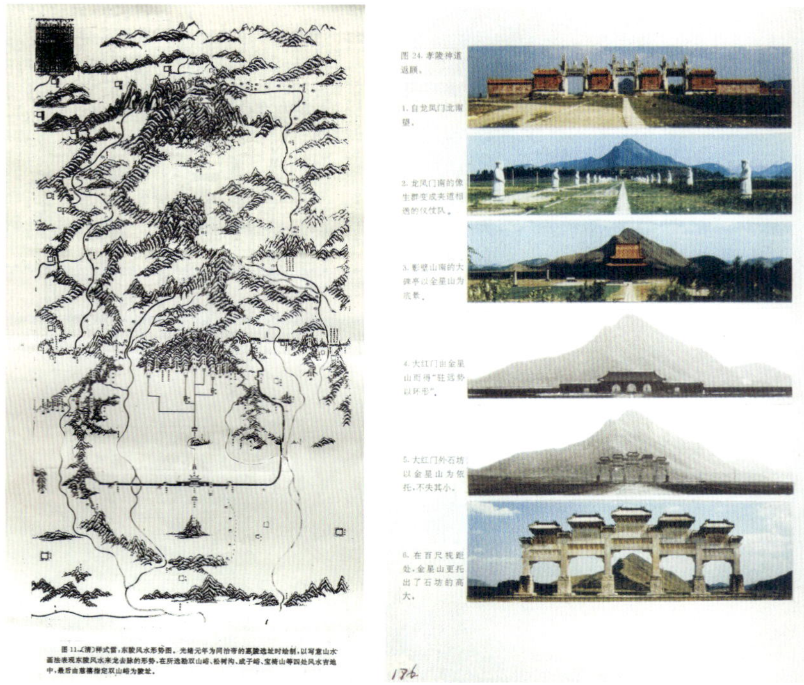

Figure 8. Left: *Feng shui* diagram of the Eastern Qing Imperial Tombs; right: views of the gates at the Xiaoling tomb of the Hongwu Emperor. Reproduced from Wang Qiheng, ed., *Fengshui lilun yanjiu / Research of Fengshui Theory* (Hebei: Tianjin University Press, 1992).

free from its constraints and rise up from its setbacks. As a young man, I went through a craze for supernatural powers, *kung fu*, and *qigong* (figure 7), that acted as my space-time tunnel. Once I walked through the door of the "opening-up," I suddenly arrived in the world as well as the cosmos. I not only went to Japan and the United States, but also "went" to outer space! It is a bizarre practice to possess cutting-edge knowledge of astrophysics in our scientific and rational modern system, while also continuing to cherish mythological and cosmological sentiments. This balance has helped me establish solidarity with the ancients and avoid being entirely consumed by the system.

*2*

The ancient Chinese did not generally portray the suffering and turbulence of the times in their art, unlike Goya, painting the darkness of massacres and cannibalism, or Pieter Bruegel's *The Triumph of Death* (1562) with its optimism. The Chinese did not paint the decay of rotting flowers, nor directly express the carnage portrayed in poetry, as in "Wine and meat spoil behind vermilion gates; human bones freeze by the roadside," or "one general's success costs thousands of corpses."[1] Instead, artists valued the distance between art and reality. I often imagine them leading luxuriant lives, gallivanting about, guzzling wine, composing poetry, with the rise and fall of their nation seeming but a distant shadow. For such people, even when life is not all roses, their spirit at least remains in a transcendental state.

Of course, we can also describe this as a form of reality. They did not paint the bereavement of heartbreak or losing a child. They did not paint worldly ambitions or the frustrations along the way. They may have used only an eagle to express ambition and the patter of rain on bamboo to express sorrow.

In terms of landscape planning, the Chinese tend to imitate the natural framework and energy of mountains and rivers, even moving toward a "cosmic pattern" (figure 8). The Great Wall of China and the Qin Tomb of Terracotta Warriors both thrilled me. I visited the Mausoleum of the Yellow Emperor, which was constructed using tens of thousands of cypress trees layered on top of each other and hills erected by heaving together the soil from flat land. It is a landscape that emphasizes its majesty and makes people feel infinitesimally small. The Forbidden Palace adopts this "the world is mine" configuration. The comprehensive aesthetic and methodology behind all these places were the work of generations of emperors.

However, there is not much "heroism" in classical Chinese painting. By comparison, Western art has exalted heroes, hormones, and muscles since ancient Greece and Rome. After the ancient Greeks inaugurated the Olympic Games, battles would come to a halt for the occasion and men would file off to compete in sports and hand-to-hand combat. Ultimately, the result of heroism was the establishment of political legislatures and the development of democracy. People actively debated and advanced philosophical thought in order for society to grow steadily and peacefully, all of which falls under the category of "action." On the other hand, Chinese art reflects the result of "inaction."

I like the idea of casually and unaffectedly contemplating the cosmos the way that the philosopher Laozi did. Of all the classical Chinese painters, I admire and respect Ni Zan (1301–1374) the most (figure 9). The sky and earth are boundless in his paintings.

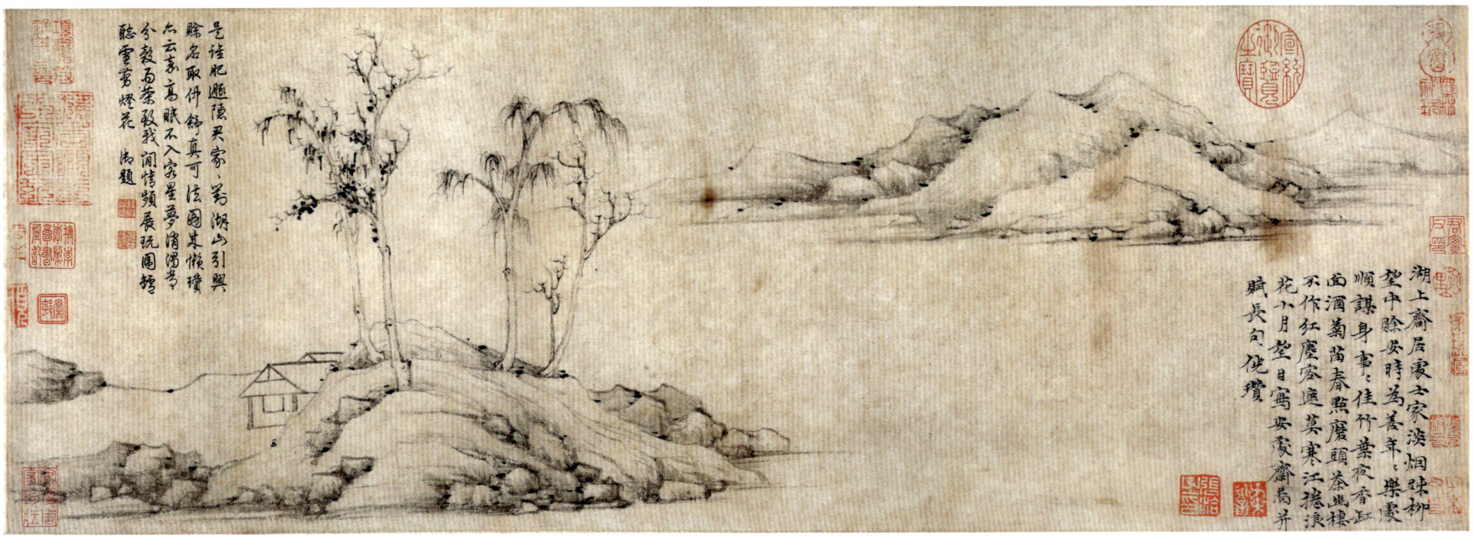

Figure 9. Ni Zan, *Cozy Abode* (*An Chu Zhai Tu*) (detail), 14th century. Handscroll, ink and wash on paper, 25.4 × 71.6 cm. Collection of National Palace Museum, Taipei

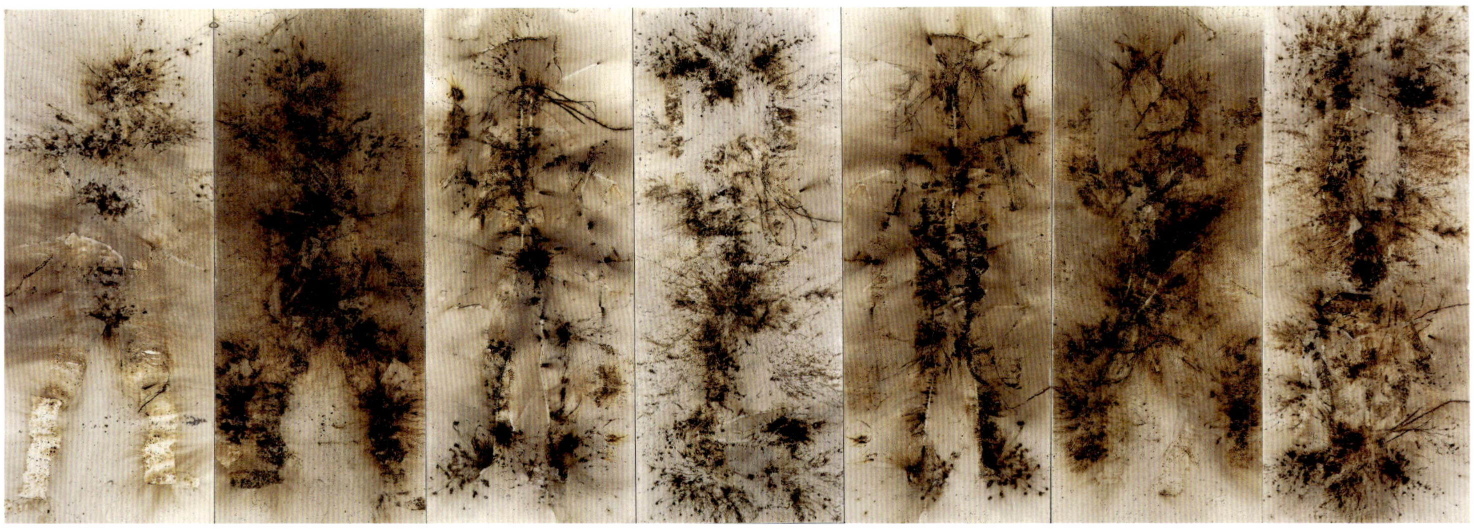

Figure 10. Cai Guo-Qiang, *The Vague Border at the Edge of Time/Space Project*, 1991. Gunpowder on paper, mounted on wood as seven-panel folding screen, 200 × 595 cm. Collection of Cartier Foundation for Contemporary Art. Photo by André Morin

They exude an abstract and aloof feeling that brings the heart and nature into a unified state of alignment. The frame of mind achieved by these classical paintings, which places the viewer in the scene and helps to ease the heart, differs greatly from the Western contexts of ancient Greece and Rome.

Chinese paintings are populated with mountains and rivers, flowers and birds, gentle breezes and radiant suns that embody the artist's heart and intention. This is innovative as it seeks to find a kind of art that transcends eras as well as the realities of the present moment.

But in the lead-up to the modern day, the West has shown a better understanding of art's value for easing the heart and establishing distance. Meanwhile, the Chinese have ended up dabbling with seemingly realist "propaganda paintings" that supposedly reflect their society and era, paintings that have become difficult to "transcend." From copying the metaphysical of the ancients to learning the physical of the Westerners, modern Chinese artists demonstrate confusion between distancing themselves from the mundane world and entering into it. Though there are exceptions, most Chinese artists study traditional realism when they seek education in the West, unlike the Japanese who learn everything from Fauvism to Dada to abstraction. Most of the time, the Chinese hope to use art to transform society and are convinced that realism is the most effective style for this purpose.

The early Chinese artists had great clarity about the position they wished to secure. While people may find their outlook somewhat narrow and express surprise that their interests were all relatively concentrated for centuries, they nevertheless had their own pride. Though they may not have had the same impact that Japanese *Ukiyo-e* had on the world, they still have their unique qualities. Whenever I visit any encyclopedic museum and go from the sculptures of ancient Greece and Rome to Leonardo and Cézanne, then onward to the gallery with classical Chinese painting and calligraphy, I can always feel their distinctive unaffectedness, dignity, confidence, and self-love ... I am always inexplicably moved. I feel consciously honored as well as ashamed and saddened, for compared to our predecessors, modern Chinese artists strive after too little. How run-of-the-mill, how middle-of-the-road.

My art is the vacillation brought on by the tug of war between so-called heroism and the spirit of inaction (figure 10).

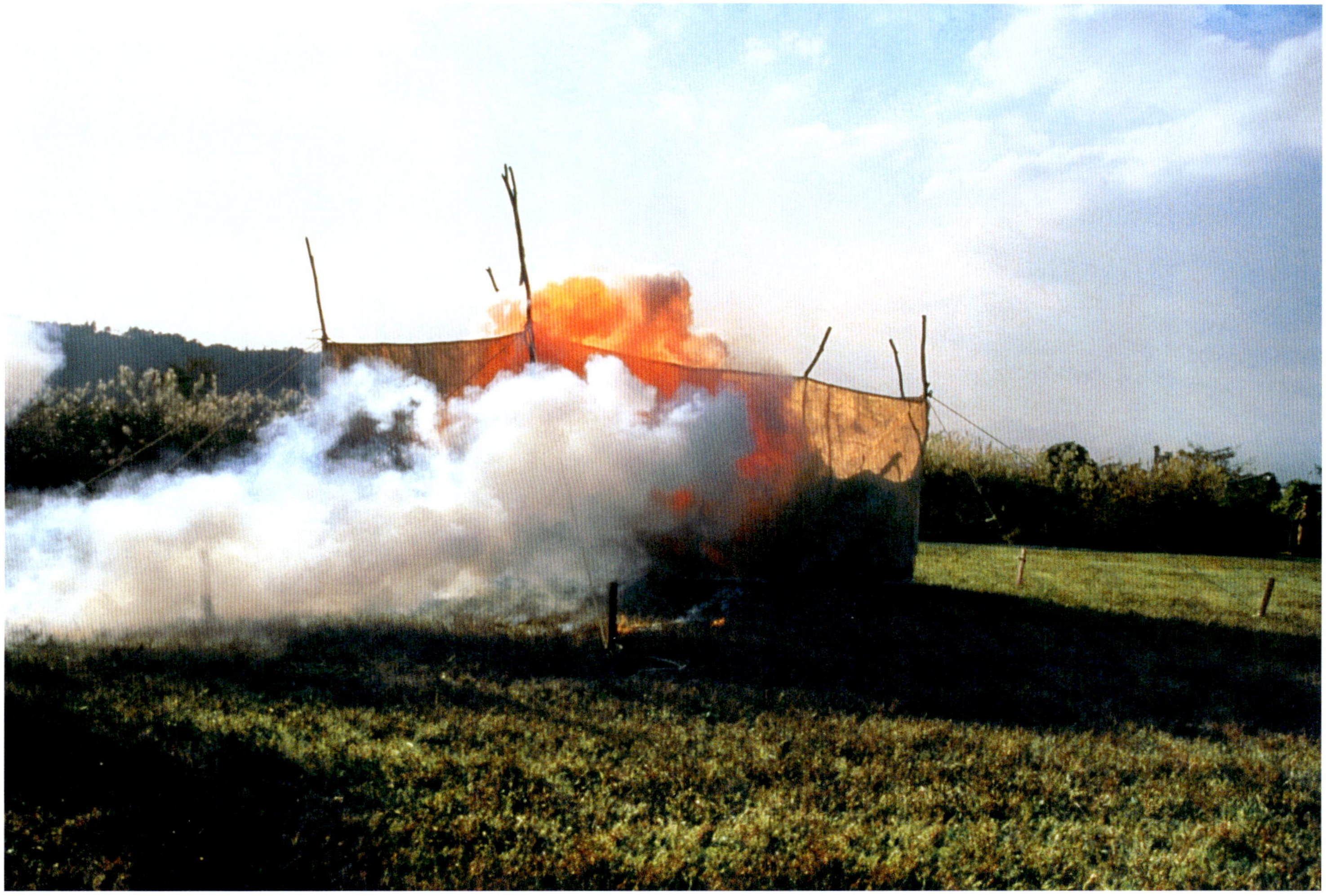

Figure 11. Cai Guo-Qiang, *Human Abode: Project for Extraterrestrials No. 1*, 1989. Explosion event realized at Fussa Minami Park and Kumagawa Shrine, Fussa, Tokyo, explosion area (size of yurt): 550 × 450 × 250 cm. Photo by Wataru Kai

## Cosmic Affections

*1*

The cosmos to scientists is, for the most part, the cosmos of astrophysics. To me, there are internal and external cosmoses. From life, *qi*, *feng shui*, the gods, to the sun, moon, and stars; from the ancestral gaze to the cosmic gaze, everything is an attempt at seeking a cosmology in which the internal and external cosmoses are one. I seek insights into connections between the internal and external cosmoses through personal cultivation and even artistic perceptions. From my very first endeavors at "cosmos projects" or painting, I have always actively considered ways to practice concepts of Chinese medicine, acupuncture points, the pulse of *qi*, and *feng shui*. In addition, I have reflected on the methodologies behind the practice of these concepts.

I can sit down with an astrophysicist and chat for a long time, but above all else I like to talk about our affection for the cosmos. Why do humans explore the cosmos? Is it only to discover scientific principles and win the Nobel Prize, or is it out of a curiosity toward our relationship with the cosmos? Do we regard ourselves as a part of the cosmos? Is an exploration of the cosmos really then an exploration of ourselves?

*2*

Since the late 1980s—all the way back in the last century—I have been expanding on the artwork series *Projects for Extraterrestrials* (figure 11). But what are "extraterrestrials" to me? I see them first and foremost as part of the unseen world, which is to say, of course, that I believe in the existence of extraterrestrials. The Earth is like a grain of sand within a vast ocean. The presumptuous claim that humans are the sole lucky survivors in the cosmos is in itself counter to science and injurious to generations of mythology, an area where I believe art has plenty to accomplish.

I also treat extraterrestrials as a source of inspiration and a partner in dialogue as I go about making art in this boundless universe. In the 1990s, while I was based in Japan, I created a work to "extend" the Great Wall of China from its endpoint.[2] Very few people were there to witness the work, and when asked about this, I always said that it was meant to be seen by the extraterrestrials observing human activity from distant planets. In my art, I have always tried to look for themes that even extraterrestrials can understand. I believed, even back then, that dialogues with extraterrestrials were more important than dialogues with different cultures. If I can interact with extraterrestrials, then interacting with different human cultures would be child's play. So even then, I was not particularly interested in the dichotomy between Eastern and Western cultures.

Then I thought, one day we humans will depart the Earth and become extraterrestrials ourselves. When we explore the cosmos, we are in fact taking steps toward turning ourselves into extraterrestrials; we begin to acquire "their" spirit. When we

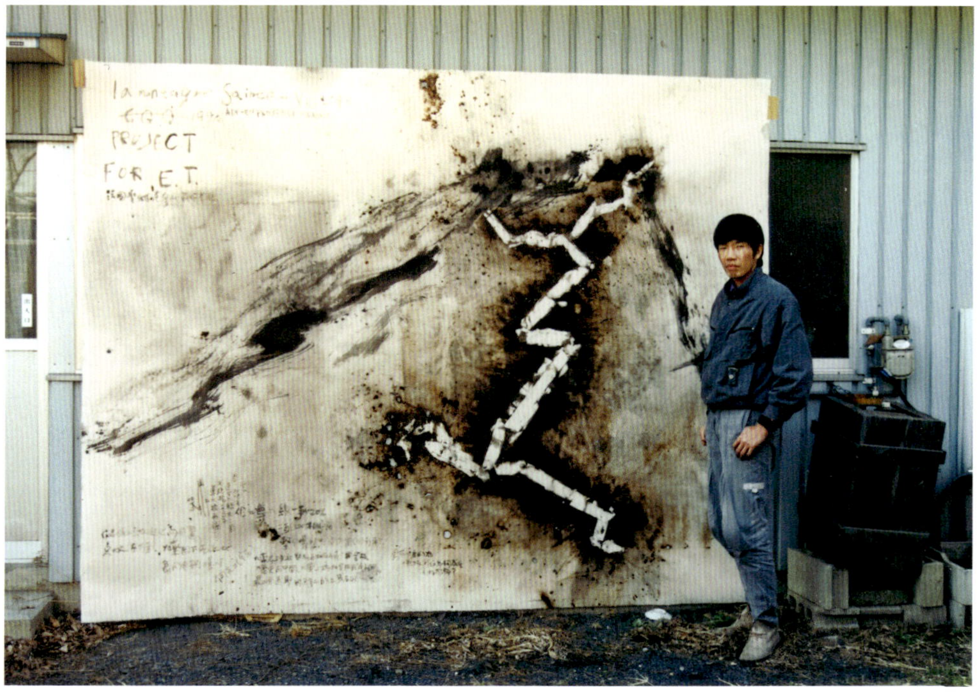


Figure 12. Cai Guo-Qiang in front of *Ascending Dragon: Project for Extraterrestrials No. 2* (no. 6.1) in Japan in 1989. Photo by Akihiko Takami

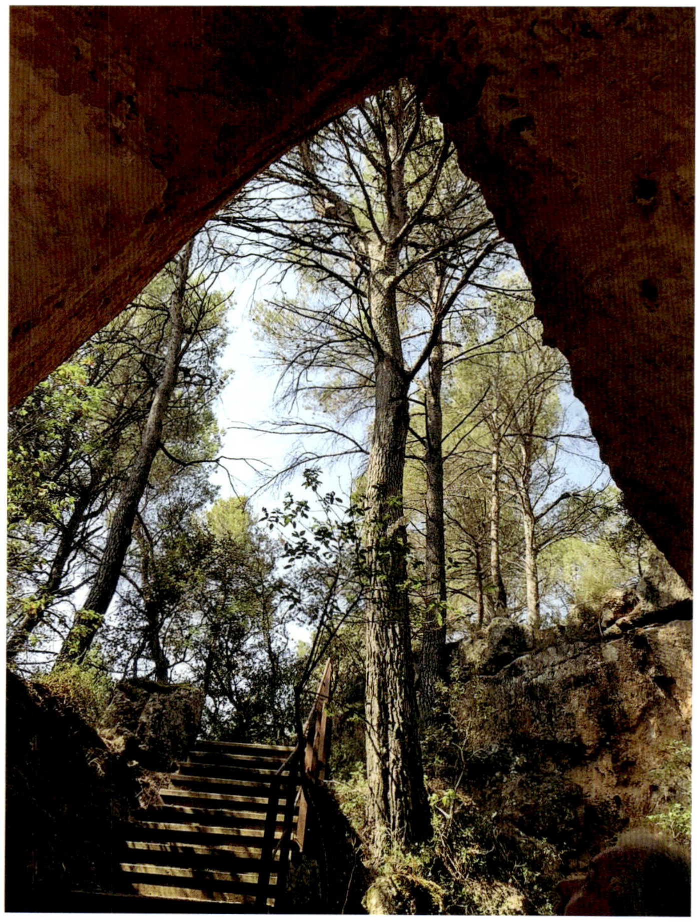

Figure 13. The Carrières de Bibémus, which influenced Cézanne's Cubist painting style, in Aix-en-Provence, France in 2019. Photo by Cai Guo-Qiang

become extraterrestrials on the Earth, we develop the feelings of "a stranger in a strange land," and such strangers learn to cherish their native land, to enjoy the heartache and tender feelings of turning into an extraterrestrial ...

## Climbing Mont Sainte-Victoire

*I*

My feelings toward Paul Cézanne are very complex. I have documented quite a few stories about my painting, but surprisingly have never written about him. Cézanne and his hometown, Aix-en-Provence, truly have this magical force that can align and connect my roots with my understanding of the world.

In 1989, I made a gunpowder drawing in Japan titled *Ascending Dragon: Project for Extraterrestrials No. 2* for the explosion project I meant to realize on Mont Sainte-Victoire. I would use a bolt of lightning to have a dialogue with Cézanne as well as with his hometown and his cosmos. The attempt to realize *Ascending Dragon* would be my first time traveling outside of Asia, and the drawing for *Ascending Dragon* would be my first work dedicated to Western art history (figure 12).

I returned to Mont Sainte-Victoire thirty years later, no longer insistent on creating the "lightning" along its slopes. Rather, like that bolt of lightning, I traveled from the foot of the mountain to its apex. Walking in Cézanne's footsteps along the mountain path, I recalled how I once longed to send a lightning bolt soaring up this mountain that symbolizes Western civilization, crying at the top of my lungs, *The dragon has arrived!* This kind of dialogue with Cézanne holds no humility; it is flamboyant posturing. And yet, back then I had a clear idea about what I wanted to achieve. Now, things are more obscure ...

At the top of the mountain, I asked Bruno Ely, the director of the Musée Granet, about Cézanne's own perceptions. Which of these Chinese sayings best captured how he felt: "the higher you

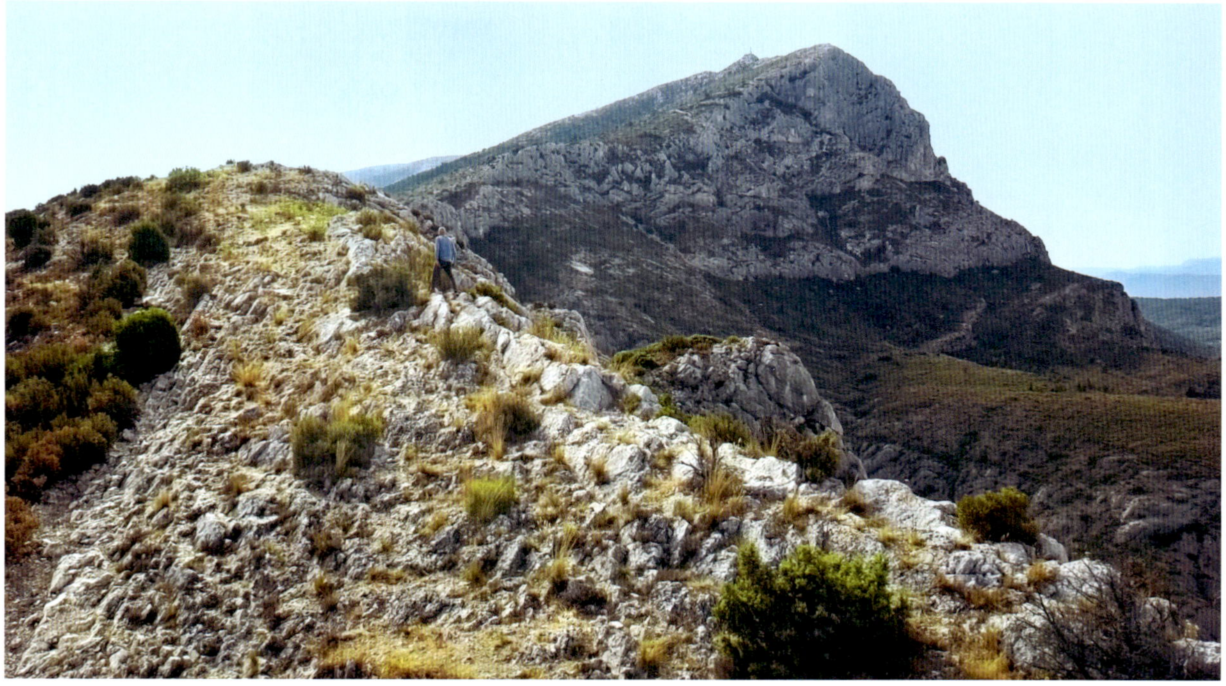

Figure 14. Cai Guo-Qiang on Mont Sainte-Victoire in Aix-en-Provence, France in 2019. Photo by 33 Studio

climb, the more unbearable the cold," or "from the utmost peak, the mountain range looks small," or "there are mountains beyond these mountains, wider skies beyond these skies"? This scholarly authority on Cézanne said, "All of the above." Cézanne was preceded by Manet, Monet, Pissarro. He used to paint *en plein air* together with Pissarro, learning how to select and frame scenes. He failed again and again to qualify for the government-sponsored Salon exhibition. He craved recognition, and perhaps even by the end of his life was unaware that he had in fact transcended those he revered to open an entirely new horizon in art. Of course, he was simultaneously aware that his work was dealing with something huge, something close to God.

A real artist retains both self-confidence and self-deprecation at the same time. Vacillation and anxiety ceaselessly erode and polish the unyielding soul and the art it creates.

*2*

We talk about Cézanne; Cézanne talked about Poussin. In Cézanne's view, the Impressionists' alterations of light and color had become too much of a florid jumble, and he longed to express the essence of forms the way Poussin did over two hundred years earlier. Fortunately, Aix-en-Provence had both the pyramid-like Mont Sainte-Victoire and a quarry at the foot of the mountain with manmade, geometric incisions (figure 13). Director Ely said, "Cézanne found the forms and the colors that correspond to his pursuit of art in his hometown." To be able to converse with the cosmos and art history from the comfort of one's hometown—that is the ultimate, ultimate happiness.

The only time that Cézanne traveled abroad was to visit the Alps in Switzerland, but he was not very inspired to paint. He never ventured farther east. There are no records of him showing any interest in China, but the three-dimensionality of his signature composition framing was akin to the "cavalier perspective" technique in classical Chinese painting, which prioritizes the essence of things without being disturbed by the flow of light and shadow. His decision to leave much of the canvas blank was also similar to the aesthetic pursuit of Eastern painting. When talking about Cézanne, most people bring up his influence on modernism, but when examining his notions of space and time from an Eastern perspective, I find that he had transcended the East-West dichotomy. The significance of discussing Cézanne is to show that anybody, from any corner of the world, can transcend the limitations of their own culture to find resonance and commonalities with other cultures.

Every artist compiles his own set of art history, one that comprises his ideal art and the artists he admires. I always say that I admire El Greco's work for "using the seen to express the unseen," but he probably never said anything of the kind. It is likewise possible that parts of Cézanne's cosmology were invented and added on to by those of us who study his work. I love El Greco, who lived five hundred years before me; Cézanne, too, loved El Greco, who lived three hundred years before him. We both see what we regard as the essence of art in "the Greek." This is the artistic essence that I wish to achieve, which may be completely different from what another artist strives for.

*3*

When I talk about Cézanne, I am ultimately talking about myself, about my awe for how much he has influenced the development of art history. A similar cosmology, or rather, something that can be described as a profoundly idealistic aesthetic, has always existed in China. Why, then, has Chinese art from the past century been in such a state of inertia? These problems are also my problems. Walking Cézanne's path is also walking my own path.

Searching for art history and journeying through art history are both acts of searching for the self. Meeting formidable people around the world allows me to distinguish my own weight,

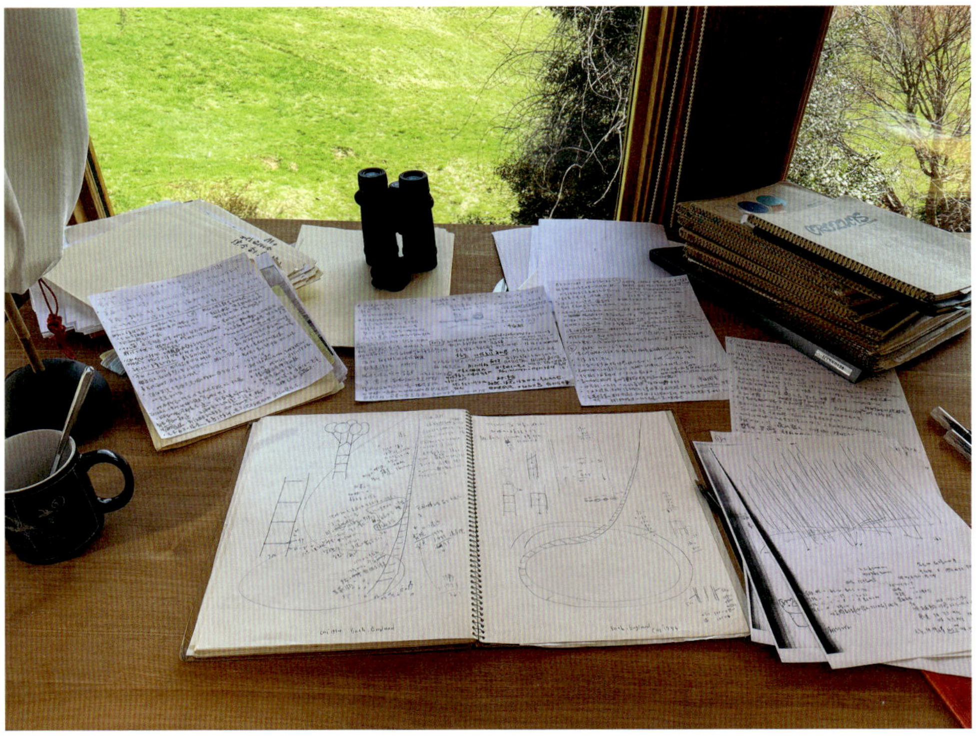

Figure 15. Cai Guo-Qiang's sketchbooks from the 1980s and 1990s at his New Jersey home in 2020. Photo by Cai Guo-Qiang

helping me to be more amenable and carefree as a person living life, and more ruthless and liberated as an artist making art.

The mountain ridge up Sainte-Victoire was not an easy hike (figure 14). With the Christian cross at the mountaintop ahead of me and steep cliffs on either side, I almost forgot whether this was Cézanne's hometown or a symbol of the West in between my heavy breaths. This is the type of aerobic exercise that cultivates a vital, expansive *qi*; to cultivate such *qi*, one must find high peaks and command oneself to surmount them.

## An Isolated *Voyage Through the Middle Ages*

Compared to other periods of art history, the extensive Middle Ages are especially difficult to summarize in a few broad strokes. This made it difficult for me to begin the project, but the mystique of the period also enticed me to find new and different ways to launch a dialogue.

The relationship that people had with God and the cosmos in the Middle Ages, as well as the relationship that artists had with their work, made me think about how I could represent the amorphous world and its spirituality. I also wanted to experience this period when human desire skidded to a crashing halt in history, and the self-exile that took place on both a spiritual plane and in daily life. Therefore, under the guidance of The Metropolitan Museum of Art's experts, I proposed the ambitious project of a *Voyage Through the Middle Ages* that would span ten countries and nearly twenty places, including Mount Athos in Greece, Mount Sinai in Egypt, Nicosia in Cyprus, and the Judaean Desert in Israel. I intended to visit the important historic sites that continue to preserve the lifestyle and monastic atmosphere of the Middle Ages, places that feel distanced from the rest of the world.

The original plan was to present the results of my dialogue with Cézanne at the end of this year at the Grand Palais in Paris. But the unexpected fire at Notre-Dame de Paris, an iconic work of medieval Gothic architecture, postponed the exhibition by several years. Soon after, the outbreak of COVID-19 put a pause on all plans for the *Voyage Through the Middle Ages*. In the midst of my research about the Black Death, its context, and the art of catastrophe, the past tense turned into the present tense … whether willingly or not, we must grow up with history.

As the pandemic grew increasingly severe around the globe and I entered into self-isolation, I made use of this time lag to also isolate from my usual busy self and current events in the art world. Instead, I revisited a dozen or so of the sketchbooks that I filled in the 1980s–90s, returning to my early resolutions in art (figure 15). I recorded the following notes while reading my "original intent notebooks." In a way, this odyssey that I undertook in isolation feels even more magical.

## Notes on My Notes

How difficult it is to again become an average person of the cosmos, to search for one's roots!

*One*

On March 23, I dug up my sketchbooks from the 1980s and the 1990s and began revisiting my original aspirations contained within them, engaging in dialogue with a version of myself from thirty years ago. How did I think about things and see things back then? What did I read and think about every day? What were the cultural structures and the pillars that formed my concepts?

At the time, I thought a lot about the human and global problems of the 20th century, including material prosperity, the degradation of human nature, environmental destruction, and the future of the cosmos. Back in the late 80s, I was already roaming the cosmos, thinking of myself as an extraterrestrial. There are still many connections between these ideas and the problems of today.

Looking back, my ideas were not all easy to accept. Some were subjective, imperious: I believed in superpowers and the supernatural and spiritual things. I believed that Eastern thought, including its methodologies of *feng shui*, *qi*, and Chinese medicine, could propel the new era of the 21st century. I felt that modern art didn't have much to it, and I was instead fascinated by the deeper, broader unknowables in life and the cosmos. I was a single-minded heretic, an argumentative and angry youth unafraid of other people's opinions. Perhaps it's impossible to go back?

Some of the ideas in my sketches were later realized and some were not. I saw that I was always copying down one quote from Laozi's *Daode Jing* (*Tao Te Ching*): "First a nebulous something was formed, born before heaven and earth." I was always arranging the sequence of my *Projects for Extraterrestrials* series, and every once in a while would copy down my project concept for *Humanity's Epitaph*.

I had odysseys in the cosmos every day back then, pondering what "language" I should use to converse with extraterrestrials. I wasn't thinking about dialogues between different cultures, because if I could communicate with extraterrestrials, I would naturally be able to converse with fellow humans.

My conceptual pillars included past and present cosmology and sorcery, the *Daode Jing*, *feng shui*, and theories in Chinese medicine. I treated the Earth as a body and sought its acupuncture points. I treated the Earth as a human life to be healed. Human acupuncture points were originally named after aspects of nature in any case.

I was fascinated with natural understandings of Earth, humankind, life, extraterrestrials, and outer space from primeval times onward. While there was plenty of what the Chinese Communist Party would have called "feudalist superstitious garbage," I still believed that science and technology cannot replace the original studies and memories of early humans on the cosmos and on life ...

*Two*

April 9: Finished reading my dozen or so sketchbooks. They contained my pursuit of drive, talent, openness, and uprightness along the way—riding on the kite of my hometown, steering the spacecraft of human childhood across romantic horizons.

I am surprised to find no record of my thoughts on or process of moving from Japan to the United States. I could only tell from the sketches for various projects that I was already in New York. I had left the place where I had put down my roots and forayed into a world then unknown to me, but from a cosmic perspective, did it look like I had simply moved houses in the same village?

At the same time, I can also see how I grew less and less metaphysical over time, redirecting my attention to sociopolitical realities. The problems of the Western world have become my own problems. In retrospect, I understand that while I was in Japan, the problems of the Eastern world were more or less my problems, too.

Starting from 1996, I became more improvisational and site-specific. This included an implementation of Eastern methodologies as part of a battle waged against the globalized art world system, which used theoretical thought as the tools of resistance. My "fiery years from strategizing tactics to charging on horseback" continued until 1997, after which the pages of the notebook were left blank.

That said, the essence, energy, and spirit from the depths of Eastern culture—"the only doctrine is the lack of doctrine," "to be free and at one's ease, to be natural and of one's self"—still continue to guide my imagination as it soars through the skies to plant seeds that blossom in different cultures across the Earth.

It's time. My original aspirations and true aspirations, my frameworks and fearlessness, my identity as a member of the cosmos, the quintessence of my work and me as an artist, my coexistence with that other unseen world ... am I still capable of embracing all these things? The sketchbooks have been read and shut; the squall surges; the deluge falls ...

June 2020
At home in New Jersey, U.S.

### Notes

1. These were quoted from the works of two Tang-dynasty poets: Du Fu, "500-Character Poem: A Reflection on the Road from the Capital to Feng Xian Town"; and Cai Song, "Two Poems Written in the Year of Ji-Hai."

2. *Project to Extend the Great Wall of China by 10,000 Meters: Project for Extraterrestrials No. 10* (1993).

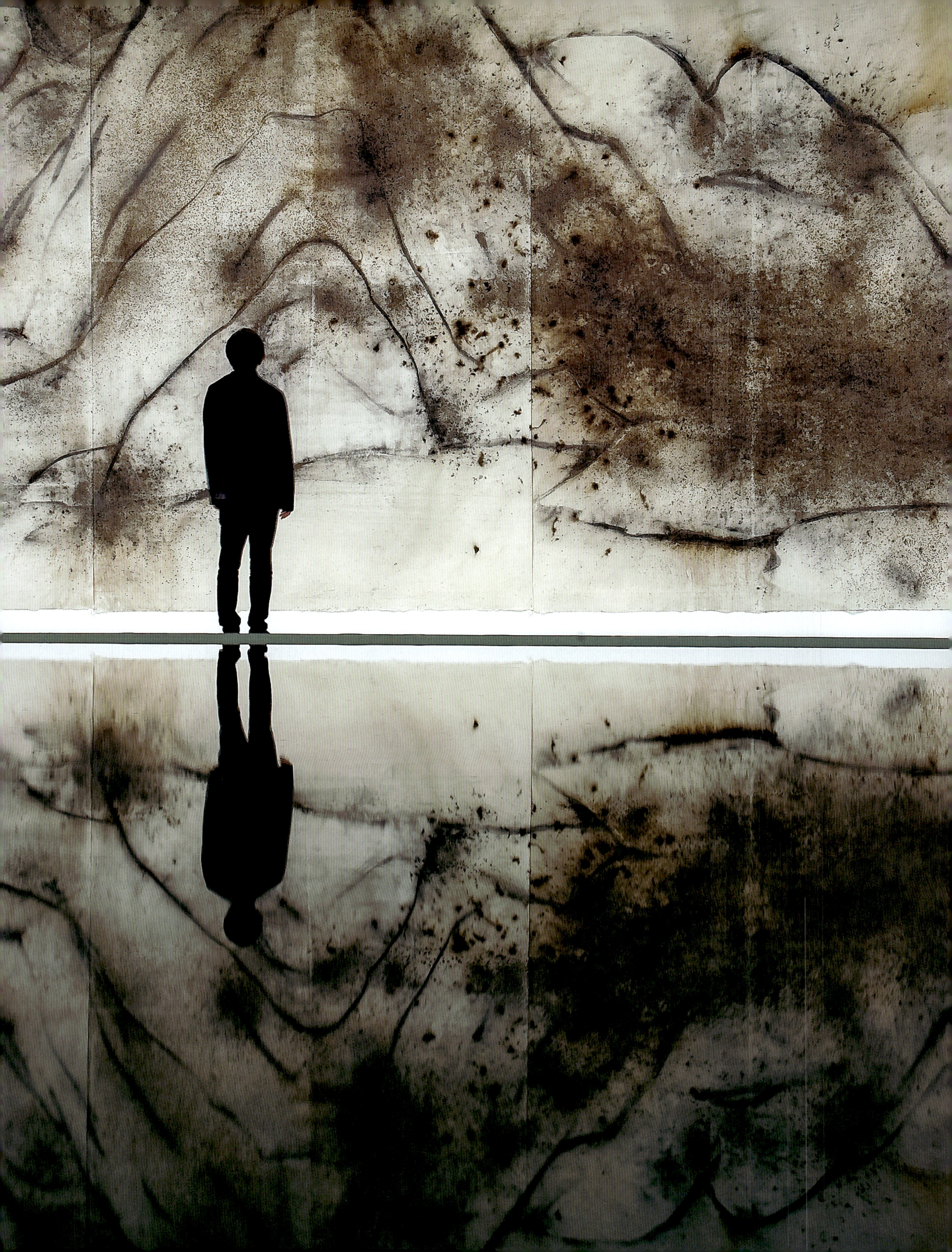

# Becoming Nature Is Poetry Itself

## *Resonances of "Plaza Art" from the Southern Song to Cai Guo-Qiang*

Yu Hui

### 1. A Historical Approach

The gunpowder art and explosion events of Cai Guo-Qiang, classified as contemporary Chinese art, are rooted in two aspects of history: the history of explosion and that of the paintbrush.

As for explosions, their origins can be traced back to the "explosion festivals," held around Chinese New Year, during the periods before the Qin dynasty (221–206 BCE). Originally a religious practice, these festivals consisted of burning bamboo poles in order to venerate the gods and drive out evil spirits. "Explosion festivals" were the third of the "Nine Festivals" recorded in the *Rites of Zhou*, but ultimately, these were nothing more than the religious ceremonies of an agricultural civilization searching for divine protection and warding off evil, not yet an art form to be appreciated. In the years following the Six Dynasties period (222–589), however, fireworks began to garner a certain admiration, as Emperor Yang of Sui (569–618) wrote in one of his poems, "A thousand lights illuminate the trees, the fireworks spread their seven-petaled flames."[1]

By the Song Dynasty (960–1279), the custom of celebrating Chinese New Year by setting off firecrackers was even more widespread, as recorded in Wang Anshi's (1021–1086) famous festival poem "New Year's Day," which observed, "Amidst the firecrackers' noise goes the departing year." During the Southern Song dynasty (1127–1279), the city of Lin'an (in present-day Hangzhou, Zhejiang Province) was the first to put on large-scale fireworks displays, which foreshadowed what I would like to call "Plaza Art" in modern times. These spectacular Song-era pyrotechnic displays and lancework designs stunned visiting Jurchen envoys. At each Lantern Festival, from the moment the lanterns were lit until the small hours of the night, high-ranking officials and wealthy merchants would compete to put on the most impressive displays. The poet Xin Qiji (1140–1207) recorded these beautiful sights vividly, writing, "The East Wind adorns a thousand trees with flowering lights / and like a shower of stars, fireworks rain down in the night."[2] While numerous methods of crafting fireworks and firecrackers were passed down and are still in use today, no records of the ancient explosions themselves, regrettably, have survived to the present.

On the other hand, the brush has been both the most beloved and most hated artists' tool. Painting developed alongside the full course of human history. At the inception of the human race, the tools by which art was created were yet to be determined. Drawings were created with whatever was available, from sharpened instruments made of stone, wood, or bone, to even bare hands. According to archeological evidence unearthed at the Xiaotun dig site in An'yang, Henan Province, brushes appeared in China at least three thousand years ago. With tips made from bound animal fur, the brushes discovered there are a specialized kind: their tubular shape marks the beginning of standardized artists' tools. This new technology would continue to improve and become ever finer, a physical manifestation of the refinement of brush techniques. By the Tang dynasty (618–907), painters developed signature brush techniques—ranging from the meticulously detailed and heavily colored technique of *gongbi* of Zhang Xuan (713–755) and Zhou Fang (c. 730–800) to the soaring, whirlwind ink washes of Wu Daozi (680–c. 760). Whether their strokes were bold or restrained, each of them achieved in their art a master's level of freedom and spontaneity.

By the latter half of the Tang dynasty, however, artists who sought to express their romantic desires began to feel the limitations the brush imposed on expressing their innermost

Figure 1. Cai Guo-Qiang, *Unmanned Nature: Project for the Hiroshima City Museum of Contemporary Art* (detail of figure 12), 2008. Photo by Seiji Toyonaga, courtesy Hiroshima City Museum of Contemporary Art

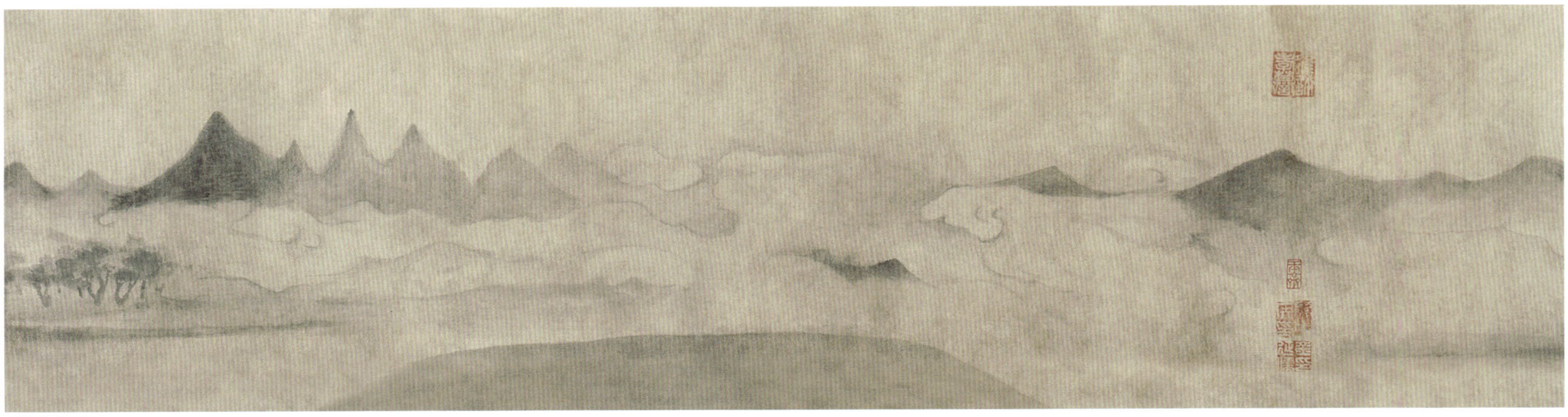

Figure 2. Mi Youren, *Rare Views of Xiao Xiang* (detail), 1135. Ink on paper, 19.8 × 289 cm. Collection of the Palace Museum, Beijing

feelings. Take for example, late-Tang painter Wang Mo (aka Wang Qia), who "studied under Xiang Rong, and was a crazed, mad drunkard who painted scenes of forests, mountains, and waters. Despite falling short of true excellence, he was still popular among the common people. After becoming drunk, he dipped his hair in ink, pressing it against tautened silk to paint."[3] Prompted by an eruption of passion, Wang Mo would use his own hair in an attempt to achieve new effects in ink painting. Zhang Zao, who specialized in similar *shanshui* (landscape) painting, thought through his actions a little more reasonably and penned the book *Huijing*, or *The Realm of Painting*. Today, only a single sentence from the book survives, though that alone has been enough to immortalize him in history: "Outside the self, make Nature one's teacher; inside the self, obtain the source of one's heart."[4] That is, through studying the foundations of the natural world, man can achieve a deep unity with nature, getting at the interconnected spiritual essence which underpins them both. Following this artistic philosophy, he painted "only with a blunt brush, hands running over tough, raw silk."[5]

The rise of literati painting in the Northern Song (960–1127) and its emphasis on a united brush technique for painting and calligraphy tied artists ever more firmly to their brushes. They strove to substitute color for ink: poet and artist Su Shi (1037–1101) went so far as to paint bamboo with cinnabar. His goal was to capture the bamboo's truest essence, leading the audience to no longer perceive the cinnabar's vermillion color. The depiction of *Cloudy Mountains* by Mi Fu (1051–1107) and by his son Mi Youren (1074–1151) reveals hazy scenes of the Xiang River, south of the Yangtze (figure 2). Vivid and lifelike, the paintings bring the viewer on a mental journey among the swelling mists, even making them forget that the landscape before them first originated from an artist's brush. Nevertheless, at the end of the Southern Song, the Buddhist monk Fachang (aka Muqi) eschewed his brush entirely, instead adopting shredded sugarcane to extraordinary effect in his daubed paintings of flowers and birds (figure 3).

It was not until the Qing dynasty (1644–1911) that artists truly broke away from the brush, as the maturing techniques of pyrography and finger painting emerged (figure 4), bringing with them new styles of art, each with their own unique effects. According to the *Da Qing Guangxu xin faling*, or the new decrees issued by the Great Qing Emperor Guangxu (1871–1908), official rewards were offered for pyrographic art: "That which each Arts and Crafts Bureau manufactures, such as ... Jiangsu pyrography, etc., are all their artisans' fine, handmade works. Presently, as advancements [in industry] are urgently sought after, rewards should be offered as appropriate."[6] The Qing painter Gao Qipei (1660–1734) was capable of finger painting in any genre (figure 5), "possessing outstanding natural talents, effortlessly creating in

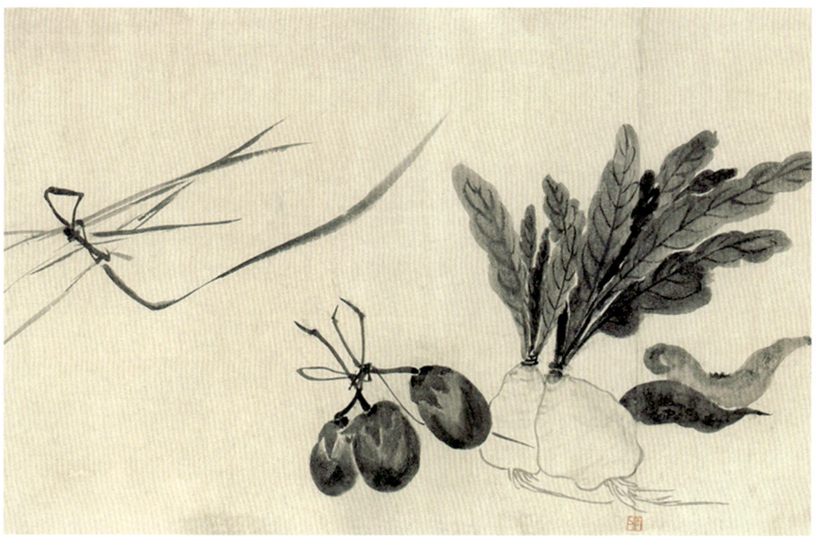

Figure 3. Fachang, *Fruit, Birds, and Fish* (detail), Song dynasty (960–1279). Ink on paper, 47.3 × 814.1 cm. Collection of the Palace Museum, Beijing

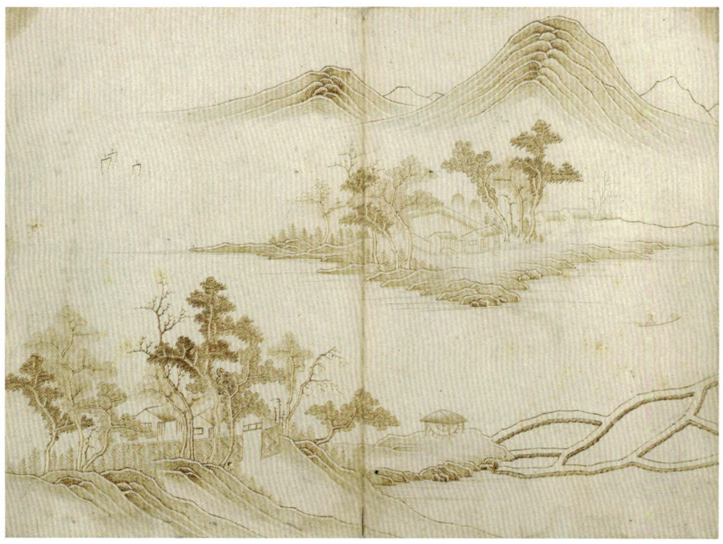

Figure 4. Wu Li, *Album of Hot Stylus Landscapes*, Qing dynasty (1644–1911). Hot stylus on paper, one of twelve leaves, 25.4 × 34 cm. Collection of the British Museum, London

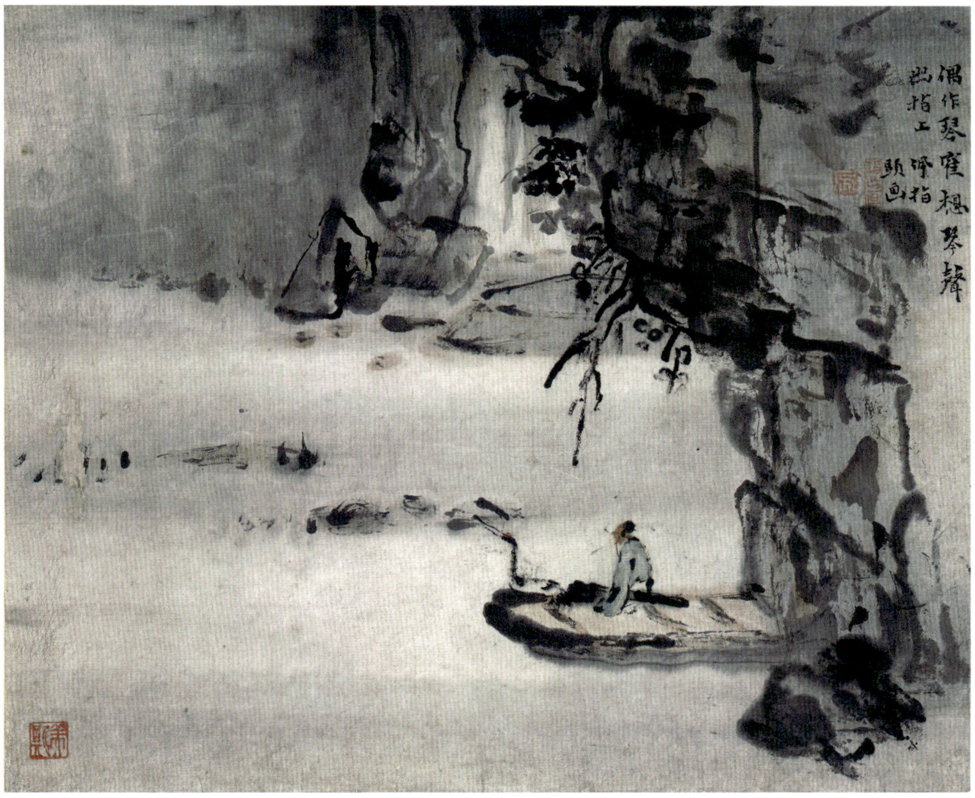

Figure 5. Gao Qipei, *Five Pines*, Qing dynasty (1644–1911). Ink on silk. 118.3 × 58.2 cm. Collection of the Palace Museum, Beijing

his works a unique mood and distinctive appeal, earning him respect from all four corners of the earth. Since people put a heavier emphasis on his finger paintings, and since his advancing age made it more convenient for him to paint with his fingers, in the end he never again picked up his brush, and thus his surviving [brush] works are few."[7]

But because finger painting—and pyrography even more so—aimed only to emulate the strokes and style of traditional brush painting, their development failed to make a dent in artists' preconceived notions of painting. Midway through the Qing dynasty, the styles of "water painting" and "fire painting" also emerged. Water paintings were created by floating ink atop a pool of water and then laying a sheet of paper down over it, whereas fire paintings were burned into a sheet of paper with a lit stick of incense, emulating traditional ink and brush line (*baimiao*) pieces.[8] Perhaps finding these works too gentle for their tastes, Qing poets likened the form of these pieces to mirages of fire: "[E]xplosions blasted from the guarded fortress as we departed the painted battlements, while amid the old temple's bell chimes and soft chanting we arrived at the pagoda. Pacing back and forth, I lingered in the past, unwilling to leave; looking back, I saw the setting sun, blurred behind mist."[9]

Originally, explosions and brushes were two completely unrelated things. Cai Guo-Qiang, by replacing the latter with the former, has brought about a fantastic world unattainable by brushes alone. Art tools have evolved from using arbitrary tools to creating specialized artistic implements, and now in the present we see a new combination of the two. But the arbitrary tools of the contemporary era are a far cry from re-creating the primitive tools of prehistory. Rather, this is the pattern of negation after negation that plays out through the course of human history. This evolution hinges upon whether or not the torrential emotions that an artist wishes to express can find an outlet in his brush; if not, another tool must rise to the occasion. As Mao Heng of the Western Han dynasty (202 BCE–9 CE) wrote in his commentary to the *Classic of Poetry*, known as the *Mao Commentary*, "In the heart, it is the will; when expressed aloud, it is poetry. Passions stir within and find form in words: when words alone are not enough, they escape us in sighs; when sighs alone are not enough, they take shape in song; and when songs alone are not enough, unconsciously our hands dance and our feet tap them out."[10]

Painting is like this as well. The evolution of tools and mediums throughout art history also follows this natural law, one that will not expire, even as art evolves into the future. Just as Laozi wrote to open the *Daode Jing*, "The Dao that can be taught is not the constant Dao; the name that can be named is not the constant name."

## 2. Forged in Reality

In the second half of the 20th century, some Chinese artists distanced themselves from the brush, seeking out new techniques of creating art. One after another, they found success, from the finger paintings of Pan Tianshou (1897–1971) in the 1950s and 60s, to the contemporary colored ink paintings of Liu Guosong (b. 1932) in the 1970s and 80s. In the Western art world, a few artistic schools attempted the same thing, the American artist Jackson Pollock's midcentury action paintings being one such example. But by the turn of this century, this tool transformation was no longer enough for some creators' artistic language to take shape. Thus, building upon the foundation of the last century, they turned their attention to transforming the mediums of their art instead, leading a practical revolution in the conceptualization of art. Breaking away from the brush was simply a superficial phenomenon. The underlying change was in the newfound understanding and exploration of the notion of art itself. As Cai Guo-Qiang said, "The significance of gunpowder is not just that it allows me to break free from the gravity and inertia

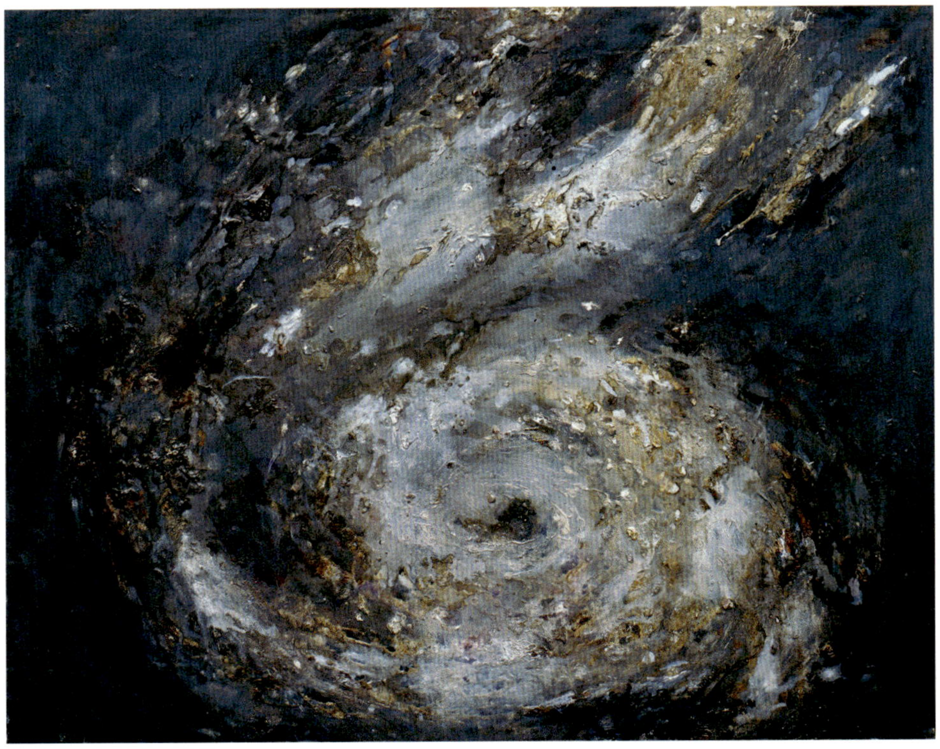

Figure 6. Cai Guo-Qiang, *Typhoon*, 1985. Oil on canvas, 78 × 100 cm

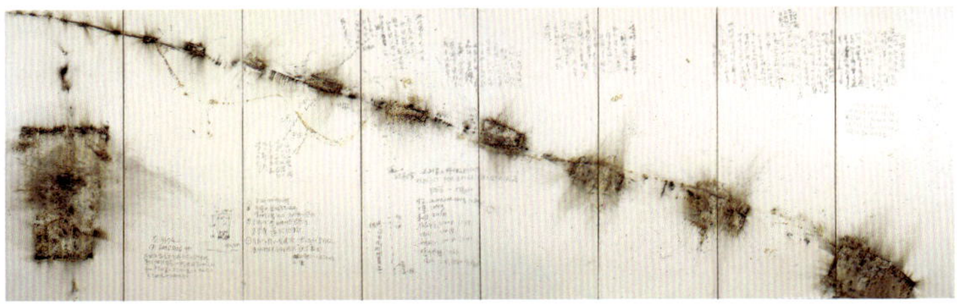

Figure 7. Cai Guo-Qiang, *Bigfoot's Footprints: Project for Extraterrestrials No. 6*, 1990. Gunpowder and ink on paper, mounted on wood as eight-panel folding screen, 200 × 680 cm. Photo by André Morin, courtesy Cartier Foundation for Contemporary Art

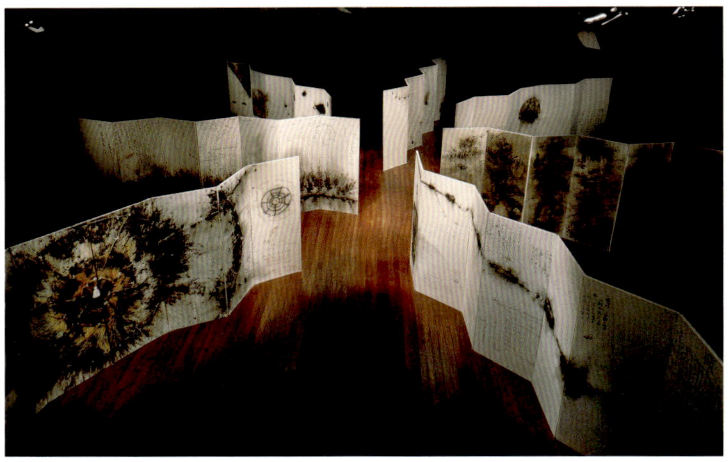

Figure 8. Cai Guo-Qiang, *Primeval Fireball: The Project for Projects*, 1991. Installation of 7 gunpowder drawings; gunpowder on paper, mounted on wood as folding screens, installation dimensions variable. Photo (at P3 art and environment, Tokyo, 1991) by Yoshihiro Hagiwara

of conventional aesthetics; it is more about helping me set up an ultimate deployment on the chessboard, encircling me with nature, and creating a situation where man is united with nature. Humans and gunpowder are both part of the natural world, and the process of painting has evolved with both material and human changes, a natural progression that conveys the reality of nature."[11]

In Cai's oil paintings from his younger days, one can almost hear through their leaping brushstrokes the dissatisfied beating of his heart (figure 6). In his youth, he had a strong sense of individuality and the courage to challenge the norm. Similarly, the few European artists he admired, such as El Greco and Cézanne, each possessed a stern exterior that hid an intensely idiosyncratic personality within. Since the 1980s, Cai has gradually completed his dual revolution of tools and mediums through "violent means": the creation of art through the detonation of black gunpowder (occasionally mixed with realgar) (figures 7 and 8). His challenge was to execute the explosion on such supports as canvas in such a way that he could control the scorchmarks left behind on the medium, which resemble the effect of ink and water, and devise a unique artistic language. Likewise, by detonating "color gunpowder" used in daytime fireworks, he creates an effect similar to that of colored ink on canvas (no. 1.7).

Cai says that he is able to control seventy percent of the blast, with the remaining thirty percent left up to chance. In his view, having complete control of the blast's outcome would not, in fact, be a good thing, for there must be an element of the unexpected, wherein lies the work of the gods. Indeed, it is precisely such an uncontrollable aspect to his work that Qi Baishi (1864–1957) pursued in his magic touch of achieving "that which is in-between resemblance and non-resemblance." Every burst point and each blast radius has already been sketched out, rationally computed, and carefully arranged before Cai and his team quietly await that hallowed, explosive boom. At that moment, they say a complete farewell to models, conservatism, and naturalism. Once the smoke clears, the scorchmarks that remain can no longer be criticized for their lack of resemblance to anything in particular; when faced with an object formed by natural processes, viewers become unusually lenient and open-minded. I believe many people will be reminded of passages from Laozi's *Daode Jing* in which conceptions of shape and sound are examined dialectically: "The vast earth has no corners," "The Great Sound has no voice," and "The Great Form has no shape." In the words of Southern Song poet Deng Chun, "Art is the epitome of culture." That "epitome," too, lies in these principles.[12]

The development of painting tools has progressed alongside the development of notions of painting itself. From the past to the present, both in China and beyond, there have been countless examples of changes in artistic conception catalyzing a revolution in artists' tools: and it is that revolution in tools that in turn realizes parallel revolutions in artistic conception. Artists are not slaves to their tools, but rather their masters. Artists, furthermore, are the creators of new tools, materials, and artistic processes. They must control their tools, commanding them to do as they ordain. The revolution of mediums and materials that Cai has undergone only confirms these principles to be true.

I once asked Cai where his brush was. He replied, "My hands are my brush." To inspect whether the explosion of the "gunpowder art" that Cai invented is dispensable, we should simply consider whether the forms and effects achieved by his artistic process can be replicated by traditional materials, such as a brush and ink: they cannot. Behind every explosion lie unique glimpses of hidden landscapes that a brush and ink have no way of conveying: waterfalls over snowy peaks, chimney smoke rising in delicate spirals, ancient cedars below the heavens, mountains of immortals rising from the sea, elegant petals glistening with moisture, and vast rivers winding through grand valleys. Not only the tangible qualities of these works but also the ways they pique their audience's interest are wholly their own, unattainable through the use of conventional brushes and ink (figures 9–11). This is an entirely new world. And yet, simultaneously, it is an ancient one,

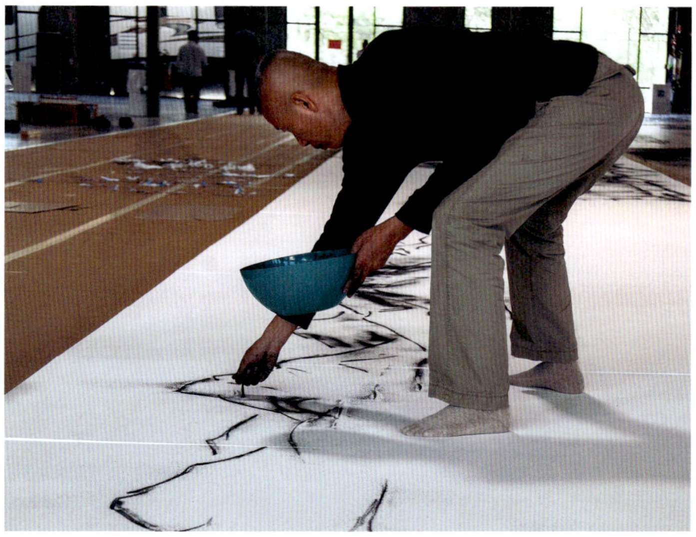

Figure 9. Cai Guo-Qiang laying gunpowder to create *Odyssey* in 2010. Photo by I-Hua Lee

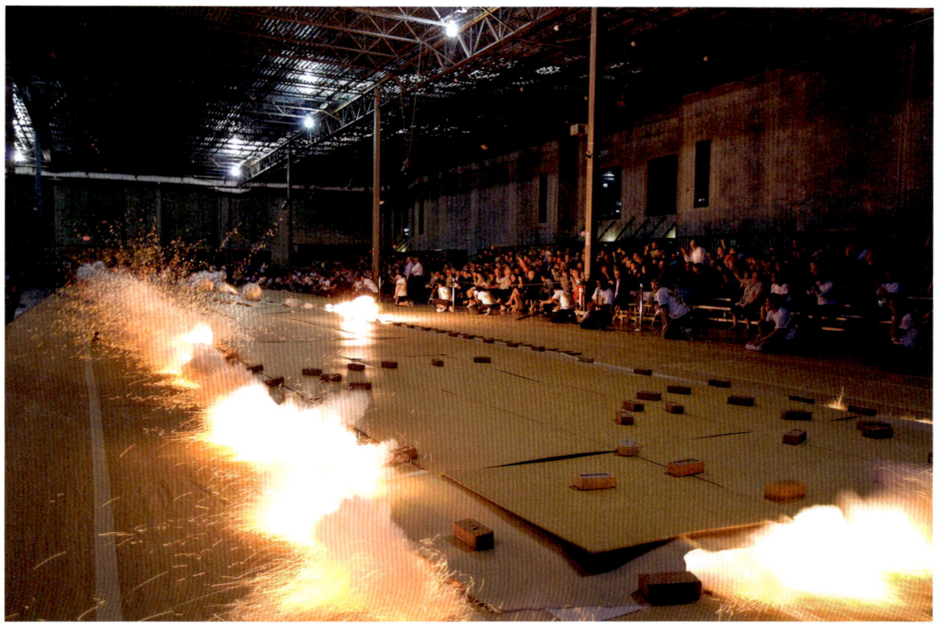

Figure 10. Ignition of *Odyssey* before the public in Houston, Texas in 2010. Photo by I-Hua Lee

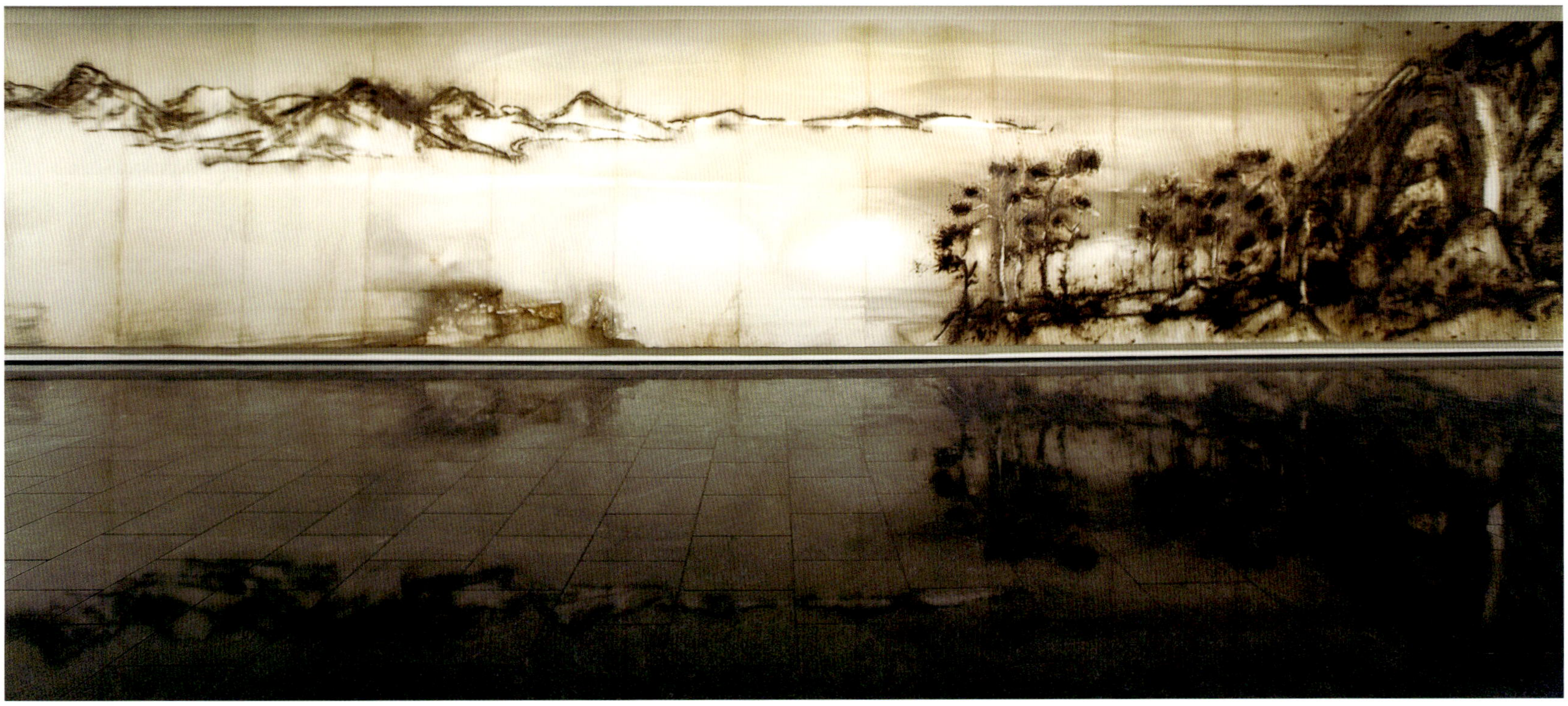

Figure 11. Cai Guo-Qiang, *Odyssey*, 2010. Gunpowder on paper, mounted on wood as forty-two-panel screen, 315 × 4938 cm. Collection of the Museum of Fine Arts, Houston (permanent installation). Photo by I-Hua Lee

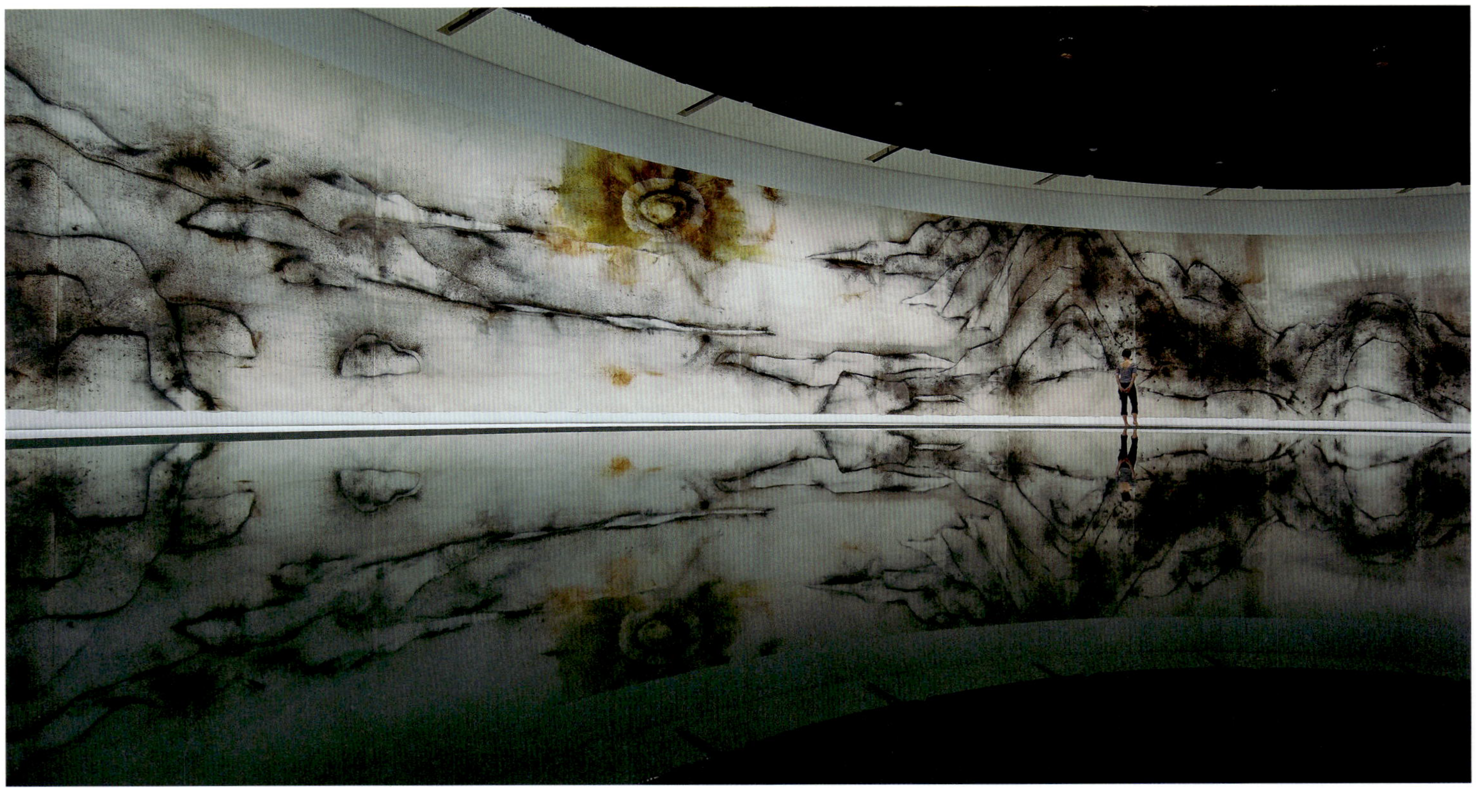

Figure 12. Cai Guo-Qiang, *Unmanned Nature: Project for the Hiroshima City Museum of Contemporary Art*, 2008. Gunpowder on paper and water pond, painting: 400 × 4500 cm. Photo by Seiji Toyonaga, courtesy Hiroshima City Museum of Contemporary Art

as if through Cai's work one could enter the profound ruminations of Laozi's *Daode Jing* once more: "Emptiness should be brought to its utmost degree, and stillness guarded with unwearying vigor. All things alike go through their own processes of activity, before we observe them returning to their original state."[13] What is revealed is a heart of veneration toward the natural world. By being formed, forged, and refined through the accomplishment of "epitomizing emptiness and guarding stillness," a single explosion can last thirty years.

This reaffirms a fundamental doctrine of art: when all is said and done, to create art is to create a certain artistic style and language. This requires the support of various tools in order to succeed, and once a certain tool becomes a pair of shackles, restraining artistic expression, then one ought to seek a new tool in its place. If this new tool fails to break through old conceptions of art, then it has fallen short of achieving true reformation.

## 3. Engaging with the West

Although Cai Guo-Qiang learned in his early years from the styles of Soviet sketches and modern Western oil paintings, the depths of his soul had always been saturated with traditional Chinese thought. From Laozi's natural philosophy to Confucius's Doctrine of the Mean, each of these classical influences stressed the balance between man and the objective world. The feelings evoked by Cai's work simultaneously encompass two diametrically opposed aesthetic results, and his work itself has a firm grasp on the equilibrium point of opposing extremes. That is, they are hot but not scorching, cold but not freezing, firm but not stiff, yielding but not weak, lively but not chaotic. And it can thus be said that within Cai's work lies the fundamental consciousness of China and its traditional philosophical thought. He possesses both a firm theoretical foundation and a unique understanding and appreciation of the arts. Because of this, he has a powerful voice, one that is more than sufficient to engage with the distant world of Western art.

In 2009, Cai Guo-Qiang followed in El Greco's footsteps, embarking on a trip to destinations such as Venice, Madrid, and Toledo. In September 2017, he began his *Individual's Journey Through Western Art History*. In his own words: "Using my techniques to re-manifest the dynamic movement and intangible energy present in Rubens, El Greco, and Goya's paintings, I have become aware of the distinction between viewing paintings and re-creating paintings. To view a painting is to observe your predecessors shadowboxing, whereas re-creating them is to directly exchange blows. Ultimately, it is for the sake of making one's own way in the world."[14]

Held at the Pushkin State Museum of Fine Arts in Moscow, *Cai Guo-Qiang: October* was his first solo exhibition on the *Journey*, engaged with Socialist Realism and avant-garde art. His next exhibition at Madrid's Prado Museum, *The Spirit of Painting. Cai Guo-Qiang at the Prado* engaged with Baroque art and the Spanish Golden Age. At the Uffizi Galleries in Florence, his exhibition *Flora Commedia: Cai Guo-Qiang at the Uffizi* engaged with the Italian Renaissance. At the National Archaeological Museum of Naples and Pompeii Archaeological Park, he engaged with ancient Greek and Roman civilization through *In the Volcano: Cai Guo-Qiang and Pompeii*. For his presentation at the Solomon R. Guggenheim Museum, *Non-Brand* 非品牌, he engaged with modernism. At the Musée Granet in Aix-en-Provence, France, he will engage with Cézanne, and at the New York Metropolitan Museum of Art, with the Middle Ages. Of these exhibitions, many of them included such works of "Plaza Art" as explosion events on a magnificent scale, in pursuit of a spirit that blends heroism and romanticism. Cai takes for his palette and canvas the open sky: his soaring fireworks transform into clouds and mist, mixing spontaneously in the air to form harmonious colors that gradually dissipate into nothingness.

Having seen his exhibitions, I cannot help but call to mind how for centuries, generations of Chinese people, time and time again, have delivered to the nomadic cultures of the West Eastern agricultural civilization's fireworks of peace and flames of enlightenment. Cai has magnified the artistic merit of these ancient elements of Chinese culture, infusing them with the conceptions of contemporary art to enable a dialogue with Western art history: this is what has won the full appreciation of artists and audiences wherever he exhibits. Finally, after achieving international success, Cai returns to where his journey began: Beijing. In the end, the significance of Cai's dialogic journey transcended that of his works themselves, illustrating perfectly how the East and the West can learn from one another through mutual conversation.

## Conclusion: Poetry Itself Is a Return to Nature

"I follow my own laws," reads the most iconic sentence in Shitao's (1642–1707) *Round of Discussions on Painting*. Shitao's "laws" are precisely the same doctrines governing heaven and earth that Laozi emphasized in the *Daode Jing*, writing that "the law of the Way is the self-so," with the heart of Laozi's "self-so" lying in the concept of "non-action." More so than ever before, all civilizations of the world are united in their common reverence for Nature's laws, seeking it out in their art. Once an artist is able to realize that goal, an inexhaustible poeticism is bestowed upon the individual by heaven itself (figures 1 and 12).

Poets of the past often fantasized about being able to control mist and explosions, transforming them into wonderful artistic forms. To pull a shroud of mist into a painting was a sight straight out of a poet's dreams. As Southern Song poet Shi Shaosong wrote, "Amidst the waves, the boats come and go; they ferry the mists and clouds to create art."[15] Ming (1368–1644) poetry also contains an assortment of similar verses, such as Yu Qian's (1398–1457) line: "The pavilion towers above the mists and clouds, truly a waste if not captured on canvas."[16] A similar quote is from Zhang Yanghe: "The vast and endless mists are captured onto canvas; lit by moonlight, the wind hisses through the waterside grasses."[17] The overwhelming majority of artists are satisfied with seeking out their own artistic language with readily available brushes. However, myriads of natural phenomena, such as the misty clouds in the sky and the raging flames of an explosion, when illustrated with a brush, will inevitably leave behind traces of artificial embellishment. Indeed, one can try to make a request of Nature's heavenly craftsmanship, returning to the natural world amidst every explosion, washing clean the pretentious and artificial ornateness of one's art and leaving only that which Nature has made, as the mother of all things: thus a state of "non-action" in the artistic world can be achieved, sublimating one's work to new poetic horizons.

---

*Yu Hui is a researcher and serves as the Director of the Institute of Chinese and Foreign Cultural Exchange at the Palace Museum, after serving as the Head of Traditional Chinese Calligraphy and Painting Department and the Head of the Research Division. He specializes in calligraphy and painting research, appraisal, and authentication, particularly renowned for establishing iconographic textology by leveraging the research methods of iconography, bibliology, and logic. He formed and theorized a unique methodology to authenticate and research ancient paintings that unveils truths of the painting's history. Major publications include* The Painted Dynasty: The Artistic Ruling House of the Song Empire *(2008),* Decoding Zhang Zeduan's "Along the River During the Qingming Festival" *(2015), and* Questions and Answers on Wang Ximeng's "A Thousand Li of Rivers and Mountains" *(2020). In 2009, he received the first China Fine Arts Prize–Theory Criticism Award.*

### Notes

1. Shi Daoxuan 释道宣, 广弘明集 [Extended collection of great brightness], vol. 30, bk. 2 in 四部丛刊 [The four branches of literature collection] (Tang period).

2. Zhou Ji 周济, 词辨 [On lyric poetry], vol. 2 (1878).

3. Zhang Yanyuan 张彦远, 历代名画记 [Notes on past famous paintings], vol. 10, in vol. 1 of 画史丛书 [Art history collection], ed. Yu Anlan 于安澜 (Shanghai: Shanghai People's Fine Arts Publishing House, 1963), 125.

4. Zhang Yanyuan, 121.

5. Zhang Yanyuan, 121.

6. Duan Fang 端方, 大清光绪新法令 [New decrees of the Great Qing Emperor Guangxu] (Shanghai: Commercial Press, 1909).

7. Duan Fang 端方, 壬寅消夏录 [Summer chronicles of the Renyin years], manuscript in 中国基本古籍库 [Database of Chinese Classic Ancient Books] (Beijing: Beijing Erudition Digital Research Center, 2011).

8. Zou Yigui 邹一桂, 小山画谱 [Xiaoshan's painting manual], vol. 2, in 粤雅堂丛书 [Yueyatang collection] (Qing period).

9. Wang Chang 王昶, 春融堂集 [Blockprint from Shunan Publishing House], vol. 4 (1808).

10. Mao Heng 毛亨, 毛诗 [Mao Commentary to the Classic of Poetry], vol. 1, in 四部丛刊 [The four branches of literature collection] (1919–36).

11. Cai Guo-Qiang, "Ramblings About Painting," in *The Spirit of Painting. Cai Guo-Qiang at the Prado* (Madrid: Museo Nacional del Prado, 2017), 70.

12. Deng Chun 邓椿, 画继 [Tradition of painting], vol. 9, in vol. 1 of 画史丛书 [Art history collection], ed. Yu Anlan 于安澜 (Shanghai: Shanghai People's Fine Arts Publishing House, 1963), 96.

13. *Daode Jing*, adapted from the translation of James Legge.

14. Cai Guo-Qiang, 76.

15. 江湖小集 [Small collection of Jianghu], vol. 9, ed. Chen Qi 陈起, in 四库全书 [The four branches of literature], Wenyuange Edition (Qing period).

16. 石仓历代诗选 [Selection of Shicang's poetry from past dynasties], vol. 331, ed. Cao Xuequan 曹学佺, in 四库全书.

17. Wang Zudi 王祖嫡, 师竹堂集 [Bamboo hall master's collection], vol. 6, Ming Tianqi Edition (Ming period).

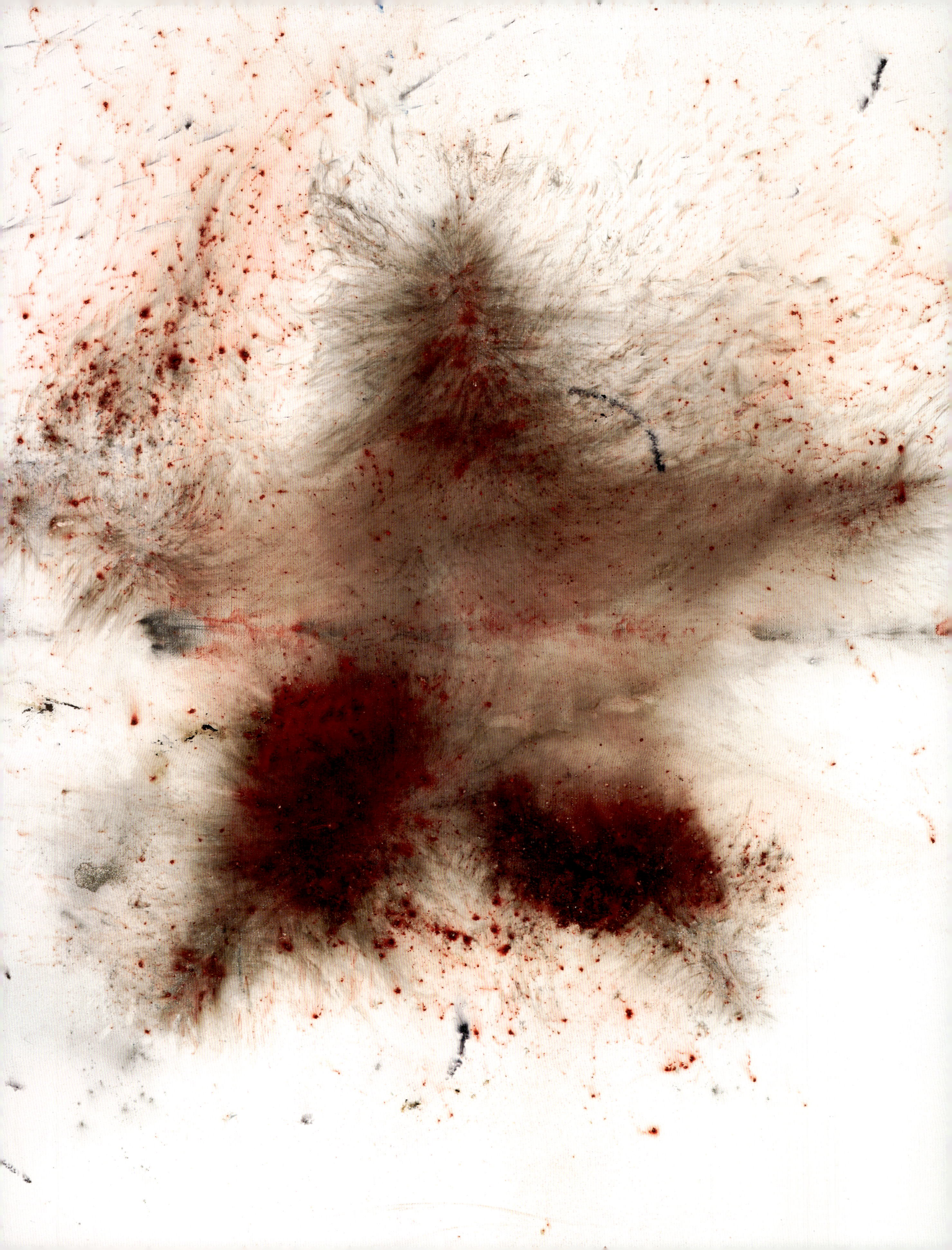

# Undercurrent
## *From Cai Guo-Qiang's* October *Project Onward*

Wang Hui

### The Faded Century of Revolution

In July 1957, shortly before the fortieth anniversary of the October Revolution, Konstantin Mefodievich Maksimov (1913–1993), a professor of painting at Moscow's Surikov Art Institute (presently Surikov Moscow State Academic Art Institute), left his two-year teaching appointment at Beijing's Central Academy of Fine Arts and returned to Moscow. He was forty-four years old that year, unaware that he stood at the starting point of the severance between China and the Soviet Union. That same year, Cai Guo-Qiang was born in Quanzhou, Fujian Province. The two did not intersect. In 1967, the year Cai turned ten and one year after the Cultural Revolution broke out in full force, soldiers from the Liberation Army based in Cai's hometown chiseled an immense portrait of Mao into the rocky surface of a hilly precipice. Fifty years later, in 2017, Cai was invited by the Pushkin State Museum of Fine Arts in Moscow to create a solo exhibition and execute a daytime fireworks event above the Red Square, both to commemorate the centenary of the October Revolution. While the explosion event was never realized, the planning process led him to return to Quanzhou and revisit the Liberation Army's 1967 cliff relief, of which he made a rubbing onto a large sheet of canvas. In Moscow, he inquired after Maksimov's burial place and surviving family, the process of which was featured in the documentary film *October: The Unrealized Century* (prod. 33 Studio, dir. Shanshan Xia) (figures 1 and 2).

In 2017, when the October Revolution had long lost its luster, a sweat-drenched Cai secured a harness around his waist to work on the rubbing of the Mao portrait. Under the scorching sun, he tapped a cotton bundle dipped in red paint against the five-pointed star on Chairman Mao's military cap to intensify the color (figures 3 and 4). Once finished, he hurled the bundle into the

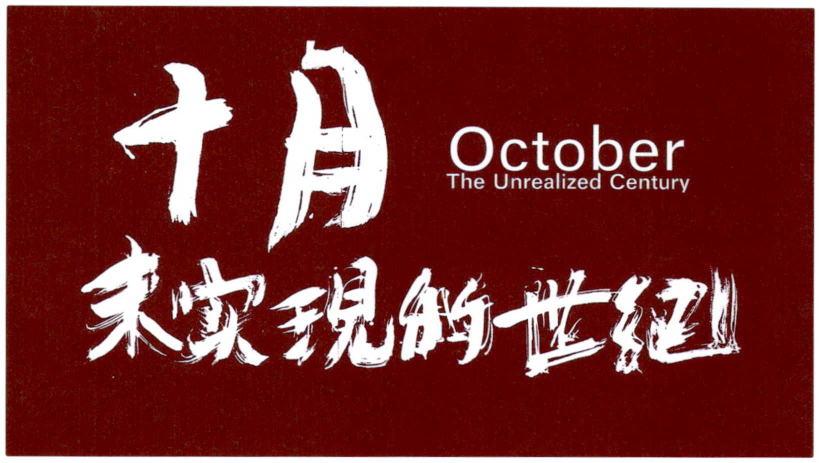


Figure 1. *October: The Unrealized Century*, 2018 (title frame). Documentary film directed by Shanshan Xia

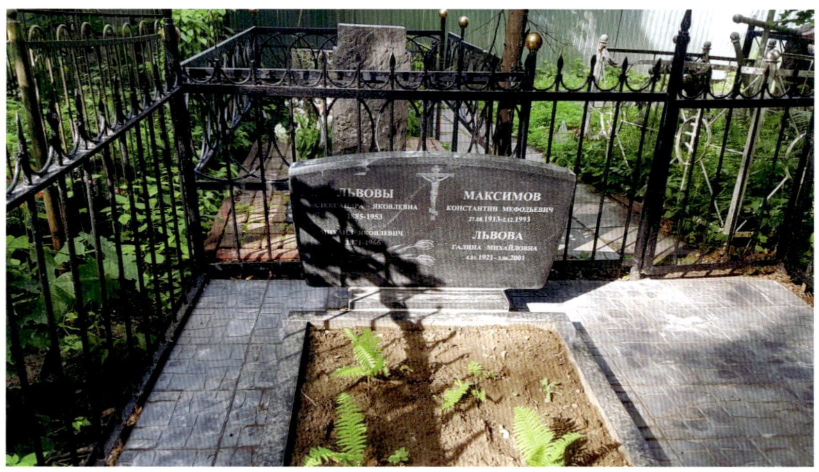


Figure 2. Grave of Konstantin Maksimov restored by Cai Guo-Qiang in 2018. Photo by Alina Selivanova

Detail of *Red Star Over Red Square* (no. 4.12)

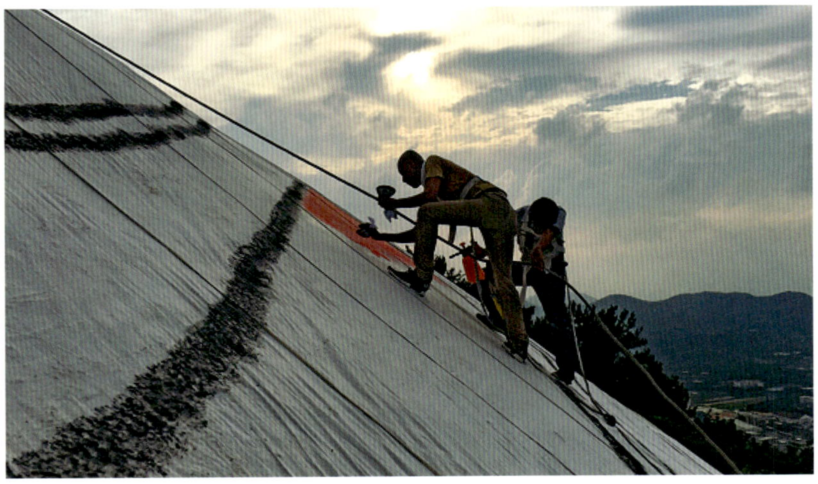

Figure 3. Cai Guo-Qiang on the cliff creating *Mao Rubbing* in Quanzhou in 2017. Photo by 33 Studio

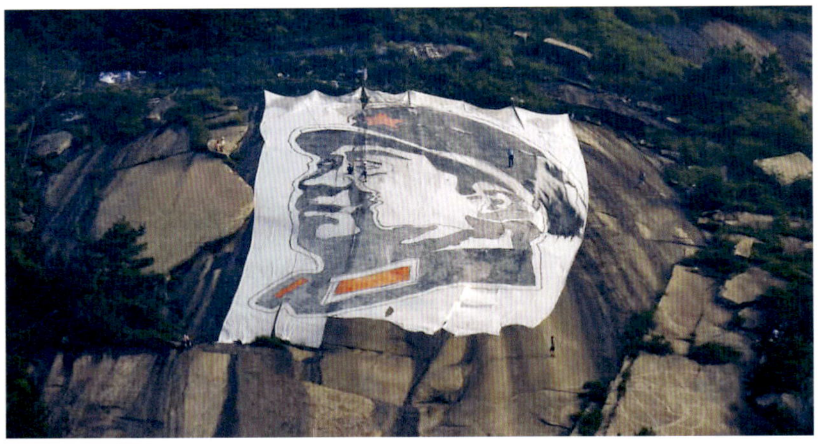

Figure 4. Cai Guo-Qiang, *Mao Rubbing*, 2017. Ink on canvas, approx. 50 × 32 m. Photo courtesy CCTV

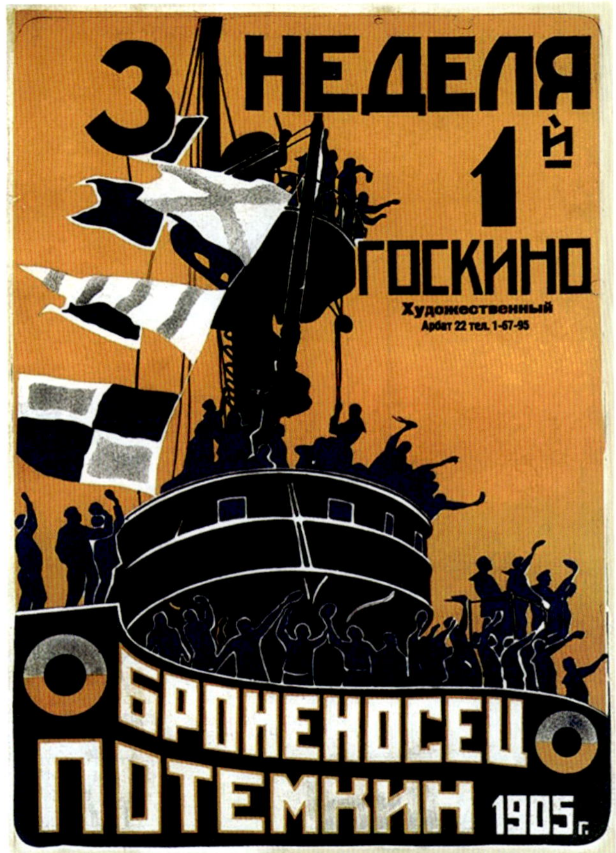


Figure 5. Sergei Eisenstein, *Battleship Potemkin,* 1925 (original Soviet release poster)

distance with all his strength. The cotton drew a red arc across the sunlit horizon as it tumbled down the hillside. Behind him, the reddened star was not particularly conspicuous, yet nevertheless left the viewer deep in thought. Narrating his own history, Cai said that this cliff portrait of Chairman Mao was the first work of "land art" he had ever witnessed. This scene of Cai coloring the cliff reminded me of an experiment conducted by world-renowned director Sergei Eisenstein: *Battleship Potemkin*, which he shot in 1925 to commemorate the twentieth anniversary of the first Russian Revolution (figure 5). Before the premiere, Eisenstein took the black-and-white film and personally hand-painted the white flag of the insurrectionary Potemkin red. In that age of black-and-white silent film, this singular color scene and the montage technique used on the Odessa Steps in this iconic picture left an eternal imprint on cinematic history.[1] Eisenstein used artistic form to directly interpose in the event's formation, expansion, and transformation of meaning. In the world of film, he facilitated a dialectical interaction between art and social event, between art and politics. In this sense, just like the Russian avant-garde, Eisenstein belongs in the ranks of the pioneers who revolutionized the great artistic tradition of the 20th century.

If all had gone according to plan, Cai would have used gunpowder to shoot this red star in a much more conspicuous fashion into the skies above Red Square, using "sky art" as a response to his childhood memory. While no one in the Chinese-speaking world in 1967 would have been familiar with the concept of land art, Cai inserts this work into the timeline of modern art by making a powerful case for naming this group-created portrait as such. There is a certain logic of reversal hidden within this—a desire to re-encode his own life trajectory in order to uncover secrets in art history. This same desire is the through line found in his *Individual's Journey Through Art History*. In Cai's artistic practice, the re-encoding of obsolete artifacts is not only inserted into the contemporary art order but also subverts it; this is not the first time this has occurred. One of the popular formulae found in Chinese contemporary art is Political Pop. In painting, sculpture, and installation art, we continue to find appearances of Mao Zedong's portrait again and again, presented with changes in color and changes in form. We might be able to see the '85 New Wave movement as the harbinger of this trend, but almost all works of Political Pop from the early 1990s that found popularity in the international market were imitations of Andy Warhol and are closer to "political kitsch." In the atmosphere of diverse contemporary exhibitions, the 1960s attempts at breaking boundaries have become a fashion trend.

Cai Guo-Qiang holds a very different attitude. From *Venice's Rent Collection Courtyard* (1999) onward (figures 6 and 7), he has bypassed Political Pop's tactic of transfiguration that has long lost any political significance. He has instead adhered to historical forms to re-encode Socialist Realism, shaping an atmosphere of ambivalence that spurs viewers to dually reflect on and observe what lies between the past and the present. Whether consciously

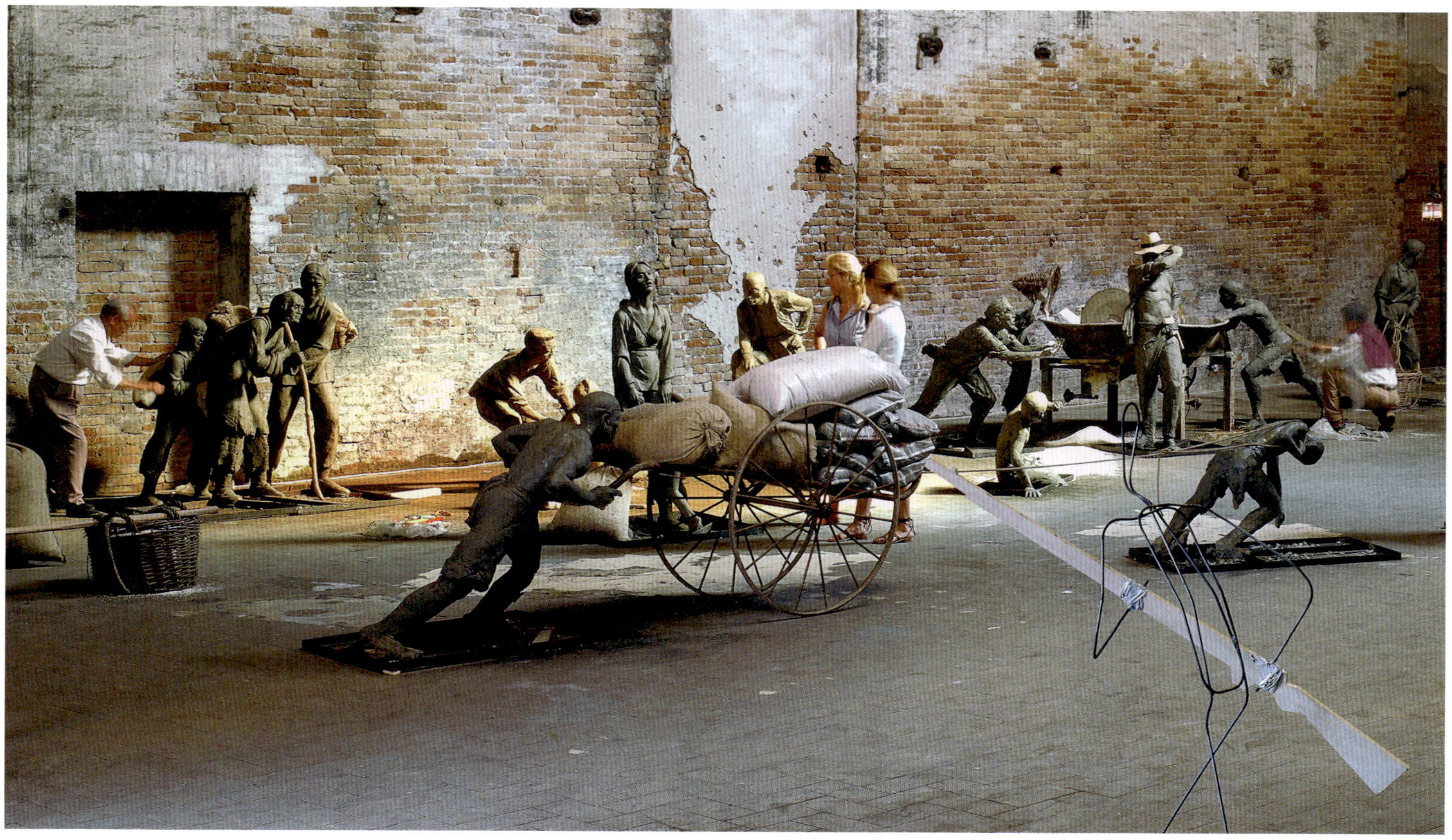

Figure 6. Cai Guo-Qiang, installation view of *Venice's Rent Collection Courtyard* at the 48th Venice Biennale in 1999. Photo by Elio Montanari

or not, Cai's replica of *Rent Collection Courtyard* highlights the context and evolution in contemporary art between two eras, and discovers temporal gulfs through the extension of form. Cai invited one of the original creators of *Rent Collection Courtyard* to join him in replicating this direct product of class politics, but this does not express a will to return to that earlier era. Needless to say, he uses an ambivalent form to incise this festival of contemporary art with a bygone era in its entirety. The precision of the copy even roused debates over copyright, but the core of the work was not its accuracy but the re-encoding of an iconic political sculpture of the past through its replication (figure 8). By inviting the original sculptors to re-create the work in front of live audiences at the Biennale, then letting it gradually crack and fracture into pieces, Cai creates a metaphor for the formation and dissolution of hierarchical politics. It also acts as a metaphor for the tortuous relationship between politics, art, and the fates of artists.

Yet it was not the throng of fashionable works that flooded the Biennale but this re-replication and re-encoding of a political artwork—originally created in 1965 and widely replicated during the Cultural Revolution—that won the Golden Lion at the final Venice Biennale of the 20th century. This perhaps hints at the true origins and eventual decline of post-1968 art. If the conscious pursuit of pioneering artists in the generations since Beuys has been to break boundaries between art and politics, between art and event, then what work can have been more effective in breaking boundaries and galvanizing the political energy of the masses through the interaction of art and politics than the original *Rent Collection Courtyard*? This also reminded me of the doubt expressed by another Chinese artist, Xu Bing, when he first came in contact with Beuys's work in the 1980s: Are not these efforts in contemporary art completely dwarfed in comparison to

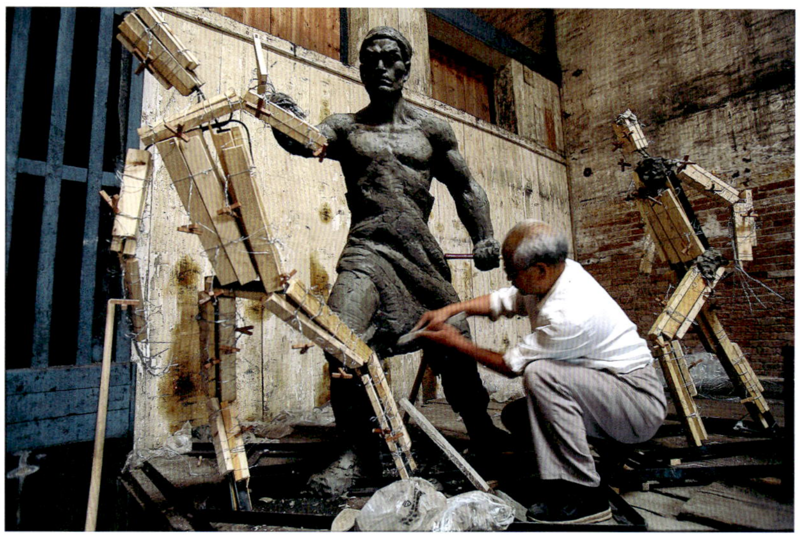

Figure 7. Sculptor Long Xuli creating a sculpture for *Venice's Rent Collection Courtyard* on site at the 48th Venice Biennale in 1999. Photo by Elio Montanari

Mao Zedong and everything he put into practice? What Cai showed was not a pure replication of *Rent Collection Courtyard*, but the entire process of its formation and crumbling. At the same time, the original sculpture offered a premise of the close interaction between art and politics, allowing Cai to accentuate the political nature in art.

## The Event and Its Sequence

The insertion of art into the sequence of events is an enduring feature that distinguishes Cai's creations. In his exploration of mutually embedding art and event into each other, he touched on

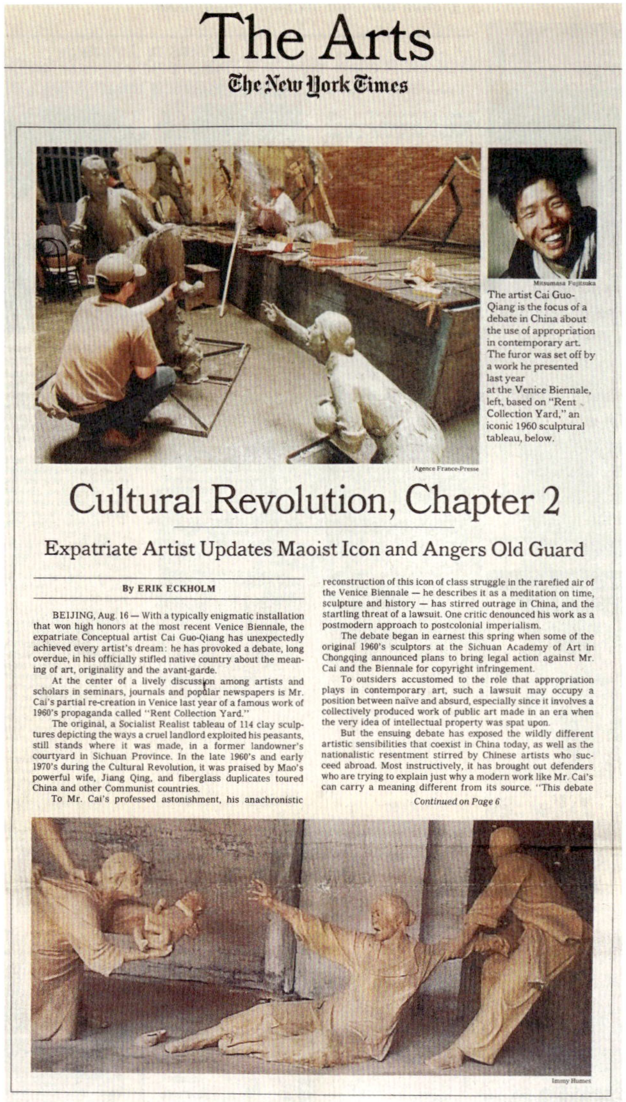

# The Arts

The New York Times

Mitsumasa Fujitsuka

The artist Cai Guo-Qiang is the focus of a debate in China about the use of appropriation in contemporary art. The furor was set off by a work he presented last year at the Venice Biennale, left, based on "Rent Collection Yard," an iconic 1960 sculptural tableau, below.

Agence France-Presse

## Cultural Revolution, Chapter 2

### Expatriate Artist Updates Maoist Icon and Angers Old Guard

By ERIK ECKHOLM

BEIJING, Aug. 16 — With a typically enigmatic installation that won high honors at the most recent Venice Biennale, the expatriate Conceptual artist Cai Guo-Qiang has unexpectedly achieved every artist's dream: he has provoked a debate, long overdue, in his officially stifled native country about the meaning of art, originality and the avant-garde.

At the center of a lively discussion among artists and scholars in seminars, journals and popular newspapers is Mr. Cai's partial re-creation in Venice last year of a famous work of 1960's propaganda called "Rent Collection Yard."

The original, a Socialist Realist tableau of 114 clay sculptures depicting the ways a cruel landlord exploited his peasants, still stands where it was made, in a former landowner's courtyard in Sichuan Province. In the late 1960's and early 1970's during the Cultural Revolution, it was praised by Mao's powerful wife, Jiang Qing, and fiberglass duplicates toured China and other Communist countries.

To Mr. Cai's professed astonishment, his anachronistic reconstruction of this icon of class struggle in the rarefied air of the Venice Biennale — he describes it as a meditation on time, sculpture and history — has stirred outrage in China, and the startling threat of a lawsuit. One critic denounced his work as a postmodern approach to postcolonial imperialism.

The debate began in earnest this spring when some of the original 1960's sculptors at the Sichuan Academy of Art in Chongqing announced plans to bring legal action against Mr. Cai and the Biennale for copyright infringement.

To outsiders accustomed to the role that appropriation plays in contemporary art, such a lawsuit may occupy a position between naïve and absurd, especially since it involves a collectively produced work of public art made in an era when the very idea of intellectual property was spat upon.

But the ensuing debate has exposed the wildly different artistic sensibilities that coexist in China today, as well as the nationalistic resentment stirred by Chinese artists who succeed abroad. Most instructively, it has brought out defenders who are trying to explain just why a modern work like Mr. Cai's can carry a meaning different from its source. "This debate

Continued on Page 6

Figure 8. Erik Eckholm, "Cultural Revolution, Chapter 2: Expatriate Artist Updates Maoist Icon and Angers Old Guard," *The New York Times*, August 17, 2000, E1

the "unrealized century" through the exhibition *Cai Guo-Qiang: October* in a way that differed from merely re-imagining these theatrical events, but rather manifesting them as the musical notes that inadvertently ring out in daily life. I once wrote, "For many of his works we can roughly specify two sequences of determinative events and their extensions: the first is the explosion of the atomic bomb and its symbolic inauguration of the Cold War era; the second is 9/11 and China's rise as a world power as symbols of the arrival of a new era. Gunpowder, explosions, ferocious animals, lethal knives and arrows, and transparent walls are among the methods and manifestations of presenting these two sequences. Cai deploys various ways to demonstrate the multivocality of an event, thereby challenging any simple grasp of it."[2]

There are two forms of "inlaying" one's art in historical events as one would set a stone in metal. One is to have the art rely on the historical event—to attain a more expansive unfolding and a more forceful impact by means of the event; the other is to rediscover the event through an artistic approach—to create the event through art and facilitate a transformation of the historical event's meaning. The 2001 Shanghai APEC (figure 9) and 2008 Beijing Olympics Opening Ceremony (figure 10) fall roughly in the first category, whereas *Golden Missile* (1998), *Borrowing Your Enemy's Arrows* (1998), and *Head On* (2006), among others, are examples of rediscovering the events and facilitating a transformation in the meaning of a given event through art. Aside from these, one of Cai's lines of pursuit that has left a deep impression on me is the series of events that comprise the broader event of "the unrealized century." This pursuit originates from the artist's life story and, because of this, has formed an endlessly undulating undercurrent. *Venice's Rent Collection Courtyard* in 1999, the Maksimov retrospective at the Central Academy of Fine Arts in 2002, and *Cai Guo-Qiang: October* and the documentary *October: The Unrealized Century* in 2017 and 2018 respectively

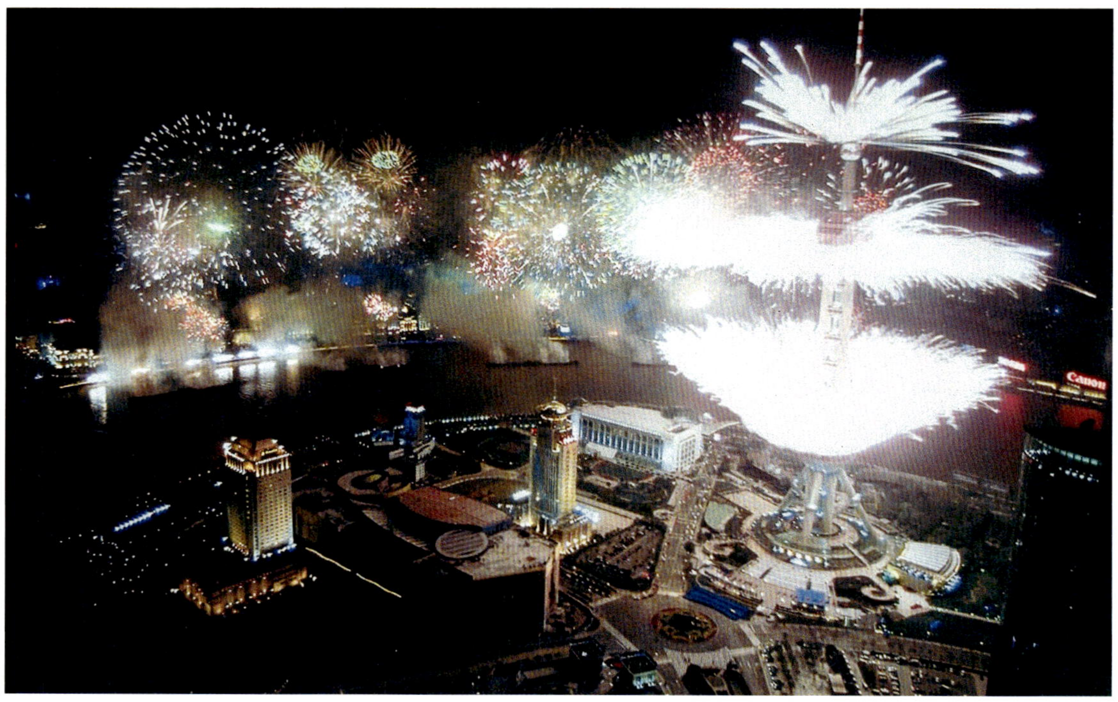

Figure 9. Cai Guo-Qiang, *Asia-Pacific Economic Cooperation (APEC) Cityscape Fireworks*, realized at The Bund, Huangpu River, and Oriental Pearl TV tower in Shanghai on October 20, 2001, at 9:00 p.m., which lasted approximately 20 minutes

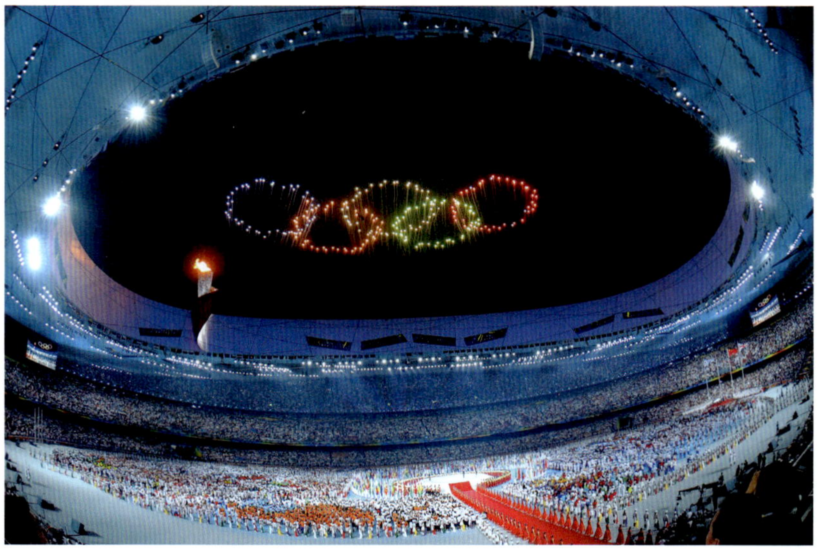

Figure 10. Cai Guo-Qiang, *Five Olympic Rings: Fireworks for the Opening Ceremony of the 2008 Beijing Olympic Games*, realized in Beijing on August 8, 2008. Photo by Lin Yi

are all moments when this undercurrent has surged up through the corners of the times. The undercurrent blends seamlessly with the century that serves as the event; by comparison, *Black Fireworks: Project for Hiroshima* (2008) and *Golden Missile* (1998) in Taipei are crashing waves roused by the upheaval of this unrealized century (figures 11 and 12). The waves and the undercurrent can be interchangeable—for instance, *Venice's Rent Collection Courtyard* received a great honor, but this great honor, much like the various dazzling ceremonies in which Cai participated over the ensuing decades, obscured the true depth of the undercurrent. The presence of an undercurrent is often natural, and its depth can even exceed the artist's self-understanding.

October 2017 was completely unlike October 1917. The ambivalent ceremony held in Moscow tellingly reveals that, even one hundred years later, 1917 remains a difficult challenge to confront. Eisenstein's color scene exceeded the conventional concept of historical realism, rewriting the stirring defeat of the Potemkin into a parable of victory—this reversal of defeat and victory could have only been realized through the lens of that October. In 2017, the Soviet Union had long ceased to exist, and Russia consolidated the celebrations of the October Revolution with the 870th anniversary of Moscow's founding. What stands out is the continuation of Russia as a multiethnic state. The national self-determination championed by the October Revolution ultimately led to the retaining or even expansion of the Tsarist Empire's land, population, and power through the formation of an alliance. This result laid the foundation for the multiethnic nation that is contemporary Russia and the path for new forms of industrialization. Following the dissolution of the Soviet Union, a series of narratives designed to "save" the October Revolution emerged in Russia. To modernists, the October Revolution cleared the obstacles to industrialization; to those who prized nationalism and patriotism, the Soviets' Great Patriotic War made eternal contributions to the resistance and crushing of Nazi Germany's offensive; to contemporary Eurasianists, the October Revolution was the turning point for the Russian Empire's resurgence. The October Revolution could not be negated in its entirety. Given this climate, the official position gradually adopted the interpretation posed in 1917 by Pavel Milyukov, founding member of the Constitutional Democratic party: that the October Revolution was a continuation of the February Revolution.[3]

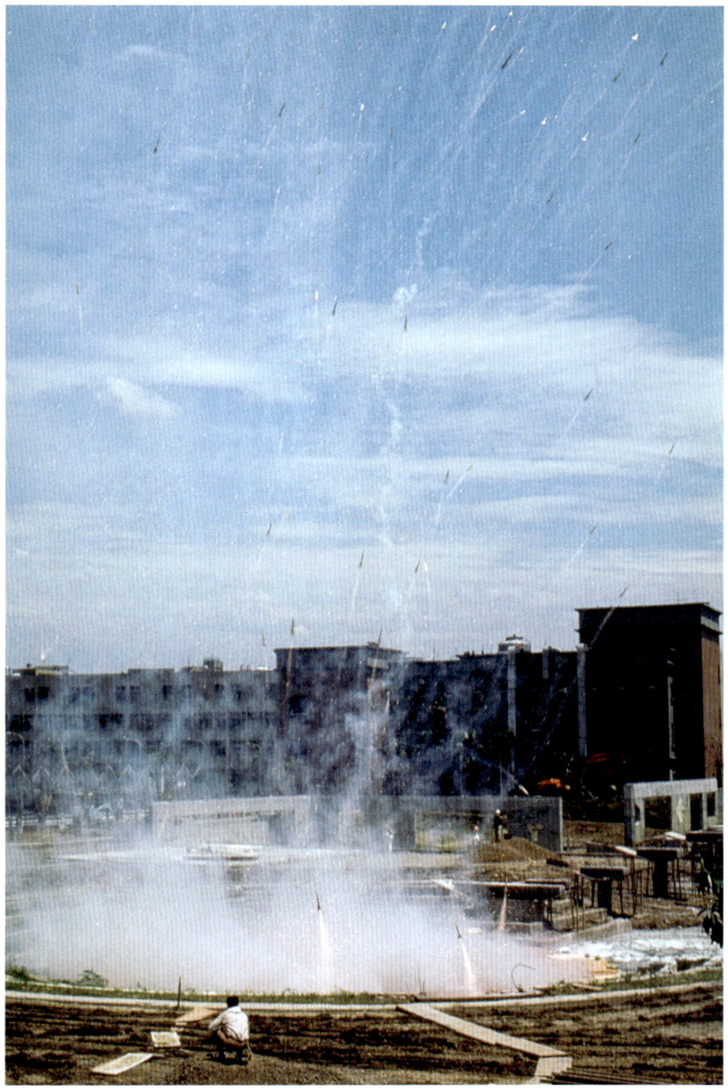

Figure 11. Cai Guo-Qiang, *Golden Missile*, realized at Taipei Fine Arts Museum in Taiwan on June 13, 1998, which lasted 53 seconds with 200 miniature missiles, with the explosion area measuring 150 × 25 × 25 m. Photo by Hongtu Chen, courtesy Taipei Fine Arts Museum

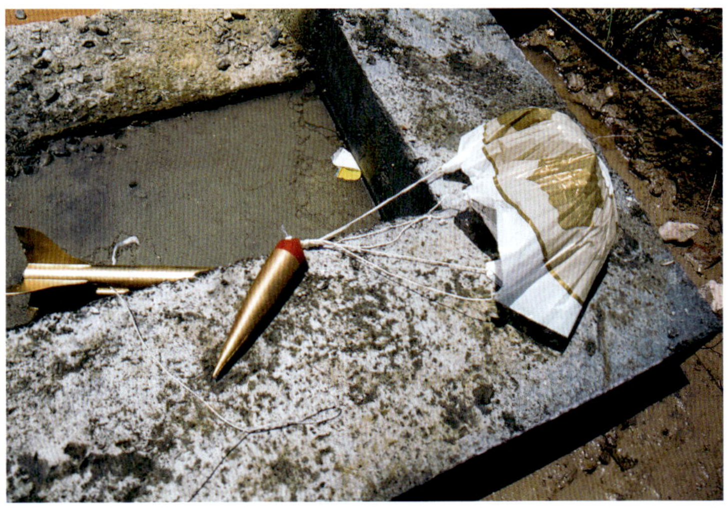

Figure 12. Miniature missile used in *Golden Missile* (1998). Photo by Tatsumi Masatoshi

Revolution, as a way of breaking away from history, must be woven into the fabric of the ever-unfolding national narrative in order to maintain its place.

We see an ambivalent approach to commemorating emerge from this complex and self-conflicting climate. On December 19, 2016, President Vladimir Putin issued the order to begin preparatory measures for commemorating the centenary of the Russian Revolution, yet at the same time noted that the commemorative

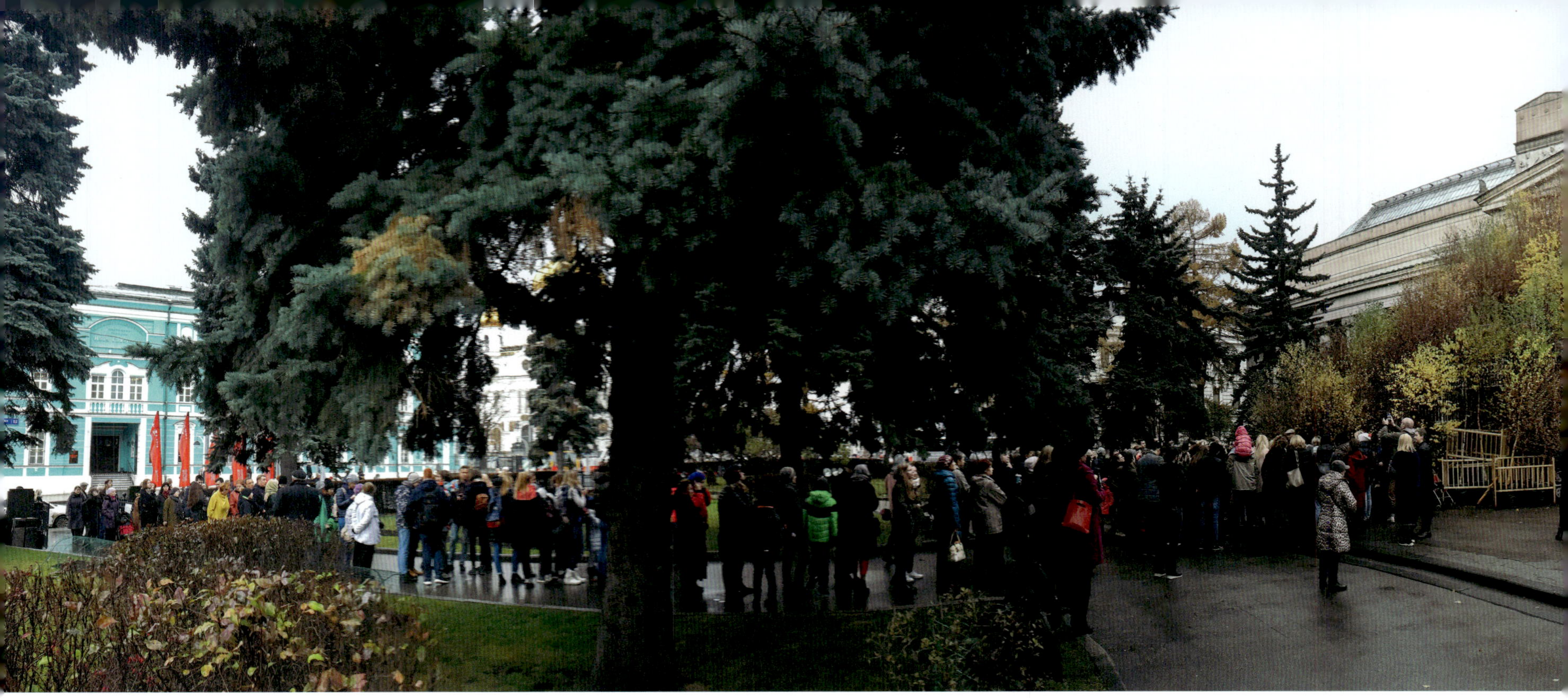

Figure 13. Crowds lining up outside the Pushkin State Museum of Fine Arts in Moscow to see Cai Guo-Qiang's solo exhibition *October* in its final week in 2017. Photo courtesy the Pushkin State Museum of Fine Arts

events would not be limited to the October Revolution but also include the February Revolution, an earlier incident in 1917.[4] The events' aim was not to reaffirm the political value of the October Revolution, but rather to achieve a compromise between the descendants of the Whites and the Reds, the defining conflict of the earlier revolution. On May 25, 2017, Putin explicitly said: "The main historical lesson that the February Revolution and the October Revolution have left us one hundred years later is to prevent the fracturing of society, to achieve harmony in society."[5] To placate the misgivings at home and abroad over commemorating the 1917 Revolution, Putin issued presidential decrees on September 30, 2015[6] and September 3, 2016[7] for enacting "the construction of an eternal monument for victims of political persecution," although "the content [of the decree] did not identify the period of Russian history in which this persecutory action took place," and, more importantly, the decree did not at all identify who the perpetrating "subjects" or the victimized "objects" were.[8] Even so, the political implications of erecting a monument were clear. It shows that the commemoration of the 1917 Revolution is not a reaffirmation of Russia's future directions, and at the same time it does not flout the "principles of human rights" widely accepted by the Western world. On October 30, 2017, the monument for victims of political prosecution was completed and named "Wall of Grief." In his closing remarks at the opening ceremony, Putin quoted Natalia Dmitrievna Svetlova, the wife of Aleksandr Solzhenitsyn: "'To know, to remember, to condemn, and only then to forgive.' I fully agree with these words. Indeed, we and our descendants must remember the tragedy of repression and what caused it. However, this does not mean settling scores. We cannot push society to a dangerous line of confrontation yet again. Now, it is important for all of us to build on the values of trust and stability. Only on this basis will we be able to achieve the goals of our society and our country, Russia, which is one for us all."[9]

October 2017 passed like any other month; it was destined not to be an earthshattering event; it did not require red stars to adorn the Moscow skies. The lights of the ceremony could only light up one corner of Red Square; other than that, it would not light up anything else. If we were to regard Cai's unrealized daytime fireworks as an event, then all it left Cai with was self-contradiction and ambivalence. His efforts ultimately evolved into a retracing of past undercurrents and their extensions. When he first began planning for his *October* project, Cai had met with the Chinese Ministry of Culture in order to seek financial support from the Chinese government. Their discussion was documented in the film *October: The Unrealized Century*. When Cai showed a Ministry of Culture official a video rendering of the *October* fireworks project, the official presciently cautioned him not to use the vibrant red star as the opening scene on Red Square. He reminded Cai, "They won't like that right now." By the summer of 2017, the Red Square explosion event had been prematurely aborted due to various causes on the Russian official side. Cai had no choice but to push this project to the background and redouble his focus on preparing for the exhibition while simultaneously searching for Maksimov's grave as the through line for his time in Moscow. Yet this latter inquiry had a long history of its own; it was no mere product of the Red Square explosion project's cancellation. I would go as far to say that, compared to the *October* solo exhibition that opened according to plan at the Pushkin Museum in September 2017 (figure 13), Cai's search for Maksimov is even more profound.

## Maksimov and a Forgotten Legacy of Realism

Cai first visited the Novodevichy Cemetery, the resting place of numerous prominent figures from Russia: Gogol, Chekhov, Shostakovich, Mayakovsky, Fadeyev, Ostrovsky, and national heroes like the sister and brother Zoya Kosmodemyanskaya and Shura (Aleksandr) Kosmodemyansky, as well as Boris Yeltsin, who personally put the Soviet Union in its grave. Cai skipped over numerous famous names from the tsarist period, but paused

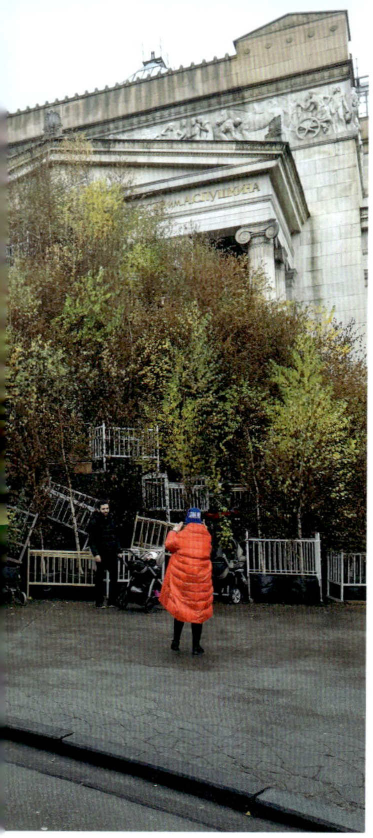

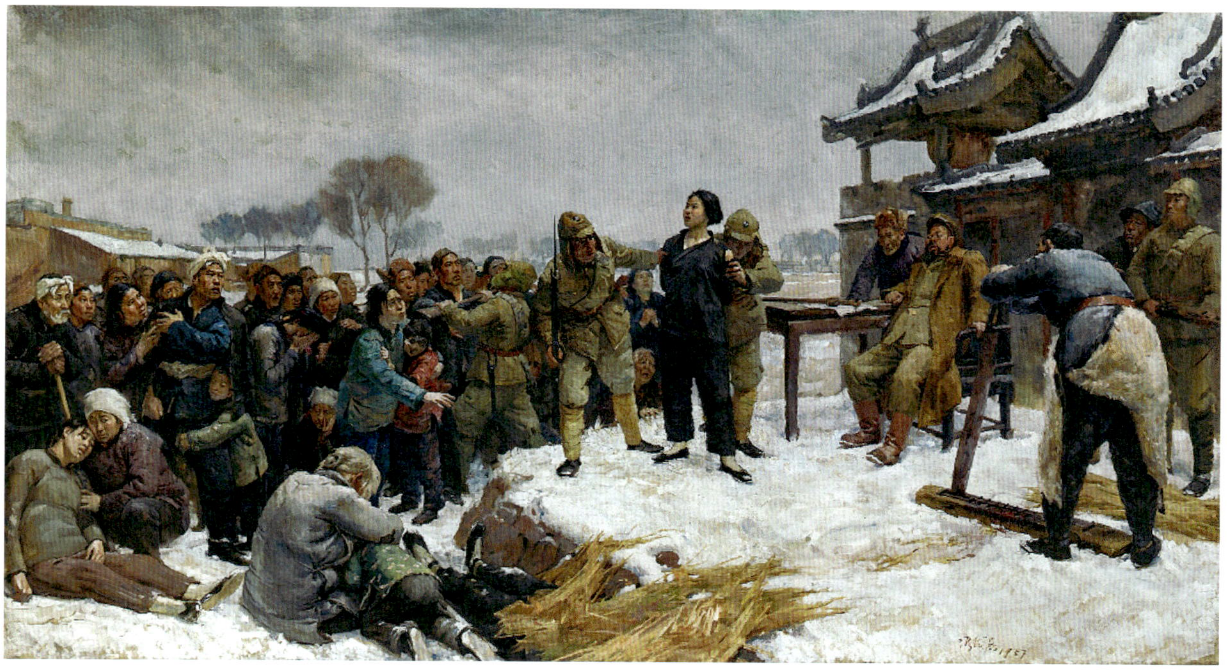

Figure 14. Feng Fasi, *The Heroic Death of Liu Hulan*, 1957. Oil on canvas, 230 × 426 cm. Collection of National Art Museum of China, Beijing

before the grave of Nikolai Ostrovsky to recite the few phrases from his book *How the Steel Was Tempered* that were so familiar to generations of people not only in Socialist countries but also in developing nations such as India. Zoya and Shura, heroes from the Patriotic War period, also drew his attention. Mao Zedong, upon first visiting the Soviet Union, also lingered at this very spot, saying: "The Soviet Union has Zoya, we have Liu Hulan." Standing there before Zoya and Shura's graves, did Cai recall that Liu Hulan was the subject of the masterpiece that brought fame to Feng Fasi (figure 14), one of Maksimov's Chinese protégés and the leader of his Central Academy class? New masterpieces of oil paintings formed a Chinese lineage within Socialist Realist oil painting: Jin Shangyi's *Climbing Muztagh Ata* and *Our Friends Are All Over the World*, Zhan Jianjun's *Five Heroes on Langya Mountain* (figure 15), and Hou Yimin's *Comrade Liu Shaoqi and An'yuan Miners* and *Young Underground Workers*. All of the above were members of Maksimov's master class.

In his own hometown, however, Maksimov's grave is far distant from the Novodevichy Cemetery. The figure who had so holistically influenced new oil painting in China was of close to no significance in the Soviet Union—not to mention in Russia today. Aside from mutually unacquainted old friends, few people, not even close neighbors, know of or remember Maksimov. He had been withdrawn to a reclusive, silent graveyard on the outskirts of Moscow, behind a large tree. The date of death on the headstone was ten years earlier than his actual date of death in 1993—an incomprehensibly hasty error that cannot but rouse suspicion. Those were the chaotic years that followed the dissolution of the Soviet Union, when the shock and inflation meant that one U.S. dollar could be exchanged for 1300–1500 rubles. In the sumptuous and elegant Mariinsky Theater, tickets to a world-class performance of the ballet *Swan Lake* cost only 50 rubles. At night, the city lights were dim and faint, leaving most regions in total darkness. In October 1993, Yeltsin, the terminator of the Soviet Union and the inaugural president of the Russian Federation, ordered a military bombardment of the parliament in the name of democracy. He forced those whom he dubbed "former Communists"—his own vice president and all the elected parliament members—to walk out from the basement of Moscow's White House while holding positions of surrender. To this day, I can recall the pallid faces and terrified, confounded gazes of those politicians who had once helped Yeltsin to overthrow the Soviet Union as they filed out of the building.

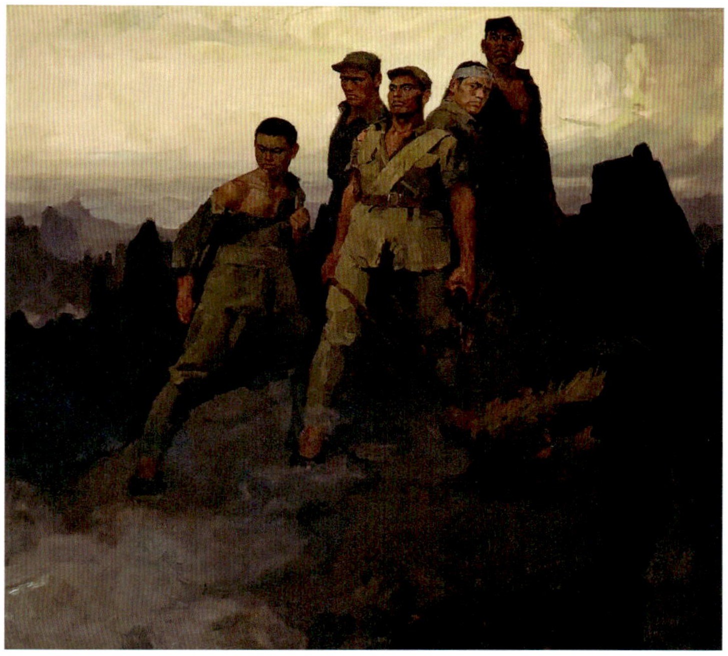

Figure 15. Zhan Jianjun, *Five Heroes on Langya Mountain*, 1959. Oil on canvas, 186 × 203 cm. Collection of National Museum of China, Beijing

In July 1993, I sailed from Stockholm across the Baltic Sea and arrived in Saint Petersburg. After getting off the ship, I bought two T-shirts for a change of clothes. They featured a portrait of Lenin splashed across the chest, with golden arcs spouting out of his vast bald head—the logo of McDonald's. The

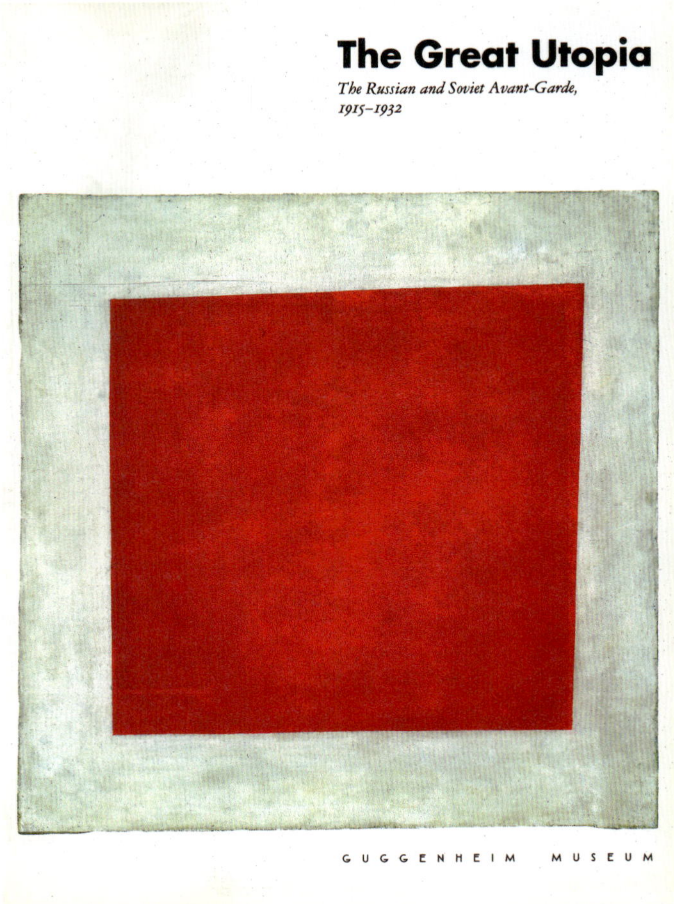


Figure 16. *The Great Utopia: The Russian and Soviet Avant-Garde, 1915–1932*, 1992 (cover). © The Solomon R. Guggenheim Foundation

curved, capital M looked just like a bridge connecting Leningrad to Saint Petersburg. With the dissolution of Soviet Eastern Europe, standard Socialist images (such as portraits of Mao or Lenin) were transformed, manipulated, and denigrated to logos for soliciting tourists in these former socialist states. The street corners and perimeter of the Palace Square where the October Revolution took place were now filled with flea markets selling artifacts like figurines of Christ and other church décor, and realist oil paintings in classical and Soviet styles at extremely low prices. Soon after, *The New York Times* began to cover China's Political Pop at length, multiplying the price of Chinese contemporary art by a hundredfold. One after another, Romanized names of Chinese artists began to appear in the media, museums, galleries, and auctions, with their prices far exceeding the classical works of exquisite craftsmanship. Chinese contemporary art was not only able to flourish in the Western art market, but also made its way through the gates of all the major museums. It is possible to see the drastic changes of the times at a glance by comparing market prices and visibility in art.

Maksimov's era had come to an end, whether in Russia or in China, but the reversals of defeat and victory were still ongoing. In the fall of 1992, only half a year after the Soviet dissolution, the Solomon R. Guggenheim Museum presented the exhibition *The Great Utopia: The Russian and Soviet Avant-Garde, 1915–1932* (figures 16 and 17). The planning process had been plodding along since 1989, but quickly came to fruition following the dissolution of the Soviet Union. Until very recently, I had been ignorant about preceding exhibitions on the Russian avant-garde, and always considered this the most stirring exhibition in the Guggenheim's history. Since the 1970s, the Western world has held many important exhibitions on the Russian avant-garde,

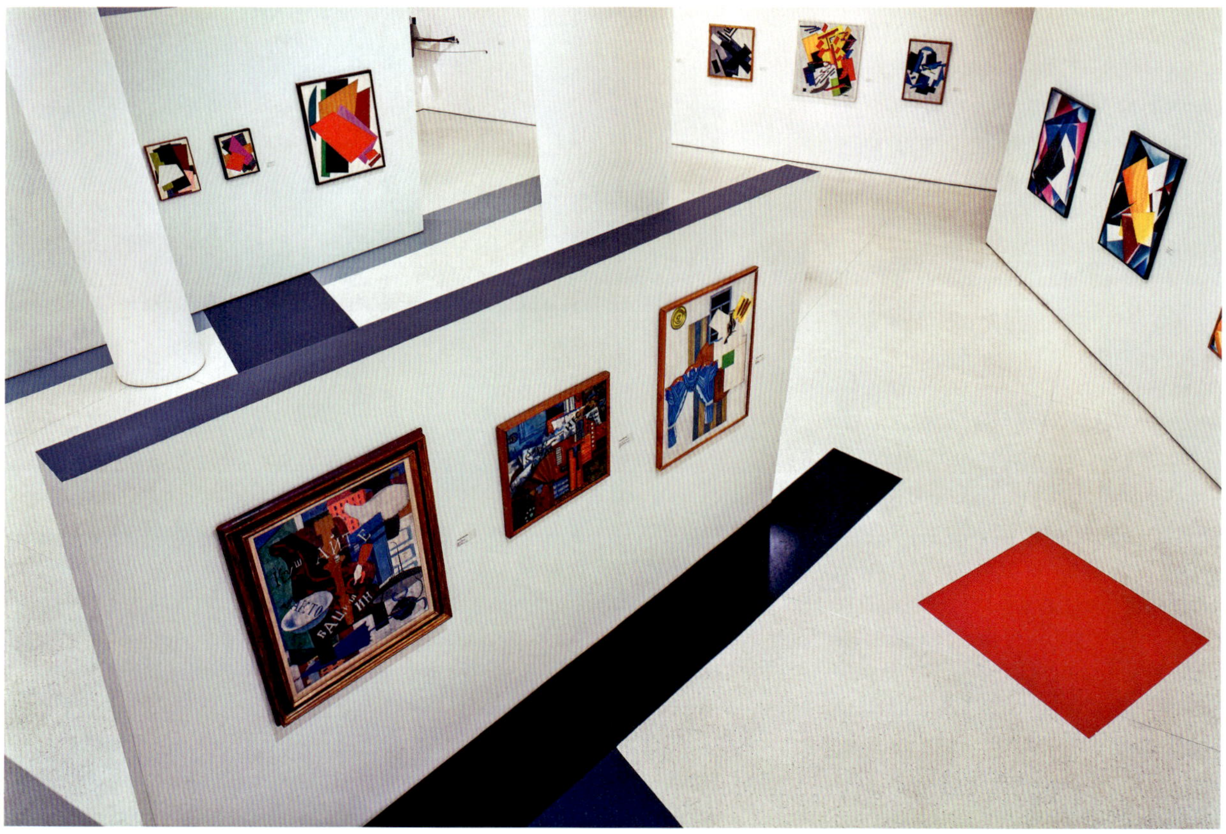

Figure 17. Installation view of *The Great Utopia: The Russian and Soviet Avant-Garde, 1915–1932*, with installation design by Zaha Hadid, held at Solomon R. Guggenheim Museum in New York in 1992–93. Photo by David Heald © The Solomon R. Guggenheim Foundation

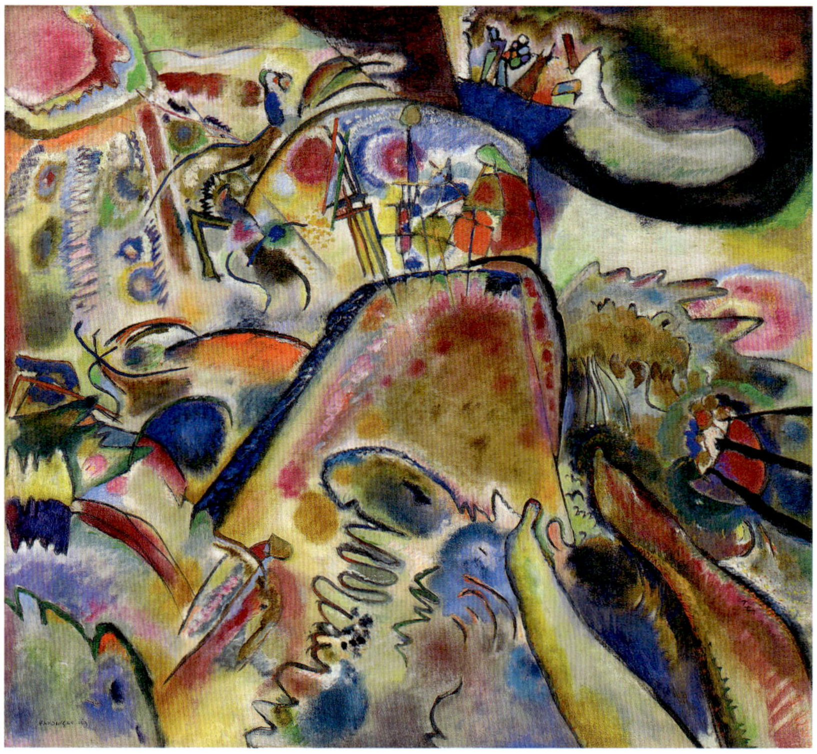

Figure 18. Wassily Kandinsky, *Small Pleasures*, 1913. Oil on canvas, 110.5 × 120 cm. © 2020 Artists Rights Society (ARS), New York

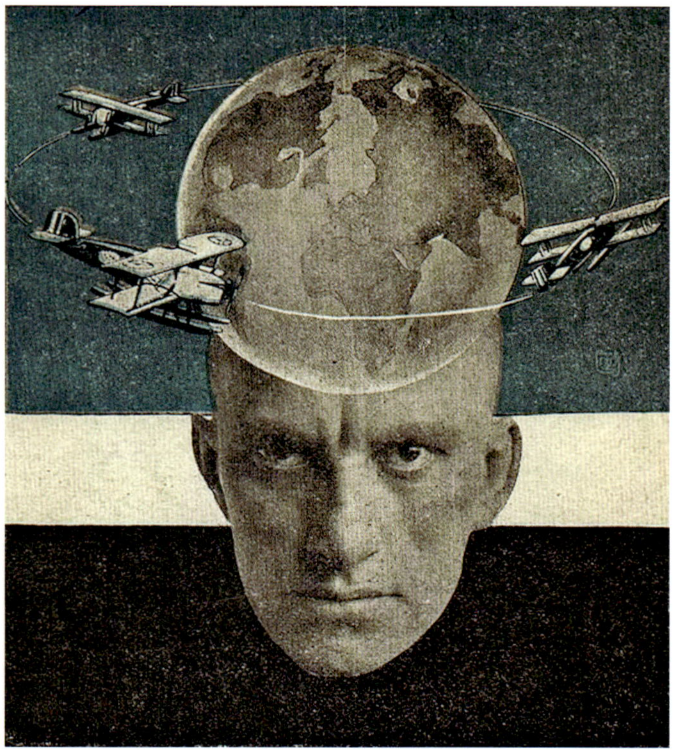

Figure 19. Alexander Rodchenko, photomontage for Vladimir Mayakovsky's *A Conversation with a Tax-Collector about Poetry*, 1926. © 2020 Estate of Alexander Rodchenko / UPRAVIS, Moscow / ARS, NY

most significantly *Paris-Moscou: 1900–1930* at Centre Pompidou, Paris, in 1979; *The Avant-Garde in Russia, 1910–1930: New Perspectives* at Los Angeles County Museum of Art and the Hirshhorn Museum in 1980; and *Art of the Russian Avant-Garde: Selections from the Costakis Collection* at the Guggenheim Museum in 1981. But for the public and the media, the timing and scale of the Guggenheim exhibition *Great Utopia* was shocking and electrifying.[10] Through the cumulative work by a few generations of art historians, curators, and museums from the 1960s to the present, it is finally possible to explore the Soviet avant-garde holistically. In this scholarship and these exhibitions, Kandinsky's colorful abstractions (figure 18) and Malevich's *Black Square* were finally vested with the spiritually and politically revolutionary connotations, and a direct connection was established between the Soviet Revolution and Constructivist art by iconic avant-garde figures like Mayakovsky and Rodchenko (figure 19). One of the major difficulties that the Guggenheim exhibition encountered during its gestation process was the question of how to standardize the transliteration of such a large number of Russian names into English. With help from numerous experts, they were able to transliterate the names of Soviet and Russian avant-garde artists within a very short period of time. People were thus able to retrace and reconsider the comprehensive and profound connections between avant-garde art and Soviet politics.[11]

Censorship and persecution of dissidents in Soviet politics had begun toward the end of the 1920s, and reached its peak in the Stalinist "Great Purge" of 1936–38. The purge spread from the political realm to the literary and artistic realm, in which

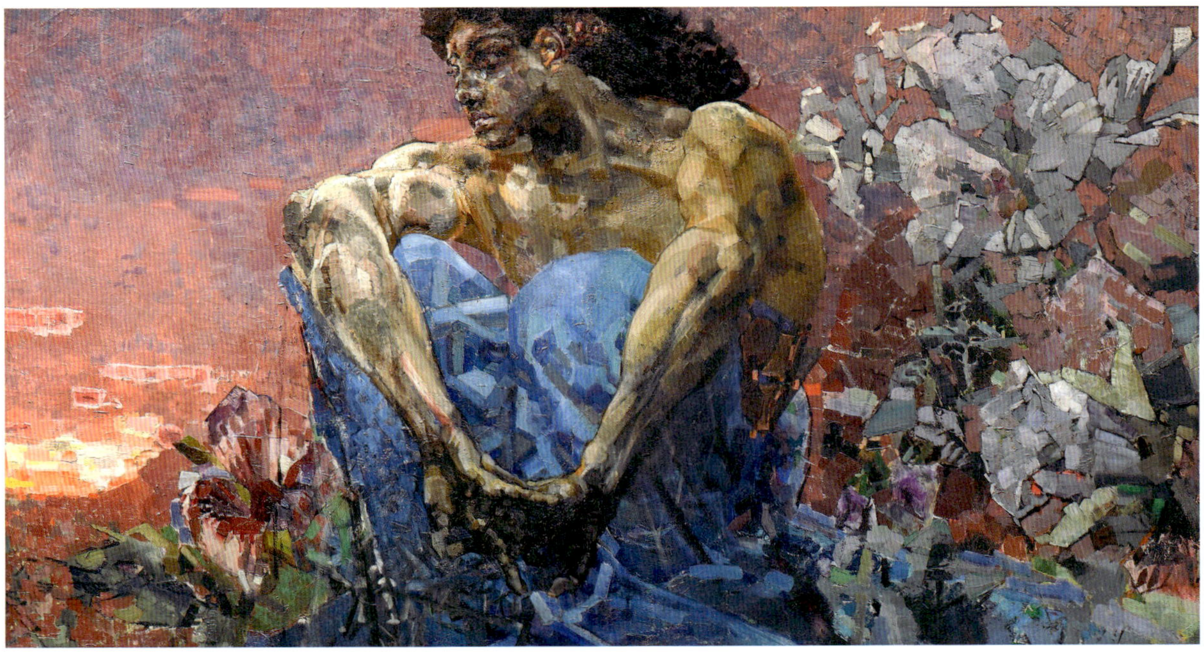

Figure 20. Mikhail Vrubel, *The Demon Seated*, 1890. Oil on canvas, 116.5 × 213.8 cm. The State Tretyakov Gallery, Moscow

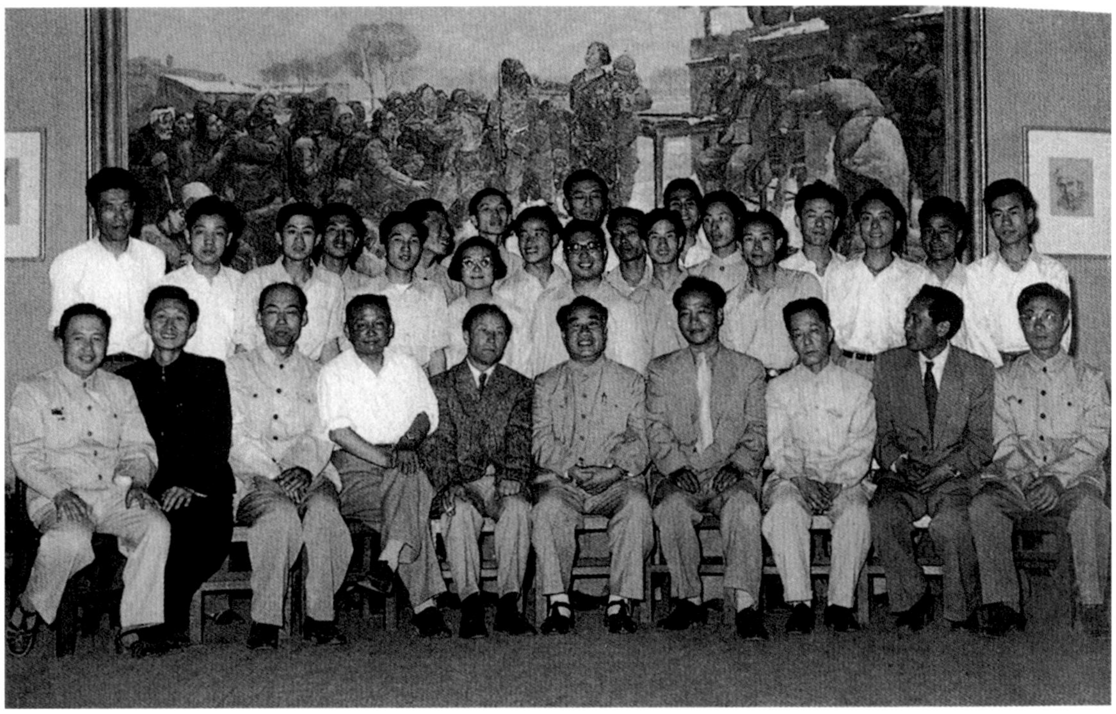

Figure 21. Konstantin Maksimov (seated first row, sixth from right), with his students at their thesis exhibition held at the end of his two-year appointment at the Central Academy of Fine Arts in Beijing. Vice-Chairman of the People's Republic of China, Zhu De (seated first row, fifth from right) made a congratulatory visit to the exhibition

along with formalism and naturalism, the avant-garde were heavily oppressed and persecuted.[12] (The theater practitioner Vsevolod Meyerhold, innovator of Biomechanics and Constructivist stage design, for instance, was executed in 1940). In contrast, Socialist Realism was recognized as the only kind of art sanctioned by the Soviet state. Maksimov's glory days in 1950s China is also proof of this contrast. In the post–Cold War context, it was difficult for Socialist Realism to earn a place in the development of contemporary art. For Maksimov in China, the context was the formation of the postwar international order, the confrontation between Eastern and Western Blocs, and the 156 projects supported by the Soviet Union during China's first "Five-Year Plan." But beyond these, there was also the great tradition of 19th-century Russian art, in particular the emphasis on social issues and political consciousness that developed in the tradition of Repin and Surikov (rather than focusing solely on formal elements like light and color). This was a lineage that developed in parallel with the modernist tradition of Mikhail Vrubel (figure 20), Kandinsky, and Malevich, among others. Contemporary art has been greatly instrumental in protesting against and criticizing the old Socialist system and its dogma of literature and art. However, in the face of increasingly severe contemporary crises—as Cai Guo-Qiang said—artists generally feel a strong sense of powerlessness. Perhaps this is not a redundant question: Is contemporary art still able to draw any energy from the long tradition of realism?

Maksimov's influence in the field of Chinese art is not an isolated event. Several scholars were sent to teach in China around the same time as Maksimov, including Assistant Professor Ivan Samoivanovich Pidarkov from Kiev University's Department of Literature, who taught at Peking University (Beijing University) in 1954–55, and Professor-Lecturer Viktor Borisovich Korzun from a now unknown university, who taught Literature and Art at Beijing Normal University in 1956–57. Their lectures were translated into Chinese, edited, and published as 文艺学引论 (*Introduction to literature and art*) in 1958 and 文艺学概论 (*Survey of literature and art*) in 1959, respectively. In 1956, when the Chinese Ministry of Education invited Nadezhda Ivanovna Gerasimova, an expert on Soviet studies, to teach an "Advanced Soviet Literature" course, the selection process of the enrolled students was similar to that of the Central Academy of Fine Arts' selection process for Maksimov's master class (figure 21). In 1954–57, at least seven experts were active at the Central Academy of Drama and its Huadong Branch (the predecessor to Shanghai Theatre Academy, Cai's alma mater). Their instruction followed the system of actor training created by Konstantin Stanislavski, a seminal Russian theater practitioner. This brought about a debate between what Stanislavksi called the "art of experiencing" and Meyerhold's school of expressionist and Biomechanical acting to Chinese theater, spurring new approaches and interpretations in the field.[13]

The later lives and theoretical teachings of these figures, who had briefly enjoyed such bursts of fame, have long vanished. However, the marks they left on contemporary Chinese literature, art, theater, and music, among other fields, have withstood the test of time. Today, it is difficult to find their full Russian names even in relevant texts on the history of academia. Like Maksimov, they only exist in the world of Mandarin Chinese.[14] Notably, Pidarkov had studied under Soviet literary theorist Leonid Ivanovich Timofeyev, whose 1948 book *Teoriya Literatury* (*Theory of literature*) was translated into Mandarin by famed translator Zha Liangzheng and published by the Shanghai publishing house Pingming in December 1953. Known for his Chinese translations of Romantic poets such as Pushkin, Byron, and Shelley, Zha was also a poet under the pseudonym Mu Dan. He was "rediscovered" as a Chinese modernist poet in the 1990s and has since

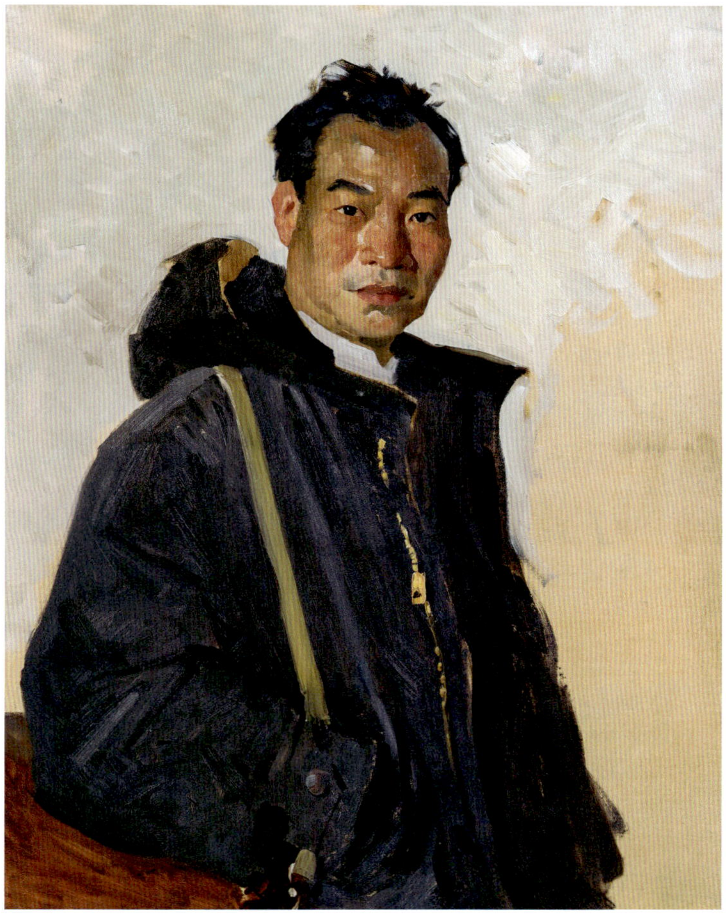

Figure 22. Konstantin Maksimov, *Man in Blue Jacket, China Series*, 1957. Oil on canvas, 80 × 65 cm. Cai Guo-Qiang Collection. Photo by Yvonne Zhao

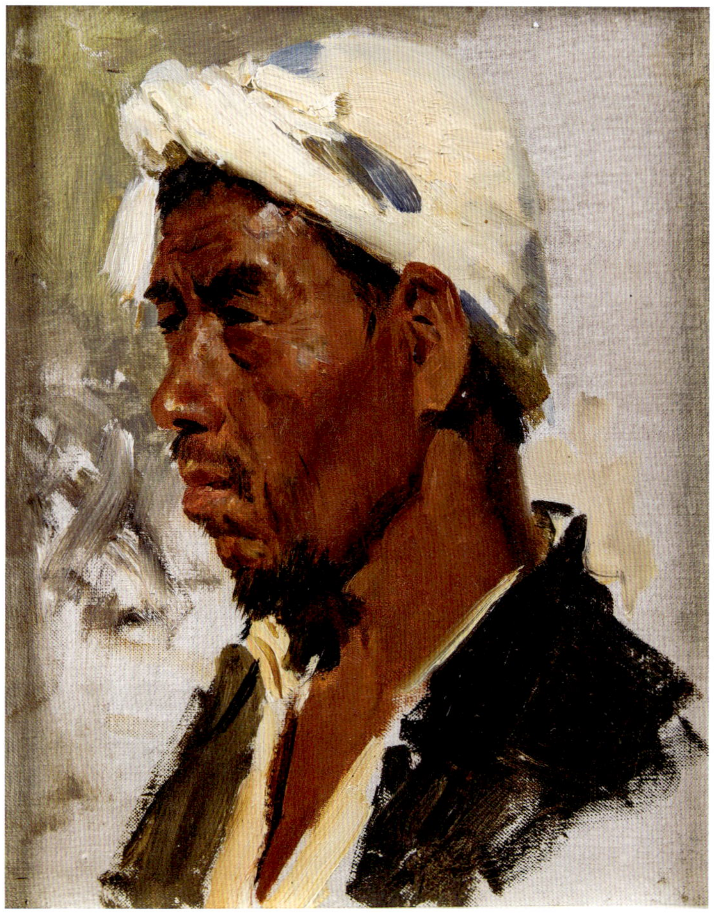

Figure 23. Konstantin Maksimov, *Portrait of a Chinese Sailor*, 1958. Oil on canvas, 25 × 20 cm. Cai Guo-Qiang Collection. Photo by Yvonne Zhao

skyrocketed in fame. His translations of Timofeyev and fellow literary critic Vissarion Belinsky have long disappeared with the arrival of modernism. Related works, such as textbooks compiled during the 1950s and 1960s for higher education, such as 文学的基本原理 (*Fundamental principles of literature*) of 1961 by Yiqun, were all produced under the influence of Soviet art theory and literary theory.

Maksimov's pedagogy in China is likewise a direct manifestation and concrete actualization of this aesthetic world in the realm of painting. As results of the large-scale dissemination of Soviet literary theory and aesthetics and as products of new Chinese literary and artistic thought, the work produced by Maksimov's class and *Rent Collection Courtyard* by the Sichuan Fine Arts Institute both directly participated in the Socialist cultural politics of the 1950s and 1960s. And because of this, they were absolutely abandoned when the Cold War came to a close. They sank from the mainstream to the bottom of the riverbed, from the popular school of thought into the shadowy realm of phantoms.

***

Will Maksimov's era make a reappearance? This question far surpasses human powers of prediction, and does not exist among Cai's curatorial motives. Standing in the century's drawn-out shadow, no one knows what its "unrealization" actually means. Cai's rediscovery of Maksimov is the post–Cold War era's pursuit of the ghost of the century. He examined this Soviet artist's life trajectory with both respect and gratitude, bringing back the good old days that have evaporated under the contemporary sun and revisiting the years of youth in this other era. In the same vein as *Venice's Rent Collection Courtyard*, his excavation has encoded Maksimov, once a symbol of the defeats suffered by Socialist cultural politics, into the timeline of contemporary art. Cai is an artist within the order of contemporary art who has no intention of reinstating the "past" into the mainstream through conducting a séance. Rather, he follows in the creative path of archivally researched exhibitions and plays the role of a collector of historical materials, casting aside the methods so widely used among artists of his generation of using the techniques of warping and satirizing to consume the "past" (revolution).

In 2000, Cai happened upon a work of Maksimov's in Amsterdam, and since then has collected nearly two hundred fifty of his paintings (figures 22 and 23). In 2000, Cai exhibited selections from his collection at the Central Academy of Fine Arts in Beijing, with many of Maksimov's old pupils in attendance (figures 24 and 25). Their impassioned remembrances of "Professor Ma" attracted the media's curiosity. Cai did not have a prior relationship with the Central Academy. His direct contact with the Russian oil painting tradition is limited to his teacher Zhou Benyi, an artist who graduated from the Soviet Union's Repin Institute and taught Cai at the Shanghai Theatre Academy. However, it was not so much Maksimov, the individual artist, as Maksimov, the ghost of an era that was once so reclusive and beyond reach, who influenced the first generation of Chinese oil painters. His fated ties with the subsequent generations of Chinese artists cannot be described in the sense of personal relationships. Cai's acts of collecting his artworks, curating his exhibition, visiting his old

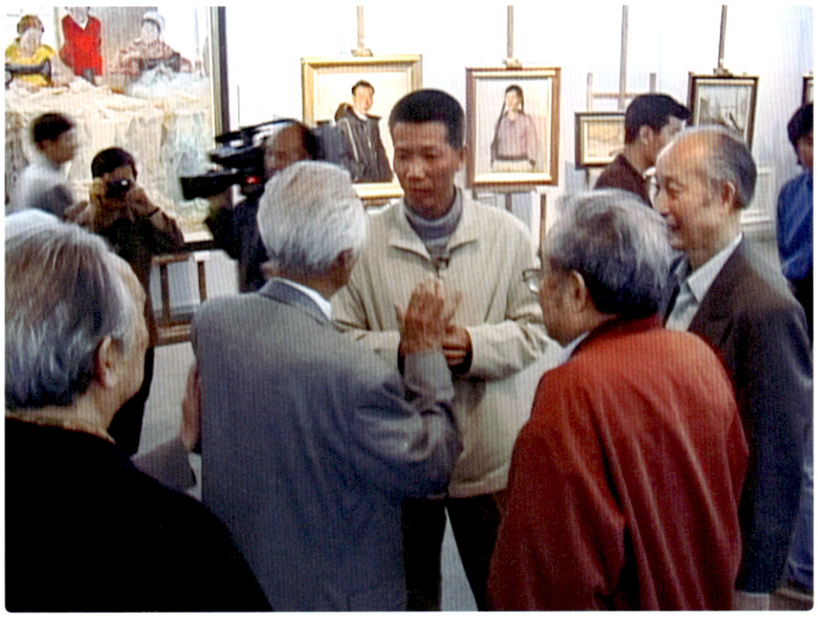

Figure 24. Maksimov's students visiting the exhibition *Cai Guo-Qiang's Maksimov Collection* at the CAFA Art Museum, Beijing in 2002

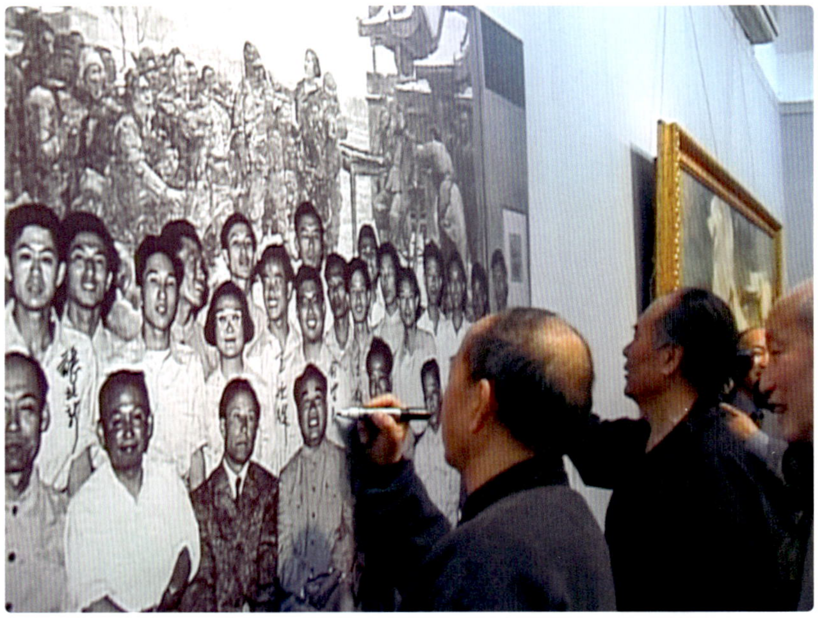

Figure 25. Maksimov's students inscribing their names next to their younger selves in a class photograph from 1957

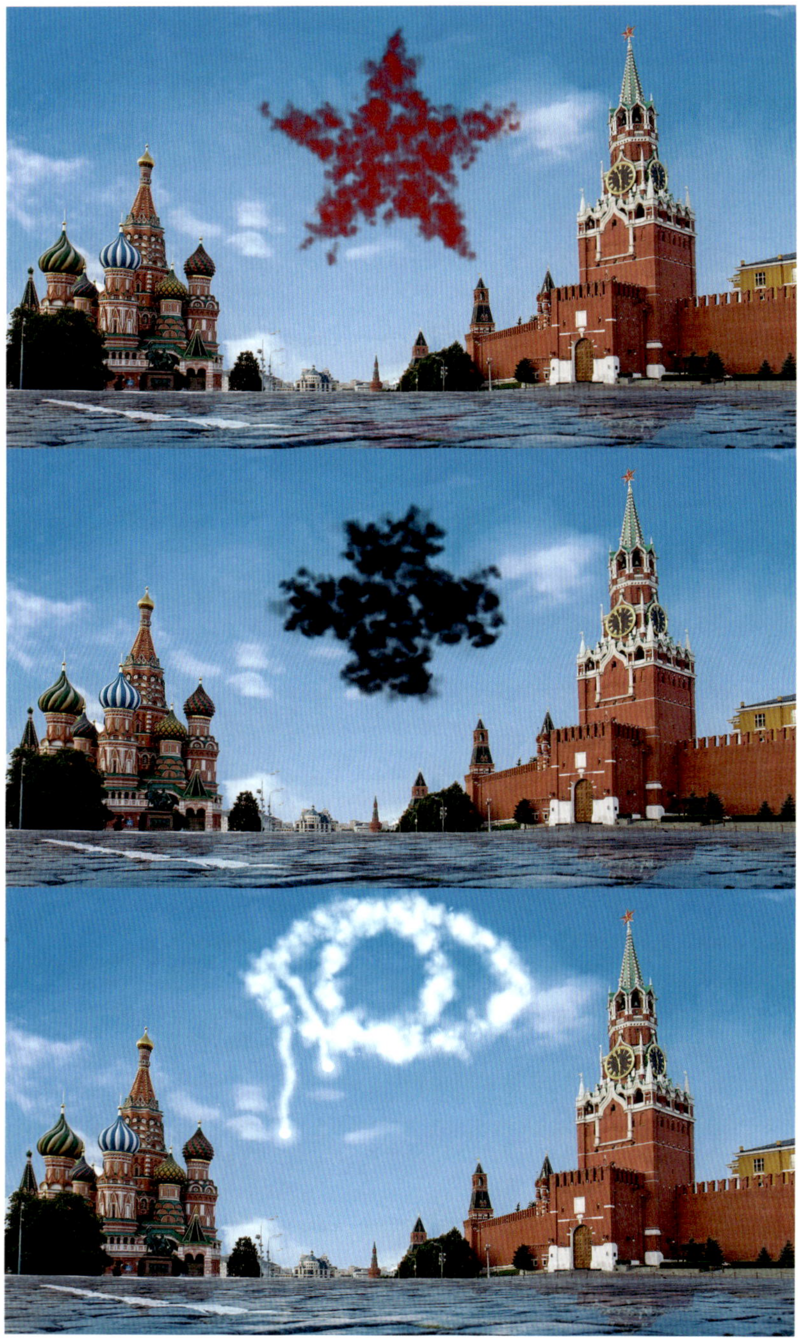

Figure 26. Still frames from animated video for unrealized work *Cai Guo-Qiang: October, Daytime Explosion Event on Red Square*, 2017 (no. 4.13)

friends, and searching for his resting place are more akin to the acts of a spiritual practitioner drawn by a ghost—before he knew it, he had ventured into the damp, dark, mystical woods.

To Cai, Maksimov, the Soviet Union, and the clashes between China and Russia are the beginnings of a new *Individual's Journey Through Western Art History* for China. This project was also the first juncture of his Journey Through World Art History. Considering Cai's own position in the contemporary art world, the Red Square explosion event, while unrealized (figure 26), presents deeper implications that deviate from the contemporary art mainstream compared to his dazzling achievements in major museums, art festivals, and ceremonies. Though the act of seeking the ghost could only exist in the form of an undercurrent, it nevertheless strikes a continuous note at the narrative of art history and shows an ardor that flows in the form of reminiscence. In my view, tides without undercurrents can only course along the shallow riverbed. No matter how violent the waves, they inevitably run dry before they reach the opposite shore. There is therefore nothing that can better manifest the "unrealized century" than this method of upstream, precarious effort.

This, too, is the dialectic of defeat and victory.

Beijing, May 4, 2020

---

*Wang Hui is Distinguished Professor of Literature and History at Tsinghua University in Beijing and the founding Director of the Tsinghua Institute for Advanced Study in Humanities and Social Sciences (TIAS). An esteemed scholar in intellectual history, social theory, and modern literature, he has lectured globally and his publications have been translated into multiple languages. Among those translated into English are* The Politics of Imagining Asia *(2010),* China from Empire to Nation-State *(2014), and* China's Twentieth Century *(2015). His four-volume work* The Rise of Modern Chinese Thought *(2004) in Chinese is regarded as one of the most important contributions to modern Chinese scholarship over the past two decades. He has received numerous awards, including the 2013 Luca Pacioli Prize, which he shared with Jürgen Habermas, and the 2018 Anneliese Maier Research Award.*

## Notes

1. Eirik Frisvold Hanssen, "Eisenstein in Colour," *Konsthistorisk Tidskrift/Journal of Art History* 73, no. 4 (2004): 212.

2. Wang Hui, "The Dialectics of Art and the Event," in *Cai Guo-Qiang: I Want to Believe* (New York: Guggenheim Museum Publications, 2008), 43.

3. This point was taken from "Reflections on the Major Incidents of the Revolutionary Period" [Russian text] by Anatoly Ivanovich Fomin, professor of Taras Shevchenko National University of Luhansk, Ukraine, published in Russia's *Free Thinking* magazine, no. 10 (1996); and also drawn from "十月"的选择—90年代国外学者论十月革命 [The "October" choice: 90s discussion of the October Revolution by scholars abroad], ed. Liu Shuchun, Zhai Mingang, and Wang Lihua (Beijing: Central Press of Editing and Translation, 1997), 367.

4. Распоряжение Президента РФ от 19.12.2016 г. No. 412-рп [Order of the President of the Russian Federation from 19.12.2016 No. 412-rp]: in Russian, http://kremlin.ru/acts/news/53503; in English, en.kremlin.ru/acts/news/53503 (accessed September 19, 2020); see also Wu Enyuan 吴恩远, "普京为什么要纪念十月革命100周年" [Why is Putin commemorating the centenary of the October Revolution?], https://www.sohu.com/a/205671938_756567 (November, 2017; accessed September 19, 2020).

5. Wu, 2017.

6. Указ Президента РФ от 30.09.2015 г. No. 487 [Decree of the President of the Russian Federation from 30.09.2015 No. 487], http://kremlin.ru/acts/bank/40063 (accessed September 19, 2020).

7. Wu, 2017.

8. Wu, 2017.

9. "Opening of the Wall of Sorrows Memorial to Victims of Political Repression" [text of Vladimir Putin's remark], October 30, 2017, in Russian: http://kremlin.ru/events/president/news/55948; in English: http://en.kremlin.ru/events/president/news/55948 (accessed September 19, 2020). For more on the commemoration of the October Revolution and its centenary, see Wang Hui, "The Prophecy and Danger of October," *Theory and Criticism of Literature and Art*, no. 1 (2018).

10. I would like to acknowledge Kathleen Friello, Project Editor of this volume, who corrected errors in my understanding of the research and existing knowledge on avant-garde art in Western art history. She provided me with a list of these exhibitions, including *Art in Revolution: Soviet Art and Design since 1917*, at Hayward Gallery, London in 1971, based on that year's reissue of Camilla Gray's *Russian Avant-Garde 1908–1922* (originally 1962); *Russian Avant-Garde, 1908–1922* at Leonard Hutton Galleries, New York, also in 1971; and *Revolution: Russian Avant-Garde, 1912–1930*, at the Museum of Modern Art, New York, in 1978. Friello also noted that there was a rare export from the U.S.S.R. in 1977: *Russian and Soviet Painting: An Exhibition from the Museums of the USSR*, presented at The Metropolitan Museum of Art, New York, and the Fine Arts Museums of San Francisco. This exhibition, organized in Russia and covering 400 years of Russian art, contained about 50 works from the Soviet period. There were also two galleries instrumental in presenting Russian avant-garde art in the West in the 1970s and 80s: Galerie Gmurzynska in Cologne (including the 1974 exhibition, *From Surface to Space: Russia 1916–1924*), and Annely Juda Fine Art in London.

11. Standard transliteration is important for the public recognition of foreign figures. In the Chinese context, Tolstoy or Gorky have standard transliteration, but there was no standard transliteration for many figures mentioned in this text.

12. Maria Silina, "Struggle against Naturalism: Soviet Arts from the 1920s to the 1950s," *RACAR: Revue d'art canadienne/Canadian Art Review* 41, no. 2 (2016): 91–104; https://doi.org/10.7202/1038074ar (accessed August 10, 2020).

13. Tian Han 田汉, "建国十一年来戏剧战线的斗争和今后的任务—在中国戏剧家协会第二次会员代表大会上的报告" [Our mission on the frontlines of the battle of theatre in the 11 years since the country's founding and onward—report for the 2nd convention of the China Theatre Association], 戏剧报 [Theater gazette], nos. 14–15. See Luo Qi 罗琦, et al., "20世纪50年代形体动作方法在中国的传播" [Spread of the method of physical action in 1950s China], 戏剧报 [Theater gazette], no. 1 (2019): 131.

14. Almost no research theses and publications specify the original Russian names of Pidarkov, Korzun, and others. I have gone to great lengths to find Korzun's full name in an essay by an academic of the time. Pidarkov was "restored" based on transliteration of the Chinese by a Russian language expert. The names of the seven theater experts mentioned are likewise only available in Chinese.

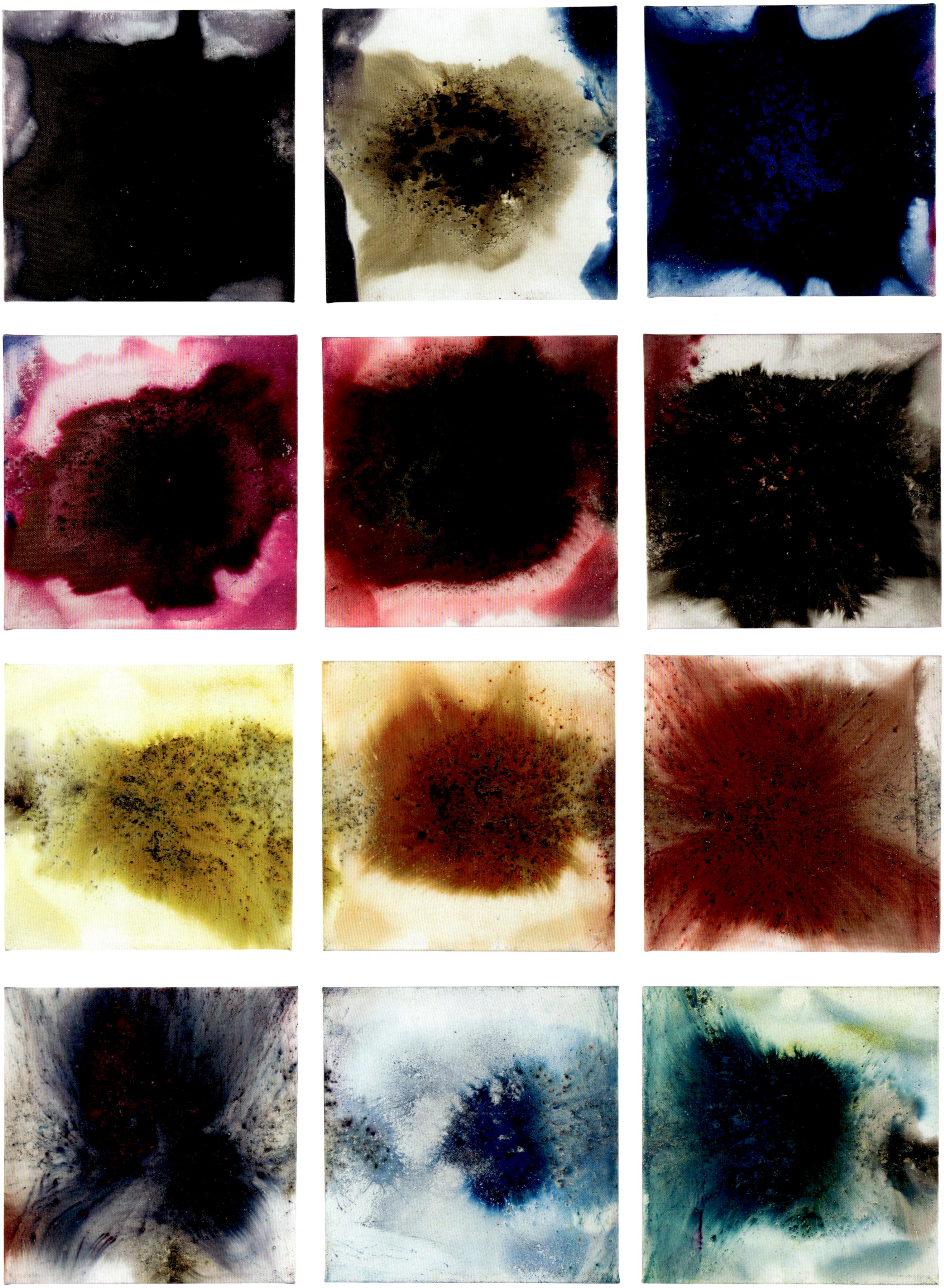

# Paradox of Entropy
## *Materials and Process in the Art of Cai Guo-Qiang*

Rachel Rivenc

### A Material Odyssey

The room falls silent. A sense of anticipation becomes palpable, perhaps even some nervousness, especially among those who have never witnessed such an event. A last call to make sure everyone is ready; silence again. Cai moves the lit incense stick closer to the fuse, fiddles with it for what seems like a very long microsecond. Then all of a sudden, the fuse is lit, igniting the gunpowder, and the flames run, they sprint at lightning speed accompanied by the violent, deafening sound of the deflagration: Boom, boom, ratatatat (figure 2). One may start to feel the sudden urge to run away, but it's already over. The room fills with smoke, eyes sting, it's hard to see. The studio team, in a well-rehearsed choreography, runs with the "pom-poms," balls of cotton rags, to smother any residual flames; the weights covering the drawing are removed, creating a thunderous rumble; finally the drawing is uncovered, everyone moves closer to see it—among them, the artist, the first to be surprised and marvel at the new creation, part his work and part the product of chance.

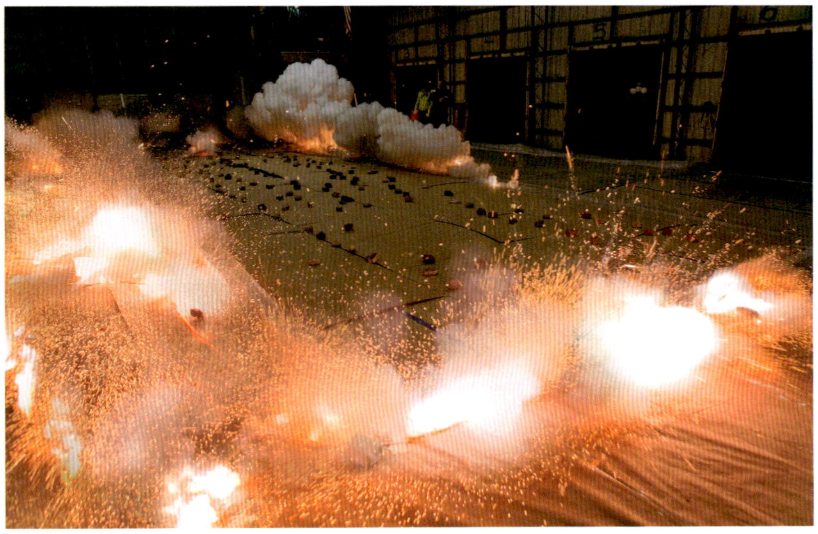

Figure 2. Ignition of gunpowder to create *White Tone* at Brookhaven, New York on April 8, 2016. Photo by Wen-You Cai

A wide-ranging, versatile artist who easily navigates between installations, ephemeral and participatory events, drawing, and painting, Cai Guo-Qiang has become best known for his use of gunpowder as an artistic material. Over his three decades of engagement with gunpowder, this explosive material has come to define Cai's work. Its partly unpredictable properties dictate the artistic process and determine the outcome. Gunpowder has successively and alternatively transformed, defined, and guided Cai's art, ensuring continuity yet disruption. It has been a dance, a dialogue, sometimes a playful wrestle between the artist and the material—the artist eager to stretch the use of the material beyond imaginable limits, and to tame it to some extent, even though the property that Cai relishes most in gunpowder is probably its uncontrollable nature.

Why gunpowder? When asked why he started using gunpowder, Cai often gives circumstantial explanations. Fireworks

Figure 1. Tests of Chinese and Japanese colored pyrotechnic powders (top two and bottom two rows, respectively) prepared by Cai Guo-Qiang in 2016 and donated to the Getty Conservation Institute for research and testing purposes. Photos by Michael Doutre, courtesy Getty Conservation Institute. © J. Paul Getty Trust

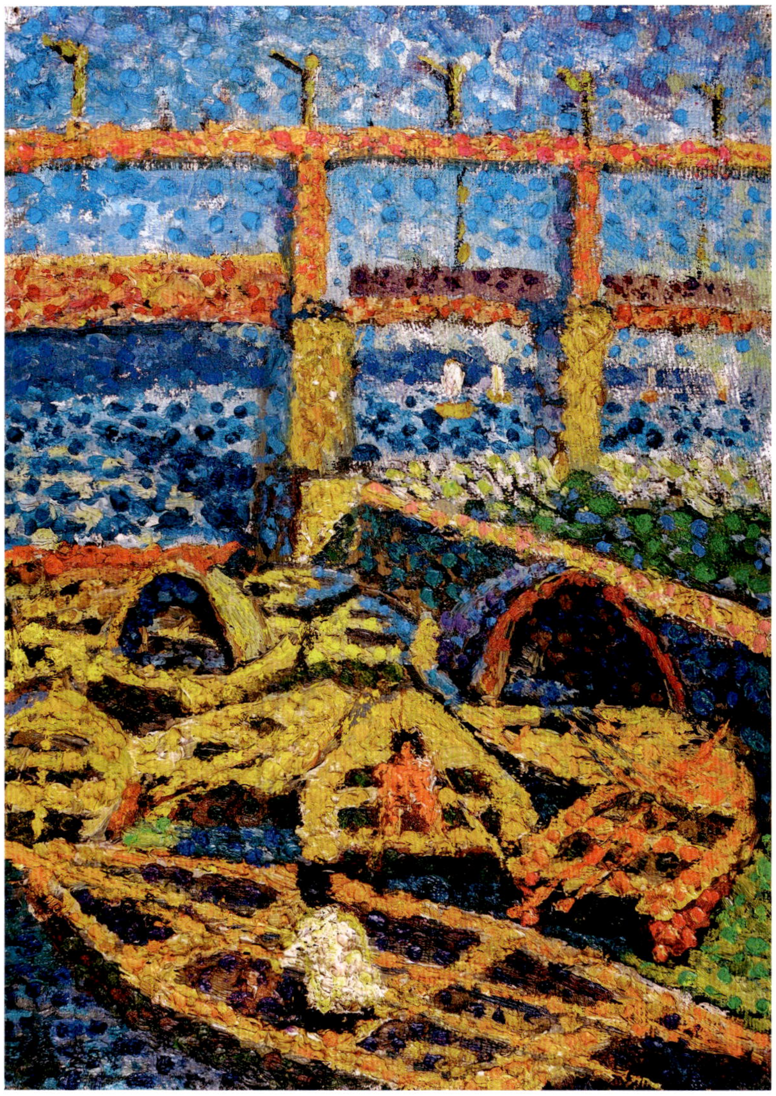

Figure 3. Cai Guo-Qiang, *Learning from Pointillism*, c. 1975–85. Oil on canvas backed with cardboard, 34.2 × 24 cm. Photo by Daxin Wu

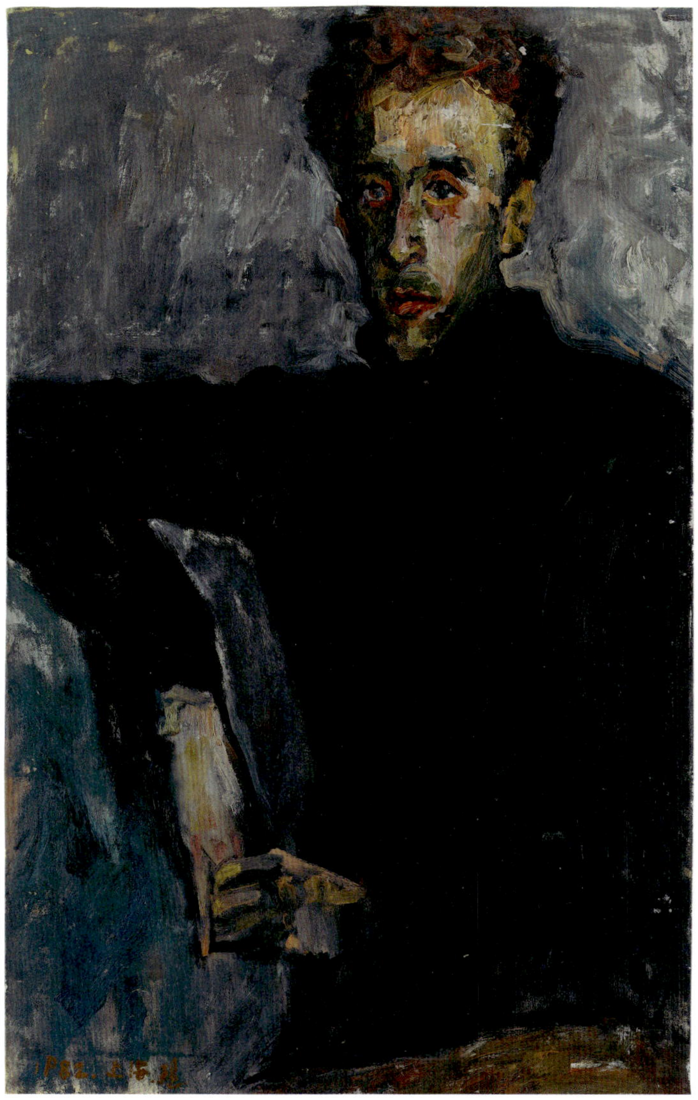

Figure 4. Cai Guo-Qiang, *Classmate*, 1982. Oil on canvas, 78.5 × 49.5 cm. Photo by Ron Amstutz

and firecrackers were everywhere in his hometown of Quanzhou, in the 1960s of his youth, for festivals, weddings, funerals, children playing. Cai even remembers how one of his cousins was maimed, and another killed, while playing with firecrackers. The danger was not a deterrent: on the contrary, it made it dangerous and forbidden, so all the more attractive to a young man looking to embolden himself. Indeed, Cai has repeatedly explained the choice of gunpowder by his desire to liberate himself from what he perceived as a timid, cautious, and overly controlling personality.[1]

Cai had been drawing and painting since his childhood. In his twenties, he painted stage sets for the Quanzhou Gaojia Opera Troupe, and then studied stage design at the Shanghai Theatre Academy. He also learned by experimenting with a wide range of Western styles, including Fauvism, Impressionism, and Pointillism, and was inspired by Cézanne, El Greco, and others. But while Cai's facility with painting enabled him to rapidly emulate and absorb these influences, it did not seem to help him find his own way, and at some point he felt lost (figures 3 and 4). To find new directions, he felt that he had to dramatically alter his painting style, and liberate his creativity; he wanted to find a way to manipulate the paint while relinquishing control over the results, and to unleash natural forces for bolder results than he was able to achieve with traditional materials and processes. So, he turned toward what he saw in his everyday life. It is hard to believe, in retrospect, that Cai's personality really was timid and cautious. He does emphasize however that not only was he cautious in general, but he was specifically scared of fireworks before he started using them for art and not used to handling them. The danger and the challenge to overcome his own fears made it all the more seductive.[2]

When Cai embarked on his long journey with gunpowder, he became curious about it and wanted to learn more. He became enamored not just with the physical potential of the material, but with its history and symbolic associations: invented by Chinese alchemists in search for the elixir of life, it is for Cai closely linked to Asian philosophies such as Daoism and *feng shui*. "Back in the days when a city was having a plague or an outbreak of disease, people might use firecrackers for special purposes, such as warding off evil spirits or the god of plague. In fact, the sulfur and flint in fireworks also helps kill bacteria and purify the air. Whether intentional or not, it becomes a sanitary measure when fireworks are used in a large-scale cultural event ... I didn't have all that in mind when I first started using gunpowder."[3]

But the main appeal of gunpowder to Cai remains its unpredictability and uncontrollability, and through this, the sensation that forces greater than the artist are at work, and contribute to the creation. Gunpowder became the means of Cai's dialogue with a source of invisible energy, and therefore an indispensable instrument of his attempts to bridge what he calls the seen and the unseen world. Gunpowder is essentially an agent of chaos. Chemically as well—for a particular mixture to be a viable pyrotechnic mixture, one of the determining factors is whether the entropy of the system increases as a result of the reaction, i.e., the randomness or disorder of the system. The greater the entropy, the greater the stability of the system, paradoxically.

For Cai, the uncontrollable nature of gunpowder and its propensity to chaos relate to the climate of the Socialist China he grew up in. Superficially, as rebellion, "[i]t was also a way for me to fight against the oppressive social climate and relatively closed environment of China at the time."[4] But perhaps more profoundly, embracing gunpowder and its uncontrollable nature might be a continuation of the Maoist spirit of rebellion. Cai has explained that the essential creed of Mao's Cultural Revolution was one of chaos and disruption: "Another influence that Mao's ideology has brought to my generation is that revolution is the truth, has the truth. Anything that is disrupting the usual, consensual rule or laws is considered a good move."[5] Mao Zedong himself is the incarnation for Cai of "the rebellious spirit, being disrespectful to authority and to the great people ... such a skeptical and rebellious spirit."[6] Eventually this very spirit of doubt and questioning preached by Mao is precisely what made Cai question and turn away from Mao's own teachings.

Not every paradox has to be reconciled: Cai often embraces contradiction, and overdetermination. Gunpowder is also for Cai a way to make peace with the violence of his upbringing, by using violence for creation. "I have totally lived in this earth-shaking age. Therefore, the times have left me with many things. Of course, the poverty of this age, there were also armed fights and conflicts and class struggle. During the Cultural Revolution, this was an age of violence with many different Red Guards, which has had an impact on me. Of course, the misfortune and sadness of this era, or the pains, poverty and lack of education of the people, many schools were shut down. This has something to do with my use of gunpowder, to create culture from such violence or using destruction to build."[7]

This aptitude of gunpowder to reconcile destruction and creation, to embrace paradoxes, and to create beauty and meaning out of chaos and violence, is probably for Cai what embodies his artistic pursuit the most.

## Early Years

Before gunpowder, the materials that Cai used for his early paintings were unremarkable—they only stood out by their paucity, lack of variety, yet the resourcefulness in their implementation. Once he started to paint stage sets for the Chairman Mao Thought Propaganda Team (which later became the Quanzhou Gaojia Opera Troupe), Cai had a small budget to purchase paints for the troupe and therefore gained access to a wider variety of material. He bought mostly cheap gouache paints, and sometimes more expensive ones for the small renderings of the final sets, destined to be reviewed by the director and leaders of the troupe. Occasionally he smuggled more than needed, to use on his own paintings. Cai also remembers that the paints he used for painting sets came in powder form and had to be mixed with water and glue, leaving one to wonder if these might have been casein based. Cai had to use all kind of ploys to mimic expensive canvases, for example gluing the gauze from facial masks or old pieces of clothing on cardboard procured from a shoe box factory. Cai also made his own white oil paint using lithopone, a white pigment composed of zinc sulfide and barium sulfate, mixed with linseed oil. The process was lengthy and labor intensive. He mostly prepared white paint, reckoning that's what he'd need in largest quantities. For colors, he purchased paint tubes made by the Shanghai Fine Arts Supply Company, sometimes sharing them with friends. "If someone has a paint of rare color, for example violet, everyone borrows some from the tube."[8]

Indeed, Cai's early paintings display a very restricted palette, predominantly white paint and very few colors: *Classmate* (1982), for example, contains large amounts of barium sulfate and zinc oxide, probably the lithopone that Cai described using (figure 3). Besides the white, the only colors are blue (imparted by the pigment Prussian blue, i.e., ferric ferrocyanide), and a few earth tones for the flesh. The medium is a drying oil, possibly linseed oil, with one sample containing fruit tree gum—perhaps an indication that Cai mixed gouache with the oil paint. Cai had to be so restrained in his use of expensive oil paints that when he wanted to achieve a thicker, more impastoed texture, he would mix all sorts of substances into the paint, including the debris from burned firewood and soil from the yard.[9]

In 1981, Cai moved to Shanghai to study at the Department of Stage Design of the Shanghai Theatre Academy (STA). His troupe in Quanzhou funded Cai to attend classes in Zhou Benyi's Department of Stage Design and receive formal training in painting. These years were very formative. Not only did Cai perfect his painting technique, but his learnings in the art of stage design profoundly influenced his practice of installation art, informing his sense of space, infusing it with theatricality and an acute understanding of how to impact the viewers. Zhou had studied in Leningrad at the Repin Institute of Arts and, having just returned from a study visit to the United States, was also familiar with Western stage design practices. He frequently took his students outdoors to sketch and paint, a habit that Cai had already developed in Quanzhou. Zhou describes these times as joyous ones: the class spent a lot of time outdoors, mingling with fishermen and workers. At the end of the day they drank together and reviewed each other's work. Zhou emphasizes that he encouraged individual development and expression, and that the training at the STA differed greatly from the very formal training dispensed at the Academy of Fine Arts. In comparison, says Zhou, the STA was freer, and put more emphasis on interdisciplinary experimentation.[10] Unfortunately, none of Cai's stage designs survived and they only exist as preliminary sketches or photographs.

## Destroying the Paint: First Experiments with Gunpowder

Cai's wife Hong Hong Wu—at the time his girlfriend—remembers vividly the creative crisis that Cai went through after a few years spent in Shanghai. "He was very unhappy and felt that his future

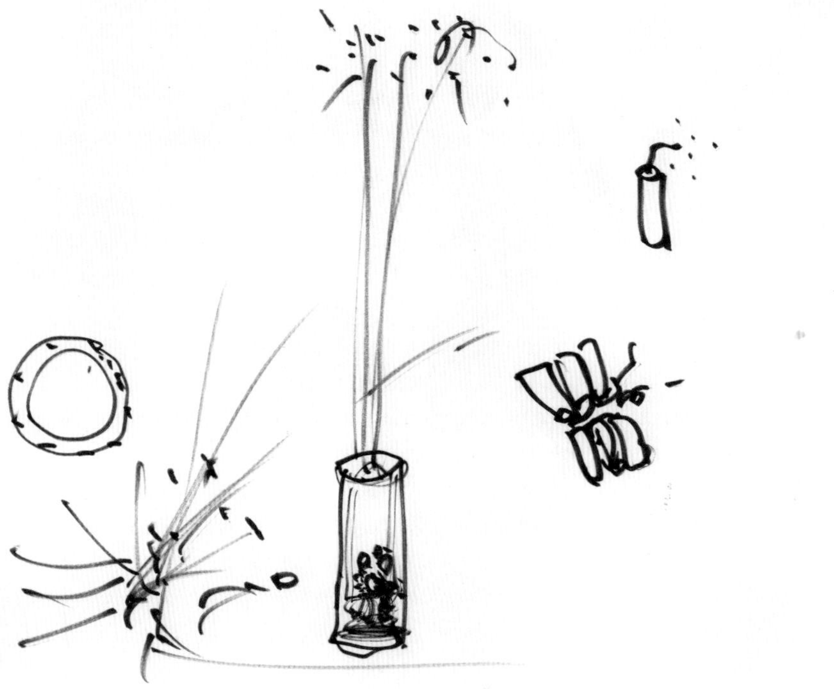

Figure 5. Structural difference between a firecracker and firework, as sketched by Cai Guo-Qiang during an interview with the author on July 22, 2016

was very bleak and he was in great pain. ... [H]e would often go to the countryside, get drunk and lie in the fields for hours ... he felt that he had no future ... he would repaint his paintings again and again, while talking to himself again and again."[11]

Looking for new sources of inspiration, Cai started making ink rubbings of ancient carvings from the Han dynasty, and of abstract natural patterns he would encounter in his surroundings, of rocks, reefs, tree roots. Cai then selected individual motifs from the ink rubbings and transformed them into paintings that looked more and more abstract—not pursuing abstraction for the sake of it, but as part of a search for new artistic horizons and individual expression. "There's no specific meaning, [except] for the pursuit of individualism and self-reliance. ... [T]o paint works that resist the social system would be the same as to praise it; it's two sides of a coin. So at that time for Chinese artists, the pursuit for abstraction is rebellion, revolution, and an act that expresses individualism."[12]

Cai was not only looking at different subject matters or sources of inspiration, he also got more and more experimental with materials around 1984–85. He looked for different ways to manipulate paint while relinquishing the control of the artist's hand. For example, he tried using a compact blower or a hair dryer to move the diluted paint around the canvas, or burning the paint directly, but felt he still had too much control.[13] This is when Cai thought of using gunpowder. In retrospect, this creative crisis was a momentous one, as it opened avenues and possibilities that Cai had barely dreamed of before.

### *Firecrackers and Gunpowder*

At first, Cai attempted to throw firecrackers or shoot toy rockets onto his paintings while they hung on the wall. To his dissatisfaction, the canvas just ended up getting burnt, so he resorted to opening the firecrackers and toy rockets to use the gunpowder that was inside. This was expensive and time consuming and eventually Cai just went to the firecracker factory to purchase bags of gunpowder. There, Cai remembers that he could simply purchase a whole bag of gunpowder that would weigh a couple of kilograms. Ironically, he recalls, gunpowder was far less stringently regulated than arts and culture. Cai then started sprinkling gunpowder on the paint and attempting to detonate it by using various means, including lit cigarettes, lighters, and incense sticks.[14]

Cai stressed that the gunpowder made for firecrackers, including the one bought directly from the firecracker factory, was different from the gunpowder used in fireworks. The gunpowder for firecrackers contained a lot of added sulfur which gave it a much yellower hue. In addition, when the firecracker was assembled, the bottom was sealed with reddish earth and the top was folded in to generate the pressure needed for the explosion. The gunpowder was in the center, creating the strong lifting charge needed to propel the toy rockets (figure 5). The gunpowder in firecrackers was much less powerful, diluted by sulfur and red earth, making it easier to create patterns in his paintings. He also used gunpowder from a firearms factory. The gunpowder used in fireworks is much purer and more powerful, but also more pricey, so Cai did not use it in bulk until later, after he moved to Japan.[15]

In the first paintings that Cai made with gunpowder, the gunpowder played little more than a supporting role. Because it was on the paint, it would not detonate properly. But Cai pursued feverishly his goal of relinquishing control and thus started drastically altering his paintings.

It is clear when looking at Cai's paintings of the time that he was still working with limited resources. However, instead of trying to disguise this fact and emulate the look of expensive art supplies, Cai started to embrace this DIY approach to making. Born out of necessity, it now served his new aesthetic. The paintings of 1984–86 look rough and unpolished, earthy, fleshy, and burnt. Cai made his own strainers or stretchers, and

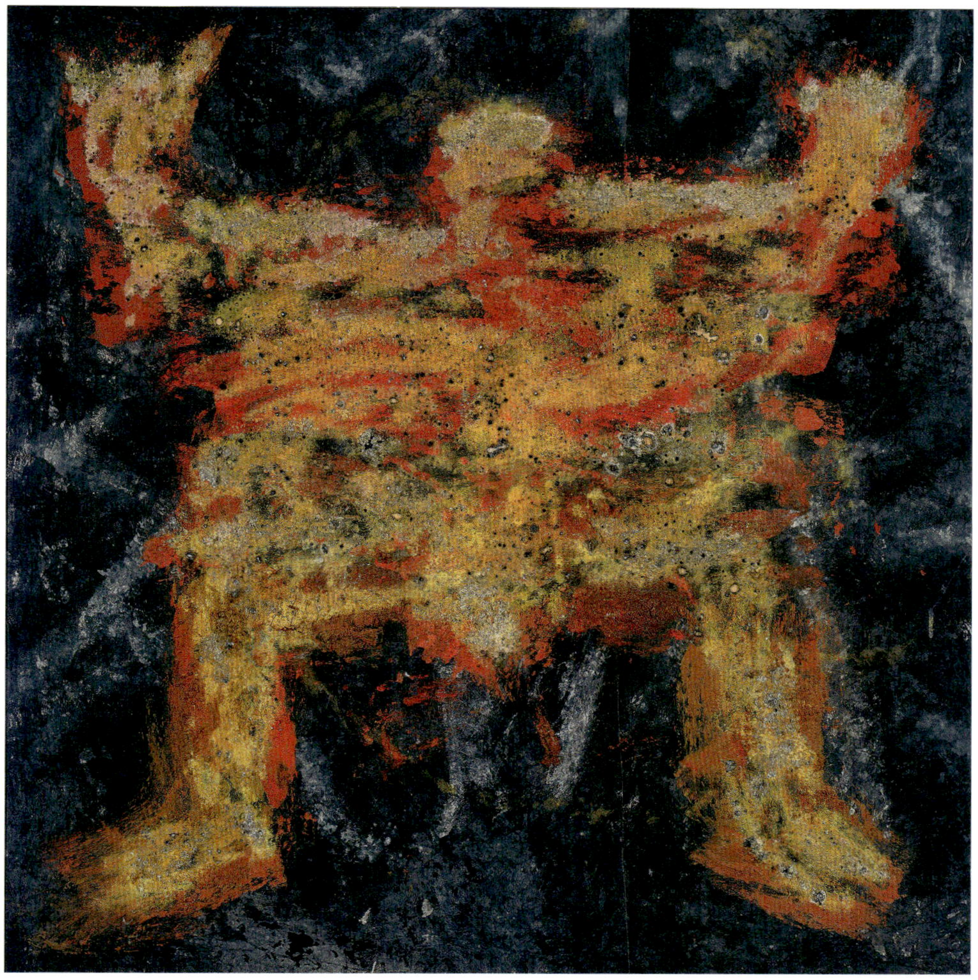

Figure 6. Cai Guo-Qiang, *Chu Ba Wang*, 1985. Gunpowder, oil, and ink on canvas, 155 × 150 cm. Photo by Hiro Ihara

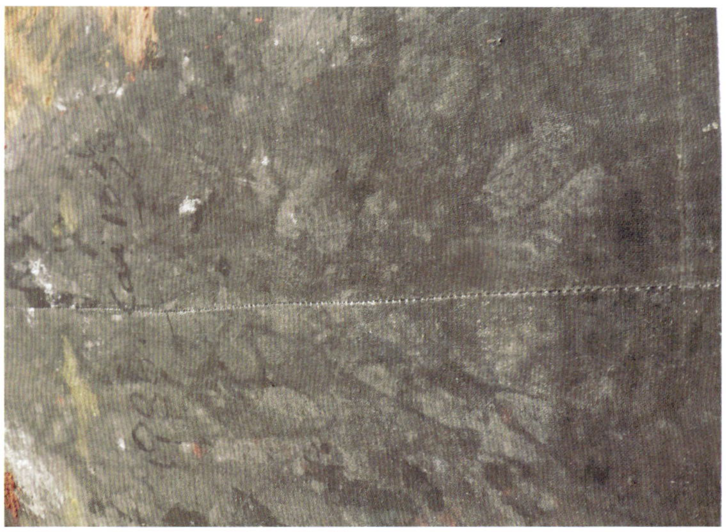

Figure 7. Detail of *Chu Ba Wang*, showing the seam visible on the front of the canvas. Photo by Rachel Rivenc

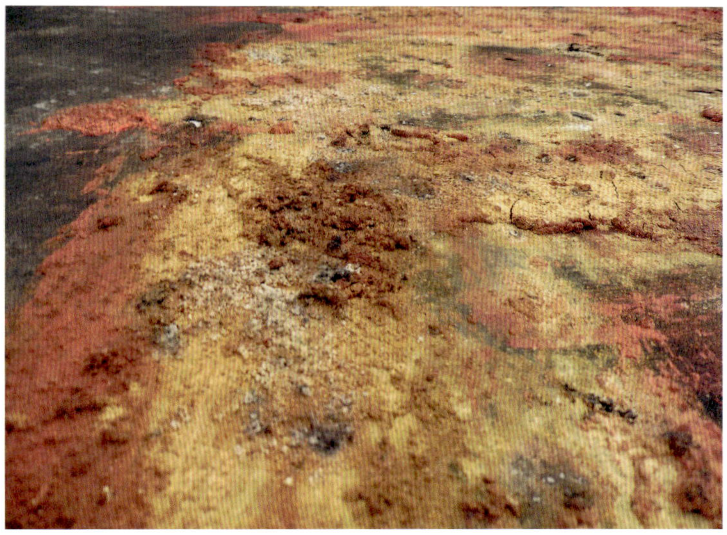

Figure 8. Detail of *Chu Ba Wang*, showing the texture of the paint. Photo by Rachel Rivenc

stretched coarse canvases over them. According to Hong Hong, he would often use sack cloth and pieces of packaging cloth from her father's department store that he'd sew together.[16] In several paintings of the time, the seam is visible and in fact quite prominently located on the front of the painting, leaving one to wonder whether this was on purpose. This is the case, for example, with *Chu Ba Wang* (1985, figures 6–8) and *Shadow: Pray for Protection* (1985–86). The paintings had no ground but Hong Hong remembers that Cai would size them, often with her help—an animal glue sizing was indeed identified on *Shadow: Pray for Protection*.[17]

In two paintings of the time, *Pillar for the Sky* (1985, figure 9) and *Chu Ba Wang*, Cai used gunpowder with an oil-based paint. He felt the paint was too bright and sprinkled sawdust and ashes from burned charcoal on top of the paint when it was still wet. Analyses of *Pillar for the Sky* do show the presence of large amounts of potassium throughout the painting, which is consistent with ashes being added to the paint, and presumably explains the overall grayish color of the paint. Analyses reveal that the yellow color of the contour lines is imparted by realgar, an arsenic sulfide compound.[18] The cross section shows a discrete

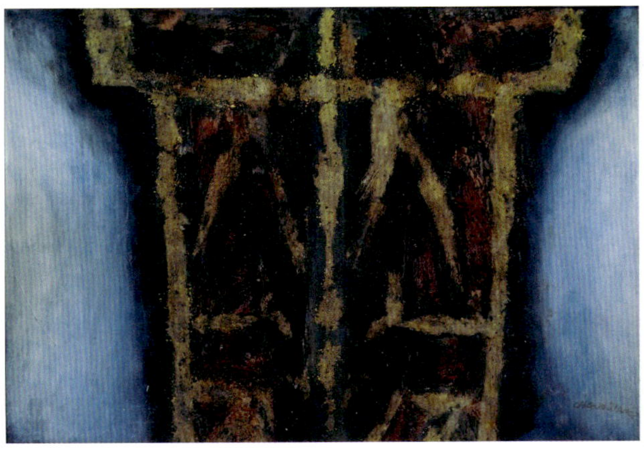

Figure 9. Cai Guo-Qiang, *Pillar for the Sky*, 1985. Gunpowder and oil on canvas, 80.1 × 116.8 cm. Photo by Tatsumi Masatoshi

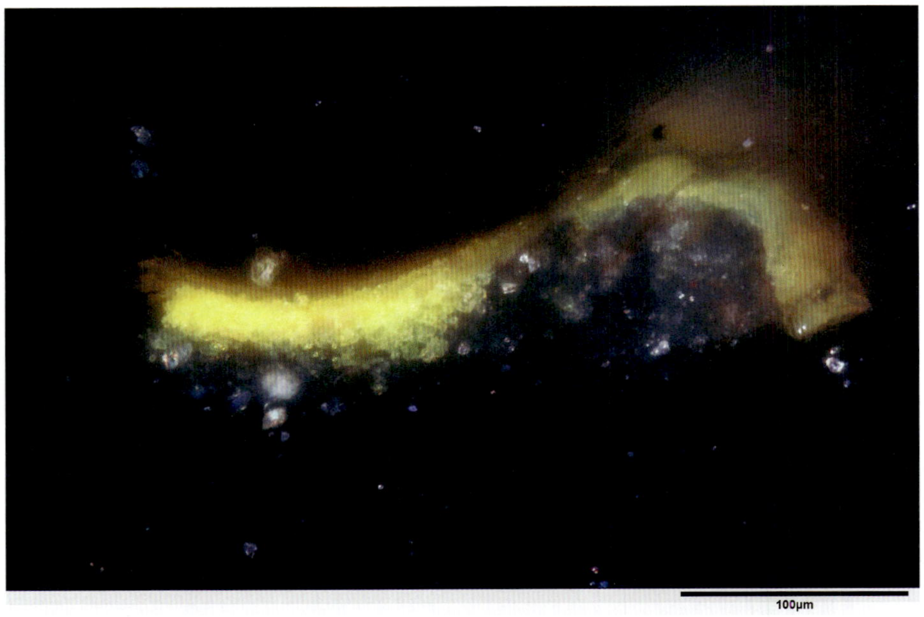


Figure 10. A cross section from *Pillar for the Sky*, observed with optical microscopy. The cross section reveals the presence of a layer of realgar on top (yellow layer). Cross section and photo by Michael Doutre, courtesy Getty Conservation Institute. © J. Paul Getty Trust

layer of paint consisting almost solely of realgar on top of a dark brown layer (figure 10). The paints that Cai used were still cheap, as indicated by the large quantities of barium sulfate, a common paint filler/extender, and the palette still very limited. In *Pillar for the Sky* the red and dark brown colors are imparted by iron oxide pigments. The dark paint appears waxy and glossy, probably as a result of the intense heat it has been exposed to. Another painting from 1985, *The Brand of Archean Era—Untitled* suggests that Cai was also experimenting with different binding media. As in *Chu Ba Wang* and *Pillar for the Sky,* realgar was used as source of yellow color, but in *The Brand of Archean Era—Untitled* it is mixed with a collagen-based glue to paint the oracle-bone symbols, while the background includes dirt and a PVA-bound paint containing Prussian blue. Prussian blue is one of the few bright and perhaps more expensive pigments to appear in Cai's early works, as in the painting *Classmate* discussed earlier.

## 35 Years of Drawing and Painting with Gunpowder

In 1986, Cai moved to Japan, and remained there for nearly ten years, mostly in Tokyo and its surroundings, except for a year spent in Iwaki in 1993–94. While in Japan, Cai was able to gain easier access to better quality gunpowder, and in 1987–88, he started exploring the use of pure black gunpowder as the sole medium for drawings, eventually dispensing with the paint altogether. He also briefly experimented with colored pyrotechnic powders from daytime fireworks around that time, but felt then that there was so much to explore with the black gunpowder, both technically and conceptually, that using paint or colored pyrotechnic powder would be distracting.[19]

Cai's exploration continued for the following three decades. During this time, Cai's process of drawing with gunpowder has essentially remained the same, but with increased refinement, mastery, and sophistication, as well as a spectacular increase in scale. In 2015, however, Cai returned to the use of colored pyrotechnic powders, sparingly at first, but soon lavishly and exuberantly (figure 11 shows one of the first paintings he made in 2015 with colored powders). Although the term is not technically accurate, they are colloquially referred to as "color gunpowder" and this terminology will be used here. Cai considers this new development in his work to be the rebirth of his painting practice, and through the use of color he has been in the past few years engaged in a fervent dialogue with Western art history. For Cai, this return to painting for its own sake started with a shift in subject matter, which he attributes to the nostalgia and longing he felt during his long absence from home while working on the Beijing Olympics ceremony:

> Before 2008 I was intrigued by the sense of the larger cosmos, the relationship between human and the universe, the Earth and land, and society. During the two years of Olympics preparation time, I started to focus more on reflecting on the Chinese culture. For the opening I was seeking the essence of Chinese culture and its significance to the world. ... The other reality is, during the two years preparing for the Olympics, I was mainly residing in Beijing. On my birthday I received a big poster written by the studio staff and hand carried by Hong Hong from New York. ... This suggested that I had left my family, my studio for a year now. So I had more emotions towards my children; without my even realizing, my eldest had graduated from high school and entered college. That's why after the Olympics I had experienced this huge change, which is focusing on florals and nature. ... [T]his change has continuously evolved to this day, from florals and slowly evolving to colors. ... Installations and large outdoor explosion events are like social activities and revolutions. But paintings are similar to making love on the bed, it's about intimacy and personal taste.[20]

Painting for Cai is not only about the subject, but also about the purpose. For decades, most of his gunpowder drawings were related to ideas that he had for explosion events: they were sketches, or preparatory drawings meant to convey the ideas he had for particular projects and events. Although the materials that he uses are far removed from traditional painting materials, Cai's current artistic practice is very much a quest for the essence or spirit of painting, which involves a thorough questioning of its traditional aesthetic tenets and relinquishing of preconceived ideas in favor of material experimentation and complete aesthetic ingenuity.[21] As Cai puts it:

> Right now I'm not rushing into mixing and pairing colors. I'm trying to avoid what I had learned when I studied art, the good color palettes and bad palettes, how colors should be paired together to achieve harmony and beauty. I'm also trying to avoid my impressions of good paintings and paintings of the Old Masters. I'm intentionally trying to put that away. ... I want to use gunpowder colors in ways that are more spontaneous, improvised, discordant, and nonrational. There are several potential objectives for this. The first is the wild and not so rational. The second is to expose the core energy of this material, including its problems. The third is the encounter with the unknown. Since now I'm returning to painting, I'm faced with the history of painting and my own art, so there is this stage where we start from the beginning to de-historicize. Sometimes it may be difficult to appreciate and it may not feel harmonized, but isn't that what you're looking forward to see?[22]

## The Materials

### *Black Gunpowder: History and Chemistry*

Gunpowder is mainly composed of black powder, i.e., a mixture of an oxidizer, a source of sulfur, and fuels. As with all combustion processes, the ignition and combustion of gunpowder requires oxygen. The oxidizer is a compound that releases oxygen as it burns, thus feeding the reaction. Saltpeter (potassium nitrate) has historically been the most commonly used oxidizer but various other nitrates, chlorates, and perchlorates can also be found in black powder formulations. Sulfur is found as elemental sulfur or sulfide minerals such as realgar and serves as fuel for the ignition reaction.

Traditional black gunpowder has had a very set composition for centuries: 75% potassium nitrate, 15% charcoal, and 10% sulfur.[23] To be reactive and properly ignite and detonate, ingredients must be brought in intimate contact, which is done by milling them with water then pressing them into a cake that then needs to be broken. The methods of preparation and conditions of use are crucial to the resulting properties and behavior. Depending on the intended use, fuels can be provided by different forms of carbon in addition to charcoal, such as resins, gums or carbohydrates.

The first firecrackers are commonly believed to have appeared in China sometime in the 2nd century BCE. They were simply bamboo stalks which, when thrown in the fire, exploded with a bang because of the overheating of the compressed air. Actual gunpowder is also thought to have originated in China, and to have been invented fortuitously in the first half of the 9th century by Chinese alchemists in search of the elixir of life. Having prepared a concoction of honey, sulfur, and saltpeter, they saw it abruptly erupt in flames, as the sulfur and honey acted as fuels and were subsequently oxidized by the saltpeter.[24]

By the 11th century, Chinese court records include texts outlining recipes for "fire medicine" to be used in incendiary bombs for warfare. Military applications continued to develop in the 12th and 13th centuries to react to the military threats posed by the Jurchens, then the Mongols. While it is not clear exactly when gunpowder appeared in Europe, it is known that chemists/alchemists by the 13th century were experimenting with different proportions of saltpeter/sulfur/charcoal, and realized that "a loose, open tray of powder was all that was needed to produce a flash, but in order to produce the bang the powder needed to be confined."[25] The use of black powder as a propellant for cannons was widespread in Europe by the 14th century and has been essential to military advances in modern Europe ever since.

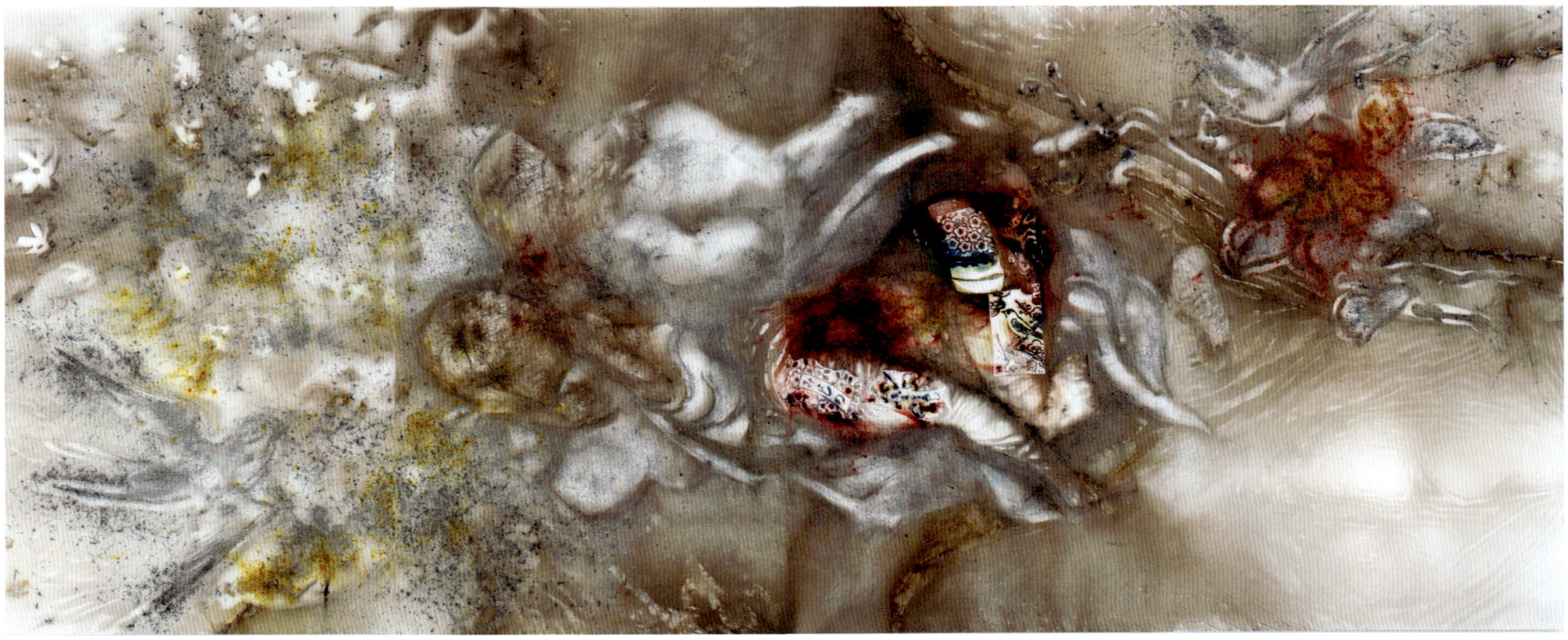

Figure 11. Cai Guo-Qiang, *Seasons of Life: Spring*, 2015. Gunpowder on canvas, 259 × 648 cm. Photo by Yokohama Museum of Art

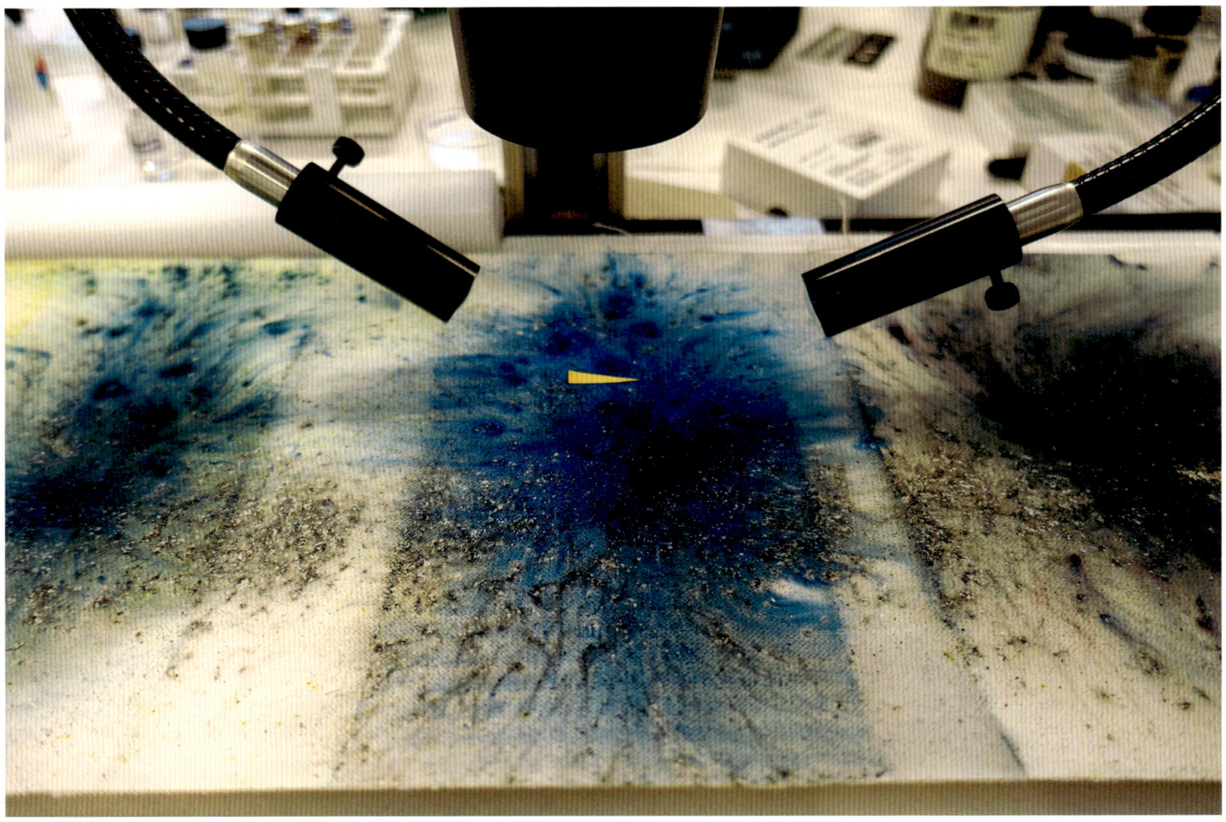

Figure 12. Test of blue colored pyrotechnic powder on canvas examined under the microscope. Photo by Andrzej Liguz, courtesy Getty Conservation Institute. © J. Paul Getty Trust

Actual fireworks were likely introduced in Europe from China and India via the Middle East, first in Italy and by the 16th century in England. Notable advances in the field of fireworks followed Claude Louis Berthollet's discovery of potassium chlorate in the 1780s, since potassium chlorate was able to produce brilliantly colored flames, thereby adding color to the effects of sparks, noise, and motion that were already available with potassium nitrate-based compositions. The latter part of the 19th century marked the beginning of modern pyrotechnic technology, with the manufacture of magnesium and aluminum metals that can produce bright white sparks and white light, and the commercial availability of strontium, barium, and copper compounds which could create vivid red, green, and blue flames.

### *Daytime Fireworks/Colored Pyrotechnics*

The colored powders that Cai started using in 2015 to create his paintings are pyrotechnic mixtures designed for daytime fireworks. The compounds used are very different from the compounds used to create colorful lights in nighttime fireworks. In daytime fireworks, a colored smoke is produced by volatilizing an organic dye which then condenses in air to form small solid particles. The dyes are strong absorbers of visible light. The light reflected off the vaporized particles is missing the absorbed wavelengths, so that the complementary hue is perceived by observers. This is the opposite from nighttime fireworks, which produce a colored flame. In this latter case the emitted wavelengths are perceived as color by viewers.

The background on the chemistry of colored pyrotechnics given below is instrumental in understanding the properties of the material used by Cai. Daytime fireworks have a number of very specific requirements. The mixture needs to produce sufficient heat to vaporize the dye and a sufficient volume and density of gas to disperse the dye into the surrounding space. At the same time, the mixture must ignite and burn smoothly at a low enough temperature to avoid decomposition of the dye. The dyes must be volatile enough to convert to the vapor state upon heating without substantial decomposition. For this reason, fairly low molecular weight dyes are generally used. They also need to be chemically stable at a high temperature, so oxygen rich functional groups are usually avoided since they easily induce oxidative decomposition of the molecule; instead, amine groups are often used. A crucial requirement is also that the smokes produced be non-toxic, since they are released into the atmosphere in proximity to the audience.

Because of these requirements, potassium chlorate, $KClO3$ is often used as an oxidizer: it provides a low ignition temperature with reliable burning at low temperatures. Coolants such as sodium bicarbonate or magnesium carbonate are often added to the mixture, in the proportions required to obtain the desired rate of burning and correct reaction temperature. Carbohydrates (i.e., sugars such as lactose or sucrose) are often used as a fuel in combination with the potassium chlorate. The amount of heat can also be controlled by adjusting the potassium chlorate to fuel ratio. Lactose is nowadays the most common fuel used for daytime fireworks. Cellulose nitrate is a common component of propellant compositions because the fuel and oxygen are combined within the same molecule.

In terms of color, the range is limited by the number of heat resistant dyestuffs that are commercially available. Anthraquinones are commonly used and can provide colors from orange to green depending on the level of conjugation—increased conjugation will cause a shift to longer wavelengths. Cai mostly works

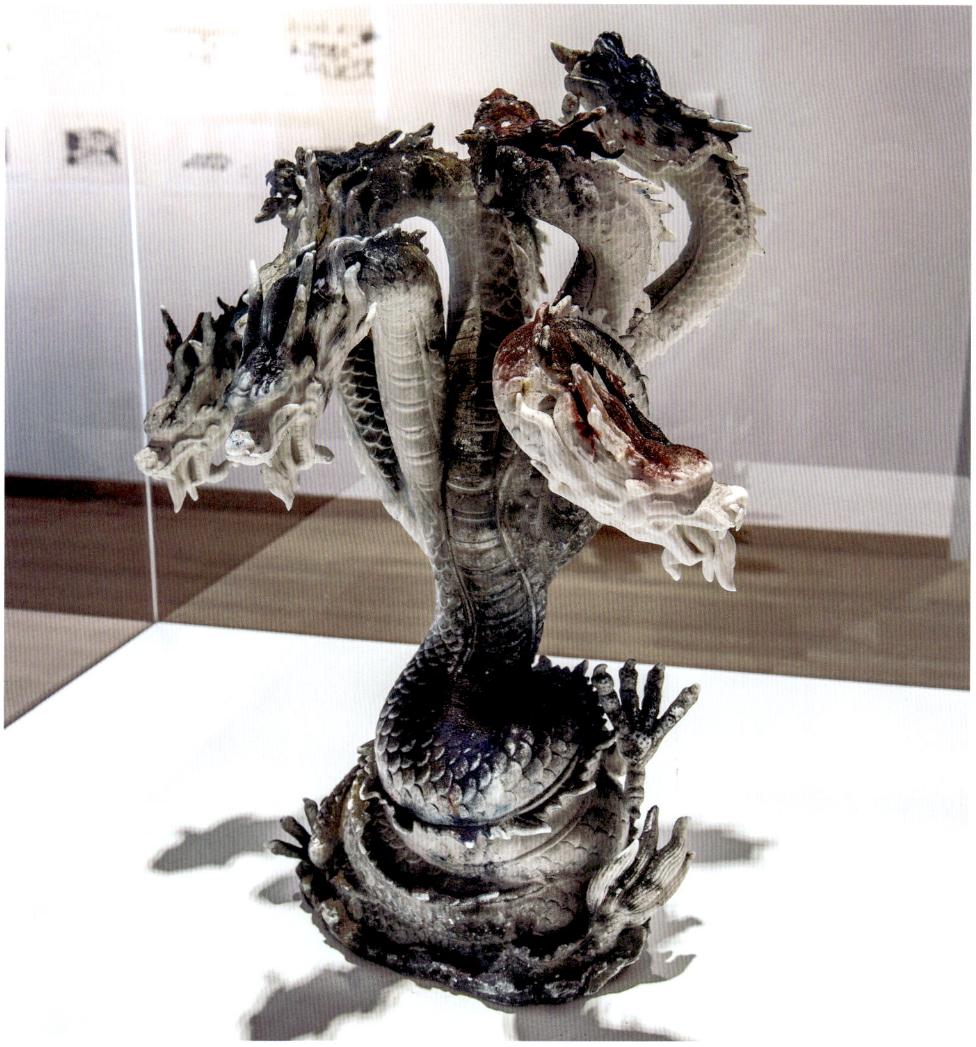

Figure 13. Cai Guo-Qiang, *Study for Seven-Headed Dragons: Project for the Vatican Museum*, 2016 (see no. 7.5). Gunpowder on porcelain, approx. 37 × 26 × 17 cm. Photo by Harry Heuts, courtesy Bonnefanten Museum

with six colors sourced from Japan and six colors sourced from China, as well as with locally sourced colors when needed. Besides its volatility, the quantity of dye present in the mixture will also affect the burning rate. The dye acts as a diluent, so the greater the quantity of dye used, the slower the burning rate. At the same time, the dye needs to be present in sufficient amount to account for the partial decomposition that inevitably occurs because of the heat. A typical colored smoke composition often contains 40–60% dye by weight. Cai generally adds black gunpowder to the colored pyrotechnic powders he uses for his paintings, to offset their slower burning rate and produce a more spectacular deflagration.

Analyses of tests prepared by Cai, with both the Japanese and the Chinese powders he is using (figures 1 and 12), confirmed that potassium chlorate or perchlorate was used as the oxidizer, and identified potassium sulfate, presumably resulting from the addition of black gunpowder to the colored fireworks by Cai to promote a more explosive reaction. A range of additives and reaction byproducts were also identified. Most of the pigments, colorants, and dyes used to impart color to the powders could also be identified. For example, analyses revealed that the blue is produced by "phthalocyanine blue" or pigment PB:15, a copper-containing pigment commonly used in paint formulations. The blue pigment was also used to produce the green and purple colors, by being mixed with, respectively, a yellow and a red dye.[26]

## Substrates

For his gunpowder drawings, Cai has mostly been using Japanese paper, preferring when possible handmade raw hemp fiber paper ordered from a traditional paper mill, Ozaki Seishijo, in Kōchi Prefecture of Japan. After 2015, Cai has used predominantly commercially prepared canvases on stretchers for his color paintings. Cai also uses rigid substrates, notably porcelain, in the form of tiles bearing intricate flowery reliefs, or of fully three-dimensional sculptures (figure 13). These are handmade by a factory in Dehua, a small town about an hour's drive from Quanzhou specializing in the craft of porcelain. The porcelain used is unglazed, hard-paste made of high purity kaolin extracted from local deposits.[27] Cai has also used silk, as well as glass and mirror, exploring the aesthetic possibilities open by the latter's transparency, and has on occasion experimented with terracotta, plaster, marble, and alabaster, among other materials.

## Application Process

Cai's drawings with gunpowder were often part of larger projects and concepts, and accompanied by a constellation of smaller artworks, including sketches, drawings, and albums. Some projects never get realized so the drawings are the only actualization of Cai's ideas. Cai always sketched extensively and kept sketchbooks where he jotted down ideas for projects as well as

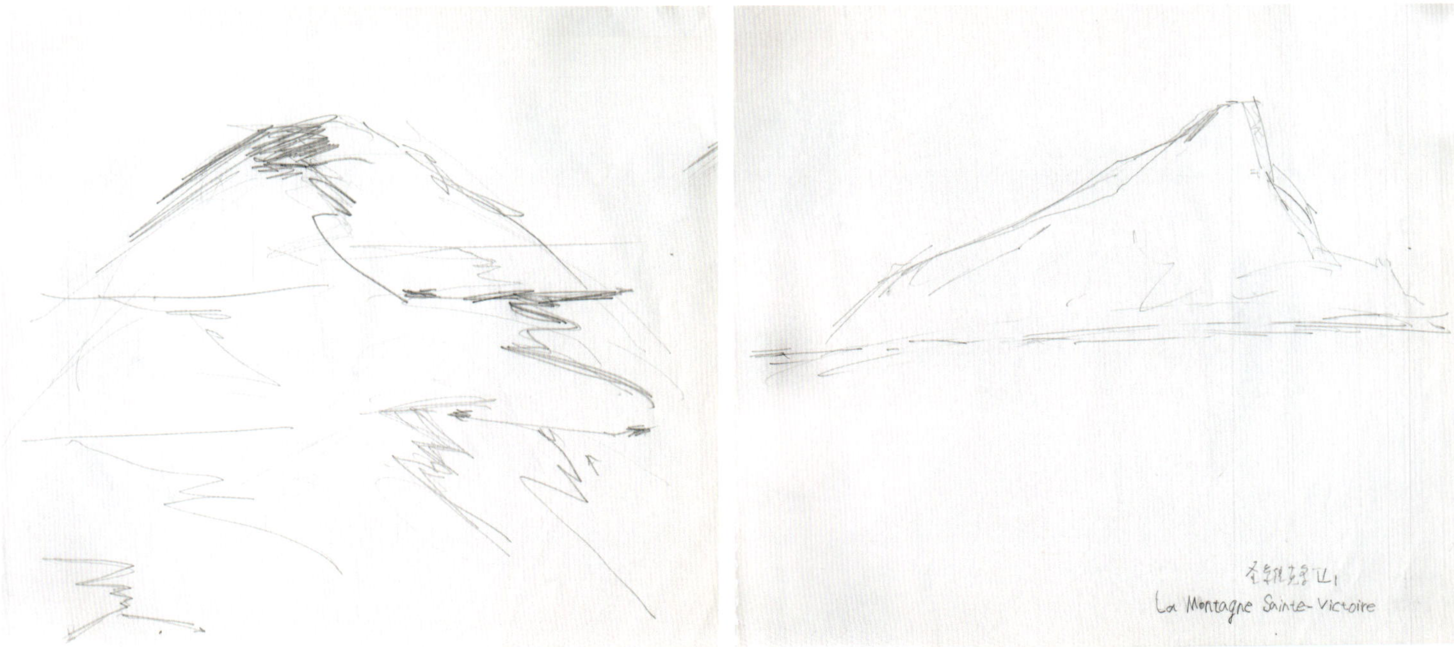


Figure 14. Cai Guo-Qiang, *Sketches for Ascending Dragon: Project for Extraterrestrials No. 2* (Mont Sainte-Victoire), 1989. Pencil on paper, 21.6 × 24.5 cm each

figurative sketches and drawings (figure 14). Cai continues to this day to sketch and draw, but the preparatory process is also often accompanied by lengthy iconographic research and the use of computer-assisted drawings.

### *Drawing and Stencil*

For a relatively simple, or abstract, drawing such as *Ascending Dragon: Project for Extraterrestrials No. 2* (figure 15) Cai lays the gunpowder directly on the paper. In addition to the gunpowder, Cai has used black sumi ink and calligraphy brushes to sign his name or, especially on earlier works, to write commentaries or draw. For more complex drawings, Cai draws a stencil first (figure 16). His studio assistants then cut the stencils. When working in different regions and cultures, Cai often tries to enlist the help of local volunteers, particularly for very large drawings.

### *Application of the Gunpowder*

Preparing the actual drawing can take up to several days, depending on the size of the painting. The floor is protected with butcher paper and the substrate laid flat over it. The stencil is laid

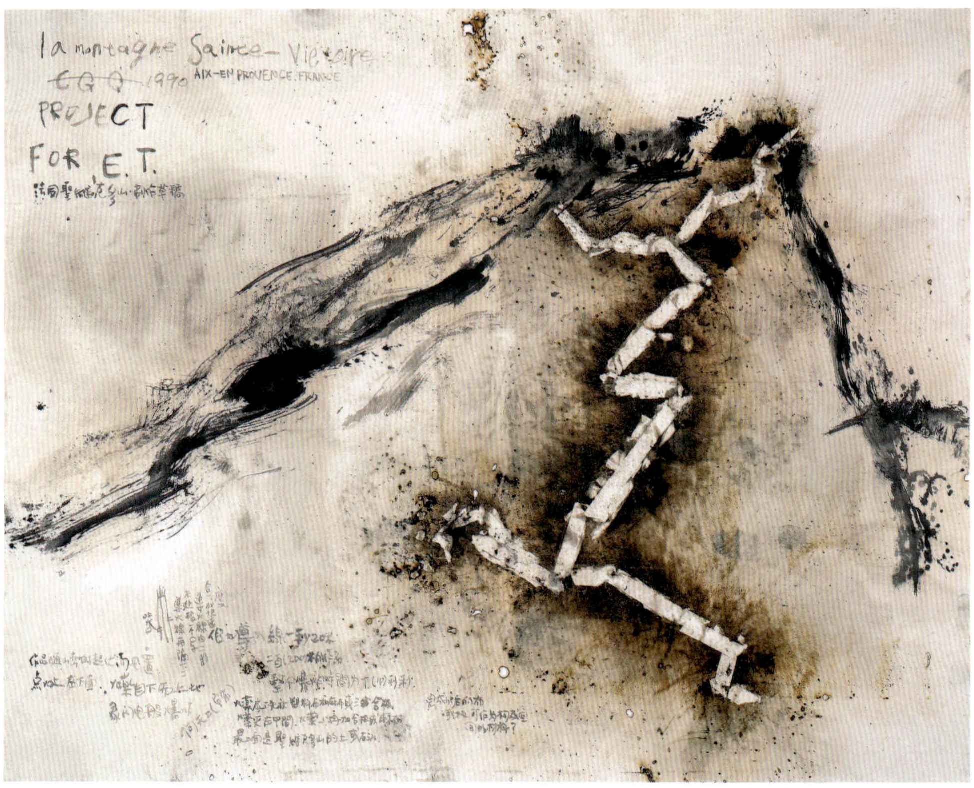


Figure 15. Cai Guo-Qiang, *Ascending Dragon: Project for Extraterrestrials No. 2* (no. 6.1), 1989. Gunpowder and ink on paper, 240 × 300 cm. Collection of Leo Shih

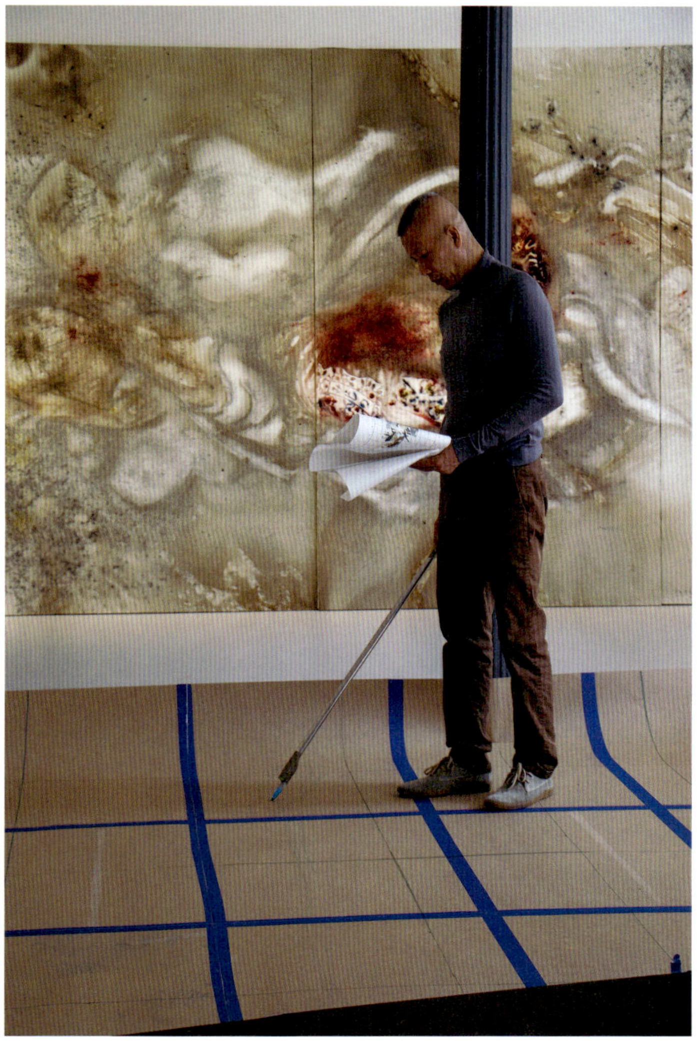

Figure 16. Cai Guo-Qiang drawing the stencil for *White Tone* in New York City on April 6, 2016. Photo by Rachel Rivenc

over the substrate, and the process of applying the gunpowder starts. Cai sprinkles and rubs the different powders slowly, deliberately, almost meditatively. The process looks deceptively simple but in fact relies on Cai's consummate knowledge of the properties, reactivity, and appearance of the different powders (figures 17 and 18). If the drawing is very large, Cai walks on it, using white socks or slippers to protect the surface of the drawing, or builds small wooden bridges over it, and might use a small broom to spread the gunpowder. Sometimes, instead of, or in addition to the stencils, Cai makes use of foliage, branches, flowers, or actual objects and garments. In *Memories* (2011), a drawing made in Doha as part of a large exhibition, Cai used local abayas[28] as stencils to create silhouettes evoking Muslim women and sprinkled gunpowder on them. Cai sprinkles the gunpowder on the objects, and the organic matter that they are made of burns and is mostly consumed during the deflagration, leaving behind charred residues, and their outline in gunpowder (figures 19 and 20).

### *Ignition*

Once Cai is satisfied with the drawing, it is prepared for the moment of ignition. The method depends on the result that Cai wants to achieve. Sometimes, the whole drawing or painting is covered with glassine; the glassine traps the smoke resulting from the ignition and creates drapery effects. The drawing is covered with cardboard and weights placed on top to contain the deflagration. This is to prevent the displacement of matter, which would disturb the drawing, and to protect the artist, his team, and the audience from projected matter. The moment of ignition is always a surprise: will the fuse behave as expected? Will the gunpowder burn through the substrate, or not even combust fully? Even though the technique is perfected, and every precaution is taken,

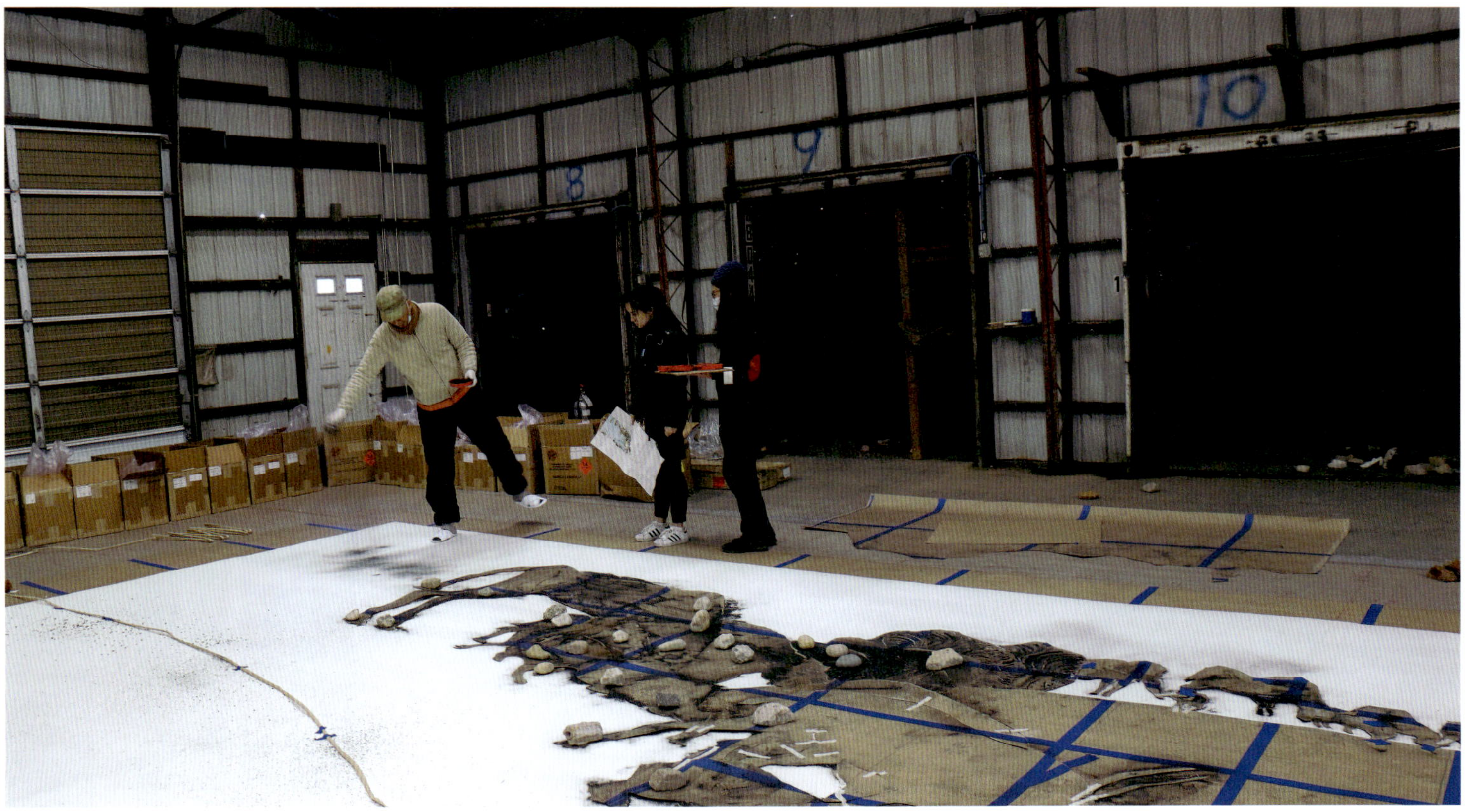

Figure 17. Cai Guo-Qiang sprinkling gunpowder to create *White Tone* in Brookhaven, New York on April 8, 2016. Photo by Rachel Rivenc

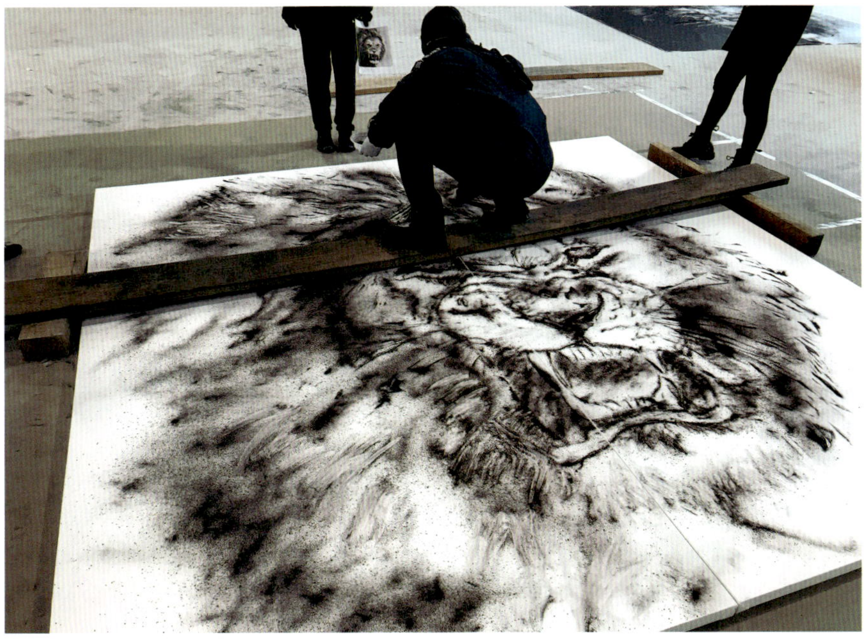

Figure 18. Cai Guo-Qiang sprinkling gunpowder to create *Study for Pompeii: Fierce Lion* (no. 3.6) in February 2018, with a bridge built over the work enabling Cai to reach all areas of the painting without staining the canvas. Photo by Sang Luo

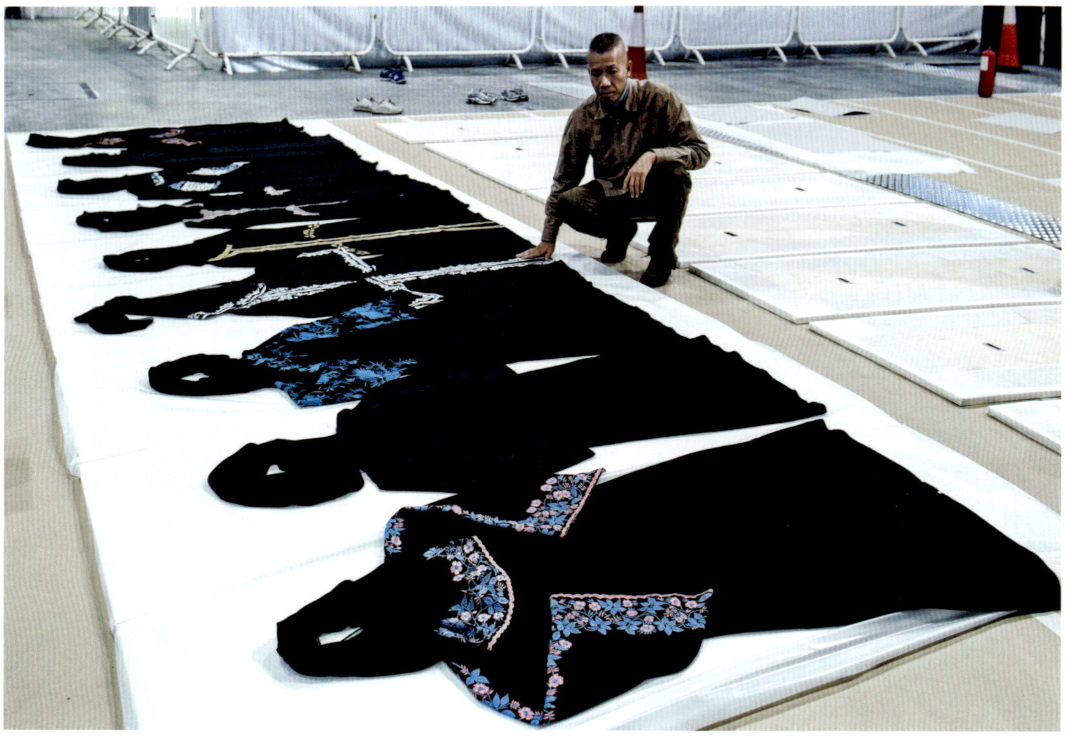

Figure 19. Cai Guo-Qiang contemplating positions of abayas for his gunpowder painting *Memories* at Al-Riwaq in Doha in 2011. Photo by Lin Yi

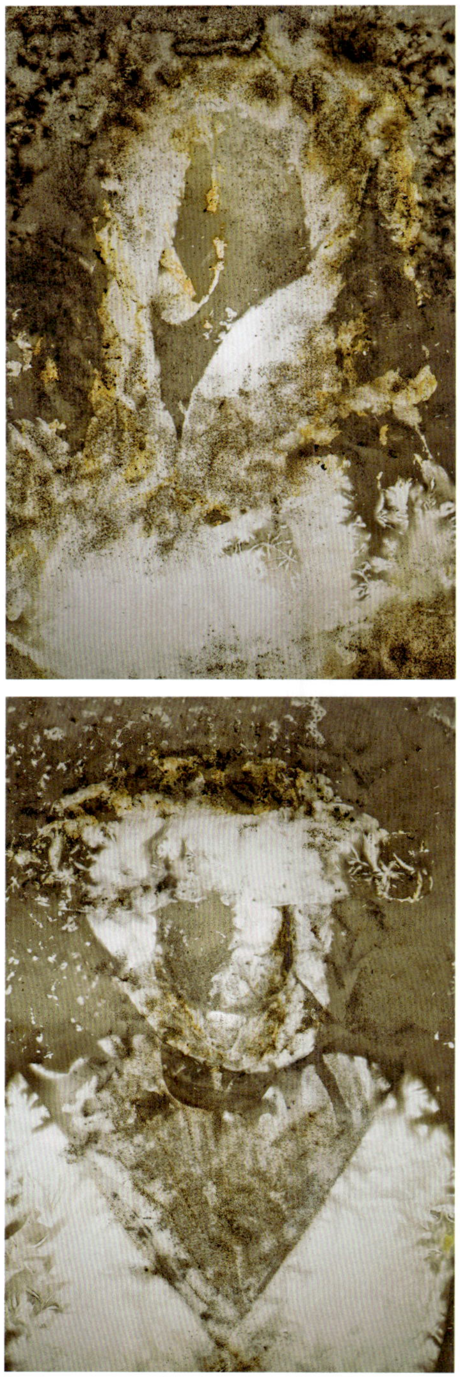

Figure 20. Details of gunpowder painting *Memories* (2011). Photo by Lin Yi

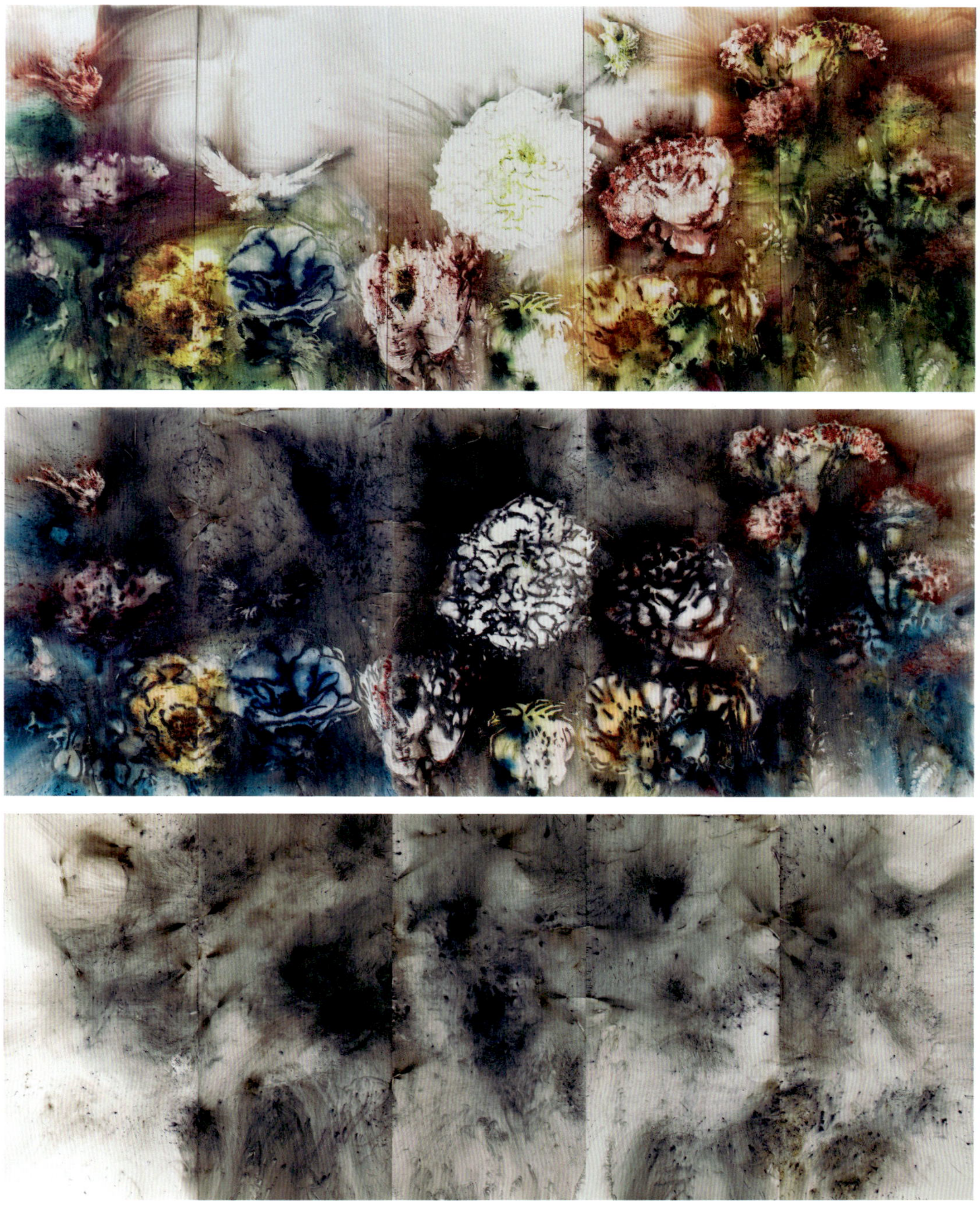

Figure 21. Top: *Heaven Complex No. 1* (no longer extant); middle: *Heaven Complex No. 1 and No. 2*; bottom: *Heaven Complex No. 3*, all 2017. Gunpowder on canvas, 300 × 750 cm each. Photos by Wen-You Cai and Yvonne Zhao

*Heaven Complex No. 1* was the result of the first ignition. Cai decided to do a second ignition: the work was returned to the floor, sprinkled with black gunpowder, and covered with a blank canvas on top. After the second ignition, *Heaven Complex No. 1* became *Heaven Complex No. 1 and No. 2*. The original *Heaven Complex No. 1* now only exists through photographs. The blank canvas placed on top became *Heaven Complex No. 3*, imprinted with a ghost image

there is always an element of danger. The studio team always has fire extinguishers on hand, and as soon as the ignition is over, rushes to extinguish any small flames remaining with "pom-poms," a studio-made device consisting of round balls made from white cotton painter's rags. Large fans are also often used to disperse the dense smoke created by the ignition.

The process for black gunpowder drawings and colored paintings is fundamentally the same, i.e., laying down on the paper, canvas, or other substrate, applying the colored powders and gunpowder to create the image, then igniting it. However, the process for colored paintings has become increasingly varied and complex as Cai's appetite for experimentation was reignited by the expansion of his color palette. Recently, Cai has experimented with a whole range of additional effects, and further explored previous techniques. For example, he's increasingly adopted the method of covering the canvas with a second, blank canvas of equal shape and size, creating a mirror painting. He started igniting a painting twice, with additional black gunpowder, creating a darker, often more ominous version of the painting, while the first version only exists as a photographic record (figure 21). He's also explored using incense sticks or fuse lines dipped into colored powders to create drawings (figure 22).

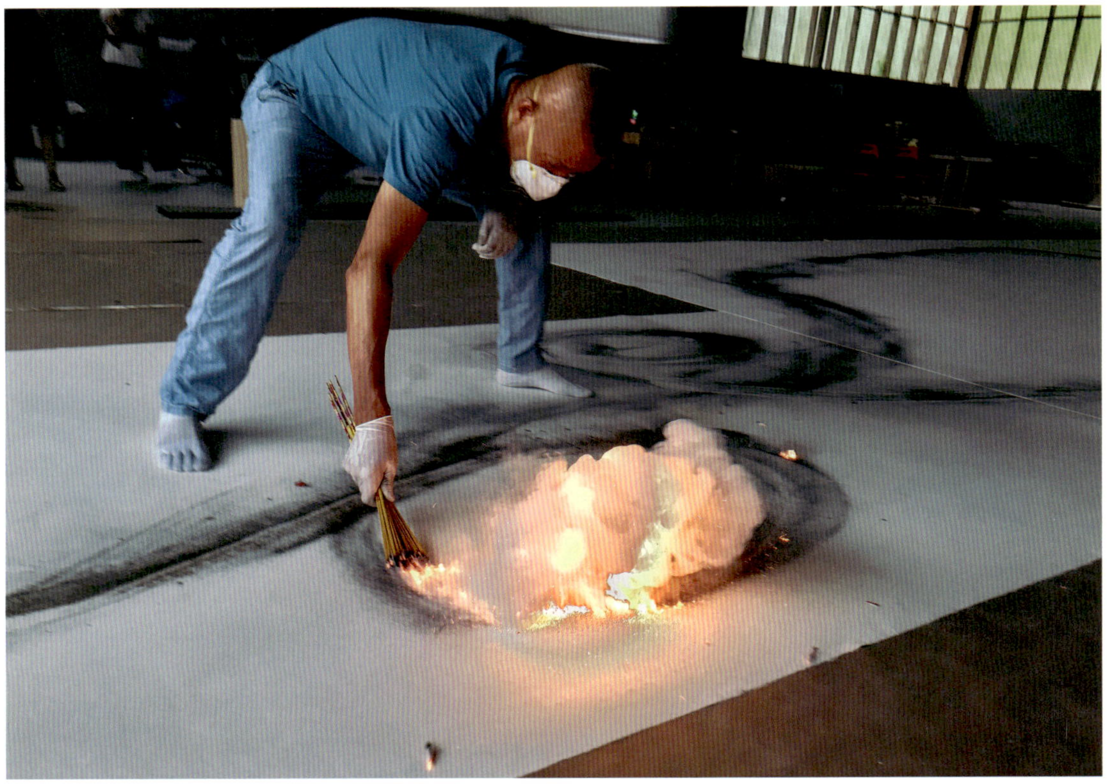

Figure 22. Cai Guo-Qiang holding ignited incense sticks to create *Color Gunpowder Drawing for City of Flowers in the Sky* (no. 2.23) in July 2018. Photo by Sang Luo

## From Here to Eternity: Conservation

When it comes to conservation, Cai's work poses concerns similar to drawings with a powdery medium, such as charcoal or pastel. The strength of the deflagration pushes the particles of powder into the fibers of the substrate, creating a mechanical anchor; the intense heat also causes them to become seared into the substrate (figure 23). However, because there is no binder, the surface remains delicate. After the ignition, when the drawing or painting is stood up, some residues from the combustion and unexploded gunpowder might fall off. Conservators in some institutions have experimented with a variety of fixatives to consolidate the charred matter—the difficulty resides in not altering the appearance or modifying the gloss, but treatments of traditional powdery drawing media can be adapted to Cai's drawings and paintings. Recently, Cai has experimented with using a handheld blowtorch to ignite the gunpowder that had not been fully combusted in the initial explosion. He found that this additional step considerably reduced or eliminated altogether the amount of loose matter susceptible to come off during the handling of the work. He has therefore taken to doing it systematically.

The dyes and pigments in the colored pyrotechnic powders that Cai uses to make his paintings have different degrees of light sensitivity. As with all works of art, adequate lighting policies are necessary to preserve the intensity of the color.[29] The most

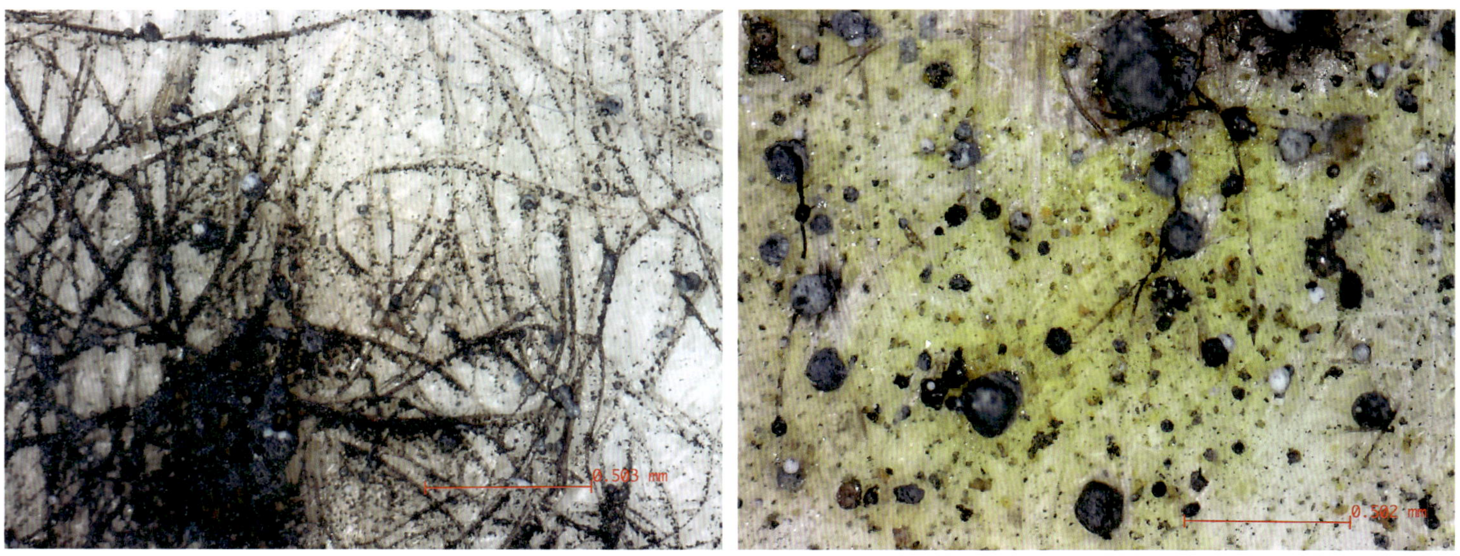

Figure 23. Cai Guo-Qiang's *Frieze* (2011) seen under the microscope, showing the gunpowder and realgar embedded in the paper fibers. Photos by Rachel Rivenc

sensitive among the colored pyrotechnic powders can be approached in a similar way to sensitive colored drawing media such as watercolor.[30] Cai has been very interested in the study and in understanding the aging properties of his material, both from a material and philosophical point of view. While he wants his work to endure, he also rightly does not want this knowledge to shackle his creativity. Ultimately, change is inevitable and time can also bring unexpected beauty.

> Even when something is eternal, you can't own it forever. Eternity and permanence are different in Chinese. Eternity transcends the existence of time whereas permanence remains in the realm of time. So when we have dialogues with, and associate with eternity through art, we don't attempt to tackle it from the permanence point of view; rather, we use the instantaneous way to grasp it. It feels like the myth of eternity, you could only taste it at the fleeting moment of chaos.[31]

---

*Rachel Rivenc is the Head of Conservation and Preservation at the Getty Research Institute, Los Angeles, the position she assumed after her work as part of the Getty Conservation Institute (GCI)'s Modern and Contemporary Art Initiative overseeing the related dissemination, training, and research activities. She initiated and led the GCI's four-year research project on Cai Guo-Qiang's artistic process and materials, whose results are presented in an upcoming new volume of the Getty Publications series* The Artist's Materials. *She is the co-curator of* A Material Odyssey, *a Palace Museum exhibition featuring the aforementioned research results.*

## Notes

All the analyses described in this essay were carried out by the Science Department of the Getty Conservation Institute (GCI), where the author worked before joining the Getty Research Institute (GRI) and where she conducted an in-depth study of the materials used by Cai Guo-Qiang. Analyses included Fourier Transform Infrared Spectroscopy (FTIR), pyrolysis-Gas Chromatography coupled with Mass Spectrometry (py-GCMS), and Environmental Scanning Electron Microscopy coupled with Energy-dispersive X-ray spectroscopy (ESEM-EDX). The author wishes to acknowledge the contributions of Michael Doutre, Vincent Dion, Alan Phenix, Joy Mazurek, Vincent Beltran Lynn Lee, and Douglas MacLennan, to the study.

1. Cai Guo-Qiang, interview with author, November 17, 2016, Cai Studio, New York; translated by Cai Studio.

2. Cai, interview with author, July 22, 2016.

3. Philip Kaiser, "Land, the Earth, and the Universe: A Conversation with Cai Guo-Qiang," in *Cai Guo-Qiang: Ladder to the Sky* (Los Angeles: The Museum of Contemporary Art and Munich/London/New York: Prestel, 2012), 79.

4. Kaiser, 79.

5. Cai Guo-Qiang, interview with Alexandra Munroe, May 2007, Cai Studio, New York; transcript by Cai Studio.

6. Cai Guo-Qiang, interview with author, April 14, 2019, Cai Studio, New York; transcript and translation arranged by author.

7. Cai, interview with author, 2019.

8. Cai, interview with author, July 22, 2016.

9. Cai, interview with author, July 22, 2016.

10. Zhou Benyi, interview with author, September 2018, Shanghai, China.

11. Hong Hong Wu, interview with author, April 18, 2017, Cai Studio, New York; transcript and translation arranged by author.

12. Cai, interview with author, July 22, 2016.

13. Cai, interview with author, July 22, 2016.

14. Cai, interview with author, July 22, 2016.

15. Cai, interview with author, July 22, 2016.

16. Cai, interview with author, July 22, 2016; Wu, interview with author, April 18, 2017.

17. Wu, interview with author, April 18, 2017.

18. Realgar is not only found as an ingredient in gunpowder as a source of sulfur, but has also a long history of use in Chinese medicine. It has also been used in European painting as a pigment.

19. Cai, interview with author, July 22, 2016.

20. Cai, interview with author, November 17, 2016.

21. *The Spirit of Painting* was the title of Cai's solo exhibition at the Prado, held from October 25, 2017 to March 4, 2018.

22. Cai, interview with author, July 22, 2016.

23. Information concerning chemical compositions of gunpowder and fireworks has been drawn from J. A. Conkling, *Chemistry of Pyrotechnics: Basic Principles and Theory* (New York/Basel: M. Dekker, 1985) and M. S. Russel, *The Chemistry of Fireworks*, 2nd ed. (Cambridge: Royal Society of Chemistry, 2009).

24. Historical information on gunpowder and pyrotechnics has been drawn from Jack Kelly, *Gunpowder Alchemy, Bombards, and Pyrotechnics: The History of the Explosive That Changed the World* (New York: Basic Books, 2004); Russel, *The Chemistry of Fireworks*; and Conkling, *Chemistry of Pyrotechnics.*

25. Russel, 5.

26. More details on these results will be published in a forthcoming book, *The Artist's Materials: Cai Guo-Qiang*, which I co-authored and which will be published by Getty Publications.

27. The composition of the porcelain was confirmed by ESEM-EDX analyses.

28. Abayas are flowy long robes that Muslim women put on top of their clothes when they leave the home, to hide the curves of their bodies.

29. Many institutions have provided guidelines for light levels appropriate for a wide range of media and sensitivities. See for example, https://www.conservation-wiki.com/wiki/PMG_Section_1.4.1_Standards,_Guidelines,_and_Recommendations_for_Light_Levels_During_Exhibition, or https://www.nedcc.org/free-resources/preservation-leaflets/2.-the-environment/2.4-protection-from-light-damage (both accessed May 23, 2020).

30. An in-depth study of the lightfastness of the main colors used by Cai has been performed by the Getty Conservation Institute. See R. Rivenc, M. Doutre, and T. Learner, "Explosive Beauty: The Art of Cai Guo-Qiang," in *Science and Art: The Contemporary Painted Surface*, ed. Antonio Sgamellotti, Brunetto Brunetti, and Constanza Miliani (Cambridge: Royal Society of Chemistry, forthcoming).

31. Cai, interview with author, November 17, 2016.

# Catalogue

Compiled by Sang Luo

Cai has a long history of both engaging with art history and using it as the subject of his works. He has lived outside his homeland China for thirty years, nomadically traversing different histories and cultures, while maintaining a deep affection for his native culture. From the outset, he has sought a cosmic framework and exercised an unbound freedom, regarding "all past and present human civilizations" as part of his own ancestry and history.

In this context, Cai's *Individual's Journey Through Western Art History* which had begun subconsciously developed consciously from 2017 onward. His dialogues have not followed the chronology of art history. In retrospect, his *Journey* is not so much one of retracing Western art history to discover breakthroughs in contemporary art, as it is one of self-dialogue and self-exploration.

Each dialogue is closely tied to the artist's personal growth, affecting those following it. It is too simplistic to characterize his dialogues according to the dichotomy of "odyssey" and "homecoming," with their developments intertwined. Their reflections are found in each other as they unfold in a vast space that encompasses all time periods: from ancient to modern times and both East and West, and even the cosmos itself. Cai's odyssey is never simply a departure, much as his homecoming remains underway.

To help our readers access basic information and facts about Cai's *Journey*, each of the following dialogues is introduced in three elements: project data, project introduction, and representative artworks. The dialogues are also roughly divided into "odyssey" and "homecoming." While the former contains projects related to *Individual's Journey Through Western Art History*, the latter encompasses Cai's engagements with traditional Chinese culture and philosophy, his original passion for painting, and the cosmos as his eternal homeland.

---

*Sang Luo is Project Director at Cai Studio. A graduate of Fudan University, China, she holds a master's degree in Arts Management from Carnegie Mellon University. During her seven years at the studio, she has directed and realized nearly twenty exhibitions and projects of varying scales the artist undertook in different cultures and regions around the world, including the explosion event* Sky Ladder *(2015), multiple exhibitions related to his* Individual's Journey Through Western Art History *(2016–19), and his solo exhibition at the Palace Museum (2020).*

Legends

1. All works are by Cai Guo-Qiang, unless otherwise noted.

2. Works in the Catalogue are referenced elsewhere in this volume with their catalogue numbers, as in "no. 1.1."

3. Unless otherwise noted, the titles of the catalogues and documentary videos are the same as the exhibitions'.

4. Measurements of artworks are given with height first, followed by width, and depth where applicable.

5. Photo credits are found in the "Copyright Notices" in the back of this volume.

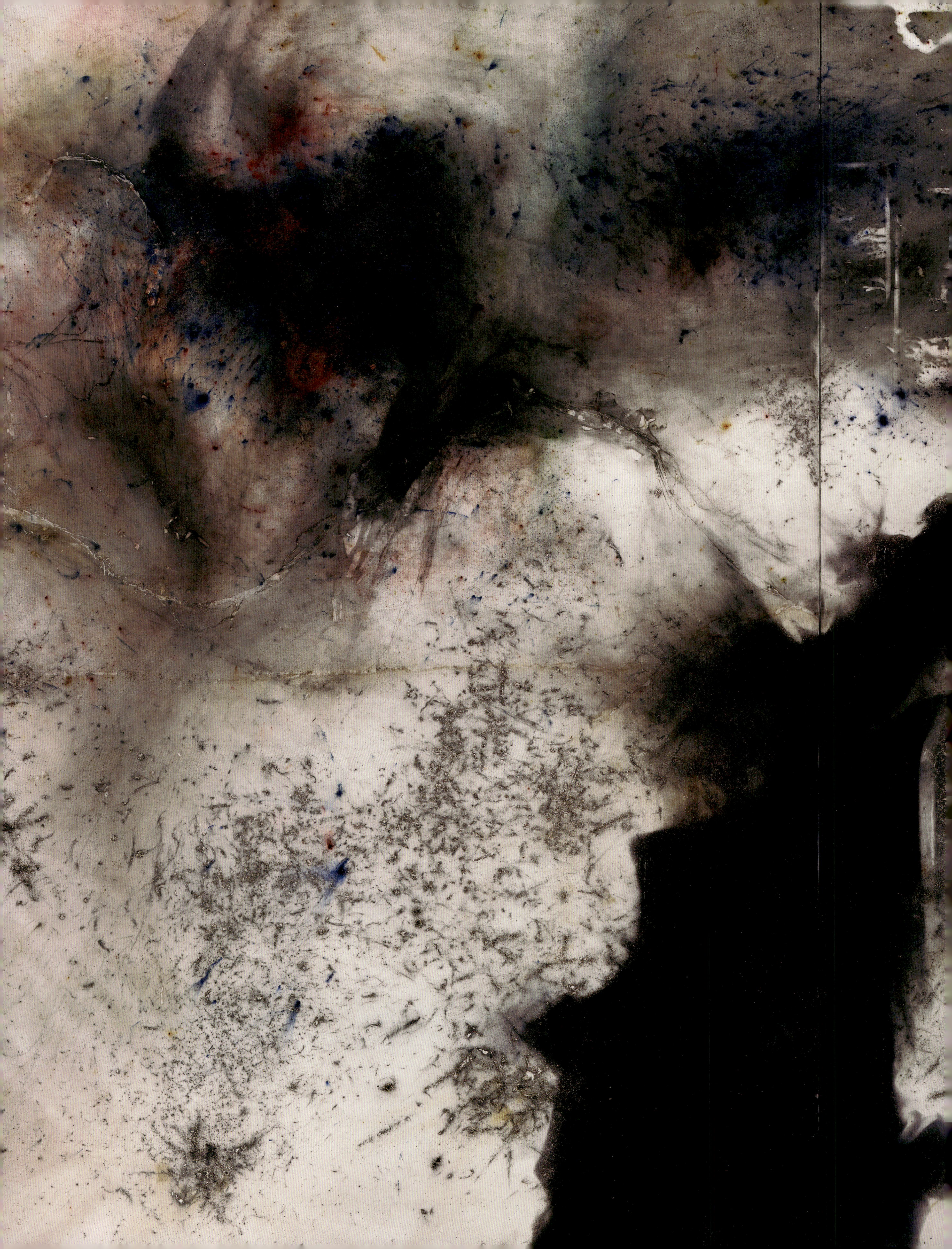

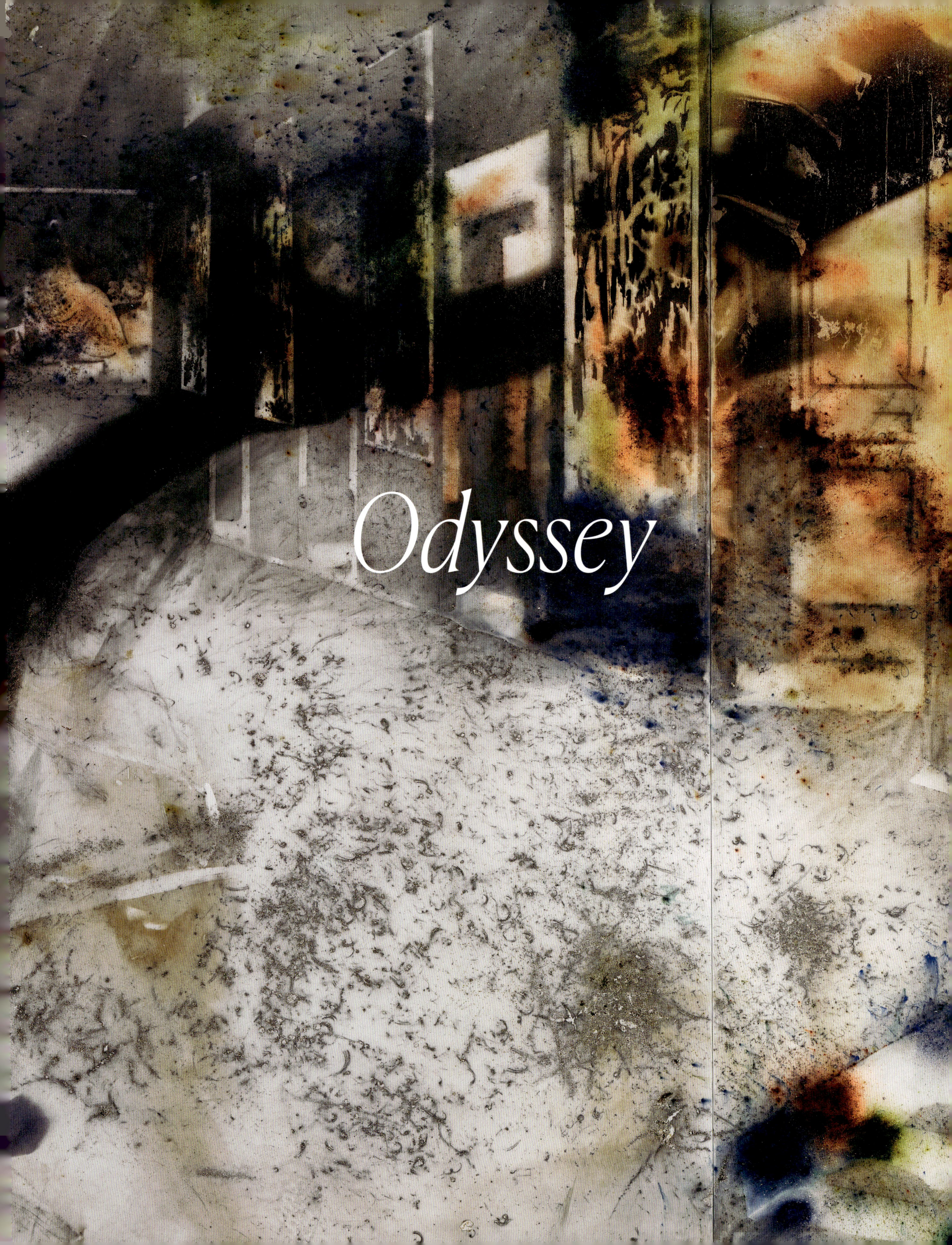
Odyssey

1

# Dialogue with Baroque Art and the Spanish Golden Age

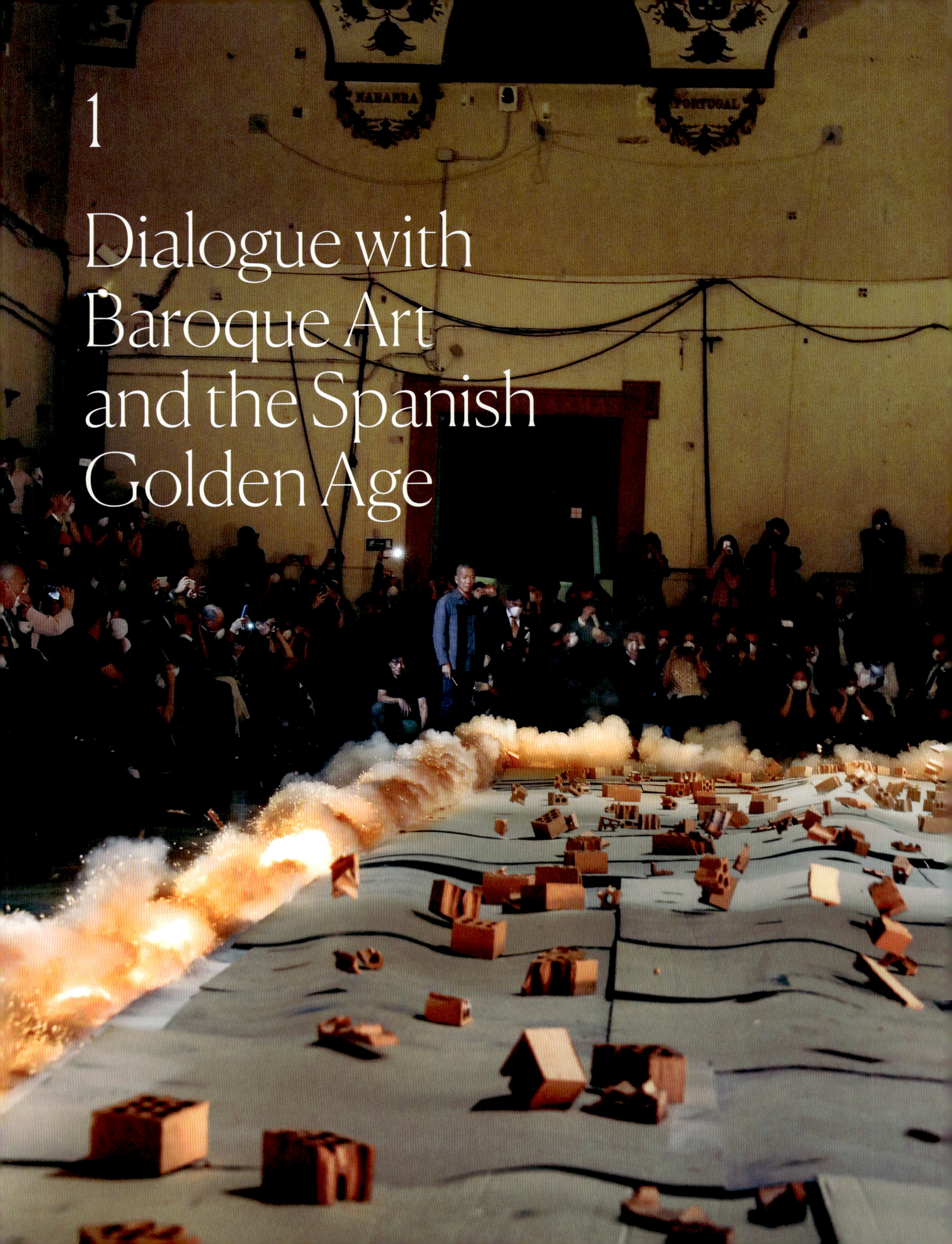

# *The Spirit of Painting. Cai Guo-Qiang at the Prado*

Prado Museum, Madrid, Spain
October 25, 2017–March 4, 2018

Curated by Miguel Zugaza Miranda, former Director, Prado Museum, and Alejandro Vergara, Senior Curator of Flemish and Northern European Paintings, Prado Museum

Public painting creation: Salón de Reinos, Madrid, October 2–23, 2017

Catalogue: English edition published by the Prado Museum and Mandarin Chinese edition published by Hunan Fine Arts Publishing House

Documentary feature: directed by Isabel Coixet, produced by Miss Wasabi Films for the Prado Museum; available in English, Spanish, and Mandarin Chinese (47:34)

*The Spirit of Painting* was the first solo exhibition for which the Prado Museum commissioned an artist to create works on site since the museum's founding in 1819. It was Cai Guo-Qiang's first exclusively painting exhibition in over ten years, for which he created more than twenty gunpowder paintings.

The exhibition consisted of four thematic spaces that naturally formed a path and rhythm similar to the Chinese compositional principle *qi cheng zhuan he* (rise, development, shift, unification). During the month prior to the exhibition, Cai used the Prado's Salón de Reinos, or Hall of Realms—where four centuries ago, Philip IV commissioned Velázquez and other preeminent artists of the time to create and exhibit masterworks such as *The Surrender of Breda*—as his studio to complete the last several paintings. The culminating piece, the 18-meter-long *The Spirit of Painting*, was ignited in front of a large audience.

The exhibition originated from Cai's exchange with the "spirit of painting" of El Greco, a conversation that has continued without interruption since his youth, when Cai's imagination was roused by blurry reprints of El Greco's works. In 2009, after Cai concluded his work on the Beijing Olympics, he went on a journey to retrace El Greco's footsteps. From El Greco's birthplace of Crete in Greece, through to Venice, Italy, on to the Prado in Madrid, and finally to Toledo, where the painter died after residing there for thirty years—Cai sought to see the things that El Greco once saw.

At the Prado, during more than two years of preparation for the exhibition, Cai benefitted from the museum's collection, deemed one of the world's greatest holdings of paintings and the most comprehensive and definitive collection of Spanish art and sculpture. He expanded his dialogue with Titian, Bosch, Rubens, El Greco, Velázquez, and Goya, through engagements with the museum's experts and collection.

Figure 1.1. Ignition of *The Spirit of Painting* (no. 1.27) at the Salón de Reinos in 2017

Pages 72–73: Detail of *Salón de Reinos ...* (no. 1.26)

His goal was not just to revisit their works and styles, but instead to recover a spirit of painting, reflected as much in the artist's sensibility and craftsmanlike capacity as the painterly quality and sense of adventure materialized on canvas. Cai's dialogue with El Greco is in fact an excavation of the self—the self who roams the world in pursuit of subjectivity, spirituality, and dialogues with the unseen world. His attempts to emulate Rubens's lust, Goya's dissociative personalities, and Velázquez's understatement and sense of eternity are likewise a layer-by-layer peeling of the self.

Cai demonstrates the ways in which a contemporary artist views his predecessors and the "spiritual fraternity" that transcends time and space, thus cementing and renewing the legacy of the Old Masters, which in turn served as a starting point for the artist, one that allows him to seek his own spirit of painting within his practices and discover possible breakthroughs in contemporary painting. In modern times, painting has been declared dead on multiple occasions and demoted to become just one of the many artistic mediums. In this context, Cai's conscious return to painting marks a significant moment in his continuing experimentations.

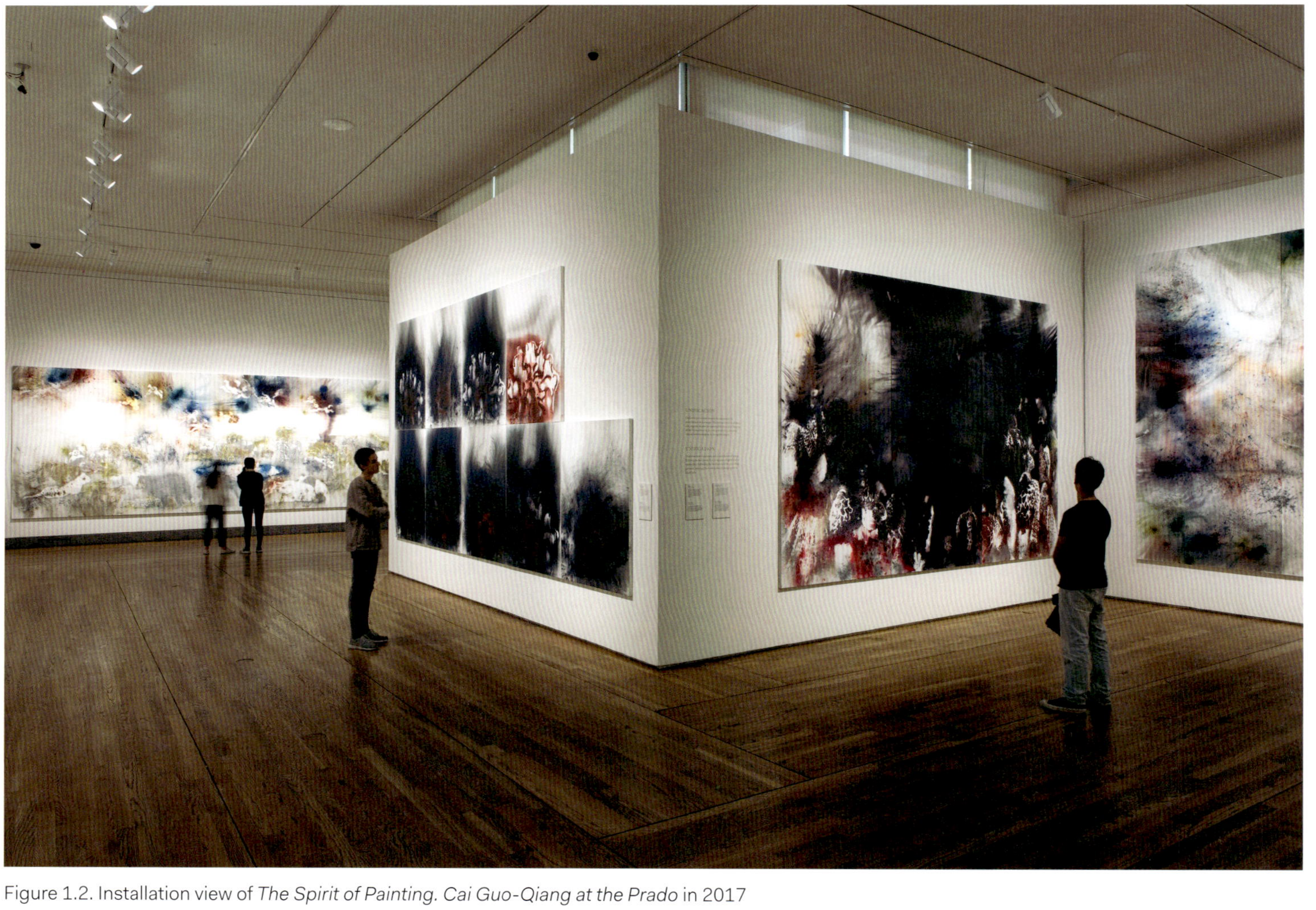

Figure 1.2. Installation view of *The Spirit of Painting. Cai Guo-Qiang at the Prado* in 2017

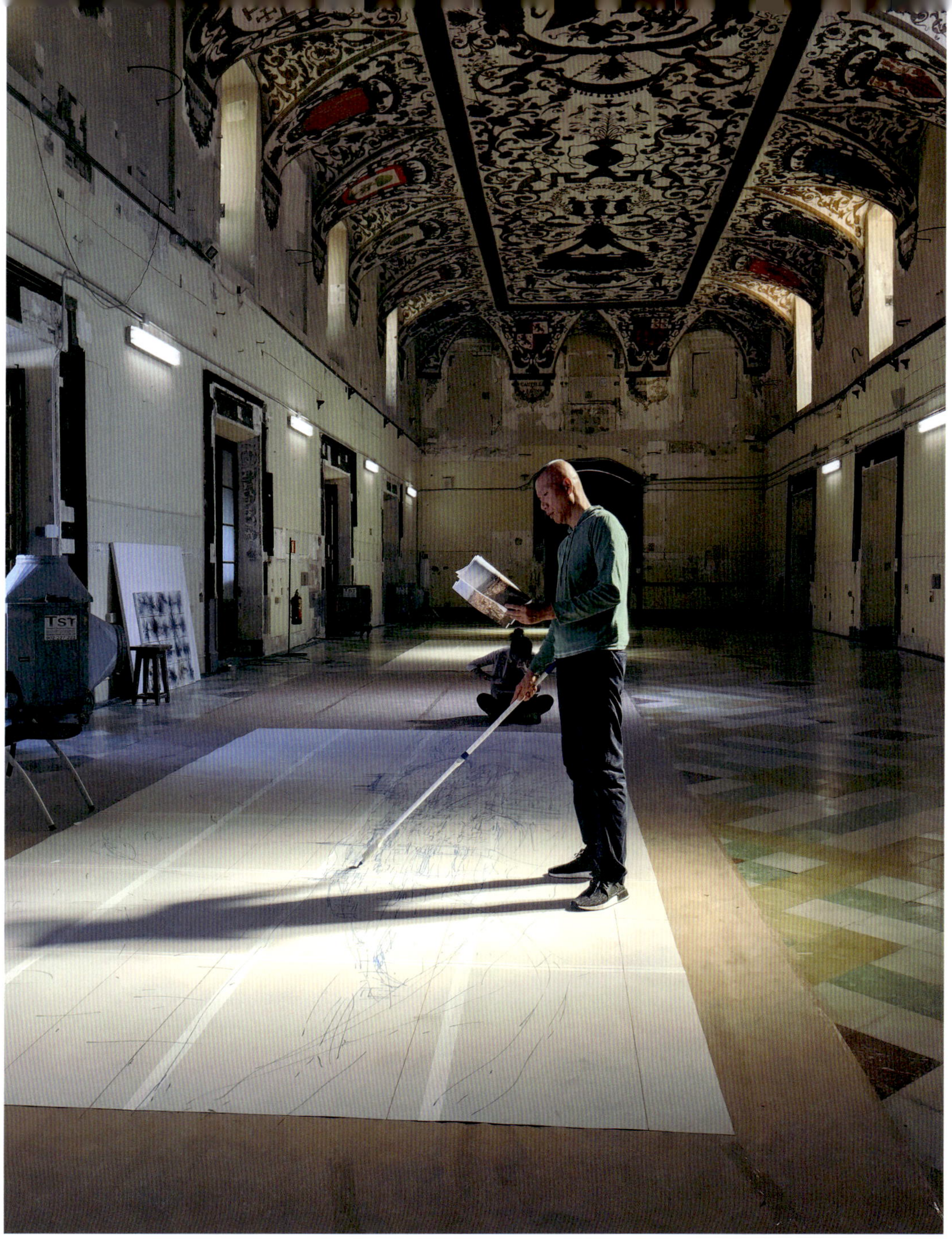

Figure 1.3. Cai Guo-Qiang drawing stencil images for *Day and Night in Toledo* (no. 1.7) at the Salón de Reinos in 2017

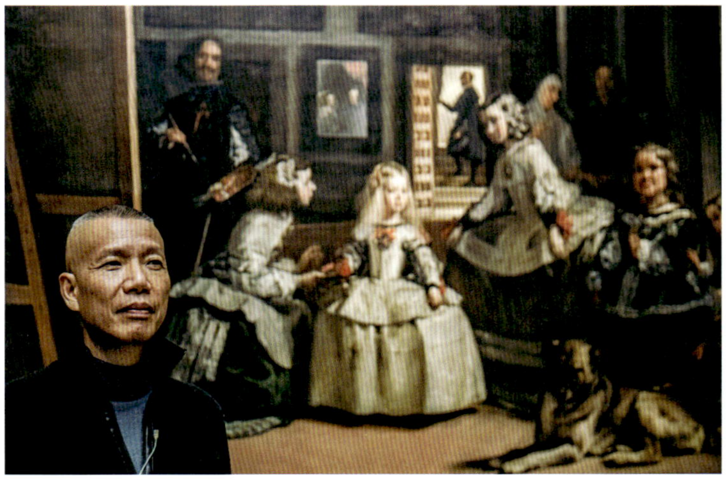

Figure 1.4. Cai Guo-Qiang in front of Velázquez's *Las Meninas* at the Prado Museum in 2017

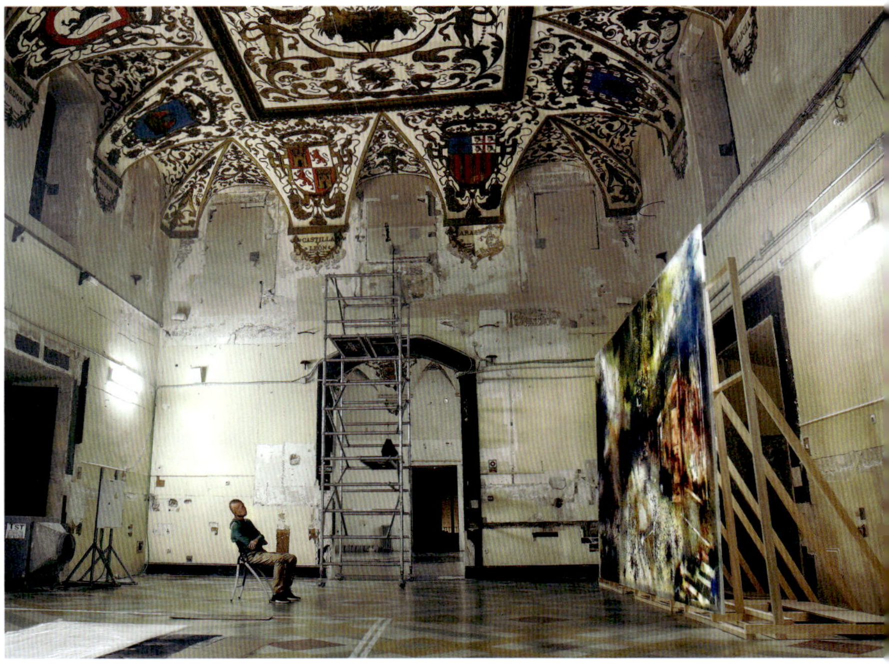

Figure 1.5. Cai Guo-Qiang seated in front of *Salón de Reinos …* after its creation at the Salón de Reinos in 2017

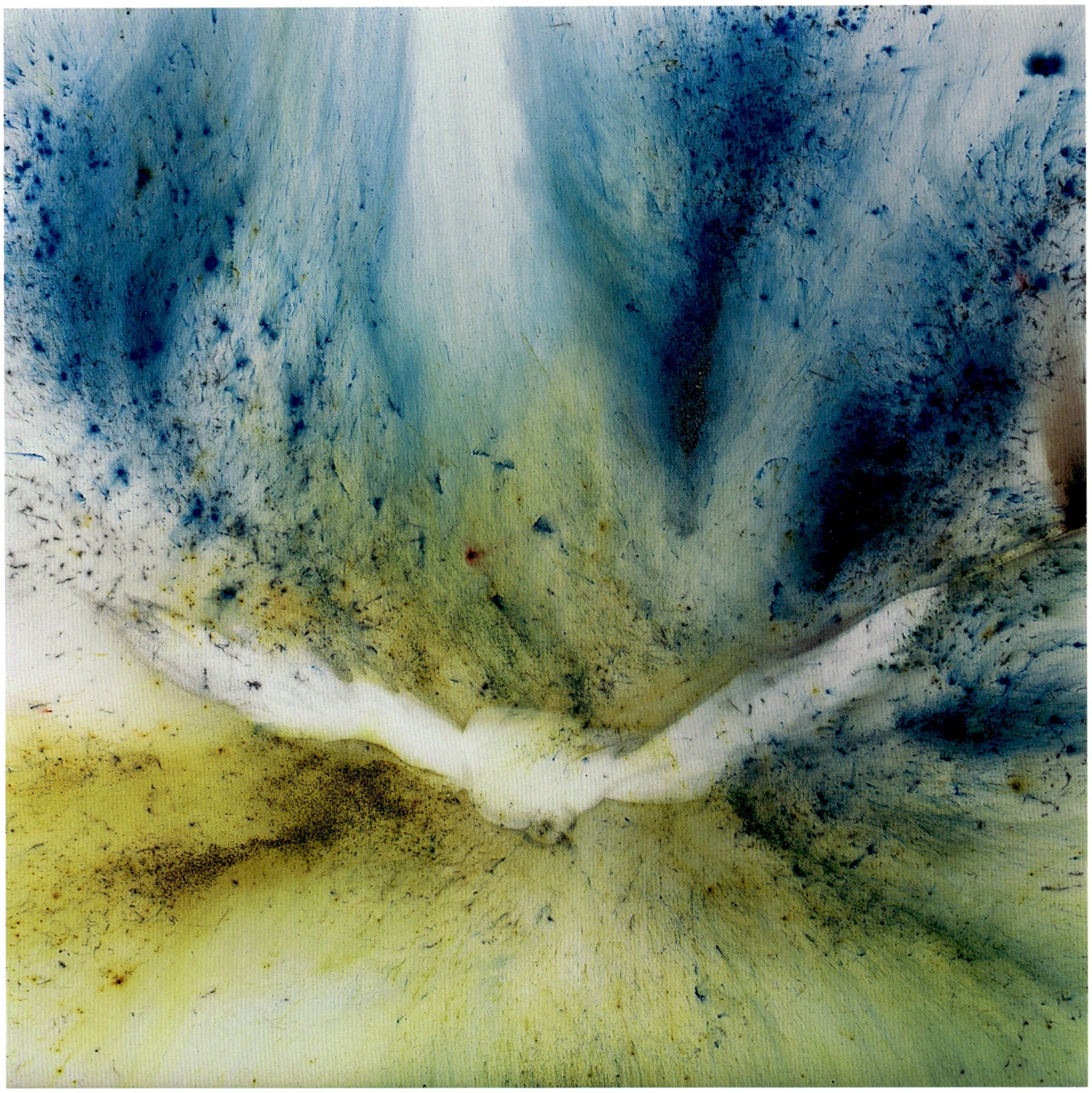

1.1 *In Search of El Greco No. 3*

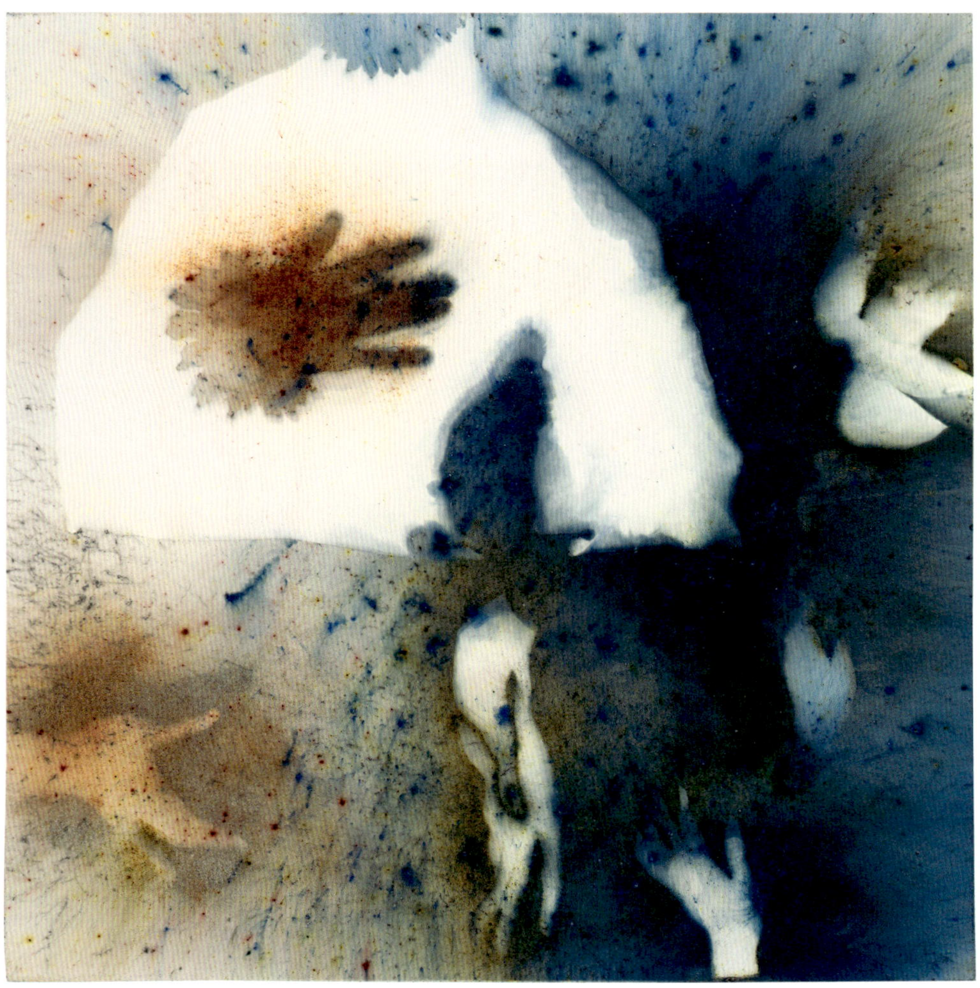

1.2 *In Search of El Greco No. 6*

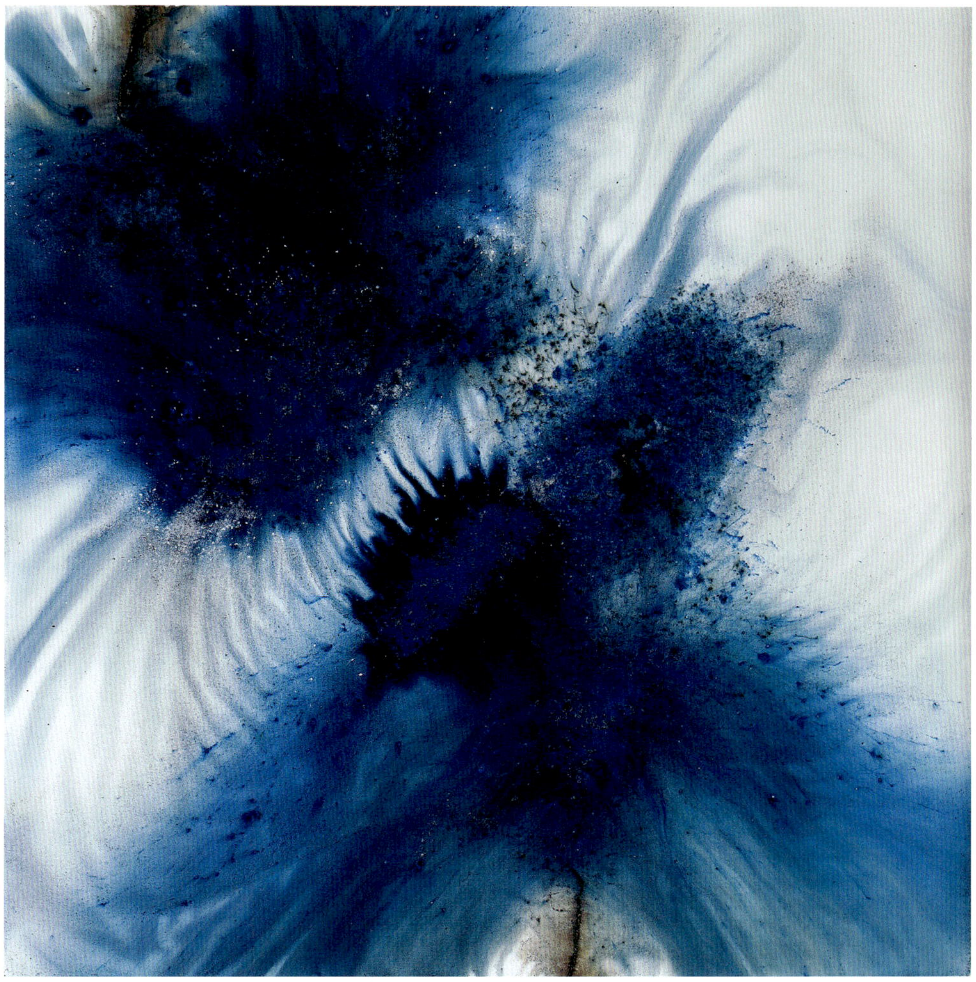

1.3 *In Search of El Greco No. 8*

1.1

*In Search of El Greco No. 3*

寻找格列柯第3号

2016

Gunpowder on canvas

122 × 122 cm

1.2

*In Search of El Greco No. 6*

寻找格列柯第6号

2016

Gunpowder on canvas

91.5 × 91.5 cm

1.3

*In Search of El Greco No. 8*

寻找格列柯第8号

2016

Gunpowder on canvas

91.5 × 91.5 cm

1.4

*Painting El Greco's The Saviour No. 1*

画格列柯“基督救世主”之一

2017

Gunpowder on canvas

152.5 × 122 cm

1.5

*Painting El Greco's Apostolado No. 3*

画格列柯“使徒”系列之三

2017

Gunpowder on canvas

152.5 × 244 cm

1.6

*Selfie*

自拍

2017

Gunpowder on canvas

183 × 304 cm

The exhibition opened with a series of works that engaged with the spirit and spirituality of El Greco (1541–1614), the Old Master who served as Cai's earliest inspiration as a painter. A major luminary of the Prado Museum collection, El Greco is regarded by Prado specialists as possibly the most representative painter of the Spanish Golden Age, and his influence remains profound today.

Through gunpowder explosions, Cai attempted to understand El Greco's painting techniques in terms of color, light, and energy flow. For *Painting El Greco's Apostolado No. 3* and *Selfie*, Cai arranged gunpowder between two canvases that were laid face-to-face on the ground. Ignited together, two paintings emerged, the lower canvas being figurative and the upper canvas abstract. Cai explained, “As though extracting an imprint of spirituality.”

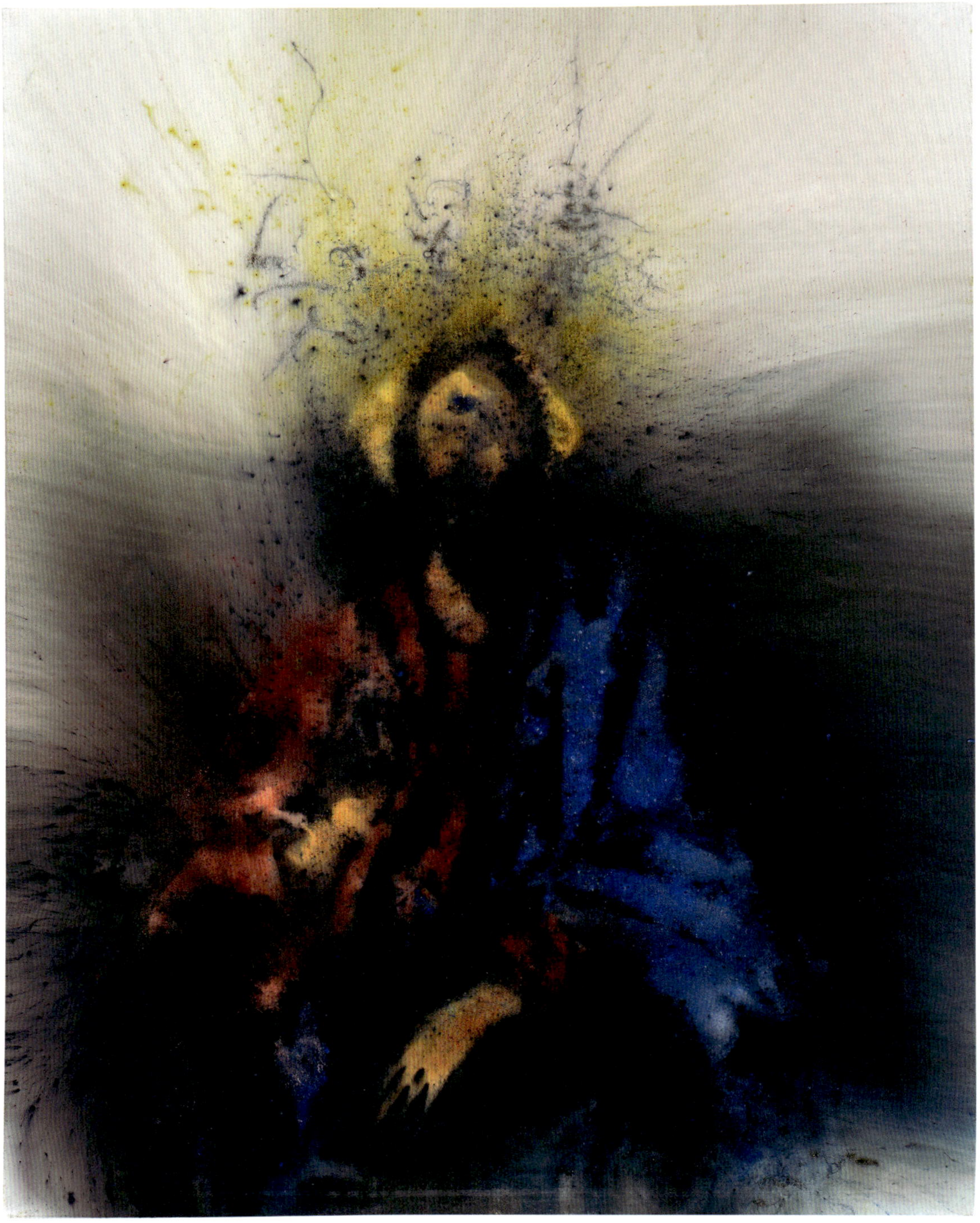

1.4 *Painting El Greco's The Saviour No. 1*

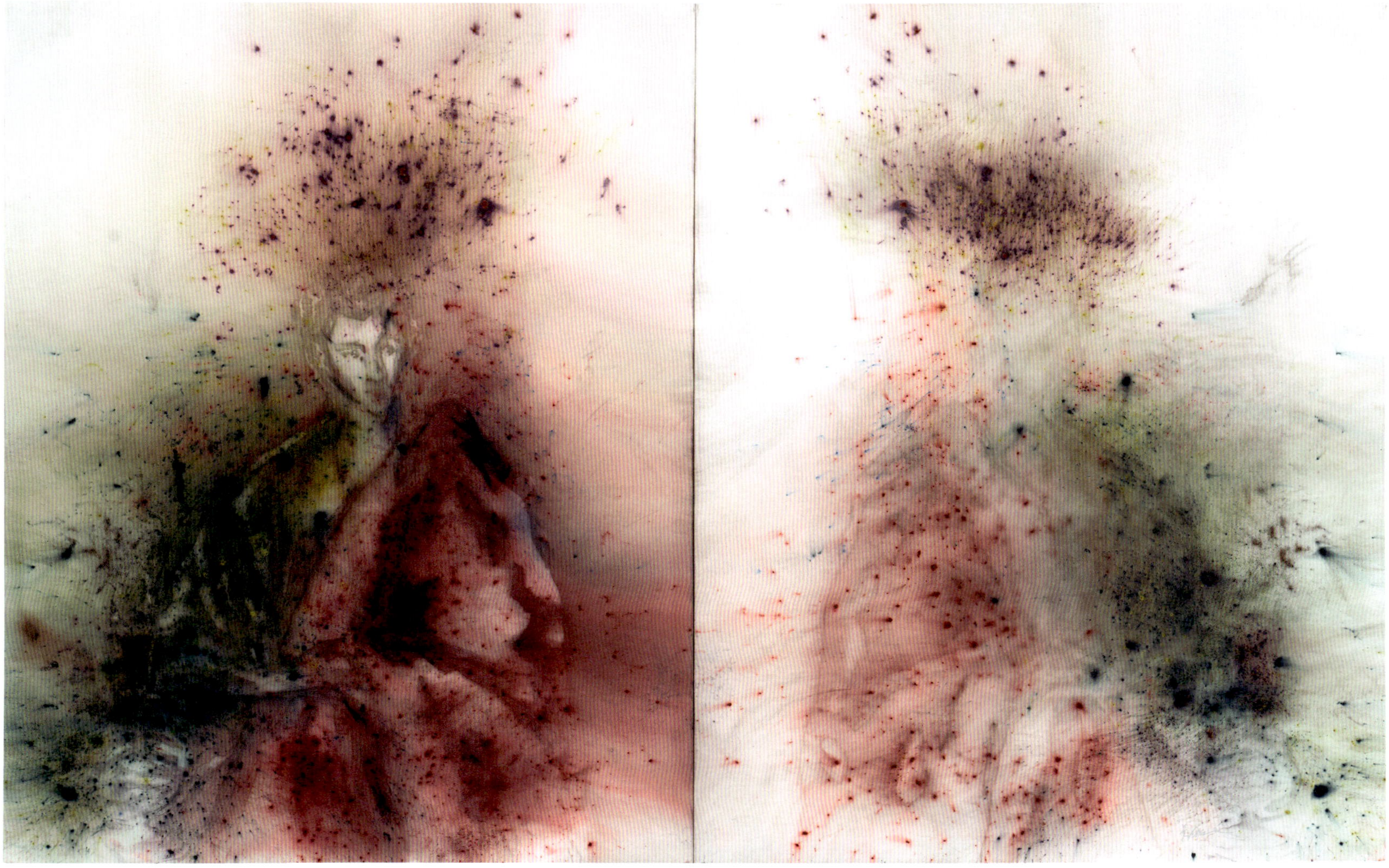

1.5 *Painting El Greco's Apostolado No. 3*

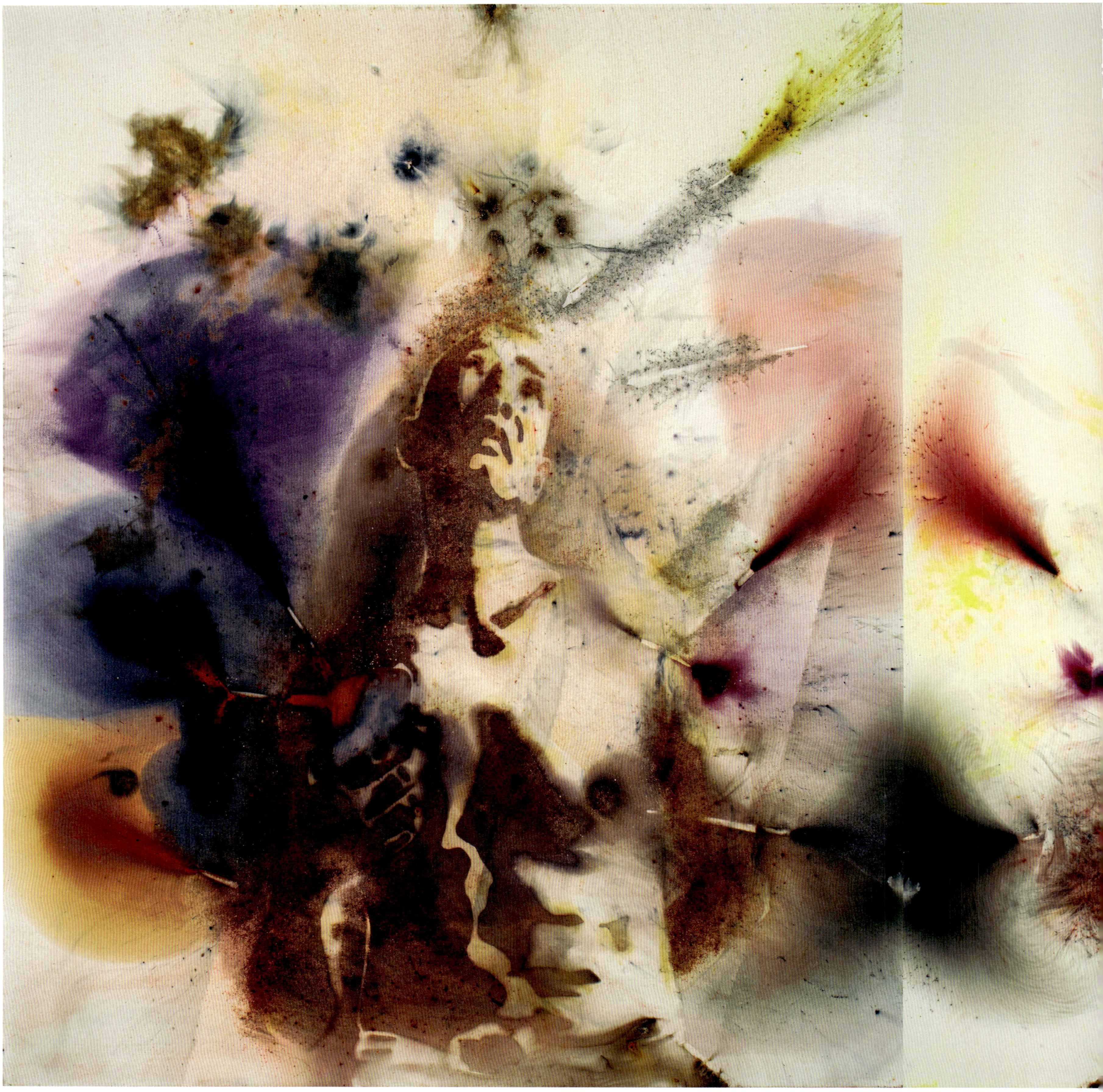

1.6 *Selfie*

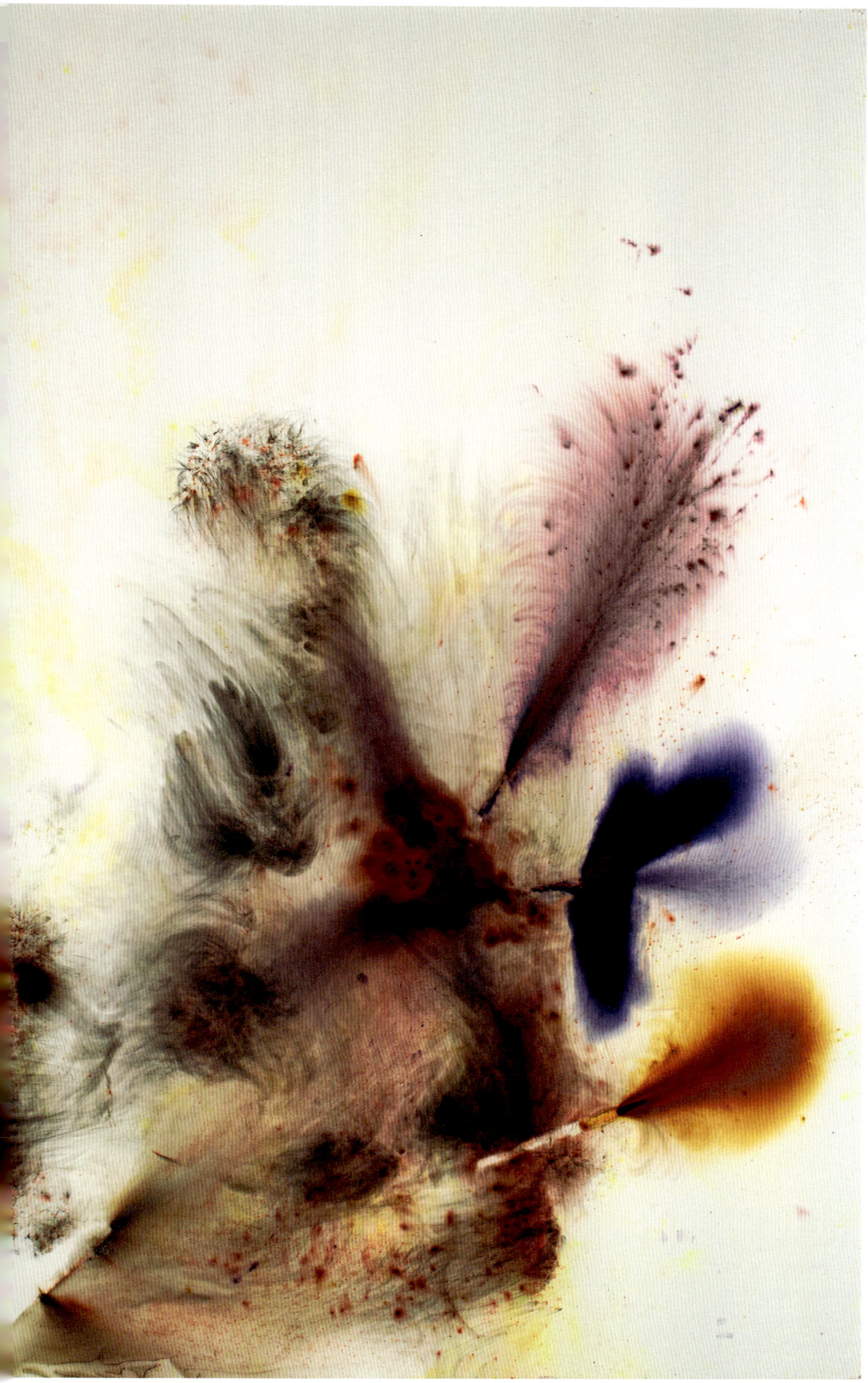

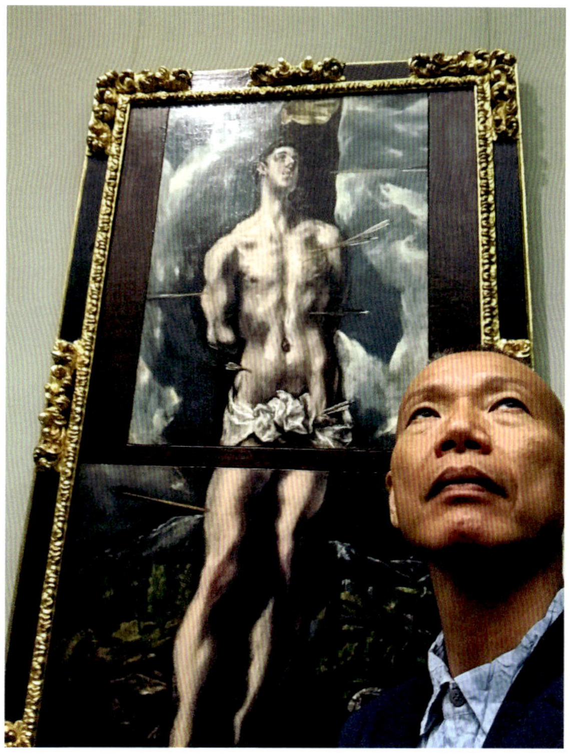

Figure 1.6. Cai Guo-Qiang's selfie with El Greco's *Saint Sebastian* at the Prado Museum in 2017

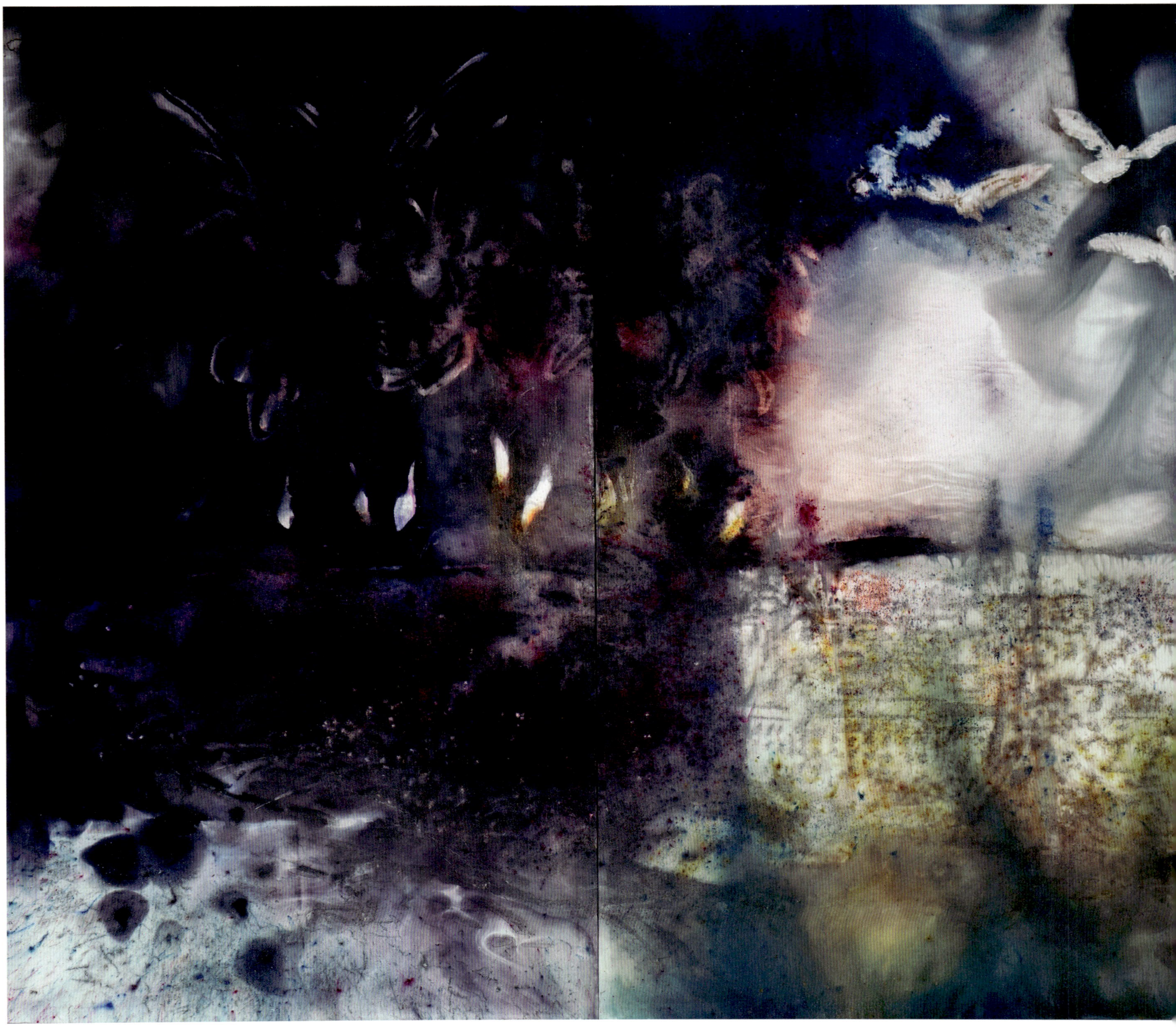

1.7

*Day and Night in Toledo*
昼夜托雷多

2017
Gunpowder on canvas
260 × 600 cm

Cai reimagined what he saw when revisiting Toledo in early 2017—the city from night to dawn, morning to sunset, and settling back into night. As the past and present intersect, the town, cathedral, valleys, and skies form a mirage on the canvas, like a homecoming of El Greco's soul. This was the first painting that Cai created at the Salón de Reinos.

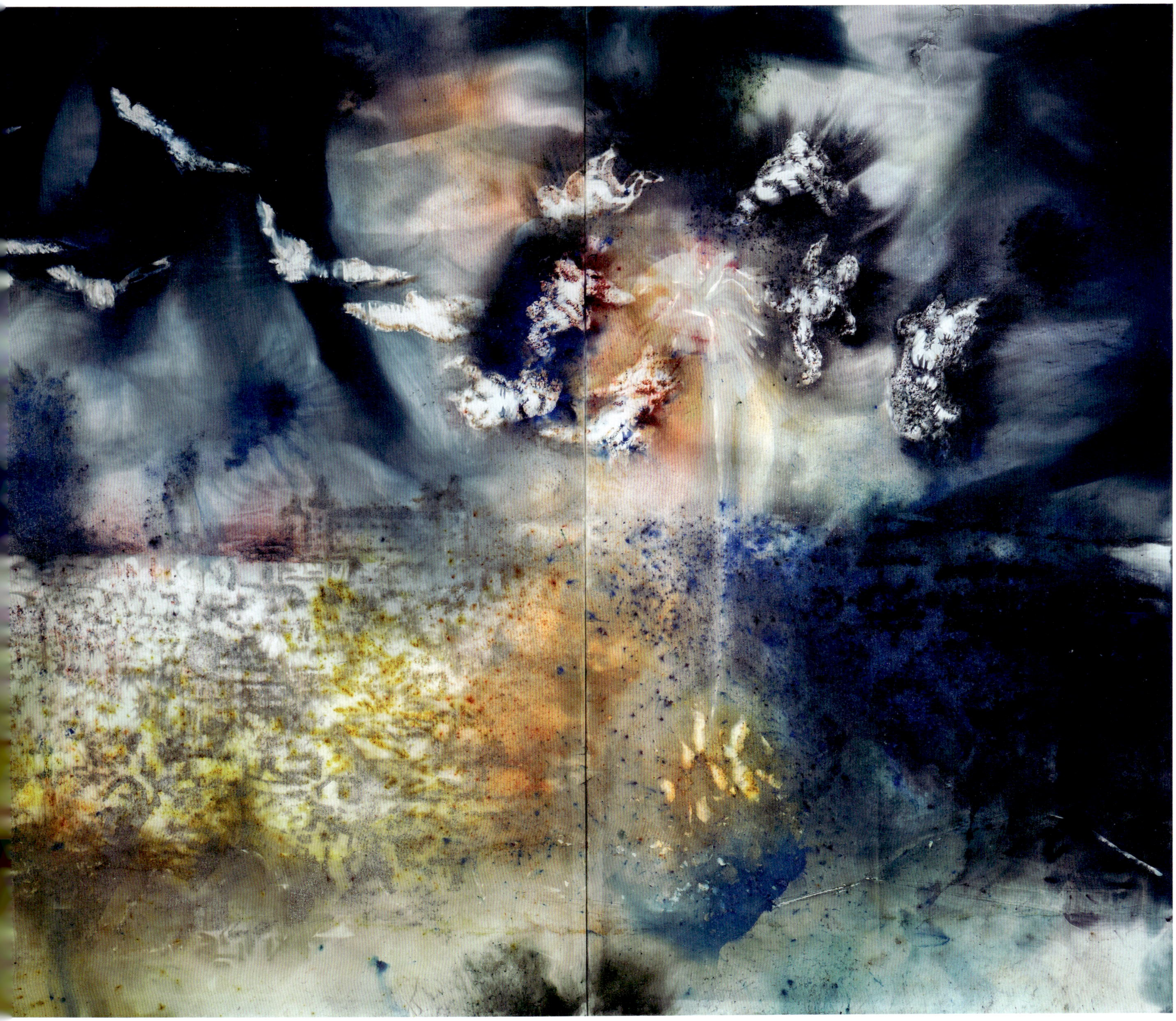

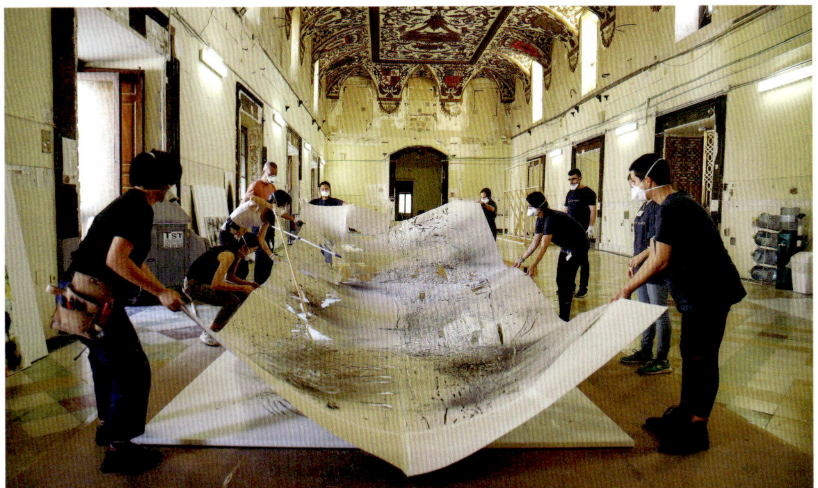

Figure 1.7. Volunteers laying stencils during the creation of *Day and Night in Toledo* at the Salón de Reinos in 2017

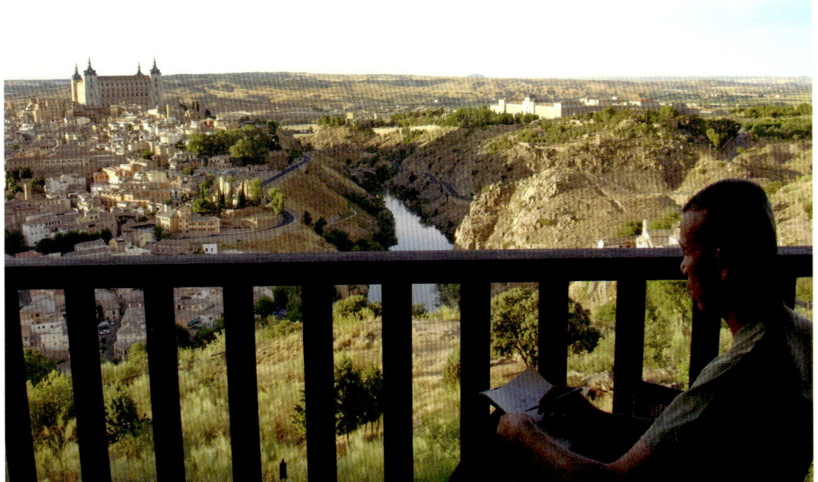

Figure 1.8. Cai Guo-Qiang sketching in Toledo in 2009

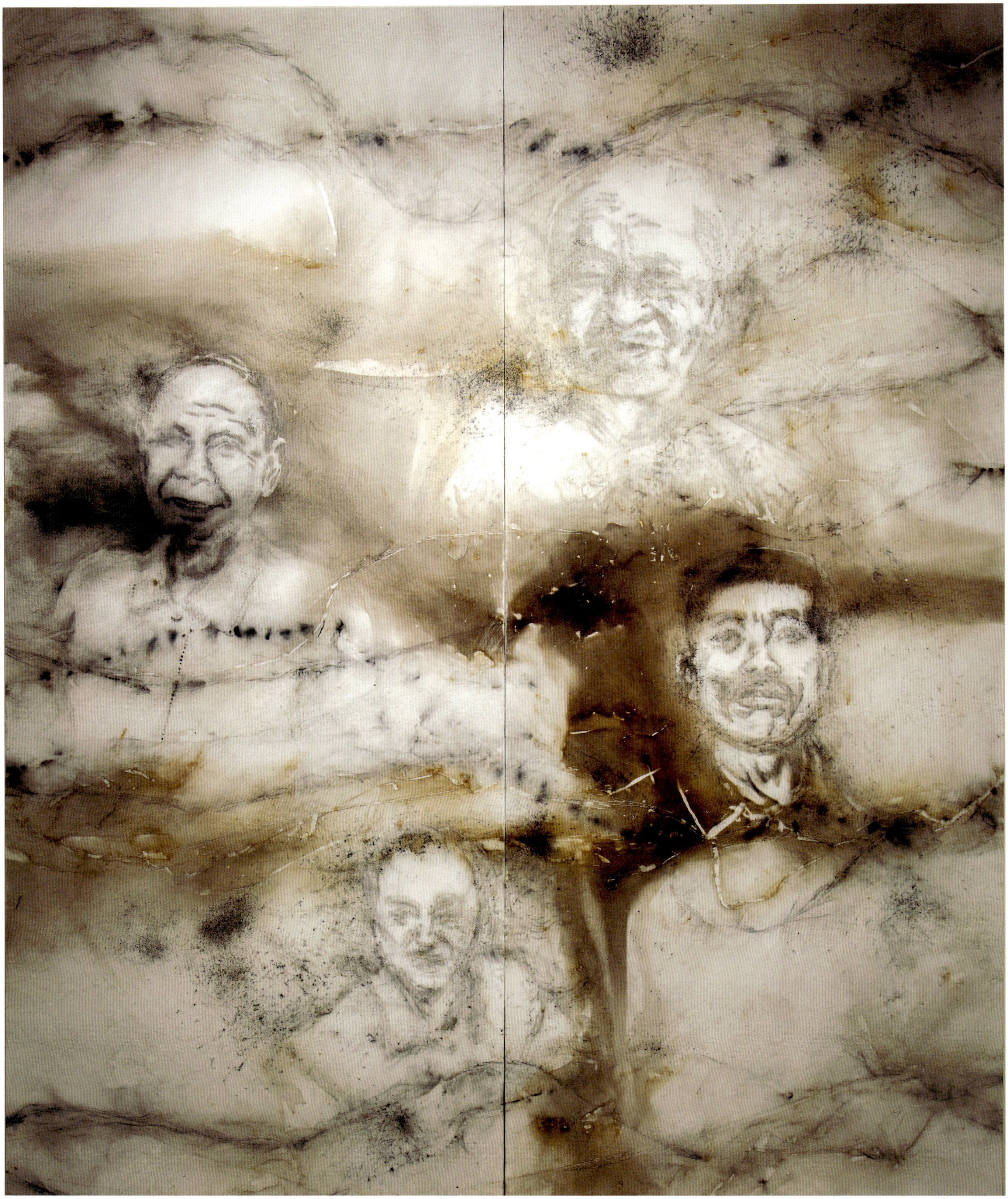

1.8 *The Distant Clouds*

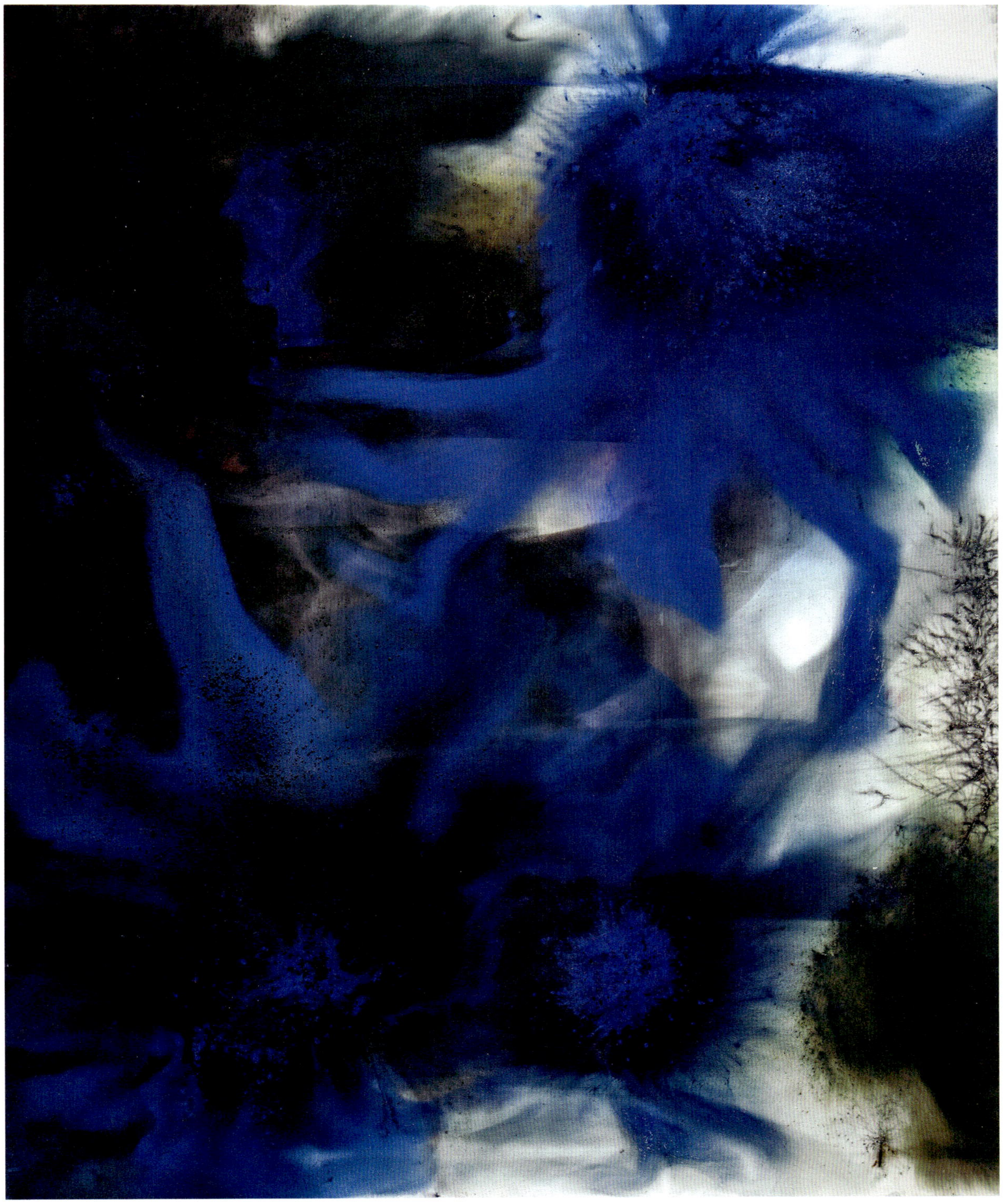

1.9 *Blue*

1.8

*The Distant Clouds*

望云

2017

Gunpowder on canvas

360 × 300 cm

Inspired by El Greco's manner of expressing spirituality, Cai used gunpowder explosions to convey his longing for and remembrance of his recently deceased grandmother, father, brother-in-law, and father-in-law. The work was realized at the Salón de Reinos.

1.9

*Blue*

蓝

2017

Gunpowder on canvas

183 × 152.5 cm

While working on site at the Salón de Reinos, the artist began exploring a new technique of "smoking." When creating a gunpowder painting, he would ignite gunpowder on an adjacent blank canvas, capture the resulting colored smoke, and channel it onto the painting's canvas. The same blank canvas would be used again and again, gradually acquiring an abstract texture, while simultaneously aiding in the creation of other paintings. The process became an exploration of a new approach to abstract painting.

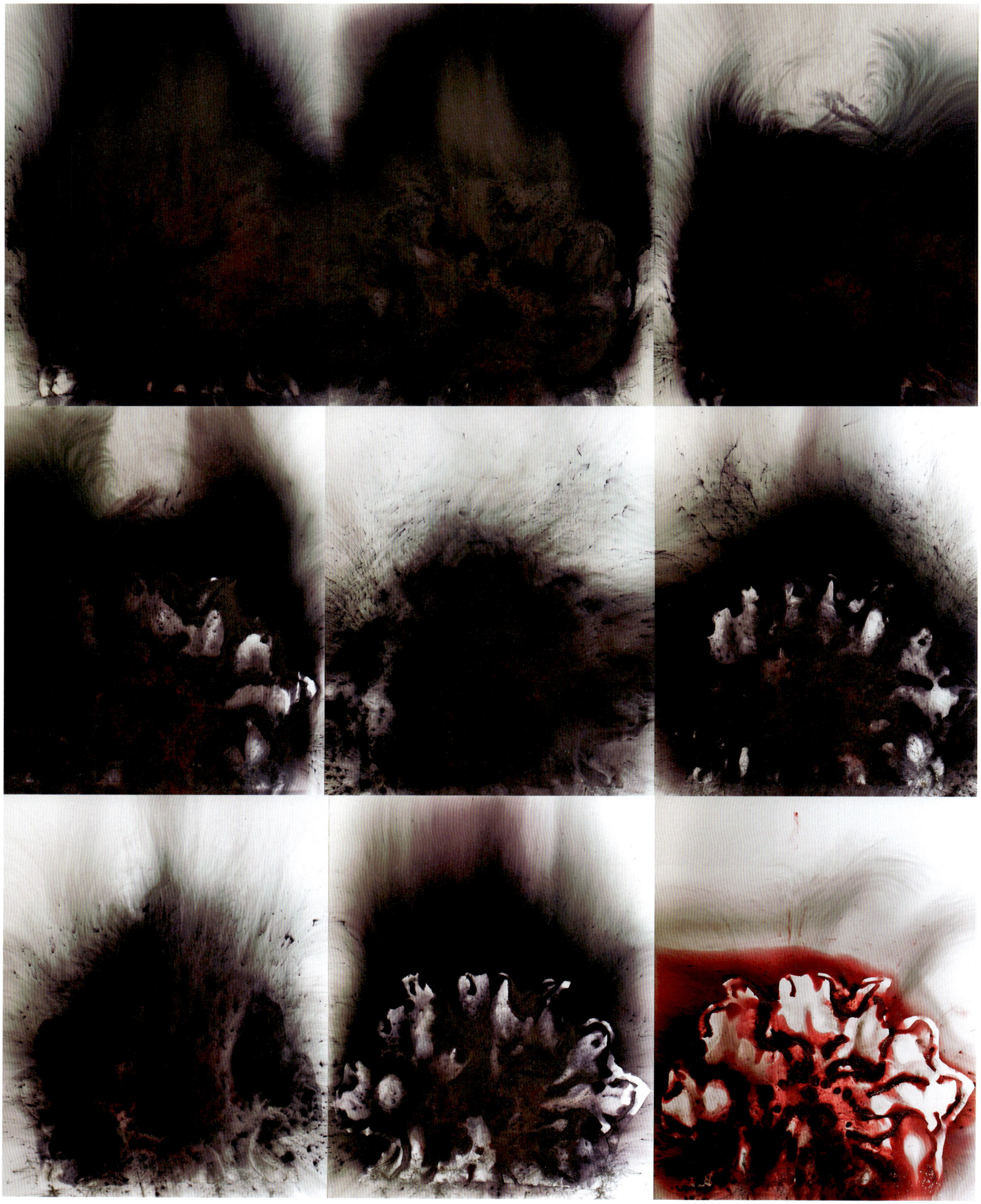

1.10 *Black Poppy*

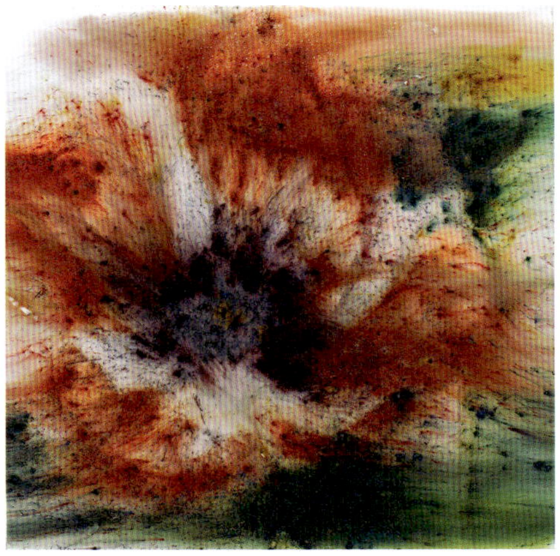

1.11 *Poppy Series: Orange*

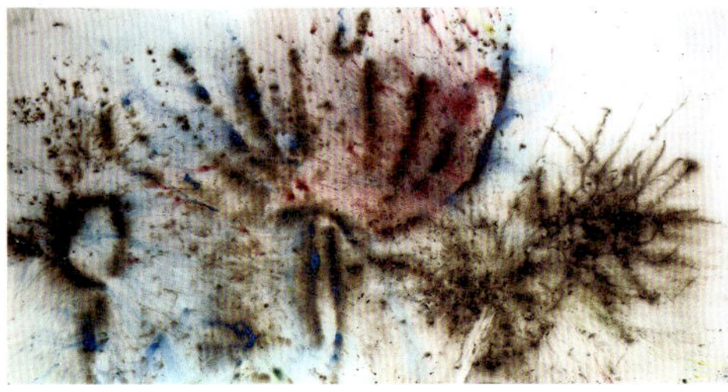

1.12 *Poppy Series: Blue and Purple*

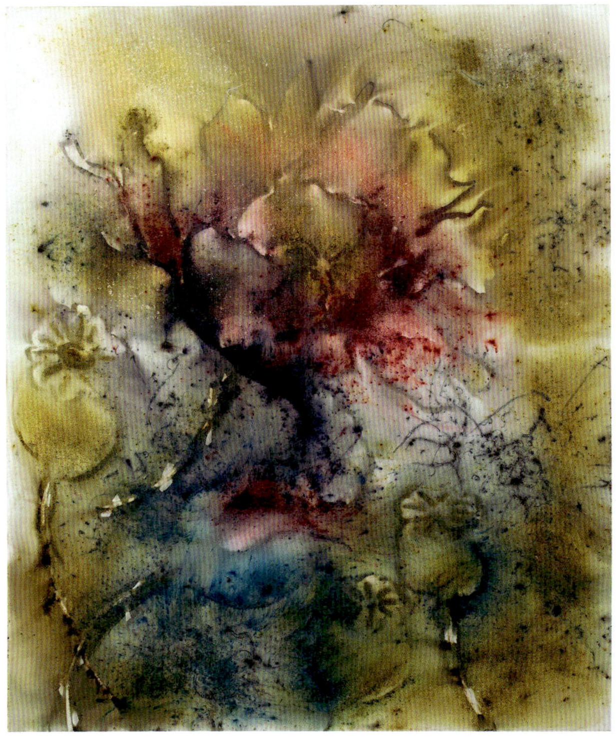

1.13 *Poppy Series: Red and Yellow*

1.10

*Black Poppy*

黑色罂粟花

2016
Gunpowder on canvas
152.5 × 1097 cm

Fresh poppy blossoms are a ubiquitous sight in Spain. On these nine canvases, Cai incrementally decreased the amount of black gunpowder to convey the passage of time and changes in energy. In the artist's view, the subjects of poppies and hallucination share an intrinsic congruence with the "loss of control" that gunpowder enables as a medium. Working together, they could potentially catalyze a greater release of energy. Over the course of one year, Cai depicted the subject of poppies through various types of color gunpowder, experimenting with ways to activate the sensuality of the medium and the subject through new applications of color.

Related Works

1.11

*Poppy Series: Orange*

罂粟系列:橙

2016
Gunpowder on canvas
122 × 122 cm

1.12

*Poppy Series: Blue and Purple*

罂粟系列:蓝和紫

2016
Gunpowder on paper
53 × 100 cm

1.13

*Poppy Series: Red and Yellow*

罂粟系列:红和黄

2015
Gunpowder on canvas
183 × 152 cm

1.14

*Poppy Series: Budding*

罂粟系列:花蕾

2016
Gunpowder on canvas
152.5 × 122 cm

1.15

*Poppy Series: Water*

罂粟系列:水

2016
Gunpowder on canvas
152.5 × 122 cm

1.16

*Pink Peony*

粉红牡丹

2017
Gunpowder on canvas
91 × 122 cm

1.17

*Chinese Poppy No. 2*

中国罂粟花之二

2017
Gunpowder on canvas
183 × 152.5 cm

1.18

*Chinese Poppy No. 1*

中国罂粟花之一

2017
Gunpowder on canvas
183 × 152.5 cm

1.19

*Poppy Series: Hallucination No. 6*

罂粟系列:幻觉第六号

2016
Gunpowder on canvas
300 × 600 cm

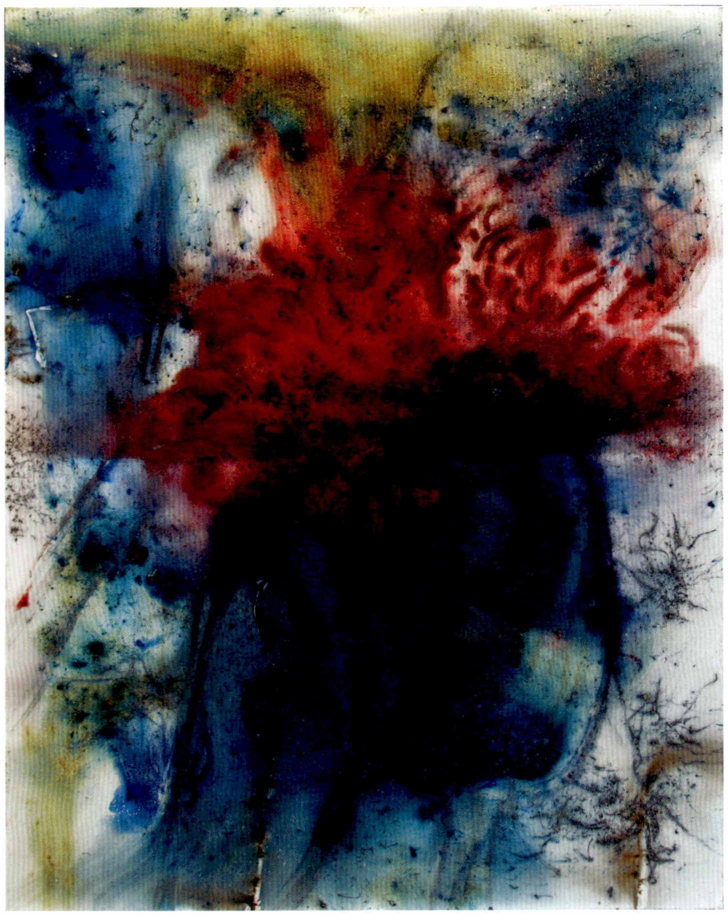

1.14 *Poppy Series: Budding*

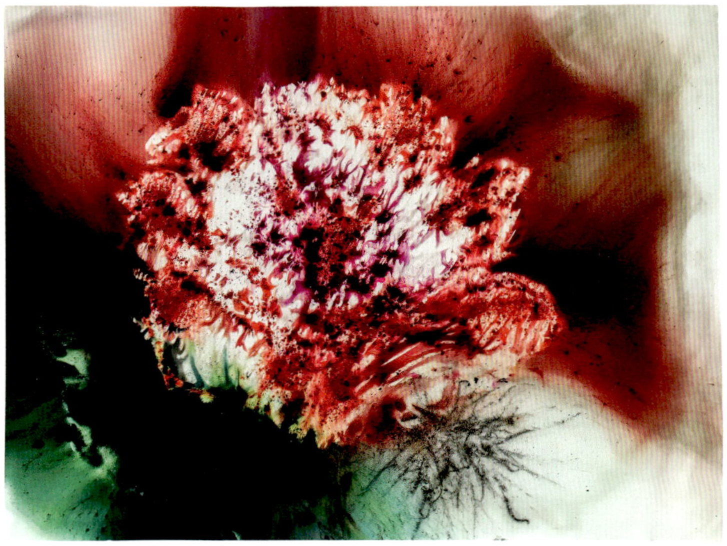

1.16 *Pink Peony*

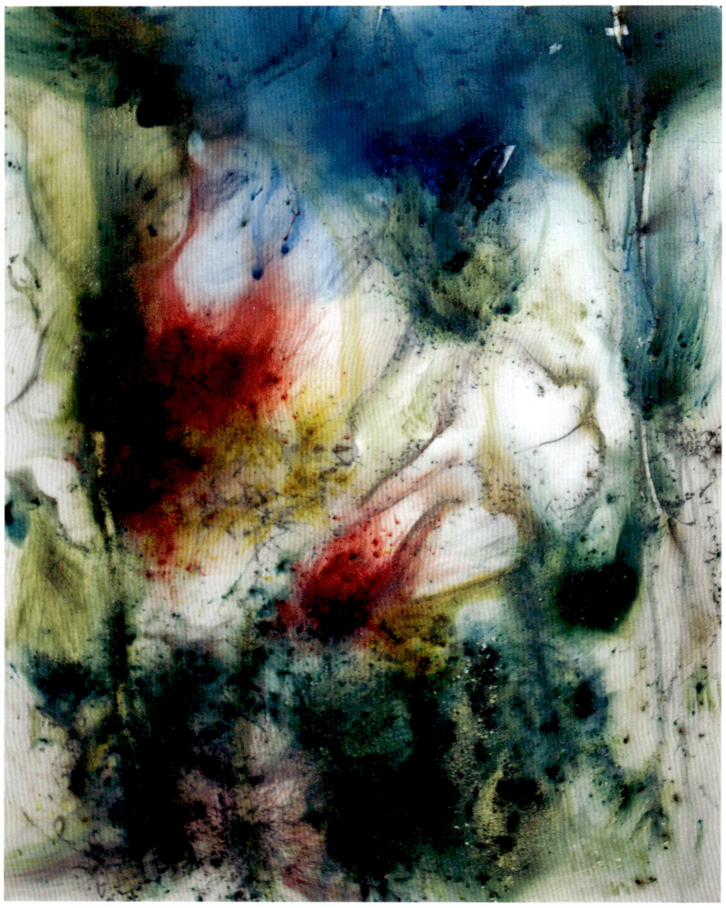

1.15 *Poppy Series: Water*

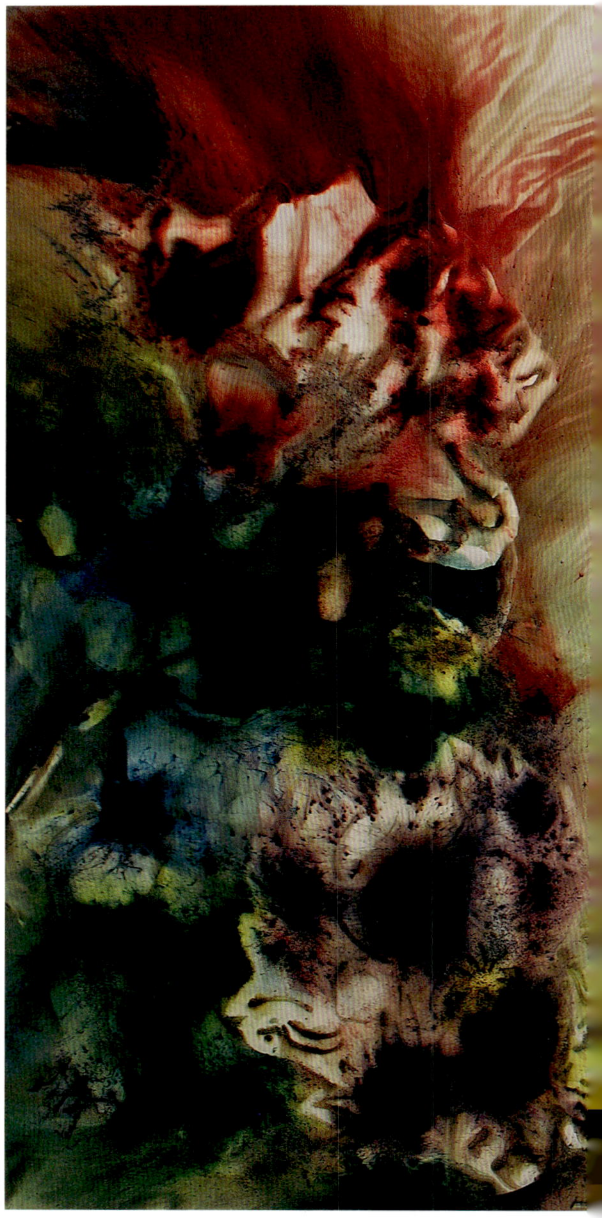

1.19 *Poppy Series: Hallucination No. 6*

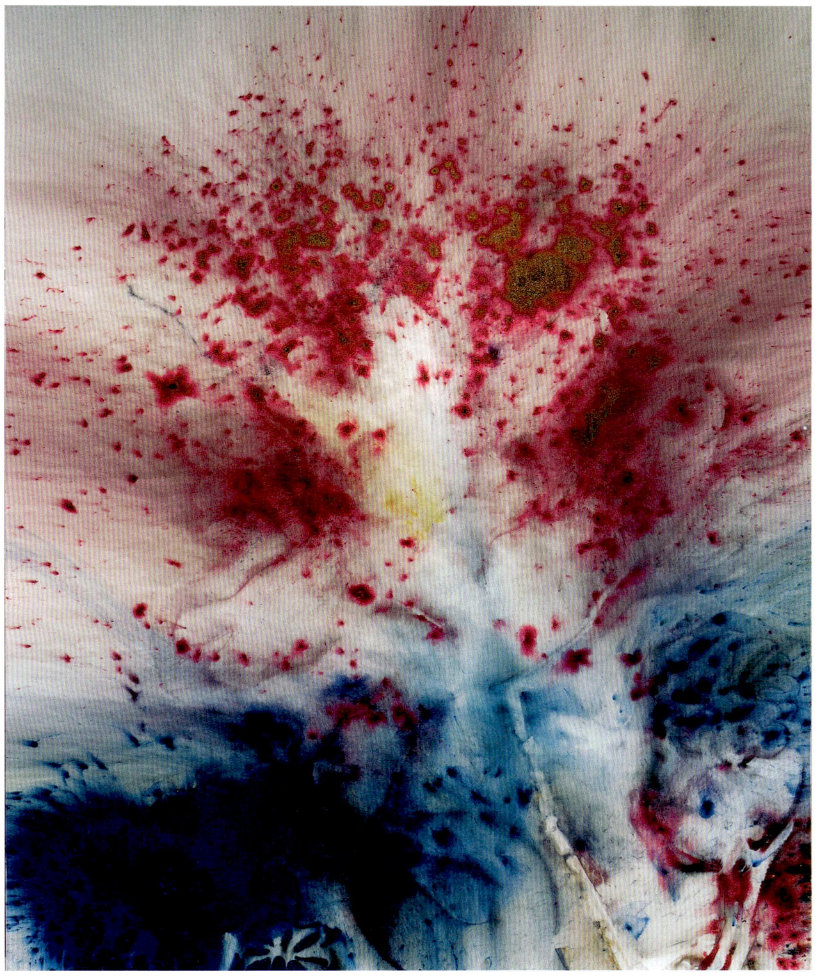

1.17 *Chinese Poppy No. 2*

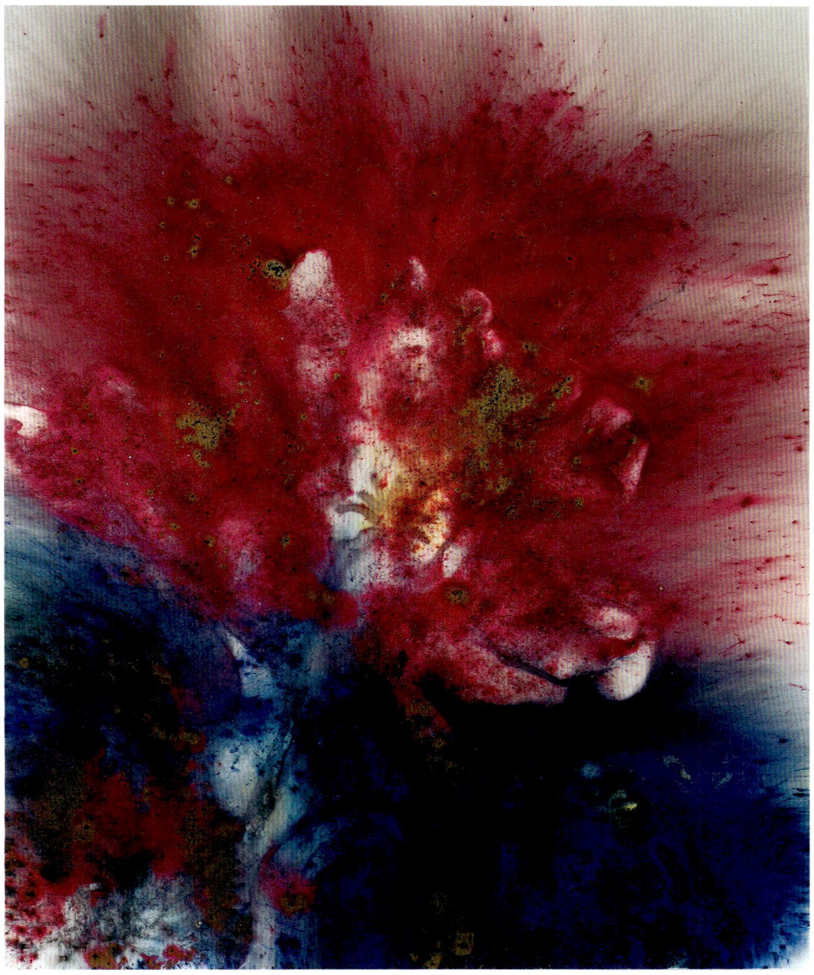

1.18 *Chinese Poppy No. 1*

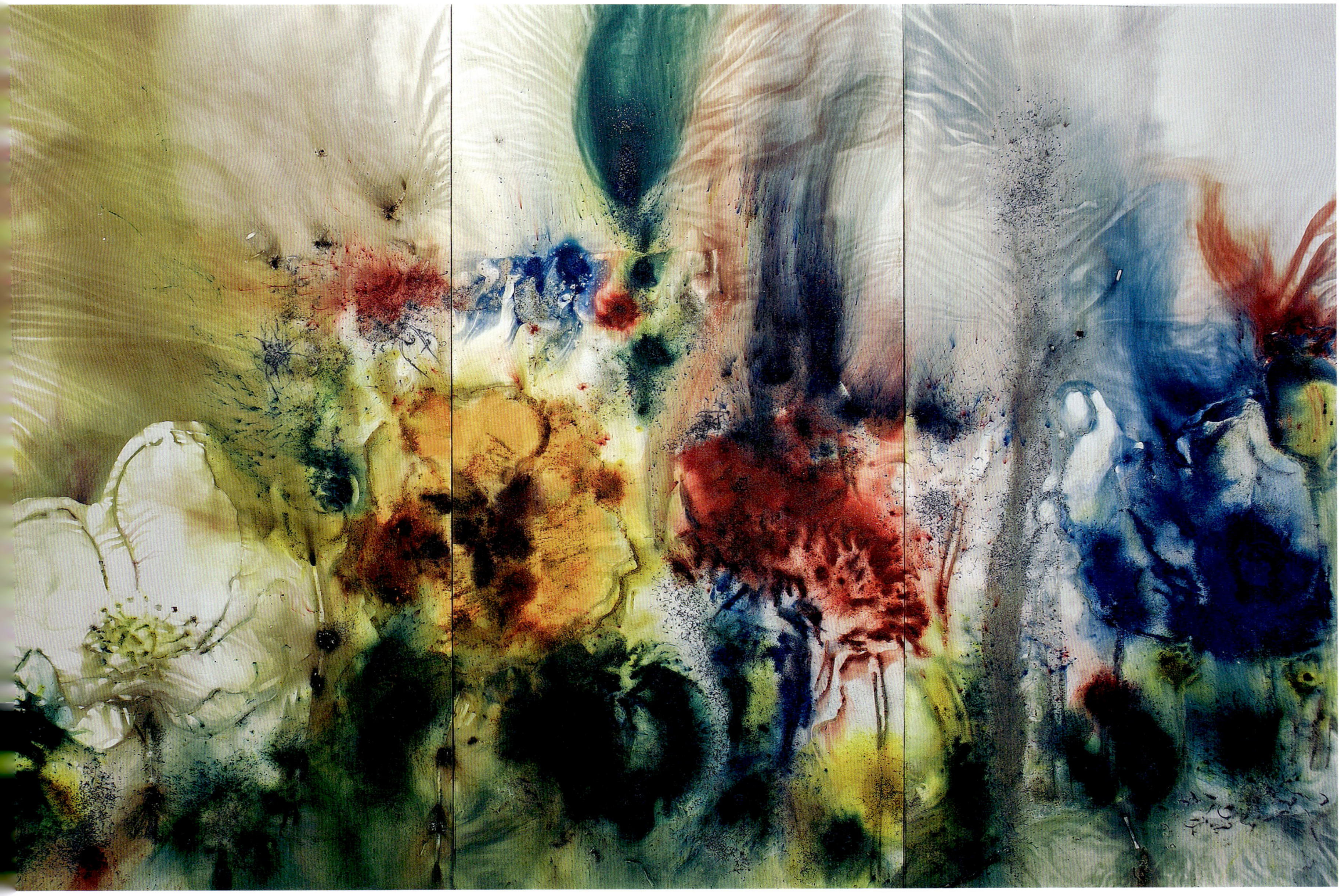

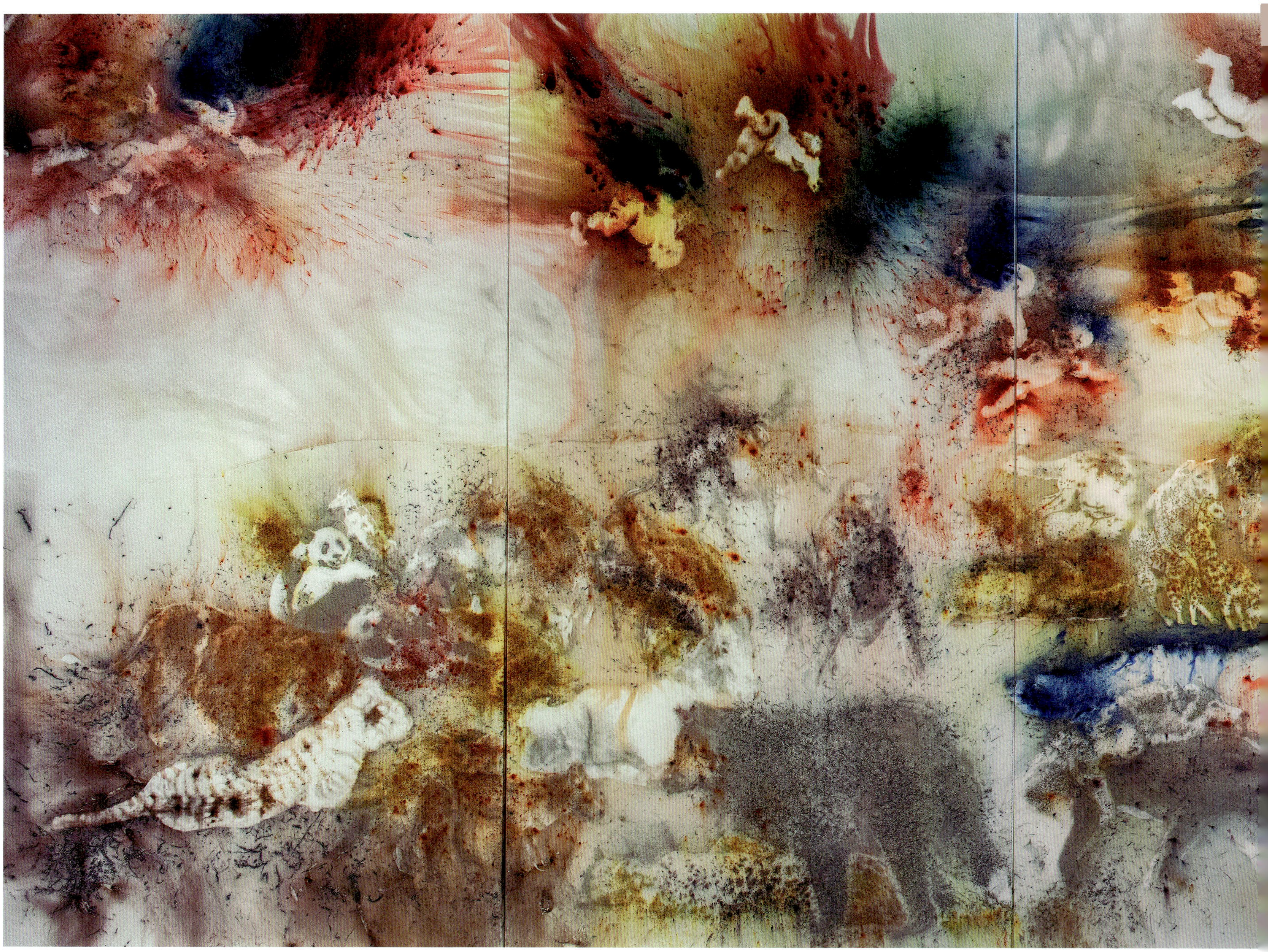

1.20 *Last Carnival*

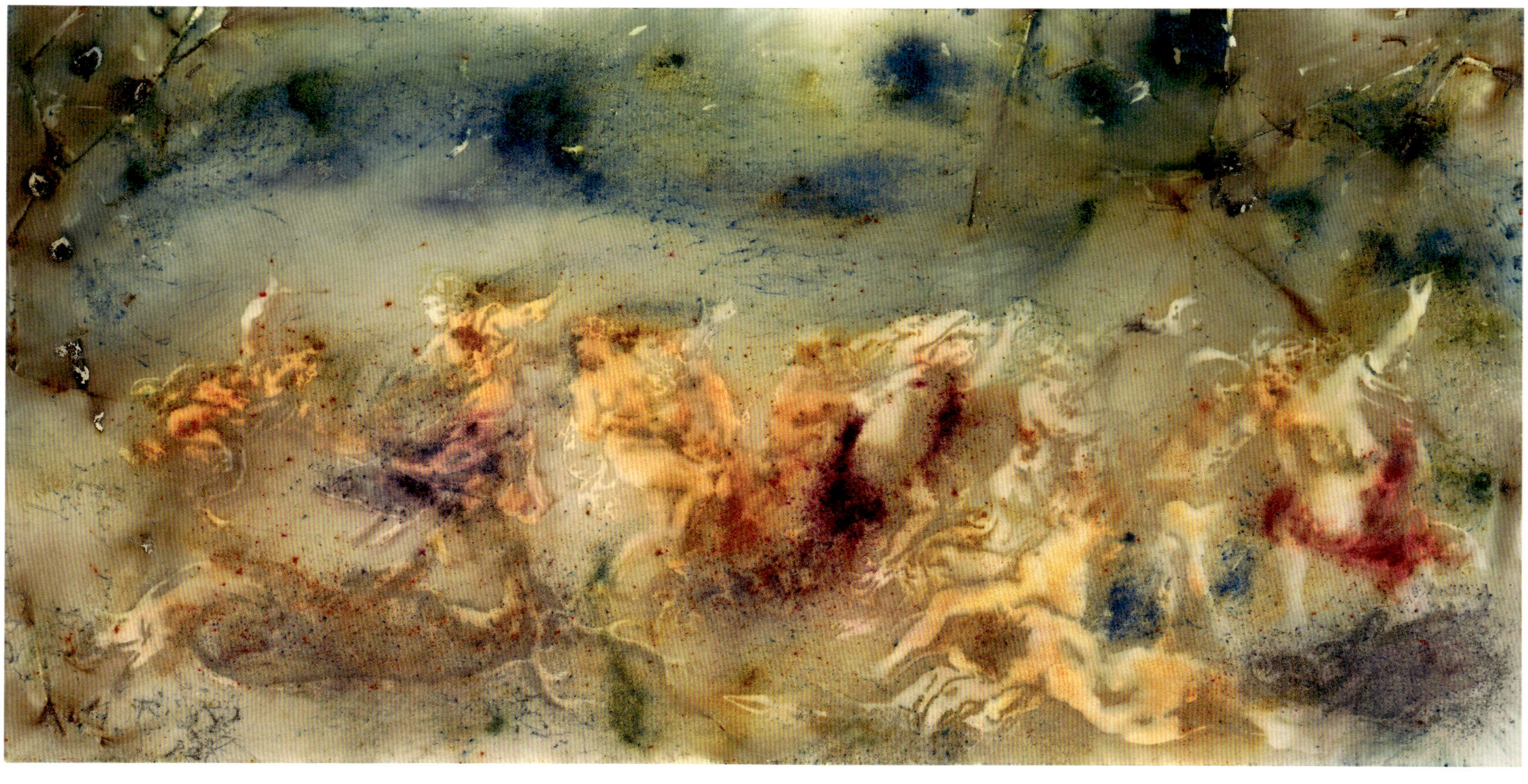

1.21 *Painting Rubens's Diana and Satyrs*

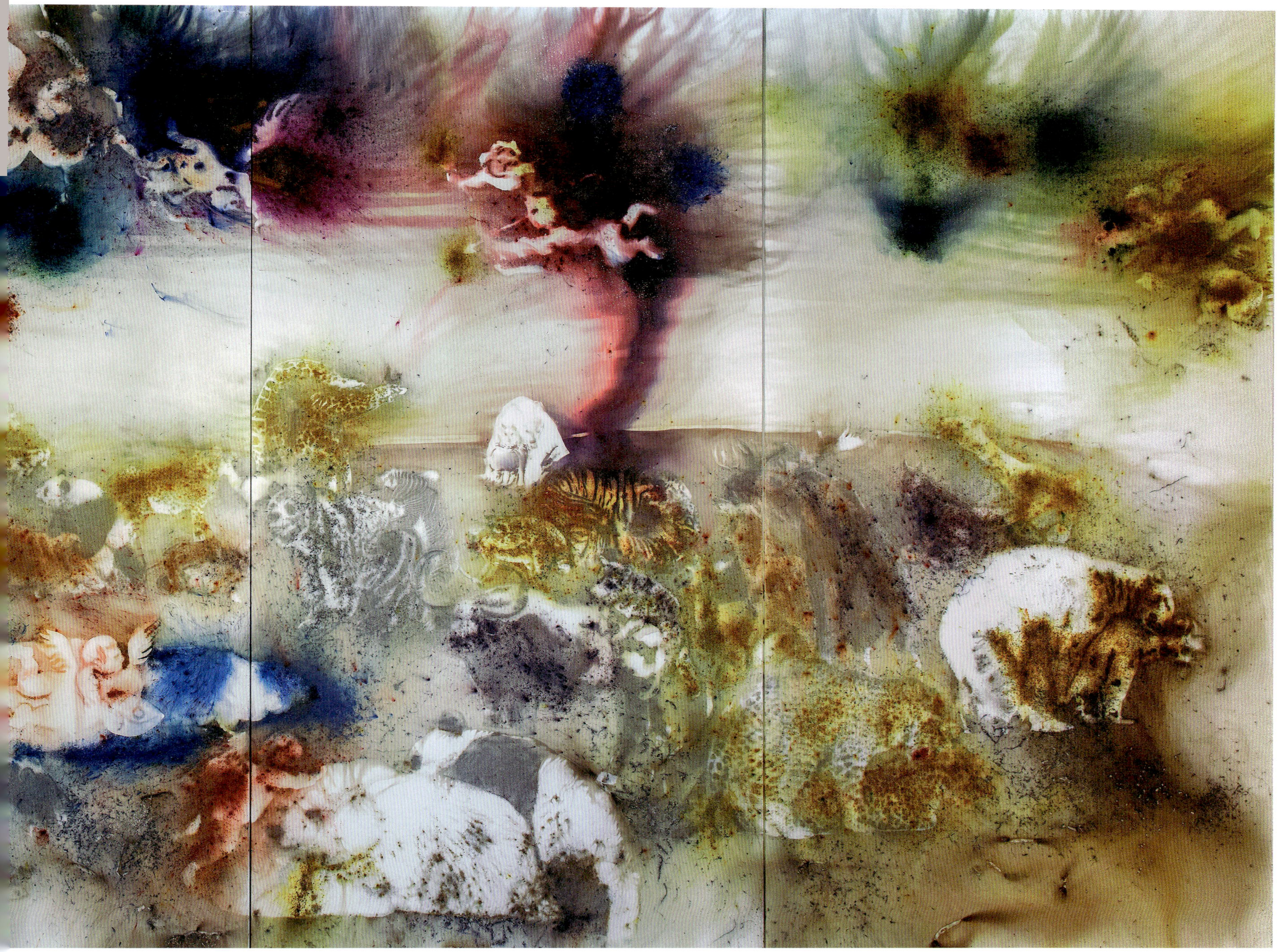

1.20

*Last Carnival*

最后的狂欢

2017

Gunpowder on canvas

280 × 750 cm

Akatsu Collection Tokyo

*Last Carnival* stems from Cai's study of Rubens's works in the Prado collection, in particular the master's ability to capture the dynamic movements of man and beast, and his methods of portraying cherubs. The piece also resonates with *The Garden of Earthly Delights*, in the Prado's collection, by Hieronymus Bosch (1450–1516), a giant from the late medieval period. Different species of animals have succumbed to interbreeding, bringing forth an environmental theme in which living beings continue to frolic even when only one single pool of water remains on the planet.

1.21

*Painting Rubens's Diana and Satyrs*

画鲁本斯“月神与公羊人”

2017

Gunpowder on canvas

150 × 300 cm

Using his unique technique and medium of gunpowder, Cai re-creates the piece *Diana and Her Nymphs Surprised by Satyrs* by the Flemish Baroque master Peter Paul Rubens (1577–1640) from the Prado collection. Through its creative process, Cai strove to capture the distinctive lust and vitality in Rubens's works.

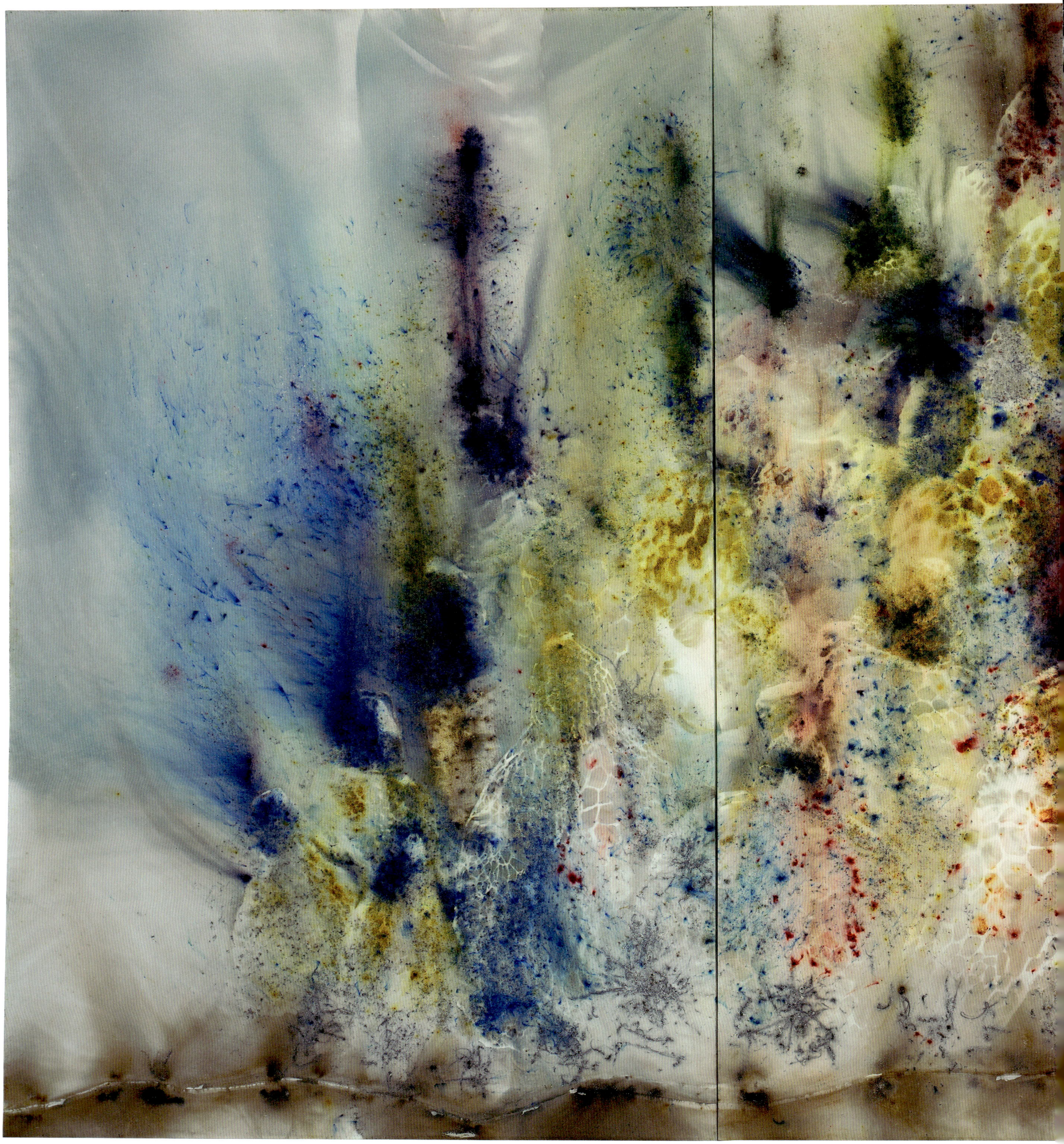

1.22 *Mountain in Heat*

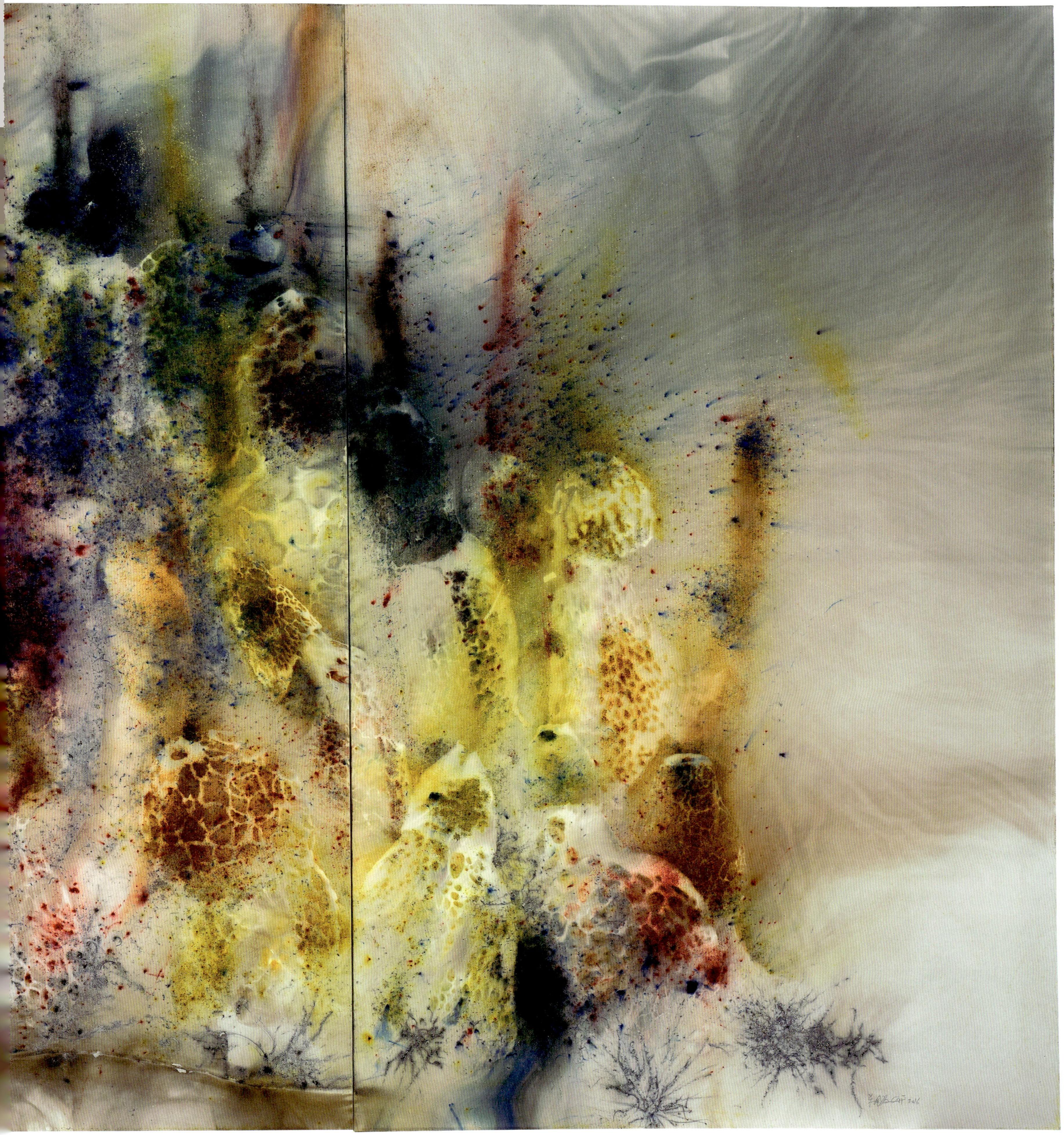

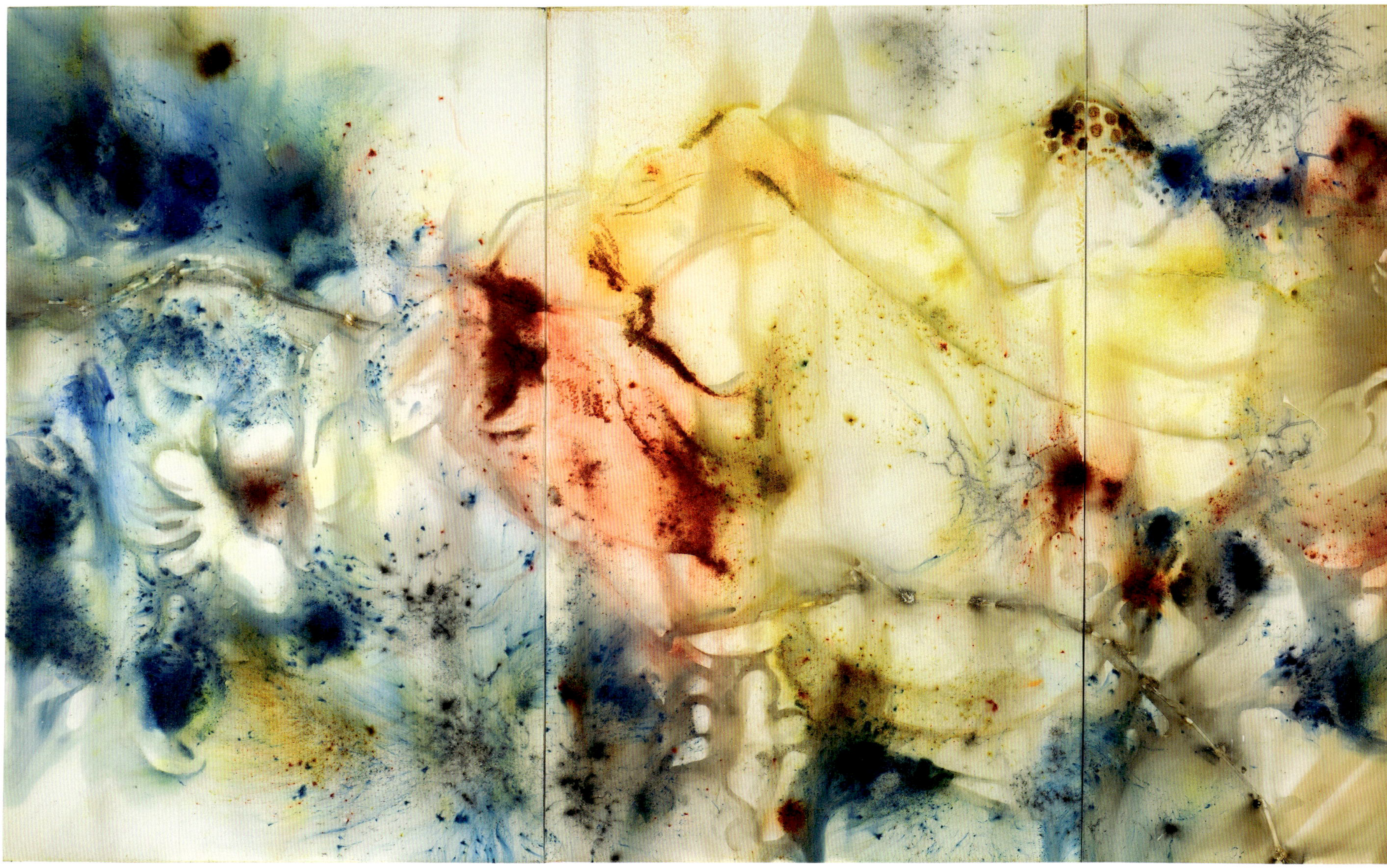

1.23 *Adolescent Fling*

1.22

*Mountain in Heat*

发情山

2016

Gunpowder on canvas

239 × 450 cm

Layer upon layer of aphrodisiac mushrooms accumulate into a mountain that bursts forth with desire. Cai strove to achieve a sense of dynamism and depth on the canvas, seeking new aesthetic possibilities between the thinness and simplicity of contemporary art and the profundity and harmony of classical painting.

Related Work

1.23

*Adolescent Fling*

青春期

2016

Gunpowder on canvas

239 × 600 cm

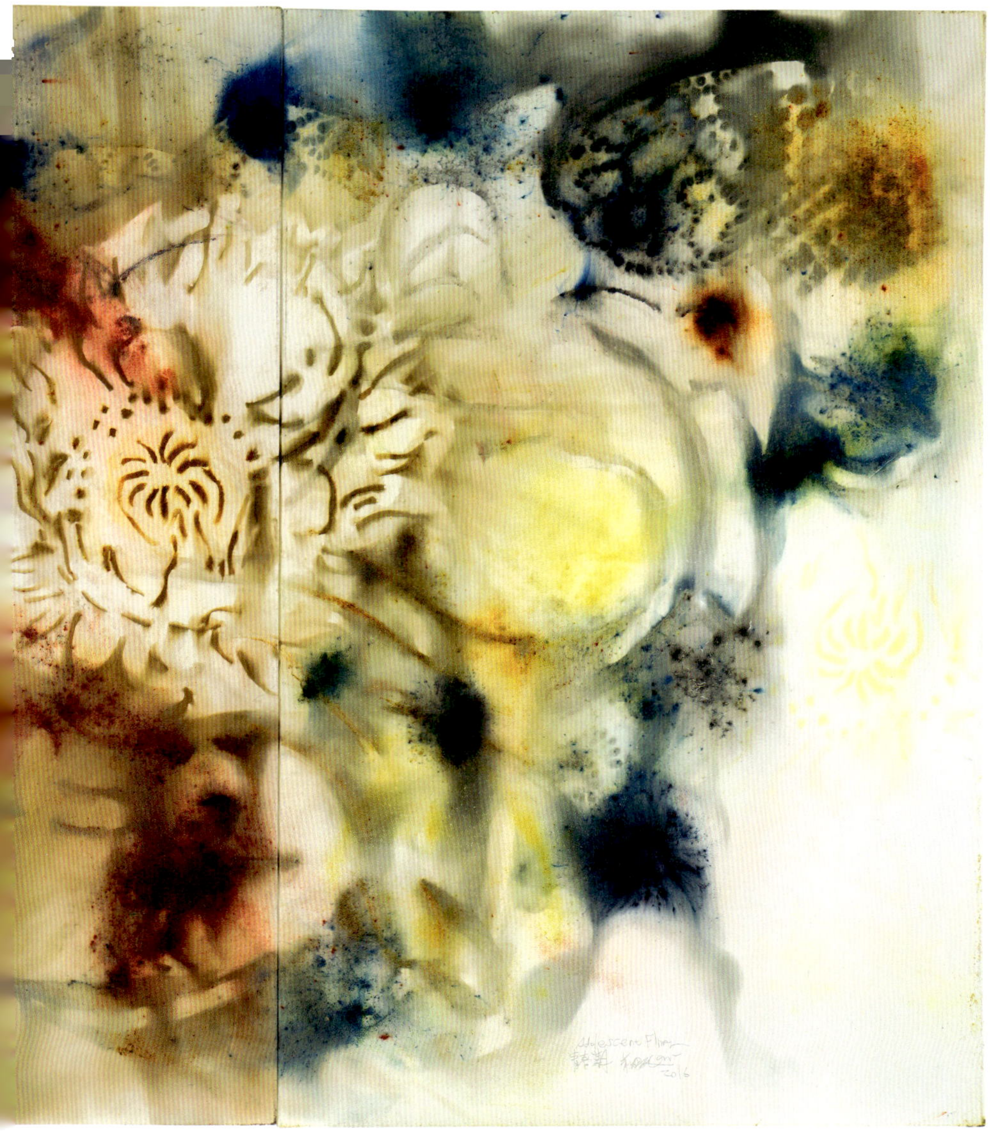

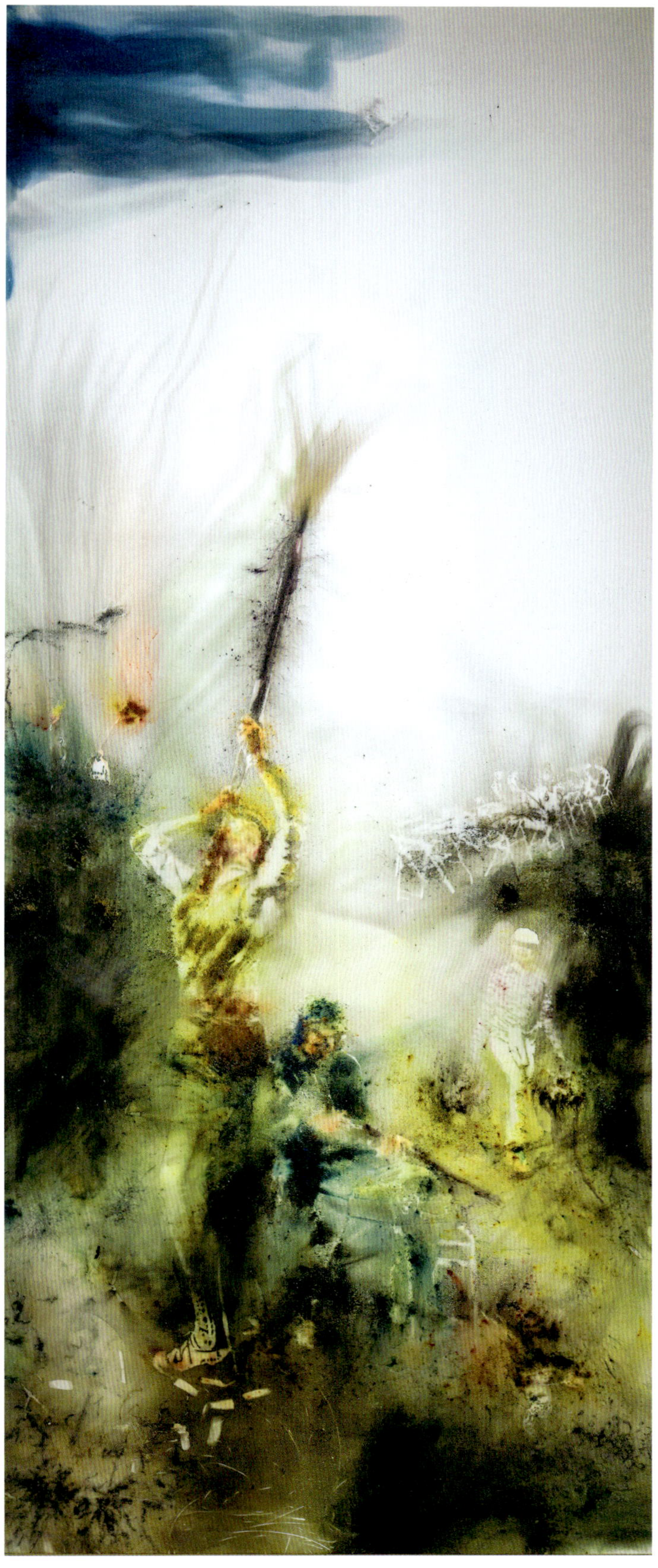

Figure 1.9. *Shooting*, 2017. Gunpowder on canvas, 360 × 150 cm

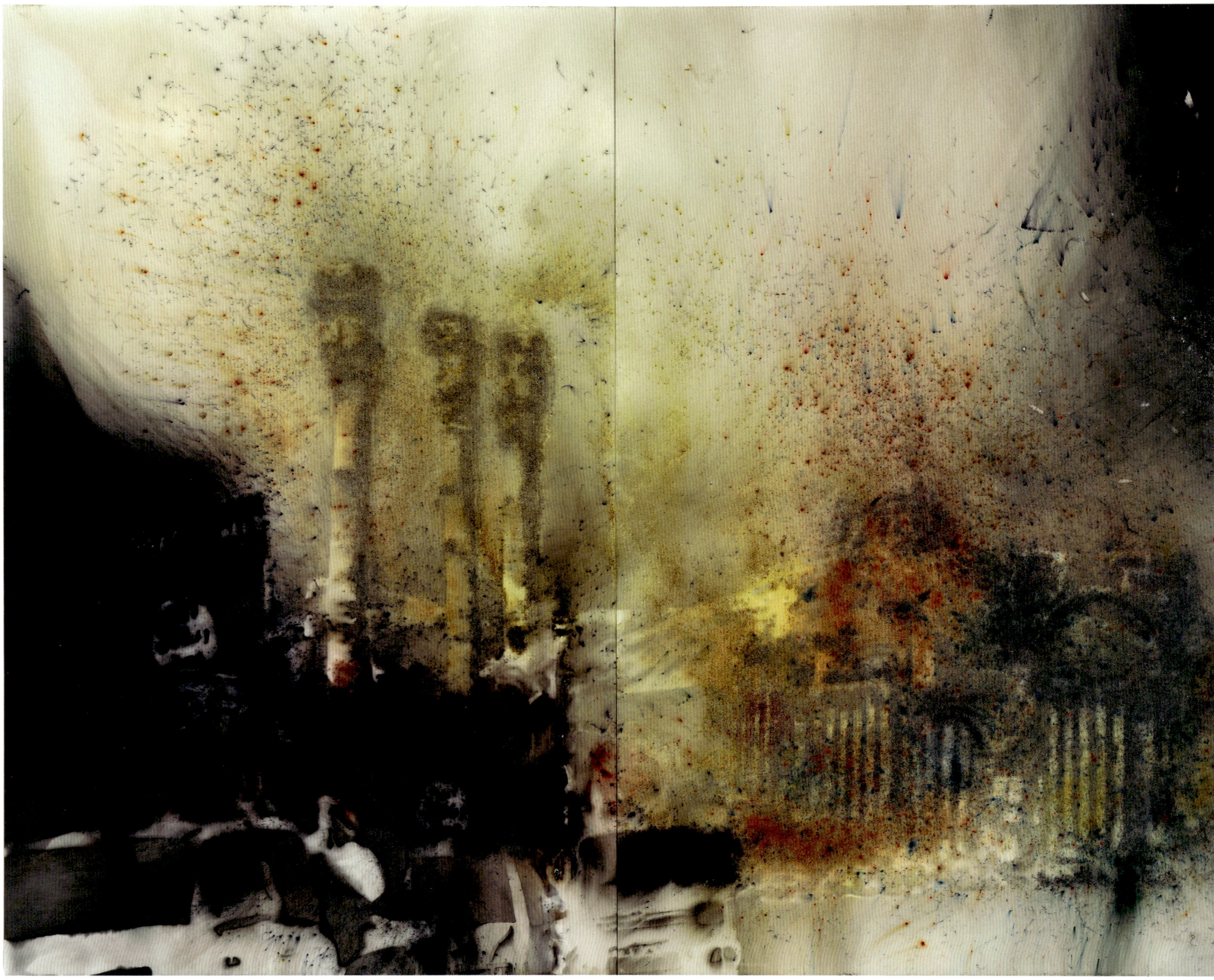

1.24 *Palmyra*

1.24

*Palmyra*

帕米拉

2017

Gunpowder on canvas

240 × 450 cm

Cai first used gunpowder to re-create *The Third of May 1808* (figure 1.10), a work in the Prado collection by the celebrated Spanish painter Francisco Goya (1746–1828), in an attempt to understand its energy and tension. Cai then crafted *Palmyra*, which offers a gesture of compassion from the Prado to that landmark of ancient civilization which has suffered in this time of misfortune. *Palmyra* was realized at the Salón de Reinos.

Related Work

1.25

*Painting Goya's The Third of May*

画戈雅 "五月三号"

2017

Gunpowder on canvas

239 × 300 cm

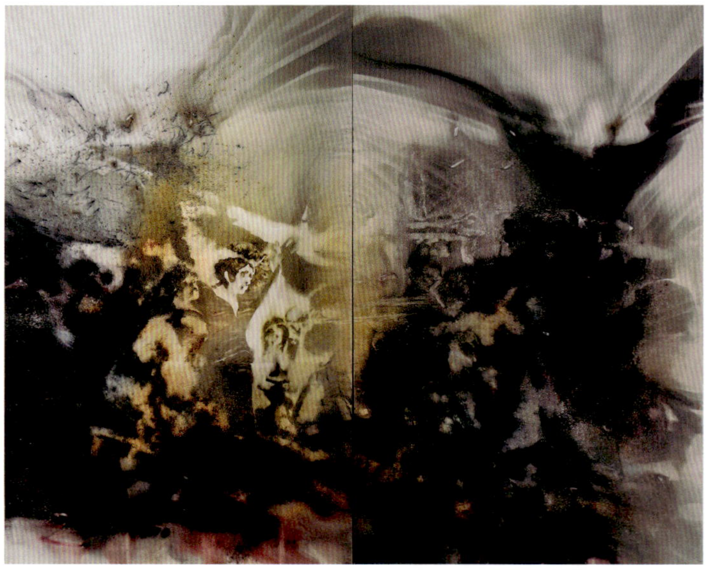

1.25 *Painting Goya's The Third of May*

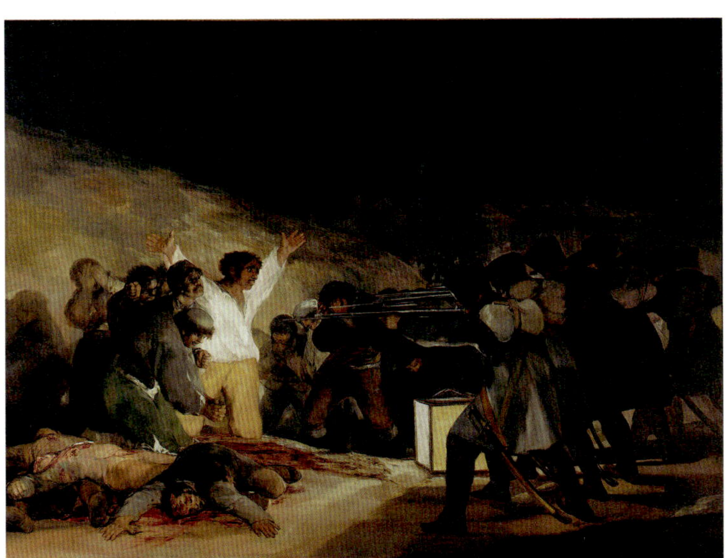

Figure 1.10. Francisco Goya, *The Third of May 1808*, 1814. Oil on canvas, 268 x 347 cm. Collection of the Prado Museum, Madrid

1.26

*Salón de Reinos ...*

万国大厅...

2017

Gunpowder on canvas

360 × 600 cm

Four hundred years ago, Philip IV of Spain received official visitors in the Salón de Reinos. There he also commissioned the best Spanish painters of the time—including Diego Velázquez (1599–1660)—to create and exhibit their works.

In the month leading up to the opening of his Prado exhibition, Cai was invited to use the same space as his painting studio and create artworks. For this painting, he attempted to capture the shadows of Old Masters such as Velázquez. The black streak pierces into an abyss, alluding to a blurring of space-time dimensions.

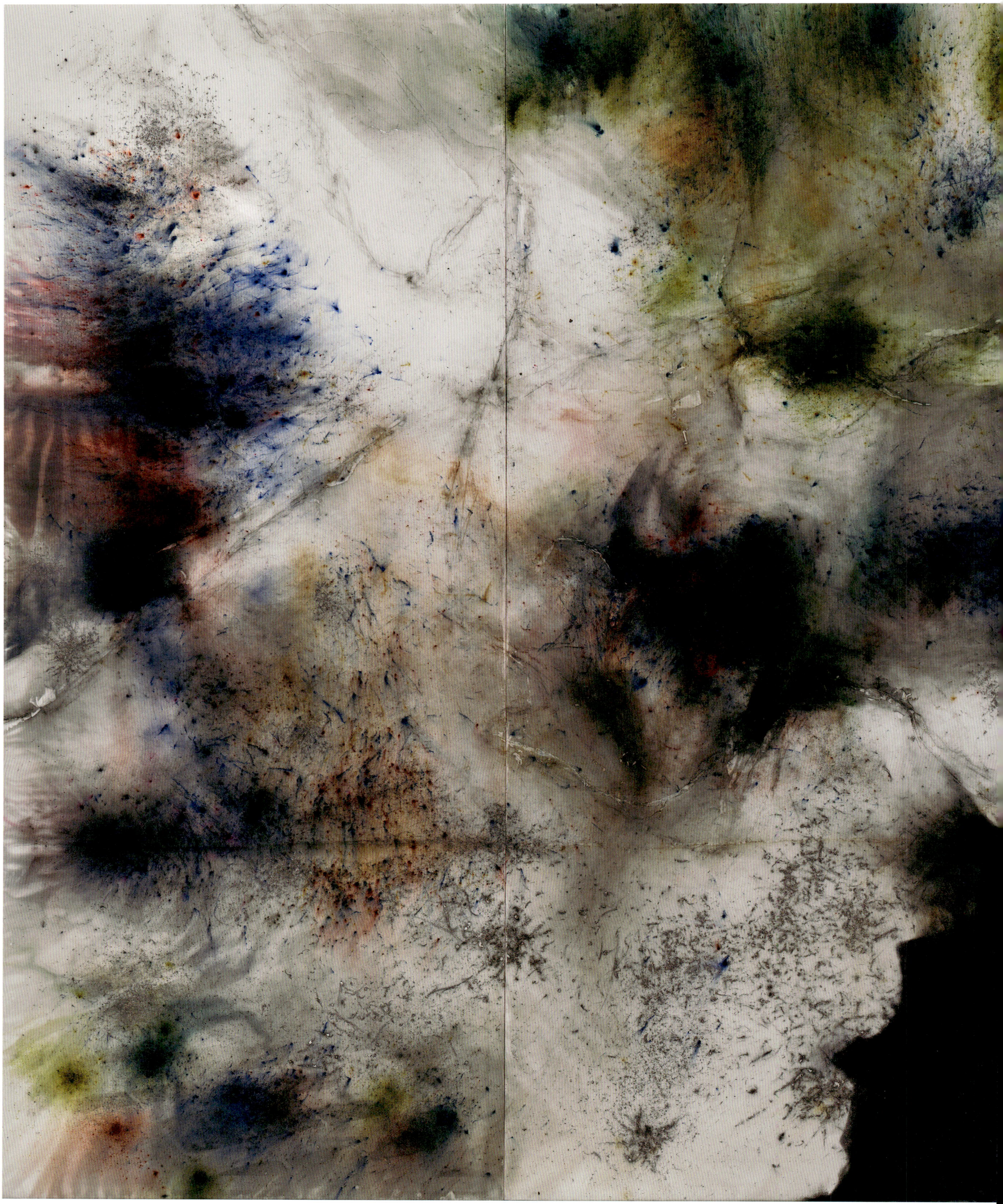

1.26 *Salón de Reinos ...*

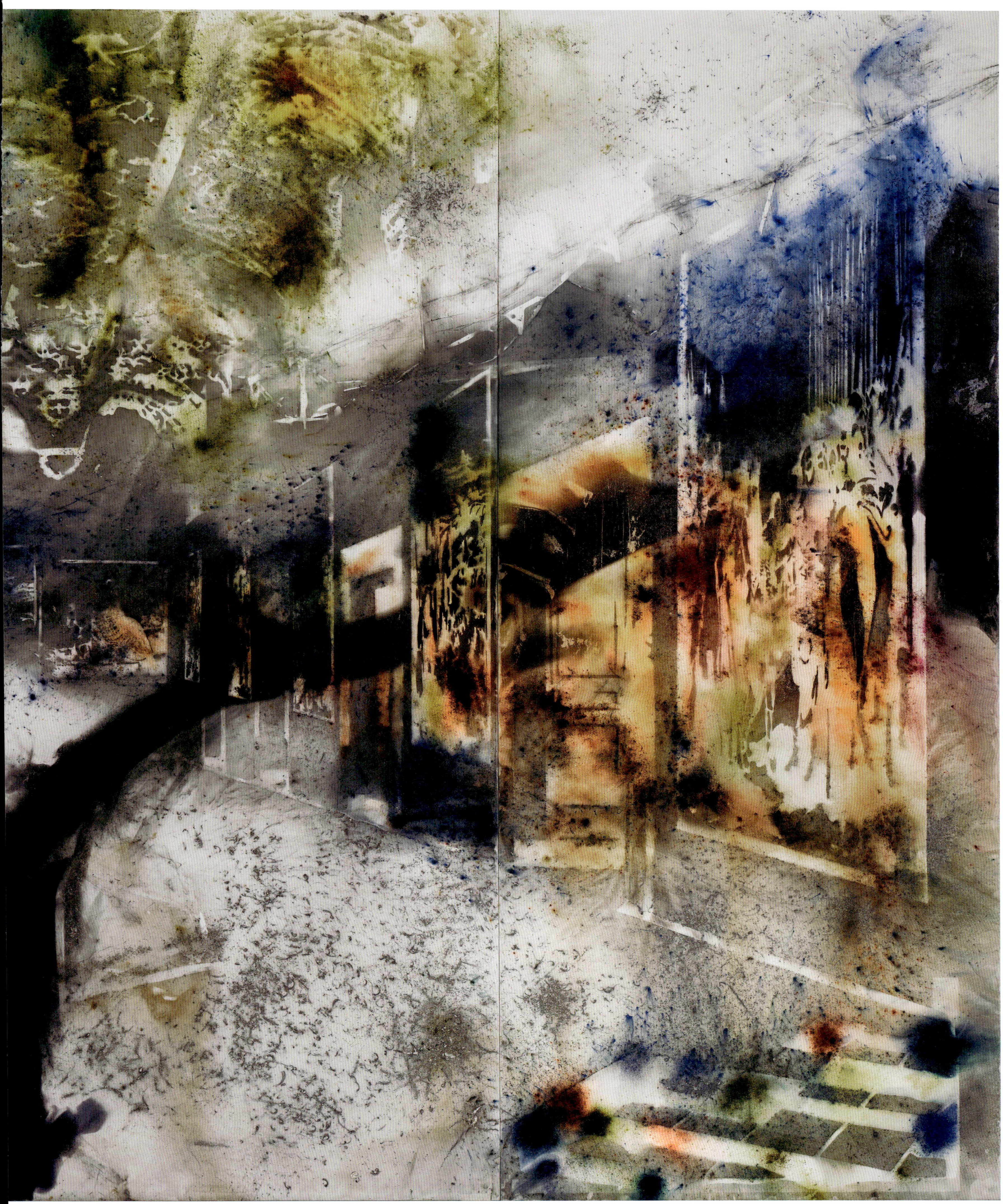

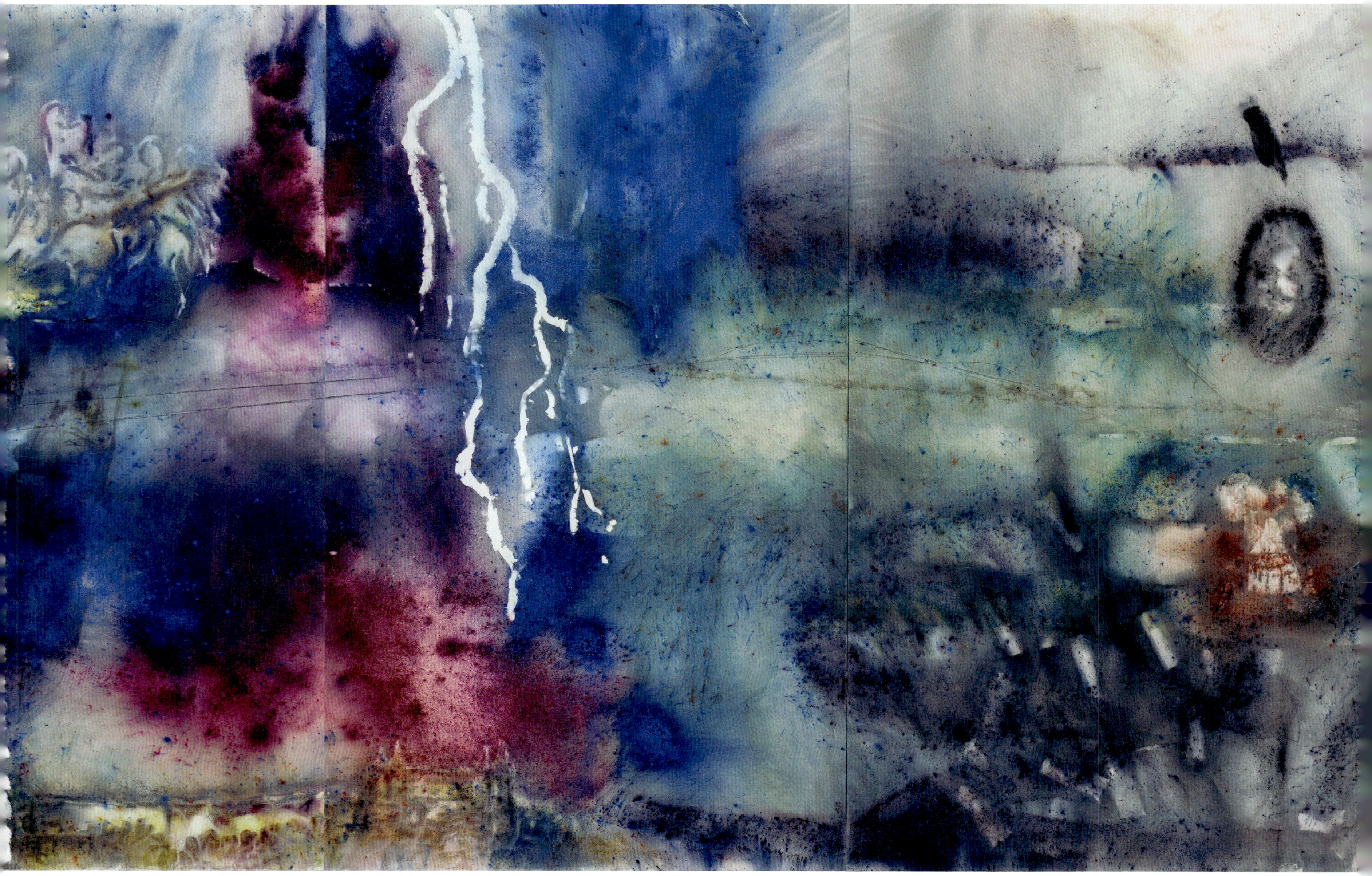

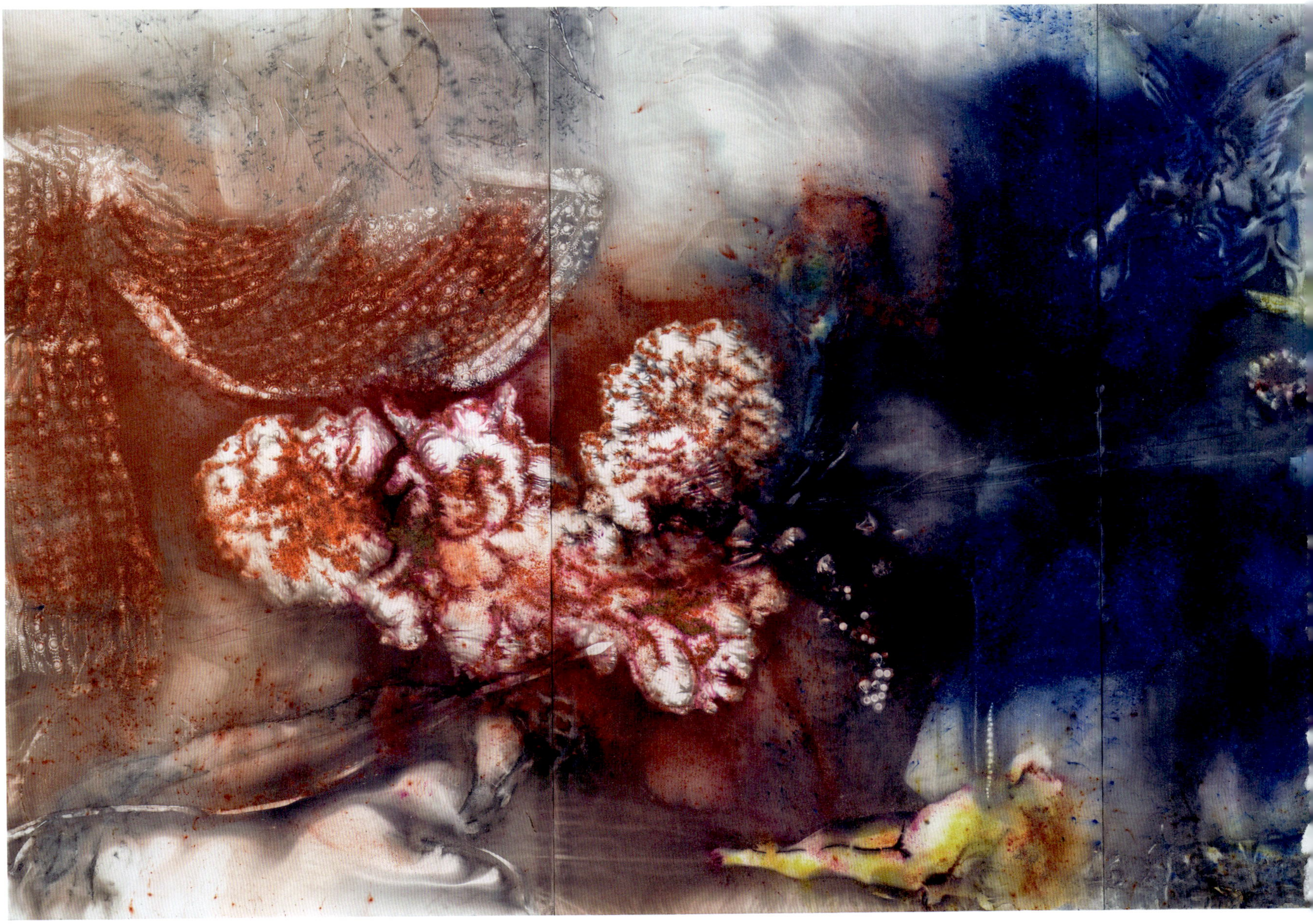

1.27 *The Spirit of Painting*

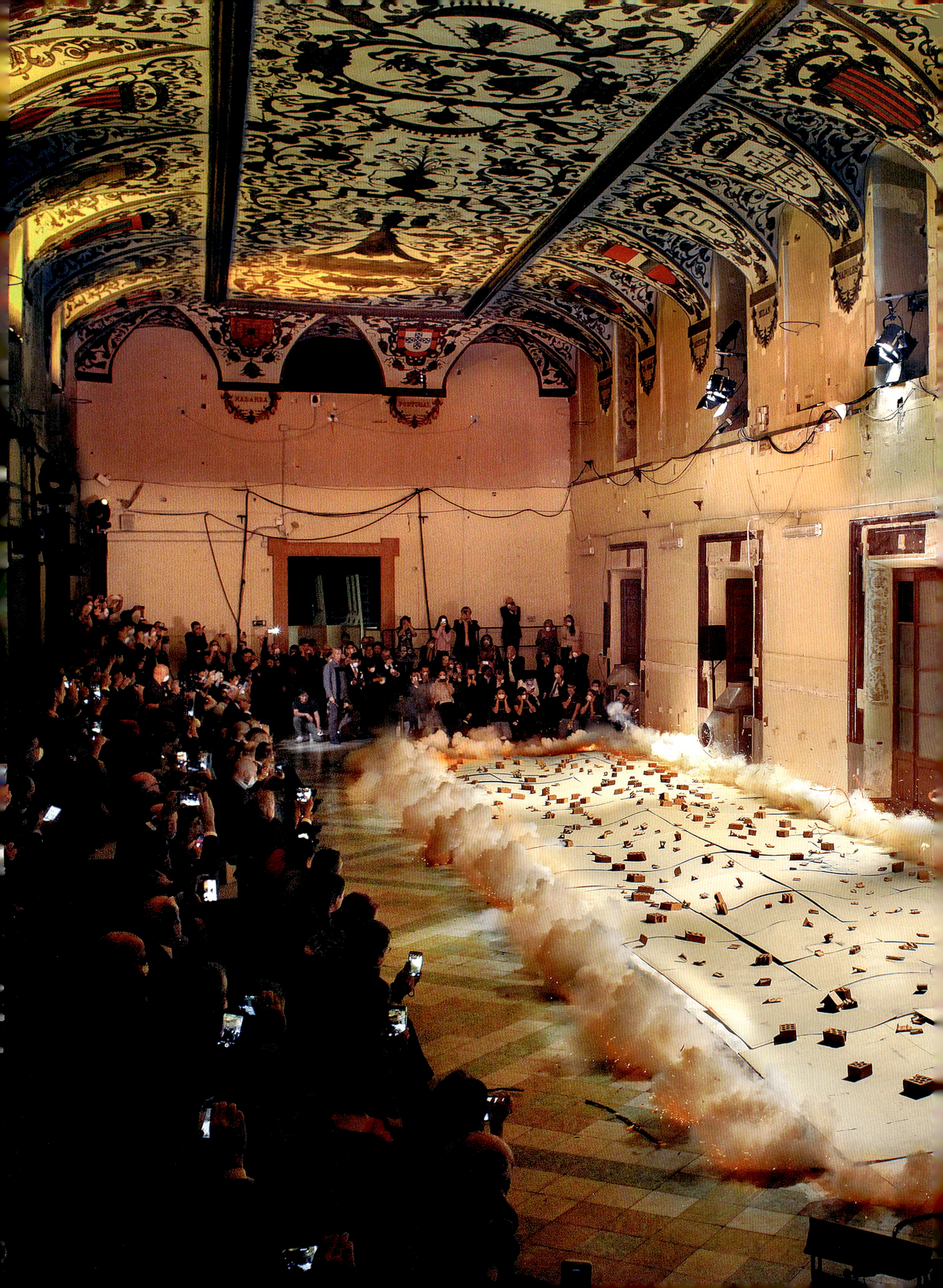
PORTUGAL

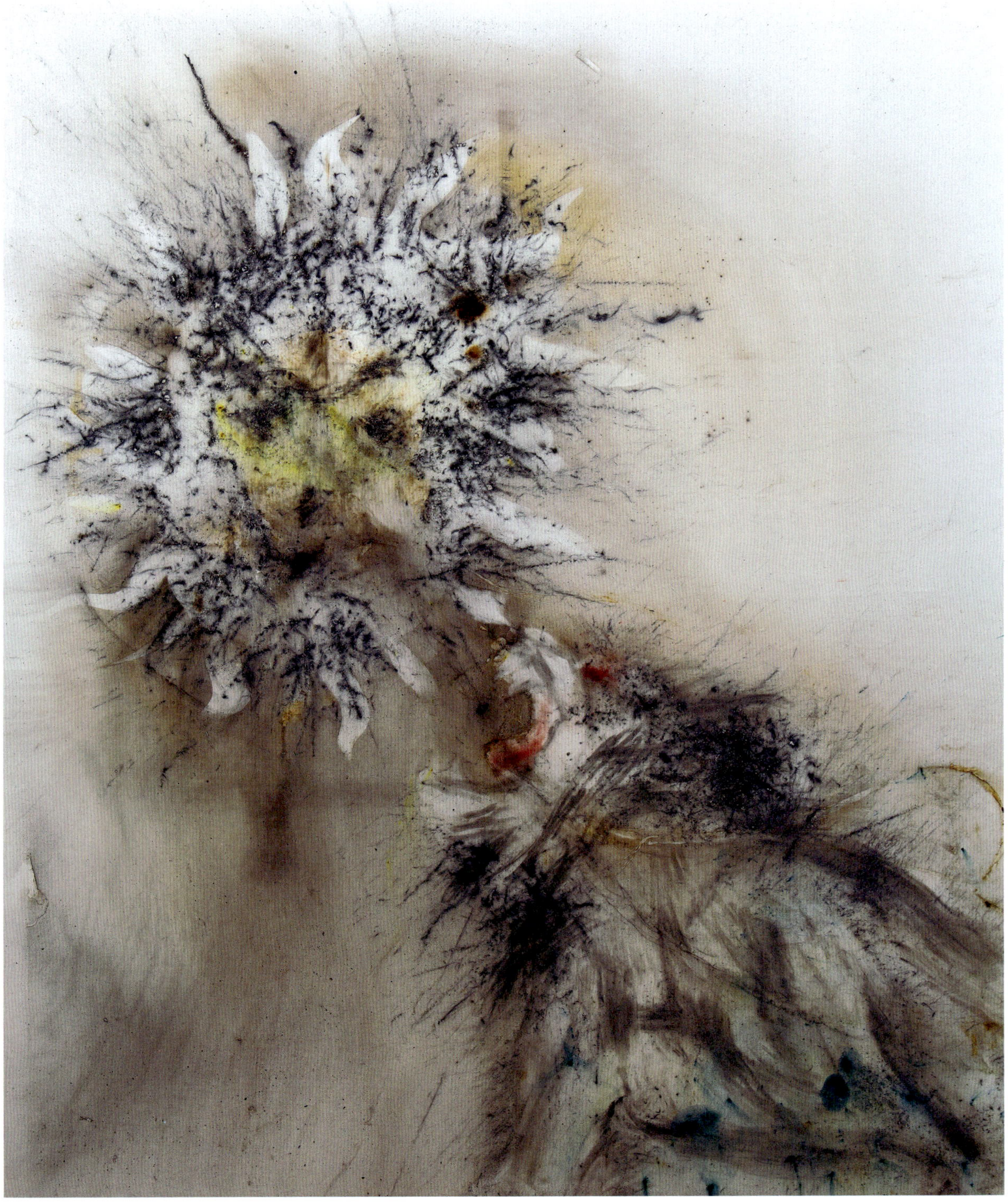

1.28

*Alchemist*

炼金师

2017

Gunpowder on canvas

240 × 200 cm

Collection of MGM Cotai, Macau

In this painting Cai returns to the basics; he discards stencils and uses his hands as paintbrushes to caress the gunpowder into various shapes. Taking ancient alchemy as its theme, the work represents its iconic symbol—the green lion. Resonating with the transformation of gunpowder as a material and the flux of energy, Cai has made it as an homage to the alchemist-like, wondrous greatness of the Prado's Old Masters. The painting was completed at the Salón de Reinos.

# 2

# Dialogue with the Italian Renaissance

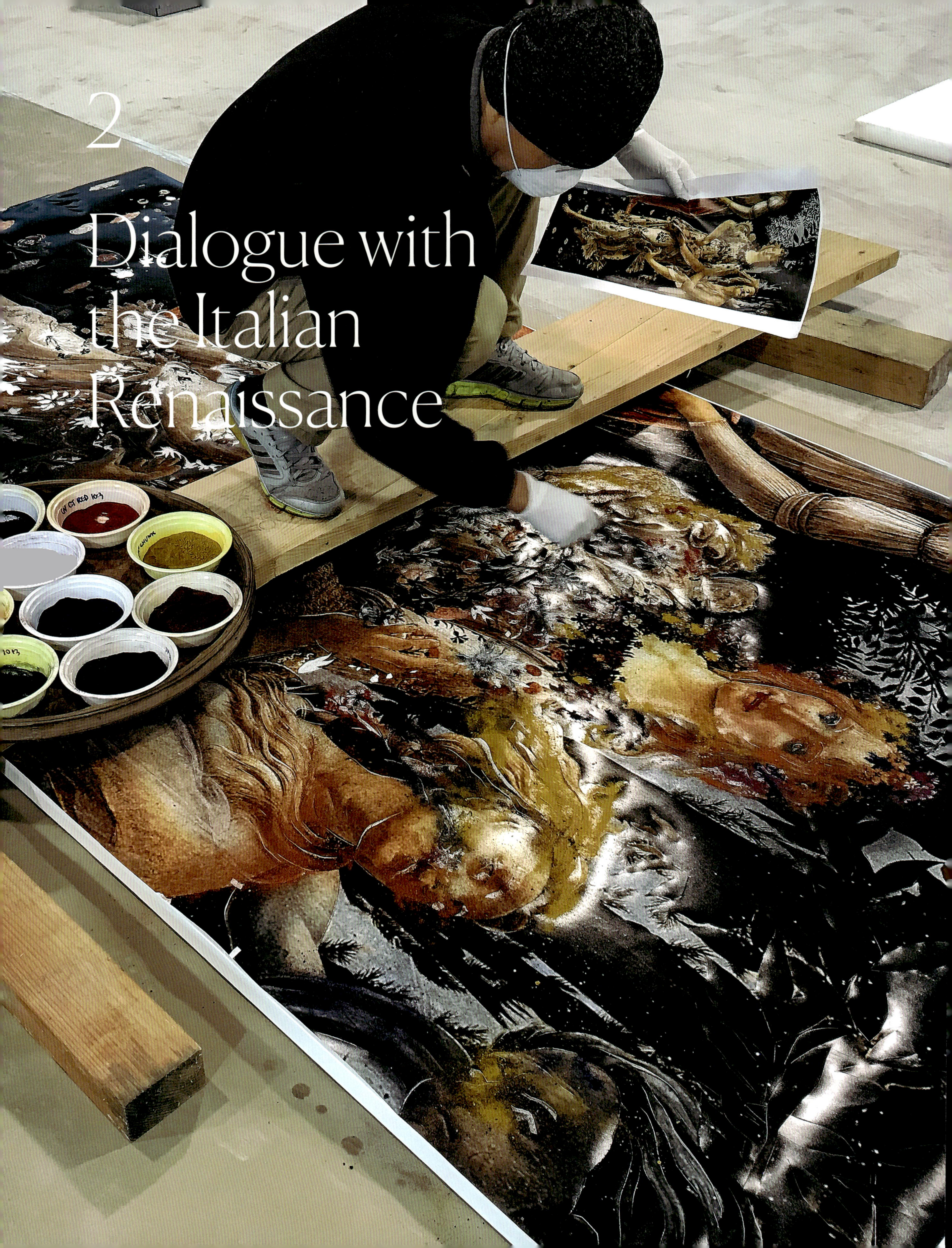

# *Flora Commedia: Cai Guo-Qiang at the Uffizi*

Uffizi Galleries, Florence, Italy
November 20, 2018–February 17, 2019

Curated by Eike D. Schmidt, Director, Uffizi Galleries, and Laura Donati, Curator, Department of Prints and Drawings, Uffizi Galleries

Daytime explosion event: *City of Flowers in the Sky*, at Piazzale Michelangelo on November 18, 2018

Catalogue: English and Italian editions published by Giunti Editore S.p.A. and Mandarin Chinese edition published by Jiangxi Fine Arts Publishing House

Documentary short: directed by Shanshan Xia, produced by 33 Studio (10:37)

*Flora Commedia* consisted of sixty gunpowder paintings and process sketches, displayed in ten interlinked special galleries in the museum's main building, with the following nine themes: *Caravaggio Garden*, *Renaissance Garden*, *Color Garden*, *Nature Garden*, *Cosmos Garden*, *White Garden, Black Garden, Erotic Garden*, and *Celestial Garden*. These galleries formed a space-time tunnel between the present and the past, as they were neighboring the galleries housing the core of the Uffizi's superb collections from the Italian Renaissance, encompassing works by Botticelli, Leonardo, and Caravaggio.

*Flora Commedia* was born of Cai's visit to the Uffizi in 2017, and developed through his subsequent returns to Florence, the "City of Flowers." Inspired by his research into the metal point drawing technique at the museum's Prints and Drawings department, he developed new techniques in gunpowder painting. He also spent time at the museum's Boboli Gardens, originally designed for the Medicis, to study the flowers and plants of the Renaissance, rare varieties of which were specially cultivated for him by the Uffizi's botanists. Cai was galvanized to use flowers and plants as the symbolic vessels through which to express the pursuit of humanity, liberation, and other spirits and characteristics of the Renaissance.

Cai felt great resonance with the Renaissance artists: Caravaggio's untamable nature as a "bad kid," Leonardo's fanciful inventions and sketches, and Botticelli's beautiful and tender flowers. He also found kindred spirits in them for their values of freedom, openness, diversity, and humanistic liberation. While he dwelled on the themes and theories of painting in the Prado exhibition, this time he began to break free from the constraints of "masterful painting," developing and realizing new techniques to his heart's content. In a sense, the Uffizi exhibition witnessed Cai's return to a state of freedom, nature, and ease, as well as a "liberation" of his own painting.

Figure 2.1. Cai Guo-Qiang sprinkling color gunpowder to create a gunpowder painting in 2018

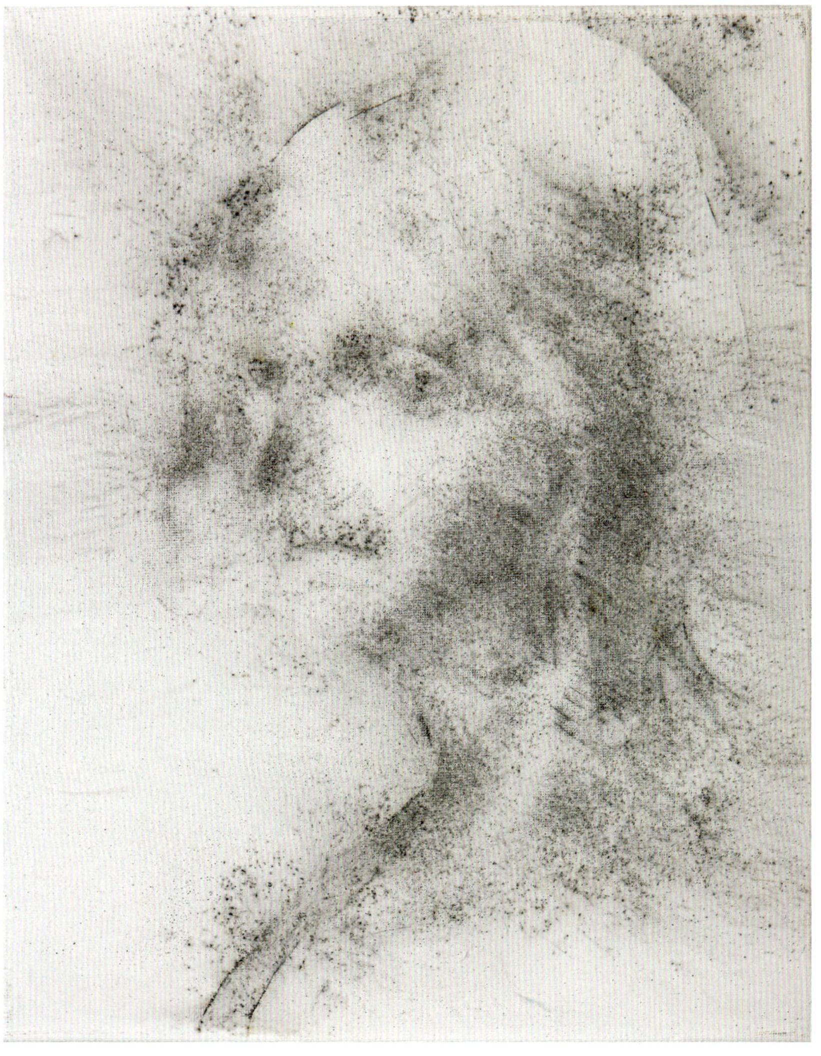

2.1 *Silverpoint Study No. 1*

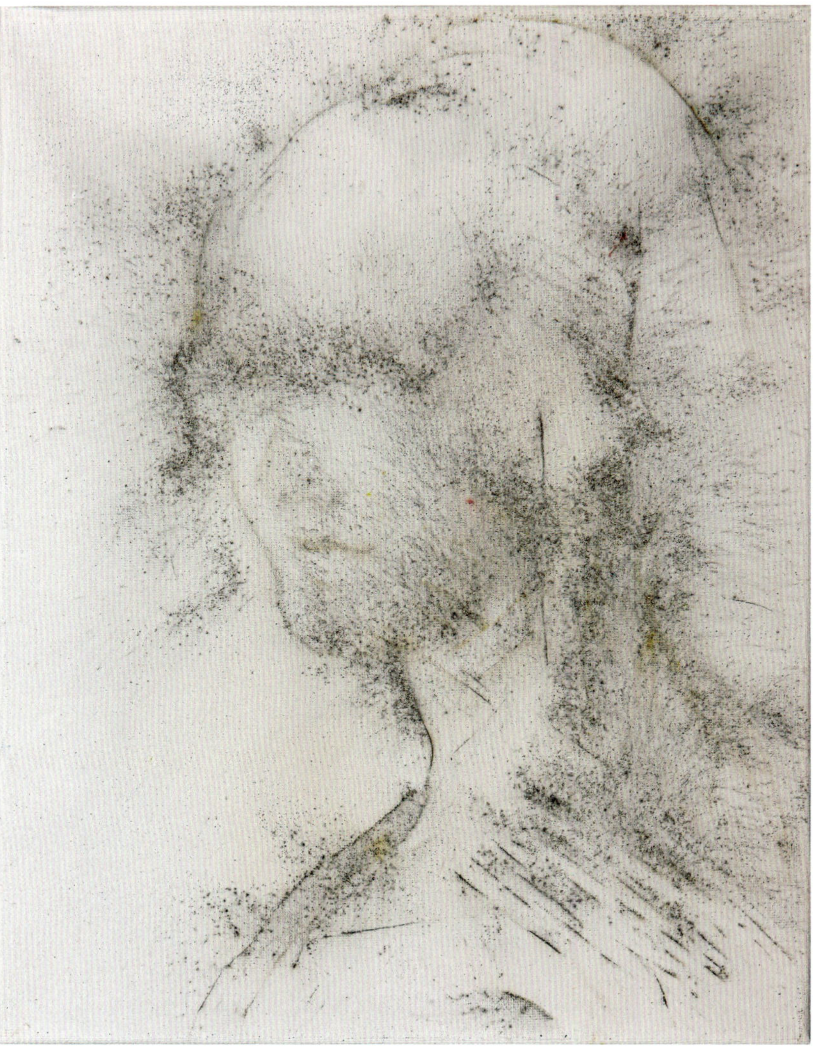

2.2 *Silverpoint Study No. 4*

2.1
*Silverpoint Study No. 1*
银尖笔研究之一
2018
Gunpowder on canvas
35.4 × 28 cm

2.2
*Silverpoint Study No. 4*
银尖笔研究之四
2018
Gunpowder on canvas
35.4 × 28 cm

2.3
*Silverpoint Study No. 5*
乌菲齐研究之五
2018
Gunpowder on canvas
30.5 × 23 cm

2.4
*Study for Uffizi: Flora No. 3*
乌菲齐研究：花神第三号
2018
Gunpowder on canvas
183 × 152.5 cm

2.5
*Study for Uffizi: Venus No. 1*
乌菲齐研究：维纳斯第一号
2018
Gunpowder on canvas
240 × 450 cm

Under the guidance of experts from the Uffizi's Prints and Drawings department, Cai studied the metal point techniques of Michelangelo, Leonardo, and Raphael. He was inspired to develop his own technique, using craft knives to slice into printed images then arrange gunpowder on top of them. This method directed the energy of detonated gunpowder to seep through the slits and imprint onto the canvas below to achieve a fine-textured effect.

*Silverpoint Studies Nos. 1, 4, 5* register Cai's first experimentation with this technique. He subsequently used it to render the goddess Flora from *Primavera*, the masterpiece of Sandro Botticelli (c. 1445–1510) in the Uffizi collection, which served as a foundation for him to create his interpretation of Botticelli's *The Birth of Venus.*

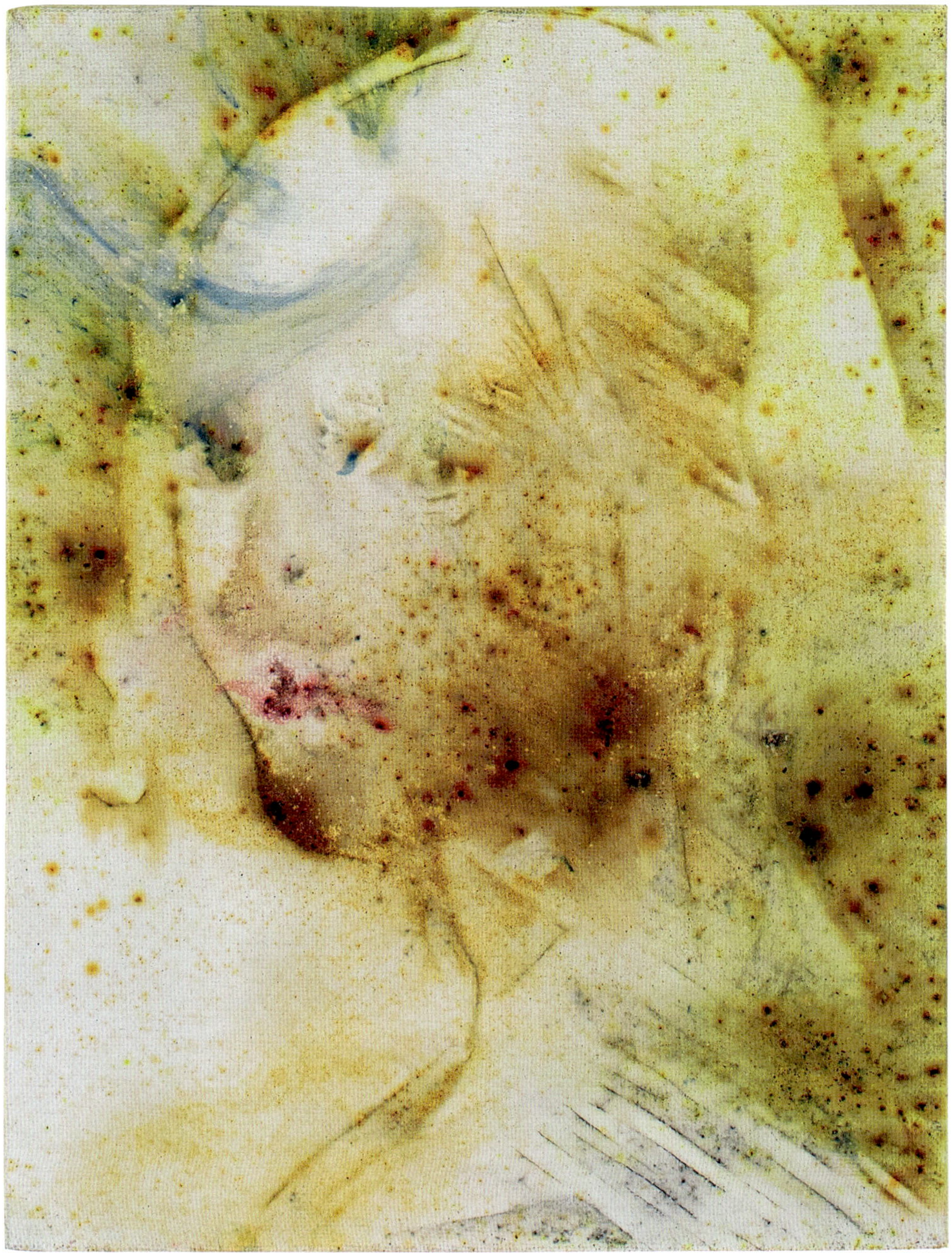

2.3 *Silverpoint Study No. 5*

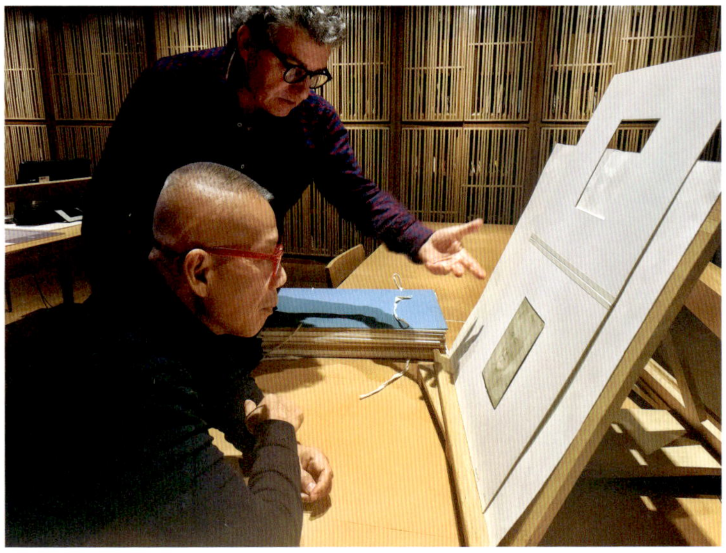

Figure 2.2. Cai Guo-Qiang studying silverpoint drawings under the guidance of an Uffizi specialist in 2018

Figure 2.3 (overleaf). Installation view of *Flora Commedia: Cai Guo-Qiang at the Uffizi* in 2018

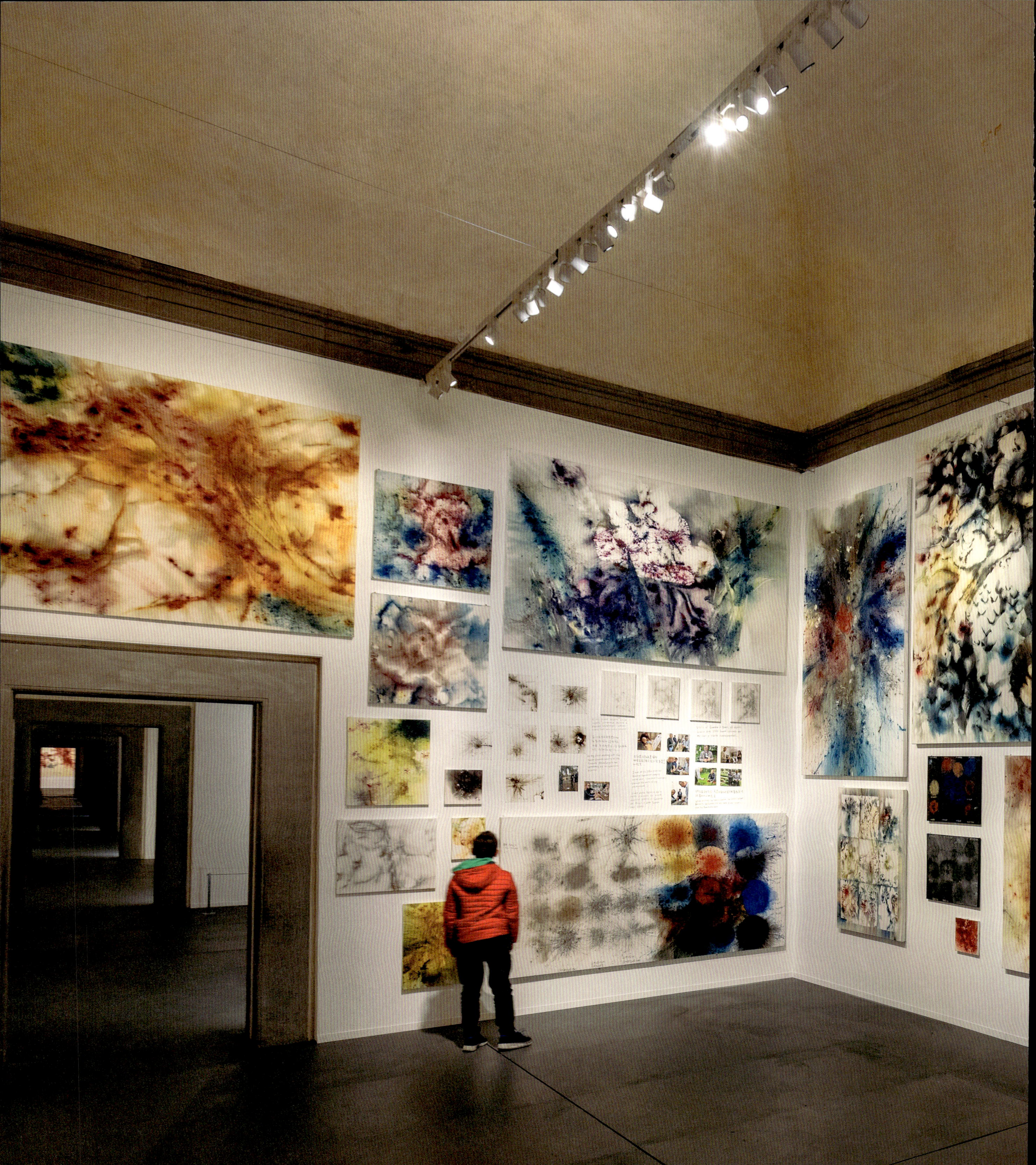

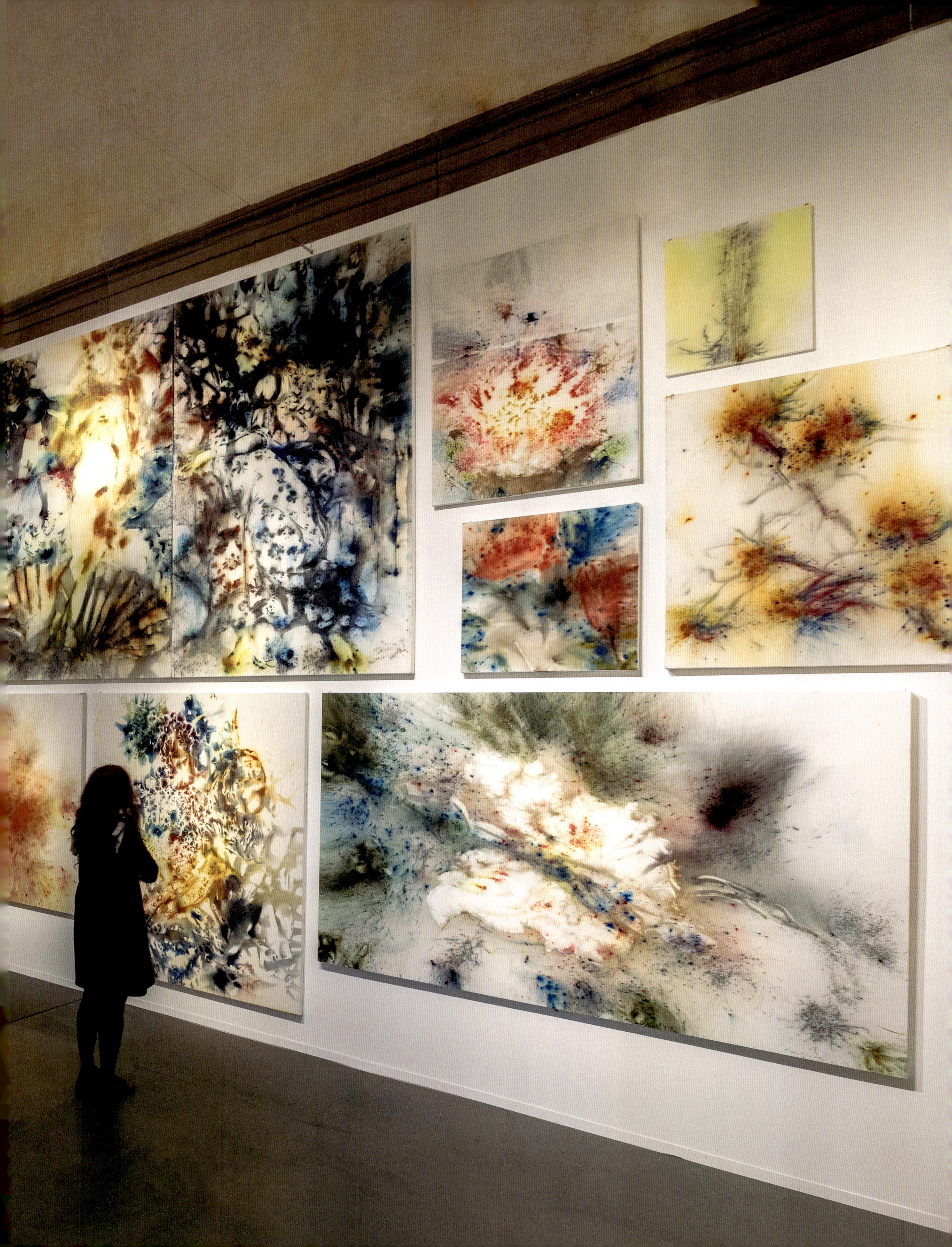

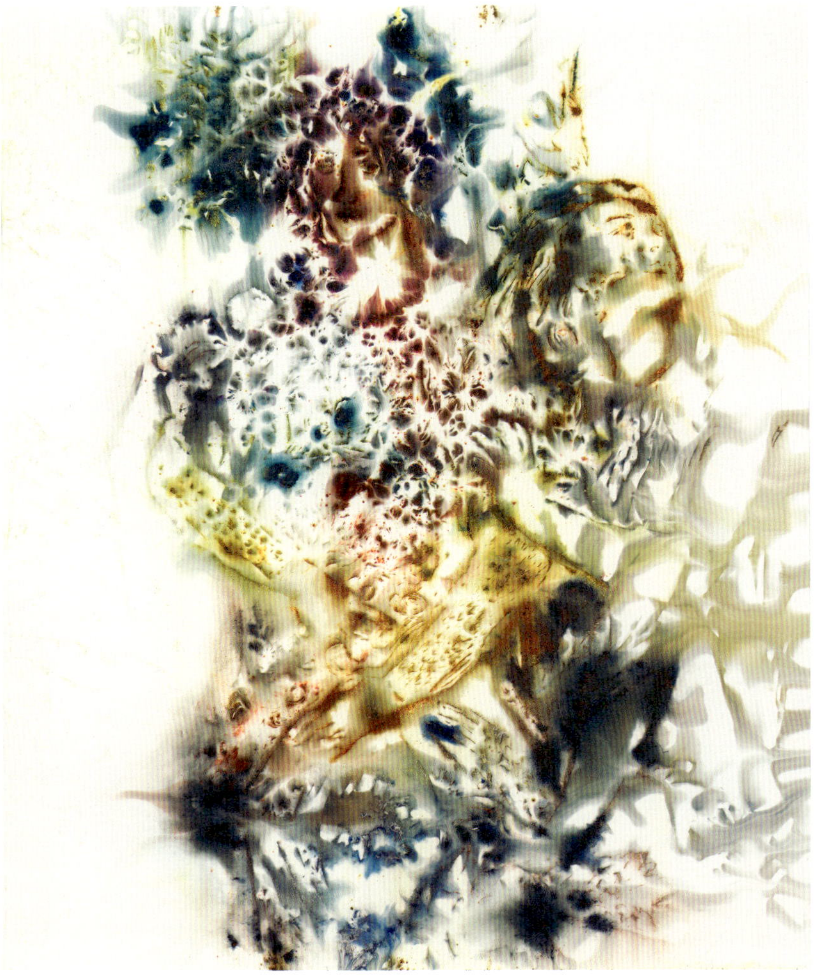

2.4 *Study for Uffizi: Flora No. 3*

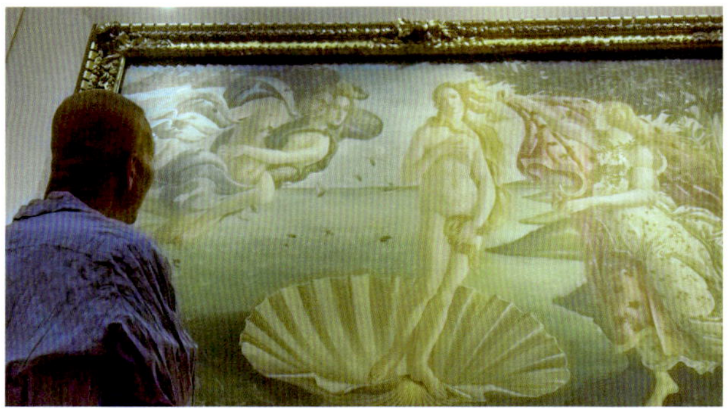

Figure 2.4. Cai Guo-Qiang looking at Botticelli's *The Birth of Venus* at the Uffizi Galleries in 2018

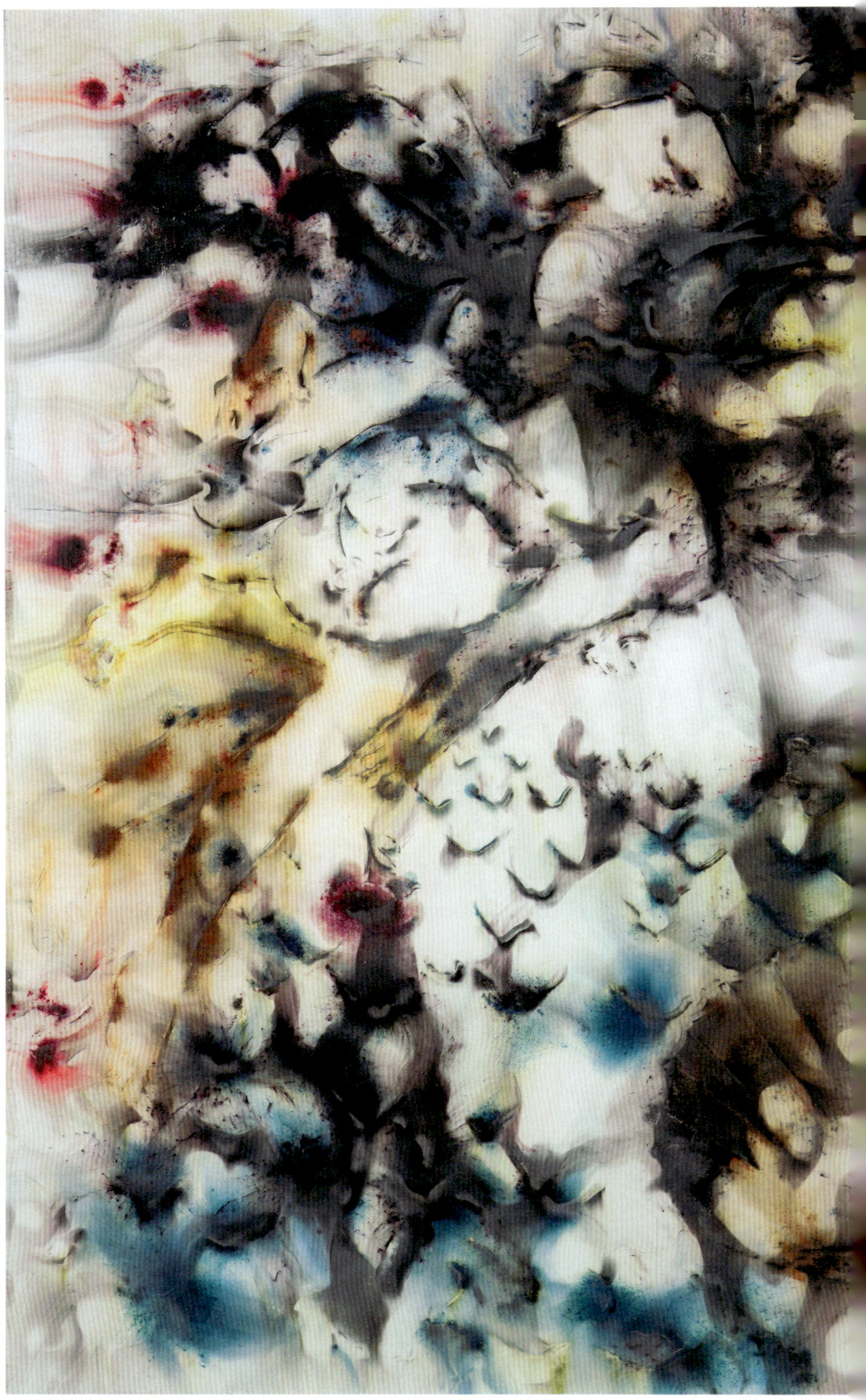

2.5 *Study for Uffizi: Venus No. 1*

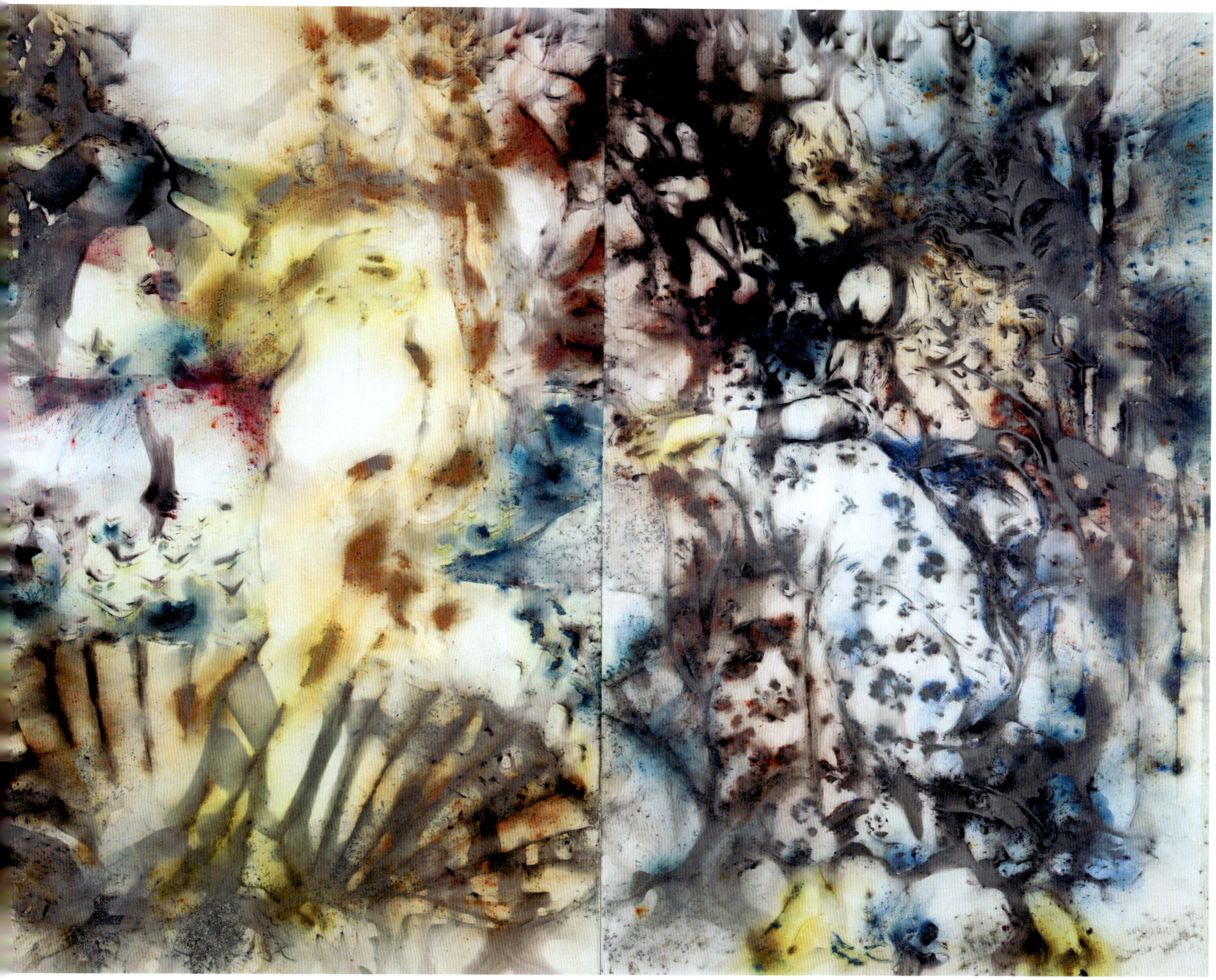

2.6
*Renaissance Flower Garden*
文艺复兴花园
2018
Gunpowder on canvas
300 × 400 cm

2.7
*Dead Roses No. 1*
蔷薇花后第一号
2018
Gunpowder on canvas
122 × 91.5 cm

2.8
*Study for Uffizi: Green Roses No. 2*
乌菲齐研究:绿玫瑰第二号
2018
Gunpowder on canvas
122 × 183 cm

2.9
*Fallen Iris*
鸢尾花掉落
2018
Gunpowder on canvas
150 × 240 cm

2.10
*Green Shrubs*
绿杂草
2018
Gunpowder on canvas
76 × 76 cm

2.11
*Daisy Field No. 1*
雏菊田第一号
2018
Gunpowder on canvas
51 × 61 cm

2.12
*Wall Plant No. 2*
墙花第二号
2018
Gunpowder on canvas
25 × 25 cm

2.13
*Maple Leaves No. 2*
枫叶第二号
2018
Gunpowder on canvas
25 × 25 cm

2.14
*Yellow Iris*
黄鸢尾花
2018
Gunpowder on canvas
61 × 51 cm

2.15
*Sweet Briar*
野玫瑰
2018
Gunpowder on canvas
122 × 152.5 cm
The East West Bank Collection

2.16
*Red Lilies*
红百合
2018
Gunpowder on canvas
122 × 122 cm

2.17
*Study for Uffizi: A Bouquet of Flowers No. 1*
乌菲齐研究:一束花第一号
2018
Gunpowder on canvas
240 × 150 cm
Collection of MGM Cotai, Macau

Cai exercised various new and tried painting techniques to depict the subject of Renaissance flowers, including wild roses, irises, and the red Florentine lily that serves as the emblem of this "City of Flowers." He explored the thorny issue of how to create good paintings with flowers, "to become free by anchoring the heart and focusing the mind," and to thereby convey the spirit and disposition of the Renaissance.

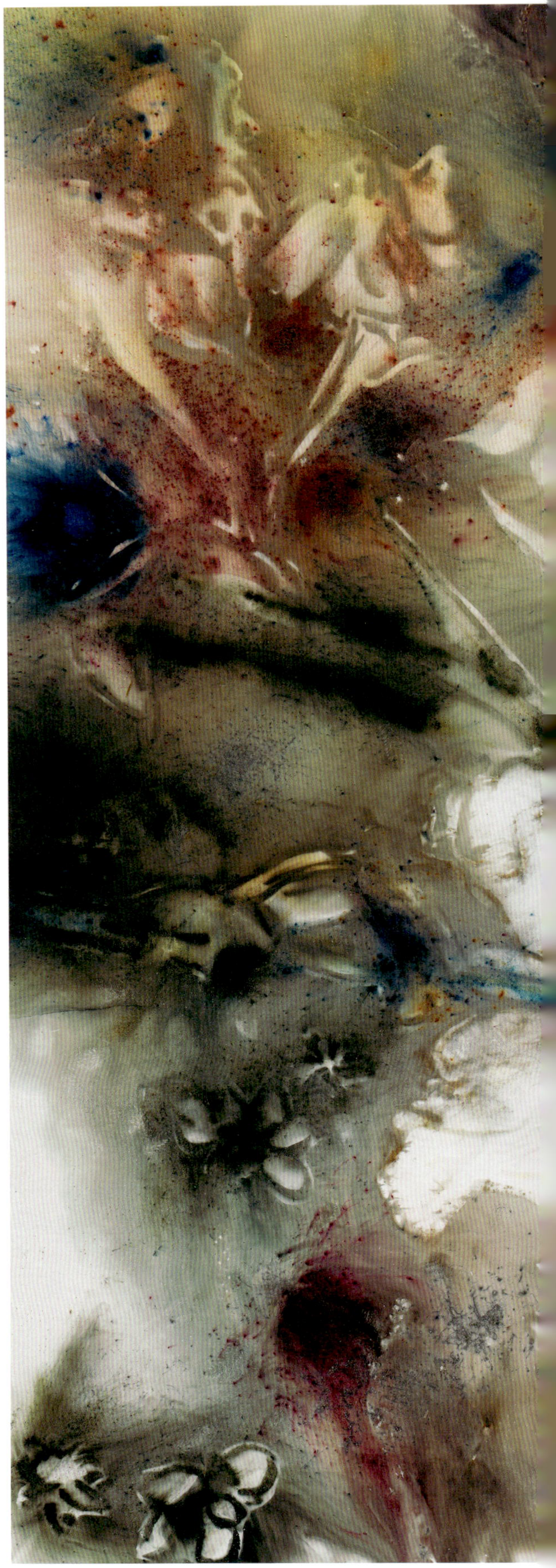
2.6 *Renaissance Flower Garden*

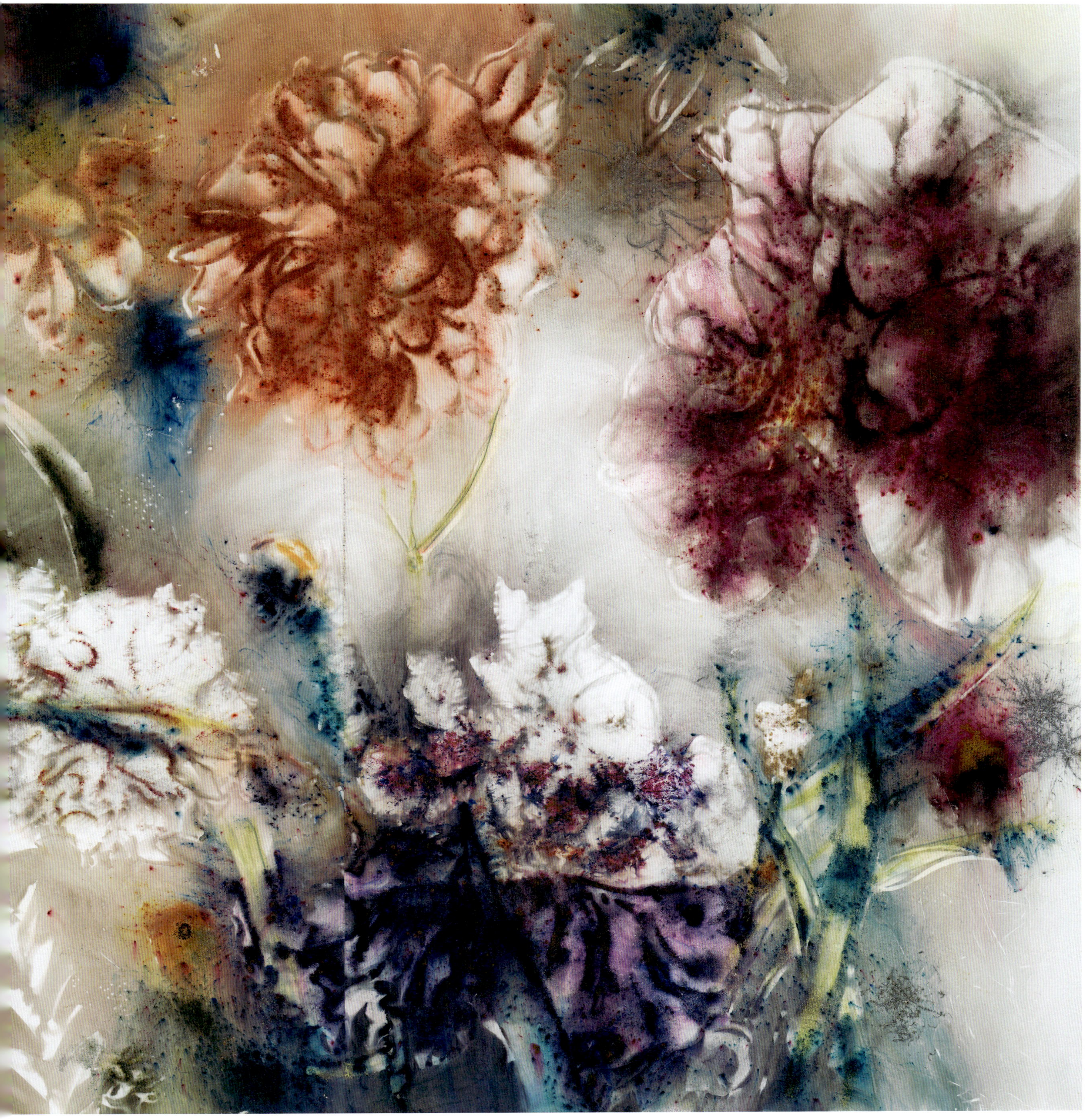

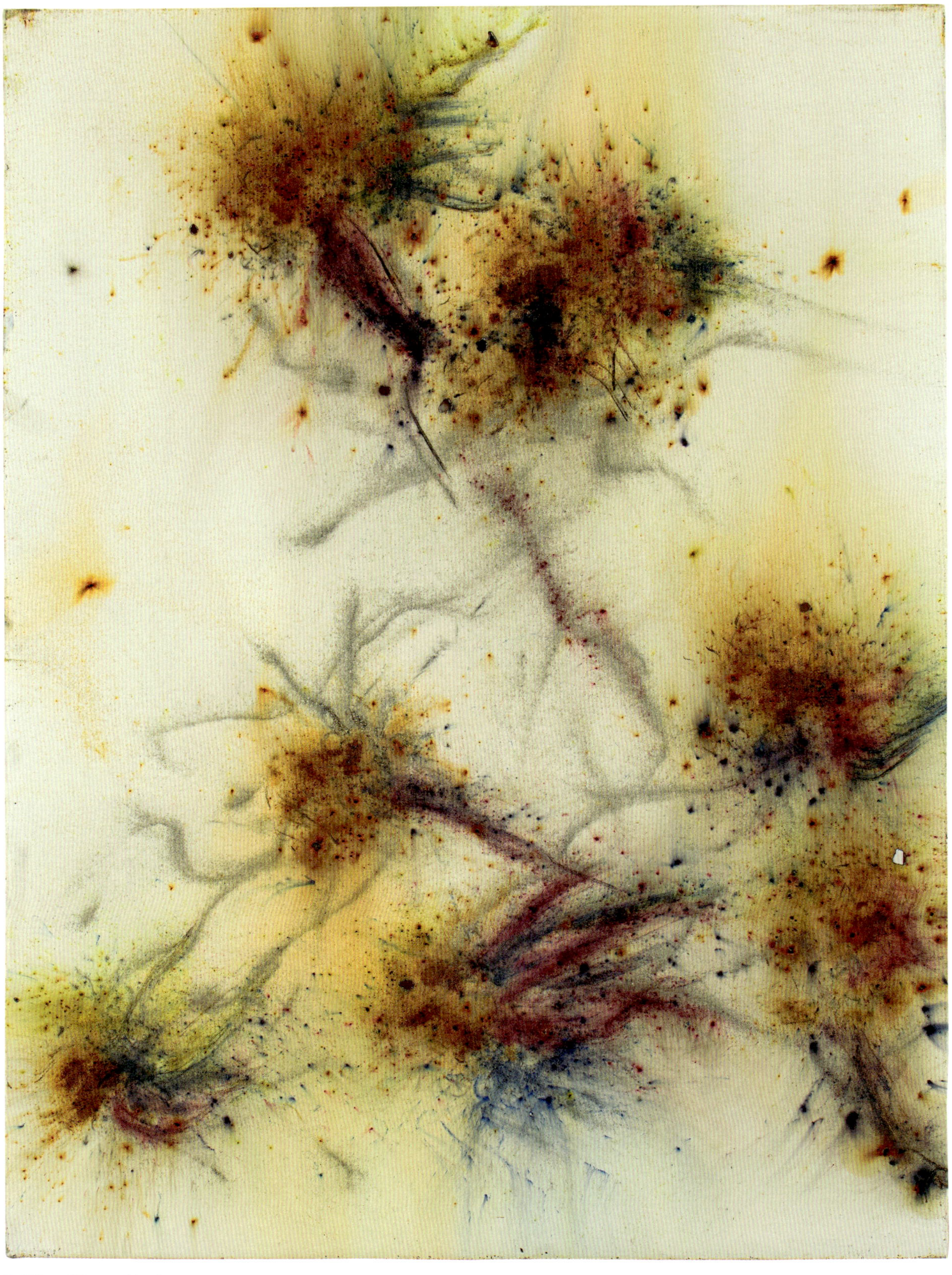

2.7 *Dead Roses No. 1*

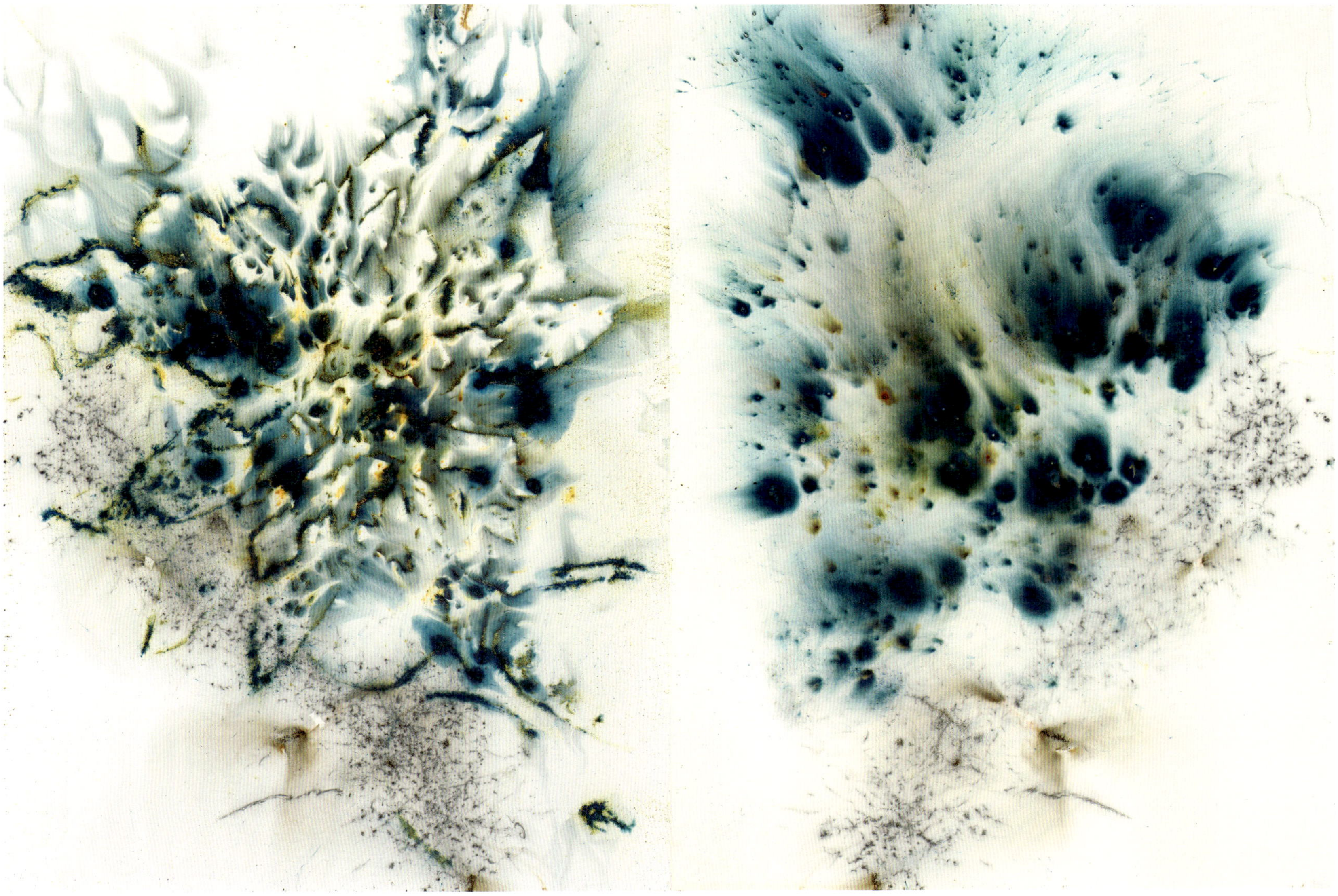

2.8 *Study for Uffizi: Green Roses No. 2*

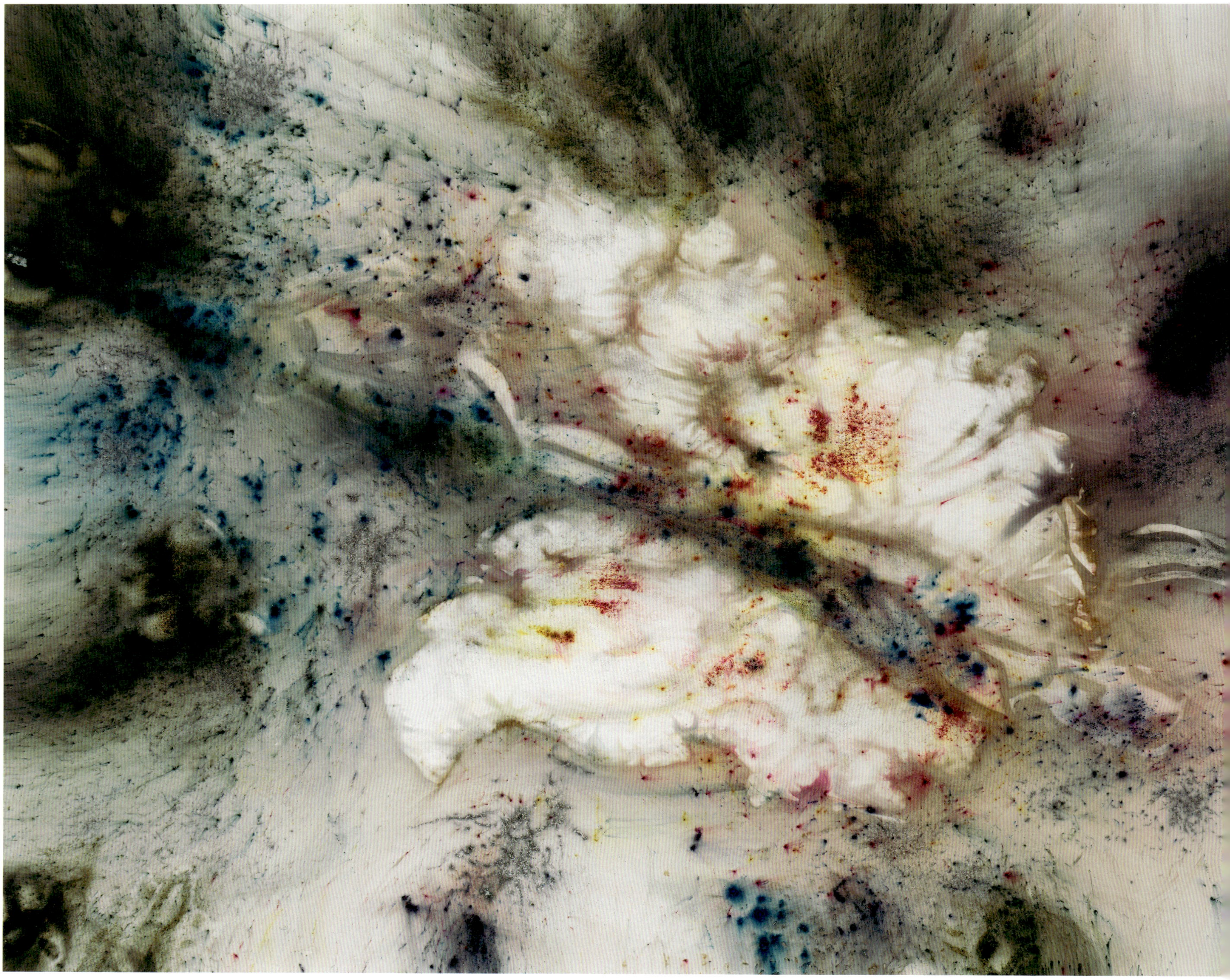

2.9 *Fallen Iris*

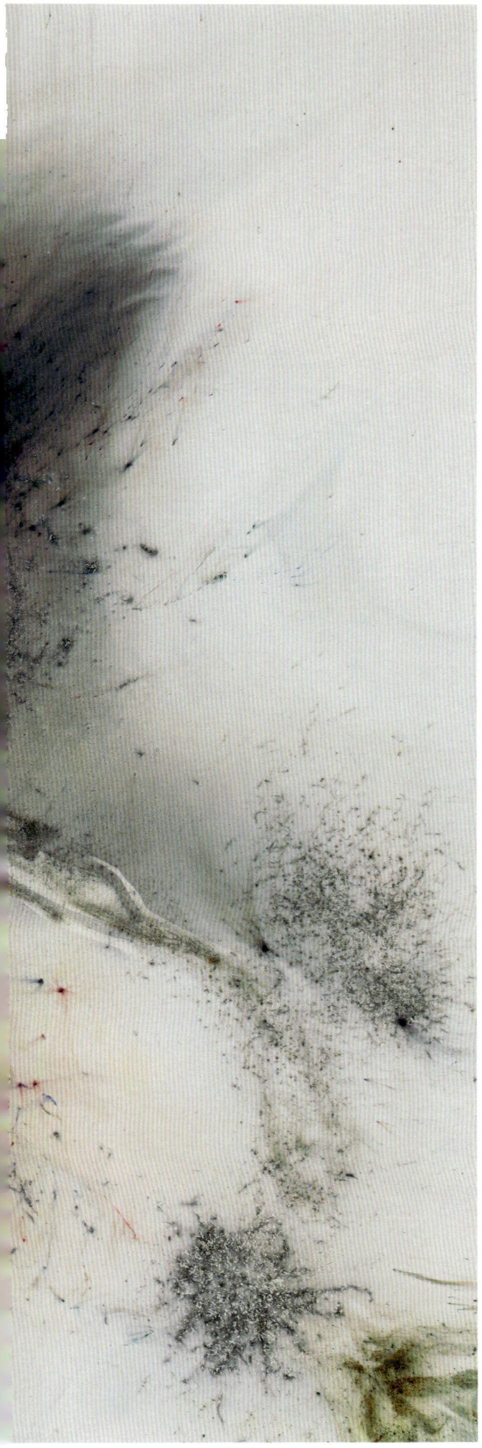

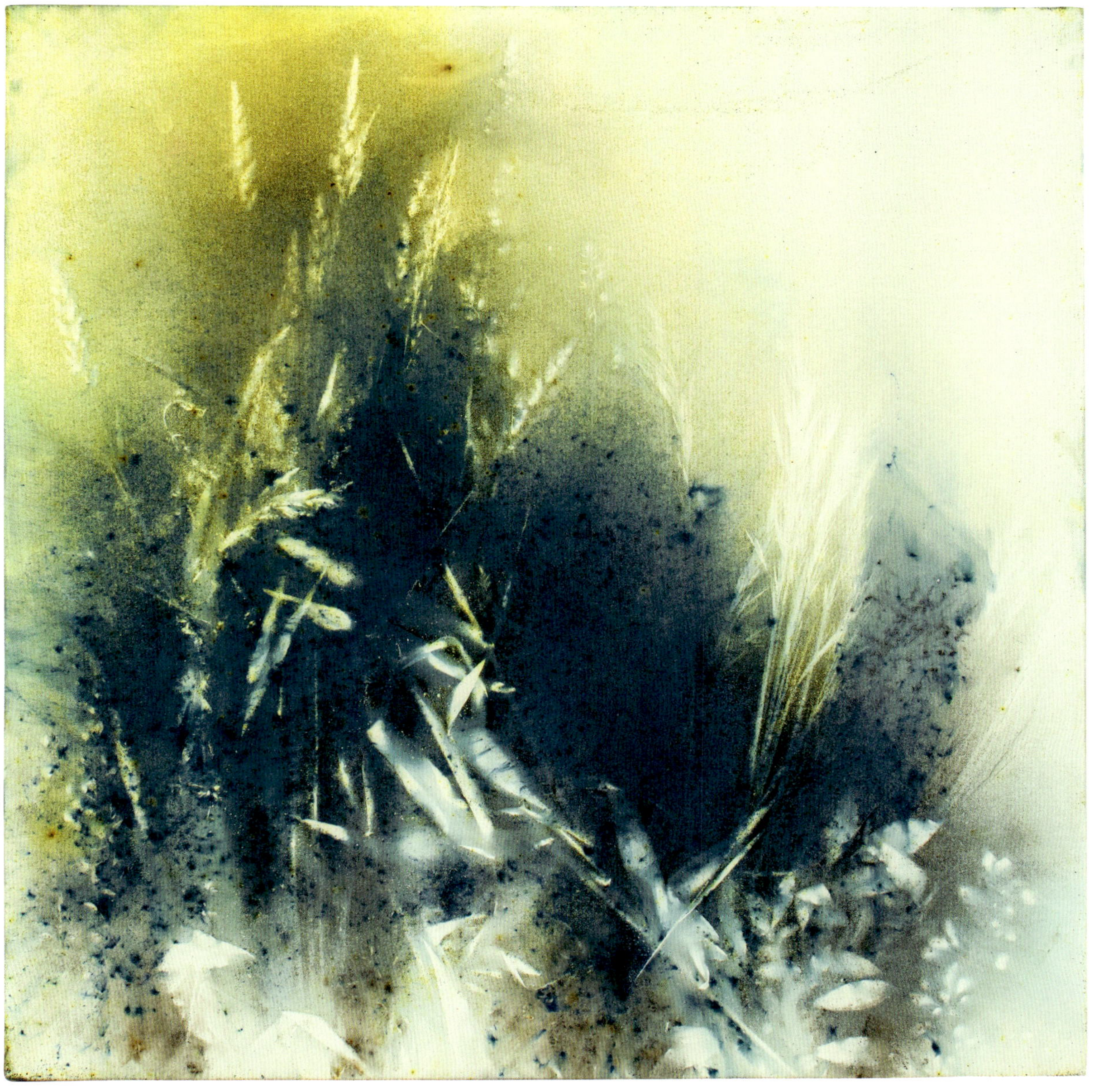

2.10 *Green Shrubs*

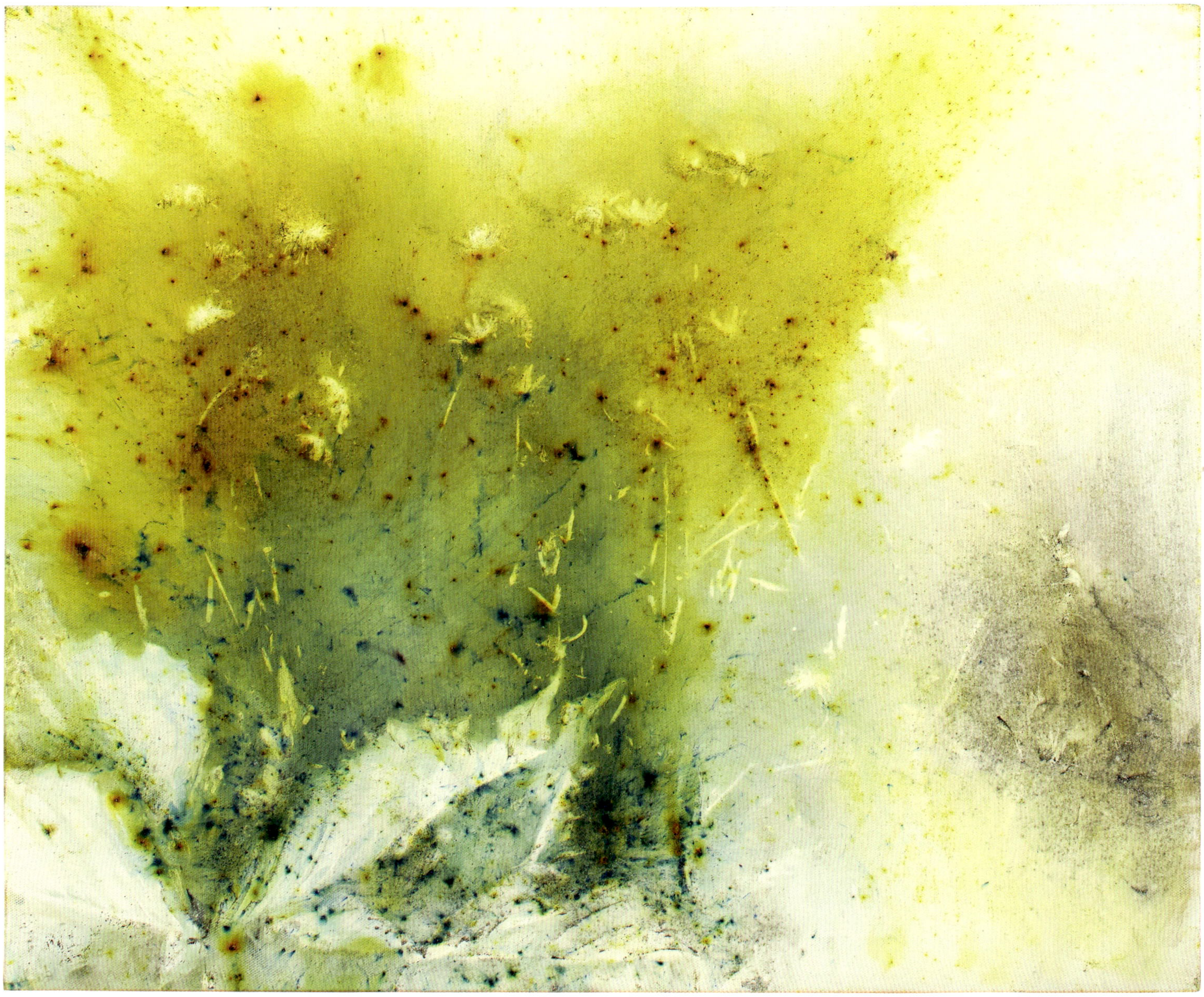

2.11 *Daisy Field No. 1*

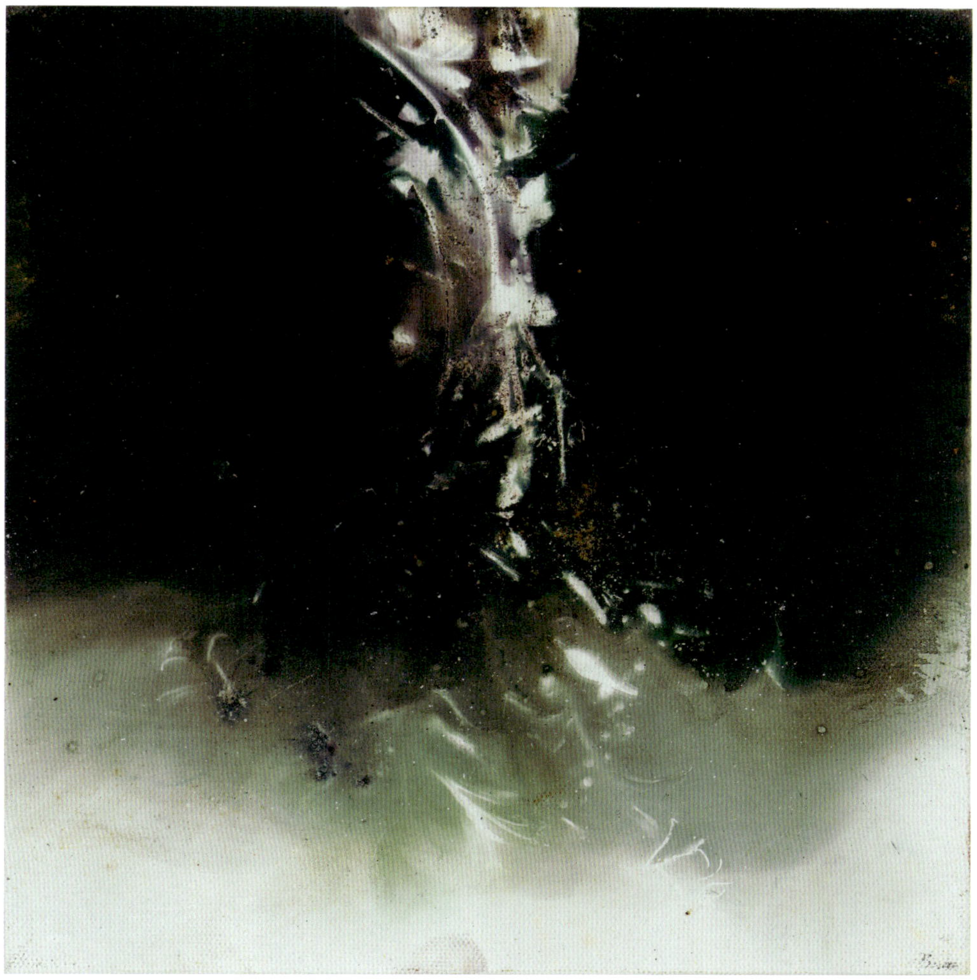

2.12 *Wall Plant No. 2*

2.13 *Maple Leaves No. 2*

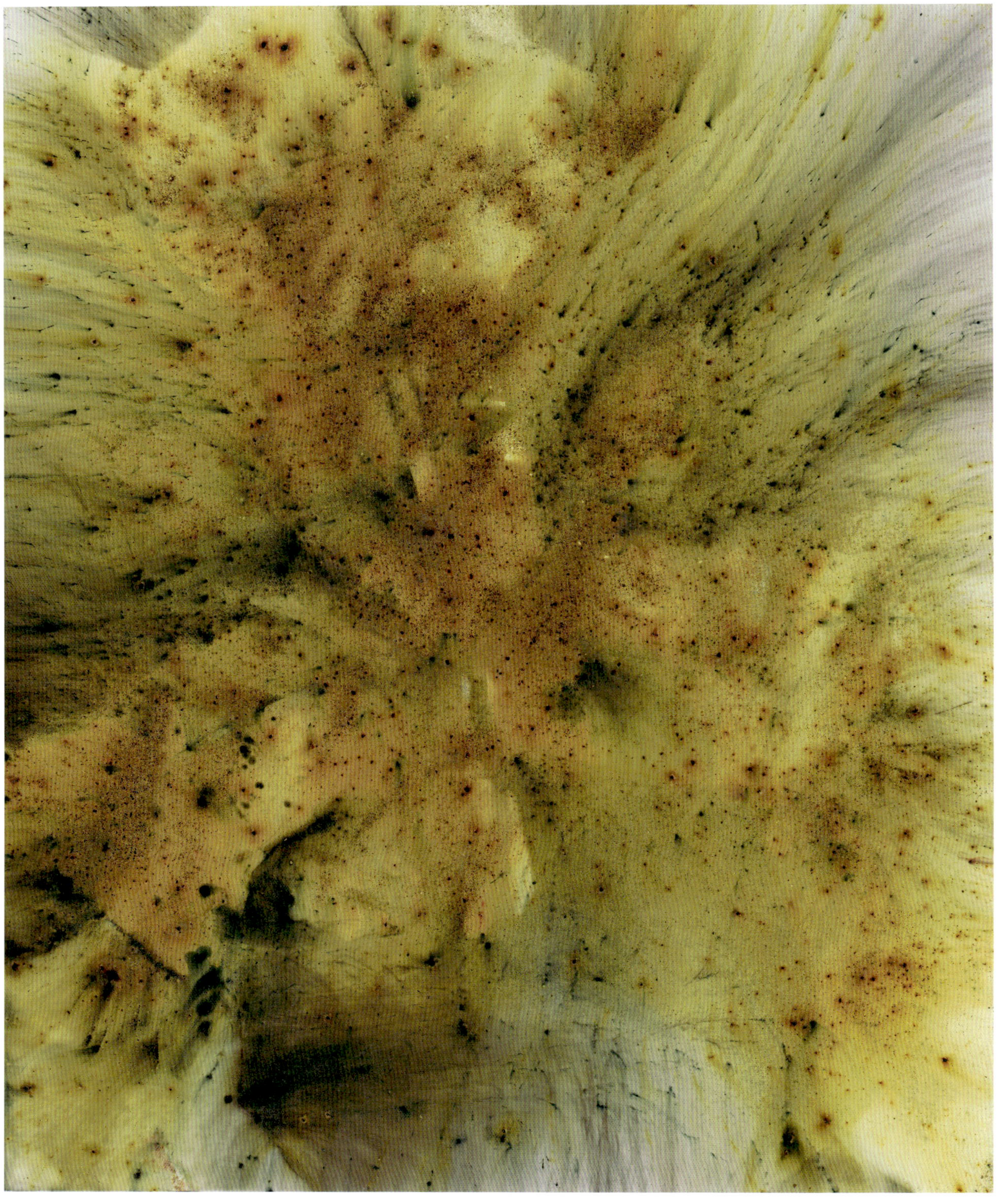

2.14 *Yellow Iris*

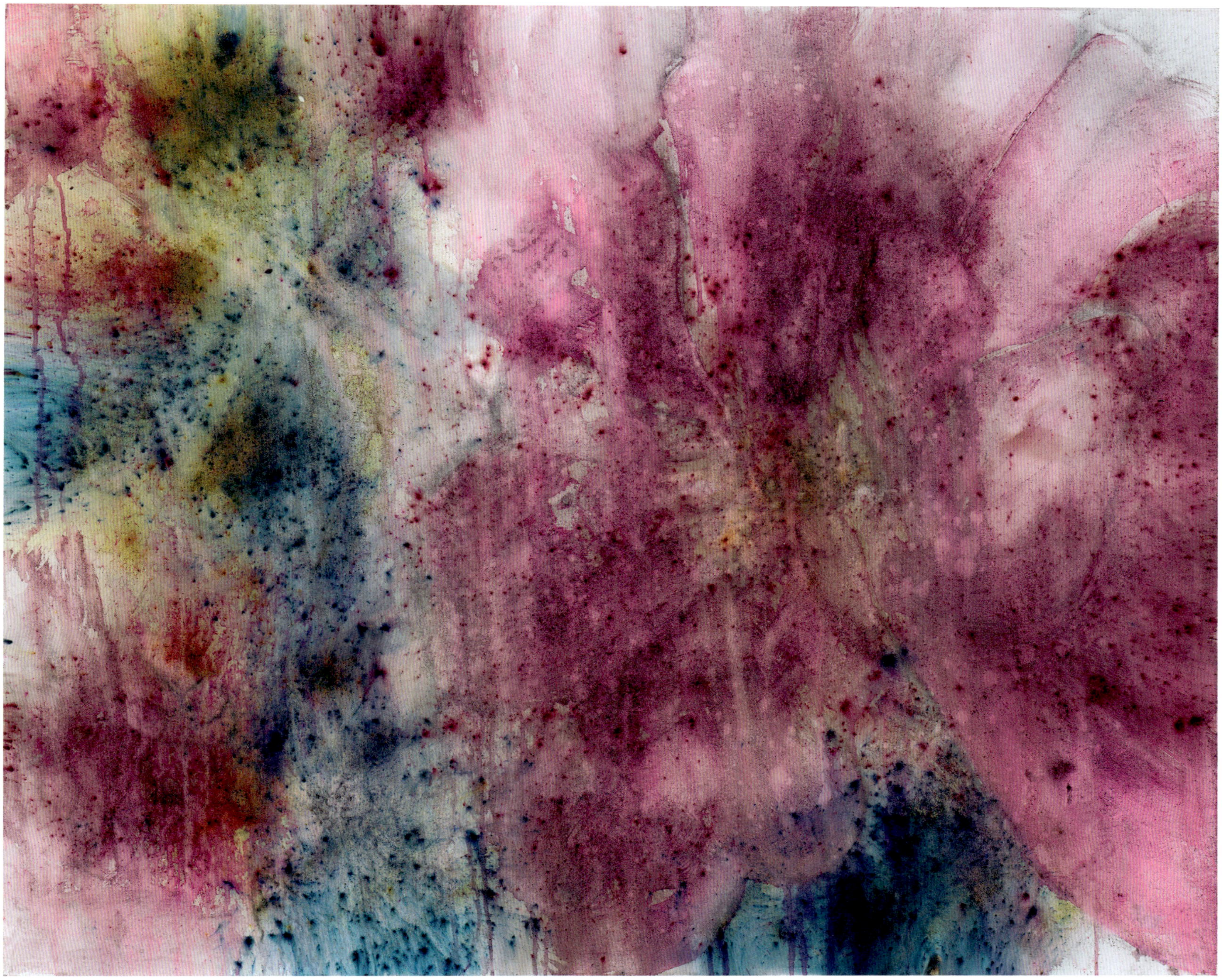

2.15 *Sweet Briar*

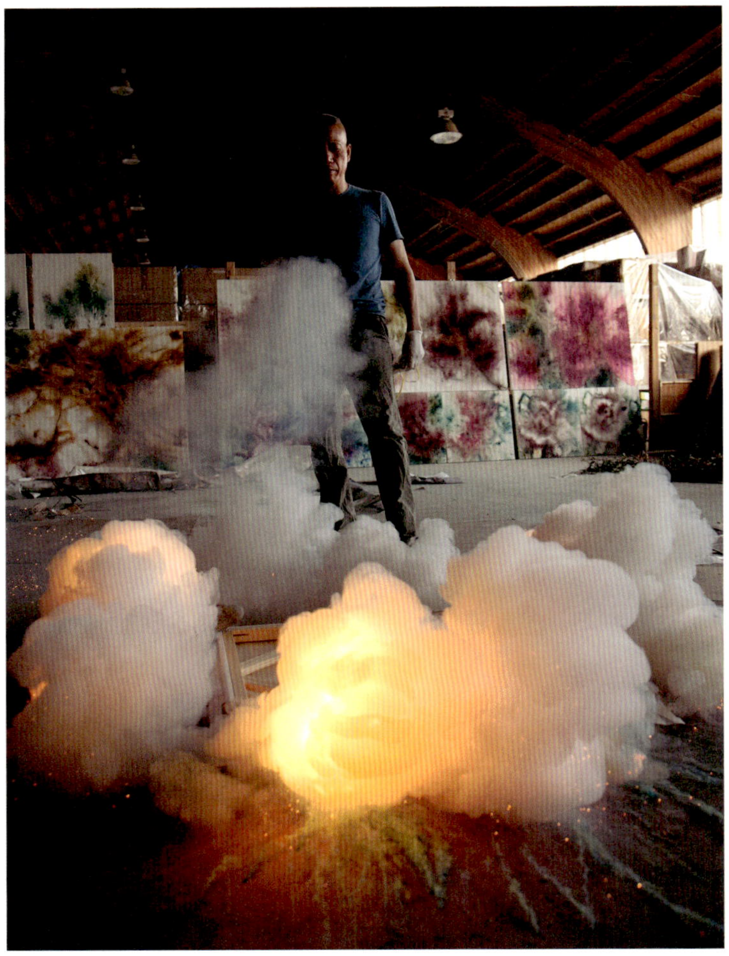

Figure 2.5. Ignition of a gunpowder painting, 2018

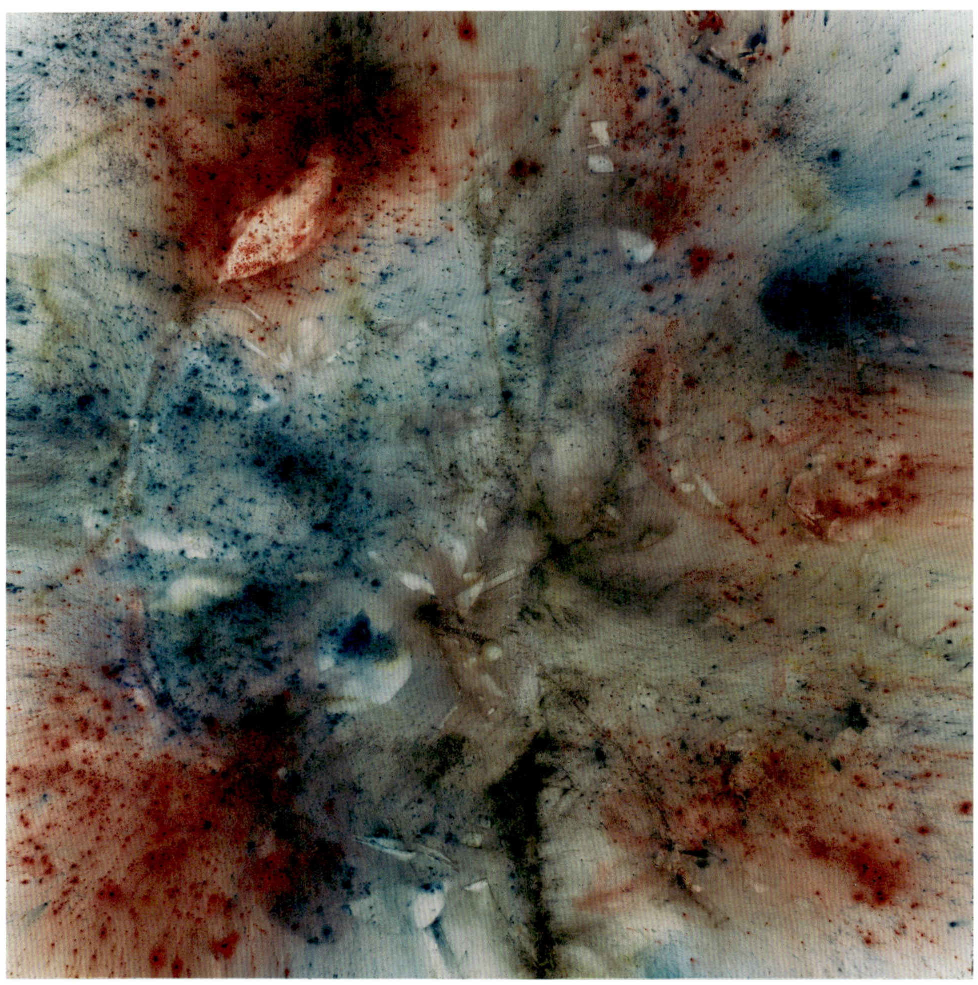

2.16 *Red Lilies*

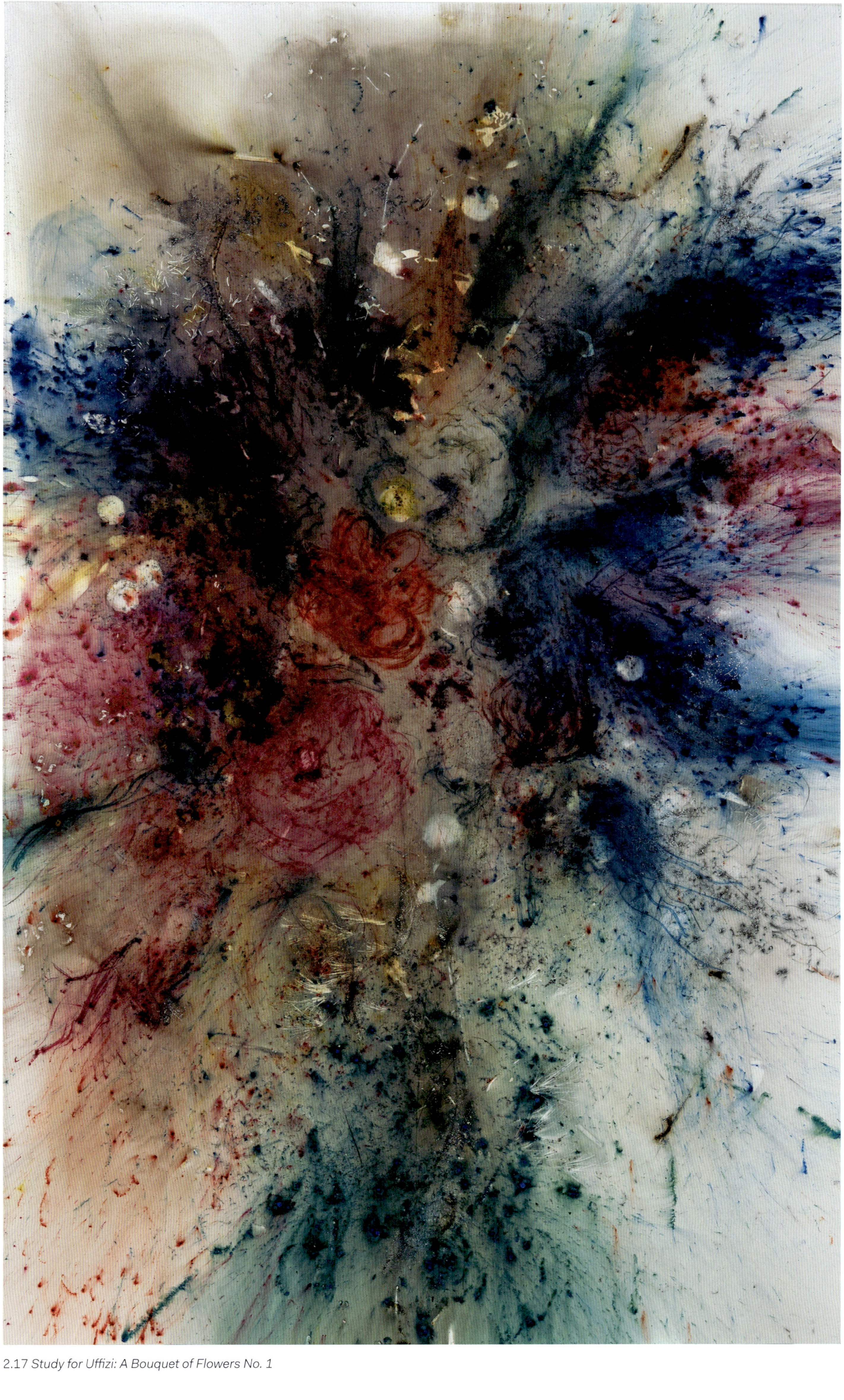

2.17 *Study for Uffizi: A Bouquet of Flowers No. 1*

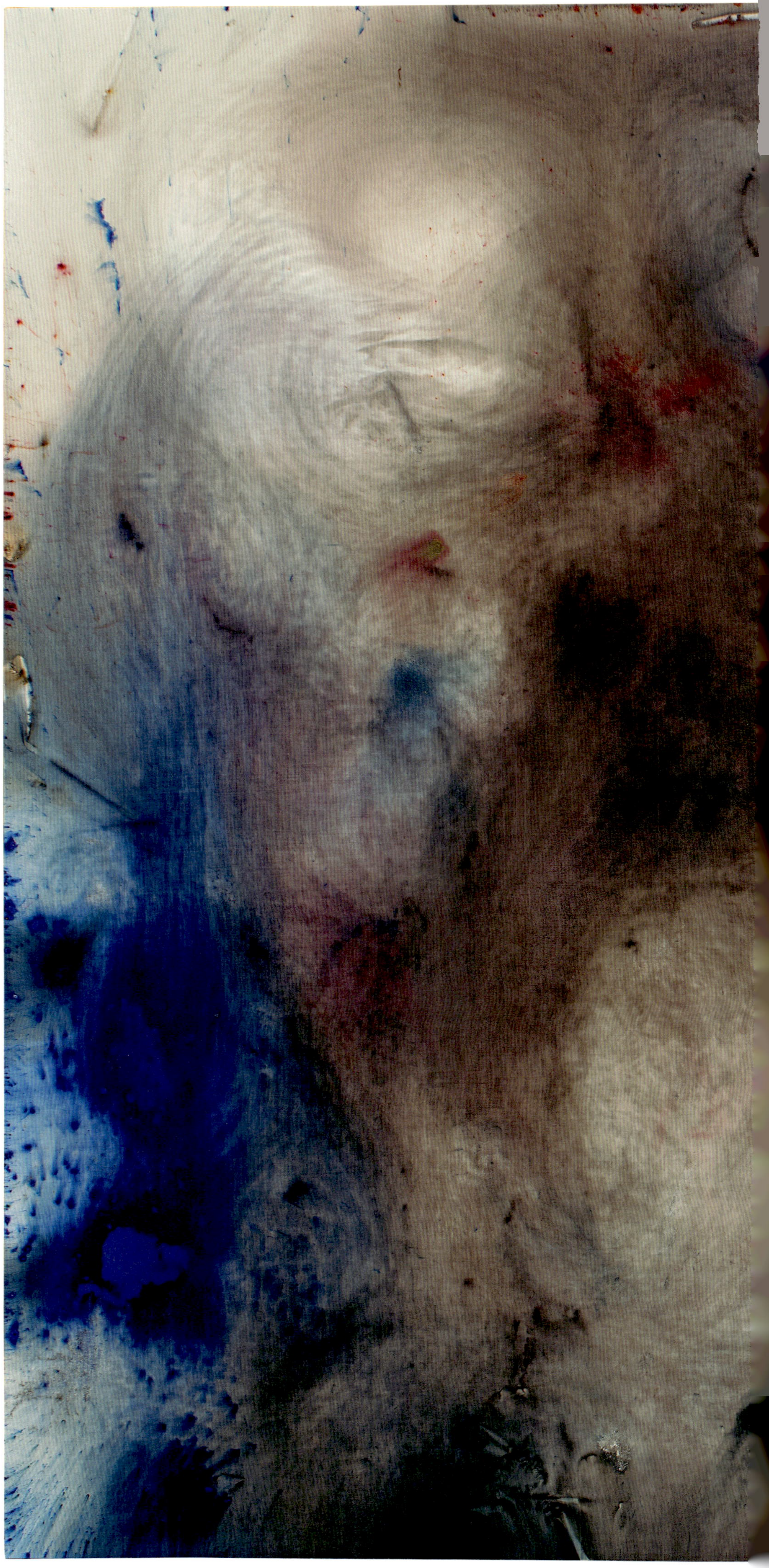

2.18

*Flower Soul No. 2*

花灵第二号

2018

Gunpowder on canvas

300 × 400 cm

Cai laid two canvases face-to-face on the ground, sandwiched gunpowder in between, then ignited them simultaneously. After the explosion, the two canvases formed an abstract effect through *yin* and *yang* counterparts, expressing the soul of Renaissance flora.

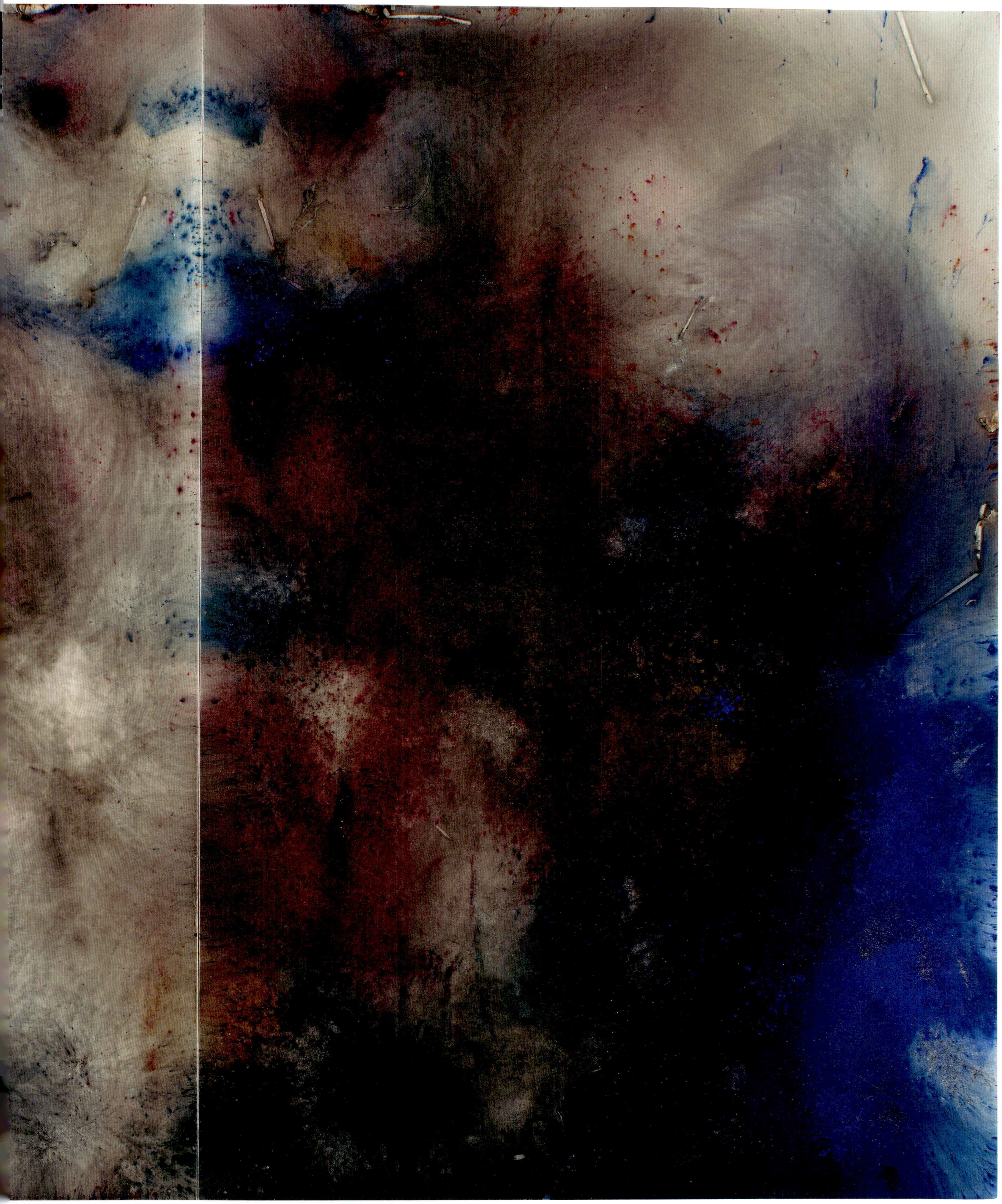

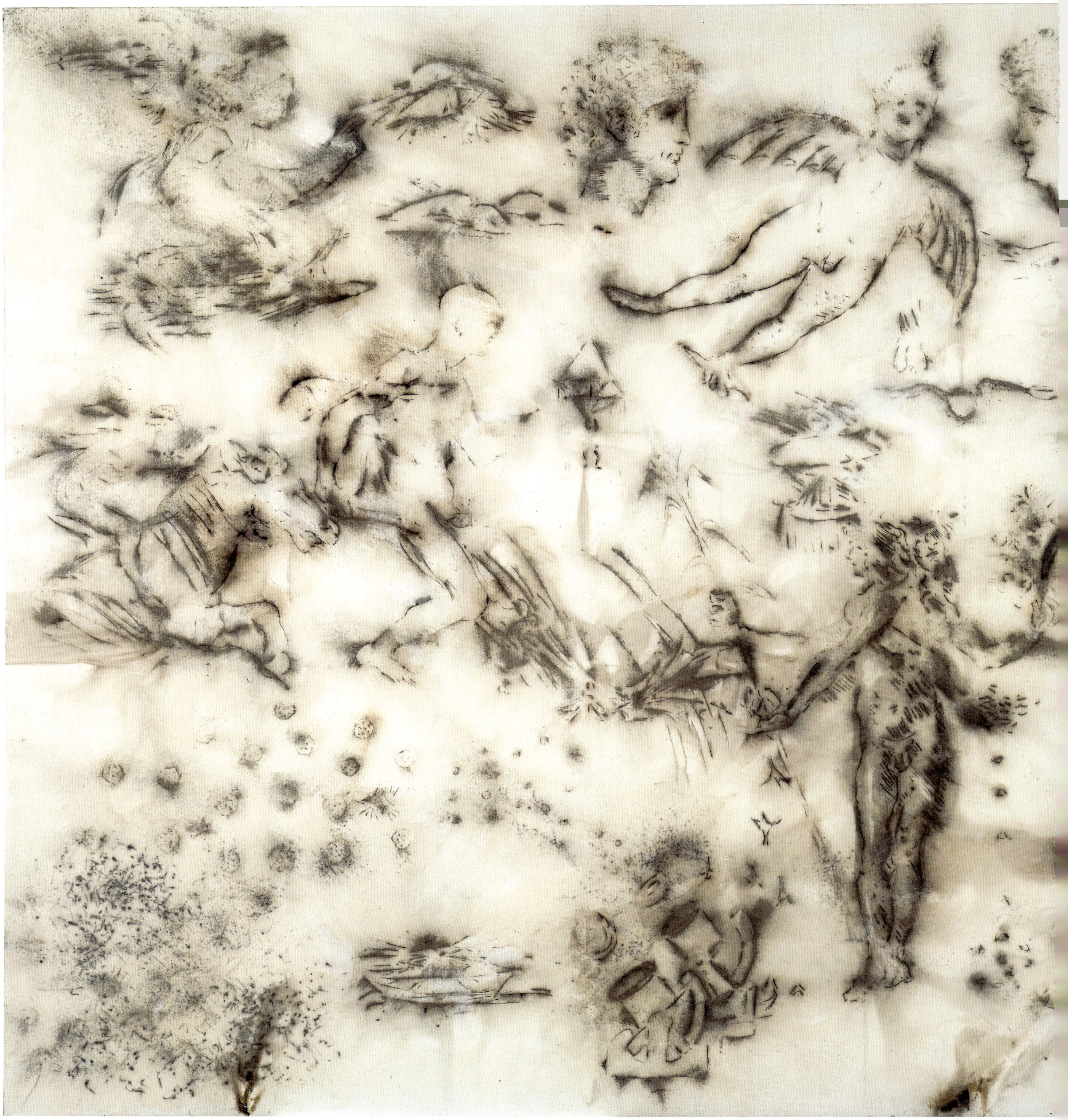

2.19

*Study of Birds*

鸟与鸟的手稿

2018

Gunpowder and oil on canvas

200 × 300 cm

The inspiration for this work was drawn from the Renaissance maestro Leonardo da Vinci (1452–1519). Cai finds Leonardo's doodles and sketches to be more charismatic than celebrated masterpieces such as *The Last Supper*. From anatomical dissections to casually penciled studies of male reproductive organs, bows, arrows, and cannons, to drafts inventing helicopters and parachutes, the sketches reflect Leonardo's ingenious imagination and childlike wonder.

For the first time, Cai coated the canvas with a base of white oil paint, applying heavy, thick brush strokes to enhance the canvas's capacity for sensual expression. The textured surface enriched the trajectories of the sparks and smoke during the explosion, alluding to Leonardo's own innovations in painting mediums.

In 2018, Cai was commissioned by Google to create this artwork for the five-hundredth anniversary of Leonardo's birth as a tribute to the trailblazer who devoted his prodigious imagination to science and art.

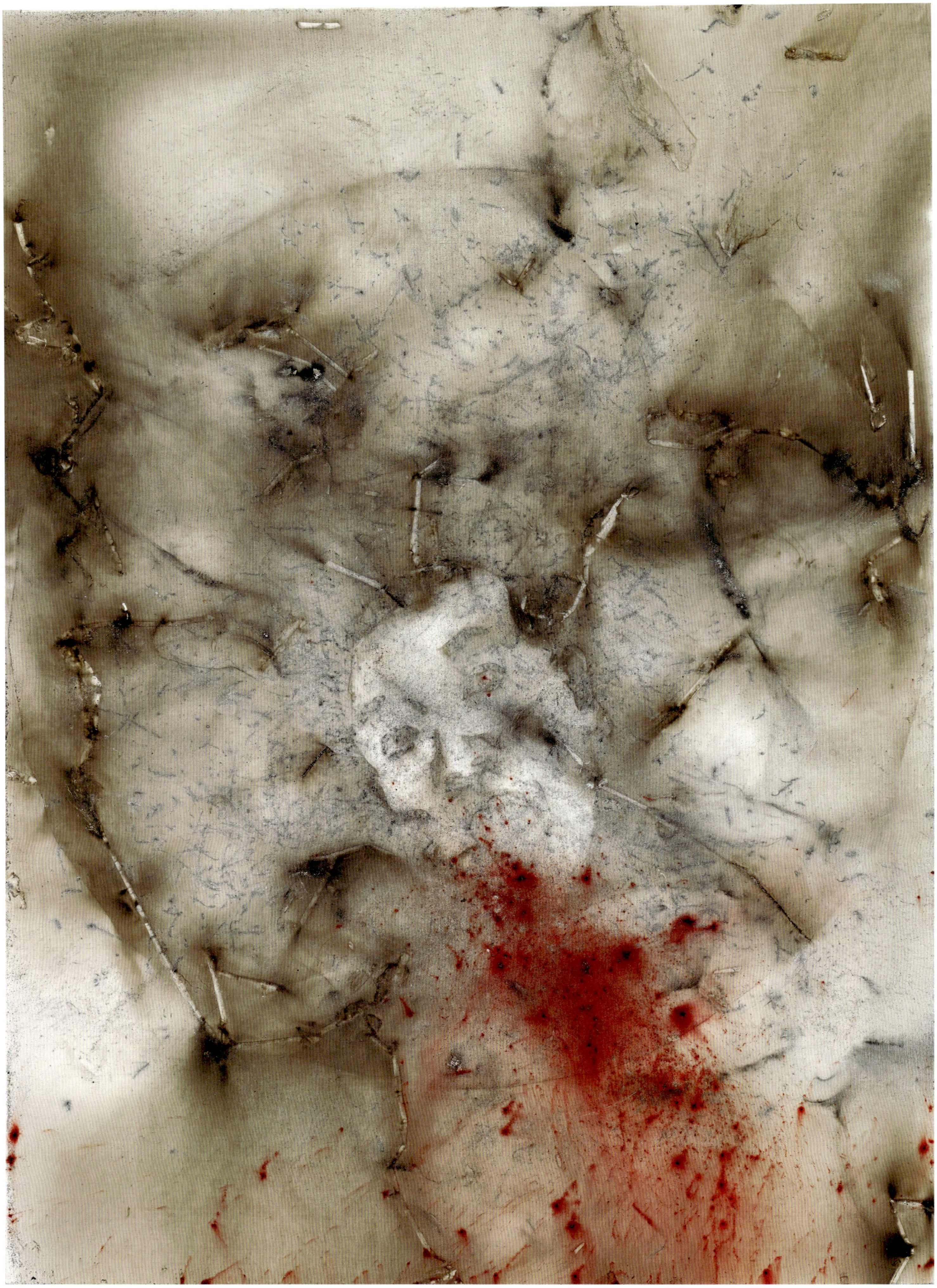

2.20 *Bad Kid!*

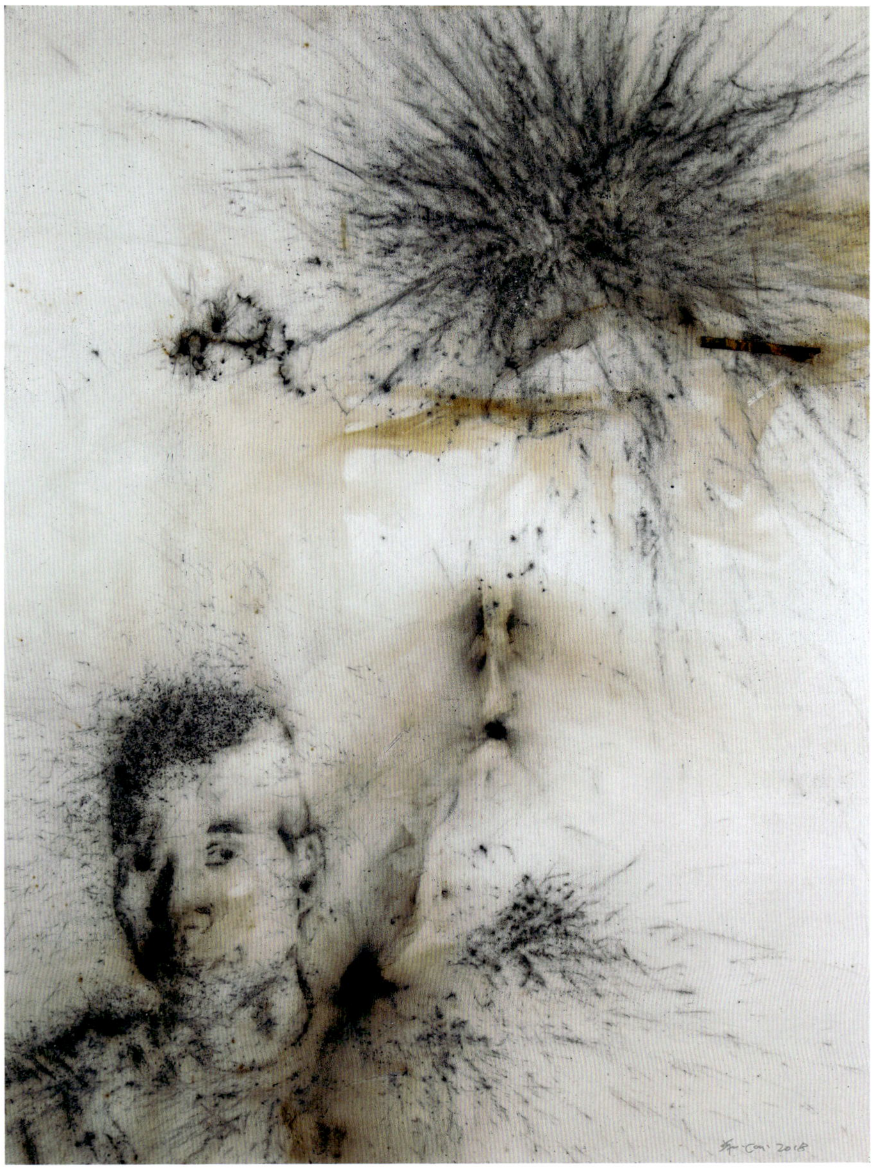

2.21 *Exploding Cai*

2.20

*Bad Kid!*

坏孩子!

2018

Gunpowder on canvas

275 × 200 cm

The artist echoed the unyielding and untamable nature of Caravaggio (1571–1610), the late Italian Renaissance painter in the Uffizi collection, by imposing a selfie on the canvas.

Related Work

2.21

*Exploding Cai*

炸蔡

2018

Gunpowder on canvas

120 × 90 cm

Collection of Uffizi Galleries

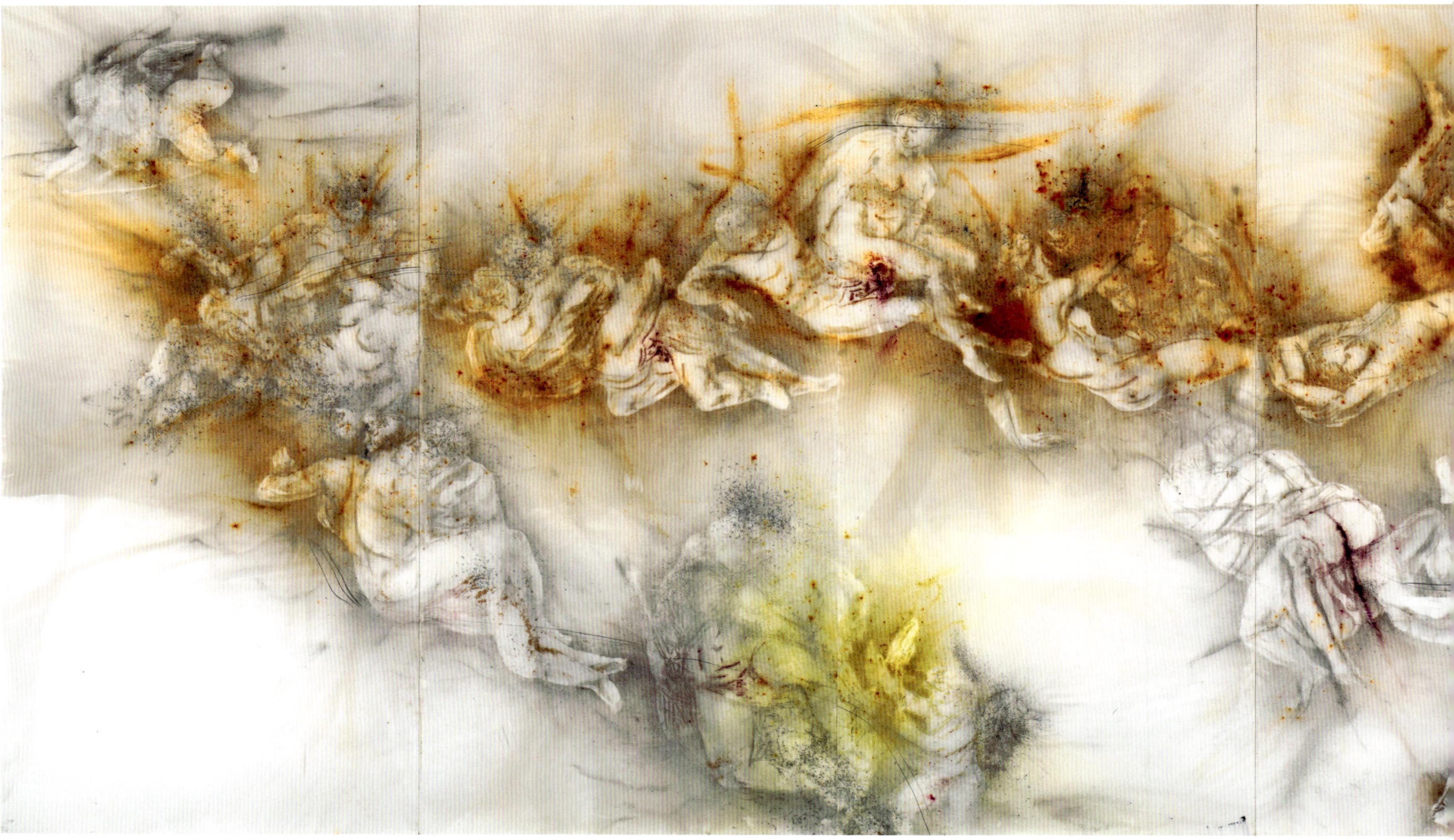

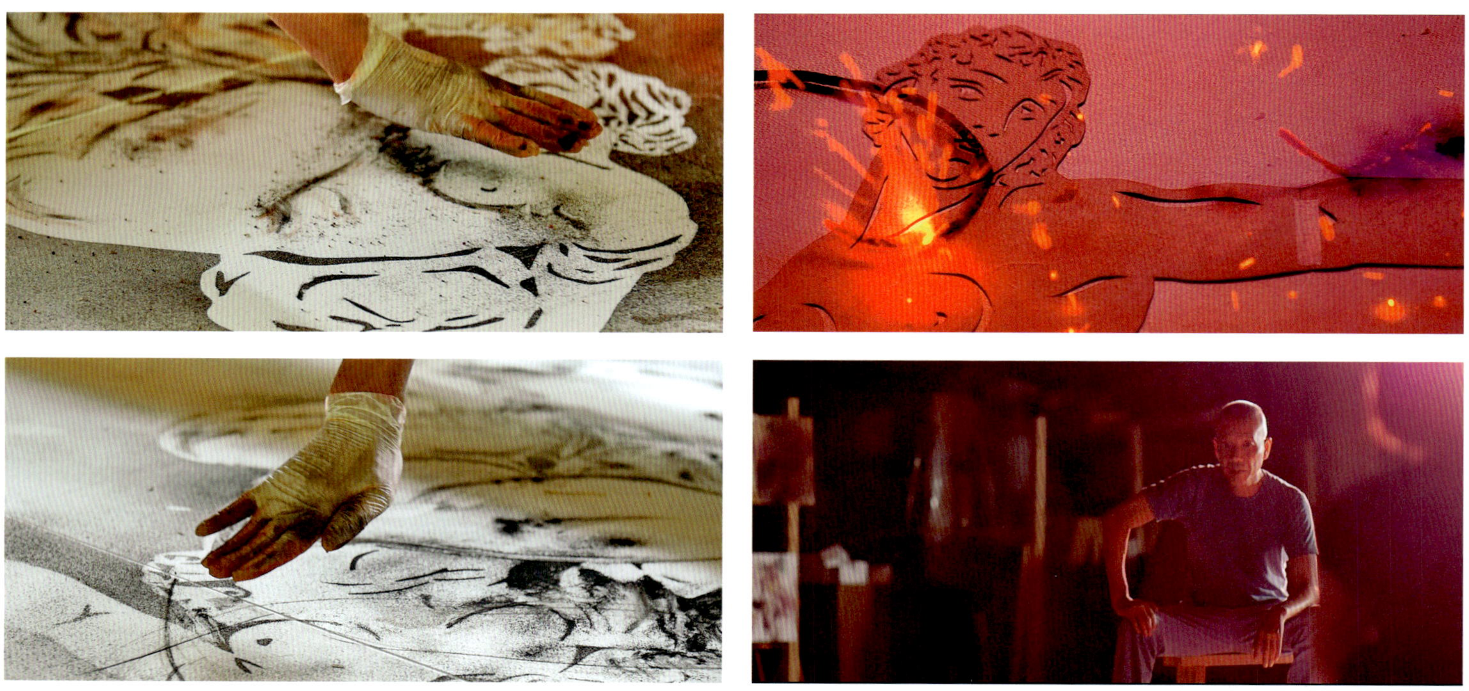

Figures 2.6a–d. Creation process of *I Modi* in 2018

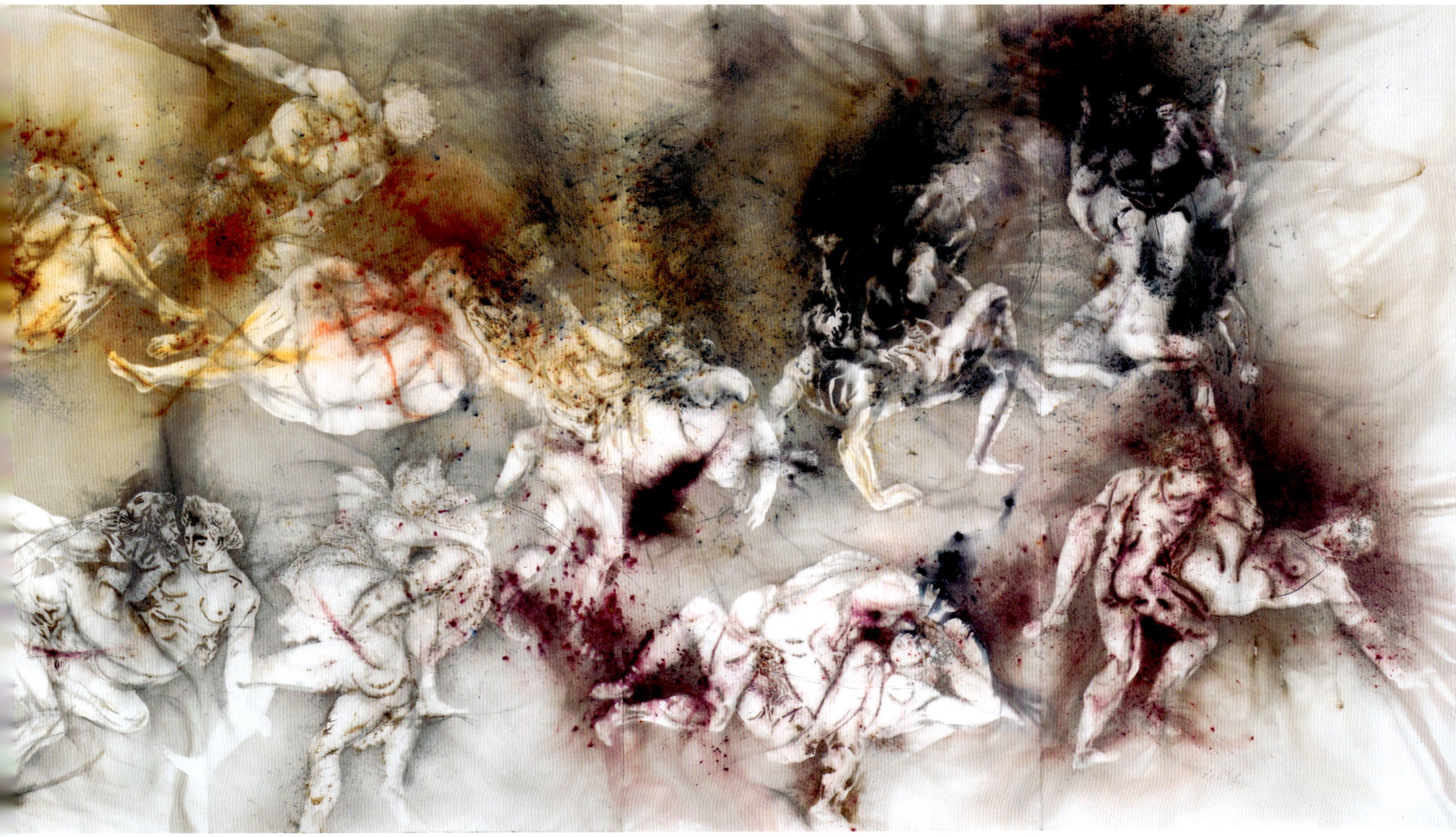

2.22

*I Modi*

技法

2018

Gunpowder on canvas

300 × 1050 cm

In 1524, the Italian engraver Marcantonio Raimondi (1480–1534) was inspired by the inventions of Giulio Romano to design and publish the erotic themed booklet *I Modi*. This booklet, containing sixteen images of different sexual positions, would become one of the first-ever banned books in Europe. Cai condensed the various scenes into one spatial-temporal plane, presenting them as the sixteen moments of a single sexual encounter. Initially, Cupid, visible in the upper-left corner, aims an arrow toward a couple, whose foreplay is illuminated by a torch-bearing angel. This is followed by back-and-forth flirtation, wildly heated climax, and ensuing reverie, concluding with fond caresses and the lingering desire for more. The work speaks to the awakening humanity and liberation unique to the Renaissance spirit.

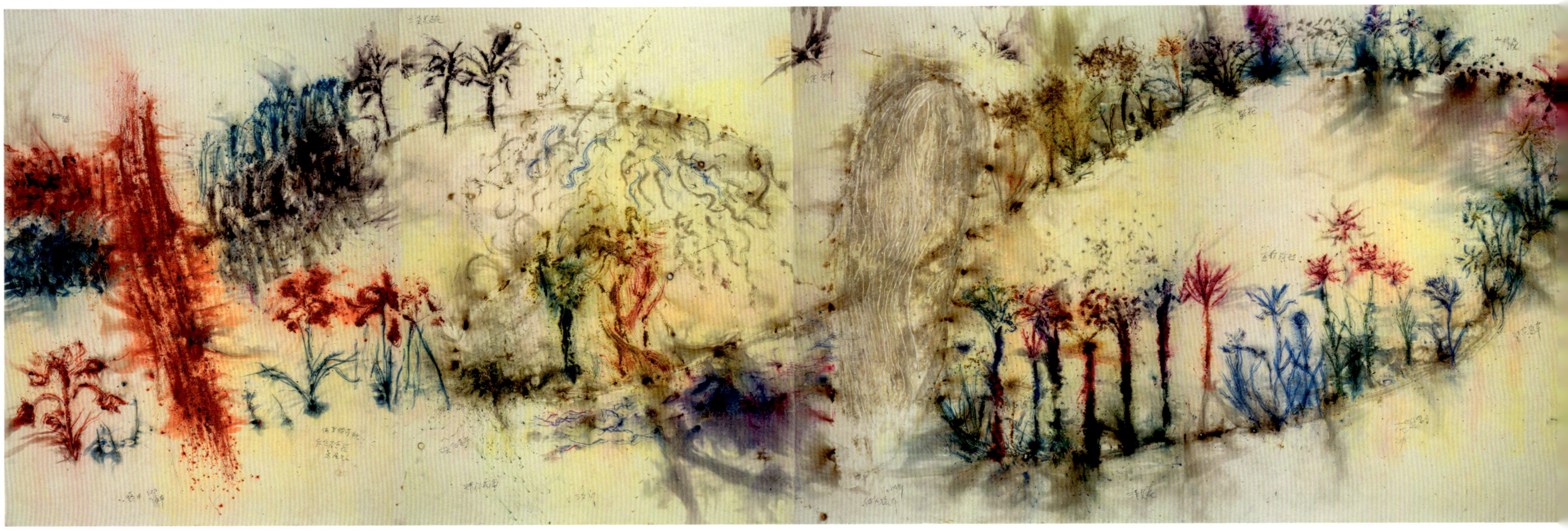

2.23 *Color Gunpowder Drawing for City of Flowers in the Sky*

2.23

### *Color Gunpowder Drawing for City of Flowers in the Sky*
### 为“空中花城”所作彩色火药草图

2018
Gunpowder on paper
4 left sheets: 400 × 300 cm each;
4 right sheets: 200 × 300 cm each

2.24

### *Sketches for City of Flowers in the Sky*
### 为“空中花城”所作手稿

2018
35 sketches; pencil and marker on paper
151 × 140 cm in total

The day before the exhibition opening, Cai's daytime explosion event, *City of Flowers in the Sky*, unfurled in the skies of the Piazzale Michelangelo overlooking Florence. Inspired by Botticelli's *Primavera*, the explosion showered thousands of fireworks of Renaissance flowers.

Cai said of this exhibition, "The Uffizi Galleries are always packed with tourists who line up for hours, with most people only interested in seeing a few famous masterpieces. The tourists raise the GDP, but the museum has become a cemetery of past culture, where local inhabitants rarely go. I dedicated this explosion event to the city of the Renaissance and her people. The rich collection of the Uffizi almost spilled over the thick walls, integrated into the city that cultivated her. Let the Renaissance artists not only live inside of the museum's ice-cold walls, but also live in the communities and the streets, just as they used to be. People from every corner of the city, even the suburbs, could see the bursts of flowers spilling out in the air, feeling the awe and intimacy of the Renaissance artworks' spirit left on today."

Inside the Uffizi exhibition gallery, the gunpowder drawing and artist sketches related to this explosion event with "the sky as its canvas" were displayed alongside video documentation of the event. Together they demonstrated how the artist drew his own horizon in painting, by enabling it to freely move between the two-dimensional support and the three-dimensional time and space.

In this gunpowder drawing, Cai adopted a new technique of "painting with ignited incense sticks." First, he sprinkled the outlines of the figures with gunpowder, then brandished sticks of burning incense as though he were holding a brush. The incense sparked an explosion wherever it made contact with the gunpowder, forging a calligraphic painting of fire.

The selected sketches were created to illustrate the artistic effects of each pyrotechnic product and of each "act" in the performance, and demonstrate the technical methods needed to realize the desired effects. They reveal how Cai conceives and creates his explosion event.

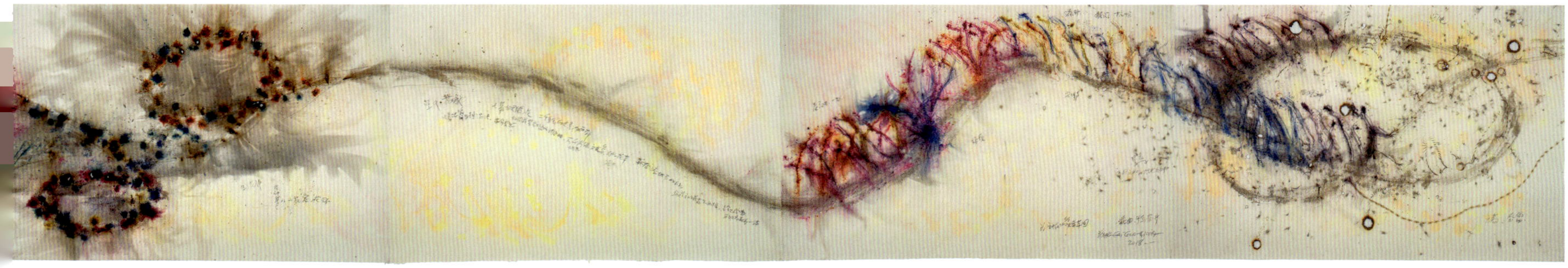

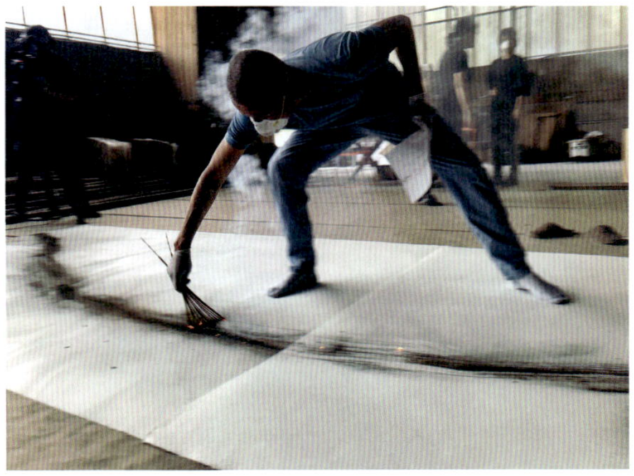

Figure 2.7. Cai Guo-Qiang holding ignited incense sticks to create *Color Gunpowder Drawing for City of Flowers in the Sky* in 2018

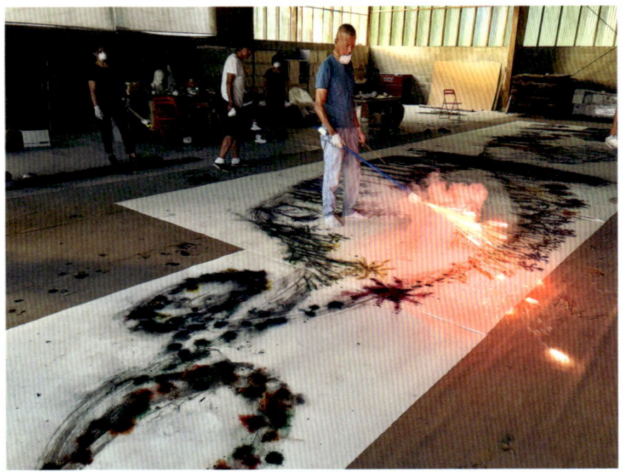

Figure 2.8. Cai Guo-Qiang holding a stick with one end connected to toy fireworks to create *Color Gunpowder Drawing for City of Flowers in the Sky* in 2018

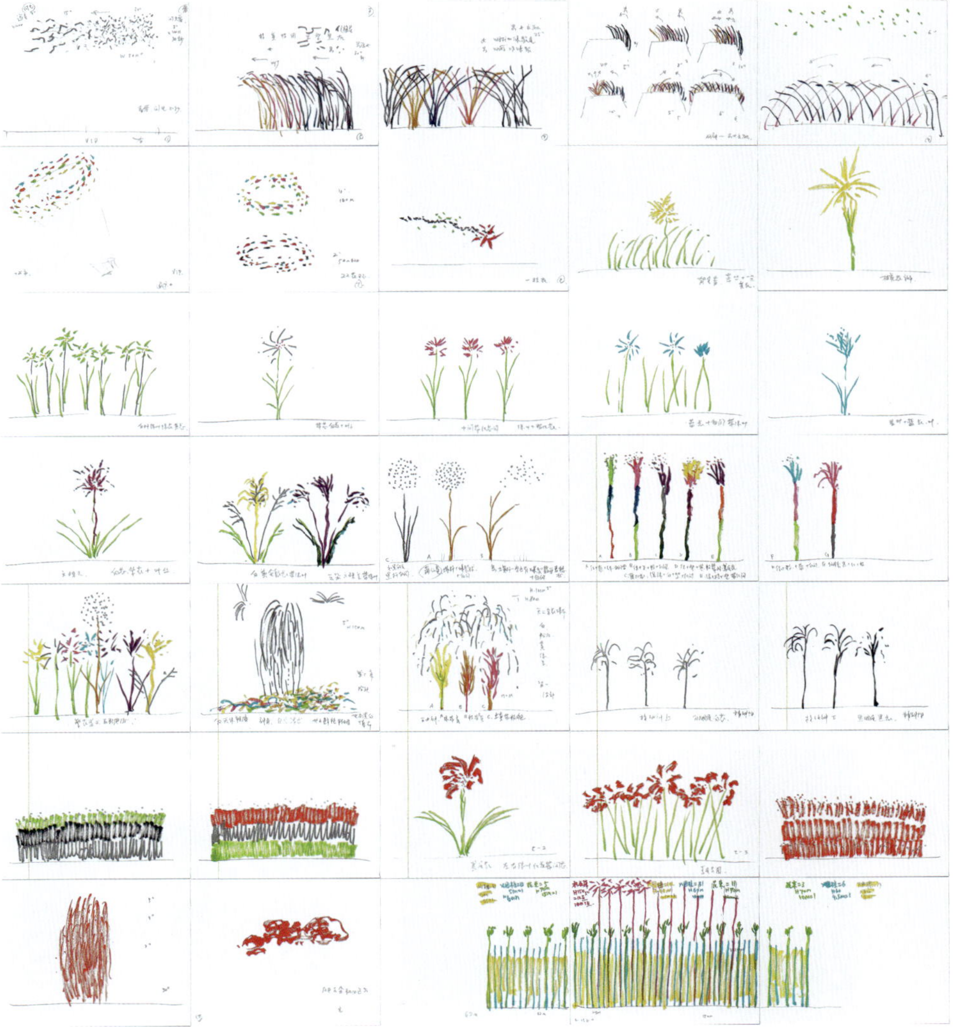

2.24 *Sketches for City of Flowers in the Sky*

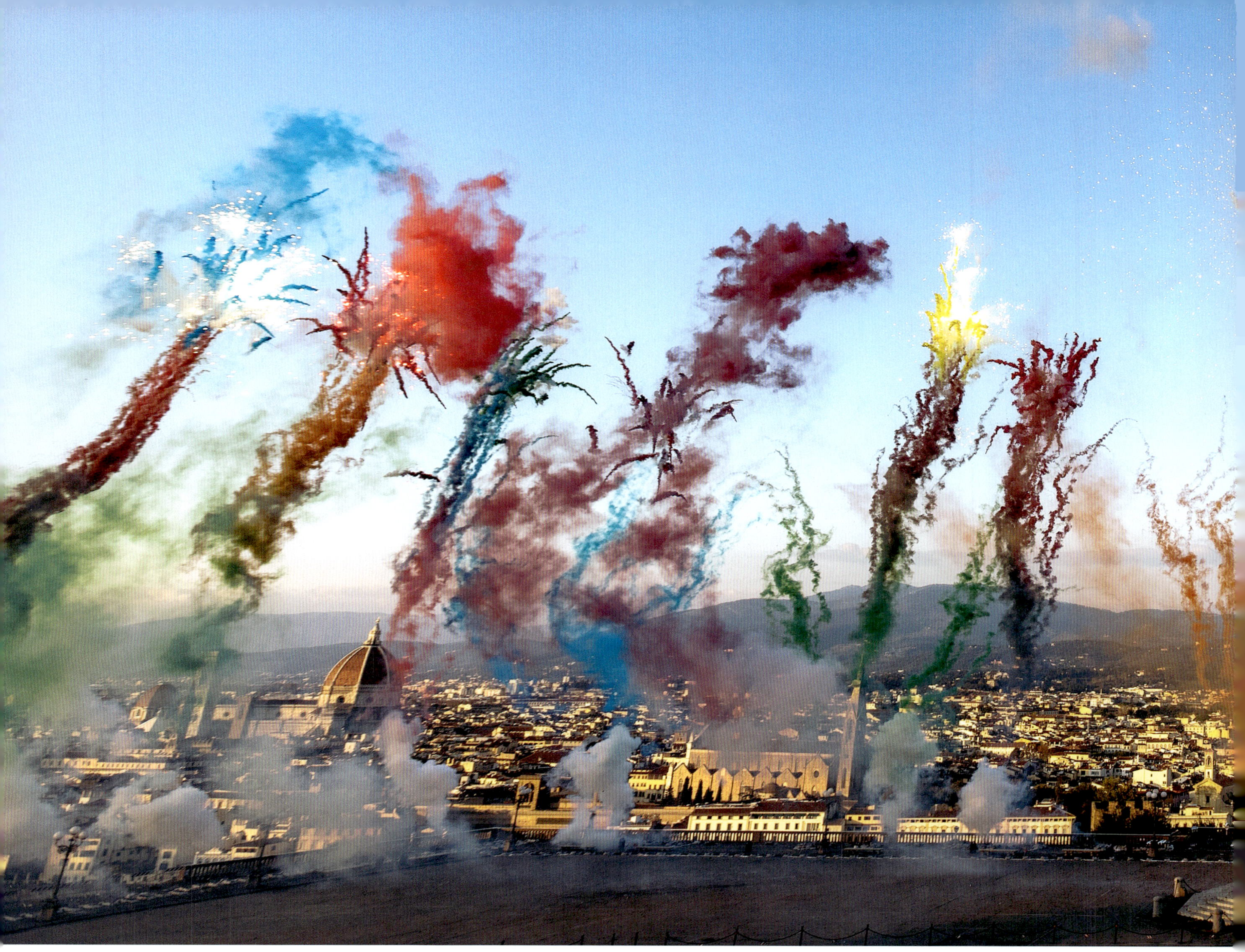

Figures 2.9a (above), 2.9b–m (below). Views of *City of Flowers in the Sky*, 2018. Daytime explosion event realized above Piazzale Michelangelo, Florence, November 18, 3:50 p.m., approx. 13:30

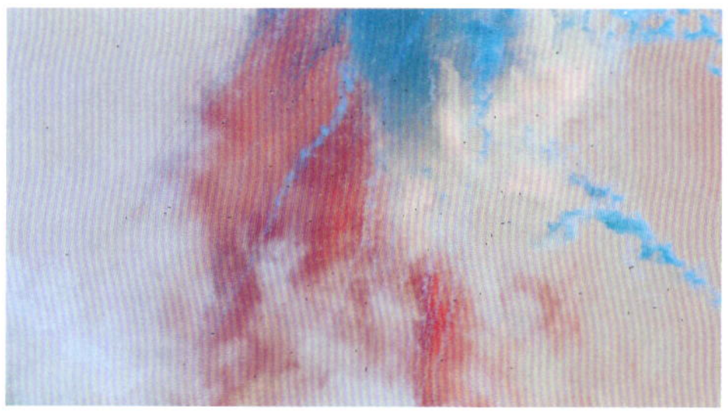

2.9b

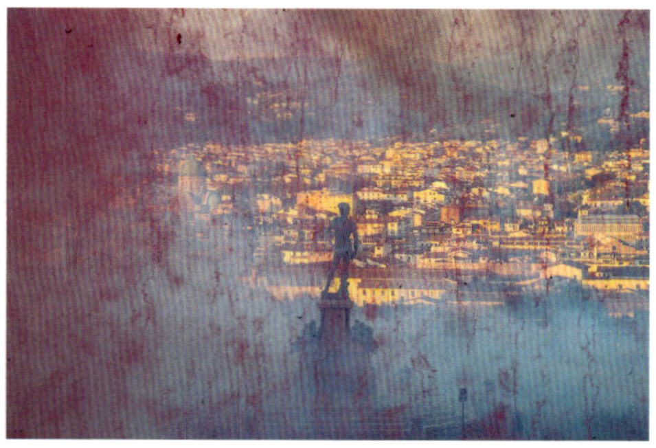

2.9c

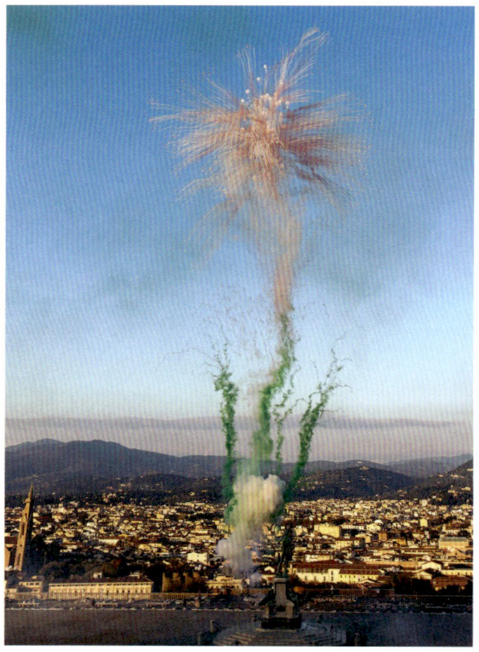

2.9d

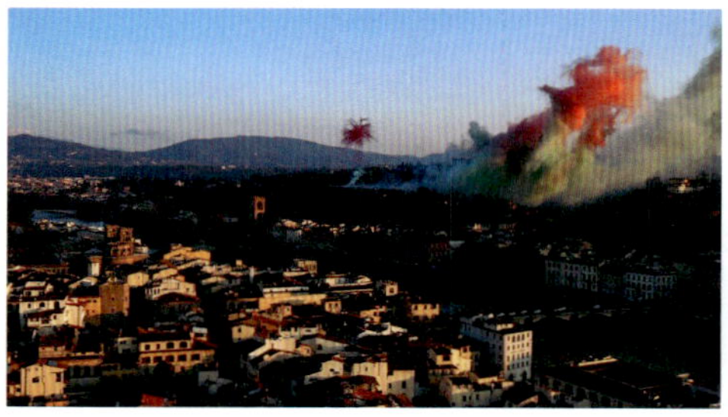

2.9e

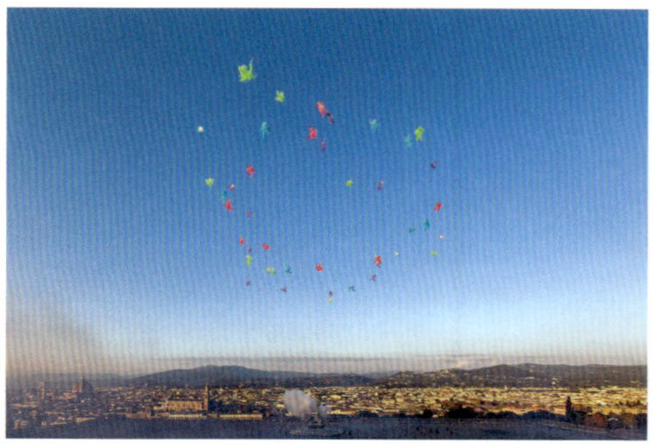

2.9f

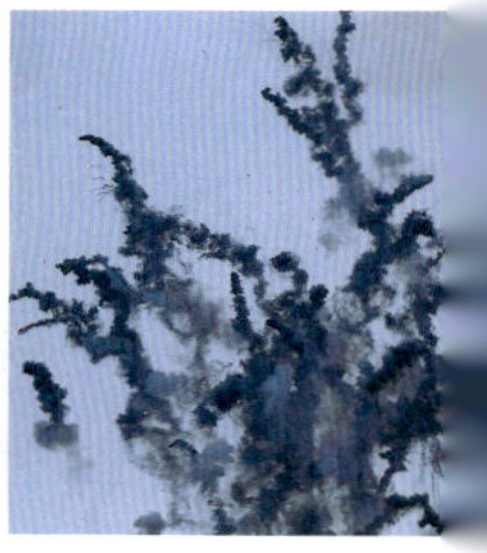

2.9g

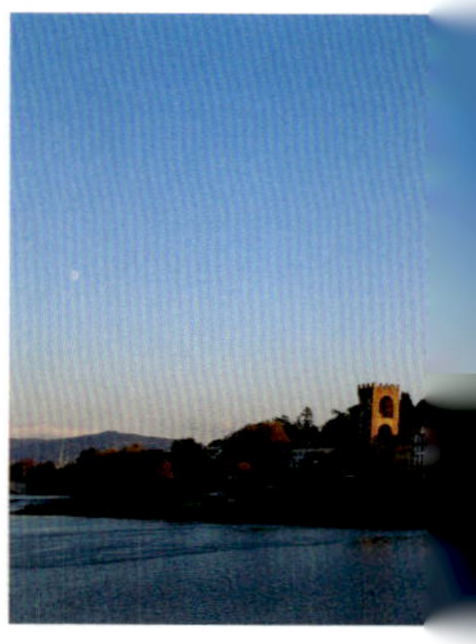

2.9h

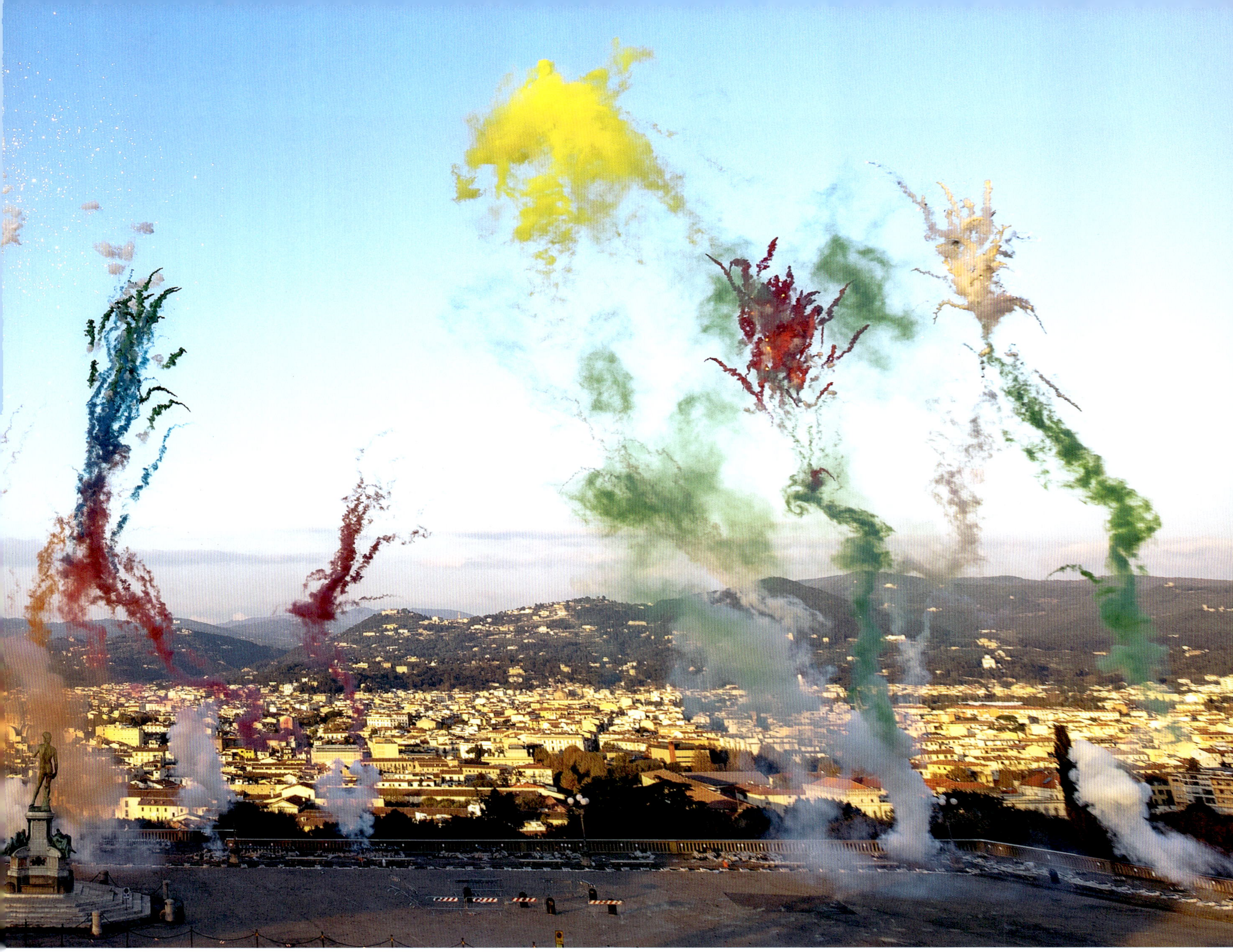

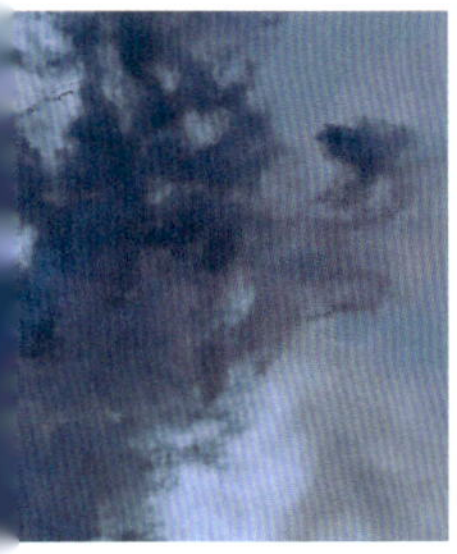

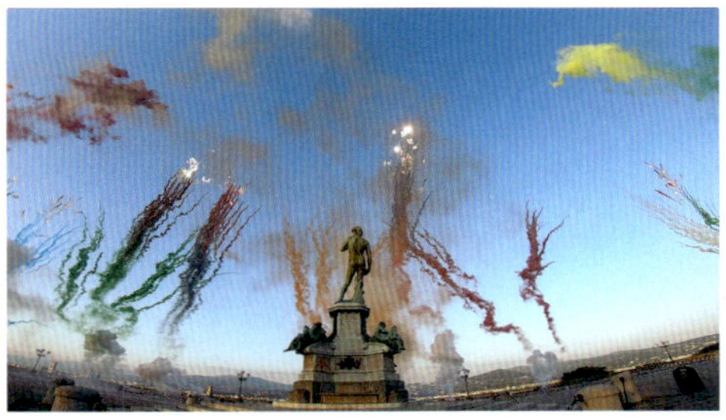

2.9i

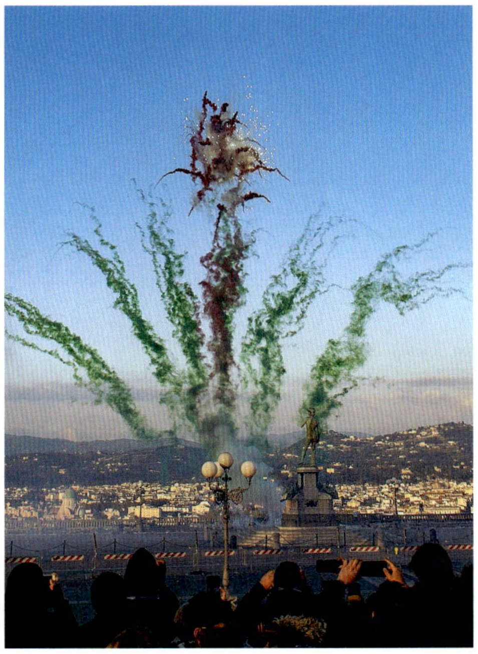

2.9k

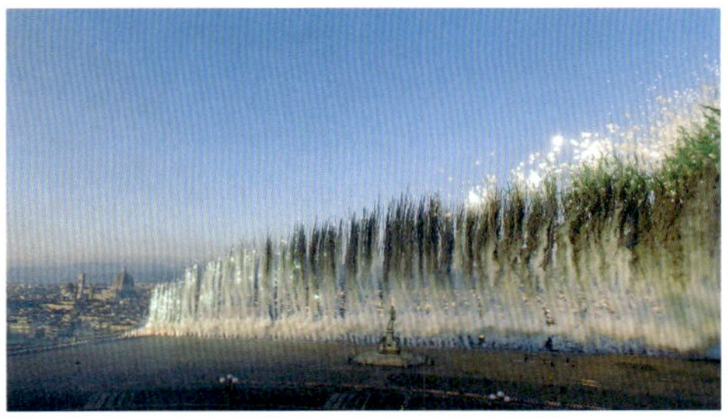

2.9l

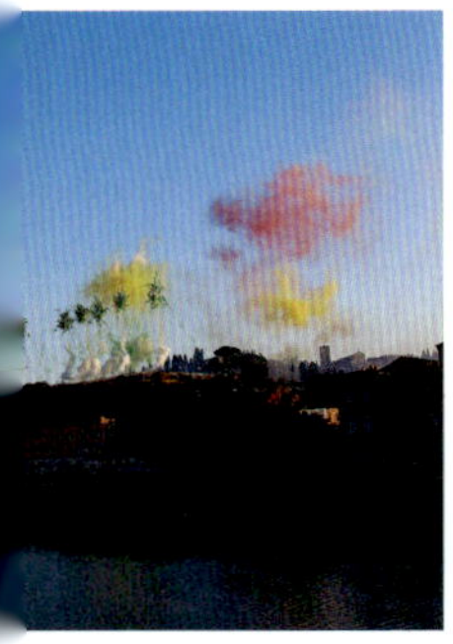

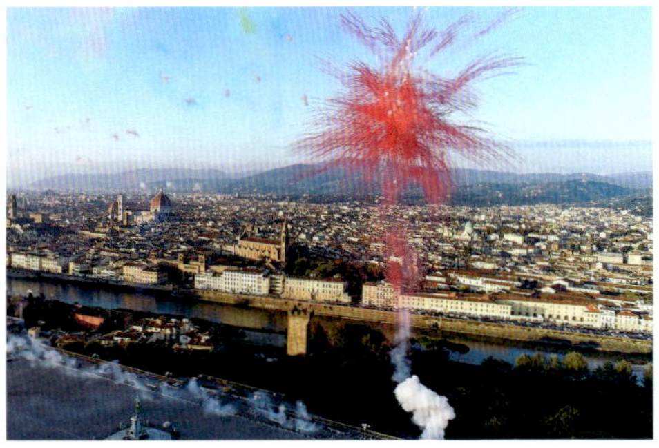

2.9j

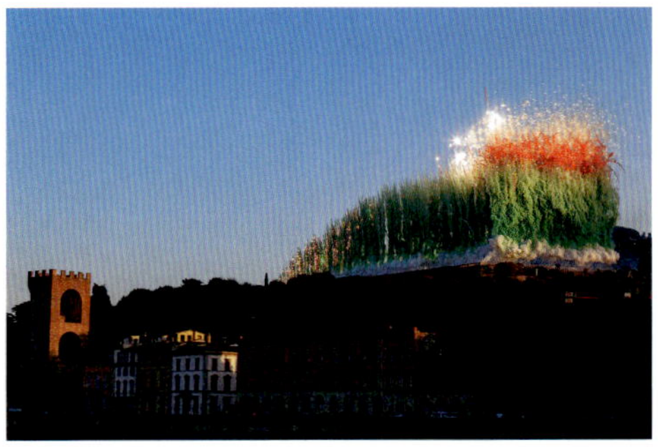

2.9m

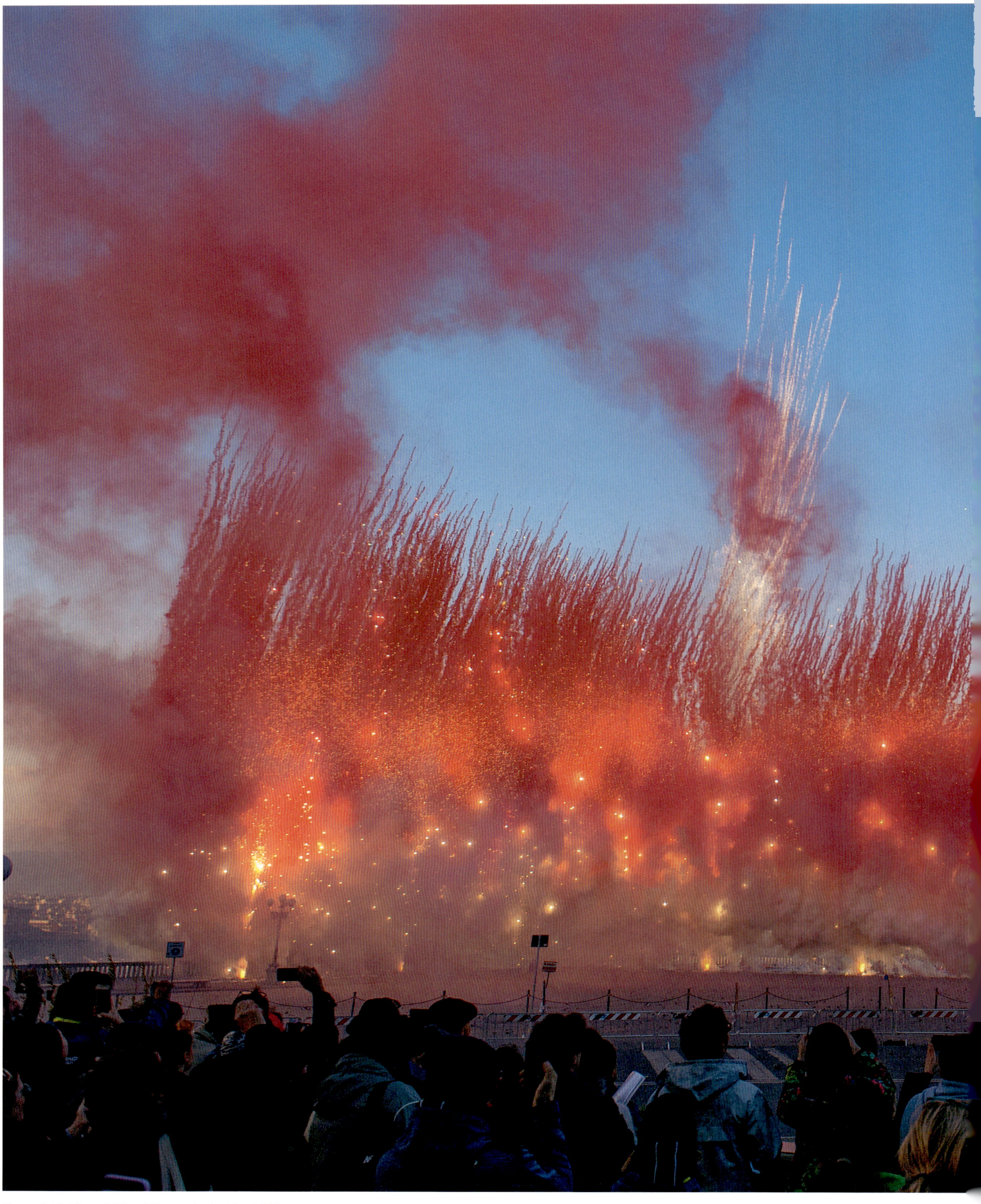

Figure 2.10. View of *City of Flowers in the Sky*, 2018

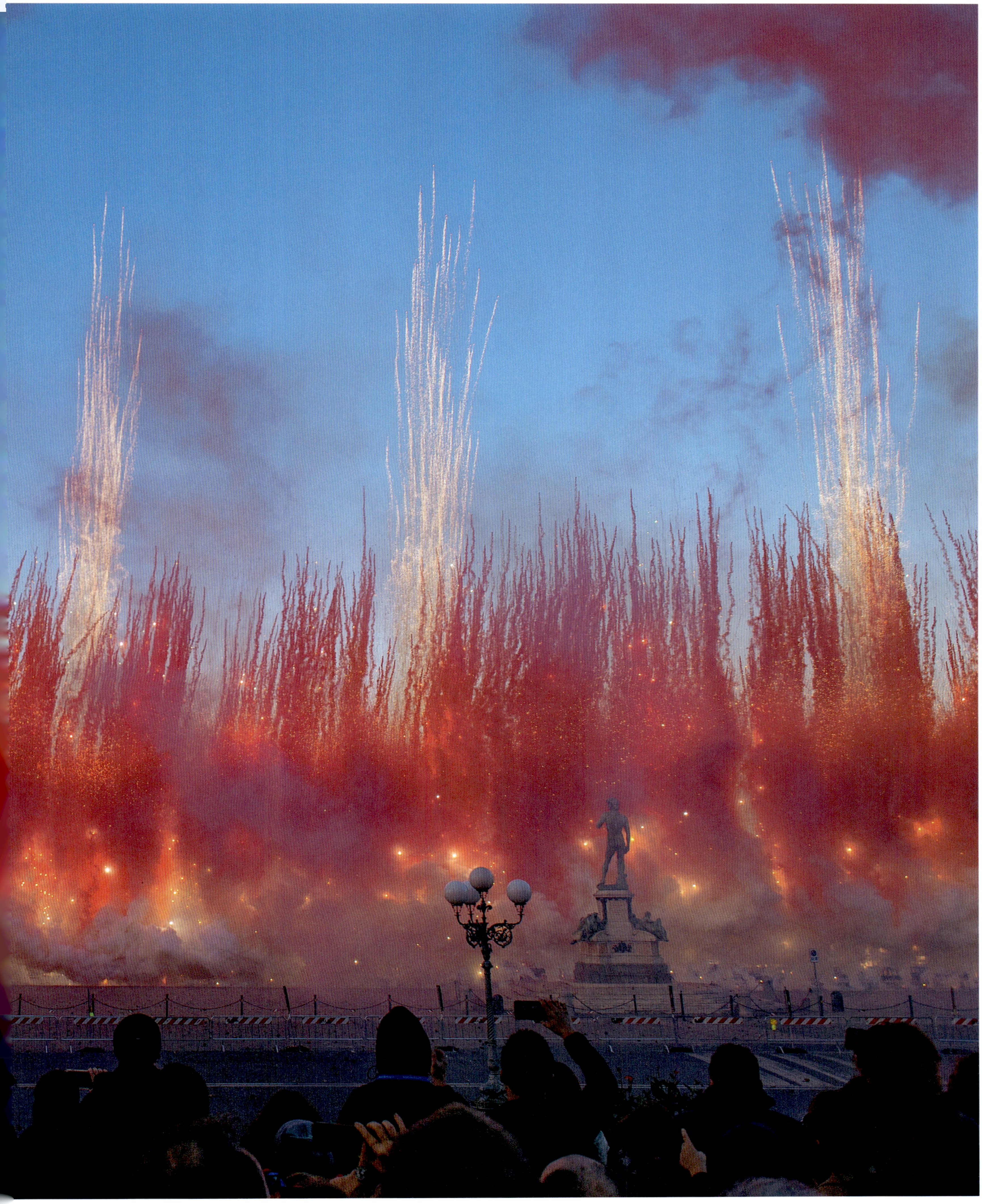

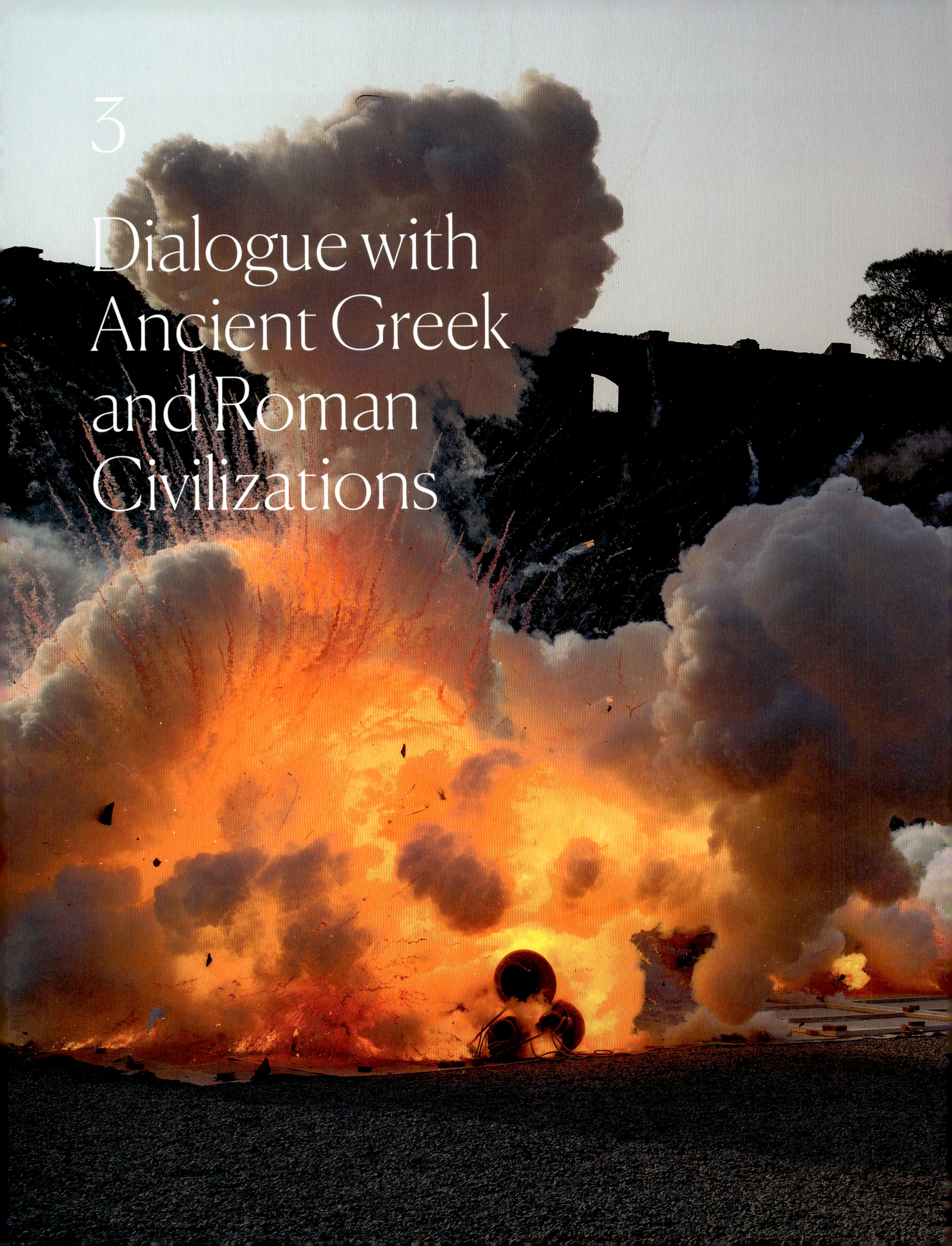

# 3

# Dialogue with Ancient Greek and Roman Civilizations

# *In the Volcano: Cai Guo-Qiang and Pompeii*

National Archaeological Museum of Naples and Pompeii Archaeological Park, Italy
February 22–May 20, 2019

Curated by Jérôme Neutres, Director of Strategy and Development, Réunion des Musées Nationaux–Grand Palais, France

Public creation: *Explosion Studio*, Pompeii Archaeological Park, February 21, 2019

Catalogue: *Cai Guo-Qiang and Pompeii: In the Volcano*, English and Italian editions published by Silvana Editoriale

Documentary short: directed by Shanshan Xia, produced by 33 Studio (15:52)

*In the Volcano* was a dialogue with ancient Greek and Roman civilizations in which Cai undertook a direct intervention of sorts, inspired as much by the catastrophe of ancient Pompeii as by the echoes of ancient Greek civilization reflected in the collection of the National Archaeological Museum of Naples (MANN), housed in a structure built in 1585. Known as one of the largest archaeological museums in the world, it holds collections centering on antiquities and sculptures from the Roman period, together with the world's most significant collection of Pompeiian art, including important mosaics and frescoes such as the *Alexander Mosaic*.

By invitation of the Pompeii Archaeological Park, Cai staged *Explosion Studio*, a public multimedia explosion event, at the world's oldest surviving Roman amphitheater, located in the Pompeii ruins at the foot of Mount Vesuvius. In the center of the amphitheater, a 30-meter-long platform was laid on the ground with canvas spread over it. Cai detonated hundreds of kilograms' worth of gunpowder along with a variety of toy fireworks, blasting and engulfing eighty-four objects in a ferocious explosion. Among them were plaster replicas of the museum's Roman statues and busts, such as *Farnese Hercules*, *Venus Callipyge*, and *Pseudo-Seneca*. There were also a large number of materials related to Pompeiian art and life two thousand years ago, including canvas, ceramics, glassware, and marble. The explosion lasted more than three minutes, after which the artist and his team excavated the exploded artworks from the ravaged "ruins" and transported them to the museum for installation. The whole process was open to the public and the press.

Cai's explosion event evoked the apocalyptic scenes from 79 CE, when the lava from the deep crevices of Mount Vesuvius first quaked, then violently erupted over the earth. Cai's explosion that conjured up the fiery consumption of the ancient city was followed by its unearthing and relocation to the museum, recalling the events that took place over two millennia in a matter of minutes.

Cai placed his exploded works throughout the museum's multistory collection galleries. Positioned next to the enduring Greek and Roman statues, they reenact Pompeii's fate for their ancient neighbors. Visitors to the museum were thus invited into an archeological and "contemporalogical" journey that emulated the principle of "cavalier perspective" in classical Chinese painting, which features multiple and shifting focal points. The visit became a labyrinthine treasure hunt in which viewers met with pleasant surprises and new encounters at every turn.

Compared to the romantic, svelte, *yin* beauty of *Flora Commedia* at the Uffizi, *In the Volcano* was forceful, virile, and *yang* in its themes of catastrophe, grief, savagery, and eroticism.

Figure 3.1. *Explosion Studio*, 2019

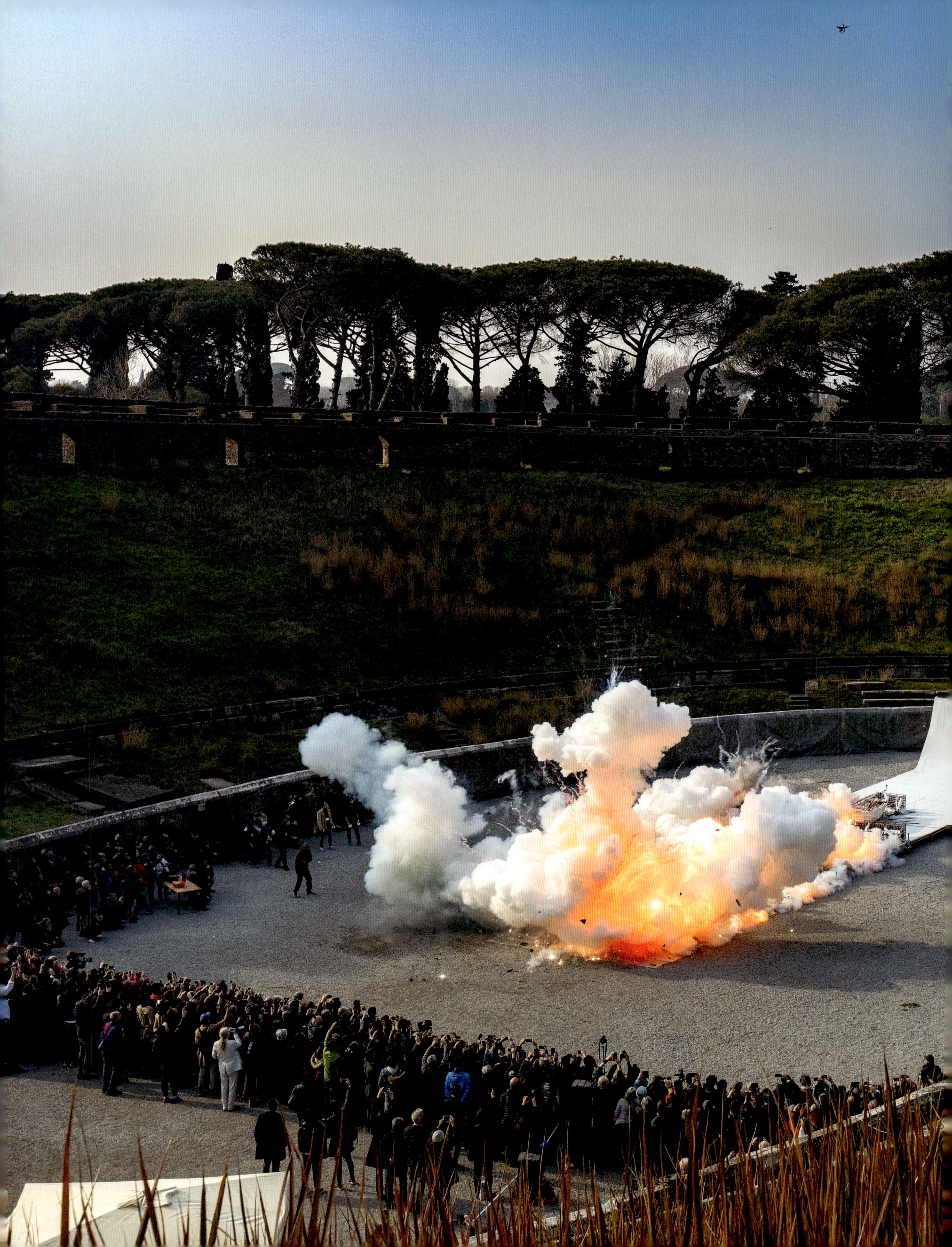

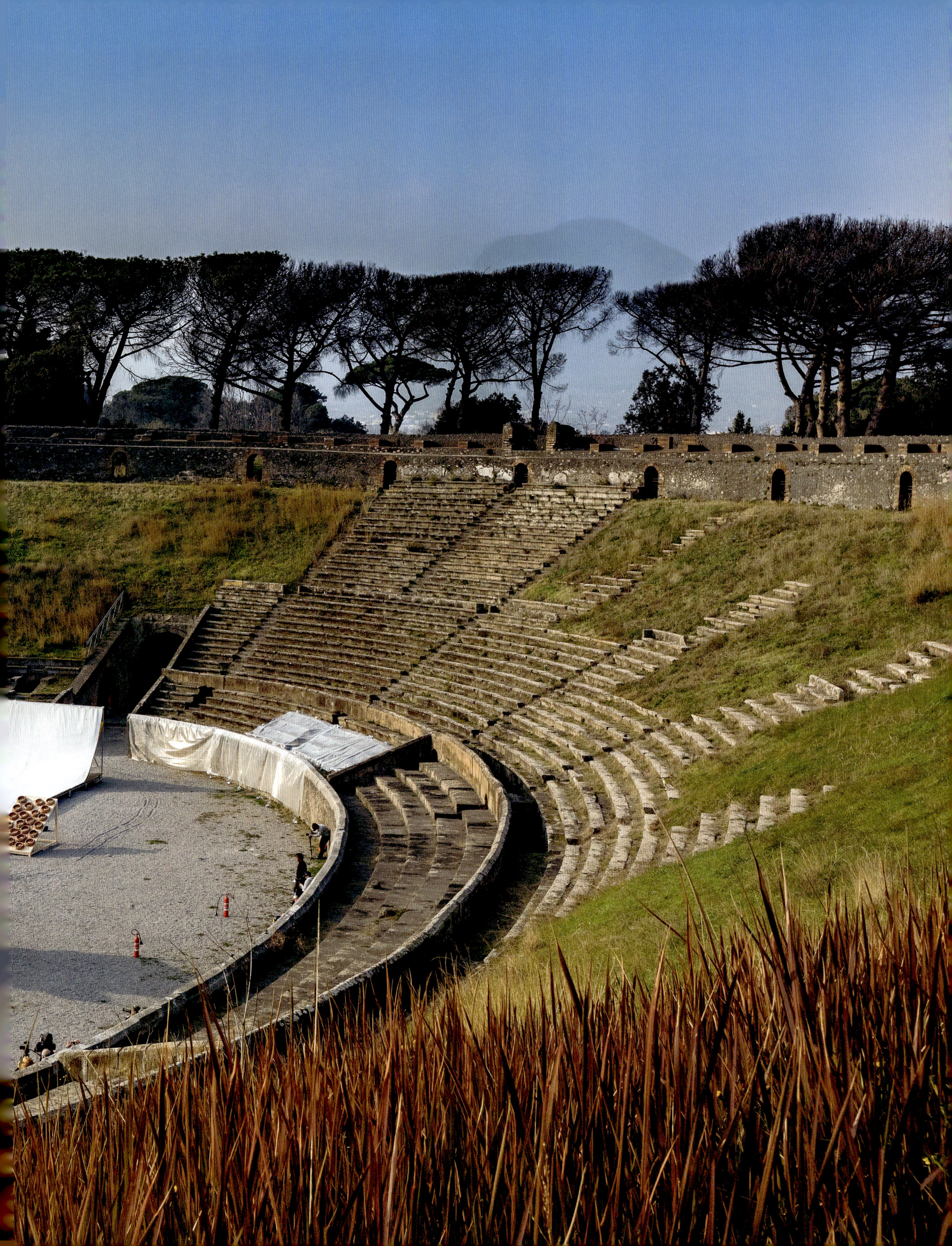

Figure 3.2 (overleaf). Cai Guo-Qiang, *Explosion Studio*, 2019. Explosion event realized at the Amphitheatre of Pompeii, February 21, 3:00 p.m. Gunpowder, canvas, silk, plaster, marble, panel for fresco, glass, terracotta, and wooden boat

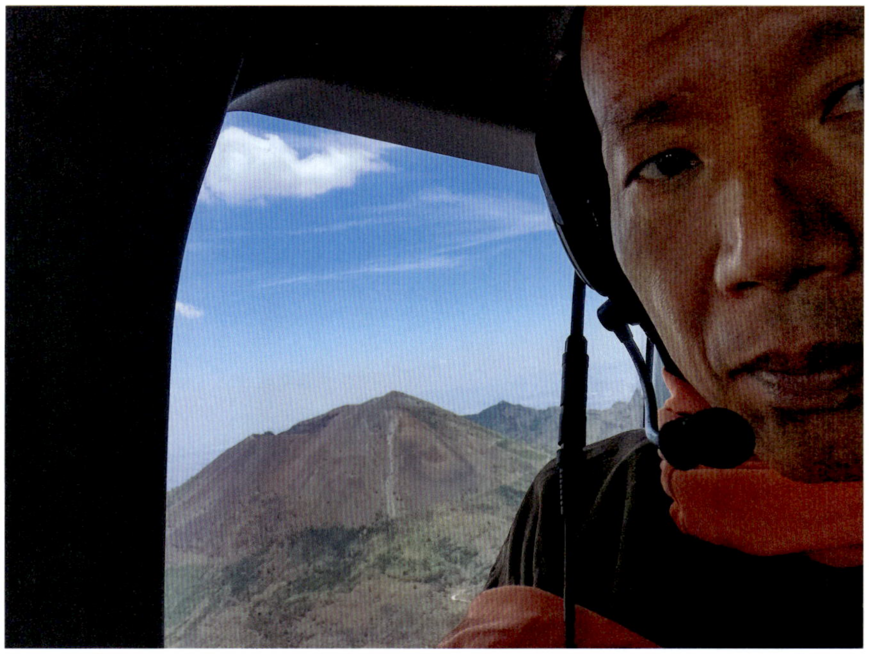

Figure 3.3. Cai Guo-Qiang visiting Mount Vesuvius via helicopter in 2018

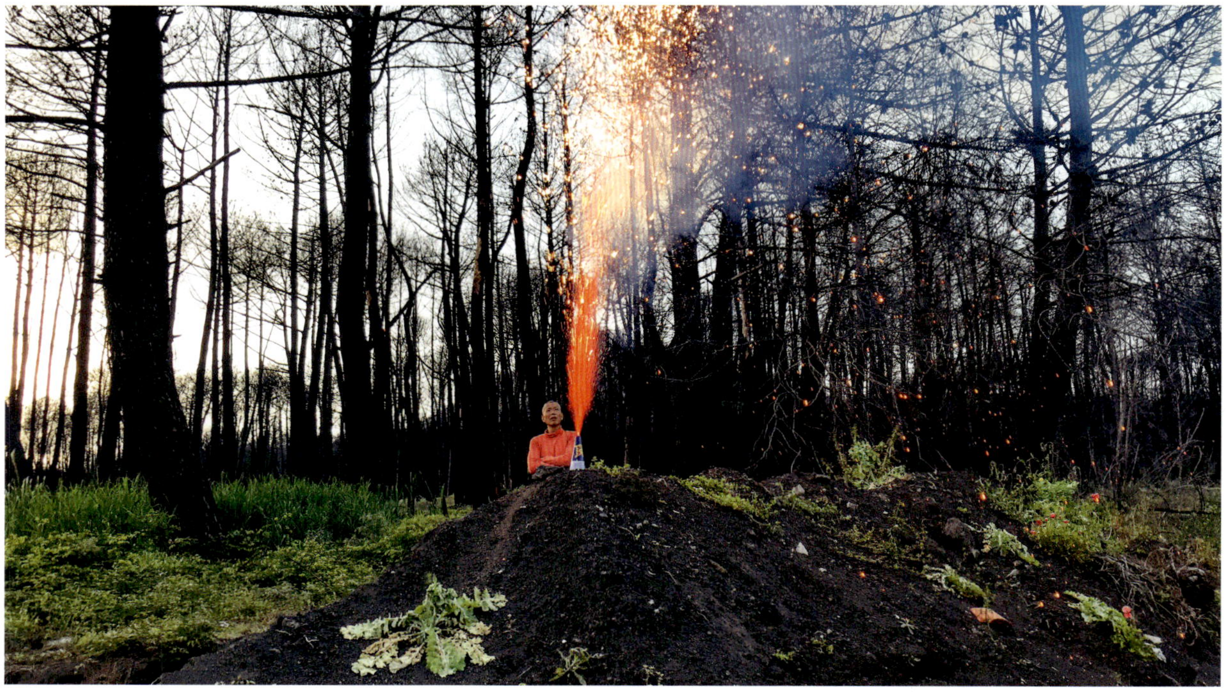

Figure 3.4. Cai Guo-Qiang testing firework products at the foot of Mount Vesuvius in 2018

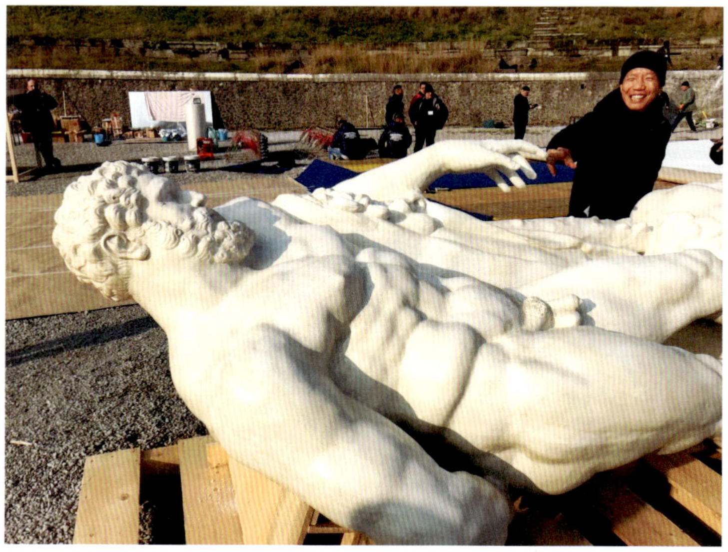

Figure 3.5. Cai Guo-Qiang and an unexploded Hercules statue prior to *Explosion Studio* at the Amphitheatre of Pompeii in 2019

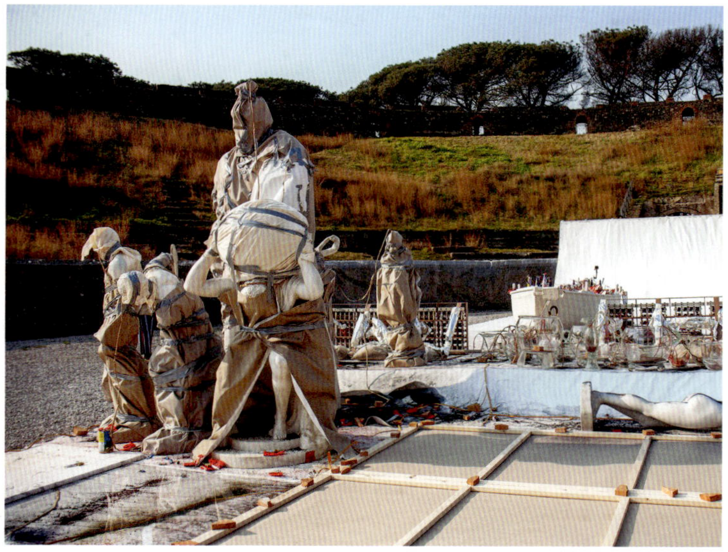

Figure 3.6. Statues and objects prior to ignition of *Explosion Studio* in 2019

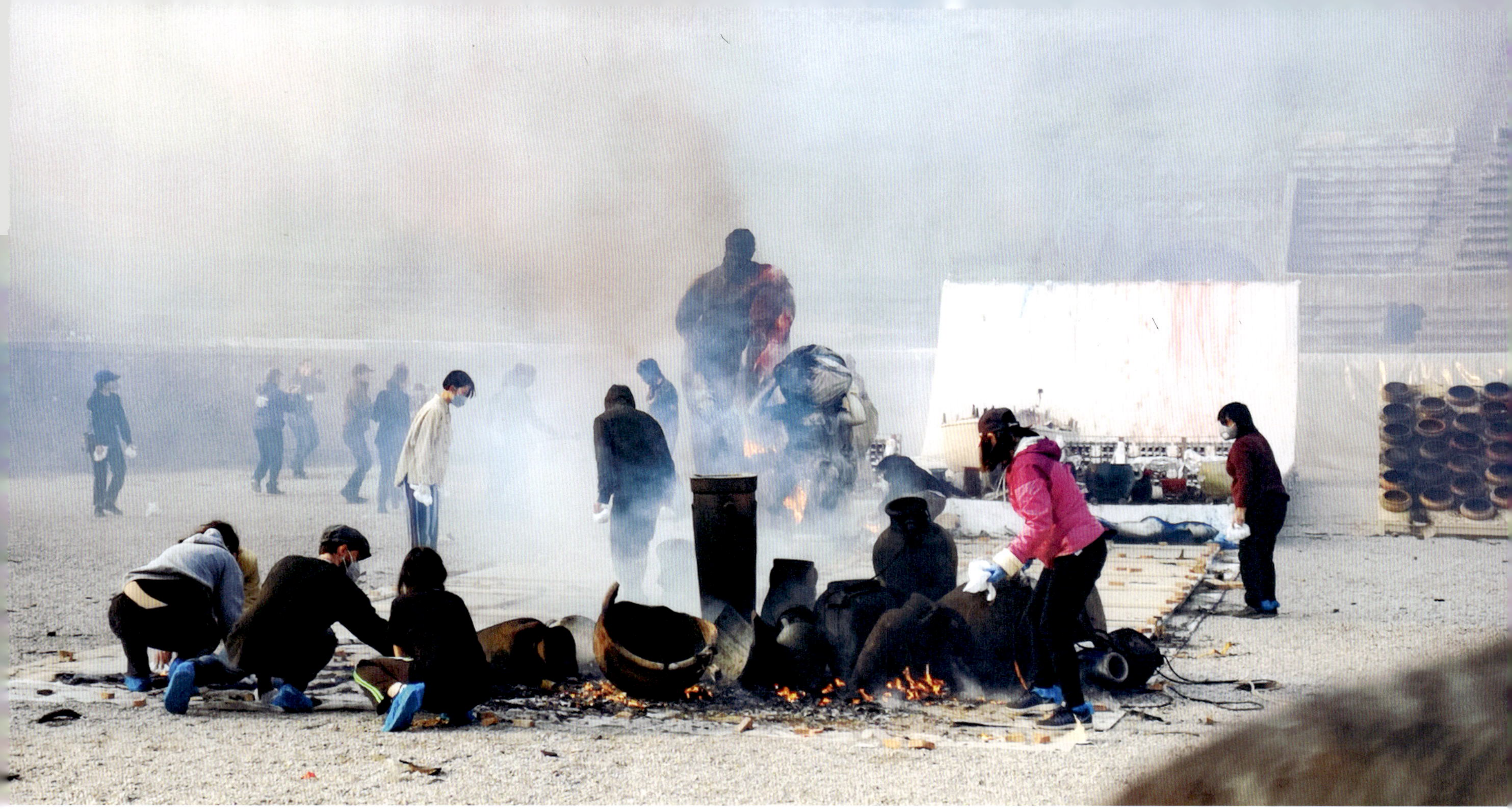

Figure 3.7. Volunteers and exhibition staff working to excavate artworks in 2019

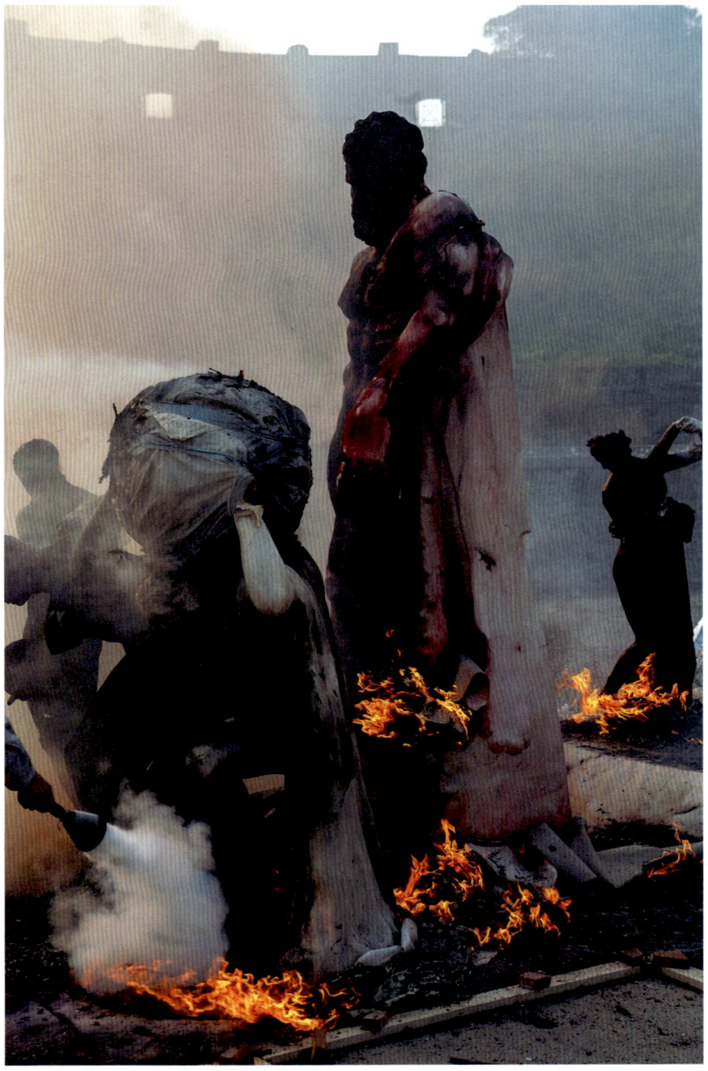

Figure 3.8. *Exploding Hercules* smoldering after its creation in 2019

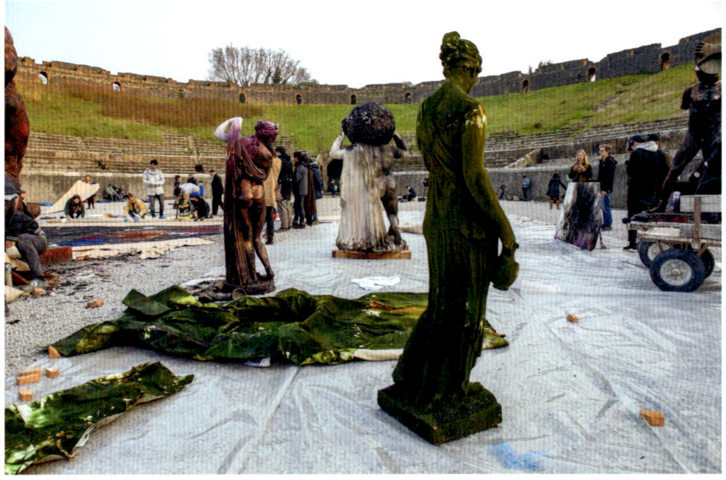

Figure 3.9. Artworks being excavated from the explosion site in 2019

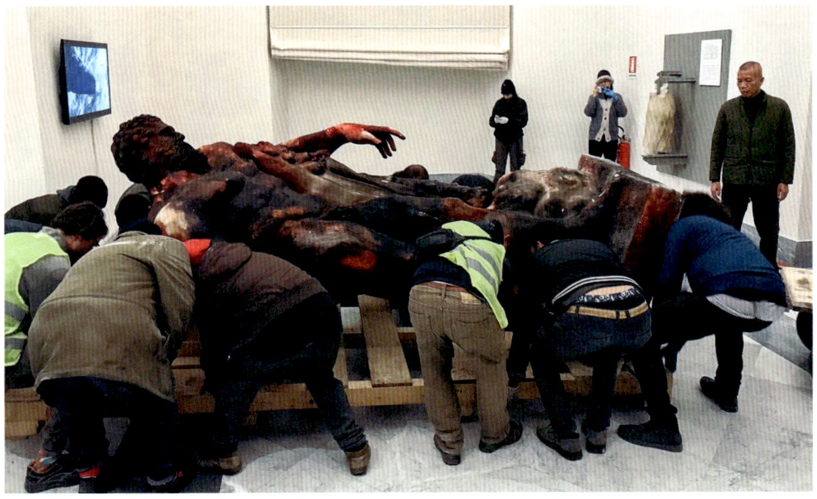

Figure 3.10. Cai Guo-Qiang and the exhibition team working overnight to install *Exploding Hercules* at the National Archaeological Museum of Naples in 2019

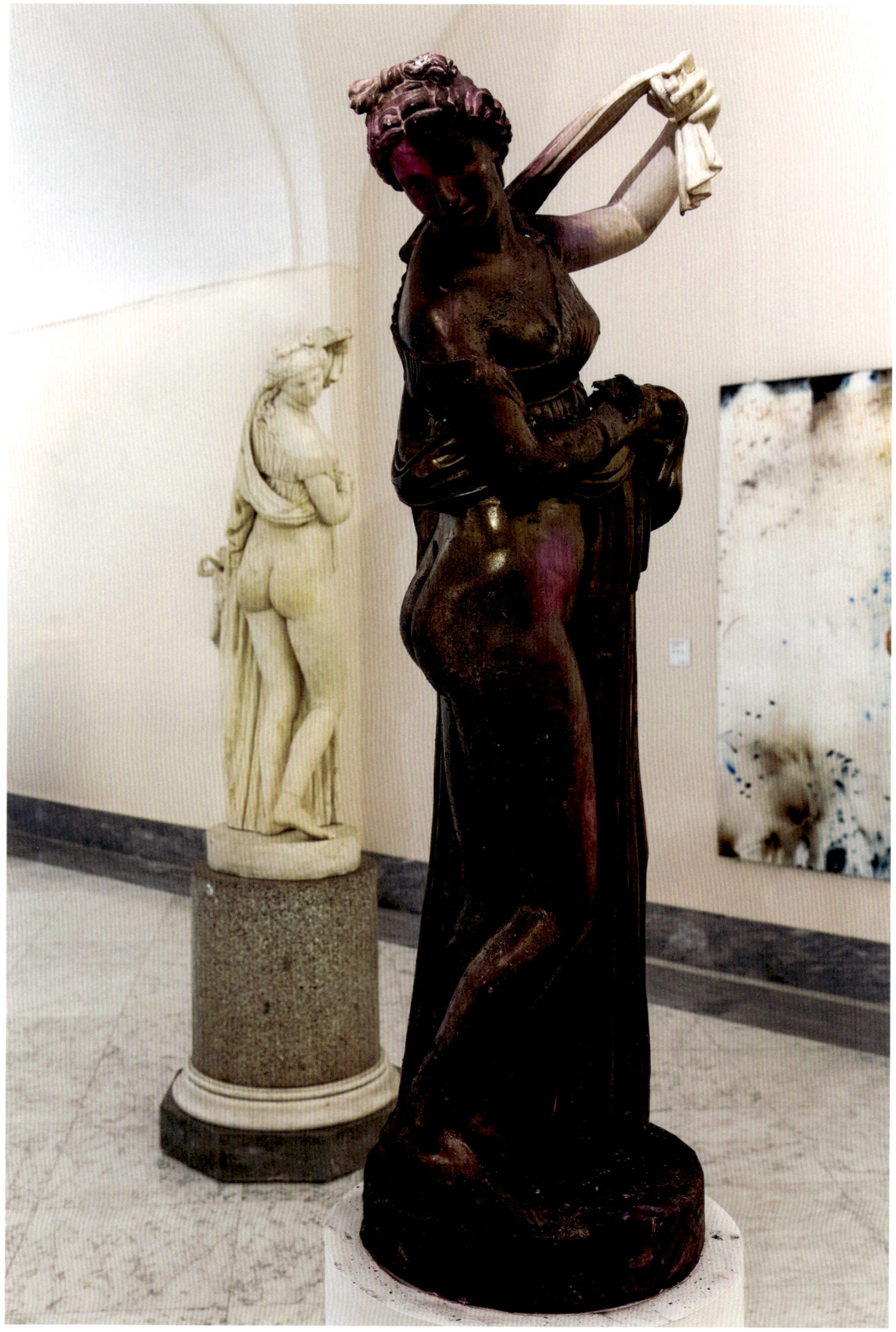

3.1 *Plum Venus*

3.1

*Plum Venus*

玫红维纳斯

2019

Gunpowder on plaster

154 × 56 × 42 cm

3.2

*Exploding Hercules*

炸大力神

2019

Gunpowder on plaster

320 × 150 × 98 cm

The artist brought plaster copies of MANN's iconic sculptures *Farnese Hercules* and *Venus Callipyge* to the Pompeii Amphitheatre, where he wrapped them with canvases, poured Chinese color gunpowder inside the wrappings, and exploded them alongside over eighty other pieces.

Cai explained, "I sketched *Farnese Hercules* when I was young, and back then I'd thought him intrepid and inimitable. Seeing him in person, I was shaken by his fatigue and helplessness—but that is precisely what makes him real and eternal. The artists of the time were pursuing something very deep."

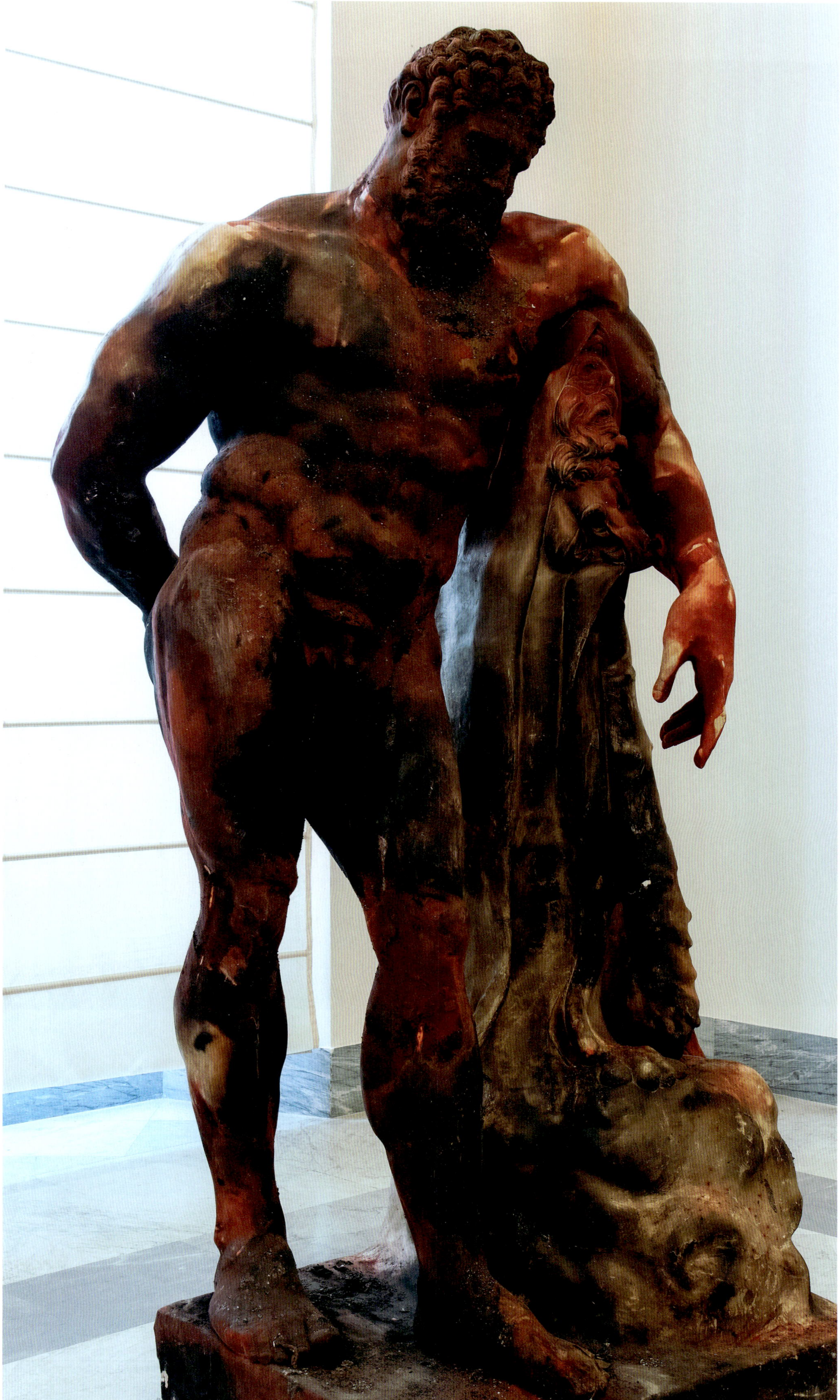

3.2 *Exploding Hercules*

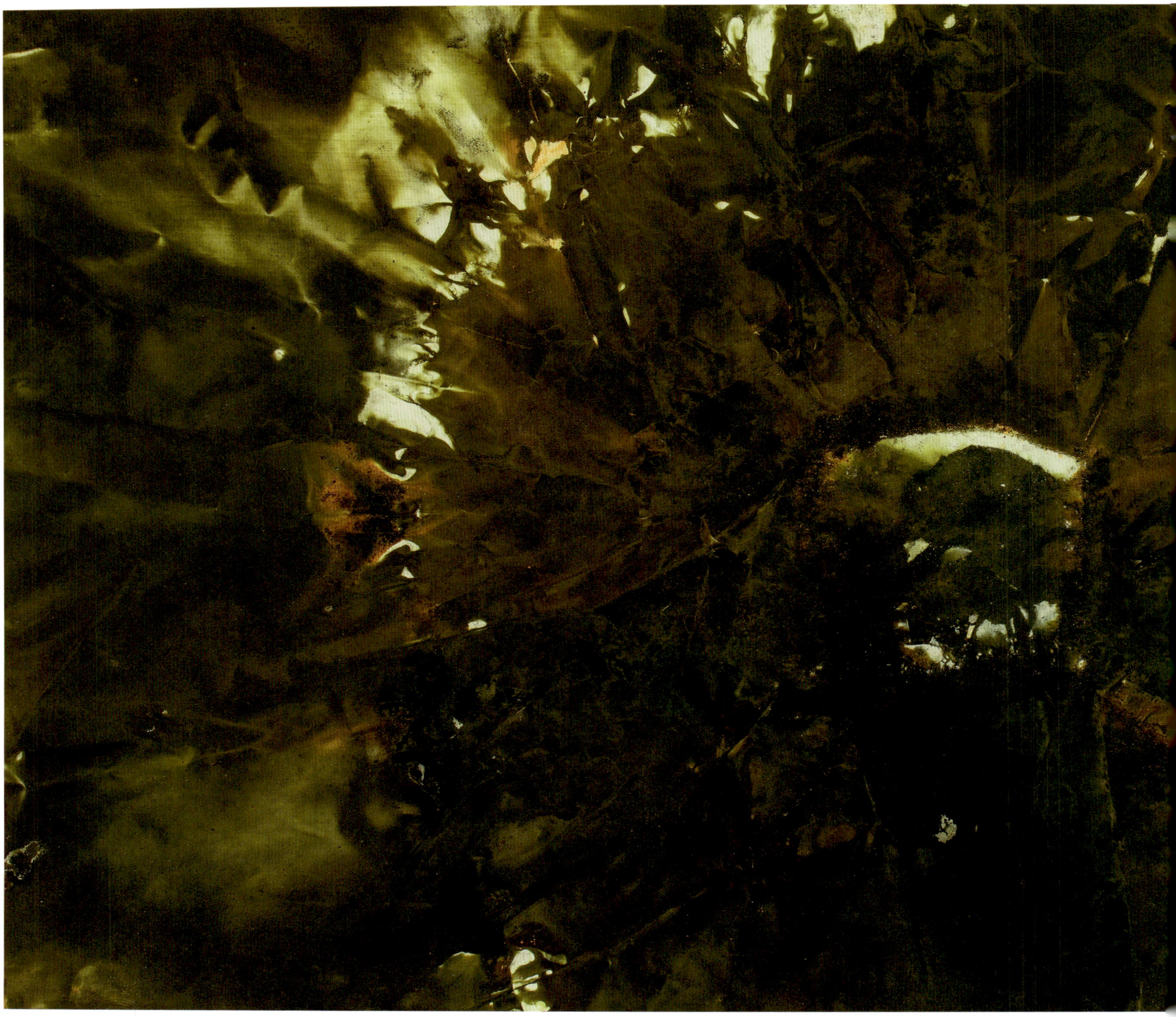

3.3
*Maid's Green No. 1*
女佣的绿色第一号
2019
Gunpowder on canvas
150 × 300 cm

One of the works from *Explosion Studio*, this canvas was wrapped around plaster replicas of the Archeological Museum's classical sculptures, and thus bears the marks of explosions and flames that the gunpowder left on the plaster. The effect evokes the act of chipping away the shell of volcanic ash that swallowed Pompeii and exposes the imprints left by the historic catastrophe.

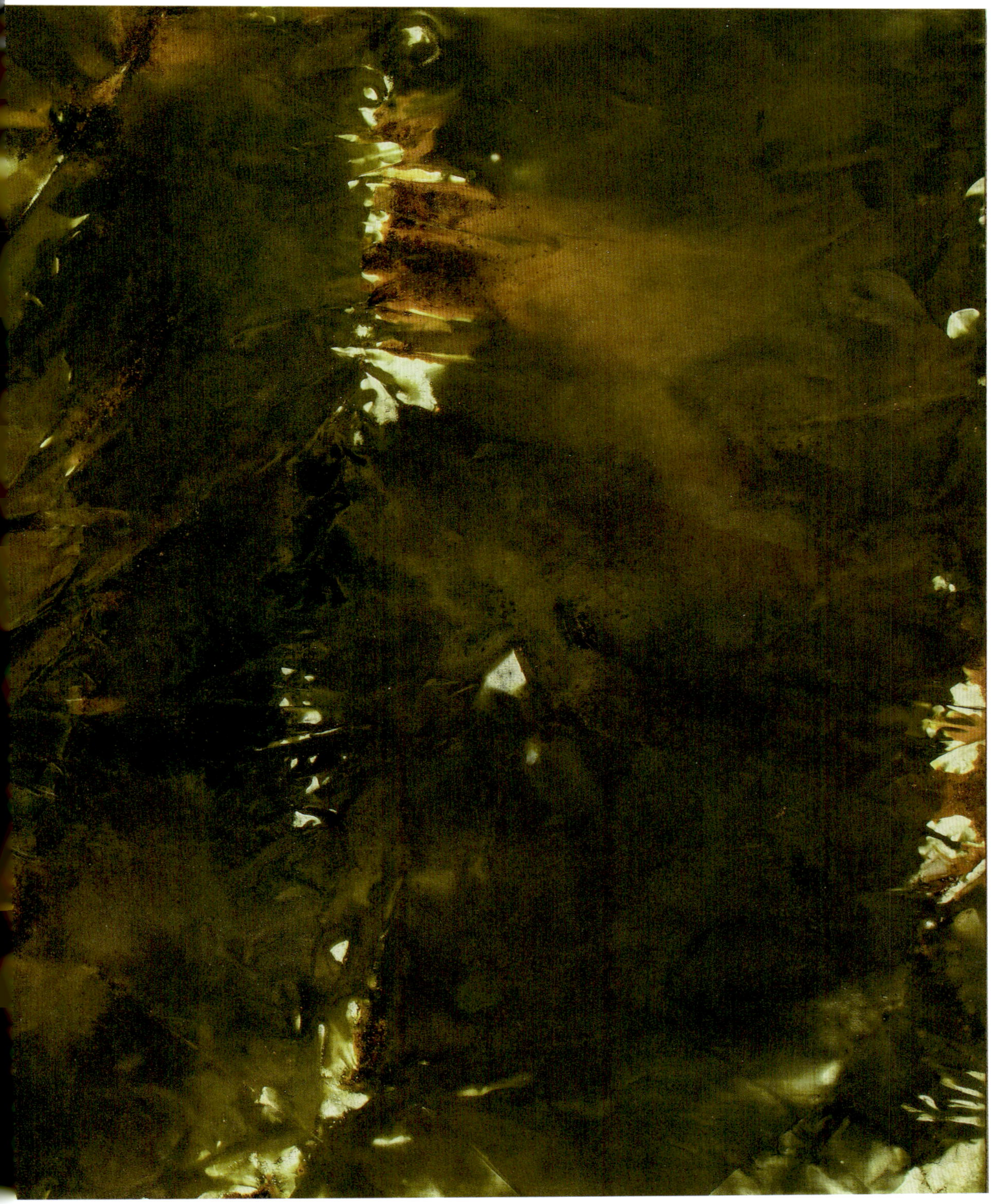

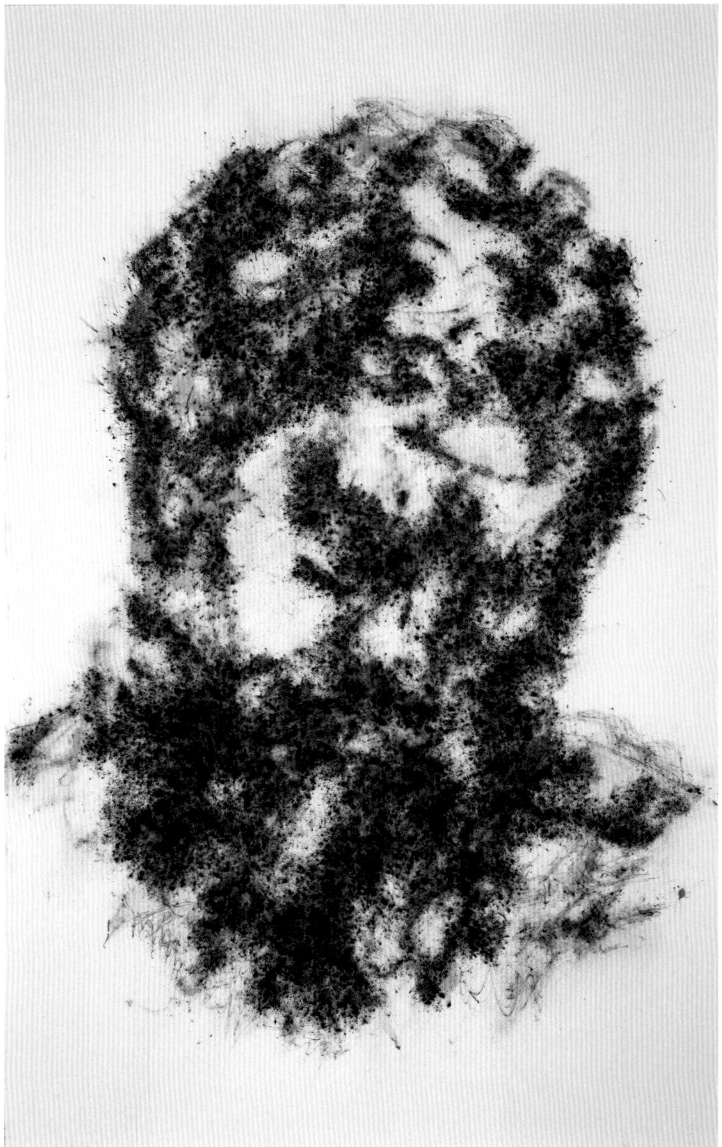

3.4 *Study for Pompeii No. 3: Hercules*

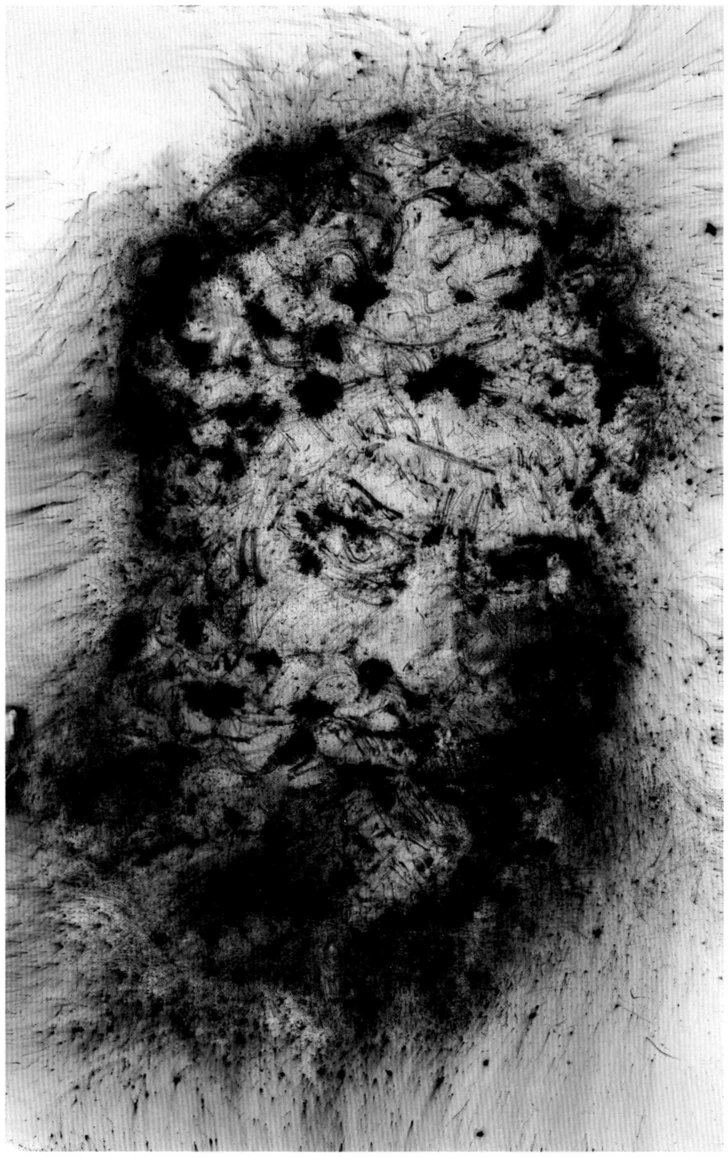

3.5 *Study for Pompeii No. 4: Hercules*

3.4

*Study for Pompeii No. 3: Hercules*

庞贝研究第三号：大力神

2018

Gunpowder on canvas

240 × 150 cm

3.5

*Study for Pompeii No. 4: Hercules*

庞贝研究第四号：大力神

2018

Gunpowder on canvas

240 × 150 cm

3.6

*Study for Pompeii: Fierce Lion*

庞贝研究：雄狮

2018

Gunpowder on canvas

300 × 300 cm

3.7

*Study for Pompeii No. 2*

庞贝研究第二号

2018

Gunpowder on canvas

122 × 122 cm

Cai introduced a new technique of "incense stick painting" while preparing for this exhibition. Cai remarked, "The sprinkling and caressing of the gunpowder to form the initial outline is dictated by my instincts and sensibilities; holding the ignited incense to trigger explosion of the gunpowder wherever it goes carries with it the inertia from my artistic training. At the end, I add more gunpowder, cover the canvas to obscure the image, and explode it with a single 'boom.' This feels like reining in all the processes with one fell swoop, returning to the energy itself."

Unlike the artist's usual gunpowder painting method of igniting the canvas with a fuse and backing away to await the explosion's result, the "painterliness" of holding the incense and igniting wherever his hand moves evoked the intimacy of sketching with charcoal from his youth.

The new technique can be observed in works in the *Studies for Pompeii* series, in which he explored the museum's iconic collection, such as fresco paintings from its "Secret Cabinet" (no. 3.7) and *Farnese Hercules* (nos. 3.4–5), as well as a lion from the history of Pompeii's amphitheater (no. 3.6).

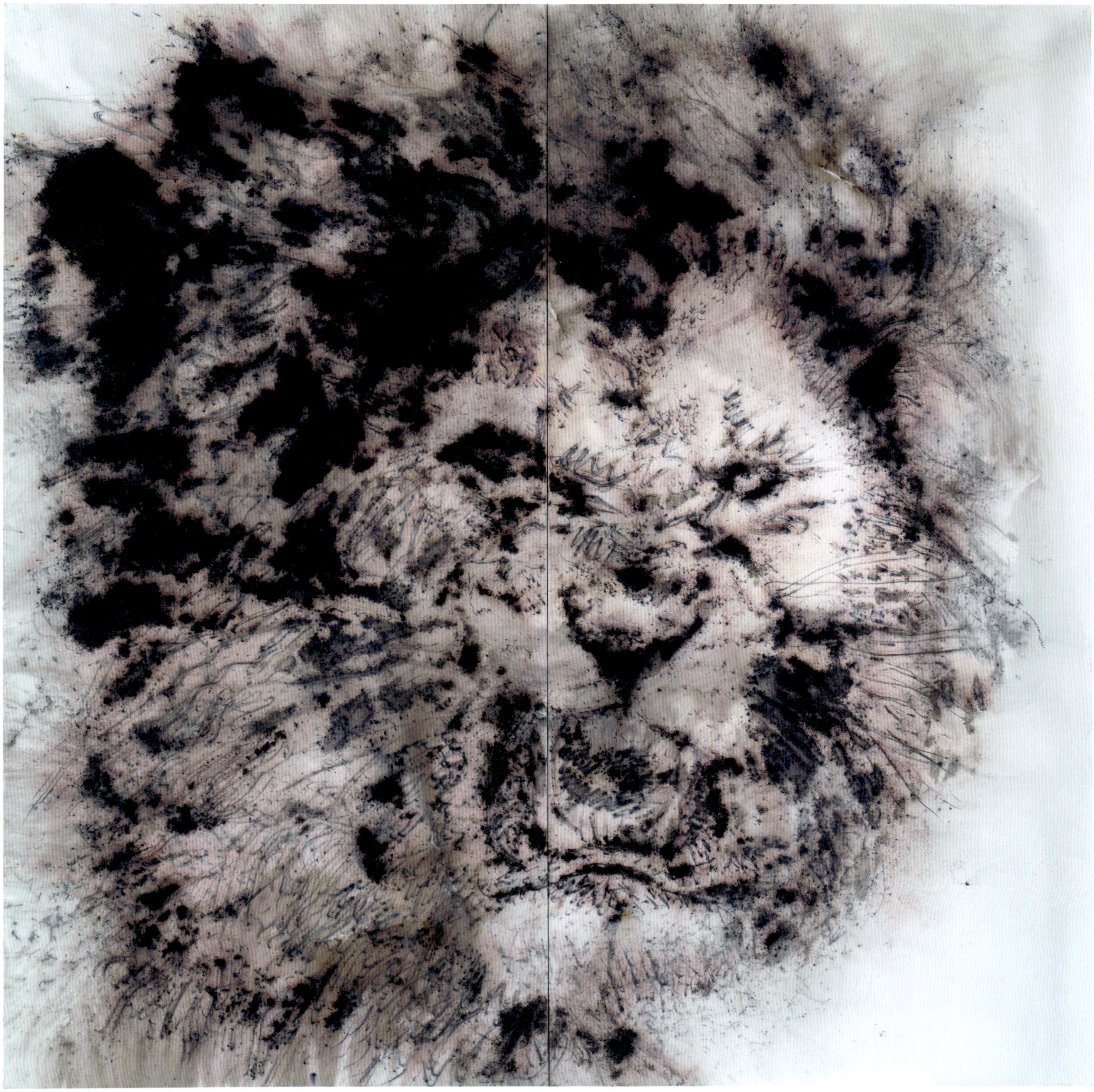

3.6 *Study for Pompeii: Fierce Lion*

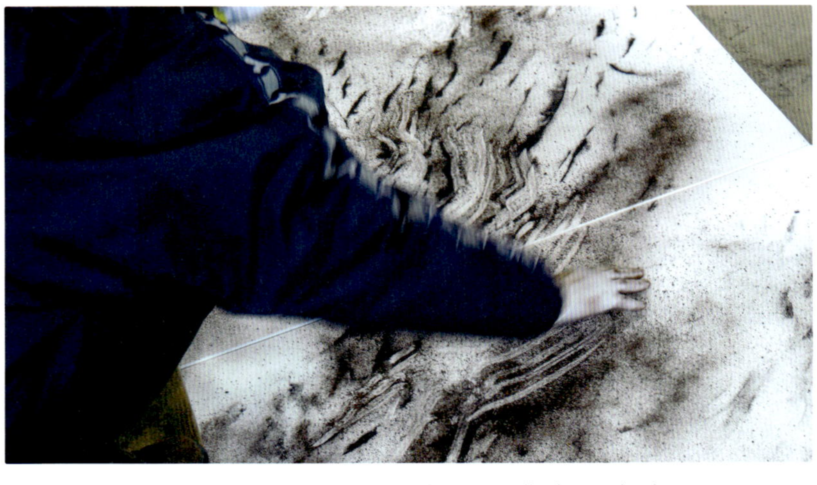

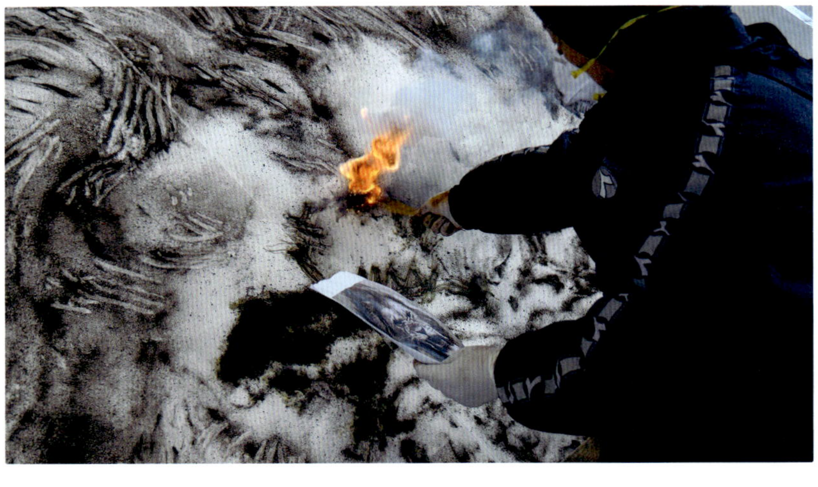

Figures 3.11a–b. Creation process of *Study for Pompeii: Fierce Lion* in 2018

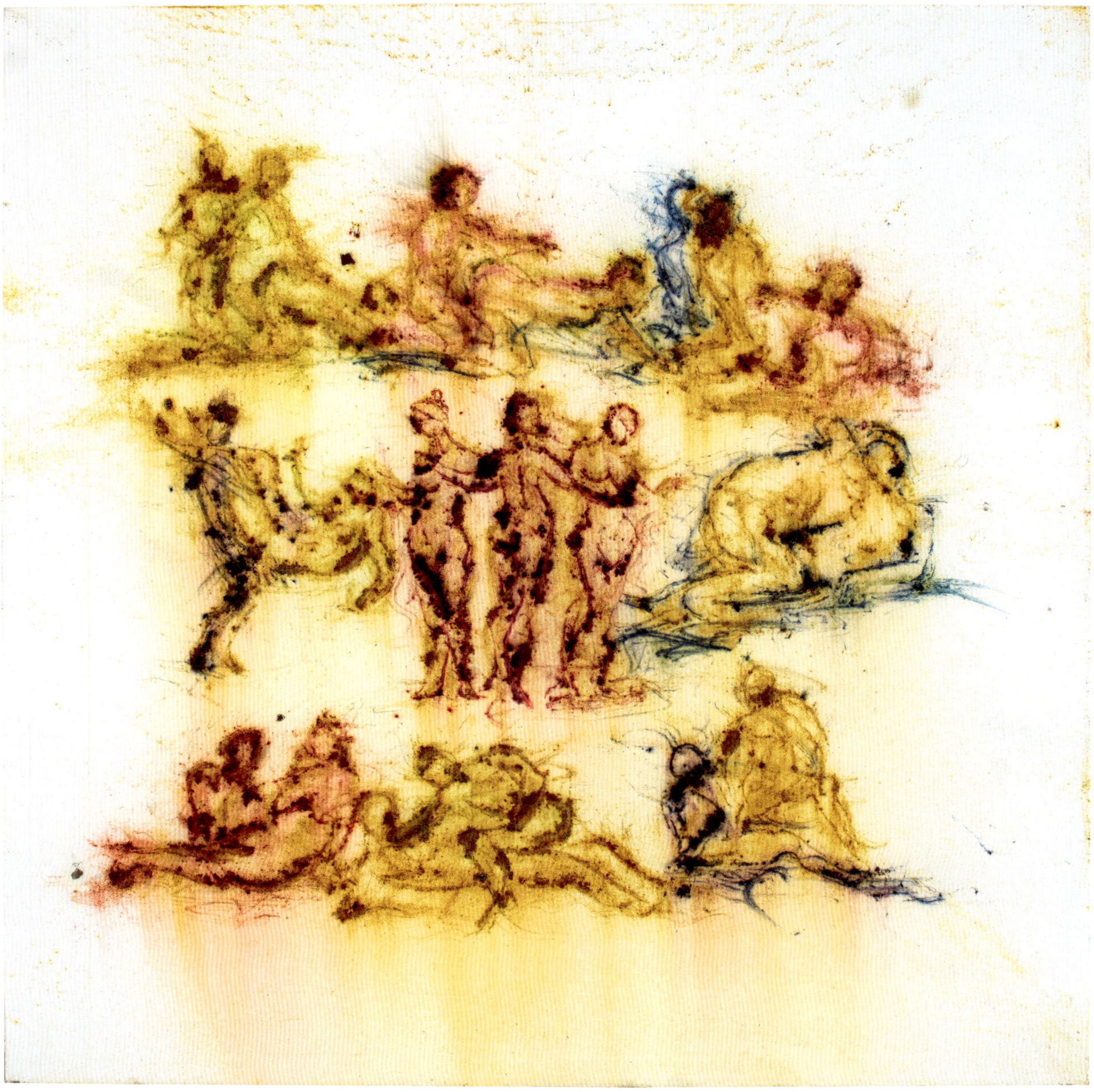
3.7 *Study for Pompeii No. 2*

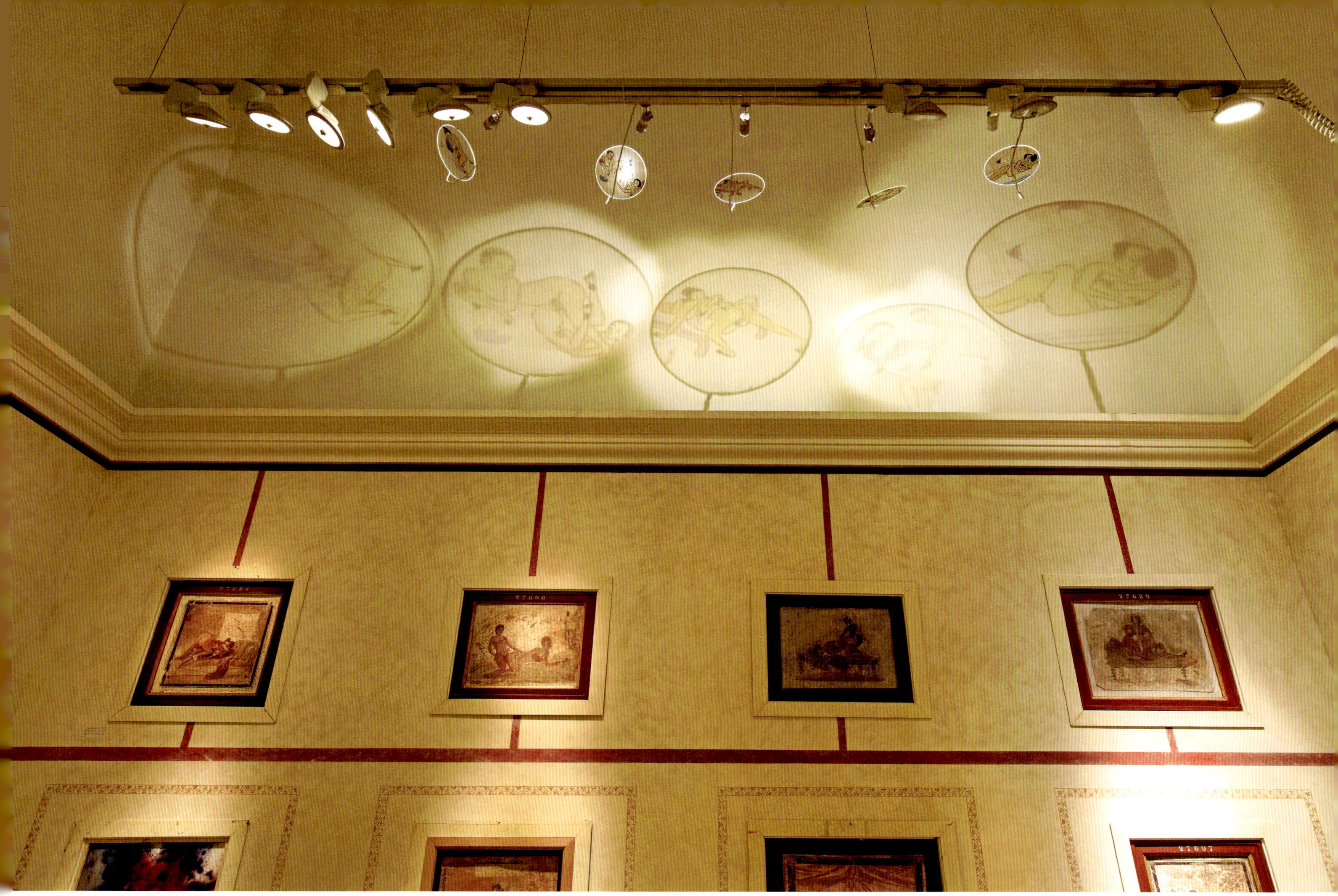

Figure 3.12. *Shunga Puppet Show*, 2019. Printed overhead projector sheets and wire, set of 5 pieces, 20 × 20 cm each

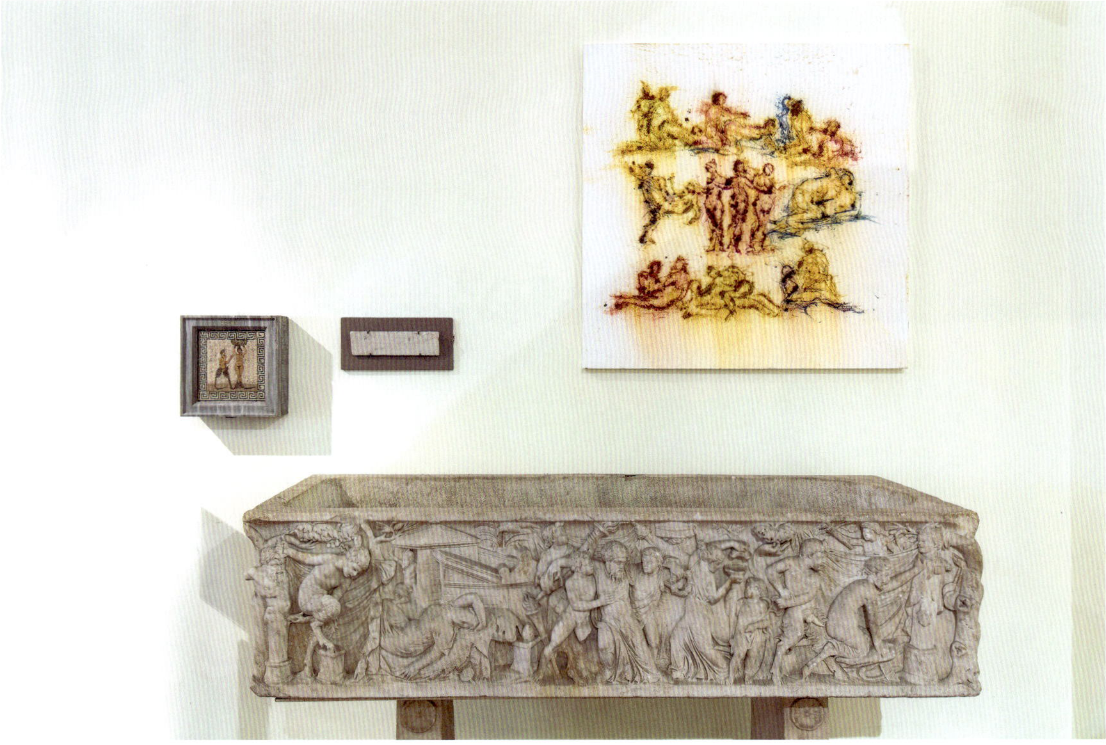

Figure 3.13. Installation view of *In the Volcano: Cai Guo-Qiang and Pompeii*

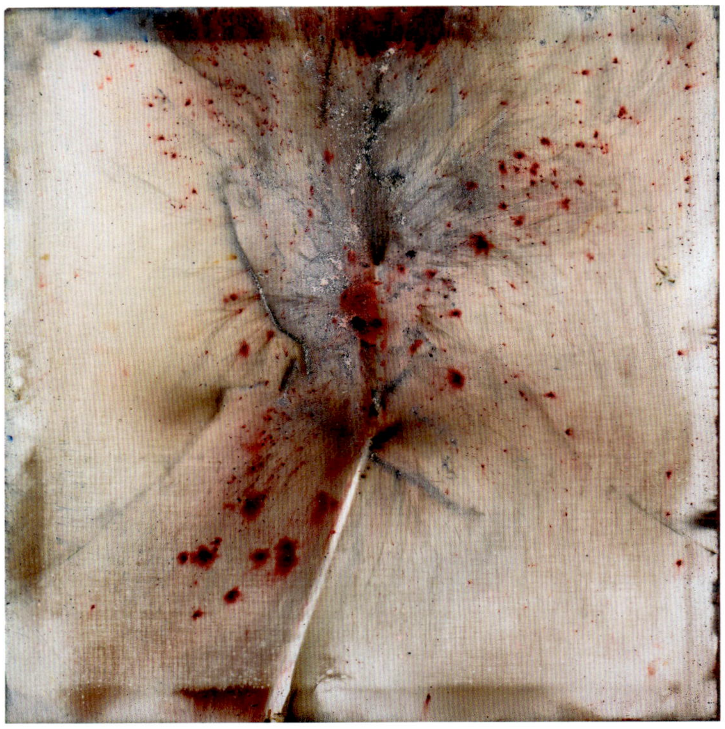

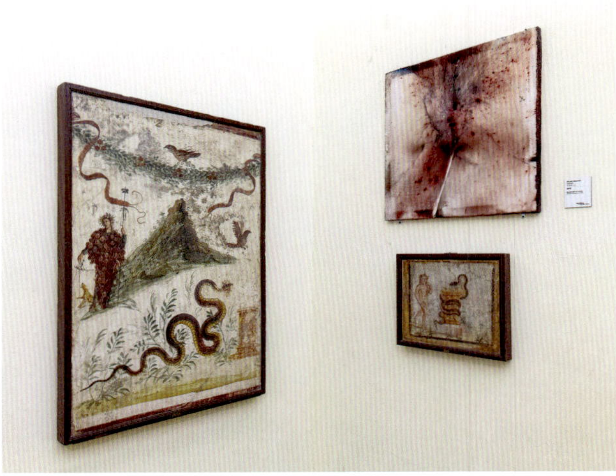

Figure 3.14. Installation view of *In the Volcano: Cai Guo-Qiang and Pompeii*

3.8 *Mount Vesuvius*

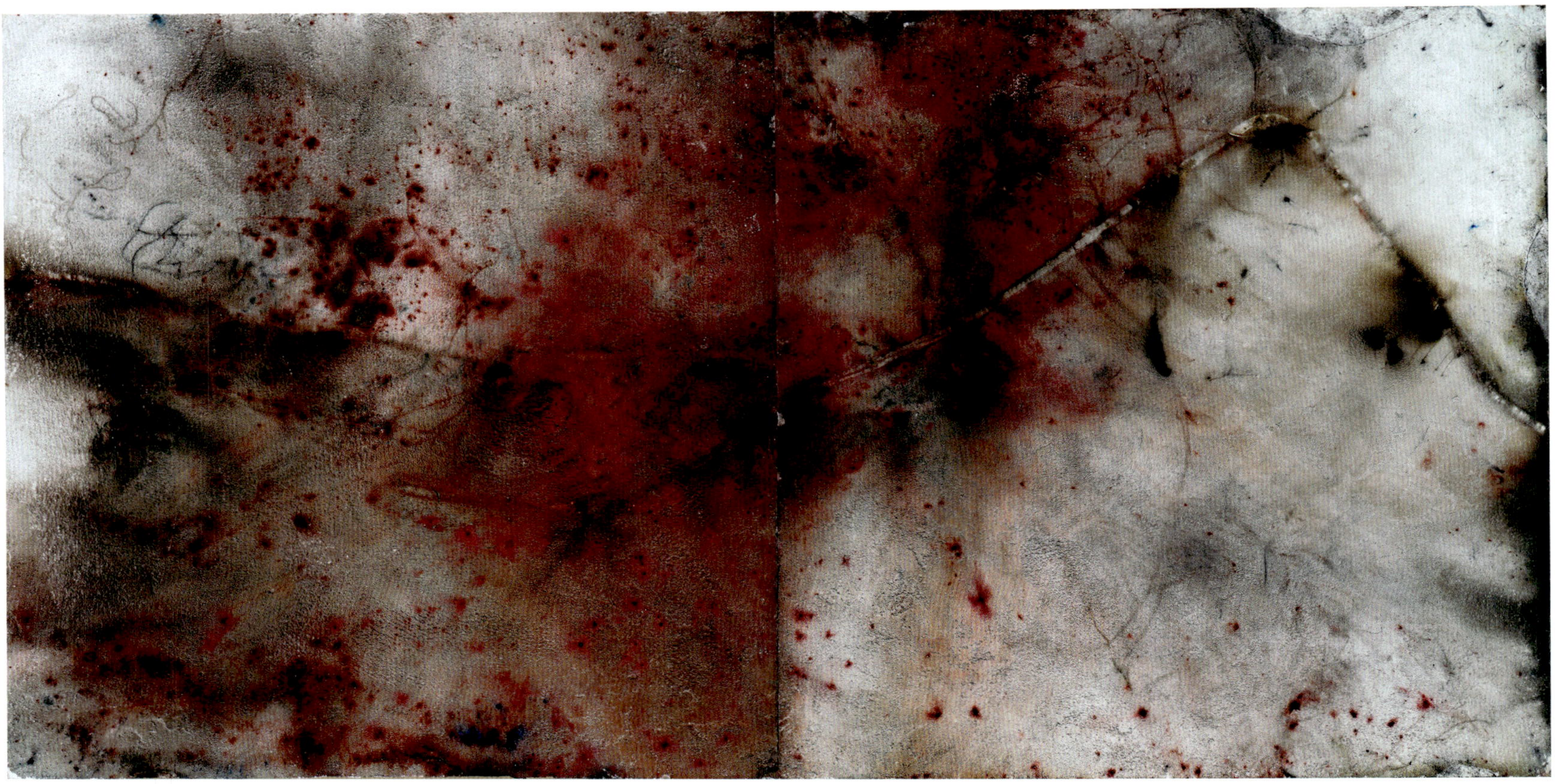

3.9 *Pompeiian Red*

3.8

*Mount Vesuvius*

维苏威火山

2019

Gunpowder on canvas

80 × 80 cm

One of the works from *Explosion Studio*, *Mount Vesuvius* captures Cai's vision of the volcano's eruption nearly two thousand years ago—a catastrophe that both devoured and preserved the ancient city of Pompeii.

3.9

*Pompeiian Red*

庞贝红

2019

Gunpowder on panel for fresco

122 × 244 cm

Part of *Explosion Studio*, this work was created on panels prepared by MANN experts using techniques from ancient Pompeiian frescoes. Over the primed panels, Cai exploded red color gunpowder from China to re-create a distinctly Pompeiian red hue.

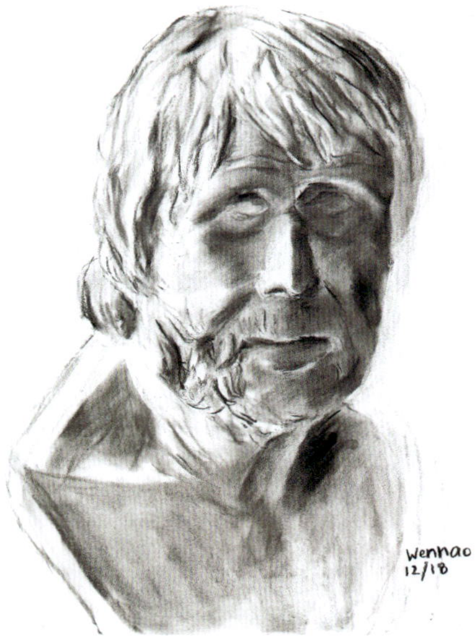


3.10 Wenhao Cai, *Wenhao's Sketch of Seneca*

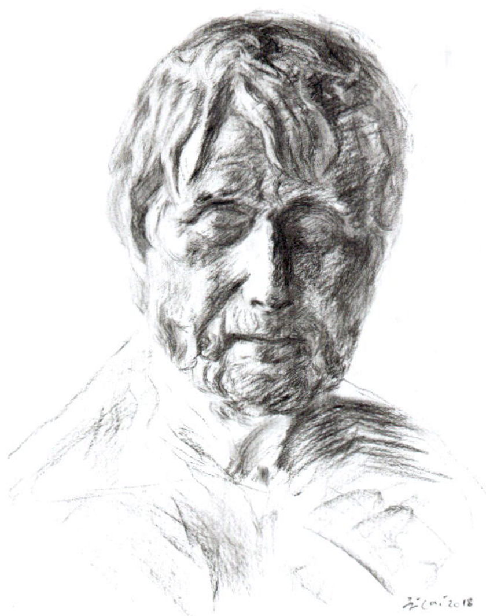

3.11 *Cai's Sketch of Seneca*

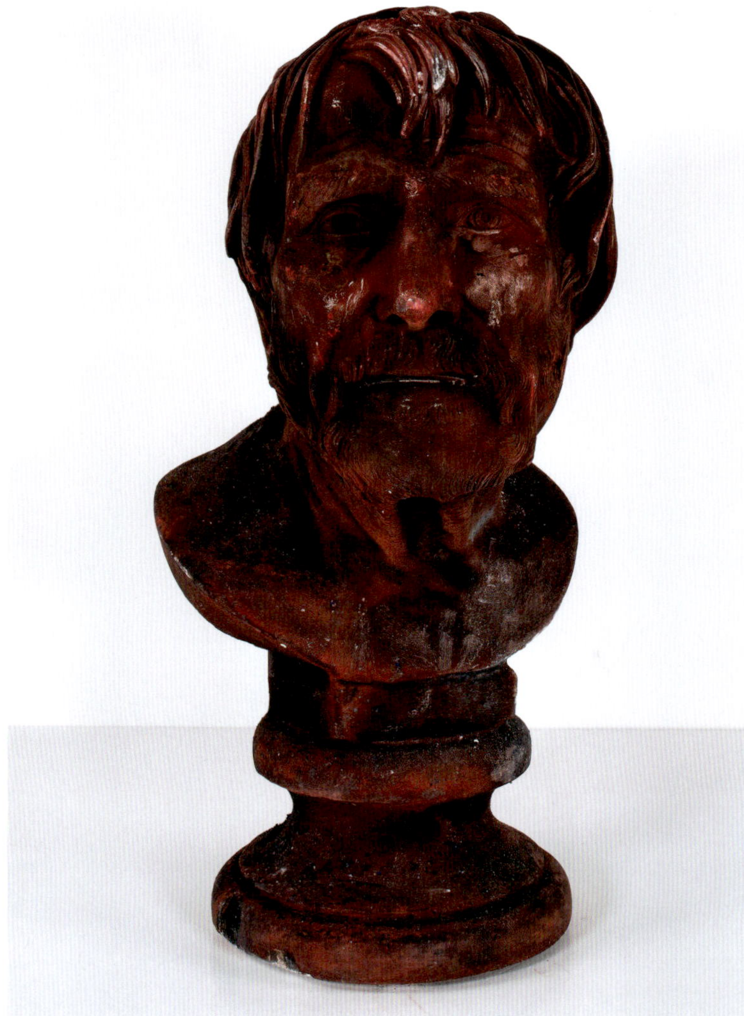

3.12 *Pseudo-Seneca: Red*

3.10

Wenhao Cai

*Wenhao's Sketch of Seneca*

蔡文浩

文浩速写塞内加

2018

Charcoal on paper

43 × 35.5 cm

3.11

*Cai's Sketch of Seneca*

蔡速写塞内加

2018

Charcoal on paper

43 × 35.5 cm

3.12

*Pseudo-Seneca: Red*

塞内加：红

2019

Gunpowder on plaster

49 × 23 × 24 cm

*Pseudo-Seneca*, an iconic sculpture in MANN's collection, was a recurring subject for the adolescent Cai while growing up in a distant, small city, as well as for other artists of his generation.

For the Naples exhibition, Cai exploded plaster copies of the *Pseudo Seneca* in the Pompeii Amphitheatre. He also asked his younger daughter, who shares his love for painting, to join him in sketching the statue and retracing the intersecting rivers of time.

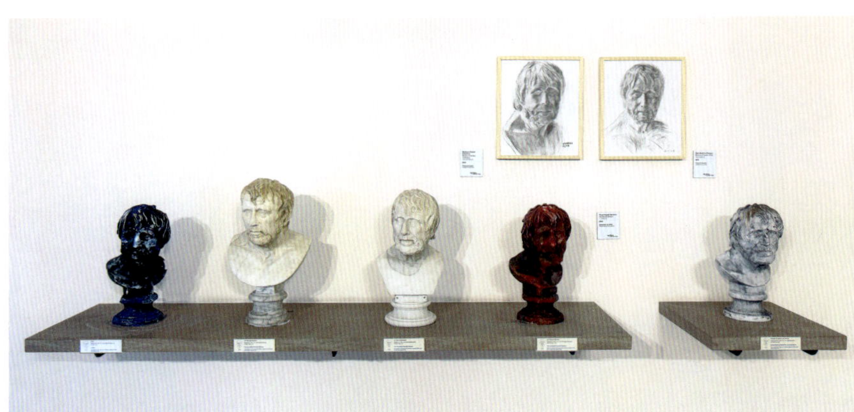

Figure 3.15. Installation view with sculptures on shelves. From left to right: *Pseudo-Seneca: Blue*, two works from MANN collection, *Pseudo-Seneca: Red*, and *Pseudo-Seneca: Gray*

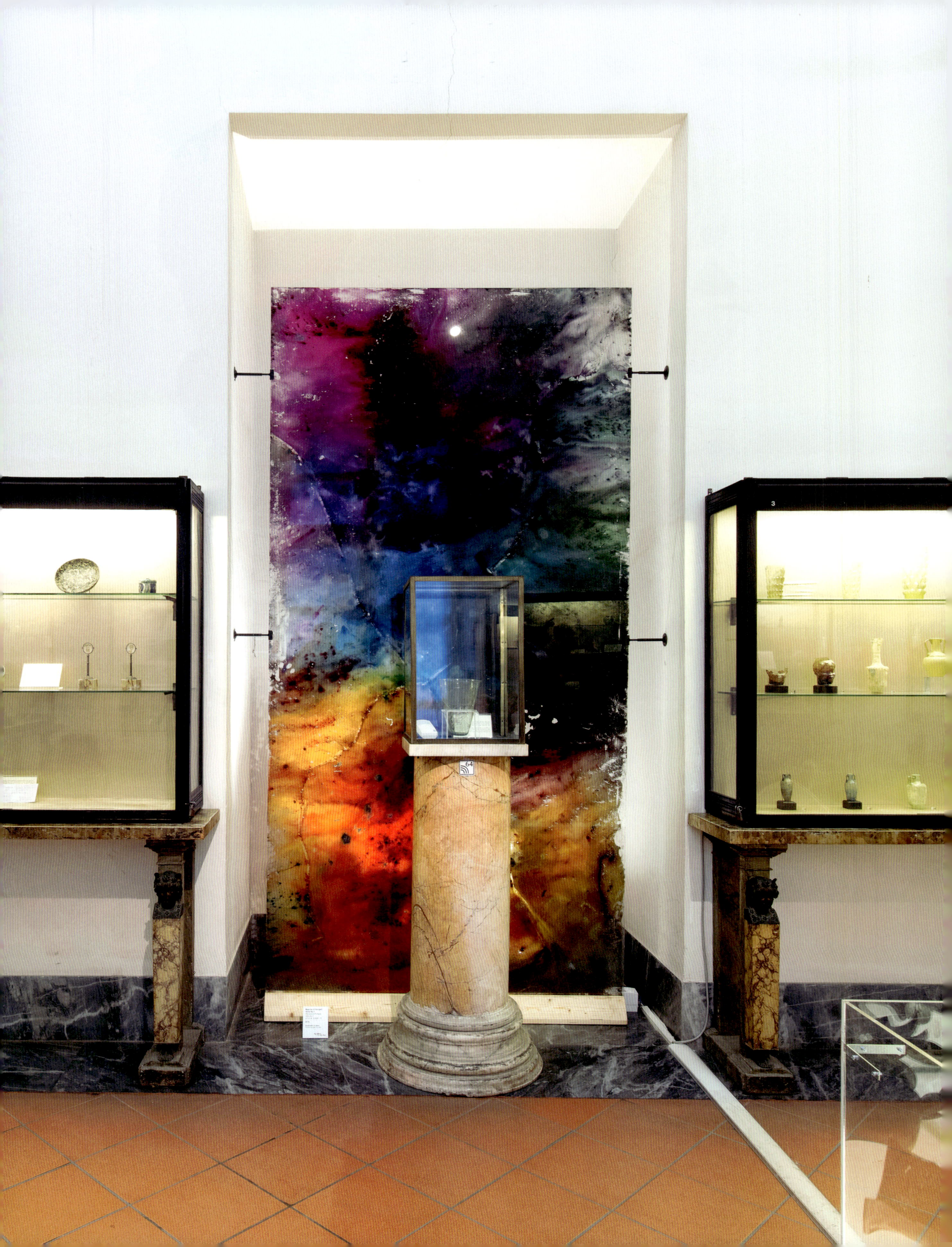

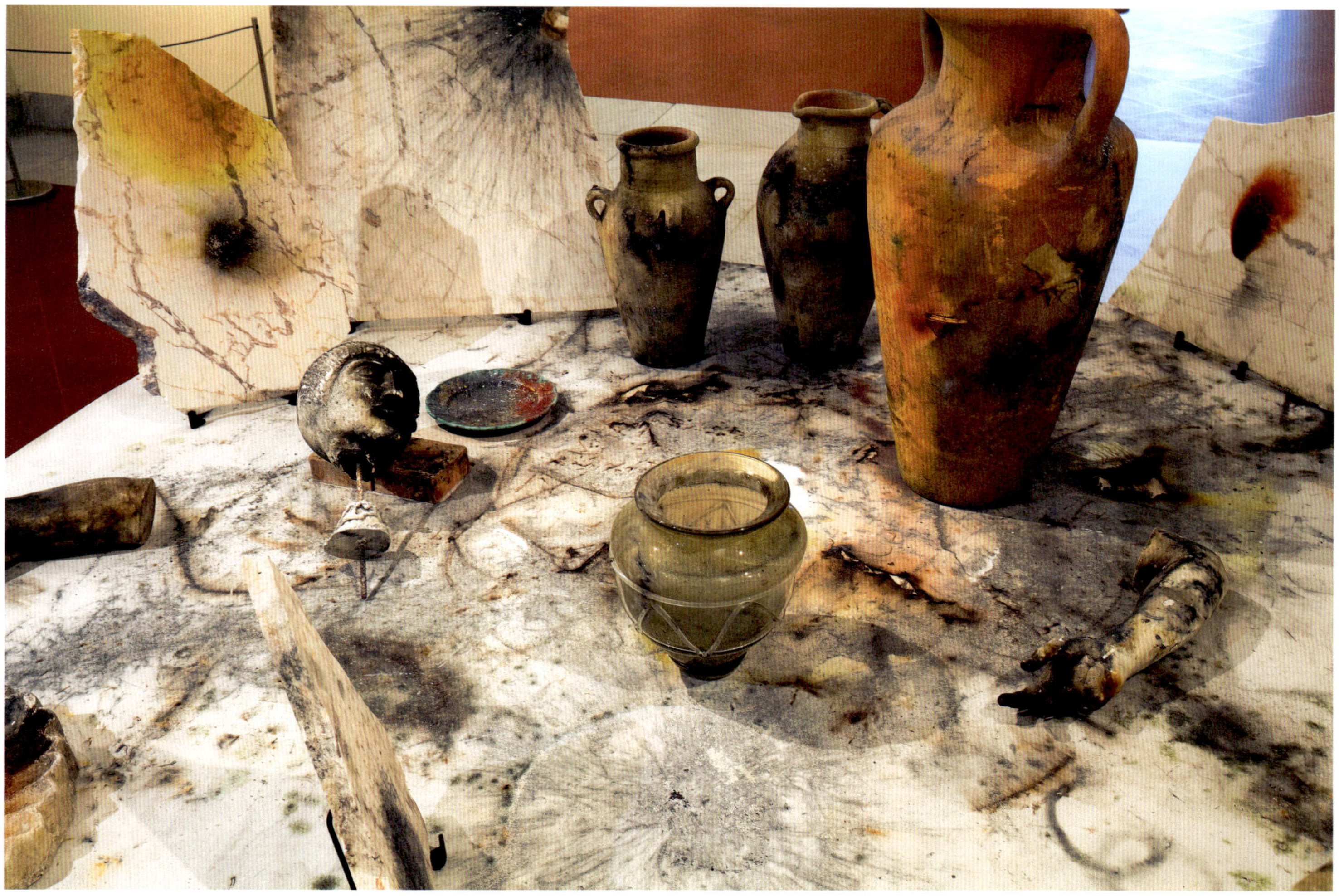

3.14 *Camorra Test*

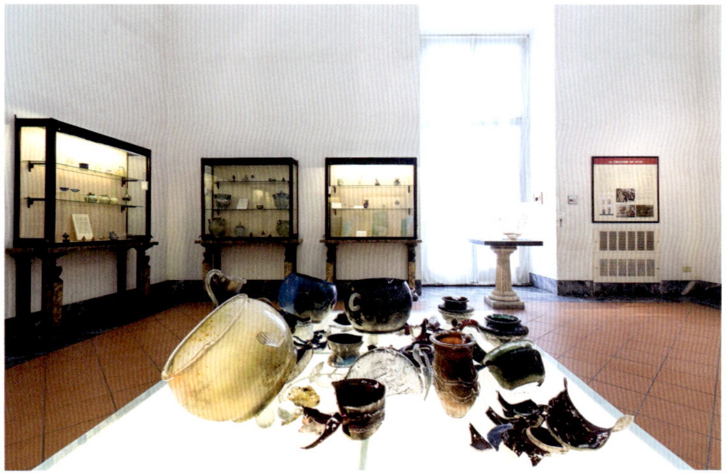

Figure 3.16. Installation view with *Memory of Pompeii: Glass No. 2* in the foreground

3.13

*Memory of Pompeii: Glass No. 1*

庞贝往事：玻璃第一号

2019

Gunpowder on glass

300 × 150 cm

3.14

*Camorra Test*

卡莫拉试炸

2018

Gunpowder on plaster, marble, glassware, porcelain, terracotta, brick, concrete, wire, and canvas

Dimensions variable

*Memory of Pompeii: Glass No. 1* was created in the explosion at the Pompeii Amphitheatre and *Camorra Test* from the explosion test at the foot of Mount Vesuvius. Thus installed, together with *Memory of Pompeii: Glass No. 2*, among MANN's collected glassware, mosaics, and murals, they engage in dialogue with the ancient pieces both in their themes and their mediums.

3.13 *Memory of Pompeii: Glass No. 1* (opposite)

Figure 3.17 (overleaf). Installation view with *Study for Pompeii No. 3: Hercules* (no. 3.4, left wall), *Explosion Studio*, a 2019 gunpowder painting (under ceiling), and *Exploding Hercules* (no. 3.2, far right)

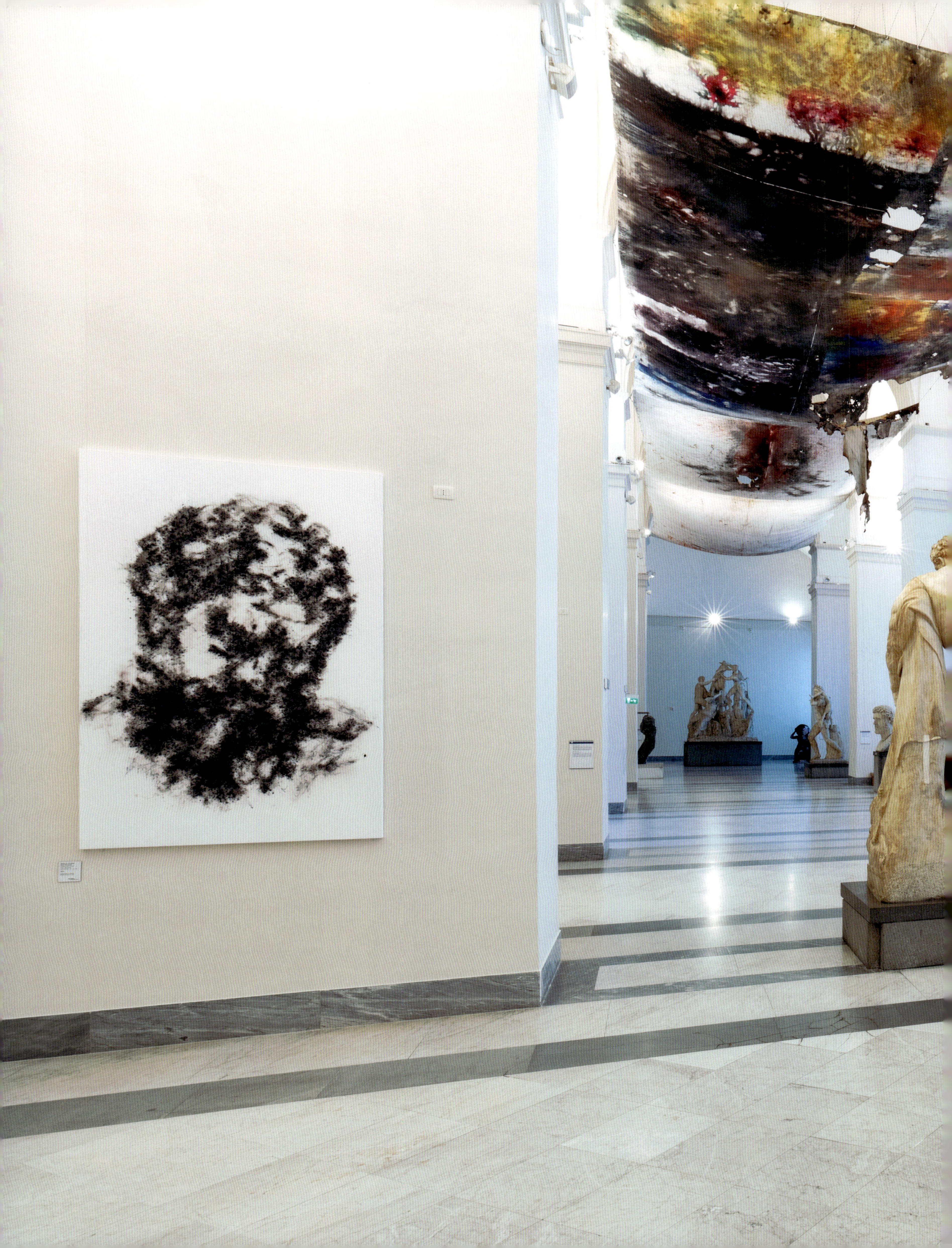

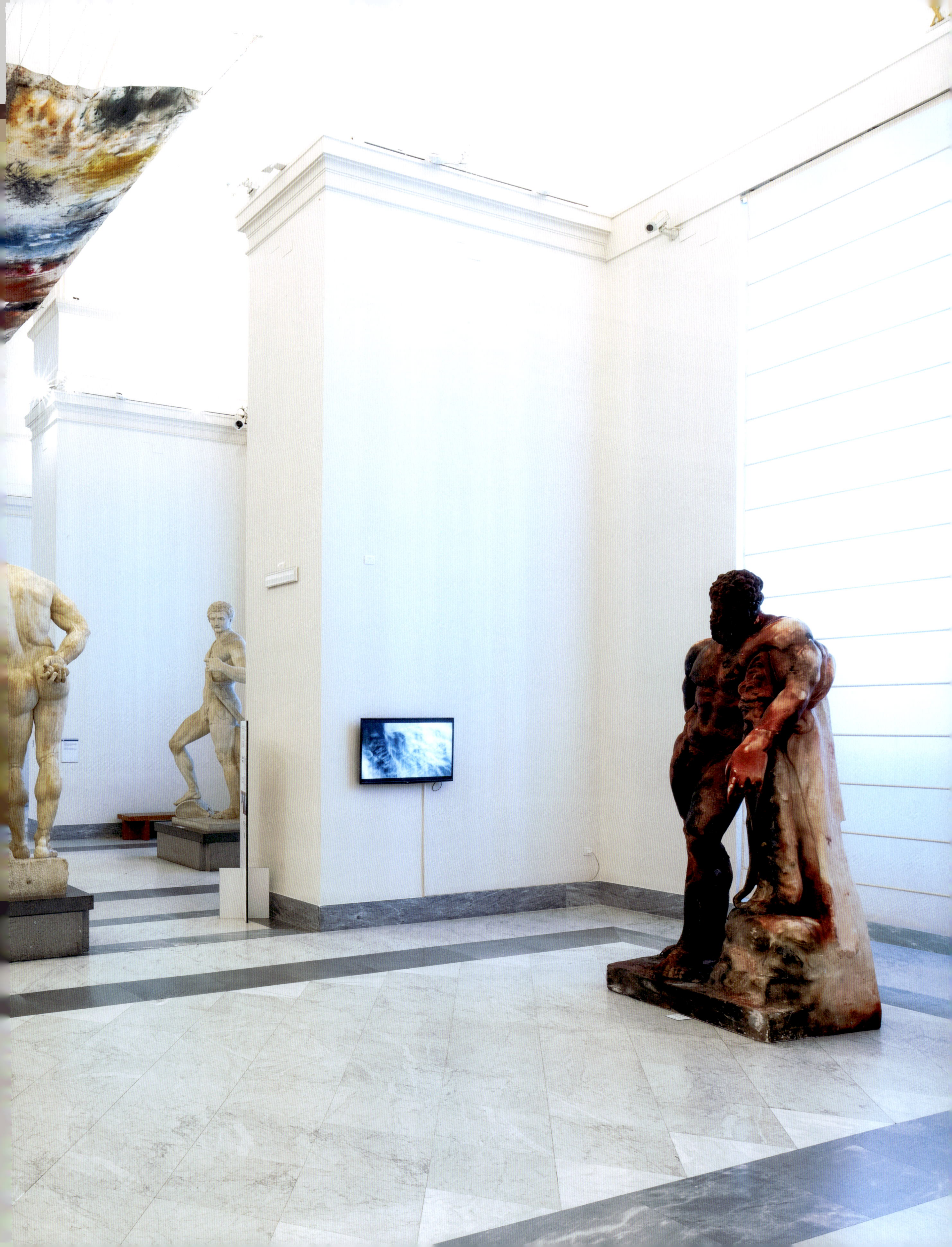

# 4

# Dialogue with Socialist Realism and Avant-Garde Art

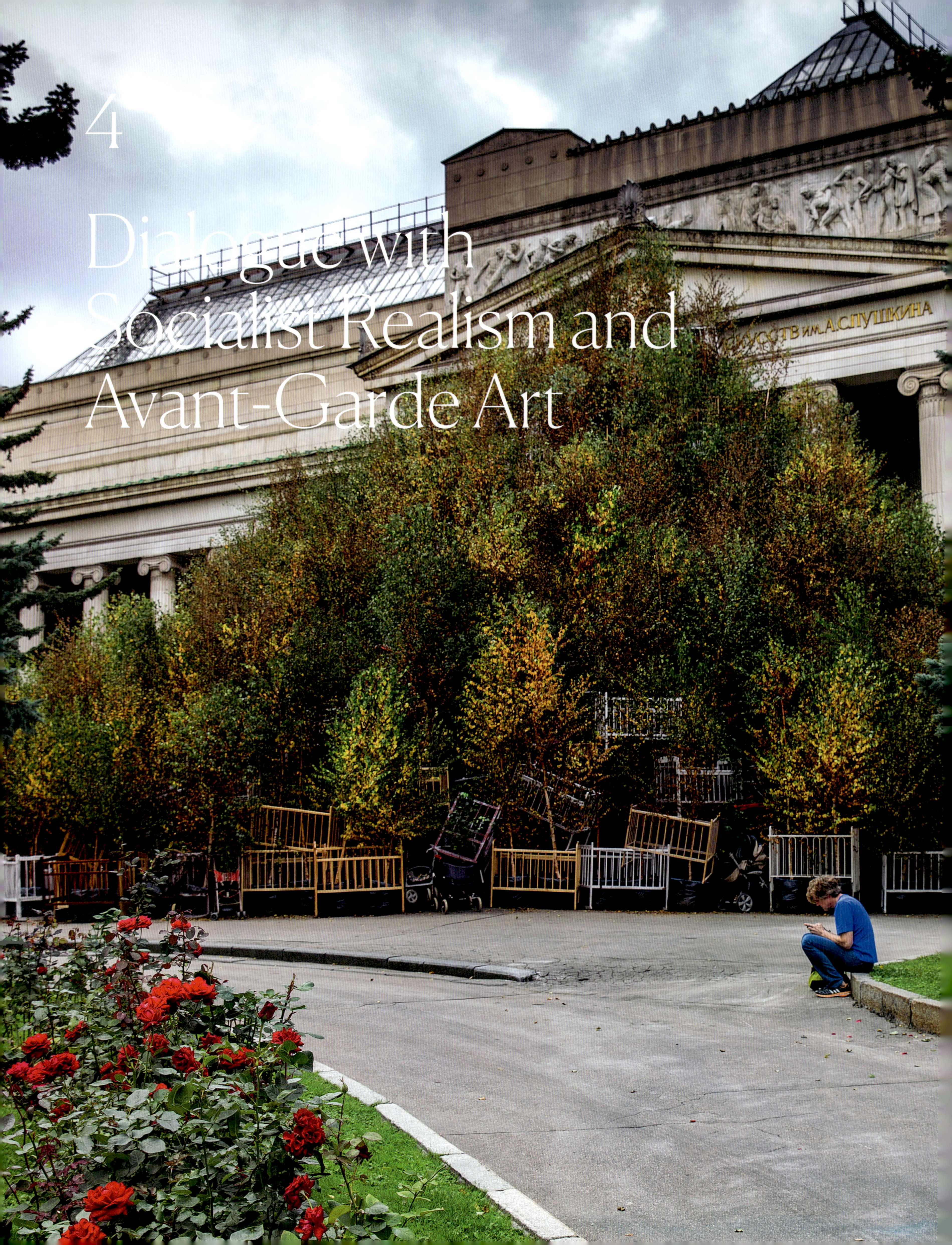

# *Cai Guo-Qiang: October*

Pushkin State Museum of Fine Arts, Moscow, Russia
September 13–November 12, 2017

Curated by Alexandra Danilova, Senior Curator, 19th and 20th Century Art, Pushkin Museum

Public painting creation: VDNKh Pavilion No. 22, Moscow, September 2–10, 2017

Catalogue: bilingual Russian-English edition published by the Pushkin Museum

Documentary film: *October: The Unrealized Century*, directed by Shanshan Xia, released by the Pushkin Museum (75:00)

Cai's first solo exhibition in Russia, *October* was a site-specific, multimedia presentation created for the Pushkin Museum, an institution established in 1912. Its holding of 700,000 works encompasses a long history from ancient Greece to the early 21st century, including one half of the modern works collected by Sergei Shchukin, a prominent Russian textile merchant and legendary art collector.

Cai grew up in a socialist culture and received his initial training in Western art through Soviet Socialist Realism. Since his youth, he has been fascinated by realist and Socialist Realist art including Pavel Chistyakov's systematized sketching, Ivan Kramskoi's *Portrait of an Unknown Woman*, Isaac Levitan's *By the Whirpool*, Boris Ioganson's bold strokes and murky gray tones, and Evsey Moiseyenko's *Sweet Cherries*. He has also studied the life of Konstantin Maksimov, a Soviet painter chosen by the Soviet Union to teach in China in the 1950s. Responsible for reshaping the entire fate of Chinese painting, Maksimov was later swiftly and thoroughly forgotten by history due to subsequent political upheaval. Cai has gone on to collect nearly two hundred fifty of Maksimov's works and, after more than a decade of labored searching, finally located the painter's grave, the tombstone engraved with an incorrect death date, on the eve of *October*'s exhibition opening.

Timed for the centenary of the October Revolution, the exhibition engaged this complex period of history by addressing the themes of revolution, idealism, and utopia. Through the combination of large-scale spectacular installations, monumental paintings, and animated video, Cai adeptly orchestrated the vast energy both inside and outside the museum's classical and palatial architecture, which has weathered the grand yet tragic history from the Revolution to World War II, from the Cold War to the dissolution of the Soviet Union. His dialogue centered on the legacy of Socialist Realism and the avant-garde, and how it was affected by the rise and collapse of utopia. His ultimate concern was the role of the individual in the changing tides of history, and how individual dreams and humanity's ideals were intersected.

The October Revolution forever altered the historical trajectory of Russia and the rest of the world. By revisiting his personal history and growth, Cai urges others to regard and reflect on this period of Russian history as the shared fate and story of humankind.

Installation view of *Autumn* (no. 4.1) outside the Pushkin State Museum of Fine Arts in 2017

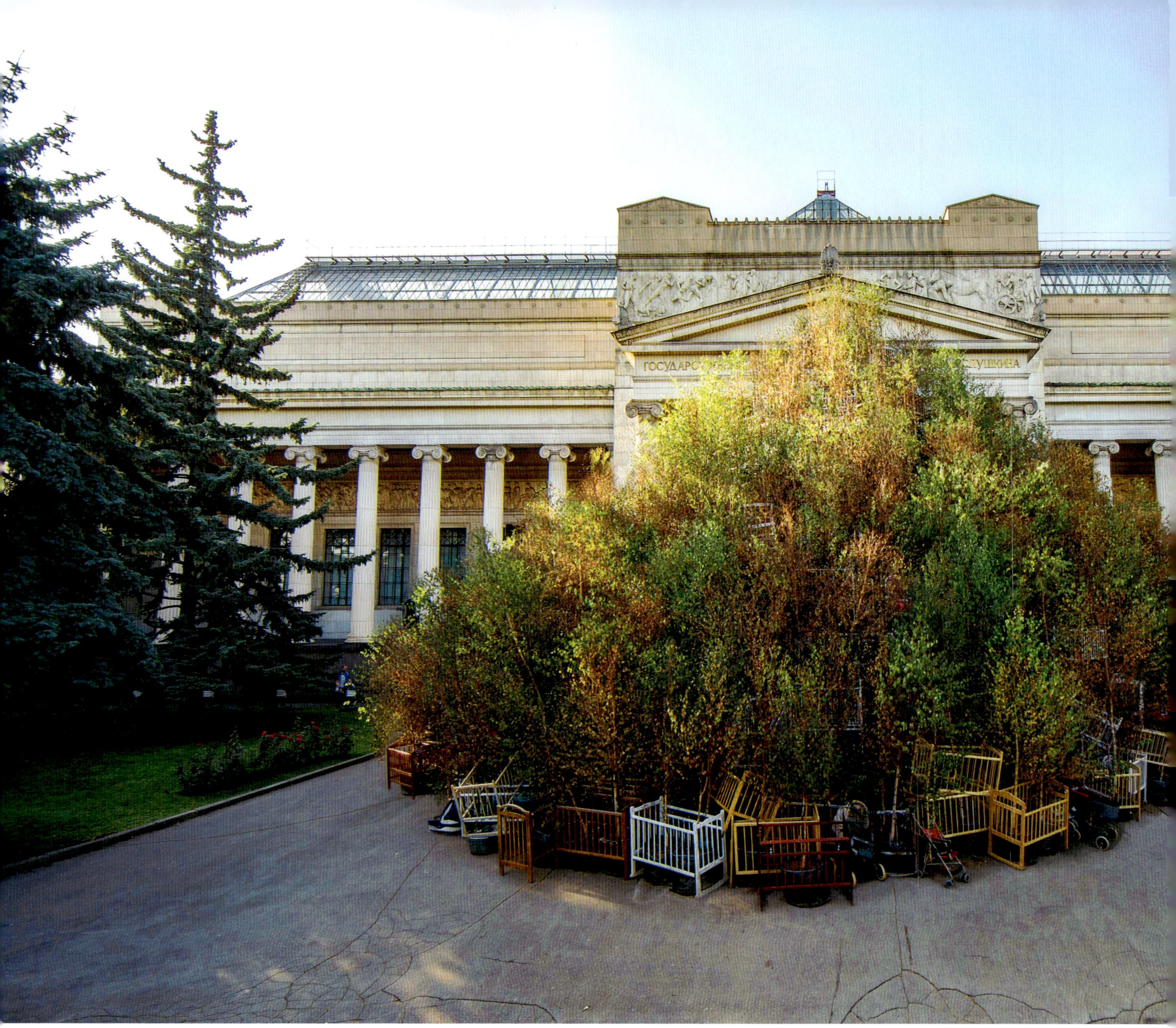

4.1

*Autumn*

秋天

2017

Installation with strollers, cribs, baby beds, and birch trees

Approx. 1500 × 2300 × 1500 cm

*Autumn* was a large mountain that blocked the palatial entrance to the Pushkin Museum's century-old halls. The installation was composed of hundreds of used baby cradles, cribs, and strollers donated by Moscow residents, like vessels carrying people's long-forgotten memories and earliest dreams. Birch trees of approximately 3 meters in height were planted in the cradles to form a lush forest. As the seasons changed from fall to winter over the course of the exhibition, the leaves changed from golden and shimmering to faded and wilted, until eventually the mountain slope was coated with fallen yellow leaves. The white birch branches and the mountain of cradles were presented as a Constructivist skeleton, narrating the vicissitudes of human fate. *Autumn* evokes a tomb of collective utopian ideals and symbolizes the beginnings of individual dreams, as well as forming a monument to the human pursuit of beautiful dreams.

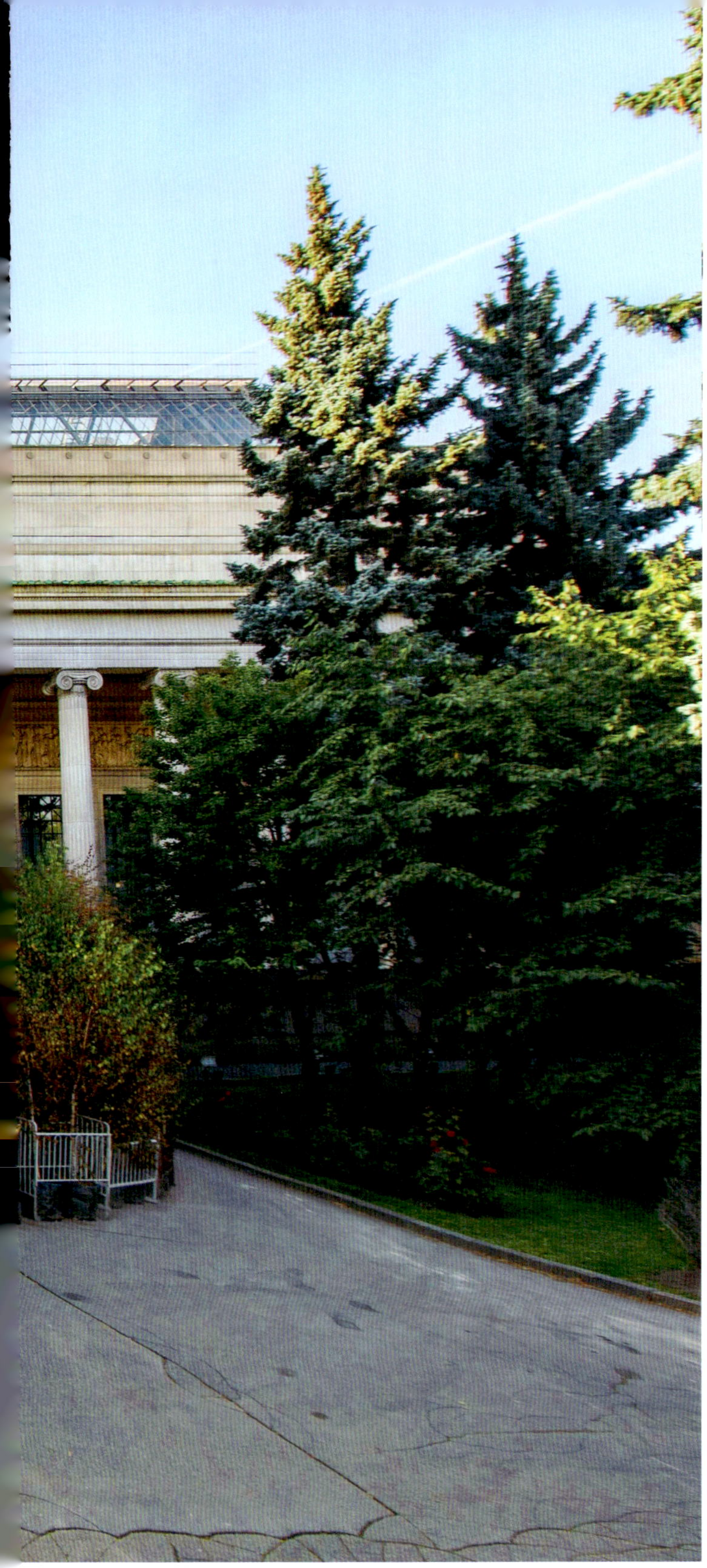

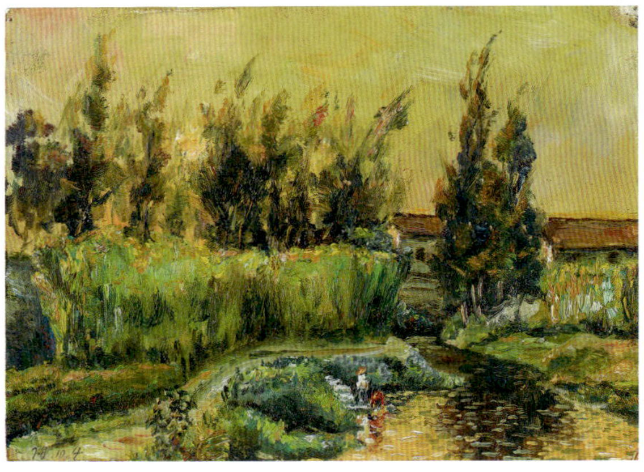

Figure 4.1. *Waterfront Sunset*, c. 1970s. Oil on cardstock, 19.3 × 27 cm

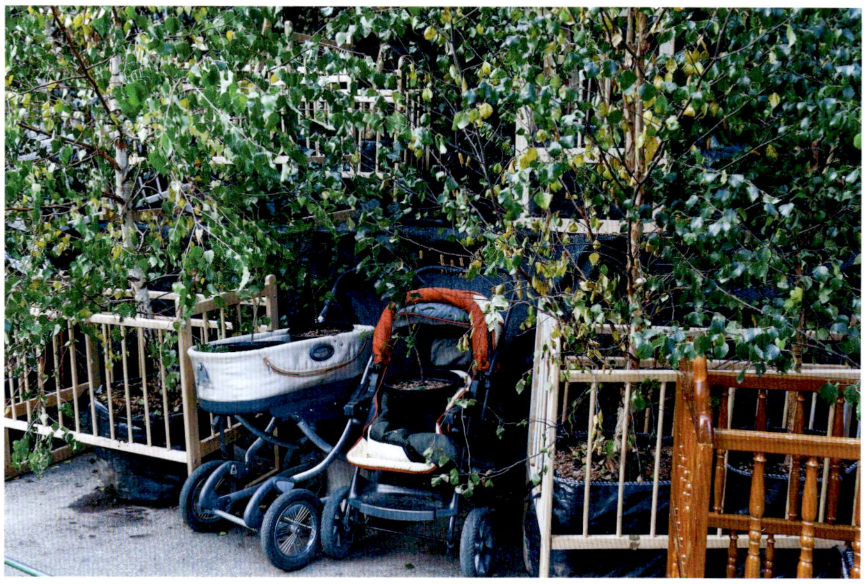

Figure 4.2. Detail of *Autumn*

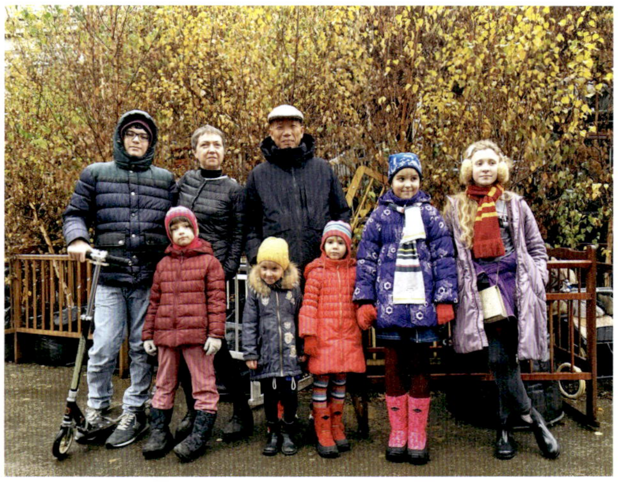

Figure 4.3. Cai Guo-Qiang with children in Moscow who donated strollers and cradles for the construction of *Autumn* in 2017

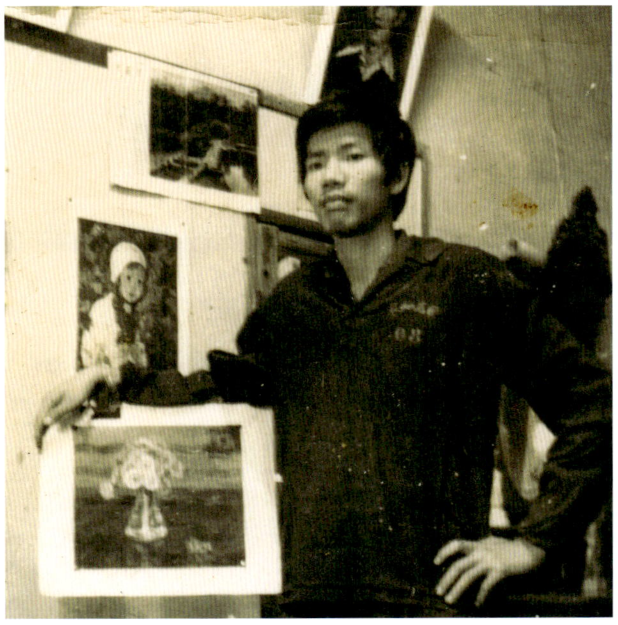

Figure 4.4. Cai Guo-Qiang in his studio in Quanzhou in 1979

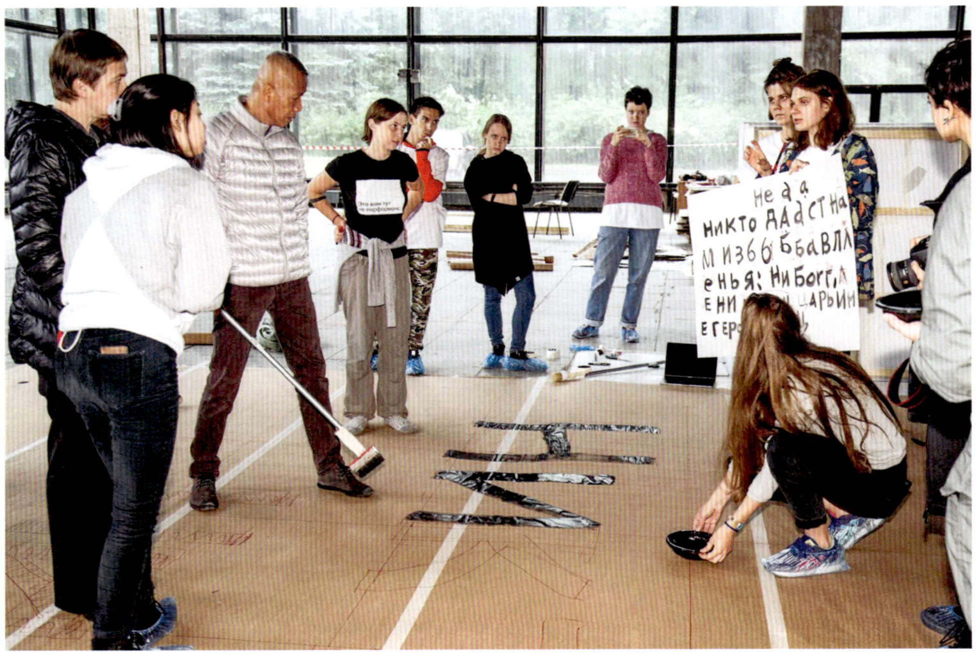

Figure 4.5. Cai Guo-Qiang and volunteers during the creation of *The Sound* in Moscow in 2017

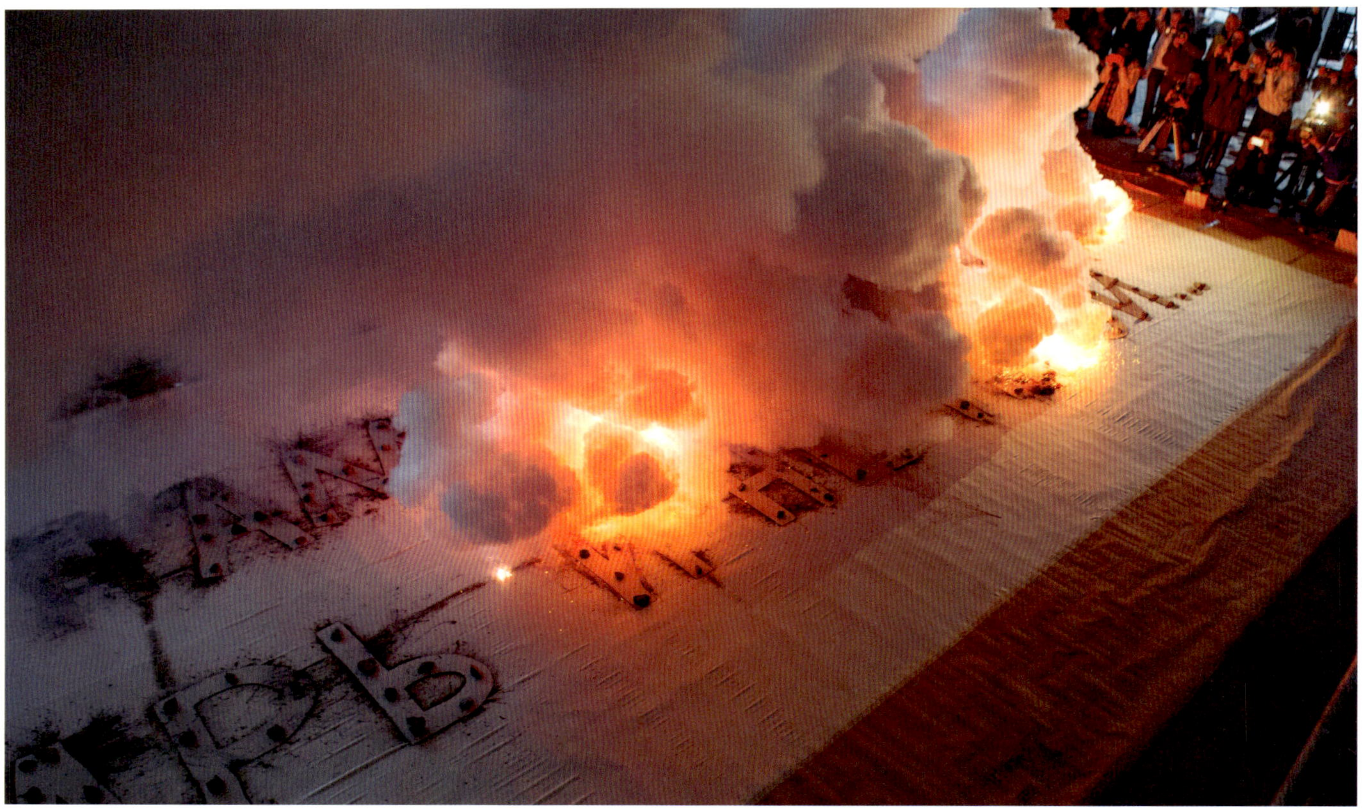

Figure 4.6. Ignition of *The Sound* in Moscow in 2017

4.2

## *The Sound*

## 声音

2017

Gunpowder on silk

470 × 2000 cm

*The Sound* is a piece of smooth white silk scorched with black gunpowder to form a cautionary Russian lyric from "The Internationale": "There are no supreme saviors: neither God, nor tsar, nor hero!" The work hangs above the Pushkin Museum's atrium along its central axis, like a vast expanse of open sky, enveloping the lofty, classical stairwell and facing visitors as they ascend its steps. The two-dimensional art of calligraphy and painting is transformed into a three-dimensional installation filled with boundless poetic majesty.

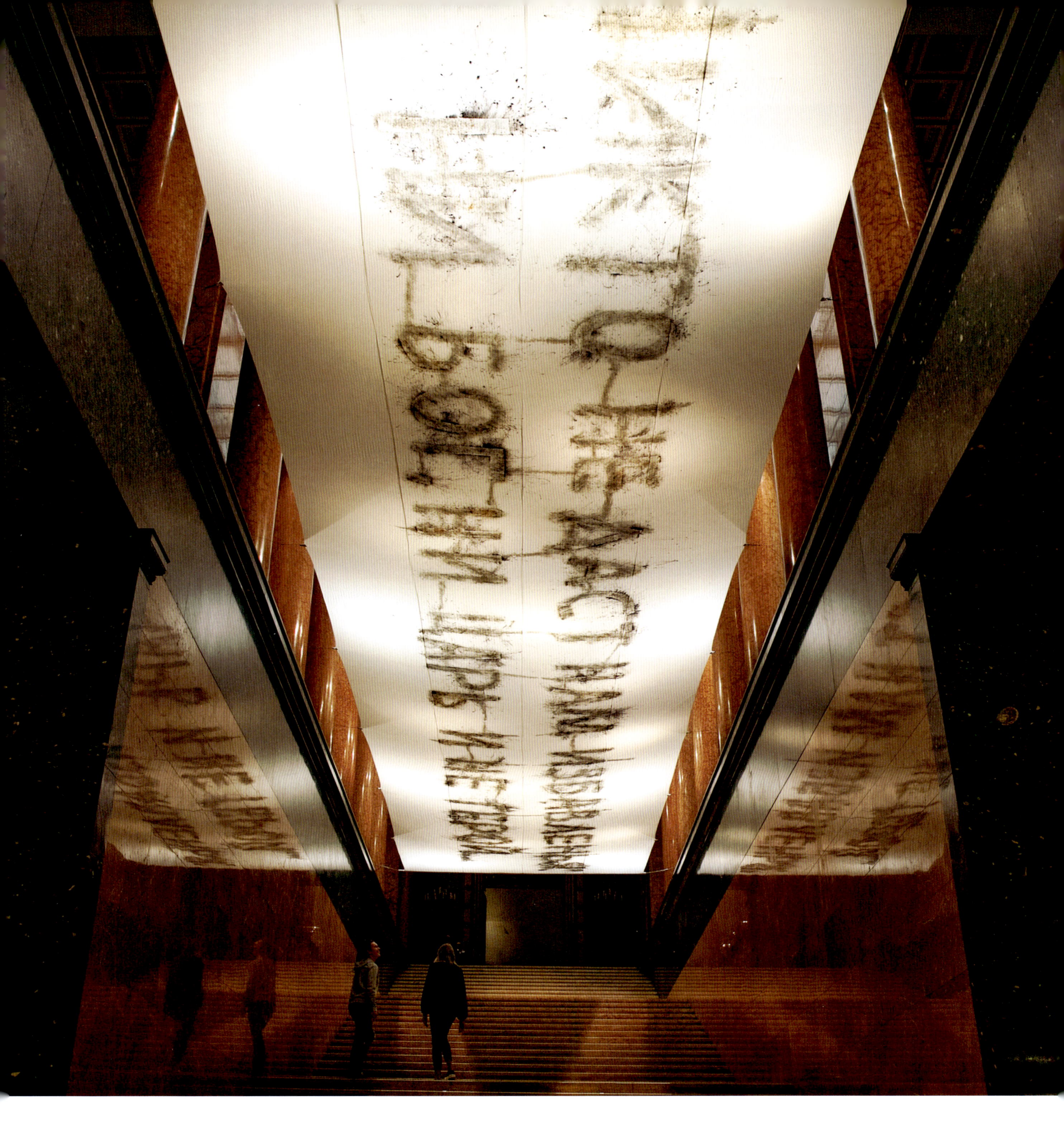
НИКТО НЕ ДАСТ НАМ ИЗБАВЛЕНЬЯ
НИ БОГ НИ ЦАРЬ И НЕ ГЕРОЙ

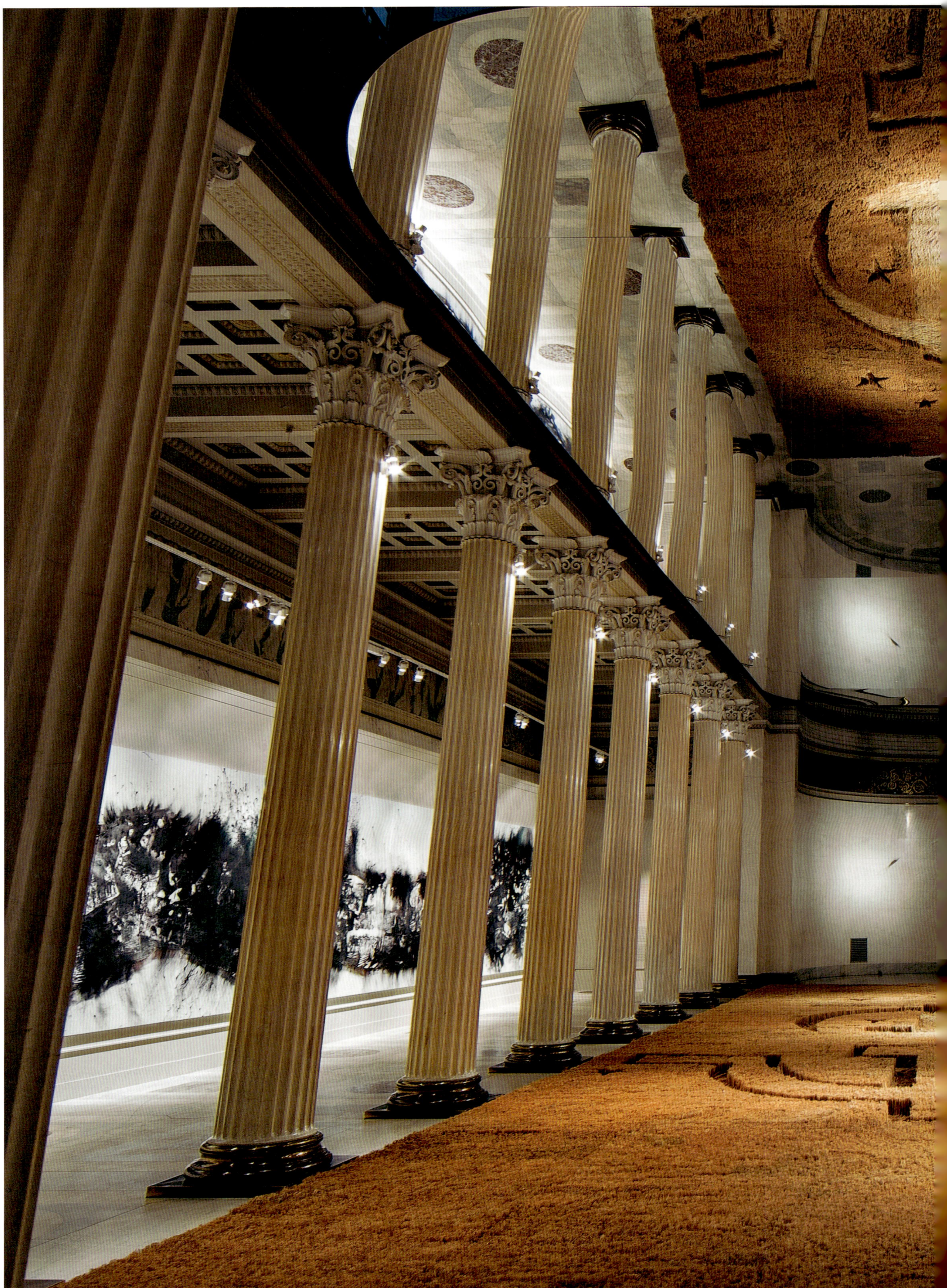

4.3 *Land*, as installed with *River* (left wall) and *Garden* (right wall) at the Pushkin State Museum of Fine Arts, 2017

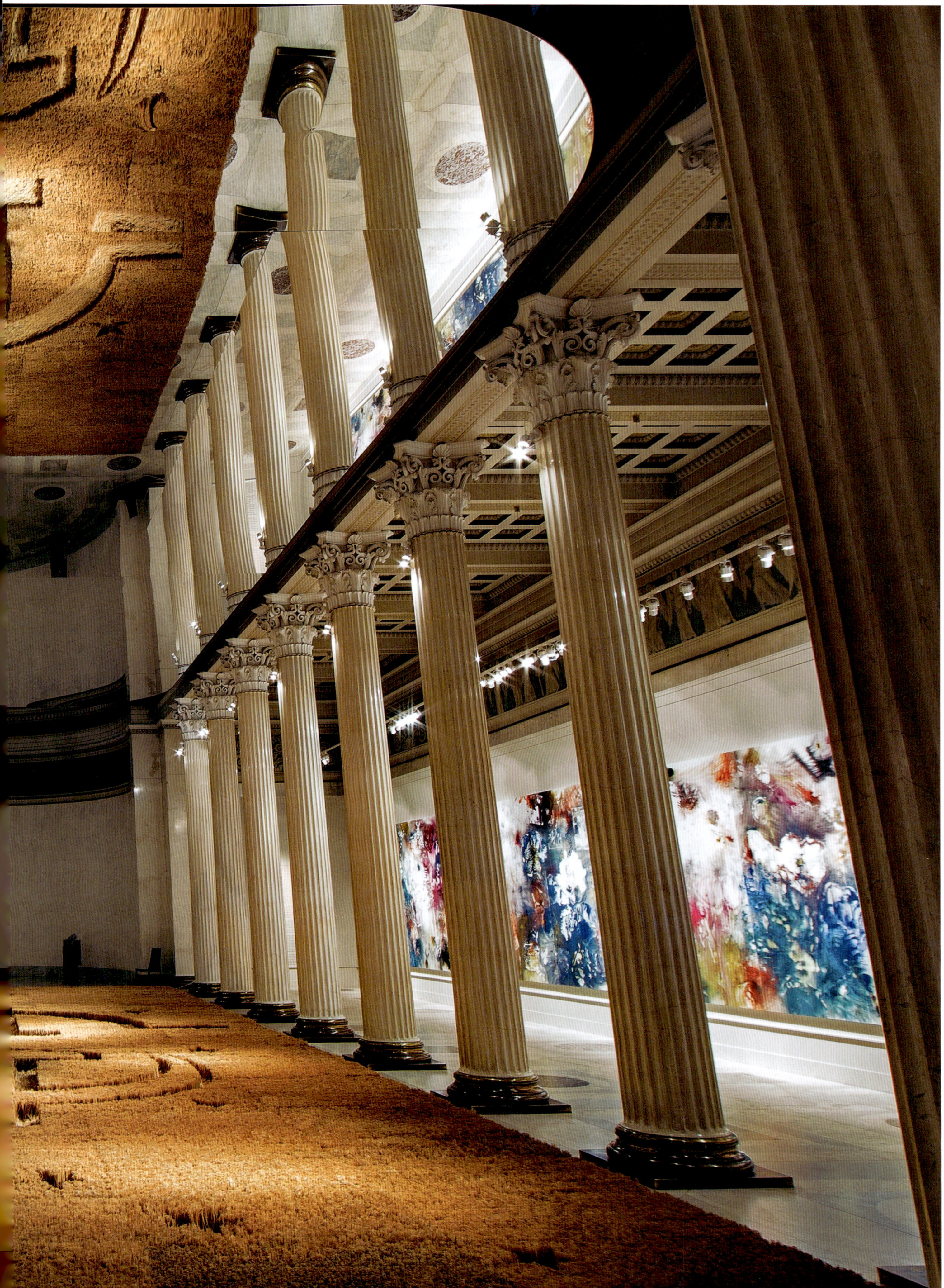

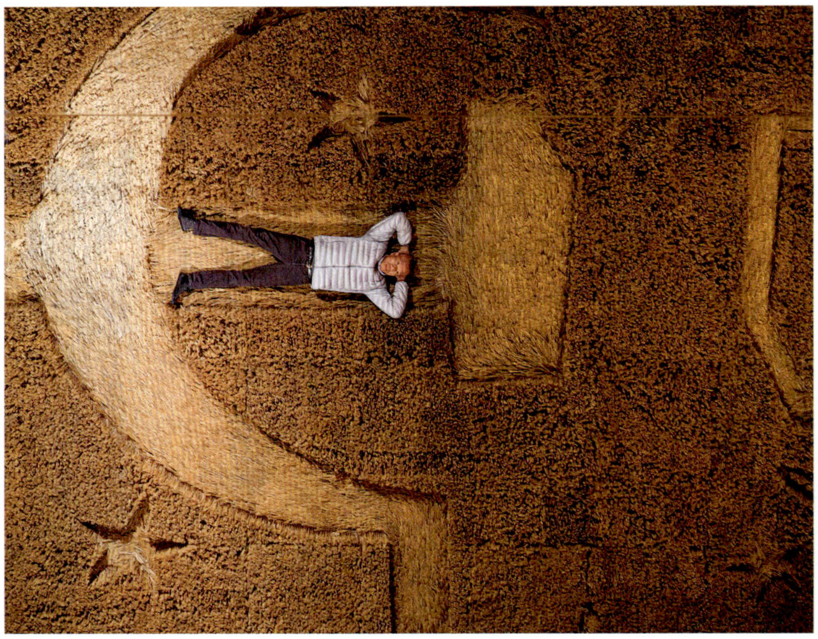

Figure 4.7. Cai Guo-Qiang lying in *Land*

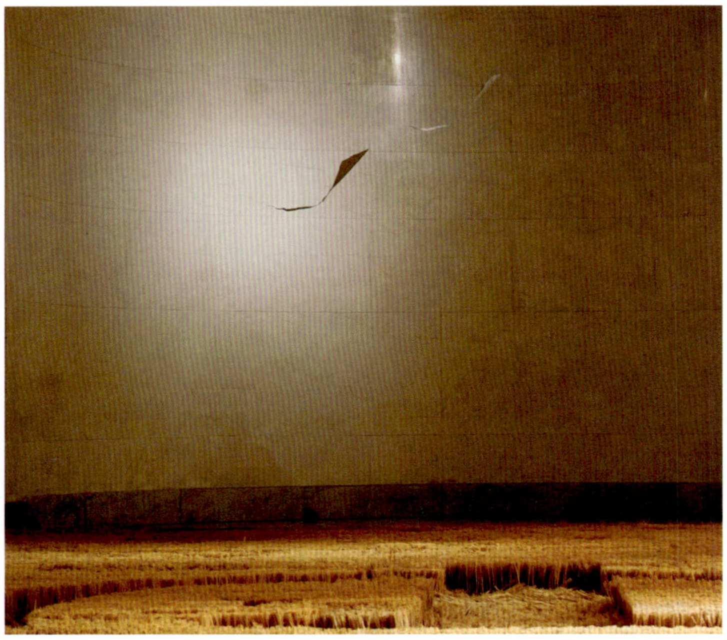

Figure 4.8. Installation view of *Kite* (2017) above *Land* at the Pushkin Museum

4.3

*Land*

大地

2017

Installation with reeds, plywood board, and reflective polymer film

Crop circle: Approx. 800 × 1980 cm; reflective polymer film: 800 × 2000 cm

4.4

*Garden*

花园

2017

Gunpowder on canvas

300 × 2000 cm

4.5

*River*

河流

2017

Gunpowder on canvas

300 × 2000 cm

Three gigantic works Cai showed on the second floor of the Pushkin Museum formed an installation group. The ceiling was covered by a silver mirror, multiplying the already expansive space. Two gunpowder paintings on the facing walls, *River* and *Garden*, surround the field of *Land* in the center of the room. With this installation, created from nearly three million stalks of golden reeds, Cai hoped to re-create the sense of mystery found in the Soviet films and Russian paintings of his childhood—the sunlight filtering through the clouds and shining on wheat fields. These images projected the romantic ideas of the freedom and beauty of life in his adolescent mind. Only through the reflection in the mirror overhead can viewers discern the symbols hidden within the crop circle. Simultaneously reflected are the countless images of civilians embedded within the turbulent history of black-and-white *River* and the colorful poppies, carnations, and Soviet posters found in the fantastical *Garden*, as well as the viewers themselves.

This inverse illusion leads viewers to reflect on their own relationships with the works.

In the painting *River*, one hundred photographs of everyday Russian life from over the past one hundred years composed a river of life. After explosion, the images created an effect reminiscent of photo negatives. This large-scale painting was created together with local Russian volunteers, conveying history and art's power of uniting people.

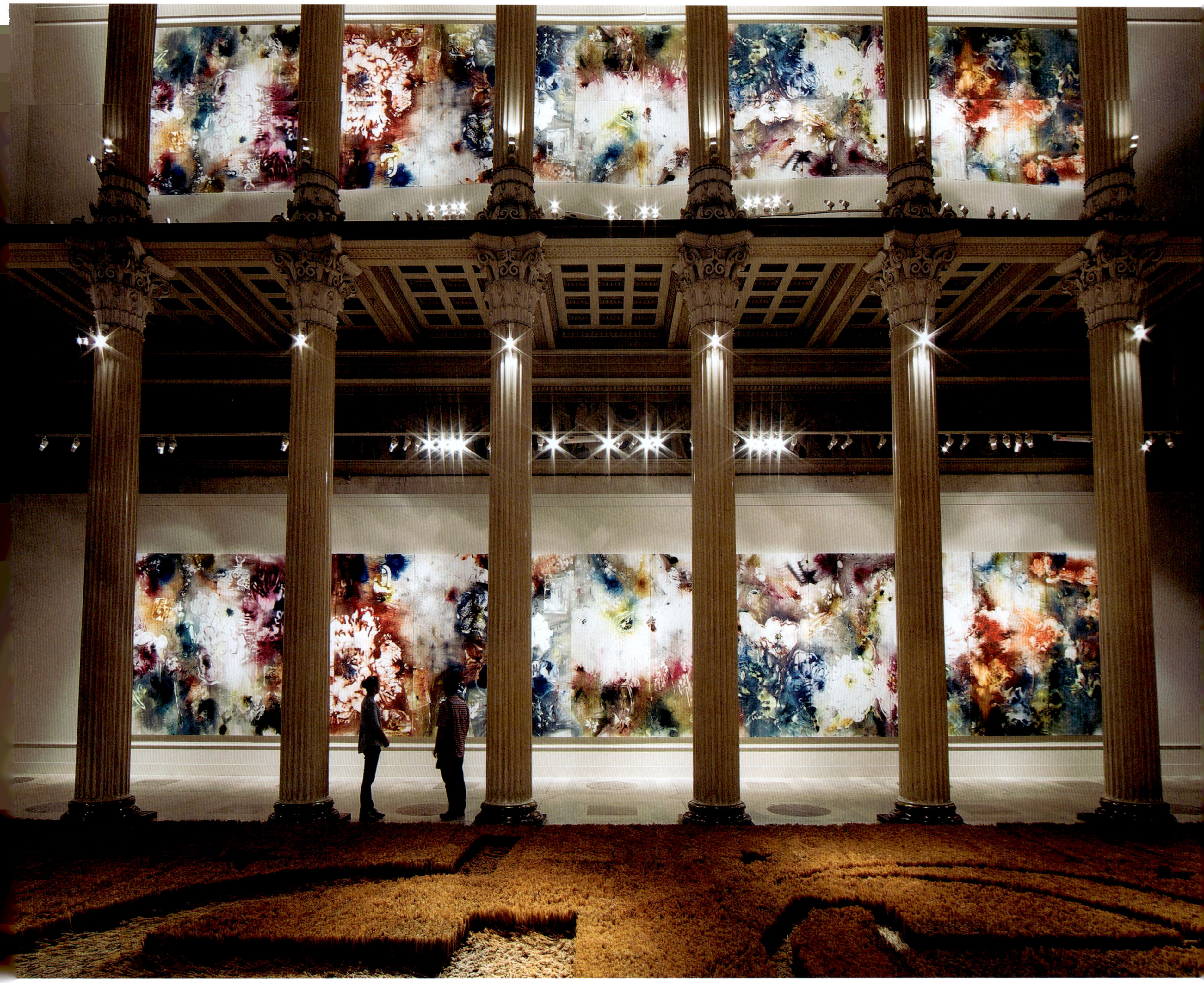

Figure 4.9. Installation view of *Garden*

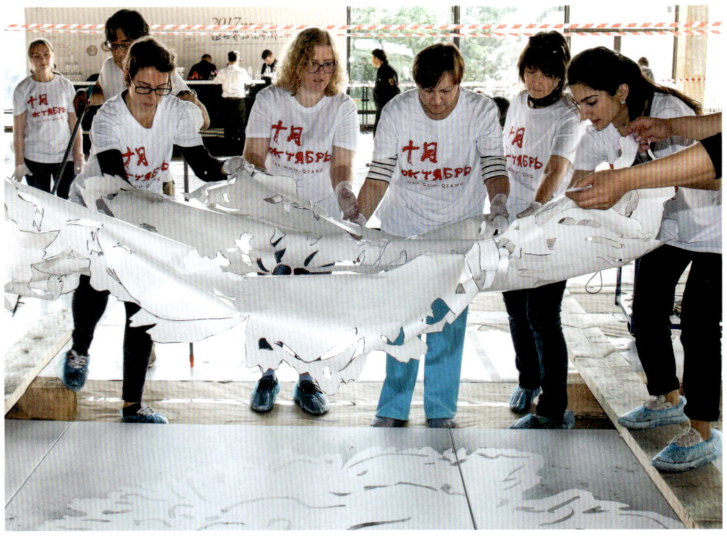

Figure 4.10. Volunteers laying stencils for *Garden* at the VDNKh Pavilion No. 22 in Moscow in 2017

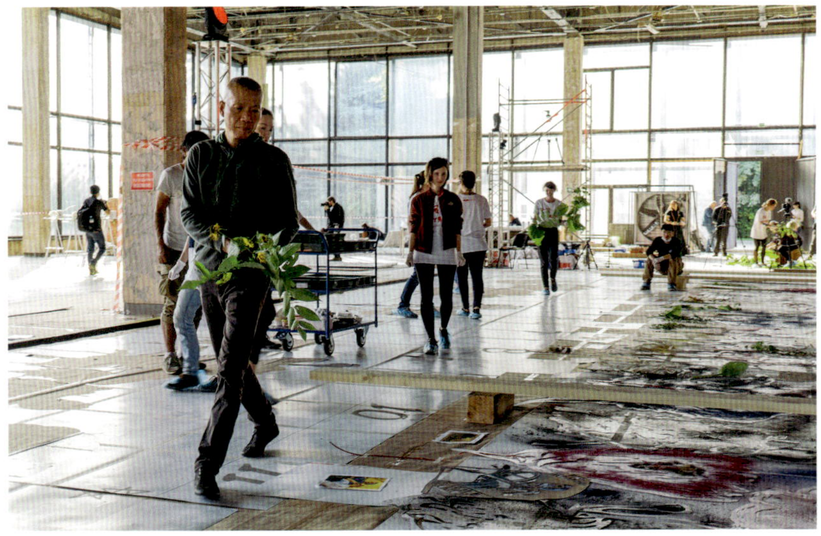

Figure 4.11. Cai Guo-Qiang and volunteers laying flowers and branches on canvas during the creation of *Garden* at the VDNKh Pavilion No. 22 in Moscow in 2017

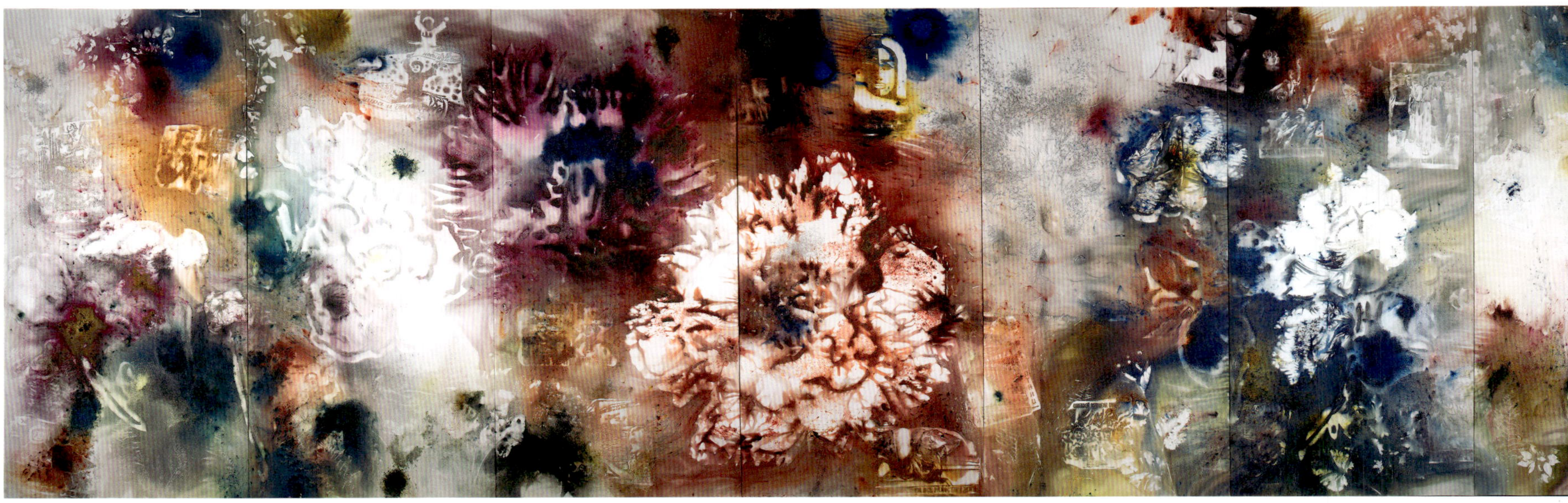

4.4 *Garden*

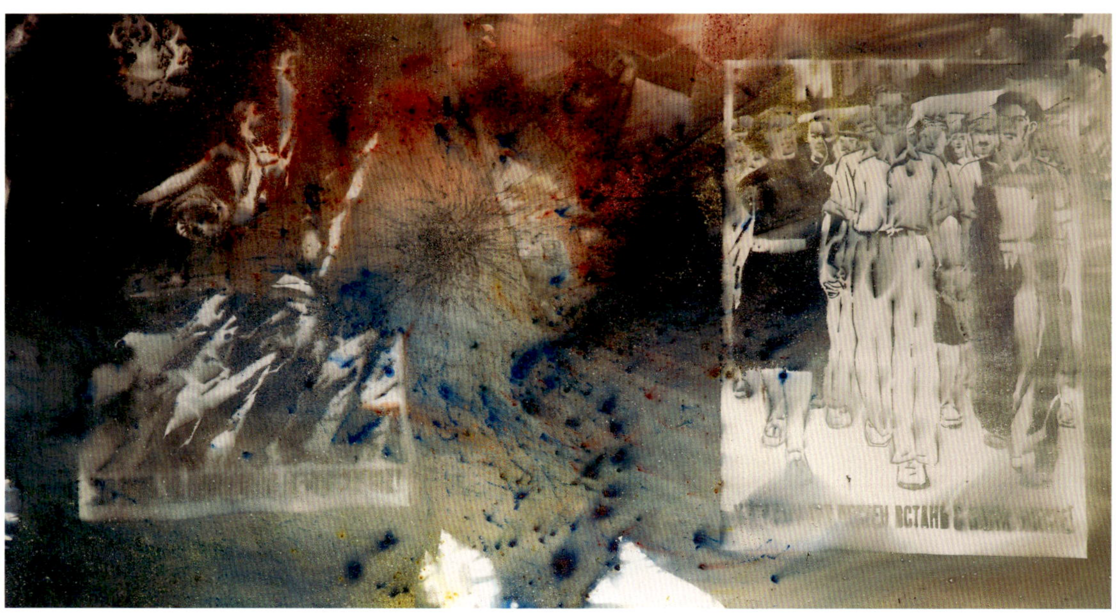

Figure 4.13. Detail of *Garden*

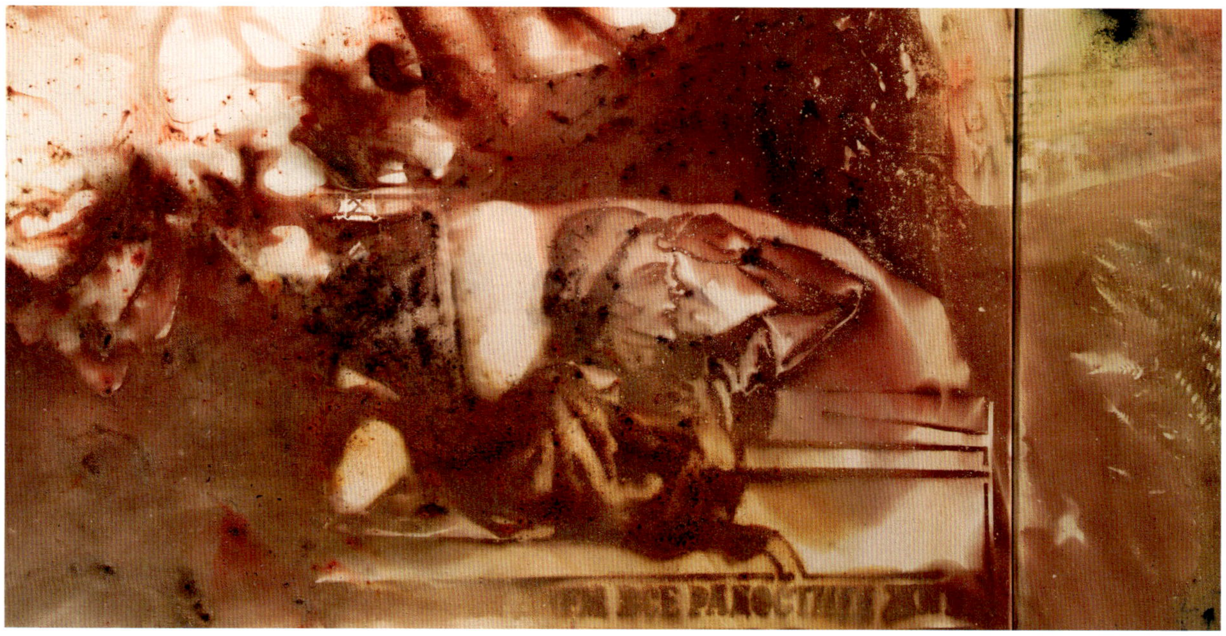

Figure 4.12. Detail of *Garden*

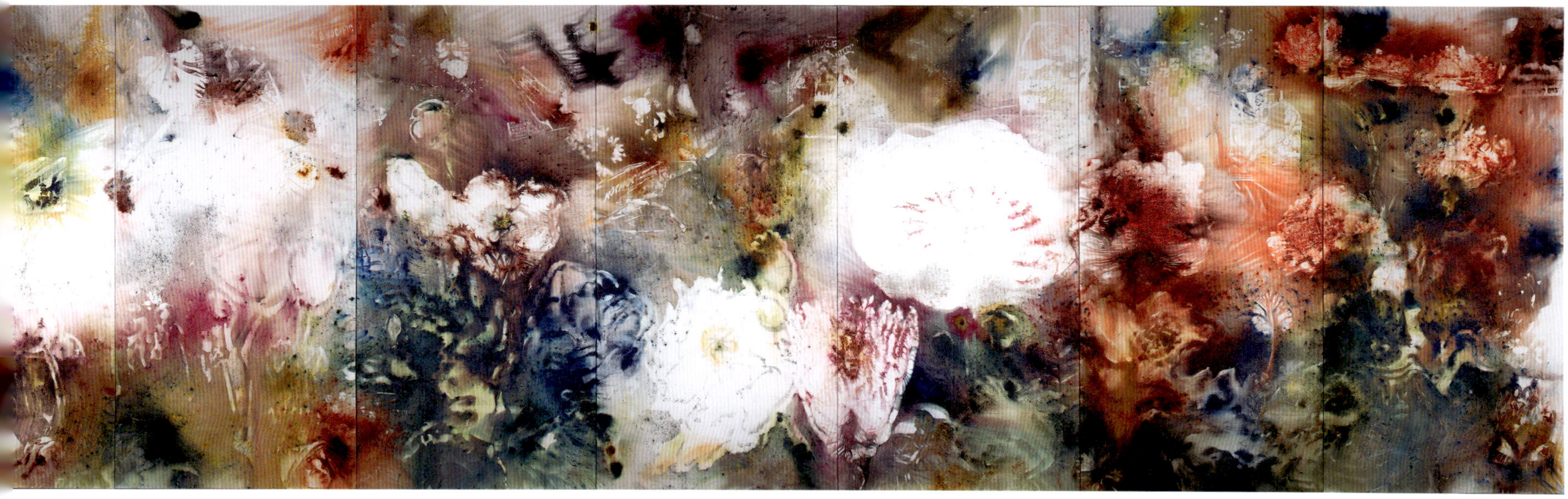

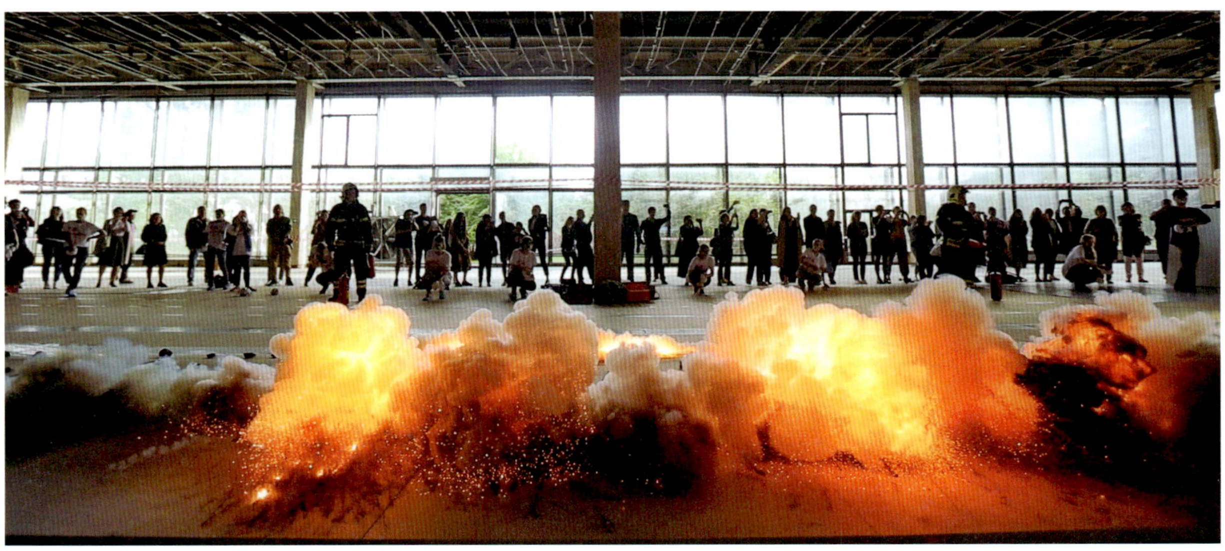

Figure 4.14. Ignition of *River* at the VDNKh Pavilion No. 22 in Moscow in 2017

4.5 *River*

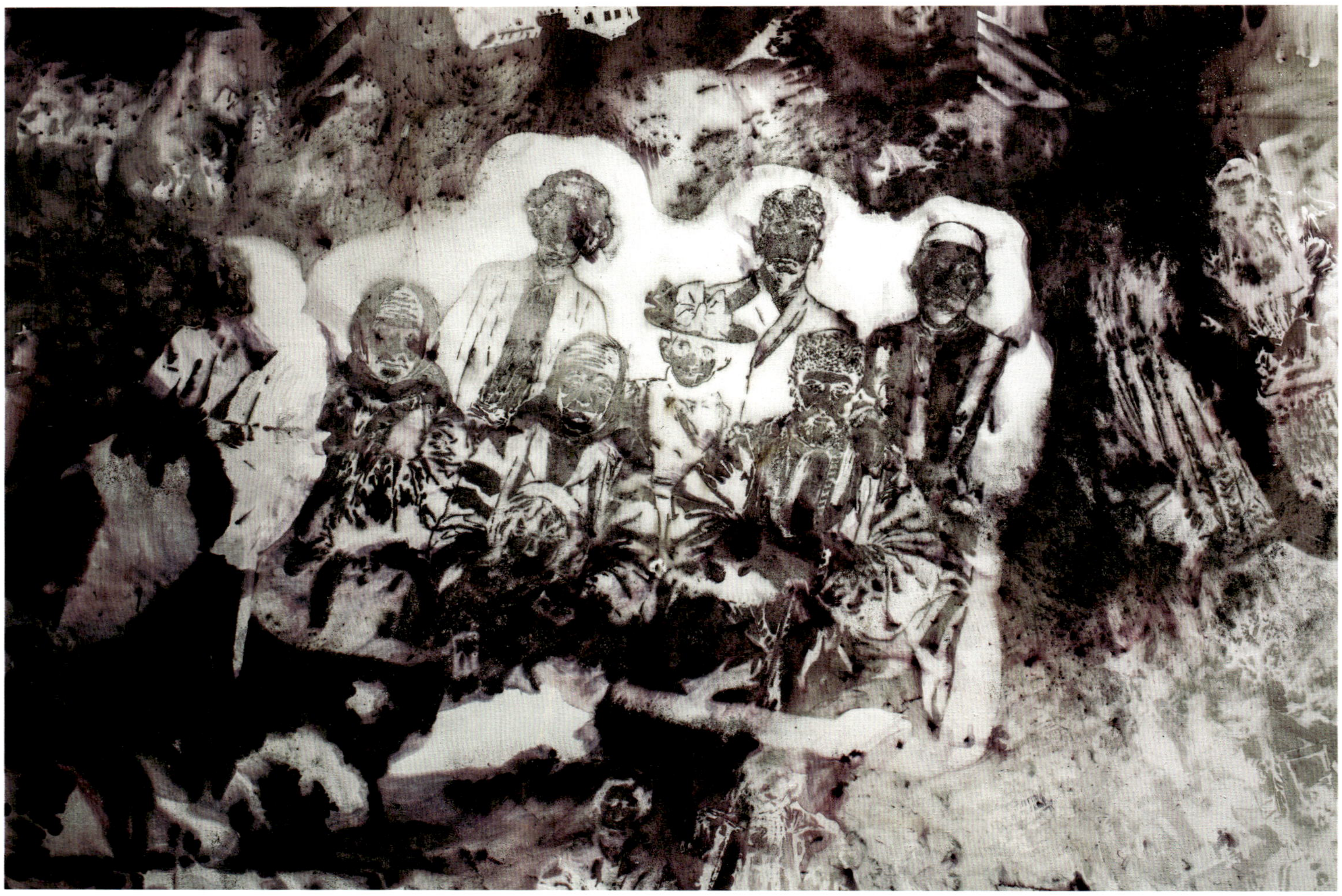

Figure 4.15. Detail of *River*

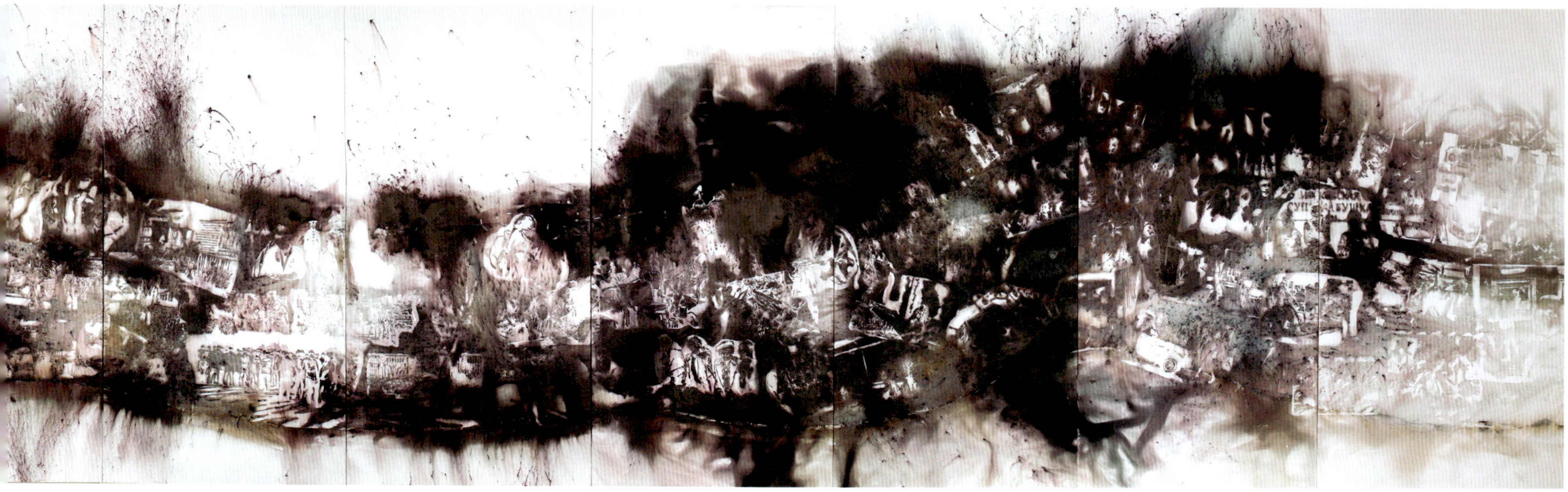

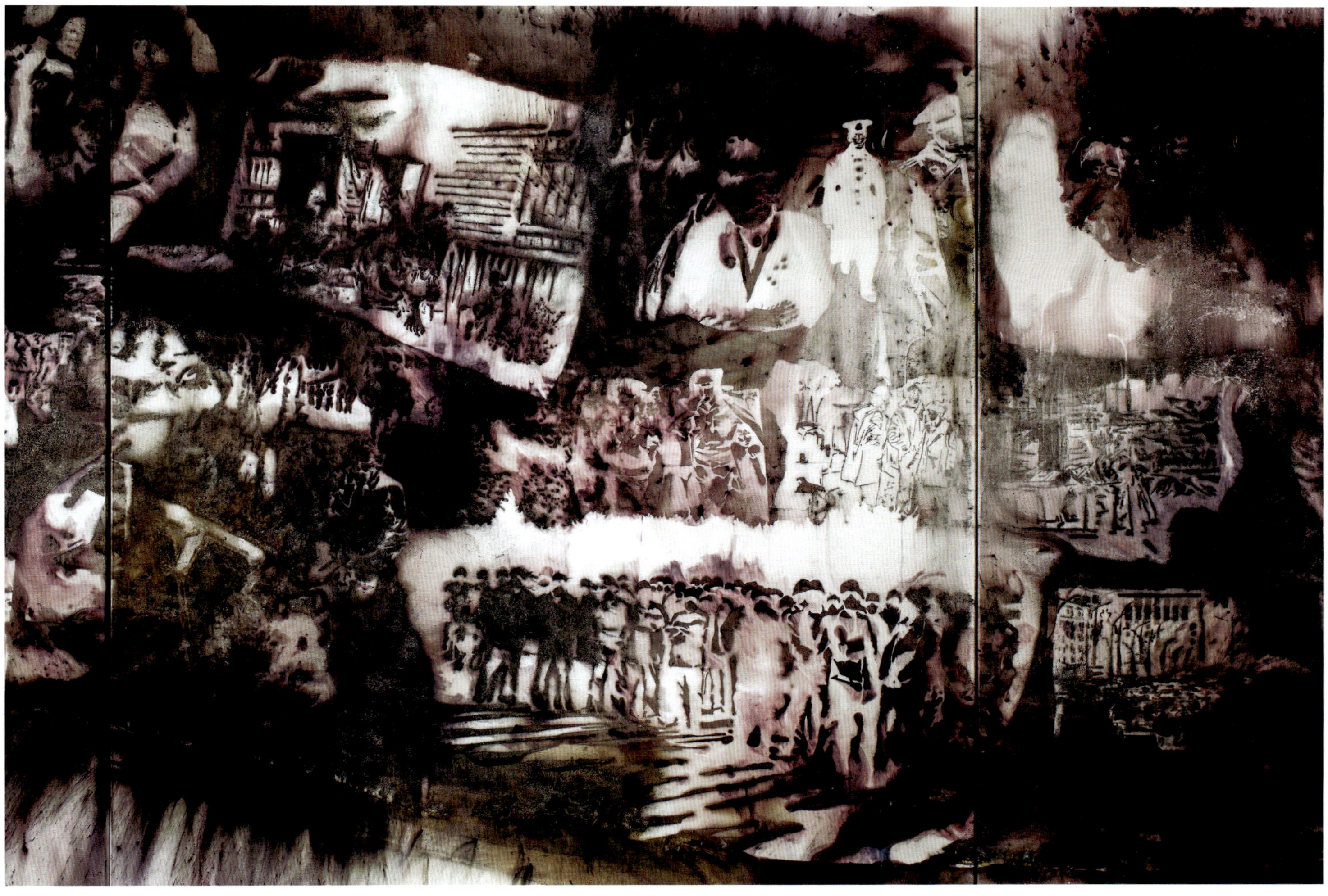

Figure 4.16. Detail of *River*

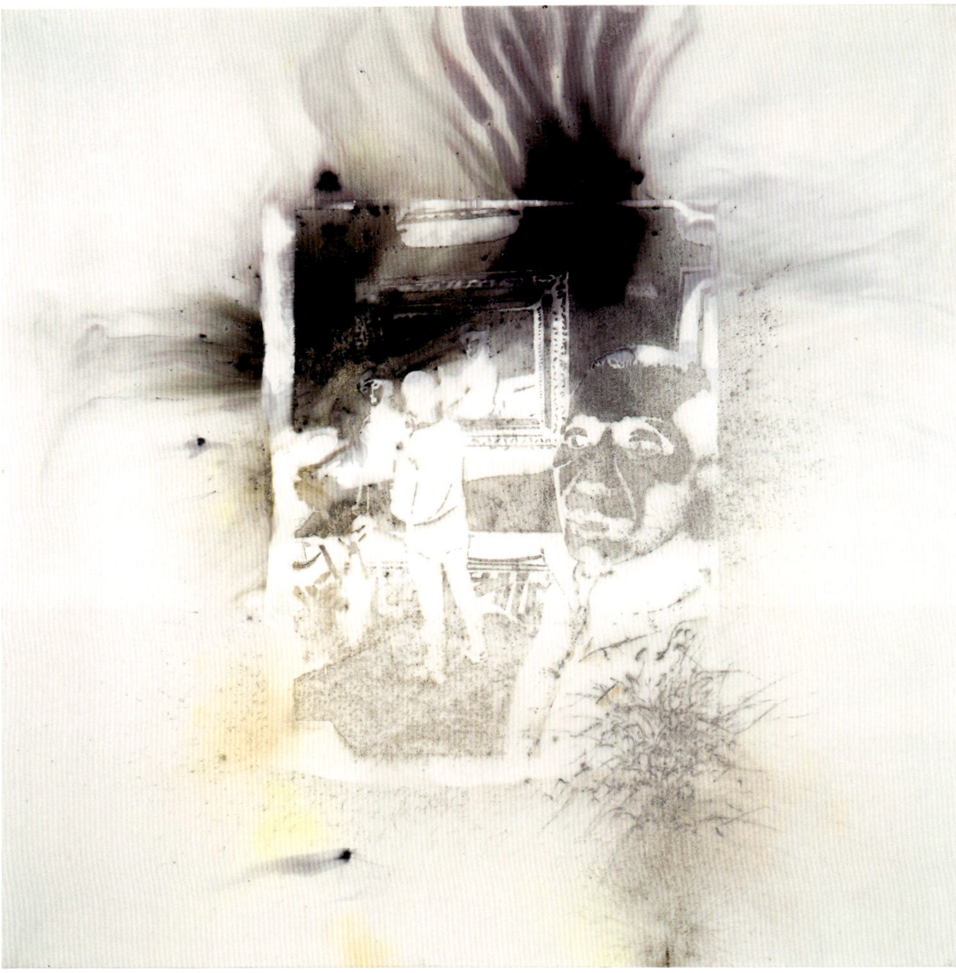

4.6 *Selfie in Front of Kramskoi's Painting (Study for River)*

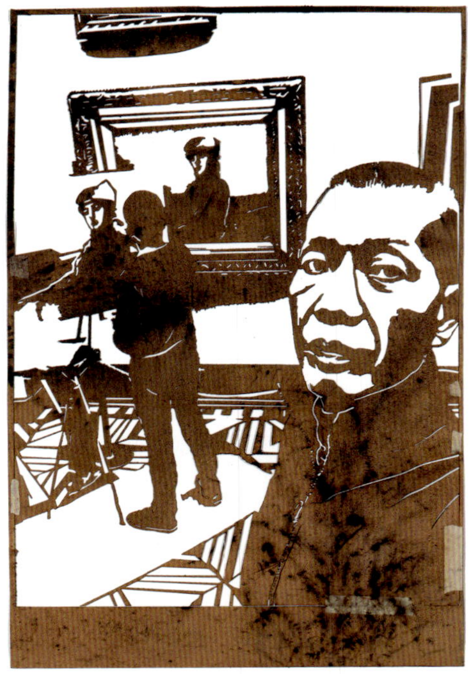

4.7 *A Stencil for River*

4.6

*Selfie in Front of Kramskoi's Painting (Study for River)*
克拉姆斯科伊画前的自拍（"河流"研究）

2017
Gunpowder on canvas
120 × 120 cm

4.7

*A Stencil for River*
"河流"纸模

2017
Laser-cut chipboard
66 × 46 cm

*The Unknown Woman* by Ivan Kramskoi (1837–1887) was a work that Cai copied again and again in adolescence. Cai used gunpowder to reproduce a selfie he took in front of the painting, housed in the State Tretyakov Gallery, as an engagement with the young painter at the bottom of his heart. It also served as a study for the large-scale gunpowder painting *River*. Select laser-cut stencils that were used during the explosion to create the painting were also exhibited.

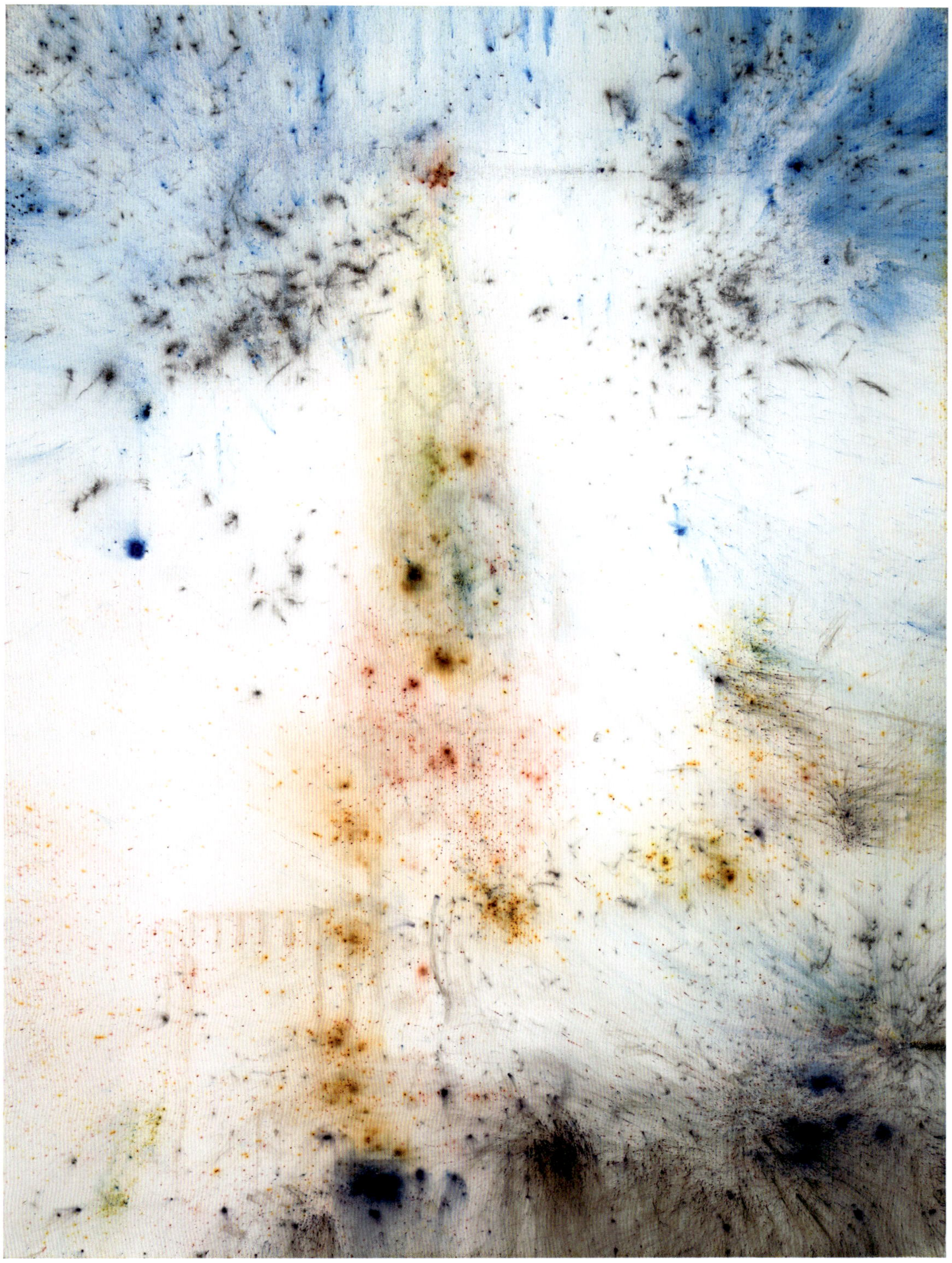

4.8 *Kremlin in the Snow*

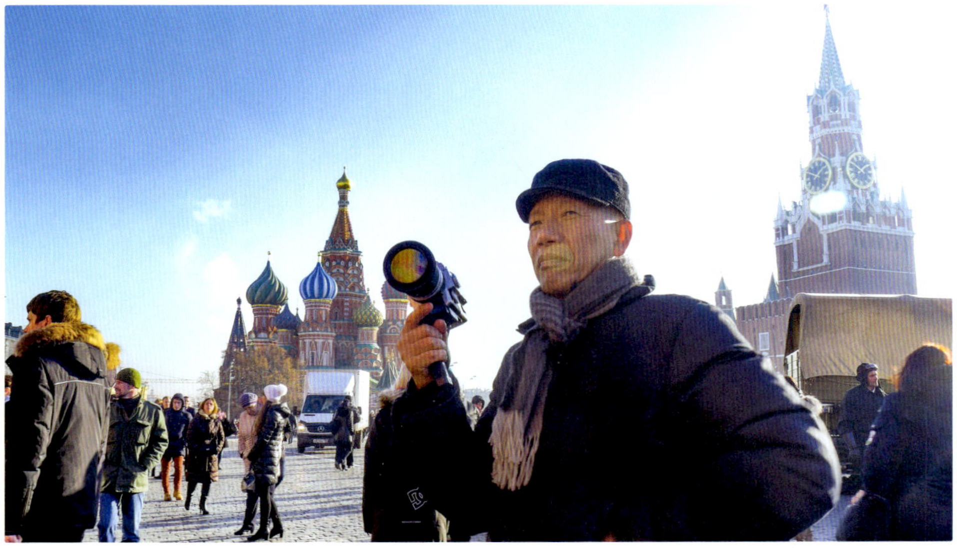

Figure 4.17. Cai Guo-Qiang shooting film on a site visit to the Red Square in Moscow in 2015

4.8

*Kremlin in the Snow*

雪中克里姆林宫

2017/2020

Gunpowder on canvas

122 × 91.5 cm

Through gunpowder explosion, Cai encapsulated on canvas the landmark structure of Red Square, along with its unique symbolic meaning.

4.9

*Malevich Over Red Square: Black Square*

红场上空的马列维奇：黑方格

2017

Gunpowder on canvas

120 × 120 cm

4.10

*Malevich Over Red Square: Black Cross*

红场上空的马列维奇：黑十字

2017

Gunpowder on canvas

120 × 120 cm

4.11

*Malevich Over Red Square: Black Circle*

红场上空的马列维奇：黑圆圈

2017

Gunpowder on canvas

120 × 120 cm

4.12

*Red Star Over Red Square*

红场上空的红星

2017

Gunpowder on canvas

120 × 120 cm

The founder of Suprematism, Kazimir Malevich (1879–1935), has left an immeasurable impression on avant-garde movements around the world and pioneered a new era in the history of art. The Suprematist triptych he created nearly a century ago, *Black Square*, *Black Cross,* and *Black Circle*, served as central images in Cai's proposed (but unrealized) daytime explosion event on Red Square. By using his unique medium to revive Malevich's revolutionary symbols in the modern-day Moscow sky, Cai aimed to pay tribute to the destiny of a generation of Russian avant-garde artists.

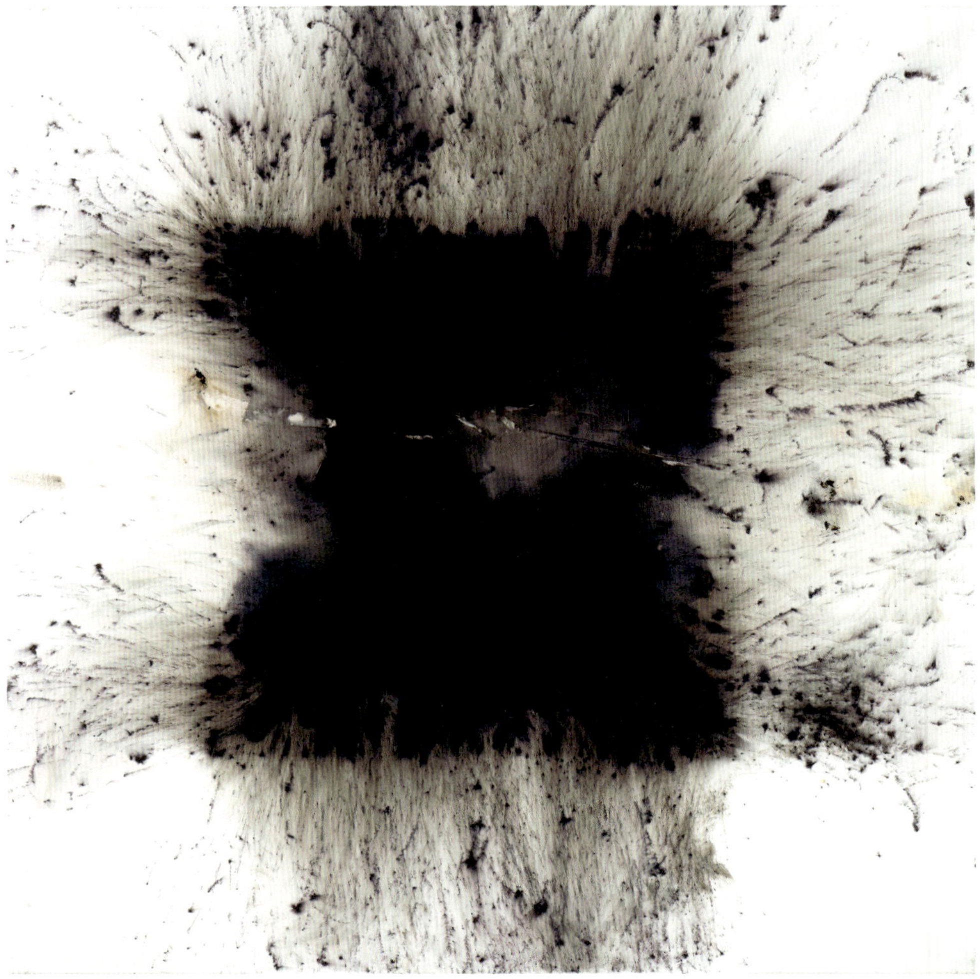

4.9 *Malevich Over Red Square: Black Square*

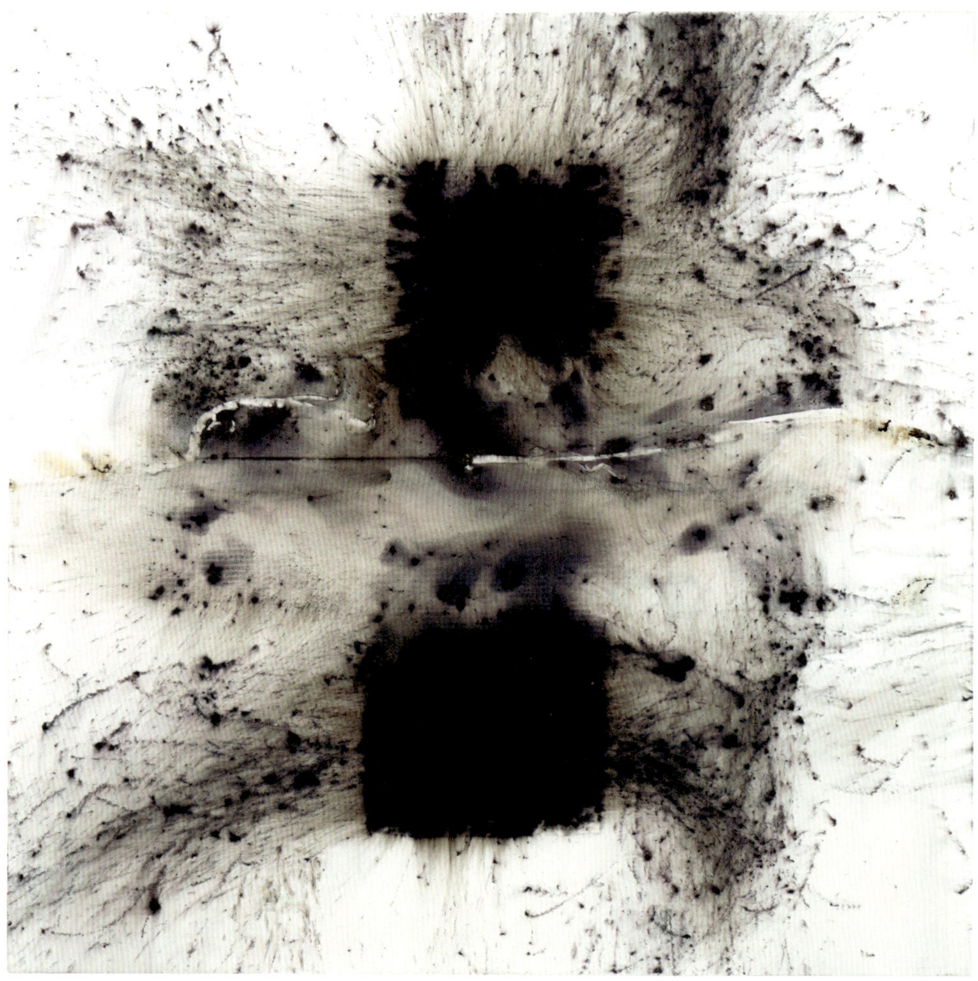

4.10 *Malevich Over Red Square: Black Cross*

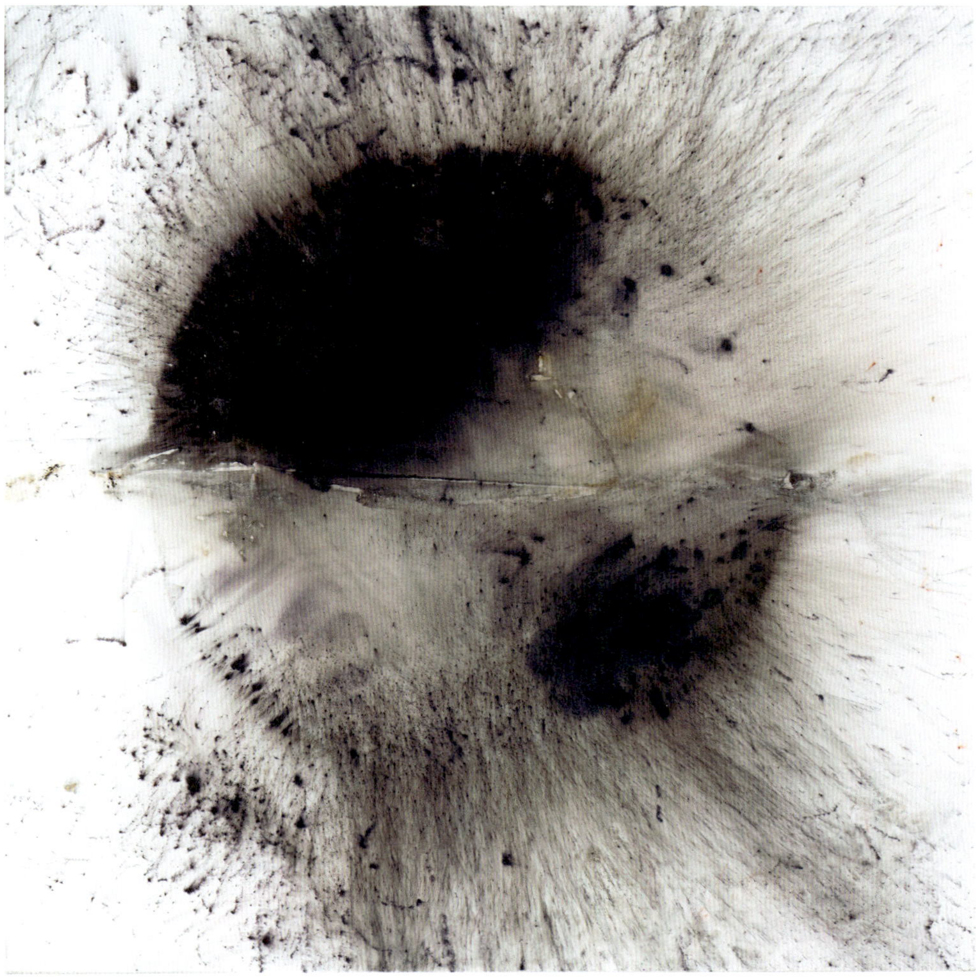

4.11 *Malevich Over Red Square: Black Circle*

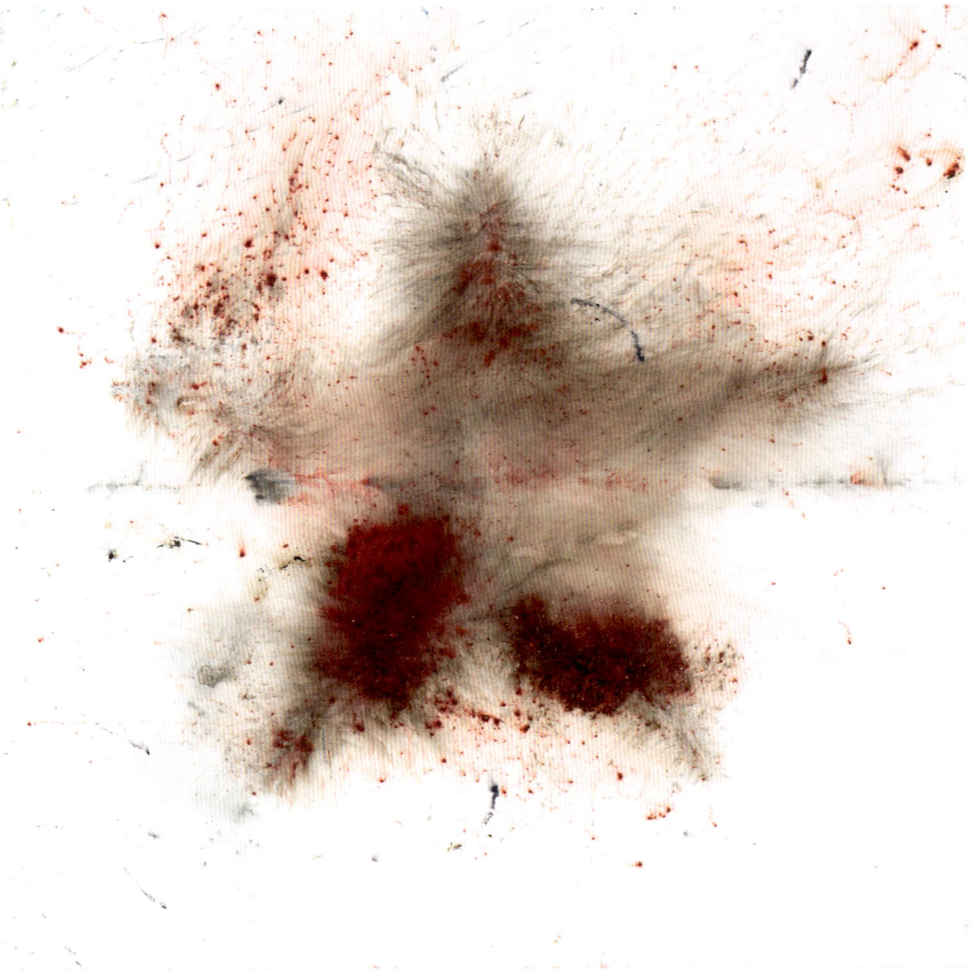

4.12 *Red Star Over Red Square*

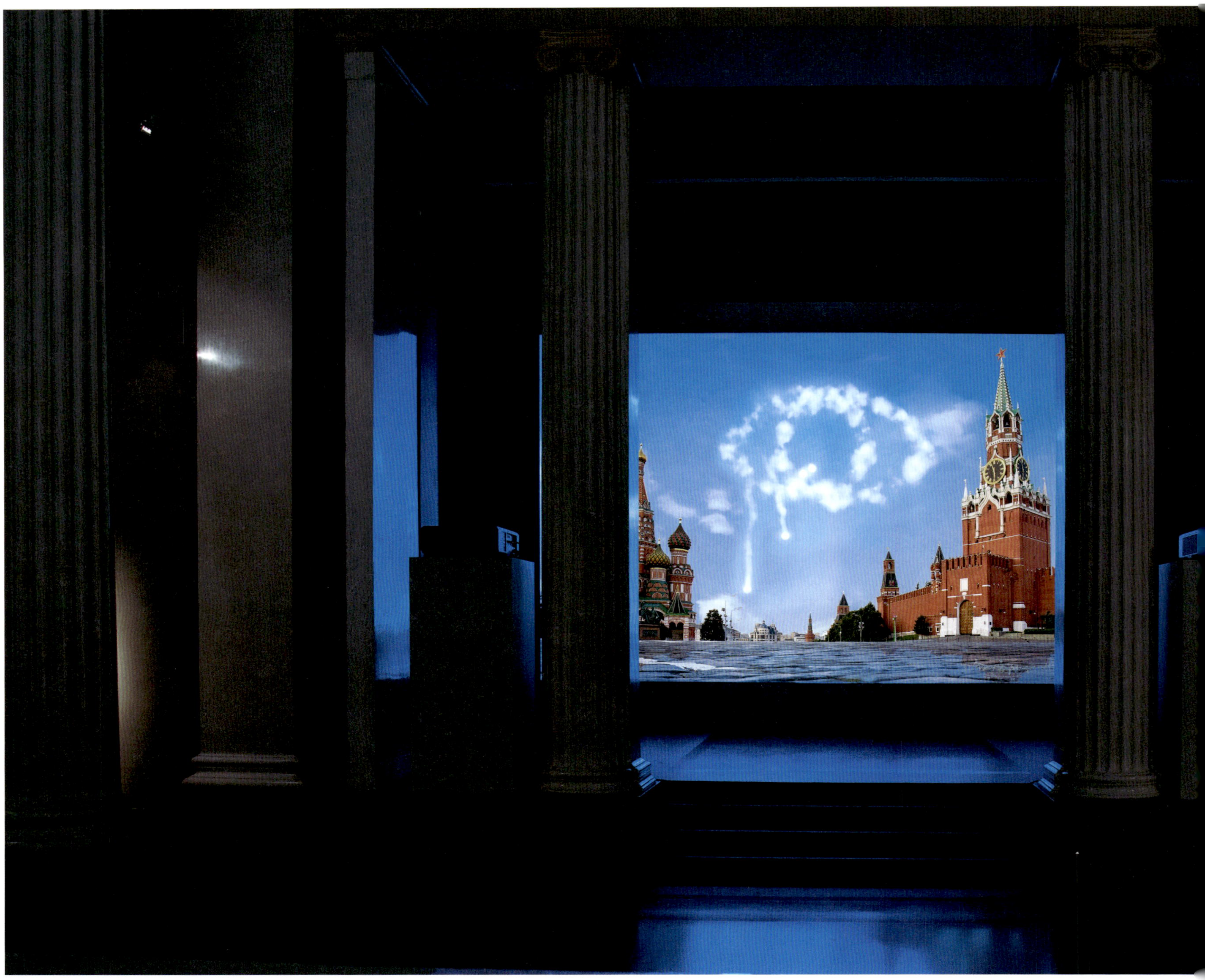

4.13 Installation view at the Pushkin State Museum of Fine Arts in 2017

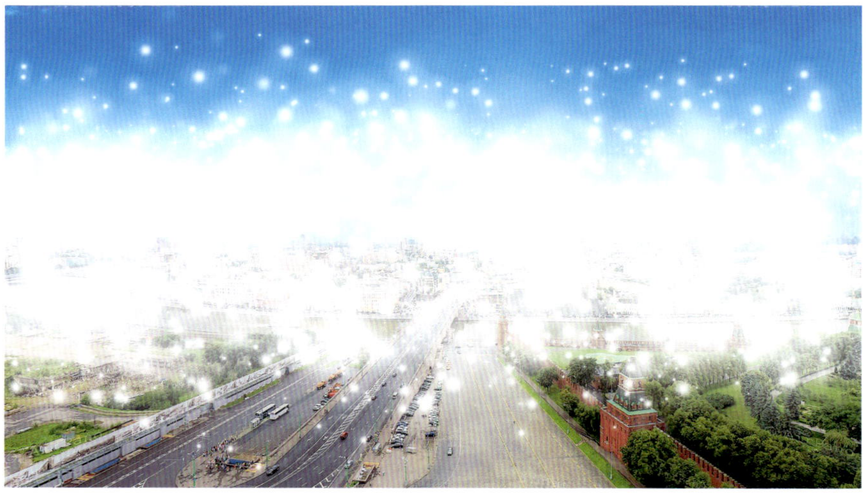

Figure 4.18. Still frame

4.13

*Cai Guo-Qiang: October, Daytime Explosion Event on Red Square*

蔡国强：十月—红场白天烟花

2017

Animated video

7:23

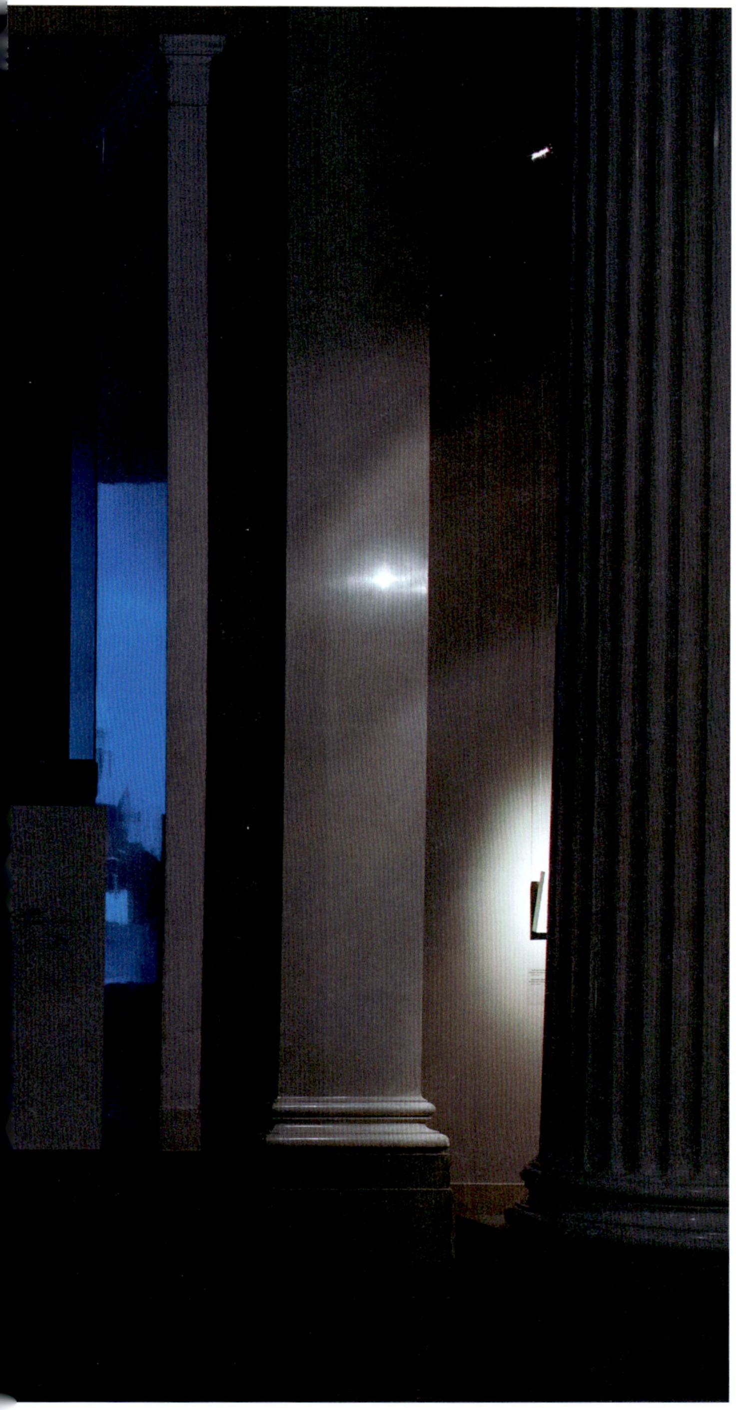

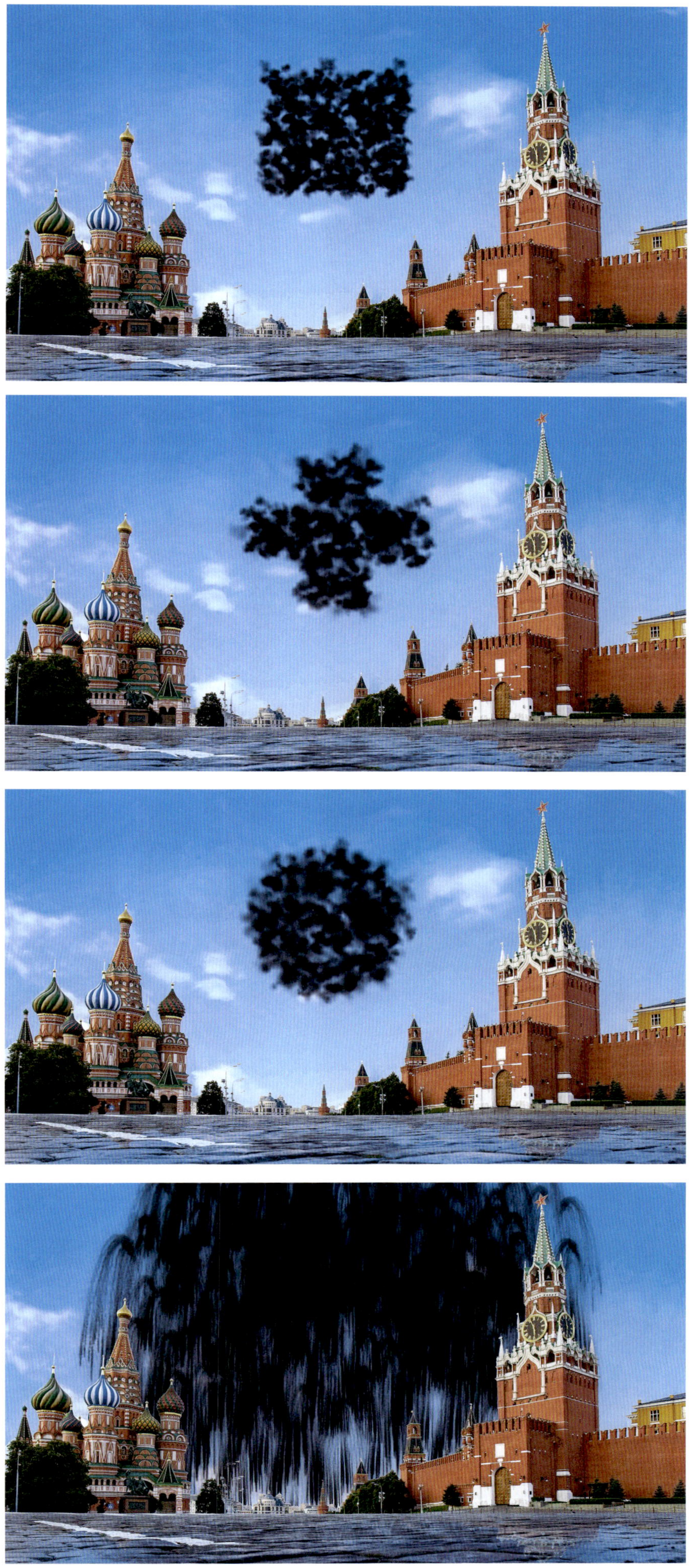

Figures 4.19a–d. Still frames

Cai was invited by the Pushkin Museum to create a daytime explosion event over Red Square on the occasion of the October Revolution's centenary. The work was unfortunately unrealized, but the artist captured the entirety of the artwork concept in animated form.

As the orchestral arrangement of Tchaikovsky sounded, a daytime explosion event would launch from Red Square and the Moskva riverbank, painting one image after another in the sky, each filled with somber sensibility. The event would conclude with one hundred seconds of earthshattering, thunderous explosions, leaving behind a blinding white flash.

# 5

# Dialogue with Modernism

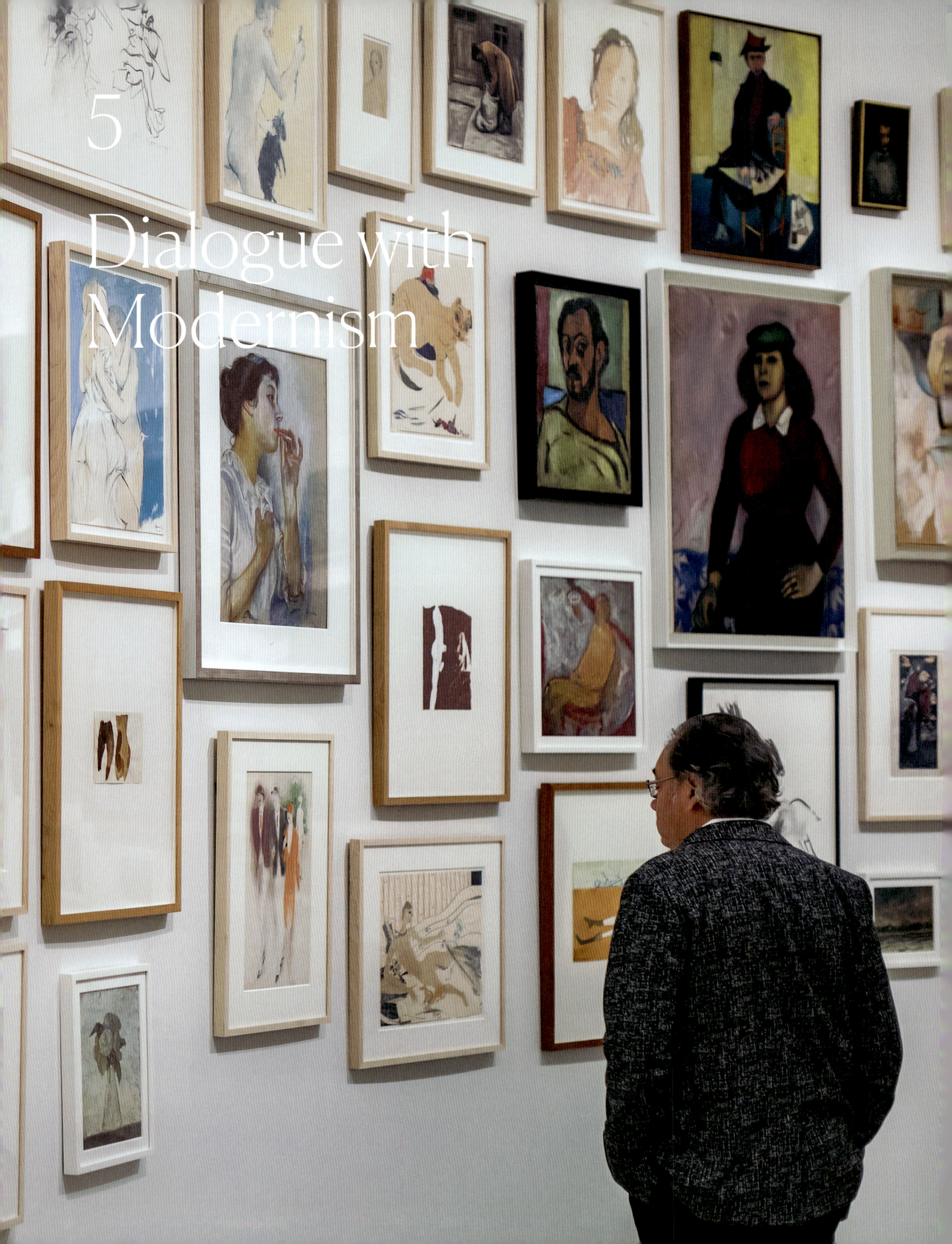

# *Non-Brand* 非品牌

Solomon R. Guggenheim Museum, New York, U.S.
May 24, 2019–January 12, 2020

Curated by Cai Guo-Qiang as part of *Artistic License: Six Takes on the Guggenheim Collection* organized by Nancy Spector, Artistic Director and Jennifer and David Stockman Chief Curator, Guggenheim Museum

Documentary short: produced by the Guggenheim Museum (2:43); edited by Shanshan Xia (4:07)

Modernism played a significant role in Cai's early introduction to painting, and to this day he feels a special attachment to the movement. In 2019, to commemorate the sixtieth anniversary of its iconic building designed by modernist master Frank Lloyd Wright, the Guggenheim Museum in New York presented its first-ever artist-curated exhibition, *Artistic License: Six Takes on the Guggenheim Collection*. The exhibition invited six contemporary artists who have shaped the Guggenheim's history through their influential solo shows, which included Cai and his landmark retrospective exhibition *I Want to Believe* in 2008.

During his research in the museum's storerooms, while revisiting modernist classics, Cai also had chance encounters with many unknown, mostly small-scale works by his modernist predecessors. For example, the museum holds early figurative works by prominent abstract painters, such as Wassily Kandinsky's landscapes, Franz Kline's self-portrait, and Piet Mondrian's chrysanthemums that he devotedly drew and redrew all his life. Cai called his presentation *Non-Brand* 非品牌, inspired by these works that seemingly lack the "brand"—that is, a coveted, easily recognizable style—associated with a particular artist.

In the High Gallery, Cai covered the main wall salon-style with over eighty figurative works by thirty artists selected from the Guggenheim collection, often dating from their early periods, along with his own early paintings. On a wall outside the High Gallery, Cai presented four newly made gunpowder paintings on glass that emulate four iconic works, associated with the Guggenheim's "brand," by four important modernist masters: Wassily Kandinsky (no. 5.1), Mark Rothko (no. 5.2), Franz Kline (no. 5.3), and Yves Klein (no. 5.4).

*Non-Brand* 非品牌 confronts the contemporary issue of "branding" faced by museums and artists alike. For Cai, artists devise distinctive stylistic "brands" that allow them to gain wide recognition and acceptance into art history. Yet, in the process, they become "brands" of cultural tourism, satiating local and foreign visitors who see the work merely to tick off a box. Moreover, they become commodities to be consumed in the "culture industry" formed by the art market and art museums. In Cai's view, most so-called groundbreaking artists do not reach the innovative stages of their careers directly. Rather, their entry points were often figuration and realism, through which they attempt to capture things as children see them when they open their eyes. Artists share a childlike innocence, which can be characterized as an eternal human "fixation on the primordial." At its root, this fixation is a reaction to nature and a fundamental love of painting. This love manifests as an unaffected essence of art that transcends any school or style. However, more often than not, these early works are dismissed as the "immature" parts of an artist's process. In a sense, the works *Non-Brand* 非品牌 displayed in a salon-style grid eliminated periodization or rank to reveal the truth of the Guggenheim's collection.

Figure 5.1. Installation view of *Cai Guo-Qiang: Non-Brand* 非品牌

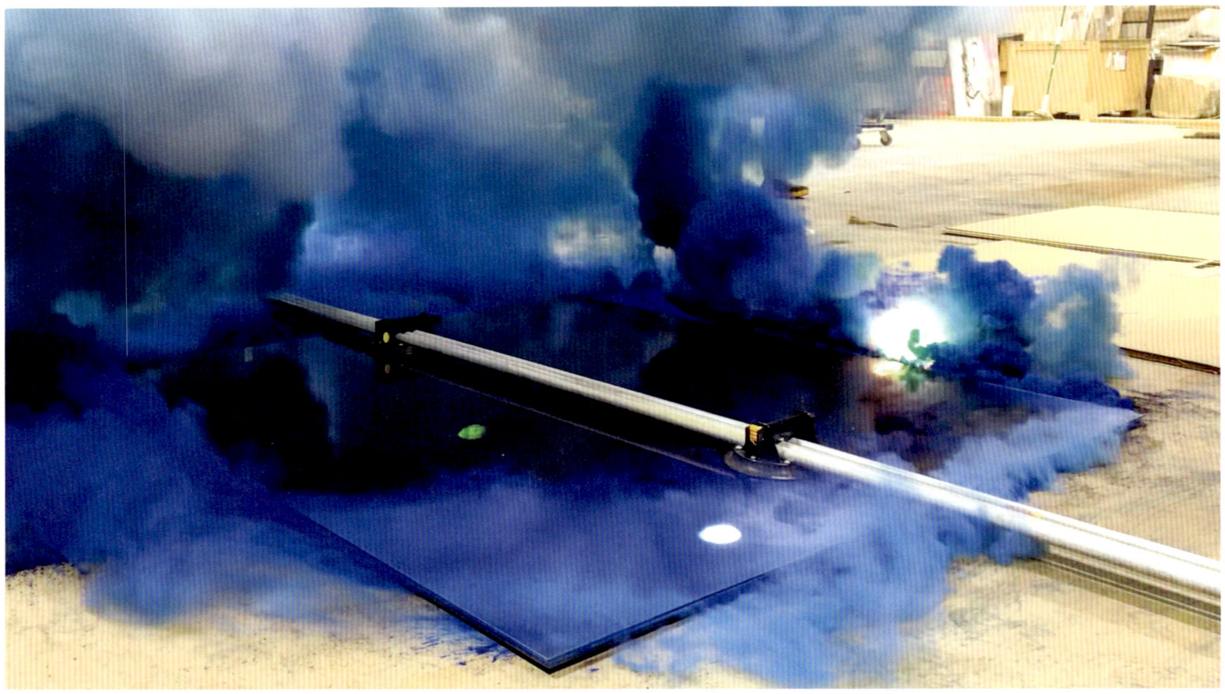

Figure 5.2. Ignition of *Non-Brand* 非品牌 *5* in 2019

5.1
*Non-Brand* 非品牌 *1*
2019
Gunpowder on glass and mirror
183 × 150 cm

5.2
*Non-Brand* 非品牌 *2*
2019
Gunpowder on glass and mirror
183 × 150 cm

5.3
*Non-Brand* 非品牌 *3*
2019
Gunpowder on glass and mirror
183 × 150 cm

5.4
*Non-Brand* 非品牌 *5*
2019
Gunpowder on glass and mirror
183 × 150 cm

Cai sandwiched gunpowder, the trademark material of his artistic "brand," between a sheet of glass and a mirror. Through explosion, the pieces emulate the masterworks of modernism that constitute the Guggenheim's "brand"—Yves Klein, Franz Kline, Mark Rothko, and Wassily Kandinsky as if they were the phantoms of those famous artworks.

The inspiration for painting with gunpowder on mirror and glass originated from Cai's childhood memories of the glass paintings in his hometown. The Guggenheim exhibition was the official debut of this new type of gunpowder painting.

Related Work

5.5
*Kung Fu*
功夫
2019
Gunpowder on glass and mirror
183 × 150 cm

5.4 *Non-Brand* 非品牌 *5*

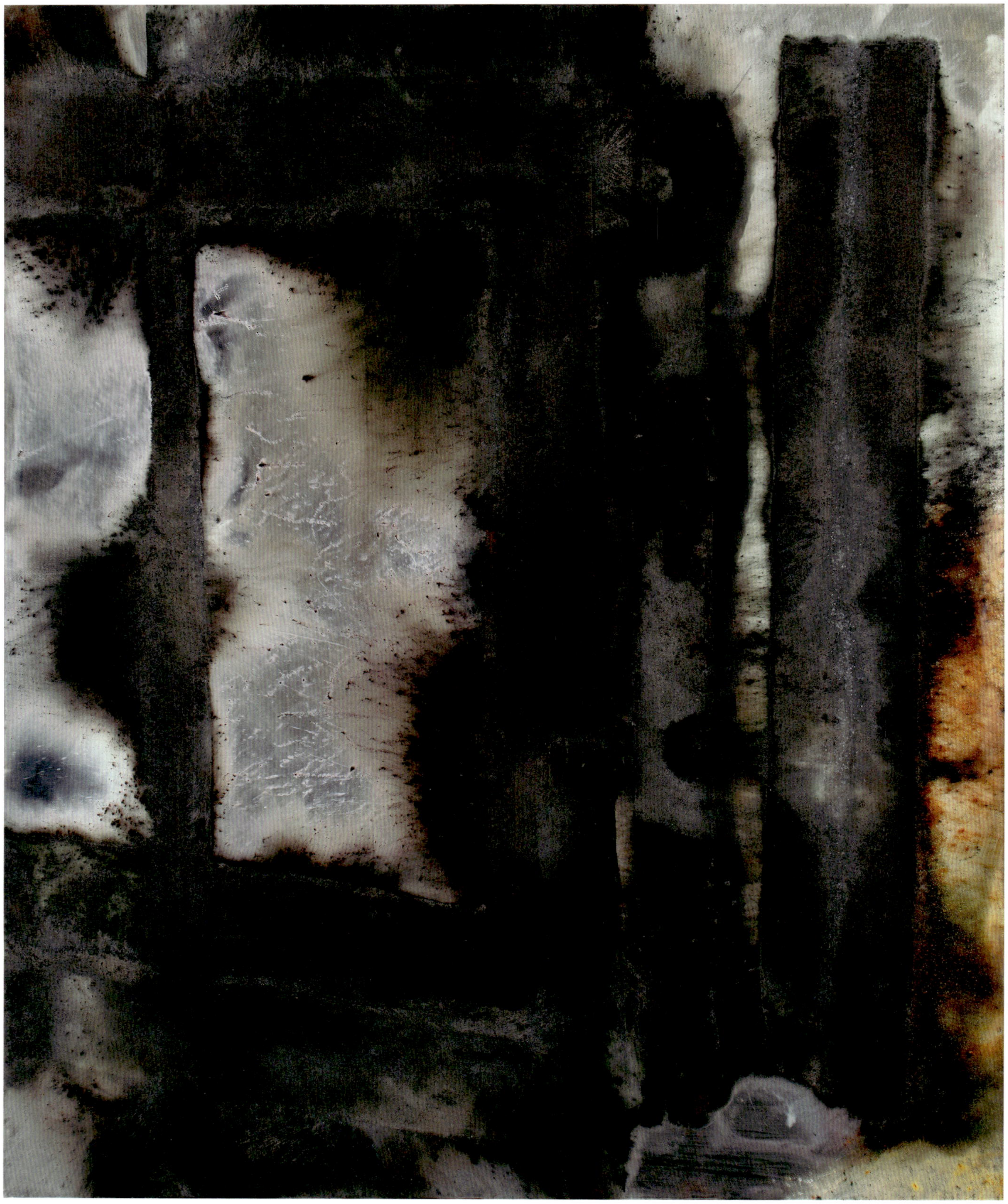

5.3 *Non-Brand* 非品牌 *3*

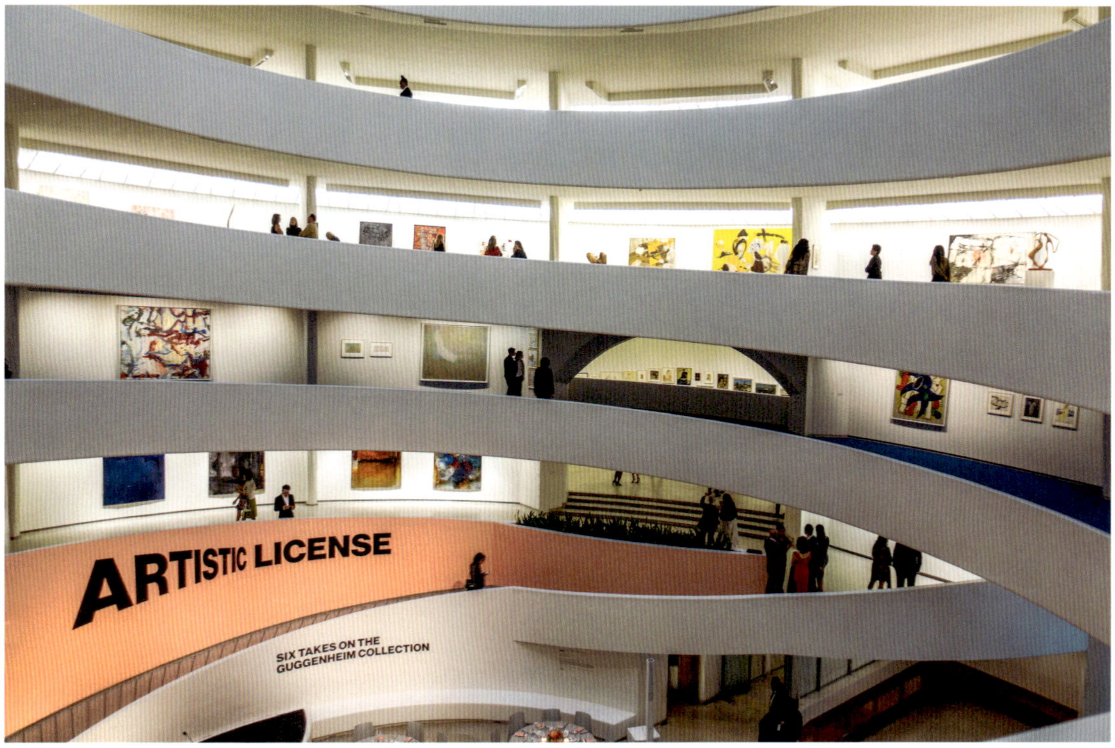


Figure 5.3. Installation view of *Artistic License: Six Takes on the Guggenheim Collection* at the Solomon R. Guggenheim Museum in 2019

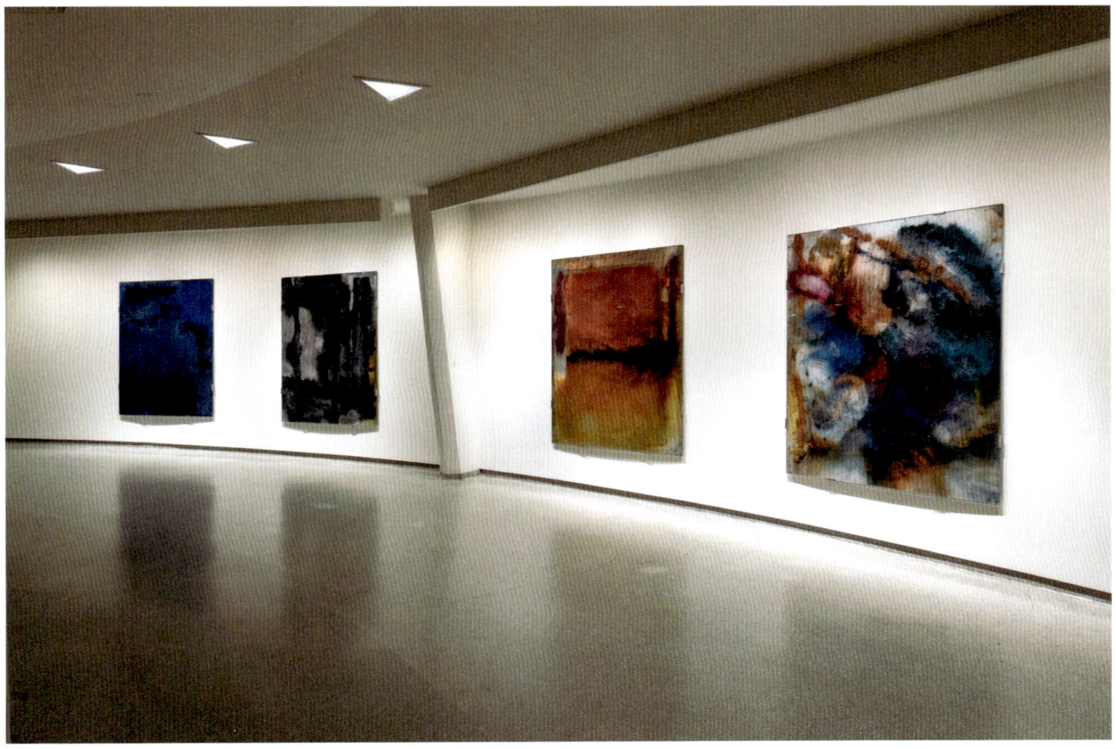

Figure 5.4. Installation view of *Cai Guo-Qiang: Non-Brand* 非品牌

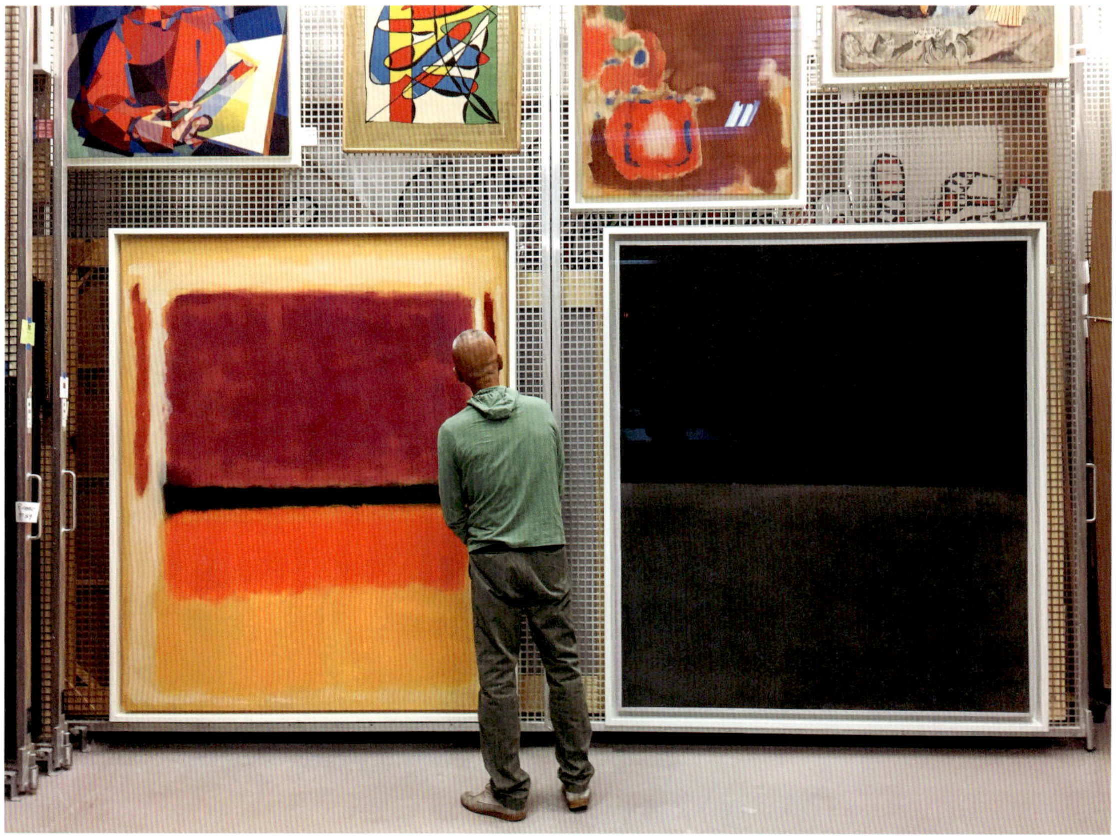

Figure 5.5. Cai Guo-Qiang examining works by Mark Rothko in the Guggenheim's collection in 2018

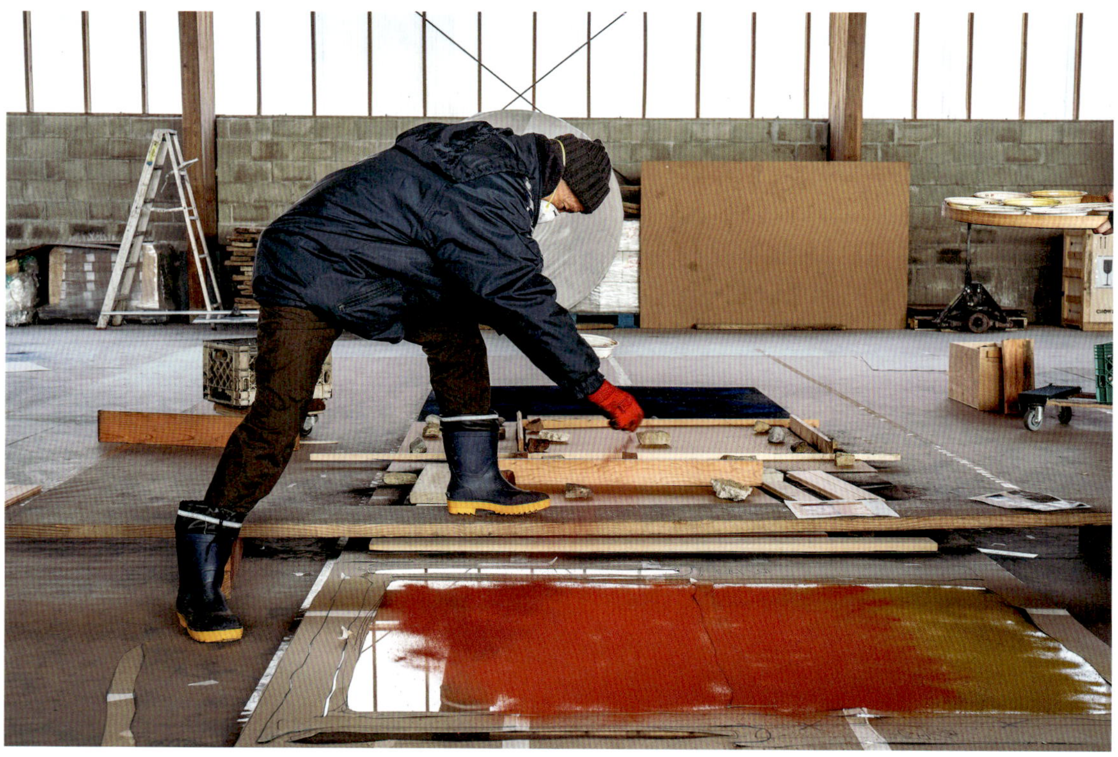

Figure 5.6. Cai Guo-Qiang at work in his studio, sprinkling gunpowder to create *Non-Brand* 非品牌 in 2019

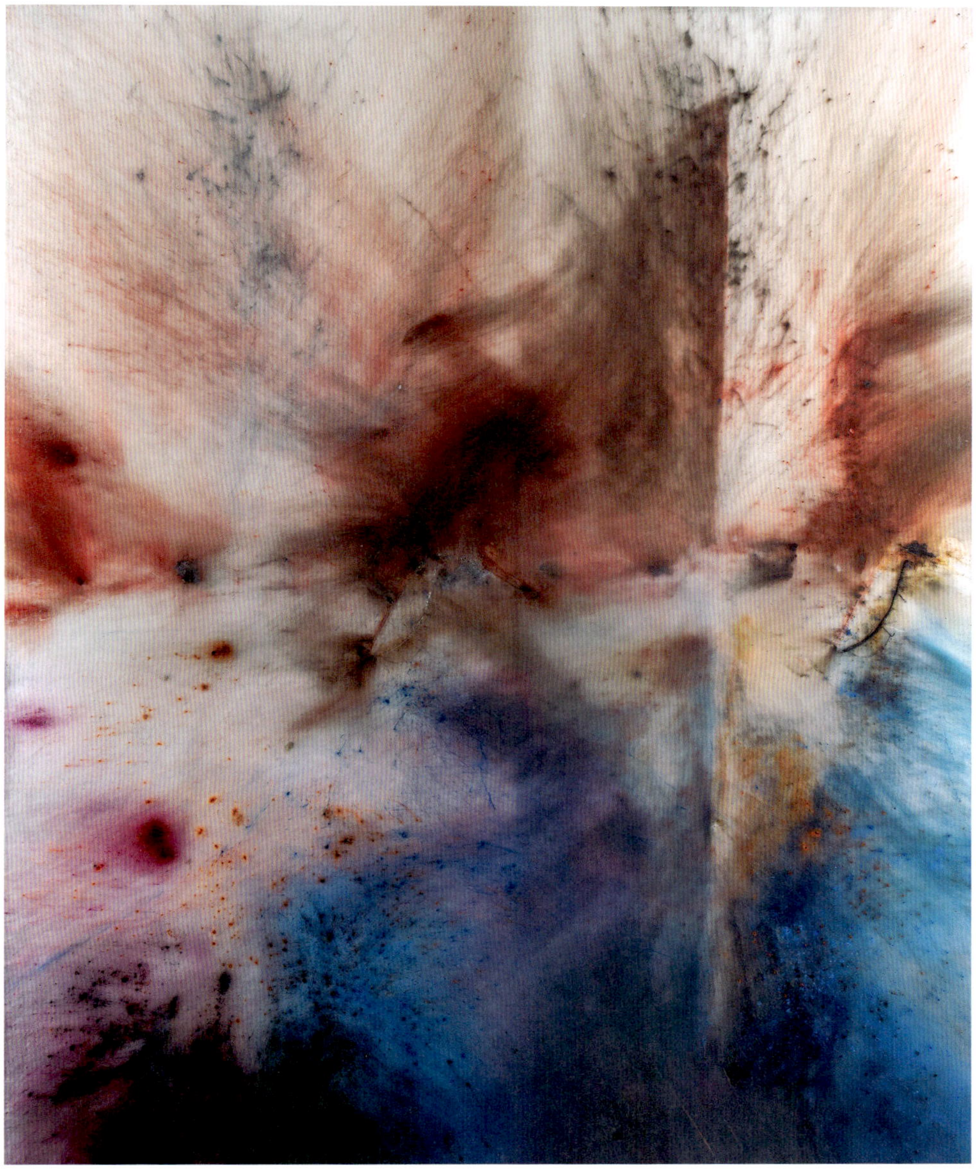

5.5 *Kung Fu*

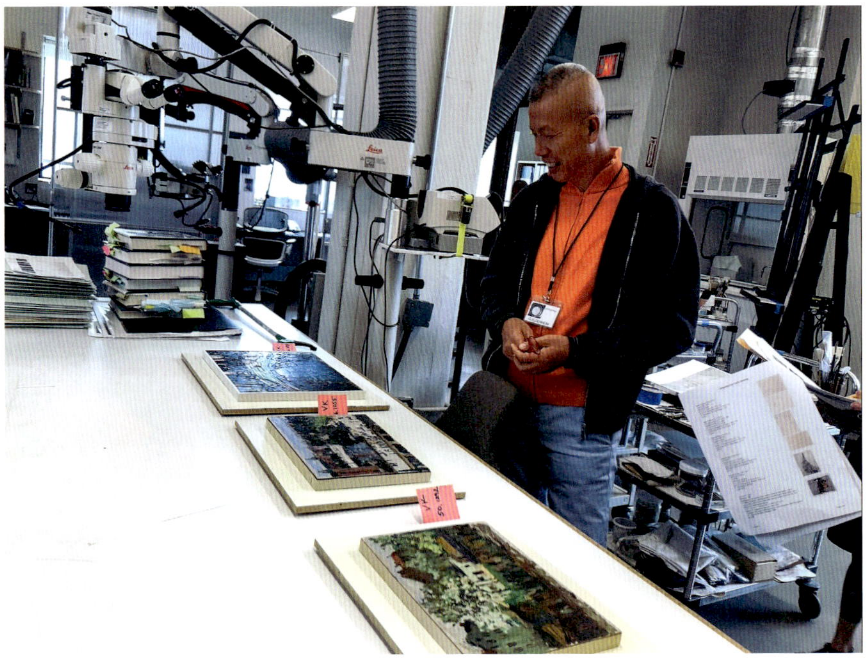

Figure 5.7. Cai Guo-Qiang selecting various artists' early works for inclusion in *Non-Brand* 非品牌 in 2019

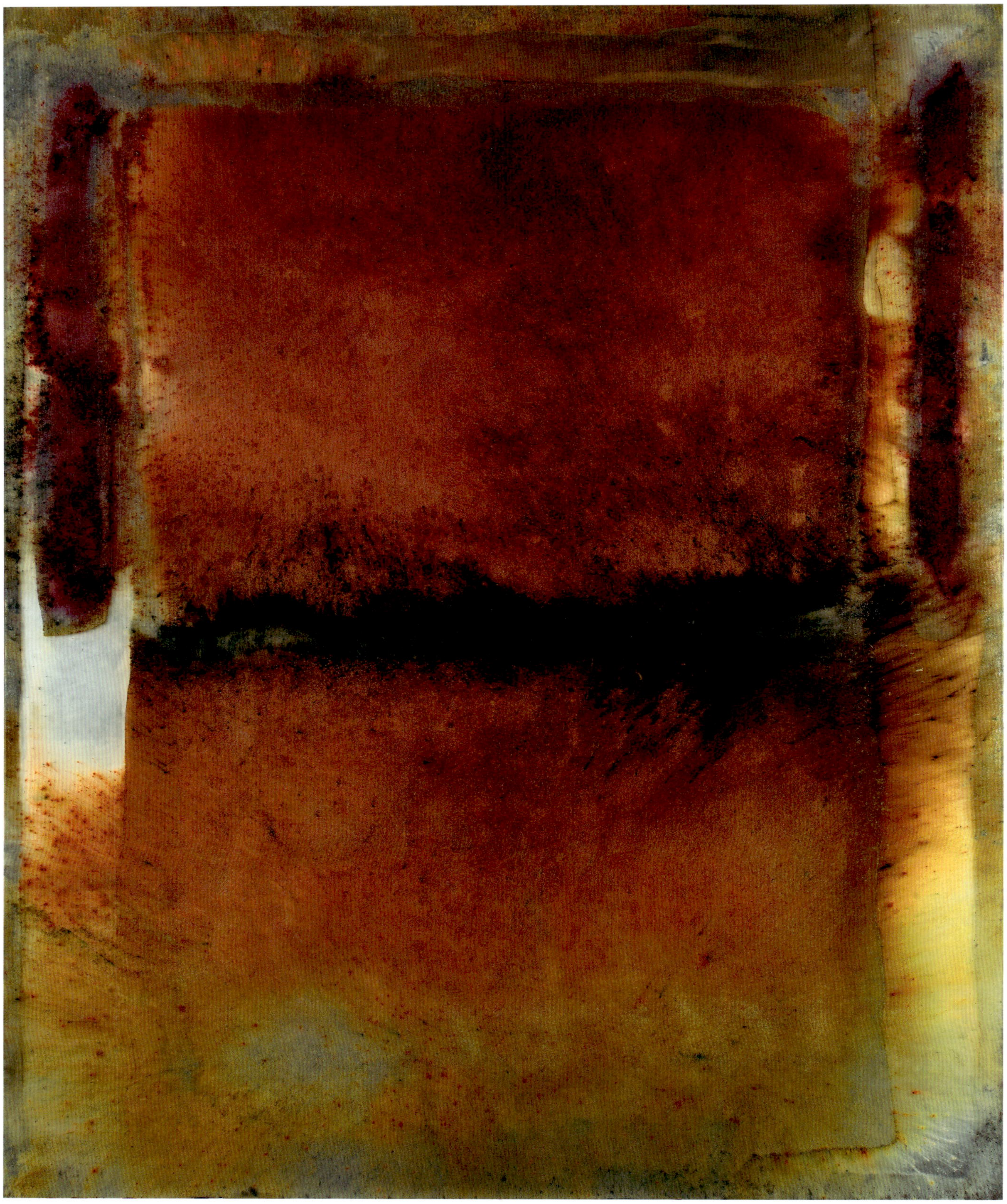

5.2 *Non-Brand* 非品牌 *2*

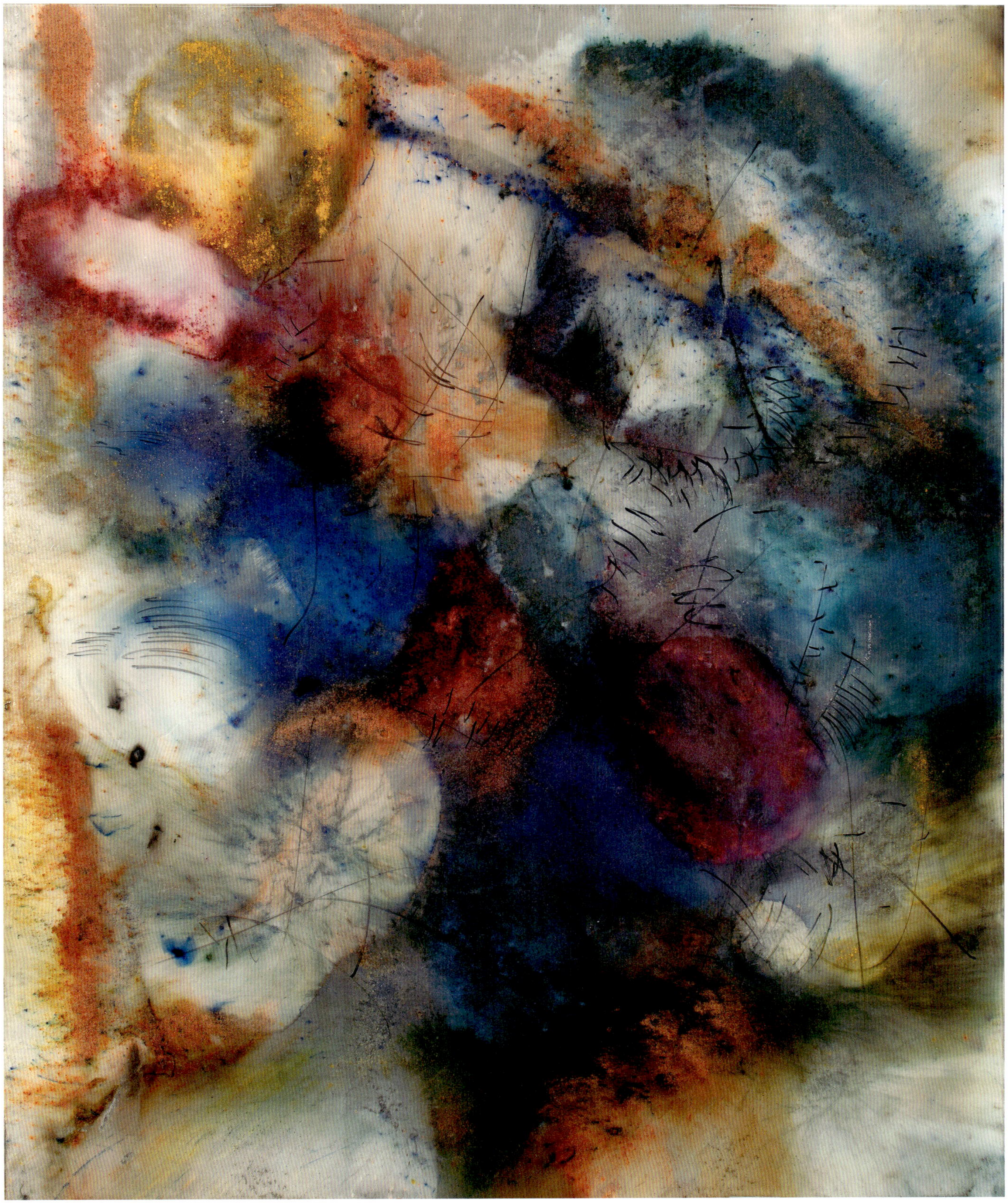

5.1 *Non-Brand* 非品牌 *1*

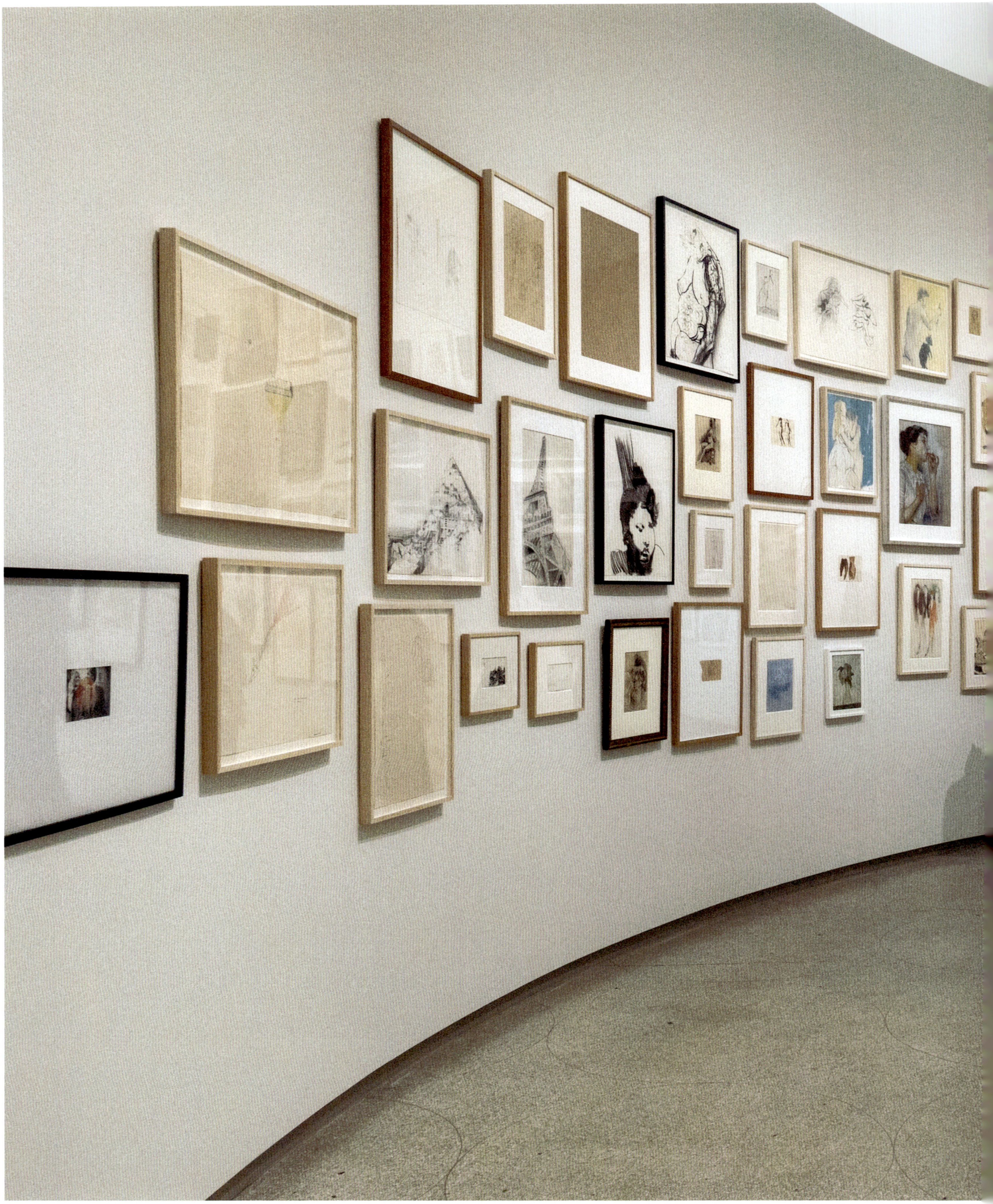

Figure 5.8. Installation view of *Cai Guo-Qiang: Non-Brand* 非品牌 in 2019

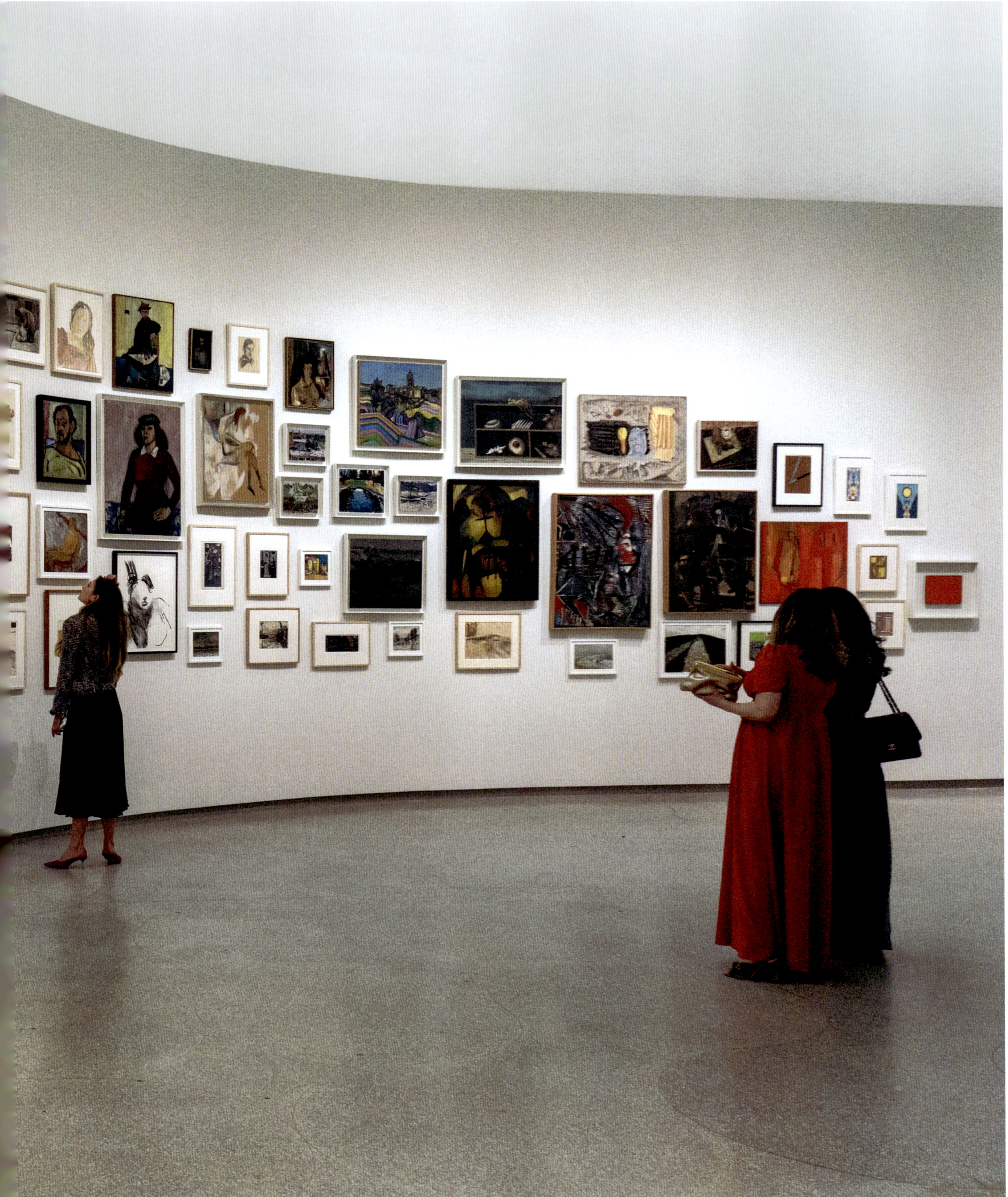

# 6

# Dialogue with Cézanne

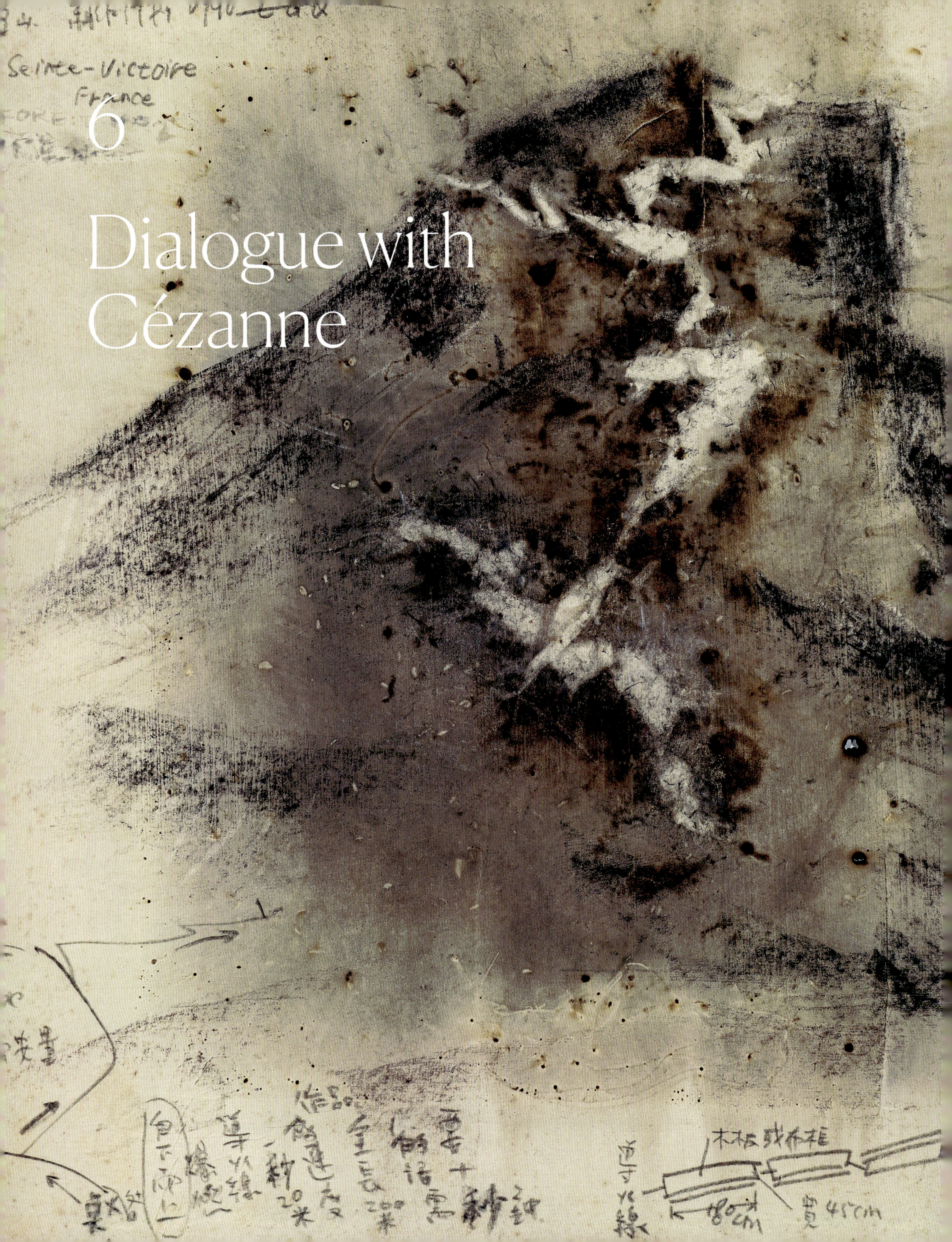

# Ongoing research

Supported by Musée Granet, Aix-en-Provence, France
1989–

Documentary short: directed by Shanshan Xia, produced by 33 Studio (11:16)

The exhibition of Cai's dialogue with Cézanne and the beginnings of modernism was originally set to take place in late 2020 at the Grand Palais in Paris. It was to include a daytime explosion event on the Champs-Élysées, marking the temporary closing of the museum's historic building for renovation. The fire at Notre-Dame de Paris in 2019 caused the postponement of the project until after the Grand Palais's reopening. Cai has nonetheless continued his dialogue with art history.

In July 2019, Cai revisited Cézanne's hometown, Aix-en-Province. Under the guidance of the Director of the Musée Granet and famed Cézanne expert Bruno Ely, he explored Mont Sainte-Victoire, which Cézanne painted again and again throughout his lifetime, the quarries at the foot of the mountain, and the local farms and fields. Cai sought to explore the relationship between Cézanne's paintings, thought, and the scenery he once gazed upon. Opened in 1838, the Musée Granet houses a number of Cézanne's prominent works and archives; Cézanne was a graduate of the Musée Granet's art school.

Cai's first time traveling from Asia to the West thirty years ago was to attempt an explosion event, *Ascending Dragon: Projects for Extraterrestrials No. 2*, at Mont Sainte-Victoire. The work aspired to engage with Cézanne and Western civilization. While the project was ultimately unrealized due to a forest fire prior to the artist's arrival, Cai's envisioning of *Ascending Dragon* was captured in a series of gunpowder drawings, studies, and sketches.

Cai is fascinated by Cézanne because the French painter "looked backward and forward." He longed for the spirit of eternality, as exemplified by masters from the past, while simultaneously thirsted to open new frontiers in art history. Cézanne looked out on his homeland and its fields and could perceive in it the essence of time and space without being tempted by the mere representation of light and shadow. In fact, Cai is fascinated by Cézanne also because he sees Cézanne's shadow within himself.

At this point along his *Individual's Journey Through Western Art History*, the dialogue has, almost miraculously, brought Cai back to key pillars of his own foundations. They comprise, above all, his affection for his hometown, where all his sentiments and artworks can find their origin; his psychological obsession with eternality that is behind his dynamic and ever-changing contemporary art creations; and his perennial exploration of the unseen world and cosmic space-time.

6.2 *Drawing for Ascending Dragon* (detail)

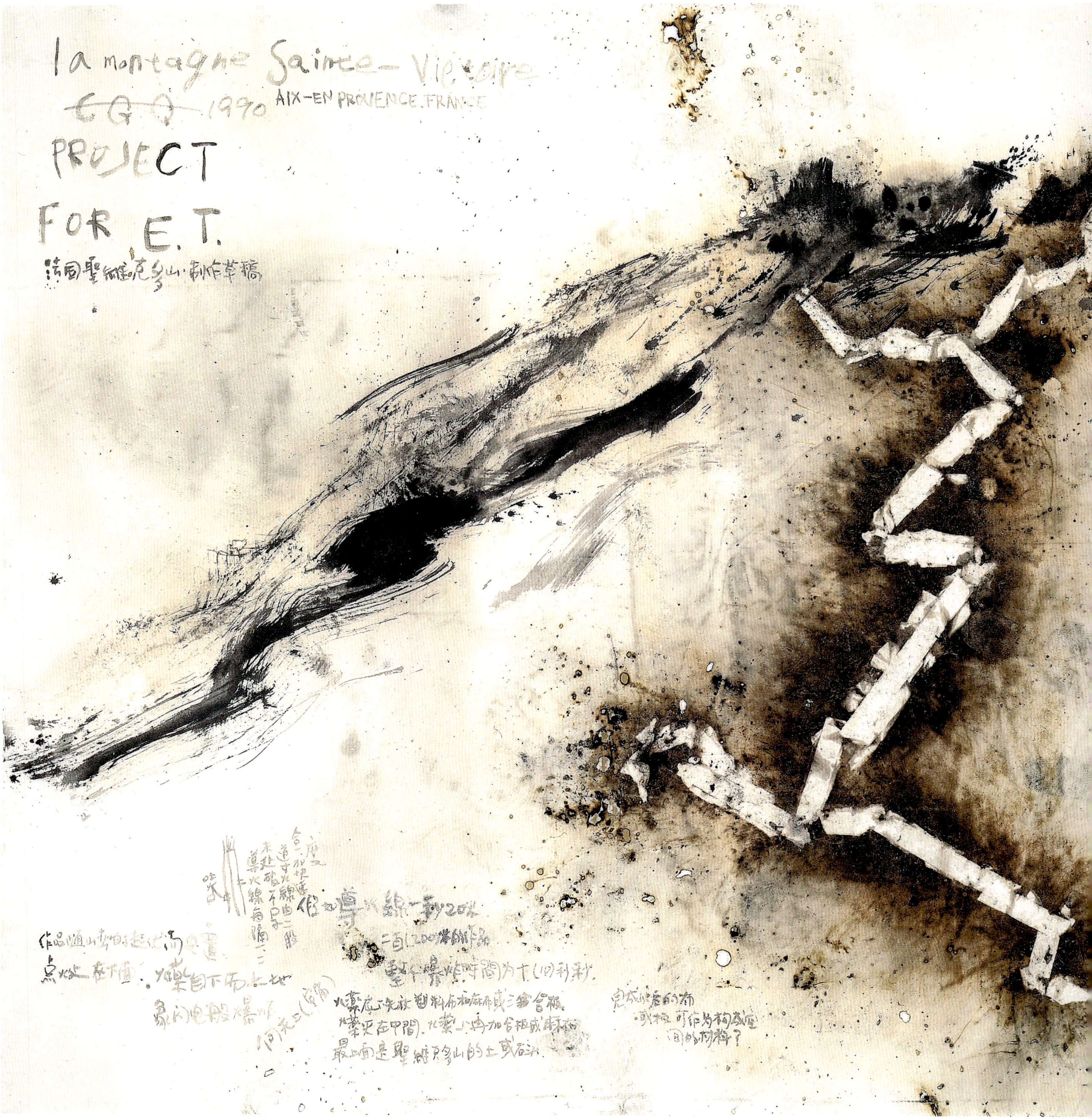


6.1 *Ascending Dragon: Project for Extraterrestrials No. 2*

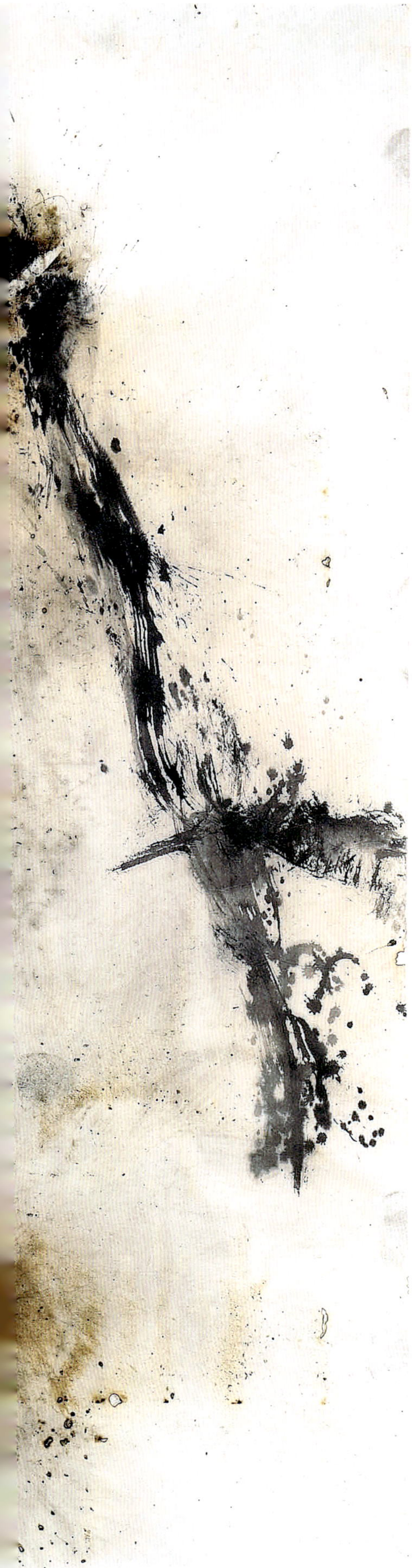

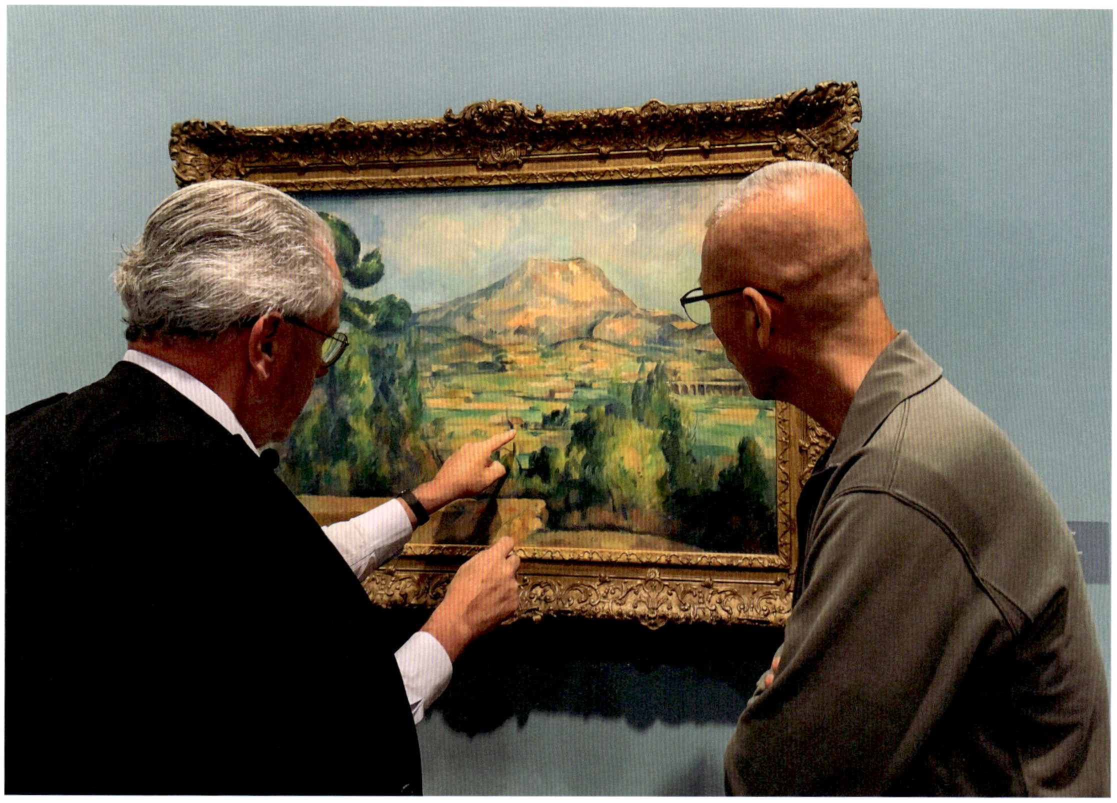

Figure 6.1. Cai Guo-Qiang and Director of Musée Granet Bruno Ely examining a work of Paul Cézanne at the museum in 2019

6.1

*Ascending Dragon: Project for Extraterrestrials No. 2*

升龙：为外星人作的计划第二号

1989

Gunpowder and ink on paper

240 × 300 cm

Collection of Leo Shih

The two gunpowder drawings from 1989 envision the unrealized explosion event *Ascending Dragon*, for which Cai had planned to use gunpowder and fuse to ignite an airborne dragon that would ascend from the foot to the summit of Mont Sainte-Victoire at dusk. The drawings were also Cai's first works dedicated to Western art history.

Related Work

6.2

*Drawing for Ascending Dragon*

为"升龙"所作草图

1989

Gunpowder and ink on paper

66.5 × 72 cm

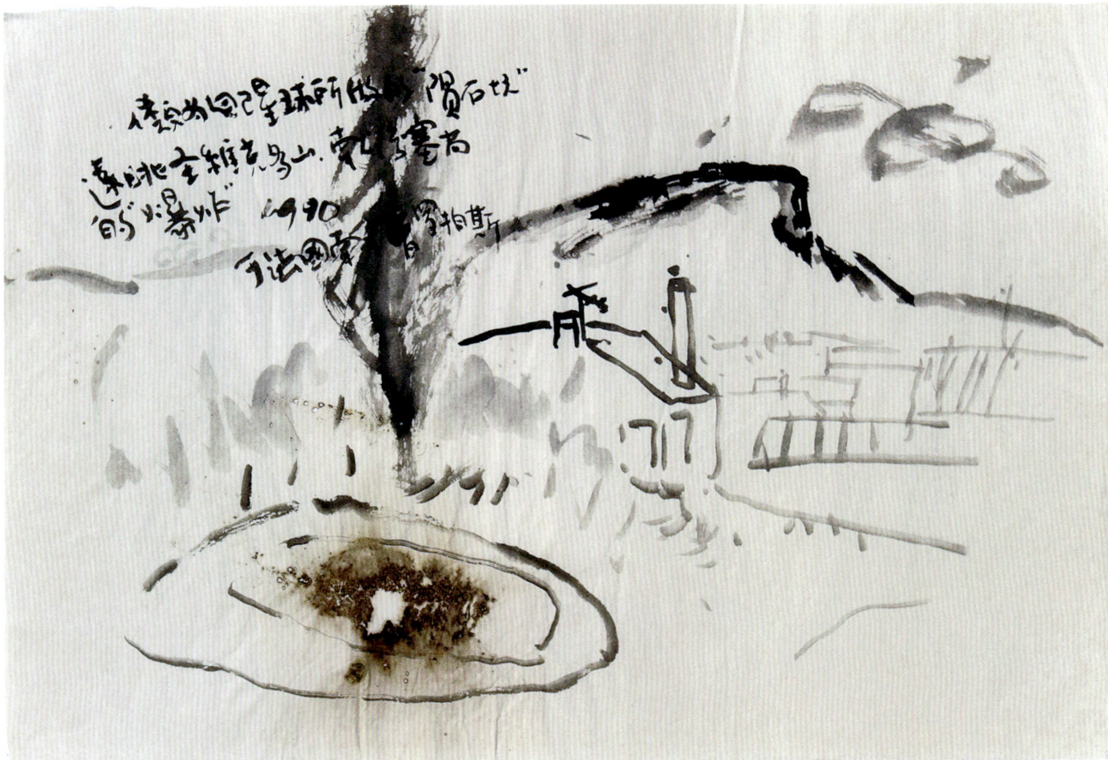

6.3 *"Craters" Made by Humans for Their Own Planet No. 1: Looking at Mont Sainte-Victoire from a Distance, the Explosion Dedicated to Paul Cézanne*

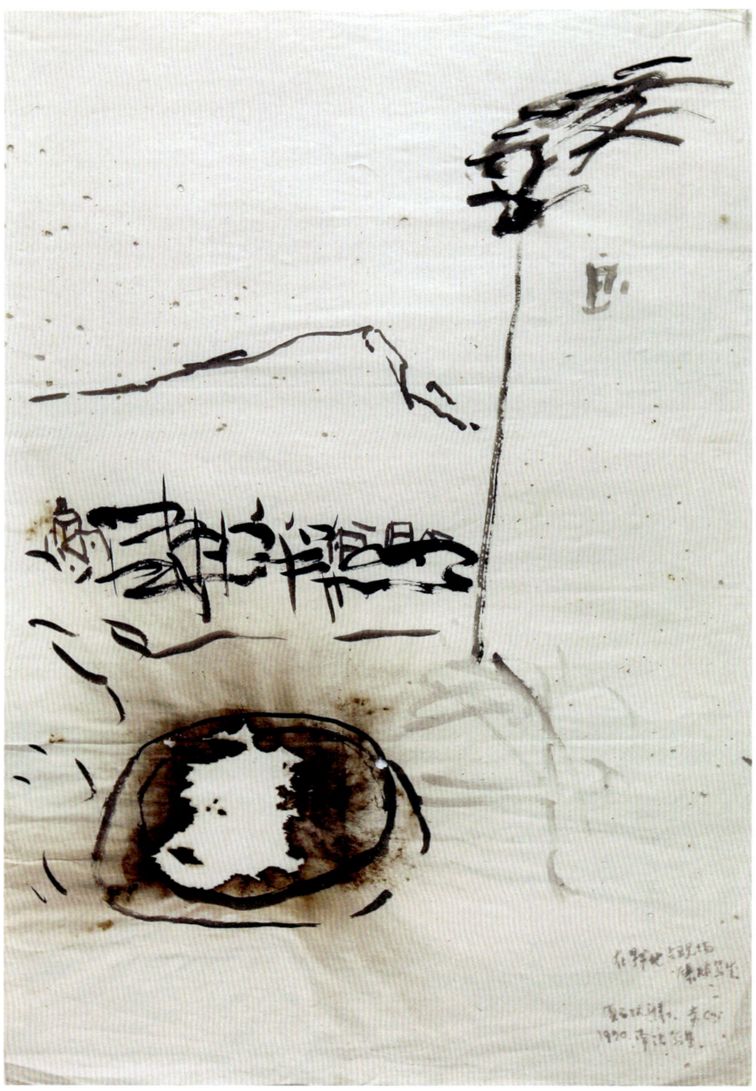

6.4 *"Craters" Made by Humans for Their Own Planet No. 11: Sketch on Explosion Site*

6.3

*"Craters" Made by Humans for Their Own Planet No. 1: Looking at Mont Sainte-Victoire from a Distance, the Explosion Dedicated to Paul Cézanne*

人类为自己星球所做的“陨石坑” No. 1:远眺圣维克多山、献给塞尚的爆炸

1990

Gunpowder and ink on paper

63.5 × 93.98 cm

6.4

*"Craters" Made by Humans for Their Own Planet No. 11: Sketch on Explosion Site*

人类自己星球所做的“陨石坑” No. 11:在野地上现场爆炸写生

1990

Gunpowder and ink on paper

92.71 × 63.5 cm

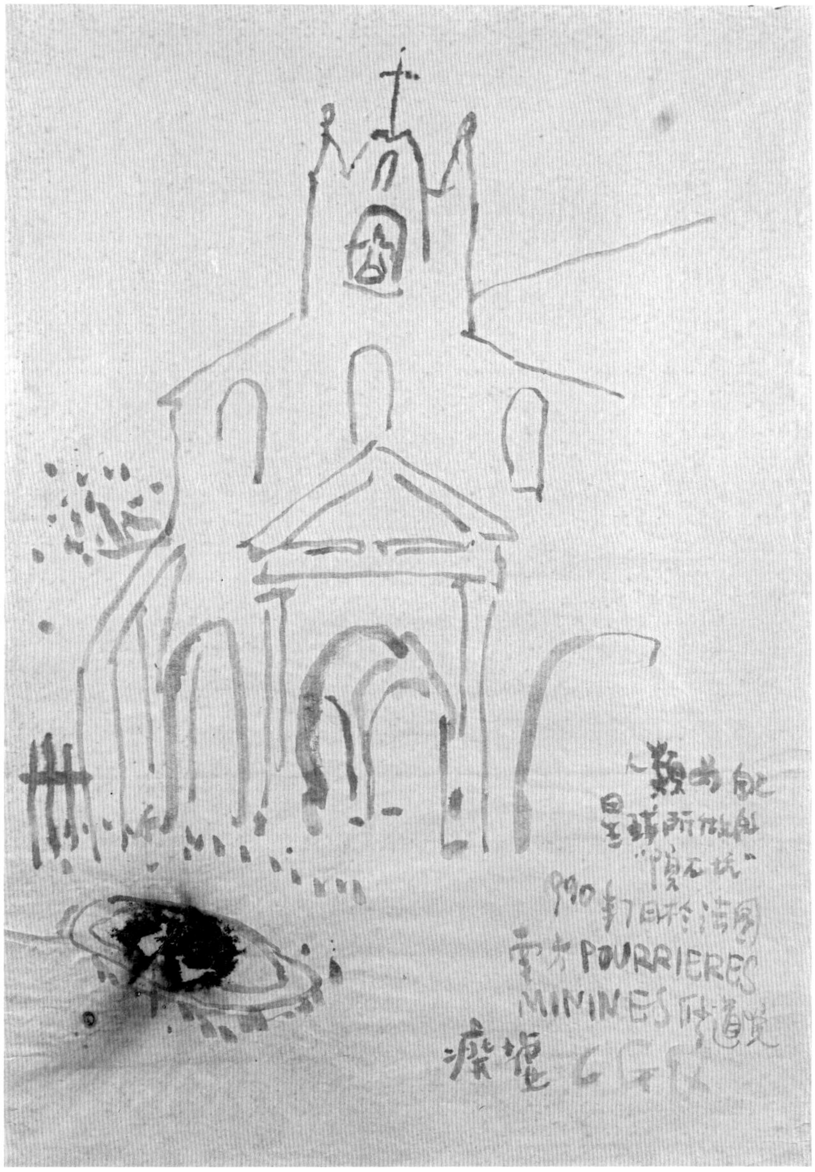


6.5 *"Craters" Made by Humans for Their Own Planet: At the Remains of the Minimes Convent*

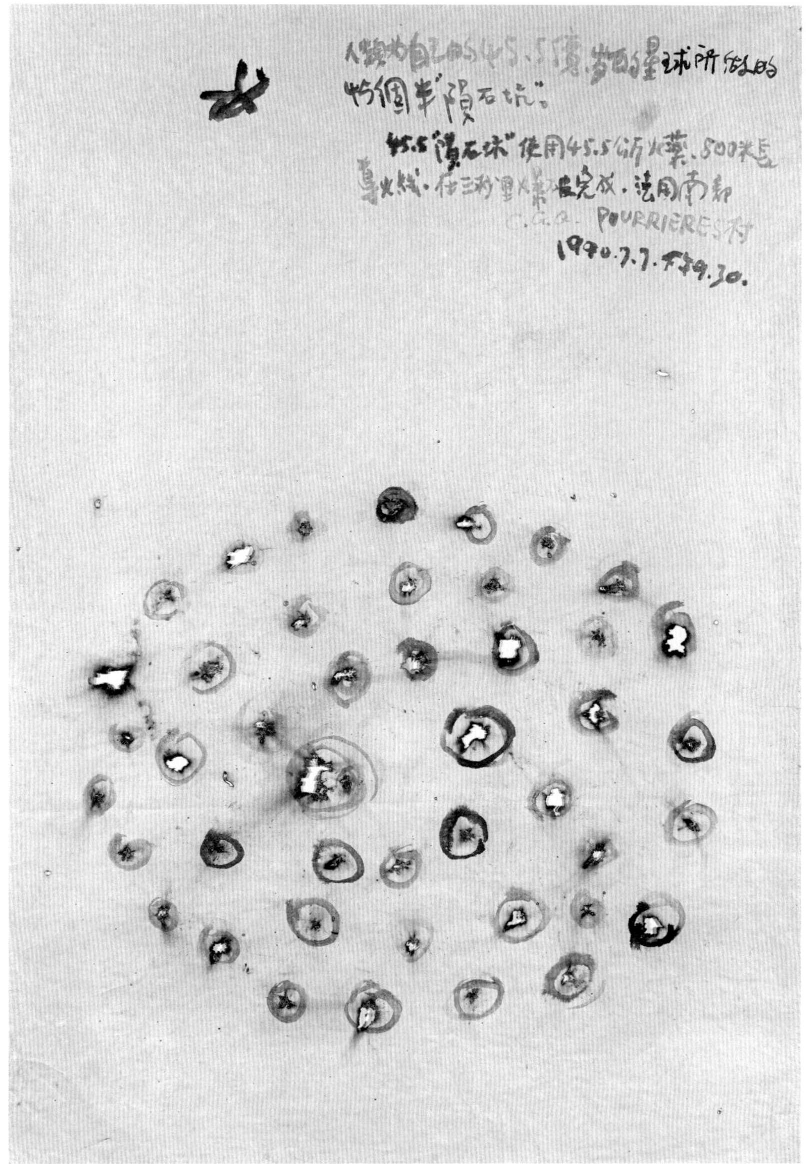


6.6 *"Craters" Made by Humans for Their Own Planet: Pourrières*

6.5

*"Craters" Made by Humans for Their Own Planet: At the Remains of the Minimes Convent*

人类为自己星球所做的“陨石坑”：Minimes 修道院废墟

1990

Gunpowder and ink on paper

92.71 × 63.5 cm

6.6

*"Craters" Made by Humans for Their Own Planet: Pourrières*

人类为自己星球所做的“陨石坑”：Pourrières

1990

Gunpowder and ink on paper

93.98 × 63.5 cm

6.7

*Crater*

陨石坑

1990

Gunpowder on papier-mâché

56 × 67 × 2.5 cm

6.8

*Crater No. 3*

陨石坑 No. 3

1990

Gunpowder on papier-mâché

Diameter: 39.4 cm

6.9

*Crater*

陨石坑

1989

Gunpowder, oil, and paper pulp on canvas

61 × 73 × 3 cm

Cai created these gunpowder drawings for a 1990 explosion event in Aix-en-Provence, *45.5 Meteorite Craters Made by Humans on Their 45.5 Hundred Million Year Old Planet: Project for Extraterrestrials No. 3*. For his first explosion event outside of Asia, Cai exploded "craters," which took one month to dig, in the blink of an eye. The explosion took on the perspective of extraterrestrial life and aspired to engage with the sense of cosmic space-time found in Cézanne's art.

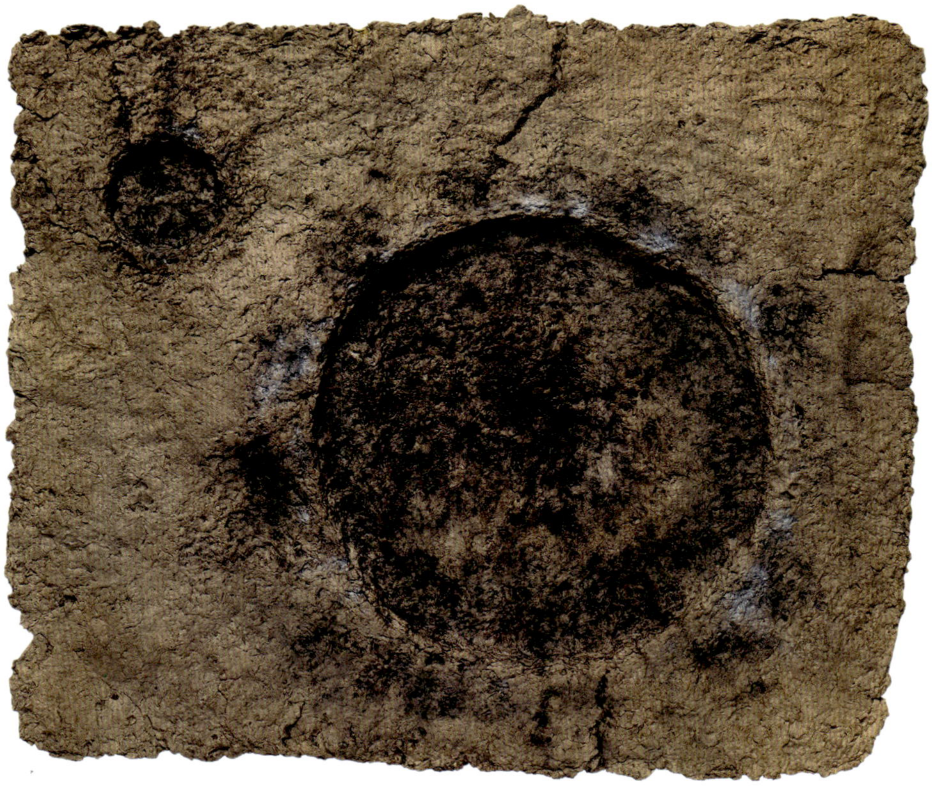

6.7 *Crater*

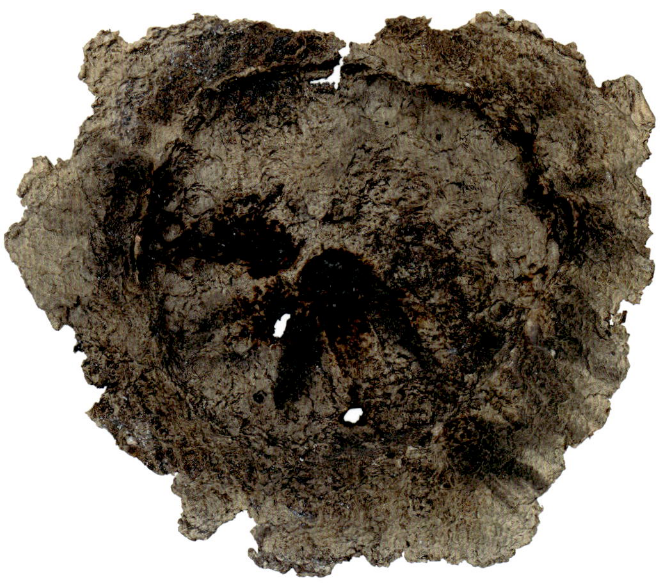

6.8 *Crater No. 3*

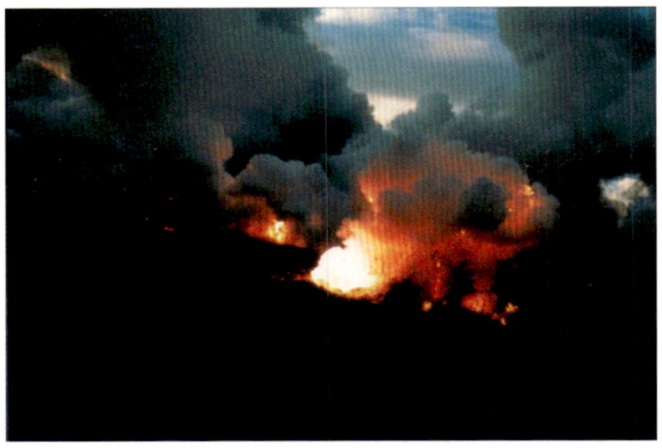

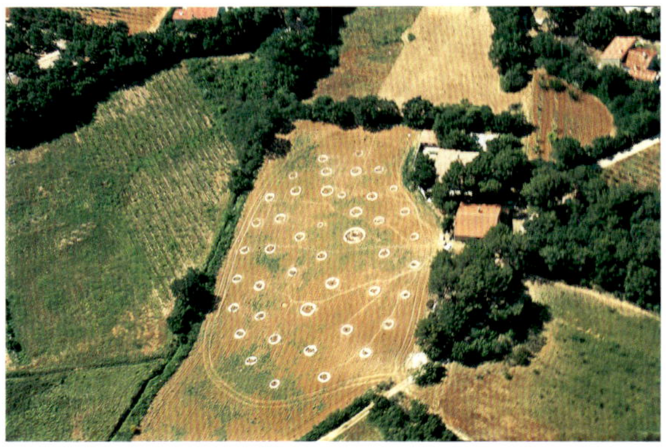

Figures 6.2 and 6.3. Ignition (top) and bird's-eye view (bottom) of *45.5 Meteorite Craters Made by Humans on Their 45.5 Hundred Million Year Old Planet: Project for Extraterrestrials No. 3* (1990)

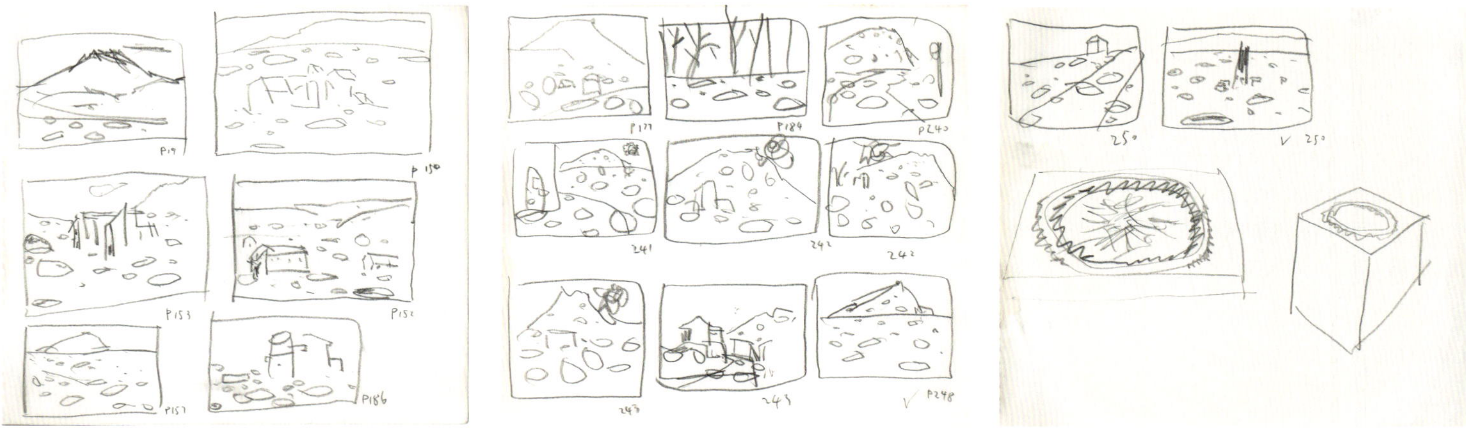

Figures 6.4a–c. *Sketches for 45.5 Meteorite Craters Made by Humans on Their 45.5 Hundred Million Year Old Planet: Project for Extraterrestrials No. 3* (1990). Pencil on paper, 21.6 × 24.5 cm each

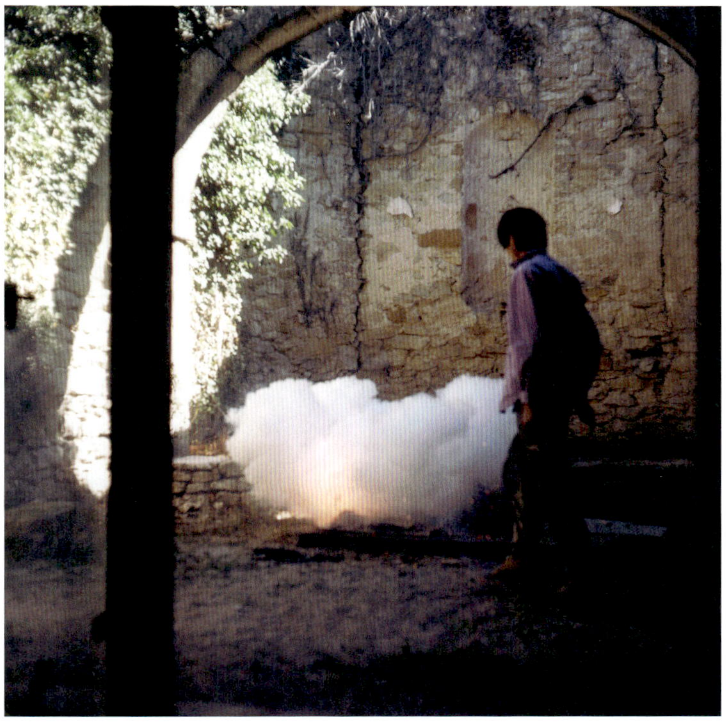
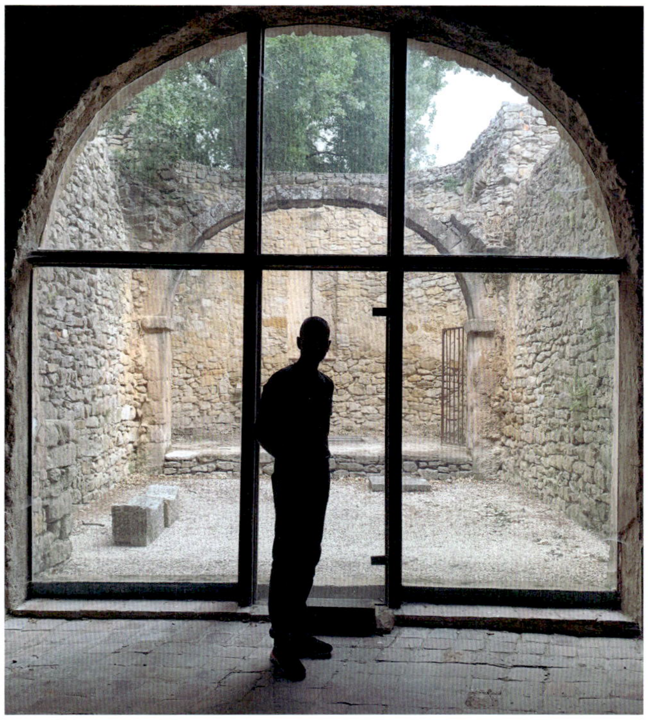

Figures 6.5 and 6.6. Cai Guo-Qiang at the Minimes Convent in Pourrières, France, nearly thirty years apart, in 1990 (left) and 2019 (right)

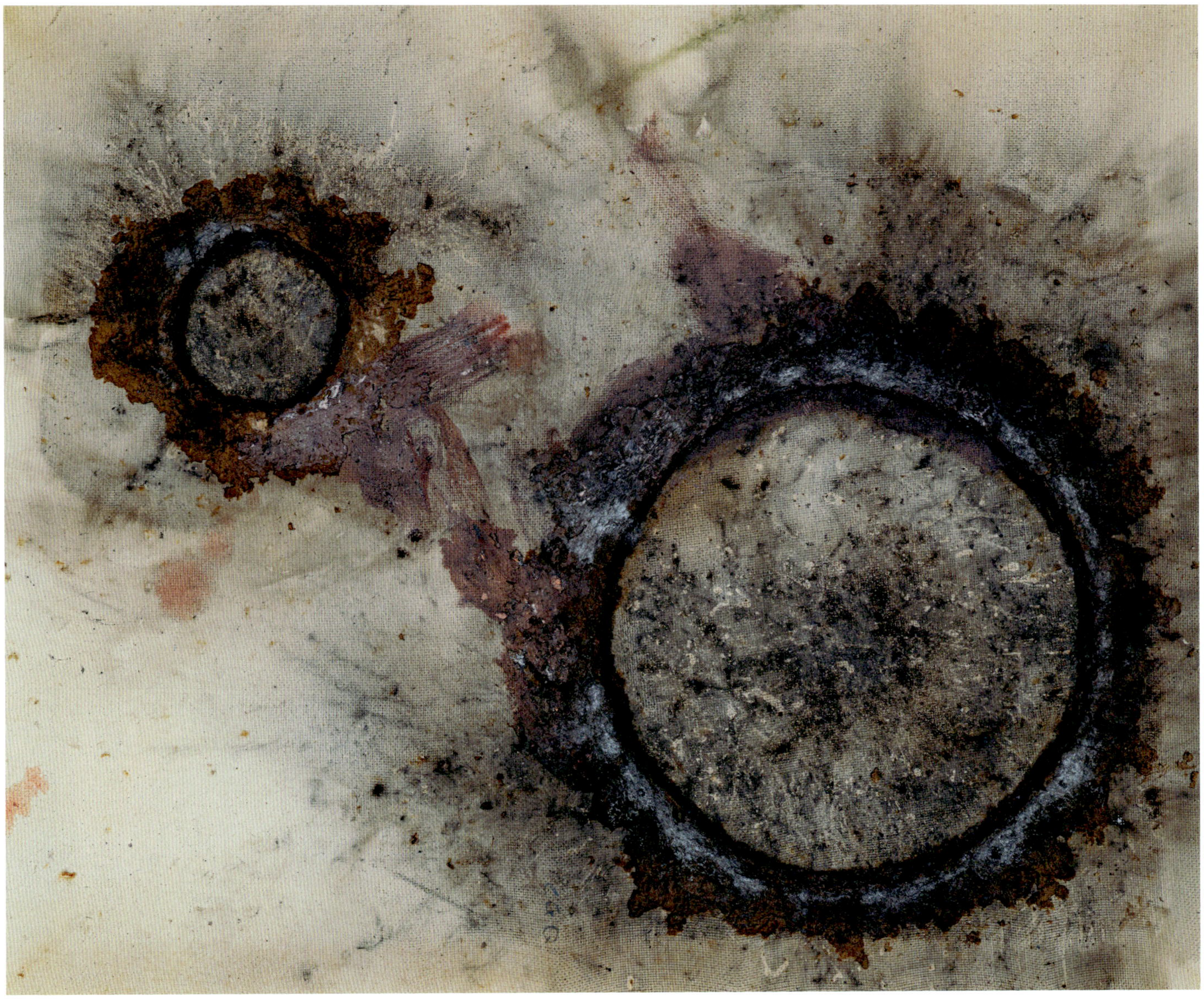

6.9 *Crater*

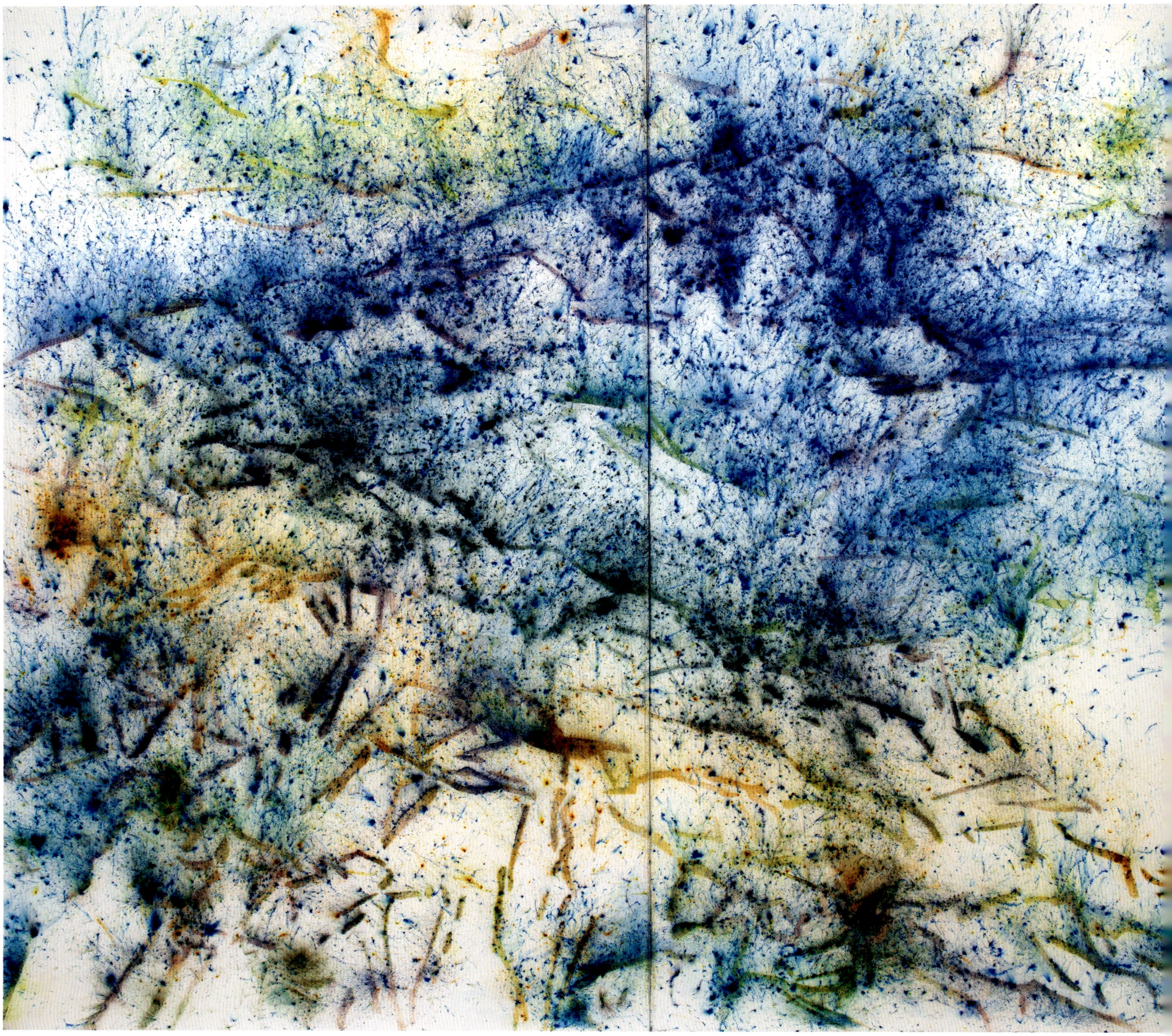

6.10 *Structure*

6.10

*Structure*

结构

2019

Gunpowder on canvas

240 × 300 cm

6.11

*Cypress of Mont Sainte-Victoire*

有松树的圣维克多山

2019

Gunpowder on canvas

275 × 200 cm

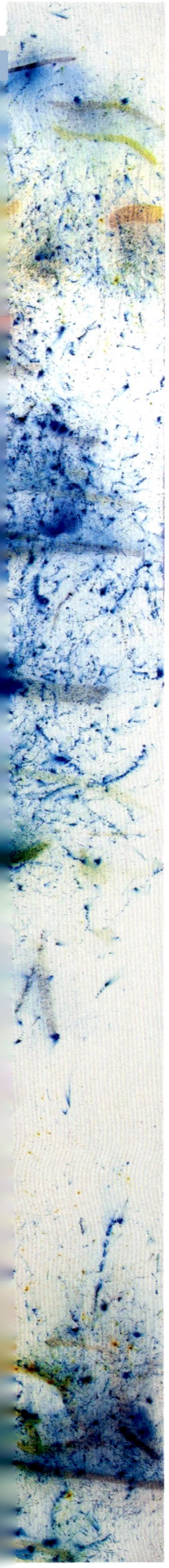

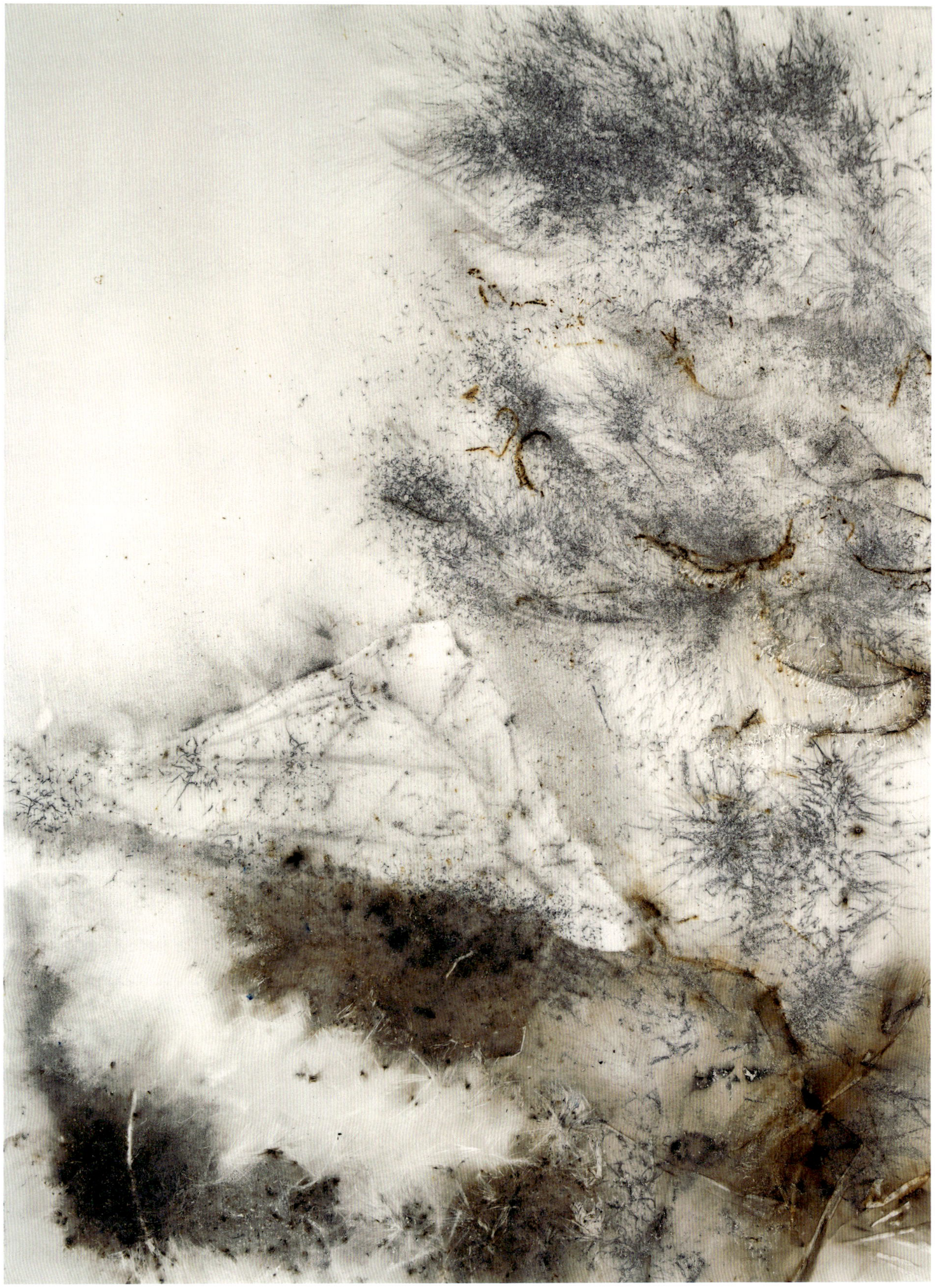

6.11 *Cypress of Mont Sainte-Victoire*

Mont Sainte-Victoire is an iconic subject in Cézanne's work. In 1989, Cai created a proposal and gunpowder drawings for a cosmos-themed explosion event based on Mont Sainte-Victoire. Thirty years later, he returned to the site to affirm his longtime feelings regarding Cézanne, which were then translated into this series of works. For Cai, Cézanne's use of light, shadow, and colors is distinct from most Impressionist paintings and his works possess a cosmology that resonates with the spatial and temporal constancy found in Chinese landscape painting. Cai uses Cézanne as a point of comparison between the aesthetics and essences of Eastern and Western art.

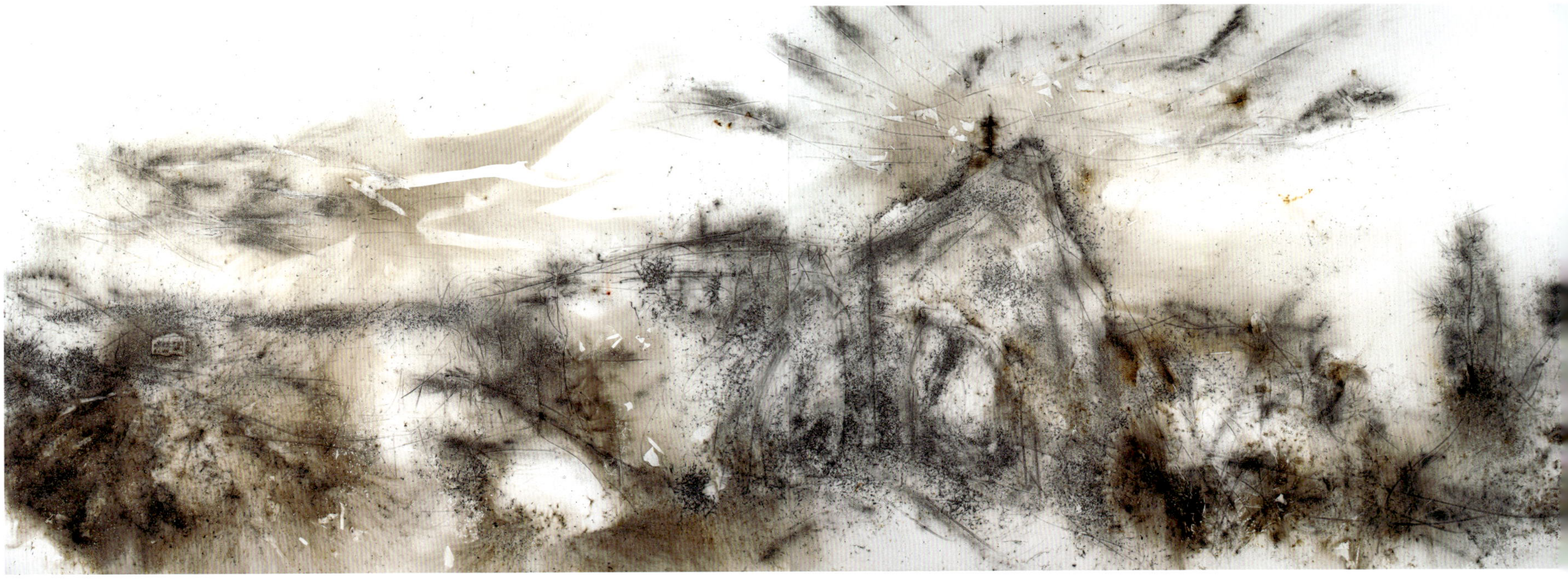

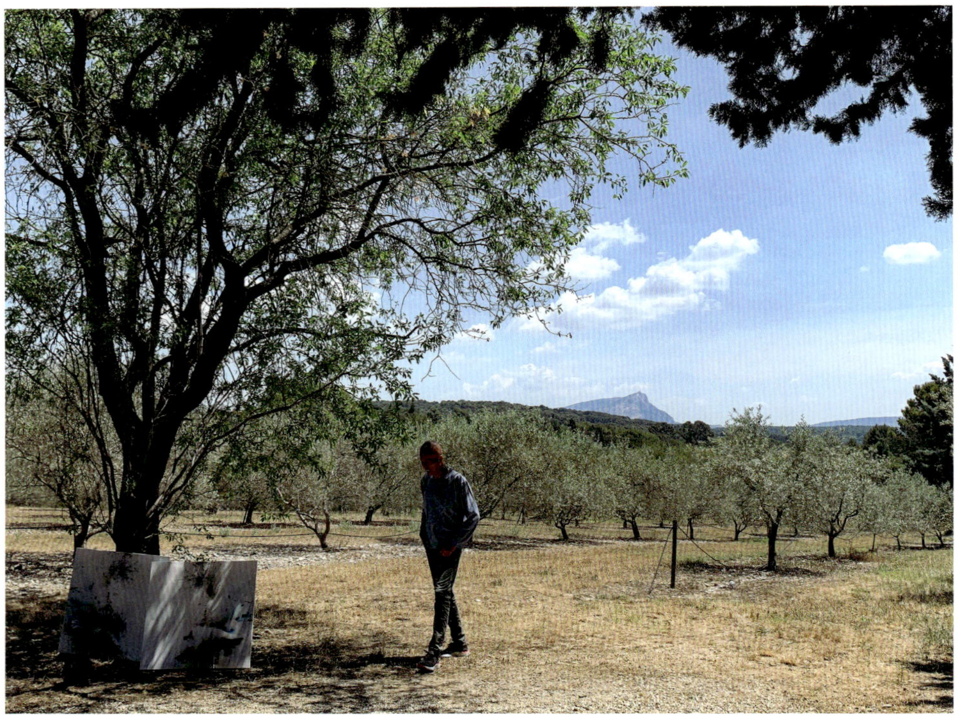

Figure 6.7. Cai Guo-Qiang painting outdoors with Mont Sainte-Victoire visible in the distance in 2019

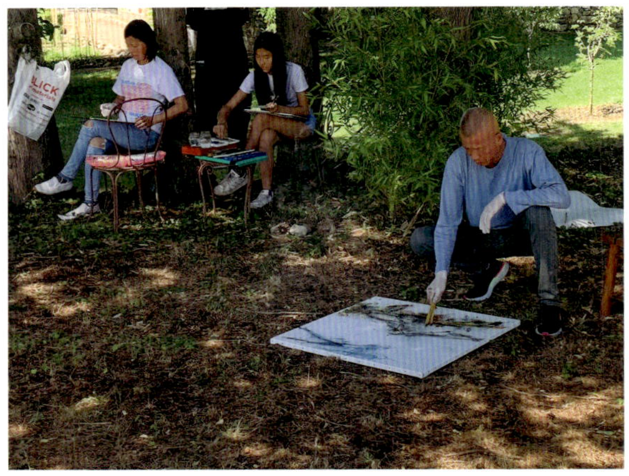

Figure 6.8. Cai Guo-Qiang paintirg with his family in Aix-en-Provence, France in 2019

6.12

## *En Route*
## 路上

2019
Gunpowder on canvas
200 × 1100 cm

In *En Route*, Cai documented his thoughts and frame of mind as he hiked Mont Sainte-Victoire in 2019, dialoguing with Cézanne across time. Cai wrote, "The mountain ridge up Sainte-Victoire was not an easy hike. With the Christian cross at the mountaintop ahead of me and steep cliffs on either side, I almost forgot whether this was Cézanne's hometown or a symbol of the West in between my heavy breaths. This is the type of aerobic exercise that cultivates a vital, expansive *qi*; to cultivate such *qi*, one must find high peaks and command oreself to surmount them."

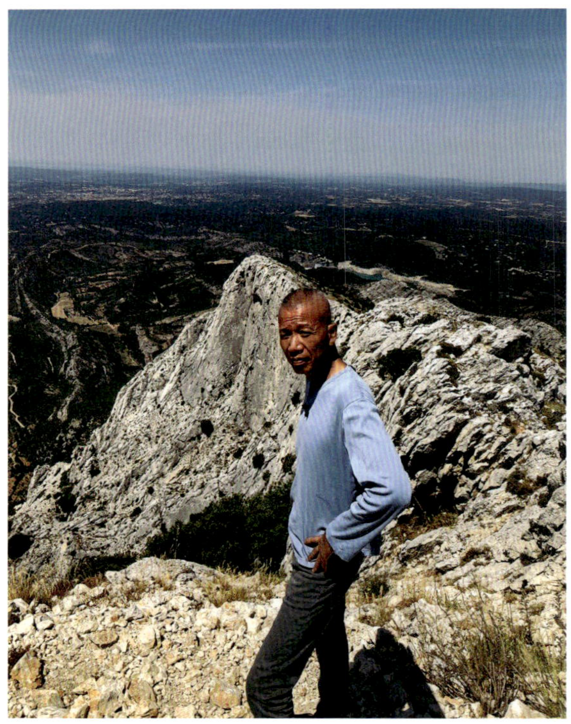

Figure 6.9. Cai Guo-Qiang atop Mont Sainte-Victoire in 2019

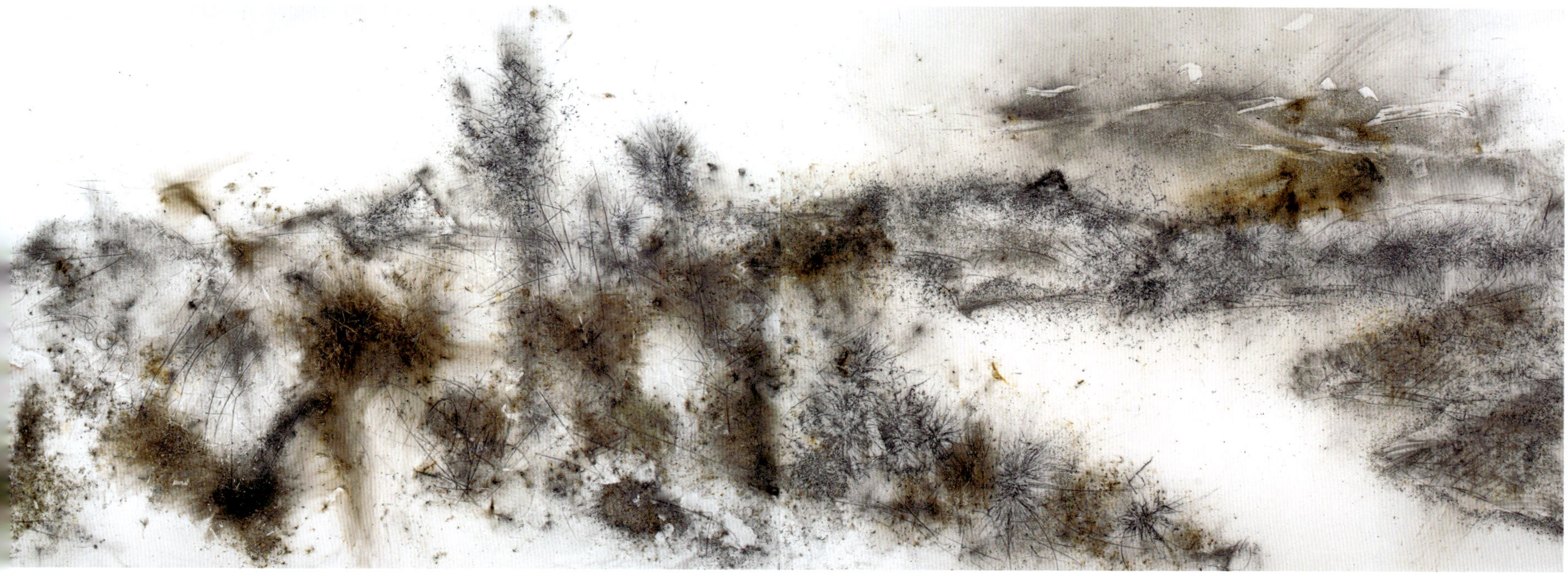

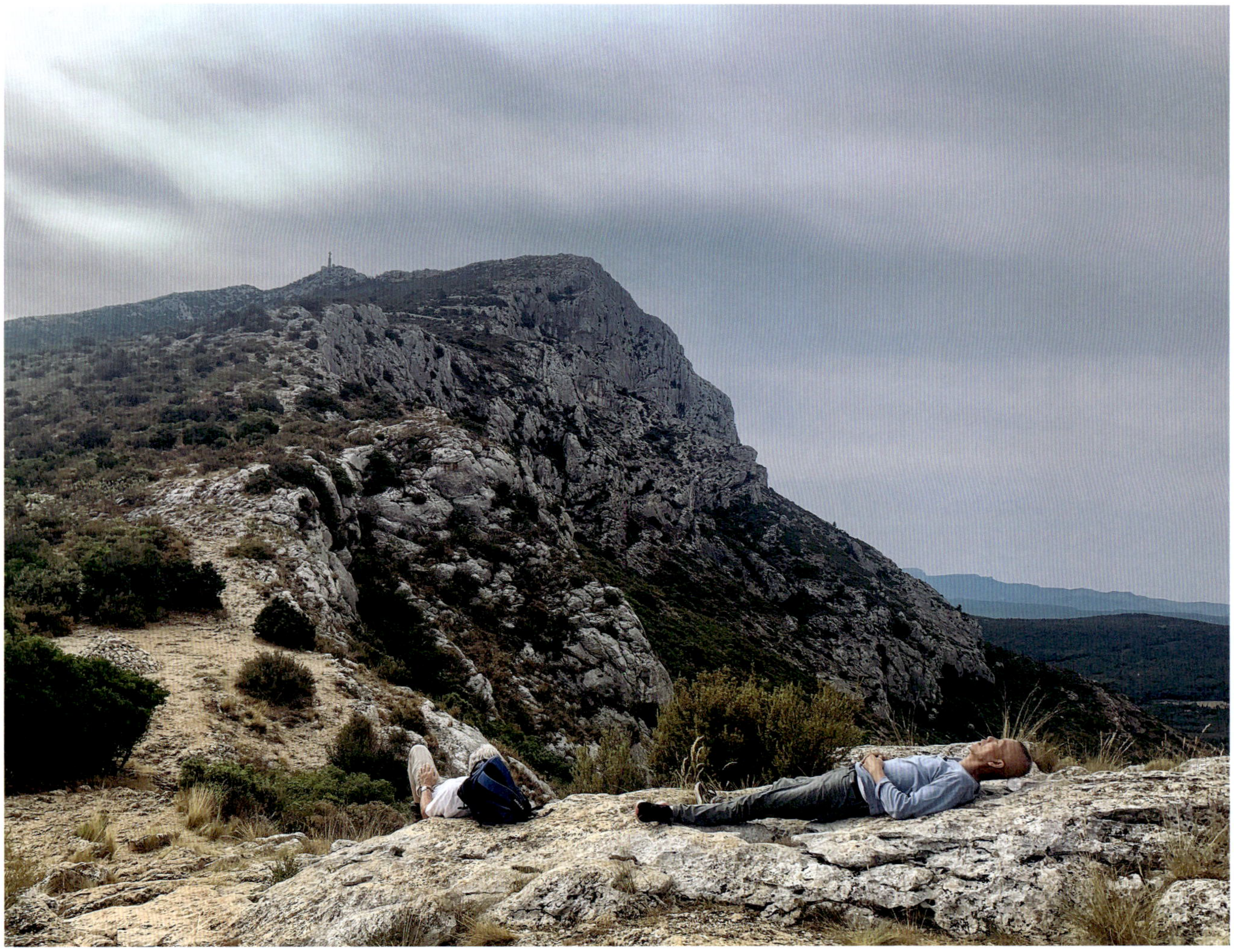

Figure 6.10. Cai Guo-Qiang lying on Mont Sainte-Victoire in Aix-en-Provence, France in 2019

# 7

# Dialogue with the Middle Ages

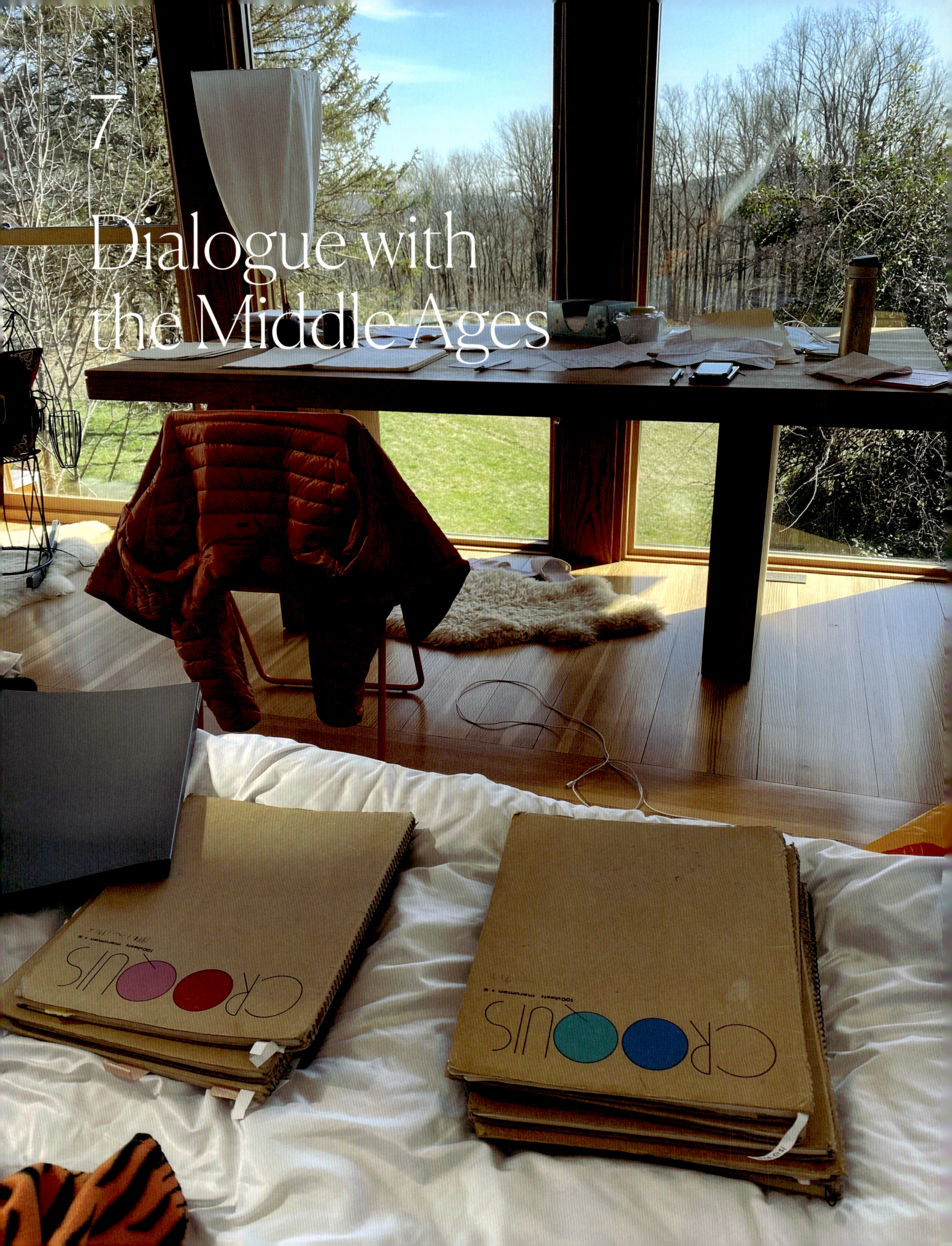

# Ongoing research

Supported by The Metropolitan Museum of Art, New York, U.S.
2018–

Documentary short: *Voyage Through the Middle Ages During the Pandemic*, directed by Shanshan Xia, produced by 33 Studio

The lengthy duration and sheer diversity of the Middle Ages once made it a difficult subject for Cai, as it offered no clear entry point. Yet, this same mystique enticed him to find alternative and unprecedented ways by which to start a dialogue.

In 2018, Cai launched extensive research on the period, under the guidance of the curatorial team of The Metropolitan Museum of Art's Department of Medieval Art. Founded in 1870, it is a paradigm of the encyclopedic museum. In particular, it holds one of the most expansive and exquisite collections of medieval art in the world. In addition to the main museum on Fifth Avenue, The Met Cloisters, located in northern Manhattan, is dedicated to exhibiting European medieval art and architecture.

For Cai, various themes of the Middle Ages—surrealism, spirituality, hell, death, conceptuality, symbolism, ornamentation, absurdities, and secularity—echo his longstanding inquiry into dark matter and energy. Cai's creativity is stimulated by the energy from another space-time. This energy comes from the impact of Eastern civilizations on the West, along with the clashes and fusions of different religions, nations, and cultures. In his view, faith in the unseen world forms another facet of existential meaning in contemporary society. This energy also originates from the beliefs, social etiquette, aesthetics, and non-secular lifestyle of the Middle Ages, as well as the symbolism and ornate styles of art from the period—the extensive use of gilded iconography with stiff and bold lines, along with a surrealism that feels distant and aloof.

Cai planned to visit a series of historically important medieval sites in the spring of 2020—a *Voyage Through the Middle Ages* that would channel the cosmicality and the exploration of the unseen world in Cai's own art. The entire trip was to focus on monasteries that preserve the medieval atmosphere, practices, and sense of isolation. He would travel to Amiens and Chartreuse in France, Ravenna and Palermo in Italy, Córdoba and Seville in Spain, Nicosia in Cyprus, Mount Sinai in Egypt, Mount Athos in Greece, and the Judaean Desert in Israel and Palestine.

In this *Voyage*, Cai had looked forward to "experiencing this period when human desire skidded to a massive stop in history, and the self-exile that took place on both a spiritual plane and in daily life." However, the sudden global outbreak of COVID-19 put a pause on all travel, and the *Voyage* was suspended. In the three months of self-isolation during which the world came to a standstill, Cai "used this time to isolate from his busy self and the art events taking place today, instead focusing on learning and self-reflection." This, in a sense, was a response to the state of mind held by people who lived in the medieval era, when the Black Death swept through the entirety of Europe six centuries ago. *Black Light No. 1* and *Medieval Study: Tower of Grotesques* (nos. 7.4 and 7.3), featured in this exhibition at the Palace Museum, were important works from Cai's isolation during the pandemic.

Figure 7.1. Cai Guo-Qiang's sketchbooks from the 1980s and 1990s at his New Jersey home in 2020

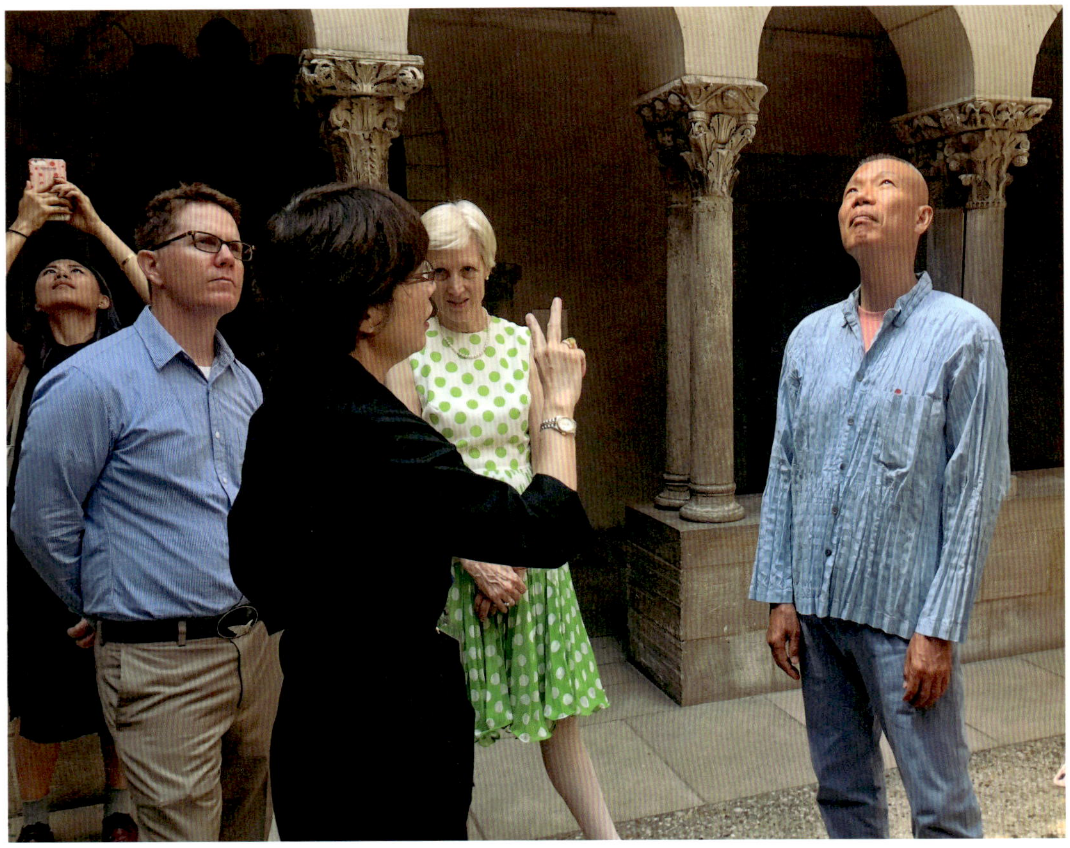

Figure 7.2. Cai Guo-Qiang studying medieval art under the guidance of the curators from The Met Cloisters in New York in 2018

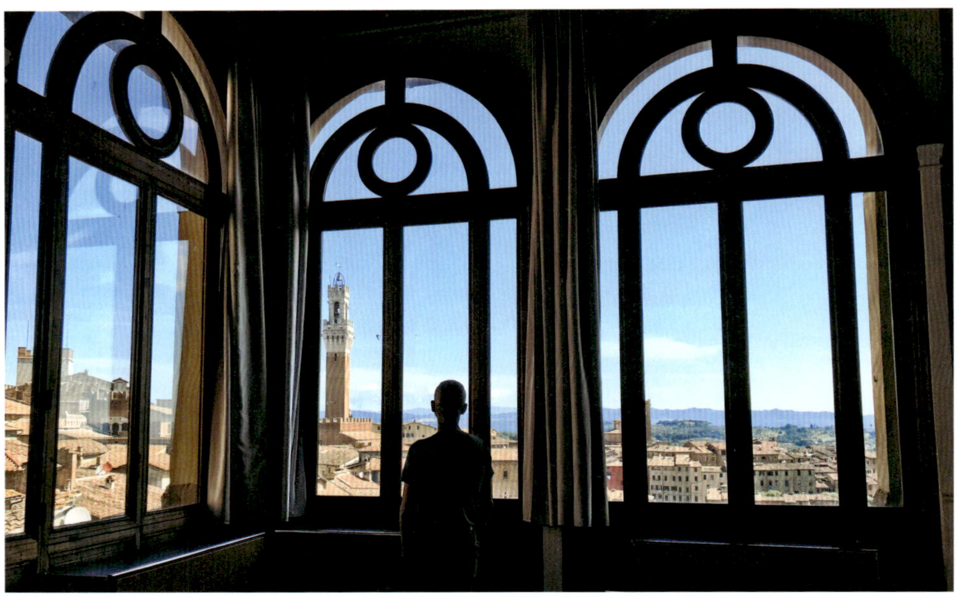

Figure 7.3. Cai Guo-Qiang looking out over Siena, Italy in 2018

7.1

*Hometown Sky Ladder*
故乡的天梯

2015
Gunpowder on paper
400 × 300 cm
PINAULT COLLECTION

This gunpowder drawing was made for Cai's explosion event *Sky Ladder* and portrays a 500-meter ladder of golden fireworks ascending off the coast of his hometown of Quanzhou at dawn. The ladder links heaven and earth while conversing with the vast infinity. The project originated from the artist's childhood dream of touching the clouds and picking the stars.

*Sky Ladder* was realized at its fourth attempt after diverse challenges and setbacks over twenty-one years in different places around the world. Smartphone footage shot by a spectator attracted over 56 million views and 1.1 million reposts on Facebook. The artwork also became the centerpiece of the Netflix documentary *Sky Ladder: The Art of Cai Guo-Qiang*, directed by Oscar-winning filmmaker Kevin Macdonald, available to stream globally in seven different languages.

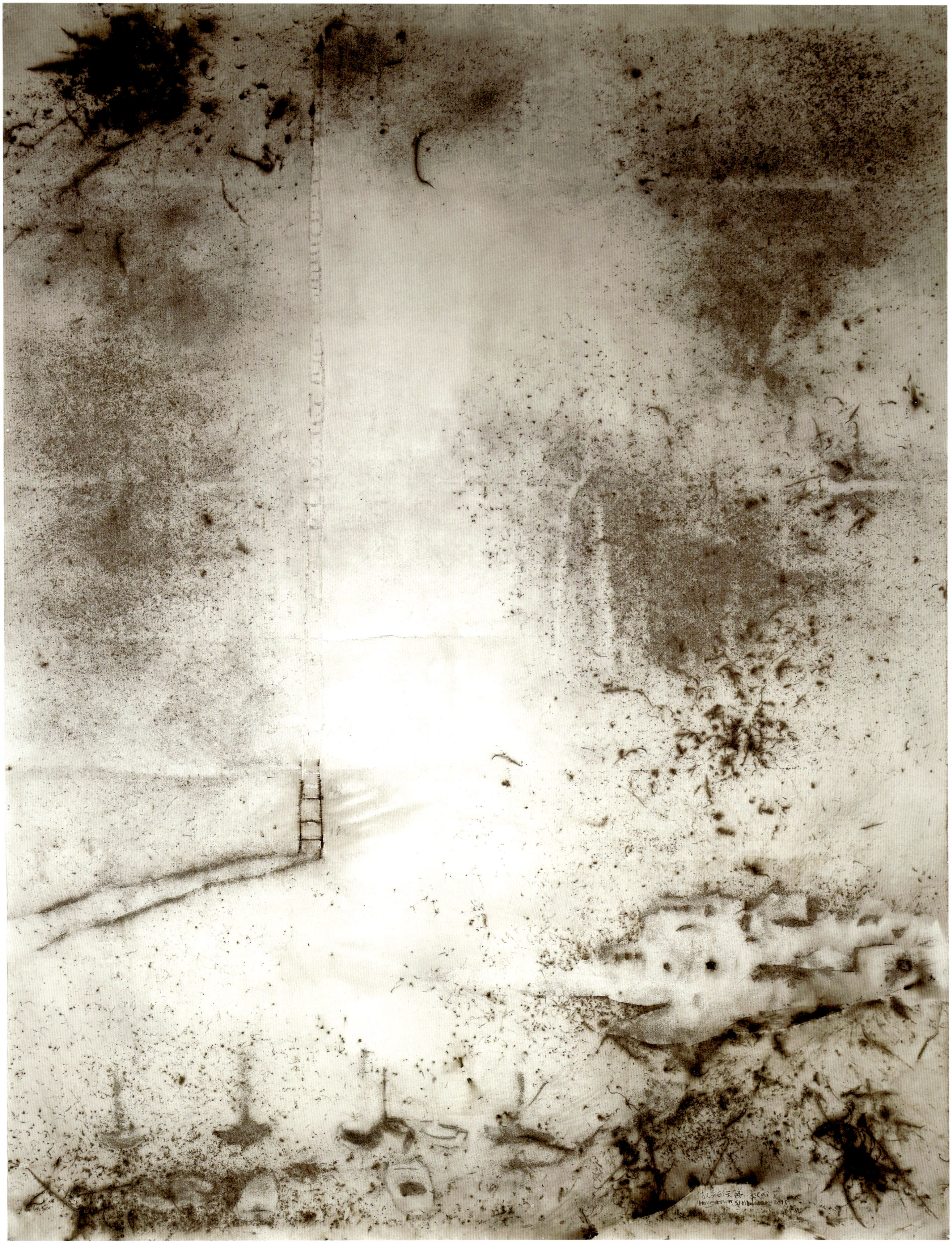

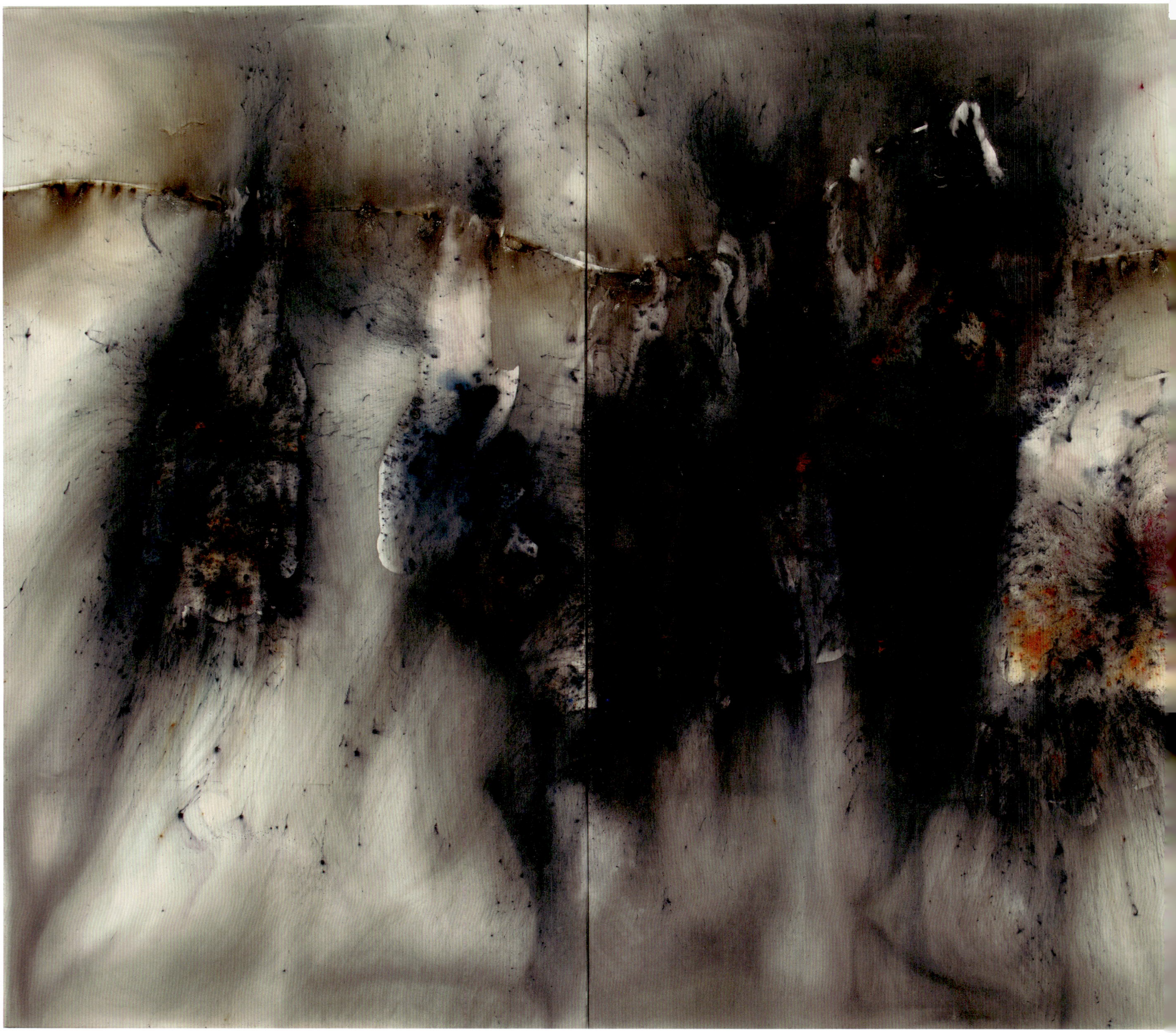

7.2

*The Bats' Eyes No. 2*

蝙蝠的眼睛 No. 2

2020

Gunpowder on canvas

263 × 450 cm

Through this image of hanging bats, Cai conveys his reaction to the natural catastrophes in the Middle Ages, including the Black Death, while pursuing themes of light, spirituality, and mysticism.

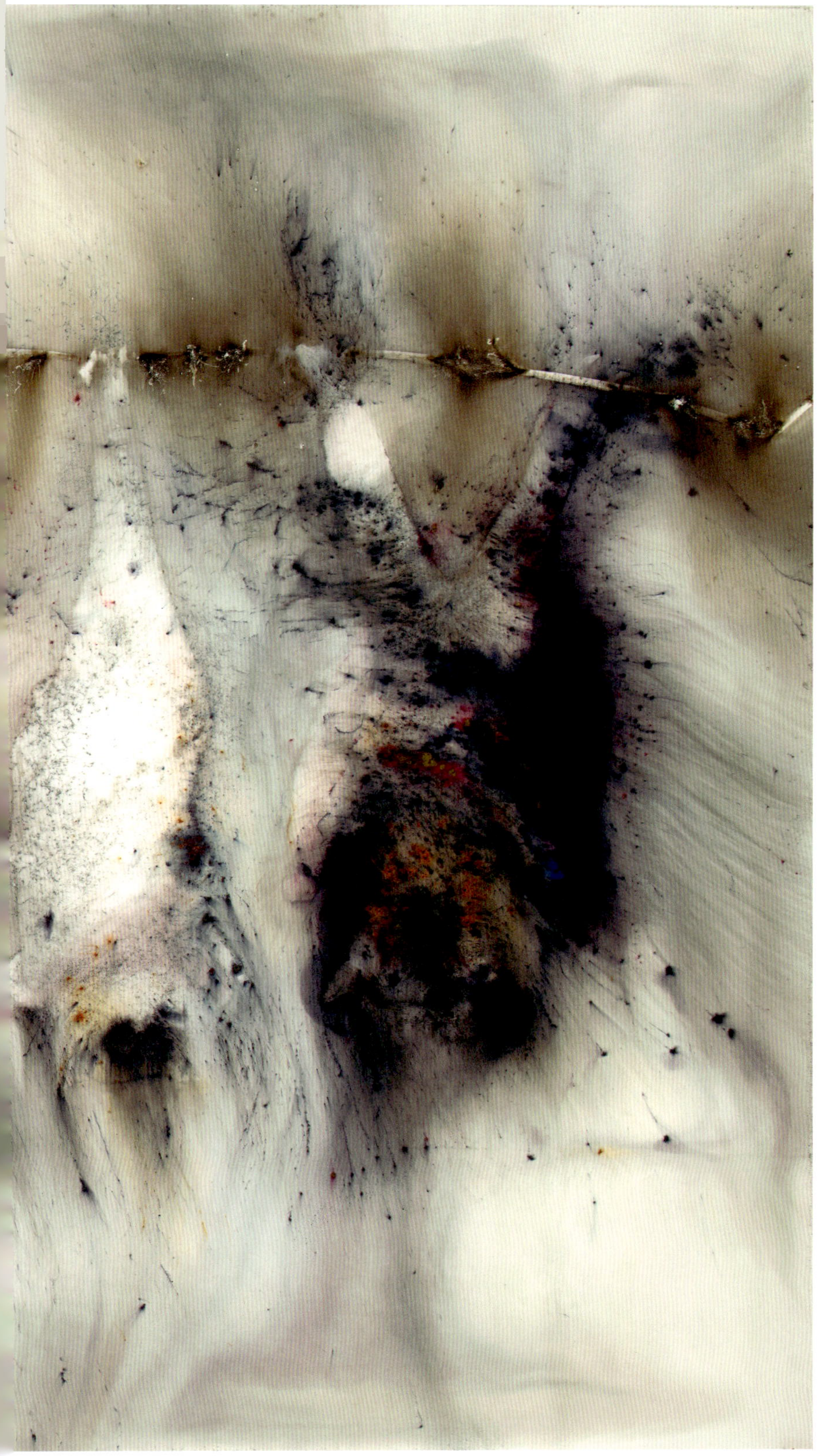

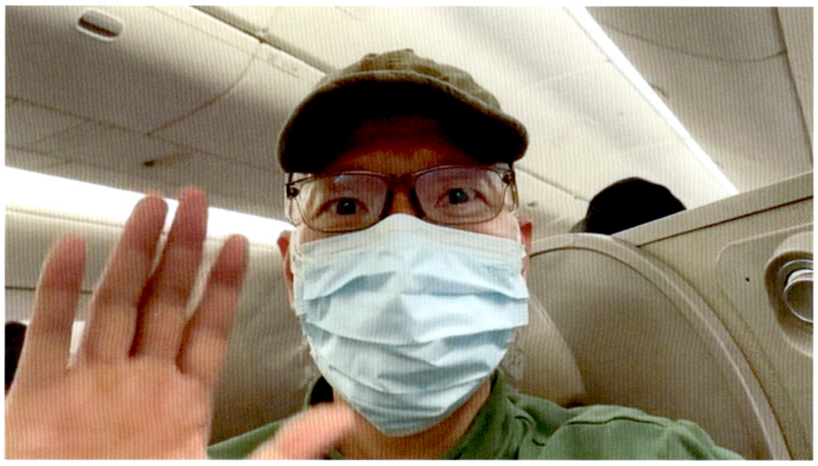

Figure 7.4. Cai Guo-Qiang's selfie on the flight back to China in the middle of COVID-19 in June 2020

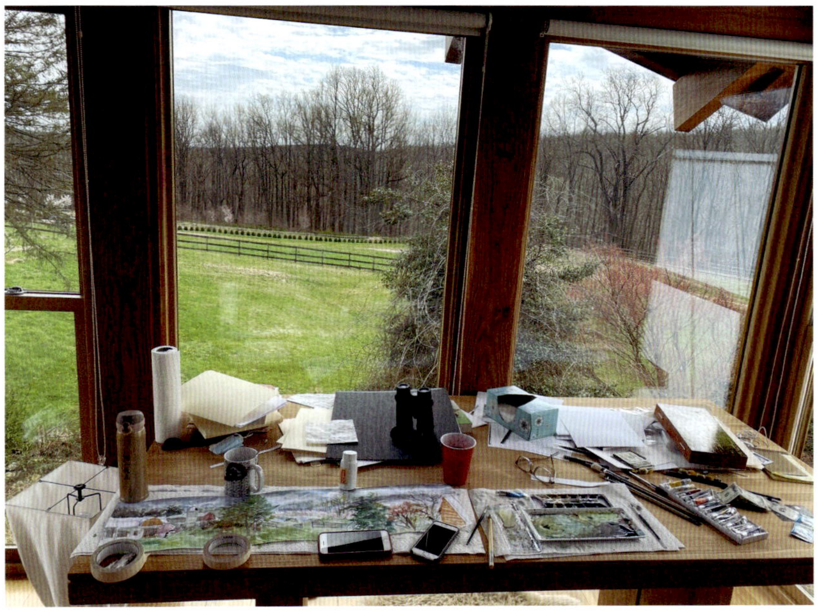

Figure 7.5. Sketches Cai Guo-Qiang created during quarantine at his New Jersey home in 2020

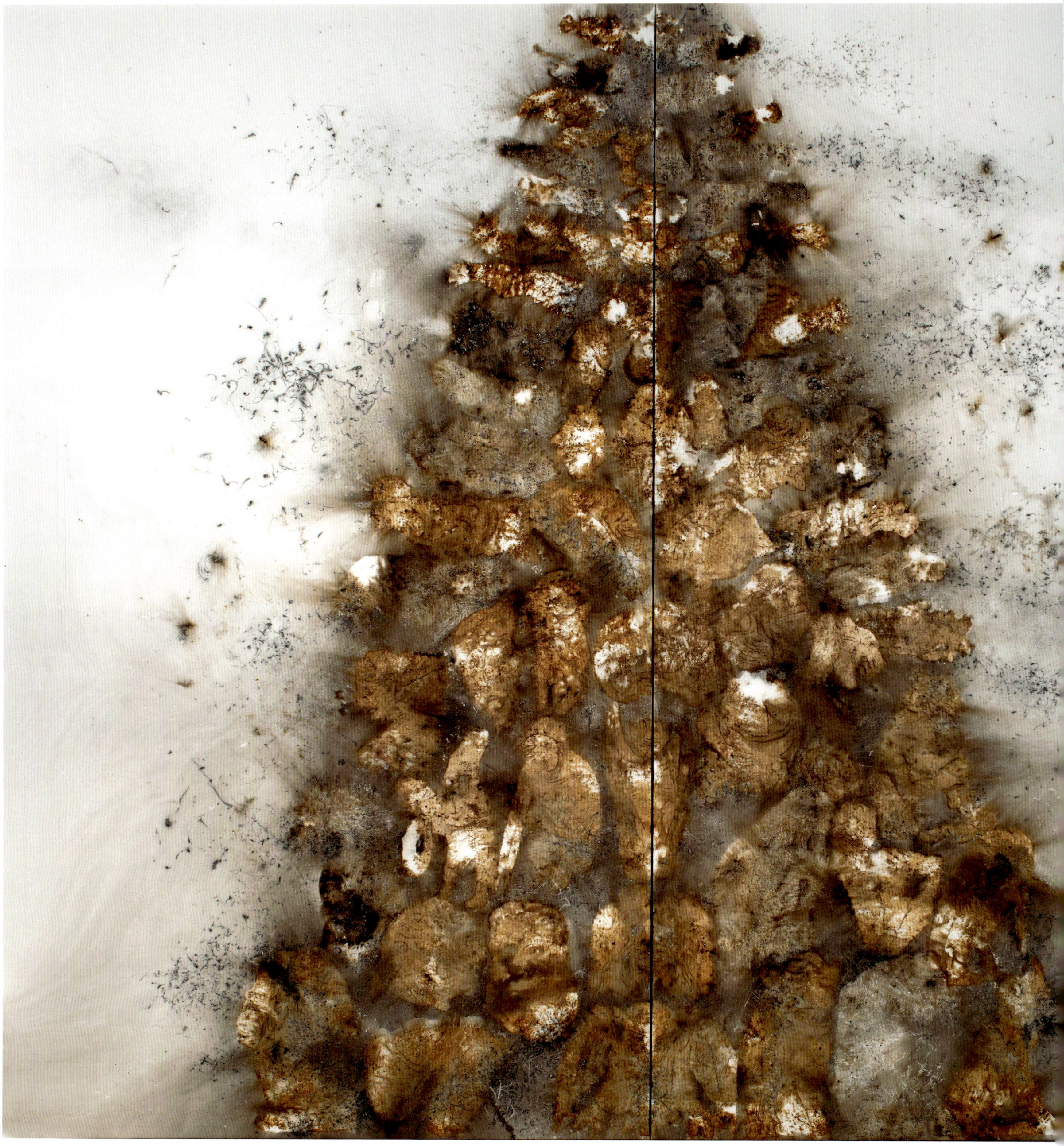

7.3

*Medieval Study: Tower of Grotesques*

中世纪研究：怪兽之塔

2020

Gunpowder on canvas

263 × 300 cm

This work, inspired by the stone grotesques common to medieval architecture like Notre-Dame de Paris, was created during the COVID-19 outbreak. Layered on top of each other, the absurd grotesques seem to reverse the flow of time, reverting the past tense of the Black Death into the present tense.

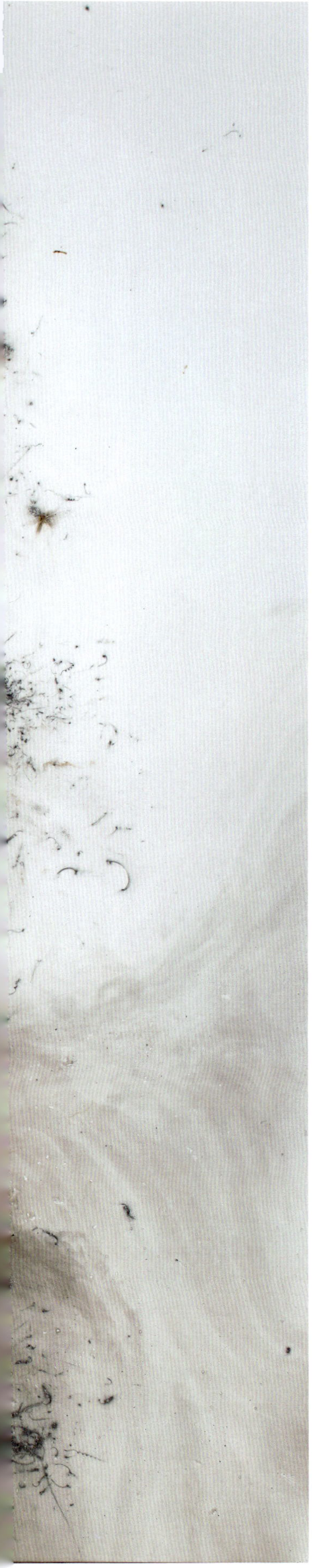

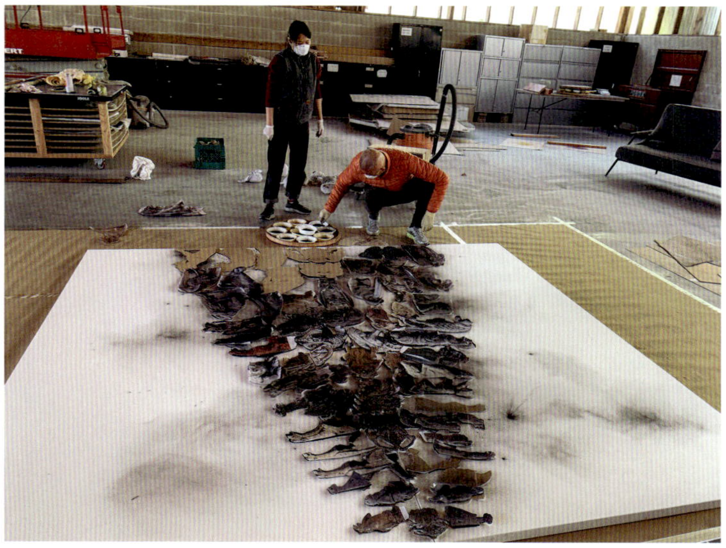

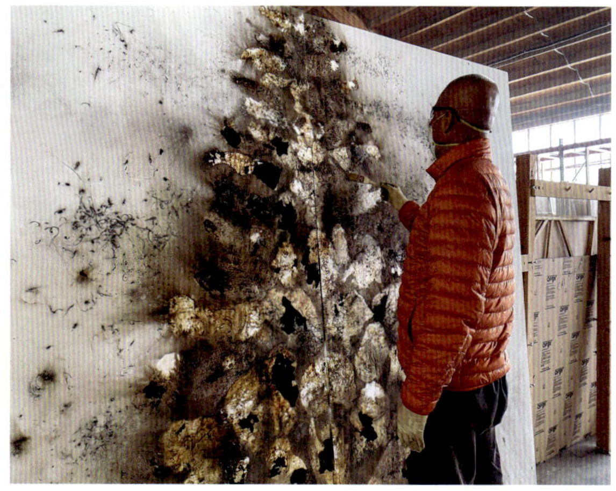

Figures 7.6 and 7.7. Cai Guo-Qiang creating *Medieval Study: Tower of Grotesques* in 2020

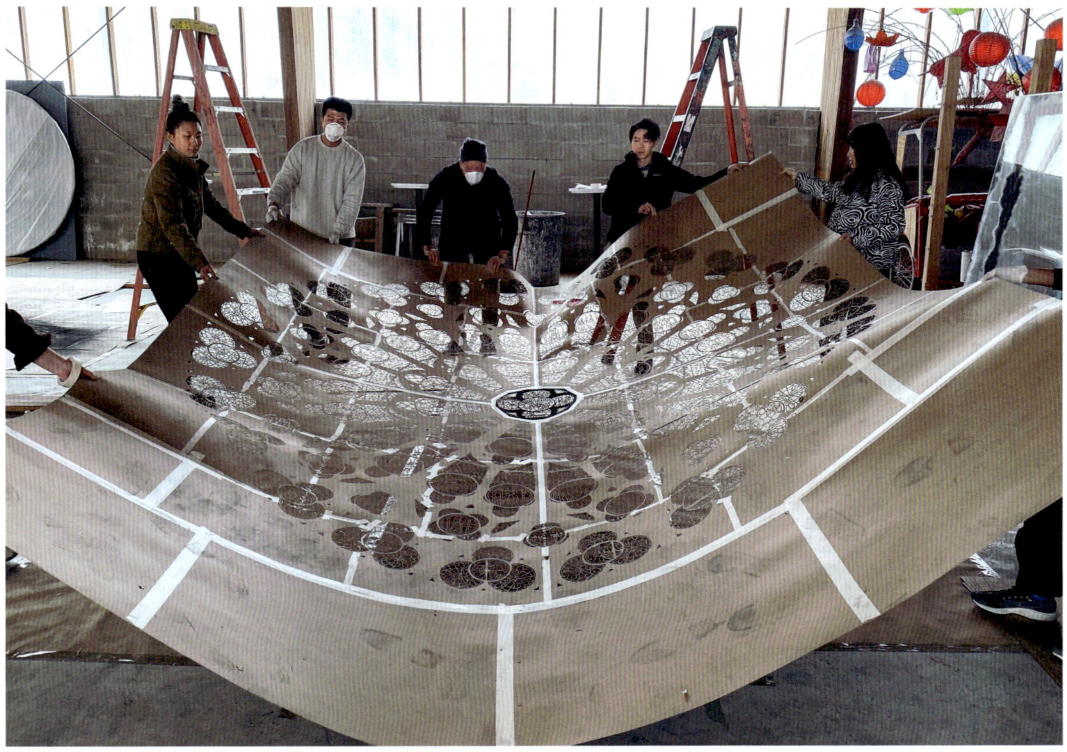

Figure 7.8. Cai Guo-Qiang and assistants lifting the stencil for *Black Light No. 1* in 2020

7.4

## *Black Light No. 1*

## 黑光 No. 1

2020
Gunpowder on canvas
360 × 600 cm

Notre-Dame de Paris is a representative work of medieval Gothic architecture. The great fire that the cathedral suffered in 2019 caused the postponement of Cai's planned 2020 solo exhibition at the Grand Palais in Paris. *Black Light No. 1* was created during the COVID-19 outbreak and used Notre-Dame's iconic rose window as its subject to convey the artist's reflections on the calamities that humanity has experienced.

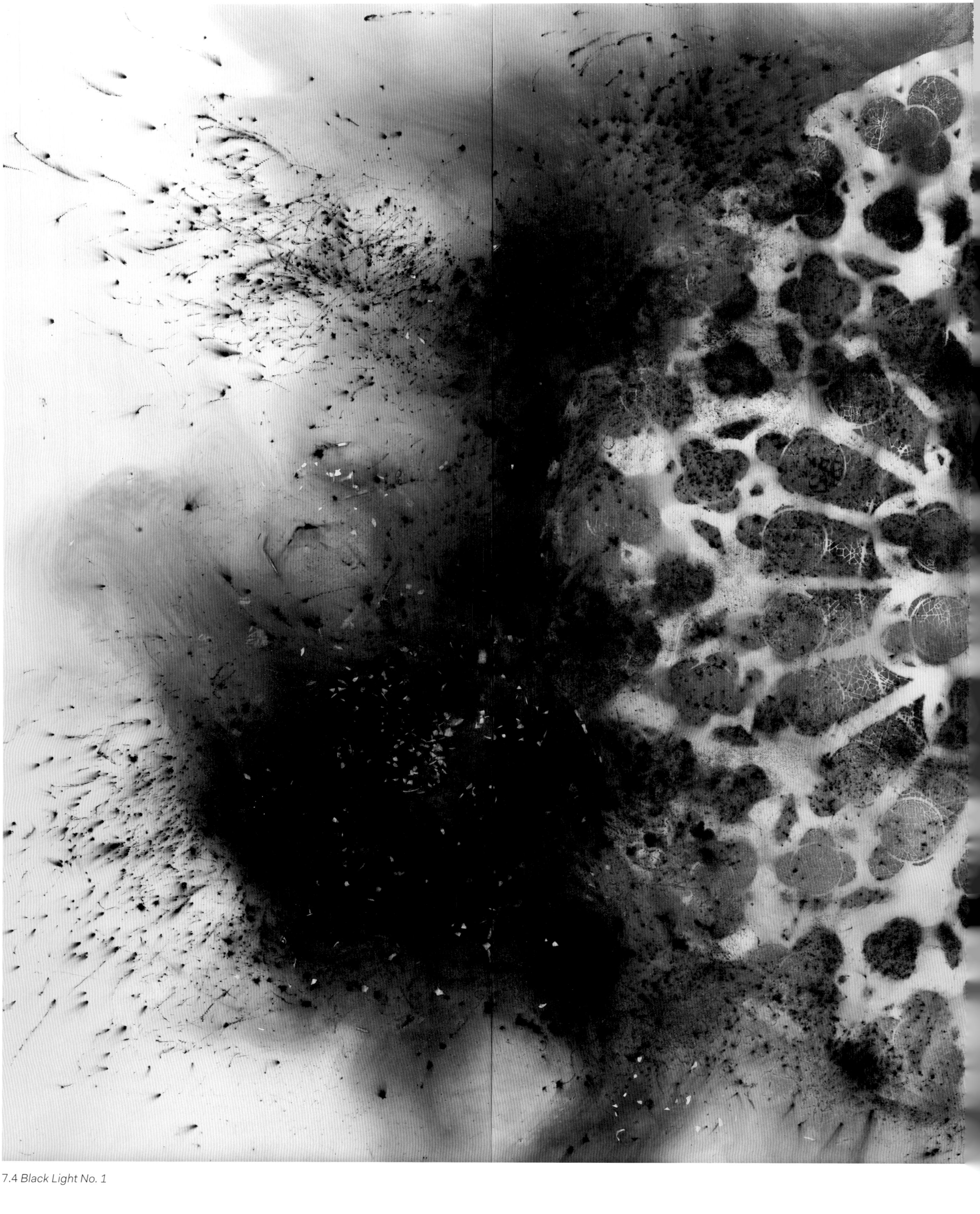

7.4 *Black Light No. 1*

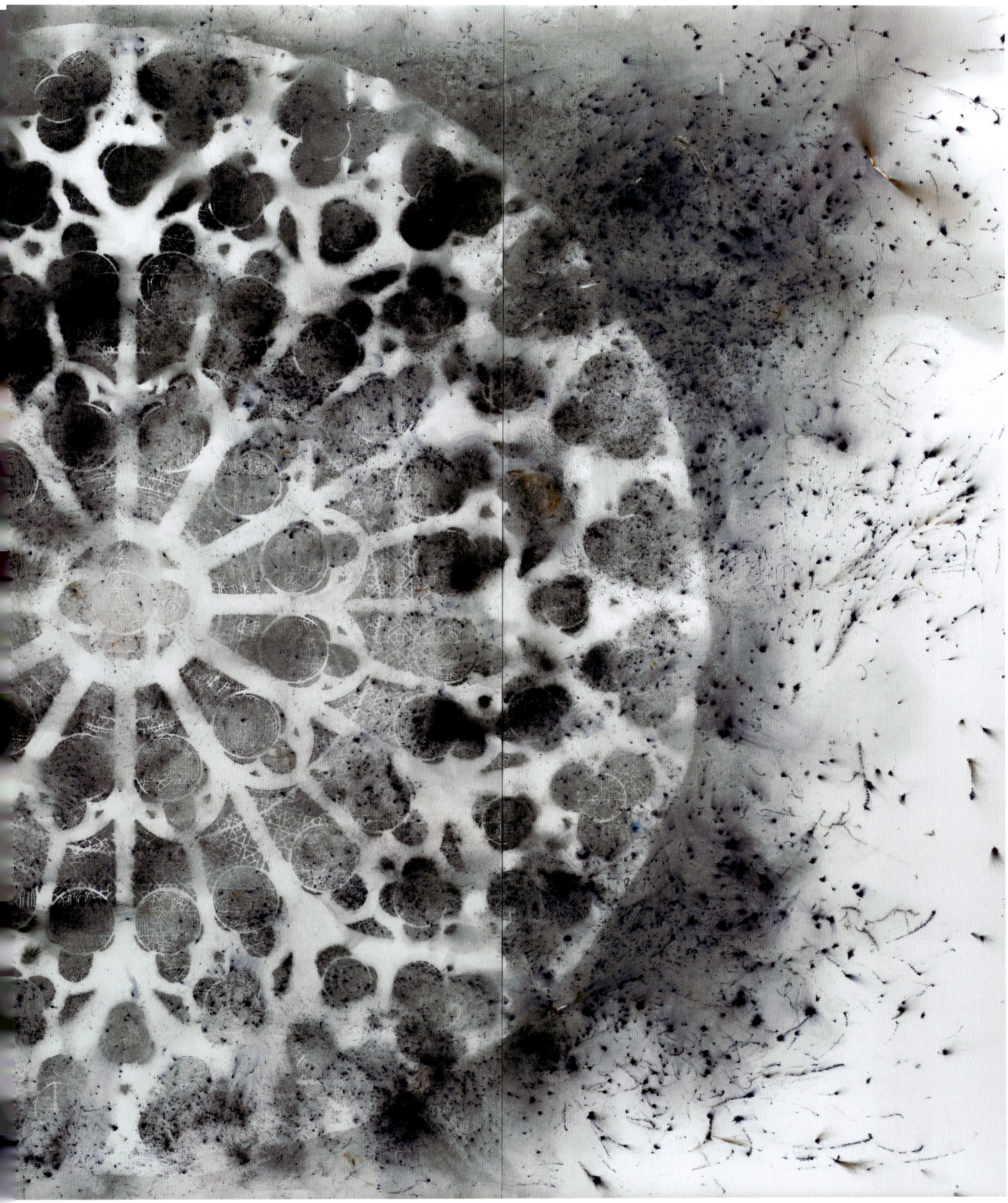

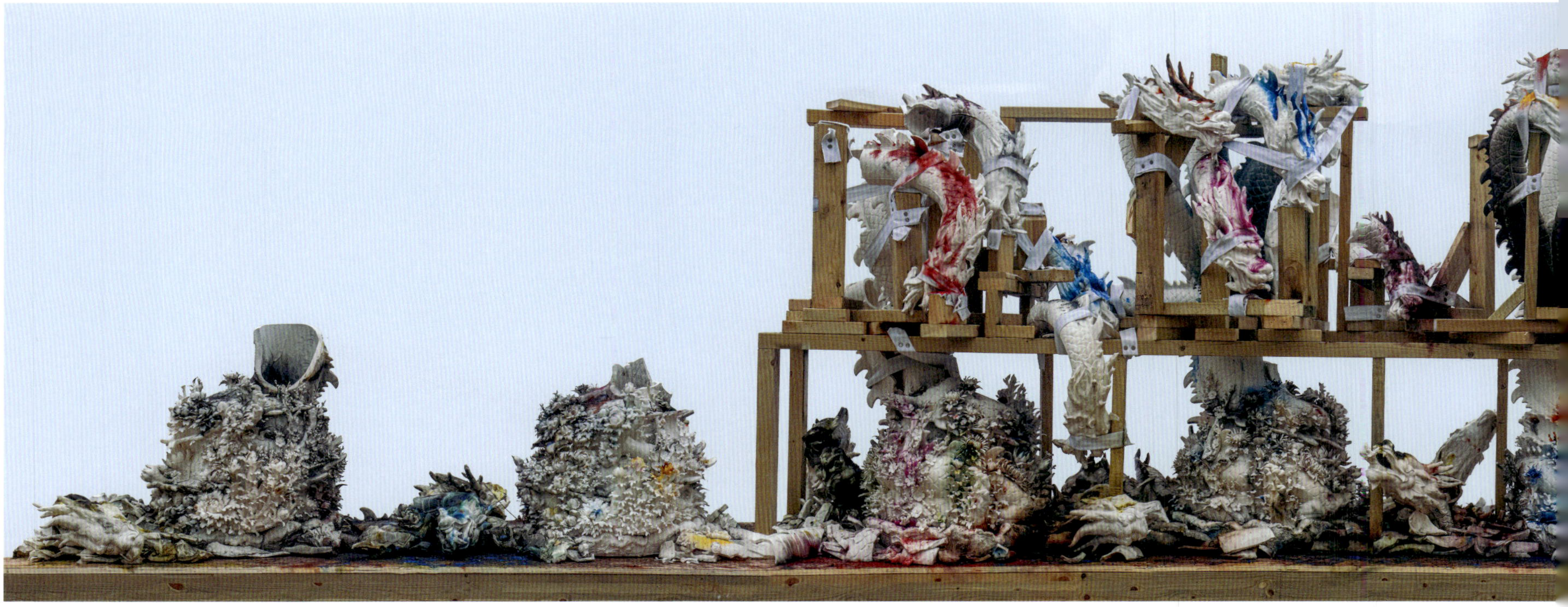

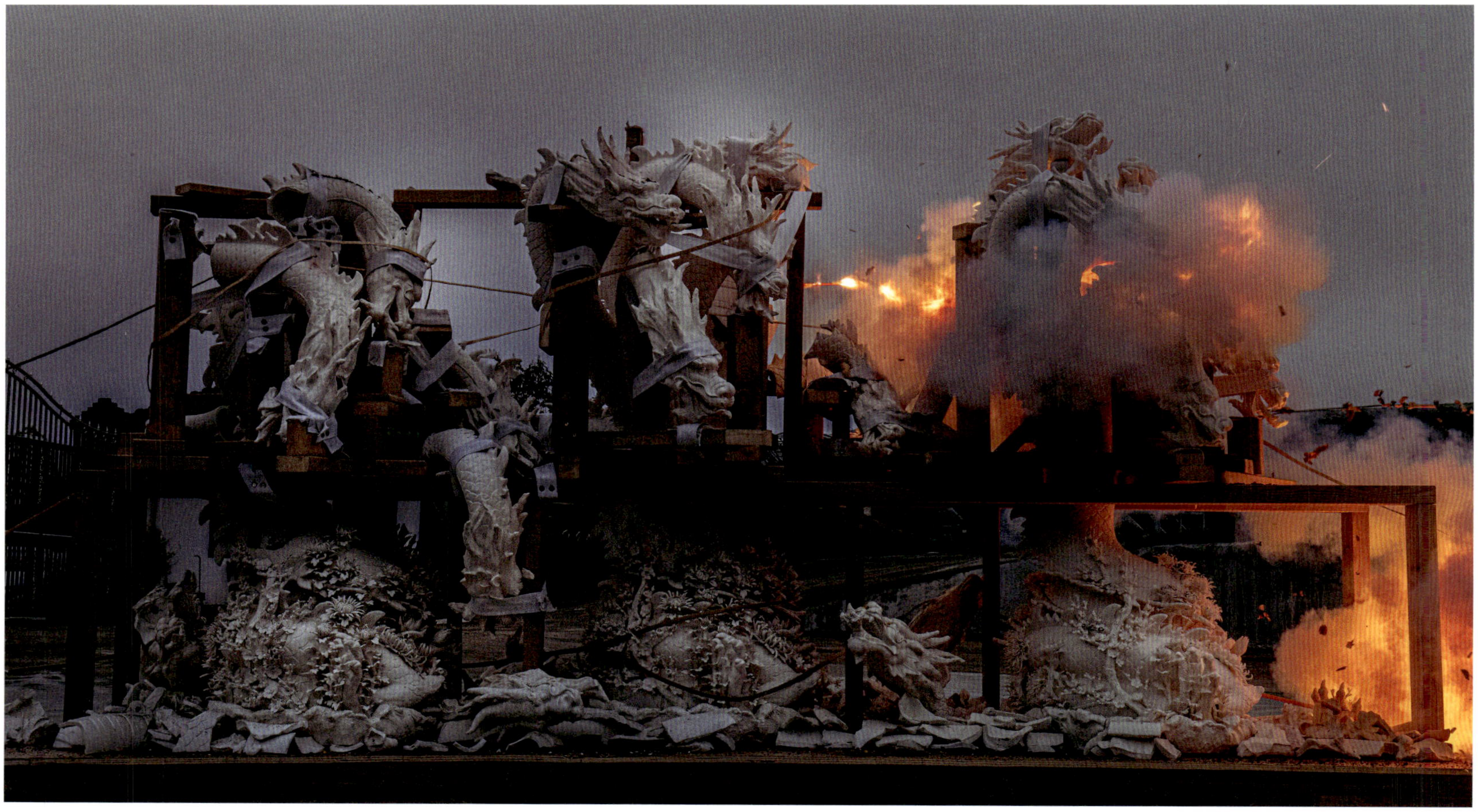

Figure 7.9. Ignition of *Seven-Headed Dragons: Project for the Vatican Museum*

7.5

*Seven-Headed Dragons: Project for the Vatican Museum*
七头龙：为梵蒂冈博物馆作的项目
2020
Gunpowder on porcelain
222 × 977 × 127 cm

In 2016, Cai was commissioned by the Vatican Museum to create the sculptural installation *Seven-Headed Dragons*. Incorporating traditional porcelain crafting techniques from his hometown, he exploded the white porcelain surface with black and color gunpowder. The work portrays a series of seven-headed dragons, which in Christianity symbolize Satan in the Book of Revelation. Each dragon emerges from a heap of flowers that represent the four seasons, including peonies, lotuses, chrysanthemums, and plum blossoms. Among the flowers, their twisting forms resonate with the seductive snake in the Garden of Eden. The work's vigorous dynamism, lifelike and intricate rendering, and romantic yet mysterious atmosphere corresponds to the eccentric theatricality of medieval sculpture.

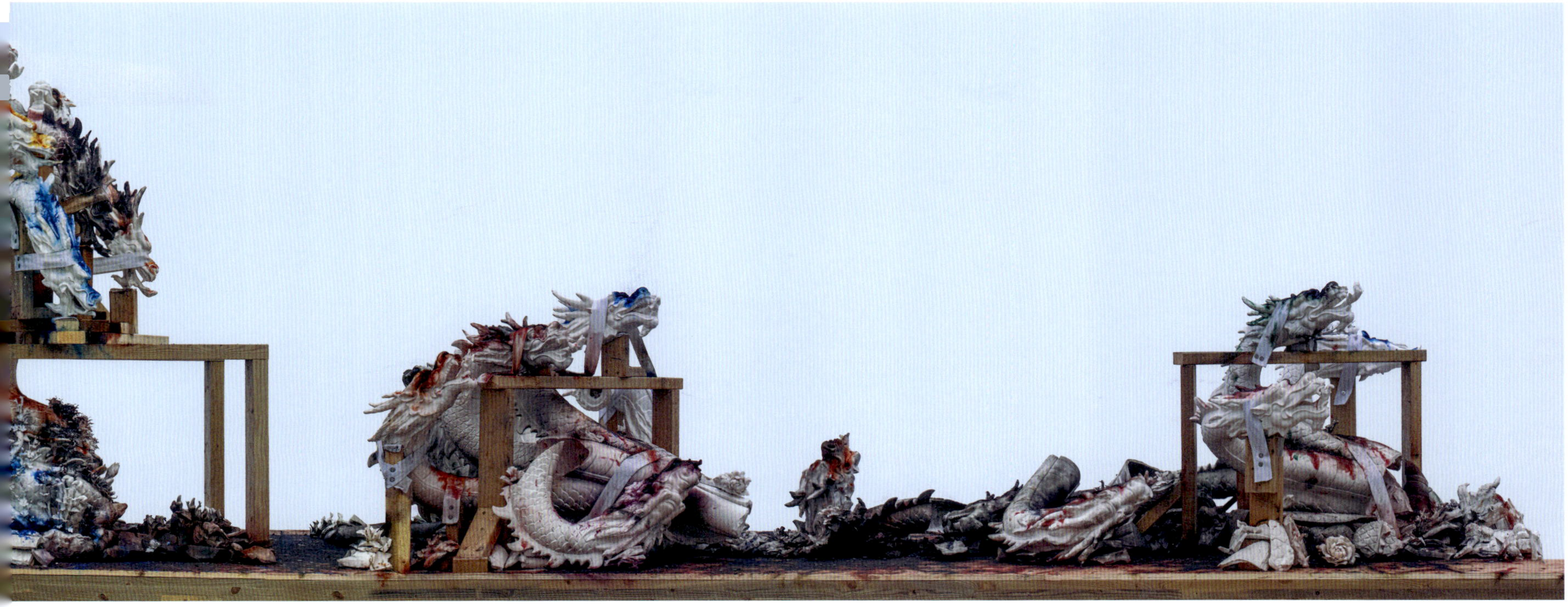

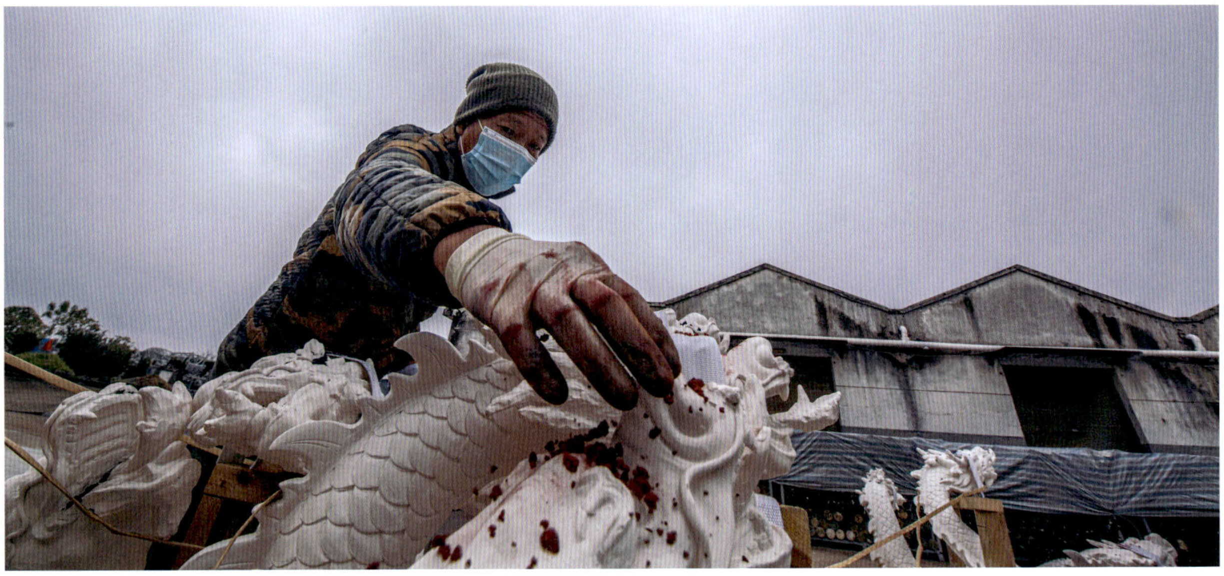

Figure 7.10. Cai Guo-Qiang sprinkling gunpowder prior to ignition

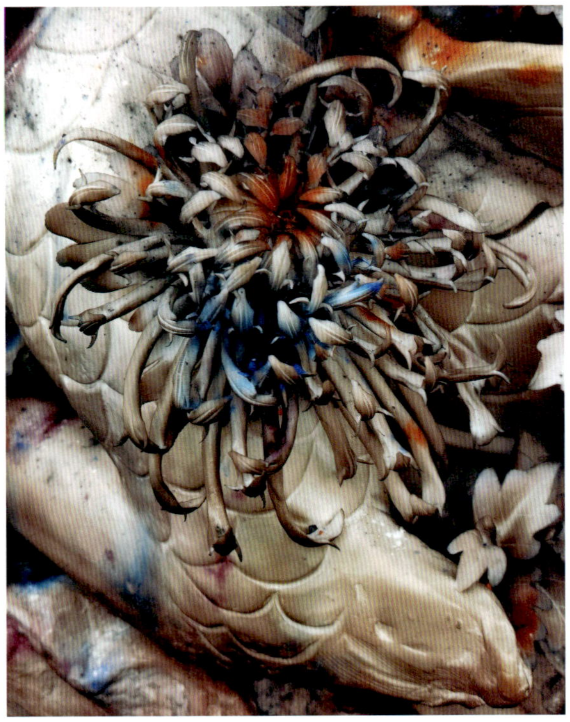

Figure 7.11. Detail of *Seven-Headed Dragons: Project for the Vatican Museum*

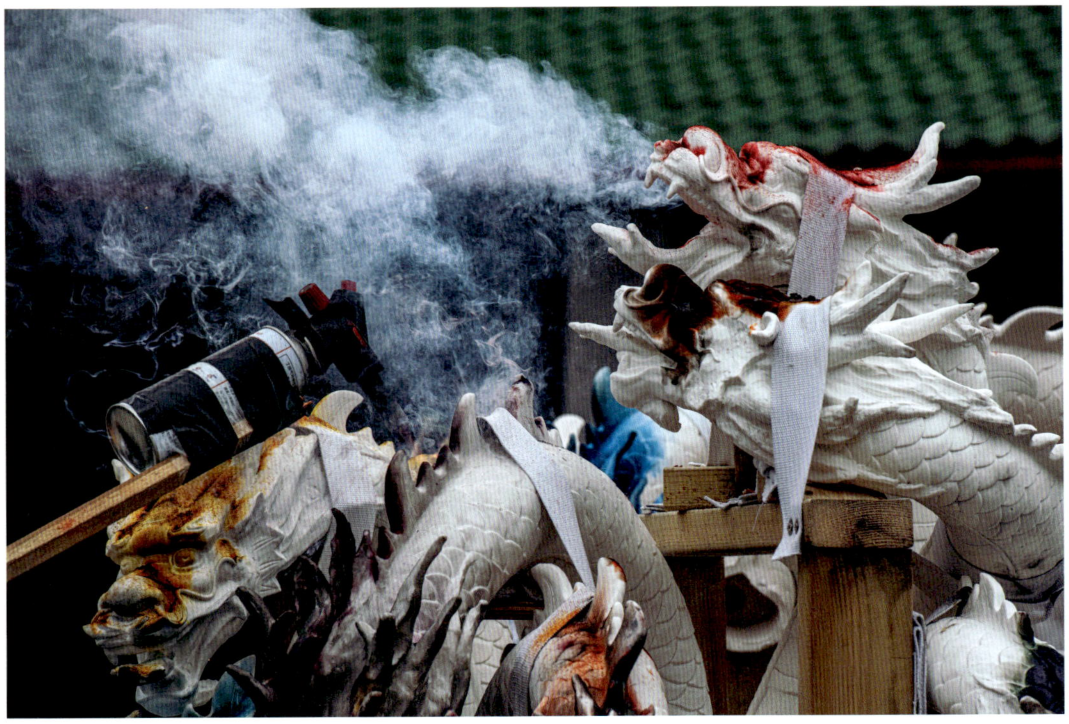

Figure 7.12. Ignition of *Seven-Headed Dragons: Project for the Vatican Museum*

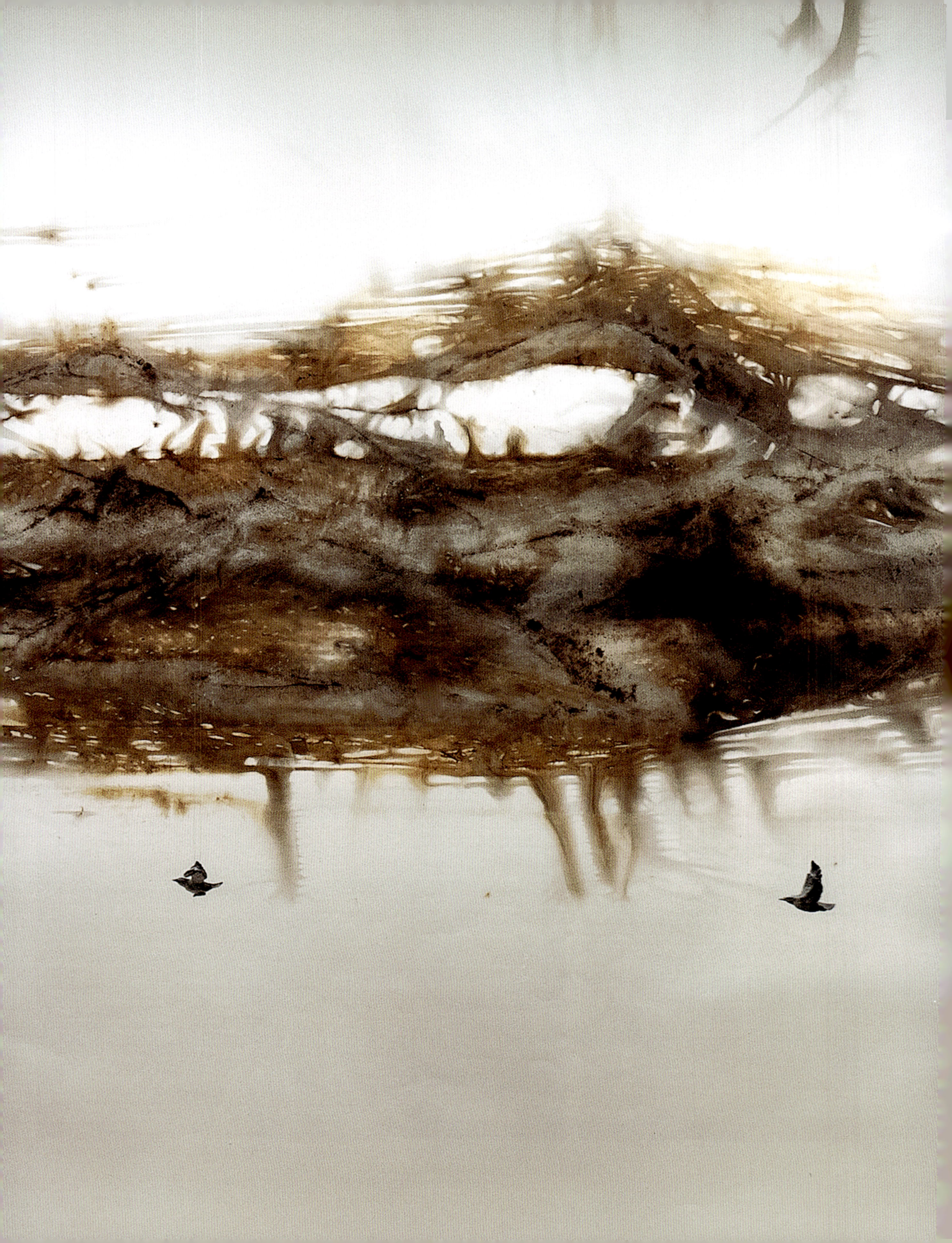

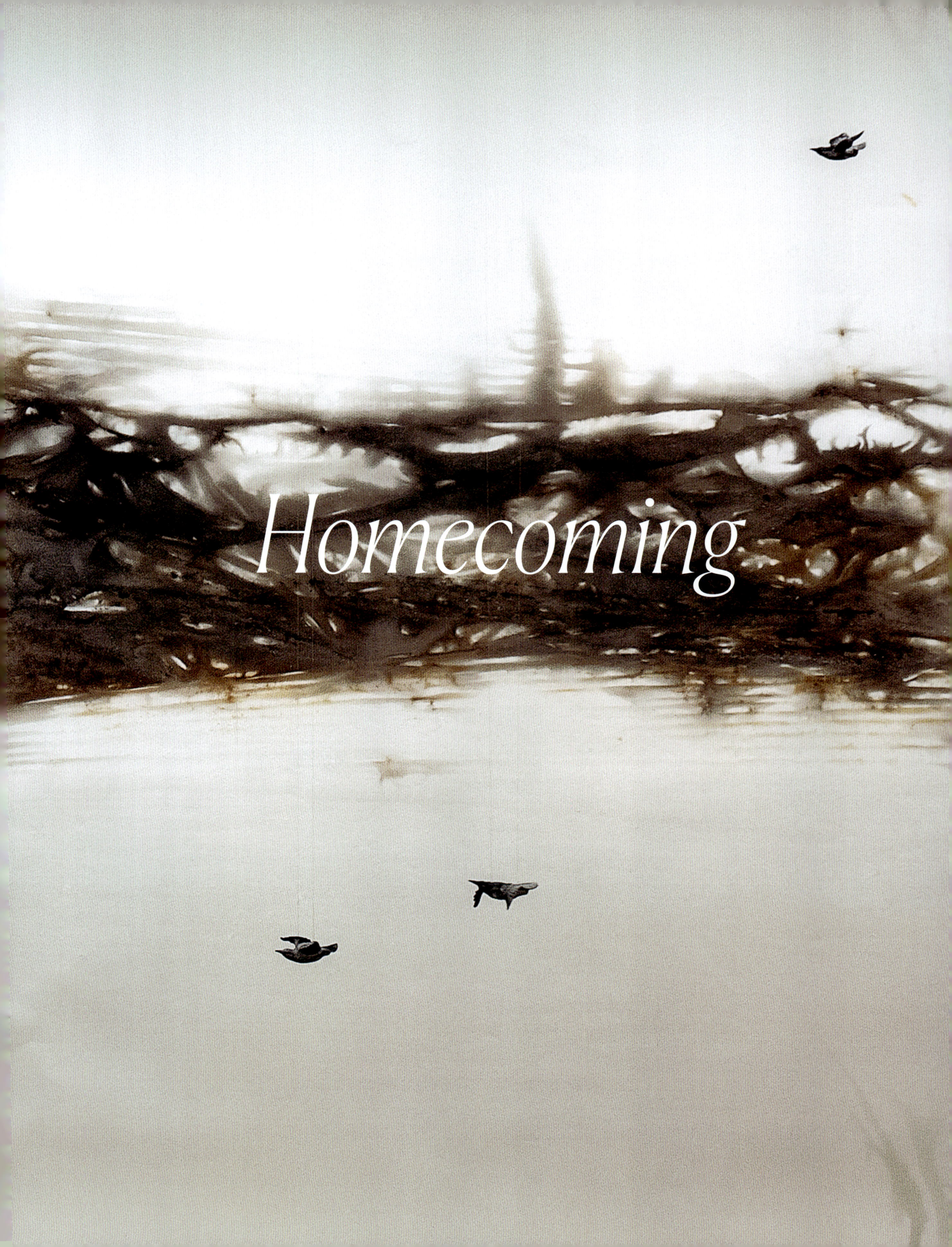
Homecoming

# 8

# Dialogue with My Original Passion for Painting

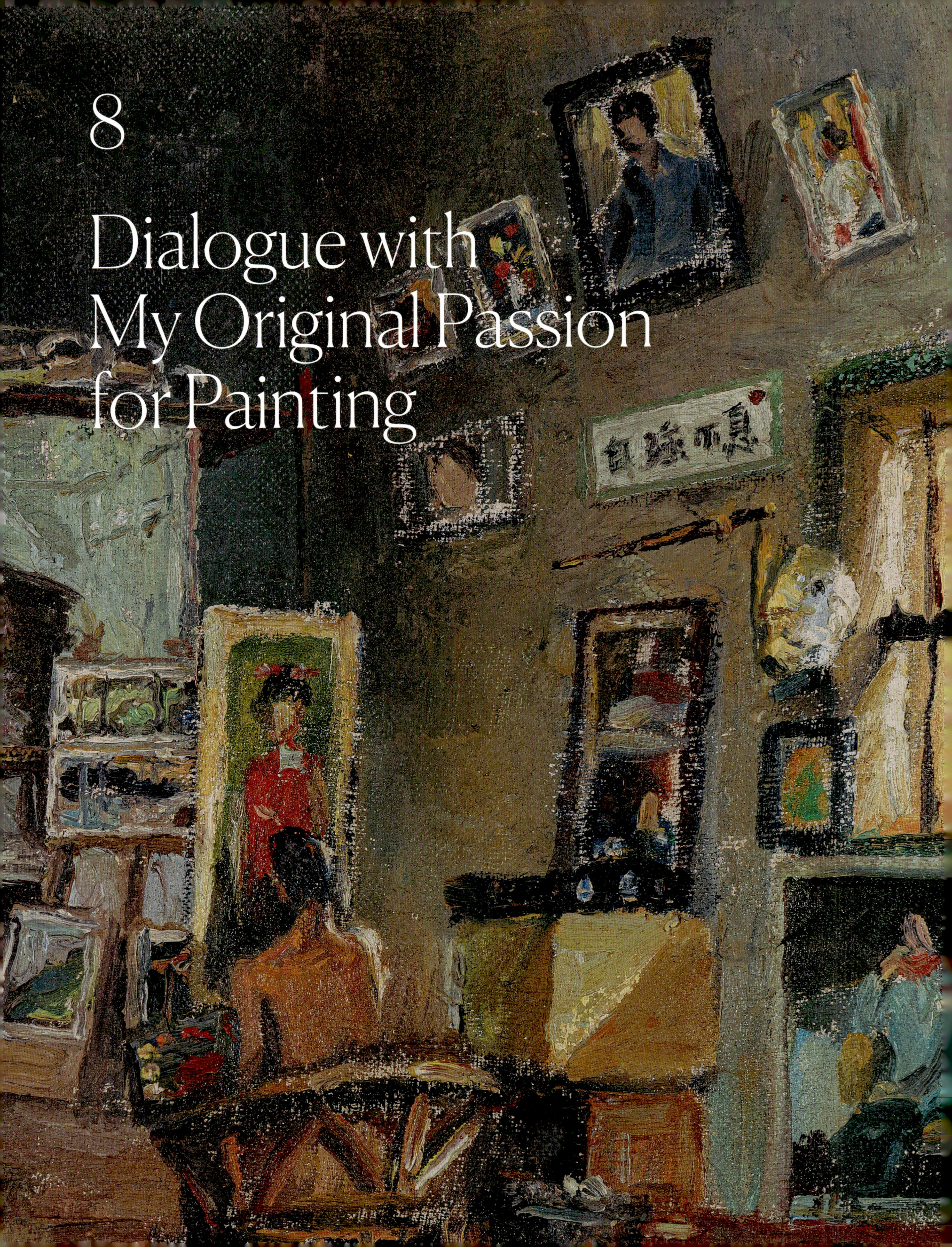

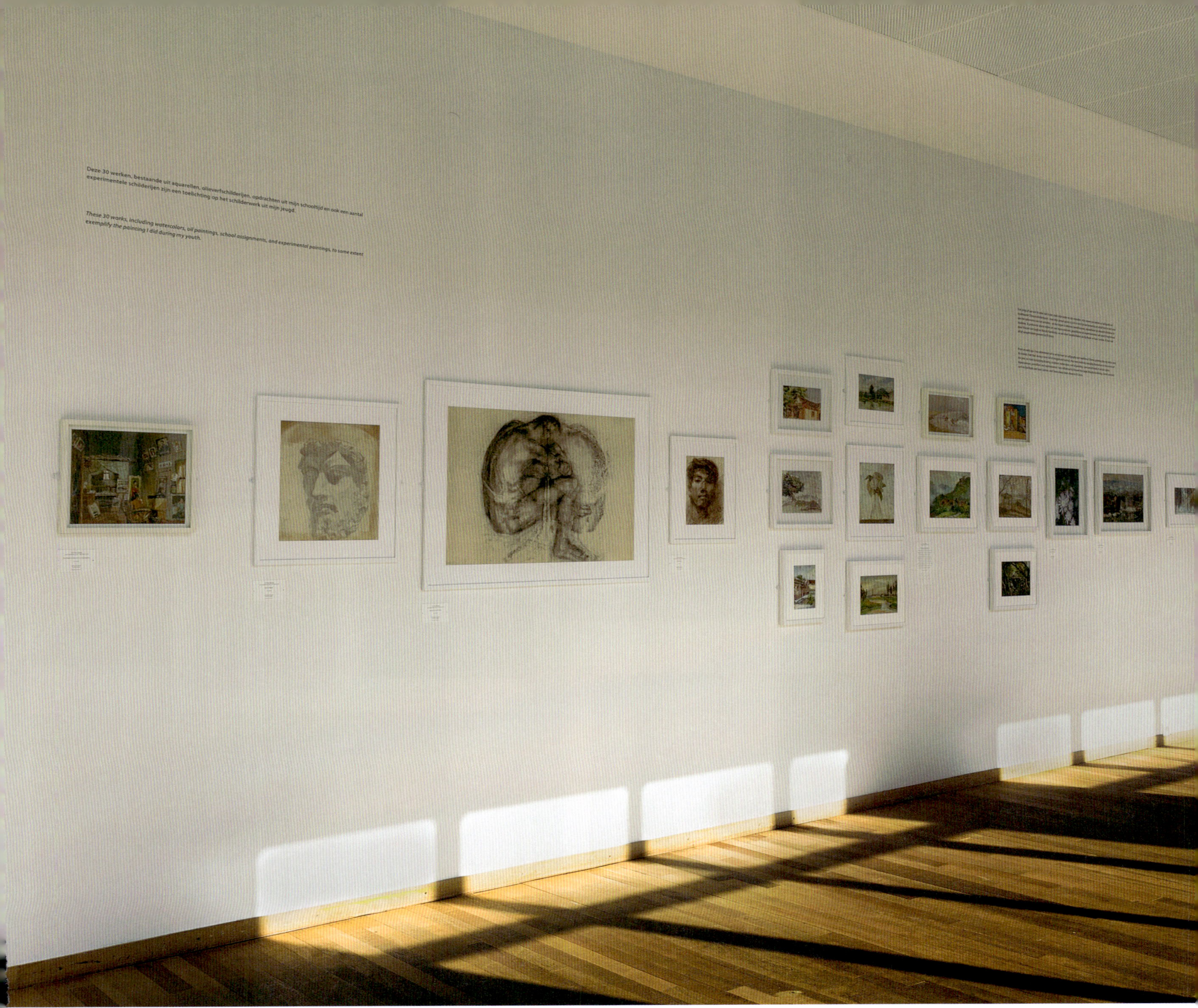

Figure 8.2. Installation view of *Cai Guo-Qiang: My Stories of Painting* at Bonnefanten Museum in Maastricht in 2016

8.1

## *Wall of Early Paintings*
## 早期作品墙

2020

87 paintings from the 1970s–80s and 2001; watercolor, oil, gouache, and acrylic on paper, canvas, cardboard, and cardstock; with Cai Ruiqin, *Untitled (Matchbox Drawings)*, dates unknown, ink, pen, and pencil on cardboard matchboxes, framed: 22.9 × 30.5 cm
Approx. 260 × 970 cm in total

This section of the Palace Museum exhibition displays around eighty small-scale works in watercolor, oil, and gouache that Cai made in the 1970s–80s and 2001, with a special appearance of *Matchbox Drawings* by Cai Ruiqin, his father. The artist's early works demonstrate the influence from the diverse styles of numerous Chinese and foreign artists on the early stages of his career. They also manifest Cai's original aspirations in art, which have their origins in a deep affection for art history and a steady love of painting that has driven him since his youth. The names of many artists that have served as Cai's influences are listed on an adjacent wall.

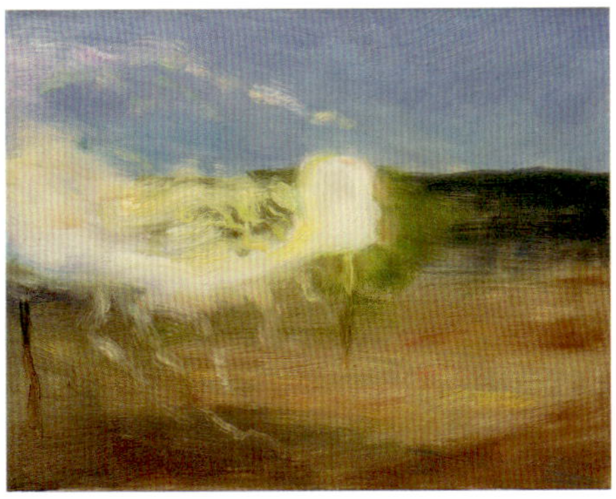
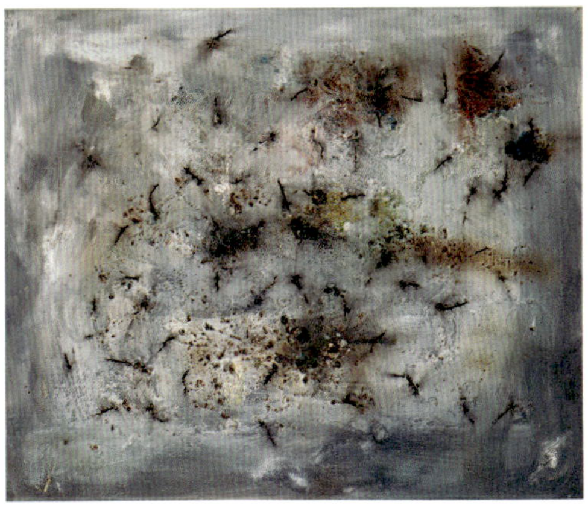
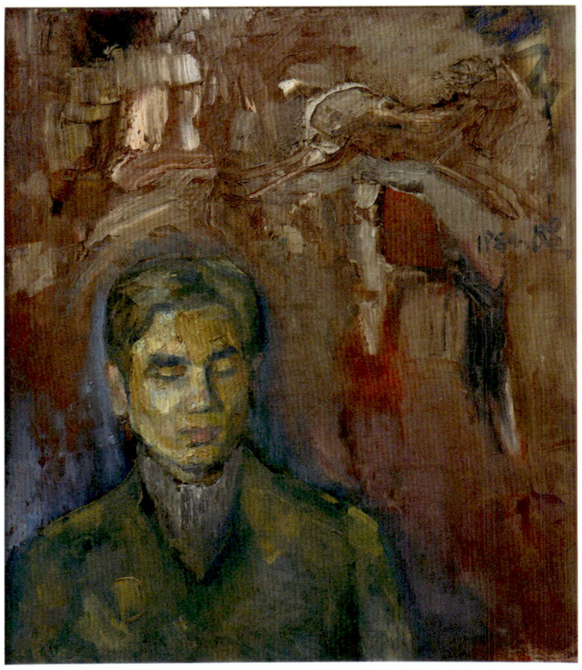
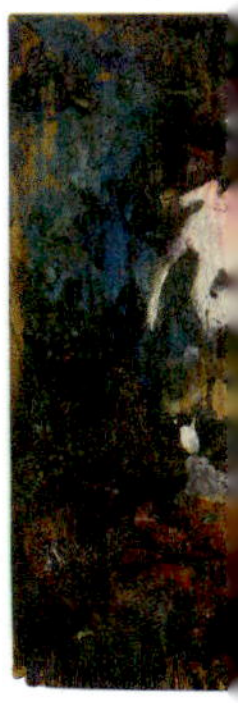
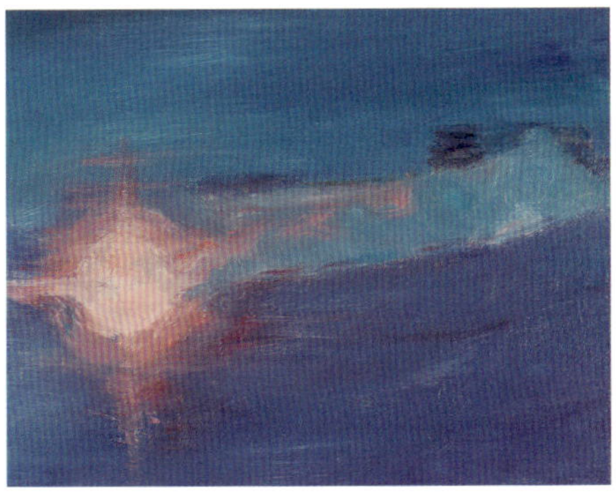
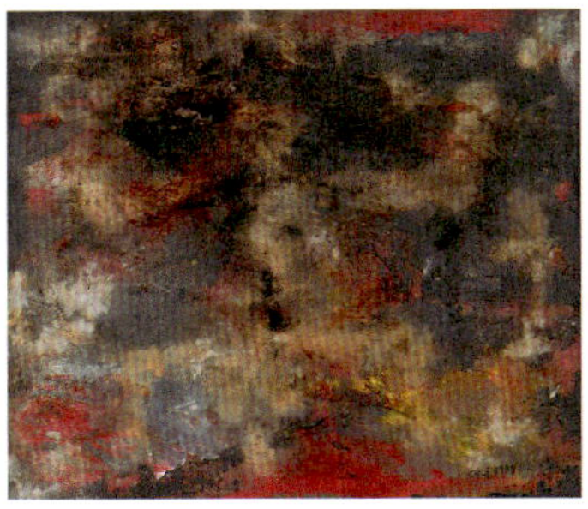
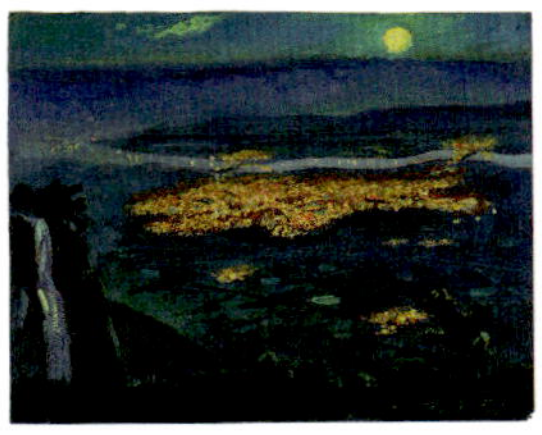
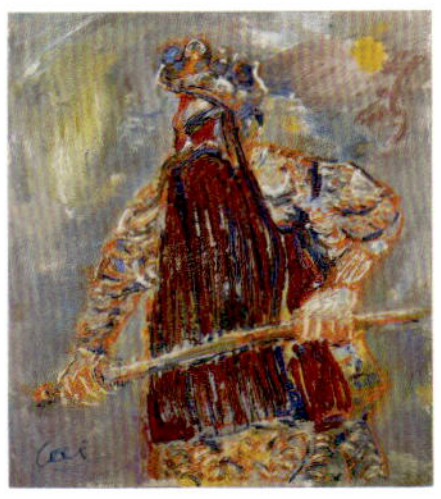
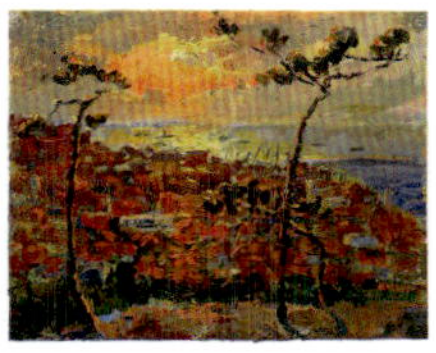
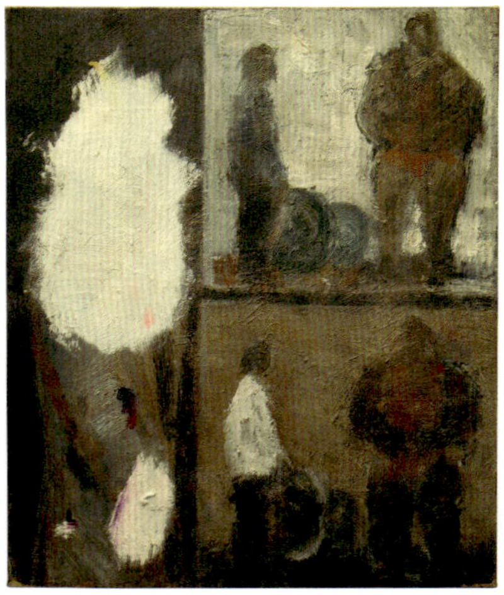
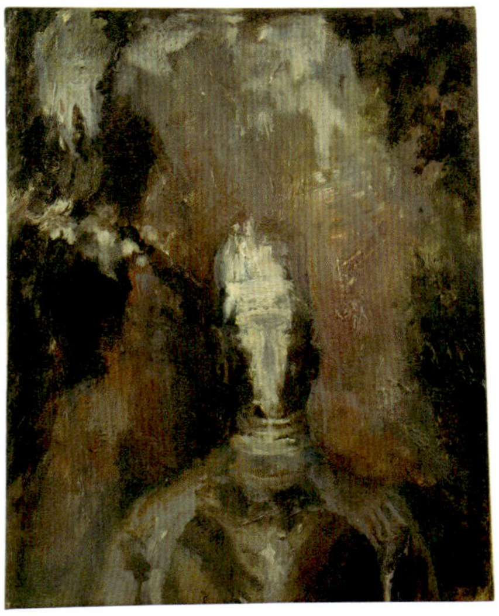
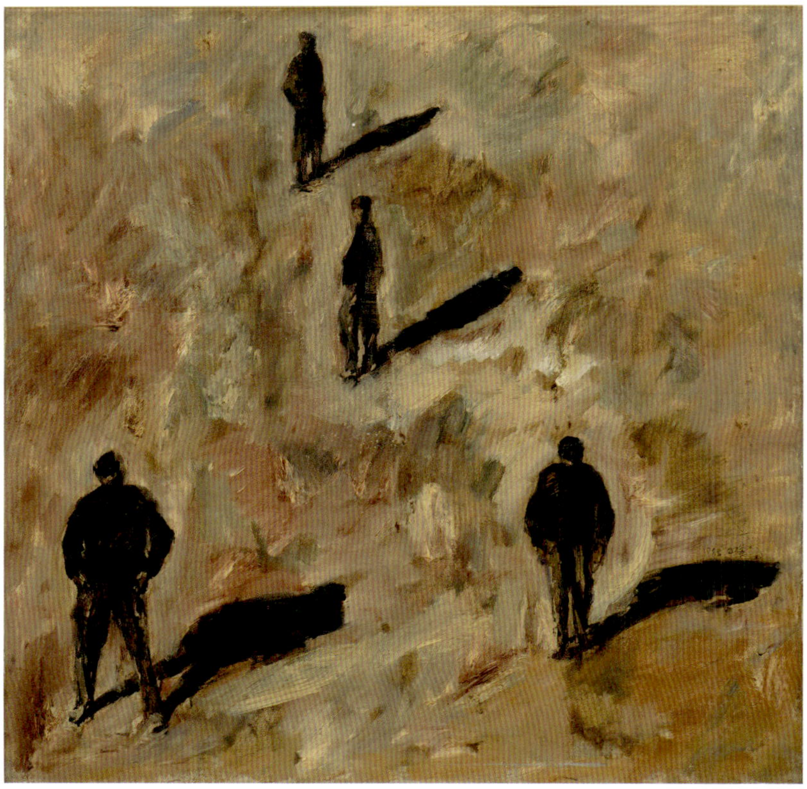
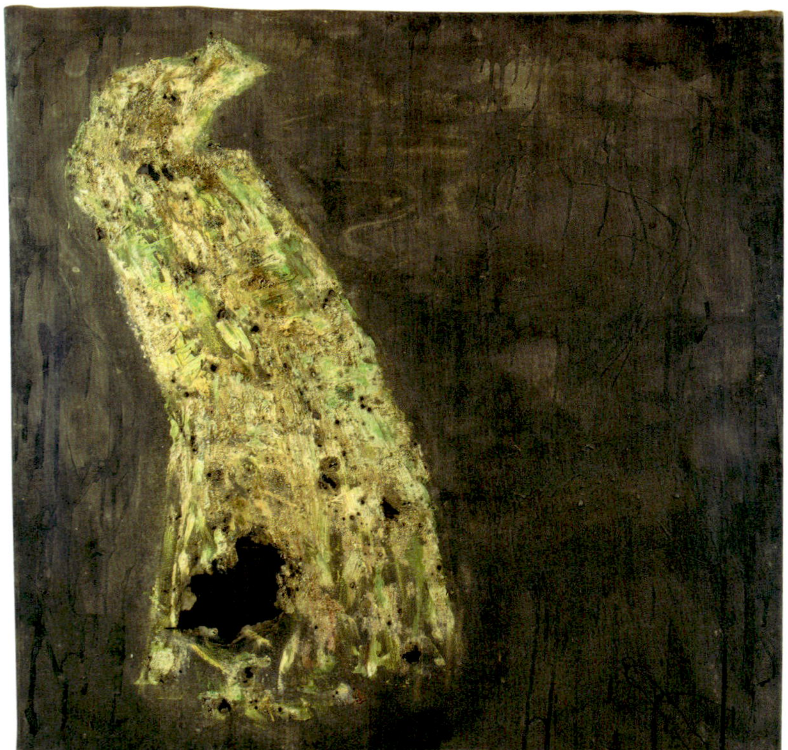
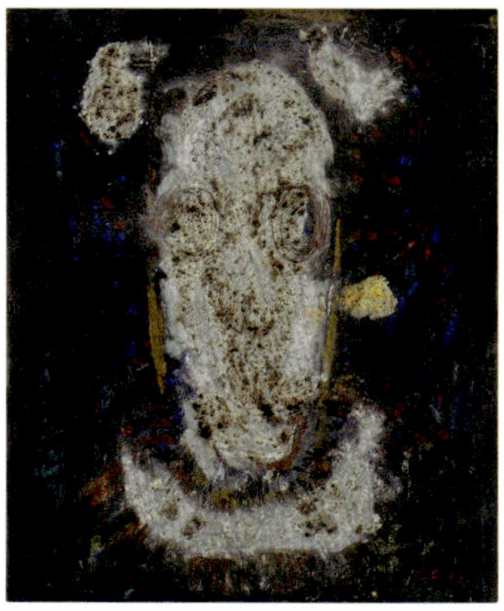

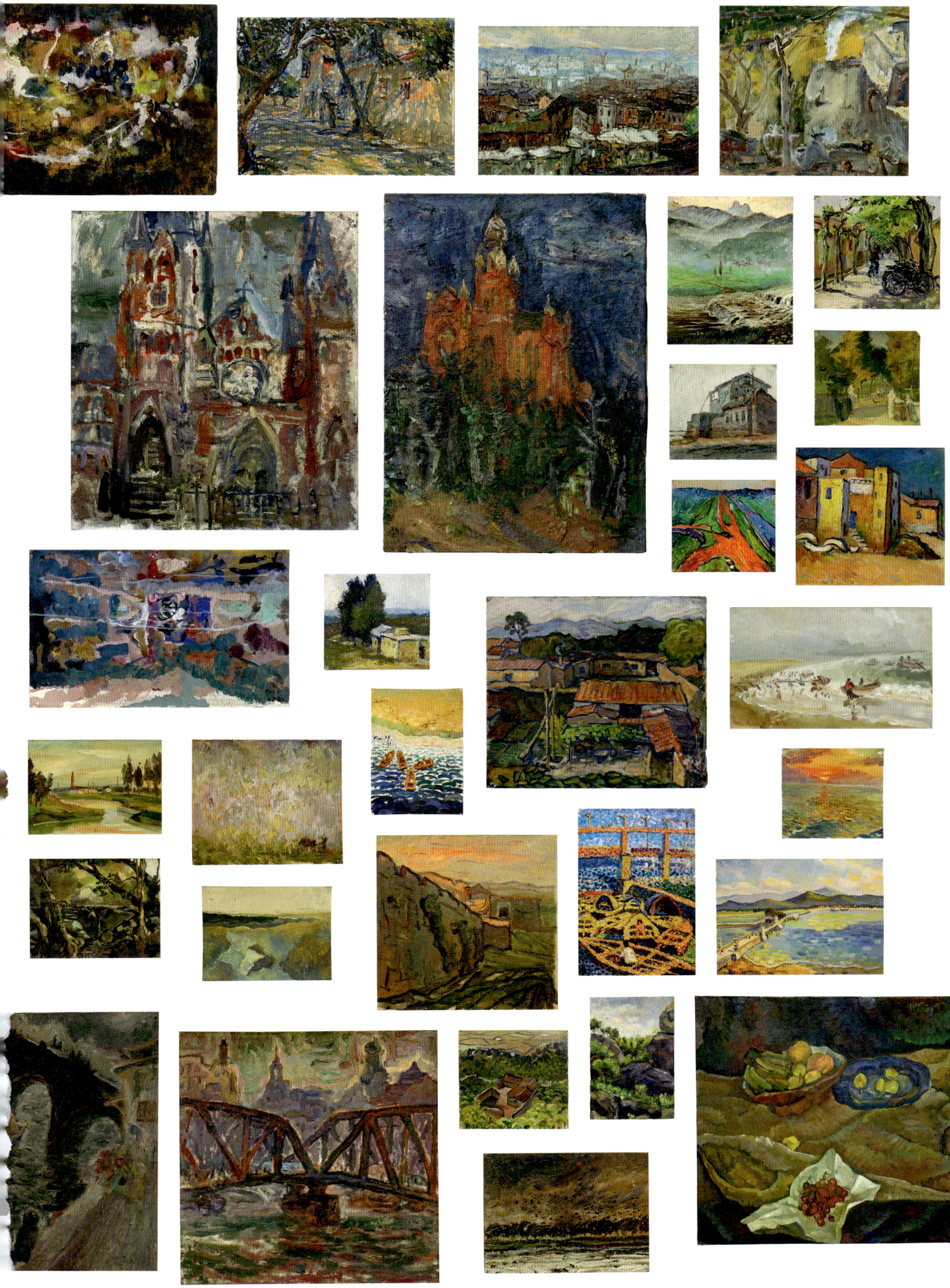

# *Cai Guo-Qiang: My Stories of Painting*

Bonnefanten Museum, Maastricht, the Netherlands
September 29, 2016–May 1, 2017

Curated by Paula van den Bosch, Senior Curator, Bonnefanten Museum

Public painting creation: Bonnefanten Museum, Maastricht, September 29, 2016

Catalogue: English and Dutch editions published by Walther König

Documentary short: *Making of Gunpowder Drawing Boy's Doodle: Drawing for the 25th Anniversary of the EU in Maastricht*, produced by Strictua for the Bonnefanten Museum (00:59)

*My Stories of Painting* was the first exhibition that reviewed Cai's multi-decade journey of painting, presented through two parallel trajectories: his consecutive explorations since childhood of painting and its evolution, and his family as a major influence on his painting journey.

Presenting hundreds of works of different periods, scales, and mediums, many of which were exhibited for the first time, the exhibition began with Cai's time in China. This section included school assignments alongside youthful experimental works in watercolor, oil, and early trials with gunpowder on oil paintings. This was followed by his time in Japan, where he developed paintings, especially abstract ones, created only with gunpowder and gunpowder drawings for explosion events. The next section dated from his time in New York and his rise on the global stage, where he continued to confront the issues and questions surrounding painting by consistently deploying and expanding his methodology. This was demonstrated by his return to create more purely independent gunpowder paintings, and his shift from using solely black gunpowder to more color gunpowder. This new stage registered the artist's unrestrained pursuit of his childhood dream to become a painter in a newly challenging context of contemporary painting, and his rebellious response to the integral challenges of contemporary painting.

The genealogical section encompassed four generations of family members: his grandmother, parents, wife, and daughters. Through their paintings, photographs, and other works, either professional or amateur, realist or spiritual, visitors came to understand how an artist's family, generation after generation, accompanied and influenced him, and vice versa.

Cai observed, "I sometimes look back on my time as a young man who loved painting and think: it really wasn't easy to have come this far, with so many people who have taught and loved me—and so many things that have broken my heart. ... *My Stories of Painting* was both an academic reconstitution of painting and as a source of resonance for people from different cultures who could witness the artist's life journey, tenderness, bitterness, and hardships."

*My Stories of Painting* was a milestone on the path of Cai's longtime pursuit of painting. A major impetus for it came from the museum which awarded Cai the 2016 Bonnefanten Award for Contemporary Art. (The award was instituted in 2000 by the Bonnefanten Museum, which, founded in 1884, holds collections of medieval, classical, and contemporary art.)

Although the exhibition's theme was not the result of long-term planning, in a sense, it paved the way for his Prado exhibition *The Spirit of Painting*, on which he was then already working and which happened one year thereafter. It enabled the artist to put in order his own stories of painting and become equipped for the next phase of his journey.

Figure 8.1. Detail of Cai Guo-Qiang's early painting *The Studio of the Artist in Quanzhou* (1979)

Pages 222–23: Detail of *Pulse (Mountain)* (no. 9.2)

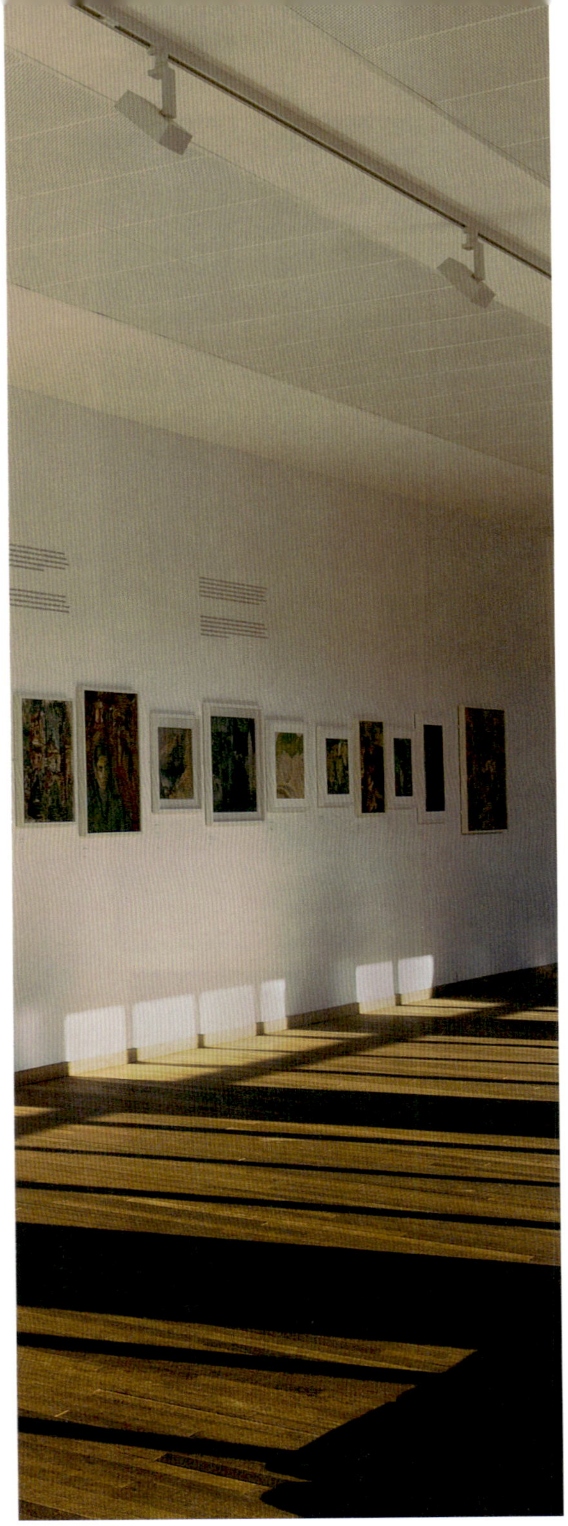

## Individuals who have influenced Cai Guo-Qiang's artistic development in his youth

*Included are painters, teachers, artisans, and preceding masters with whom he dialogues along his Individual's Journey Through Western Art History*

*In alphabetical order, by most commonly used name. In East Asian names, surnames indicated by underline*

Corneliu Baba
Thomas Hart Benton
Pierre Bonnard
Hieronymus Bosch
Sandro Botticelli
Cai Ruiqin
Michelangelo Merisi da Caravaggio
Paul Cézanne
Chen Yiting
Jean Baptiste Camille Corot
Willem de Kooning
Edgar Degas
André Derain
Fang Shicong
Paul Gauguin
Alberto Giacometti
Francisco de Goya
El Greco (Doménikos Theotokópoulos)
Guan Liang
Hu Xiangcheng
Huang Gongwang
Wassily Kandinsky
Kawaguchi Tatsuo
Ivan Kramskoi
Leonardo da Vinci
Isaac Levitan
Lin Fengmian
Konstantin Maksimov
Kazimir Malevich
Henri Matisse
Evsey Moiseyenko
Claude Monet
Giorgio Morandi
Ni Zan
Pablo Picasso
Jackson Pollock
Qi Baishi
Mark Rothko
Peter Paul Rubens
Egon Schiele
Valentin Serov
Sesshū Tōyō
Georges Seurat
Titian
Joseph Mallord William Turner
Vincent van Gogh
Diego Velázquez
Maurice de Vlaminck
Mikhail Vrubel
Wu Guanzhong
Yan Wenliang
Yang Zhenrong
Zhang Chongren
Zhou Benyi

## Cai Guo-Qiang was also influenced by the following in his youth

Quanzhou arts: folk art glass painting, lacquer painting, stone carving, wood carving, puppetry, Chinese opera, and more
New Year pictures (*nianhua*)
Dunhuang mural paintings
ancient grottoes
ancient petroglyphs
ceremonies and shamans
Yongle Palace murals
Mexican murals

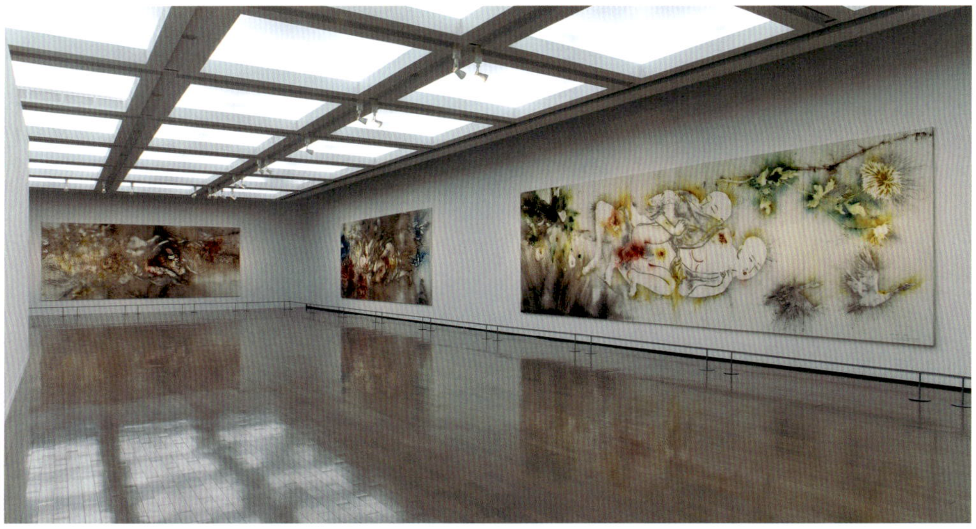

Figure 8.13. Installation view of *Seasons of Life* at Yokohama Museum of Art in Japan in 2015

8.2

*Seasons of Life: Spring*

人生四季：春

2015

Gunpowder on canvas

259 × 648 cm

8.3

*Seasons of Life: Summer*

人生四季：夏

2015

Gunpowder on canvas

259 × 648 cm

In 2015, Cai created *Seasons of Life* for his solo exhibition *There and Back Again* at the Yokohama Museum of Art. It marks his first series of color gunpowder paintings on canvas since the 1980s. Cai first attempted to work with color gunpowder soon after he arrived in Japan—however, he then felt that the medium was unsuitable for expressing his desired spiritual pursuit in art, and began working only with black gunpowder for many years.

The central theme of the Yokohama exhibition was painting. Through the medium of color gunpowder, Cai manifested a sensuality that had been brewing for years. The usage of color evoked an unexpected excitement within the artist, setting off a new stage in his unadulterated exploration of painting.

*There and Back Again* was also Cai's first major exhibition in Japan after leaving the country as a young artist thirty years prior for his long journey around the world—and therein lay the incipient spark for what would become *Odyssey and Homecoming*, a culmination of his return to the East from the West.

*The Artist's Statement*

I exploded four gunpowder paintings on canvas, a series titled *Seasons of Life*. The subjects in the paintings are dressed in neutral colors, as though to mask any indication of time. The tattoos on the bodies were inspired by Japanese *hanafuda* and correspond to the different seasons as well as their respective flora and fauna. Exploded, they seem to peel back the layers of human desire. *Spring* is gentle and hazy: swallows call to each other and desire is palpable as that of a sprightly young deer. *Summer* is clearer and displays lilies and peonies. One can almost hear cuckoos cheering with bursts of joy.

This is the first group of paintings I created after starting to work more with color gunpowder in 2015. The exploded scarlet reminds me of Francis Bacon's oil paintings with their wild sense of abuse. Small areas of dense and strong color drastically contrast with vast expanses of the earth tones resulting from black gunpowder, which brings an unexpected thrill as if a wild beast were released, in turn revealing a different side of myself. I experimented with the raw power of black gunpowder and the color of the daytime fireworks to convey sentiments and desire, as well as the loss and aspiration in a life's journey, which for me points to a variety of new possibilities.

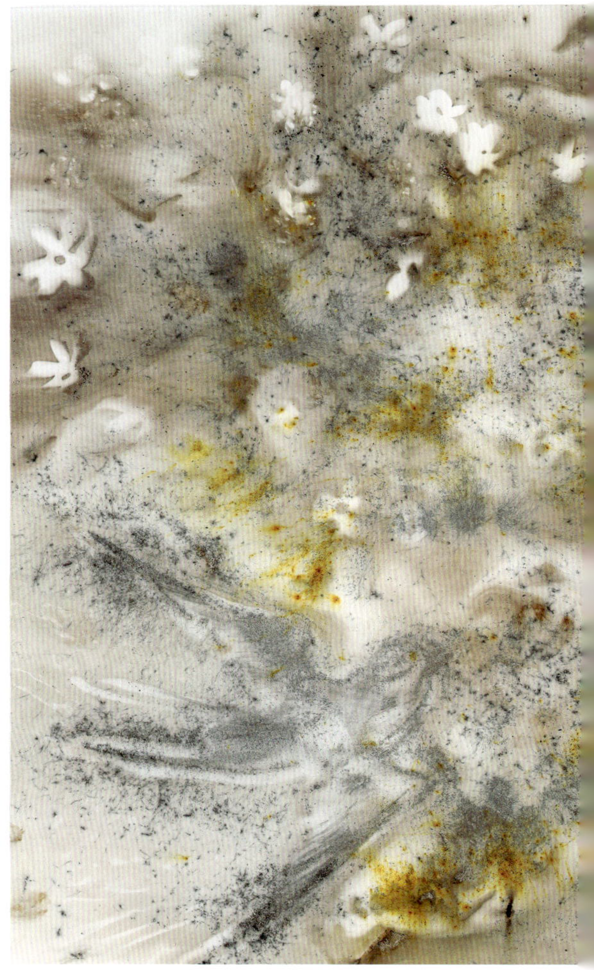

8.2 *Seasons of Life: Spring*

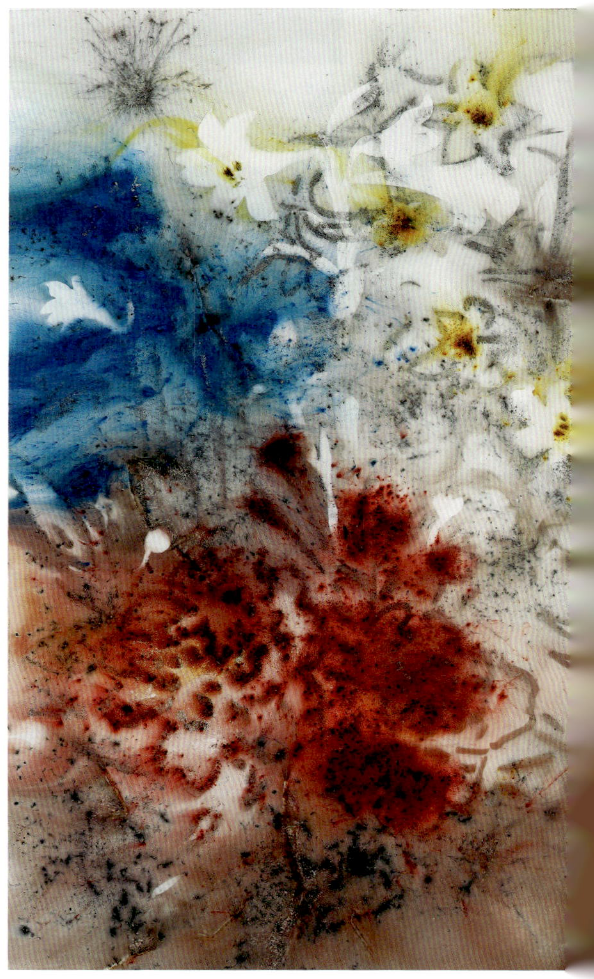

8.3 *Seasons of Life: Summer*

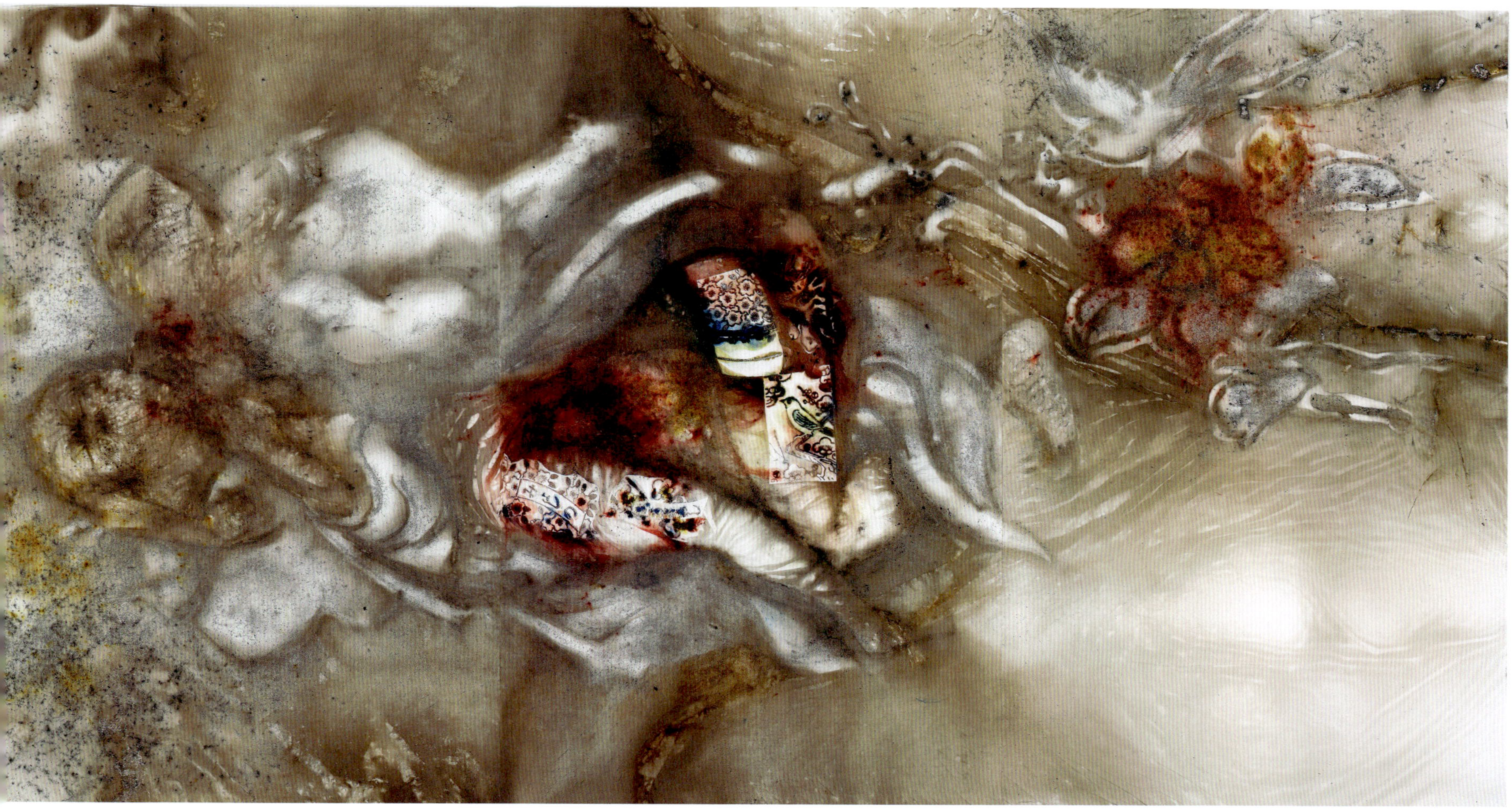

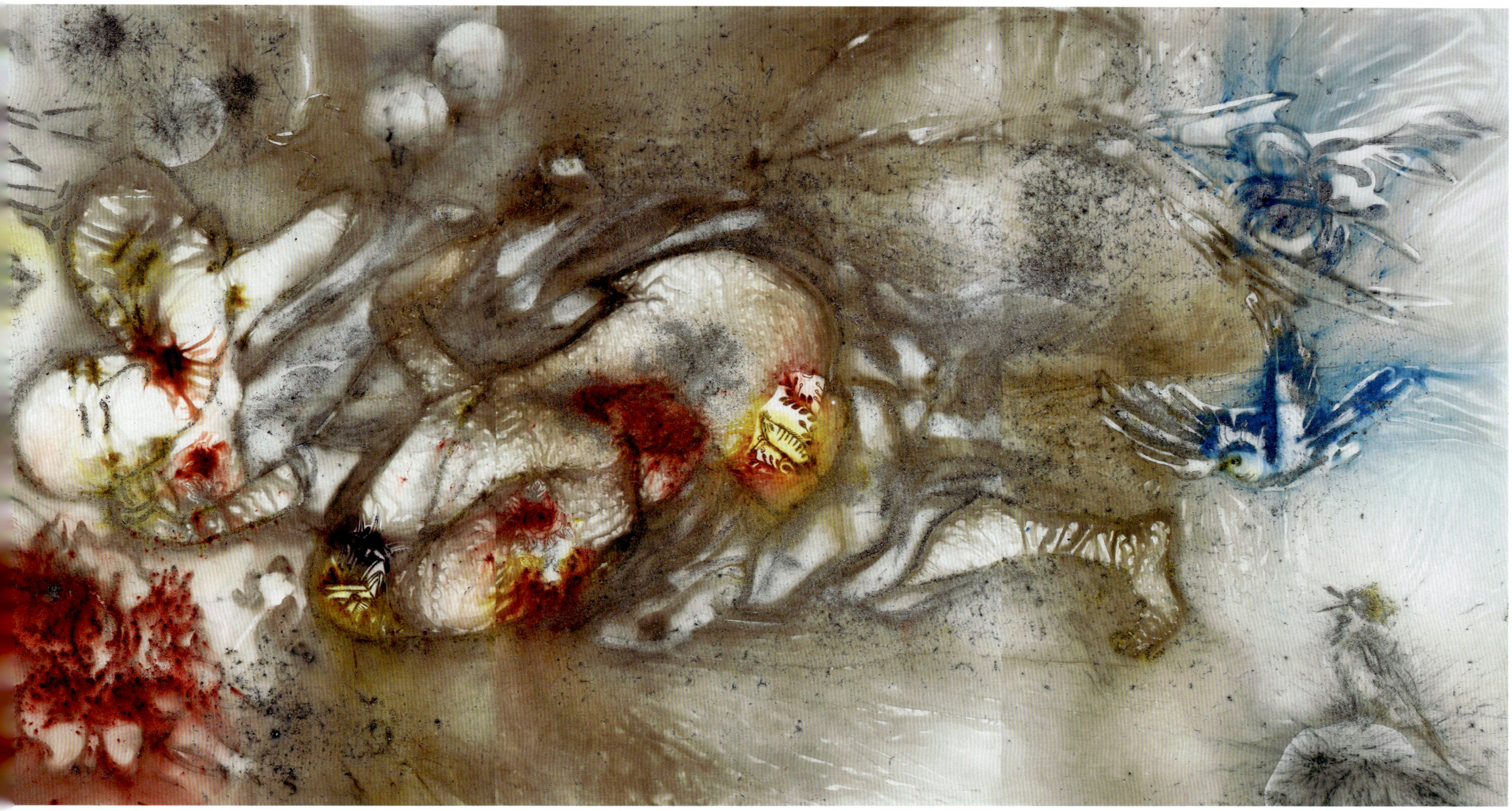

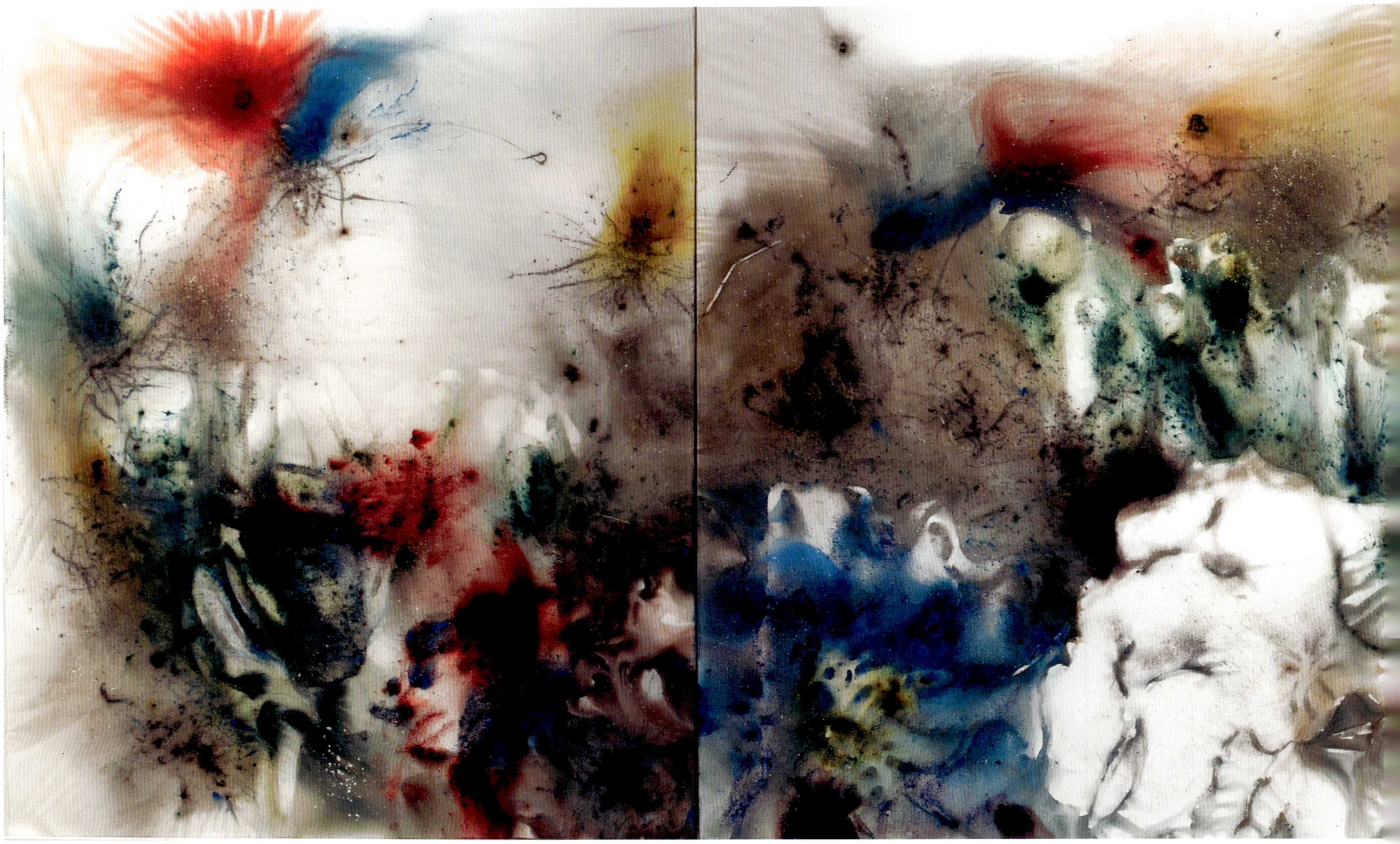

8.4

*Poppy Series: Hallucination No. 1*

罂粟系列:幻觉第一号

2015

Gunpowder on canvas

183 × 608 cm

Using poppy flowers as a motif to express lust and hallucination—forces that wield the same uncontrollability as a gunpowder explosion—the work challenged the artist to unleash the sensual energy of both the artist and the materials themselves. This is a significant work from 2015 when Cai began to reintroduce color gunpowder into his oeuvre.

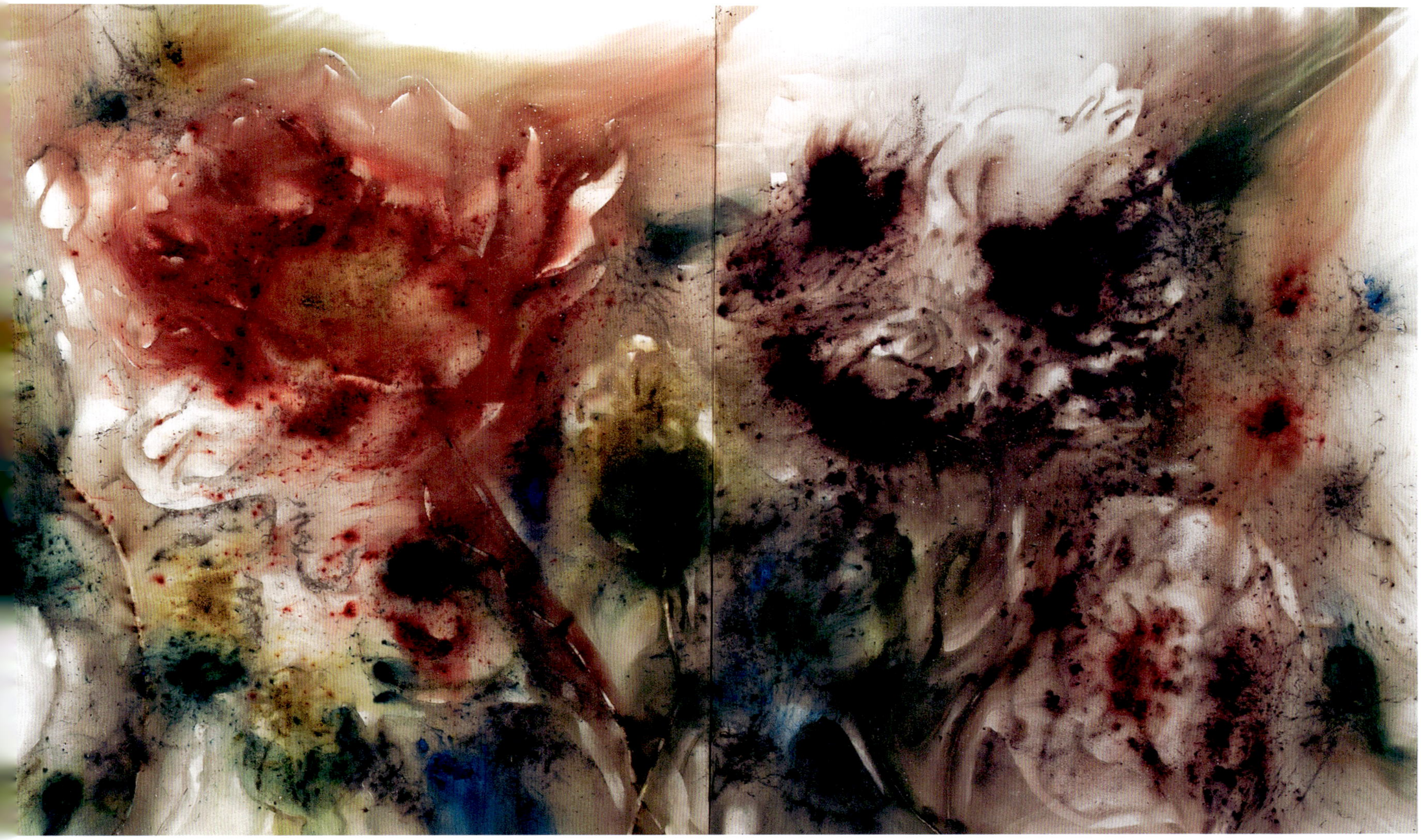

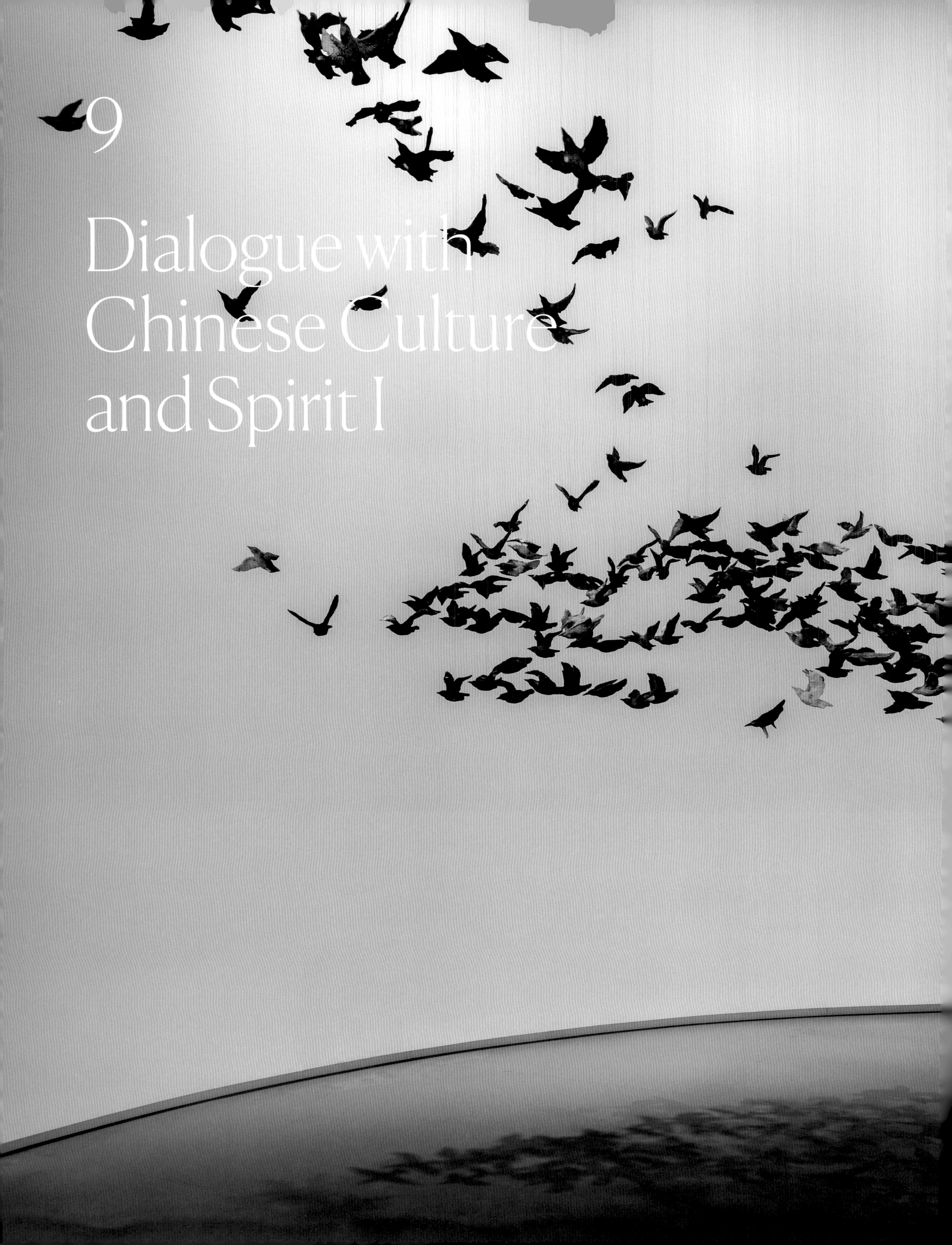

9

# Dialogue with Chinese Culture and Spirit I

# *Cai Guo-Qiang: The Transient Landscape*

National Gallery of Victoria (NGV), Melbourne, Australia
May 24–October 13, 2019

Curated by Wayne Crothers, Senior Curator of Asian Art, National Gallery of Victoria

Public painting creation: Williamstown warehouse, Melbourne, March 11–16, 18–22, 2019

Catalogue: English edition published by NGV

Documentary short: directed by Benjamin Ducroz, released by NGV (1:08)

In 2019, the National Gallery of Victoria (NGV), the oldest, largest, and most visited art museum in Australia, hosted *Terracotta Warriors: Guardians of Immortality*, a historical exhibition centering on major artifacts from the tomb of Qin Shi Huang, China's "First Emperor" (259–210 BCE). NGV concurrently presented *Cai Guo-Qiang: The Transient Landscape* to build a larger context with a contemporary exhibition, in line with its mission as a general-interest institution whose holdings range from the continent's aboriginal art and artifacts to global contemporary art, as well as antiquities of ancient Egypt and Greece and classical paintings in between. This opportunity enabled Cai to dialogue with the cultural tradition of his homeland. This was the first exhibition where the Terracotta Warriors, one of the "Eight Wonders of the World," was shown in combination with contemporary art.

In each room of *Terracotta Warriors*, Cai had his works—a series of large-scale, site-specific gunpowder paintings and installations—coexist with the ancient works and artifacts. His exhibition accordingly was intermeshed with *Terracotta Warriors*, generating a multidimensional dialogue with the past on conceptual, material, and pictorial levels. Conceptually, both Qin Shi Huang and Cai sought to secure and visualize the unseen world. Whereas the emperor prepared his tomb for his afterlife, the artist demonstrated his cosmology engaging both the external and internal realms. Materially, Cai exploded gunpowder on porcelain, handmade hemp paper, and silk, in correspondence to the Terracotta Warriors and other artifacts unearthed from the emperor's mausoleum. Pictorially, the imagery in Cai's works, such as mountain ranges, cypress trees, and peony blossoms, are symbolic of Chinese history and culture. The somber tones of the artist's expression allude to the colors of life, nationhood, and empire. Taken together, the juxtaposition invites the viewer to confront history and consider the present in a multivalent way.

Detail of *Murmuration (Landscape)* (no. 9.1)

Cai remarked, "*The Transient Landscape* and *Guardians of Immortality* are two exhibitions, akin to two rivers of time separated by two millennia, which course simultaneously but separately in the same space. Herein, the ancient and the contemporary signify two surges of energy, a tension between them crisscrosses and tugs at each other, mutually attracting and repelling. I hoped to give a new relevance to objects conventionally defined as cultural artifacts and make them into art through this intervention as a contemporary artist. Ultimately, the 'guardians of immortality' could not preserve the emperor's land or power. Like the Qin dynasty itself, they will eventually become a transient part of history. 'Transience' is the true eternity."

Cai's visit to Melbourne in March 2019 to create the gunpowder artworks took place only one month after his presentation of *In the Volcano* in Pompeii and Naples. Cai's dialogue with the origins of Western civilization now seemed to naturally segue into his dialogue with the artery of his own Eastern land that has been pulsing for thousands of years. The unbridled violence of the explosion at Pompeii and the destruction and rebirth evoked by the volcano grew into a powerful and deep serenity found in the Eastern spirit. It was as though the brute force was joined with the force of life and death, of transience and eternity, each realizing the other into being.

*All entries in this section are adapted from from Wayne Crothers's writings for the exhibition.*

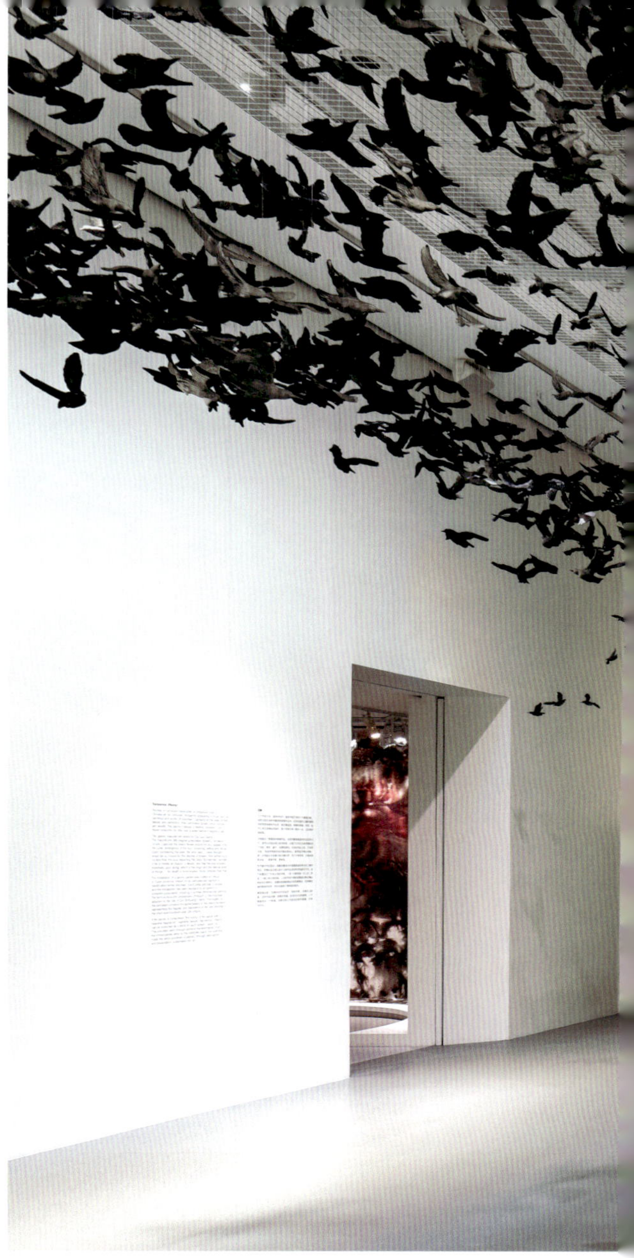

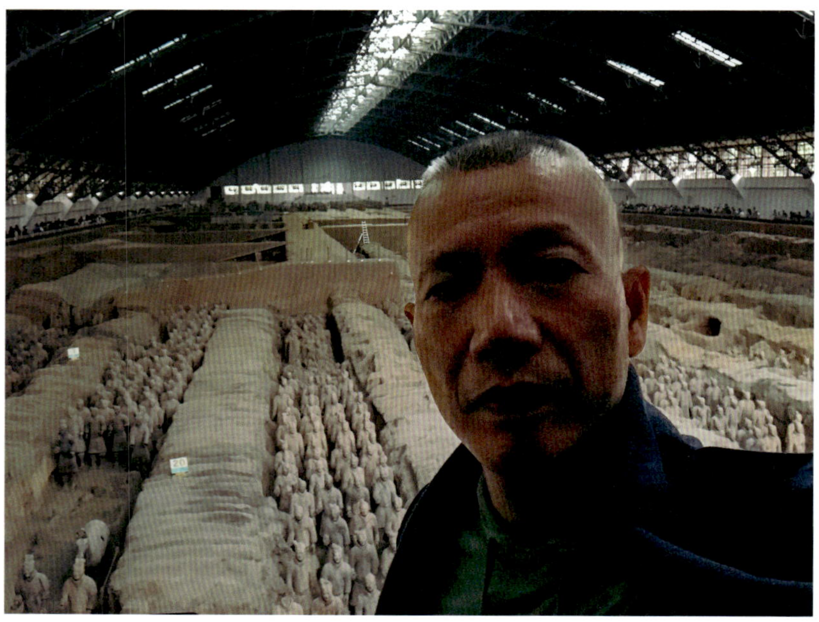

Figure 9.1. Cai Guo-Qiang visiting the Terracotta Warriors pit in Xi'an in 2018

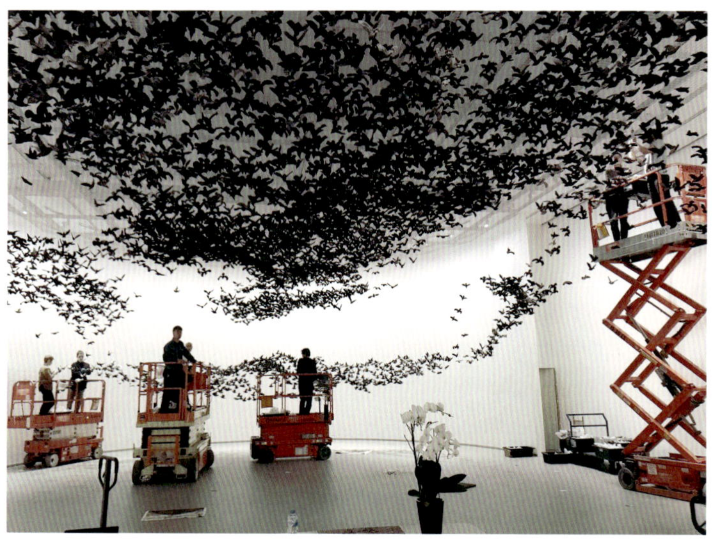

Figure 9.2. NGV and Cai Studio staff working to hang 10,000 exploded birds of *Murmuration (Landscape)* in 2019

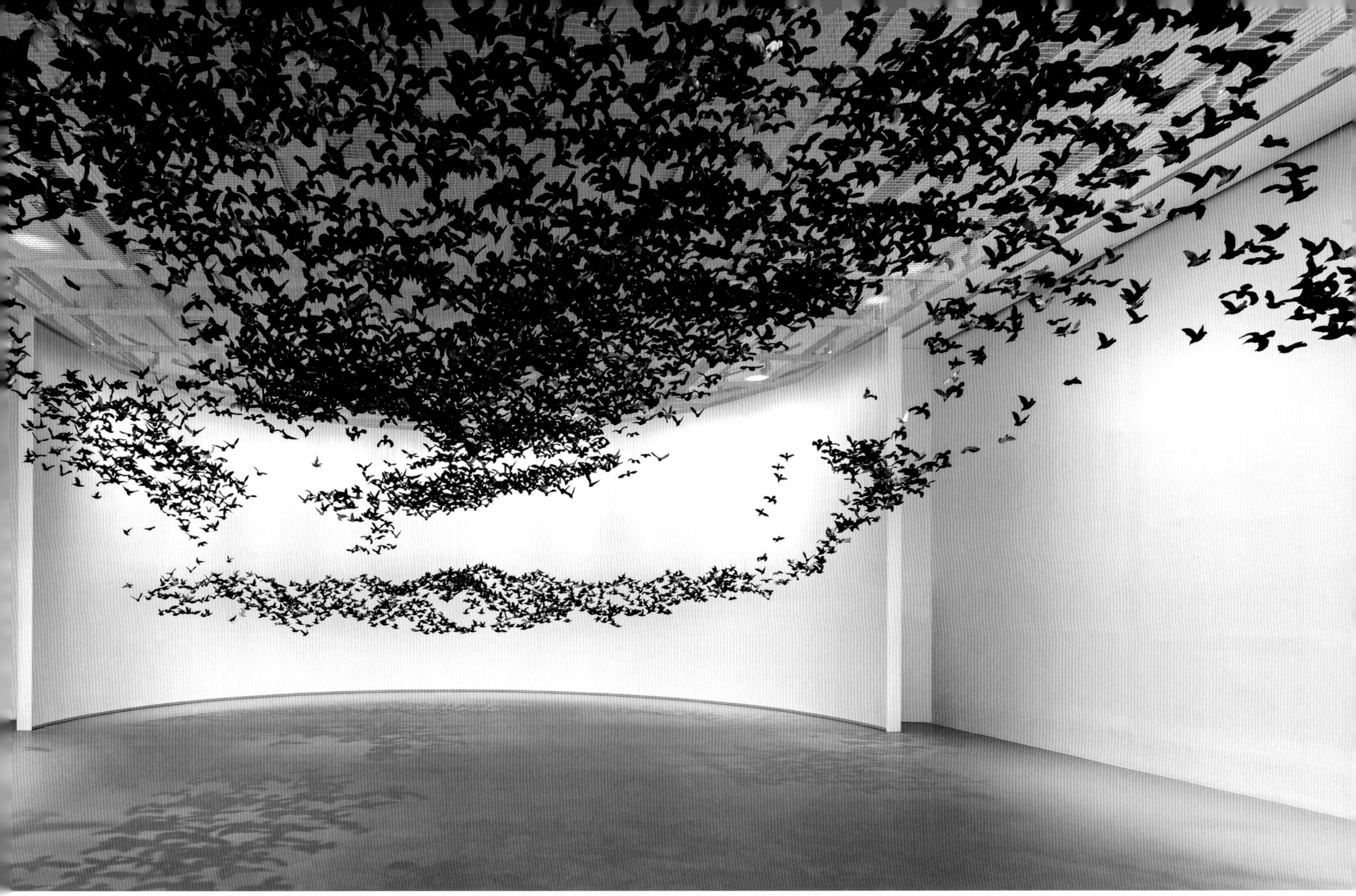

9.1

*Murmuration (Landscape)*

鸟云

2019

Gunpowder on porcelain

Dimensions variable

Collection of the National Gallery of Victoria

Ten thousand porcelain birds thread the two exhibitions from the beginning to the end, appearing as a lingering spirit or a haunting shadow. At times, the birds appear in a small flock; at times, they gather to form stormy clouds hovering high above our heads like an imposing infantry; at times, their configuration conjures up the undulation of Mount Li around the mausoleum of China's First Emperor. These birds of distinct features are made of porcelain to respond to the material of the Warriors. They were first hand-crafted in Cai's hometown and later scorched by gunpowder explosion in Melbourne, to achieve expressive patterns akin to ink-wash painting.

The inspiration of *Murmuration* comes from a visit to the Terracotta Warriors in Cai's youth. Overlooking the infantry of terracotta figures in the vast pits across the epic site, he was in awe of the momentous and majestic presence and astonished by the concept of creating eight thousand sculptures only to be buried. Cai comments, "Exhibitions of Terracotta Warriors overseas often display only a few sculptures, taking part in the exoticized promotion of a distant culture. These exhibitions can't communicate the grandeur of Qin and Han dynasties, nor can they speak of today's China and its relationship with the rest of the world—its momentum, energy, complexity, and chaos. The ever-changing formation of ten thousand porcelain birds seems to embody the lingering spirits of the underground army, or perhaps the haunting shadow of China's imperial past."

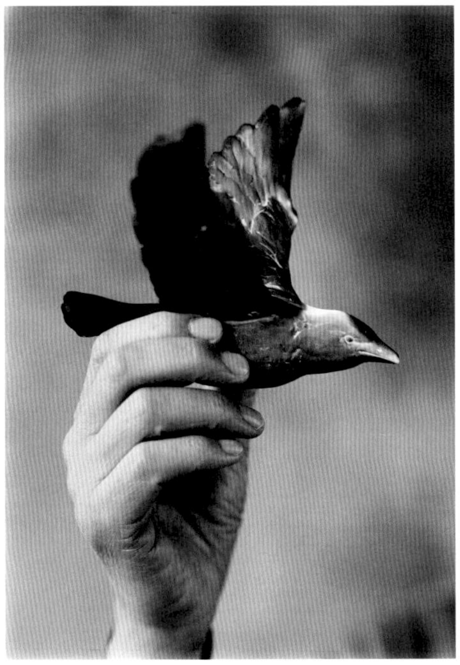

Figure 9.3. Cai Guo-Qiang holding an exploded porcelain bird from *Murmuration (Landscape)* in 2019

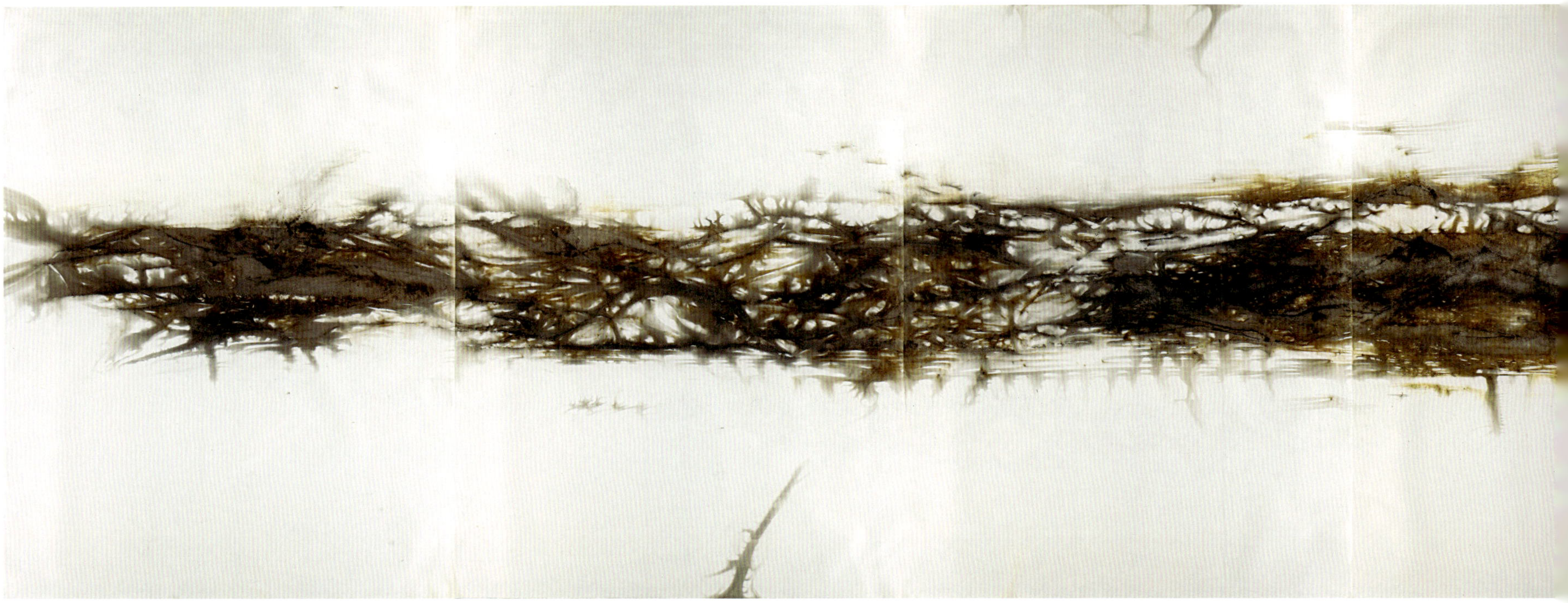

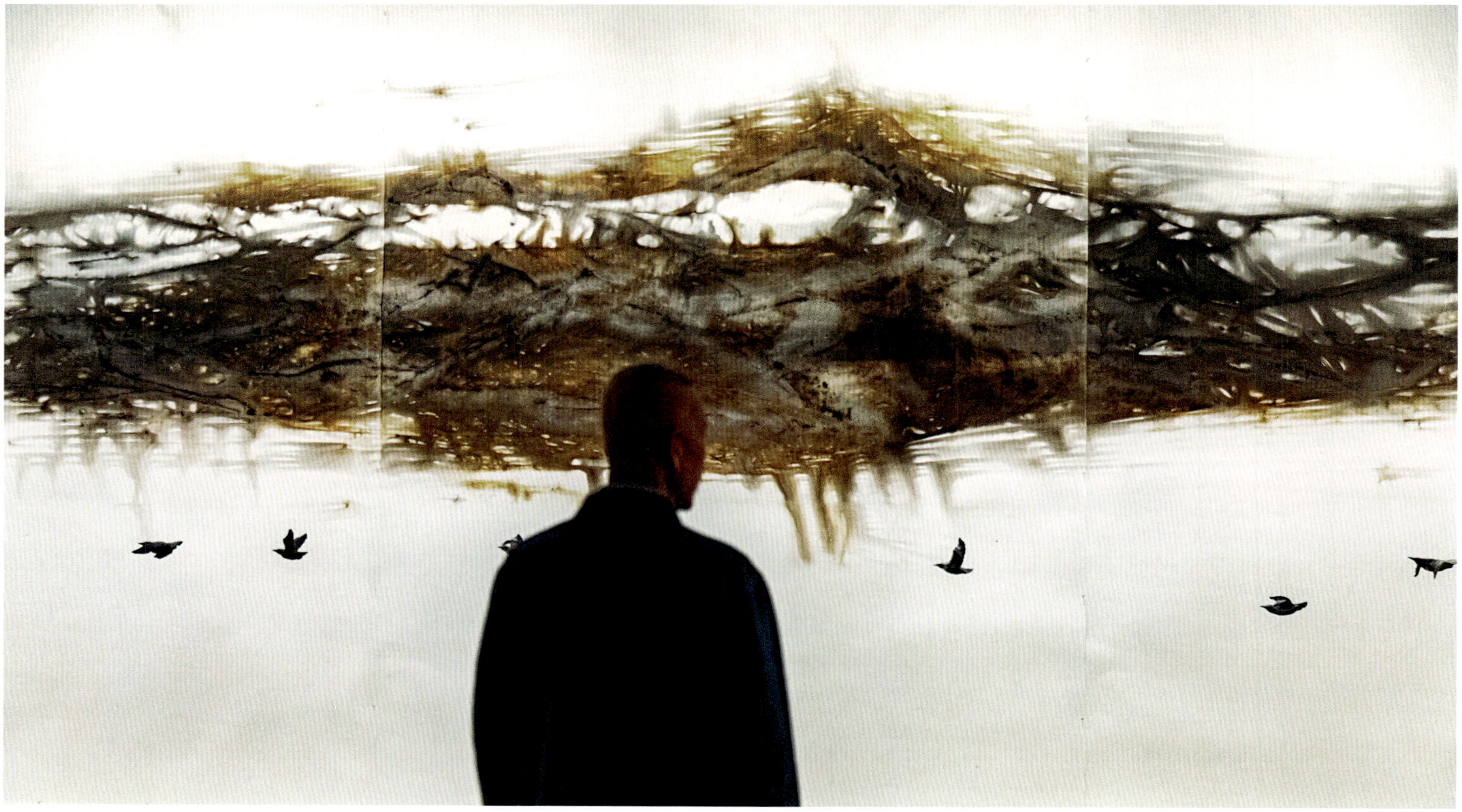

Figure 9.4. Cai Guo-Qiang in front of *Pulse (Mountain)* in 2019

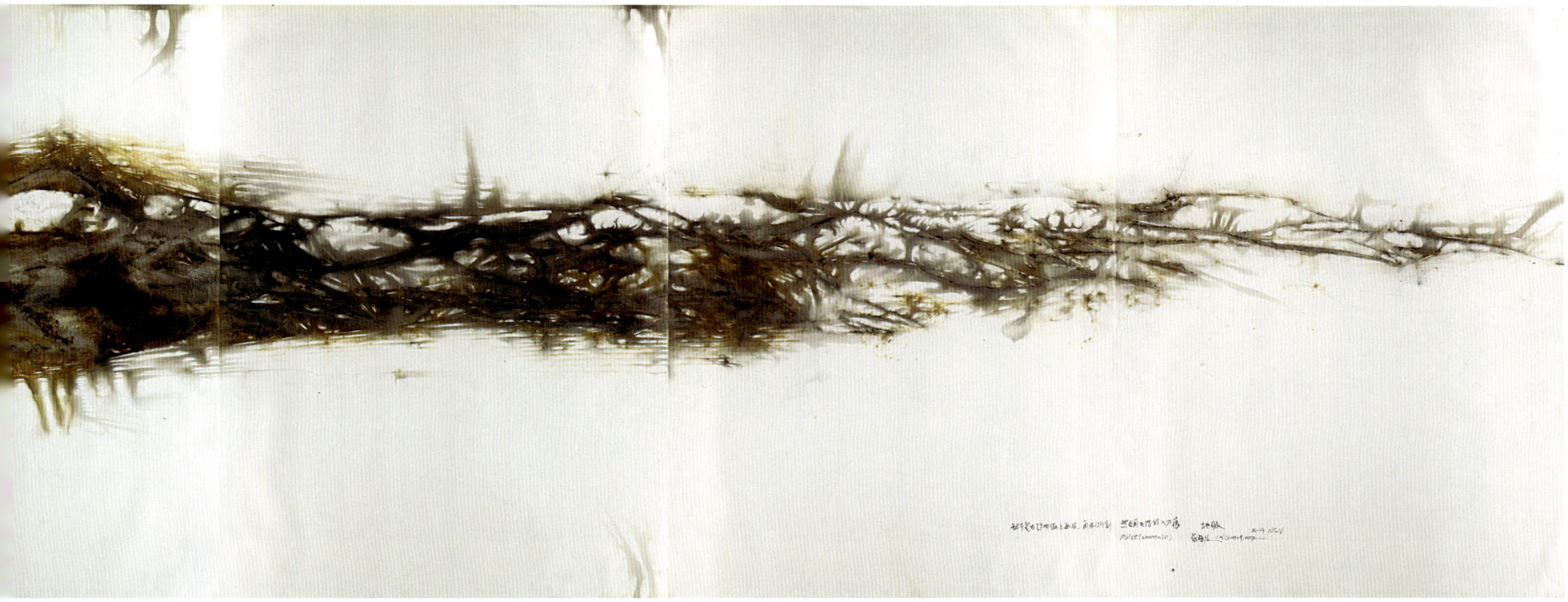

9.2

*Pulse (Mountain)*

地脉

2019

Gunpowder on paper and porcelain

Gunpowder painting: 400 × 2100 cm;

16 porcelain birds: 10 × 20 × 30 cm each

*Pulse (Mountain)* depicts the vast chain of mountains and the tranquil horizon of the Central Plains. The rusty yellow color resulting from the explosion happened to resemble the Loess Plateau of China. Cai thinks that in *feng shui*, the ancient Chinese study of energy forces, geographical contours like ridges and valleys denote the earth's veins and the flow of *qi*, or life force. The excessive amount of gunpowder pushed the smoke to break through the chain of mountains meticulously carved on the glassine paper. In the end, the trace of smoke imbued the painting with an elevating air.

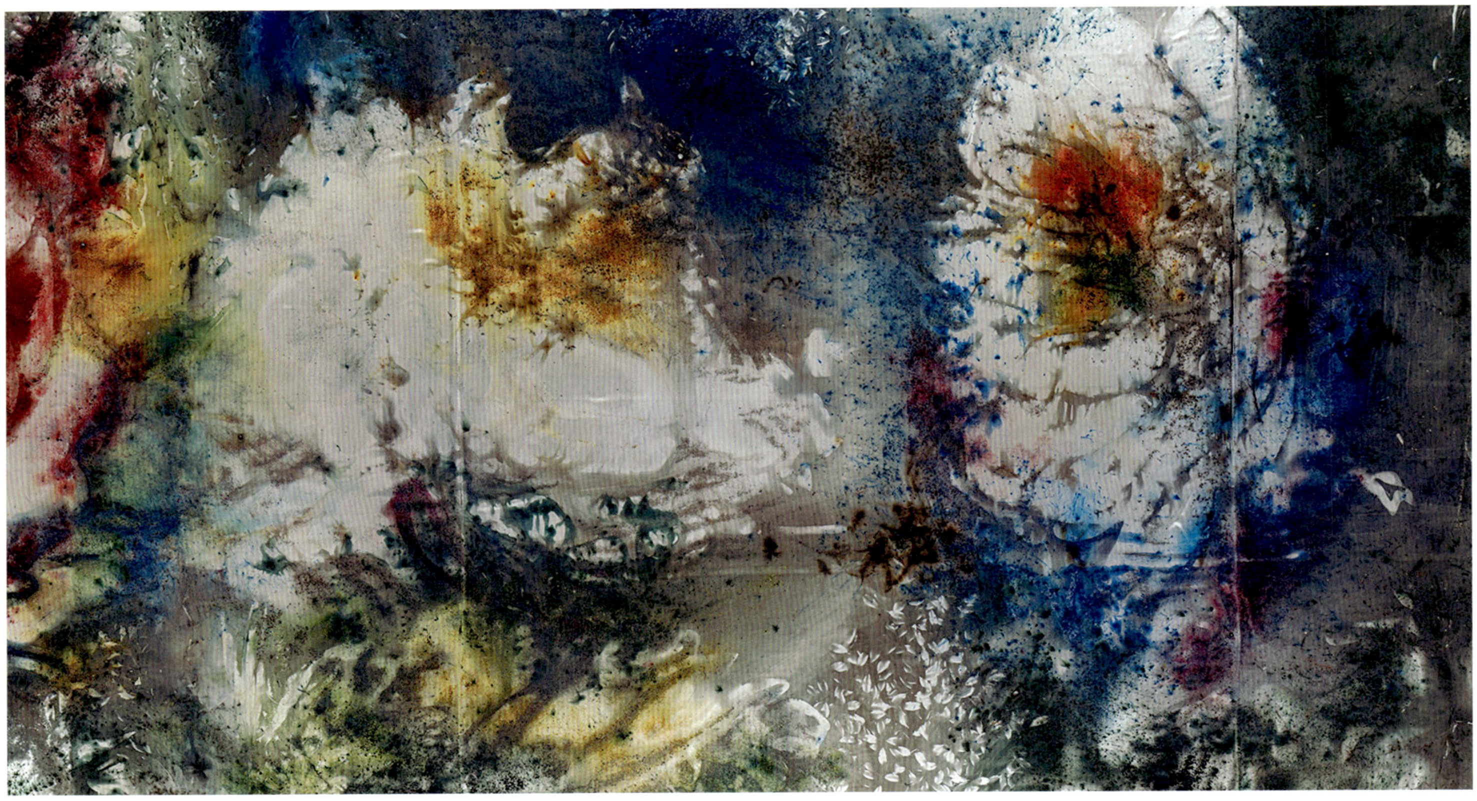

Figure 9.5. Detail of *Transience II (Peony)*

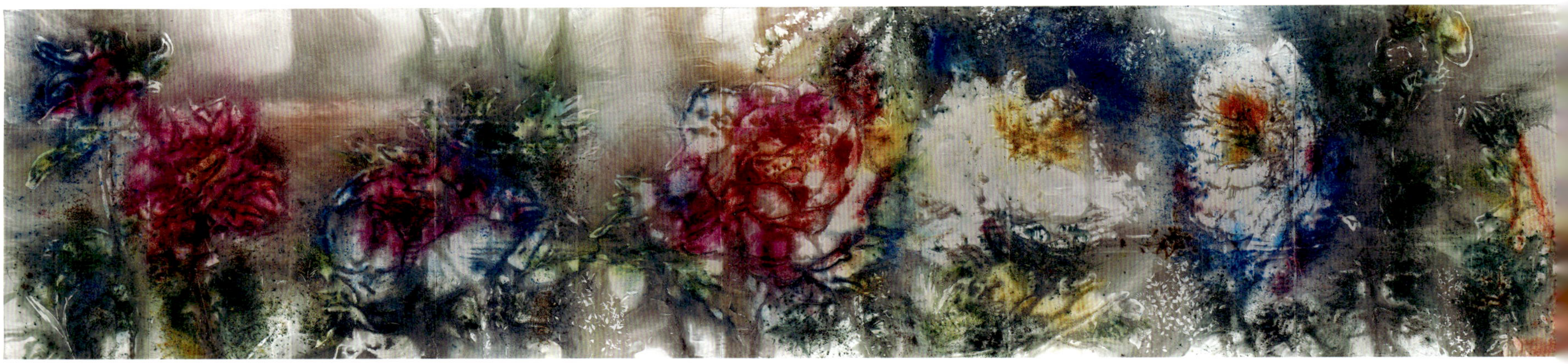

9.4 *Transience II (Peony)*

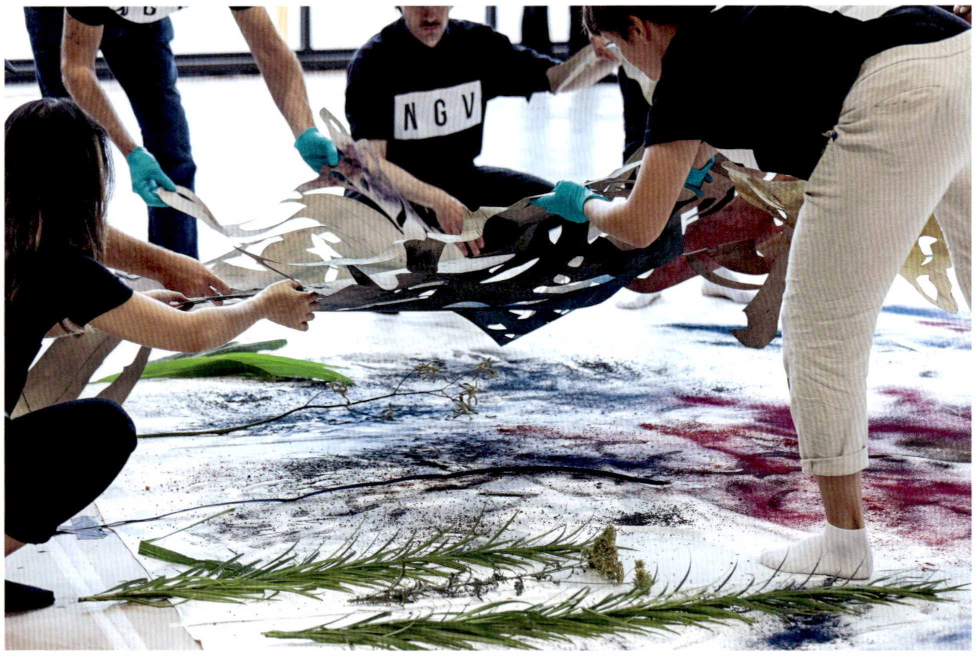


Figure 9.7. Volunteers laying stencils during the creation of *Transience II (Peony)* in 2019

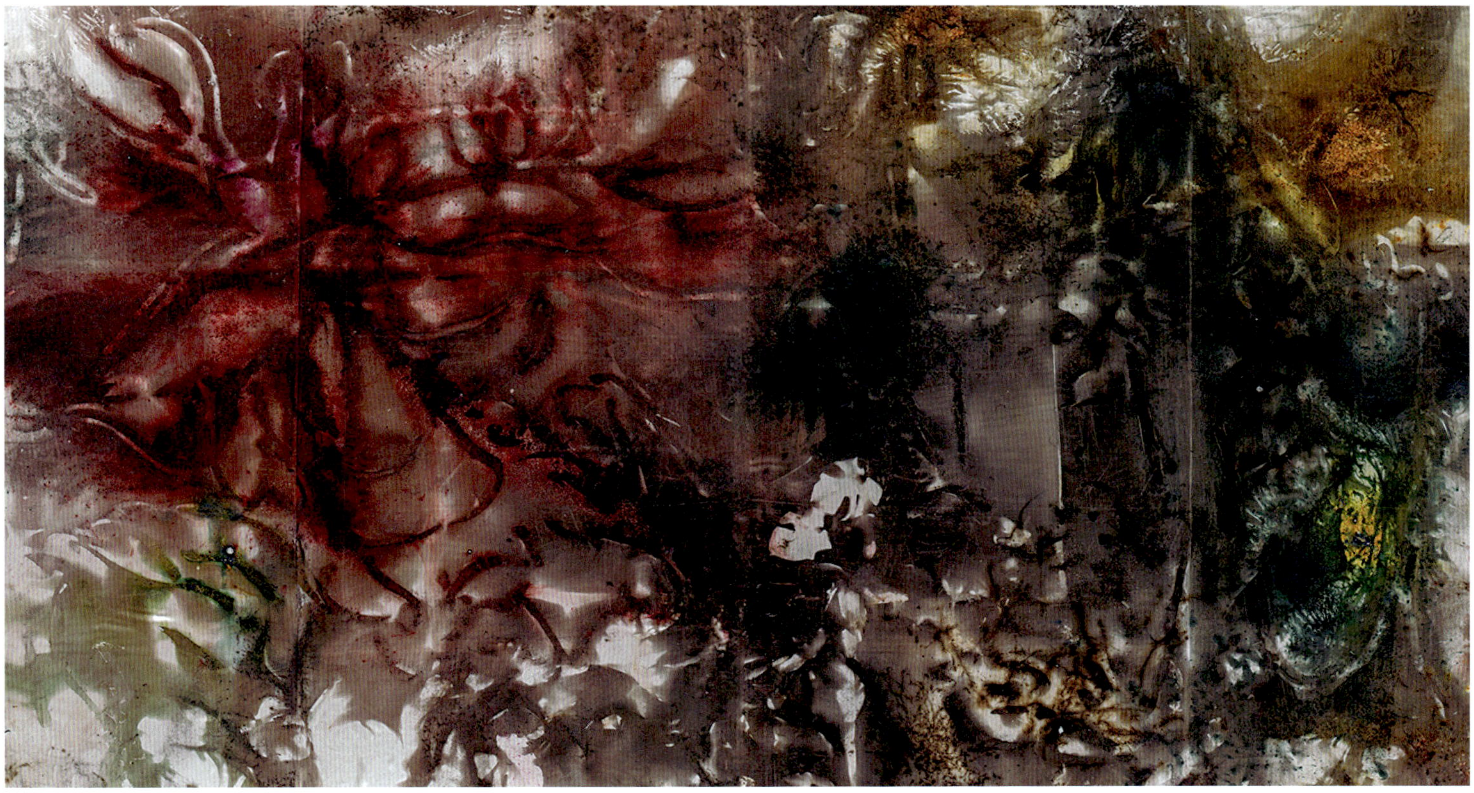

Figure 9.6. Detail of *Transience II (Peony)*

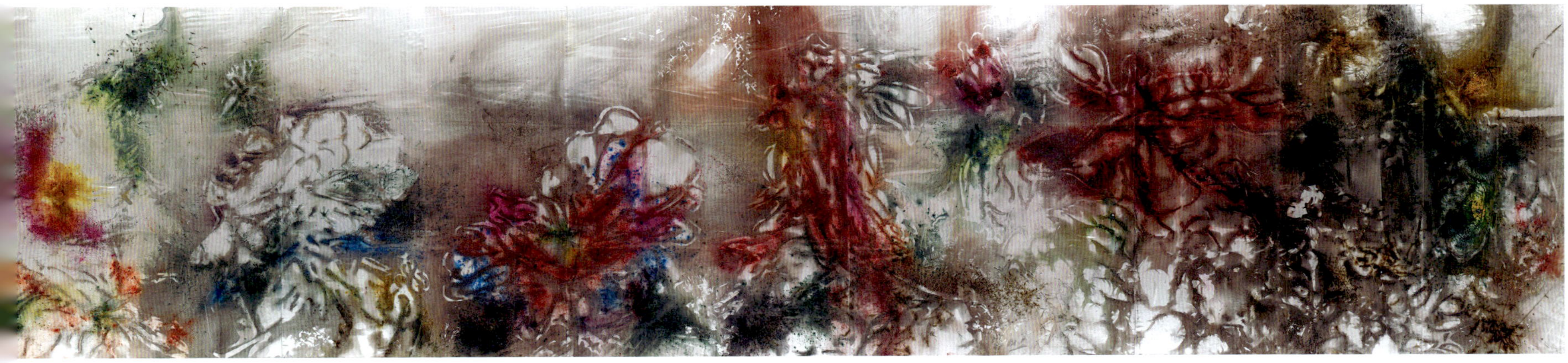

9.3

*Transience I (Peony)*

花瞬一

2019

Gunpowder on porcelain

90 × 100 × 200 cm

9.4

*Transience II (Peony)*

花瞬二

2019

Gunpowder on silk

350 × 3080 cm

Two works both center on the theme of the peony flower. *Transience I (Peony)* is a gunpowder on white porcelain sculpture. A stunningly crafted white porcelain sculpture is sublimated into art through destruction and devastation. The artist comments, "If the peony is considered 'the color of the nation with a heavenly fragrance,' deemed to symbolize supreme beauty, this work can be considered a burial for such beauty. Chinese painting masters often depict flowers in prosperity but neglect to face the equally authentic state of life that is death and decay. The ancient painters lack the all-embracing vision of the poets who praise not only the blossoming flowers but also the fallen petals."

*Transience II (Peony)* is a gunpowder painting on silk covering an entire wall of the exhibition space. It aims to express the beauty in the life and death of peony flowers—from sprouting of bud to full bloom, wilt, and decay—to manifest the fragility of life and culture. Cai said, "I never thought I would be so moved by the wilting of flowers. Their withering is no less than the soul departing the body! Sometimes I wonder if life is merely an illusion, a dream, and that the soul actually manifests upon dying, which is the origin and the eternal state of things."

9.3 *Transience I (Peony)* on the floor and 9.4 *Transience II (Peony)* on the wall (overleaf)

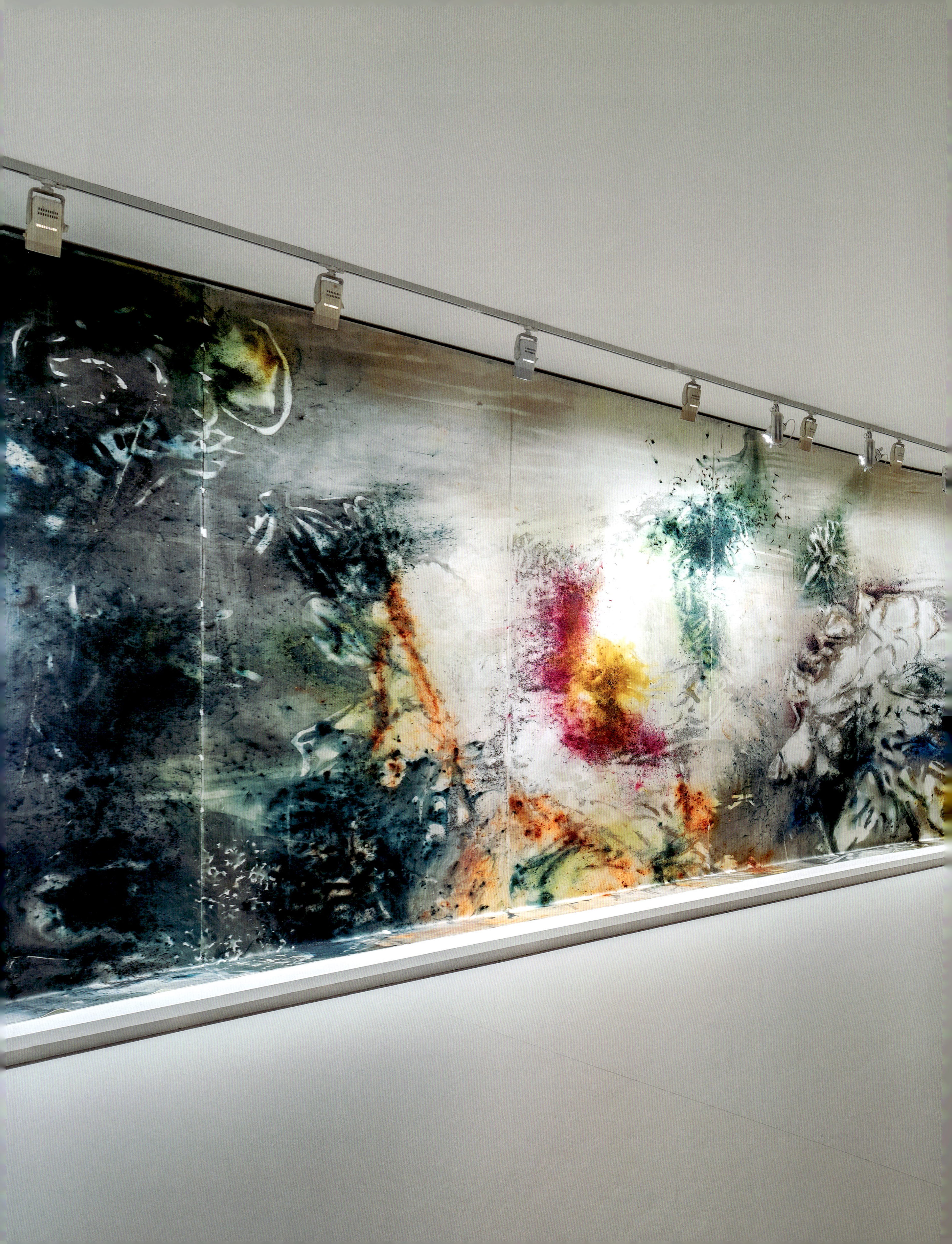

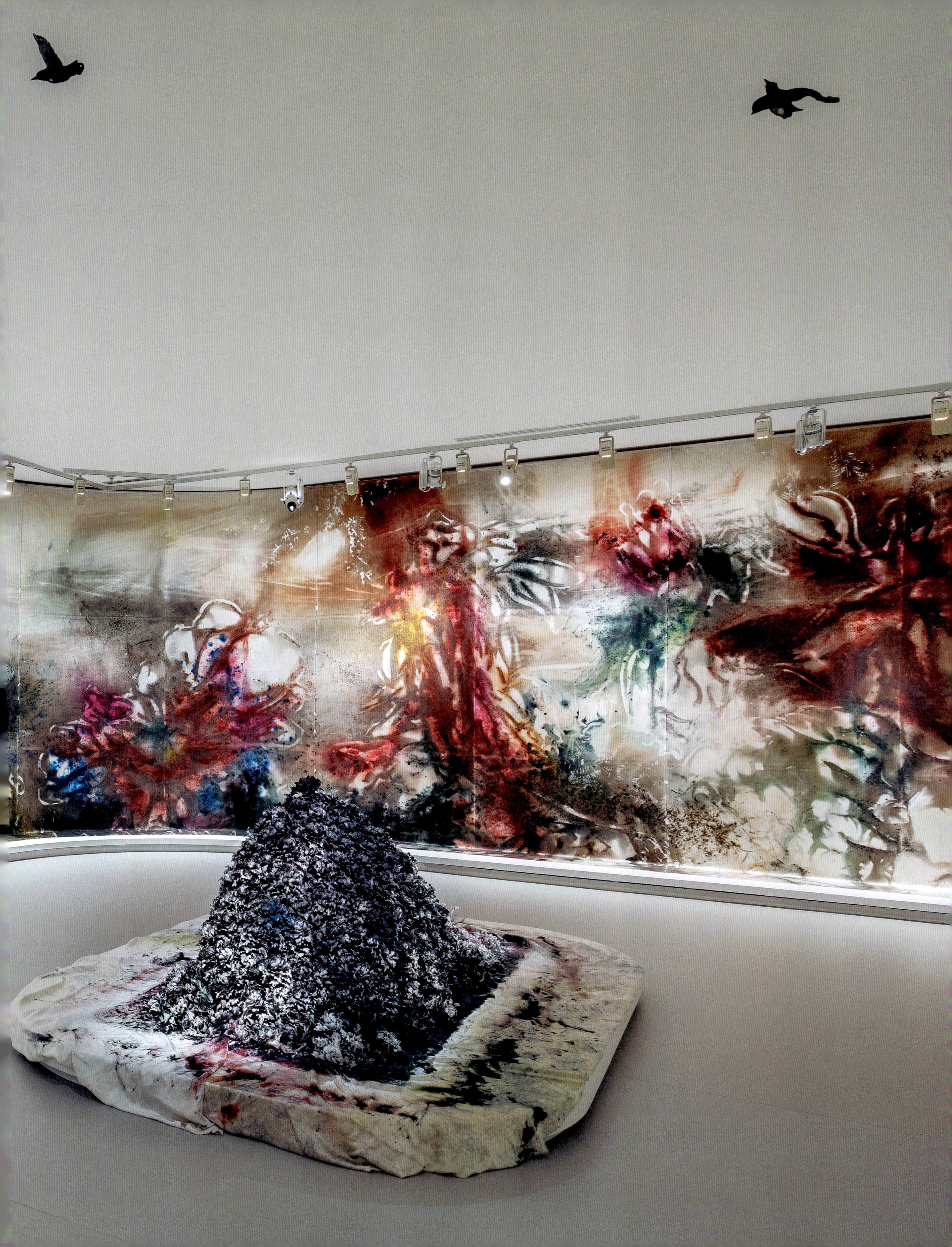

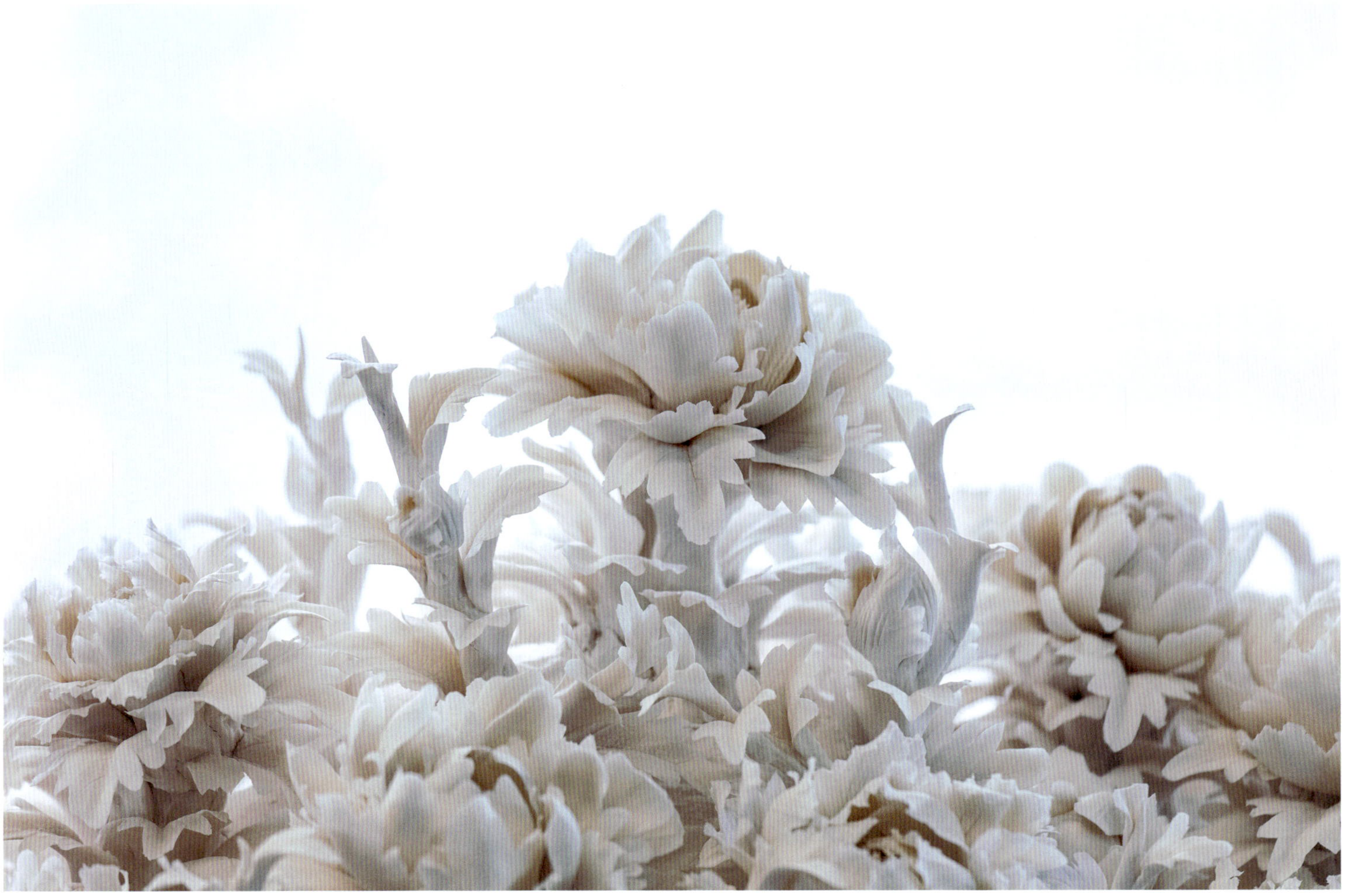

Figure 9.8. Unexploded porcelain peonies in 2019

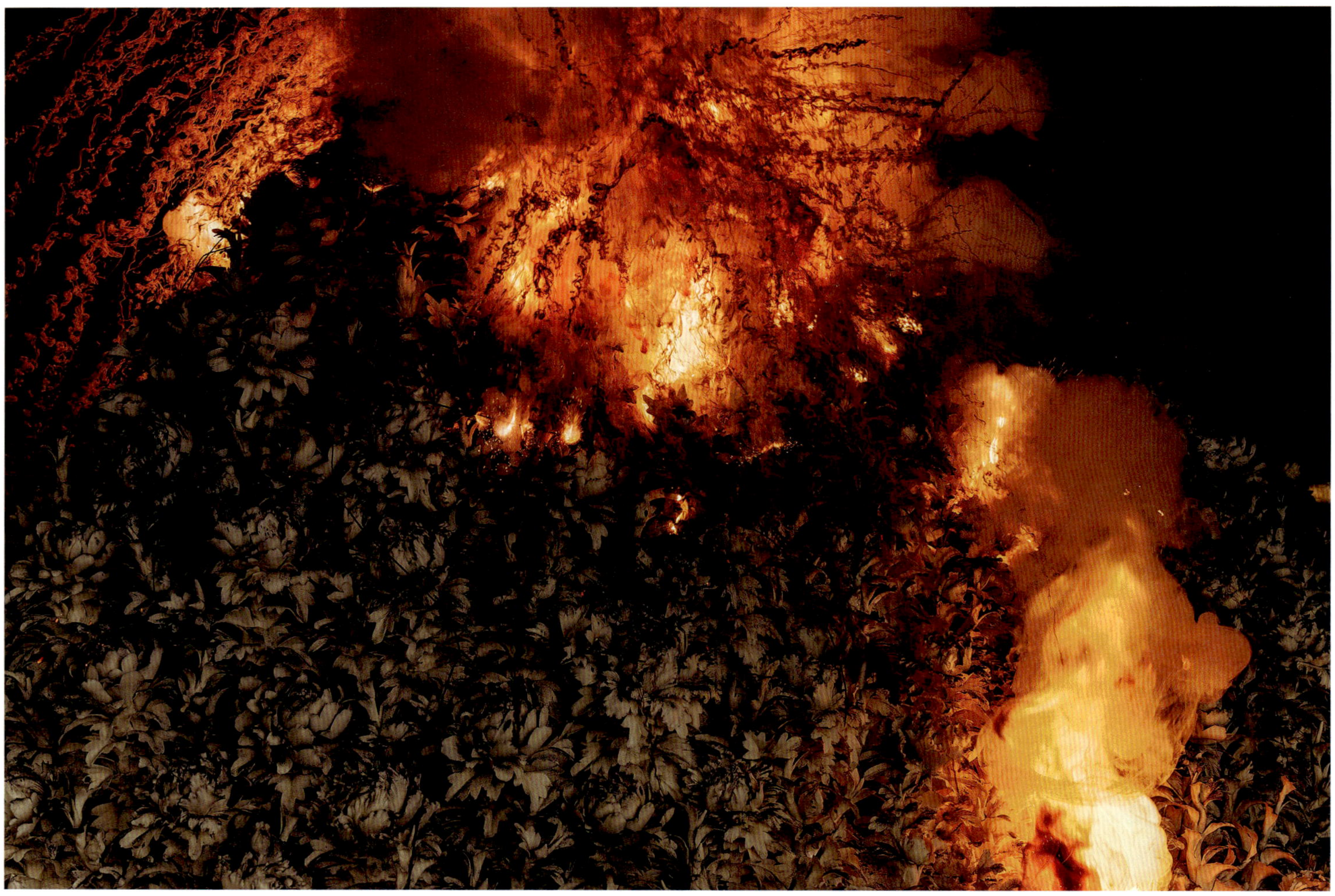

Figure 9.9. Ignition of *Transience I (Peony)* in 2019

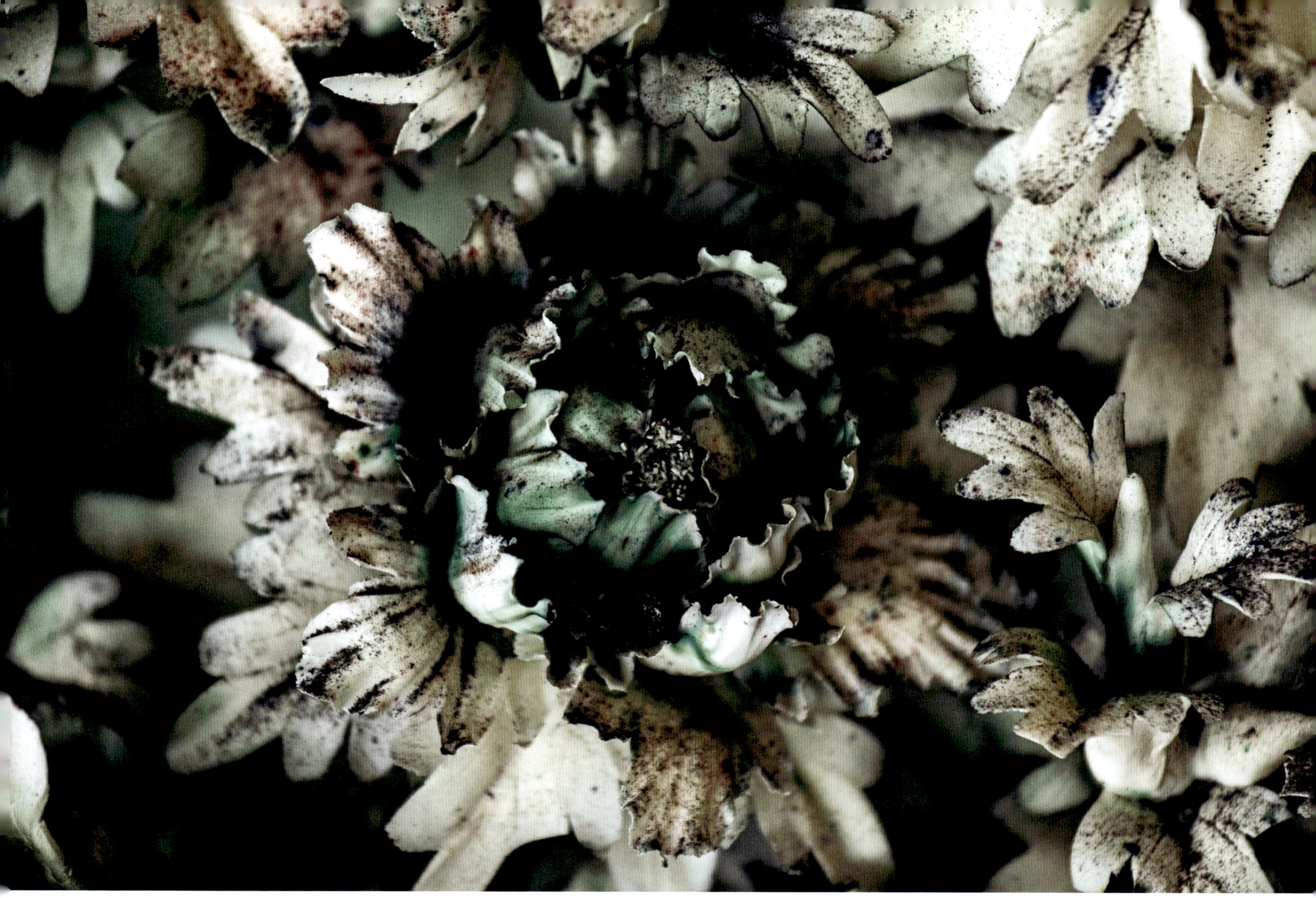

Figure 9.10. Detail of *Transience I (Peony)* (no. 9.3)

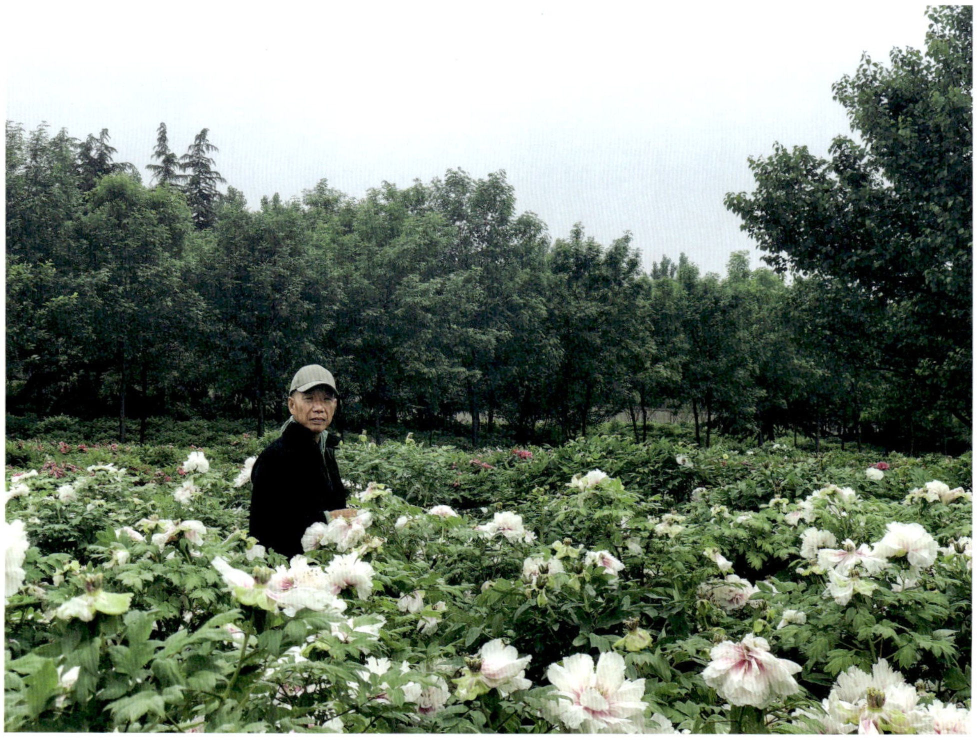

Figure 9.11. Cai Guo-Qiang in a peony field in Luoyang in 2018

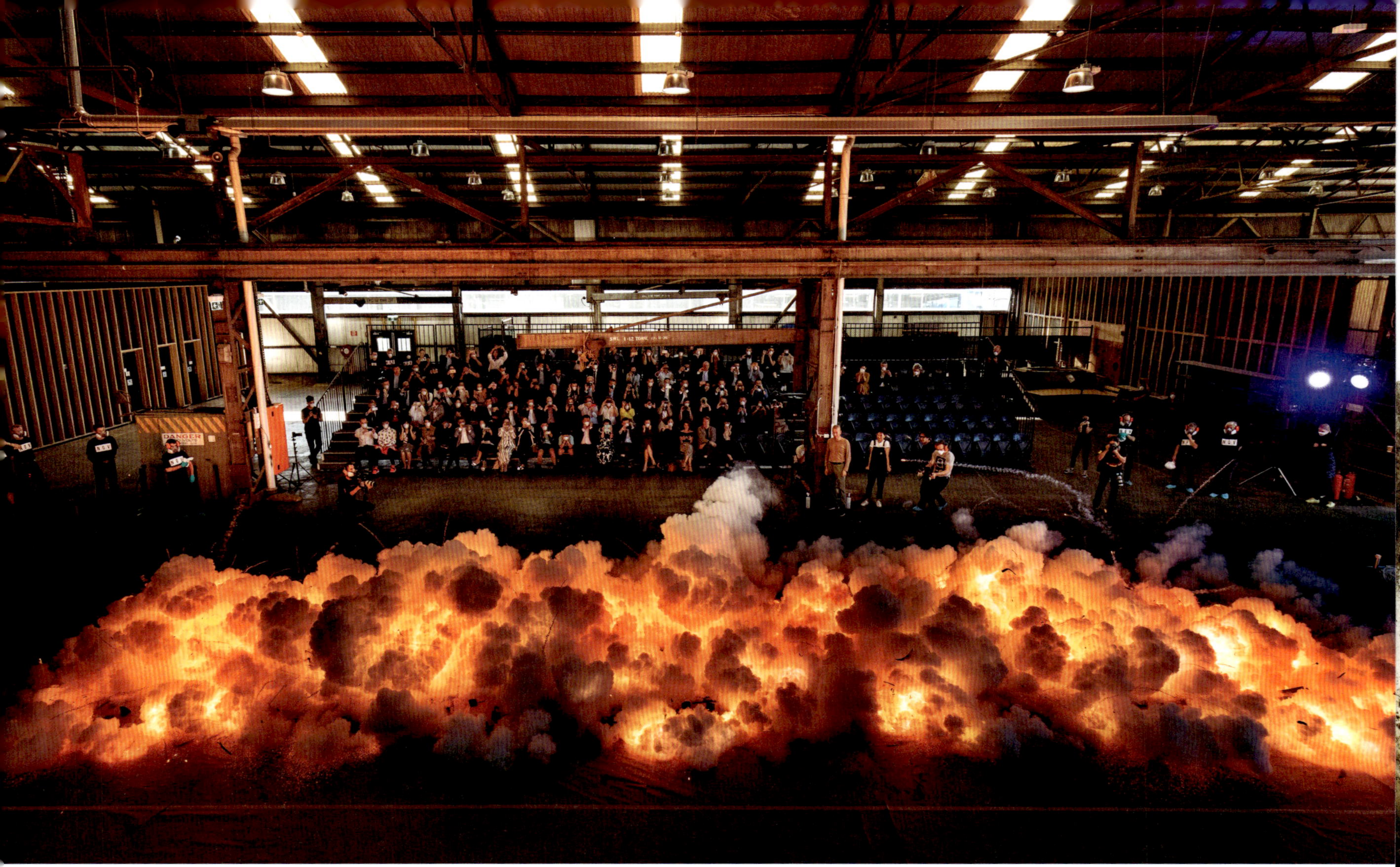

Figure 9.12. Ignition of *Flow (Cypress)* in Melbourne in 2019

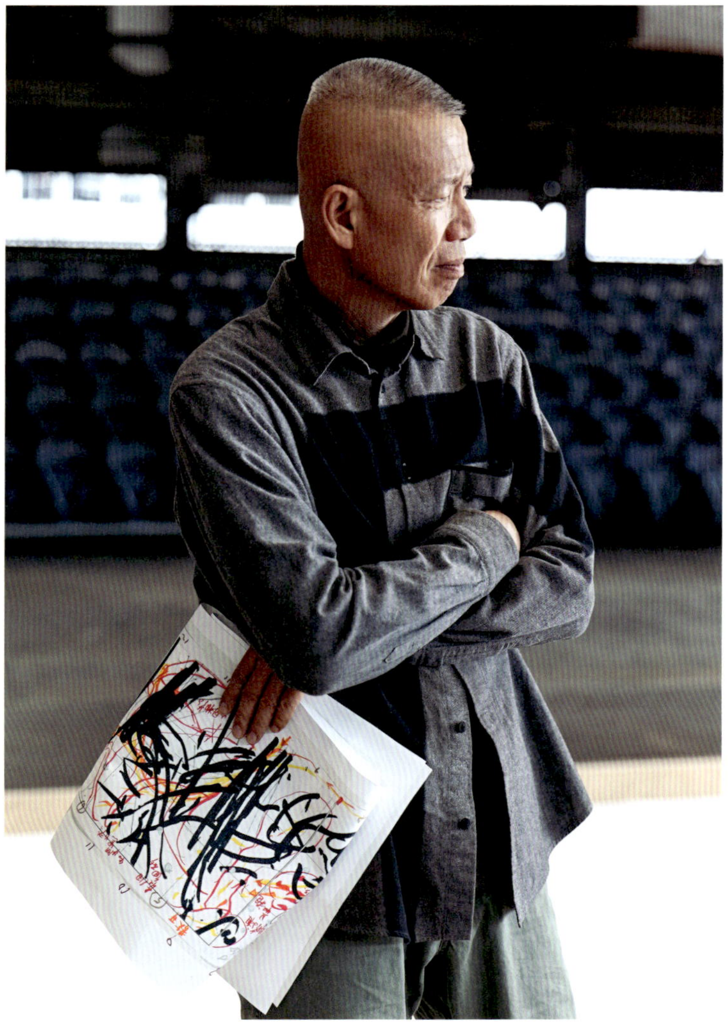

Figure 9.13. Cai Guo-Qiang during the creation of *Flow (Cypress)* in 2019

9.5

## *Flow (Cypress)*
## 柏风

2019
Gunpowder on paper
300 × 1600 cm

*Flow (Cypress)* was inspired by the energy field of the cypress forest around the mausoleum of the mytho-historical Yellow Emperor (2712–2599 BCE). The cypress has symbolized longevity and resilience. The smooth bark of the cypress is chiseled with lines running from the root to the crown, leaving upon the paper a rhythmic trace punctuated by series of twists and turns, as well as an embodiment of an unyielding spirit. In traditional Chinese painting, the composition and spatial arrangement of cypress and pine trees is believed to provide insight into the artist's character. Exploded with gunpowder of various granular sizes and fuses of different lengths, the work seems to be achieved in one breath.

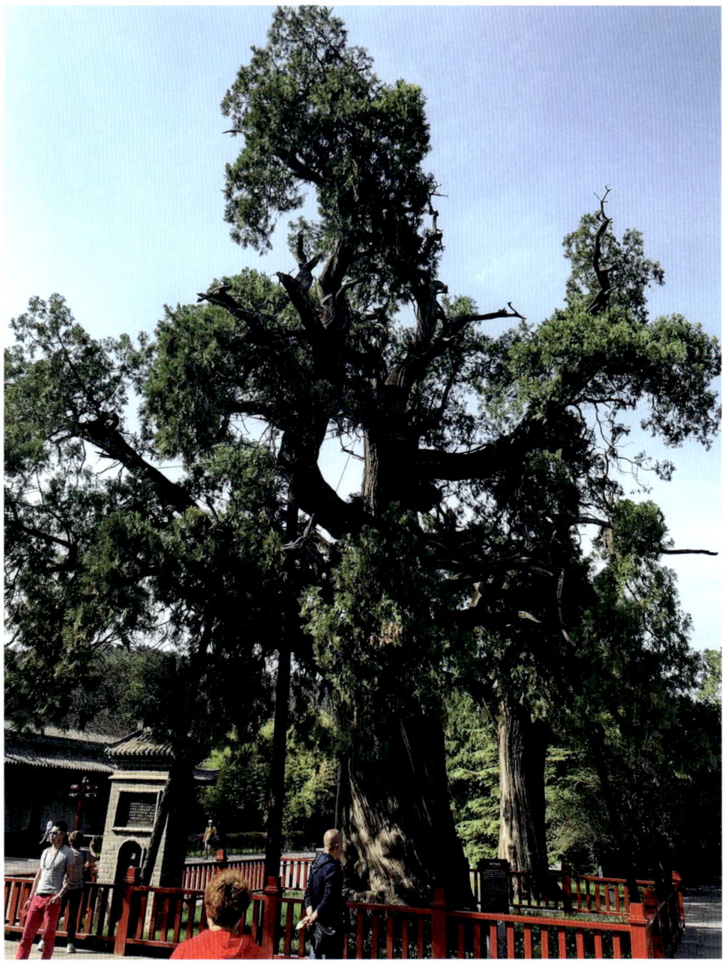

Figure 9.14. A cypress tree in the Mausoleum of the Yellow Emperor in Xi'an in 2019

Figure 9.15. Museum staff and volunteers assisting in the creation of *Flow (Cypress)* in 2019

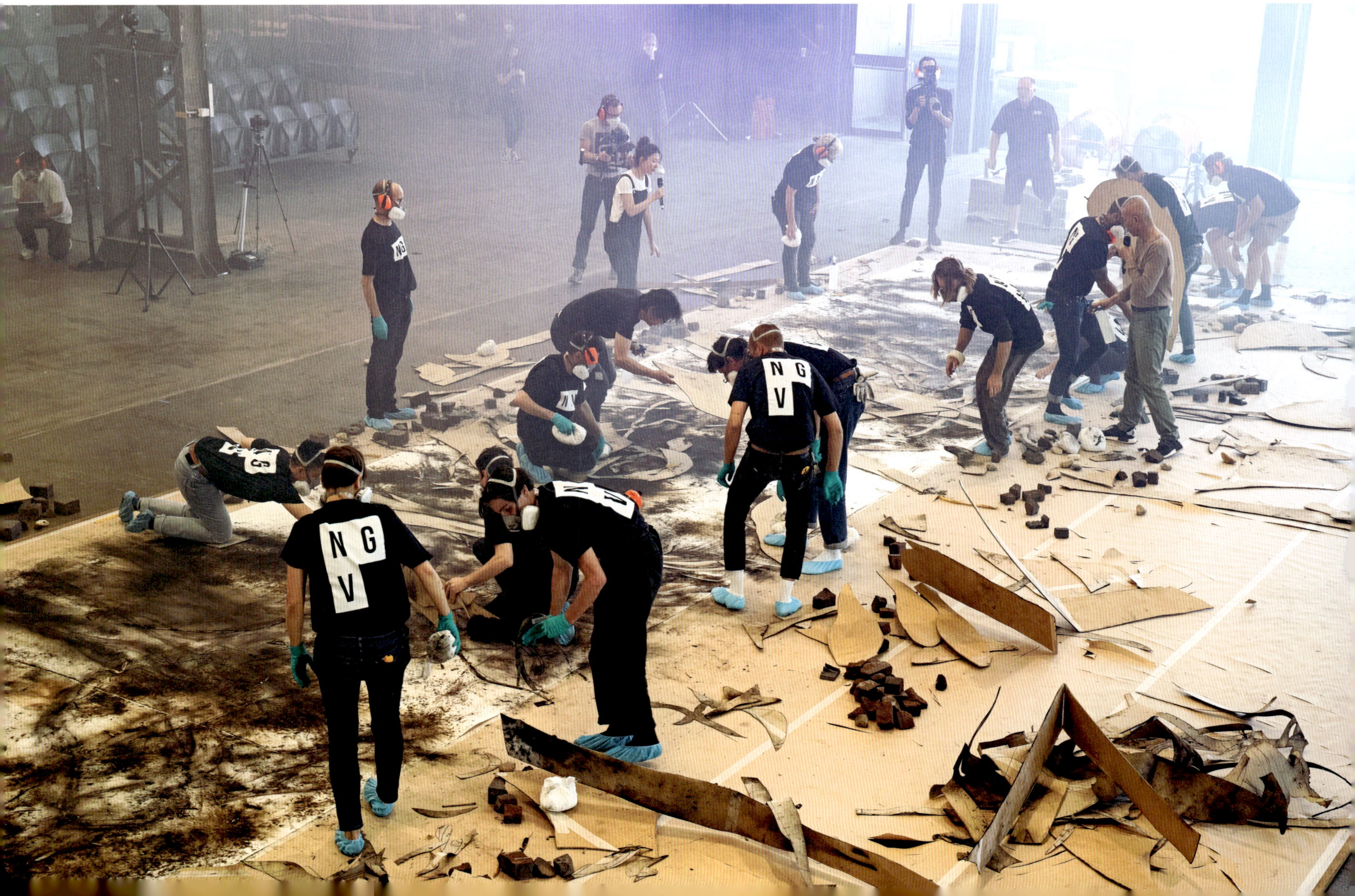

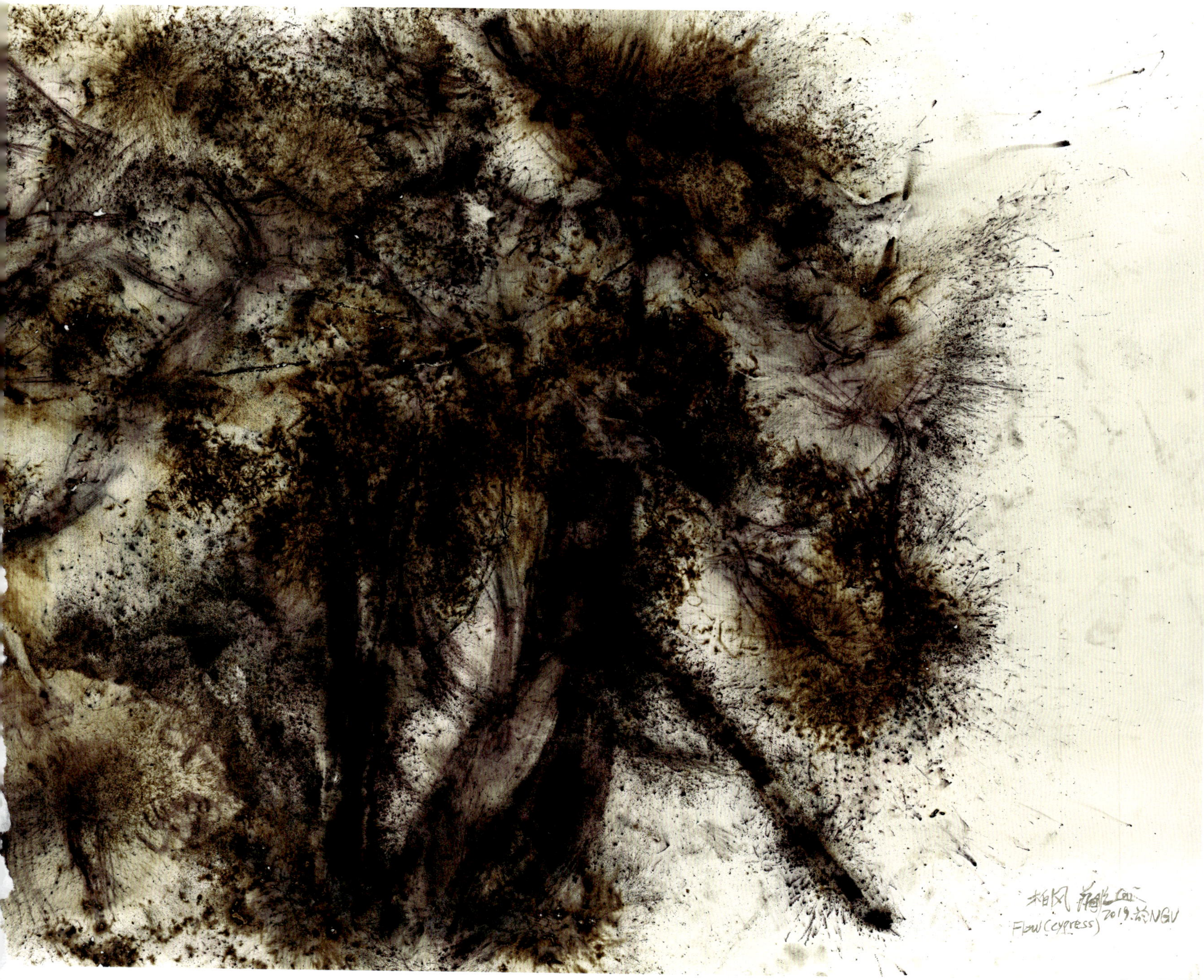
柏风
2019.於NGV
Flow (cypress)

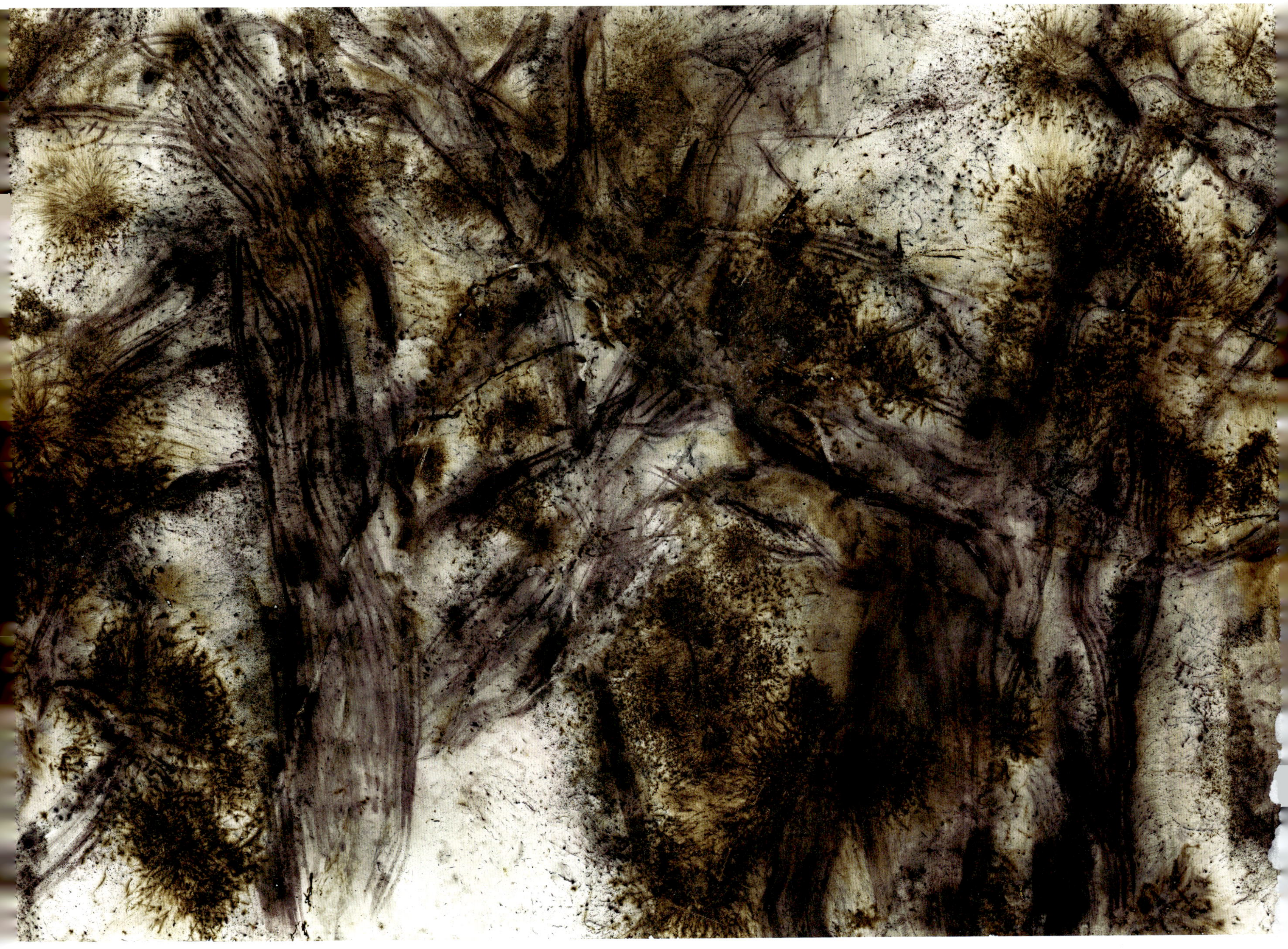

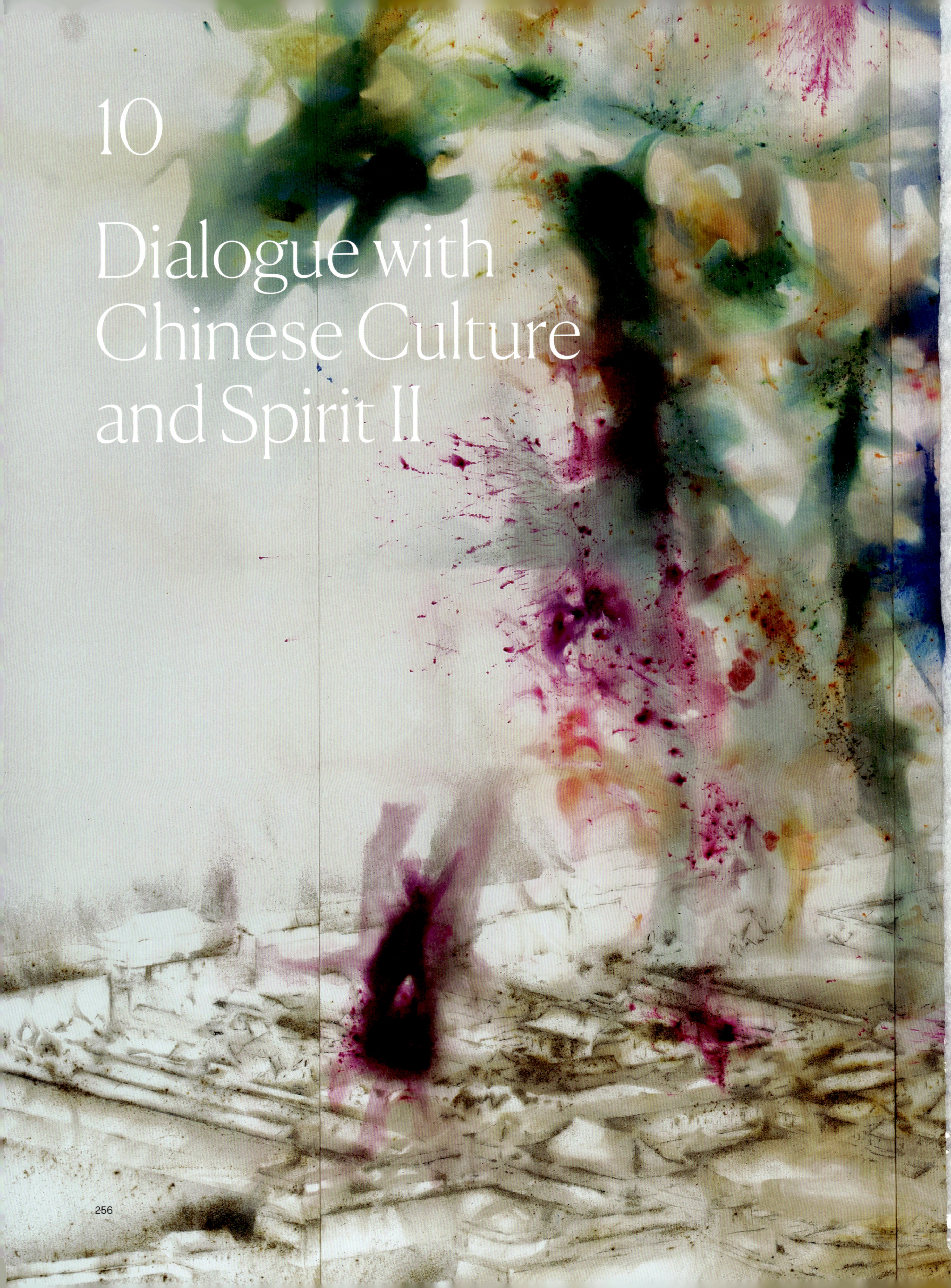

# 10

# Dialogue with Chinese Culture and Spirit II

# *Odyssey and Homecoming*

The Palace Museum, Beijing, China
December 15, 2020–February 28, 2021

Curated by Simon Schama, Professor of Art History and History at Columbia University, New York

Catalogue: Mandarin Chinese and English editions to be published

Documentary short: *Homecoming*, directed by Shanshan Xia, produced by 33 Studio, released by the Palace Museum. Footage courtesy Cai Studio and the National Gallery of Victoria, Melbourne

At the end of 1986, Cai left his homeland for the first time and journeyed to Japan with the support of his friends at the Palace Museum. From there, he relocated to New York and stepped onto the international stage. Today, following this "odyssey," he has returned to the museum in an act of "homecoming" to dialogue with the spirit of Chinese culture that the museum symbolizes. It deepens and complicates the significance of this exhibition and makes the artist both eager and wary. This is an entirely different kind of dialogue from those Cai has had with artists and works from different historical periods along his *Individual's Journey Through Western Art History*.

Completed in 1420, the Palace Museum was once the imperial Forbidden Palace of the Ming and Qing dynasties (1368–1644 and 1644–1911). It houses the largest collection of preserved ancient wooden structures in the world. The collection consists of over 1.8 million groups of works, including paintings, calligraphy, correspondence, and stone rubbings. All are priceless pieces of cultural heritage for all humankind.

For decades, Cai Guo-Qiang's art has spanned numerous forms and mediums, engaged with widely varying themes, and grown with nourishment from different cultures. Despite this, his foundation remained rooted in Eastern philosophy and the spirit of Chinese culture, as exemplified by such ideas as "the only doctrine is the lack of doctrine," and "to be free and at one's ease, to be natural and of one's self." This foundation is likewise reflected in his *Individual's Journey Through Western Art History*.

The exhibition blends and presents works from Cai's "odyssey" in dialogues with different world civilizations within the realm of Chinese civilization, as superbly exemplified by the Palace Museum. It demonstrates the artist's political stance of

Detail of *Gunpowder Drawing for Sleepwalking in the Forbidden City* (no. 10.3)

"treating himself as an heir to all human cultural heritage, of treating masters from all cultures as his own predecessors." The exhibition is also an extension of the spirit of confidence, openness, and tolerance found in Chinese culture, which upholds that "the sea is broad enough to embrace hundreds of rivers," just as the human mind is broad enough to embrace whatever comes its way. Cai adopted this spirit in his dialogue with the Palace Museum. He further explores "How may the Palace Museum not only act as a cultural guardian of the past, but also become an agent of cultural ignition for new eras, one that can spark boundless creativity in today's artists?"

As the exhibition coincides with the six-hundredth anniversary of the Forbidden Palace, Cai has created a grand "ceremony" for the palace through a set of works, *Sleepwalking in the Forbidden City*. The primary inspiration came from the use of virtual reality (VR), which tangles space and time, allowing the audience to feel as though they are sleepwalking between the celebration and the reality at the Forbidden City. Cai also created several new paintings in which he engages with the frame of mind of the painters behind the museum's collection.

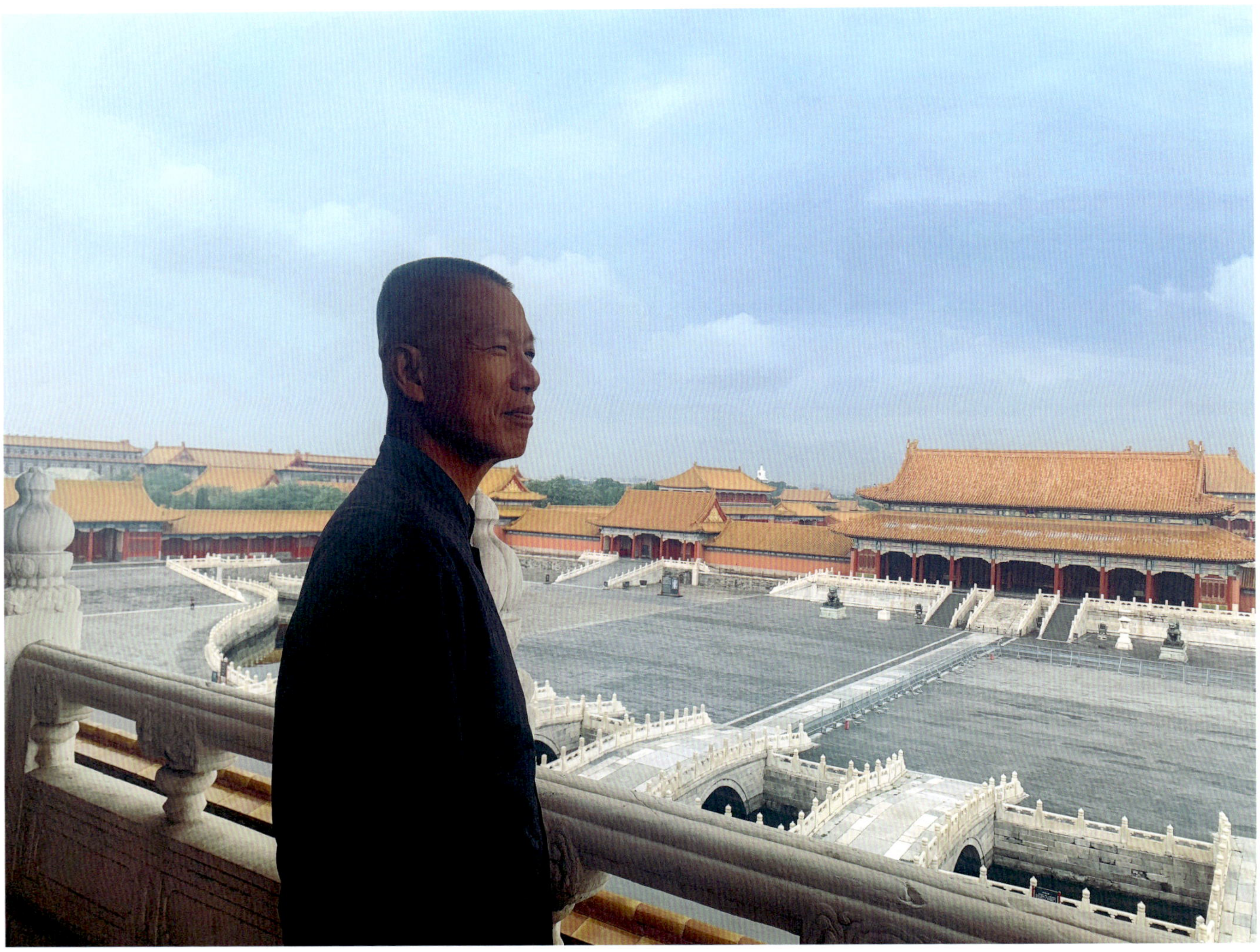

Figure 10.1. Cai Guo-Qiang visiting the Palace Museum in Beijing in 2019

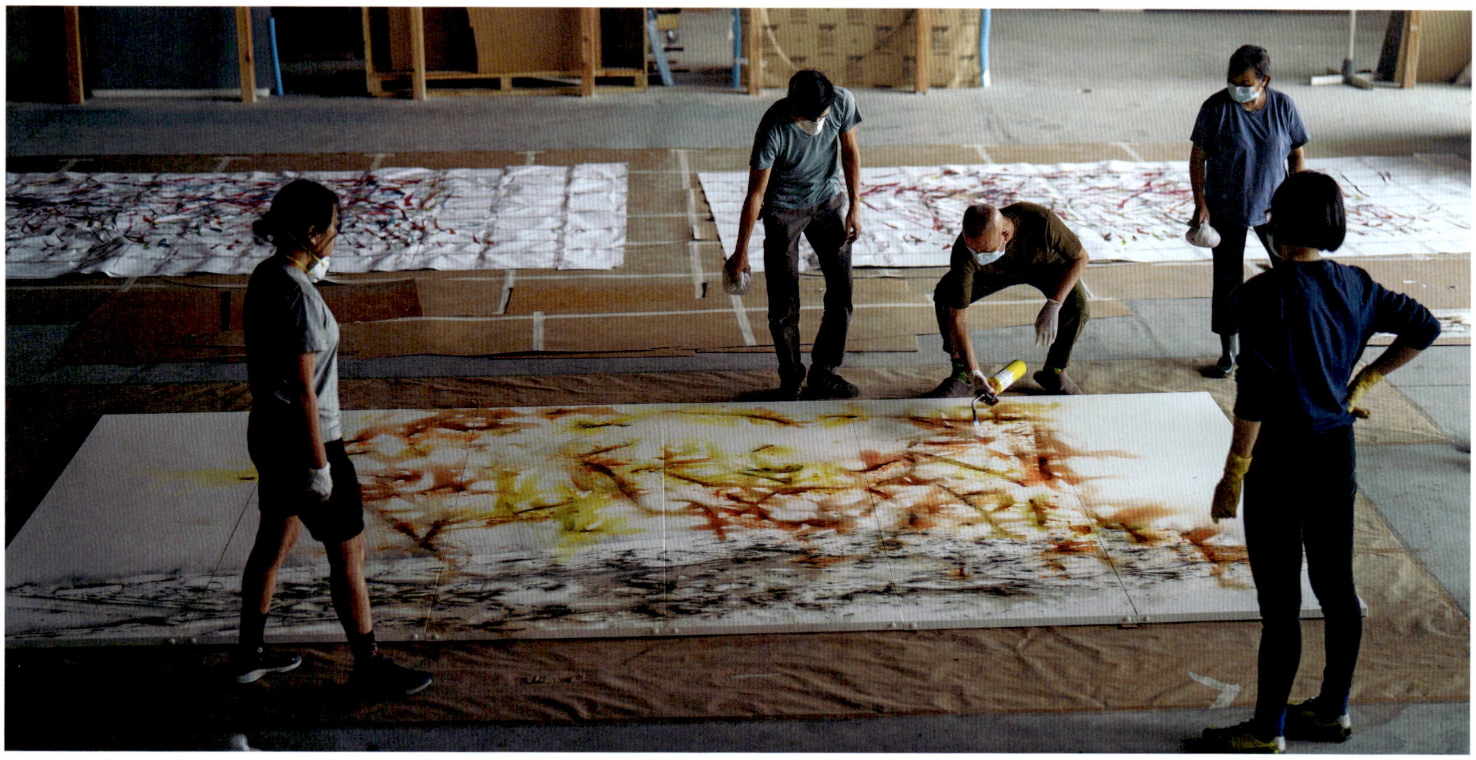

Figure 10.2. Cai Guo-Qiang creating *Gunpowder Drawing for Sleepwalking in the Forbidden City* in 2020

10.1

### *Gunpowder Drawing for Sleepwalking in the Forbidden City*
### 为“梦游紫禁城”所作火药草图

2020
Gunpowder and ink on paper, mounted on wood as six-panel screen
230 × 465 cm

10.2

### *Sleepwalking in the Forbidden City: After the Fireworks*
### “梦游紫禁城”烟花之后

2020
Gunpowder on alabaster
39.8 × 472.3 × 663.3 cm

10.3

### *Sleepwalking in the Forbidden City*
### 梦游紫禁城

2020
Fireworks ceremony in virtual reality experienced through VR headsets
Approx. 5 minutes
Virtual Reality in partnership with HTC VIVE Arts

In the set of works *Sleepwalking in the Forbidden City*, Cai highlights traditional Chinese aesthetics and the bold spirit of "the world is mine" felt within the Forbidden City. On the shores of the Liuyang River in Hunan Province, he created a resplendent fireworks ceremony that he imagined would have taken place at the palace six hundred years ago. This ceremony can be experienced through three distinct works in the Palace Museum exhibition.

For *Gunpowder Drawing for Sleepwalking in the Forbidden City*, the artist first constructed, by exploding black gunpowder on a hemp paper screen, the Forbidden City at the work's base, as if resting in the depths of time. Similar to a color-separated screen print, explosions using gunpowder of different colors were then detonated, one color at a time, atop the screens to complete the piece. The work conveys the artist's thoughts while "sleepwalking" back through six centuries of history.

For *Sleepwalking in the Forbidden City: After the Fireworks*, craftsmen from Cai's hometown were invited by the artist to collaborate, and spent five months hand carving an alabaster model of the Forbidden City. The model was then showered with a "daytime explosion event ceremony" in Liuyang and transformed into a work of three-dimensional painting. Through the snow-white marble, the builders of the Forbidden City and the craftsmen of the artist's hometown have been connected, linked over six centuries by their shared warmth of artisanship and the spirit of craftsmanship.

*Sleepwalking in the Forbidden City* marks the artist's first time integrating virtual reality (VR) into his works. Upon donning a VR headset, the viewer embarks on a dreamy journey alongside the artist back to a grand ceremony in the distant past. In the interweaving of past and present, time and space grow hazy until the visitor barely knows where the present lies. The fireworks last approximately five minutes: "Scene I: Ceremony" is a majestic opening with gold, silver, and red fireworks flashing forth from all corners of the Forbidden City. "Scene II: Song and Dance" reveals strands of sparkling color smoke congregating, separating, and whirling like the flowing sleeves of Chinese court dancers. "Scene III: Illumination" shows sunlight reflecting on the palace's layered roofs as the morning sun rises in the east. "Scene IV: Revelry" fills the sky with fireworks, bursting into color and stirring the viewer's soul among the reverberating cracks and bangs of the fireworks' detonation, reaching an explosive climax! Finally, the smoke slowly dissipates, and the artist wakes up from his dream ...

Since their invention by the Chinese in the 10th century, fireworks have been used in grand ceremonies and events. Historically, the Forbidden City would hold fireworks celebrations for the Lunar New Year, setting off fireworks simultaneously with the lighting of the Aoshan lanterns. For this exhibition, the artist uses leading VR technology to create a wondrously magnificent fireworks ceremony dedicated to the Forbidden Palace and its majestic history.

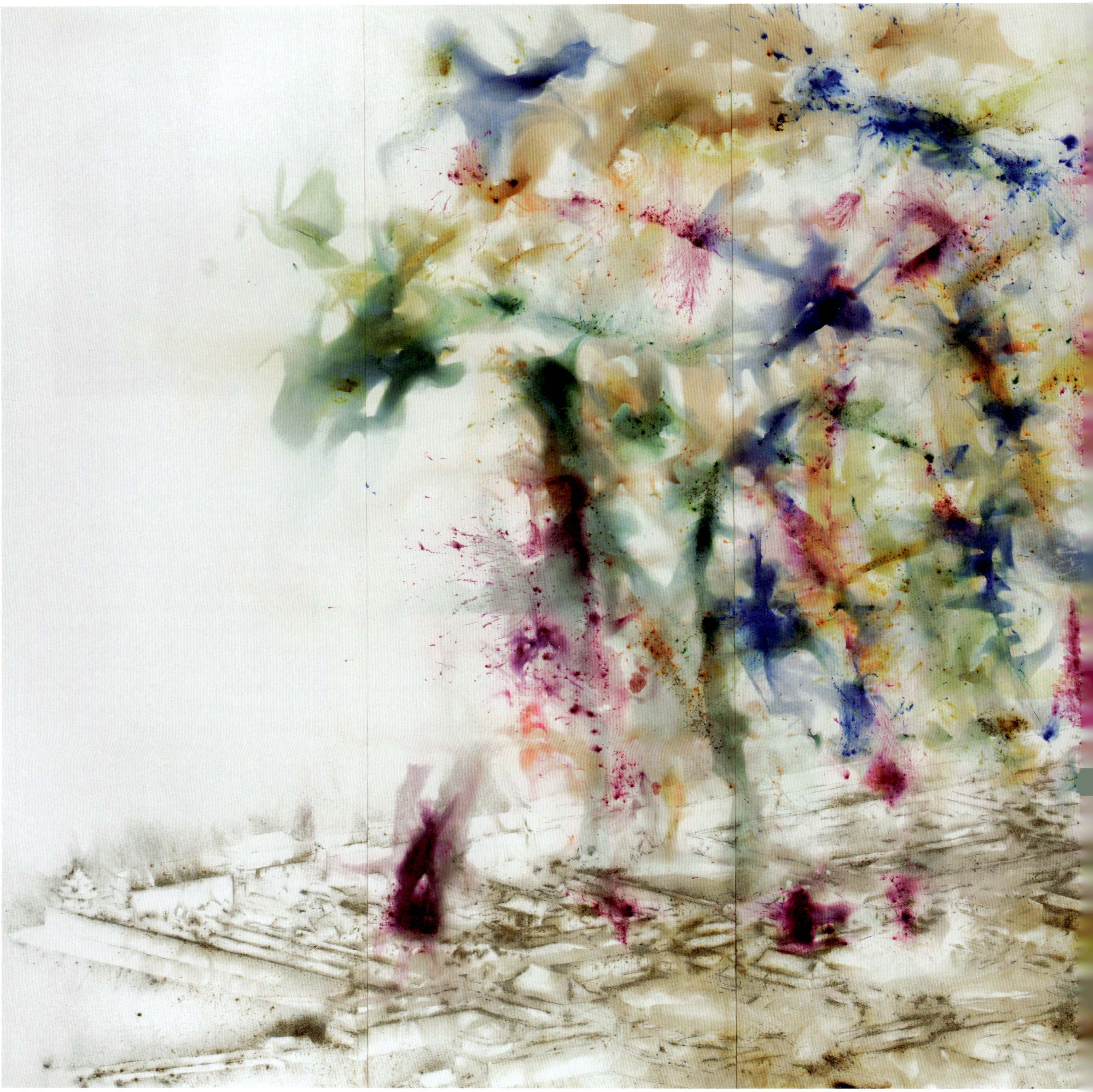

10.1 *Gunpowder Drawing for Sleepwalking in the Forbidden City*

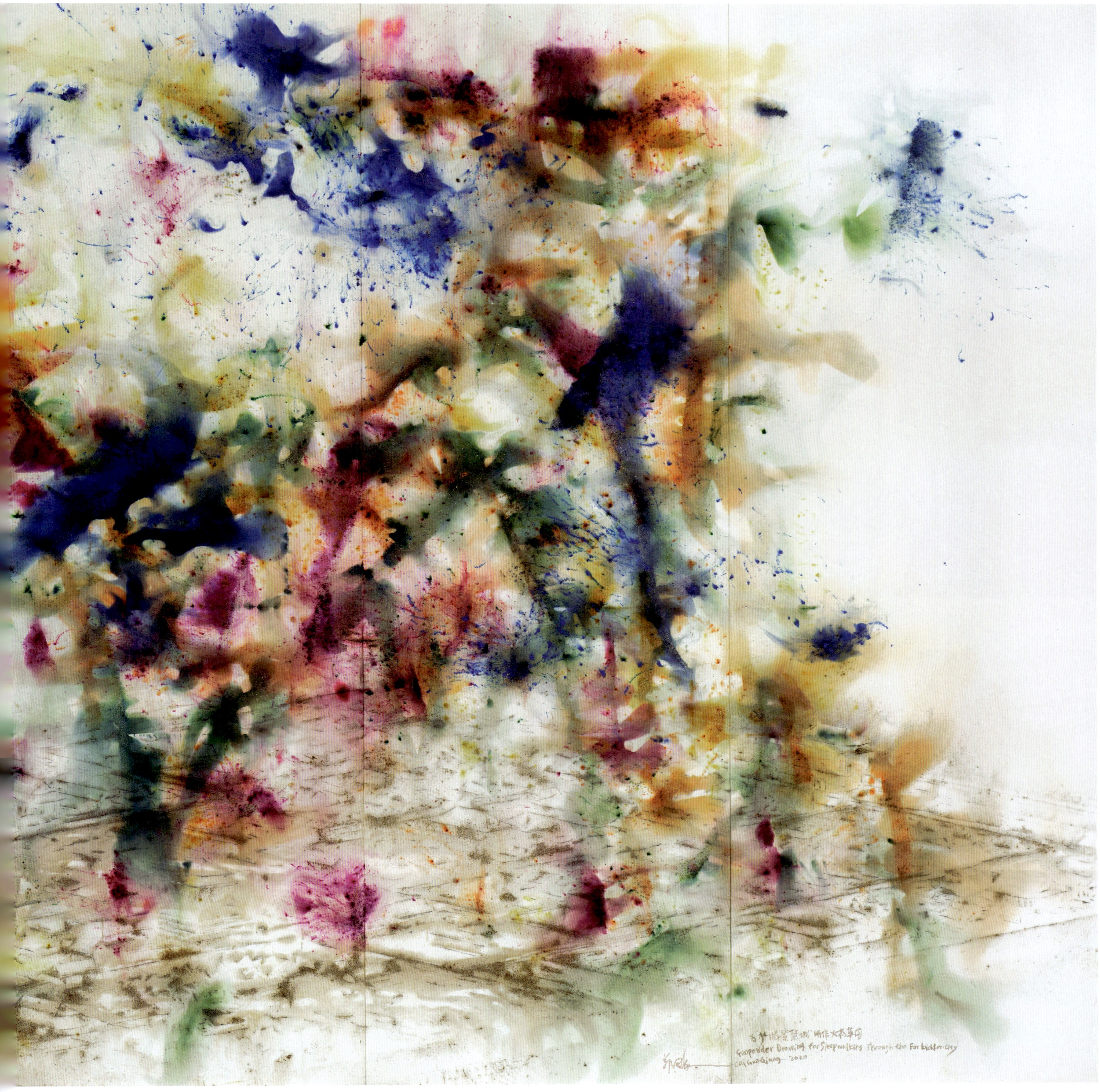
为"梦游紫禁城"所作火药草图
Gunpowder Drawing for Sleepwalking Through the Forbidden City
Cai Guo-Qiang 2020

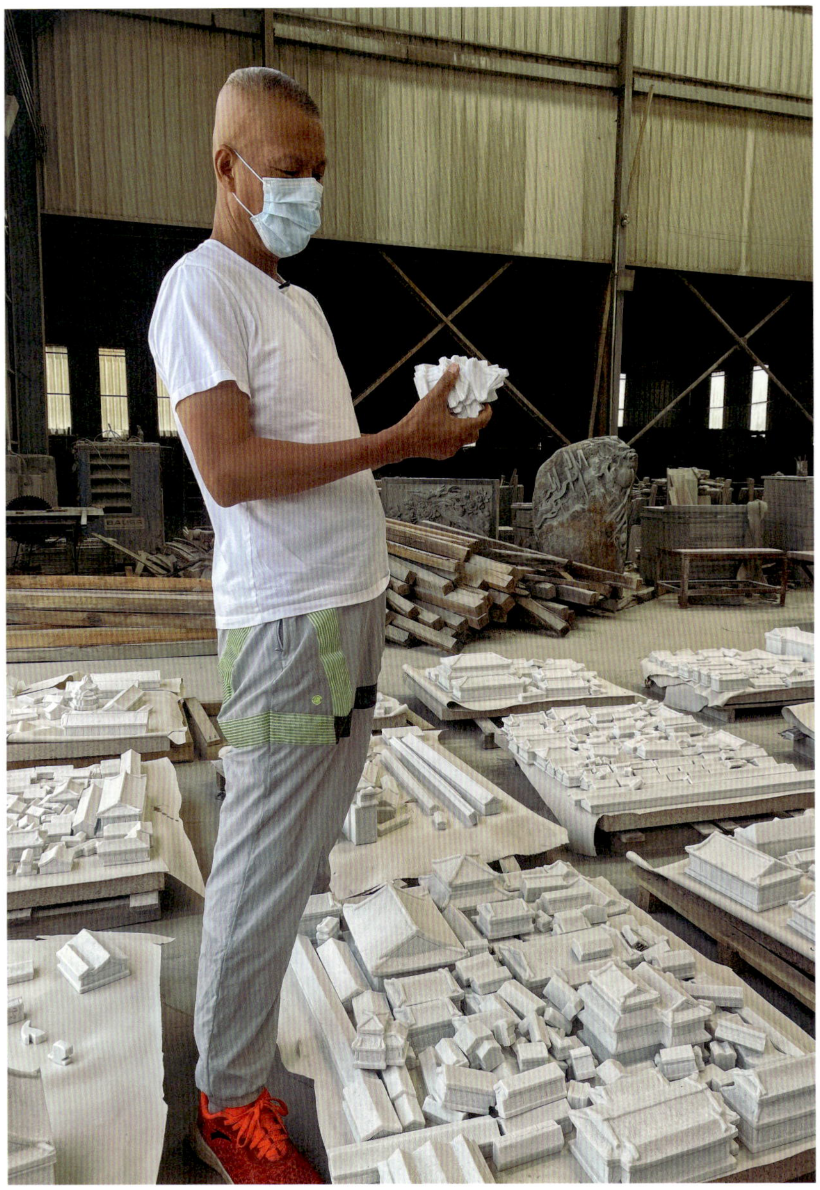
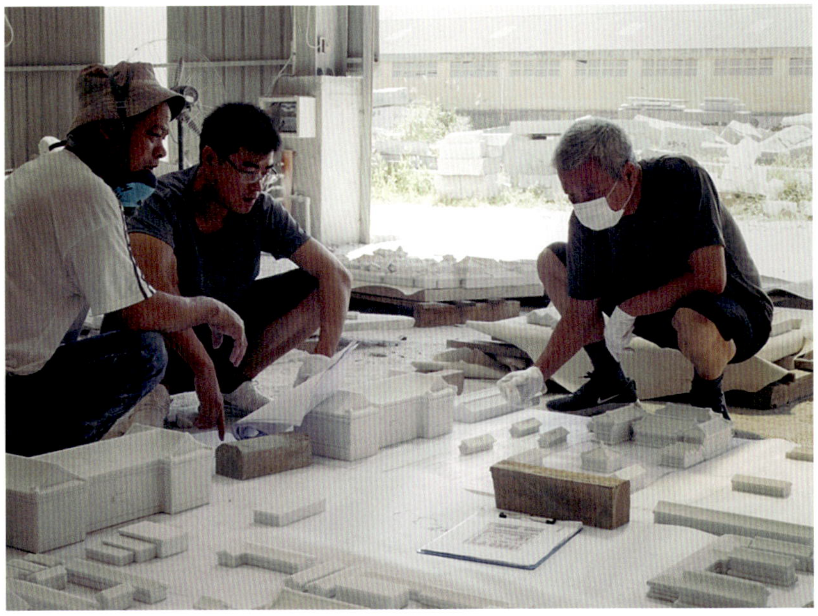
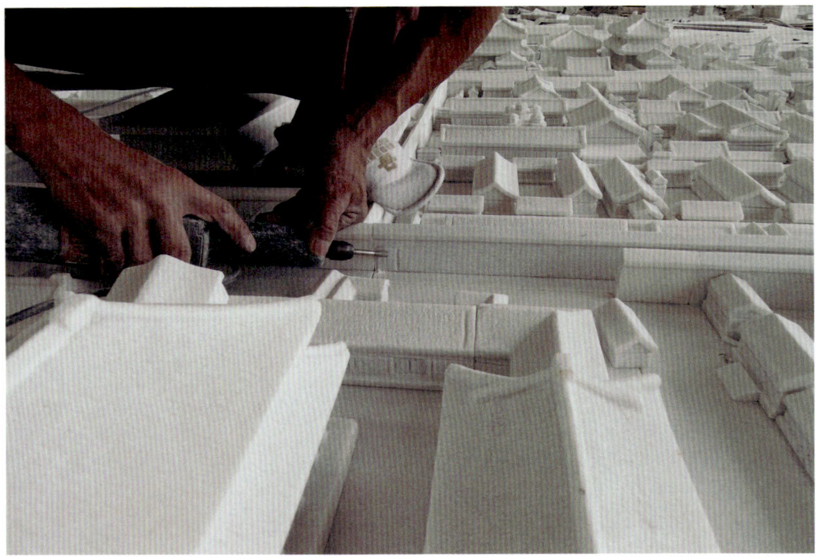

Figures 10.3a–d. Production of the alabaster model for *Sleepwalking in the Forbidden City: After the Fireworks* in Quanzhou in 2020

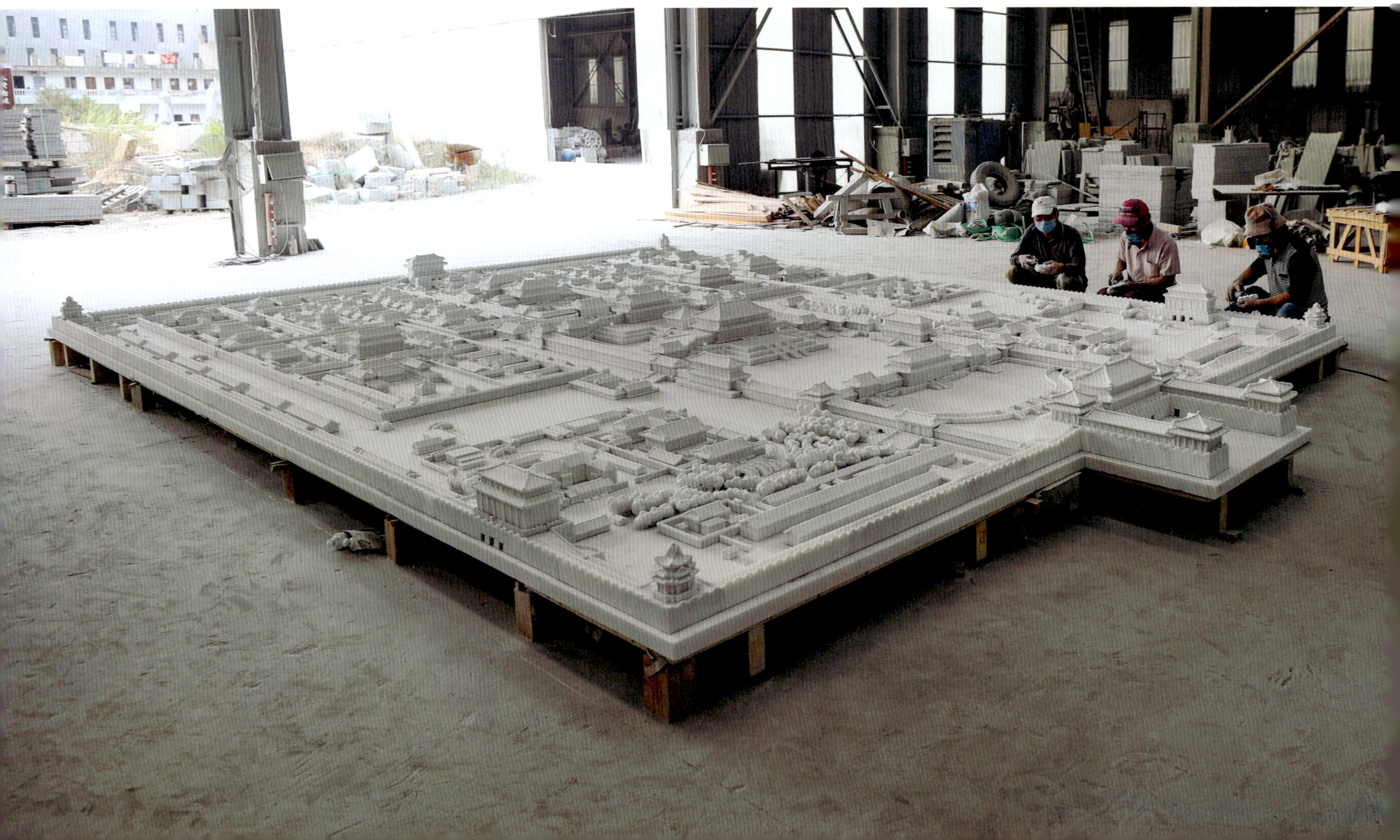

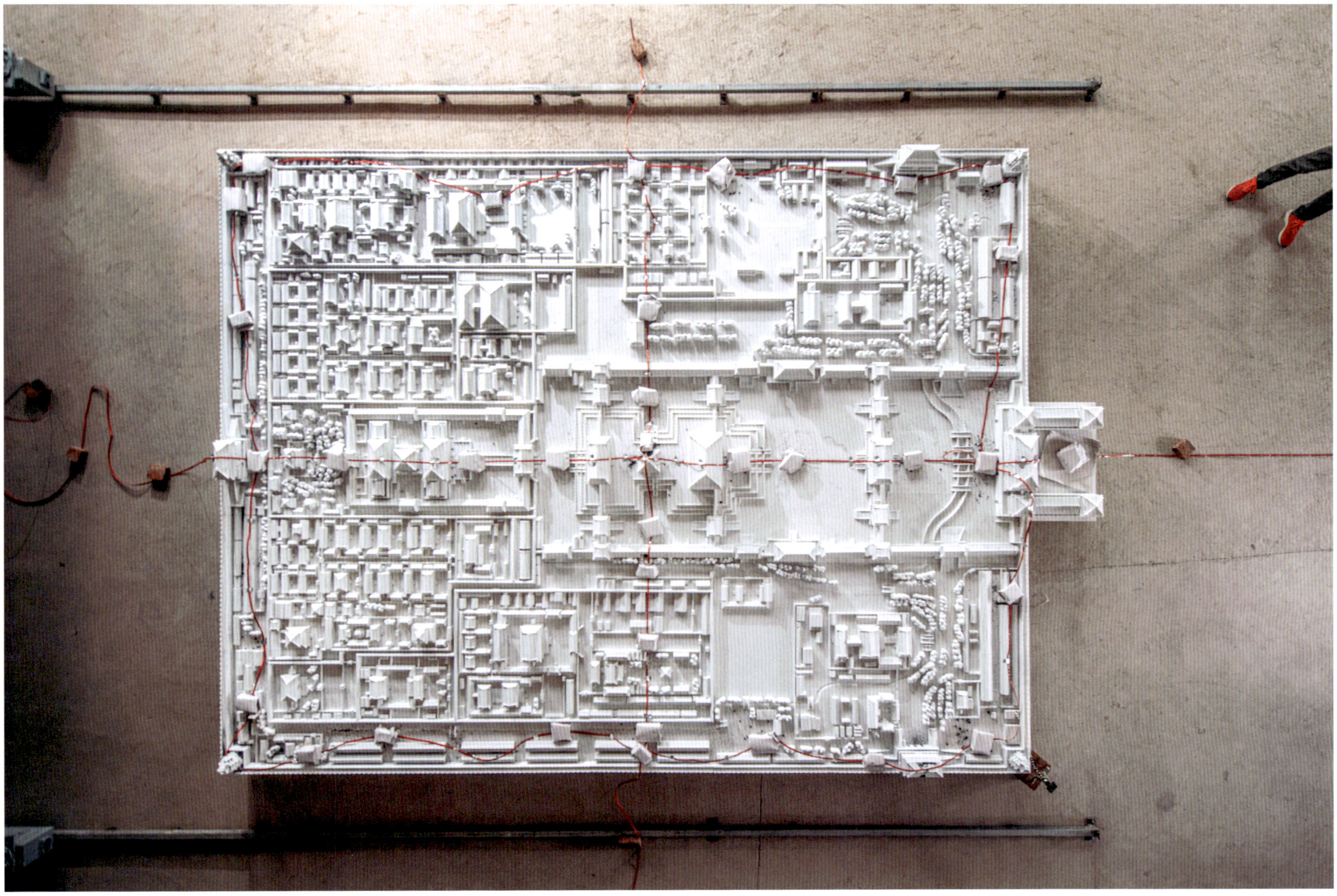

Figure 10.4. The alabaster model with gunpowder fuse atop prior to ignition

Figure 10.5. Cai Guo-Qiang overseeing ignition of *Sleepwalking in the Forbidden City: After the Fireworks*

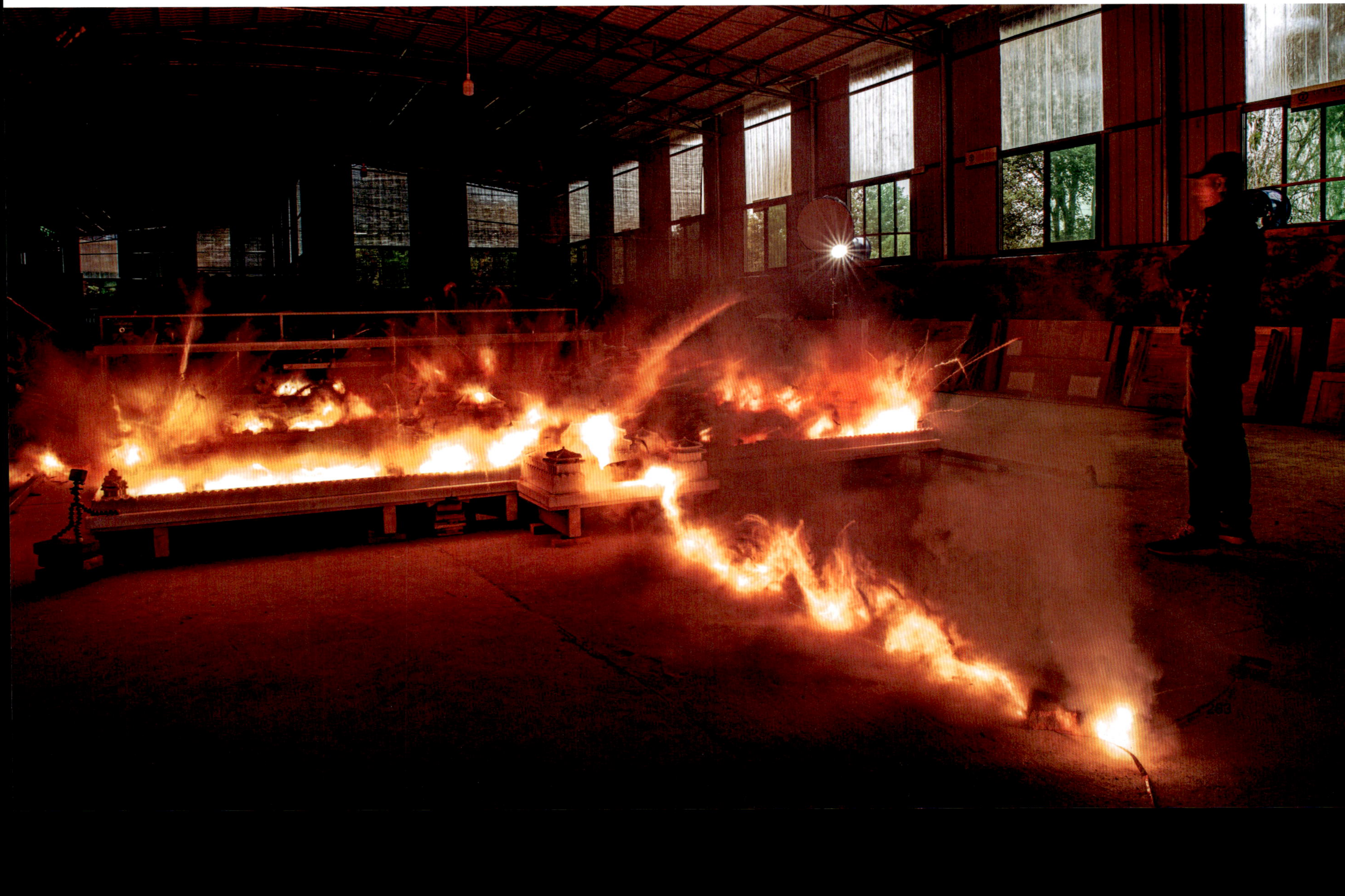

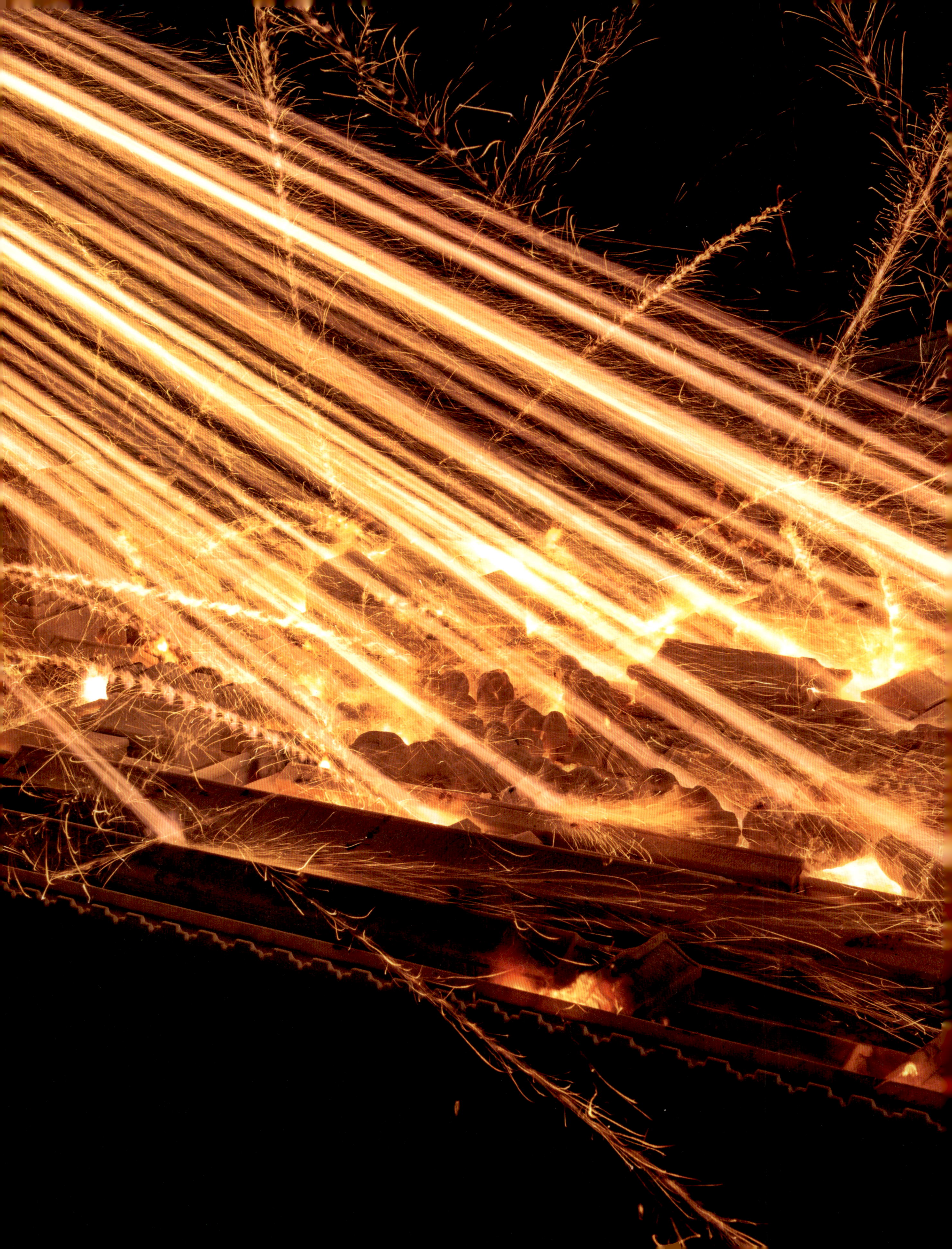

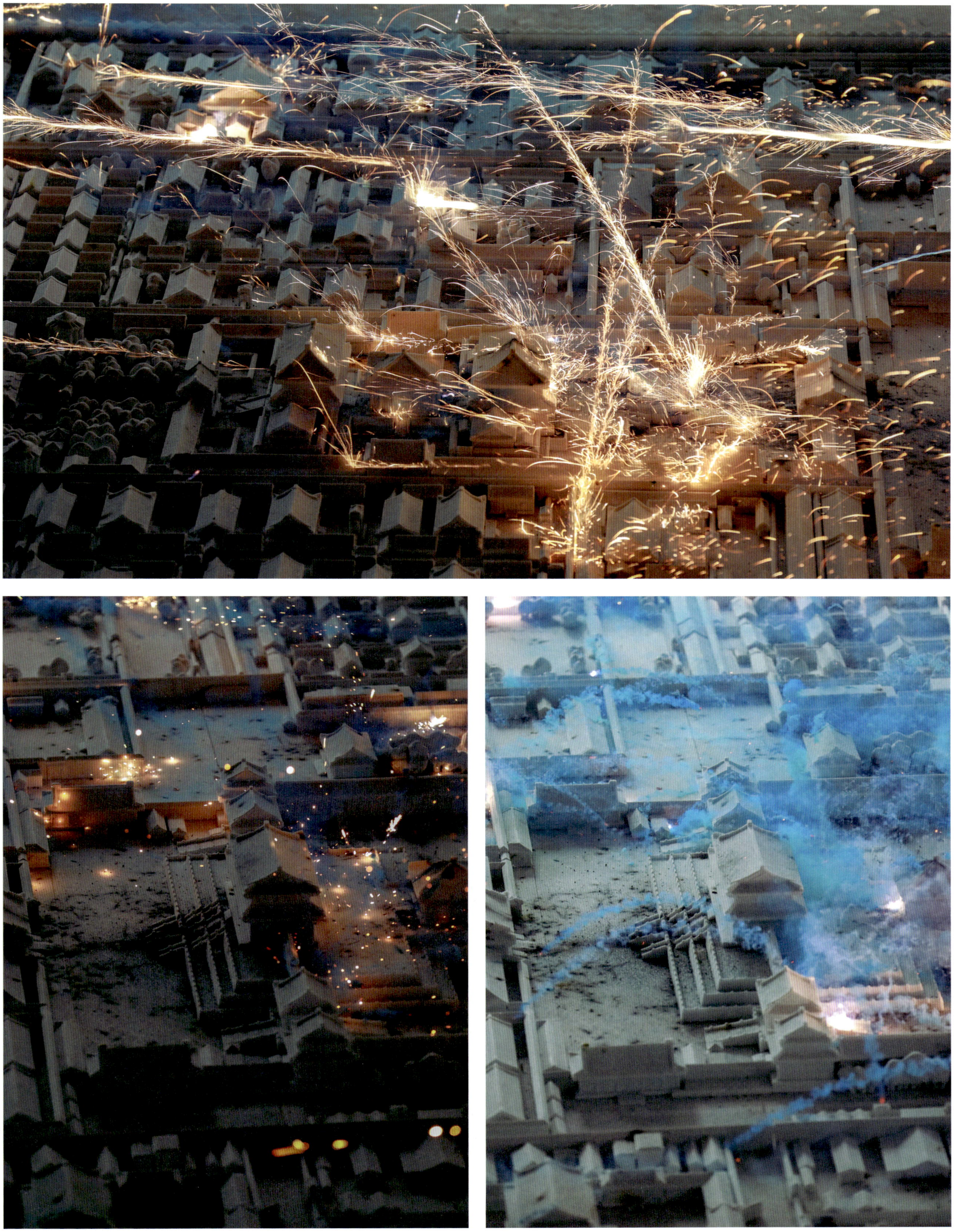

Figures 10.6a–d. Ignition of *Sleepwalking in the Forbidden City: After the Fireworks* in Liuyang, China in 2020

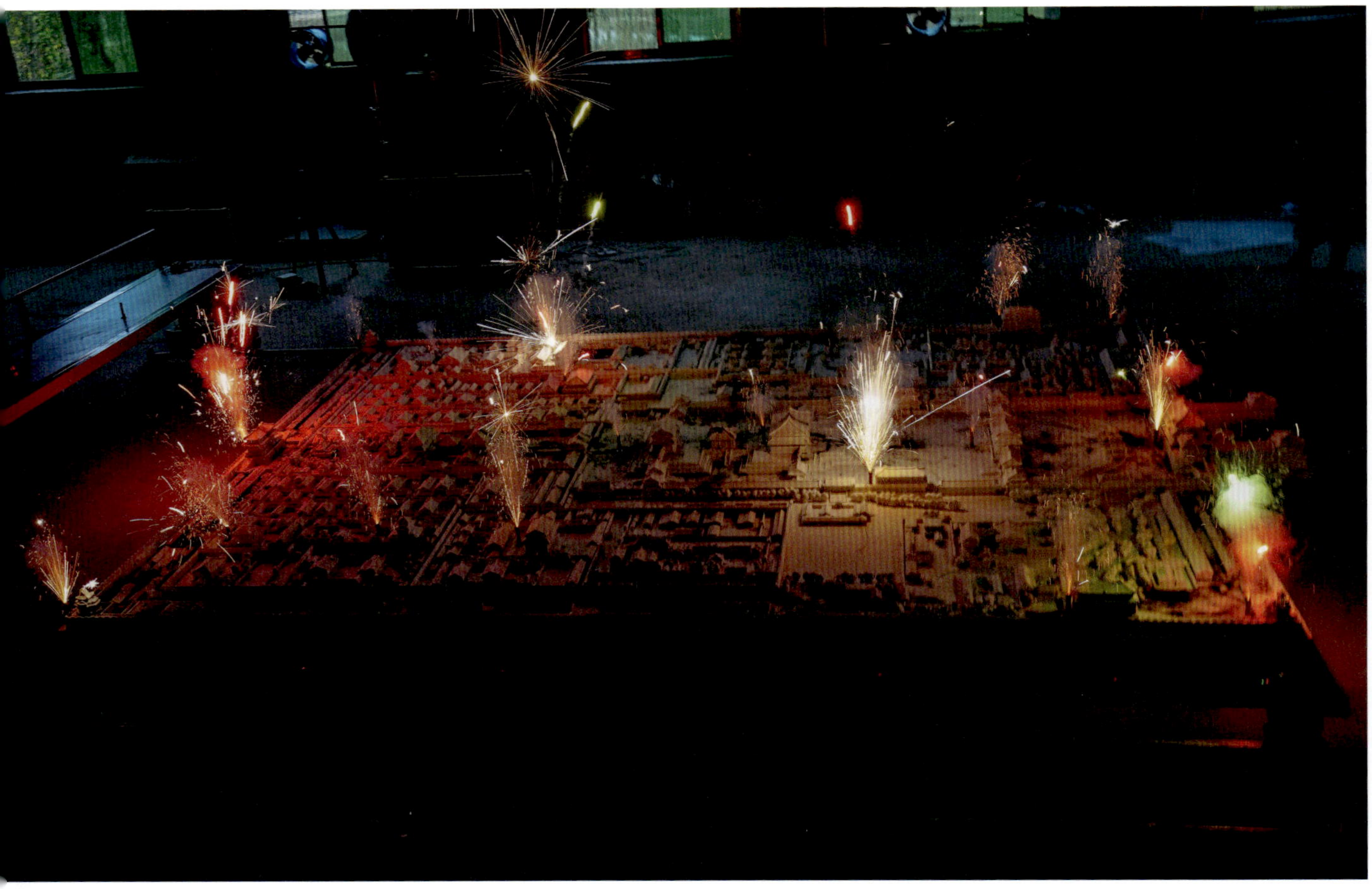

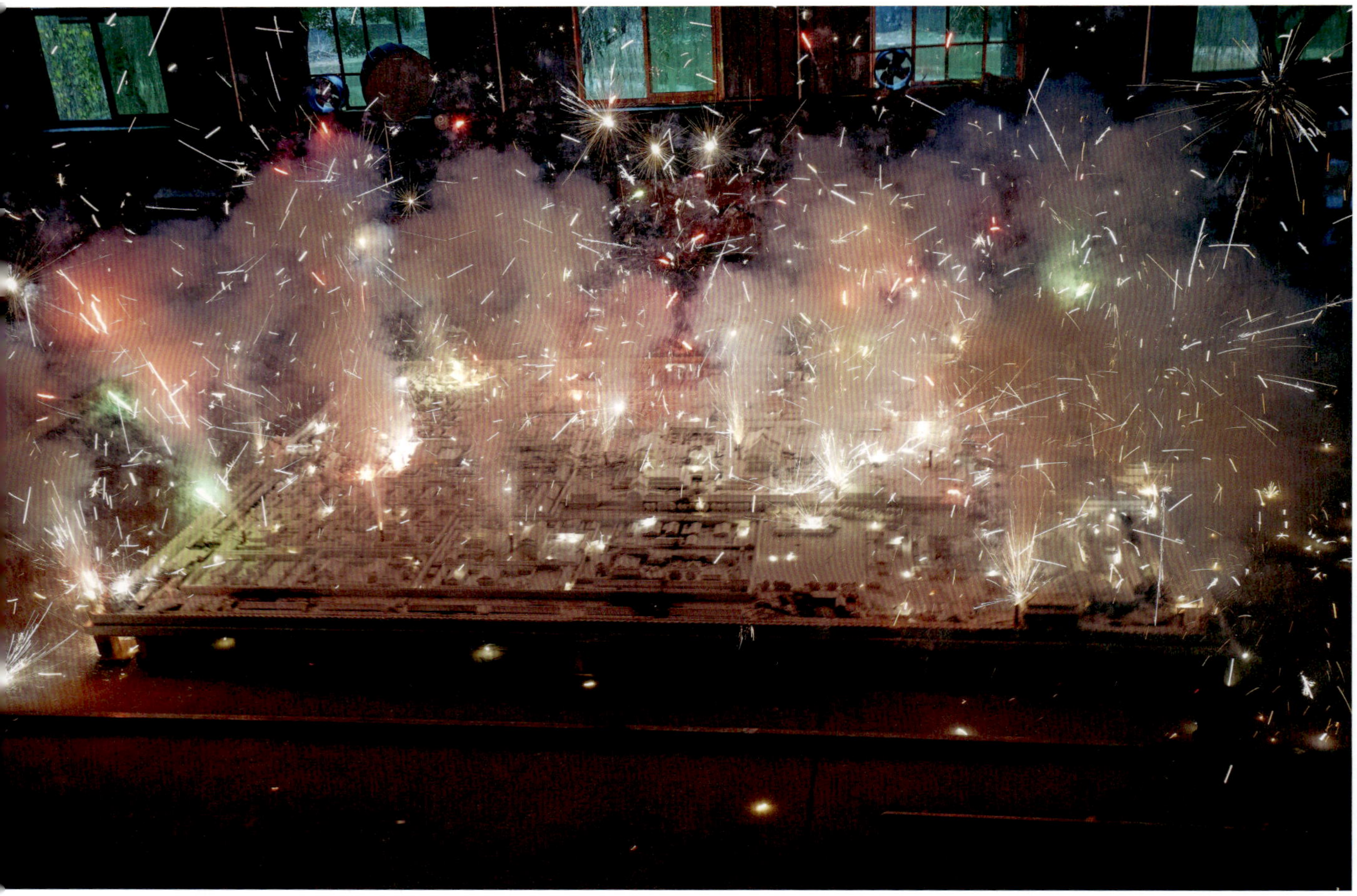

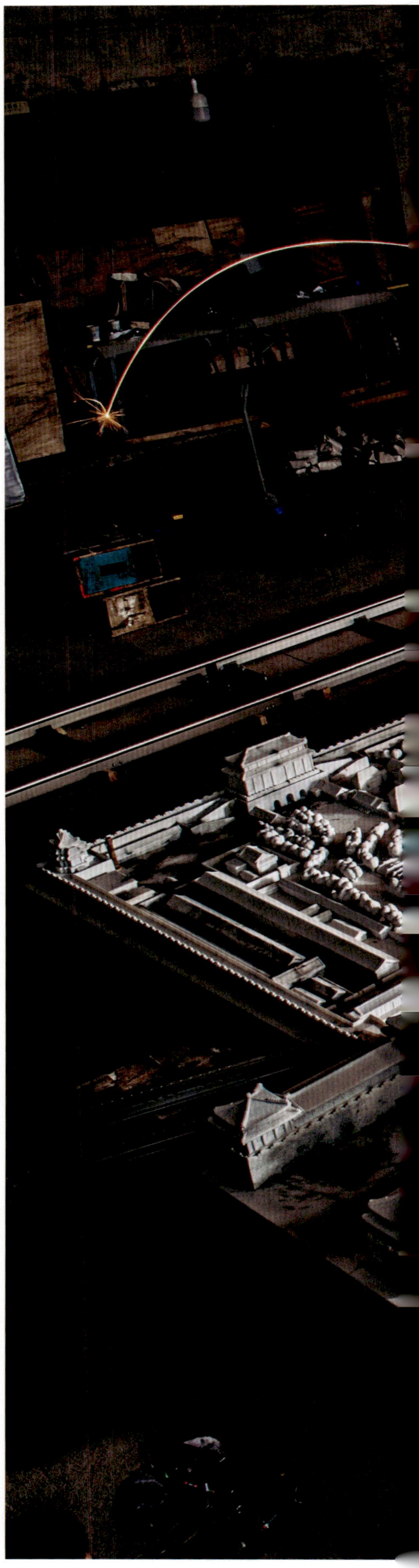

Figures 10.7a–c. Ignition of *Sleepwalking in the Forbidden City: After the Fireworks* in Liuyang, China in 2020

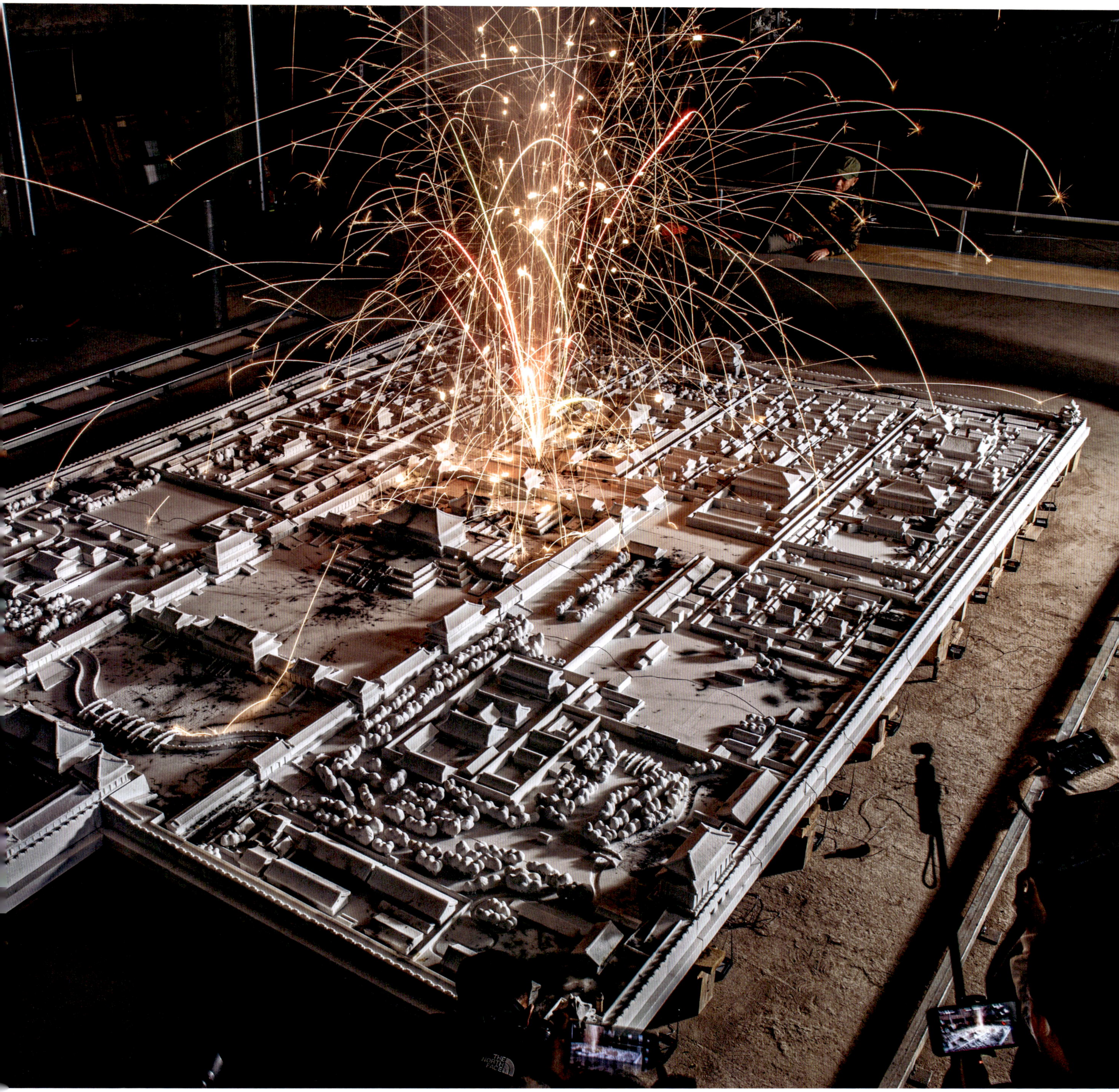

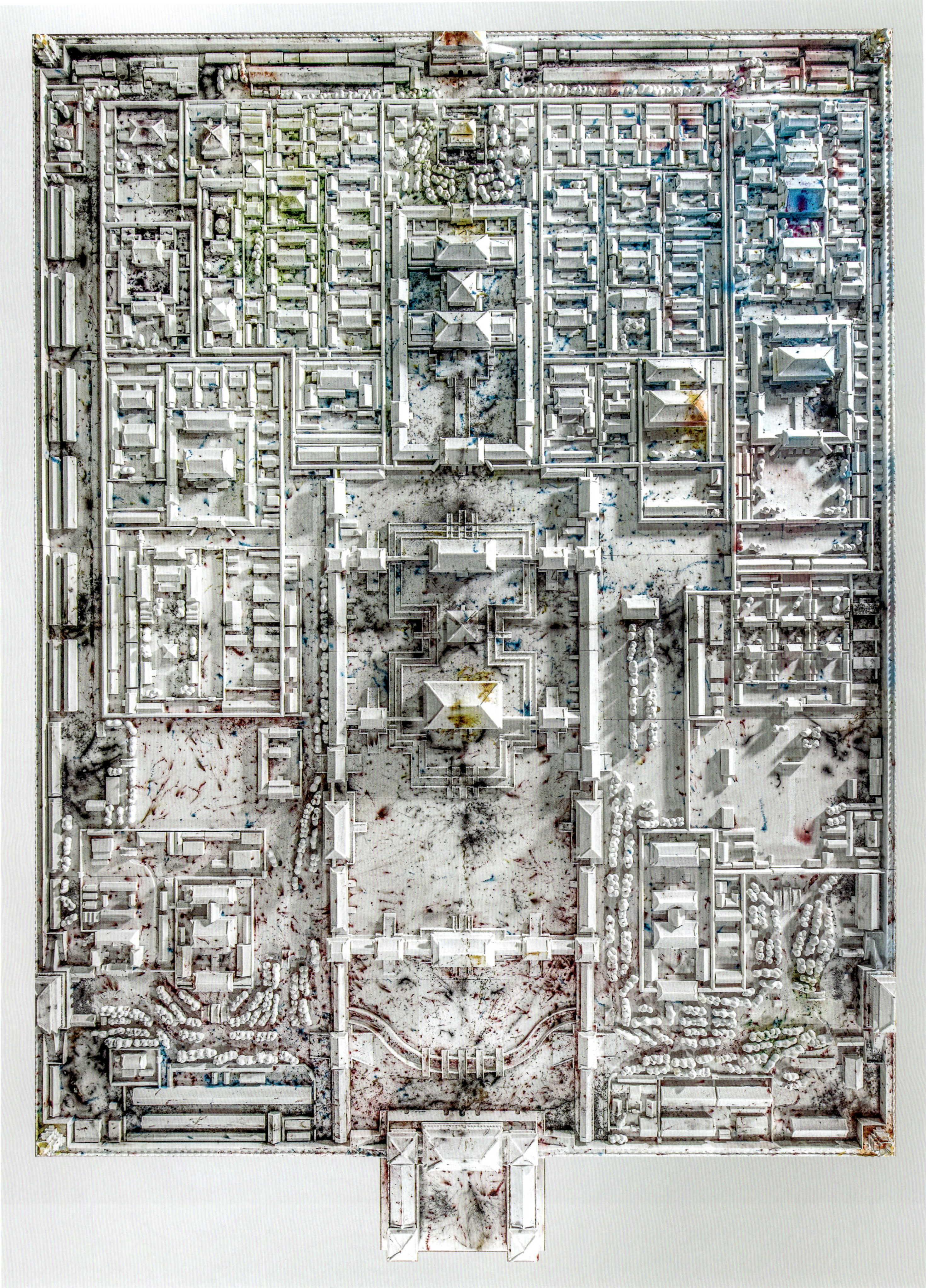

10.2 *Sleepwalking in the Forbidden City: After the Fireworks*

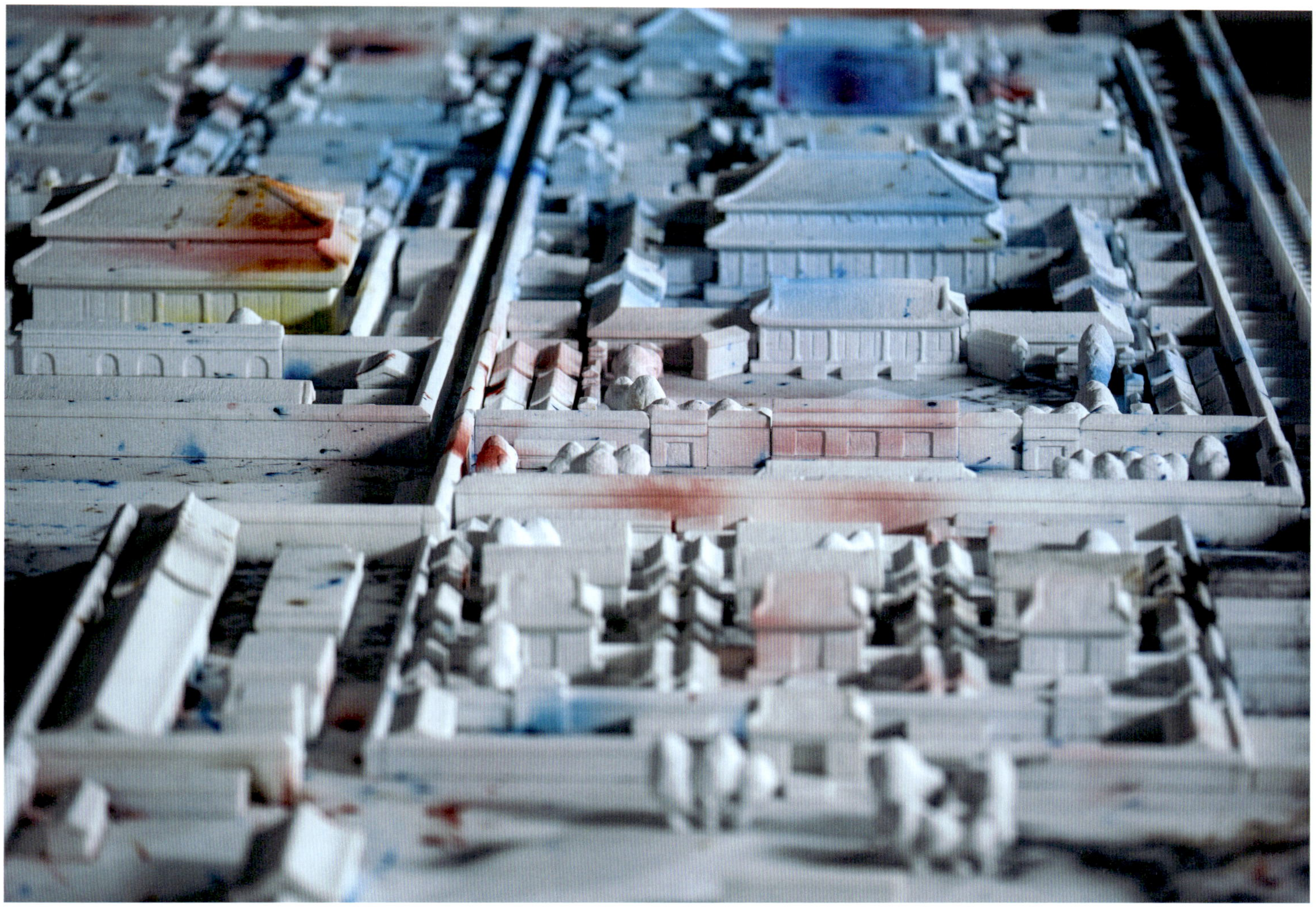

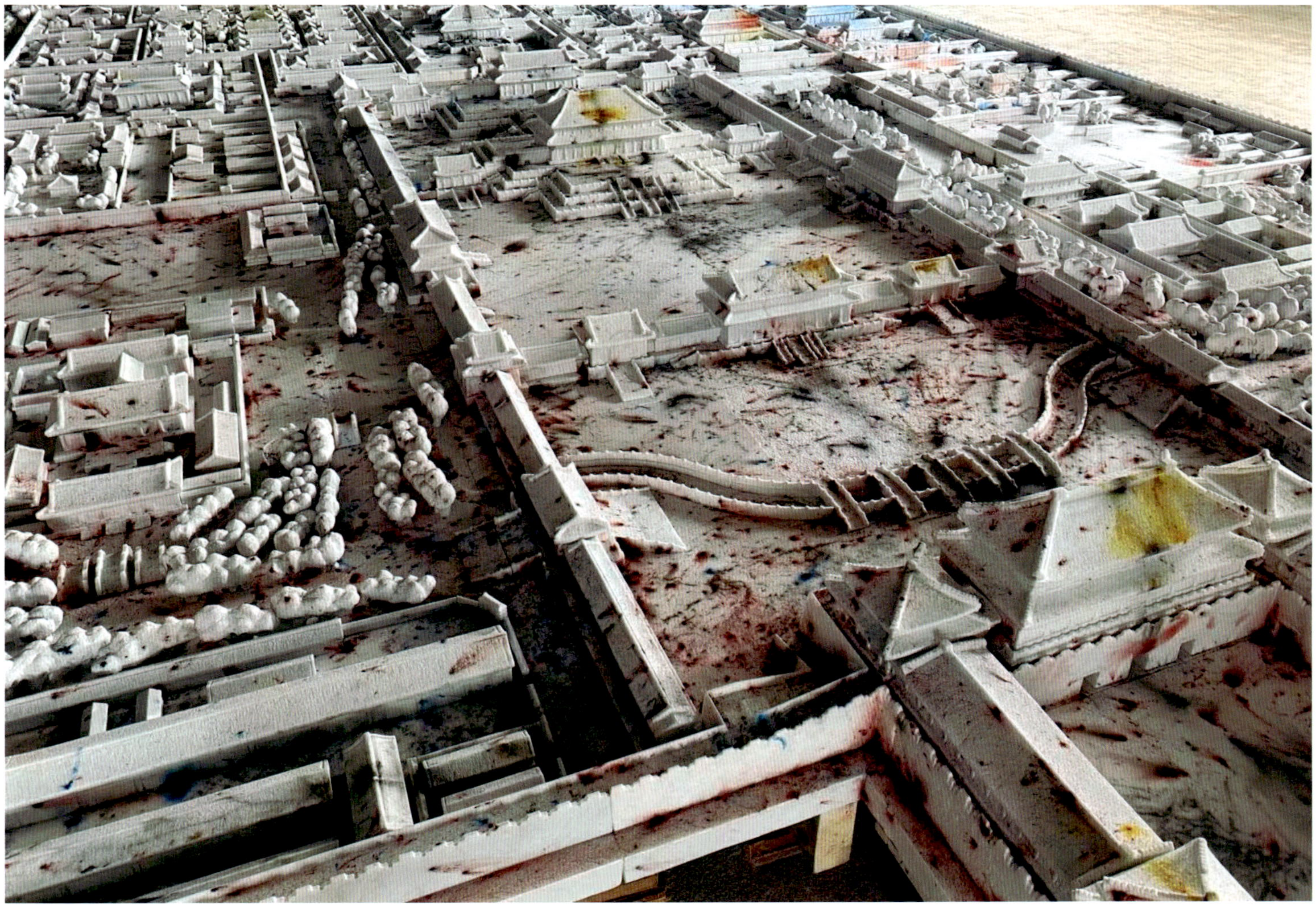

Figures 10.8a–b. Details of *Sleepwalking in the Forbidden City: After the Fireworks*

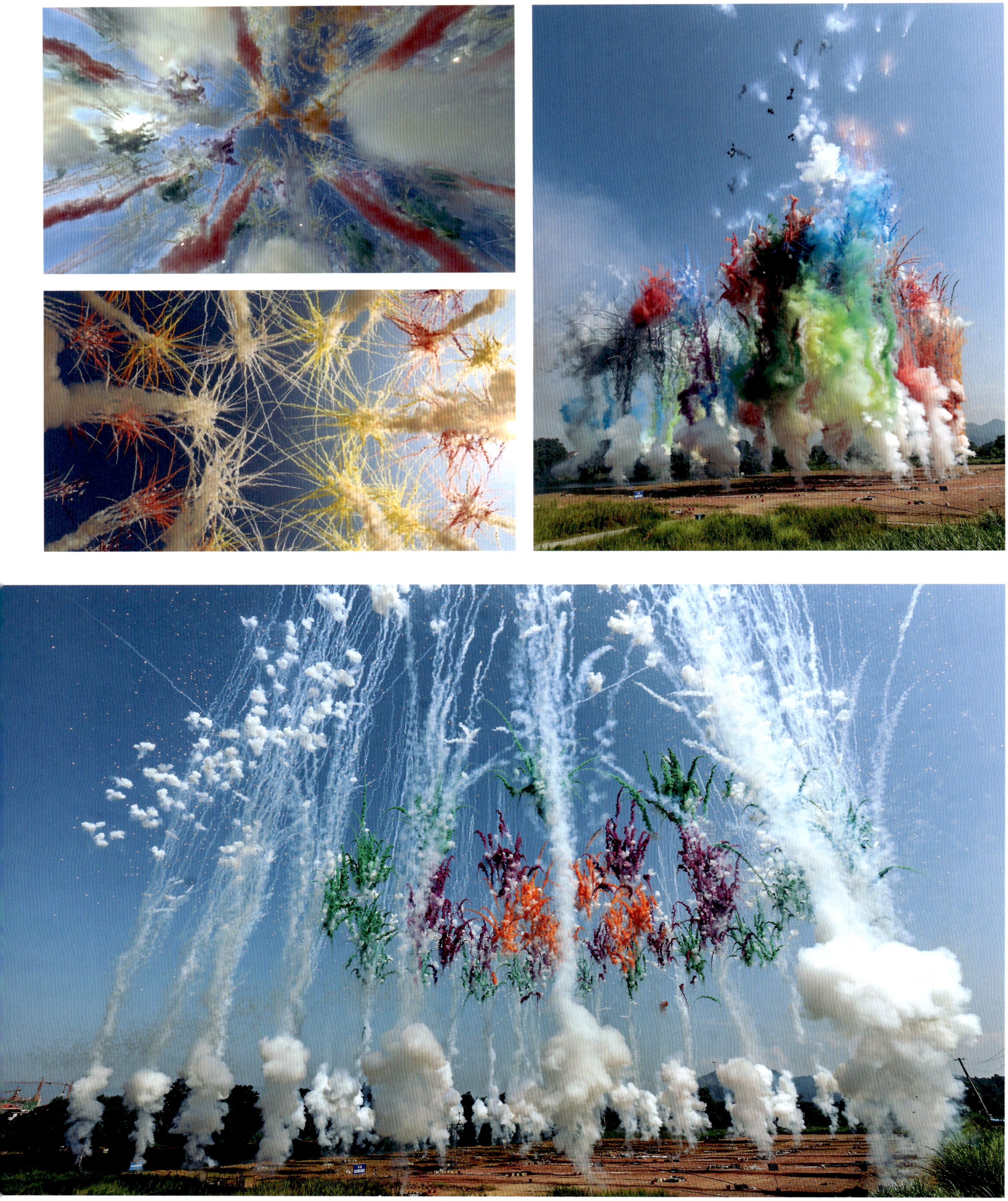

Figures 10.9a–d. Fireworks for *Sleepwalking in the Forbidden City* in Liuyang, China in 2020

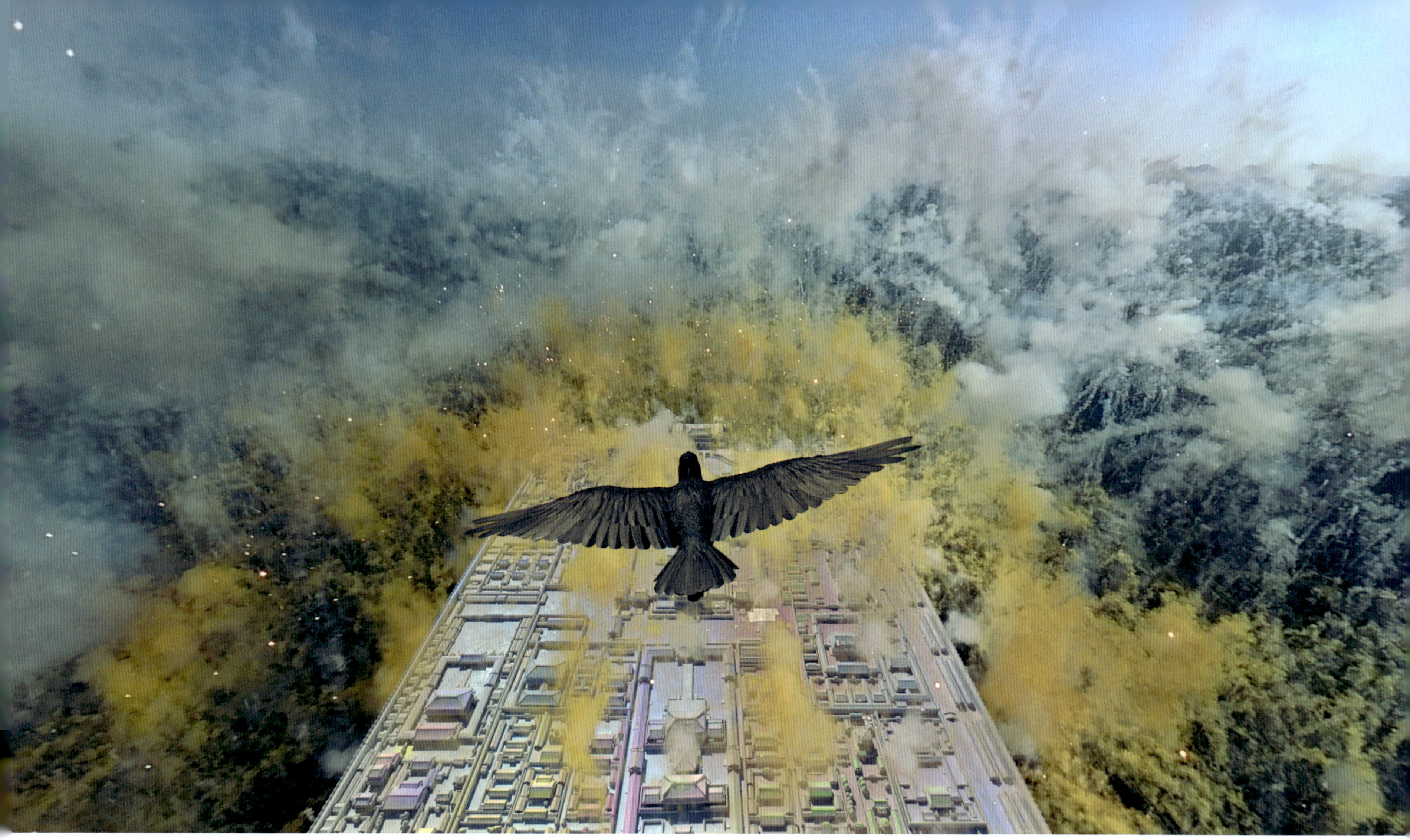

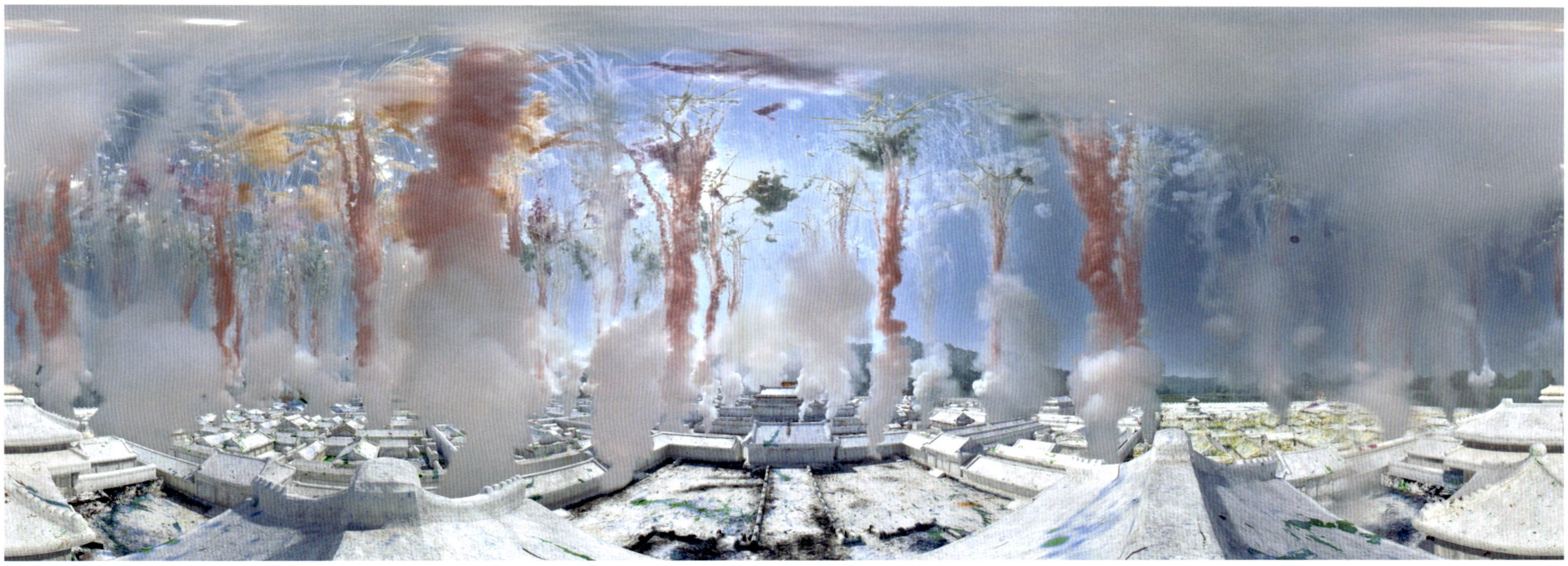

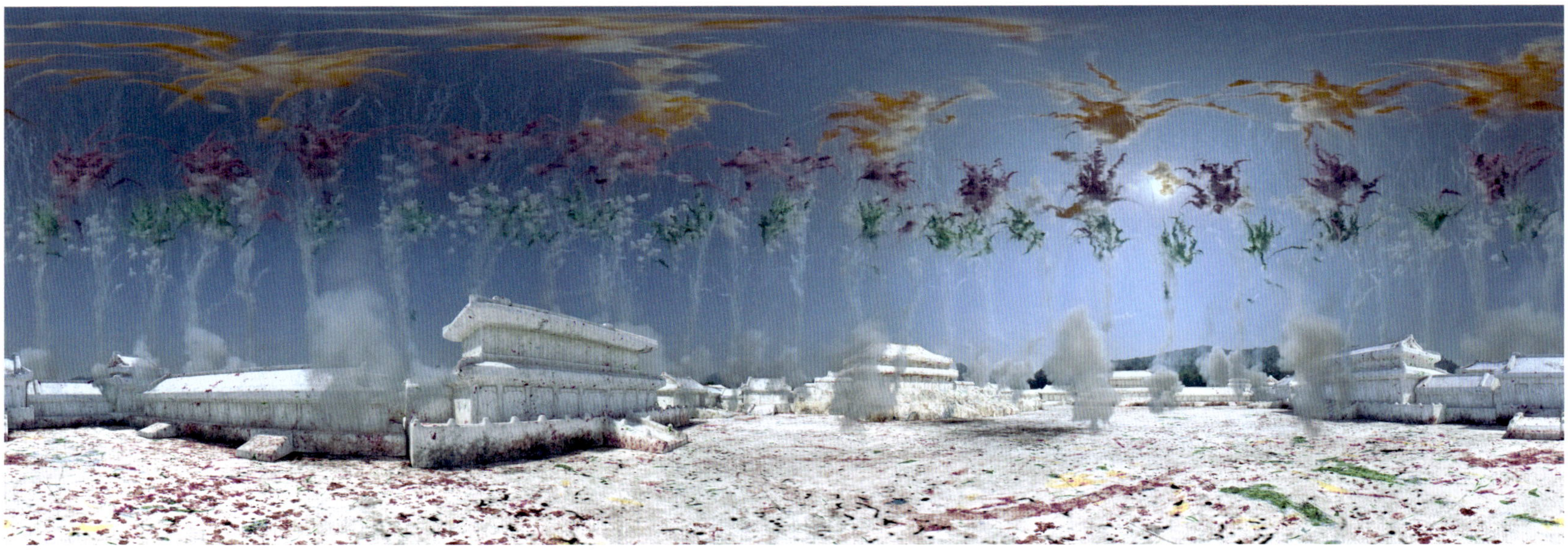

10.3 *Sleepwalking in the Forbidden City* (stills)

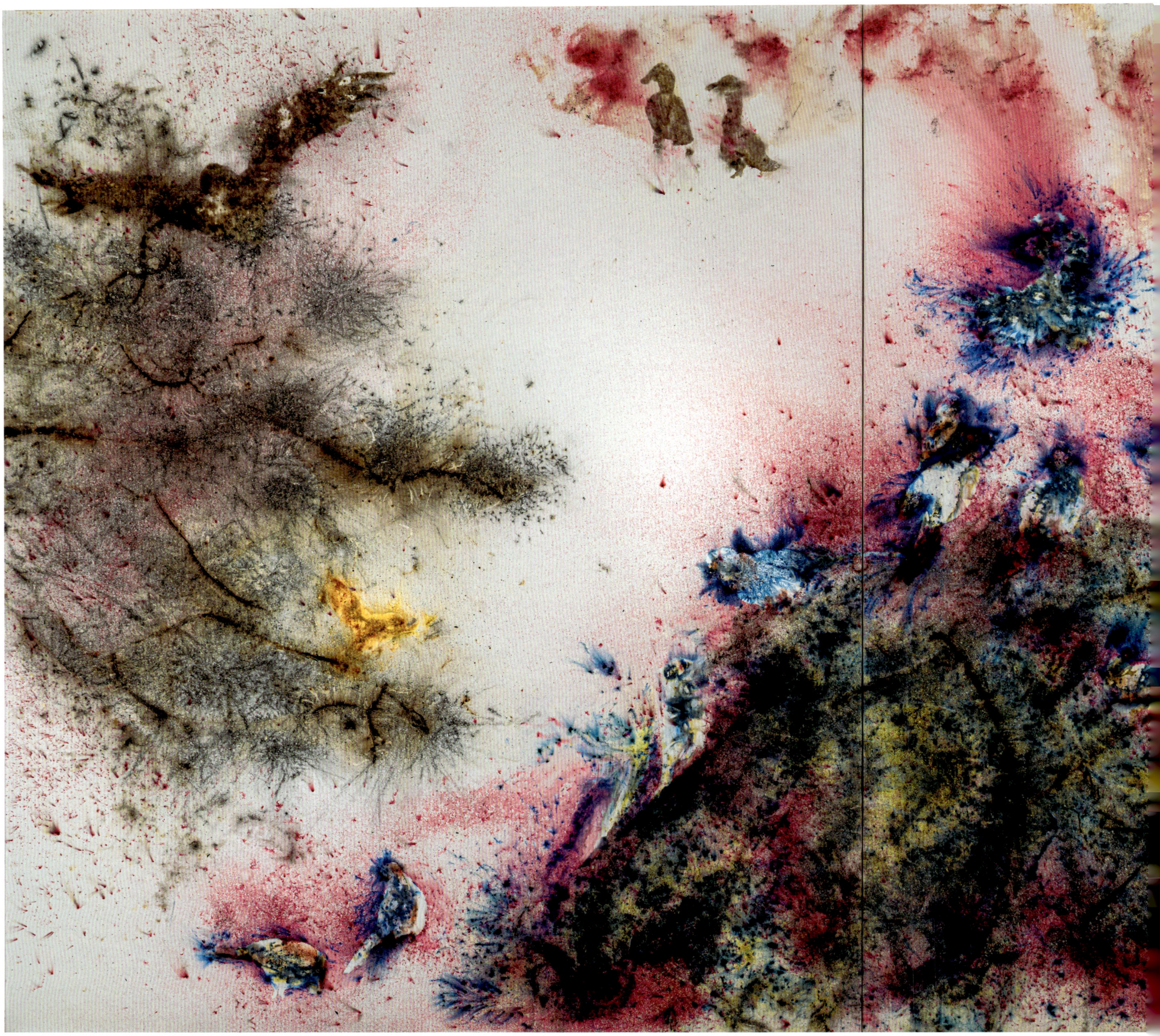

10.4 *Outside My Window: April in the Year of Gengzi*

10.4

*Outside My Window: April in the Year of Gengzi*

窗外:庚子四月

2020

Gunpowder on canvas

183 × 305 cm

While quarantining in the countryside of New Jersey during the 2020 COVID-19 outbreak, Cai captured his thoughts and frame of mind through the birds and flowers outside his window. This was a dialogue with his predecessors in ancient China, who also used nature to express their hearts and minds in painting, that transcended space and time.

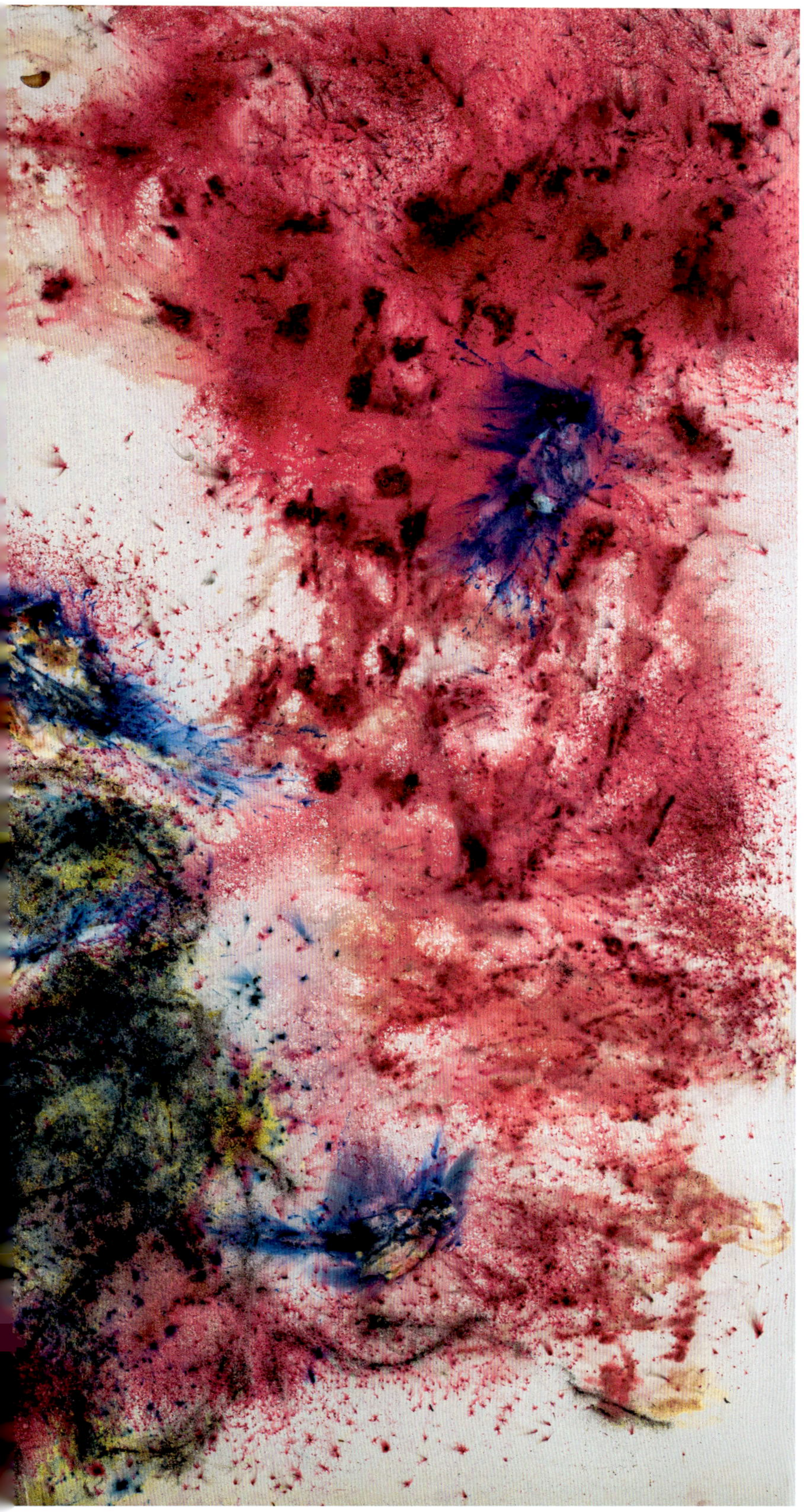

Related Work

10.5

*Study for Outside My Window: April in the Year of Gengzi No. 1*
为“窗外：庚子四月”所作研究 No. 1

2020
Gunpowder on canvas
122 × 92 cm

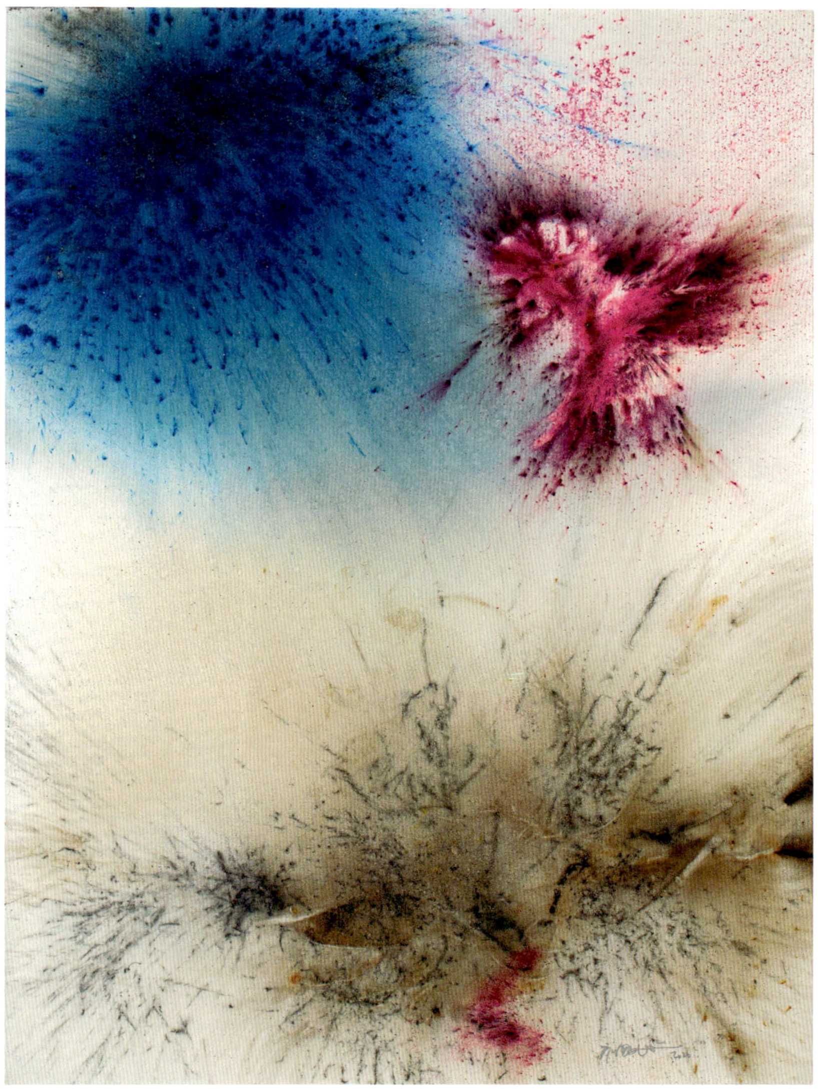

10.5 *Study for Outside My Window: April in the Year of Gengzi No. 1*

# II

# Dialogue with the Cosmos

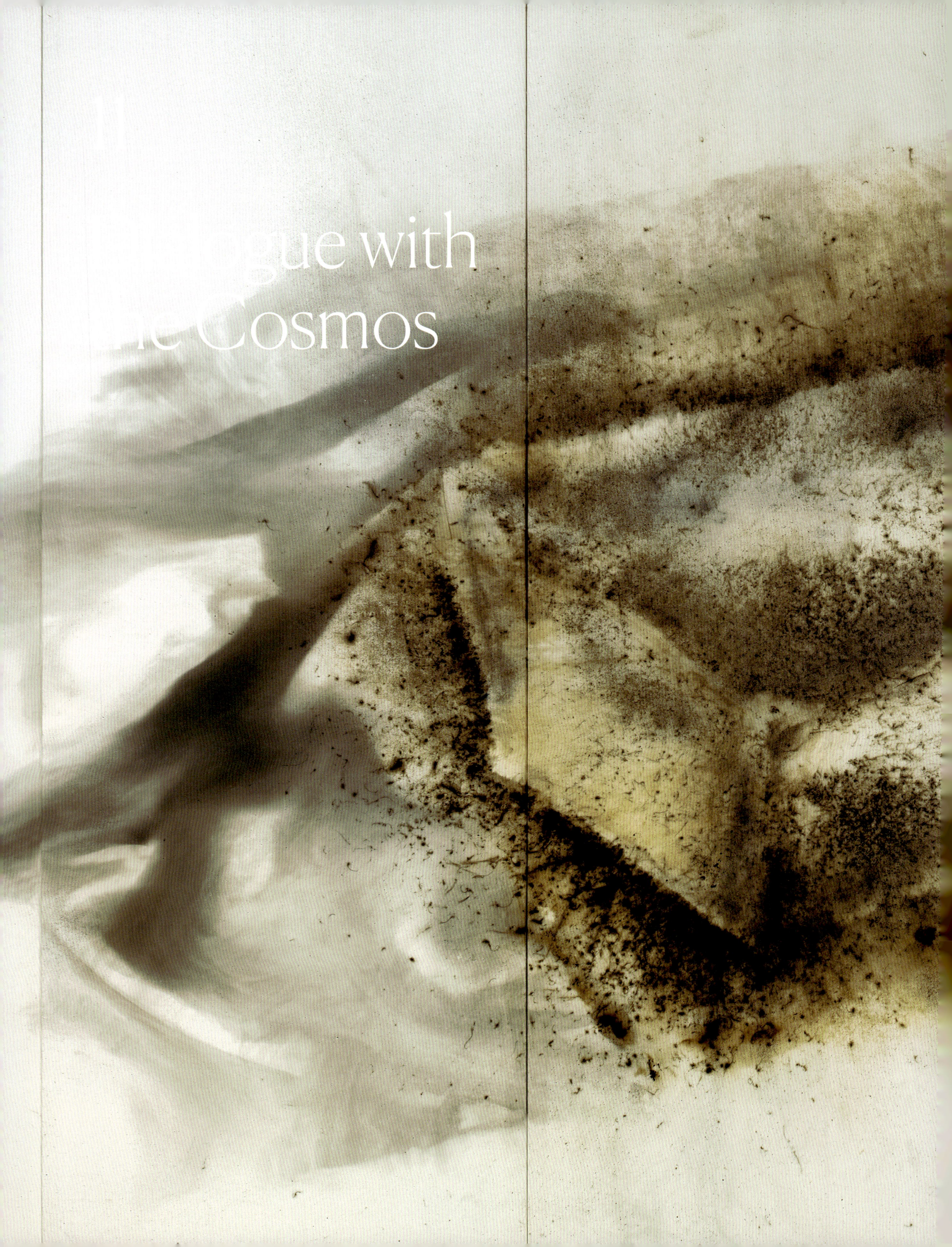

# Ongoing engagement

1957–

As a child in his homeland, Cai would frequently gaze up at the stars. Moving to Japan at the end of 1986, he soon went beyond the East-West dichotomy, and developed his fascination with observing humankind from the perspective of the cosmos. In the late 1980s, he initiated the series of explosion events *Projects for Extraterrestrials*, alongside which he created a large number of related gunpowder drawings. For a long time, the cosmos remained the primary theme of his work. After moving to New York, however, Cai began to create art for a broader, international society. While he still created such works as *Sky Ladder*, the cosmos as an explicit theme faded away from his practice, although his unique cosmology has served as a pillar of his artistic framework.

While quarantining during the COVID-19 pandemic, Cai revisited his sketchbooks from the 1980s and 90s and wrote "Notes on My Notes" (see his essay in this volume for the full text): "I had odysseys in the cosmos every day back then, pondering what 'language' I should use to converse with extraterrestrials. I wasn't thinking about dialogues between different cultures, because if I could communicate with extraterrestrials, I would naturally be able to converse with fellow humans. ... Riding along on the kite of my hometown, steering the spacecraft of human childhood across romantic horizons. ... My original aspirations and true aspirations, my frameworks and fearlessness, my identity as a member of the cosmos, the quintessence of my work and me as an artist, my coexistence with that other unseen world ... am I still capable of embracing all these things?"

The Palace Museum exhibition includes three gunpowder drawings for the *Projects for Extraterrestrials* series and one gunpowder drawing for the related series *Projects for Humankind*, all made during Cai's quarantine based on unrealized projects rediscovered in his sketchbooks. And so, he resumed making drawings for the *Projects for Extraterrestrials* after a twenty-year hiatus. In those explosive instants of creation, he was coming face to face with his past self, returning to the bosom of the cosmos—the eternal homeland of this "young painter." The exhibition also features *Frolicking on Ice in the Galaxy*—a piece inspired by the Qing-era painting *Frolic on the Ice* (*Bing Xi Tu*) in the Palace Museum's collection—which connects to the theme of the 2022 Beijing Winter Olympics, imagining the romantic scene of ice-skating against the Milky Way's celestial rim.

Every time Cai uses gunpowder, a Chinese invention, as a medium to create art on the theme of the cosmos, it seems as though all the winding, sweeping roads he has taken have only led him home.

Detail of *Humanity's Epitaph: Project for Extraterrestrials No. 13* (no. 11.4)

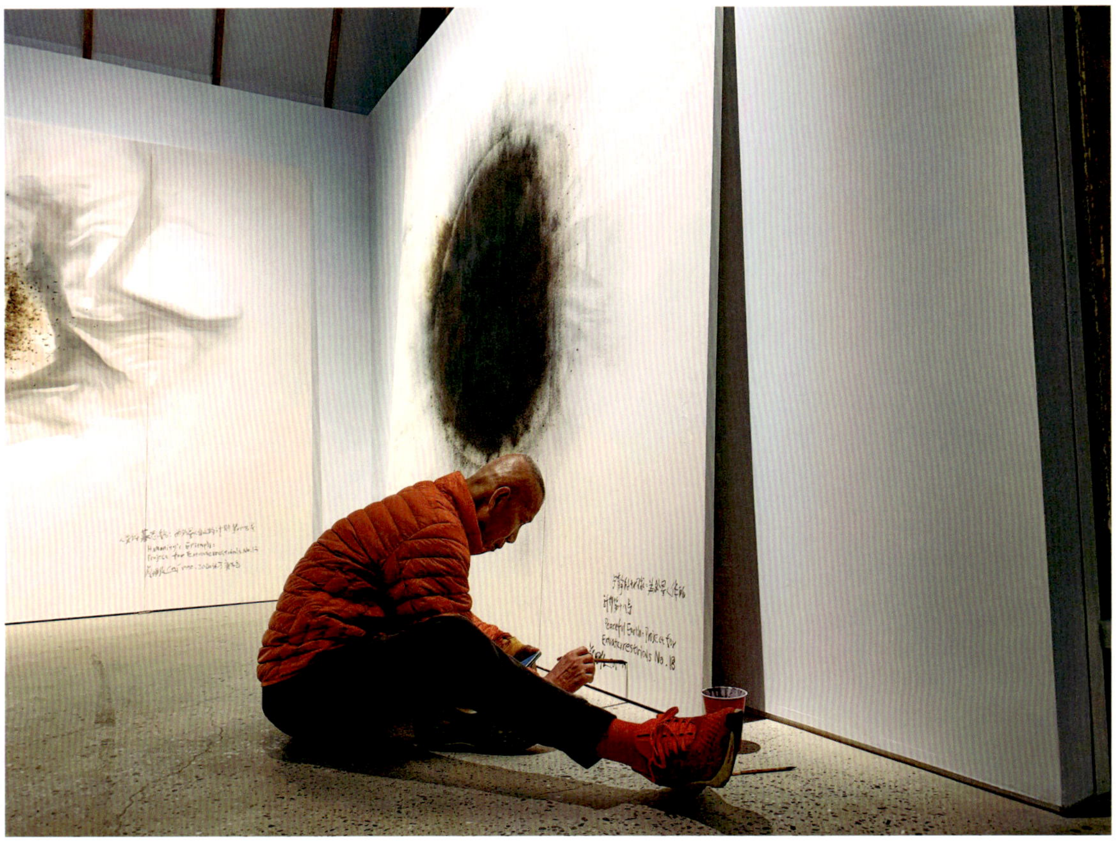

Figure 11.1. Cai Guo-Qiang signing *Peaceful Earth: Project for Extraterrestrials No. 18* in 2020

11.1

## *Peaceful Earth: Project for Extraterrestrials No. 18*
## 宁静的地球：为外星人作的计划第十八号

2020

Gunpowder and ink on paper, mounted on wood as three-panel screen

230 × 232.5 cm

*The Artist's Statement*
*(inscribed text in English translation)*

In 1993, I was invited by UNESCO to create this proposal. If realized, the project would require the participation of everyone on Earth. By turning off their lights, they would be able to see the entire world in momentary complete darkness via a live television broadcast. Because of time-zone differences, each country would coordinate to turn off all their lights one after another at the moment they cross over from one millennium to the next. Through this act, people would become aware that there is no true center stage in this world and that societies are connected to one another. Ultimately, organizing such an event was beyond our capacity, and the project never saw fruition, which was a great pity. It takes countless generations to experience the turn of the millennium.

People expected me to light up fireworks for the new millennium, but all I wanted to do was switch the lights off. At the time, I wrote, "Seen from space, the Earth glitters each night. At the last second of this millennium, and the first of the new, the residents of planet Earth each turn off their lights to be part of this creative process and 'take away the colors' of the world. In the last century, humanity has consumed enormous resources to light up the world. Hence, at such an important moment as we enter the new millennium, humanity should let the Earth rest, return it to the universe, and revert to the same darkness and peace as other planets. This will also allow the planet to step across time and space, and connect to its past self from one thousand years ago, or even its primordial origins."

1993 and 2020 (Year of *Gengzi*),
during the global lockdown
and in the silence ...

宁静的地球：为外星人作的计划第十八号
Peaceful Earth: Project for Extraterrestrials No. 18
蔡国强 Cai 1993.2020庚子年全球隔离寂静时……

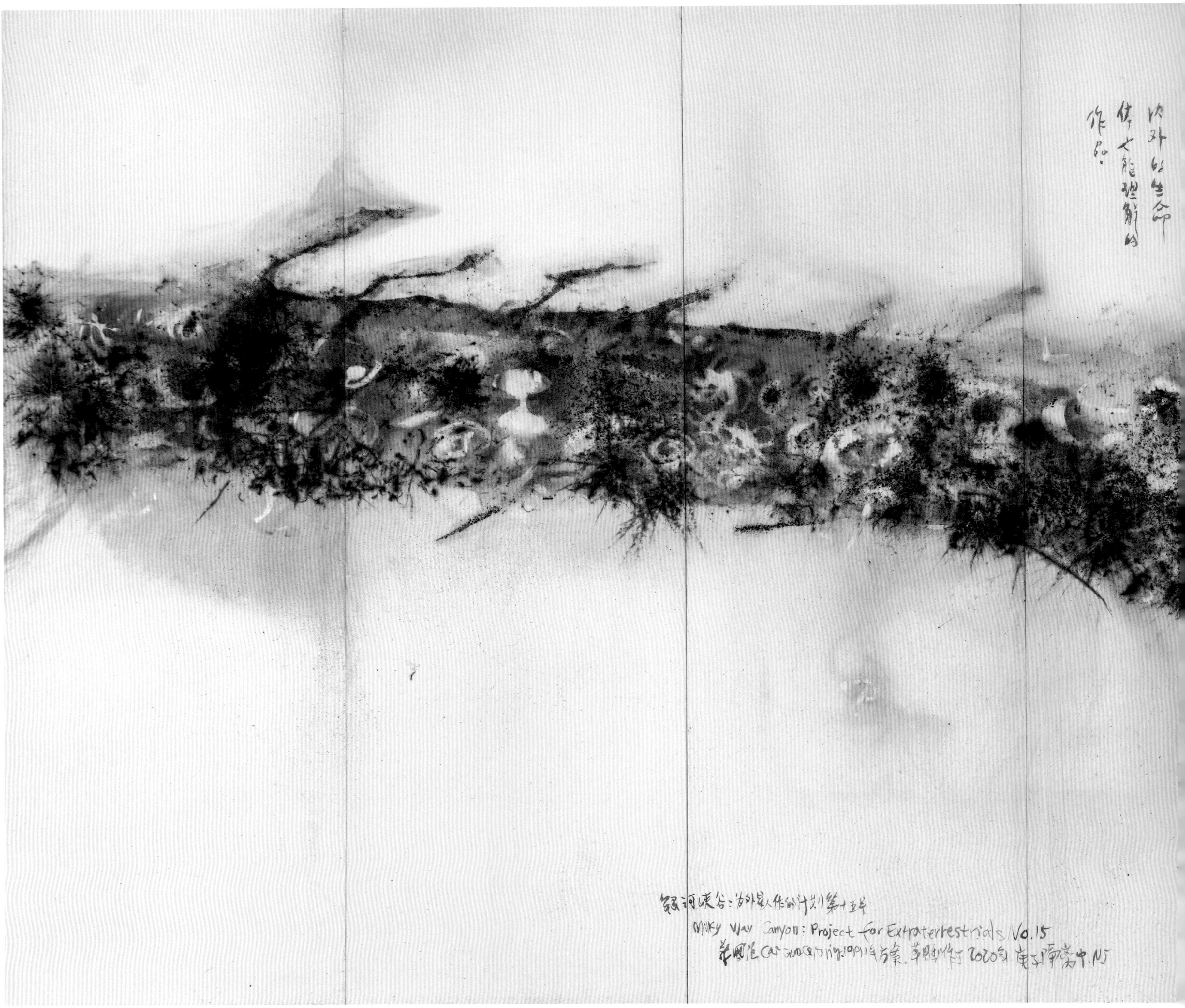


11.2

*Milky Way Canyon: Project for Extraterrestrials No. 15*

银河峡谷：为外星人作的计划第十五号

2020

Gunpowder and ink on paper, mounted on wood as seven-panel screen

230 × 542.5 cm

*The Artist's Statement*
*(inscribed text in English translation)*

Ten thousand cosmic star-shaped fireworks are launched simultaneously from the bottom of the 2000-meter-deep Grand Canyon. The audience above takes on the perspective of the extraterrestrials who watch the Earth from outer space—looking down from the top of the Grand Canyon as it is transformed into a dazzling, splendid Milky Way.

*Milky Way Canyon* symbolizes mankind's Cosmic era, which is in its "drawing" phase—albeit a monumental one. Mankind's understanding of the universe, when compared with the vast mystery of our relationship with the universe, is in the same initial stage.

The moment we [human beings] look downward, it's as if we have become extraterrestrials. At the same time, we are exhibiting our galaxy to the extraterrestrials. By taking the form of the Milky Way, the work can be appreciated by creatures native and foreign to the Galaxy alike.

Proposal from 1991,
drawing created during lockdown in
2020 (Year of *Gengzi*), in New Jersey

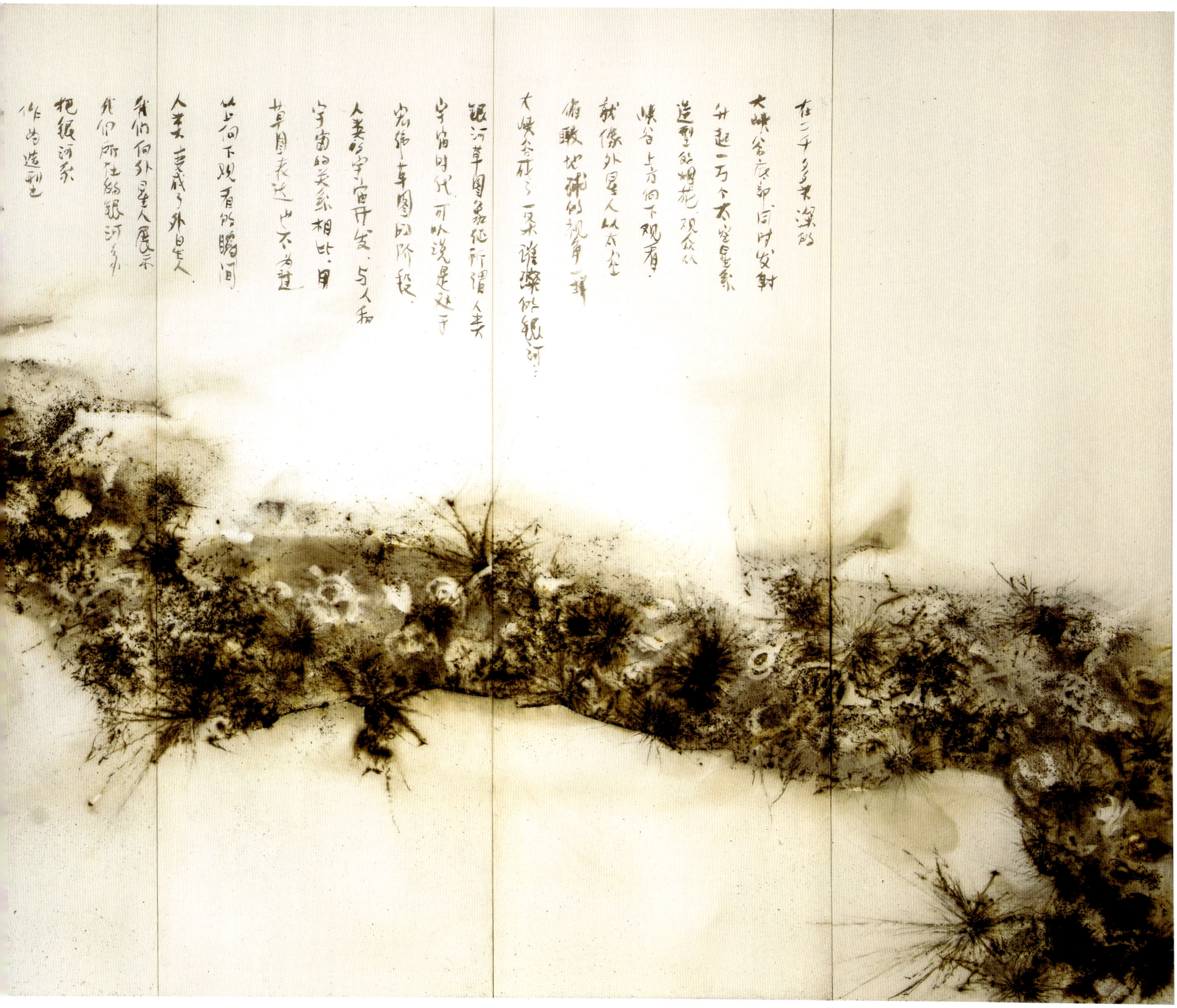
在二千多米深的
大峡谷底部同时发射
升起一万个太空星系
造型的烟花，观众从
峡谷上方向下观看，
就像外星人从太空
俯瞰地球的视角一样
大峡谷形成了一条璀璨的银河：
银河草图象征所谓人类
宇宙时代，可以说是处于
宏伟草图的阶段，
人类的宇宙开发，与人和
宇宙的关系相比，用
草图表达也不为过
从上向下观看的瞬间
人类变成了外星人
我们向外星人展示
我们所在的银河系
把银河系
作为造型。

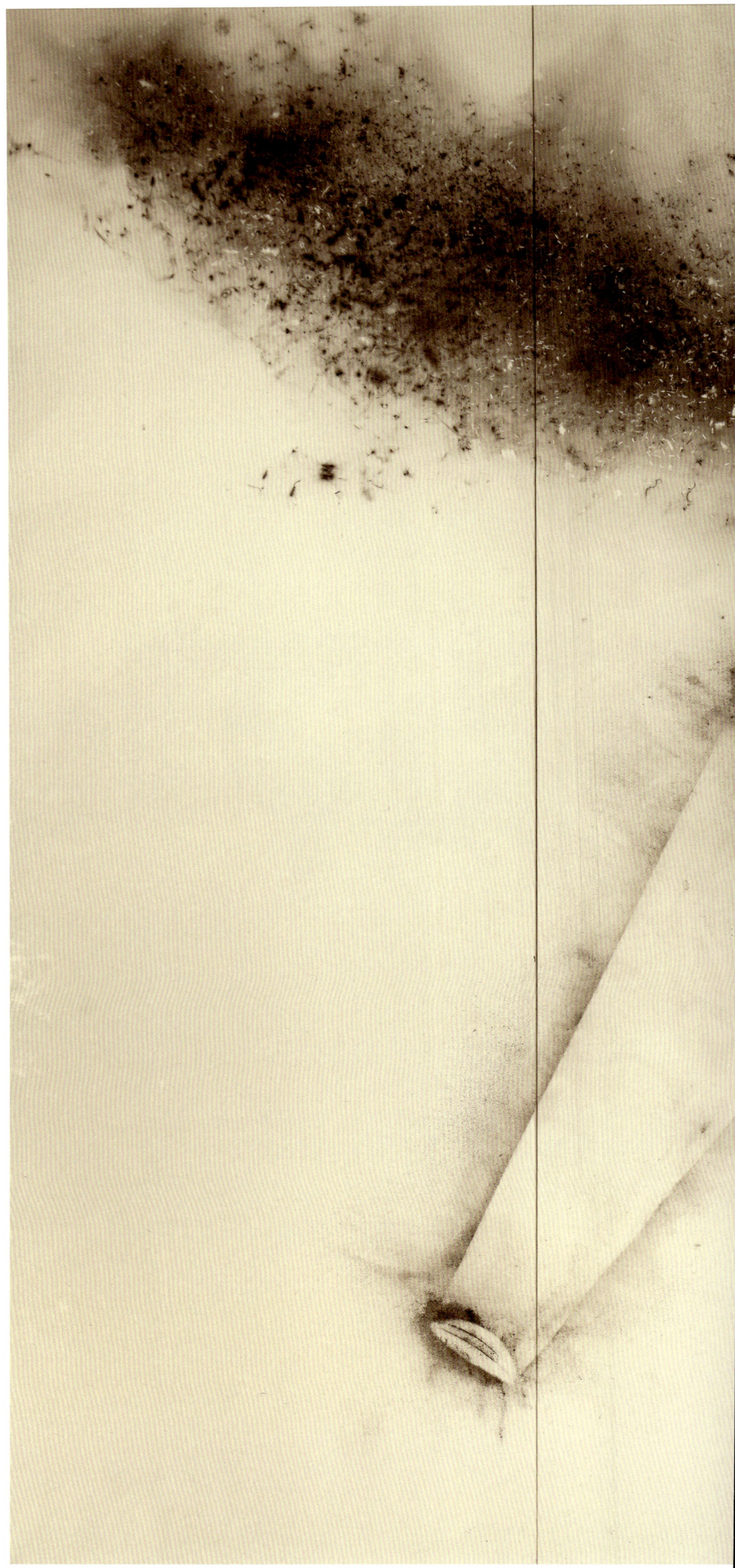

11.3

*Nostalgia for Homeland: Project for Humankind No. 4*
望乡：为人类作的计划第四号
2020
Gunpowder and ink on paper, mounted on wood as four-panel screen
230 × 310 cm

*The Artist's Statement (inscribed text in English translation)*

Since 1990, I've been dreaming of building a cosmic telescope by constructing two gigantic lenses. People passing by could look up and transcend light years instantaneously. That is the Galaxy and even the Universe—the homeland of itinerants. There and back again.

2020 (Year of *Gengzi*),
re-creating the proposal from the 1990s

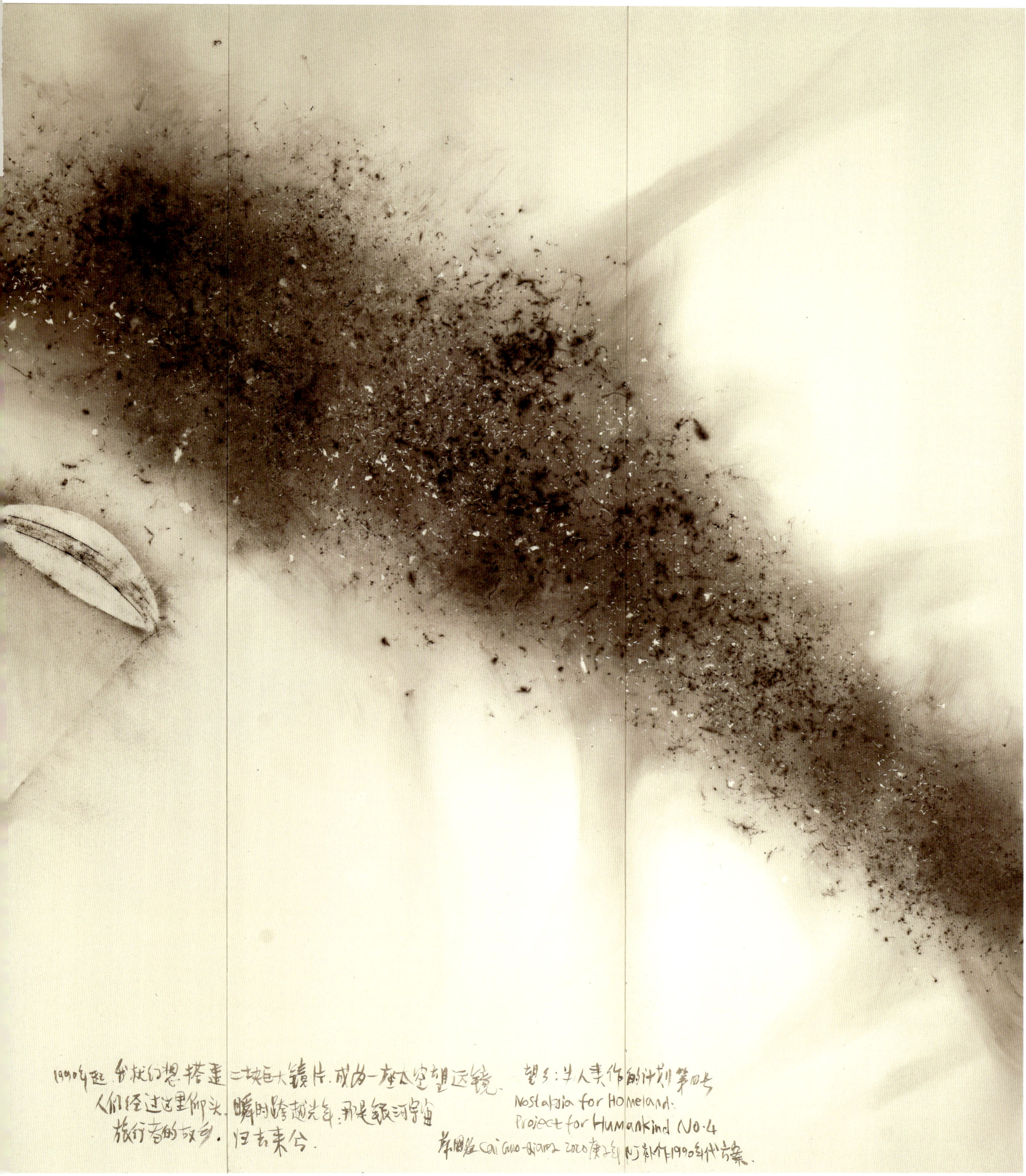
1990年起，我就幻想搭建二块巨大镜片，成为一座太空望远镜。
人们经过这里仰头，瞬时跨越光年，那是银河宇宙
旅行者的故乡。归去来兮。
望乡：为人类作的计划第四号
Nostalgia for Homeland:
Project for Humankind No.4
蔡国强 Cai Guo-Qiang 2020庚子年 新作1990年代方案.

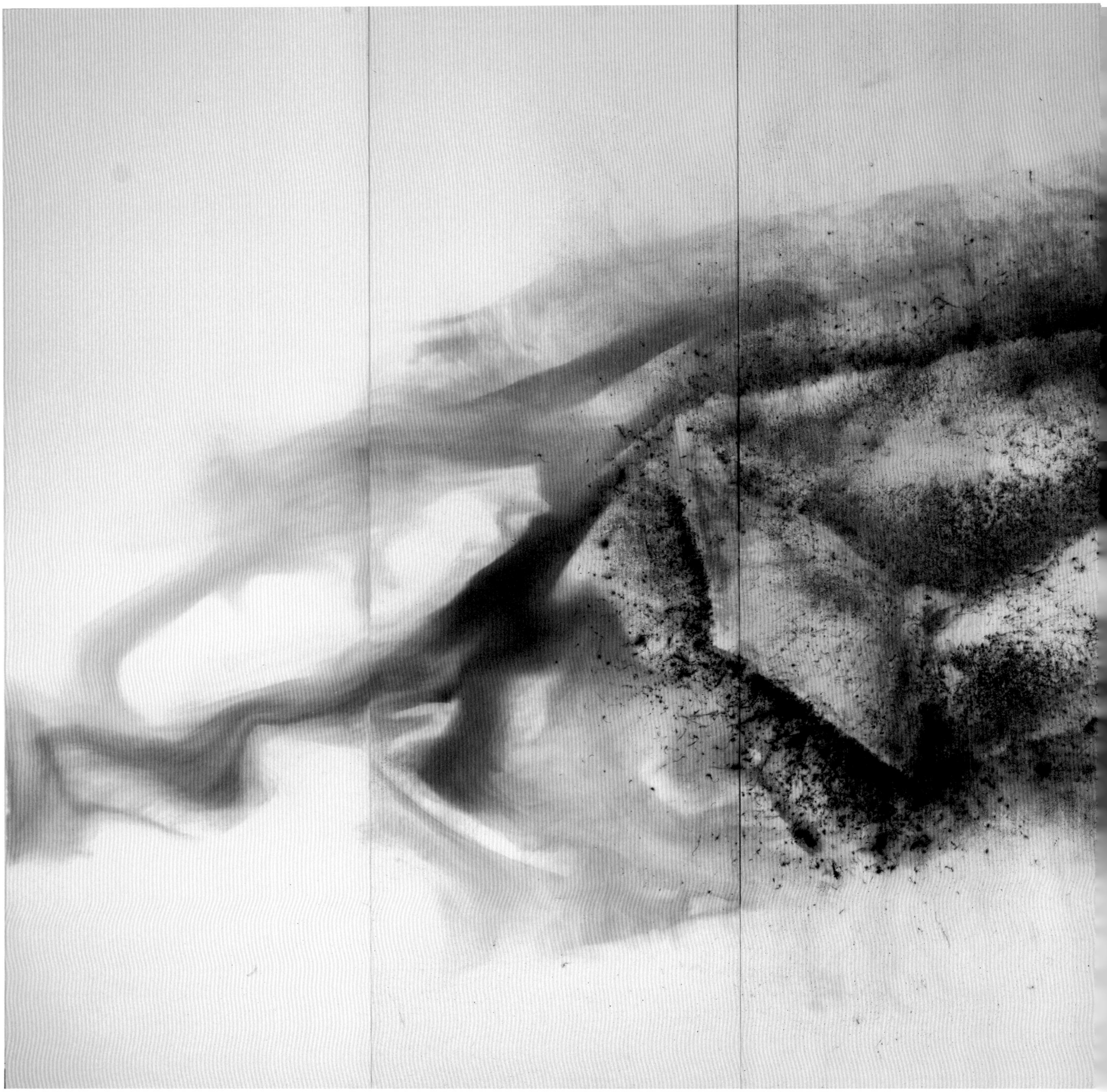

11.4

*Humanity's Epitaph: Project for Extraterrestrials No. 13*
人类的墓志铭：为外星人作的计划第十三号
2020
Gunpowder and ink on paper, mounted on wood as six-panel screen
230 × 465 cm

*The Artist's Statement*

This is my project from 1990. I wanted to construct a coffin-shaped block of frozen sea water containing microorganisms and then send it off to wander the cosmos containing the bio-information of Earth.

I have transcribed the work's description several times. Every time, it was as if I were floating through the cosmos alongside it.

*In the Dark and Freezing Universe*

An ice cube, pure white, wanders through the boundless expanse of space-time; it contains the code condensing the composition and history of life in Earth's seas. The ice melts when it encounters another distant planet, making the cosmos its new home. The light from another sun holds its funeral.

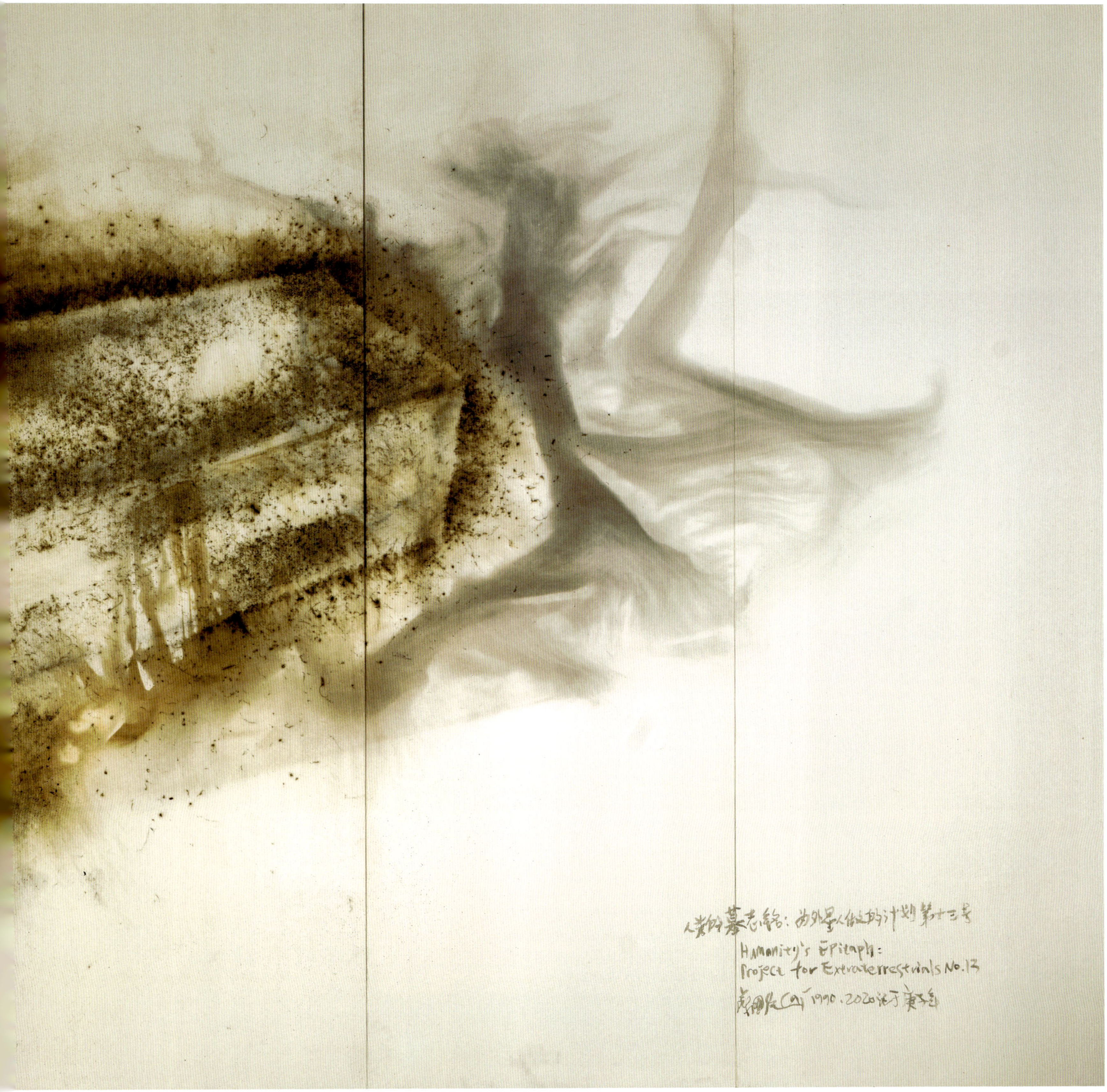


When it meets with comets that fly forth, it will be deeply drawn by these new companions—perhaps marrying one of them with embraces and loving caresses, perhaps becoming the beloved of another star, perhaps being reduced to a bead of sweat on the body of a giant, perhaps bearing children and helping a society to prosper. If it breaks into another civilization, if it finds guidance and makes its way into another atmosphere unharmed, settling into a new abode, then it will become the darling of that other world's thinkers.

Everything will be understood, nothing will be said. The efforts and anxieties of its friends, the ones who originally lifted this gift out of the atmosphere and sent it on its lengthy and turbulent journey—how their work will profoundly shake that other noble society!

Of course, even if this one-in-a-trillion chance is not realized, it will rest quietly alongside the cosmic rays, occasionally receiving a greeting from another star's glimmer and deriving some comfort. It will drift hither and thither in the ever-expanding universe, recalling memories of all that has transpired since 4.5 billion years ago. (Re-transcribed in the dead of night on May 6, 1992)

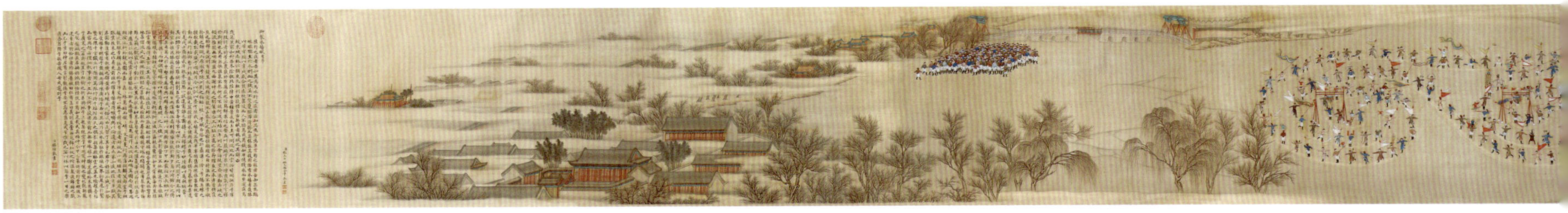

11.6 Zhang Weibang, Yao Wenhan, et al., *Frolic on the Ice* (*Bing Xi Tu*)

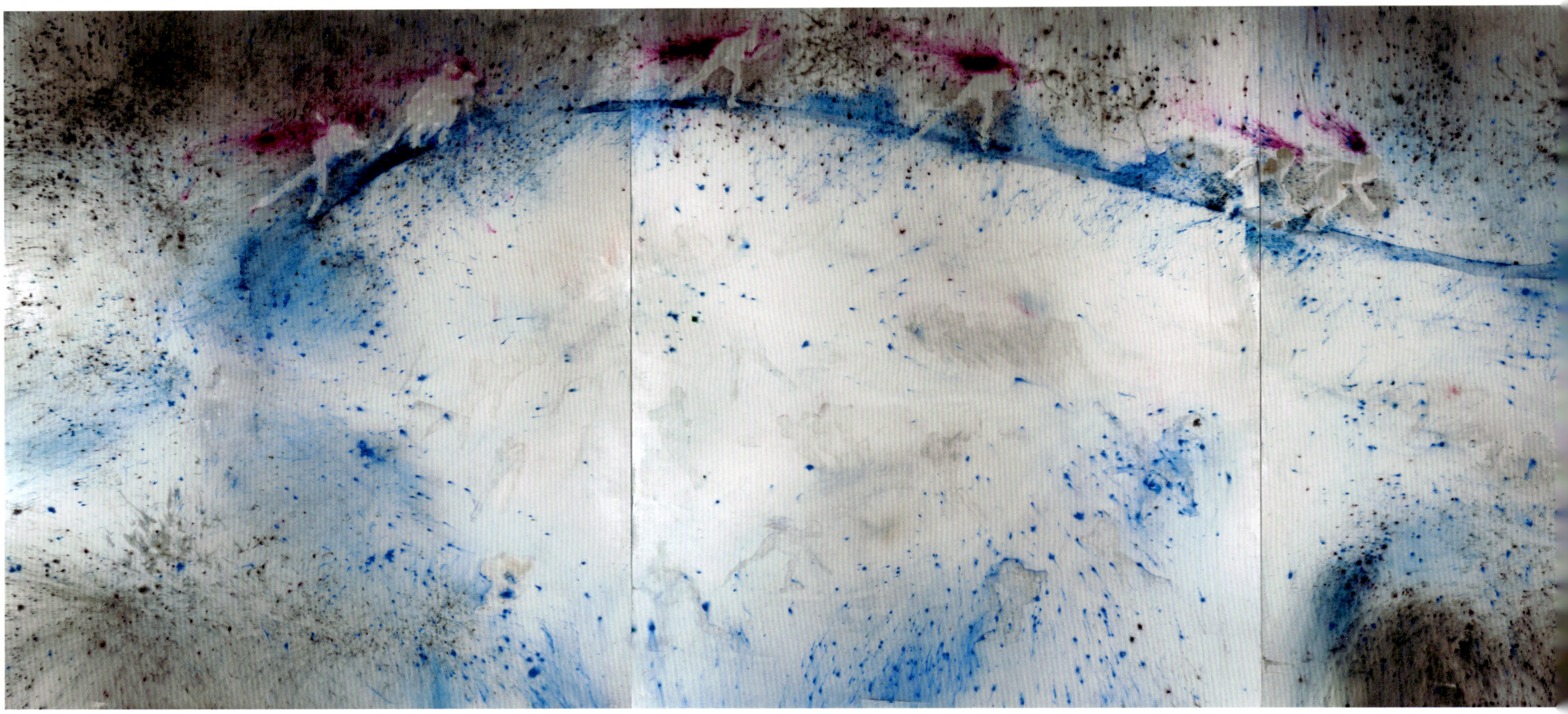

Figure 11.2. Exploded mirror sheets, which, combined with the exploded glass sheets in its front, form the complete work *Frolicking on Ice in the Galaxy*

11.5

*Frolicking on Ice in the Galaxy*

银河嬉冰

2020

Gunpowder on glass and mirror

205 × 915 cm

11.6

Zhang Weibang,
Yao Wenhan, et al.

*Frolic on the Ice* (*Bing Xi Tu*)

张为邦、姚文翰等合绘

冰嬉图卷

Qing dynasty (1644–1911)

Ink and colors on silk

36.8 × 563.4 cm

Collection of the Palace Museum

Inspired by *Frolic on the Ice* (*Bing Xi Tu*), a Qing-period painting in the collection of the Palace Museum, Cai created *Frolicking on Ice in the Galaxy* that echoes the theme of the 2022 Beijing Winter Olympics. This painting marks the artist's first time detonating gunpowder atop glass and mirrors on such a large scale, while deploying a new technique especially developed to allow for detonations on the glass and mirror panels to occur at different scales respectively. After the detonation, a final large explosion merged the upper and lower half of the piece into one complete image, depicting a profoundly magical scene that envisions skaters gliding across the vast Milky Way. As for the exploded mirrors, the smoky effect evokes a romantic vision of the vast ice and snow, a pleasant surprise hidden in the work.

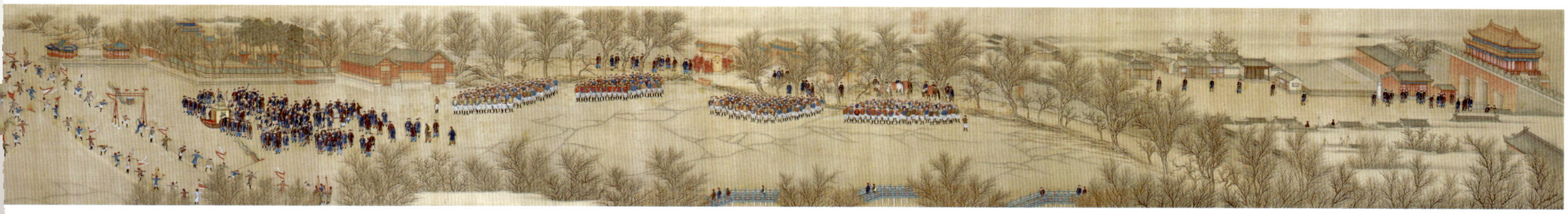

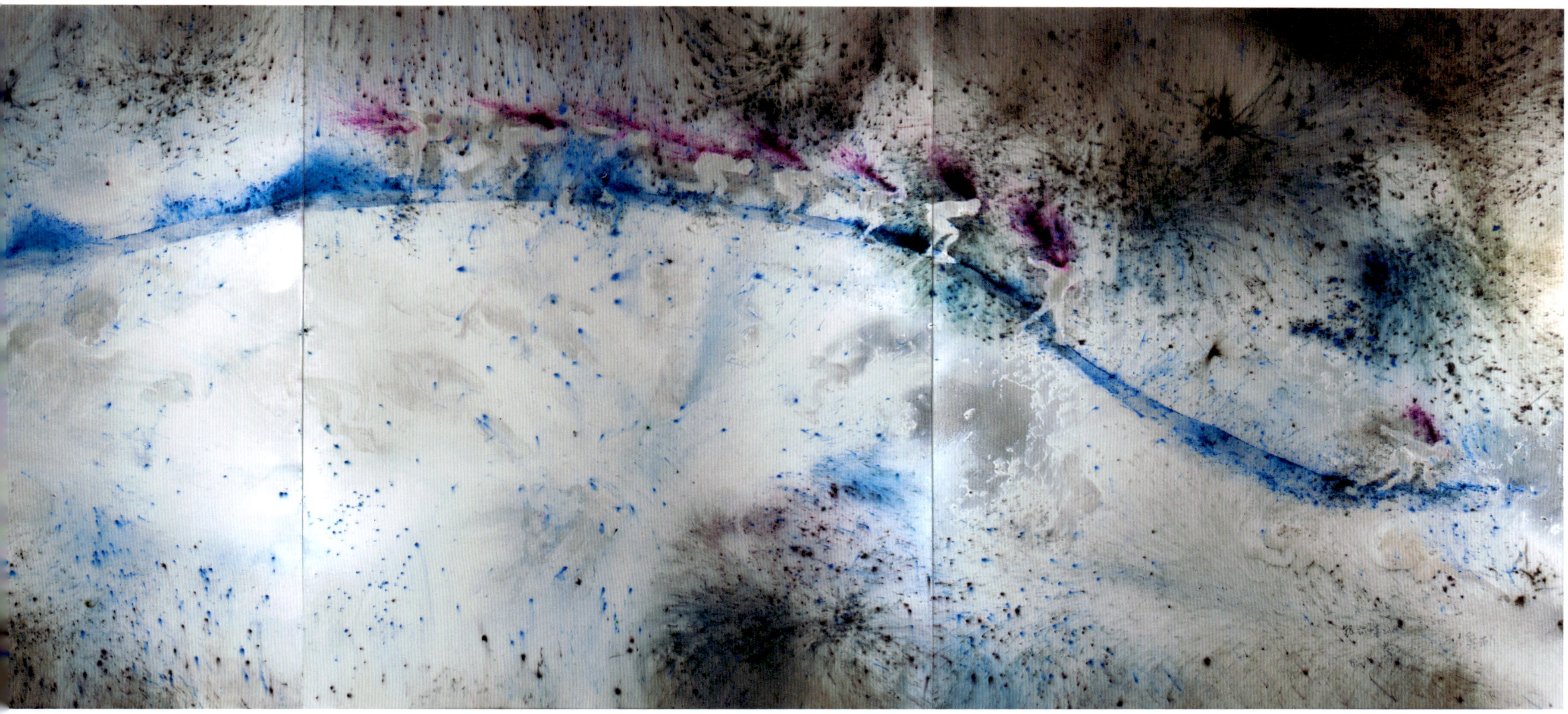

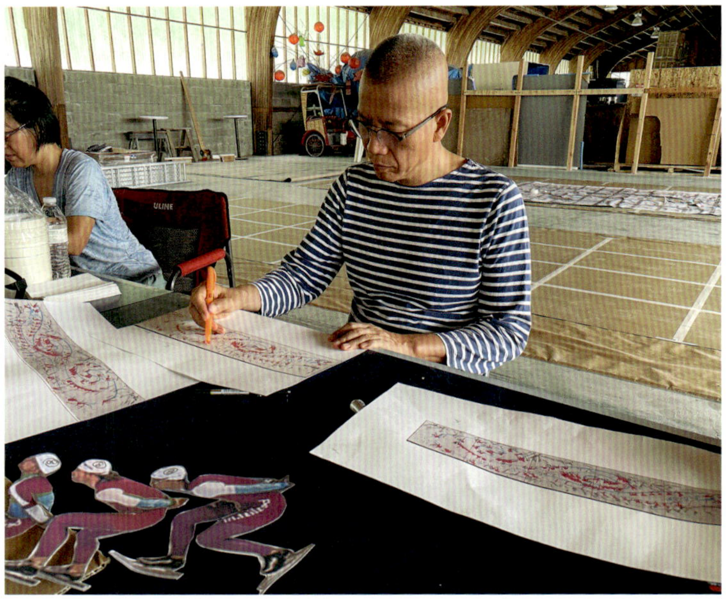

Figure 11.3a. Cai Guo-Qiang sketches images of ice-skaters in dynamic poses for the painting's composition

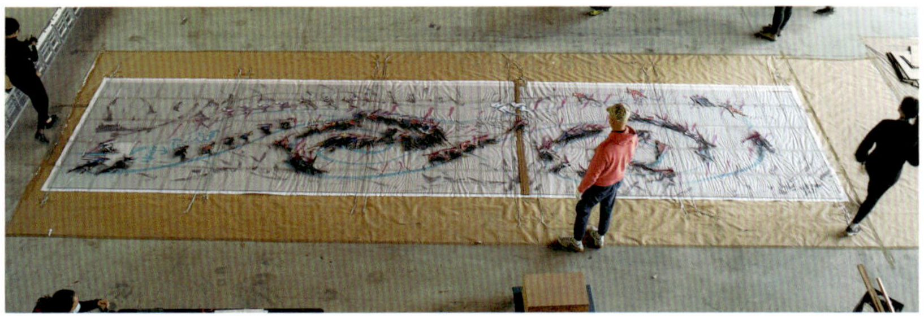

Figure 11.3b. An enlarged reproduction of the sketch is laid on the floor and covered by glass sheets (hereafter "glass"). Over the glass, carefully numbered paper figures of ice-skaters are placed in their designated spots. Cai sprinkles gunpowder over the glass and paper figures

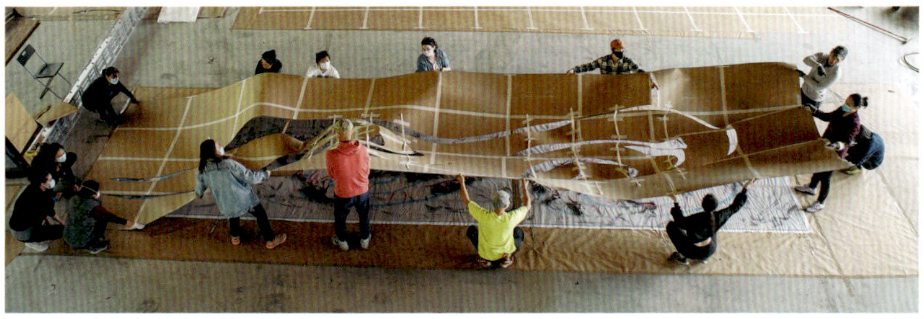

Figure 11.3c. Assistants place a cardboard stencil over the glass, paper figures, and gunpowder

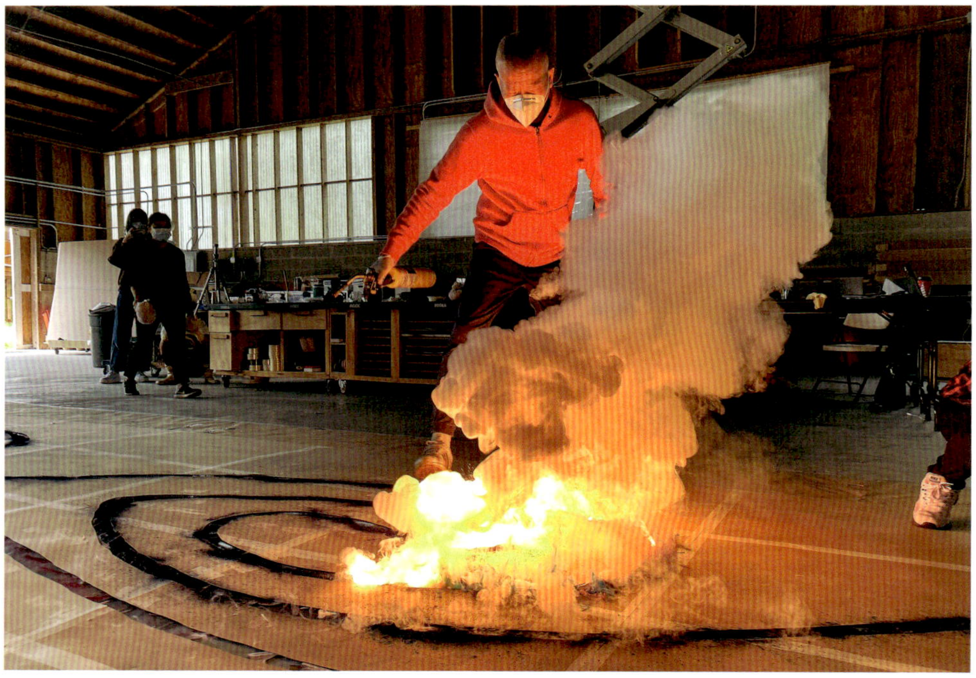

Figure 11.3d. Cai ignites gunpowder to produce exploded imagery on the glass

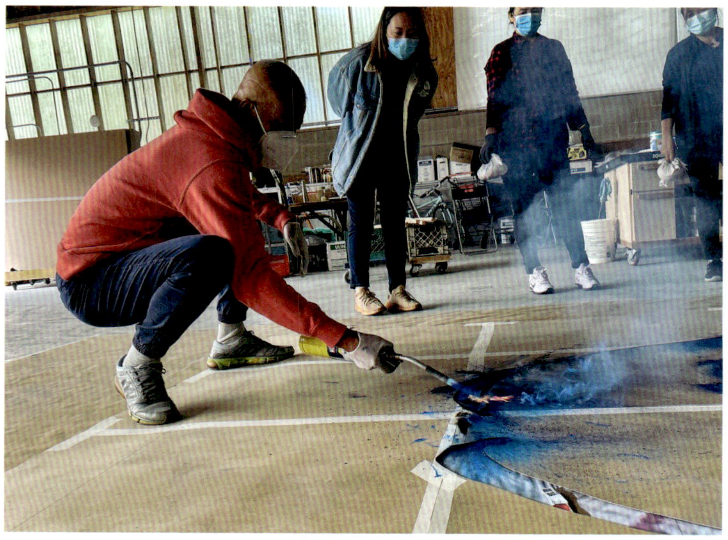

Figure 11.3e. Cai ignites the gunpowder that was not fully exploded

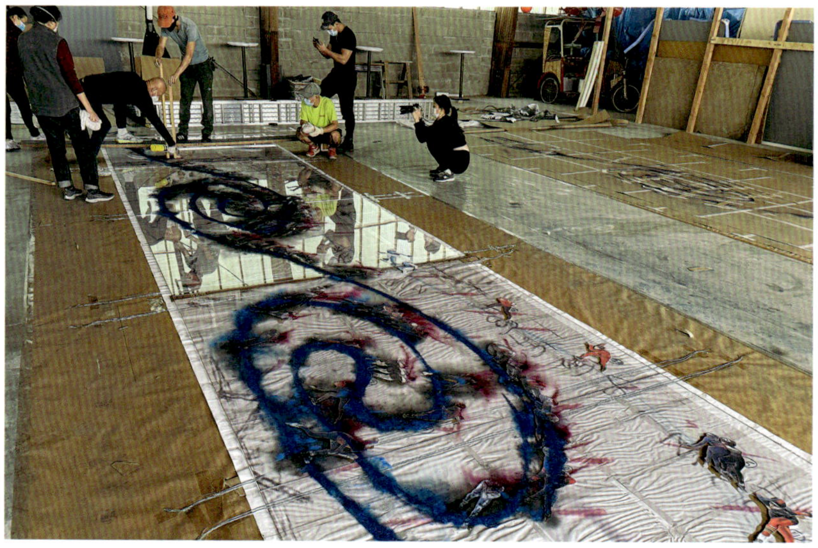

Figure 11.3f. After removal of the stencil, Cai re-ignites the unexploded gunpowder, area by area, for a desired result

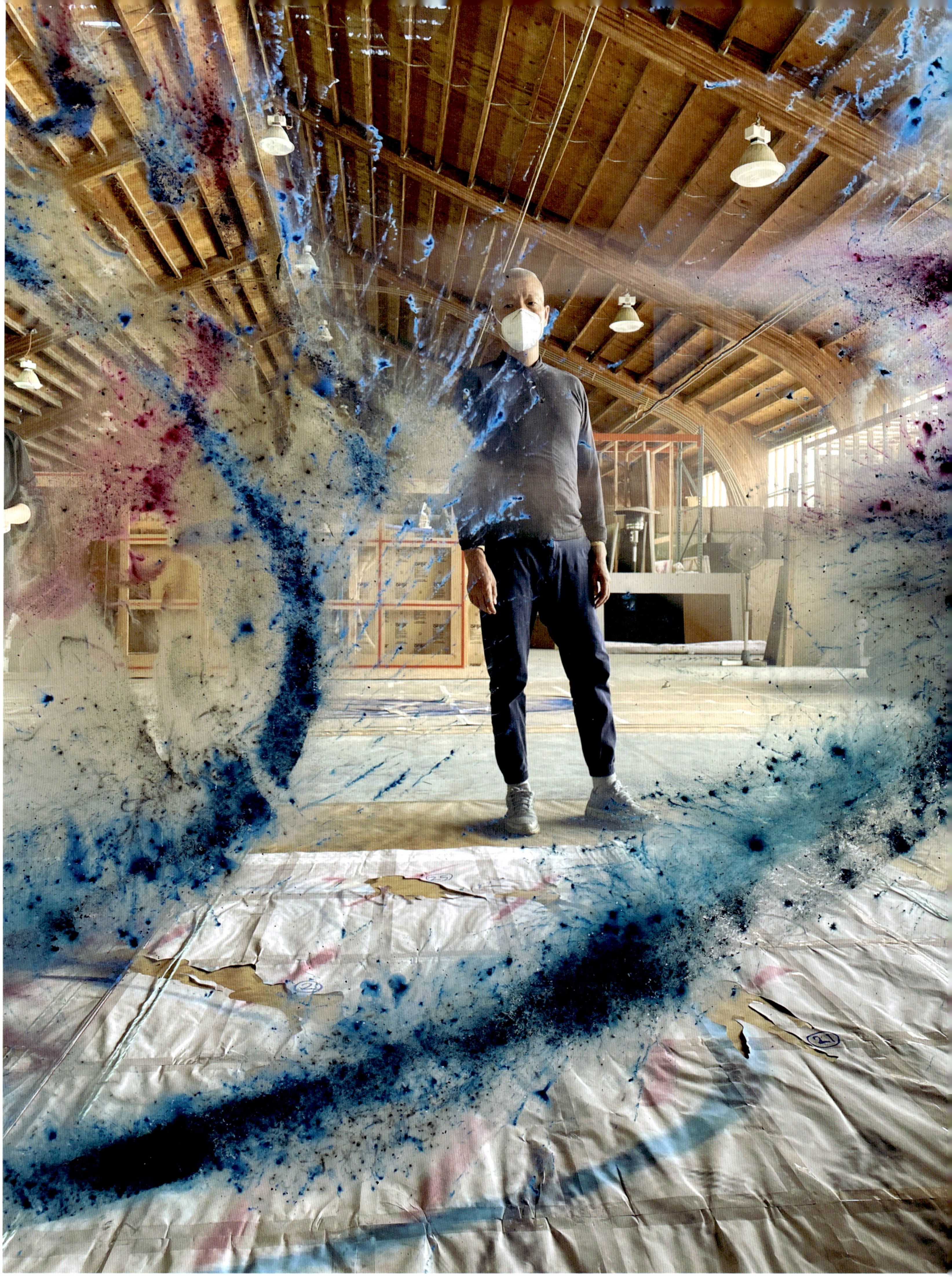

Figure 11.3g. Each sheet of the exploded glass is erected for Cai Guo-Qiang's inspection

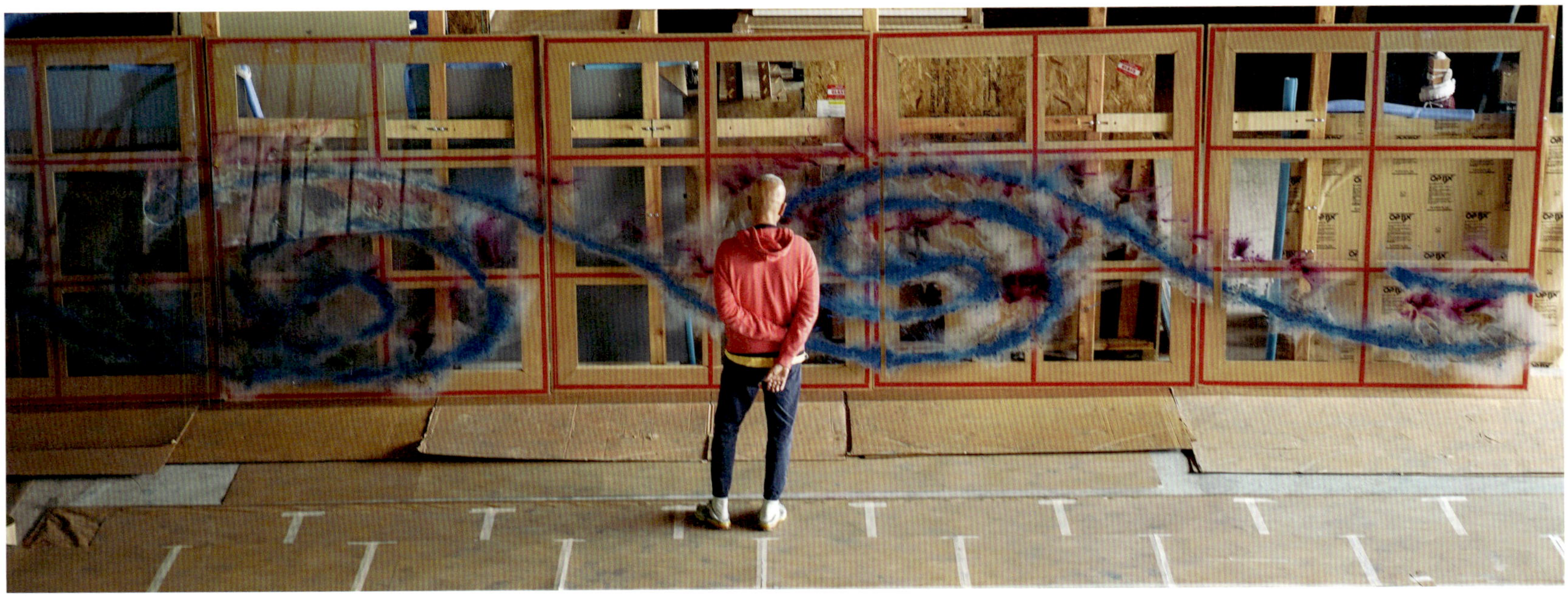

Figure 11.3h. Cai Guo-Qiang examines the general effect of the exploded glass

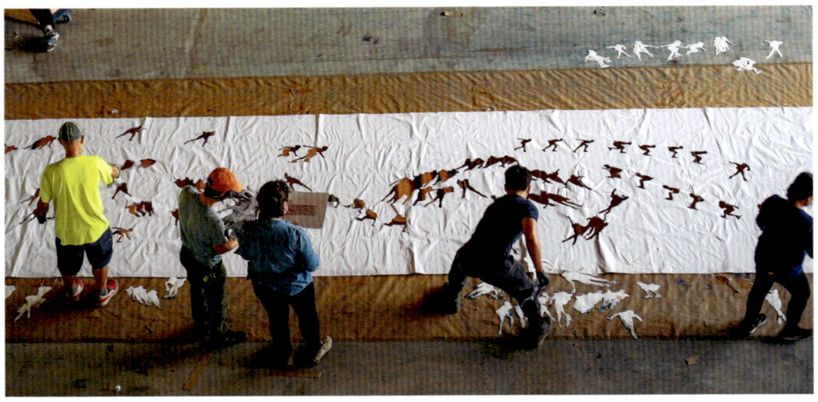

Figure 11.3i. Mirror sheets (hereafter "mirror") are placed on the ground and another stencil, from which reversed images of the ice-skaters are cut out, is placed over them. The cut-out paper figures are placed in the corresponding empty parts of the stencil

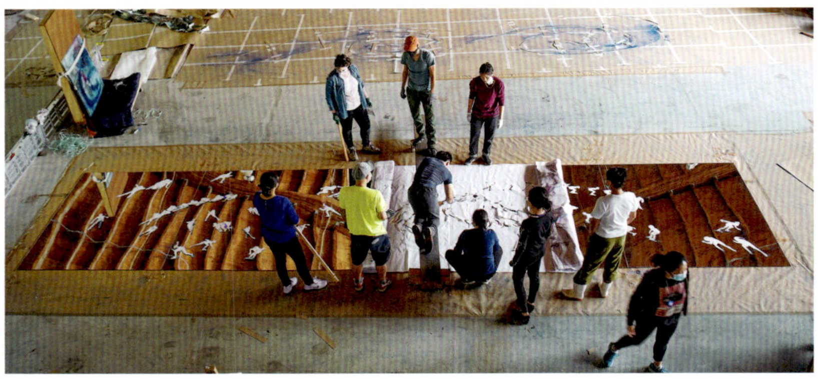

Figure 11.3j. The stencil is removed and only the paper figures are kept on the mirror

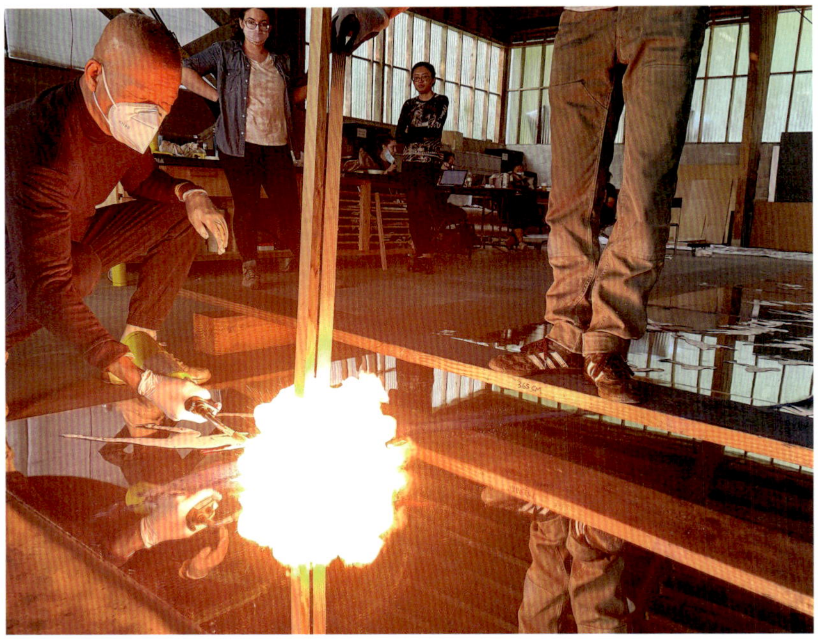

Figure 11.3k. Cai sprinkles gunpowder on paper skaters and ignites them

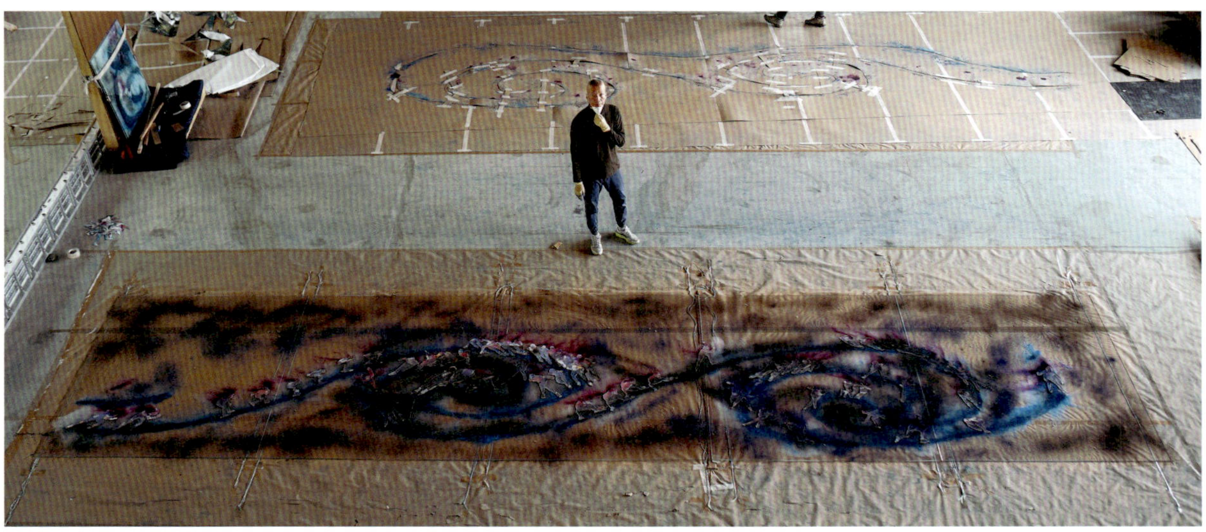

Figure 11.3l. The exploded glass is put back on the floor. Cai sprinkles gunpowder over the glass

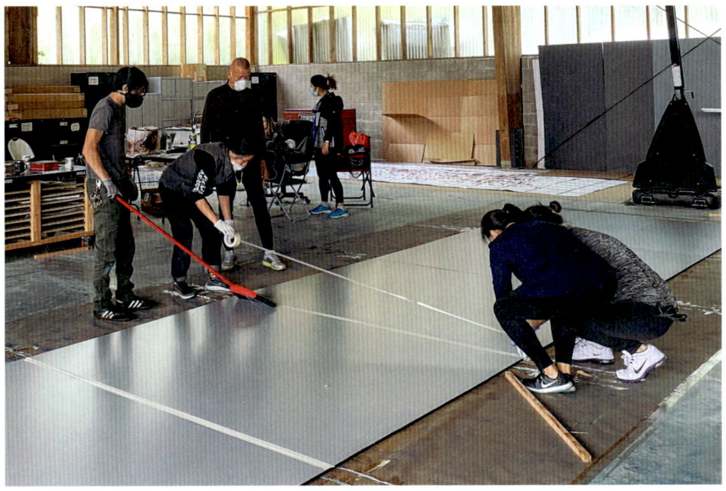

Figure 11.3m. The exploded glass with gunpowder is covered by the exploded mirror sheets. Seams between mirror sheets are sealed with tape. This makes a "sandwich" of gunpowder between the mirror and the glass

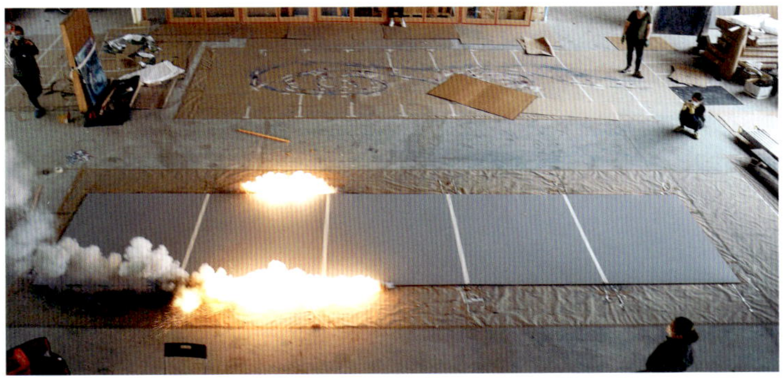

Figure 11.3n. The "sandwich" is ignited. Bang!

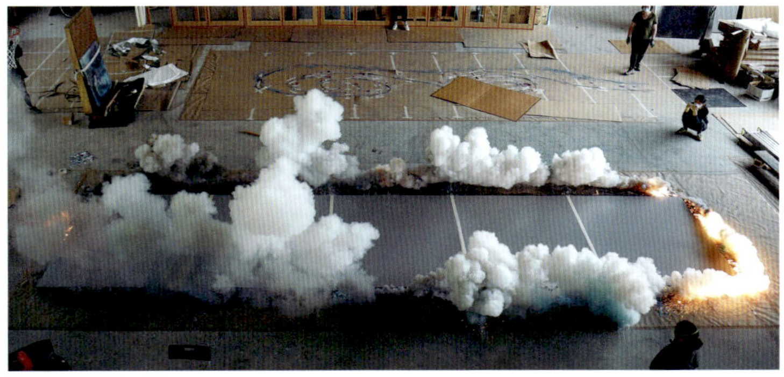

Figure 11.3o. Bang!

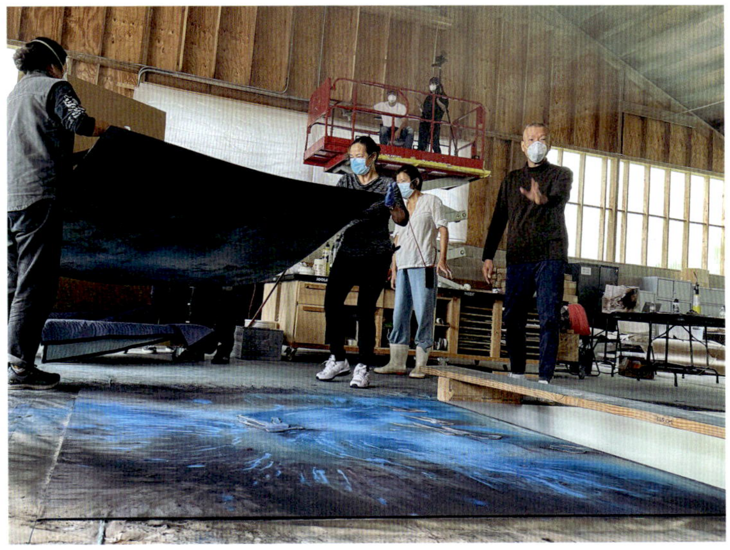

Figure 11.3p. The mirror is taken away for Cai to inspect the results

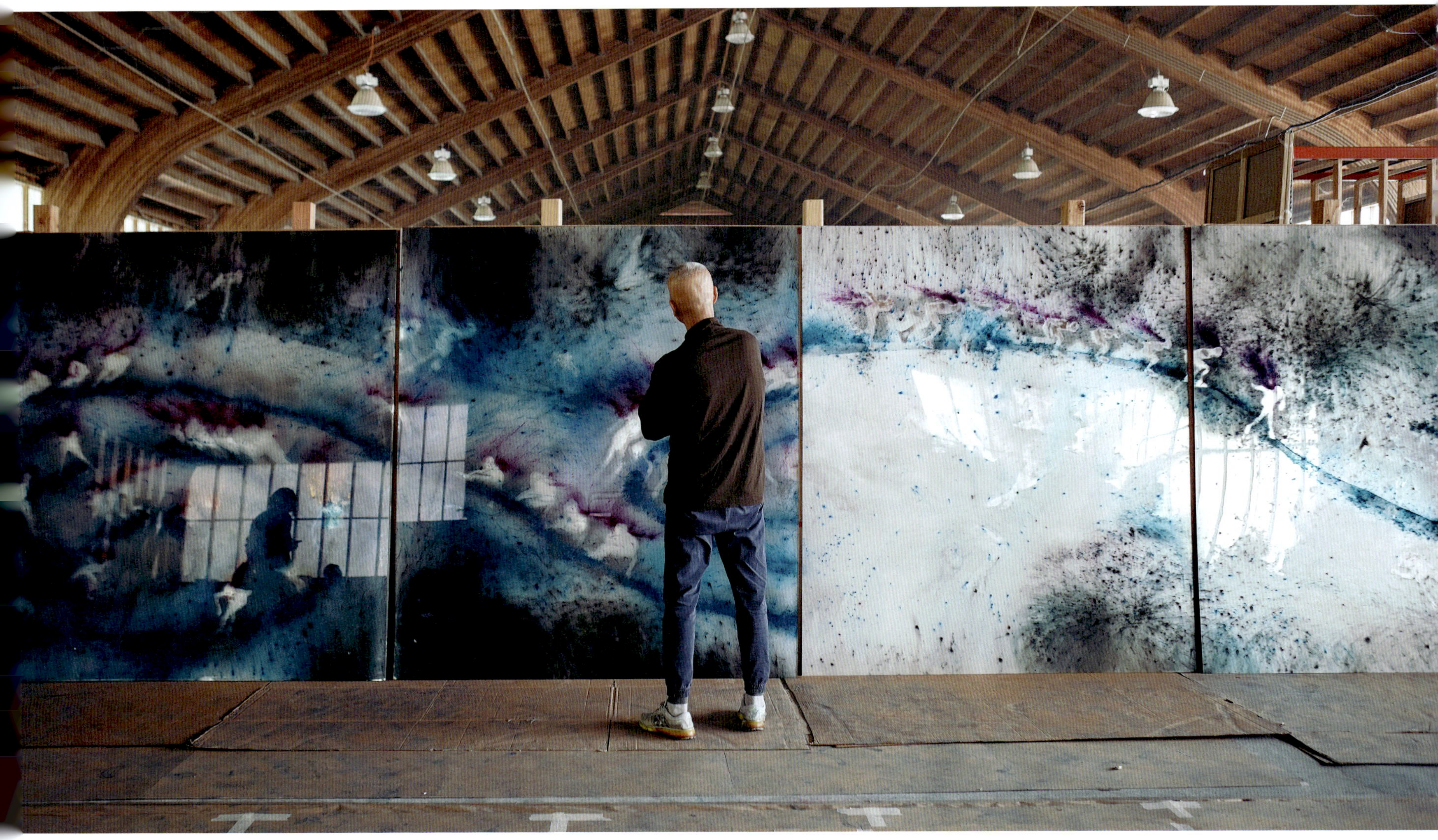

Figure 11.3q. Cai Guo-Qiang inspects the result as the exploded sheets of glass and mirror are being combined

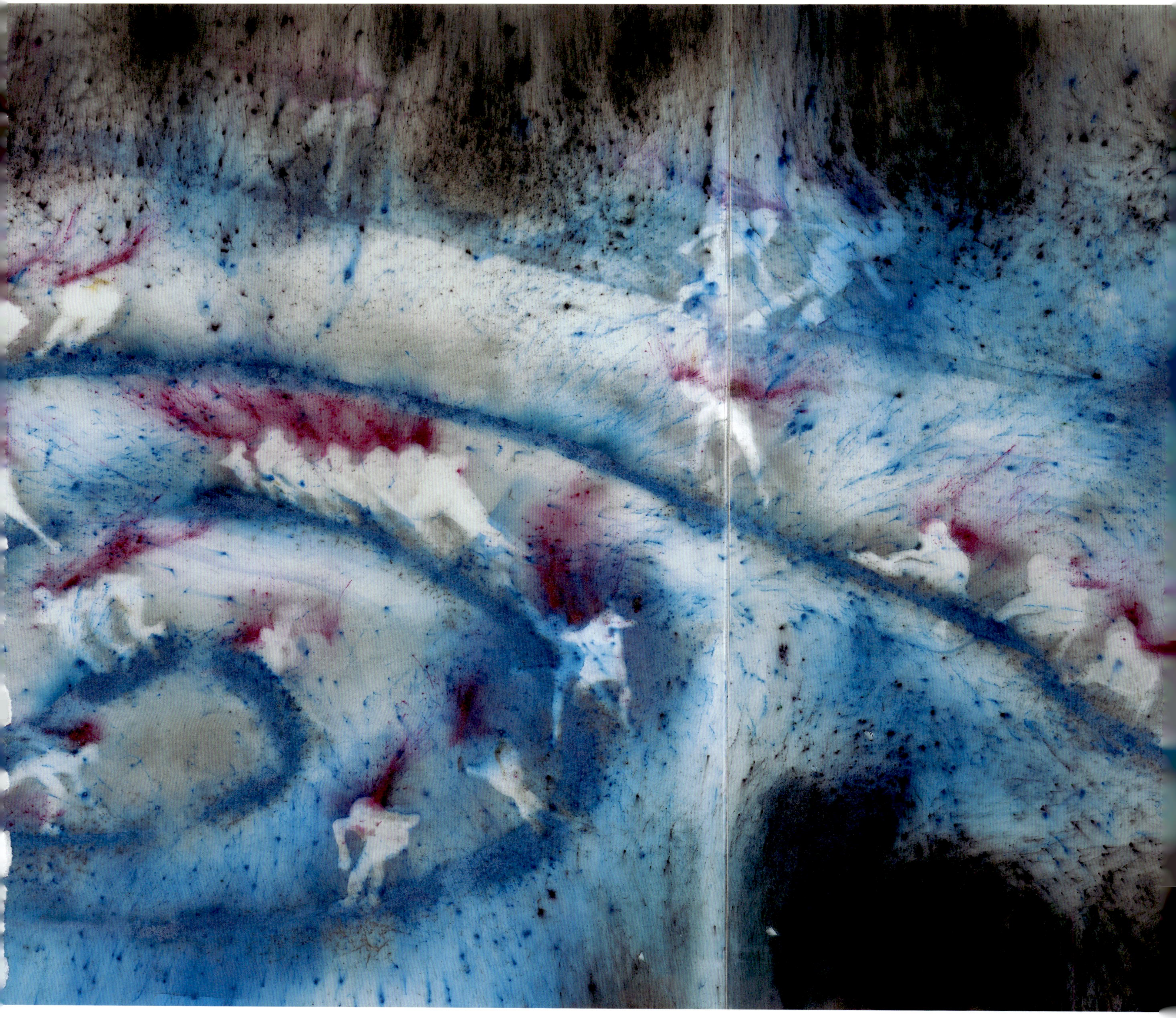

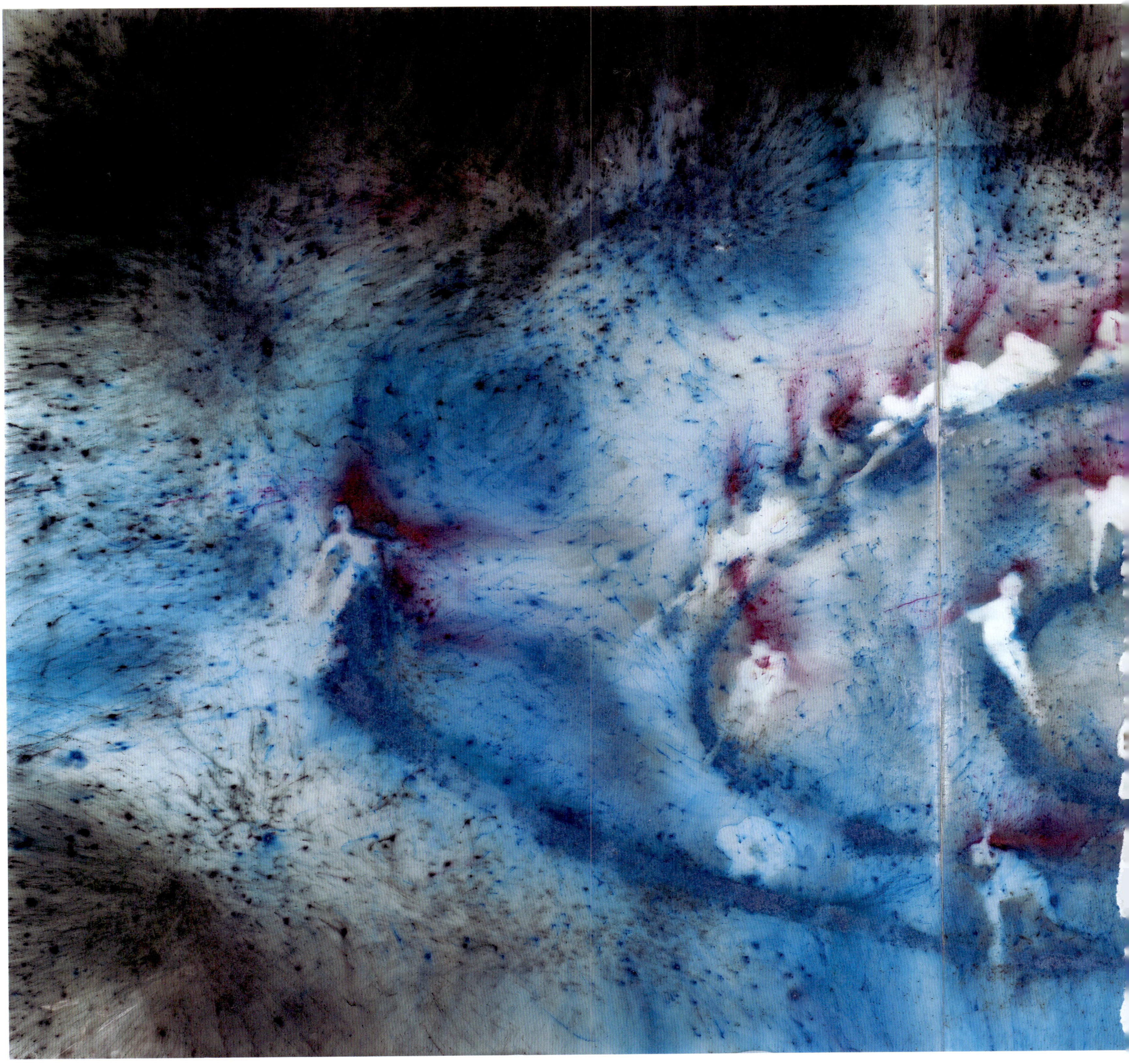

11.5 *Frolicking on Ice in the Galaxy*

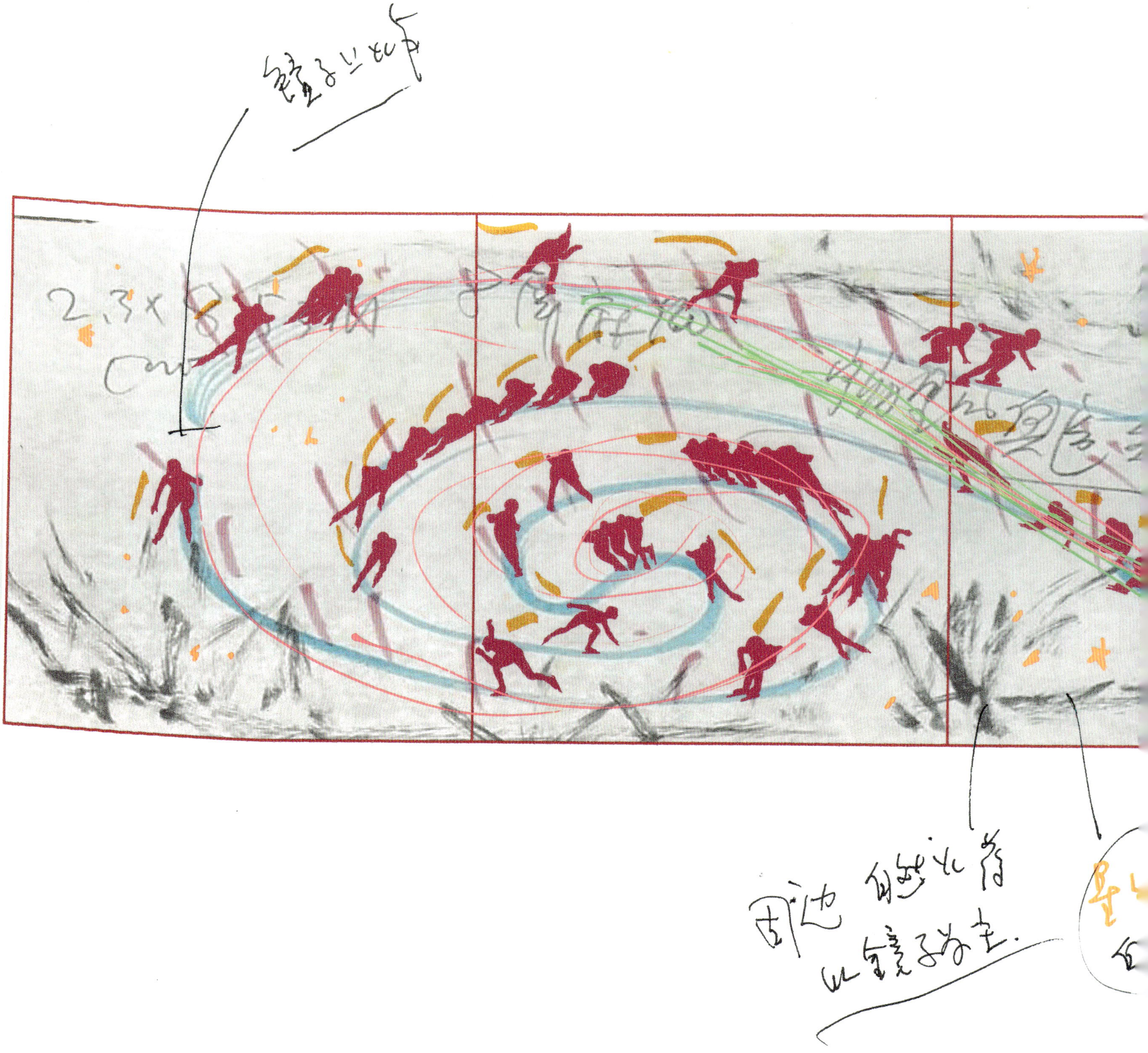

Figure 11.4. *Sketch for Frolicking on Ice in the Galaxy*, 2020. Pencil on printed paper, 28 × 43 cm

“嬉冰”

205 X 915 CM.

正

蓝线 镜子上绘.
及人

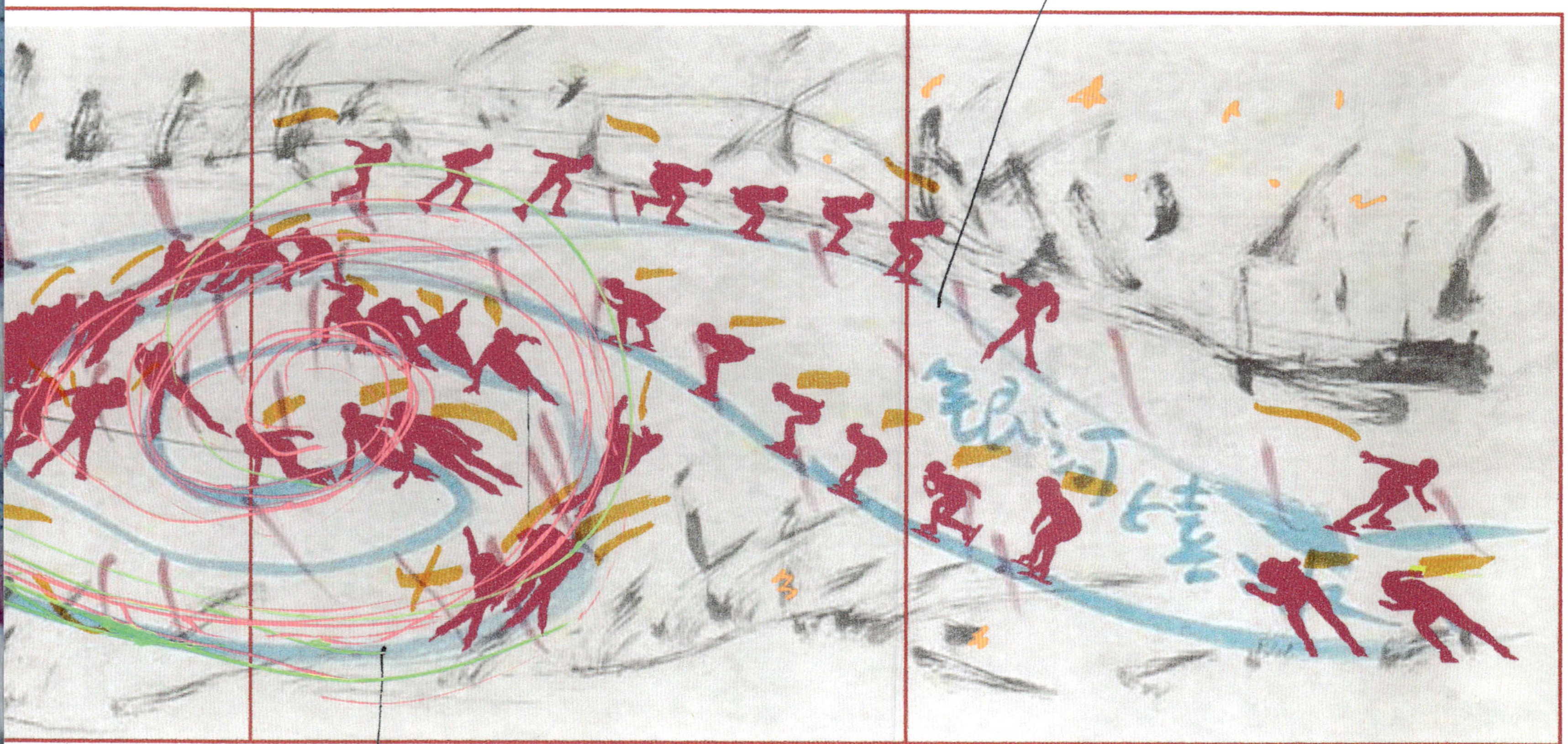

蓝线及人 玻璃上绘.

H 44CM — 50CM

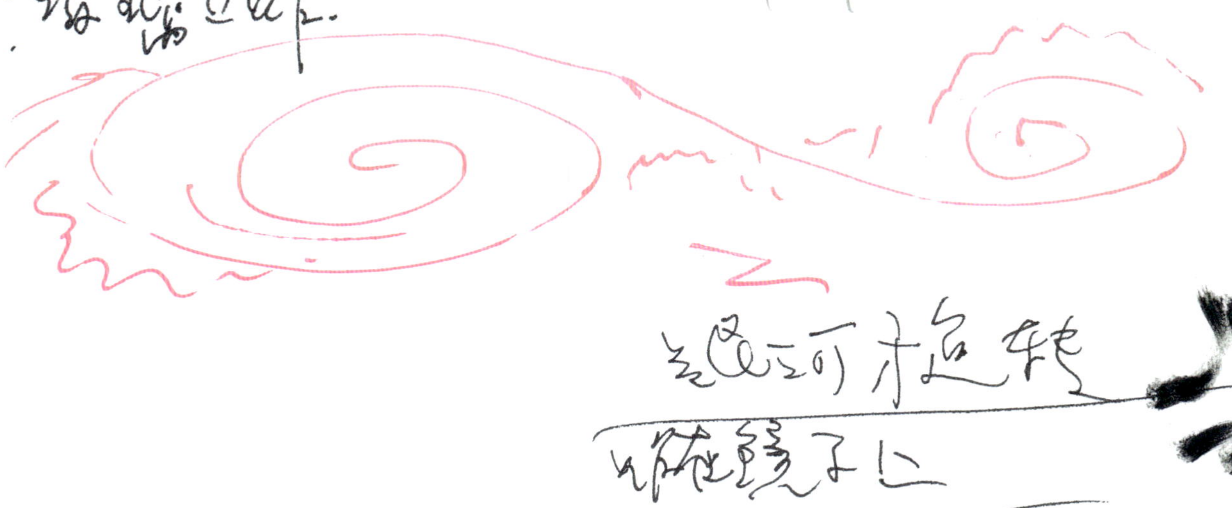

银河旋转

绘镜子上

# Exhibition

*Odyssey and Homecoming*
The Palace Museum, Beijing, China
December 15, 2020–February 28, 2021

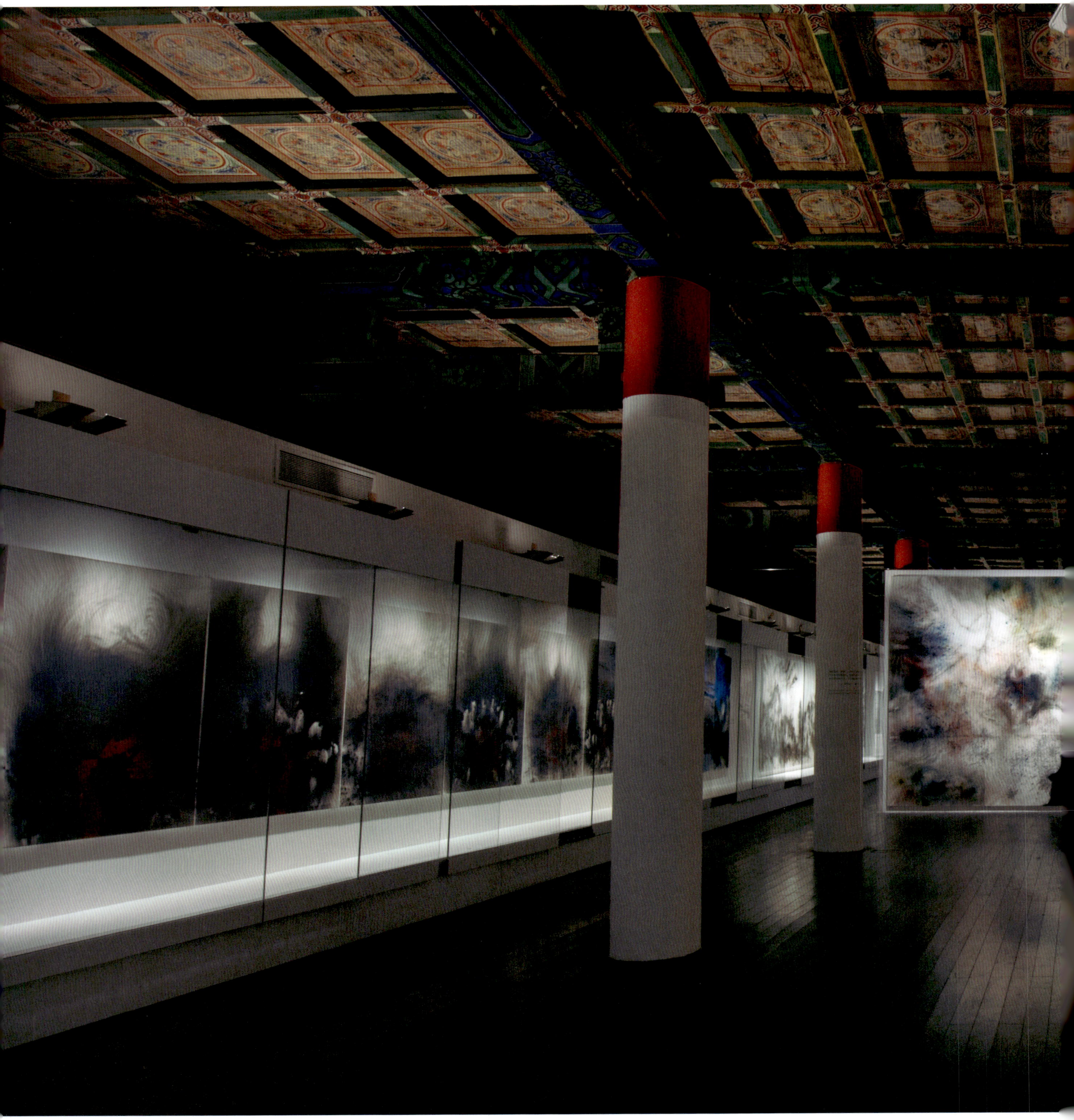

Figure E1. Exhibition view of West Wing Gallery, showing works from Cai Guo-Qiang's Dialogue with Baroque Art and the Spanish Golden Age.
Left to right: nos. 1.10, 1.26, 1.6, and 1.5

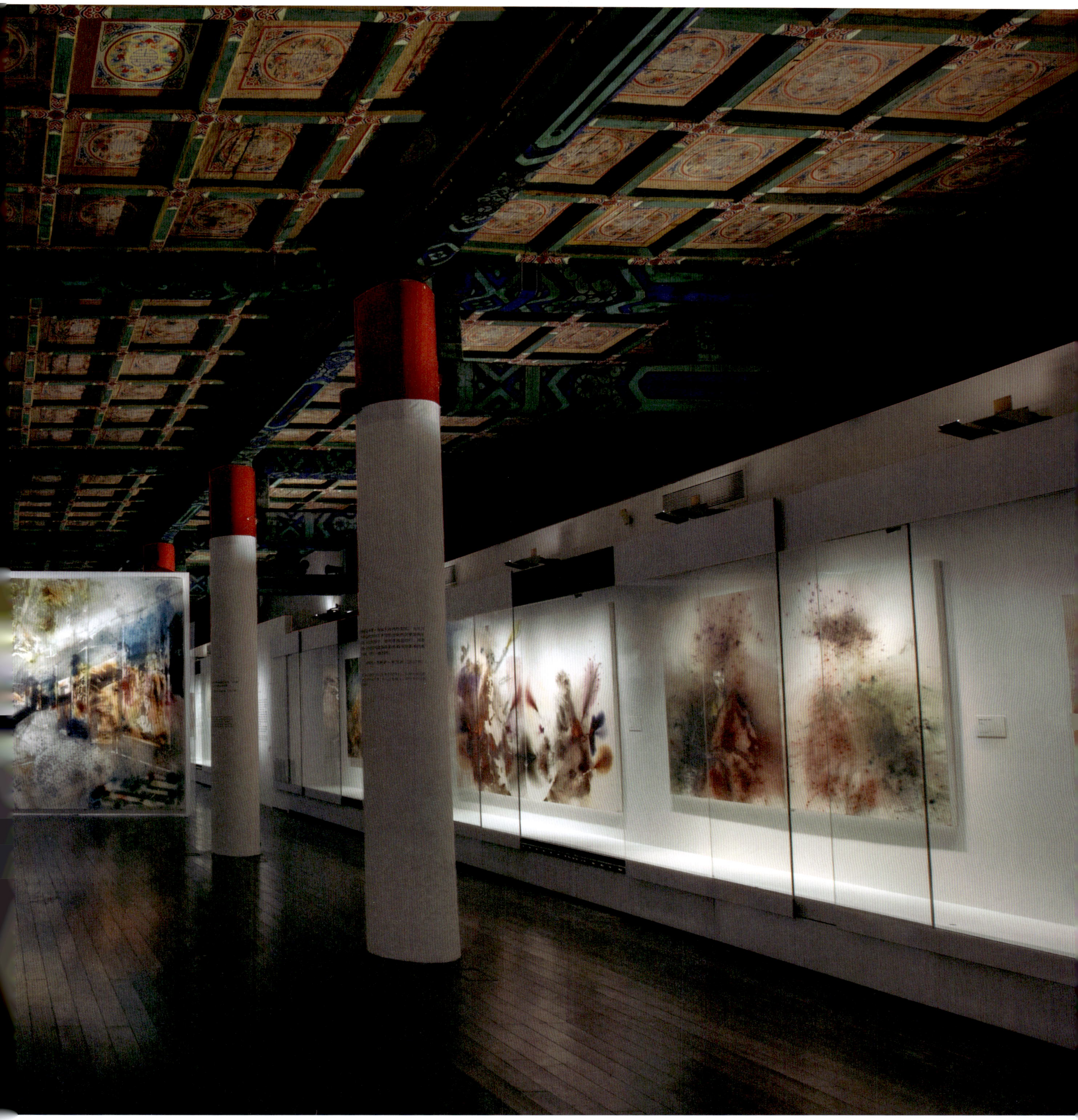

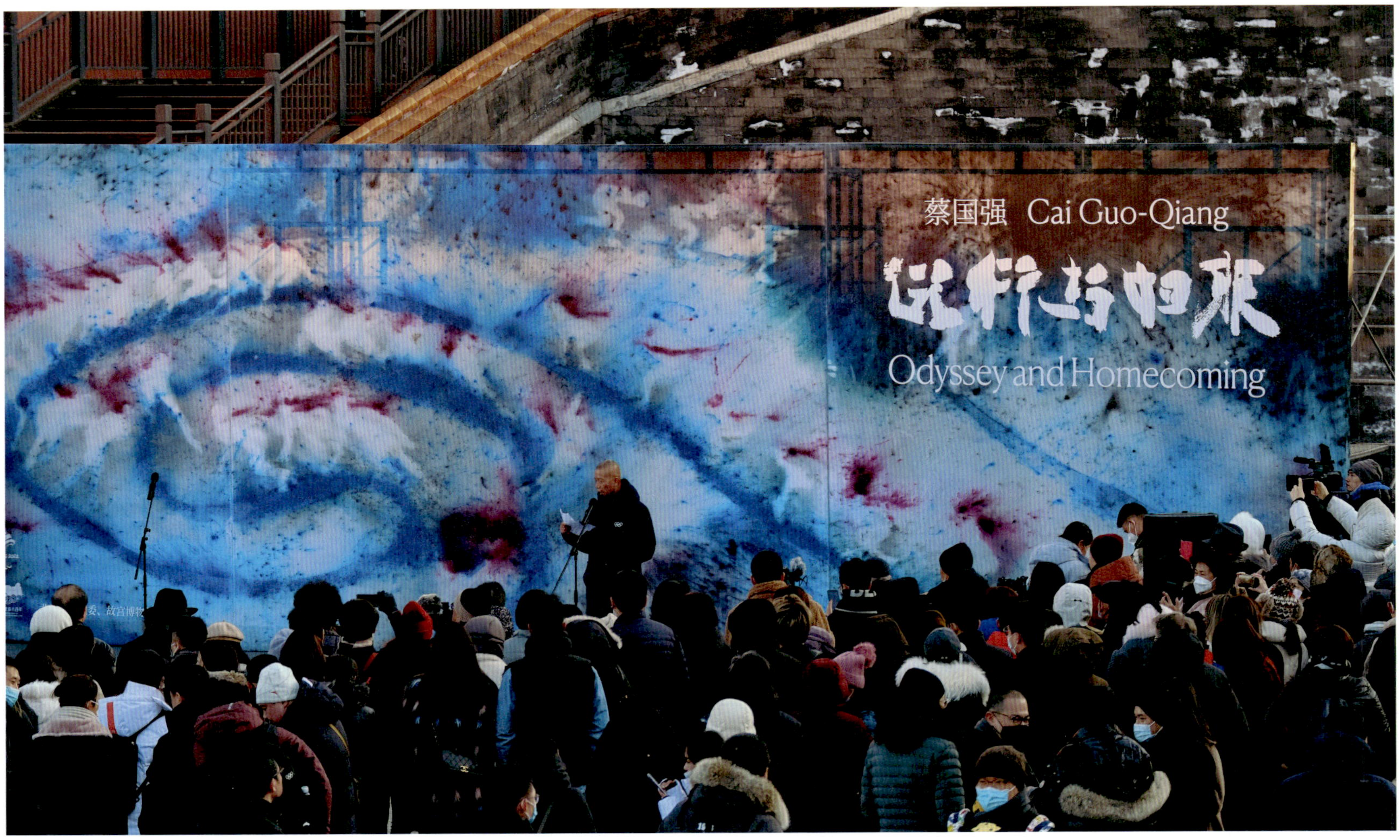


Figure E2. Cai Guo-Qiang speaking at the exhibition opening

Figure E4. Exhibition billboard overlooking the Palace Museum, Beijing

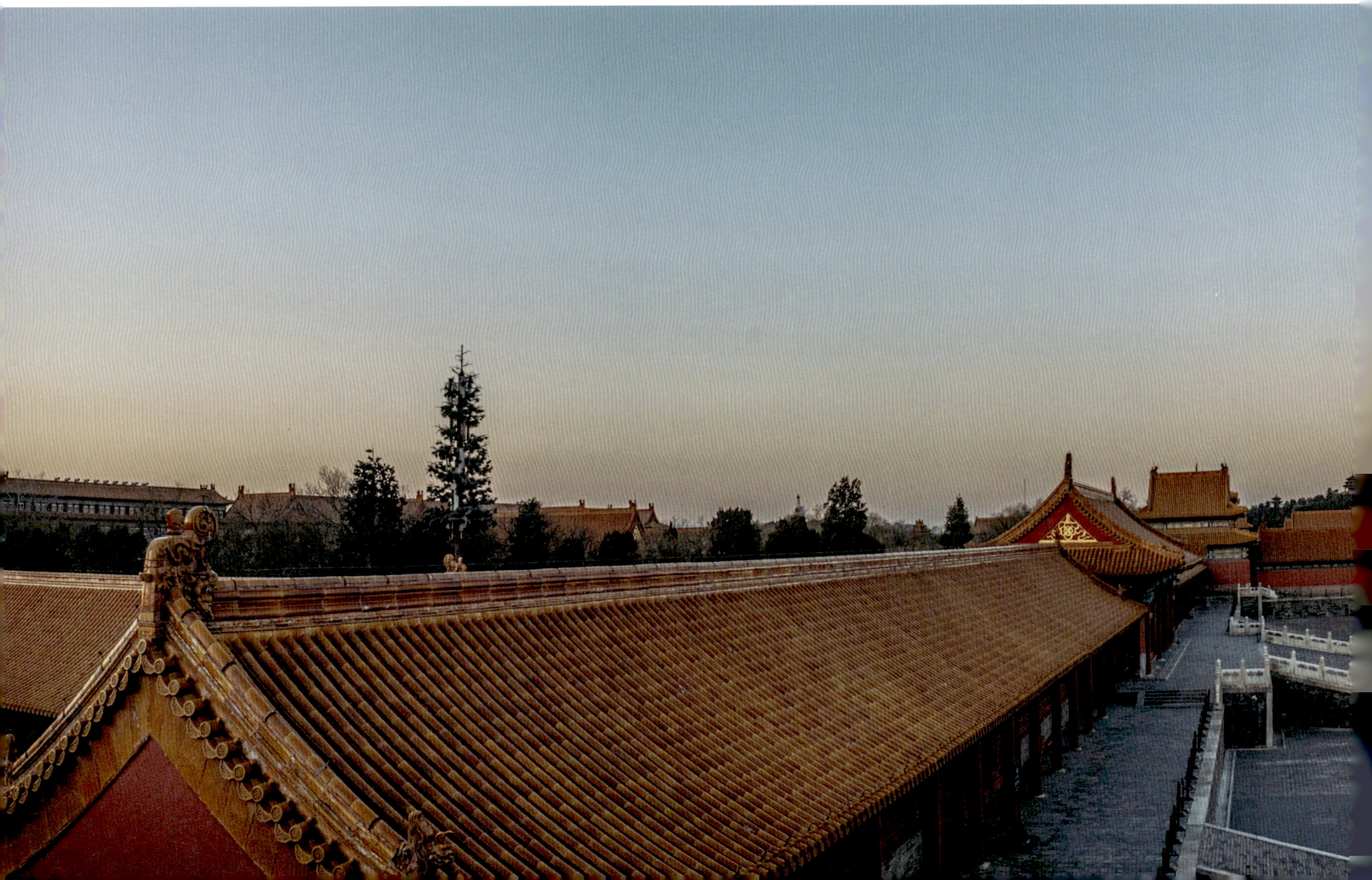

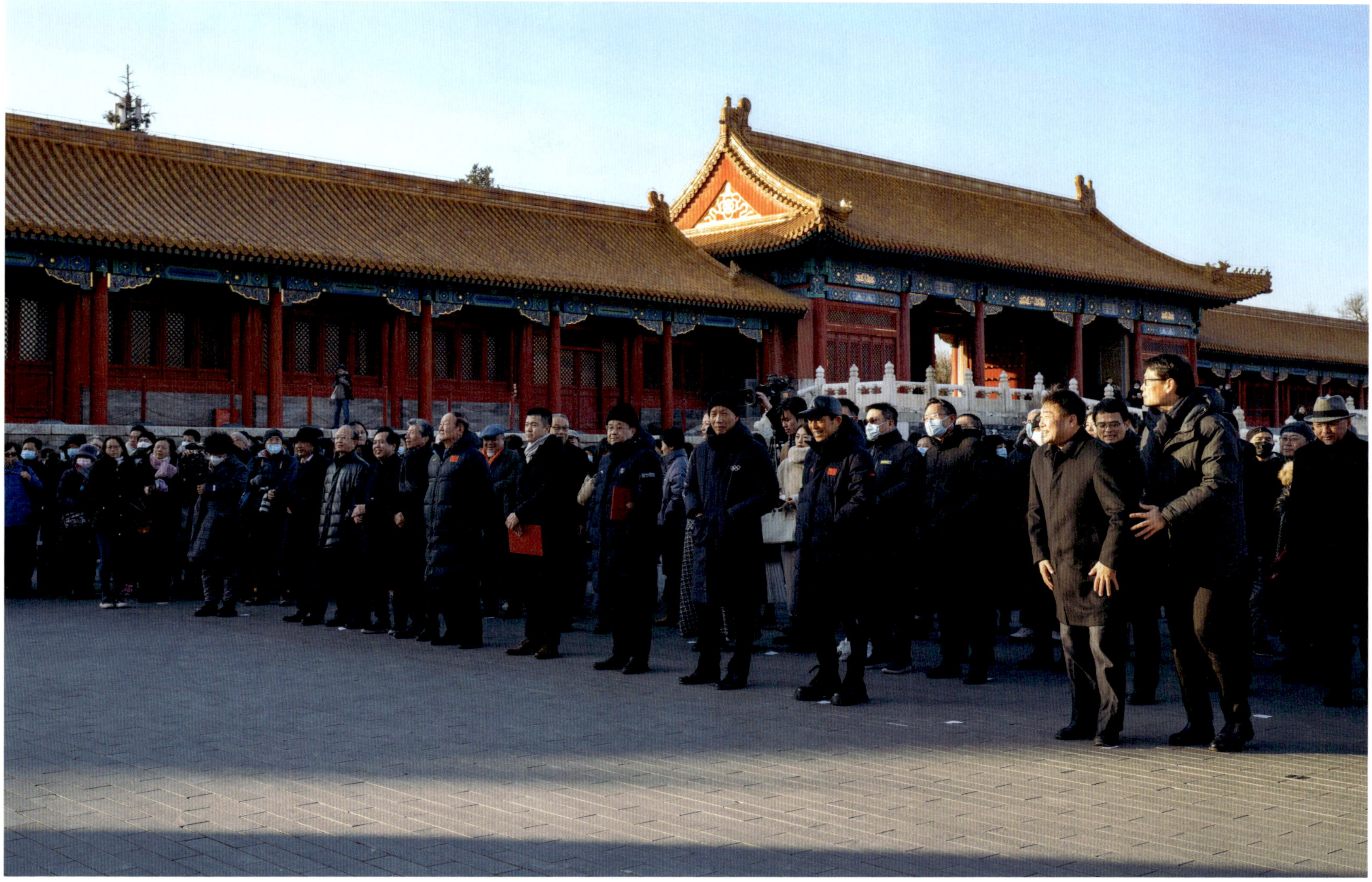

Figure E3. Cai Guo-Qiang and special guests at the exhibition opening

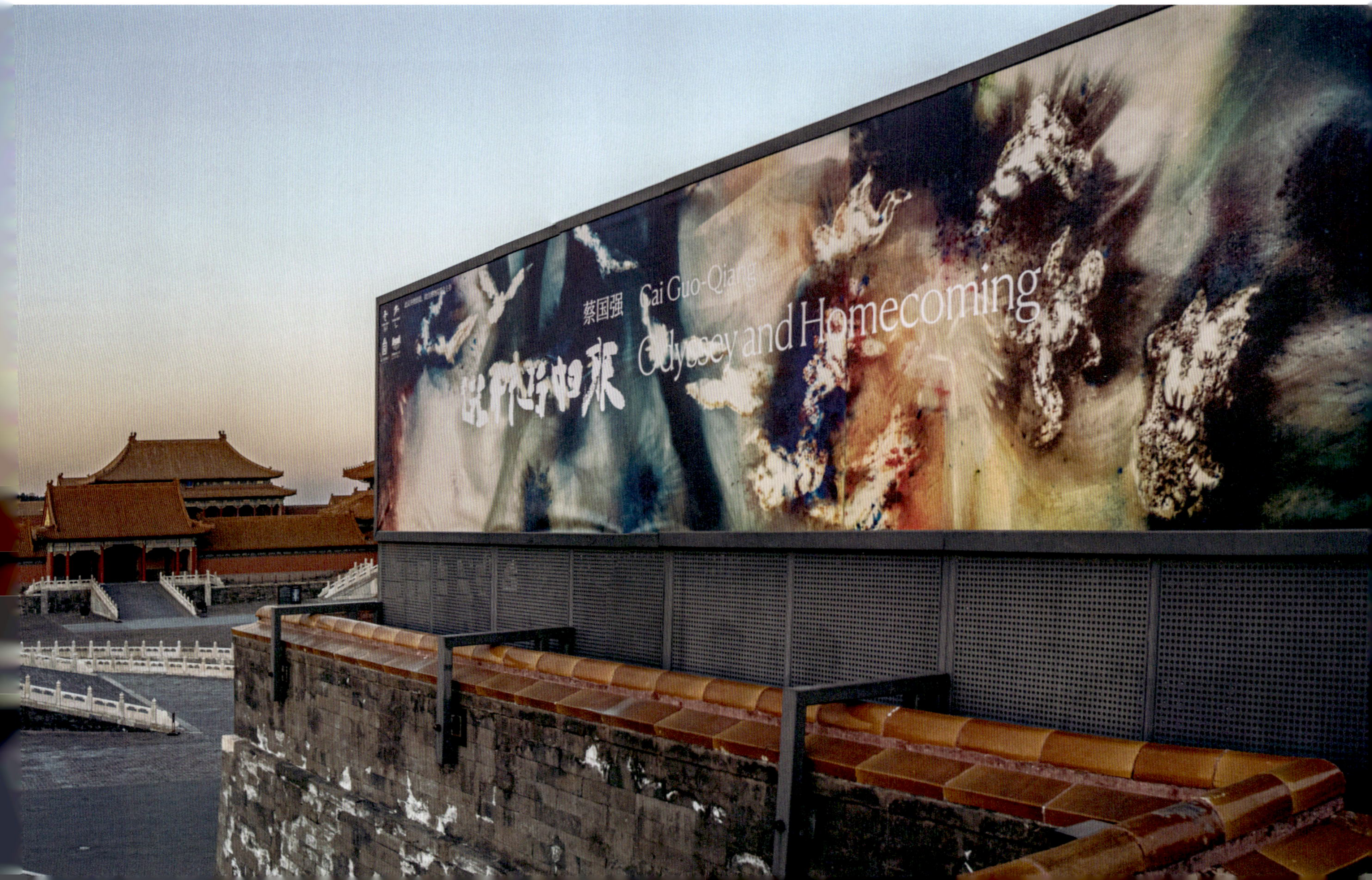

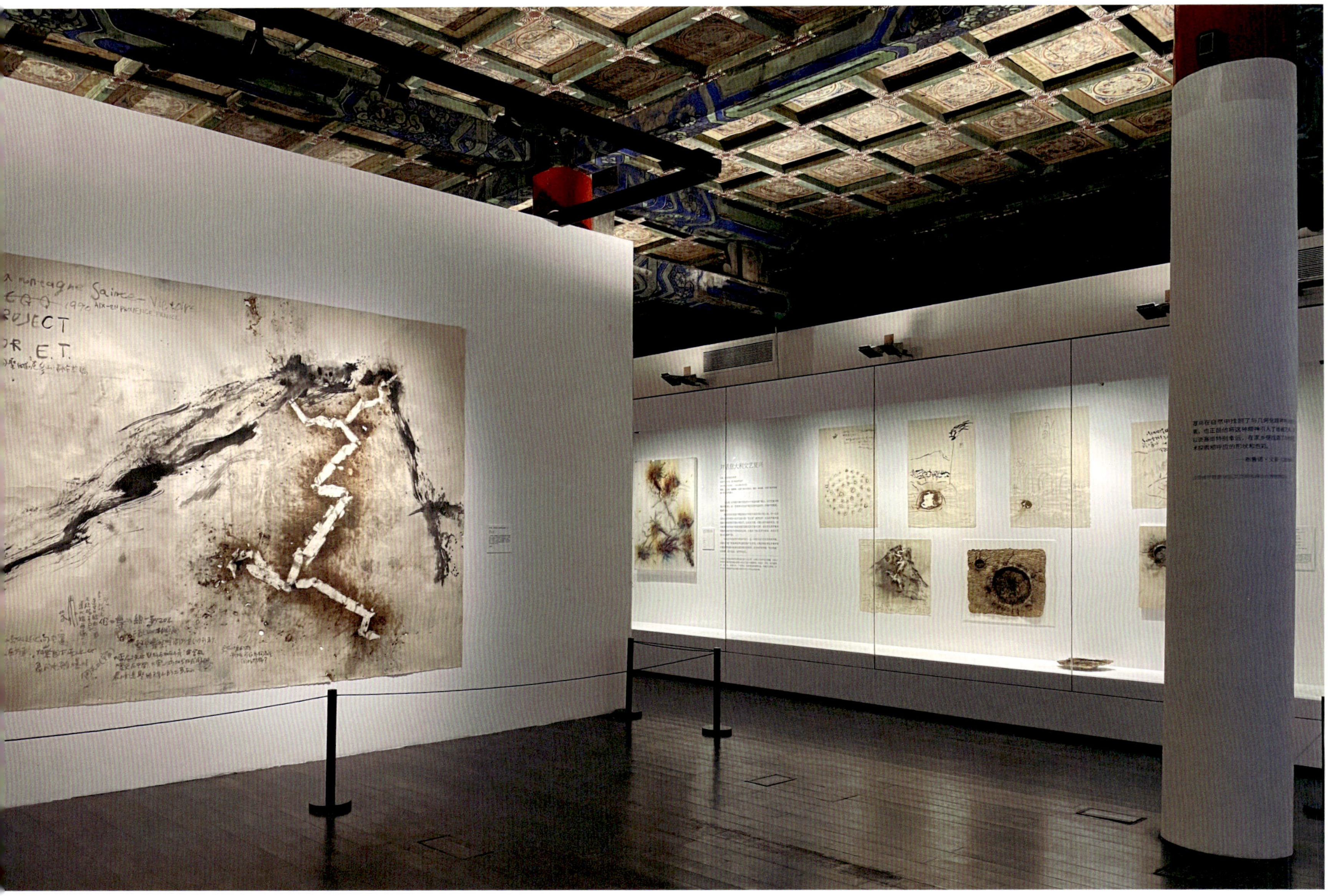

Figure E5. Exhibition view of West Wing Gallery, showing works from Cai Guo-Qiang's Dialogue with Cézanne and Dialogue with the Italian Renaissance. Left to right: nos. 6.1, 2.7, 6.6, 6.4, 6.5, 6.2, and 6.7

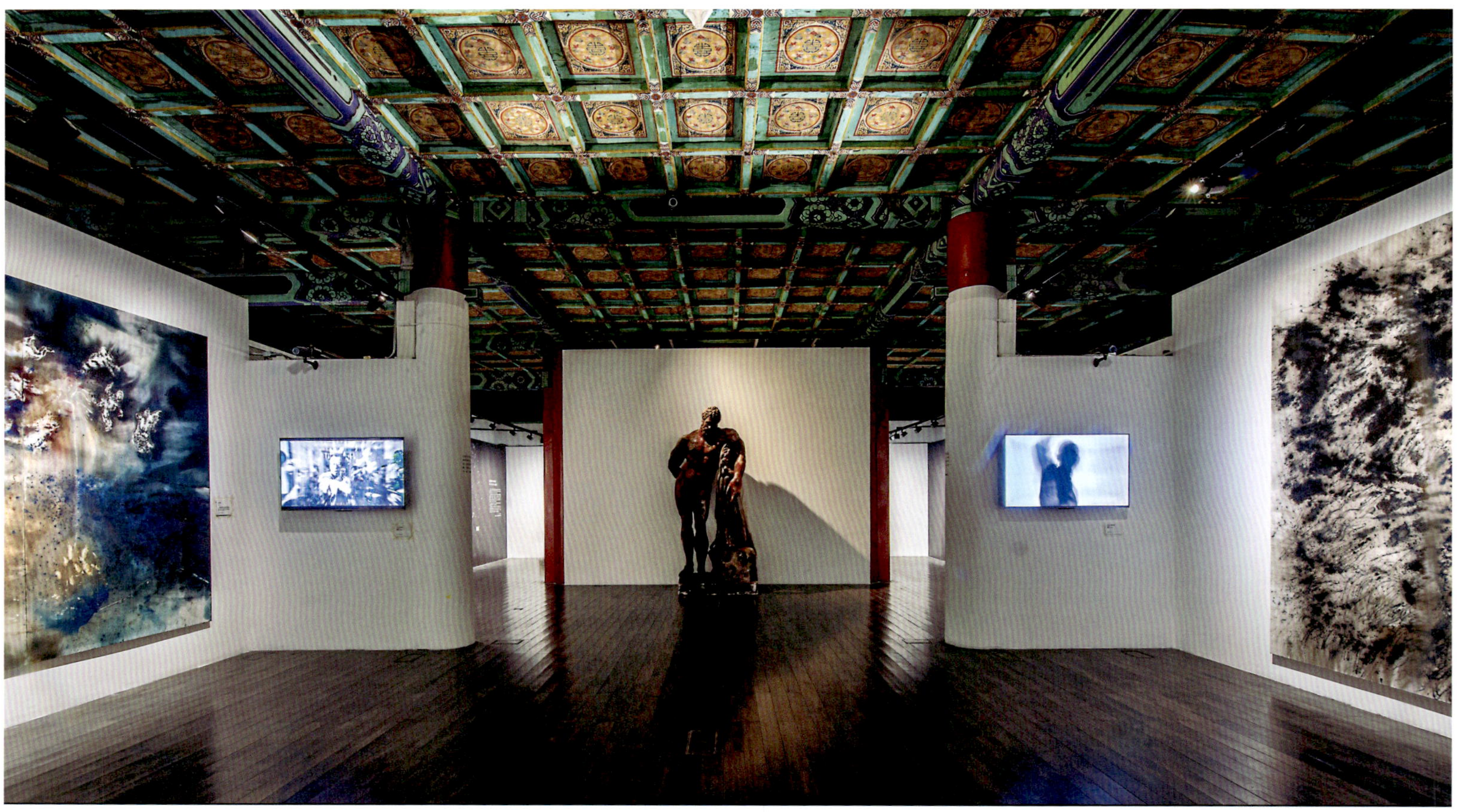

Figure E6. Exhibition view of East Wing Gallery. Left to right: nos. 1.7, 3.2, and 3.6

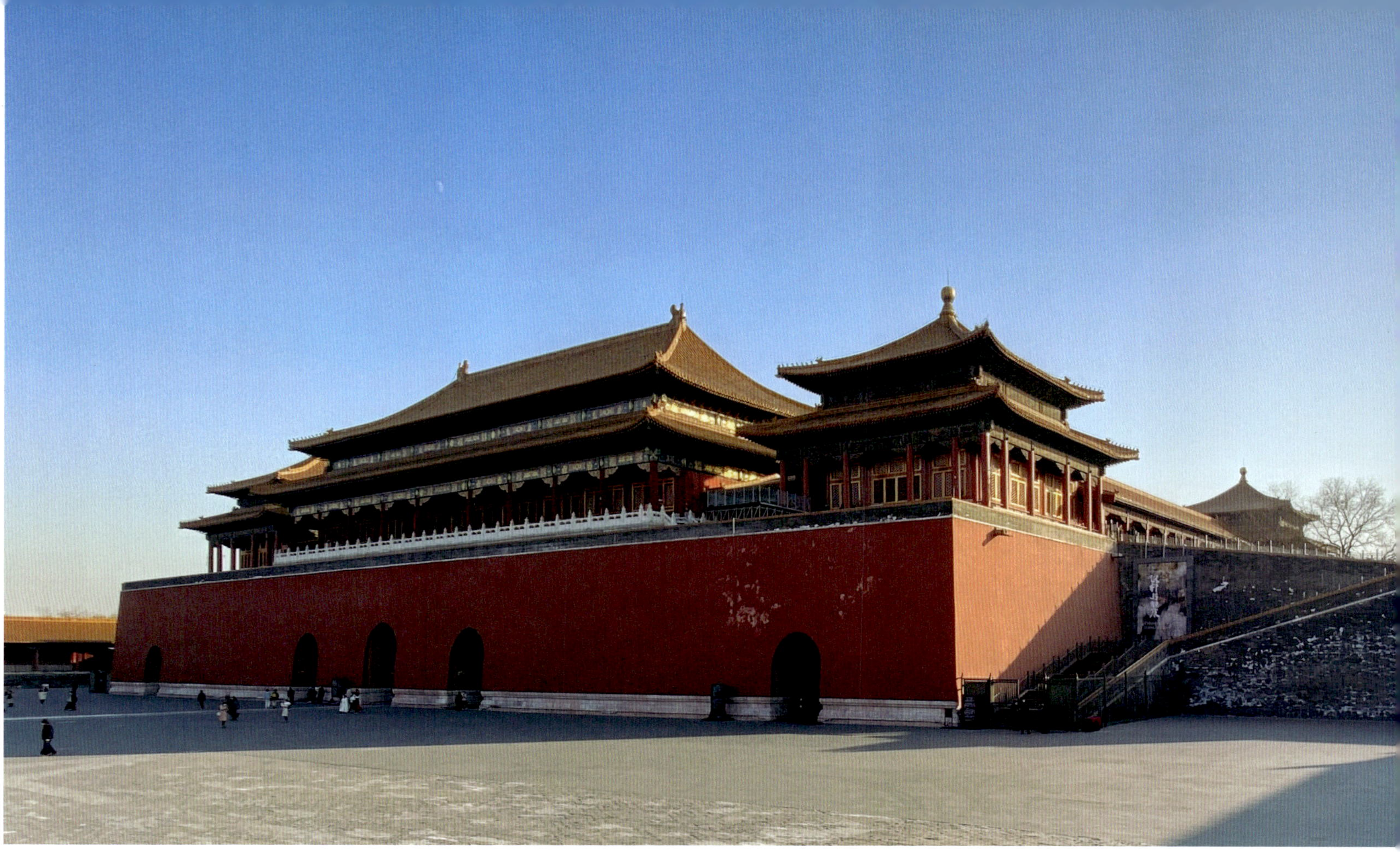

Figure E7. Meridian Gate galleries of the Palace Museum, Beijing and exhibition poster

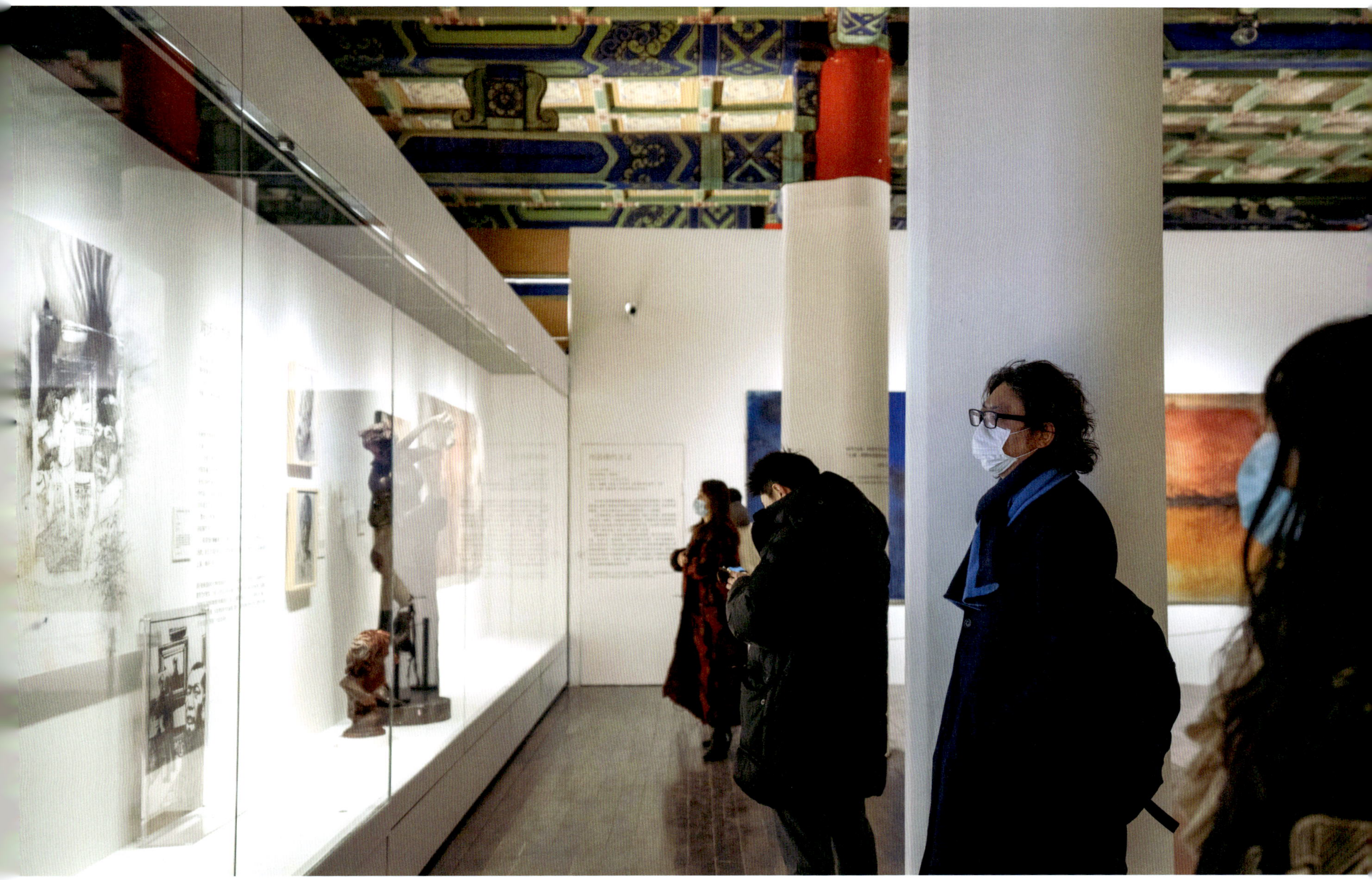

Figure E8. Exhibition view of West Wing Gallery

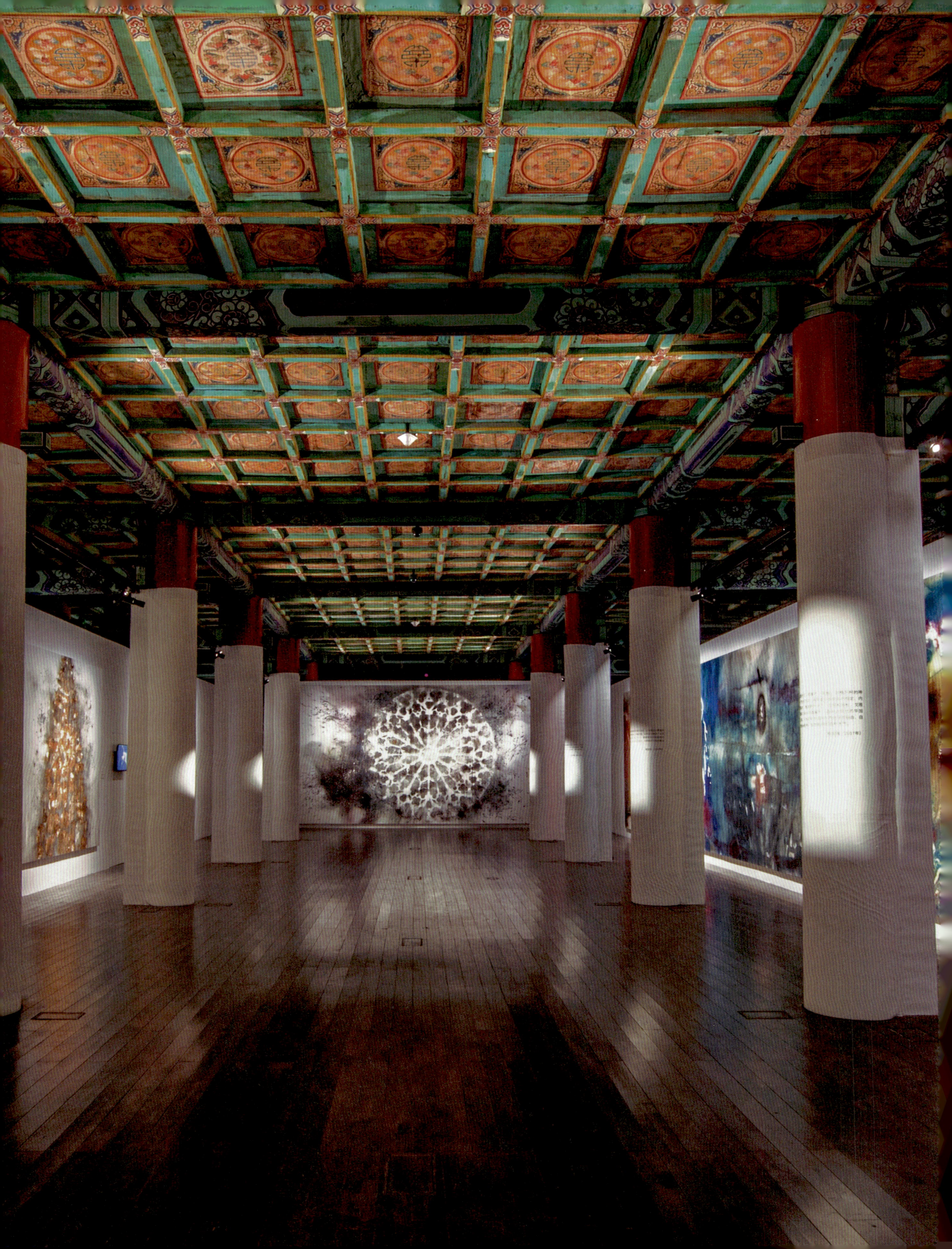

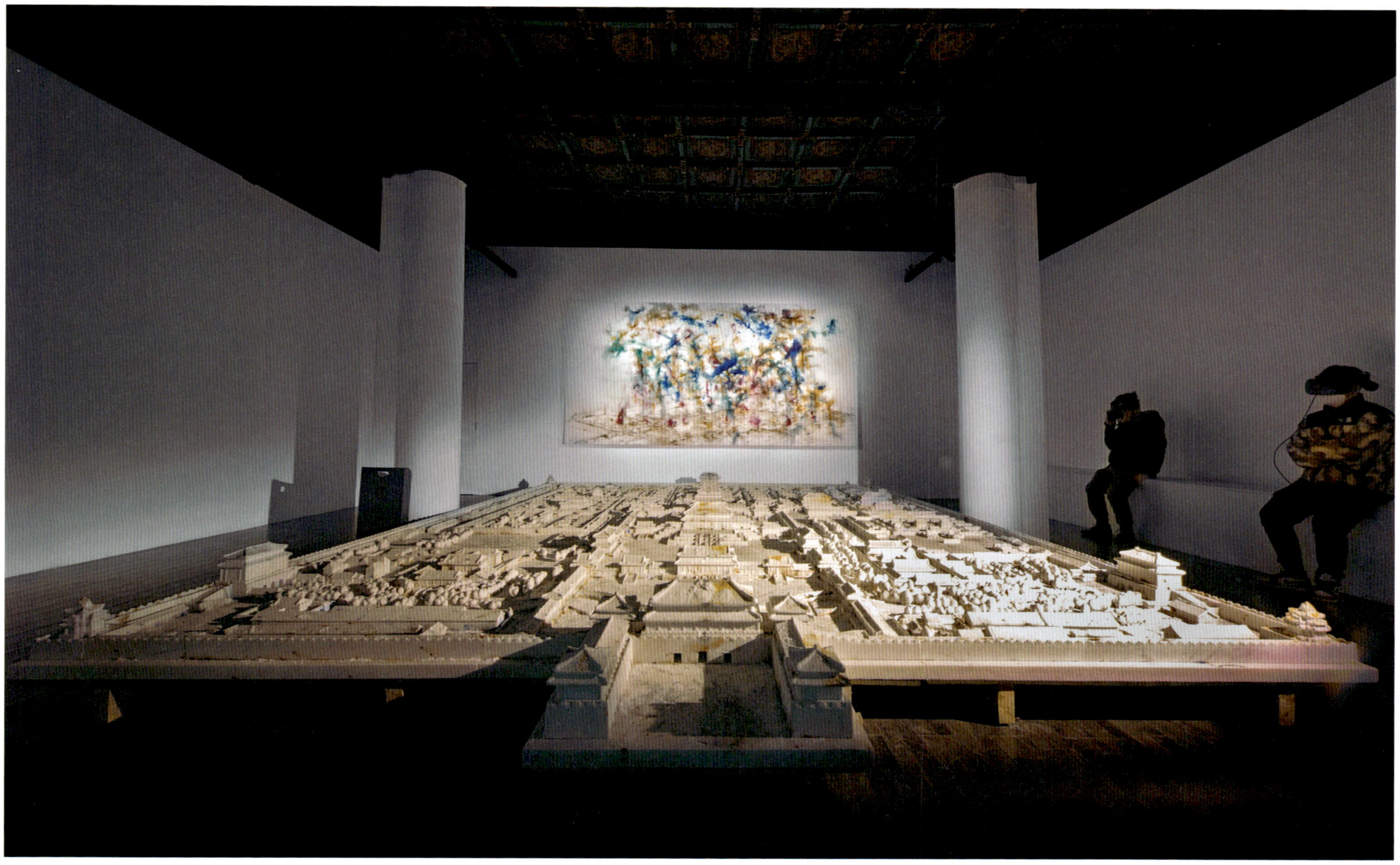

Figure E10. Trio of *Sleepwalking in the Forbidden City* works (nos. 10.1–3) in East Wing Gallery

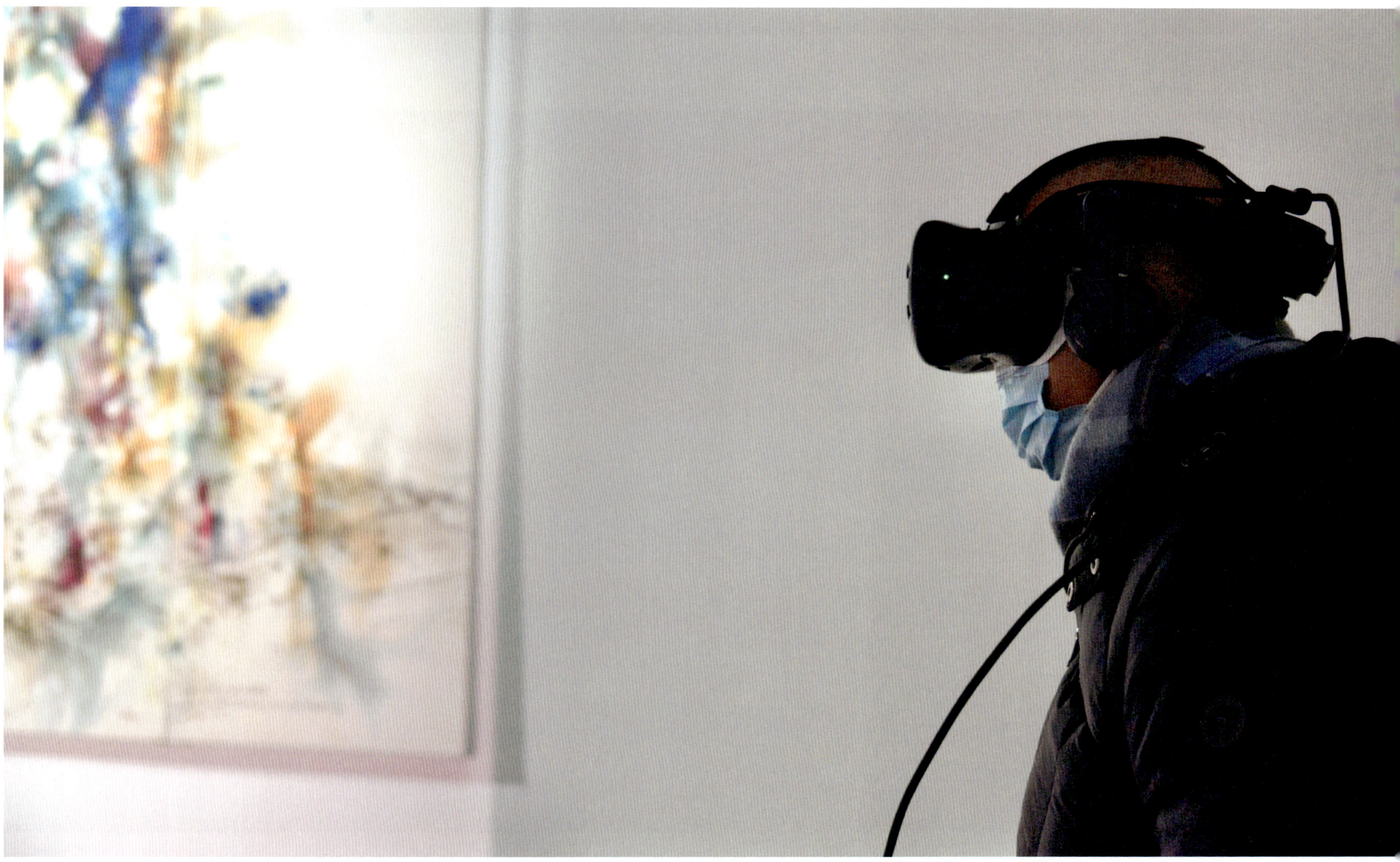

Figure E11. An exhibition visitor experiencing Cai Guo-Qiang's VR work *Sleepwalking in the Forbidden City* (no. 10.3) in 2020

Figure E9 (opposite). Exhibition view of East Wing Gallery, showing works from Cai Guo-Qiang's Dialogue with the Middle Ages and Dialogue with Baroque Art and the Spanish Golden Age. Left to right: nos. 7.3, 7.4, and 1.27

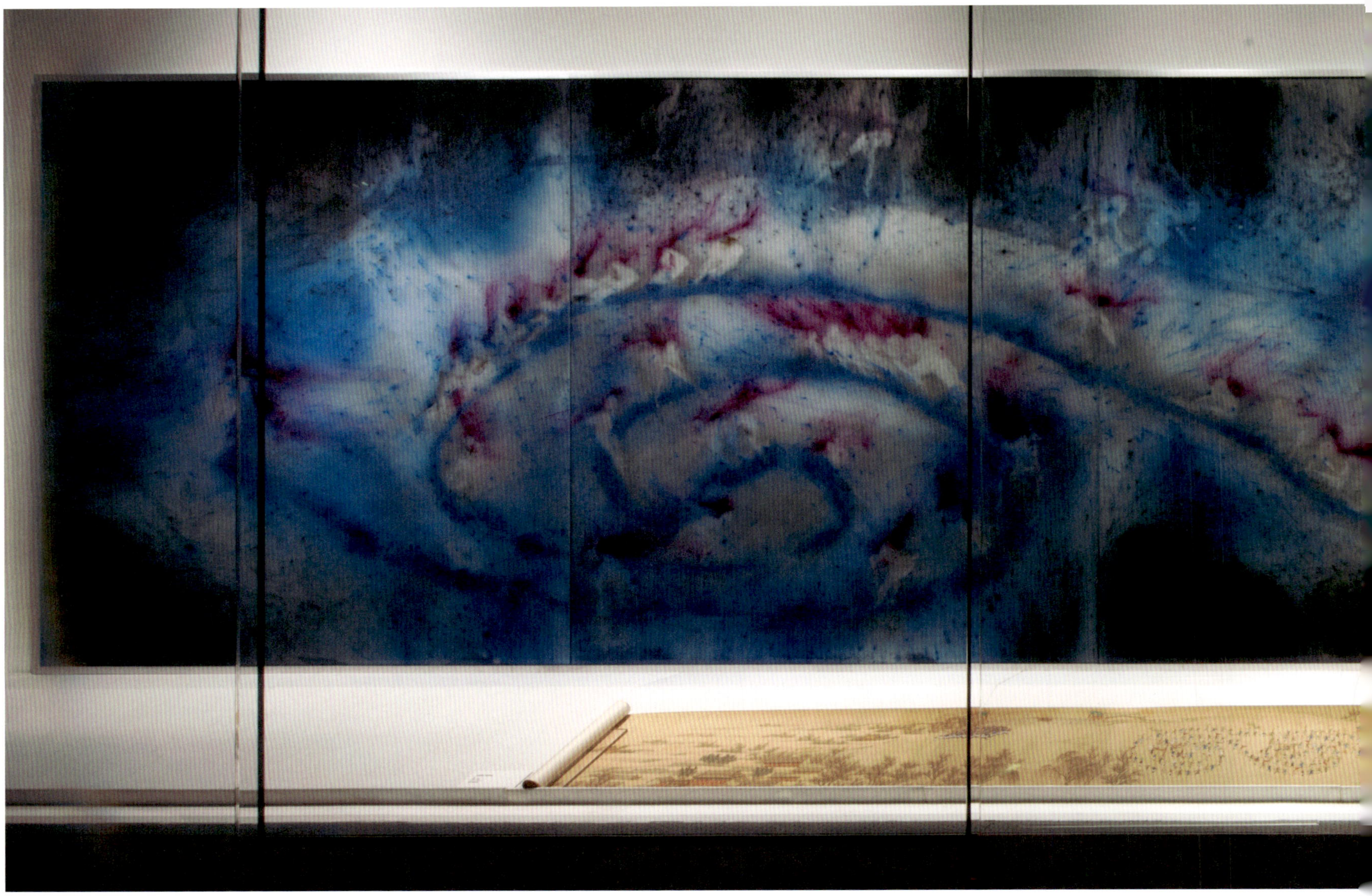

Figure E12. Installation view of no. 11.5 (above) and no. 11.6 (below) from Cai Guo-Qiang's Dialogue with the Cosmos in Central Tower Gallery

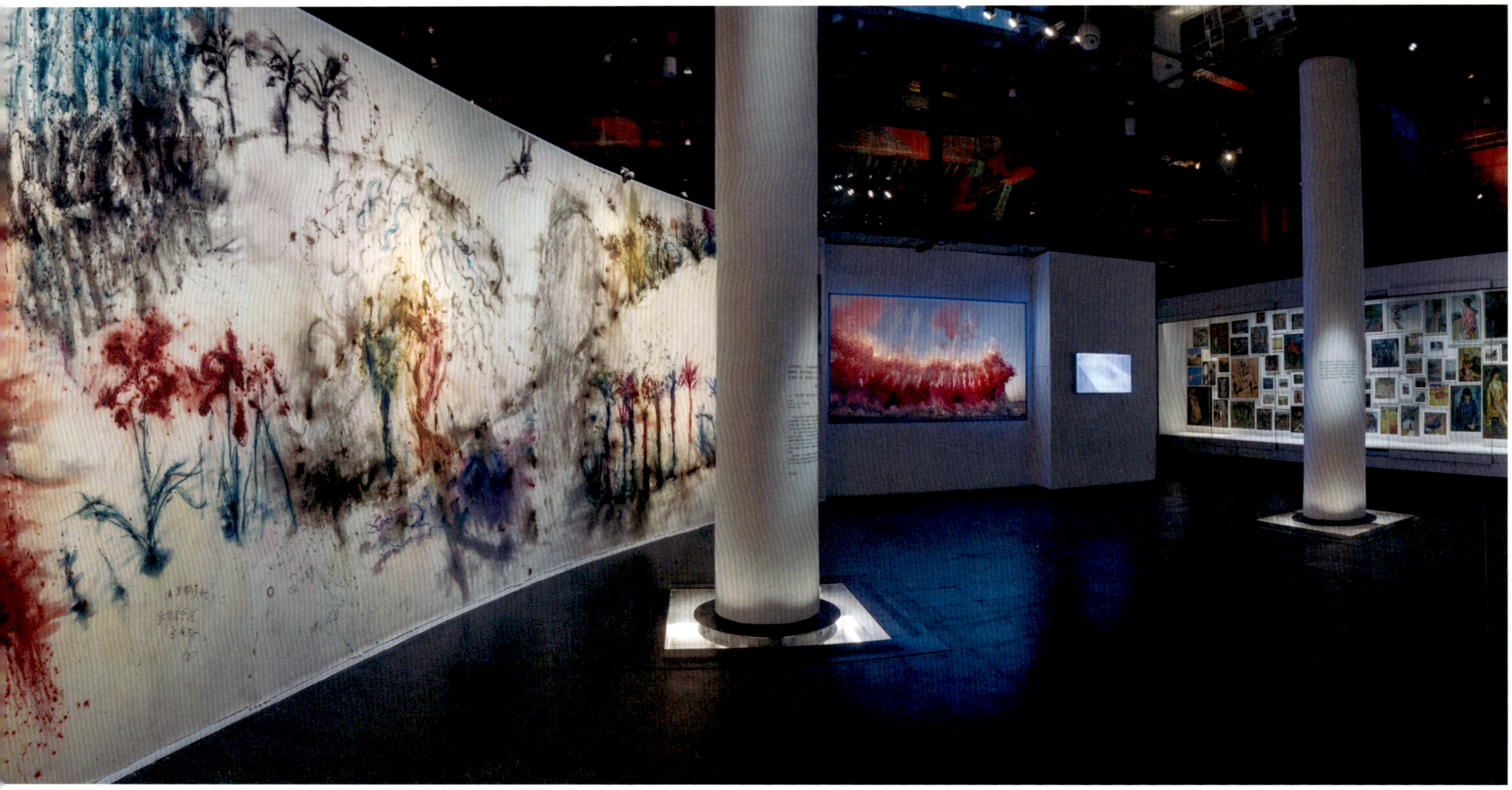

Figure E13. Exhibition view of Central Tower Gallery, showing works from Cai Guo-Qiang's Dialogue with the Italian Renaissance and Dialogue with My Original Passion for Painting. no. 2.23 (far left) and no. 8.1 (far right)

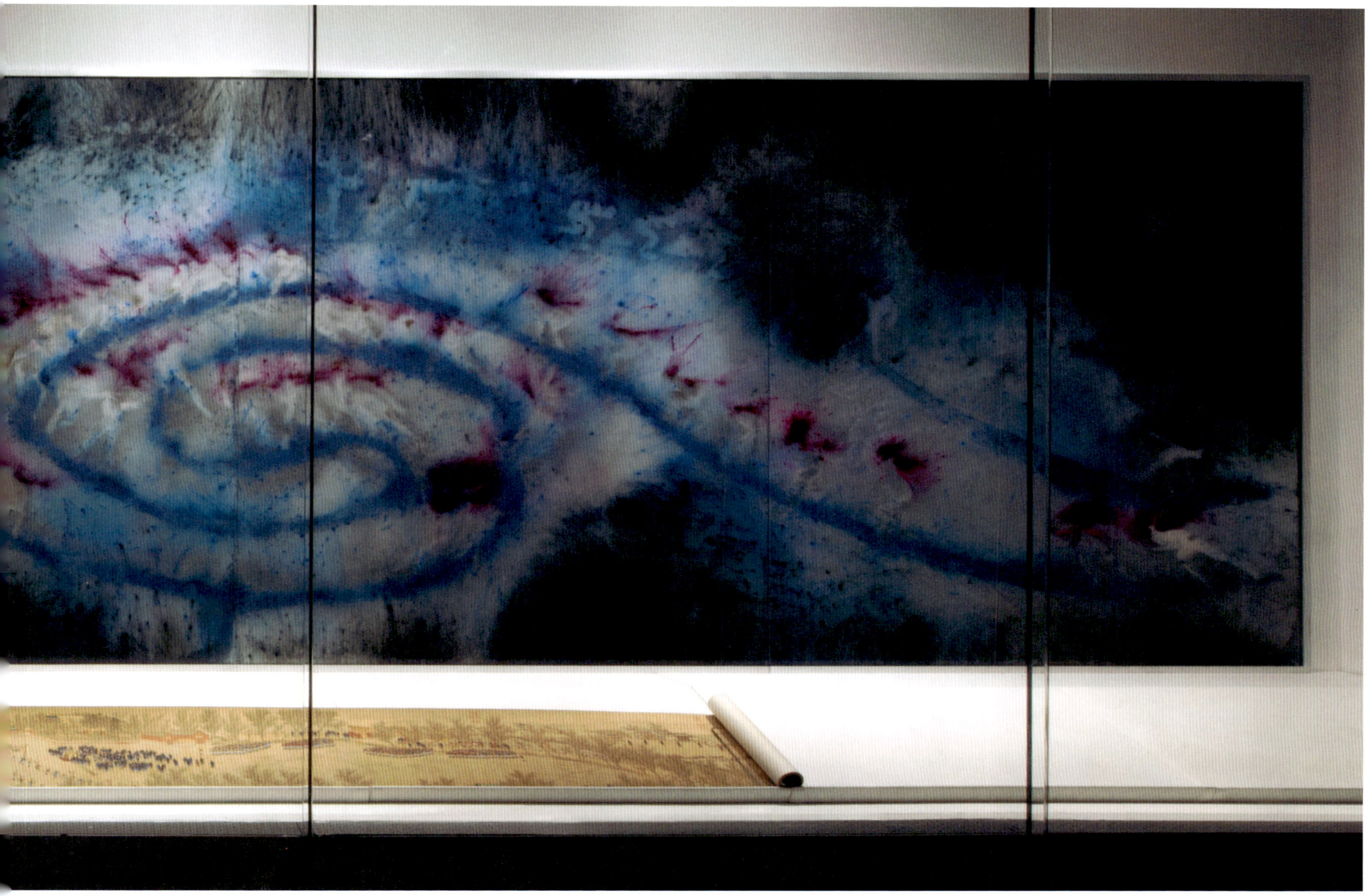

Figure E14. Installation view of no. 8.1 from Cai Guo-Qiang's Dialogue with My Original Passion for Painting

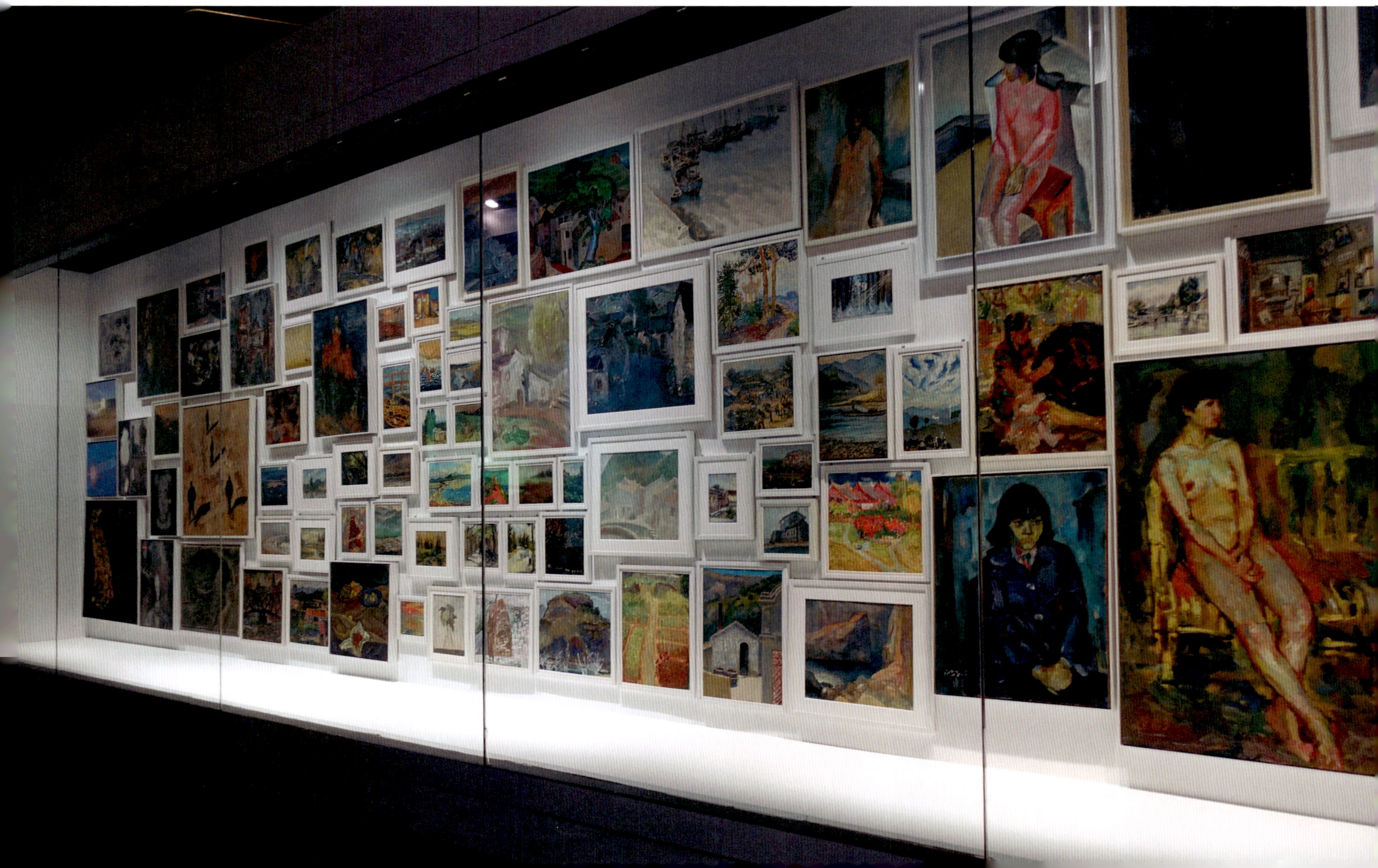

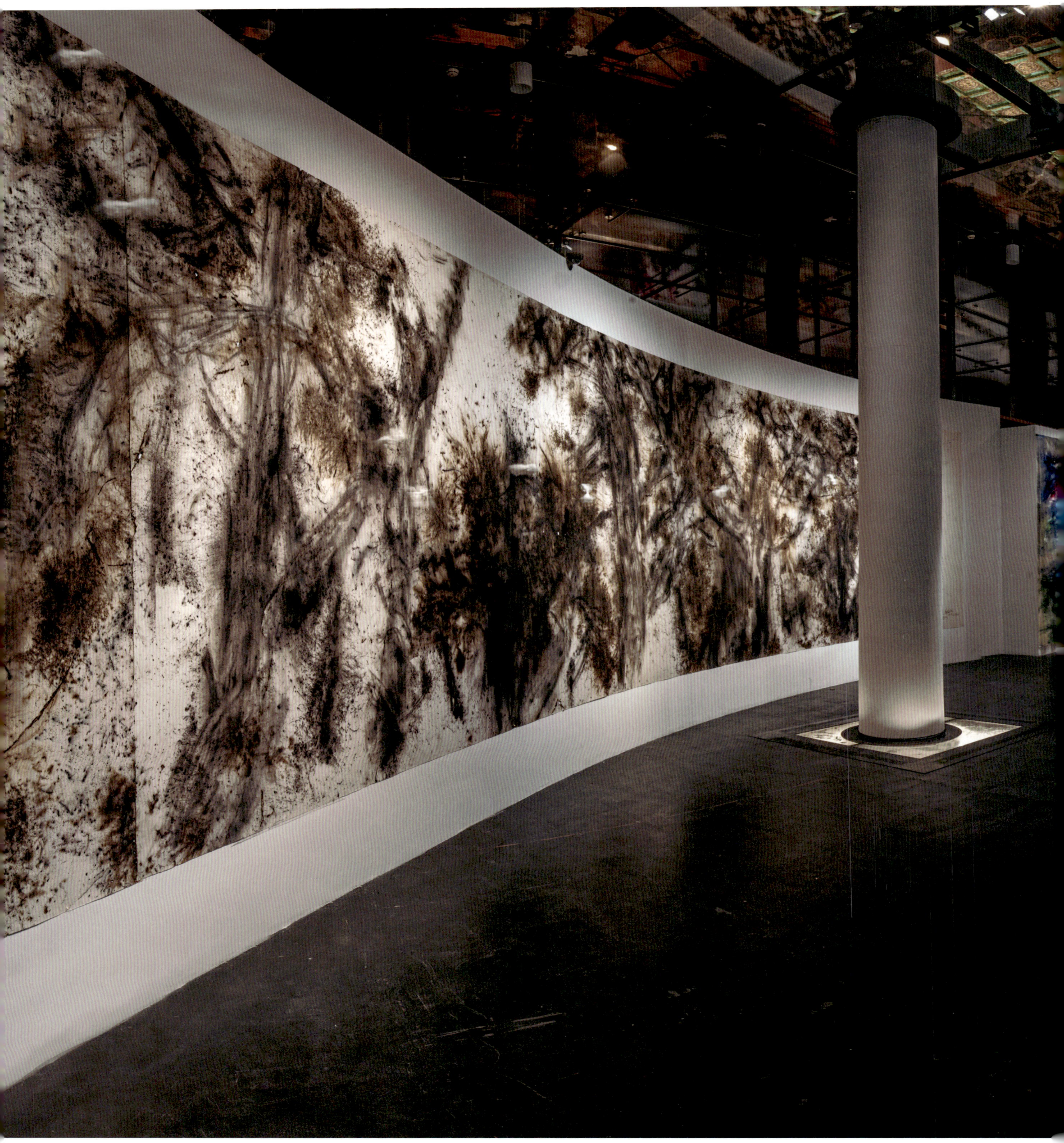

Figure E15. Exhibition view of Central Tower Gallery, showing works from Cai Guo-Qiang's Dialogue with Chinese Culture and Spirit and Dialogue with the Cosmos. Left to right: nos. 9.5, 9.4, and 11.5

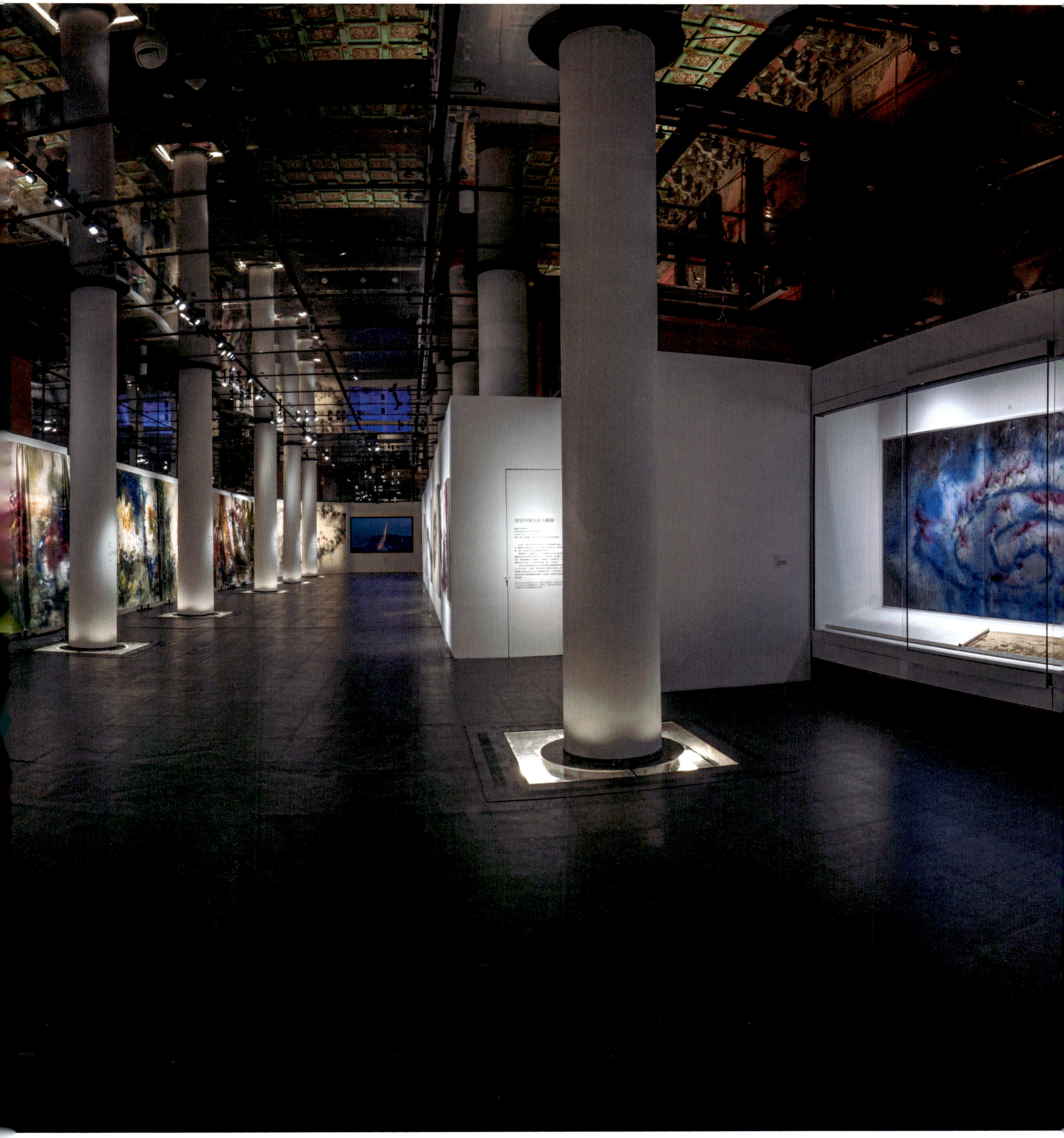

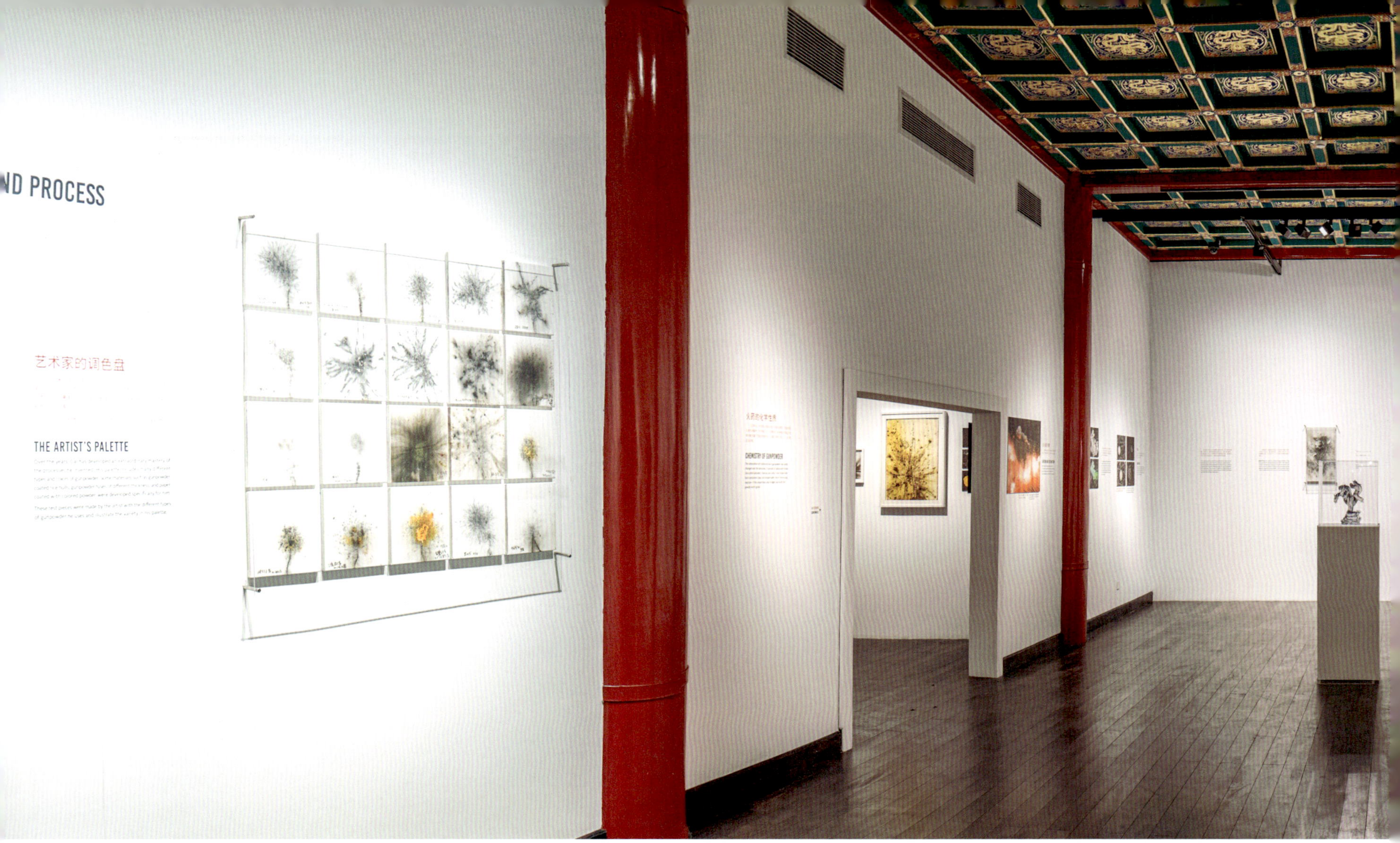


Figures E16a–c. Exhibition views of *A Material Odyssey* at the Palace Museum

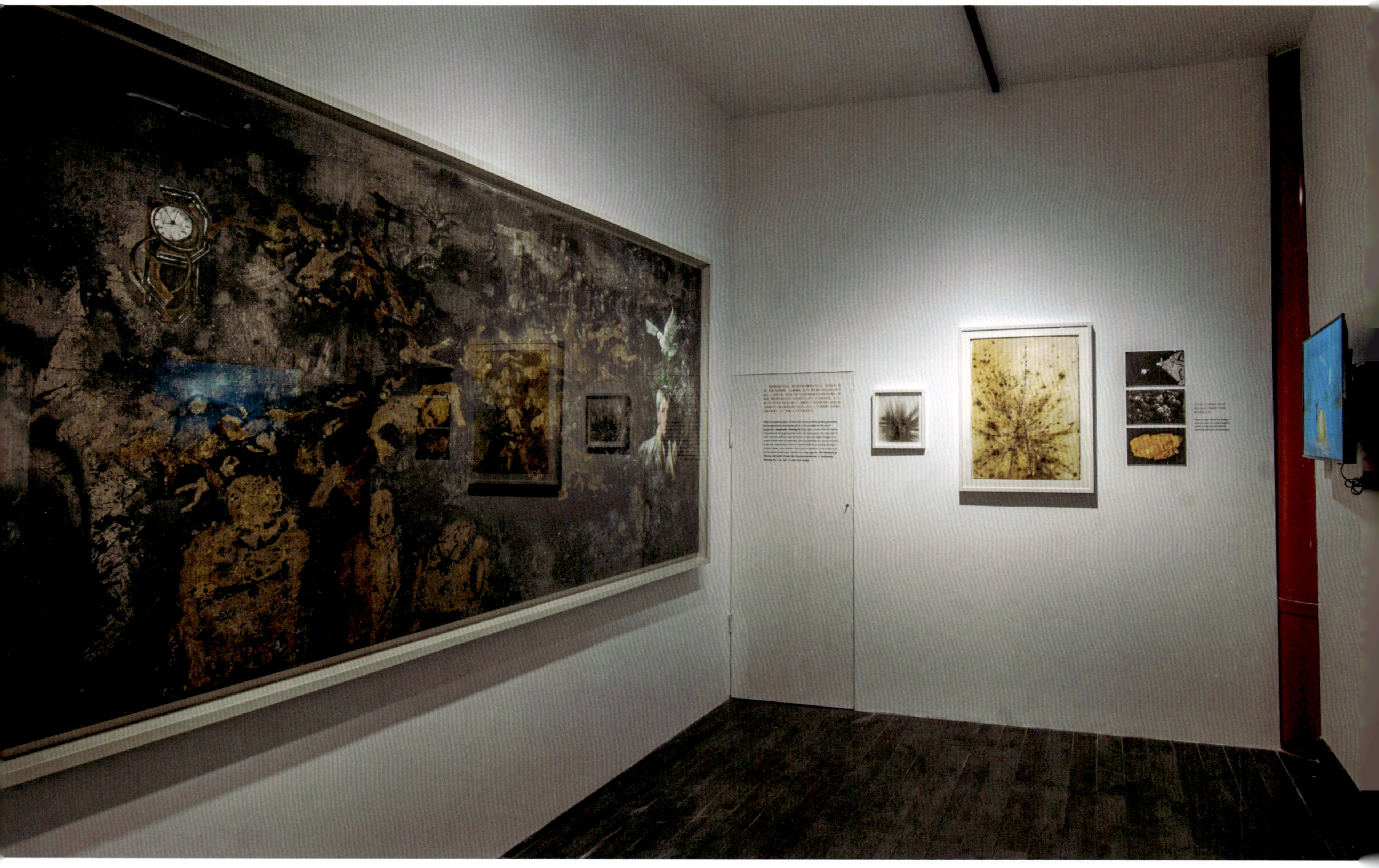

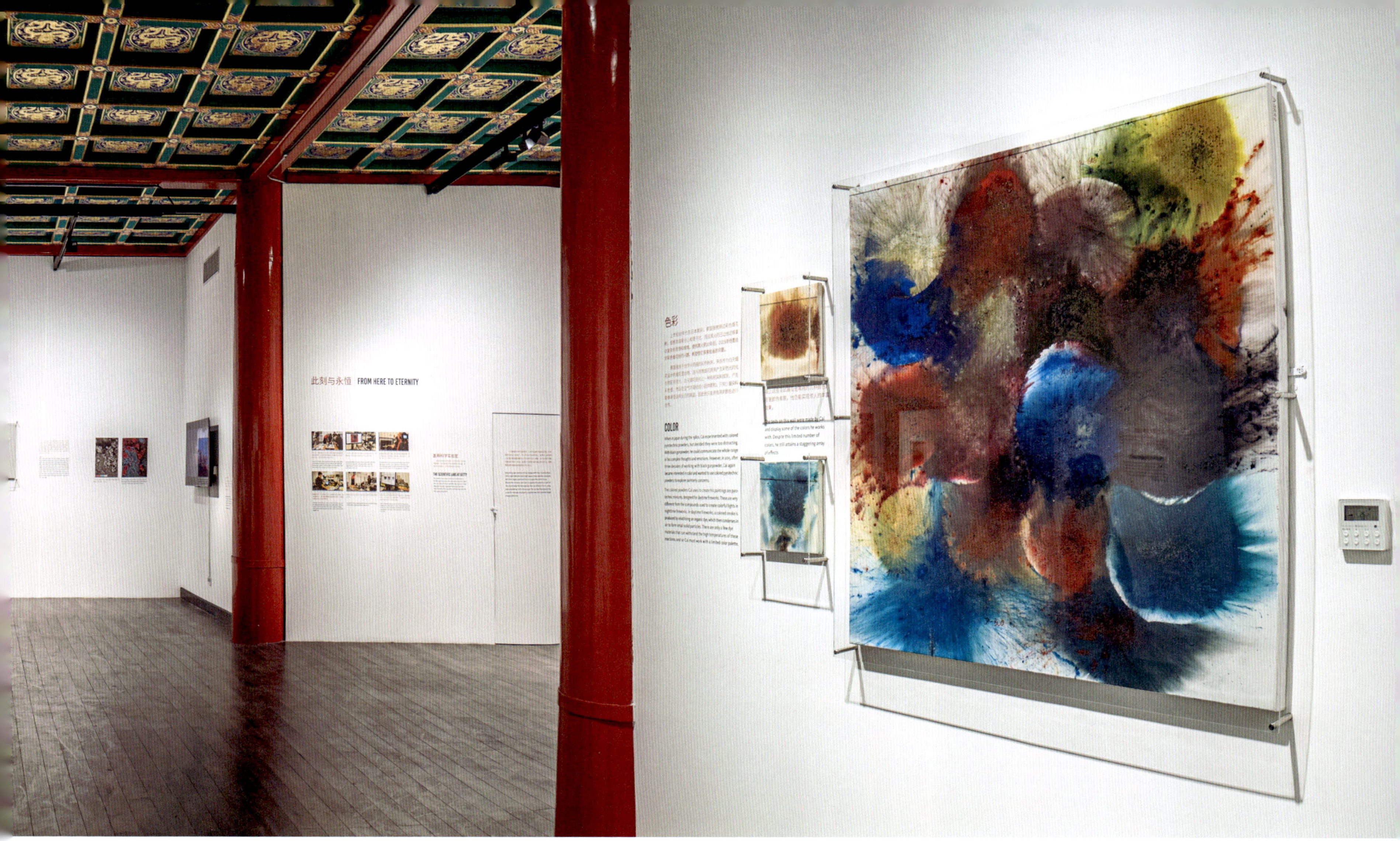


## *A Material Odyssey*

As part of the exhibition *Odyssey and Homecoming*, *A Material Odyssey* is organized by the Getty Conservation Institute (GCI), Los Angeles, and curated by Dr. Rachel Rivenc and Dr. Thomas J. S. Learner.

In 2016, GCI embarked on a large-scale study of the materials and processes of Cai's oeuvre. Through the prisms of the chemical and physical makeup of his work, the study discusses relevant conservation questions, and contemplates Cai's career evolution. Cai is the first living artist chosen for this research series. Other artists include Willem de Kooning and Lucio Fontana. The findings of the study will be published as a book in the GCI series *The Artist's Materials*.

The display at the Palace Museum presents some of the key findings from CGI's research, with a focus on gunpowder. It explores the medium's nature and properties, chronicles its use by the artist, and even peers into the future by studying the aging properties of gunpowder and pyrotechnics.

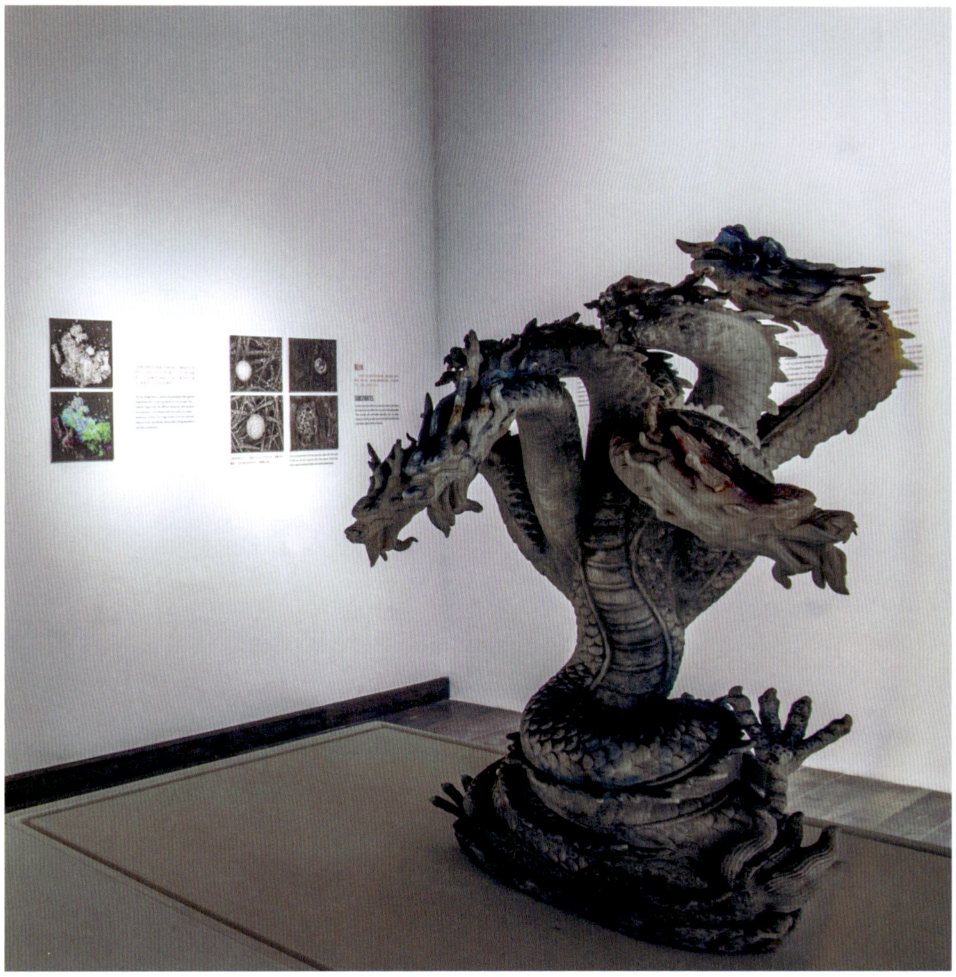

*Even when something is eternal, you can't own it forever. Eternity and permanence are different in Chinese. Eternity transcends the existence of time, whereas permanence remains in the realm of time. So when we have dialogues with, and associate with, eternity through art, we don't attempt to tackle it from the permanence point of view. Rather, we use an instantaneous way to grasp it. It feels like the myth of eternity—you could only taste it at a fleeting moment of chaos.*

— Cai Guo-Qiang (2016)

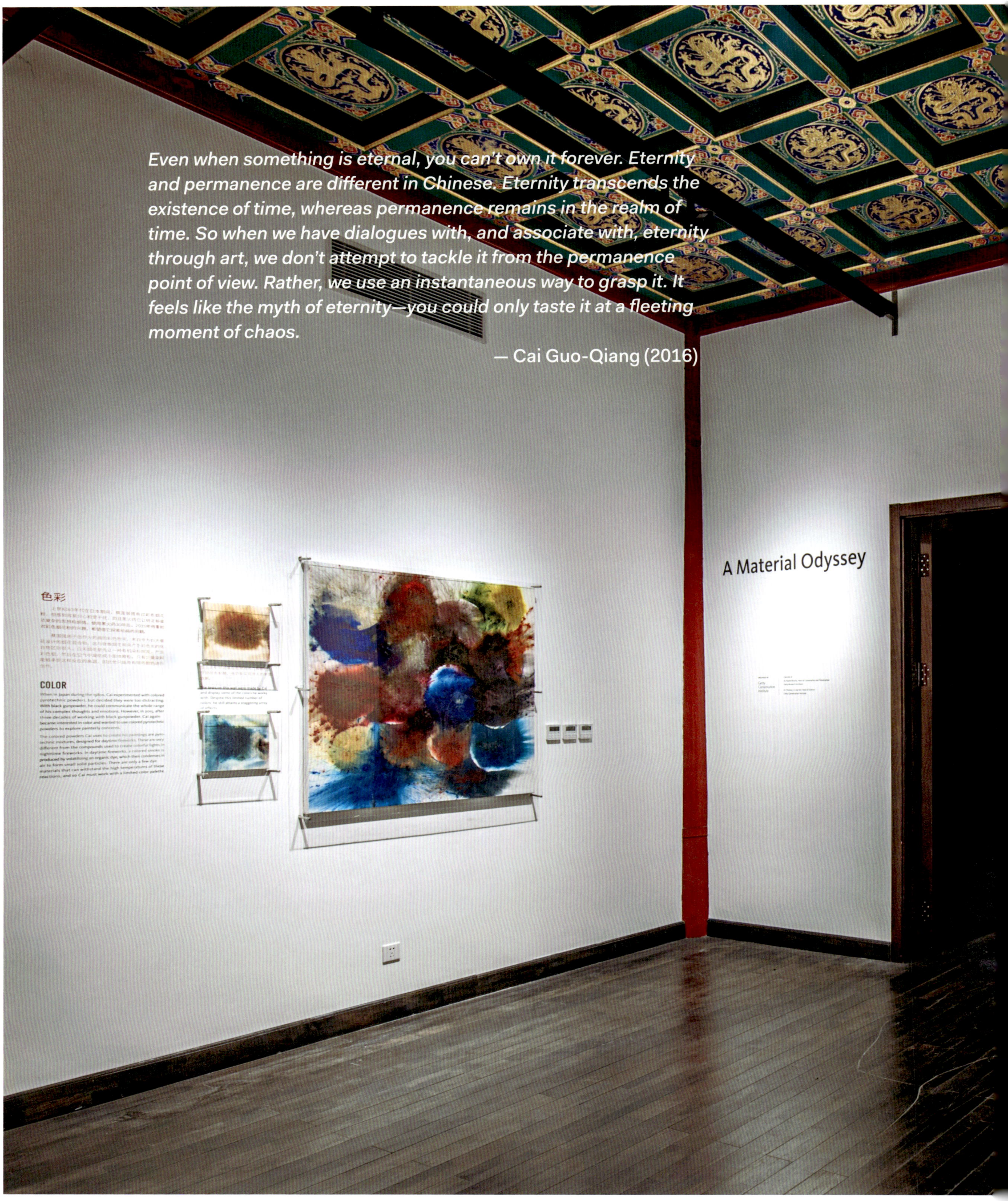


Figure E17. Exhibition view of *A Material Odyssey* at the Palace Museum

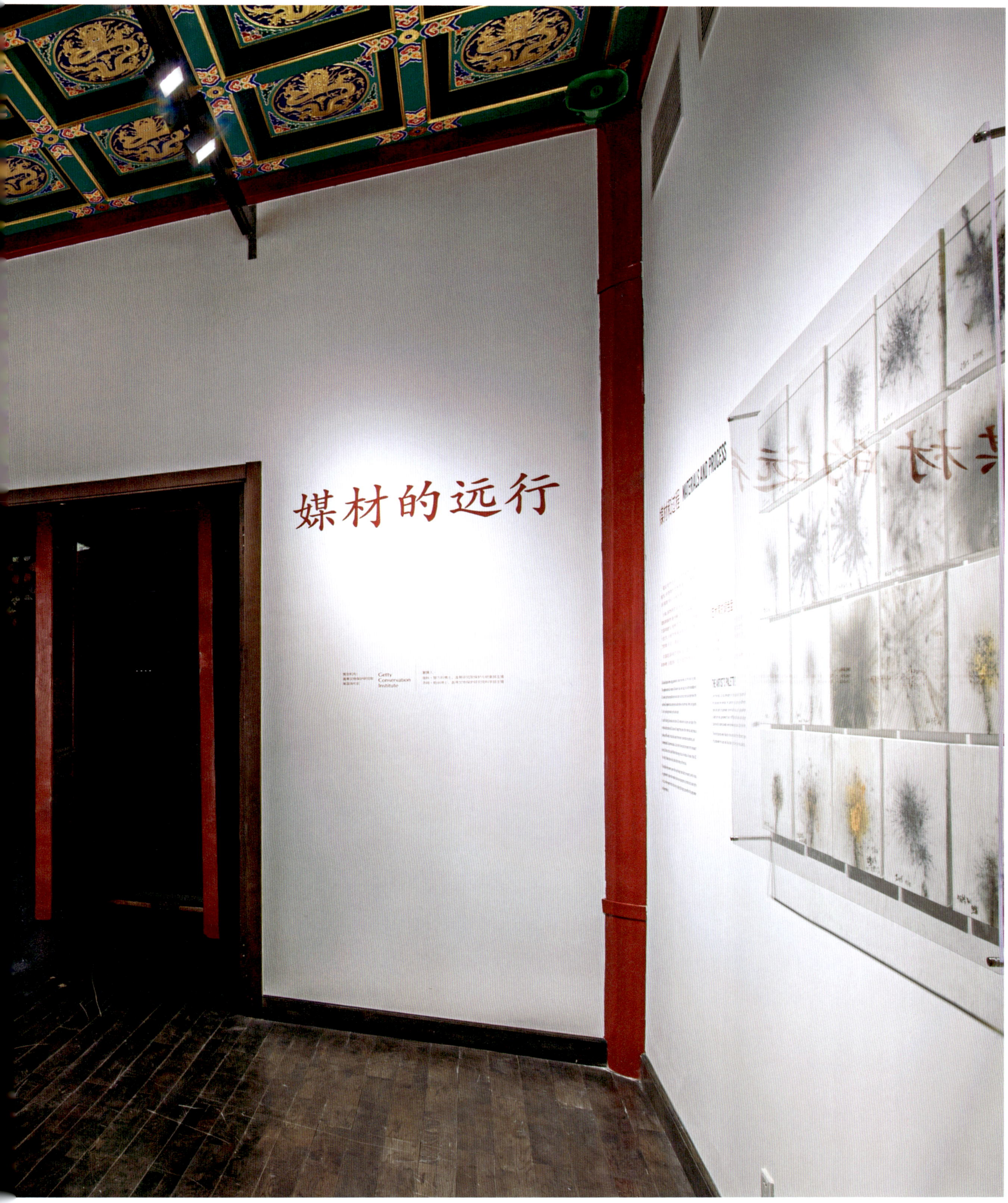
媒材的远行
Getty Conservation Institute

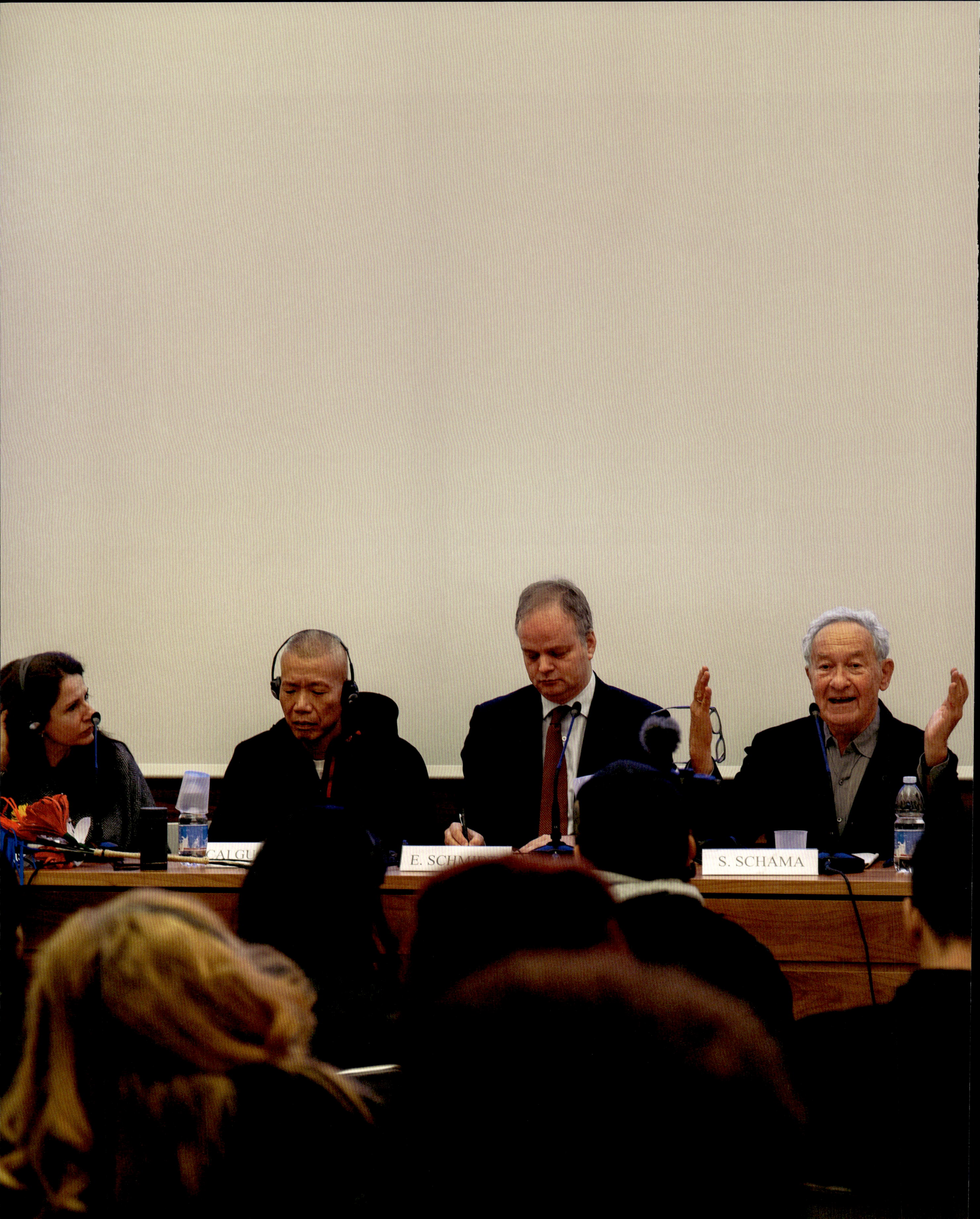
E. SCHM
S. SCHAMA

# Anthology

## Selected by Sang Luo

This anthology consists of two sections, "On the Artist" and "By the Artist," with texts selected from Cai Guo-Qiang's solo exhibition catalogues produced over the past four years that engage the theme of this exhibition, *Odyssey and Homecoming.* The "On the Artist" section reflects the unique inquiries, views, and analyses of museum directors and art history experts regarding Cai's art and exhibitions. The "By the Artist" section aims to reveal the questions, reflections, and frames of mind that he had in each dialogue, articulating the internal and external forces that shaped the distinctive characters of these exhibitions. This section also offers a glimpse into his biography, as narrated by himself, to contextualize his art.

Each project, realized through the years of preparation, offers an opportunity with the artist for pursuing a new dialogue with the museum directors, curators, and art historians on a broad range of topics, ranging from the contemporary mission of centuries-old Western museums to the essence of each period of Western art history, which have converged and collided with the work and thoughts of this contemporary artist from the East. And novel insights into his art came into being.

At the heart of the selection criteria was the idea of "raising questions." Especially in today's contemporary art, where the possibilities seem almost limitless, the artist himself believes that "questions" are the lighthouses that lead artists out of their haze and toward a clear-headed progress, without getting swept away by the popular tides. A key to unlocking Cai's artistic thinking is understanding how, in a time when so many questions have been asked about art, he has consistently sought to raise questions about the fundamentals of today's art, including his own, seeing through its gilded façade and actively putting his resulting thoughts into practice.

The artist's writings, presented here in chronological order, reflect his state of being at that particular moment in time. For example, his essay for the Prado exhibition marked the commencement of his *Individual's Journey Through Western Art History*, thus revealing his frame of mind at the time when he was especially immersed in the study and contemplation of painting: he was at once humble and proud, as he sought to break open the secrets of the pivotal moments throughout the history of painting. The reader will also recognize the development and maturation in his own response to such questions as *why* he embarked on his *Journey* over the past four years.

---

*Sang Luo's biography can be found in the introduction to the Catalogue section.*

### Legends

1. Sources include exhibition catalogues:

*Cai Guo-Qiang: My Stories of Painting*. Maastricht: Bonnefanten Museum, 2016
*Cai Guo-Qiang: October*. Moscow: Pushkin State Museum of Fine Arts, 2017
*The Spirit of Painting. Cai Guo-Qiang at the Prado*. Madrid: Prado Museum, 2017
*Flora Commedia: Cai Guo-Qiang at the Uffizi*. Florence: Uffizi Galleries, 2018
*Cai Guo-Qiang and Pompeii: In the Volcano*. Naples: National Archaeological Museum of Naples and Pompeii Archaeological Park, 2019
*Cai Guo-Qiang: The Transient Landscape*. Melbourne: National Gallery of Victoria, 2019

2. Each selected text is accompanied by a citation with an abbreviated title of its source and page numbers.

Panel discussion of Cai Guo-Qiang's Uffizi exhibition. From left to right: Laura Donati, Cai Guo-Qiang, Eike D. Schmidt, and Simon Schama. Photo by Yvonne Zhao

# On the Artist

*So much can be and has been said about his work. ... A lot of detailed commentary and interpretation can be meaningful—but only for a moment. Cai then moves on and undermines the conclusion that one has come to. The next, equally thoughtful, comment cancels out the previous one. What remains is the ever-expanding work. One that is captivating and full of wonder, the work of a truly great artist of our time.*

— Lars Nittve (2016)

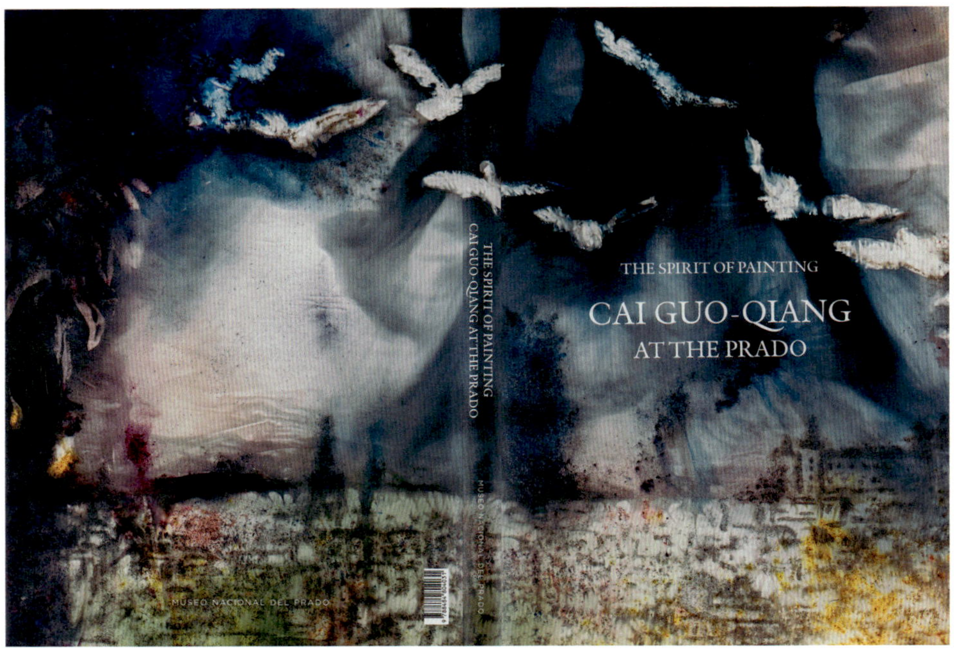


*The Spirit of Painting. Cai Guo-Qiang at the Prado*, 2017 (front and back cover)

Miguel Falomir

## Director's Foreword

From *The Spirit of Painting* (2017), page 13

Phrases such as "connecting the visible with the invisible world" or concepts such as "the mind's eye" remind us that artistic creation is a spiritual endeavor which an artist must undertake with ambition and ingenuity. Familiar to anyone with a knowledge of the history of art, attitudes and expressions of this type recall those of earlier artists who left a record of their ideas. Cai is an artist with an innovative approach who constantly seeks to work with new techniques and materials and who enjoys discussing how he uses them. [...]

Among Cai's intentions in *The Spirit of Painting* is that of understanding and connecting with the creative spirit of some of the artists of the past whom he admires. By doing so he also brings us closer to the paintings and artists in the Prado, giving them a new voice. [...] When Cai refers to the uncertain nature of artistic creation and the fear it arouses he reminds us of something obvious but easy to forget: painting and art in general are the work of men and women who take conscious risks in order to transcend the everyday. [...]

The Museum, and not just its collections, nourish Cai Guo-Qiang, just as he brings new energy to the art of the past. His reaction to the works in the Prado is in fact comparable to that of other great artists of the past such as Manet, and it is that capacity to inspire living artists which must provide the focus for the Prado's interaction with contemporary art.

*Miguel Falomir is Director of the Prado Museum.*

---

Miguel Zugaza Miranda

## Cai Guo-Qiang in the Prado

From *The Spirit of Painting* (2017), pages 18–20

Ultimately, the road to self-reflection in art is an endless one and however often its death is announced, an artist will emerge who adds another twist and turn. This is the context for locating the great artist from China Cai Guo-Qiang. [...] Cai's artistic adventure is a journey from East to West and hence runs in the opposite direction to the crucial and modernizing influence of the Eastern aesthetic on modern and contemporary European art. A journey against the tide which Cai Guo-Qiang has not undertaken alone, as he has followed in the wake of another artist from the East who was fundamental to the modernization of painting in the contemporary world: Doménikos Theotokópoulos. [...]

It has often been said that the Prado is more a museum of artists than of art history, and this is true. The artists represented in its rooms created their works for royal patrons, the monarchy and the Church, competing [...] not only with other artists of the day but also with examples from the past in a line of succession that creates the context for the very history of art narrated by the Museum. [...] It is within this context that the great artist Cai Guo-Qiang is giving a new identity to the former Buen Retiro Palace, subsequently the Museo del Ejército (Army Museum), and now the site of the Museo del Prado's imminent bicentenary extension.

*Miguel Zugaza Miranda was Director of the Prado Museum from 2002 to 2017, when he initiated Cai's solo exhibition at the Prado and acted as its chief curator. Currently he is the Director of the Bilbao Fine Arts Museum.*

---

Kosme de Barañano

## Cai Guo-Qiang: Tradition and the Individual Talent

From *The Spirit of Painting* (2017), pages 37–39, 42, 55–56

[Cai] embarks upon the oeuvre of others, by exploring through those navigations a crossing of his own device; or as through a previously played score that deep down seeks to discover the spirit of his own painting. [...] Cai has traveled extensively from continent to continent, from millenary culture to millenary culture, but unlike Picasso or Matisse, he delved into Chinese and Japanese culture first [...] and only then into European culture and its composition. The artist himself states that this quality derives from his stay in Japan, which helped his work develop in a more spontaneous, more refined, and more subtle manner, unlike that of his peers in China, which appears to be more acerbic or "naked" in its expression. Cai's oeuvre is striking in its dialectic ability to bring together elements that originate from traditional Chinese culture, Western contemporary art, as well as European painting tradition. [...]

El Greco is a painter that inspired Cai from early on. Not only because of his immersion into different cultures, or the sense of mystery in his oeuvre, or out of a certain pride or solitude in the studio, as Cai has confessed. Like El Greco, Cai works from intuition and with that technical ability that is condensed in the form of grace. In Cai's drawings, the handling of volumes works in a volatile manner, with hardly any definition; managing ethereal spaces. We also find in Cai a rejection of the classical principles of size and proportion, always seeking the subjective representation of creation. [...] Through the use of gunpowder Cai has succeeded in giving a special velvetiness to the black line in his drawings. [...]

Cai's aesthetic experience is a journey to the unknown, or rather a search for an epiphanic manifestation of the unknown, of images or metaphors that pounce on the archetype that makes of the unknown a game of representations. This is why his aesthetic, which does not stem from any specific religious theory, reaches a form of pantheism, an aesthetic collection of geographically remote visions of the world, both in technical and in historic-cultural terms, in which common roots converge. [...] As T. S. Eliot wrote, the genuine artist moves between "Tradition and the *Individual* Talent."

*Kosme de Barañano is a renowned art historian, curator, and professor of art history. Formerly the Executive Director of Institut Valencià d'Art Modern (IVAM) in Spain, he has been following the development of Cai's painting for over fifteen years since their first collaboration in 2005.*

---

Alejandro Vergara

## Cai Guo-Qiang and the Energy of Painting

From *The Spirit of Painting* (2017), pages 24, 31–32

The fireworks of Cai are blasts of energy that have a paradoxical delicacy—reminiscent of the delicacy of touch in a painting or a drawing. The critic Peter Schjeldahl has written about the artist that "he understands gunpowder as Velázquez understood oil paint." [...] The idea of ascension that *Sky Ladder* expresses connects with a tradition of idealism for which the primary goal is the evocation of a place beyond the visible world. This idea defines much of the history of Western art. [...] In this wondrous work, Cai takes on the metaphysical role that philosophers have assigned to artists. [...]

He uses the term "shaman" to refer to the curators at the Prado whom he has had the opportunity to talk to. It is a term that I like: it implies that we are mediators between him and the art and artists of the past. [...] In the 19th and 20th centuries many artists have come to the Prado looking for inspiration—they are Cai's predecessors. The list is too long to reproduce in its entirety. It includes Courbet, Manet, Degas, Renoir, Ilya Repin, Mary Cassatt, Eakins, Sargent, Toulouse-Lautrec, Picasso, Gustav Klimt, Edward Hopper, Georgia O'Keeffe, Francis Bacon, Helen Frankenthaler, Robert Motherwell, Rauschenberg, Twombly, and many others. [...] Cai relishes the idea of being part of this sequence.

*Alejandro Vergara, Senior Curator of Flemish and Northern European Paintings at the Prado Museum, co-curated Cai's solo exhibition at the Prado in 2017–18.*

---

Eike D. Schmidt

## Make Art Not War. Cai Guo-Qiang's Pyrotechnic Tachygraph

From *Flora Commedia* (2018), page 12

With good reason the artist himself says that "managing a fireworks display is like making love," this similarity being intended not only for the paroxysmal and almost rapturous aspect of the act, but also for its generative purpose: in Renaissance art theory, artistic production is actually often compared with an act of creation-procreation, especially about the gestation and birth of the work of art.

*Eike D. Schmidt is Director of the Uffizi Galleries and chief curator of Cai's solo exhibition at the Uffizi in 2018–19.*

---

Germano Celant

## A Pyrotechnic Vision: Cai Guo-Qiang

From *Flora Commedia* (2018), pages 15, 23–25, 28

[T]he insistence on his exploration of traditional art runs the risk of presenting him as a philologist who enriches the comprehension of "texts," such as the configurations of El Greco and the formless images of Willem de Kooning, without making clear his involvement in and linguistic reflection on contemporary research, on the art of the present day. Whereas his practice, with its independent perspective, does not just hark back to the past but aspires to broaden the modes of transmission of art through the use of media that, even though they have their roots in antiquity, appear radical and surprising today, such as fireworks. [...]

[Cai] aspired to integrate a classical and traditional vision with experimentation on the level of material and chemistry, performance and deconstruction, criticism and politics. ... It was a propensity for a dialectic of opposites, in an effort to establish an osmosis that would overcome the polarities. [...]

The decision to make use of gunpowder and accept the visual and formal consequences of igniting it and letting it explode is very important to an understanding of the contribution Cai has made to art. It indicates an "all-round" vision of artistic practice, one that was not shared by previous generations,

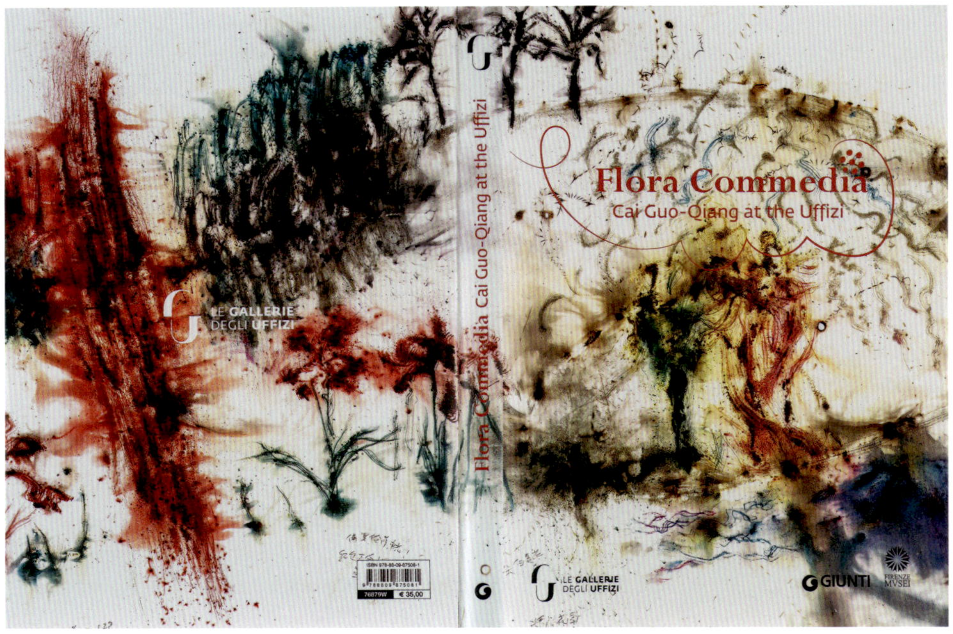


*Flora Commedia: Cai Guo-Qiang at the Uffizi*, 2018 (front and back cover)

generally focused on a specific approach in which one material excluded another, one procedure excluded another. The adoption of this ancient process of intervention in a contemporary language, painting, [...] implied a taste for innovation. [...] It was a rebirth of art from within, fed by tradition and memory, but it happened through a process of alchemical reunification of opposites. One in which destruction was transformed into creation, where the flow of heat and matter, making the transition to psyche and spirituality, arrived at a mystical union. This was an attainment of that invisible element so dear to Asian culture, the *qi*, the circulation of the vital force and the breath, in art. [...]

The whole of his practice turns around the formulation of a passage between distinct moments, so that everything is in evolution: from the drawing to the event, from the image to reality, from darkness to light. [...] The subject of a transition and dialogue that outline the passage between primary entities also finds expression, in Cai's work, through the recourse to images drawn from the history of art. But this is not a practice of appropriation, an extolling of a return to classical iconography; rather, it is a mental and corporeal transfer, made manifest in references to the imagery of the Old Masters.

*Germano Celant (1940–2020) was a prominent Italian art historian, critic, and curator, known for coining the concept of Arte Povera. Formerly the Artistic and Scientific Superintendent of the Fondazione Prada, and a Senior Curator of Contemporary Art at the Solomon R. Guggenheim Museum in New York, he followed Cai's art closely since the 1990s and curated and contributed essays for several of Cai's projects, including the Venice Biennale of 1997.*

---

Laura Donati

## "To Light A Fire Is Not Enough." Cai Guo-Qiang Dialogues with the Masterpieces in the Uffizi

From *Flora Commedia* (2018), pages 35, 40, 44–45

Cai Guo-Qiang's extreme multiplicity of themes, forms, and creative and exhibition techniques makes it difficult at first glance to identify the underlying theme of his nearly four decades of artistic research. And yet, the coherent and continuous return to certain fundamental concepts is a definite and distinctive feature of his oeuvre that ranges from installations to paintings, to pyrotechnical events in which the formal results only seem to contradict each other. Some of these essential artistic principles are present in the works created specifically for the Gallerie degli Uffizi. These pieces, inspired by some of the museum's most iconic paintings such as the *Allegory of Spring* or *Primavera* by Botticelli and Caravaggio's *Medusa* are evidence of his interest in the early techniques in the Uffizi collections. [...]

The execution [of Cai's works] deserves as much admiration as the result, since the transformation of the material represents the eternal process of change in nature. [...] The attempts at releasing the energy of the cosmos by using the potential of gunpowder, inevitably moved apace with thoughts on the individual since he is an expression of cosmic force. [...] [I]n Florence, flowers mark the moment when we recognize and collect the legacy of those who no longer live, whether they are unknown people or great artists of the past. The flowers shorten the distance between life and death and between past, present, and future, emblematically representing the search for temporal and cosmic continuity that distinguishes the production of Cai Guo-Qiang.

*Laura Donati is Curator of the Department of Prints and Drawings of the Uffizi Galleries and co-curator of Cai's solo exhibition at the Uffizi in 2018–19.*

---

Simon Schama

## Heavenly Complexities

From *Flora Commedia* (2018), page 53

Cai Guo-Qiang inspected all this in a state of happy exhilaration but also with an expression of wonder, as if he had not been the maker of this stunning work at all but just the enabler of some immanent vision powered by the flowing *qi* of the universe. But then again, that's pretty much what Michelangelo felt about marble when he sought to free forms trapped within the carapace of stone. For that matter, all great art is the result of a hard negotiation between the conceiving artist and the resistance of materials. Though Cai in his modest fashion likes to stress the ways in which powder, smoke, fire, and light can and should get away from his designing hand, the fact remains that, as with every bona fide genius, his mind is the only source of the kindling spark.

*Sir Simon Schama is an esteemed historian, art historian, and professor of Art History and History at Columbia University. He composed and hosted the globally acclaimed BBC documentary series* Simon Schama's Power of Art *and* Civilisations. *He is curator of* Odyssey and Homecoming *and editor-in-chief of the exhibition catalogue.*

---

Paolo Giulierini

## Preface

From *In the Volcano* (2019), page 35

Projecting this extraordinary gaze, *In the Volcano: Cai Guo-Qiang and Pompeii* is about rediscovering the inevitable links between the classical past and the modern sensibility. The persistent links have opened up a new, disquieting, and surprising dialogue between the visitor and the museum's masterpieces (among them the *Venus Callipyge*, the

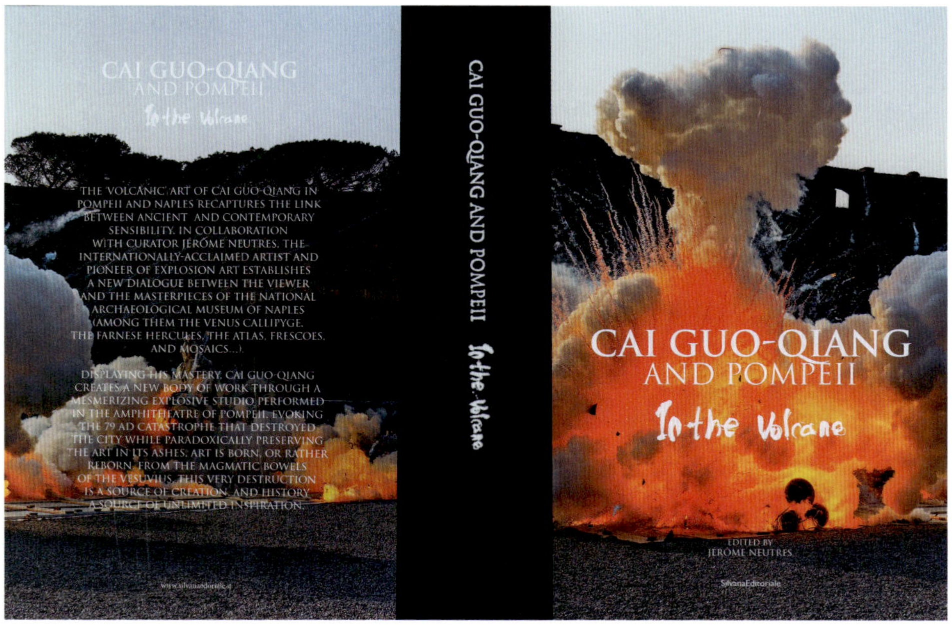


*Cai Guo-Qiang and Pompeii: In the Volcano*, 2019 (front and back cover)

*Farnese Hercules*, the *Atlas*, and the bust of the *Pseudo-Seneca*). [...] Folklore, the influence and power of Eastern traditions insert themselves compellingly into the rooms of MANN, showing that cultural exchange is the result of a shared capacity to look at the world with the *curiositas* referred to by the ancients.

*Paolo Giulierini is Director of the National Archaeological Museum of Naples (MANN).*

---

Massimo Osanna

## Cai Guo-Qiang: A Pompeiian "Palingenesis"

From *In the Volcano* (2019), page 39

Cai Guo-Qiang is also part of the contemporary history of Pompeii—a constantly evolving site and a welcoming collective legacy of human knowledge. [...] The energy released bursts forth like a generative force celebrating the beauty and joy, typical not of destruction but of creation, not of the end but of the beginning, not of inflicted violence but of ideas and intuitions developed and shared. Rather than works as such, Cai Guo-Qiang's pieces are symbolic manifestations of the tenacity of identity and the resilience of the past, despite being immersed in the flow of change and transformation.

The paintings and sculptures that derive from them are also palimpsests of the free movement of ideas and the natural circulation of materials, understood as uncontrollable reactions, like propelling bursts of enthusiasm.

*Massimo Osanna is General Director of Italian state museums, Director of the Pompeii Archaeological Park, and a specialist in Italian classical archaeology.*

---

Loredana Troise

## Cai and Naples

From *In the Volcano* (2019), page 37

[Cai] unleashes an amazing and destabilizing force, balanced on a perfect, hieratic structure. Filled with a potent psychic and emotional charge, his performances are the ideal place to experience extreme disorientation as revelation, the culmination of a journey as aesthetic as it is cognitive. The unquestionable reference to Eastern spirituality in his work is combined with a variation on the themes of transhumanist thought: "Not the pervasive aestheticization of the undertaking, but the performance itself, which is like an initiation process leading to a higher and enlightened state of collective consciousness," Giuseppe Morra, the founder of Fondazione Morra, explains. [...]

It is a theater of social memory. A kind of "second navigation" in the Platonic sense, aimed at understanding sensitive phenomena by placing them in a meta-phenomenological dimension, which are not self-explanatory. We are asked to observe and listen to what happens outside and within us. Neither within the limits of the prisoners in the cave, unable to understand what they saw, or like the enlightened man who returned to the cave with all his convictions. As Morra states, "We must inhabit the middle ground, the space in between what we perceive on the wall and the form that is impressed on our retina and, following the movement of the images, recognize their meanings by delving into our history with our senses, with levity and no illusions. It is not always possible to grasp the ultimate meaning, or identify the signifiers with certainty, because it is an ephemeral art beyond the conventional. But even though fleeting it is a channel for ideas, icons, and a space in which to perform extraordinarily fascinating experiments."

*Loredana Troise is an art historian, curator, and writer. She is a member of the board of directors and head of the department of visual arts of the Fondazione Morra, Naples, which provided organizational support for Cai's solo exhibition in Naples and Pompeii in 2019.*

---

Jérôme Neutres

## Portrait of the Artist as Volcano

From *In the Volcano* (2019), pages 45–46

Every work becomes the story of some catastrophe orchestrated by the artist in order to discover something new. [...] Cai Guo-Qiang's works are placed at the core of the permanent collection, creating a sort of treasure hunt vacillating between past and present, as well as mirror effects between the aesthetic of Pompeii and that of the 1st century and the imminently contemporary art of Cai Guo-Qiang. [...]

The living performance's specificity is to share with life itself its fugitive character. It is also this fragility that gives beauty and meaning to the performance. No other site better embodies this fragility than Pompeii. Pompeii is essentially an ephemeral city, and at the same time it is eternal thanks to art and the memory of art. In my opinion, a whole part of Cai Guo-Qiang's painterly work is to give continuity to performance. Each canvas is like the memory card of a performance. Not only its memory, but its prolongation, its destiny and its destination.

*Jérôme Neutres is Director of Strategy and Development for the Réunion des Musées Nationaux–Grand Palais (until 2020) and curator of Cai's solo exhibition in Naples and Pompeii in 2019.*

---

Jürgen Schilling

## Detonations in Arcadia

From *In the Volcano* (2019), page 81

This kind of structure reveals marked discrepancies—not due solely to the materials or the aesthetic perception of a past period—but also surprising similarities. With the energy and independence that set him apart,

Cai Guo-Qiang appropriates the visual language of a distant civilization and activates his individual myth in relation to auratic phenomena of the past. "Great things are done when men and mountains meet ..."

*Jürgen Schilling is a German art historian, theorist, and curator. He is the former Director of the Kunstverein Braunschweig and Director of the German Academy Villa Massimo in Rome.*

---

Achille Bonito Oliva

## Erotic Catastrophe in the Work of Cai Guo-Qiang

From *In the Volcano* (2019), pages 51–52, 54, 57

Cai Guo-Qiang's art has gone beyond the decorative beautiful form and moved towards the drifting phantasmatic apparition. Technical expertise is programmatically eschewed by impelling inner images which, in order to acquire the evident light of form, demand blindness and abandon, inward gaze and feverish disattention, by adopting *intelligent chance* during the creative process. This disattention emerges from the need to overcome or avoid the pride of reason, the pathetic optimism of the Project, always the symptom of a logocentric condition. [...]

There are no backgrounds in Cai Guo-Qiang's paintings, a kind of impermeable wall retains the dueling signs that explode on the picture surface, traced with colors reminiscent of abstract sidereal heights and dizzying marine depths. The painting becomes the scene of an archaic battle between forces never to be placated, between energies that can be evoked but never blocked. For this reason the artist uses a language that is part organic and part figurative, between informal and quasi-figurativeness. [...]

In this sense catastrophe and eroticism are linked in Cai Guo-Qiang's work and at the same time, they are alternating and often intertwining movements that define the meaning of the image that is never Manichean, tending to a simple denouncement. The artist is well acquainted with the deep workings of the psyche, the shifting, indeterminate paths of the unconscious. He can depict the area and limit within which visual trajectories occur. The area where the height of designing reason (the anthropoids) and the height of instinctive drives (the war between the elements) are expressed. [...]

Cai Guo-Qiang has succeeded in simultaneously combining the organic and automatic systems, which both compete in the search for a conflictual solution.

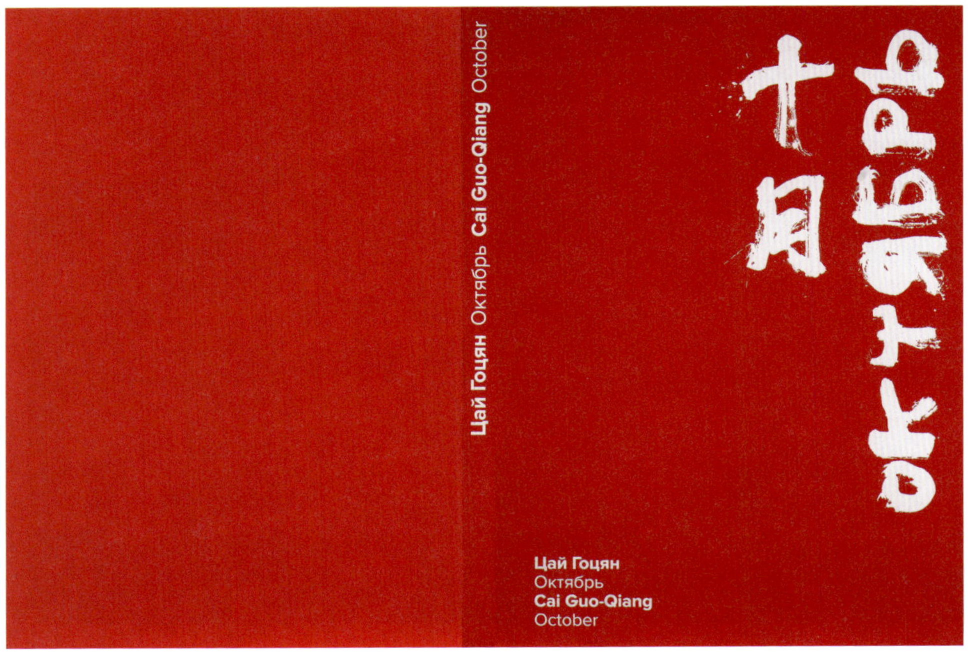


*Cai Guo-Qiang: October*, 2017 (front and back cover)

*Achille Bonito Oliva is a distinguished Italian art critic, contemporary art historian, and curator, who originated the term* Transavanguardia. *He organized numerous major exhibitions, including serving as artistic director of the Venice Biennale in 1993.*

---

Marina Loshak

## Director's Foreword

From *October* (2017), page 9

On the occasion of the centenary of the 1917 October Revolution, it is very important for us to make a statement that both sums up the past and demonstrates our openness towards the future. Together with our colleagues, we thought a lot about what our museum should be like and what role contemporary art should play. This exhibition may seem a lot like 1917 because of its revolutionary character. Our academic institution provided a contemporary artist with the opportunity to turn the museum into a huge installation.

*Marina Loshak is Director of the Pushkin State Museum of Fine Arts.*

---

Alexandra Danilova

## October: The Personal Dimension of History

From *October* (2017), page 36

Like Dante's Virgil, Cai guides viewers through the metaphorical pages of the past, evoking reflection about the history and fate of their country, about the present and the future. Cai's installations are always filled with inner drama, where the spectacular coexists with the philosophical.

*Alexandra Danilova is Senior Curator of 19th and 20th Century Art at the Pushkin State Museum of Fine Arts and curator of Cai's solo exhibition at the Pushkin Museum in 2017.*

---

Alexander Etkind

## Work of Memory, Work of Fire

From *October* (2017), page 48

Cai's grand, political, and international art is best implemented in his fireworks. Requiring no words, these large-scale performances cater directly to our senses, affecting several of them at once: vision, hearing, and even our sense of balance. Moreover, they engage with another sense that is akin to amazement: I will call it the experience of scale. It is akin to Kant's term "sublime."

*Alexander Etkind is a historian, cultural scientist, and professor of history and the Chair of Russia-Europe Relations at the European University Institute.*

---

Lars Nittve

## Cai Guo-Qiang: In Praise of Uncertainty

From *October* (2017), pages 54–55, 71

One of the world's most celebrated artists, [Cai] is also one of the hardest to categorize. I mean, what is Cai Guo-Qiang? [...] [Y]ou will notice the phenomenon of all the categories canceling each other out, so that they in a way become meaningless. Simply by doing everything an artist can do, in the end Cai evades categorization. At the same time, he is amazingly consistent over the years, assiduously building up a body of work that opens up a wonderful free space between categories and beyond definitions. [...]

Playfully but without irony, he can deal with the symbols, rituals, and sometimes touching absurdities of a post-revolutionary society—which can be critical but also nostalgic. After all, those difficult times gave him the tools he now uses so well: his attraction to volatility, instability and risk, and his complete understanding of uncertainty as the basis of art.

*Lars Nittve is a curator, art critic, and writer. He was the founding director of Tate Modern in London and M+, museum of visual culture in Hong Kong, and director of several major museums including the Moderna Museet in Stockholm and the Louisiana Museum of Modern Art in Humlebæk, Denmark.*

---

Boris Groys

## Avant-Garde Memories: A Conversation Between Cai Guo-Qiang and Boris Groys

From *October* (2017), page 80

I think it's very important what you're trying to do, to go back to a different memory, not to a nationalist memory, but an internationalist memory, like *The Internationale*. Because it goes against this kind of nationalist discourse. [...]

[B]ecause you're not Russian, you come from outside, from a different culture, from a different trajectory, of China; but at the same time, your personal history is part of the same history as the history of Russia: the history of Communism, revolution, Marxism. I think it's interesting to say that, because speaking about memory, I think Chinese and Russians tend to think about history as their very own history, as closed history that is specific to them. I think in your project it's important that you show—that you also belong to this history. It's not that you're really an outsider, it's not like you're really coming from a completely different cultural sphere or space. You experienced the same ideas, the same problems, the same utopian aspirations, the same delusions that the Russians also experienced. So you come from the outside and the inside at the same time.

[Editor's Note: The second part of the above is not included in the published catalogue, but the artist decided to include it in this anthology.]

*Boris Groys is an art critic, media theorist, philosopher, and Global Distinguished Professor of Russian and Slavic Studies at New York University. He re-evaluated Socialist Realist art by expanding on Walter Benjamin's art theory.*

---

Lars Nittve

## Cai Guo-Qiang: The Amazing Freedom In Between

From *My Stories of Painting* (2016), pages 17–18, 21

Critical and affirmative, political and not, ironic and absolutely honest—even when entering the most sensitive of arenas for a contemporary artist on the stage of major world politics, for example [...] the 2008 Beijing Olympic Games [...] the skeptic may say, Cai Guo-Qiang is obviously very canny and calculating. In a certain way he probably is, and he has to be. If you want to realize projects at the level of ambition that he has shown around the world—out in the desert, in big cities, in the world's greatest museums—you don't have much choice. He is also smart, diplomatic, charismatic, and extremely well organized. [...]

So much can be and has been said about his work. ... A lot of detailed commentary and interpretation can be meaningful—but only for a moment. Cai then moves on and undermines the conclusion that one has come to. The next, equally thoughtful, comment cancels out the previous one. What remains is the ever-expanding work. One that is captivating and full of wonder, the work of a truly great artist of our time.

*Author's biography appears above.*

---

Lesley Ma

## History, in a Flash

From *The Transient Landscape* (2019), pages 20, 26–27

[Cai] pivoted the conversation from celebrating the glorious past of a civilization to exposing questions around cultural politics, albeit rather implicitly and with a sense of humor. [...]

In the design and architecture of Qing dynasty imperial tombs, built in the 17th century, and their surroundings, Cai saw "the unity of aesthetics and philosophy of the highest order." With the awestruck feeling came a desire for self-determination: "Whenever I recall the design [...] I can feel agitation and uneasiness stirring within me." Facing the divine arrangement, he sought to develop his own anchor. In some ways, Cai's artistic language is a direct translation of his personal cosmology. Just as Cho-yun Hsu sees folk rituals and customs such as Chinese medicine, *feng shui* and divination practices as ways for ordinary Chinese people to exercise proactivity (*zhudongquan*) in the universe, Cai, with his gunpowder explosions, performative actions, dramatic installations, and ritualistic scenarios is inserting a voice into established historical, cultural or artistic narratives. His art becomes his way to address and release the "agitation and uneasiness" he felt under larger structures of order. This perhaps explains why,

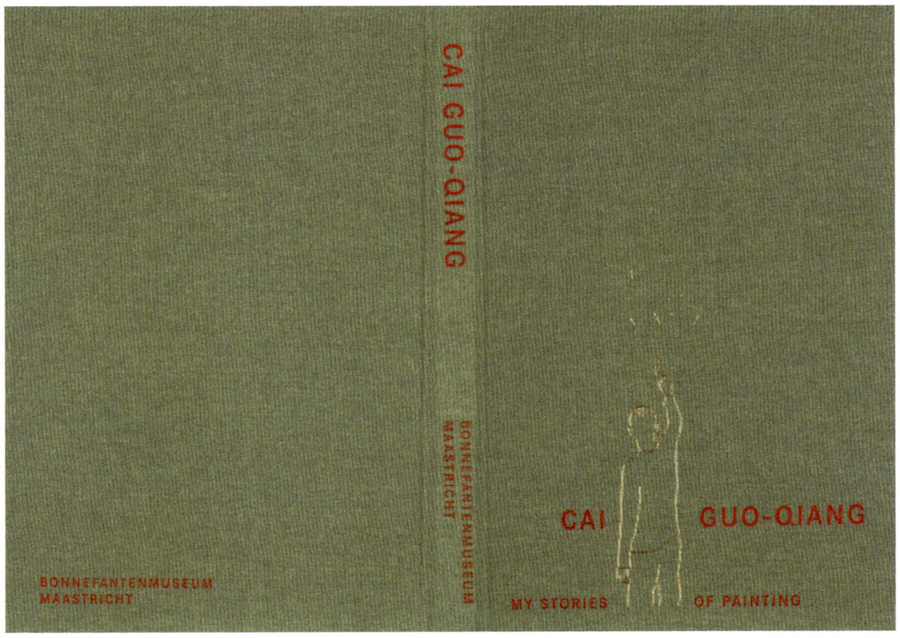


*Cai Guo-Qiang: My Stories of Painting*, 2016 (front and back cover)

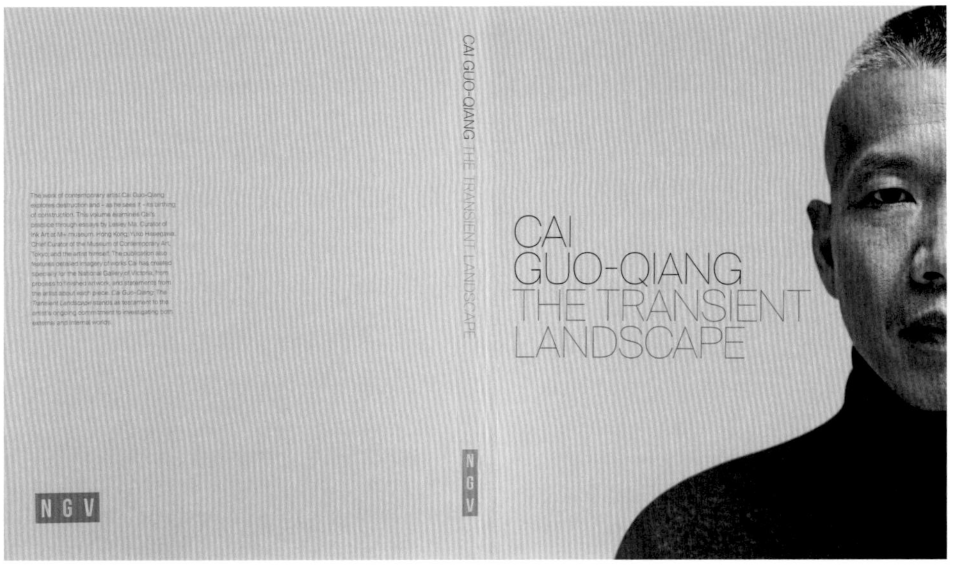


*Cai Guo-Qiang: The Transient Landscape*, 2019 (front and back cover)

among his expatriate peers, Cai is the most obsessed with the imperial legacy. Yet it is important to understand that the engagement with the dynastic narrative in his work is never blind worship, but a proactive assertion of his own cultural identity. [...]

The spiritual life and customs of the Chinese, often dismissed as superstitions and as backward by Westerners, held the key, in Cai's mind, to understanding the people and the culture. Cai's dedication to bringing forth the spirit of humanity has allowed him to take his cosmology to foreign sites and find resonance in local contexts.

*Lesley Ma is Curator of Ink Art at M+, museum of visual culture, Hong Kong.*

Yuko Hasegawa

## New Order Out of Chaos

From *The Transient Landscape* (2019), pages 61–64, 68, 71

[Cai's] works go inside the viewer, break down conventional systems, and produce chaos, releasing the potential energy of life. [...] He makes full use of natural conditions in order to stimulate the natural vitality of cities and people. [...]

It is difficult to claim these "regulatory techniques"—actual collaborative projects performed with the help of professional Chinese doctors and geomancers—as art. Cai's "art" is achieved by creating "rituals" which connect these techniques to internal structures of people and land, making them effective in the present age. [...] Form in Cai's works is found in the object as event. Its eternity can be described as "momentary eternity." [...]

[Cai] presents situations of conflict, chaotic values, and cultural destruction which occurred in a number of different historical periods when old ideas and cultural forms were replaced by new ones. Cai is not necessarily criticizing these particular events. He accepts what has happened and places everything in a system of chaos. [...] He has discovered the secret of "action in non-action"; the fact that refusing to criticize contains the greatest criticism. [...]

The state of chaos, neither monist nor dualist, created by Cai produces violent motions and vibrations between *yin* and *yang*. He reminds us of the angel who races at high speed through a special zone between heaven and earth, where eternity and the present exist without contradiction, a Daoist destroying and creating life.

*Yuko Hasegawa is a prominent curator, Artistic Director of the Museum of Contemporary Art, Tokyo (MOT), and professor at Tokyo University of the Arts. Her various roles and positions include: curator of the 7th Moscow Biennale (2017) and the 11th Sharjah Biennial (2013), and co-curator of the 29th São Paulo Biennial (2010), among others. She curated Cai's solo exhibition* Chaos *at Setagaya Art Museum, Tokyo, in 1994.*

# By the Artist

## Talk Talk My Stories of Painting

From *My Stories of Painting* (2016), pages 23–24, 31, 39, 129, 134, 138

I don't recall whether or not Quanzhou has ever produced any great painters, but the city certainly has its own painterly pursuit—namely, literati painting. I remember that everybody painted, though very few strived to realize any so-called "creative feats." It was difficult and impressive enough to be occasionally selected for the National Fine Arts Exhibition, let alone to win an actual award. This is not to say that everyone would envy those who did win awards or attempt to imitate them, because people understood that while painting should reflect one's era, and in order to be truly interesting, it also has to transcend said era. This quality depends on the painters' individual tastes, natural dispositions, as well as their own little inventions in technique or material. [...]

[E]veryone was an amateur; people painted for their own amusement, learning from each other in organic and symbiotic ways. I think this must have been similar to how people painted in ancient times. Later, when I went abroad, I realized that most people painted in more or less the same way, largely by themselves. [...]

The specific conditions surrounding my upbringing in my hometown were very good for me. It was a multifaceted and open place: a free, individualistic, leisurely, carefree place—a corner of the world left untouched by the struggles and strife of society.

***

[...] In my memory, our house was always filled with local scholars and poets who came to read, paint, or practice calligraphy with Father. They would even bring over wine to pair with Grandmother's seafood dishes. Father was such a man even in those times of poverty. Our home became a cultural salon, and that was my upbringing.

***

[...] I had my own studio from a very young age, taking up two whole [connected] rooms of the house by myself. I sometimes painted people, but portraiture was largely used for themed creations wanted by the government; meanwhile, landscapes allowed for more individual creative freedom. I therefore grew to prefer painting landscapes, especially those of my hometown. When Mother went to do laundry by the river, I would paint on the riverbank; when she secretly visited a temple in the mountains before dawn, I would sit outside and paint the sun's first rays; when I traveled with the theater troupe to the mountains and countryside for performances, I would paint the high peaks and vast seas; when we had to transport stage sets by boat because some of the rural areas didn't have paved roads, I would paint at the helm, washing my brushes in the river. [...]

***

[...] Through seeking the liberty and natural force of gunpowder, I was able to free myself, create an art form, and find enjoyment in it. I also seized every opportunity to travel within China, conversing with ancient cultures and the natural world. [...]

Starting in 2006, I devoted myself to the Beijing Olympics opening and closing ceremonies. The themes were all about countries and the great cultures in history. I was away from home for more than two years while working on this project, growing a bit older and a little bit more sentimental in the meantime. Because of this, after the Olympics, I began to include more flowers and plants in my drawings, allowing the pieces to be closer to my surroundings and feelings. [...]

[Some say there are no real questions] left in painting today. Painting has gone from objective, literal sketches to subjective, important vessels for conveying emotion—it seems to have already undergone every method and concept imaginable. Some might even say that painting cannot possibly suit every era; it's the general opinion that multimedia art is more suited to the Internet age. So can painting evolve and cultivate new features unique to the present time? Or perhaps it's precisely because we belong in this current era that we should cherish and emphasize all the more the glory and dignity inherent in painting? And what exactly is it that we should be cherishing? If it's sentimentality, then how can we create a sentimentality of the present that differs from that of the past? All in all, I've grown increasingly aware of the difficulties in painting, but the more difficult I find it, the more excited I become, to the point where it all brings me to a sort of "high." Moreover, no matter what I've done, I have never outgrown my love for painting.

Reviving my explorations of color gunpowder has created a new stage in my painting. I feel as though I've "returned to paint after fighting a hundred battles." This is a continuation of my unrealized dream of becoming a painter from my youth, as well as my rebellion against the predicament of contemporary painting.

## A Boy's October + The Boy of October

From *October* (2017), pages 13–14, 26–27

These were the paintings found in the little booklet from which the Boy learned to paint; each painting was a home to which the Boy returned in his dreams. Meanwhile, outside the world of the painting, the fates of Soviet artists became the Boy's early awakening.

How expansive Russian culture seemed in the eyes of Chinese people then! So expansive that, to us, it was the definition of foreign culture; it was the West to the East. Outside of traditional Chinese painting, Western painting was equated to Russian painting. Although the word "Russia" suddenly vanished from the cultural lives of Chinese people after relations between the U.S.S.R. and China soured, Russian culture continued to exist as a steadfast foundation from which the Boy of Art continued to absorb nutrition. In this persisting state of scarcity, the Boy awaited the arrival of another West.

At last, China's reform and opening-up began. All of a sudden, everything—from Impressionism to contemporary art—came coursing into the country. The Western masters suddenly dominated the world art history in the Boy's mind: Monet, Cézanne, Picasso, Duchamp, Warhol, Beuys ... all began giving the Boy master classes! Ilya Repin, Vasily Surikov, and Isaac Levitan quickly became like teachers from elementary school—though near and dear to the heart, they existed somewhere farther away down the lane of memory.

The Boy also vaguely intuited that the world—the Western world—may have been somewhat unfair to his former teachers. They were great painters, they were likewise intent on the representation of light and color, and they had been so early to kindle Abstraction, not to mention Suprematism ...

What exactly happened to the Boy's teachers—those groundbreaking, heroic mentors of enormous talent—at the cruel hands of history? It is said that times of trial give birth to enduring art. If this is correct, and even tsarist times birthed artists whose enduring work influenced the world, then what about those artists who came afterwards? In the end, all these minds of creativity only composed a Fate Motif with no enduring trace in Art History, leaving behind an unfading requiem in the Boy's heart.

***

As a participant in this endeavor, I am also revisiting my personal experiences and emotional journey in this exhibition. I am not discussing this period of history as an outsider. Throughout the process of developing this exhibition, I have worked towards a better understanding of myself, China, Russia, and the human race. A hundred years ago, this Revolution began with the ideal of striving for a better societal system and life. In the end, is this ideal just an eternally condemned path of suffering that ultimately leads to nothing but a laughingstock of utopia to be regretted by later generations? Or are we still striving after this ideal today? The ups and downs we are experiencing on the path to globalization, the frustrations we are facing in the pursuit of democracy and freedom ...

---

## Ramblings about Painting

From *The Spirit of Painting* (2017), pages 62, 64, 66–67, 69–71, 73, 75–76, 78

My childhood dream of being an artist was actually one of becoming a painter. There is something wondrous about exhibiting at the Prado; it is as though I was strolling along a little path next to the field of painting, filled with admiration for the history of art, and suddenly I hear a voice saying, "Go ahead, plant some seeds, join in the fray." It is miraculous. As a young painter who loved classical art, but who grew up to become a contemporary artist working in all forms and mediums, I suddenly feel privy to the honors and self-realization associated with being a painter of past generations. This is the homecoming that I have been awaiting my entire life!

***

[...] I have come to discover that El Greco has been a mirror in which I can see myself. His pursuit of intangible and mythical worlds, his stubborn love for the culture of his homeland, and his outsider and nomadic spirit all resonate within me. To reflect on my own experiences: I had virtually no presence in China's '85 New Wave movement; in Japan I roamed as a wolf outside the artistic system, inciting revolution in a fishing village outside of Tokyo and stirring up trouble in the Japanese art world. By the time I left Japan, I had made my way into just about every museum that exhibited contemporary art in the country. After moving to the United States, I have played both inside and outside the system while wandering across five continents. A free spirit, I have sought a Monkey King–esque path to mischief and rebellion, believing that no rule is the rule. [...]

My understanding of the spirit of Spanish painting is that it embodies the painters' sensibilities in the adventure of painting on the spot and the charismatic genius effused while standing before the canvas. The paint and color, the control over depth and light, tension and ease are all clearly preserved in the brushstrokes, each one as vivid and lifelike as it was hundreds of years ago. The charms of such *painterliness* are irreplaceable.

Compared to Italian Renaissance painting, Spanish works possess a greater sense of immediacy and confrontation. Their form of naturalism derives from the traces of reality revealed in the painter's process and the scenes from everyday life. This, in no small amount, was inherited from Titian—Spanish painters chose Titian. At the time, the Italians were more reverential of the scientific techniques of Renaissance masters and their conceptions of an eternal and supreme spiritual world. Titian's worlds were more naturalistic, closer to daily life. His textures and brushstrokes are an easy expression of the artist's passions and sensibilities.

From Titian's intimate and steady fine brushwork to El Greco's exaggerated and fluid mysticism; from Velázquez's constancy, understatement, and nobility to Rubens's dynamism, sensuousness, and looseness; and from Goya's sweet splendor and somber violence, through to Picasso, the freedom and naturalness of these works express the spirit of painting prevalent in Spain with a distinctly sensual and down-to-earth magnanimity.

Such expressions of *painterliness* are not unlike the thrill of the "ignite, explode, and extinguish" that accompanies painting with fire. Each technique conveys the charms of process and illuminates traces of experience that have been present in art since cave painting, evincing the power of reality captured in painting.

***

Gunpowder painting is linked to the spirit of painting. My sensibilities and that of the material make up the painting's sensuality. Conducting tests on canvas allows the gunpowder to naturally express its sensibility, its capacity for creation. The results of such a straightforward manifestation of sensibility can be quite enchanting, but I cannot and do not stop there. A painting created with gunpowder is seared with my own sensibilities and attempts to capture the core of our time. I hope that gunpowder can free the spirit of an elevated dimension; this newly liberated world is determined by the painter's integrity and spiritual attainment. [...]

When I am painting, from choosing different types of gunpowder to the amounts used, or deciding how they are deployed to make lines or how the stencils are cut, even the weight of the stones or their placement on the canvas—all of these choices reveal contradictions between my dictatorial will as creator and my attempts to liberate the materials. There is a sense of gratification and release that I enjoy with every explosion, but I am also anxious about the tension between the gunpowder and myself. Democracy and autocracy ... there is no such perfect dialectical relationship in art.

I vacillate between gunpowder's freedom and constraint. I indulge its latent ability to expand. I release its energy, making it freer yet harder to control; but I also require it to contract, to contain its inner force, otherwise it will become too flimsy. Having a harmonious balance of freedom and restraint tends to result in an overly traditional appearance. Canvases that are simple, legible, and direct will appear more contemporary. Therein lies the paradox. Artists of every era oscillate between the need to confront the issues of their day and a desire to engage with the eternal. The artworks they leave behind are the result of that struggle. [Am I the same?] [...]

Artists have wild imaginations. They are often keen to tell their paintings what they should be, when sometimes they should just wait and let the paintings say what they are. Sometimes my painting produces miracles that scare me. The results are not entirely dependent on me, but on that magical moment when I become intertwined with the gunpowder and the spirit of painting. We become linked with nature and the intangible world—then miracles will transpire.

The significance of gunpowder is not just that it allows me to break free from the gravity and inertia of conventional aesthetics; it is more about helping me set up an ultimate deployment on the chessboard, encircling me with nature, and creating a situation where man is united with nature. Humans and gunpowder are both part of the natural world, and the process of painting has evolved with both material and human changes, a natural progression that conveys the reality of nature. The Chinese word for nature (*ziran*) is brilliant. It simultaneously embraces the cosmos, the natural world, and a sense of ease and spontaneity.

Art alone cannot resolve the issues of art, yet ultimately the issues in art must be resolved by art itself. Since my youth, I have been quietly asking myself: is art a chess game that encompasses life, society, the cosmos, and nature? If it is, what are its possibilities? What are its possibilities in a globalized world that oscillates between prosperity and decline? Ultimately we need to identify the artistic forms and languages of our time. From gunpowder painting to outdoor explosion events, from large-scale installations to social projects, I have roamed the entire globe seeking to overcome cultural boundaries, realizing projects through public participation, believing that no rule is the rule, going with the flow, and learning from nature and gunpowder. The same principles apply to my explorations in painting.

***

[...] Creating with gunpowder is significant only if it can be adopted as an artistic methodology to be expanded upon by myself or other artists. If gunpowder painting only exists to resolve issues of gunpowder painting, then it has little significance. It needs to address the issues in painting; if it cannot, then it can hardly solve its own problems.

My approach to painting has several levels. First is the visual legibility of the work, such as the style, technique, and materials apparent at first glance. The work must also possess a penetrating force, simply put: the painting must have appeal. These are all related to "how to paint." Second is the correspondence of content, including subject matter; this is "what to paint." Generally speaking, these two concerns are the foundation of painting. Third are the issues of painting, or "why do we paint?" This concerns one's contributions to the advancement of the painterly discipline, driven by an artistic attitude towards painting and its conception. Why you paint can in turn help you think and further develop how you paint and what you paint. Painting has been declared dead on several occasions, but as long as painting continues to have issues to resolve, the spirit remains and painting may live on contentedly. What questions are posed to painting today? Even if artworks are rooted in social issues, we need to transform content-based issues into painterly ones.

When an artist attains a certain level, formulating ideas or an individualistic style is not too difficult. The challenge is in transcending this and bringing individualism to an appreciation and understanding of life to reach new heights in art history. This is ultimately determined by whether or not the artist is capable of posing such inquiries to painting, and also the types of questions that are posed. Sometimes one needs to induce the collisions of painting history and contemporary reality before more profound issues or questions at a more fundamental level can be revealed. Once you have posed questions, you must also find ways to solve them.

Good art is ultimately determined not by the quality of the questions put forth, but by the individual sensibility of the painter and the natural and charismatic way his or her questions are expressed. [...]

Artists are consistently preoccupied with how to paint, what to paint, and why we paint. But when we ask ourselves why we continue to paint in this day and age, we often come short of a rational answer. The simple answer is: we love to paint. [...]

With every generation, individuals arise to seek out the fundamental reality of their time and pursue new possibilities. If photography relieved painting of its centuries-old documentary obligation, making way for the Impressionists, Expressionism, and abstract art, then has the immediacy of television precipitated new types of innovation in painting? [...]

As we consider painting and the spirit of painting today, we rediscover the innate appeal of the medium. We must face our times, our changing ways of life, and ourselves. Only through confronting these issues and giving them due importance can we choose to abandon or continue with the craft. [...]

Can painting capture the crux of evolving human relationships and our changing perceptions of time and space in the digital age? Can we find new expressive possibilities in today's shifting lifestyles and aesthetics? Perhaps it is precisely because of the strong reaction to the digital age that we begin to contemplate history, and consider the value of its vestiges. For tens of thousands of years, human lives have carried a sense of eternity. While human lifestyles and social relations are consistently evolving, feelings of love, fear, and loneliness as well as our bodies have not dramatically changed. Many of our predecessors expressed a sense of the eternal that transcends time, and managed also to express their today. Confronted with an increasingly virtual world, should we be more determined in our painterly approaches to capture the reality of painting in the moment? Should we reclaim the sensual spirit of painting?

With these struggles in mind, the decision to return to painting today seems almost pioneering.

***

For my large-scale installations, social projects, outdoor explosions, or gunpowder drawings, I have worked in cooperation with people that represent the world's various cultures and fields. The hardships and joys that stem from the complex external factors are attractive to me, and while they become important factors in the artworks themselves, they also obscure certain issues. The most touching aspect of painting is how it allows for a direct confrontation with an understanding of the self. It is less about the accumulation of knowledge or a rational self-knowledge, and more about the recognition of your own sensibility and your place as a part of nature. [...]

The two years I spent studying and experimenting with painting for this exhibition became the foundation for its centerpiece, *The Spirit of Painting*. My explorations into the spirits of master painters seemed like mere foreplay, a long and seductive period of self-restraint and patience that caused me to finally stand in front of the 18 meters of blank canvas, raise my weapons, and exclaim "*FUCK IT!*"—directly manifesting a vibrant expression of spirit. My interminable search for direction was, in fact, a way to lose myself; endless experiments whose goal was to lose control. I felt that emancipating the gunpowder was my path to liberation, when in fact I had to free myself before the gunpowder could be released. When the gunpowder rips loose, it subverts my past, present, logic, and sensibilities, and mingles the powers of heaven and earth in a corrupt form of crossbreeding. Art creation opens a window for artists; it cultivates both good and evil. The gods favor children who throw banana peels at their feet, those who both revere and dare to tease them. Without these children, everyone would be bored. [...]

The qualities unique to my early black gunpowder drawings and their pursuit of a lofty and cosmological spirit, together with my later process of secularization, act as two ends of a pendulum dragging me back and forth. Is my artistic journey one of retreat and struggle? In retrospect, indulging in painting today seems to be moving counter to the trend. It seems as if I have lost myself, or perhaps I have done so intentionally. Euphemistically it is the building of a ladder, or walking a lonely treacherous path to art history.

## Talk Talk My Loss of Direction

From *Flora Commedia* (2018), pages 62–64, 67, 70–72, 78, 80

These museums comprise various critical periods in art history; their collected artists and artworks, as well as the cultural history of the respective periods, often become the basis for my thematic and technical pursuits. They are the origin, inspiration, and material for my artworks. Yet as a contemporary individual coming from a different cultural perspective, I am more concerned with a new journey and reflection on Western art history that can disrupt the creative paths and processes that have grown increasingly familiar to me over the years—a new journey that broadens new horizons. [...]

[A]t each museum, my aim is not to consume the subject matter and components of the masters and transform these into an exhibition, but to discover the points at which my energy can collide with theirs, and then redefine my own goals accordingly. [When asked] "Is the use of [Old Masters'] images for you a connection that makes them contemporary?" I answered: Perhaps a little. "Contemporary" did indeed free us from the necessity of realism, allowing for modern technology to transform some iconic imagery into stencils that directly replace my personal labor. But the question is not whether or not I use this imagery; the important thing is that the paintings themselves need to raise questions, including questions about art history and about painting today. Supposing that there are still questions remaining in painting today, they would be contemporary ones. So the crucial thing is: Do my paintings raise questions?

Paintings are not like installations, whose concept and material sometimes speak for themselves. When I make installations, social projects, gunpowder explosion projects, or even gunpowder drawings for the sake of explosion projects, I barely think of art history at all—perhaps I feel that there is not much art history to think about in these cases. But when it comes to painting, I am as obedient as a little kid—all those generations of early painters were truly fucking fantastic! After the Prado exhibition, I felt humbler than ever—and I am not a modest guy by nature! Thinking back to my installations such as *Head On* with 99 replica wolves, or my explosion projects such as *One Night Stand* with its sensual romance, and those poignant daytime explosion events, that 500-meter ladder of fireworks rising into the dawn sky ... with these, I felt that even the Old Masters would have given me many 'Likes' in their turn. But when it comes to embracing master painters on this journey through art history, I am constantly agonizing over how I can better release my sensuality and audacity, how I can unleash my energy on canvas, as they did ... I often resent myself for overthinking, for not having the guts. This makes me anxious and restless, and at times even makes me feel that I am inflicting humiliation upon myself. The question of 'how' that arises whenever I face a blank canvas never fails to awaken and challenge the timidity that I felt as a young painter. But this is also honest; it is beautiful.

In this digital age of artificial intelligence overrun with images, we are reminded to consider: Why do we want art? What is the art of this era? Does art have an intrinsic principle or reason that allows it to survive generations? What will we have left by the time A.I. can achieve almost everything? No matter how advanced A.I. may be, it will never be an animal; no matter how civilized we are, we will always be animals. Sensibility, lust, hormones ... the surprises or dejection of these accidental and uncontrollable factors, as well as the improvisational serendipity that occurs on the canvas—all of these intrinsically stem from the wild nature of animals.

Maybe we might as well play up our animal nature even more freely in painting, reversing the course of cultural development and going backward? The rewinding through art history will eventually connect with the origin of painting in primeval society—that is, our original animal nature. [...]

Sometimes, journeying through art history and engaging in dialogue with classic masterpieces from different cultures and eras, I feel that despite being able to provide extensive reasoning on the surface, I may not actually have much clarity underneath. But I am also aware that the inability to see the road ahead, the feeling of being lost, can likewise help arouse my survival instinct within art. Disorientation stirs in people a sense of panic and danger, and can in turn help them to discover themselves; it is only when you cannot find your way in the mountains that you can face your own fears and mortality. [...]

***

To paint the cosmos as nature, to paint souls as the cosmos; the soul is the cosmos, the cosmos is nature at its most expansive. To transform chaos into energy and make gunpowder into chaos!—perhaps gunpowder is my cosmos.

My assistants joke that I am "B.Y.O. Cosmos." The fact is, people are all a part of the cosmos, so if you open yourself up, you naturally bring your own cosmos with you. If you could embrace self-contradiction as much as the Grand Unification Theory of the Cosmos, then you would dare to do absolutely anything and you would do so without a care. Ultimately, it is about realizing your personal stance. My tiny "Grand Unification Theory of Art" may embrace many forms, including installations, paintings and drawings, explosion events, social projects, and more, but it needs to adopt a stance of an even higher level: can I work on this or that or whatever else, including the cosmos, without a care? To build an individual world of the artist, to be a pioneer of the times—these lofty goals are all but a jest. No matter how remarkable something is, it is for the sake of fun—for the sake of having fun, playing, getting a thrill. If I can reach this level of existence, then I am truly at ease, natural, free ... *that* would be so-called B.Y.O. Cosmos. Haha! [...]

***

And thus this work [*The Spirit of Painting*] continued to evolve through complexity and chaos. In the end, the result was not what I was after, but then again I had not been clear on what exactly I was after. For many years, I have used self-contradiction and ambivalent vacillation as forces of conflict and tension, believing that power rested in raising problems and questions. This is the reflection of a personal tendency: when faced with the choices of safety or risk, I tend to get more excited about risk. We can be generous and call this my youthful impetuousness, but in reality, at the end of this incomparable "Golden Journey" at the Prado, there is a sense of my loss of direction. I love this painting deeply. It truly preserves the chaotic parts of my methodology. Scorched within it are an artist's struggle with confusion and disorientation; a bittersweet work is always the artist's favorite.

The Prado was my first exhibition that centered on paintings that employ large quantities of color gunpowder, which I focused on creating beginning in 2015. I have always felt that color was difficult to use well and could easily appear over-harmonized and picturesque. There are many examples of this in traditional aesthetics, which have made me feel that the pursuit of color could be a little sinful and ugly, even a little unseemly. I do not use color in the gunpowder to paint perfect flowers. In fact, I sometimes feel that I can use color more stiffly and dissonantly, pushing the envelope of "ugly" into even more uncomfortable territory—perhaps this can transform into something distinctively subversive? We cannot say that an artwork has "venom" by relying on color gunpowder to depict sex, lust, hallucination, or drugs. If we can turn the color itself into the viper, as though the viper itself is painting on canvas, seducing and poisoning on its own accord ... how difficult that is!

The Uffizi exhibition is a continuing exploration of the problems from the Prado, but at the same time has its separate pursuits. At the Prado, there were more themes and dialogues centered on the Old Masters, as well as more of a desire to display different facets of my own. For the Uffizi, I want to purify things—purity is the attitude. Focusing on one theme redirects us to the question of what else can be done with painting. To concentrate on painting good paintings through flowers, to become free and unrestrained by anchoring and centering the heart and mind—this is the concept and goal of the Uffizi. Once you have purified things, it becomes even more difficult to avoid the difficulties of painting! [...]

The development of color painting and the innovation of various materials and techniques have brought so much fascinating novelty that I am over the moon at work! Art is, in essence, *wan wu sang zhi*—fixating on the indulgence of material goods at the expense of losing one's life goals. Inventing new techniques can bring about new explanations to painting, but is not necessarily the goal of painting itself. As such, I often have to remind myself to backtrack, bringing the "particularity" back into the common. The "how to paint" that prompts "what to paint" as well as the "what to paint" that prompts "how to paint" will address the question of: "why paint?" [...]

***

The Renaissance saw a great intermingling of thought and philosophy, including the cosmos, religion, democracy, and human rights; the achievements of visual art is a testament to this merging of thought. How were the Old Masters influenced by their times and how did they absorb and process this in their own art? We, too, are living in extraordinary times—what is its essence? What kind of art will act as the testament to our time? When people discuss this period decades from now, they will be able to discern where we stand in history. [...]

The goal: forward. The method: backward. My aim lies in the future, yet I am rewinding through art history and the cosmos. [...]

The journey of Western art history has unsettled me. I always call out it's difficult to paint, it gives me anxieties. But this is not pain, it is enjoyment. Every time I go back to my country studio I am reluctant to leave. Painting gives me a moment of pause, and allows me to calmly focus on what one can face. Avoiding the many people and things, travels and meetings, and stay away from the hustle and bustle of the outside world.

The character "busy" (*mang*) in Chinese is a compound of "heart" (*xin*) and "death" (*wang*). Painting is never busy. It is fun, and nobody is too busy while having fun.

Taking the journey of Western art history, it is exciting to challenge today's difficulty in painting. Perhaps it is not about opening up daring new roads, but rediscovering my sweet dreams of looking at the poor reproductions in a Western art book as a boy. Pursuing the state of mind of my predecessors in the process of painting ...

[...] [I have asked] "Looking at these masters' paintings, there is still this warmth and feeling from creating art and from creating art in the past. Are we passing this warmth on to our own successors today?"

## In the Volcano, I

From *In the Volcano* (2019), pages 64–69

Volcanic eruptions are the climaxes of nature. Its natural spontaneity is similar to the human condition and that of society; it also intersects with my realization of and attitude toward gunpowder explosions over the past decades.

Mount Vesuvius buried the civilization of Ancient Rome, as though nature herself created an enormous time capsule with one stroke of calamity. I want to engage in a dialogue with catastrophe, to discuss the modern day—terrorism, artificial intelligence, space exploration, and all kinds of anxieties toward the unknown—through the lenses of nature and past civilizations.

Sometimes I think: After doing so much, do I still have my volcano today? Do I still erupt with energy? In the 80s, many vanguard Chinese artists—no matter their genre—were like little volcanoes. It was an era full of ferocity and power. Beneath individual style and talent there must also be the pressure of magma ready to erupt.

This time, I tried my best to leave behind primal traces by letting my hormones take the lead. We always appear to be so full of wisdom, acting so civilized, meticulously fine-tuning the work at hand, trying to comb even artwork concepts into neat, clean explanations. It would be better to have a straight eruption that pours forth directly—like a volcano, like the apocalypse of Pompeii! There shouldn't be so much rationalizing. This is the essential nature of a volcano: when it's time to fire, fire; when it's time to go wild, go wild ...

***

I am curious about how the Ancient Romans copied the Ancient Greeks and remade those Grecian bronzes into marble sculptures. Did they do so sitting next to the original statues, or did they do so by memory? I think about the Ancient Chinese who made copies of the paintings by their predecessors; they had no printed materials or photographs to rely on, and often times had to rush home for brush and paper after seeing the original, while the memory was still fresh. In the West, most artists, whether working in sculpture or painting, cannot rely on models alone to express human bodies in flight or in battle—they cannot rely on hanging people up on wires, but must instead utilize their understanding of human anatomy, of movement and aesthetic. In the East and West alike, oftentimes our imaginations are more freeing, and their products may appear realistic but in fact differ from real proportions. Good painters have always held inside their hearts mountains and human figures, whose spirit and energy are extracted from the painters' own spiritual inner life. [...]

***

My past explosion events have ended in seconds. This time there was an inferno that could not be subdued with mere fire extinguishers in the howling wind. But this was precisely the animalism and loss of control that I wanted. It wasn't only explosion art, but also fire art, wind art. The mediums that represent civilization stand burning in the towering flames, allowing them to better convey the language of the everyday and of contemporary society—the language that generates political discussion. [...]

We cannot compete with the volcano or with Pompeii; we can only borrow and redirect the force of their space and time. I have been seeking the critical point of artistic expression and its capacities, but it is a search that requires many serendipitous coincidences.

The union strike was the greatest surprise this time around, but it was also a coincidence. I like controlling things, and am always seeking a conduit through which to lose control and find release. The strike and ensuing negotiations were entirely out of control yet also entirely legal. Of course I had to respect their freedom of democracy—isn't that the entire point of people like me making contemporary art? Since my creative process had been affected by democratic freedom, then I should also create more "democratically," more "freely"! [...]

Seeing as my art shares close ties with nature, politics, society, and historical eras, I need to be able to change according to whatever changes come my way. Much of this outcome did not go according to my plan, but overall it has surpassed my imagination with its spontaneity, brazenness, and ferocity. I have always felt that if an artist feels *something might go wrong this time* while creating an artwork, it may very well lead to a miracle. [...]

The "ferocious" nature of the explosion is interconnected to that of the volcano. A volcanic eruption does not allow for much preparation; the unexpected union strike caught me equally unawares. At first, the strike was an intrusion, but later it became part of the artwork itself, helping me to be more spontaneous. My spontaneity and compromise do not show a lack of principle, but rather the ability to discover greater freedom and wider potential in the midst of difficulty. This is precisely the concept of "Inner *qi* gives rise to life, outer *qi* gives rise to form" in *feng shui*—if you can find a mutual harmony between the inner and outer, "*feng shui* gives rise to itself." In other words, a new *feng shui* is achieved.

***

[...] I do not shy away from acknowledging the chaotic nature of the goal and significance of this journey, but I am certain that it has allowed me to soar and play freely within the vast landscape of art history, of nature, and of my predecessor artists' hot-blooded ferocity. This experience has allowed me to "nurture" myself—a different version of self within me. It has nurtured a particular *something* that will remain unwavering and constant against the vicissitudes of time and history. It has nurtured my *qi*, my "spirit"—which cannot presume to be called "noble," but can perhaps claim the name of a "budding spirit" instead.

---

## Shadow of the Empire

From *The Transient Landscape* (2019), pages 40–41, 44, 47–50

In classical Western paintings, light and shadow represent both an analytical and emotional understanding of the natural world, and the order of the myriad beings within it. In classical Chinese paintings, it is the internal and external *qi* (life force) that unifies the composition and energy. According to the system of natural laws governing *qi*, also known as *feng shui*, "internal *qi* gives rise to life, external *qi* gives rise to form; when internal and external *qi* are reconciled, *feng shui* is generated." This concept is fundamentally rooted in the classical Chinese aesthetic. Many concepts in Chinese culture are related to *qi*: vulgarity (*su qi*), seductiveness (*mei qi*), malice (*xie qi*), perniciousness (*du qi*), righteousness (*zheng qi*), grandeur (*da qi*), heroism (*hao qi*). The mountain peaks, rivers, and waterfalls fashioned by outer *qi* rely on the invisible inner *qi* for their vitality and life. When the painter works harmoniously with the ink and brush so the external and the internal resonate, a fine work is born! Indeed, the harmony of the inner and outer worlds creates good *feng shui*. This principle is applicable to the making of gardens, the construction of buildings, the design of urban spaces, and so on. [...]

Exhibitions of my work have been held all over the world, not necessarily because people are moved by the grand history of China or the contemporary vitality of Chinese culture, but rather because in some way my work speaks to them. They see a childlike innocence and playfulness, a self-liberation in cosmic space and time, as well as my commentaries on current social issues of common concern. [...] My work, though it has numerous other resonances, inherently embraces a Chinese aesthetic. For example, the installation *Head On*, 2006 [...] seems to show a circuit of ninety-nine wolves hitting a wall and returning to the starting point, before starting the cycle again. But, in fact, the installation describes one wolf's movement over a period of time. This references the conception of time prevalent in the Chinese aesthetic and can be compared to the process of reading a Chinese scroll over the course of time, or putting figures in different places in a composition to indicate distinct moments in time—a principle known as multi-viewpoints perspective. I apply the epistemology of internal and external qi, guided by my own methodology, to my current artistic practice.

***

[...] This project was a challenge to me from the outset, because I am personally not very fond of exhibitions of ancient artifacts. In today's so-called globalized world, a lot of historical artifact exhibitions take part in the widespread phenomenon of cultural tourism, especially through the lens of exoticism. The captions tend to be vague and insubstantial in the actual analyses of the ancient objects. The artifacts end up being treated as mere symbols, promoting a greater cultural narrative, and in turn are not examined for their artistry nor artistic merit. Contemporary issues in the arts and in society are not discussed, and there is a lack of a deeper level of active, self-reflective engagement with the objects, and the manner in which they are displayed.

These tendencies are not limited to exhibitions of Asian artifacts in the West—Western artifacts, such as those of Pompeii, would face the same predicament when shown in China. These are phenomena worth interrogating and contemplating in the context of our current times. After many years of globalization, there are inextricable conflicts and obstacles, and these concerns triggered the formation of the critical framework behind my exhibition. [...]

***

For *The Transient Landscape* exhibition at the NGV, I visited the mausoleum of the Yellow Emperor (Huangdi). Emperors have been honouring their ancestors at this site since the Spring and Autumn, and Warring States periods (770–c. 475 BCE and c. 475–221 BCE) more than 2500 years ago. During the War of Resistance against Japan (1937–45), Mao Zedong and Chiang Kai-shek came to worship; in the 1980s, Deng Xiaoping and Jiang Zemin also paid their respects—the captivating energy of the Yellow Emperor's mausoleum is indeed unparalleled! When I visited, the lofty mountain range stretched across the landscape and the tens of thousands of cypress trees extended towards the sky, each embodying a sense of rising spirituality while returning the gaze of passing travelers in the thousands of years gone by. Following other tourists, I took my plastic bottle and collected some water as a memento. I came to experience the unbending vigor, the immensity of the pines and cypress trees, just as depicted in the paintings of the ancient masters. They stirred within me a strong feeling about the noble character and temperament of our ancestors. Gazing into the tranquil horizon of the Central Plain, I felt as if I had been pulled into boundless realms of space and time, and heard cries and sighs echoing in the abyss.

During the same trip I also visited Luoyang to see the peonies. Since it was late in the season, many had already begun to fall. Layers of red and white petals, like snowflakes, created such a mess on the ground, but the scene touched me deeply! I asked myself: why do Chinese painters always portray these flowers either in bud or in full bloom? Prosperity and decline, life and death all have their own charm. A weak painting is the result of a weak painter with a weak spirit. If we say the peony is a symbol of China, it is only interesting if we also incorporate the flower's decay and withering return to the earth in our representations. Immaculate porcelains are fragile just as silk is flammable; creating peonies on these materials using gunpowder explosions can be seen as an attempt to convey the fragility of life and culture. [...]

I do not consider individual terracotta figures to be independent works of art. Compared to the unique classical sculptures in Western art history—such as the statue of Venus, or Hercules, even the Roman replicas of ancient Greek originals—these mass-produced terracotta figures, typically discovered and excavated by the thousands, are in my view part of an immense installation, epitomizing the essential ideas of life, death, and power. In this way, the mega-installation can be understood as a single conceptual work.

On my recent visit to Xi'an, I had a closer look at the individual sculpted figures, and in them detected the optimism of their creators. People of the Qin dynasty were in fact meticulous in their pursuit of high-quality life. They paid attention to their appearances, molding their hair and beards into different and distinctive styles. When imagining the Terracotta Warriors during the time of their creation, I see a vivacious assembly of figures painted with various colours, exhibiting endless combinations of characteristic features—it must have been an ancient equivalent of Pop Art! Yet, when each figure becomes integrated into military configurations and deployed as units in different spaces, the conceptual approach of the whole endeavor becomes apparent. [...]

The earth does not move; it is the sky that is revolving. The first Qin emperor, like Emperor Liu Bang of the Han dynasty and the many who followed, must have looked up at the birds soaring across the sky, empathising with the hero's ambition and innermost solitude. Their visions were global and all-embracing, and in their hearts they must have sensed the abstract spirit of the cosmic—what I envision to be the ultimate ritual between heaven and earth.

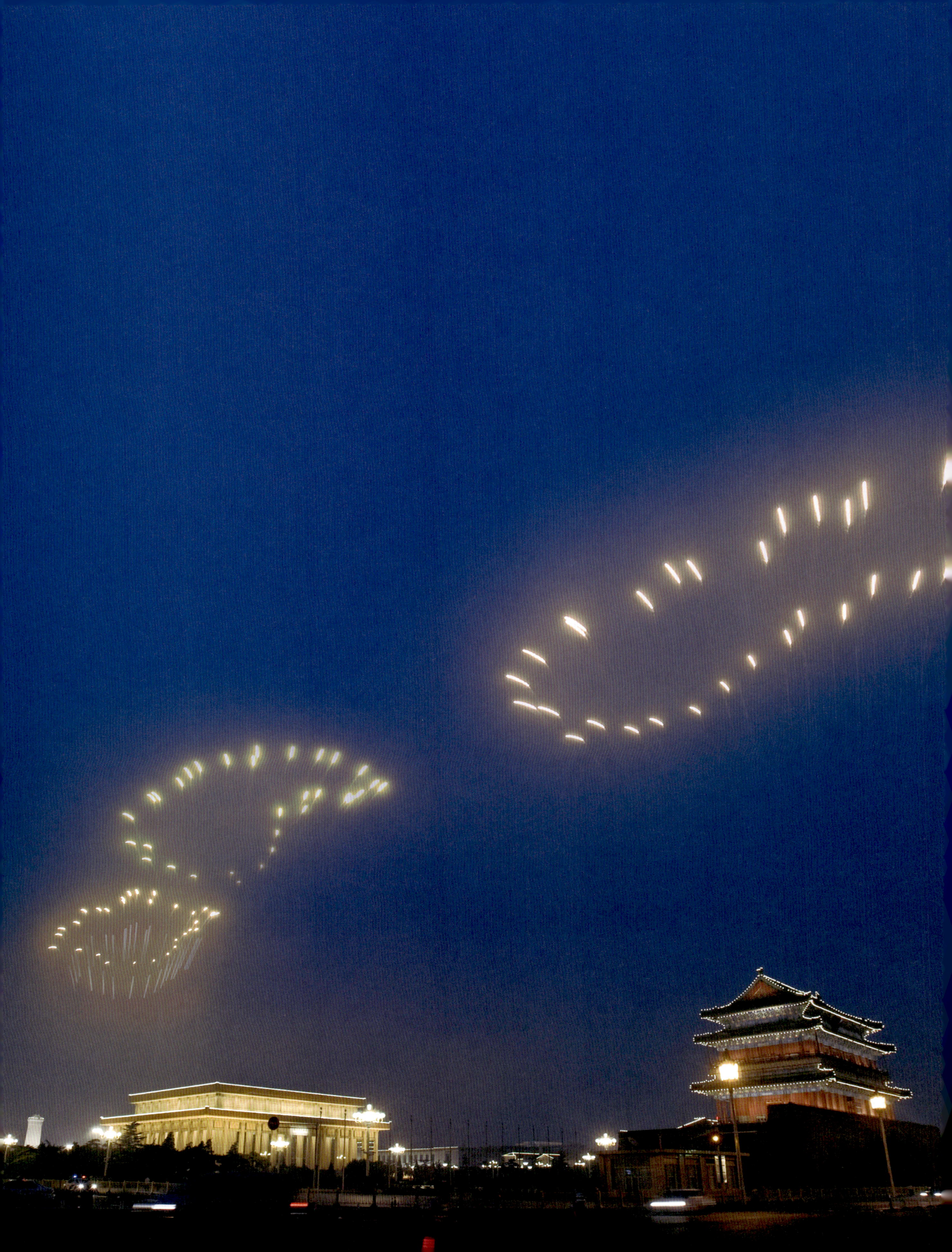

# A Guide to Cai Guo-Qiang's Dialogues
## *99 Projects and Keywords*

Compiled by Reiko Tomii
Researched by Hsiu-man Lin

What is one key idea that can decipher the concepts underlying Cai Guo-Qiang's vast body of work? The artist himself would respond with a deceptively simple idea: to "present the unseen world through visible means." This has defined his conceptual and methodological pursuit through the years, and serves as the cornerstone of his cosmology.

For many decades, Cai's art has shuttled between the seen and unseen worlds, spanning multiple forms, mediums, and fields, including painting, installation, video, and performance art shown in almost all major art institutions across five continents. Using Eastern philosophy and the issues of contemporary society as the foundation for his artistic concepts, he responds to local cultures and histories, and adopts them into his work in site-specific, multilayered manners.

This section offers a guide to Cai's massive output in three parts: Footprint, Chronology, and Notes on Keywords. "Footprint" maps the artist's outputs geographically, while "Chronology" orders representative works year by year. "Notes" explains "keywords" that signal the underlying ideas and themes behind Cai's countless dialogues to help readers better understand the trajectory and essence of the artist's career from the 1980s to the present (2020).

Since a living artist is a moving target, this guide by no means pretends to be precisely characteristic or comprehensive. The number 99, a repdigit of 9, invoked in the subtitle symbolically implies "infinite" in Chinese thought. The artist himself often uses this number in this manner, as in his autobiographical text "Ninety-Nine Tales: Curious Stories from My Journey Through the Real and Unseen Worlds," as well as a large number of artworks that make use of the number 99. The following selected keywords, and by extension the artist's related conceptual thinking and representative projects that exemplify them, each adopt a different approach and level to highlight Cai's fundamental conceptual and methodological pursuit.

Cai describes himself as a seed from his hometown. In order to blossom in different cultures, he has to believe that he is special yet universal—natural, unaffected, free. He regards art history, both Eastern and Western, as part of his "genes." In my view, this regard is vital to creating a new art not just for the present but for the future, and for the whole of humanity—and perhaps even for extraterrestrials.

### Legends

1. "Project Footprint" plots geographic locations of Cai's projects, exhibition activities (including solo exhibitions and Cai-curated exhibitions, as well as participation in group exhibitions), and permanent public works (as of September 2020).

2. "Chronology" captures Cai's works, projects, and solo exhibitions that embody his dialogue in terms of "keywords." Each entry consists of year; title of work/project/solo exhibition; occasion/venue/location; and keywords. In some instances, more than one work is listed from a single solo exhibition. Unrealized works and projects are so noted. Titles of solo exhibitions are abbreviated by omitting the artist's name. For example, *Cai Guo-Qiang: Chaos* (1994) is given as *Chaos*.

3. "Notes on Keywords" is organized alphabetically, with cross-references, if any, given at the end of each note. The artist's words, quoted without attribution here, are gathered from his past writing and interviews, as well as in-person and e-mail conversations with the compiler. Works underlined are found in Chronology.

Cai Guo-Qiang, *Footprints of History: Fireworks for the Opening Ceremony of the 2008 Beijing Olympic Games*, 2008. Photo by Hiro Ihara

# Project Footprint

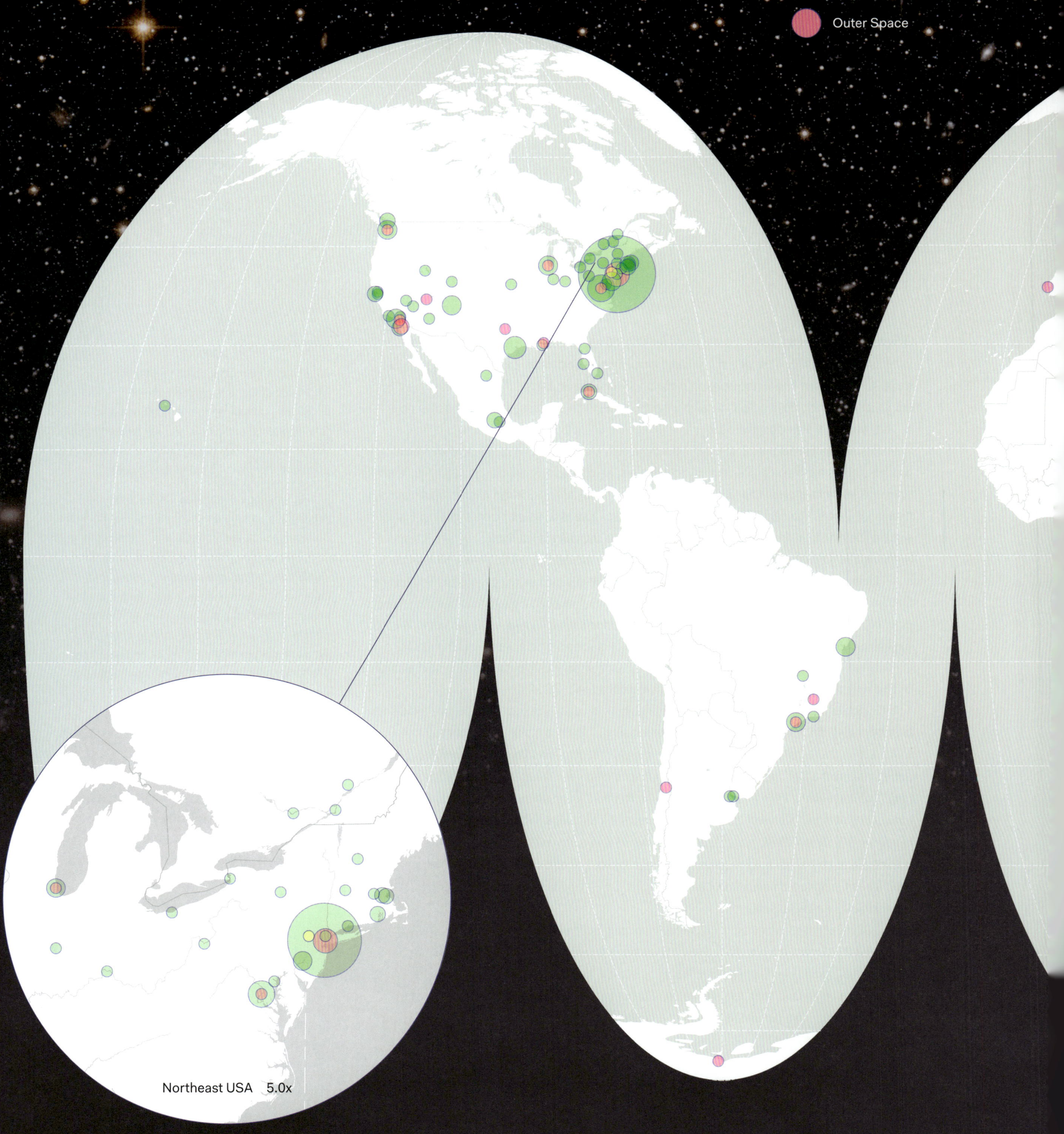

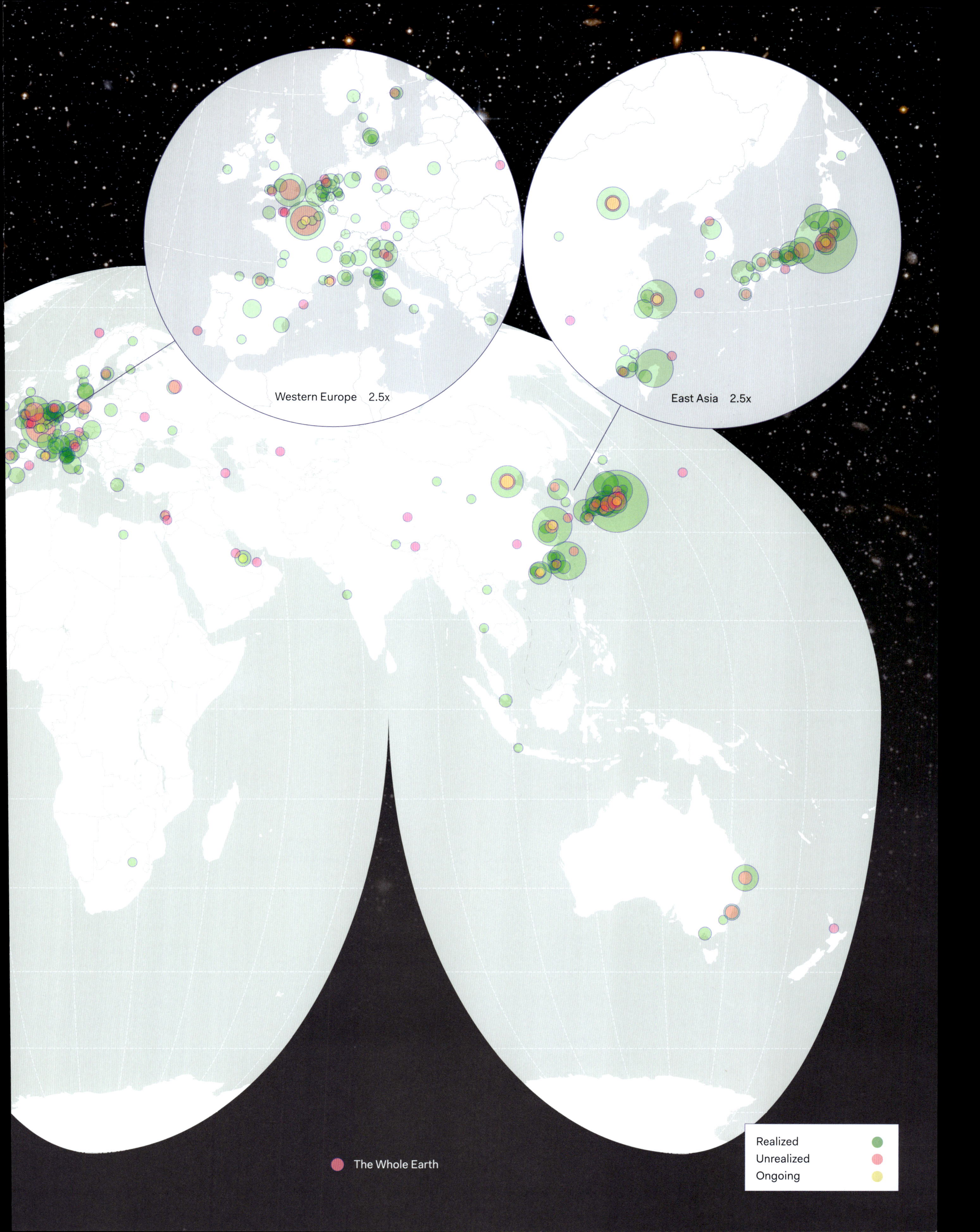

Western Europe 2.5x
East Asia 2.5x
The Whole Earth
Realized
Unrealized
Ongoing

# Asia

*Azerbaijan*
Baku 1

*Bhutan*
Himalayas 1

*China*
Beijing 12 3 2
Changsha 1
Fuzhou 1
Guangzhou 1
Hangzhou 4
Hong Kong 6 1 1
Jiayuguzan City 1
Nanping 1
Quanzhou 7
Shanghai 18 2 1
Shenzhen 3
Suzhou 2
Tibet 1
Yan'an 1
Kinmen, Taiwan 2 1
Taichung, Taiwan 2
Taipei, Taiwan 17

*India*
Mumbai 1

*Indonesia*
West Jakarta 1

*Israel*
Jerusalem 1
Tel Aviv 1 1

*Japan*
Chiba 1
Fukuoka 6
Fussa 1
Hakone 1
Hiroshima 4 1
Iwaki 12 1
Kagoshima 2
Kasama 1
Kawasaki 1
Kōbe 3
Kōka 1
Kumamoto 1
Kyoto 7
Mito 2 1
Mount Fuji 1
Nagoya 8 3
Naoshima 3
Nara 1
Niigata 7
Obihiro 1
Ōita 1
Oku District, Okayama 2 1
Osaka 5 1
Ōtsu, Shiga Prefecture 1
Saitama 3
Sakura Island 1
Tōkamachi 1
Tokyo 45 4 1
Ube 1
Utsunomiya 1
Yokohama 5 1

*Kazakhstan*
Baikonur 1

*Laos*
Luang Prabang 1

*Nepal*
Kathmandu 1

*Qatar*
Doha 3 1

*Russia*
Moscow 2 2

*Saudi Arabia*
Dhahran 1

*Singapore*
Singapore 2

*North Korea and South Korea*
Military Demarcation Line 1

*South Korea*
Gwangju 1
Seoul 5

*Thailand*
Bangkok 1

*Turkey*
Istanbul 1

*United Arab Emirates*
Abu Dhabi 1

# Europe

*Austria*
Salzburg 1
Sankt Veit an der Glan 1
Vienna 4

*Belgium*
Antwerp 2
Brussels 1
Ghent 6
Leuven 1

*Channel Islands*
Guernsey 2

*Denmark*
Copenhagen 4
Humlebæk 3

*Finland*
Helsinki 1
Rovaniemi 1

*France*
Aix-en-Provence 1 1 1
Arles 1
Boissy-le-Châtel 1
Bordeaux 1
Cognac 1
Jouy-en-Josas 1 1
Le Havre 1
Lyon 3
Nice 3
Paris 18 10 1
Reims 1

*Germany*
Berlin 2 2
Bonn 1
Cologne 1
Dresden 1
Düsseldorf 1
Hannover 1
Herford 3
Leipzig 1
Nordhorn 1
Stuttgart 1

*Greece*
Athens 2

*Ireland*
Limerick 1

*Italy*
Carrara 1
Codroipo 1
Colle di Val d'Elsa 3
Florence 1
Milan 3
Naples 1
Pistoia 1
Prato 1
Rivoli 1
Rome 4
San Gimignano 2
San Giovanni Valdarno 1
Siena 1
Trento 2
Turin 3
Tuscany 2
Venice 9 2
Vicenza 1

*Luxembourg*
Luxembourg 1

*Monaco*
City of Monaco 1

*Norway*
Lofoten 1
Oslo 2

*Poland*

| | | | |
|---|---|---|---|
| Warsaw | 2 | | |

*Portugal*

| | | | |
|---|---|---|---|
| Lisbon | | 1 | |

*Spain*

| | | | |
|---|---|---|---|
| Barcelona | | 1 | |
| Bilbao | 3 | 1 | |
| Córdoba | 1 | | |
| Donostia-San Sebastián | 1 | | |
| Gijón | 1 | | |
| Madrid | 4 | | |
| Valencia | 3 | | |

*Sweden*

| | | | |
|---|---|---|---|
| Gothenburg | 1 | | |
| Stockholm | 3 | 1 | |

*Switzerland*

| | | | |
|---|---|---|---|
| Basel | 1 | | |
| Lausanne | 1 | | |

*The Netherlands*

| | | | |
|---|---|---|---|
| Amsterdam | | 1 | |
| Arnhem | 1 | | |
| Maastricht | 1 | | |
| Otterlo | 4 | | |
| Rotterdam | 1 | | |
| Tilburg | 1 | | |
| Utrecht | 1 | 1 | |

*Ukraine*

| | | | |
|---|---|---|---|
| Donetsk | 1 | | |
| Kiev | | 1 | |

*United Kingdom*

| | | | |
|---|---|---|---|
| Bath | 1 | 1 | |
| Bristol | 1 | | |
| Edinburgh | 1 | | |
| London | 12 | 4 | |
| Manchester | 1 | | |
| Oxford | 2 | | |

## Africa

*Egypt*

| | | | |
|---|---|---|---|
| Siwa Oasis | 1 | | |

*South Africa*

| | | | |
|---|---|---|---|
| Johannesburg | 1 | | |

## North America

*Canada*

| | | | |
|---|---|---|---|
| Montréal | 1 | | |
| Ottawa | 1 | | |
| Shawinigan | 1 | | |
| Vancouver | 2 | | |

*Cuba*

| | | | |
|---|---|---|---|
| Havana | 2 | 1 | |

*Mexico*

| | | | |
|---|---|---|---|
| Cholula | 1 | | |
| Mexico City | 2 | | |
| Monterrey | 1 | | |

*United States*

| | | | |
|---|---|---|---|
| Aspen | 1 | | |
| Baltimore | 1 | | |
| Berkeley | 1 | | |
| Boston | 2 | | |
| Buffalo | 1 | | |
| Cambridge | 2 | | |
| Chester, NJ | | | 1 |
| Chicago | 3 | 1 | |
| Cincinnati | 1 | | |
| Claremont, CA | 1 | | |
| Cleveland | 1 | | |
| Fort Worth | | 1 | |
| Gainesville, FL | 1 | | |
| Grand Canyon | | 1 | |
| Greencastle, IN | 1 | | |
| Hanover, NH | 1 | | |
| Hayward, CA | 1 | | |
| Honolulu | 1 | | |
| Houston | 4 | | |
| Ithaca | 1 | | |
| Kansas City, MO | 1 | | |
| Los Angeles | 3 | | |
| Miami | 1 | | |
| Mormon Mesa, NV | 1 | | |
| Nevada Test Site | 1 | | |
| New Haven | 1 | | |
| New Orleans | 1 | 1 | |
| New York | 49 | 5 | |
| North Adams, MA | 1 | | |
| Orange County, CA | | 1 | |
| Philadelphia | 3 | | |
| Pittsburgh | 1 | | |
| Providence | 2 | | |
| Ridgefield, NJ | 1 | | |
| Salt Lake | 1 | | |
| San Diego | 2 | 2 | |
| San Francisco | 2 | | |
| Santa Barbara | 1 | | |
| Santa Fe | 3 | | |
| Sarasota | 1 | | |
| Scottsdale | 1 | | |
| Seattle | 3 | 1 | |
| Waltham | 1 | | |
| Washington, D.C. | 6 | 1 | |

## South America

*Argentina*

| | | | |
|---|---|---|---|
| Buenos Aires | 2 | | |

*Brazil*

| | | | |
|---|---|---|---|
| Belo Horizonte | | 1 | |
| Brasília | 1 | | |
| Rio de Janeiro | 1 | | |
| Salvador, Bahia | 3 | | |
| São Paulo | 3 | 1 | |

*Chile*

| | | | |
|---|---|---|---|
| Santiago | | 1 | |

## Australia and Oceania

*Australia*

| | | | |
|---|---|---|---|
| Brisbane | 8 | 2 | |
| Canberra | 1 | | |
| Melbourne | 2 | | |
| Sydney | 3 | 2 | |

*New Zealand*

| | | | |
|---|---|---|---|
| Auckland | | 1 | |

## Antarctica

| | | | |
|---|---|---|---|
| Antarctica | | 1 | |

## On the Sea

| | | | |
|---|---|---|---|
| East China Sea | | 3 | |
| North Pacific Ocean | | 1 | |

## The Whole Earth

| | | | |
|---|---|---|---|
| The Whole Earth | | 2 | |

## Outer Space

| | | | |
|---|---|---|---|
| Outer Space | | 7 | |

## Total

| | | | |
|---|---|---|---|
| Realized | 538 | | |
| Unrealized | | 101 | |
| Ongoing | | | 9 |

Background image of "Project Footprint" (pages 328–29): Stars in the Andromeda Galaxy's disk, as seen through the NASA/ESA Hubble Space Telescope. Photo by NASA, ESA, and T. M. Brown (STScI)

# Chronology

## 1985

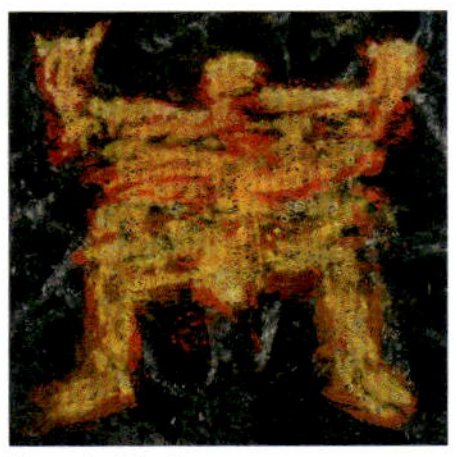

Photo by Hiro Ihara

### *Chu Ba Wang*

Painting presented in solo exhibition *Cai Guo-Qiang's Painting* at the Foreign Correspondents' Club of Japan, Tokyo, Japan

KEYWORDS: CHINESE HISTORY, ANCIENT

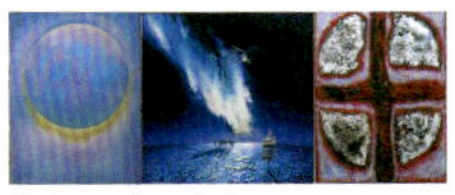

Photo by Chen Yi-Li

### *The Earth Is Our Common Home*

Painting presented in group exhibition *The Shanghai and Fujian Youth Modern Art Joint Exhibition* at Fuzhou Museum, Fuzhou, China

KEYWORDS: ECOLOGY

## 1985–86

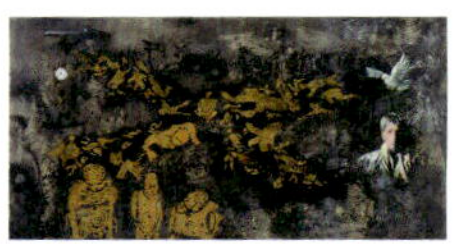

### *Shadow: Pray for Protection*

Painting presented in solo exhibition *Cai Guo-Qiang's Painting* at the Foreign Correspondents' Club of Japan, Tokyo, Japan

KEYWORDS: WAR AND PEACE

## 1989

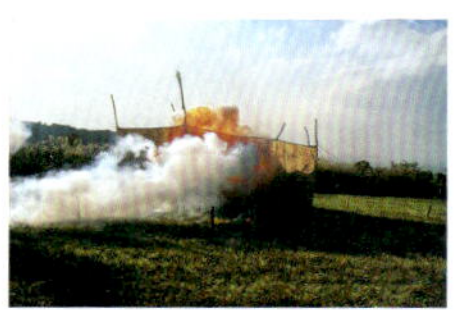

Photo by Wataru Kai

### *Human Abode: Project for Extraterrestrials No. 1*

Explosion event realized for group exhibition *'89 Tama River Fussa Outdoor Art Exhibition* at Fussa Minami Park and Kumagawa Shrine, Tokyo, Japan

KEYWORDS: CHINESE CULTURE AND CRAFTS; COSMOS; EXTRATERRESTRIALS; JAPAN; MYTHOLOGY AND RELIGION; ROMANTIC

## 1990

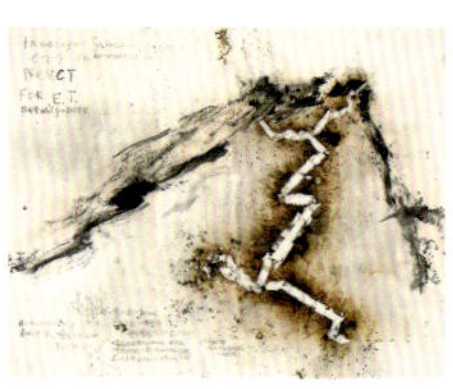

### *Ascending Dragon: Project for Extraterrestrials No. 2*

Explosion event proposed but unrealized for group exhibition *Chine demain pour hier* at Pourrières, Aix-en-Provence, France

KEYWORDS: ART HISTORY; CÉZANNE; DRAGON; EXTRATERRESTRIALS; GUNPOWDER DRAWING AND GUNPOWDER PAINTING

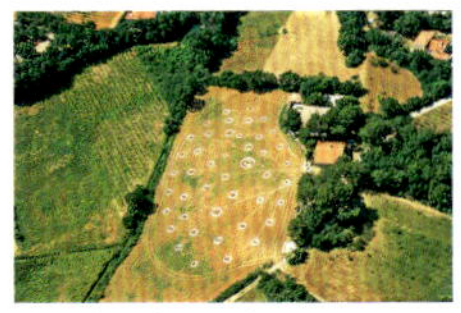

Photo by Cai Guo-Qiang

### *45.5 Meteorite Craters Made by Humans on Their 45.5 Hundred Million Year Old Planet: Project for Extraterrestrials No. 3*

Explosion event realized for group exhibition *Chine demain pour hier* at Pourrières, Aix-en-Provence, France

KEYWORDS: COSMOS; EXTRATERRESTRIALS

## 1991

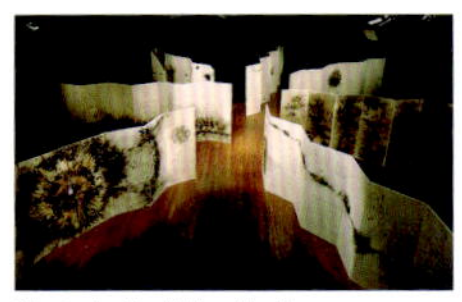

Photo by Yoshihiro Hagiwara

### *Primeval Fireball: The Project for Projects*

Solo exhibition at P3 art and environment, Tokyo, Japan, comprising 7 gunpowder drawings on folding screens below

KEYWORDS: COSMOS; EXTRATERRESTRIALS; GUNPOWDER DRAWING AND GUNPOWDER PAINTING; ROMANTIC

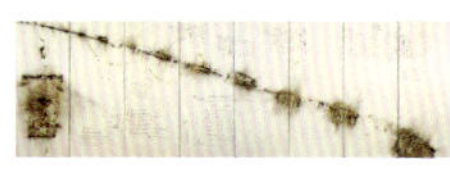

*Bigfoot's Footprints: Project for Extraterrestrials No. 6* (1990)

KEYWORDS: BIGFOOT

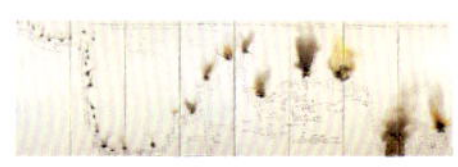

*Reviving the Ancient Signal Towers: Project for Extraterrestrials No. 8* (1990)

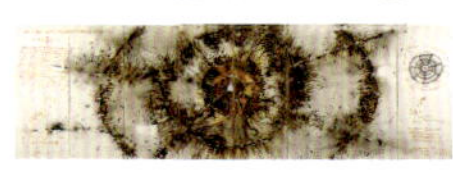

*Fetus Movement II: Project for Extraterrestrials No. 9* (1990)

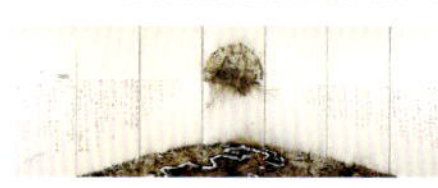

*A Certain Lunar Eclipse: Project for Humankind No. 2* (1991)

KEYWORDS: COSMOS

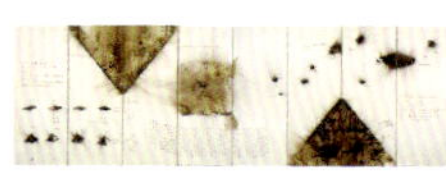

*Inverted Pyramid on the Moon: Project for Humankind No. 3* (1991)

KEYWORDS: COSMOS

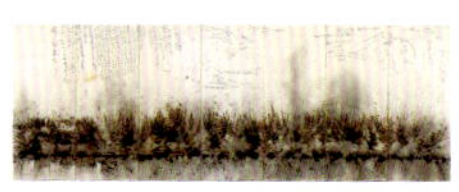

*Rebuilding the Berlin Wall: Project for Extraterrestrials No. 7* (1991)

KEYWORDS: CURRENT EVENTS

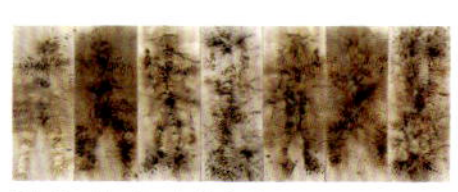

*The Vague Border at the Edge of Time/Space Project* (1991)

Photos by André Morin, courtesy Cartier Foundation for Contemporary Art

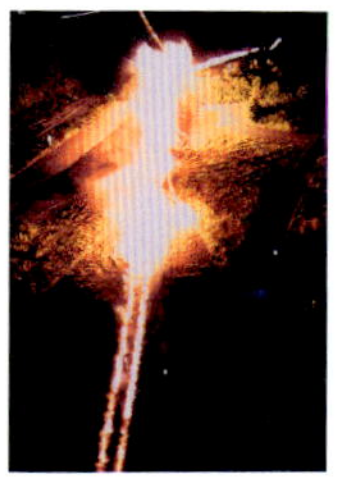

## *The Immensity of Heaven and Earth: Project for Extraterrestrials No. 11*

Explosion event realized at Kashii former train yard, Fukuoka, Japan

KEYWORDS: COSMOS; EXTRATERRESTRIALS

### 1992

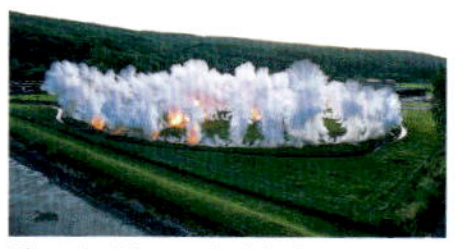

Photo by Masanobu Moriyama

## *Fetus Movement II: Project for Extraterrestrials No. 9*

Explosion event realized at the German Army's water exercise area in Hann. Münden, Germany

KEYWORDS: COSMOS; EXTRATERRESTRIALS; *FENG SHUI*

### 1993

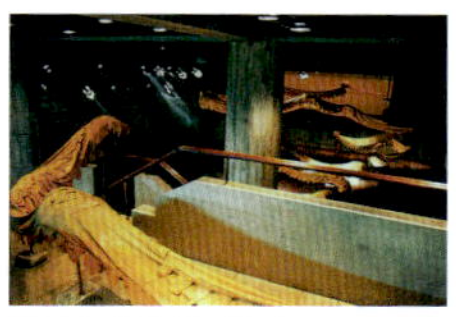

Photo by Yoshihiro Hagiwara

## *Long Mai: The Dragon Meridian*

Solo exhibition at P3 art and environment, Tokyo, Japan

KEYWORDS: CHINESE MEDICINE AND NATURAL HEALING; DRAGON

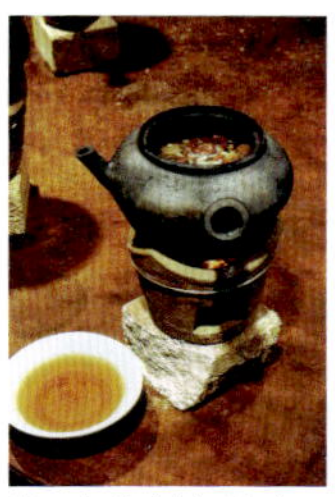

Photo by Yoshihiro Hagiwara

## *Secret Recipe for Japan: Fan Pu Gui Zhen Tang and Zeng Shou Ning Shen Tang: Project for Humankind No. 5*

Installation presented in solo exhibition *Long Mai—The Dragon Meridian* at P3 art and environment, Tokyo, Japan

KEYWORDS: CHINESE MEDICINE AND NATURAL HEALING

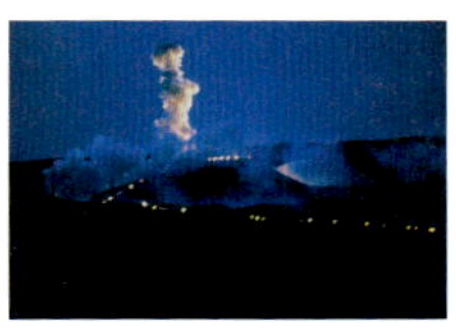

Photo by Masanobu Moriyama

## *Project to Extend the Great Wall of China by 10,000 Meters: Project for Extraterrestrials No. 10*

Explosion event realized at the Gobi Desert, Jiayuguan, Gansu Province, China

KEYWORDS: CHINESE HISTORY, ANCIENT; COSMOS; DRAGON; EXTRATERRESTRIALS

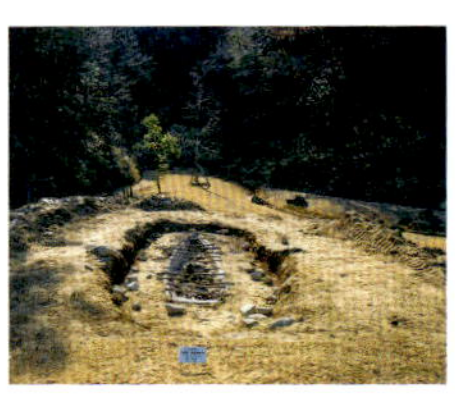

## *Buried Civilization—Field Firings*

Project realized at Sun Plaza and Spring Square, Shigaraki Ceramic Cultural Park, Shiga, Japan

KEYWORDS: BOAT; JAPAN

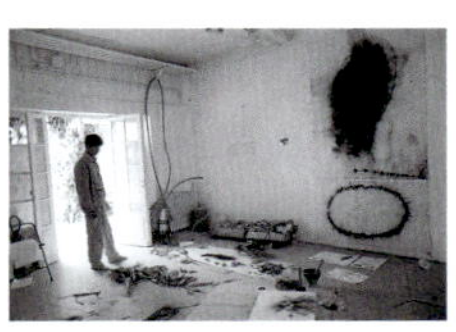

Photo by Hugues Colson, courtesy Cartier Foundation for Contemporary Art

Residency at the Cartier Foundation for Contemporary Art for three months in Jouy-en-Josas, France

KEYWORDS: CHINESE MEDICINE AND NATURAL HEALING

### 1994

Photo by Kazuo Ono

## *The Horizon from the Pan-Pacific: Project for Extraterrestrials No. 14*

Explosion event realized on the Pacific Ocean near Iwaki, Fukushima, Japan

KEYWORDS: COSMOS; IWAKI; ROMANTIC

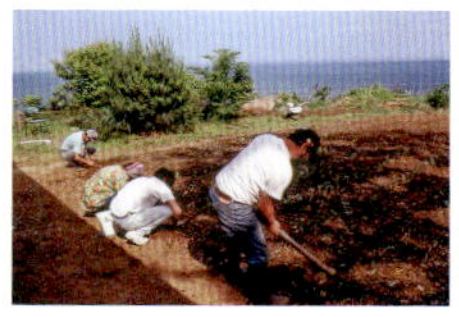

## *Chrysanthemum Tea*

Installation presented in solo exhibition *From the Pan-Pacific* at Iwaki City Art Museum, Fukushima, Japan

KEYWORDS: CHINESE MEDICINE AND NATURAL HEALING

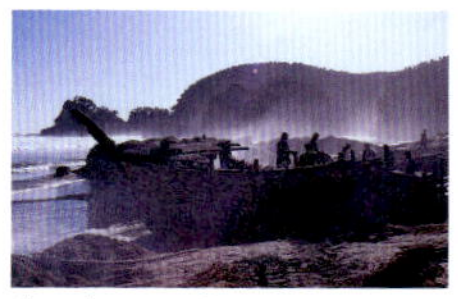

Photo by Kazuo Ono

## *Kaikou—The Keel (Returning Light—The Dragon Bone)*

Installation presented in solo exhibition *From the Pan-Pacific* at Iwaki City Art Museum, Fukushima, Japan

KEYWORDS: BOAT; IWAKI

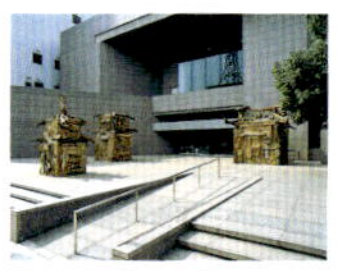

Photo by Kazuo Ono

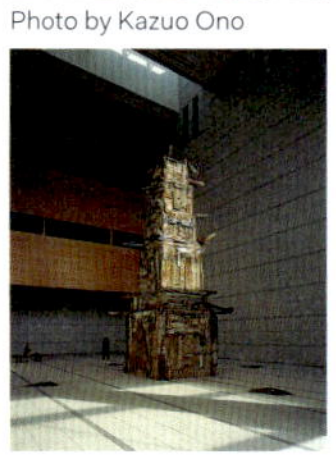

Photo by Norihiro Ueno

## *San Jō Tower*

Installation presented in solo exhibition *From the Pan-Pacific* at Iwaki City Art Museum, Fukushima, Japan

1995: reconfigured as *The Orient (San Jō Tower)* presented at the Museum of Contemporary Art, Tokyo, Japan

KEYWORDS: IWAKI; TOWER

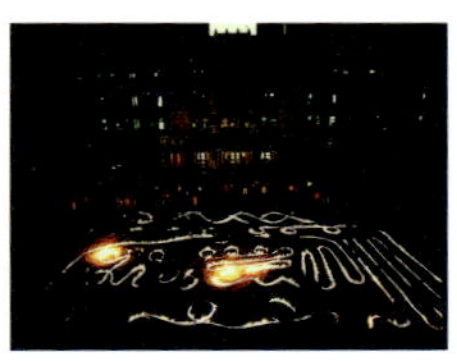

Photo by Masanobu Moriyama

## *Project for Heiankyō 1,200th Anniversary: Celebration from Chang'an*

Project realized at City Hall plaza, Kyoto, Japan

KEYWORDS: CHINESE HISTORY, AND JAPAN

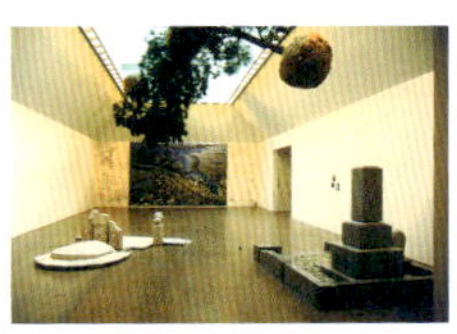

Photo by Cai Guo-Qiang and Taku Saiki

## *Universal Design: Feng Shui Project for Mito: Chang Sheng*

Installation presented in group exhibition *Mito Annual '94: Open System* at Art Tower Mito Contemporary Art Center, Mito, Japan

KEYWORDS: *FENG SHUI*

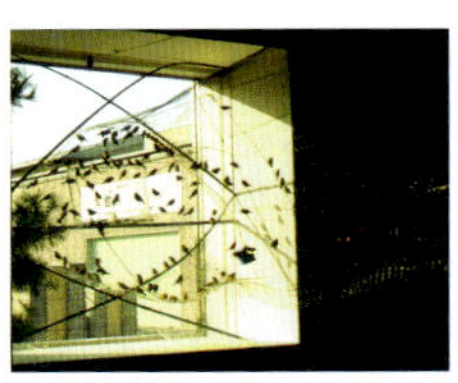

Photo by Cai Guo-Qiang and Taku Saiki

## *Fang Sheng*

Installation presented in group exhibition *Mito Annual '94: Open System* at Art Tower Mito Contemporary Art Center, Mito, Japan

KEYWORDS: FAUNA AND FLORA; *FENG SHUI*; MYTHOLOGY AND RELIGION

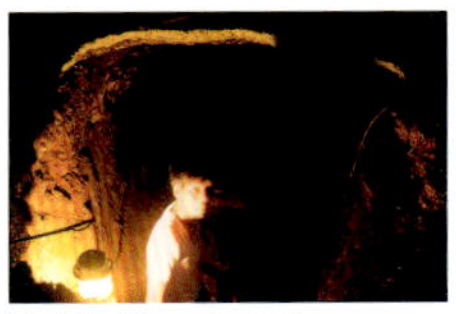

Photo by Masanobu Moriyama

### *Grave Robbing*

Installation presented in solo exhibition *Chaos* at Setagaya Art Museum, Tokyo, Japan

KEYWORDS: CHINESE HISTORY, ANCIENT

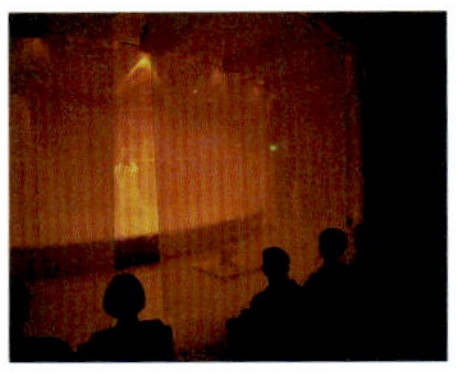

### *Elixir of Immortality*

Immersive theater realized for solo exhibition *Chaos* held in conjunction with *Qin-Dynasty's First Emperor and His Age* at Setagaya Art Museum, Tokyo, Japan

KEYWORDS: CHINESE HISTORY, ANCIENT; CHINESE MEDICINE AND NATURAL HEALING

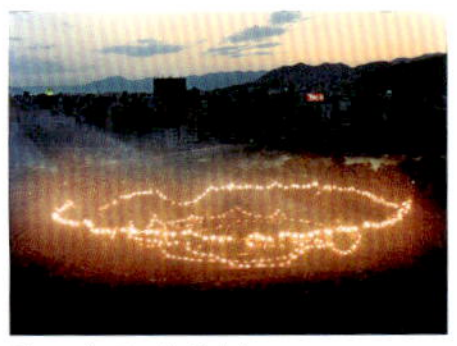

Photo by Kunio Ōshima

### *The Earth Has Its Black Hole Too: Project for Extraterrestrials No. 16*

Explosion event realized at Hiroshima Central Park near the Atomic Bomb Dome ruins and a former Japanese military headquarters, Hiroshima, Japan

KEYWORDS: COSMOS; EXTRATERRISTRIALS; WAR AND PEACE

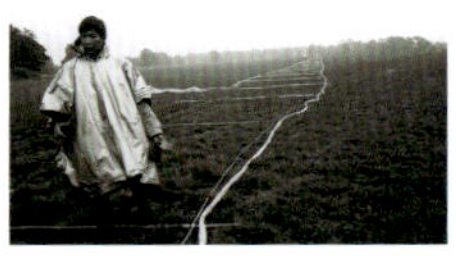

### *Making a Ladder to the Earth: Project for Extraterrestrials No. 20*

Explosion event proposed but unrealized for the Bath Festival, Bath, U.K.

KEYWORDS: COSMOS; EXTRATERRISTRIALS; GRANDMOTHER

## 1995

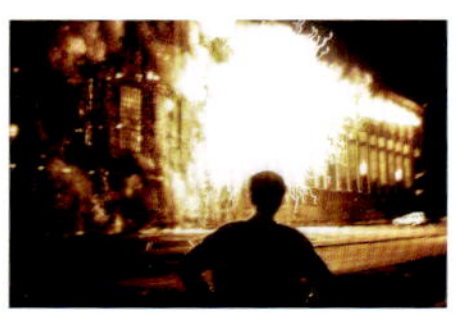

Photo by Takashi Shinkawa

### *Restrained Violence—Rainbow: Project for Extraterrestrials No. 25*

Explosion event realized for group exhibition *The Ever-Changing, Drifting Heat: The First Johannesburg Biennale*, on the façade of Tribune Hall, the Electric Workshop (former power generating station), Johannesburg, South Africa

KEYWORDS: CURRENT EVENTS; SHAMAN

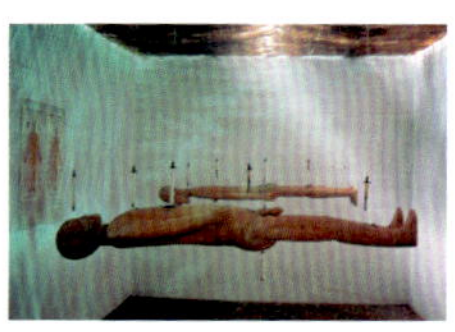

Photo by Cai Guo-Qiang

### *Moxacautery—For Africa*

Installation presented in group exhibition *The Ever-Changing, Drifting Heat: The First Johannesburg Biennale,* the Electric Work-shop (former power generating station), Johannesburg, South Africa

KEYWORDS: CHINESE MEDICINE AND NATURAL HEALING

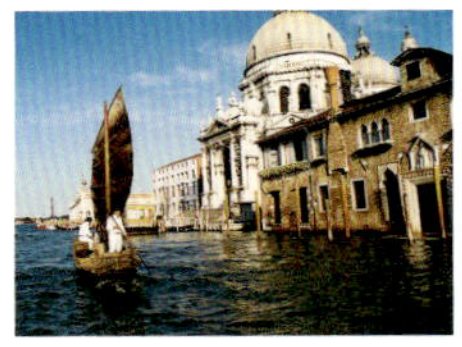

Photo by Yamamoto Tadasu

### *Bringing to Venice What Marco Polo Forgot*

Social project realized for group exhibition *46th Venice Biennale: TransCulture* at Palazzo Giustinian Lolin and Grand Canal, Venice, Italy

KEYWORDS: BOAT; CHINESE MEDICINE AND NATURAL HEALING; GLOBALIZATION IN HISTORY; QUANZHOU

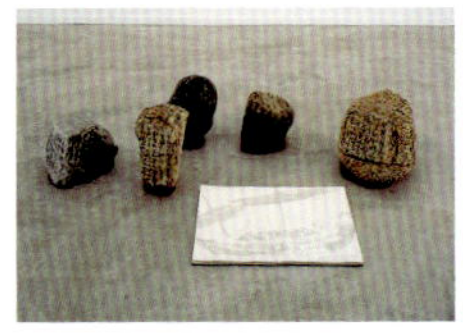

### *Wakō: Japanese Pirates of the Middle Ages*

Project proposed but unrealized for group exhibition *TransCulture Homecoming Report: To Distant Japan* at Naoshima Contemporary Art Museum (presently Benesse House Museum), Naoshima, Japan

KEYWORDS: CHINESE HISTORY, AND JAPAN; GLOBALIZATION IN HISTORY

## 1996

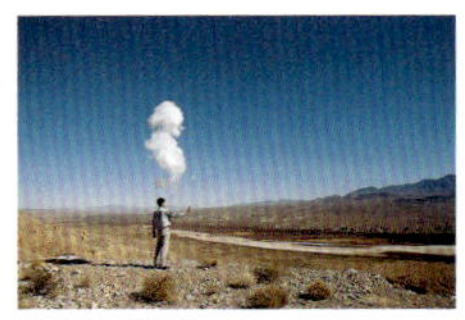

Photo by Hiro Ihara

### *The Century with Mushroom Clouds: Project for the 20th Century*

Explosion event realized at various sites in the Nevada Test Site (presently Nevada National Security Site); Mormon Mesa, Nevada; Salt Lake, Utah; and various sites in New York and New Jersey, U.S.

KEYWORDS: UNITED STATES; WAR AND PEACE

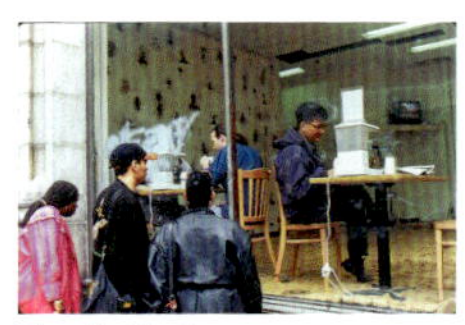

Photo by Hiro Ihara

### *Crab House*

Installation presented in group exhibition *In the Ruins of the Twentieth Century: The 20th Annual International Studio Artist Exhibition* organized at P.S.1 Contemporary Art Center (presently MoMA PS1), New York, U.S.

KEYWORDS: CHINESE MEDICINE AND NATURAL HEALING; WAR AND PEACE

### *Guanyin*

Paintings presented in solo exhibition *Guanyin* at Gallery APA, Nagoya, Japan

KEYWORDS: MYTHOLOGY AND RELIGION

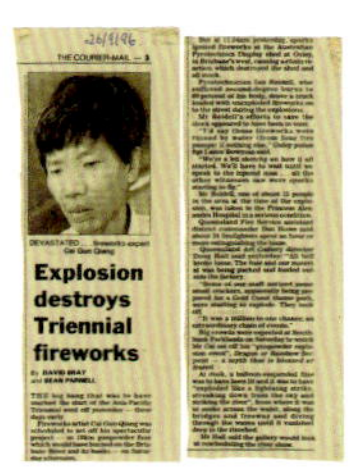

**Explosion destroys Triennial fireworks**

*The Courier Mail* (Brisbane), September 26, 1996

### *Dragon or Rainbow Serpent: A Myth Glorified or Feared: Project for Extraterrestrials No. 28*

Explosion event proposed but unrealized for group exhibition *The Second Asia-Pacific Triennial of Contemporary Art* at Queensland Art Gallery, South Brisbane, Australia

KEYWORDS: DRAGON; MYTHOLOGY AND RELIGION

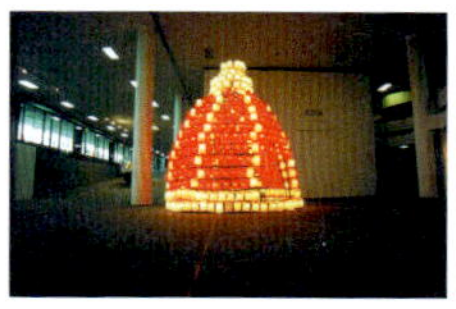
Photo by Tatsumi Masatoshi

### *Dome*

Installation presented in group exhibition *Universalis: 23rd International Biennial of São Paulo*, at Ibirapuera Park, São Paulo, Brazil

KEYWORDS: ART HISTORY; CHINESE CULTURE AND CRAFTS

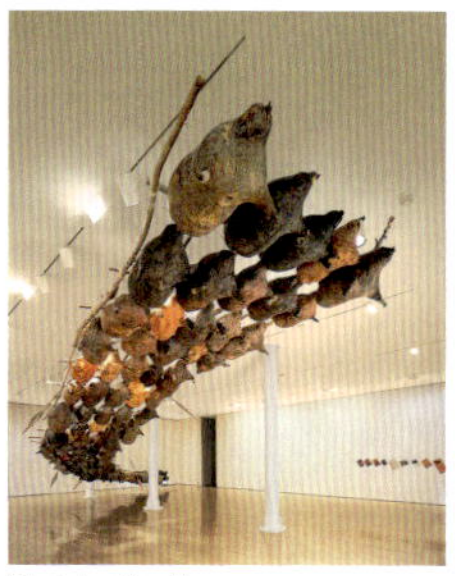
Photo by Hiro Ihara

### *Cry Dragon/Cry Wolf: The Ark of Genghis Khan*

Installation presented in group exhibition *The Hugo Boss Prize 1996* at Guggenheim Museum SoHo, New York, U.S.

KEYWORDS: DRAGON; GLOBALIZATION IN HISTORY; UNITED STATES

## 1997

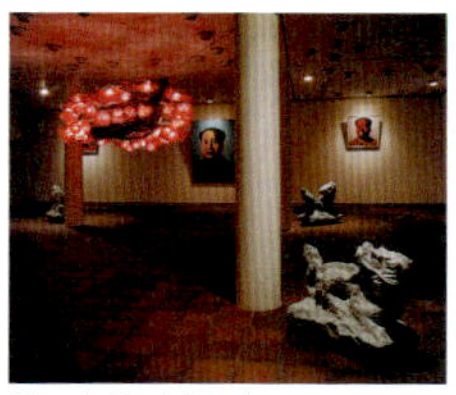
Photo by Daniel Kowitz

### *Mao*

Installation presented in solo exhibition *Flying Dragon in the Heavens* at Louisiana Museum of Modern Art, Humlebæk, Denmark

KEYWORDS: CHINESE CULTURE AND CRAFTS; CHINESE HISTORY, POST-1949; DRAGON

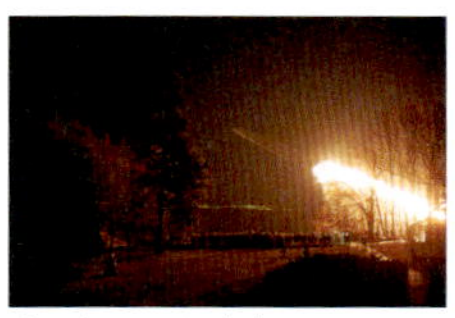
Photo by Jens Frederiksen

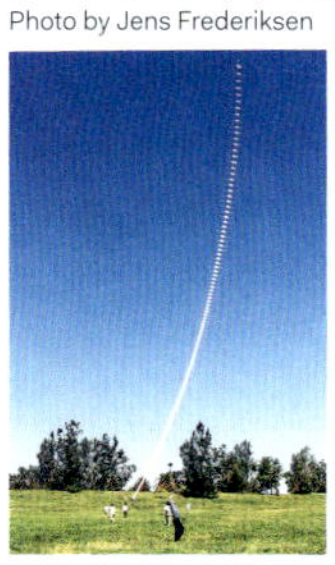

### *Flying Dragon in the Heavens: Project for Extraterrestrials No. 29*

Explosion event realized for solo exhibition *Flying Dragon in the Heavens* at Louisiana Museum of Modern Art, Humlebæk, Denmark

1998: partially realized for group exhibition *Crossings* at National Gallery of Canada, Ottawa, Canada

KEYWORDS: CHINESE CULTURE AND CRAFTS; DRAGON

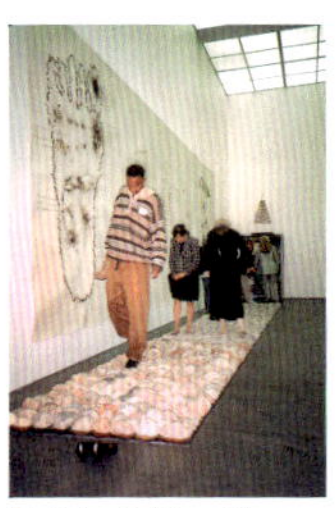
Photo by Cai Guo-Qiang

### *A Cure When Ill, A Supplement When Healthy*

Installation presented in group exhibition *Performance Anxiety* at the Museum of Contemporary Art Chicago, Illinois, U.S.

KEYWORDS: CHINESE MEDICINE AND NATURAL HEALING

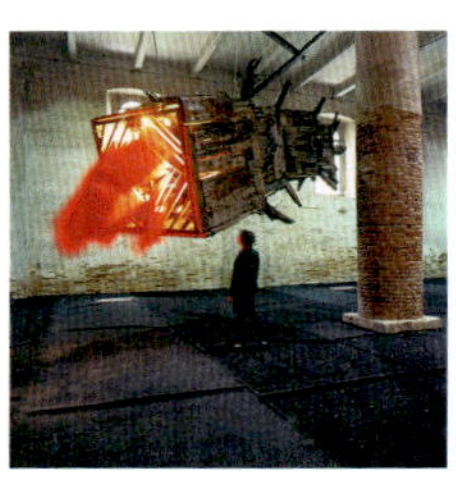
Photo by Elio Montanari

### *The Dragon Has Arrived!*

Installation developed from *San Jō Tower* (1994), presented in group exhibition *47th Venice Biennale: Future, Past, Present* at Arsenale, Venice, Italy

KEYWORDS: DRAGON; GLOBALIZATION IN HISTORY; IWAKI

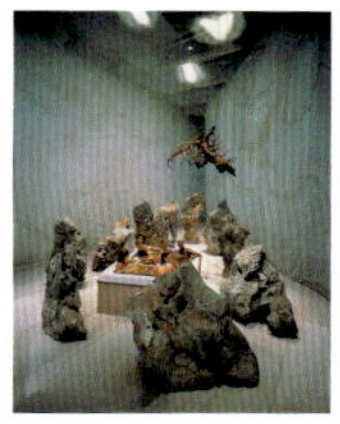
Photo by Hiro Ihara

### *Cultural Melting Bath: Project for the 20th Century*

Installation presented in solo exhibition of the same title at the Queens Museum of Art (presently the Queens Museum), New York, U.S.

KEYWORDS: CHINESE MEDICINE AND NATURAL HEALING; *FENG SHUI*; GLOBALIZATION IN HISTORY

## 1998

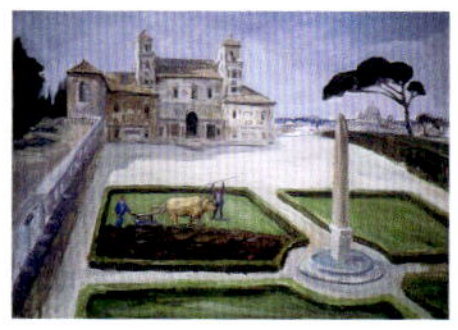

### *Summer Tilling at Villa Medici*

Oil drawing presented in group exhibition *La Ville, le Jardin, la Memoire* (1998–2000) at the French Academy in Rome, Rome, Italy

2000: *Till by Blade, Sow by Fire*
Associated explosion event realized at the same location

KEYWORDS: DRAWING

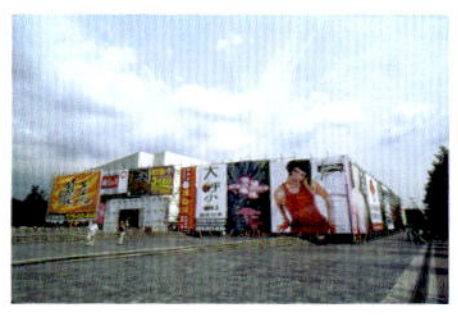
Photo by Tatsumi Masatoshi

### *Advertising Castle*

Installation presented in group exhibition *1998 Taipei Biennial: Site of Desire* at Taipei Fine Arts Museum, Taipei, Taiwan

KEYWORDS: MUSEUM AS MEDIUM

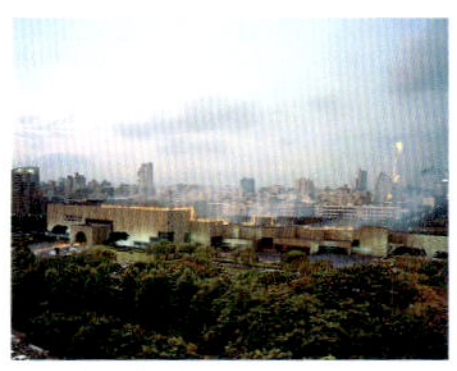
Photo by Hiro Ihara

### *No Destruction, No Construction: Bombing the Taiwan Province Museum of Art*

Explosion event realized at Taiwan Province Museum of Art (presently National Taiwan Museum of Fine Arts), Taichung, Taiwan

KEYWORDS: DRAGON; MUSEUM AS MEDIUM

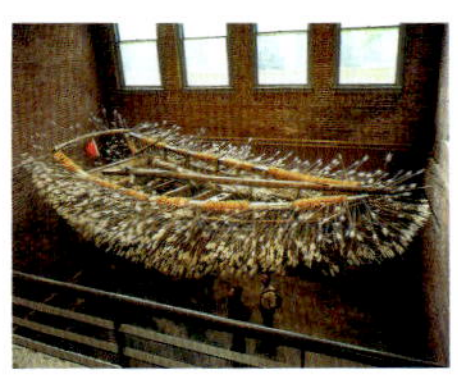
Photo by Hiro Ihara

### *Borrowing Your Enemy's Arrows*

Installation presented in group exhibition *Inside Out: New Chinese Art* at P.S.1 Contemporary Art Center (presently MoMA PS1), New York, U.S.

KEYWORDS: BOAT; CHINESE HISTORY, ANCIENT; GLOBALIZATION IN HISTORY

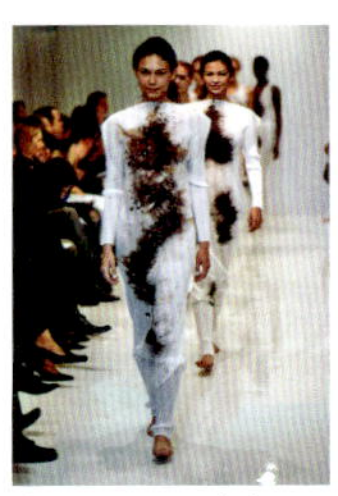
Photo courtesy Miyake Design Studio

### *Issey Miyake Making Things*

Project in collaboration with fashion designer at the Cartier Foundation for Contemporary Art, Paris, France

KEYWORDS: CONTEMPORARY CULTURAL FIGURES; DRAGON

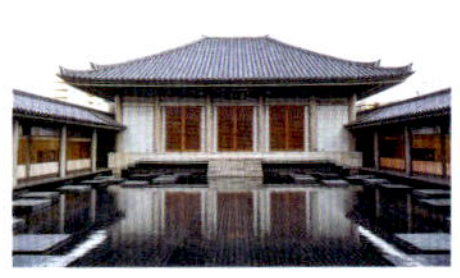
Photo by Shigeki Ogasawara/Kelham Photograph

### *Four Seasons and Four Phases*

Public art at Tōchōji temple, Tokyo, Japan

KEYWORDS: CHINESE CULTURE AND CRAFTS; MYTHOLOGY AND RELIGION

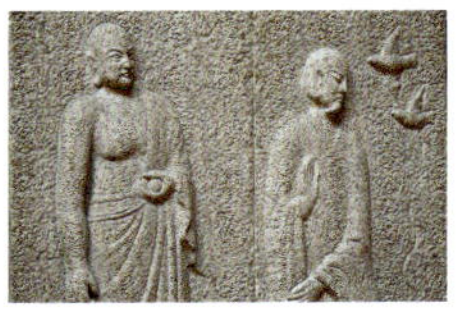

Photo courtesy Tōchōji

### *Ten Great Disciples*

Sculptures at Tōchōji temple, Tokyo, Japan

KEYWORDS: MYTHOLOGY AND RELIGION

## 1999

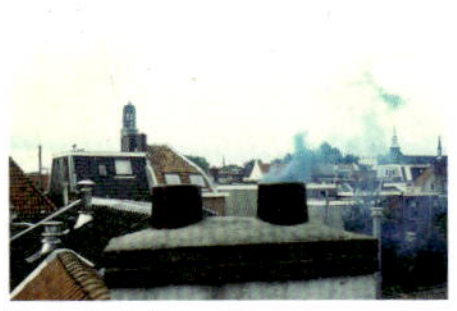

Photo by Cai Guo-Qiang

### *The Last Supper: Project for Extraterrestrials No. 31*

Participatory explosion event realized for group exhibition *Panorama 2000: Art in Utrecht Seen from the Dom Tower* at Centraal Museum, Utrecht, the Netherlands

KEYWORDS: CURRENT EVENTS

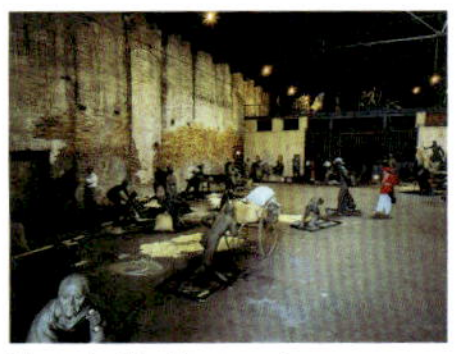

Photo by Elio Montanari

### *Venice's Rent Collection Courtyard*

Project presented in group exhibition *48th Venice Biennale: dAPERTutto* at Venice, Italy

KEYWORDS: ART HISTORY; CONTEMPORARY CULTURAL FIGURES; *FENG SHUI*; SOCIALISM

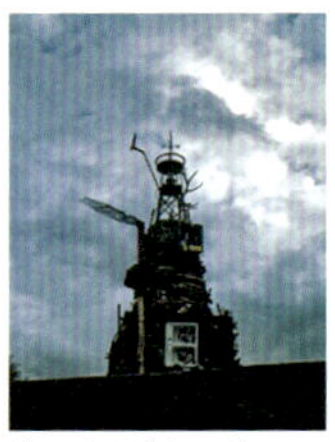

Photo by Cai Guo-Qiang

### *Calling*

Installation presented in group exhibition *Looking for a Place: The Third International SITE Santa Fe Biennial* at SITE Santa Fe, New Mexico, U.S.

KEYWORDS: TOWER

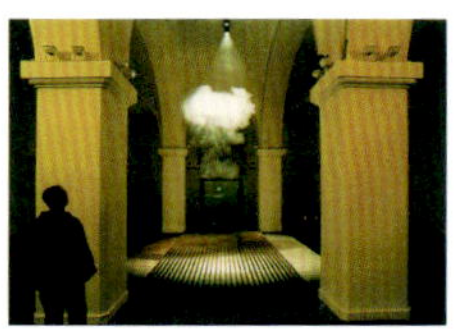

Photo by Fritz Simak

### *I Am the Y2K Bug*

Solo exhibition at Kunsthalle Wien, Vienna, Austria

KEYWORDS: CURRENT EVENTS

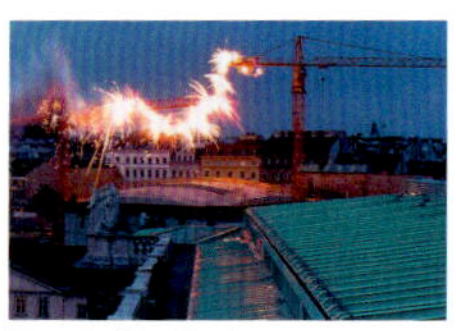

Photo by Fritz Simak

### *Dragon Sight Sees Vienna: Project for Extraterrestrials No. 32*

Explosion event realized for solo exhibition *I Am the Y2K Bug* at Kunsthalle Wien, Vienna, Austria

KEYWORDS: DRAGON; GLOBALIZATION IN HISTORY

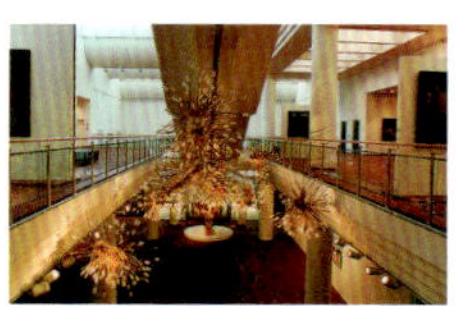

Photo courtesy Museum Ludwig

### *The Age of Not Believing in God*

Installation presented in group exhibition *Art-Worlds in Dialogue* at Museum Ludwig, Cologne, Germany

KEYWORDS: MYTHOLOGY AND RELIGION

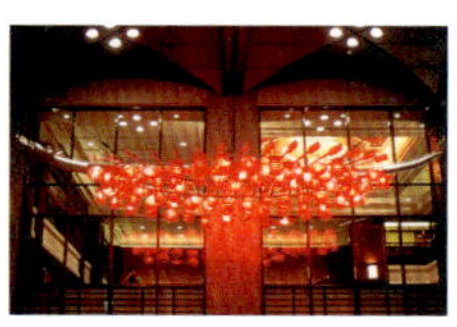

### *Dragon Boat*

Public art at Hakataza Theater, Fukuoka, Japan

KEYWORDS: BOAT; CHINESE CULTURE AND CRAFTS; DRAGON

## 1999/2000

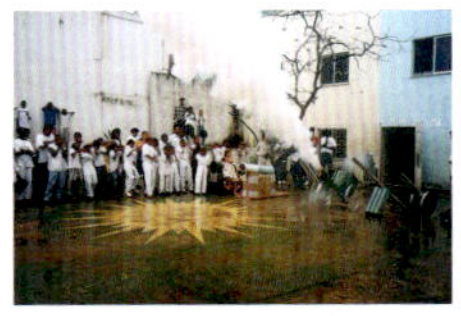

Photo courtesy France Morin and Cai Guo-Qiang

### *Salute*

Social project in collaboration with local juvenile offenders, realized through Projeto Axé at Casa de Cultura (presently Casa de Somes) (1999), and Museu de Arte Moderna da Bahía (2000), Salvador, Bahia, Brazil

KEYWORDS: CENTRAL AND SOUTH AMERICA; ROMANTIC; WAR AND PEACE

## 2000

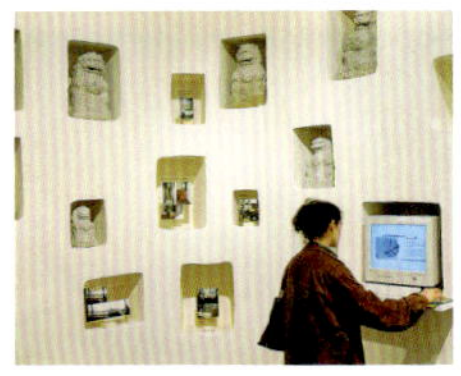

Photo by Hiro Ihara

### *How Is Your Feng Shui?: Year 2000 Project for Manhattan*

Installation presented in group exhibition *Whitney Biennial: 2000 Exhibition* at Whitney Museum of American Art, New York, U.S.

KEYWORDS: *FENG SHUI*

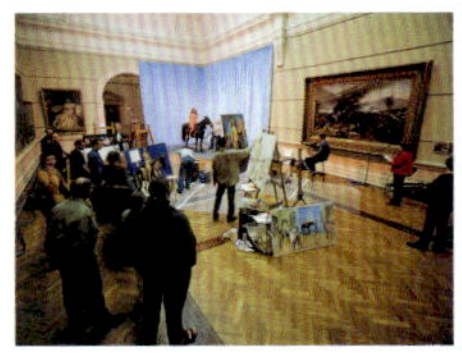

Photo by Jenni Carter

### *Still Life Performance*

Performance in group exhibition *Biennale of Sydney 2000* at Art Gallery of New South Wales, Sydney, Australia

KEYWORDS: ART HISTORY; DRAWING

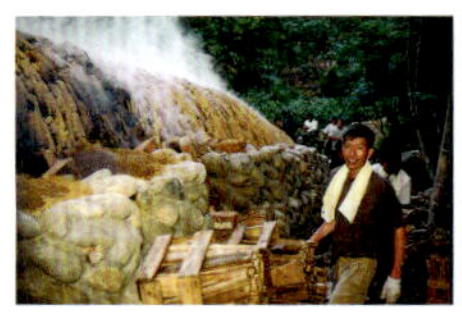

Photo by Shinji Murakami

### *DMoCA (Dragon Museum of Contemporary Art)*

Space established and curated by Cai Guo-Qiang in Tsunan Mountain Park, Niigata, Japan, initiated in conjunction with *Echigo-Tsumari Art Triennial*

KEYWORDS: MUSEUM AS MEDIUM

## 2001

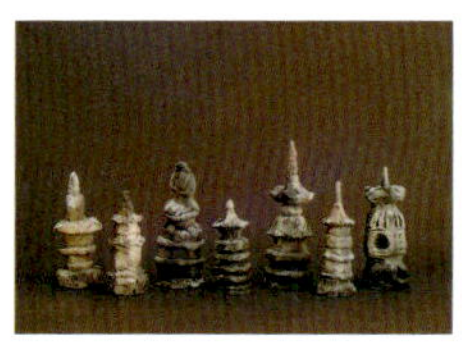

### *Iwaki Ninety-Nine Towers*

Solo exhibition in Gallery Iwaki, Fukushima, Japan

KEYWORDS: TOWER

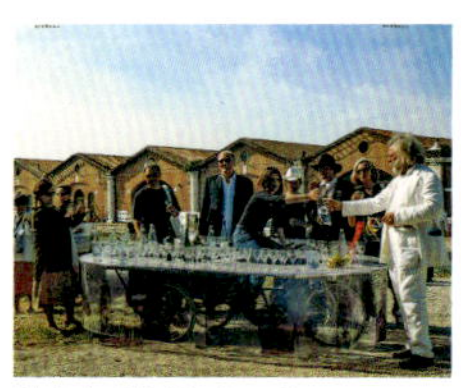

Photo by Elio Montanari

### *Service for the Biennale!*

Project realized for group exhibition *49th Venice Biennale: Plateau of Humankind* at Venice, Italy

KEYWORDS: CONTEMPORARY CULTURAL FIGURES

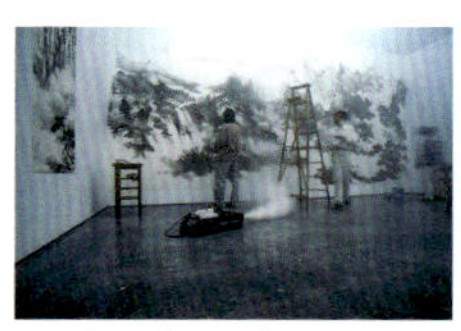

Photo by Carlos Mendes

### *Performing Chinese Ink Painting*

Performance presented in solo exhibition of the same title at Contemporary Art Gallery and Dr. Sun Yat-Sen Classical Chinese Garden, Vancouver, Canada

KEYWORDS: CHINESE PAINTING, TRADITIONAL

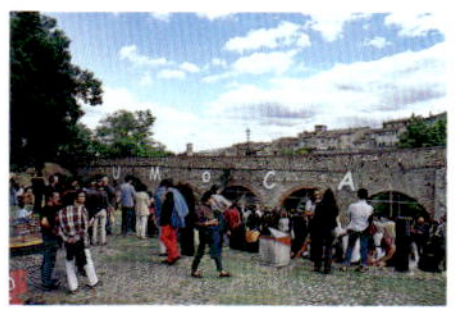

Photo by Galleria Continua

### *UMoCA (Underground Museum of Contemporary Art)*

Space established and curated by Cai Guo-Qiang under St. Francis Bridge, Colle di Val d'Elsa, Tuscany, Italy, initiated in conjunction with *Arte all'Arte*

KEYWORDS: MUSEUM AS MEDIUM

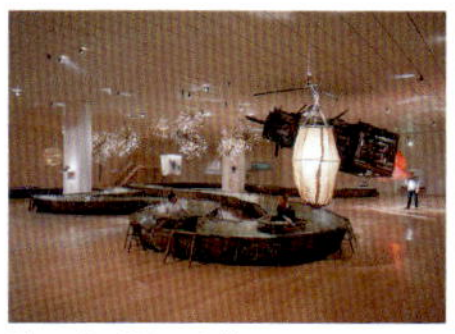

Photo by Blaise Adilon, courtesy Museum of Contemporary Art in Lyon

### *An Arbitrary History: River*

Installation presented in solo exhibition *An Arbitrary History* at Museum of Contemporary Art in Lyon, France

KEYWORDS: ART HISTORY

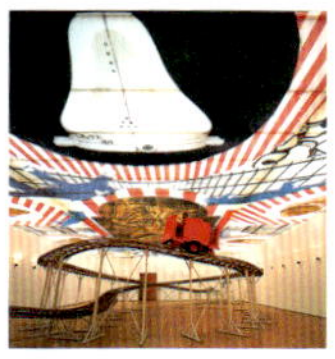

Photo by Blaise Adilon, courtesy Museum of Contemporary Art in Lyon

### *An Arbitrary History: Roller Coaster*

Installation presented in solo exhibition *An Arbitrary History* at Museum of Contemporary Art in Lyon, France

KEYWORDS: ART HISTORY

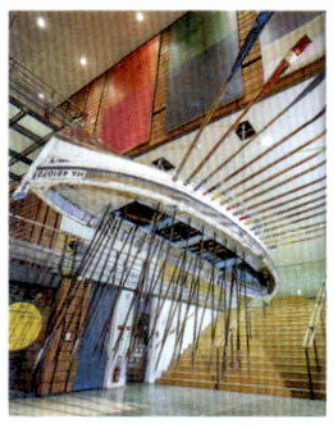

Photo by Blaise Adilon, courtesy Museum of Contemporary Art in Lyon

### *The Eagle Has Arrived!*

Installation presented in solo exhibition *An Arbitrary History* at Museum of Contemporary Art in Lyon, France

KEYWORDS: BOAT; CURRENT EVENTS

## 2002

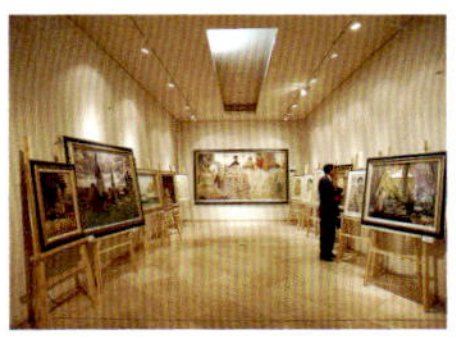

### *Cai Guo-Qiang's Maksimov Collection*

Exhibition curated by Cai Guo-Qiang at Shanghai Art Museum, Shanghai, China

KEYWORDS: ART HISTORY; MAKSIMOV

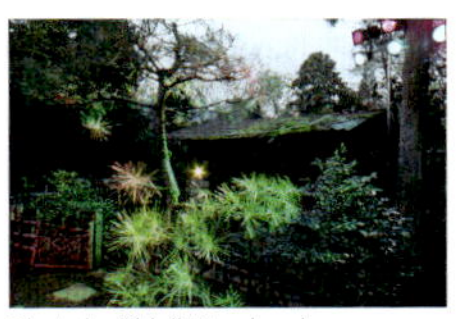

Photo by Shinji Murakami

### *Cai Guo-Qiang's CHADO Pavilion—Homage to Tenshin Okakura*

Installation presented at Hakone Open-Air Museum, Kanagawa, Japan

KEYWORDS: JAPAN

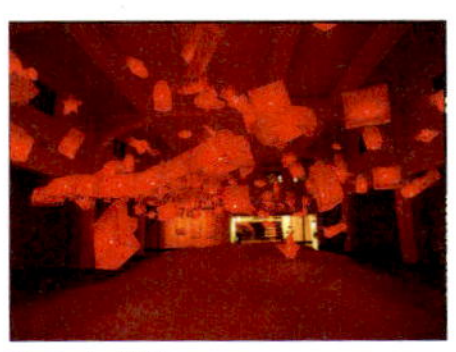

Photo by Ni Yan

### *Dream*

Installation presented in solo exhibition *Cai Guo-Qiang* at Shanghai Art Museum, Shanghai, China

KEYWORDS: CHINESE CULTURE AND CRAFT

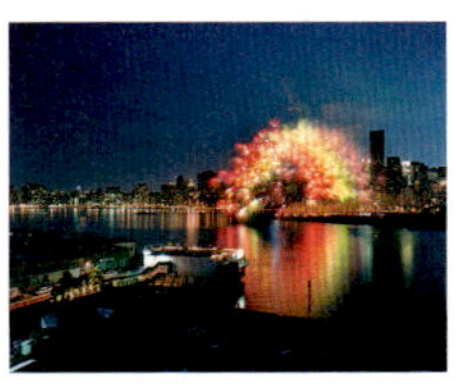

Photo by Hiro Ihara

### *Transient Rainbow*

Explosion event commissioned by the Museum of Modern Art, New York, over the East River, New York, U.S.

KEYWORDS: CURRENT EVENTS

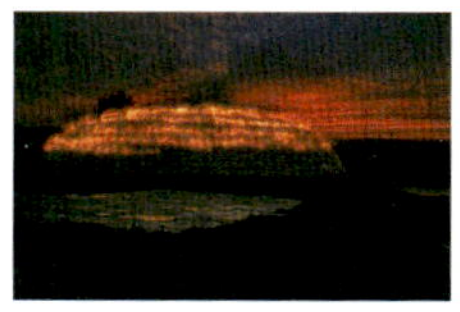

Photo by Tatsumi Masatoshi

### *Sky Bound UFO and Shrine*

Explosion event realized for group exhibition *Tokachi International Contemporary Art Exhibition: Demeter* at Obihiro Racetrack, Hokkaidō, Japan

KEYWORDS: COSMOS; MYTHOLOGY AND RELIGION

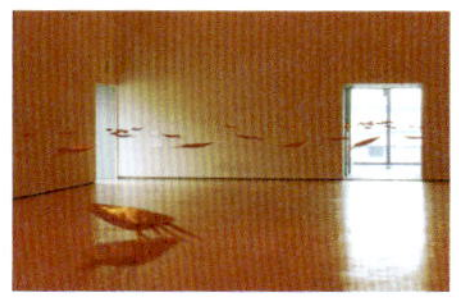

Photo by Izumiya Gensaku

### *99 Golden Boats*

Installation presented in group exhibition *The Power of Art: The 2nd Inaugural Show of the Prefectural Museum of Art* at Hyōgo Prefectural Museum of Art, Kōbe, Japan

KEYWORDS: BOAT; JAPAN

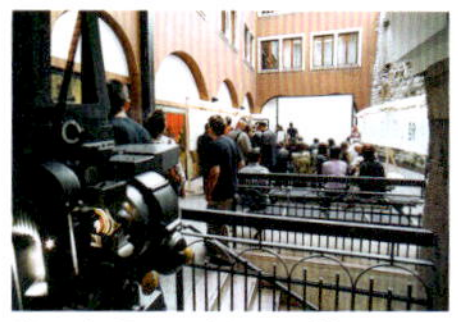

Photo by Tatsumi Masatoshi

### *Daylight Screen, Big White Truth*

Installation presented in solo exhibition *Ethereal Flowers* at Galleria Civica, Trento, Italy

KEYWORDS: CHINESE HISTORY, POST-1949

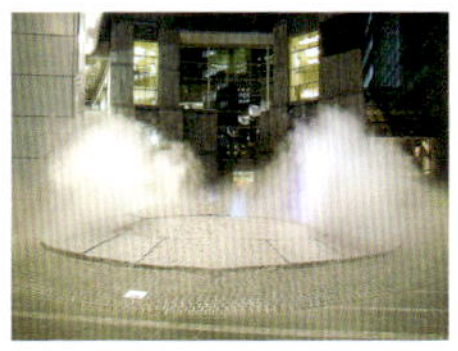

### *Turtle Fountain*

Public art at Dentsū Inc. Headquarters, Tokyo, Japan

KEYWORDS: CHINESE THOUGHT AND PHILOSOPHY, ANCIENT; JAPAN

## 2003

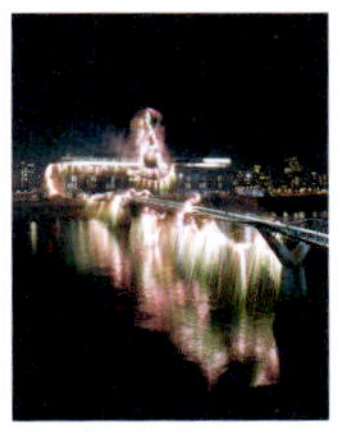

Photo by Hiro Ihara

### *Ye Gong Hao Long (Mr. Ye Who Loves Dragons) for Tate Modern*

Explosion event realized at Millennium Bridge and Tate Modern, London, U.K.

KEYWORDS: DRAGON; MUSEUM AS MEDIUM

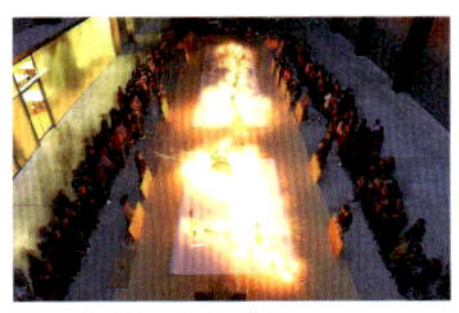

Photo by Martin Godwin

### *Ye Gong Hao Long (Mr. Ye Who Loves Dragons)*

Gunpowder drawing created for explosion event of the same title at Tate Modern, London, U.K.

KEYWORDS: DRAGON; PUBLIC PAINTING CREATION

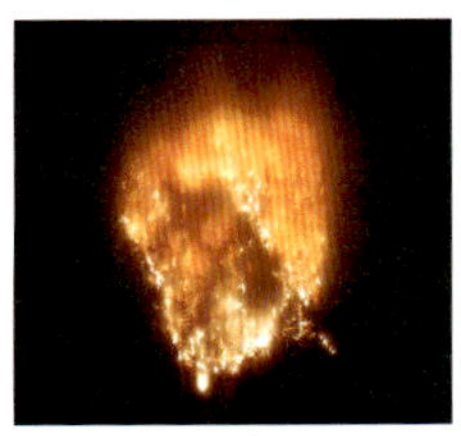

Photo by Dirk Pauwels, courtesy S.M.A.K. Museum of Contemporary Art

### *Inheritance: Exploding Jan Hoet's Portrait*

Explosion event realized for solo exhibition *An Arbitrary History* at S.M.A.K. (Stedelijk Museum voor Actuele Kunst), Ghent, Belgium

KEYWORDS: CONTEMPORARY CULTURAL FIGURES

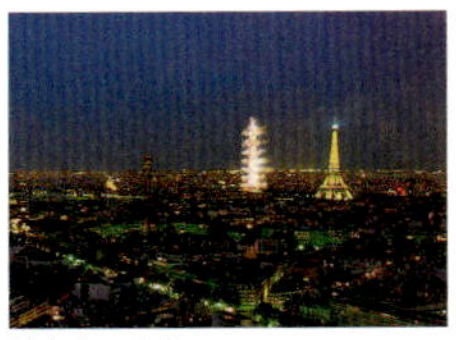

Digital rendering

### *Proposal for Building a Chinese Tower in Paris*

Explosion event proposed but unrealized for group exhibition *Alors, la Chine?* at Centre Pompidou, Paris, France

KEYWORDS: TOWER

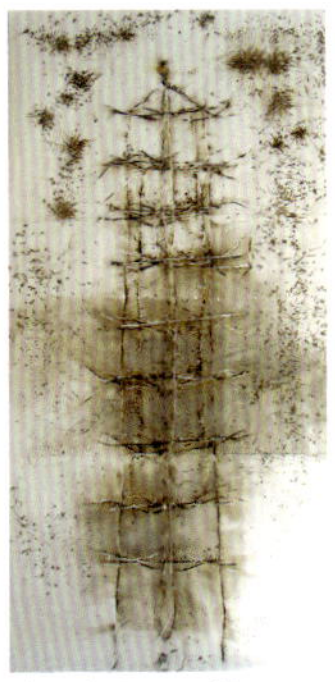

Photo by Bertrand Prevost

### *Drawing for Building a Chinese Tower in Paris*

Gunpowder drawing presented in group exhibition *Alors, la Chine?* at Centre Pompidou, Paris, France

KEYWORDS: PUBLIC PAINTING CREATION; TOWER

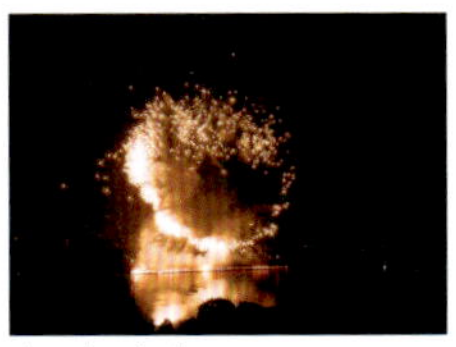

Photo by Hiro Ihara

### *Light Cycle for Central Park*

Explosion event realized at Central Park, New York, U.S.

KEYWORDS: SHAMAN

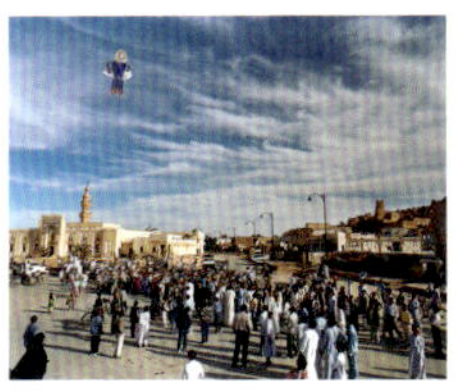

Photo by Hiro Ihara

### *Man, Eagle, and Eye in the Sky: Kite Project for Siwa*

Social project commissioned by Siwa Art Project and realized at Siwa Oasis, Egypt

KEYWORDS: CHINESE CULTURE AND CRAFTS; GLOBALIZATION IN HISTORY; ROMANTIC; SHAMAN

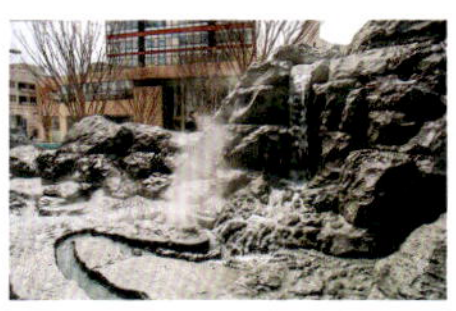

### *High Mountain Flowing Water: 3-D Landscape Painting*

Public art at Mori Art Museum, Tokyo, Japan

KEYWORDS: CHINESE PAINTING, TRADITIONAL; JAPAN

## 2004

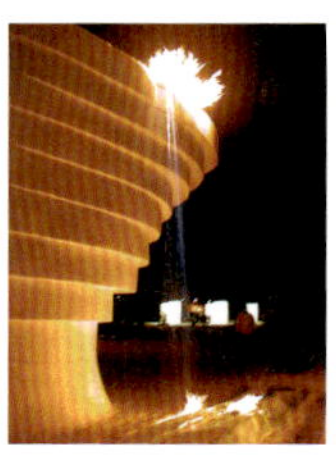

### *Caressing Zaha with Vodka*

Explosion event realized for group exhibition *The Snow Show* at Rovaniemi, Finland

KEYWORDS: CONTEMPORARY CULTURAL FIGURES

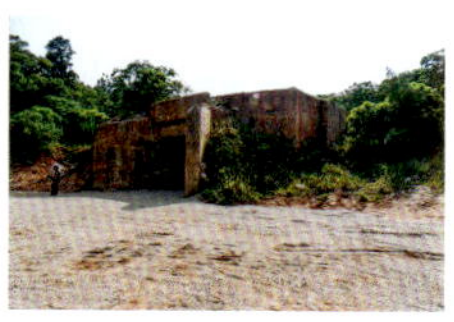

Photo by Hiro Ihara

### *BMoCA (Bunker Museum of Contemporary Art)*

Space established and curated by Cai Guo-Qiang in Kinmen Island, Taiwan

KEYWORDS: CHINESE HISTORY, POST-1949; MUSEUM AS MEDIUM

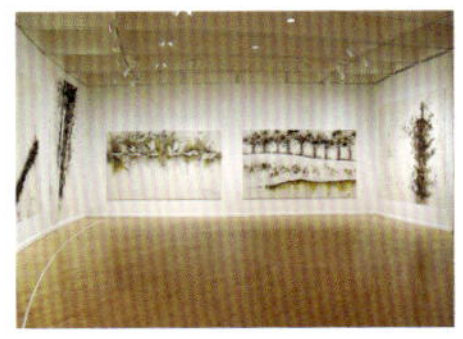

### *Unlucky Year: Unrealized Projects from 2003–2004*

Gunpowder drawings and sketches presented in solo exhibition *Traveler* at Arthur M. Sackler Gallery and Hirshhorn Museum and Sculpture Garden, Smithsonian Institution, Washington, D.C., U.S.

KEYWORDS: GUNPOWDER DRAWING AND GUNPOWDER PAINTING; SHAMAN

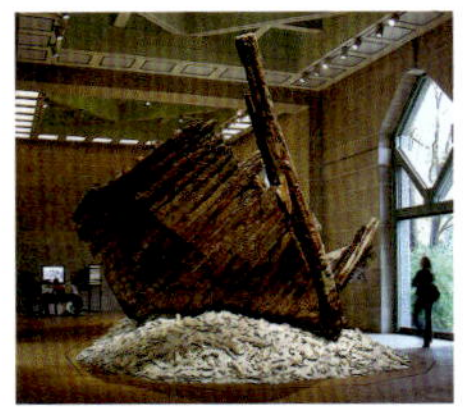

Photo by Cai Guo-Qiang

### *Reflection—A Gift from Iwaki*

Installation presented in solo exhibition *Traveler* at Arthur M. Sackler Gallery and Hirshhorn Museum and Sculpture Garden, Smithsonian Institution, Washington, D.C., U.S.

KEYWORDS: BOAT; IWAKI

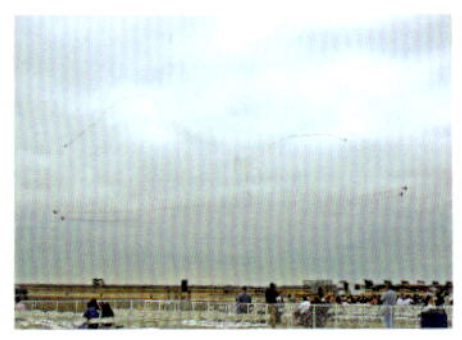

### *Painting Chinese Landscape Painting*

Performance commissioned by San Diego Museum of Art for *2004 Miramar Air Show* in conjunction with group exhibition *Past in Reverse: Contemporary Art of East Asia* and realized at Marine Corps Air Station Miramar, San Diego, California, U.S.

KEYWORDS: CHINESE PAINTING, TRADITIONAL; WAR AND PEACE

## 2005

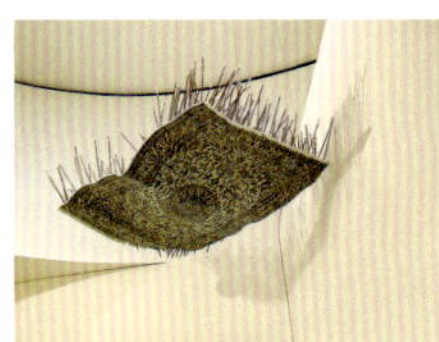

Photo by Cai Guo-Qiang

### *Flying Carpet*

Installation presented in group exhibition *(My private) Heroes* at MARTa Herford, Herford, Germany

KEYWORDS: MIDDLE EAST

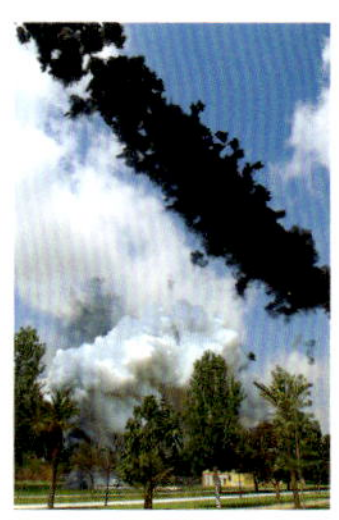

Photo by Juan García Rosell, © Institut Valencià d'Art Modern. Generalitat Valenciana, España, 2005

### *Black Rainbow for Valencia*

Daytime explosion event realized in solo exhibition *On Black Fireworks* at Old Turia Riverbed Park, Valencia, Spain

KEYWORDS: CHINESE PAINTING, TRADITIONAL; GUNPOWDER

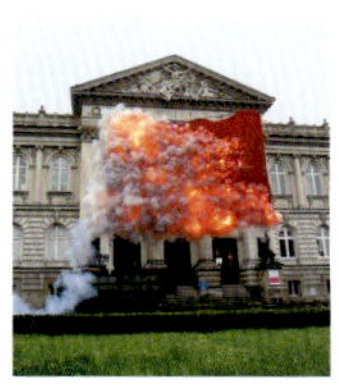

Photo by Tatsumi Masatoshi

### *Paradise*

Solo exhibition at the Zachęta National Gallery of Art, Warsaw, Poland

KEYWORDS: SOCIALISM

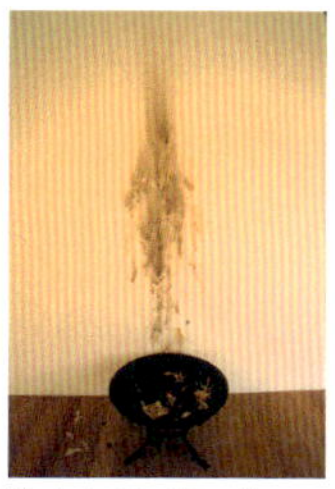

Photo by Alan Dimmic

### *Life Beneath the Shadow*

Installation presented in solo exhibition of the same title at Fruitmarket Gallery, Edinburgh, Scotland

KEYWORDS: SHAMAN

## 2006

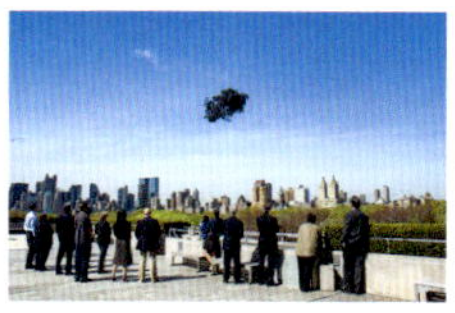

Photo by Hiro Ihara

### *Cai Guo-Qiang on the Roof: Transparent Monument*

Solo exhibition at Metropolitan Museum of Art, New York, U.S.

KEYWORDS: CURRENT EVENTS

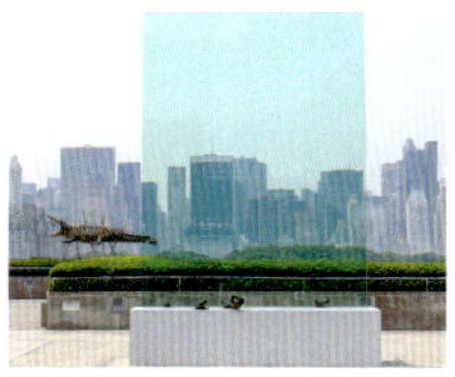

Photo by Hiro Ihara

### *Transparent Monument*

Installation presented in solo exhibition *Cai Guo-Qiang on the Roof: Transparent Monument* at Metropolitan Museum of Art, New York, U.S.

KEYWORDS: CURRENT EVENTS; GLOBALIZATION IN HISTORY

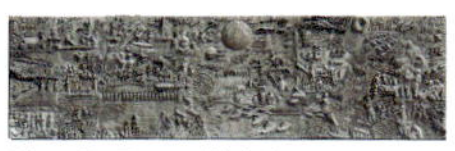

Photo by Teresa Christiansen, courtesy The Metropolitan Museum of Art

### *Nontransparent Monument*

Sculpture presented in solo exhibition *Cai Guo-Qiang on the Roof: Transparent Monument* at Metropolitan Museum of Art, New York, U.S.

KEYWORDS: CHINESE CULTURE AND CRAFTS; CURRENT EVENTS

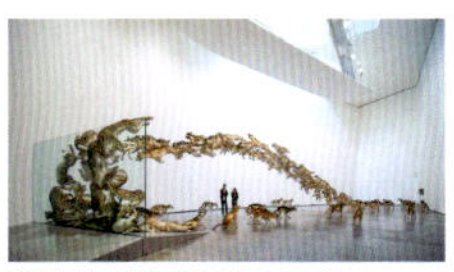

Photo by Erika Barahona-Ede, ©FMGB Guggenheim Bilbao Museoa, 2009

### *Head On*

Installation presented in solo exhibition *Head On* at Deutsche Guggenheim, Berlin, Germany. Photo as shown at Guggenheim Museum Bilbao, 2009

KEYWORDS: CURRENT EVENTS; FAUNA AND FLORA

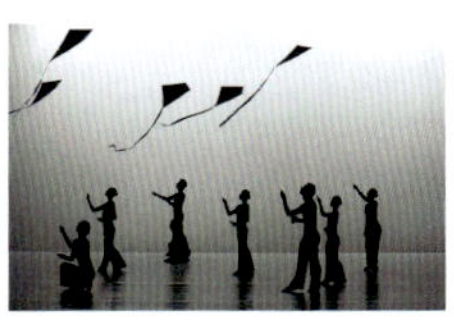

### *Wind Shadow*

Project in collaboration with Cloud Gate Dance Theatre of Taiwan, presented in National Theater, Taipei; Kaohsiung Cultural Center; and Chiayi Performing Arts Center, Taiwan

KEYWORDS: CONTEMPORARY CULTURAL FIGURES

## 2007

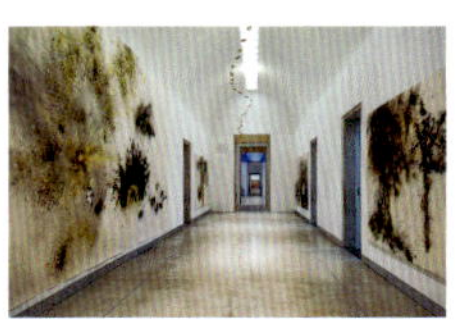

Photo by Constance Mensh, courtesy Philadelphia Museum of Art

### *Light Passage*

Four gunpowder paintings presented in solo exhibition *Cai Guo-Qiang & Shiseido* at Shiseido Gallery, Tokyo, Japan. Image: Exhibition view at Philadelphia Museum of Art, 2009

KEYWORDS: CHINESE PAINTING, TRADITIONAL

## 2008

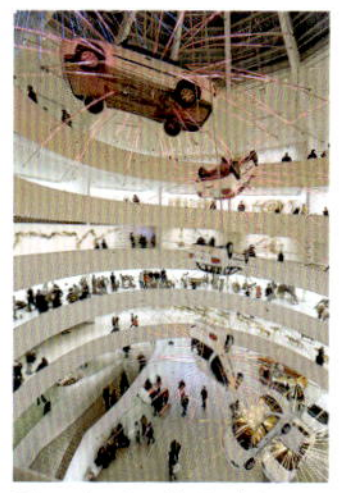

Photo by David Heald. © SRGF, NY

### *I Want to Believe*

Solo exhibition at Solomon R. Guggenheim Museum, New York, U.S.

KEYWORDS: CURRENT EVENTS

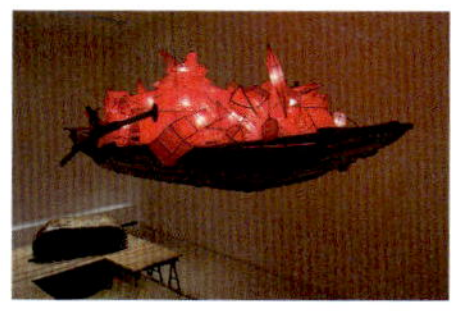

Photo by Hiro Ihara

### *A Boat with Dreams*

Installation presented in solo exhibition *I Want to Believe* at Solomon R. Guggenheim Museum, New York, U.S.

KEYWORDS: CHINESE CULTURE AND CRAFTS

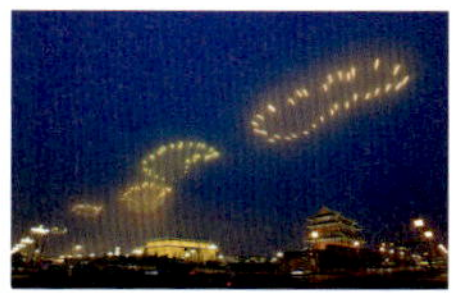

Photo by Hiro Ihara

### *Footprints of History: Fireworks for the Opening Ceremony of the 2008 Beijing Olympic Games*

Fireworks realized in Beijing, China

KEYWORDS: BIGFOOT; WAR AND PEACE

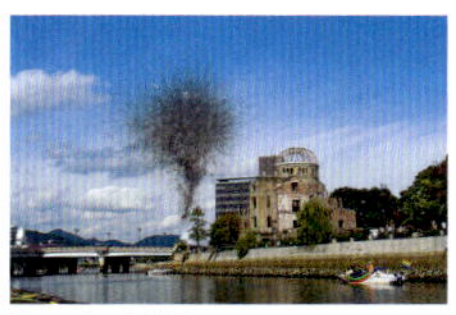

Photo by Seiji Toyonaga, courtesy Hiroshima City Museum of Contemporary Art

### *Black Fireworks: Project for Hiroshima*

Daytime explosion event realized for solo exhibition *The 7th Hiroshima Art Prize* at Hiroshima Peace Memorial Museum, Hiroshima, Japan

KEYWORDS: WAR AND PEACE

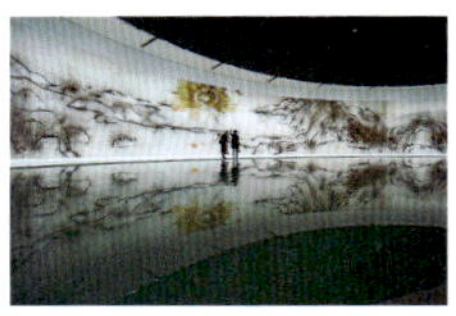

Photo by Seiji Toyonaga, courtesy Hiroshima City Museum of Contemporary Art

### *Unmanned Nature: Project for the Hiroshima City Museum of Contemporary Art*

Painting-installation presented in solo exhibition *The 7th Hiroshima Art Prize* at Hiroshima City Museum of Contemporary Art, Hiroshima, Japan

KEYWORDS: CHINESE PAINTING, TRADITIONAL; ECOLOGY

## 2009

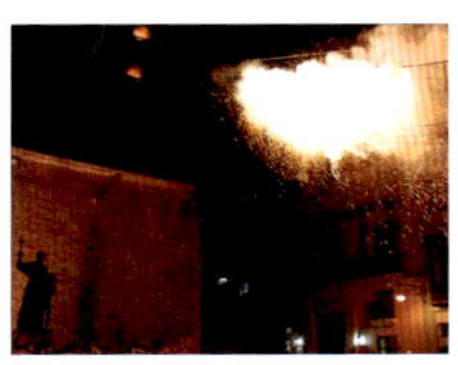

Video still courtesy Havana Radio

### *Sketch of a Boat*

Explosion event realized for group exhibition *Meeting Point: 10th Havana Biennial* at Plaza de San Francisco de Asís, Havana, Cuba

KEYWORDS: CENTRAL AND SOUTH AMERICA; SKETCHING

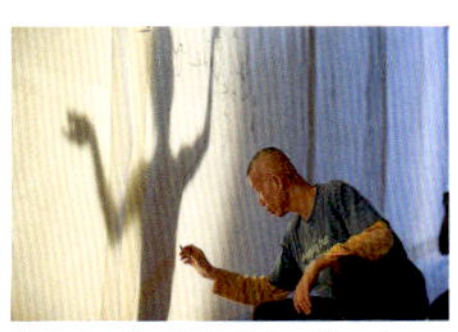

Photo by On-Works International Multimedia Co., Ltd.

### *Day and Night*

Gunpowder painting presented in solo exhibition *Hanging Out in the Museum* at Taipei Fine Arts Museum, Taipei, Taiwan

KEYWORDS: PUBLIC PAINTING CREATION

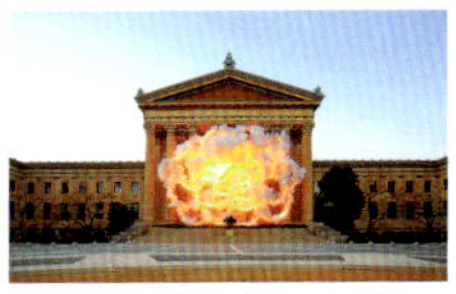

Photo by Lonnie Graham, courtesy The Fabric Workshop and Museum

### *Fallen Blossoms*

Explosion event realized for solo exhibition of the same title at Philadelphia Museum of Art, Pennsylvania, U.S.

KEYWORDS: CHINESE PAINTING, TRADITIONAL

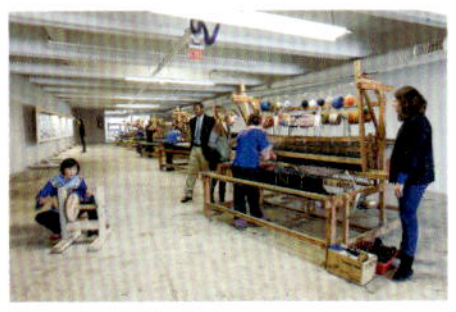

Photo by I-Hua Lee

### *Time Flies Like a Weaving Shuttle*

Project realized for solo exhibition *Fallen Blossoms* at Philadelphia Museum of Art and The Fabric Workshop and Museum, Pennsylvania, U.S.

KEYWORDS: CONTEMPORARY CULTURAL FIGURES

## 2010

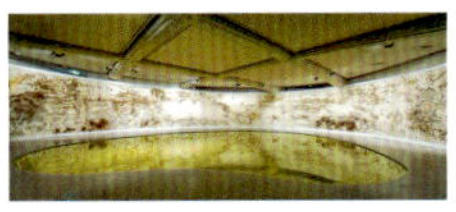

Photo by Muriel Assens, courtesy MAMAC-Nice

### *Travels in the Mediterranean*

Painting-installation presented in solo exhibition *Travels in the Mediterranean* at Museum of Modern and Contemporary Art, Nice, France

KEYWORDS: PUBLIC PAINTING CREATION

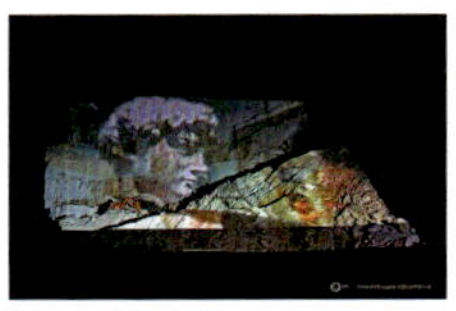

Photo by Valerio Brambilla, courtesy Biennale Internazionale di Scultura di Carrara

### *One Thousand Youngsters Drawing David*

Installation presented in group exhibition *Post Monument: XIV Biennale Internazionale di Scultura di Carrara* at Cave Michelangelo in Carrara, Italy

KEYWORDS: ART HISTORY; DRAWING

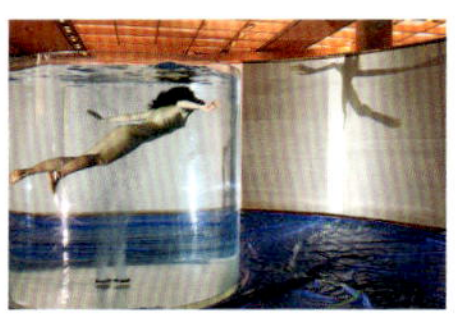

Photo courtesy Kanako Hayashi

### *Mermaid: Project for the 2010 Aichi Triennale*

Gunpowder painting presented in group exhibition *Arts and Cities: Aichi Triennale 2010* at Aichi Prefectural Museum of Art, Nagoya, Japan

KEYWORDS: PUBLIC PAINTING CREATION

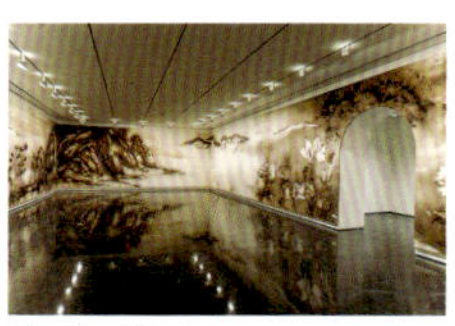

Photo by I-Hua Lee

### *Odyssey*

Painting-installation at the Museum of Fine Arts, Houston, Texas, U.S.

KEYWORDS: CHINESE PAINTING, TRADITIONAL; PUBLIC PAINTING CREATION

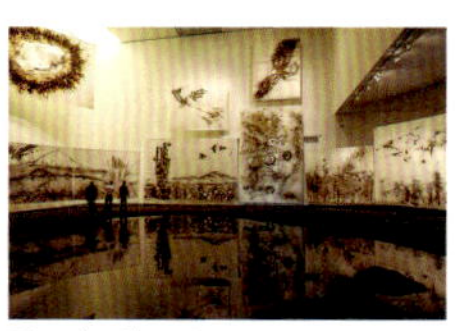

Photo by Diego Berruecos, courtesy MUAC

### *Sunshine and Solitude*

Solo exhibition at Museo Universitario Arte Contemporáneo, Mexico City, Mexico

KEYWORDS: CENTRAL AND SOUTH AMERICA; MYTHOLOGY AND RELIGION

## 2010/2013/2015

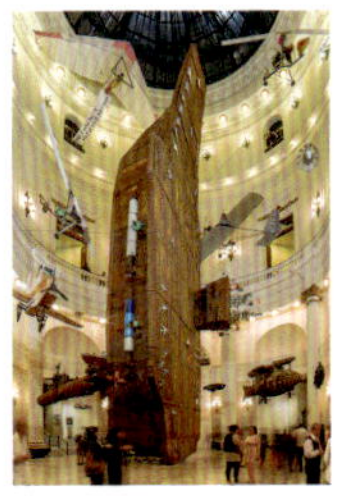

Photo (Rio de Janeiro) by Joana França

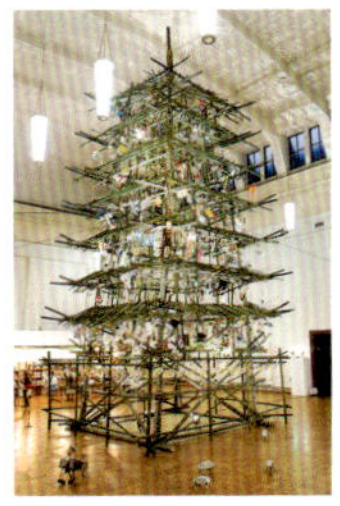

Photo (Kyoto) by Kenryou Gu

### *Peasant Da Vincis*

Solo exhibition first presented at Rockbund Art Museum, Shanghai; traveled to Centro Cultural Banco do Brasil in Brasília, São Paulo, and Rio de Janeiro, Brazil (2013); traveled to Leonardo da Vinci National Museum of Science and Technology, Milan, Italy (2015); partially presented in group exhibition *Parasophia: Kyoto International Festival of Contemporary Culture 2015* at Kyoto Municipal Museum of Art, Japan (2015)

KEYWORDS: PEASANT DA VINCIS; ROMANTIC; TOWER

## 2011

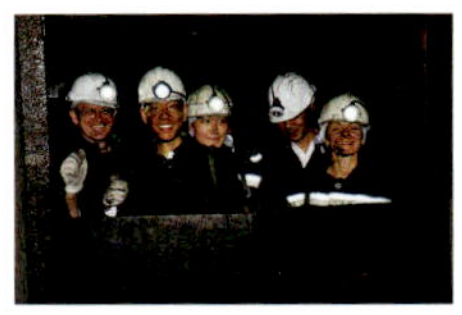

Photo by Dima Sergeev, courtesy IZOLYATSIA. Platform for Cultural Initiatives

### *1040M Underground*

Solo exhibition at IZOLYATSIA. Platform for Cultural Initiatives, Donetsk (presently in Kiev), Ukraine

KEYWORDS: SOCIALISM

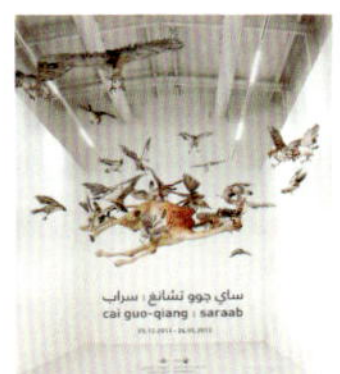

Exhibition poster

### *Saraab*

Solo exhibition at Mathaf: Arab Museum of Modern Art, Doha, Qatar

KEYWORDS: BOAT; GLOBALIZATION IN HISTORY; MIDDLE EAST; MYTHOLOGY AND RELIGION; QUANZHOU

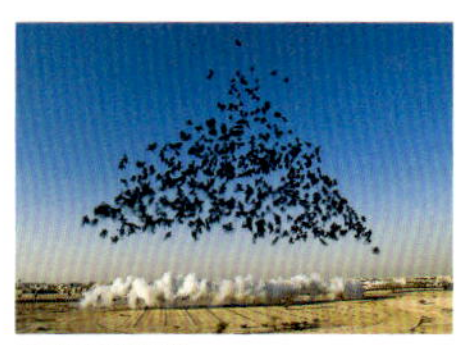

Photo by Lin Yi

### *Black Ceremony*

Daytime explosion event for the opening of solo exhibition *Saraab*, outside Mathaf: Arab Museum of Modern Art, Doha, Qatar

KEYWORDS: GUNPOWDER; MIDDLE EAST; SHAMAN

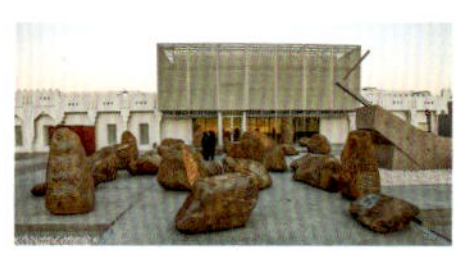

Photo by Hiro Ihara

### *Homecoming*

Installation presented in solo exhibition *Saraab* at Mathaf: Arab Museum of Modern Art, Doha, Qatar

KEYWORDS: MIDDLE EAST; QUANZHOU

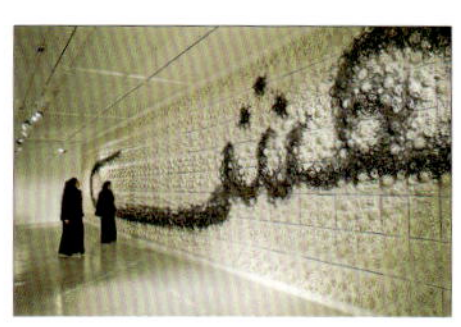

Photo by Lin Yi

### *Fragile*

Installation presented in solo exhibition *Saraab* at Mathaf: Arab Museum of Modern Art, Doha, Qatar

KEYWORDS: CHINESE CULTURE AND CRAFTS; MIDDLE EAST

## 2012

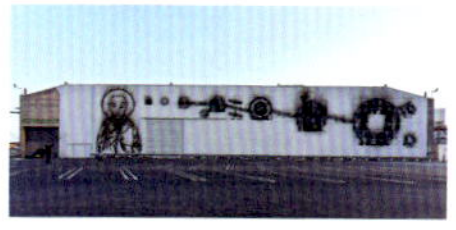
Photo by Joshua White/JWPictures.com, courtesy The Museum of Contemporary Art, Los Angeles

### *Sky Ladder*

Solo exhibition at Museum of Contemporary Art, Los Angeles (MOCA), California, U.S.

KEYWORDS: COSMOS; EXTRATERRISTRIALS; PUBLIC PAINTING CREATION

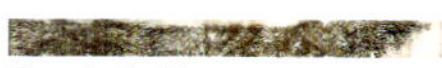
Photo by Lin Yi

### *Tides*

Gunpowder painting presented in solo exhibition *Spring* at Zhejiang Art Museum, Hangzhou, China

KEYWORDS: CHINESE PAINTING, TRADITIONAL

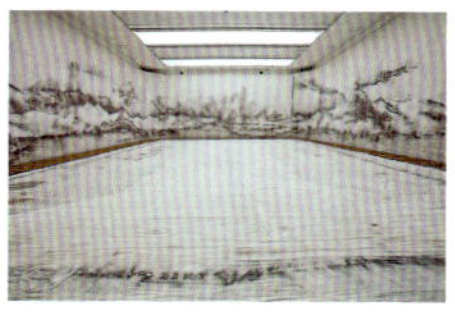
Photo by Rohsuan Chen

### *West Lake*

Painting-installation presented in solo exhibition *Spring* at Zhejiang Art Museum, Hangzhou, China

KEYWORDS: CHINESE PAINTING, TRADITIONAL; PUBLIC PAINTING CREATION

## 2013

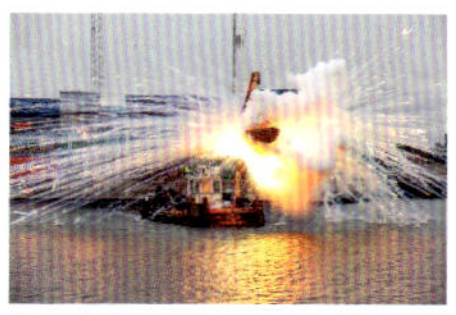
Photo by Wen-You Cai

### *A Clan of Boats*

Solo exhibition at Faurschou Foundation, Copenhagen, Denmark

KEYWORDS: BOAT

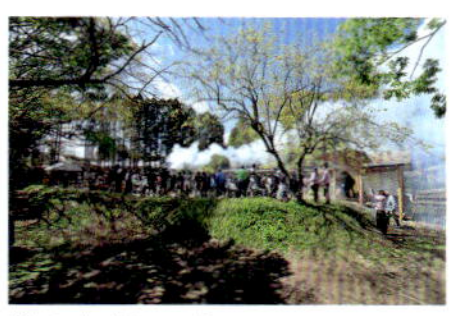
Photo by Kazuo Ono

### *SMoCA (Snake Museum of Contemporary Art)*

Space established and curated by Cai Guo-Qiang in Iwaki, Fukushima, Japan, collaboration of Cai Studio and the Iwaki Board for the Project to Plant Ten Thousand Cherry Blossom Trees

KEYWORDS: IWAKI; MUSEUM AS MEDIUM; TOWER

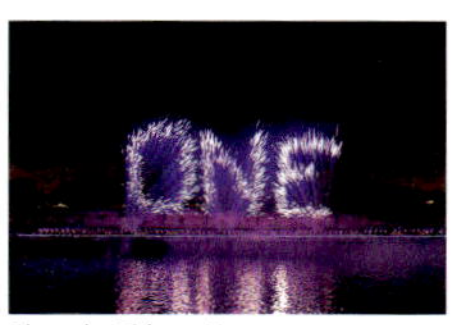

Photo by Thierry Nava

### *One Night Stand for Nuit Blanche*

Explosion event realized on the Seine, between Musée du Louvre and Musée d'Orsay, Paris, France

KEYWORDS: ROMANTIC

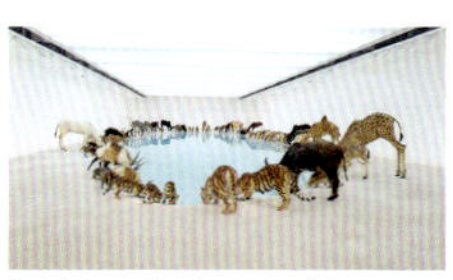
Credit found in the "Copyright Notices" in the back

### *Heritage*

Installation presented in solo exhibition *Falling Back to Earth* at Queensland Art Gallery of Modern Art, Brisbane, Australia

KEYWORDS: ECOLOGY; FAUNA AND FLORA; ROMANTIC

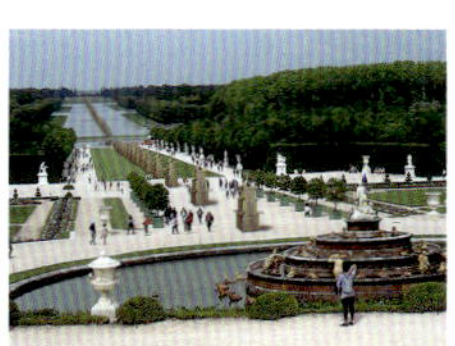
Digital rendering

### *Ninety-Nine Chinese Pagodas at Château de Versailles*

Explosion event proposed but unrealized at the Palace of Versailles, France

KEYWORDS: TOWER

## 2014

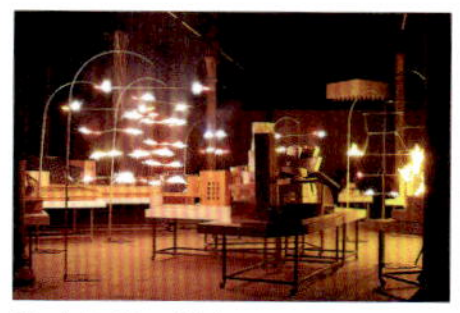
Photo by Tweaklab, ©2014 LUMA Foundation

### *Hanabi: Sparks of Inspiration*

Explosion event realized for *Frank Gehry: Solaris Chronicles* at LUMA Foundation, Arles, France

KEYWORDS: CONTEMPORARY CULTURAL FIGURES

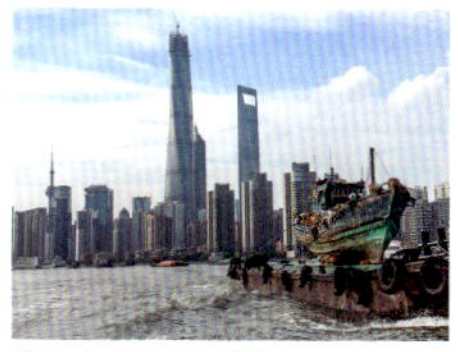
Photo by Wen-You Cai

### *The Ninth Wave*

Project realized for solo exhibition of the same title at Power Station of Art, Shanghai, China

KEYWORDS: BOAT; ECOLOGY

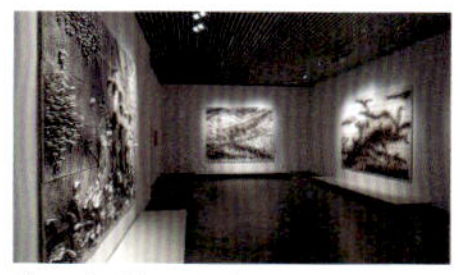
Photo by Zhang Feiyu

### *Spring, Summer, Fall, Winter*

Installation presented in solo exhibition *The Ninth Wave* at Power Station of Art, Shanghai, China

KEYWORDS: CHINESE CULTURE AND CRAFT

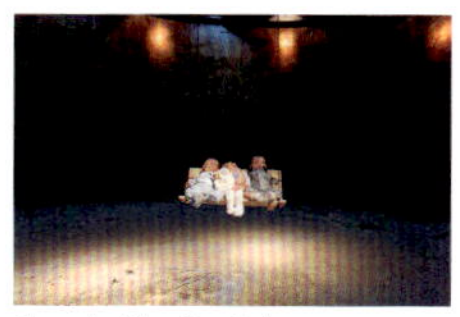
Photo by Wen-You Cai

### *Air of Heaven*

Installation presented in solo exhibition *The Ninth Wave* at Power Station of Art, Shanghai, China

KEYWORDS: ECOLOGY

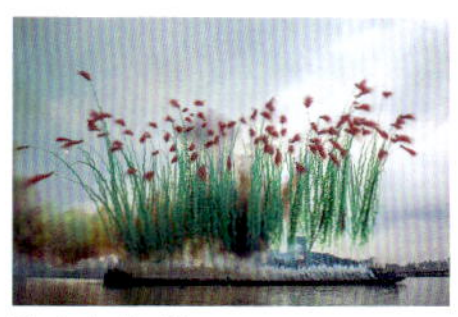
Photo by Lin Yi

### *Elegy*

Daytime explosion event realized for the Opening of solo exhibition *The Ninth Wave* on the riverfront of Power Station of Art, Shanghai, China

KEYWORDS: ECOLOGY; GUNPOWDER

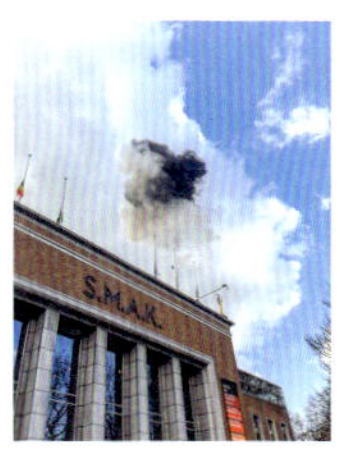
Photo by Jan Hoet, Jr.

### *Cloud for Jan Hoet*

Explosion event realized at S.M.A.K. (Stedelijk Museum voor Actuele Kunst), Ghent, Belgium

KEYWORDS: CONTEMPORARY CULTURAL FIGURES

## 2015

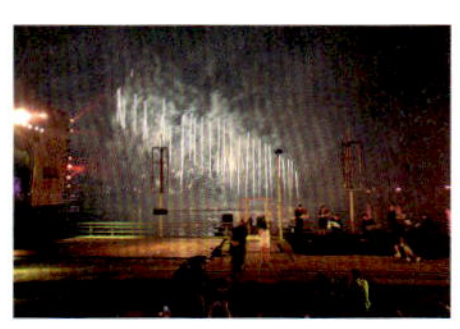
Photo by Wen-You Cai, © Fundación Proa & Cai Studio

### *Life Is a Milonga: Tango Fireworks for Argentina*

Explosion event realized at Vuelta de Rocha outside Fundación Proa, Buenos Aires, Argentina

KEYWORDS: CENTRAL AND SOUTH AMERICA; CONTEMPORARY CULTURAL FIGURES

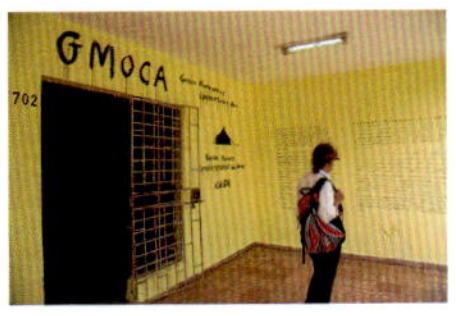
Photo by Wen-You Cai

## *GMoCA (Green Museum of Contemporary Art)*

Space established and curated by Cai Guo-Qiang at Museo Orgánico de Romerillo (MOR), Havana, Cuba

KEYWORDS: CENTRAL AND SOUTH AMERICA; MUSEUM AS MEDIUM

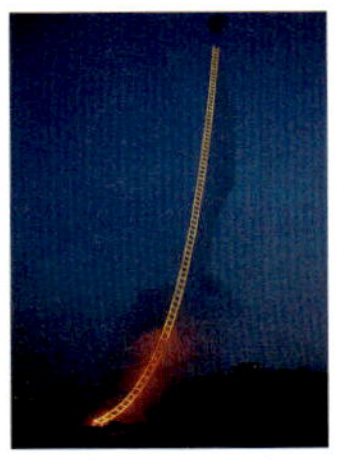
Photo by Wen-You Cai

## *Sky Ladder*

Explosion event realized off Huiyu Island, Quanzhou, China

KEYWORDS: COSMOS; GRANDMOTHER; ROMANTIC

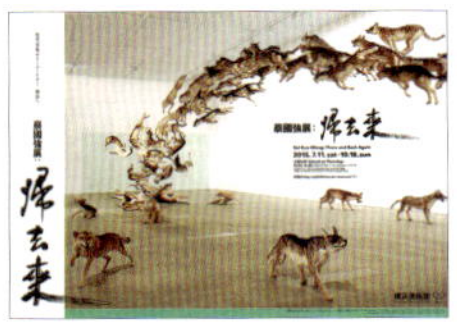
Exhibition poster

## *There and Back Again*

Solo exhibition at Yokohama Museum of Art, Kanagawa, Japan

KEYWORDS: GUNPOWDER DRAWING AND GUNPOWDER PAINTING; JAPAN

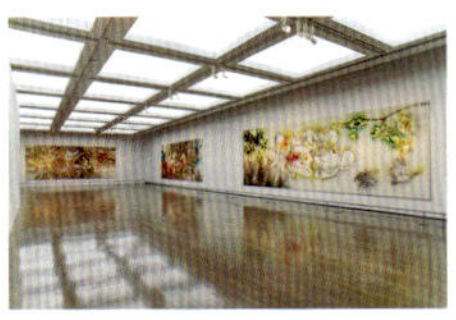
Photo by Wen-You Cai

## *Seasons of Life*

Four gunpowder paintings presented in solo exhibition *There and Back Again* at Yokohama Museum of Art, Kanagawa, Japan

KEYWORDS: GUNPOWDER; GUNPOWDER DRAWING AND GUNPOWDER PAINTING; JAPAN

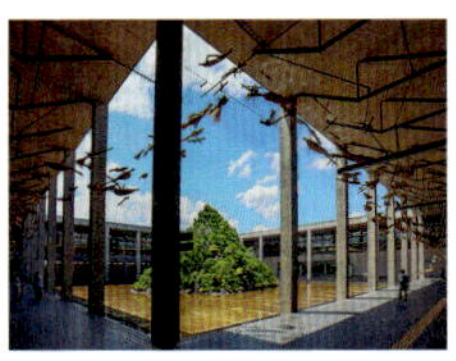
Photo by Kenryou Gu

## *Penglai / Hōrai*

Installation presented in solo exhibition *Penglai / Hōrai*, Echigo-Tsumari Satoyama Museum of Contemporary Art, KINARE, Niigata, Japan

KEYWORDS: CHINESE HISTORY, AND JAPAN; CHINESE THOUGHT AND PHILOSOPHY, ANCIENT; CURRENT EVENTS

# 2016

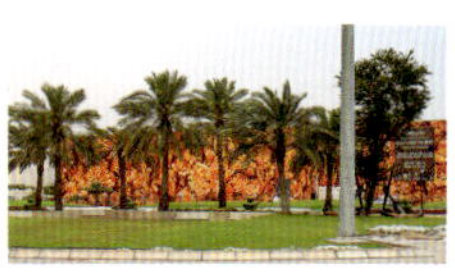
Photo by Wen-You Cai

## *What About the Art? Contemporary Art from China*

Exhibition curated by Cai Guo-Qiang at QM Gallery Al Riwaq, Doha, Qatar

KEYWORDS: MIDDLE EAST

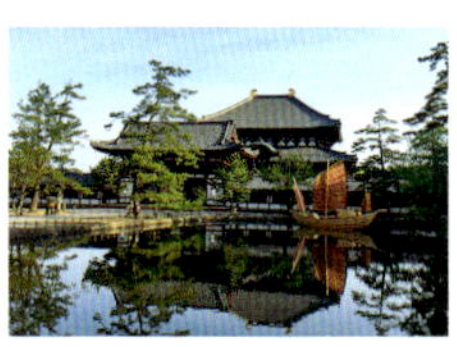
Photo by Art Front Gallery

## *To Build a Ship: Project for Nara Culture City of East Asia 2016*

Installation presented in group exhibition *Culture City of East Asia 2016* at Tōdaiji temple, Nara, Japan

KEYWORDS: BOAT; CHINESE HISTORY, AND JAPAN

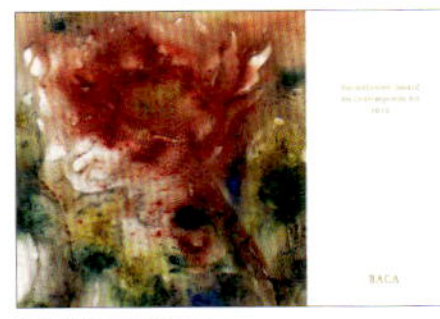
Exhibition poster

## *My Stories of Painting*

Solo exhibition at Bonnefanten Museum, Maastricht, the Netherlands

KEYWORDS: PAINTING

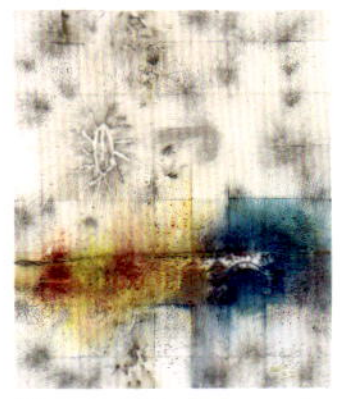
Photo by Peter Cox, courtesy Bonnefanten Museum

## *Boy's Doodle: Drawing for the 25th Anniversary of the EU in Maastricht*

Gunpowder drawing presented in solo exhibition *My Stories of Painting* at Bonnefanten Museum, Maastricht, the Netherlands

KEYWORDS: CURRENT EVENTS

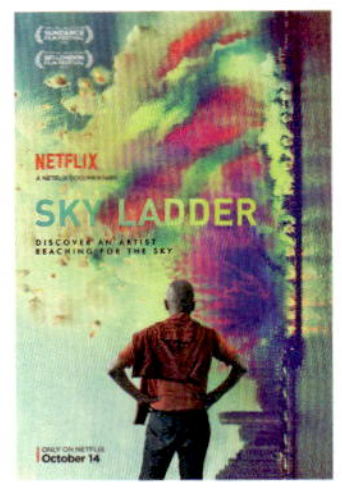
Film poster

## *Sky Ladder: The Art of Cai Guo-Qiang*

Documentary film directed by Academy Award winner Kevin Macdonald and distributed globally by Netflix

KEYWORDS: GRANDMOTHER

# 2017

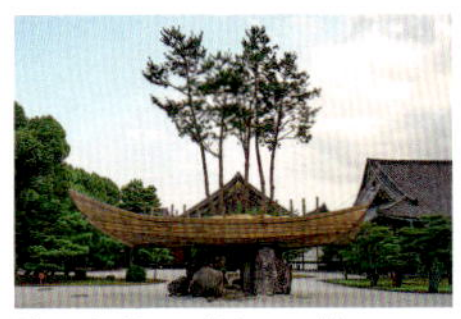
Photo by Tatsumi Masatoshi

## *Bonsai Ship*

Installation presented in group exhibition *Asia Corridor Contemporary Art Exhibition* as part of *Culture City of East Asia 2017, Kyoto* at Nijō Castle, Kyoto, Japan

KEYWORDS: BOAT; CHINESE HISTORY, AND JAPAN; FAUNA AND FLORA

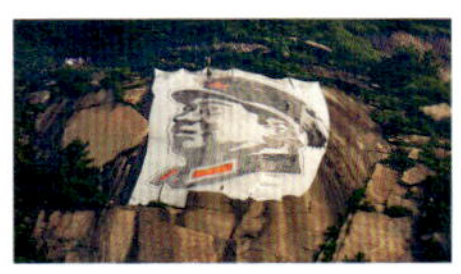
Photo courtesy CCTV

## *Mao Rubbing*

Ink rubbing on canvas, 1967 Mao Zedong portrait carving on the cliffs of Quanzhou

KEYWORDS: CHINESE HISTORY, POST-1949

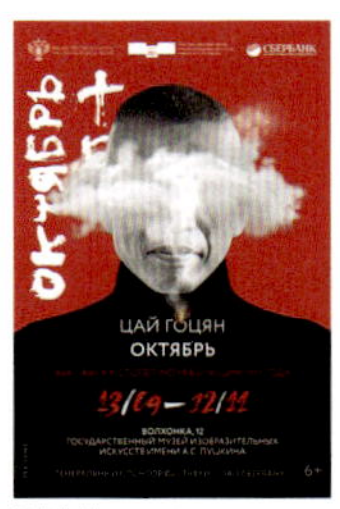
Exhibition poster

## *October*

Solo exhibition at the Pushkin State Museum of Fine Arts, Moscow, Russia

KEYWORDS: ART HISTORY; PUBLIC PAINTING CREATION; SOCIALISM

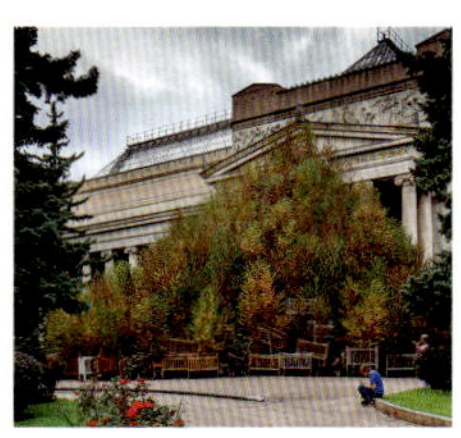
Photo courtesy the Pushkin State Museum of Fine Arts

## *Autumn*

Installation presented in solo exhibition *October* at the Pushkin State Museum of Fine Arts, Moscow, Russia

KEYWORDS: FAUNA AND FLORA; SOCIALISM

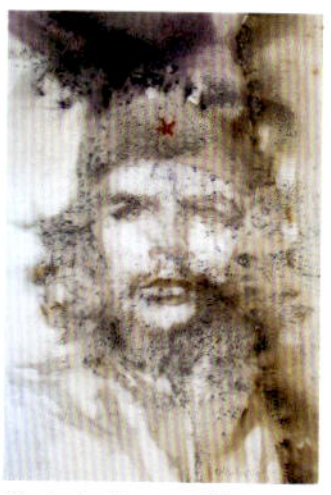

Photo by Yvonne Zhao

## *Che Guevara*

Gunpowder painting created as a study for solo exhibition *October* at the Pushkin State Museum of Fine Arts, Moscow, Russia

KEYWORDS: CENTRAL AND SOUTH AMERICA; SOCIALISM

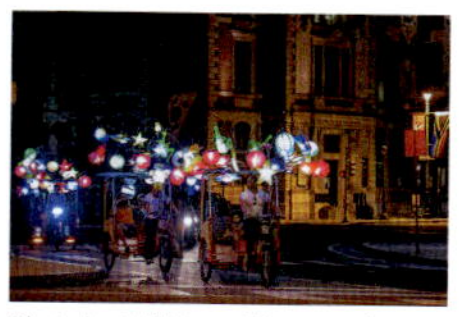

Photo by Jeff Fusco Photography, courtesy Association for Public Art

## *Fireflies*

Public art project realized on the centennial of Benjamin Franklin Parkway, Philadelphia, U.S.

KEYWORDS: CHINESE CULTURE AND CRAFTS; ROMANTIC

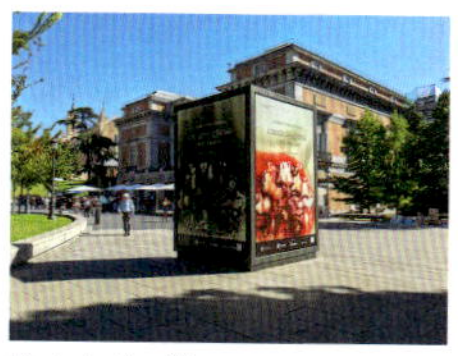

Photo by Anqi Xu

## *The Spirit of Painting. Cai Guo-Qiang at the Prado*

Solo exhibition at the Prado Museum, Madrid, Spain

KEYWORDS: ART HISTORY; EL GRECO; PAINTING; PUBLIC PAINTING CREATION

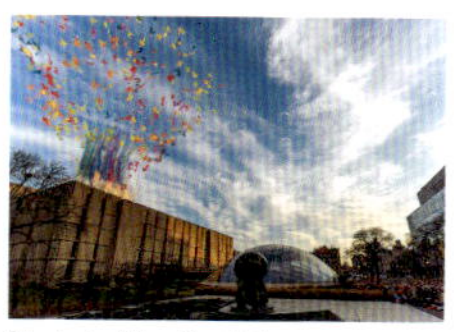

Photo by Wen-You Cai

## *Color Mushroom Cloud*

Daytime explosion event realized at the University of Chicago for the 75th anniversary of the first controlled self-sustained nuclear chain reaction, Illinois, U.S.

KEYWORDS: WAR AND PEACE

# 2018

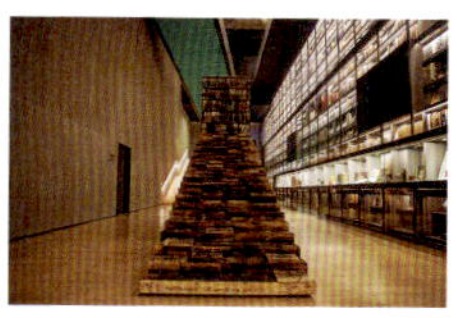

Photo courtesy Artron Art Center

## *Book Burning*

Explosion event realized for *Artron 25th Anniversary: A Special Art Project by Cai Guo-Qiang* at Artron Art Center, Shenzhen, China

KEYWORDS: CHINESE HISTORY, POST-1949

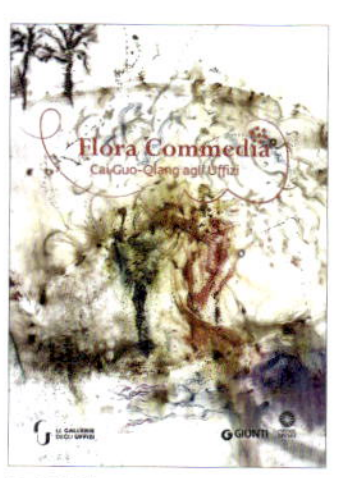


Exhibition poster

## *Flora Commedia: Cai Guo-Qiang at the Uffizi*

Solo exhibition at the Uffizi Galleries, Florence, Italy

KEYWORDS: ART HISTORY; FAUNA AND FLORA

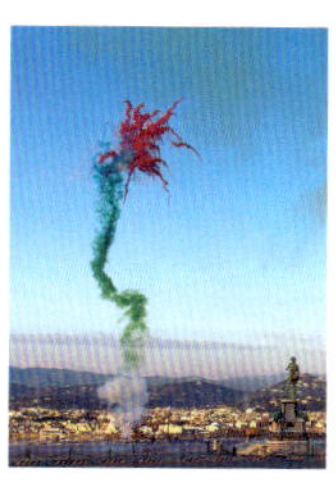

Photo by Lin Yi

## *City of Flowers in the Sky*

Daytime explosion event realized for solo exhibition *Flora Commedia* at the Uffizi Galleries, Florence, Italy

KEYWORDS: FAUNA AND FLORA

# 2019

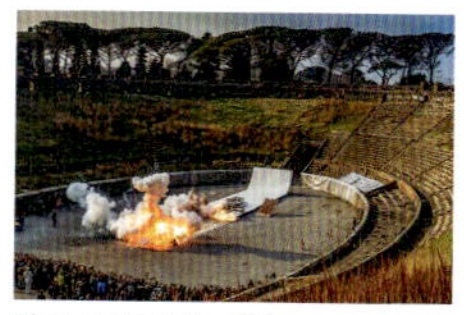

Photo by Wen-You Cai

## *In the Volcano: Cai Guo-Qiang and Pompeii*

Solo exhibition at National Archaeological Museum of Naples and Pompeii Archaeological Park, Italy

KEYWORDS: ART HISTORY; PUBLIC PAINTING CREATION

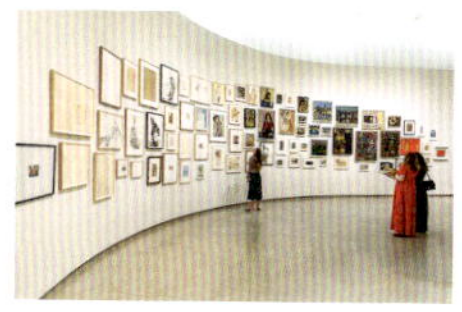

Photo by Wen-You Cai

## *Non-Brand* 非品牌

Exhibition curated by Cai Guo-Qiang as part of *Artistic License: Six Takes on the Guggenheim Collection* at Solomon R. Guggenheim Museum, New York, U.S.

KEYWORDS: ART HISTORY; CHINESE CULTURE AND CRAFTS; PAINTING

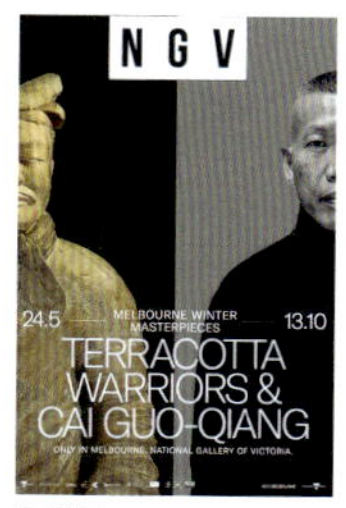


Exhibition poster

## *The Transient Landscape*

Solo exhibition at National Gallery of Victoria, Melbourne, Australia, in conjunction with *Terracotta Warriors: Guardians of Immortality*

KEYWORDS: CHINESE HISTORY, ANCIENT; FAUNA AND FLORA

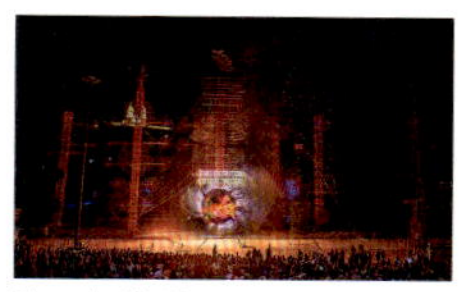

Photo by Lin Yi

## *Encounter with the Unknown: Cosmos Project for Mexico*

Explosion event realized at San Pedro Cholula, Mexico

KEYWORDS: CENTRAL AND SOUTH AMERICA; COSMOS; SHAMAN

# 2020

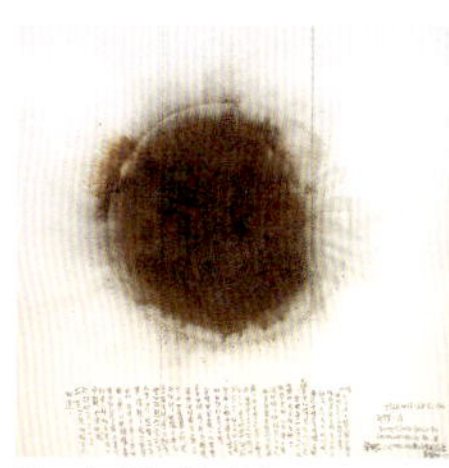

Photo by Wen-You Cai

## *Peaceful Earth: Project for Extraterrestrials No. 18*

Gunpowder drawing created during the 2020 quarantine, New York, U.S.

KEYWORDS: CURRENT EVENTS; EXTRATERRESTRIALS; GUNPOWDER DRAWING AND GUNPOWDER PAINTING

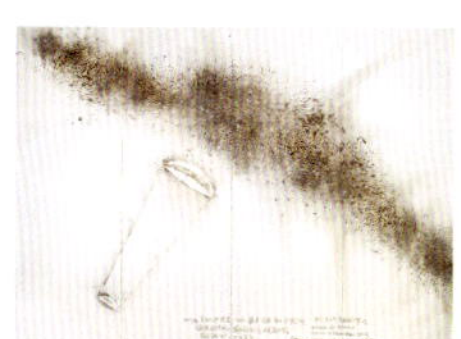

Photo by Wen-You Cai

## *Nostalgia for Homeland: Project for Humankind No. 4*

Gunpowder drawing created during the 2020 quarantine, New York, U.S.

KEYWORDS: COSMOS; EXTRATERRESTRIALS; GUNPOWDER DRAWING AND GUNPOWDER PAINTING

# Notes on Keywords

## ART HISTORY

Cai has dialogued with his predecessors in art history as part of his studies since his youth. He went from sketching a plaster bust from Michelangelo's *David* and experimenting with Soviet styles, to pursuing myriad styles and artists including Van Gogh, Kandinsky, Impressionism, Pointillism, and Expressionism, and later to engaging with art history as an artistic theme in concrete forms. Early examples include *Ascending Dragon: Project for Extraterrestrials No. 2* of 1990, an unrealized explosion event proposed for Aix-en-Provence through which he aspired to dialogue with Cézanne, and *Dome* of 1996, the shape of which Cai borrowed from the Renaissance cathedral Santa Maria del Fiore in Florence.

His dialogue with art history came to the fore in 1999 with *Venice's Rent Collection Courtyard*, presented at the Venice Biennale, which re-created the canonical Socialist Realist group sculpture in front of live audiences. This was followed by other projects that are inextricably tied to his youthful experiences in Socialist China, such as *Cai Guo-Qiang's Maksimov Collection* (2002) and *One Thousand Youngsters Drawing David* (2010), among others.

Since 1999, his commitment to art history has grown in diversity and intensity. As he recovers, retraces, and reinterprets art history, his goals are unlike an art historian's: he studies the past in order to address his own questions and challenges. This spirit is most spectacularly embodied in two installations at Museum of Contemporary Art in Lyon in 2001, *An Arbitrary History: River* and *An Arbitrary History: Roller Coaster*. The viewer is invited to see an out-of-context montage of various works while paddling a boat in a canal or riding on a roller coaster set up within the museum; the two works respectively chart art history and Cai's personal history.

In 2017, Cai embarked on his project *Individual's Journey Through Western Art History*, which is a primary subject of the present exhibition and publication. This includes *October* at the Pushkin State Museum of Fine Arts in Russia, which was followed by *The Spirit of Painting. Cai Guo-Qiang at the Prado* in the same year. Individual projects are extensively explored in other sections in this volume.

SEE ALSO: CÉZANNE; CHINESE PAINTING, TRADITIONAL; DRAWING; EL GRECO; MAKSIMOV; PAINTING; SOCIALISM

## BIGFOOT

Cai's unrealized project, *Bigfoot's Footprints: Project for Extraterrestrials No. 6* of 1990, embodies his prescient vision for transcending national borders. The work would require two hundred "footprints," each 2 meters long, to be placed and exploded along the border between France and Germany for a stretch of more than 2000 meters. The project proved not feasible due to the difficulty of obtaining visas from the two countries.

Notably, his interest in "footprints" dates back to his youth in Quanzhou, when he frequented the Water Flow Pit in the forest up in the mountain to sketch and paint *en plein air*. He recalls seeing "magically indented footprints on the rock, which the locals named 'Immortal's Footprints.'"

It was not until 2008, on the occasion of the Beijing Olympic Games, that Cai realized *Bigfoot's Footprints* as part of the opening ceremony, under the title *Footprints of History: Fireworks for the Opening Ceremony of the 2008 Beijing Olympic Games*. To celebrate this global event, the artist deployed his signature fireworks to have an unseen living being sprint in a fleetingly borderless night sky along the axis of the city of Beijing, across the 15 kilometers from Yongdingmen, through Tiananmen and the Forbidden City, and finally reaching the Bird's Nest. Over 1.5 billion people worldwide witnessed this historic moment in the stadium or through livestream.

## BOAT

Boats and ships figure in many of Cai's works, ranging from *Dragon Boat* (1999), adorned with red paper lanterns and suspended in midair, to *Kaikou—The Keel (Returning Light—The Dragon Bone)* (1994), excavated from a beach in Japan.

Born and raised in the port city of Quanzhou, Cai developed a "special complex" about the vessels. Since his youth, he has frequently drawn and painted boats, which in his mind are "the sailboats that could leave behind 'gravity' to journey to distant lands and strive toward the cosmos." Having departed his own hometown, Cai too is like a boat. In 2012, he held a solo exhibition devoted to the theme, *A Clan of Boats*, at Faurschou Foundation in Copenhagen, Denmark, which is physically located on a dock.

Boats symbolize mutual connections between different cultures and regions. As he began to work as an artist on the global stage, the boat came to assume a greater significance. He pondered on the relationship between China and the world in a number of boat-based works, including *Bringing to Venice What Marco Polo Forgot* (1995) and *Borrowing Your Enemy's Arrows* (1998), among others. In *The Eagle Has Arrived!* (2001), he selected a local boat from Lyon and refurbished it in the style of a warship from the ancient Roman Empire. In 2002, he created *99 Golden Boats* (2002) for Hyōgo Prefectural Museum of Art in Kōbe, to commemorate the Great Hanshin Earthquake of 1995.

SEE ALSO: CHINESE HISTORY, AND JAPAN; IWAKI; QUANZHOU

## CENTRAL AND SOUTH AMERICA

Cai's engagement with this region began long before Cai had the chance to visit it in person. As a young artist, he was interested in Mexico's post-revolution mural movement, propelled by such giants as Diego Rivera, José Clemente Orozco, and David Alfaro Siqueiros, which was embraced by the Chinese government, together with Soviet Socialist Realism. Chinese artists were deeply moved by the Mexicans' passionate and creative endeavors to bring art to the masses while incorporating the tradition of European painting into their native culture to express the spirit of their era. They also saw freedom and charm in how Central and South American artists applied the vocabulary of Western modernism, such as Cubism, to propagandistic art.

In 1996, he finally had a chance to visit Mexico, when his work was included in *Between Earth and the Heavens: Aspects of Contemporary Japanese Art II*, a group exhibition held at Museo Tamayo in Mexico City. He was mesmerized by its landscape, but saddened to contemplate the rise and fall of its unique ancient civilizations of the Maya and Aztecs. These sentiments informed his solo exhibition *Sunshine and Solitude* in 2010 in Mexico City, in which he presented the largest gunpowder painting production to date.

In his 2019 project *Encounter with the Unknown: Cosmos Project for Mexico*, Cai reflected on the complex history following the Spanish arrival in the Aztec Empire five centuries ago, which brought about an encounter between the cosmologies of ancient and modern civilizations. In the moment of explosion, he seemed to spiritually return the land to the forebears of Mexico.

In 2015, he presented *Life Is a Milonga: Tango Fireworks for Argentina*, an explosion event in Buenos Aires, into which he incorporated livestreamed commentary and a tango orchestra in rhythm with the fireworks. Tango dancers, along with hundreds of thousands of audience members, danced together to the music in order to enhance the impassioned sense of improvisation in the Argentine tango.

## CÉZANNE

Born in Aix-en-Provence, France, Paul Cézanne frequently painted his hometown landscape with Mont Sainte-Victoire. In 1990, Cai participated in the group exhibition *Chine demain pour hier* curated by Fei Dawei in Cézanne's hometown. This was the first group exhibition to present the work of Chinese artists residing overseas and the first to present Cai's work in the West. Cai proposed *Ascending Dragon: Project for Extraterrestrials No. 2* in which a lightning-like gunpowder explosion would soar up from the foot to the peak of Mont Sainte-Victoire. Trusting the dragon to carry his aspiration for creativity and freedom, Cai hoped to initiate a dialogue between a young artist from East Asia and a great master of modernism. Unfortunately, the project was unrealized due to opposition from local people who had suffered from sudden wildfires just before the artist's arrival.

SEE ALSO: DRAGON

## CHINESE CULTURE AND CRAFTS

Chinese culture and crafts are an important inspiration and material for Cai. In *Human Abode: Project for Extraterrestrials No. 1* (1989), Cai uses a yurt to reference the wandering nomads in Central Asia, who for him embody the freedom of humankind that transcends borders. This was his first outdoor explosion event, and the nomadic spirit thus became the symbol of the artist's journeys around the world and the cosmos.

His hometown Quanzhou has been known for an impressive array of craftsmanship, encompassing shipbuilding, temple architecture, Buddhist sculpture, stone carving, ceramics, puppetry, paper-cut art, and decorative lanterns, among others. Foundational to all these crafts, Cai believes, was painting. Of several painterly forms practiced in Quanzhou, he was especially influenced by polished lacquer painting and glass painting that represent the kind of craftsmanship manifested in household objects. He incorporated the former into the permanent installation *Four Seasons and Four Phases* (1998), and was inspired by the latter to create a new series of glass and mirror gunpowder paintings presented in *Non-Brand 非品牌* at the Guggenheim Museum in 2019.

Associated with his childhood memories of red paper lanterns are such works as *Dream* (2002) and *A Boat with Dreams* (2008), all the way up to the public art project *Fireflies* (2017) in Philadelphia where he used nearly a thousand lanterns of various shapes and colors manufactured in Quanzhou.

Porcelain from Dehua, located in Quanzhou city, appeared in *Reflection—A Gift from Iwaki* (2004) in the form of Guanyin, the Buddhist goddess of mercy. He subsequently used Dehua porcelain in combination with gunpowder explosion to create a relief panel *Black Peony* (2008) and further developed the technique with *Fragile* (2011) and *Spring, Summer, Fall, Winter* (2014).

Various sculpting techniques that Quanzhou excels in are also deployed. Traditional masonry carving was used to depict events from and aspects of our lives after the 9/11 attack in *Nontransparent Monument*, part of *Cai Guo-Qiang on the Roof: Transparent Monument*, his rooftop solo exhibition at The Metropolitan Museum in New York in 2006. For the present exhibition at the Palace Museum, he invited Dehua craftsmen to create an alabaster model of the Forbidden City and colored it with fireworks to celebrate the six-hundredth anniversary of the Forbidden City.

Like gunpowder, kites originated in China two to three thousand years ago. For Cai, kites are an imaginative means to reach out to the sky. They represent humanity's earliest sense of breaking away from gravity, as he demonstrated in *Flying Dragon in the Heavens: Project for Extraterrestrials No. 29* (1997), for which the artist exploded a dragon-shaped intricate kite, and *Man, Eagle, and Eye in the Sky: Kite Project for Siwa* (2003), for which he invited the local children to draw on three hundred kites so that their mothers, who were not allowed to leave their households, could see from their yards the children's hopes that were flying high.

SEE ALSO: BOAT; GUNPOWDER; QUANZHOU; TOWER

## CHINESE HISTORY, ANCIENT

Cai came to appreciate the immensity of history through reading Sima Qian's *Shiji*, or *Records of the Grand Historian*, from his father's book collection. The spirit and philosophy of Chinese history and tradition have served as the foundation for Cai's art. Qin Shi Huang (259–210 BCE) was the first emperor to unify China. Among his numerous legacies were the construction of the Great Wall of China and his army of life-size terracotta soldiers and horses. Cai's first engagement with this major historical figure was through *Project to Extend the Great Wall of China by 10,000 Meters: Project for Extraterrestrials No. 10* (1993). This was followed by a more direct dialogue in 1994, when he held the solo exhibition *Chaos* at the Setagaya Art Museum in Tokyo concurrently with its blockbuster exhibition *The First Qin Emperor and His Times*. Among the works he created was *Elixir of Immortality*, a performance piece that thematized Qin Shi Huang's obsession with immortality.

In 2019, he had the solo exhibition *The Transient Landscape* at the National Gallery of Victoria, Melbourne, Australia, in conjunction with *Terracotta Warriors: Guardians of*

*Immortality*, the two exhibitions taking place side-by-side in the same exhibition spaces. Cai writes, "They are like two rivers separated by the passage of two millennia, each coursing at their individual pace through the galleries. The ancient and the contemporary—the tension between two surges of energy crisscrossing, pulling ... each attracting and rejecting the other."

Other early history-related works include *Chu Ba Wang* (1985), or *Hegemon King of Chu*, which refers to Xiang Yu (232–202 BCE), a warlord who revolted against the Qin dynasty. A 1998 installation, *Borrowing Your Enemy's Arrows*, alludes to a tale about Zhuge Liang (181–234 CE), a shrewd strategist from the Three Kingdoms period (220–280 CE).

## CHINESE HISTORY, POST-1949

The history of Chinese society since 1949 is an integral part of Cai's biography and work. In 1997, Cai created *Mao*, using memories from the Red ages as a humorous response to Western Pop art. As part of his installation, he hung Andy Warhol's famous Mao portrait high and slanted downward like Mao's portrait used to hang in Chinese elementary classrooms. In 2006, at the exact location where Mao held the "Yan'an Forum on Literature and Art," Cai organized the four-day "Yan'an Forum on Contemporary Art Education." He invited art and education experts from various perspectives to discuss the present and future of contemporary art education in China in a rapidly changing global art world and market. It was at this conference that Cai first unveiled his "Two Year Curriculum for Graduate Studies in Contemporary Art."

In 2017, on the occasion of his *October* exhibition in Moscow, he retraced the Red memories from his boyhood: the unfinished carving of a gigantic Mao portrait on a cliff in Quanzhou, measuring roughly 50 by 32 meters. He climbed onto the cliff and made a rubbing on canvas of this long-deserted stone carving. The process of *Mao Rubbing* was recorded in the documentary film *October: The Unrealized Century*.

In 2018, Cai realized a live explosion work, *Book Burning*, at Artron Art Center in Shenzhen, China. This drew on his childhood memory of helping his father burn banned books through the night in the early stage of the Cultural Revolution, and echoed similar incidents in the history of China and other civilizations.

Cultural misunderstanding is the subject of *Daylight Screen, Big White Truth* (2002), which Cai presented in Trento, Italy by holding an outdoor daytime screening of *Chung Kuo, China*, a 1972 documentary directed by Michelangelo Antonioni. The film was made with the consent of the Chinese government but was then banned for many years; in Cai's interpretation, the censorship was due to the stylistic discrepancy between China's Socialist Realism and Italy's Neorealism.

Cai's hometown of Quanzhou is located in proximity to Taiwan in both culture and geography. This fact led him to develop a deep interest in the region and cross-strait relations since childhood. *BMoCA (Bunker Museum of Contemporary Art)* of 2004 was sited on Kinmen Island in Taiwan, which for decades was in the center of military conflict between Taiwan and Mainland China due to its geopolitically strategic location. Cai commissioned contemporary artists from both sides of the strait to create site-specific works and performances in and around the many bunkers.

## CHINESE HISTORY, AND JAPAN

Since at least the first century BCE, Japan has varyingly maintained a diplomatic relationship with China. Chang'an (present Xi'an), which was China's capital from the Han to the Tang dynasty (202 BCE–907 CE), served as a model for Japan's ancient capitals, Nara and Kyoto.

In 1994, Cai responded to the city of Kyoto's invitation with *Project for Heiankyō 1,200th Anniversary: Celebration from Chang'an*. He carried the invitation letter from Kyoto to its sister city Xi'an, requesting the Xi'an government to send 1,200 liters of its famed *xifeng* liquor to Kyoto as a congratulatory gift. In Kyoto, he dug trenches in the shape of auspicious archaic Chinese emblems on the City Hall plaza, filled the trenches with the liquor, and set them ablaze at nightfall. The brilliant blue flames burned for over an hour as the rich perfume of liquor connected the distant pasts, presents, and futures of the two cities.

In 1995, Cai envisioned the project *Wakō: Japanese Pirates of the Middle Ages* for Naoshima Contemporary Art Museum (presently Benesse House Museum) in Japan. *Wakō* (倭寇) was originally a pejorative given by the Chinese and Koreans to Japanese pirates who plundered along the coasts of these two countries in the 13th–16th centuries. Cai's project would highlight the multivalent readings of a shared history; to the Japanese, these pirates in effect promoted trade in Asia. However, the project remains unrealized due to its politically sensitive content.

*To Build a Ship: Project for Nara Culture City of East Asia 2016* was inspired by Jianzhen (Ganjin in Japanese), a Tang-dynasty Chinese monk who propagated Buddhism in Japan and facilitated Sino-Japanese cultural exchange when he managed to reach Japan after many grueling attempts. The artist invited a team of shipbuilders from China to collaborate with Japanese craftsman to build a traditional East Asian junk on site in front of Tōdaiji's main temple hall, which had been built by craftsmen that Jianzhen brought to Nara. The work seemed to reenact the story of how Buddhism arrived in Japan 1200 years ago. The artist strove to ask, "Does this spiritual ship still exist on the East Asian seas of today? Can these seas still tolerate such a ship? Can people from different regions of East Asia still build this ship together? Is the annual 'Culture City of East Asia' an attempt at creating this ship, or is it merely a once-a-year 'one-night stand'?"

The following year, for the Culture City of East Asia event in Kyoto, Cai transformed the ship that asked whether the nations of East Asia are capable of "staying in the same boat" into the absurdist *Bonsai Ship* (2017), joining the pines and boulders of Kyoto's gardens to create the impression of a skyship alighting on Nijō Castle. Once again, the artwork takes on a humorous tone to ask, "The spirit of Eastern philosophy and the ambitions of peace embodied by the Culture City of East Asia—are these simply an immense bonsai display?"

SEE ALSO: BOAT

## CHINESE MEDICINE AND NATURAL HEALING

In Cai's cosmology, traditional Chinese medicine encapsulates a system of methodology to achieve the unity of the external universe and the internal universe.

Cai routinely consults with specialists in Chinese medicine to obtain precise prescriptions for a specific project, as in his first use of herbal infusion in the solo exhibition *Long Mai—The Dragon Meridian* (1993), which took place prior to his explosion event *Project to Extend the Great Wall of China by 10,000 Meters: Project for Extraterrestrials No. 10* (1993). For those who joined him on his trip to the Gobi Desert, he prepared *Secret Recipe for Japan: Fan Pu Gui Zhen Tang and Zeng Shou Ning Shen Tang: Project for Humankind No. 5*, consisting of two medicinal soups made from Chinese medicine as prescribed by a local doctor in Jiayuguan. One concoction, taken in advance of the project, would provide the participants strength and courage and lift their spirit, whereas the other, taken afterwards, would calm their spirit and produce tranquility.

At his 1994 solo exhibition at the Iwaki City Art Museum in Japan, he offered visitors *Chrysanthemum Tea*—which he had cultivated himself in Iwaki—to cleanse their hearts and clear their eyes. That same year, for the solo exhibition *Chaos* at the Setagaya Museum in Tokyo, he grilled poppy seeds with charcoal, making participants swoon and falter with the pungent scent. In 1996, at P.S.1 Contemporary Art Center in New York, he offered *lingzhi* mushroom tea as a detox (humorously countering "mushroom clouds" with "mushroom tea") in the installation *Crab House*. In 1997, for the installation *Cultural Melting Bath: Project for the 20th Century*, he devised a modern American delivery method for Chinese herbal medicine through a hot tub with hydrotherapy jets.

As part of his study of natural healing, in 1993, he experimented with local herbs to extract medicines and balms during a residency at the Cartier Foundation for Contemporary Art in France. He considers alchemy a Western counterpart to Chinese medicine, with the two sharing the ultimate goal of discovering an elixir of immortality.

In his pursuit of the unseen world, Chinese medicine embodies the "Eastern spirit" that Marco Polo "forgot" to bring back to Europe, as he demonstrated in his 1995 project *Bringing to Venice What Marco Polo Forgot* for the Venice Biennale. Cai filled a traditional junk with Chinese medicines and sent it from Quanzhou to Venice, and sailed the boat on the latter's canals on the day of the Biennale's opening. The work echoed the Italian's voyage to Venice, his hometown, from Quanzhou, the artist's hometown, seven hundred years before. In this project, Cai installed a vending machine of varying bottled herbal infusions that met different visitors' needs; another installation symbolically applied an acupuncture treatment to Venice's waters, clearing and cleansing it of blockages.

Also in 1995, he made an indoor work, *Moxacautery—For Africa*, for the inaugural Johannesburg Biennale. He invited a local artist to carve two human forms in wood as a metaphor for the South African landscape mired by social and political issues. He then gave the sculptures a moxa treatment to induce soothing and relaxing effects.

Both moxibustion (moxa-cautery) and acupuncture are built on the Chinese understanding of meridians, or invisible "energy paths," which can be mapped on a human body, with numerous acupuncture points located along them. For the 1997 installation, *A Cure When Ill, A Supplement When Healthy* at the Museum of Contemporary Art Chicago, he invited viewers to walk barefoot on a path paved with stones of varying sizes to stimulate the meridians on their soles. Alongside, he displayed a gunpowder drawing of meridian diagrams of the body and the foot, which viewers could consult to minister to their bodies accordingly.

SEE ALSO: COSMOS

## CHINESE PAINTING, TRADITIONAL

Cai had no formal training in Chinese painting, but his father Cai Ruiqin was devoted to traditional Chinese ink painting and calligraphy. As a child, Cai would watch his father smoke cigarettes while drawing tiny landscapes on matchboxes. The drawings were allegedly of the small fishing village that Cai's father was from, but the images were grand and imposing, complete with mountains, rivers, boundless seas, hundreds of boats, and waterfalls. As Cai grew older and began making art himself, he came to appreciate that the matchboxes embodied "a particularly Chinese poetic expression of the pursuit of aesthetic beauty, encompassing a boundless horizon in a mere square inch." He recalls, "My father was my first artistic influence."

In 2001, he staged *Performing Chinese Ink Painting* at the Contemporary Art Gallery in Vancouver, inviting three traditional ink painters to create ink painting sketches live on site at the nearby Dr. Sun Yat-Sen Classical Chinese Garden. In 2003, for *High Mountain Flowing Water: 3-D Landscape Painting* outside of Mori Art Museum in Tokyo, he created a three-dimensional landscape installation counterpart to the famed *View of Ama-no-hashidate* (c. 1501–6) by Sesshū, a Japanese monk-painter who had studied ink painting in China.

Traditional Chinese painting uses monochromatic black ink to richly express light and shade. Cai's black daytime explosion events, which he introduced in 2005, evoke the strewing of black ink across a canvas of blue sky.

Among the painters he has dialogued with in the exploration of ink painting is Qi Baishi (1864–1957), a painter with a modern bent and known for his depictions of flowers, birds, fish, and shrimp. Cai is interested in Qi's concept of "swinging between resemblance and dissimilarity" in order to capture the essence of a subject, and applied this principle in the 2007 series *Light Passage* and his 2009 explosion event *Fallen Blossoms*.

In his Hiroshima project in 2008, *Unmanned Nature: Project for the Hiroshima City Museum of Contemporary Art*, Cai broke new ground by creating a 45-meter-long "mountains and waters" painting-installation with actual water in the center of a gallery space. (In Chinese art, "mountains and waters," or *shanshui*, means "landscape.") The inspiration came from Huang Gongwang's (1269–1354) revered masterpiece *Dwelling in the Fuchun Mountains*. The work was exhibited in his solo exhibition *Unmanned Nature* at The Whitworth art gallery in Manchester, U.K. in 2015.

In 2010, he drew inspiration from his favorite Chinese painter, Ni Zan (1301–1374), to create the gunpowder scroll painting *Odyssey*, now on permanent display at the Museum of Fine Arts, Houston. In 2012, for his solo exhibition at Zhejiang Art Museum, he built a stage at the center of West Lake in Hangzhou, China and used gunpowder to sketch the lake's shimmering waters in 360 degrees on silk as *West Lake*. He then used the gunpowder painting *Tides* (2012) to explore the free-spirited expressiveness and the rare sense of abstraction that he saw in traditional paintings such as *Water Image Scroll* by Ma Yuan (1160–1225).

## CHINESE THOUGHT AND PHILOSOPHY, ANCIENT

Ancient Chinese thought and philosophy, which encompasses Confucianism and Daoism with syncretization of Buddhism, plays a significant role in Cai's artistic endeavor. Almost every aspect of Chinese culture he dialogues with and deploys in his work—be it the mythic dragon, traditional Chinese medicine, or *feng shui*—reflects Chinese thinking on harmony (和諧) and moderation (中庸), the binary of *yin* and *yang* (陰陽), the unity of heaven and man (天人合一), and the principle that "things reverse themselves upon reaching an extreme" (物极必反).

From *Yijing* (*I Ching*), or *Book of Changes*, an ancient text on divination that has codified Chinese thought, Cai has been most influenced by the concept of *yi*, or "changes." Cai made use of *Yijing* in *Turtle Fountain* (2002), which referenced the ancient mythic association of the turtle's back to the Eight Trigrams, or *Bagua*.

*Penglai / Hōrai* (2015), meanwhile, referenced the mythical island Penglai (in Japanese: Hōrai), a legend widely shared in East Asia, which is informed by Chinese mythology and Daoism. The fabled island is inhabited by immortals and embodies an ideal world free of desire and conflict. Cai materialized this myth by constructing a large mountain in a museum's shallow pool. The frontal view is covered with greenery, stones, waterfalls, and an otherworldly mist. Circling around to the back, however, the viewer sees that it is an empty mountain held up by scaffolding. The work alludes to the contemporary dispute between China and Japan over islands in the East China Sea, which, geopolitically speaking, is perhaps also only a façade.

## CONTEMPORARY CULTURAL FIGURES

Interdisciplinary in spirit, Cai has befriended a number of contemporary figures. In addition to collaborating with museum curators, Cai also works with contemporary thinkers, *feng shui* masters, Chinese medicine practitioners, artists, designers, architects, and scientists, always trying to stimulate and challenge both the collaborator and himself to have a new breakthrough. With Issey Miyake, Cai exploded gunpowder to draw dragon-inspired motifs on the Japanese designer's signature *Pleats Please* garments for Miyake's *Making Things* exhibition in Paris in 1998.

In 1999, as part of the 48th Venice Biennale, Cai for the first time collaborated with the curator Harald Szeemann, when the artist presented *Venice's Rent Collection Courtyard* and won the Golden Lion award. In 2001, Szeemann again organized the 49th Venice Biennale and invited Cai back. A self-proclaimed "troublemaking kid in the big family of art," Cai responded to the invitation by "playing a joke on the curator" with *Service for the Biennale!*, for which he asked Szeemann to sell bottled water to visitors in the blazing heat of the Biennale. Something that Szeemann once said has had a lifelong impact on Cai: "You are an artist, you should decide yourself what you want to do. Be bold."

For *The Snow Show* in Lapland, Finland in 2004, Cai was invited to collaborate with Pritzker Architecture Prize winner Zaha Hadid. Cai produced *Caressing Zaha with Vodka*, in which he poured nine tons of the hard liquor on Zaha's intricately built ice and snow castle, setting it aflame and letting it melt and vanish in the blue flames.

In 2006, he collaborated with Lin Hwai-min, a dancer and founder of the dance company Cloud Gate, to create *Wind Shadow*. Afterward, Cai observed, "In the future, my art won't necessarily use dance directly, but this collaboration may have a subtle, silent effect on my understanding of 'time' and approach to controlling on-site effects."

His 2009 project, *Time Flies Like a Weaving Shuttle*, thematized the friendship between two female directors in Philadelphia, who jointly invited the artist to have solo exhibitions at their institutions: Anne d'Harnoncourt of the Philadelphia Museum of Art and Marion "Kippy" Boulton Stroud of The Fabric Workshop and Museum. By the time the artist began his preparation for the exhibition, d'Harnoncourt had passed away, and Cai decided to create a work based on Boulton Stroud's memories of her. He invited five traditional weavers from the minority Tujia ethnic group, native to the western Hunan Province of China, to Philadelphia to interpret Boulton Stroud's memories of d'Harnoncourt into pieces of tapestries of the lifelong friendship.

In 2009, Cai's retrospective exhibition went on tour to the Guggenheim Museum Bilbao designed by Frank Gehry. Gehry was overjoyed to see how Cai had understood and utilized his spaces, and the two formed a lasting bond. In 2014, Cai made a whimsical contribution, the mini explosion event *Hanabi: Sparks of Inspiration*, for the exhibition *Frank Gehry: Solaris Chronicles* at the LUMA Foundation in France. Cai's collaborations with the architect also include the latter's design of the artist's studio in New Jersey in the U.S., and a joint plan to build a Quanzhou Museum of Contemporary Art.

Also in 2014, Cai memorialized Jan Hoet, his longtime collaborator and the founder of S.M.A.K. (Stedelijk Museum voor Actuele Kunst) in Ghent, Belgium, with *Cloud for Jan Hoet*, at his funeral. The posthumous collaboration became the tenth between artist and curator, who had worked together since 1995. One of their memorable collaborations took place in 2003, when Cai exploded Hoet's portrait on the wall of S.M.A.K. for an explosion work titled *Inheritance: Exploding Jan Hoet's Portrait*. Hoet was about to retire from his role as S.M.A.K.'s director, and with this work, the artist dared Hoet to erase his own likeness and let his successors completely take over.

## COSMOS

In Cai's cosmology, the cosmos consists of two aspects: the external universe and the internal universe, informed by both Western literature and Eastern thought. The external universe encompasses planet Earth and the general understanding of outer space, as well as the natural environments we live in. The internal universe refers to the life imbedded in our bodies.

His reverence for the universe, both internal and external, was nurtured from his childhood, especially under the influence of his grandmother. Later, he developed a broader understanding of the internal universe as he learned more about *feng shui* and Chinese medicine. His interest in the external universe originated from his childhood experience of looking up to the starry sky and learning about mythology and folklore; he later studied various works on cosmology, ranging from books by Chinese contemporary astrophysicist Fang Lizhi to Stephen Hawking's *A Brief History of Time: From the Big Bang to Black Holes* (1988). For a long time, Cai always carried with him Carl Sagan's book *Cosmos* (1980) on his long journeys.

The external and internal universes loosely correspond to the seen and unseen worlds, the visible and the invisible. The crux of Cai's creative endeavors as an artist is the effort to connect the two and bridge communication among nature, humankind, and the cosmos. The gunpowder explosion events he began devising in 1989 can thus be grouped into two series directed at two kinds of audiences, humans and extraterrestrials: thirty-three works, from No. 0 to No. 32, of *Projects for Extraterrestrials* and six works, from No. 1 to No. 6, of *Projects for Humankind*. Cai uses the Earth as his canvas in the former, intended for extraterrestrials to view from outer space, while he uses outer space as his canvas in the latter, intended for humans to view from the Earth.

While some works in the *Projects for Extraterrestrials* series make direct references to astrophysics, as with *45.5 Meteorite Craters Made by Humans on Their 45.5 Hundred Million Year Old Planet: Project for Extraterrestrials No. 3* (1990), many others thematize historical and art-historical episodes, as demonstrated in 1993 by *Project to Extend the Great Wall of China by 10,000 Meters: Project for Extraterrestrials No. 10*, through which he made an ephemeral westward addition to the sprawling structure said to be the only manmade product on the Earth visible from outer space. The adoption of an extraterrestrial perspective enabled Cai to break free from conventional ideas and question the alleged progress of human civilization.

The *Projects for Humankind* series consists of mostly unrealized ideas, such as *A*

*Certain Lunar Eclipse: Project for Humankind No. 2* and *Inverted Pyramid on the Moon: Project for Humankind No. 3*, both made into gunpowder drawings in 1991 and included in his *Primeval Fireball* exhibition. In 2020, while under quarantine in New Jersey from the COVID-19 outbreak, Cai drew from his early sketchbooks to create *Nostalgia for Homeland: Project for Humankind No. 4* as a gunpowder drawing.

SEE ALSO: EXTRATERRESTRIALS; GRANDMOTHER

## CURRENT EVENTS

Back in elementary school, Cai would secretly tune in to "enemy stations" (broadcasts from outside of Mainland China) under the covers. Since then, he has been an avid consumer of news on current affairs, especially international politics. In his work, Cai dialogues with the present as much as with the past. On the one hand, he responds to current events and social issues through his work; on the other hand, he derives energy for living and working in a complex, multicultural state by thinking broadly about rapidly changing international situations.

In 1995, he created the project *Restrained Violence—Rainbow: Project for Extraterrestrials No. 25* for *The Ever-Changing, Drifting Heat: The First Johannesburg Biennale*, curated by Jean-Hubert Martin. In this explosion event, Cai thematized the situations in South Africa, which had just held its first universal election in the previous year. In particular, he referenced President Nelson Mandela's tactics of assaulting only economically vital sites with "restrained violence" during his time as a guerilla leader, and his goal of building "a rainbow nation" during his time as leader of the country.

For many years, Cai wanted to create a work based on the Berlin Wall. In *Rebuilding the Berlin Wall: Project for Extraterrestrials No. 7*, an unrealized idea from 1989, Cai envisioned creating an ephemeral wall on the Berlin Wall site through gunpowder explosion, alluding to the invisible walls that continue to divide human beings. In 2006, he finally realized a concept inspired by the Berlin Wall with the invisible wall in *Head On*, an installation of 99 replica wolves repeatedly colliding into a glass wall. The work dissects the human tendency to be blinded by hero worship and herd mentality.

Another major development in the late 20th century was the establishment of the European Union in 1993, to which Cai has responded through multiple works. In 2016, when Cai had a solo exhibition *My Stories of Painting* at the Bonnefanten Museum in the E.U. signatory city Maastricht, he created *Boy's Doodle: Drawing for the 25th Anniversary of the EU in Maastricht*, an unrealized concept for a daytime explosion event centered on a bridge, implying that the member states and the E.U. have a couple-like relationship, loving and hating (or competing) at the same time.

Symbolically marking the start of the new millennium, the year 2000 was also known as Y2K, a shorthand used to describe the potential havoc caused by a computer programming glitch related to the two-digit year format. Cai humorously pondered on a kind of "magic power" that the computer has in contemporary society in his solo exhibition *I Am the Y2K Bug* (1999), in which the combination of a computer and a manual act would trigger a small mushroom cloud explosion. Earlier in 1993, Cai was invited by UNESCO to conceptualize a project in anticipation of the new millennium and proposed *Peaceful Earth: Project for Extraterrestrials No. 18*. If realized, this project would have required everyone on the Earth to participate, turning off their lights one time zone after another at the moment they crossed over from the last millennium to the next. (The idea transitioned from his sketchbook to a gunpowder drawing in 2020.) Another project, *The Last Supper: Project for Extraterrestrials No. 31* (1999), took place on the last day of 1999 in Utrecht, the Netherlands, where the artist distributed small fireworks tubes to all local residents. Once ignited, they sent smoke drifting up the city's long-unused chimneys, as though rewinding time through this last supper of the millennium.

The 9/11 attacks led Cai, who had been living in New York for many years, to feel more than ever that "New York is my home." His explosion event *Transient Rainbow* (2002) commissioned by MoMA, New York, was the first pyrotechnic event permitted in the city—or even the entire United States—since the attack. This was also the debut of the fireworks smoke shells fitted with a computer chip.

A more somber response to the tragedy was found in his solo exhibition *Cai Guo-Qiang on the Roof: Transparent Monument* at The Metropolitan Museum of Art in New York in 2006. In particular, the titular work *Transparent Monument* consists of a 5-meter-high piece of glass erected to face the direction of the World Trade Center's site. He explains, "In the multidimensional world of reality, the contents behind the glass become two-dimensional; the moment a bird crashes into the glass and falls, time and space seem to shift and morph, creating chaos. Airplanes cannot cross to the other side and crumble before the two-dimensional plane. This piece of glass is like a giant scroll painting slotted into the middle of our era. I keep thinking about the ambiguous and convoluted connotations of this work. The only thing clear to me is that, though I have made installations of cars, tigers, and crocodiles following 9/11, I stopped working with this subject matter after making *Transparent Monument*."

## DRAGON

The dragon, an auspicious mythic creature, represents an expansive iconography in Cai's work. Its conceptual significance is twofold. First, viewed from Western cultures, the dragon is a monster with powers of destruction and embodies the modern nation of China as a globalizing force. Second, in the ancient understanding of Eastern cultures, the dragon embodies the forces of nature that reign on earth and in the heavens and the universe. Cai has used this symbol with such culturally disparate connotations as a theme for numerous works, often using the dragon as a symbol of energy or *qi*, especially in relation to the principles of *feng shui* and Chinese medicine. As an extension, Cai sees the dragon as "humankind's dream to break through its own physical limitations, to freely roam about between the sky and the sea. As the dragon leaps into the sky, it carries humankind's desire to communicate with life forms outside the Earth, as well as its attempt to return to the open arms of the universe." This was the foundation for *Ascending Dragon: Project for Extraterrestrials No. 2* (1989).

In the explosion events *Dragon Sight Sees Vienna: Project for Extraterrestrials No. 32* (1999) and *Ye Gong Hao Long (Mr. Ye Who Loves Dragons) for Tate Modern* (2003), the Vienna project can be said to represent China as a threat in the Western view, including the future ubiquity of Chinese tourists, while the Tate Modern project was a humorous interpretation of "Ye Gong Hao Long," which derives from a story of a Mr. Ye in ancient times who loved dragons and painted them all the time and everywhere. But one day when Mr. Ye saw a real dragon, he was so frightened that he ran for his life. There are a few possible interpretations of this allegory found in Cai's piece. The most familiar is the Western attitude toward the East, especially modern-day China. The other is the artist's self-deprecating humor on his own history of tirelessly using dragons as a symbol and subject matter.

## DRAWING

Drawing has a particular significance for Cai beyond his signature gunpowder works, as drawing and sketching were an essential part of his painting training under the official regimen of Socialist Realism. Cai's drawing in this sense has developed and evolved conceptually, for example in 1998 at the French Academy in Rome where he created a number of oil drawings inspired by the beautiful setting. One of them was *Summer Tilling at Villa Medici* (1998). It depicts his idea for a performance work, in which the curator Hans Ulrich Obrist would plow a field in suit and dress shoes. This project was later realized in 2000 as *Till by Blade, Sow by Fire*.

Cai's use of the term "sketch" derived from *suxie* (速写), or "quick sketch," as customarily used in China's Western-derived art practice and education. To "sketch" is to draw using simple tools to create images of people and objects in concise lines within a limited time. He applied this form to his 2009 explosion event *Sketch of a Boat*.

The academic studio exercise of drawing and painting a nude model was turned into a live event in Cai's 2000 work, literally entitled *Still Life Performance*, in which he set up a makeshift studio, hired a nude model, and had her pose atop a horse, within a 19th-century painting gallery of the Art Gallery of New South Wales in Sydney, Australia. The painting "performance" was undertaken by Cai and three other painters from different backgrounds and styles for two hours every day over a week.

His multi-element work of 2010, *One Thousand Youngsters Drawing David*, directs our attention to the common classroom experiences among post-1949 generations of Chinese art students. Cai filmed over a thousand Chinese art students drawing plaster busts from *David* by Michelangelo, then projected the video onto the rock wall of the Michelangelo cave in Carrara, Italy. Notably, the Renaissance master worked with marble from this locale to create *David*. In the video, Cai commented on the shared tradition: even today, Chinese art students must undergo lengthy training in sketching, with strict criteria imposed on pictorial form and shadowing. While this deprives countless students of letting their personalities run free, if students are able to go beyond mere mimesis in order to thoroughly understand objects and their relationships to their surroundings, develop command over details as well as the holistic picture, and clearly distinguish between primary and ancillary subjects, this training will significantly affect both their studies and their lives.

SEE ALSO: GUNPOWDER DRAWING AND GUNPOWDER PAINTING

## ECOLOGY

Cai thematizes climate change, nature, and ecology in multiple works. This includes *The Earth Is Our Common Home* (1985), a triptych of oil paintings that depicts the Earth full of water, an arctic station where scientists of various nations cohabit harmoniously, and the burnt Earth.

*Heritage* (2013) and *The Ninth Wave* (2014) are works that employed 99 life-sized replicas of animals, including pandas, tigers, and leopards, fabricated in Fujian Province, China. In *Heritage*, ferocious and gentle animals coexist peacefully and drink water together from a pond surrounded by white sand. The work evokes the question: If such a scene of "paradise" is only possible when only one pool of water remains in the world, then this is a scene of apocalyptic heritage that humans hope never to achieve. For *The Ninth Wave*, Cai loaded 99 animals on an 18-meter-long fishing boat, which departed from Quanzhou and traveled along the Huangpu River, passing by architectural landmarks emblematic of modernism and progress on either side, to arrive at Power Station of Art in Shanghai. Reminiscent of Noah's Ark, the animals appeared exhausted from the long trip, as though seasick from the currents of our time. The work was inspired by *The Ninth Wave* (1850) by the Russian marine painter Ivan Aivazovsky.

On a lighter note, also at Power Station of Art, Cai created *Air of Heaven*, an installation housed inside its chimney of the former power plant. He placed three lifelike baby dolls on a swing, continually disturbing the air inside the 100-meter chimney and rousing people's neuroticism about air pollution.

Cai has long been dedicated to sustainability in fireworks. Harnessing compelling artistic concepts and effects, he pushed for the development of air-powered firework launching, microchips for precise positioning, and computer ignition technology to drastically reduce the quantity of fireworks needed to effectively produce an event and the smoke generated by ignitions. With the help of such large international events as the Olympics, he has been able to develop and promote toxin-free, little-smoke, low-sulfur pyrotechnic products and explosion techniques by capitalizing on national resources and technologies. When China supplies 90% of the world's fireworks via export, the efforts of a single artist can have a tangible effect on the progress of environmental awareness in the pyrotechnics industry.

## EL GRECO

Cai has named El Greco as his favorite painter since his youth. Aside from the parallel between the two artists' nomadic life trajectories, there are also similarities in their approaches to art. In Cai's view, El Greco's "art became a conduit, able to transmit the spirit and connect to a mystical world," just like he himself aspires to do in his pursuit of "shuttling freely between the seen and the unseen, between the ancient and the avant-garde."

After the work on the 2008 Beijing Olympics came to an end, Cai longed to "return to the embrace of the world." He therefore made a trip to trace El Greco's footsteps from Crete, where he was born, to Rome, Venice, Madrid, and finally Toledo, where he died as an expatriate. Cai returned to Toledo in 2017, where he revisited his earlier inspirations and created a large number of works that he presented at his solo exhibition *The Spirit of Painting* at the Prado Museum later that year.

## EXTRATERRESTRIALS

In Cai's cosmology, extraterrestrials still belong to the unseen world. He believes in their existence, because, he reasons, "humankind cannot possibly be the only survivor in the vast universe. [If so, that] violates science and disrupts the space of mythology." For him, extraterrestrials are a source of inspiration, and he dialogues with them in infinite Time and Space. Hence, the series title *Projects for Extraterrestrials*. These explosion events are acts undertaken by humankind on Earth for extraterrestrials to view from above. In other words, Cai's goal is to make a kind of art that extraterrestrials would understand. To him, being capable of dialoguing with extraterrestrials means he can certainly dialogue with different cultures on Earth.

In Cai's view, in a distant future, earthlings will eventually depart from their homeland on Earth and become extraterrestrials. A majority of human civilization will be left behind on Earth in a state of ruin. Cai imagines that, when extraterrestrials come to visit Earth or when humans later return as extraterrestrials, they can find traces of life in a big frozen block of seawater, thereby reawakening or giving birth to a new indigenous civilization. Cai materialized a part of this scenario in *The Immensity of Heaven and Earth: Project for Extraterrestrials No. 11* (1991). In addition to an aboveground explosion event, he created an "underground" part by burying a coffin-shaped ice block made from 600 kilograms of seawater and sealed it with stones at an abandoned train yard in Fukuoka, Japan. A more elegiac work is *Nostalgia for Homeland: Project for Humankind No. 4*, which is set in a boundless galaxy and expresses the longing gaze back at the homeland from light years away. This unrealized idea was transferred from his sketchbook to a gunpowder drawing in 2020.

## FAUNA AND FLORA

Plants and animals often carry local cultural or historical significance, opening a space for dialogue. The animal species frequently featured in Cai's gunpowder drawings, paintings, and installation works include turtles, crocodiles, eagles, birds, tigers, horses, and spiders. Plants often used are peonies, sunflowers, poppy flowers, chrysanthemums, vines, mushrooms, pines, and cypresses. Among them, the poppy flower appeals to Cai in particular because of its hallucinatory effect, in which he finds resonance with the "out of control" nature of gunpowder. He created around forty paintings on the subject in 2015–17, and went all the way to one of the world's few licensed poppy fields near Toledo, Spain to further study the flower.

Included in his solo exhibition *October* in 2017 was *Autumn*, an installation work of an artificial mountain sited at the entrance of the Pushkin Museum. Small trees were planted in hundreds of cradles, which signify the birthplace of innocent dreams. As the exhibition progressed, the tree leaves turned yellow and withered. The installation as a whole stood as a monument to the collective longing for a better society, but was also a tomb for generations of utopian ideals.

In his solo exhibition *Flora Commedia: Cai Guo-Qiang at the Uffizi* in 2018, Cai focused on Renaissance flowers and the Roman goddess Flora, famously portrayed by Botticelli in *Primavera* in the museum's collection, in order to capture the spirit of Renaissance, its connection with nature, and the awakening of humanity. Prior to the exhibition's opening, Cai created the daytime explosion event *City of Flowers in the Sky*, which took place at the Piazzale Michelangelo that overlooks the city of Florence. Using *Primavera* as inspiration, Cai ignited thousands of Renaissance flowers, "So that people from all corners of the city, even the suburbs, could witness it and feel the impact and intimacy of the Renaissance painters and their works in today's context."

## *FENG SHUI*

*Feng shui* is an ancient Chinese tradition of geomancy that orchestrates unseen energy forces (*qi*) to create a harmonious environment. Cai is a practitioner of *feng shui* both in art and in life. In *feng shui*, there is the credo of "Inner *qi* gives rise to life, outer *qi* gives rise to form. When inner meets outer, *feng shui* gives rise to itself." To Cai, this means going along with the flow of nature and maintaining balance. In 1992, he first used *feng shui* in an explosion event with *Fetus Movement II: Project for Extraterrestrials No. 9*, in which he redirected river water into the military base in Germany, where the work was realized. In 1994, he made *feng shui* an explicit theme of his multi-element presentation *Universal Design: Feng Shui Project for Mito: Chang Sheng* at Art Tower Mito, in Japan. It included a "cosmic diagram" in which he simulated a prescription to correct the energy flow of the city of Mito. He hung a pine tree inside the gallery, under which he created stone graves for himself and the curator. Outside, in the area considered by *feng shui* as the "dragon head" of Mito, located next to the mountain pass that had been cleaved by train tracks, he placed a large stone lion sculpture to symbolically preside over negative energies.

As with his use of Chinese medicine, the artist often consults with specialists to incorporate the principles of *feng shui* in his work. In 2000, when he was invited to the Whitney Biennial, he created *How Is Your Feng Shui?: Year 2000 Project for Manhattan*, in which he presented viewers with computer software to assess the *feng shui* of their homes or offices. To remedy bad *feng shui* situations, the visitors might acquire one (or more) of 99 stone lions which the artist would personally install.

In a less conspicuous way, *feng shui* helps Cai to grasp unseen energy flow in a given space and plan his project in situ. Upon entering any exhibition space, he immediately feels the energy flow and direction within it, based on which he can plan his exhibition layout, determine, and even envision works that would go well in this space. In other words, *feng shui* is an integral part of his artistic methodology. For example, in 1997, he created an interactive large-scale installation *Cultural Melting Bath: Project for the 20th Century* for his first solo exhibition in the United States, held at Queens Museum of Art in New York. In a spacious entrance hall, he placed strangely shaped Taihu rocks according to *feng shui* principles and optimized the natural flow of energy, wherein the visitors might take a Chinese herbal bath on the most advantageous spot—the acupuncture point of the space—in terms of *feng shui*.

Another example of Cai's *feng shui* application is *Venice's Rent Collection Courtyard* in 1999. For this live installation, he chose the worst *feng shui* spot on the grounds of the Venice Biennale, where the wind can easily blow in, where the space looks especially desolate, and where sculptures easily dry and crack. But since his intention was to revisit the tragic turn of events surrounding the landmark sculpture *Rent Collection Courtyard* by re-creating it on site, the selected space worked well. His decision proved correct, and the work won Cai the Golden Lion grand prize that year.

## GLOBALIZATION IN HISTORY

Before modern times, China played a central role in the early phase of globalization. The Maritime Silk Road, which connected China with Europe via the Middle East, starting from Cai's hometown Quanzhou, is an appealing subject for Cai. This is demonstrated in his 1995 project *Bringing to Venice What Marco Polo Forgot* and his 2011 solo exhibition *Saraab* in Doha, Qatar.

Asia's economic rise in the wave of 1990s globalization has featured as a theme in several of Cai's works. With his 1996 installation *Cry Dragon/Cry Wolf: The Ark of Genghis Khan*, he relativized the Western fear of the invading dragon that is contemporary China with the Mongols' historical conquests across Eurasia. His 1997 work *The Dragon Has Arrived!* has a dappled, Eastern, wooden pagoda-cum-rocket with a fan blowing at ten or so Chinese flags at the base of the rocket, sending them fluttering like mock jet flames. The two installations were both accompanied by a compendium of news magazines on China's rapid ascent displayed on the adjacent walls.

Warfare that accompanies the desire for territorial expansion was another vital force in human globalization. In 2003, commissioned by Siwa Art Project in Egypt, Cai dialogued with Alexander the Great in *Man, Eagle and*

Eye in the Sky: Kite Project for Siwa. Alexander was known for his far-ranging conquests, his formation of the largest territorial empire in the world at the time, and his facilitation of the growth of ancient Greek civilization and of cultural diffusions between East and West. Cai focused on an episode of Alexander traversing the Sahara Desert to seek out an oracle in Siwa Oasis. In the work's title, "man" signifies humankind as an agent of history, "eagle" represents Alexander the Great, and "eye in the sky" alludes to eyes of the unseen powers.

SEE ALSO: QUANZHOU

## GRANDMOTHER (CHEN AIGAN)

As a child, Cai would sleep in the same bed as his grandmother, listening to her stories about Grandfather, who died before she reached her thirties. Grandmother's recollections included how, after Grandfather's death, an extraordinary experience with a local shaman led her away from her Christian faith in favor of worshipping traditional Chinese deities and practicing folk customs. The encounter also spurred her to leave Dongtou Village for the city of Quanzhou. Cai's reverence for the unseen world thus took deep root in his childhood to form a singular foundation of his creative endeavor.

When Cai first started experimenting with gunpowder on canvas in the 1980s, it was Grandmother who first made him realize that, while it was important to light fires, it was more important to know when to put them out. A tireless supporter of her grandson's aspiration, Grandmother never saw any of his works around the world in person, in the decades after Cai left their hometown. In 2015, Cai decided to realize the explosion event Sky Ladder in the harbor of Quanzhou's Huiyu Island, and dedicated it to his one-hundred-year-old Grandmother.

*Sky Ladder* began as Making a Ladder to the Earth: Project for Extraterrestrials No. 20. The earliest attempt to realize it was in 1994 for the Bath Festival. The idea—to raise a 500-meter ladder by a hot air balloon and set the ladder on fire—failed due to bad weather. The project was attempted two more times in vain, first in Shanghai then in Los Angeles, as documented in the film *Sky Ladder: The Art of Cai Guo-Qiang* (2016, dir. Kevin Macdonald, available on Netflix). An act of dialoguing with the unseen world, *Sky Ladder* was finally realized after twenty-one years at his fourth attempt. Grandmother passed away one month later. A phone video of *Sky Ladder* uploaded onto Facebook attracted over thirty million views in just two days.

## GUNPOWDER

One of the "four great inventions" of China, gunpowder has become Cai's signature material, which he has used to produce explosion events and two- and three-dimensional works (such as drawings, paintings, and installations). His earliest experiments with gunpowder were undertaken in an effort to identify a method of painting that enabled him to liberate his cautious and controlling nature and break from the social constraint at the time. There were many firecracker factories in his hometown, so it was relatively easy to acquire gunpowder.

After relocating to Japan in 1986, he continued his exploration of gunpowder. Beginning in 1987, he completely replaced paint with gunpowder, using the latter to create drawings or paintings on handmade hemp paper. In 1989, he realized his first outdoor explosion event, which has since enabled him to "create through destruction" in a broader social and natural realm. "All beings forget the self, time-space stops or returns to the primeval moment of beginning. All merges with the cosmic *qi*." Gunpowder's explosion catalyzes the artist's ability to achieve an eternity in a flash, bridging the seen and unseen worlds.

Over the years, Cai has continued developing his repertoire of ways to use gunpowder both in explosion events and in painting. Black Rainbow for Valencia (2005) marked his first time realizing a daytime explosion event. The use of daytime explosion events in multiple colors began with Black Ceremony (2011) in Doha, and subsequent significant projects include Elegy for the opening of his solo exhibition *The Ninth Wave* in Shanghai (2014). Since 2015, with his solo exhibition at Yokohama Museum of Art in Japan, Cai has worked more with color gunpowder in painting. He had come in contact with color gunpowder when he first relocated to Japan in the 1980s, but felt at the time that, "In Eastern culture, 'one' can express all. It is ideal if I can reach my goals using black gunpowder alone." Color seemed impure and disruptive to his spiritual pursuit. He therefore only used different types of black gunpowder to paint for many years.

## GUNPOWDER DRAWING AND GUNPOWDER PAINTING

Gunpowder drawing and gunpowder painting are among Cai's signature practices. The difference between the two is that the former is created for other projects, including indoor and outdoor explosion events and installation works. In contrast, a "gunpowder painting" is created for its own sake. The first gunpowder drawings were made in 1989 for the series Projects for Extraterrestrials, when he began using gunpowder on handmade Japanese hemp paper to represent the series's large-scale, outdoor explosion events, both realized and unrealized. The drawings were sometimes records of live events and sometimes a means to articulate his ideas through images and texts. Both functioned as a kind of concept drawing.

His solo exhibition Primeval Fireball: The Project for Projects (1991) consisted of a compendium of seven concept drawings. The unrealized projects they presented among these included Rebuilding the Berlin Wall: Project for Extraterrestrials No. 7 (1991) and Reviving the Ancient Signal Towers: Project for Extraterrestrials No. 8 (1990), as well as A Certain Lunar Eclipse: Project for Humankind No. 2 (1991) and Inverted Pyramid on the Moon: Project for Humankind No. 3 (1991).

A more unusual instance of gunpowder drawing is The Vague Border at the Edge of Time/Space Project (1991). Cai did not create it for any project, but considers it a "drawing" for his philosophy and thinking. It concerned a set of fundamental questions he was pondering at the time: "Is there a world where material and spirit are united? If there is, where is it? Is this a place where this work is situated?"

Another exhibition focused on gunpowder drawing was Unlucky Year: Unrealized Projects from 2003–2004, which was featured in his solo exhibition at Arthur M. Sackler Gallery and Hirshhorn Museum, both part of the Smithsonian Institution. Cai's presentation consisted of a large group of gunpowder drawings in which the artist envisioned explosion events around the world that had been underway but ended up unrealized over the past year.

In 2015, when he presented the series Seasons of Life at his solo exhibition *There and Back Again* at Yokohama Museum of Art in Japan, Cai advanced the new terminology upon the museum's suggestion. The museum wanted to introduce two categories into Cai's works universally referred to as gunpowder drawings since *Primeval Fireball* in order to differentiate "gunpowder paintings" from "gunpowder drawings." Cai felt that it was the right timing, all the more so because the newly prepared pieces, made on canvas with color gunpowder to bring forth more dynamic techniques as well as fuller hues and emotions, were a type of painting in a purer sense. It was no longer fitting to continue calling them "drawings."

SEE ALSO: DRAWING

## IWAKI (FUKUSHIMA PREFECTURE, JAPAN)

Cai lived in Japan for almost nine years, from December 1986 to September 1995. But Iwaki, a coastal town east of Tokyo, has a special place in Cai's life and art almost as a second hometown. The artist first visited the city in 1988 and soon became friendly with its people. In 1993, he decided to rent a studio there, in particular to prepare for his exhibition at Iwaki City Art Museum. He would ask himself, "Why does Iwaki need art from me?" This reflection led him to the motto: "To create work here, to have a dialogue with the universe from here, to create a story of the era with the people living here." Together with many local volunteers, he realized the explosion event *The Horizon from the Pan-Pacific: Project for Extraterrestrials No. 14* (1994) and a concurrent solo exhibition *From the Pan-Pacific* at Iwaki City Art Museum.

*Horizon* exploded a 30,000-meter-long gunpowder fuse across a pitch-black sea, using the flame to illustrate the boundary between Earth and outer space. The local residents contributed to this project by purchasing 1 meter of gunpowder fuse each, and they even volunteered to turn off their lights so that the outline of Earth would be clearer and more beautiful.

For the exhibition, he worked with local residents to excavate an abandoned fishing boat on the beach, from which he fashioned two works: *San Jō Tower* and *Kaikou—The Keel (Returning Light—The Dragon Bone)*. In 1997, the tower was reconfigured into a propelling rocket in *The Dragon Has Arrived!*. In 2004, the same team of Iwaki volunteers excavated and gifted a larger fishing vessel to Cai for his solo exhibition *Traveler* at Arthur M. Sackler Gallery in Washington, D.C. Cai combined it with white porcelain fragments of Guanyin deities from his hometown to form *Reflection—A Gift from Iwaki*. *Reflection* has subsequently toured the world, including appearances at the National Gallery of Canada in Ottawa, the Guggenheim Museum in New York, Guggenheim Museum Bilbao in Spain, Taipei Fine Arts Museum, and the Museum of Modern and Contemporary Art of Nice. Each time, his friends from Iwaki participated in the ship's assembly and installation. The invisible friendship and passing years have become the core of the work.

The city of Iwaki was gravely affected by the 2011 Tōhoku earthquake and the Fukushima Daiichi nuclear accident. Countless residents were left without a home. To help his friends, Cai raised funds for them to rebuild their homes, but they instead decided to use the money to make *Project to Plant Ten Thousand Cherry Blossom Trees*, to express their lament and responsibility of their generation's destruction of nature. In conjunction, Cai initiated *SMoCA (Snake Museum of Contemporary Art)* in 2013, inviting Iwaki's residents to build a 99-meter-long winding corridor from trees that were unsellable due to radiation contamination. The corridor winds through the forest of cherry blossom trees, becoming a space where adults and children can hold exhibitions and performances, have emotional exchanges, and let their dreams fly free. The "museum" has since been extended to 160 meters, and now boasts two towers as well as a bridge.

## JAPAN

From 1986, Cai spent almost nine years living in Japan, which was a crucial formative phase in the development of his art and career. Japan led him to focus his studies on the pure beauty of materials and forms. It was in Japan that he began working with outdoor explosion events, initiating *Projects for Extraterrestrials*. He also began taking advantage of delicate yet sturdy Japanese handcrafted paper to create gunpowder drawings with dynamic methods. As he presented his ideas for the unseen world through his gunpowder works, he found a sympathetic audience in Japan and was able to cultivate friendships as well as ties with a number of cultural institutions.

An earlier Japan-themed project was *Buried Civilization—Field Firings* (1993), staged in Shiga Prefecture, where one of the Six Ancient Kilns is located. Cai reflected on pottery as a shared trait among different civilizations that nonetheless reveal diversities and variations. He made small replicas of artifacts from such ancient civilizations as Egypt, China, and Japan, and placed them all in a wooden boat, together with computer chips, symbolic of contemporary civilization. He buried the wooden boat and set it on fire, leaving a boat-shaped mark in the pit after the entire boat was burnt to ashes. The burnt terracotta objects blended with the fired earth, which took on the texture of terracotta, and became an integrated whole.

In 2002, he created *Cai Guo-Qiang's CHADO Pavilion—Homage to Tenshin Okakura*, in tribute to Okakura, whose *The Book of Tea* (1906) made him a pioneer in facilitating dialogues between Eastern and Western cultures.

Cai was especially interested in Okakura's advocacy for the significance of Eastern aesthetics and value systems in the global context at a time when Japan was undergoing extreme Westernization. Okakura's stance influenced subsequent directions in *Nihonga* (Japanese-style painting). The inquiries of Okakura and the *Nihonga* painter Yokoyama Taikan inspired Cai to thematize painting in his 2015 solo exhibition at Yokohama Museum of Art. Furthermore, Japanese *shunga* and *hanafuda* gambling cards roused the theme of lust on which he has been ruminating for years, resulting in *Seasons of Life*. "In *shunga*, life flows like a river and strives to correspond to the changes of nature. It is more inclusive of the concept in Eastern culture that space and time are one, and also seems closer to contemporary art." Experimenting with *shunga* and tattoos, he was surprised with the excitement brought about by the usage of colors. This led him to launch an impassioned pursuit of painting.

## MAKSIMOV (KONSTANTIN)

Soviet painter Konstantin Maksimov (1913–1993) had a complex and profound influence on Cai, who received art education and training shaped by the Soviet model.

Maksimov was awarded the State Stalin Prize twice, and in 1955, the Soviet government sent him to China, where he was commissioned to establish a master painting class in the Central Academy of Fine Arts in Beijing. The class, known as "Ma Xun Ban," or "Maksimov's Training Class," gathered the most accomplished young oil painters in China at the time and introduced them to the education system of Socialist Realist style oil painting. In 1957, "Ma Xun Ban" graduation exhibition caused a sensation in the culture and art world of China. That same year, the relationship between China and the Soviet Union cooled, and Maksimov returned to his homeland. He suffered setbacks both in his life and career, with his name practically unknown in Russia today. But his students from "Ma Xun Ban" went on to become the most important figures in the history of modern Chinese art. Maksimov thus influenced several generations of Chinese painters, including the young Cai.

Since the end of 1999, not only has Cai collected nearly two hundred fifty works by Maksimov, but also received his painting tools and archival materials as a gift from his family. Cai is probably the biggest Maksimov collector in the world. In 2002, Cai brought his collection to the Central Academy of Fine Arts where Maksimov had taught, to be exhibited at the same Academy Museum where he had held his farewell exhibition. Members of "Ma Xun Ban" came from all over the country to participate in the symposium. Cai recalls, "My eyes filled with tears seeing these gentlemen, now over sixty years old with many accomplishments to their names, gather together for the first time since their graduation to mourn their late teacher and bravely praise his achievements. History has cheated so many generations of Chinese and Soviet artists. I feel deeply for their fates, so entangled with political ups and downs as they were." For Cai, to collect Maksimov is to collect the fates of a generation of artists who lived through the political and social turmoil of their time, as well as to collect his own history.

## MIDDLE EAST

A sympathetic and anxious follower of the Middle East's political relationship with the West, Cai has been fascinated by Islamic culture and tradition such as Arabic miniature paintings. The Middle East first became Cai's subject in 2005, when he created *Flying Carpet*, fashioning a blue and white Persian carpet into a gigantic abstract shape of bird wings, pierced by five hundred arrows, which at once look like aggressive weapons and like feathers floating in midair.

In 2011, his solo exhibition *Saraab* at Mathaf: Arab Museum of Modern Art in Doha, Qatar was the country's first time hosting a solo exhibition by a foreign artist. Arab culture has been inextricably linked to Quanzhou, Cai's hometown, through trade via the Maritime Silk Road since the Tang dynasty (618–907 CE), and was the source of inspiration for the exhibition. Hundreds of years ago, large numbers of Muslims came to Quanzhou from the Middle East, including Thabit ibn Qays and Sa'd ibn Waqqas, two of Prophet Muhammad's disciples who are known as the Third and the Fourth Sages in China and were buried there after their deaths. Cai created *Homecoming*, which used Koran-inspired inscriptions taken from the tens of thousands of Arabic tombstones and steles, such as "To die in a foreign land is to die a martyr," carved onto rocks from Quanzhou. These rocks were transported to Doha and installed both inside and outside the museum, bringing the souls of these Muslim figures and their descendants home.

The Arab Spring spread across the Arab world during the preparation stages of the Doha exhibition. In response, Cai presented *Black Ceremony*, an explosion event for the exhibition opening, which was also intended to be a "spiritual funeral for Arab people who had died far away from home."

With the mutual trust and friendship born of *Saraab*'s success in 2011, Sheikha Al-Mayassa, Chairperson of Qatar Museums, invited Cai to return to collaborate in 2016, for which he curated a group exhibition *What About the Art? Contemporary Art from China*. He has been invited to create another exhibition at Mathaf in 2021.

Cai has engaged in dialogues with other regions of the Middle East. They include a proposal for the F1 opening ceremony in Abu Dhabi in 2009, and two site visits that resulted from an invitation to create a large-scale museum opening project in Saudi Arabia in 2015 (unrealized).

## MUSEUM AS MEDIUM

The first project that Cai devised to explicitly use the museum as a medium was his 1998 explosion event, *No Destruction, No Construction: Bombing the Taiwan Province Museum of Art*. Responding to the vision of Ni Tsai-Chin, the newly appointed director, to "rejuvenate" the ten-year old institution, Cai threaded gunpowder fuse through the museum from the rooftop through the skylight into the inside. Once lit, it blasted through the building like a fiery dragon of light and noise, permanently leaving charred traces on two interior columns.

Another museum intervention, at Taipei Fine Arts Museum was *Advertising Castle*, which he produced for *1998 Taipei Biennial: Site of Desire*. He created a gigantic scaffolding of advertising billboards that shrouded the museum, helping the project to attract advertiser funding while simultaneously using irony to highlight the self-contradiction in the exhibition's theme.

In 2000, Cai began the *Everything Is Museum* series, whereby establishing museums and holding exhibitions in regions where it is more difficult to do so, despite the waves of museum-building. *DMoCA (Dragon Museum of Contemporary Art)* was created in Niigata Prefecture, Japan, by bringing a dragon kiln from Quanzhou and reassembling it locally. Cai has since curated seven solo exhibitions of contemporary artists there. *DMoCA* was followed by *UMoCA (Underground Museum of Contemporary Art)* under St. Francis Bridge, Colle di Val d'Elsa, Tuscany, Italy in 2001; *BMoCA (Bunker Museum of Contemporary Art)* on Kinmen Island, Taiwan in 2004; *SMoCA (Snake Museum of Contemporary Art)* in Iwaki, Japan, in 2013; and *GMoCA (Green Museum of Contemporary Art)* in Havana, Cuba, in 2015.

The series of *Everything Is Museum* embodies the artist's intent of offering alternatives to the institutionalized museum culture. Cai states, "It's important to me that the project not only brings artworks to a community, but also erects a stage on which other artists can continue to exhibit their work in the community afterward, furthering conversations between artists and locals ... Many of these contemporary museums lack essential facilities such as running water, electricity, security, and insurance. They are non-elitist and non-systemized. When other artists agree to participate in my projects, their participation is in a sense rooted in the willingness to reconsider the meaning of art, as well as the origins of our own passion and love for art."

## MYTHOLOGY AND RELIGION

Cai believes that mythology is an area where artists have much to accomplish. In Cai's work, mythology is often tied to a local culture, and serves as an entry point for his dialogue. A salient example is *Dragon or Rainbow Serpent: A Myth Glorified or Feared: Project for Extraterrestrials No. 28* (1996, unrealized). The idea was to ignite a fuse in midair over the Brisbane River, where the flame would fall down on the river's surface like lightning, then snake along the surface of the water, crawl up the riverbank, cross the highway and bridge, and finally disappear underneath the bridge. Its winding trajectory would resemble the dragon of Chinese myth, and would even more resemble the Rainbow Serpent of aboriginal myth.

To Cai, the UFO is a myth of modern times. While the series *Projects for Extraterrestrials* is latently couched in the spirit of this contemporary mythology, examples of more explicit references include *Flying Saucer in the Sky* (1998) and the explosion event *Sky Bound UFO and Shrine* (2002).

Quanzhou, a place where almost all religions of the world are represented, has a tremendous influence on Cai. Many of Cai's works encompass various religions, including Confucian and Daoist ideology. A work from his residence in Japan, *Human Abode: Project for Extraterrestrials No. 1* (1989), brought the remnants of an exploded yurt to the nearby Kumagawa Shrine for display under the protection of a nature god.

Cai came in contact with Buddhism early, and his mother would regularly take him to worship the Buddha. He has made several gunpowder paintings that thematize the Buddha with light and shadow. His feeling toward Buddhism was particularly embodied by *Guanyin* from 1996, which he made for a Japanese friend who had fallen terminally ill. Cai painted a series of Blanc de Chine Guanyin statues on Japanese paper with oil paint, then covered it with another layer of the same kind of Japanese paper. Under regular lighting, the work looks like a blank piece of paper; but when seen obliquely from the corner of the eye, there seems to be an indistinct presence of a deific shadow.

In 1998, he received a commission to create a permanent installation at Tōchōji temple in Tokyo and produced *Four Seasons and Four Phases* (1998), which narrates Buddha Shakyamuni's biography and the destiny of contemporary life through lacquer paintings, in addition to his stone sculpture *Ten Great Disciples*. In *The Age of Not Believing in God* (1999), he placed Christian and Buddhist iconographies side by side in the Museum Ludwig located next to the massive Cologne Cathedral. The work showed the crucified Christ with angels and Bodhisattva Guanyin with flying attendants. Both are pierced with arrows and hanging in midair, seemingly symbolizing pain while hinting at their ascensions to heaven.

## PAINTING

Cai often says, "My childhood dream of being an artist was actually one of becoming a painter." Over the decades, his art forms have spanned gunpowder drawings, installations, explosion events, videos, and social projects, but he has never ceased to paint.

Cai's training in painting and his lifelong dedication to the medium are demonstrated by two recent exhibitions. *My Stories of Painting* (2016) was the first exhibition in which Cai reviewed his journey of painting, tracing the decades of his exploration in painting in varying scales and across various mediums, along with the stories behind them. The exhibition also showed how his family has influenced each other through their painting, and featured works by his grandmother, parents, wife, and daughters. In the following year, *The Spirit of Painting*, his solo exhibition at the Prado Museum, marked a milestone as the artist's first exhibition of pure paintings.

*Individual's Journey Through Western Art History*, which Cai launched in 2017, is a journey through the history of Western painting. His exploration of painting began with the excitement and toils of his Prado exhibition, followed by the freedom and abandon of his Uffizi exhibition. It then took a form of ferocity at the Pompeii Archeological Park and the National Archeological Museum, Naples, leading to the "encounter with an old friend in a foreign land" in his dialogue with Cézanne, as much as the "return to the original aspiration" in his dialogue with the Middle Ages. Throughout the *Journey*, the artist rediscovers and excavates himself. The series is therefore a true reflection of his existence across past eras and the turmoil of the contemporary world.

When curating *Non-Brand 非品牌* for the Guggenheim Museum in 2019, Cai combined his own youthful figurative works side by side with those of modern and contemporary painters known for their abstract or conceptual practices, as well as those by little-known painters. In an age where museums and artists engage in "branding," Cai reflects on the primordial passion that ignited the act of creating paintings, as well as an "essence of painting that transcends any school or style."

In 2012, Cai won the Praemium Imperiale, known as the Nobel Prize of the art world, for Lifetime Achievement in the Arts (Painting). At the award ceremony, John Elderfield, former Chief Curator of Painting and Sculpture at the Museum of Modern Art, New York, said: "Cai Guo-Qiang uses the sky as his canvas."

SEE ALSO: ART HISTORY; CENTRAL AND SOUTH AMERICA; CHINESE PAINTING, TRADITIONAL; DRAWING; SOCIALISM

## PEASANT DA VINCIS

China is a millennia-old agrarian society. By distributing land to the people, Mao Zedong mobilized the agrarian peasants to join the revolution and bring it to fruition, building a new China. After the liberation, however, peasants continued to suffer from the economic stagnation brought about by the mismanagement of industrialization policies.

Beginning in 2004, Cai spent six years traveling nine provinces and cities in China to visit peasant inventors and seek out stories of individuals pursuing their dreams. He coined the term *Peasant Da Vincis* and curated an exhibition of the same name at the Rockbund Art Museum in Shanghai, showing his collection of over forty peasant-invented works. In the context of the Shanghai Expo's slogan, "Better City, Better Life," the artist proposed such catchphrases as, "Never Learned How to Land," "What's Important Isn't Whether You Can Fly," and "Peasants—Making a Better City, a Better Life." The exhibition examines the peasants' contribution to the modernization and urban development. Their works demonstrate the unrestrained creativity of the individual peasant independent of collective will and action. The touching stories of each and every life show the wish of a nation pursuing a fair and democratic society.

The exhibition traveled to Brasília, São Paulo, and Rio de Janeiro in 2013. It drew an estimated one million visitors, with the stop at Rio de Janeiro becoming the world's most-visited exhibition by a living artist that year. In 2015, part of the collection appeared in *Parasophia: Kyoto International Festival of Contemporary Culture*. During the Milan World Expo that same year, the inventions made a "homecoming" of sorts to the Leonardo da Vinci National Museum of Science and Technology in Milan—the homeland of their namesake.

## PUBLIC PAINTING CREATION

It is one of Cai's distinctive practices to open his painting creation process to an audience. This allows the audience to gain firsthand experience in close proximity to the creation process of a gunpowder painting or drawing and thus form a closer "connection of destiny" with the artist. The earliest example is *Ye Gong Hao Long (Mr. Ye Who Loves Dragons)* in 2003 at the Tate Modern in London.

Cai continued developing a more collaborative mode of creation, and in 2009, he collaborated with a modern dancer from Taipei to create *Day and Night*. Cai set up a 32-meter-long paper screen and asked the dancer to physically express her emotions every hour during a twelve-hour period. Cai situated himself on the other side of the screen and sketched her silhouette onto it, then exploded the silhouettes with gunpowder. For *Mermaid: Project for the 2010 Aichi Triennale* in 2010, he sketched a local synchronized swimmer and a koi swimming in a water tank. That same year for *Travels in the Mediterranean*, he brought a female student from his alma mater, Shanghai Theatre Academy, to Nice, France, where he created paintings based on her verbal description of her travels. In each work, Cai prioritized his collaborator's agency, following her spontaneous and unpredictable acts.

In recent decades, Cai has more frequently created large-scale works in public as special projects within exhibitions. Following the public creation, the artworks would be featured in the exhibitions. These projects include artworks such as *Drawing for Building a Chinese Tower in Paris* (2003) at the Centre Pompidou, and those created at solo exhibitions *Odyssey* (2010) in Houston, *Sky Ladder* in Los Angeles (2012), *October* in Moscow (2017), *The Spirit of Painting* in Madrid (2017), and *In the Volcano* in Naples and Pompeii (2019).

Cai differentiates live public creation from performance art. In his public creations, he is not performing, but rather sharing the process of creation with the audience. He writes, a live creation allows the audience to "experience together the moments of uncertainty and anxiety after the fuse is lit, to share the consequences of a small act of fate." Among his painting-related works, Cai considers the following as "performance art": *Still Life Performance* (2000), *Performing Chinese Ink Painting* (2001), and *Painting Chinese Landscape Painting* (2004).

## QUANZHOU

Cai's hometown, Quanzhou, Fujian Province, is a small coastal town in southern China. It served as the starting point of the Maritime Silk Road, and by the Yuan dynasty (1271–1368 CE), it was the largest seaport in the world, from which Marco Polo made his voyage home to Venice. Quanzhou was a node of global trade and exchange, which made it a richly multicultural city where diverse ethnicities and cultures coexisted. Known as a "museum of religion," Quanzhou is where almost all the religions of the world coexist peacefully—Daoism, Buddhism, Christianity, Islam, and Manichaeism, as well as local faiths as in the goddess Mazu and the warlord Guan Yu.

Quanzhou's historical confidence, openness, tolerance, and spirit of diversity have nurtured Cai's art. In current times, the city's geographical distance from Beijing, the nation's political center, enabled the artist to maintain relatively more personal freedom and space in the midst of the Socialist system. Most significantly, these historical contexts helped Cai develop a globalized multilateral perspective.

Cai's hometown has continually influenced his art. He once said, "Not every work is necessarily inspired by my hometown, but it serves as a ruler or mirror in my work, helping me to feel and understand the allure of different cultures." How his "mirror" works can be understood though his 1995 work *Bringing to Venice What Marco Polo Forgot* at the Venice Biennale and his 2011 solo exhibition *Saraab* in Doha, Qatar, both inextricably informed by his hometown, as discussed elsewhere.

SEE ALSO: BOAT; CHINESE CULTURE AND CRAFTS; MIDDLE EAST

## ROMANTIC

Cai sees art history in two lineages, "hot" and "cold." The "hot" lineage consists of "ancient cave paintings, Impressionism, Expressionism, 'hot' abstract painting, and spectacular installation art, etc. In a sense, all have a thread of 'romance' running through them, emotionally charged." In contrast, the "cold" thread "focuses more on the scientific approach, from strict perspectival analysis to cold abstraction and formalism, stressing the use of lines to convey a rigid and aloof beauty." Cai considers himself aligned with the "hot" lineage, demonstrating a natural "romantic" sensibility and an essential characteristic of "human childhood" that does not seek maturity. Instead, he strives after a spirit of the accidental and the loss of control. He is not interested in distinguishing between so-called "absurdity" versus "reason," "reality" versus "myth."

Cai's works express the artist's unwavering "romantic" disposition. These include: explosion events from the *Projects for Extraterrestrials* series that began in 1989, to *Sky Ladder* (2015), to the daytime explosion events of recent years; large-scale installations from *Peasant Da Vincis* (2010) to *Heritage* (2013); and social projects from *Man, Eagle, and Eye in the Sky: Kite Project for Siwa* (2003) to *Fireflies* (2017).

In 2013, Cai created the explosion event *One Night Stand for Nuit Blanche*, a contemporary art event organized by the City of Paris. On the Seine between the Louvre and Musée d'Orsay, he used twelve minutes of fireworks to express the flirtation, foreplay, climax, and savoring of lovemaking. Fifty couples from around the world were invited to board a tourist boat and, when enlivened by the fireworks display, to venture inside individual tents. When they were satisfied, they would press a button that triggered spontaneous bursts for fireworks launched from small boats nearby. For the finale, the fireworks spelled the English words "Sorry Gotta Go." In the artist's view, the museums on the two banks of the Seine are home to France's romantic tradition, bringing together world-renowned masterpieces that once challenged the social customs of their times and expanded the horizons of art. Creating *One Night Stand* was like administering a dose of rousing "aphrodisiac" to France's contemporary art scene.

In Cai's work, this defining characteristic of primal emotion shared among humankind serves as a glue between the artist and his collaborators in practice, unleashing their imagination to merge with his. This shared feeling also galvanizes people from different cultures to help Cai realize one project after another, each complex yet romantic.

## SHAMAN

Art forms such as theater, performance, and dance all originate from shamanism. Cai believes that an artist is a kind of shaman, for he aspires to coalesce "the mystery in the process of artistic creation," seeks "encounters with the unseen which he respects," and follows "the fate to be an artist." He feels that the spiritual and supernatural aspects of shamanism help practitioners in the arts to counter the confines of rationalism and modern science.

On occasion, Cai seeks out a local shaman to pray for and foretell the outcome of a forthcoming project. As he recalls in his autobiographical text, "Ninety-Nine Tales: Curious Stories from My Journey Through the Real and Unseen Worlds" (2012), he has encountered shamans during the preparation for or culmination of projects including *Restrained Violence—Rainbow: Project for Extraterrestrials No. 25* in *The First Johannesburg Biennale* in 1995; the explosion event *Light Cycle for Central Park* in New York in 2003; *Man, Eagle, and Eye in the Sky: Kite Project for Siwa*, a social project in the Egyptian Sahara Desert, also in 2003; and *Encounter with the Unknown: Cosmos Project for Mexico* in 2019.

For his 2005 installation *Life Beneath the Shadow* created in Edinburgh, Scotland, he was inspired by local history that involved the medieval Black Death and the legends of witches.

## SKETCHING

SEE: DRAWING

## SOCIALISM

Cai was a grade-school pupil when several students of Sichuan Academy of Fine Arts created the legendary Socialist Realist group sculpture *Rent Collection Courtyard* in 1965. With its powerful propaganda value of exposing landowners' exploitation of peasants, the work was copied, reproduced, and exhibited extensively throughout China. Cai recalls weeping while viewing the work and listening to the account of suffering in the pre-1949 China. In 1999, at the Venice Biennale, he decided to have the Socialist Realist sculptures re-created on site by Long Xuli, one of the original artists, and a group of young sculptors under the title *Venice's Rent Collection Courtyard*. By letting the audience watch the artists make the sculptures, the artists became the subjects of the piece, and their fates within history became the theme of the piece.

In his solo exhibition *Paradise* at the Zachęta National Gallery of Art in Warsaw, Poland in 2005, Cai tapped into the Soviet-influenced experiences shared by China and Poland through works including the explosion event *Red Flag*. In 2011, for his solo exhibition *1040M Underground* in Donetsk, Ukraine, he went down a coal mine 1040 meters underground, and invited local painters, all of whom had undergone Socialist Realist training, to sketch with him the portraits of twenty-seven coalminers. Cai then exploded gunpowder paintings using the different styles of these artists' portraits, and the twenty-seven portraits were erected in the exhibition gallery on top of a black mound of coal and a white mound of salt, much in the way the likenesses of Soviet leaders used to be held high during parades.

His solo exhibition *October* at Moscow's Pushkin State Museum of Fine Arts in 2017, the centennial of the Russian Revolution, became a major opportunity for him to reflect on history, in particular on the role of individuals in history and the relationship between individual dreams and collective ideals. The Russian avant-garde and Soviet Socialist Realism, both inspired by the Revolution, were Cai's subject of artistic study as a "young man learning to paint."

SEE ALSO: MAKSIMOV

## TOWER

For Cai, the tower is an emblem of humankind's conversation with the cosmos. As such, the tower is an important icon in Cai's oeuvre. It probably began with his childhood affection for the landmark "East and West Towers" in his hometown Quanzhou, which are the tallest extant stone towers in China.

His 1994 work *San Jō Tower*, initially created in Iwaki, Japan, is reminiscent of the Buddhist pagoda ubiquitous in Japan as well as the light tower (lighthouse), an important facility for the coastal city of Iwaki. The version that he realized for the Museum of Contemporary Art, Tokyo was titled *The Orient (San Jō Tower)*, which was equipped with seismographic meters on all four sides, spurring the audience to experience the ongoing precariousness of the earthquake-prone city and also inspiring reflection on the relationship that people of the East have with the planet as well as nature.

In 1999, at SITE Santa Fe, in New Mexico, he built *Calling*, a tower constructed from branches collected from the nearby desert as well as unused materials from other artists' exhibits. At the top of his tower, he placed a lighted beacon, as though the tower on a desert plateau was summoning distant memories of the seas.

In 2001, he titled his solo exhibition at Iwaki Gallery *Iwaki Ninety-Nine Towers* and presented an installation with numerous terracotta towers. This was followed in 2003 by his *Proposal for Building a Chinese Tower in Paris* to orchestrate a dialogue with the Eiffel Tower by using computer chip-embedded firework shells to create an instantaneous Chinese tower; in 2013, he made another proposal to create *Ninety-Nine Chinese Pagodas at Château de Versailles*, but both projects are yet to be realized. In 2015, for *Parasophia: Kyoto International Festival of Contemporary Culture*, he built a site-specific, large-scale bamboo tower and installed on it small *Peasant Da Vincis*–inspired inventions created by local children. In 2016, he expanded his *SMoCA (Snake Museum of Contemporary Art)* in Iwaki with two wooden towers built in collaboration with Iwaki's residents: *Ink Tower* and *Rebirth Tower*.

## UNITED STATES

Cai first came to the United States on an Asian Cultural Council (ACC) grant in September 1995 and used the studio in the P.S.1 Contemporary Art Center for one year. The ACC's support enabled him to bring his wife and daughter to the U.S., conduct research and produce work without worry, gain exposure to American life and art, and most important, to address head-on the 20th- and 21st-century human problems of East versus West, Cold War, globalization, and high-tech development.

His first project in the United States was a visit to the Nevada Test Site (presently Nevada National Security Site), where he exploded little mushroom clouds using powder extracted from firecrackers that he had acquired in New York's Chinatown. Other sites of the miniature mushroom cloud included two works of American Earthworks, Michael Heizer's *Double Negative* (1969) in Nevada and Robert Smithson's *Spiral Jetty* (1970) in Salt Lake City. The project was also realized in Manhattan. Together, these constituted the work *The Century with Mushroom Clouds: Project for the 20th Century* (1996).

The move to the U.S. catalyzed a turning point in Cai's art. While he maintained his interest in the cosmos and the relationship between humankind and nature that was his focus while in Japan, he began to pay closer attention to global and local socio-political issues. With this transformation, his work not only shifted in theme and philosophy, but also became more diverse in style and form, in particular with the creation of more large-scale installations. In part because of his linguistic difficulty with English, he began to place more emphasis on visual power and connotative complexity.

Cai received numerous invitations for exhibitions in the U.S. within the first year of his stay. He therefore acquired a green card with help from the ACC and settled permanently in New York, establishing his studio. Soon he was exhibiting in many major museums in the U.S., beginning with his participation in *Hugo Boss Prize 1996* at Guggenheim Museum SoHo, a 1997 solo exhibition at the Queens Museum of Art in New York, *Whitney Biennial: 2000 Exhibition*, a 2004 solo exhibition at MASS MoCA (Massachusetts Museum of Contemporary Art), a 2006 solo exhibition at The Metropolitan Museum of Art in New York, and a 2008 retrospective exhibition at the Guggenheim Museum, New York. In Cai's view, the generosity, openness, and tolerance of American culture allowed him to take root and blossom on U.S. soil. Cai feels blessed to have come to the U.S. at the right moment: as "multiculturalism" was embraced and buoyed by globalization, the West was simultaneously engaged in self-reflection in an expanding world. This, he believes, enabled him to realize works that touched on sensitive topics of political and cultural difference without much resistance.

## WAR AND PEACE

Through his work, Cai transforms gunpowder, a material often deployed in war and violent acts, into artwork and a creator of beauty. This is an ethical position that the artist has taken with a sense of social significance and responsibility.

For *Salute*, an educational program he organized from 1999 to 2000 for underage criminals in Brazil, Cai asked the children to design and make cannons. He hoped that they could understand how the energy contained in both gunpowder and humans can be used either to violate or benefit society, and can be transformed into art.

Nuclear weapons have attracted Cai's attention from early on. He first used the atomic bomb as a theme in his painting *Shadow: Pray for Protection* from 1985–86, in which a clock indicates the time when the bomb was dropped on Nagasaki. A large X-shape in the center of the canvas represents the shadow cast by the U.S. military plane, superimposed and surrounded by disfigured bodies of victims; a white peace dove flies over the artist's self-portrait, embodying his desire for world peace. In 1994, he realized *The Earth Has Its Black Hole Too: Project for Extraterrestrials No. 16*, at the Hiroshima Central Park near the Atomic Bomb Dome ruins and a former Japanese military headquarters.

Cai sees the mushroom cloud's iconic form as the most impactful symbol of the 20th century; as a victorious representation of scientific development, its visual impact has had an immense physical and spiritual influence on human society. In 1996, he undertook *The Century with Mushroom Clouds: Project for the 20th Century*, for which he created gunpowder explosions at the Nevada Test Site as well as various places in New York and New Jersey overlooking Manhattan, in reference to the Manhattan Project that produced the first atomic bombs. Later in 1996, he created postcards bearing images of his mushroom cloud explosion events and sold them for $1 apiece at *Crab House*, a multi-component installation at P.S.1. In this installation, he also presented a book of mushroom-cloud images and a gunpowder drawing with numerous tiny mushroom clouds. He served tea from *lingzhi* mushroom, known for its detoxification effect. It bears some resemblance to the shape of the mushroom cloud, hinting that objects of destructive power can be curative. An incongruous presence of three hundred live crabs points to an unexpected and hidden hazard of the nuclear power in human civilization.

The Olympic Games were originally a "festival of peace," when the ancient Greeks would cease warfare to participate in the sports competitions. Cai took on the role of the Director of Visual and Special Effects for the 2008 Beijing Olympics Opening and Closing Ceremonies, using creative firework pieces such as *Footprints of History* to catalyze the climax of these events; the images of this event have become classic. That same year, he received the Hiroshima Art Prize, which lauded his contributions to the world through the material of gunpowder. For the award ceremony, he exploded *Black Fireworks: Project for Hiroshima* against the sky above the Hiroshima Peace Memorial and the Atomic Bomb Dome, a skeletal remnant from the historic A-bomb dropping by the U.S. in 1945.

2017 was the seventy-fifth anniversary of the first controlled self-sustained nuclear chain reaction. Cai was invited to commemorate the event above the former CP-1 site at the University of Chicago, where, using the positioning technology of computer chip-embedded fireworks shells, he exploded a 75-meter-high *Color Mushroom Cloud* at the same time of the first reaction. The work was an exploration of the complex legacy left to human society by this historic experiment.

---

*Reiko Tomii is an independent scholar and curator. Co-Director of PoNJA-GenKon, a scholarly listserve group of postwar Japanese art history, she has widely published on the topic and made pioneering contributions by positioning 1960s Japan in world art history of modernism. Her recent publication* Radicalism in the Wilderness: International Contemporaneity and 1960s Art in Japan *(2016) received the 2017 Robert Motherwell Book Award. She received the 2020 Commissioner for Cultural Affairs Award from the Japanese government. She has known Cai Guo-Qiang since 1995 and worked with him on several projects, including solo exhibitions at the Queens Museum of Art (1997) and the Solomon R. Guggenheim Museum (2008) in New York.*

*Hsiu-man Lin is an archivist at Cai Studio. A graduate of National Taiwan Normal University with a B.F.A. in Fine Arts, she holds a master's degree in Library and Information Science and an advanced certificate in Conservation and Digital Curation from Pratt Institute, New York. She is responsible for running and maintaining Cai Guo-Qiang's archives and database, as well as preserving the artist's works and collections.*

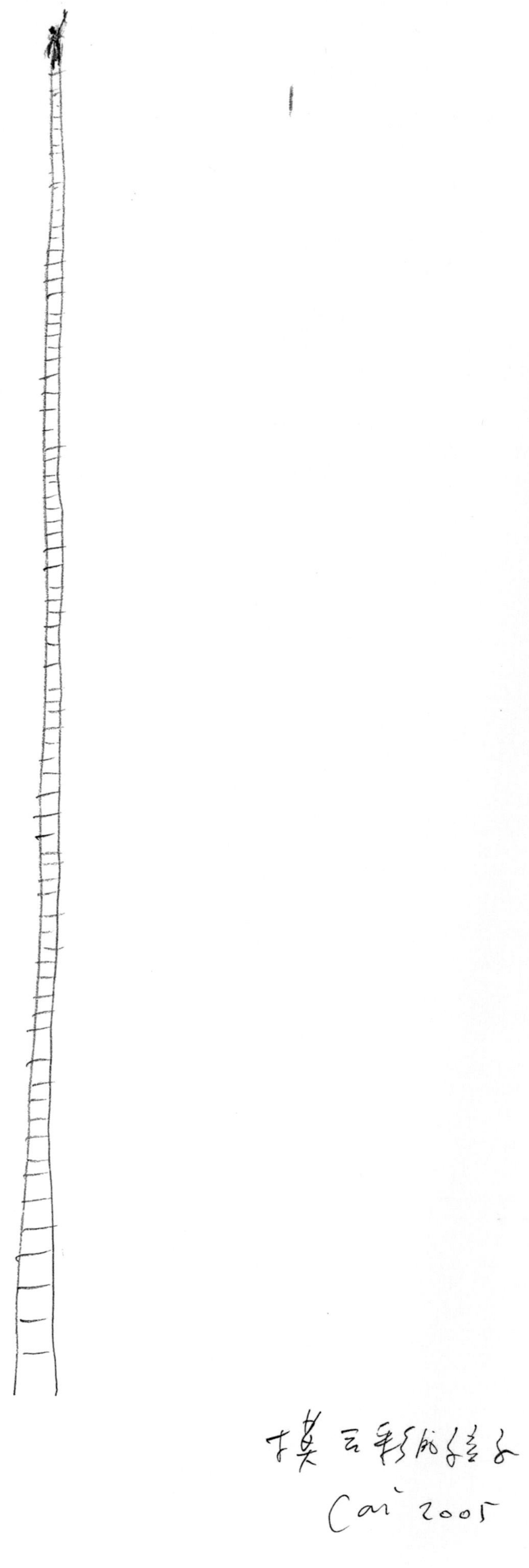


Cai Guo-Qiang, *Child Touching the Clouds*, 2005. Pen on paper, 31 × 37 cm

# Checklist

Grouped by dialogues within each gallery, and generally arranged according to the exhibition display. Unless otherwise noted, all works by Cai Guo-Qiang

## West Wing Gallery: *Odyssey*

*In Search of El Greco No. 8*
2016
Gunpowder on canvas
91.5 × 91.5 cm

*In Search of El Greco No. 6*
2016
Gunpowder on canvas
91.5 × 91.5 cm

*Painting El Greco's Apostolado No. 3*
2017
Gunpowder on canvas
152.5 × 244 cm

*Selfie*
2017
Gunpowder on canvas
183 × 304 cm

*Painting Rubens's Diana and Satyrs*
2017
Gunpowder on canvas
150 × 300 cm

*Black Poppy*
2016
Gunpowder on canvas
152.5 × 1097 cm

*Blue*
2017
Gunpowder on canvas
183 × 152.5 cm

*Salón de Reinos ...*
2017
Gunpowder on canvas
360 × 600 cm

*Hometown Sky Ladder*
2015
Gunpowder on paper
400 × 300 cm
PINAULT COLLECTION

*"Craters" Made by Humans for Their Own Planet: Pourrières*
1990
Gunpowder and ink on paper
93.98 × 63.5 cm

*"Craters" Made by Humans for Their Own Planet No. 11: Sketch on Explosion Site*
1990
Gunpowder and ink on paper
92.71 × 63.5 cm

*"Craters" Made by Humans for Their Own Planet: At the Remains of the Minimes Convent*
1990
Gunpowder and ink on paper
92.71 × 63.5 cm

*"Craters" Made by Humans for Their Own Planet No. 1: Looking at Mont Sainte-Victoire from a Distance, the Explosion Dedicated to Paul Cézanne*
1990
Gunpowder and ink on paper
63.5 × 93.98 cm

*Drawing for Ascending Dragon*
1989
Gunpowder and ink on paper
66.5 × 72 cm

*Crater*
1989
Gunpowder, oil, and paper pulp on canvas
61 × 73 × 3 cm

*Crater*
1990
Gunpowder on papier-mâché
56 × 67 × 2.5 cm

*Crater No. 3*
1990
Gunpowder on papier-mâché
Diameter: 39.4 cm

*Ascending Dragon: Project for Extraterrestrials No. 2*
1989
Gunpowder and ink on paper
240 × 300 cm
Collection of Leo Shih

*Cypress of Mont Sainte-Victoire*
2019
Gunpowder on canvas
275 × 200 cm

*Structure*
2019
Gunpowder on canvas
240 × 300 cm

*En Route*
2019
Gunpowder on canvas, 3 out of 4 panels shown
200 × 275 cm each

*Dead Roses No. 1*
2018
Gunpowder on canvas
122 × 91.5 cm

*Fallen Iris*
2018
Gunpowder on canvas
150 × 240 cm

*Silverpoint Study No. 1*
2018
Gunpowder on canvas
35.4 × 28 cm

*Silverpoint Study No. 4*
2018
Gunpowder on canvas
35.4 × 28 cm

*Silverpoint Study No. 5*
2018
Gunpowder on canvas
30.5 × 23 cm

*Green Shrubs*
2018
Gunpowder on canvas
76 × 76 cm

*Daisy Field No. 1*
2018
Gunpowder on canvas
51 × 61 cm

*Wall Plant No. 2*
2018
Gunpowder on canvas
25 × 25 cm

*Maple Leaves No. 2*
2018
Gunpowder on canvas
25 × 25 cm

*Yellow Iris*
2018
Gunpowder on canvas
61 × 51 cm

*Study for Uffizi: Green Roses No. 2*
2018
Gunpowder on canvas
122 × 183 cm

*Study for Uffizi: Flora No. 3*
2018
Gunpowder on canvas
183 × 152.5 cm

*Sweet Briar*
2018
Gunpowder on canvas
122 × 152.5 cm
The East West Bank Collection

*Study of Birds*
2018
Gunpowder and oil on canvas
200 × 300 cm

*Poppy Series: Hallucination No. 1*
2015
Gunpowder on canvas
183 × 608 cm

*Cai Guo-Qiang: October, Daytime Explosion Event on Red Square*
2017
Animated video
7:23

*Kremlin in the Snow*
2017/2020
Gunpowder on canvas
122 × 91.5 cm

*Malevich Over Red Square: Black Square*
2017
Gunpowder on canvas
120 × 120 cm

*Malevich Over Red Square: Black Cross*
2017
Gunpowder on canvas
120 × 120 cm

*Malevich Over Red Square: Black Circle*
2017
Gunpowder on canvas
120 × 120 cm

*Red Star Over Red Square*
2017
Gunpowder on canvas
120 × 120 cm

*Selfie in Front of Kramskoi's Painting (Study for River)*
2017
Gunpowder on canvas
120 × 120 cm

*A Stencil for River*
2017
Laser-cut chipboard
66 × 46 cm

Wenhao Cai
*Wenhao's Sketch of Seneca*
2018
Charcoal on paper
43 × 35.5 cm

*Cai's Sketch of Seneca*
2018
Charcoal on paper
43 × 35.5 cm

*Pseudo-Seneca: Red*
2019
Gunpowder on plaster
49 × 23 × 24 cm

*Plum Venus*
2019
Gunpowder on plaster
154 × 56 × 42 cm

*Mount Vesuvius*
2019
Gunpowder on canvas
80 × 80 cm

*Pompeiian Red*
2019
Gunpowder on panel for fresco
122 × 244 cm

*Non-Brand 非品牌 1*
2019
Gunpowder on glass and mirror
183 × 150 cm

*Non-Brand 非品牌 2*
2019
Gunpowder on glass and mirror
183 × 150 cm

*Non-Brand 非品牌 3*
2019
Gunpowder on glass and mirror
183 × 150 cm

*Non-Brand 非品牌 5*
2019
Gunpowder on glass and mirror
183 × 150 cm

*The Spirit of Painting. Cai Guo-Qiang at the Prado*
2017/2020
Video documentation
Original video *The Spirit of Painting* (2017) © Miss Wasabi Films; directed by Isabel Coixet, produced by Miss Wasabi Films for the Prado Museum
Re-edited by 33 Studio

*Cai Guo-Qiang: Returning to Mont Saint-Victoire*
2020
Video documentation
Directed by Shanshan Xia, produced by 33 Studio

*Flora Commedia: Cai Guo-Qiang at the Uffizi*
2018/2020
Video documentation
Directed by Shanshan Xia, produced by 33 Studio

*Cai Guo-Qiang: Non-Brand 非品牌*
2019/2020
Video documentation
Footage by Shanshan Xia, 33 Studio, Sijia Yang, and Sang Luo (courtesy Cai Studio) and installation views of *Artistic License: Six Takes on the Guggenheim Collection*, at Solomon R. Guggenheim Museum, New York, May 24, 2019–January 12, 2020, with additional footage © The Solomon R. Guggenheim Foundation. All artworks © the artists
Edited by 33 Studio

## East Wing Gallery: *Odyssey*

*Exploding Hercules*
2019
Gunpowder on plaster
320 × 150 × 98 cm

*Study for Pompeii No. 3: Hercules*
2018
Gunpowder on canvas
240 × 150 cm

*Study for Pompeii No. 4: Hercules*
2018
Gunpowder on canvas
240 × 150 cm

*Study for Pompeii: Fierce Lion*
2018
Gunpowder on canvas
300 × 300 cm

*Day and Night in Toledo*
2017
Gunpowder on canvas
260 × 600 cm

*Mountain in Heat*
2016
Gunpowder on canvas
239 × 450 cm

*Palmyra*
2017
Gunpowder on canvas
240 × 450 cm

*The Spirit of Painting*
2017
Gunpowder on canvas
300 × 1800 cm

*Medieval Study: Tower of Grotesques*
2020
Gunpowder on canvas
263 × 300 cm

*The Bats' Eyes No. 2*
2020
Gunpowder on canvas
263 × 450 cm

*Black Light No. 1*
2020
Gunpowder on canvas
360 × 600 cm

*Sleepwalking in the Forbidden City*
2020
Fireworks ceremony in virtual reality
experienced through VR headsets
Approx. 5 minutes
Virtual Reality in partnership with
HTC VIVE Arts

VR experience demonstration of
*Sleepwalking in the Forbidden City*
2020
Video
Approx. 5 minutes
Virtual Reality in partnership with
HTC VIVE Arts

*Gunpowder Drawing for Sleepwalking in the Forbidden City*
2020
Gunpowder and ink on paper, mounted on
wood as six-panel screen
230 × 465 cm

*Sleepwalking in the Forbidden City: After the Fireworks*
2020
Gunpowder on alabaster
39.8 × 472.3 × 663.3 cm

*In the Volcano: Cai Guo-Qiang and Pompeii*
2019/2020
Video documentation
Directed by Shanshan Xia, produced by
33 Studio

*October: The Unrealized Century*
2017/2020
Video documentation
Directed by Shanshan Xia, produced by
33 Studio

*Voyage Through the Middle Ages During the Pandemic*
2020
Video documentation
Directed by Shanshan Xia, produced by
33 Studio

## Central Tower Gallery: *Homecoming*

*Wall of Early Paintings*
2020
89 Paintings from the 1970s–80s and 2001;
watercolor, oil, gouache, and acrylic on paper,
canvas, cardboard, and cardstock
Approx. 260 × 970 cm

Cai Ruiqin
*Untitled (Matchbox Drawings)*
Dates unknown
Ink, pen, and pencil on cardboard matchboxes
22.9 × 30.5 cm framed
(shown with *Wall of Early Paintings*)

*Color Gunpowder Drawing for City of Flowers in the Sky*
2018
Gunpowder on paper, 4 out of 8 sheets shown
400 × 300 cm each

*Sketches for City of Flowers in the Sky*
2018
Pencil and marker on paper, 35 sketches in total
151 × 140 cm

*Flow (Cypress)*
2019
Gunpowder on paper, shown with 9 porcelain
birds from *Pulse (Mountain)*, 2019
Painting: 300 × 1600 cm; birds: 10 × 20 ×
30 cm each

*Transience II (Peony)*
2019
Gunpowder on silk
350 × 3080 cm

*Outside My Window: April in the Year of Gengzi*
2020
Gunpowder on canvas
183 × 305 cm

*Peaceful Earth: Project for Extraterrestrials No. 18*
2020
Gunpowder and ink on paper, mounted on
wood as three-panel screen
230 × 232.5 cm

*Nostalgia for Homeland: Project for Humankind No. 4*
2020
Gunpowder and ink on paper, mounted on wood as four-panel screen
230 × 310 cm

*Milky Way Canyon: Project for Extraterrestrials No. 15*
2020
Gunpowder and ink on paper, mounted on wood as seven-panel screen
230 × 542.5 cm

*Humanity's Epitaph: Project for Extraterrestrials No. 13*
2020
Gunpowder and ink on paper, mounted on wood as six-panel screen
230 × 465 cm

*Frolicking on Ice in the Galaxy*
2020
Gunpowder on glass and mirror
205 × 915 cm

Zhang Weibang, Yao Wenhan, et al.
*Frolic on the Ice* (*Bing Xi Tu*)
Qing dynasty (1644–1911)
Ink and colors on silk
36.8 × 563.4 cm
Collection of the Palace Museum

*Homecoming*
2020
Video documentation
Footage courtesy Cai Studio and National Gallery of Victoria, Melbourne
Directed by Shanshan Xia, produced by 33 Studio

*Sky and Land as Canvas: Selected Explosion Events*
2020
Video compilation
Directed by Shanshan Xia, produced by 33 Studio

## Lofty Pavilion: *A Material Odyssey*

Presentation organized by Getty Conservation Institute
Arranged according to the exhibition display

*Test 2017.1-1A (Black gunpowder)*
2017
Gunpowder on canvas, 2 out of 18 panels shown
25.5 × 25.5 cm each

*Test 2017.1-1B (Black gunpowder)*
2017
Gunpowder on canvas, 18 panels
25.5 × 25.5 cm each

*Study for Seven-Headed Dragons: Project for the Vatican Museum*
2016
Gunpowder on porcelain
Approx. 37 × 26 × 17 cm

*Black Peony*
2020
Gunpowder on porcelain
66.8 × 37.3 × 5.7 cm

Unexploded peony porcelain panel
2008
Porcelain
66.8 × 37.3 × 5.7 cm

*Making a Gunpowder Painting*
2020
Video documentation
Footage provided by Cai Studio and 33 Studio, edited by Ava Porter for Getty

*Color Gunpowder Test in Moscow*
2017
Gunpowder on canvas
120 × 120 cm

*Test 2016.11-2A (Japanese gunpowder)*
2016
Gunpowder on canvas, 2 out of 6 panels shown
25.5 × 25.5 cm each
Collection of Getty Conservation Institute

*Rubbing of Archean Era*
early 1980s
Ink and gunpowder on canvas
140 × 60 cm

*Pillar for the Sky*
1985
Gunpowder and oil on canvas
80.1 × 116.8 cm

*Shadow: Pray for Protection*
1985–86
Gunpowder, ink, candle wax, and oil on canvas, mounted on wood
155 × 300 cm

*Gunpowder Drawing No. 8-27*
1988
Gunpowder on paper
27 × 24 cm

*The Immensity of Heaven and Earth: Project for Extraterrestrials No. 11, Preliminary Drawing No. 3*
1991
Gunpowder and ink on paper
74.9 × 55.9 cm

*Test 2016.11-1A (Chinese gunpowder)*
2016
Gunpowder on canvas, 6 panels with a piece cut out from each
25.5 × 25.5 cm each
Collection of Getty Conservation Institute

*Test 2016.11-1A (Chinese gunpowder)*
2016
Gunpowder on canvas, 6 cutout pieces from 6 panels
14 × 7 cm each
Collection of Getty Conservation Institute

*Color Gunpowder Test for Getty*
2016
Gunpowder on canvas, 6 cutout pieces from 1 scroll
14 × 7 cm each

*Color Gunpowder Test for Getty*
2016
Gunpowder on paper, 6 cutout pieces
14 × 7 cm each
Collection of Getty Conservation Institute

# Acknowledgments

*A Few Final Thoughts*

The pandemic allowed us to recognize the value of breathing freely. Breath usually belongs to the subconscious. It was also subconsciously that I, with the passing of the years, have gone from breathing with my chest to breathing with my abdomen. This book addresses the wonder of my encounters with the West, the struggle over my unrequited love for my predecessor painters, and, moreover, the deep breaths that I have taken in their hometowns and in the gardens of their art. This homecoming to my native culture and the stories of painting from my youth has reawakened the traditional Chinese breathing technique of *dantian*—breathing with the core—that I studied slightly as a young man. But after such an odyssey, how can I possibly come home and immediately clear the orbit of *qi* around my body, just like that?

All those who paint have dialogues with their predecessors, with the masters. Most do this through art catalogues or by visiting the works they revere in exhibition galleries. There's a Chinese saying that every stretch of soil gives rise to its own kind of people; people are the products of their environments, and artworks are the products of their peoples. So, I ventured out—to ancient Greek and Roman civilizations, to the Renaissance, the Spanish Golden Age, and the avant-garde, going door-to-door. What great fun we've had! I regard museums, artworks, and the pioneers of art history as my creative materials and concepts. I've set myself an aspiration as big as the sky, just as I did for my *Projects for Extraterrestrials* series. Naturally, the distant predecessors cannot raise any objections—they have no choice but to let me make as much mischief as I wish. They have no time to bother with the millions of things that have been inspired by them since their own time. Our predecessors are like the stars overhead; whatever we do, we're just romping around for our own amusement under the night sky.

Because this publication contains ambivalent questions about my odyssey and homecoming, it includes some of the avant-garde and therefore some of its risks. It also therefore contains something a little feral. Sometimes I feel that, thanks to the pandemic, I have had time to stop, think, and paint. I was unable to carry out my journey to explore medieval spirituality as planned, but was able to embark on another journey altogether: rereading the "notes on the heart and spiritual formation" that I wrote as a young man. Speedy transportation and easy communication don't signify that the exchange with our predecessors and with the unseen world has become more fluid. It likewise doesn't mean that the interchange with our inner selves and souls has become more fluid.

After a period of self-isolation, I began to resist the idea of being busy. In Chinese, the character for "busy" (忙) can be broken down into "heart" (心) and "death" (亡)—we can lose our hearts by being too busy. Adding the character for "center" (中) on top of "heart" (心) makes "devotion" (忠), whereas adding two "centers" to "heart" makes the character for "peril" or "affliction" (患). Whether making art, doing work, or living life, we must always be whole-hearted: centered, focused, undivided. Right now, we are both "busy" and "afflicted": afflicted with gain, with loss, with illness, with trouble. Busy hearts breed great afflictions.

Eastern and Chinese culture have helped support my journey of art, but I have never made many distinctions between the cultures of others and my own. The legacies of all human civilizations and countless ancestors flow in my blood, nurturing me. We can commune with the spiritual by being open-minded and whole-hearted; spiritual connections bring human connections. This may sound like I'm just "talking big," but the pursuit of achieving interflow with unseen forces, of reaching an ideal natural state without the blockades of nationalism or blind superiority complexes ... that pursuit is, in itself, "big."

In the blink of an eye, I've spent more than half a century studying art. When I was young, I swelled with wonder and thrill when entering a celebrated museum. Today, I bury my sentiments deep inside my heart. More and more, I understand that no painting or exhibition is easily created. Though my journey hasn't been easy and I do feel lonely and have fears, no matter how wavering and fragile I've been, there are always so many mentors, directors, and curators who've told me, "You can do it." Even when new directors took over the Palace Museum and the Prado Museum, the preparations for my exhibitions persisted through all the changes. To realize an exhibition of this scale and an accompanying book of this size during the pandemic—what a feat! I am especially grateful for Mr. Wang Xudong, Director of the Palace Museum, who hacked through all difficulties to realize this exhibition. I am especially heartened by his remarks that the exhibition "is an exact extension of the open and inclusive spirit, heart, and self-confidence of Chinese culture. Not only artworks are on display, but also the artist's experiences and understanding of world civilizations ... Through this exhibition, we look forward to driving further international cultural exchange, with the Palace Museum as an exemplar of Chinese culture, strengthening and inspiring the interchange and mutual learning among different civilizations."

Have I received preferential treatment from the forces of fate by dialoguing with the unseen world? Or has it only ever been chance and coincidence? Whatever it is, it has brought me to so many corners of the world, and also returned me to the home where I began my journey. The Palace Museum! I'm making myself emotional just thinking about this. This is my fairy tale.

I often boast that I'm a darling of the gods. What this really means is that the gods have always brought me endless angels to lend me their strength. The supporters and patrons of each and every one of my projects are like my Medici and Philip IV. This note was originally meant to express my gratitude to all those who have advocated for me, but while writing entry after entry, I realized that there are simply too many angels to count. I can only give my thanks briefly through the list of names and institutions at the end of this hefty tome. Please forgive me—there is just too much to tell, too much to feel.

If artists are like ships, stopping at one port after another, then the Palace Museum, the Prado Museum, the Uffizi Galleries, so on and so forth, are all major ports, the significant milestones in my artistic career. But ports are not where ships ultimately belong. Their place is the star-studded seas, the blue horizon, even the ocean floor ...

Cai Guo-Qiang
December 2020

*The realization of the exhibition* Odyssey and Homecoming *and this publication is indebted to the extraordinary commitments of the following organizations and individuals.*

## Hosts

The Palace Museum, Beijing
Beijing Winter Olympics Committee

## Support

Ministry of Culture and Tourism of the People's Republic of China
General Administration of Customs of the People's Republic of China

## Sponsors

Principle Sponsor: ANTA
With the Precious Support of: Hennessy
Special Support: Guardian Art Center

Artron Art Group
Shanghai International Culture Association
Zhaotai Group
YF Life Insurance International Ltd.
Beijing Zixin Yongle Culture Co., LTD
Mr. and Mrs. Thomas & Linda Lau
Pansy Ho

Virtual Reality Partner: HTC VIVE Arts

## Special Thanks

Mimi Gardner Gates
Wei Zhao
Xiaofang Zhong
Ning Wang
Wei Li
Heping Zhang
Xiaoyu Jiang
Mr. and Mrs. Silas Chou
Wendi Murdoch
Xin Li
Qiru Mu
Frank Gehry
Yihua Li
Guosheng Cai
Lan Yang
Mingxian Wang
Xinping Su
Zikang Zhang
Michael Aidan
Ling Weng
Chuanfeng Wang
Zijiao Jiao
Xiujun Wang
Yifei Wang
Kai Sun
Yumeng Du
Consulate General of the People's Republic of China in New York
Consulate General of the People's Republic of China in Osaka
Museum of Art Pudong, Shanghai
The Ashmolean Museum of Art and Archaeology, Oxford, England
Akatsu Collection Tokyo
The East West Bank
Getty Conservation Institute (GCI)
Leo Shih
PINAULT COLLECTION
Mr. and Mrs. Cheung Chung Kiu
Mr. and Mrs. Yaping Ou
Thomas S. Smith Jr Revocable Trust
Quan Wang
Michael Hess
Steven Murphy

## *Exhibition Team*

## Sir Simon Schama, Curator

## The Palace Museum, Beijing

*Special Thanks*
Xudong Wang
Haijiang Du
Jixiang Shan
Xin Yang

*Exhibition Manager*
Yuegong Wang

*Exhibition Execution*
Miao Sun
Bo Wang
Ning Gu
Tong Yu
Shanzhuo Wang

*Exhibition Coordination*
Zhaoren Wang
Shaoyi Li
Bin Li
Siying Wang
Yingxuan Yang

*Catalogue Publishing*
Xiaojun Song

*Text Contribution*
Yu Hui

## Getty Center, Los Angeles

James Cuno, President and CEO of the J. Paul Getty Trust
Rachel Rivenc, Head of Conservation and Preservation, GRI
Tom Learner, Head of Science, GCI
Tim Whalen, John E. and Louise Bryson Director, GCI
Michael Doutre, Research Lab Associate, GCI
Kevin Young, Senior Mount Maker, GRI
Nicole Onishi, Staff Assistant, GCI
Irma Ramirez, Getty exhibition design, independent
Ava Porter, video editing, independent

## Cai Studio, New York and Beijing

Sang Luo, Project Director
Canhuang Cai, Project Manager
Siqiao Lyu, Project Manager
Rui Tang, Project Assistant
Mengjia Zhao, Project Assistant
Tatsumi Masatoshi, Technical Director
Yi-Boe Huynh, Technical Manager

Lydia Ohl, Head of Archives
Frannie Trempe, Digital Archivist
Hsiu-man Lin, Archivist

Silin Chow, Registrar
Jacqueline DeLuca, Collection Manager

Guirong Jin, Finance
Dongxia Wu, Logistics
Zhanhuan Zhou, Assistant
Xiaohong Zhou, Assistant
Ziyao Zhao, Assistant
Xiaoyu Lyu, Assistant
Baoduan Huang, Assistant
Yonggang Zhang, Assistant

Lulu Zhang, Studio Manager
Hong Hong Wu, Financial Manager

*Interns*
Zhijun Cai
Mei Liu
Weihang Dear Liu
Xinyi Liu
Siwei Yu
Zijun Wen
Chengru Eric Yu
Xingyan Cai
Wenhao Cai

*Special Thanks*
Yi Zhou, On-site Coordination
Wenting Chen
Honggang Luo
Boying Su
Ruyi Dai
Deyu Wu

## Exhibition Catalogue

*Contributors*
Sir Simon Schama
Cai Guo-Qiang
Yu Hui
Wang Hui
Rachel Rivenc
Reiko Tomii
Sang Luo
Hsiu-man Lin (research)

*Special Thanks*
The Palace Museum Publishing House

*Editing*
Sir Simon Schama, Editor-in-Chief
Sang Luo, Executive Editor
Reiko Tomii, Managing Editor and Consulting Scholar
Kathleen M. Friello, Project Editor

Hsiu-man Lin, Editor
Lydia Ohl, Editor
Frannie Trempe, Editor
Mengjia Zhao, Editor
Jacqueline DeLuca, Editor
Rui Tang, Editor

*In Asian names, surnames are indicated by underlines.*

*Translation*
Lin King
Jay Zhang
Boliang Shen
Silin Chow
Mengjia Zhao
Thomas Garbarini
Hsiu-man Lin
HI-COM (Shanghai) Consulting Co., Ltd.

*Design*
Miko McGinty
Julia Ma

*Image Management*
Frannie Trempe
Yi-Boe Huynh
Lydia Ohl

## Documentary

33 Studio
Shanshan Xia, Director/Producer
Hailun Xue, Videographer
Shouxi Liu, Videographer
Lingzhi Wu, Videographer
Wei Wang, Videographer
Xiaoyu Wei, Videographer
Huilin Zhu, Videographer
Li Xiong, Videographer

Special Thanks: Lei Chen

## Photography

Wen-You Cai
Mengjia Zhao
Lin Yi
Sang Luo
Christopher Burke Studio

## Chinese Media

Concord Communications Co., Ltd.
Yifei Hong, China Affairs
Limin Zhong, Project Director and Media Chief
Mengling Yu, Project Manager and Media Coordinator
Xiaodong Yu, Project Manager
Lihua Zhou, Administrator

## Fabrication of *Sleepwalking in the Forbidden City* artwork group

Virtual Reality Partner: HTC VIVE Arts
Beijing Blackbow Co., Ltd.
Shanghai Leshan Information Technology Co., Ltd.
33 Studio
Quanzhou Xinwen Craft Co., Ltd.
Liuyang Tang Hua Fireworks Co., Ltd.

## Fabrication of *Seven-Headed Dragons*

Quanzhou Xinwen Craft Co., Ltd.

## Transportation and Exhibition Installation

ZHC Art Center
Huaxie Int'l Fine Art Freight Services Co., Ltd.
Transcon
Masterpiece International, Ltd.
JA Conservation-Restoration of Art

## Merchandise Design

Special Special Productions

*Heartfelt thanks go to the following institutions and individuals, who made critical contributions to the exhibitions or research leading to the exhibition* Odyssey and Homecoming.

## Museums

Pushkin State Museum of Fine Arts, Moscow, Russia
Prado Museum, Madrid, Spain
Uffizi Galleries, Florence, Italy
National Archaeological Museum of Naples, Italy
Pompeii Archaeological Park, Italy
Solomon R. Guggenheim Museum, New York, U.S.
Musée Granet, Aix-en-Provence, France
The Metropolitan Museum of Art, New York, U.S.
National Gallery of Victoria (NGV), Melbourne, Australia
Bonnefanten Museum, Maastricht, the Netherlands

## Museum Directors

Miguel Falomir
Eike D. Schmidt
Paolo Giulierini
Massimo Osanna
Marina Loshak
Richard Armstrong
Bruno Ely
Max Hollein
Tony Ellwood
Stijn Huijts

## Curators

Miguel Zugaza Miranda
Alejandro Vergara
Eike D. Schmidt
Laura Donati
Jérôme Neutres
Alexandra Danilova
Nancy Spector
C. Griffith Mann
Wayne Crothers
Paula van den Bosch

## Catalogue Contributors

Miguel Falomir
Miguel Zugaza Miranda
Kosme de Barañano
Alejandro Vergara
Eike D. Schmidt
Germano Celant
Laura Donati
Simon Schama
Paolo Giulierini
Massimo Osanna
Loredana Troise
Jérôme Neutres
Jürgen Schilling
Achille Bonito Oliva
Marina Loshak
Alexandra Danilova
Alexander Etkind
Lars Nittve
Boris Groys
Lesley Ma
Yuko Hasegawa

## Documentary

Isabel Coixet
Miss Wasabi Films
33 Studio

## Patrons

Mondriaan Fund
VSBfonds
Municipality of Maastricht
ACCIONA
PJSC Sberbank
Luzhoulaojiao National Cellar 1573
Mr. and Mrs. Silas Chou
Mr. and Mrs. Cheung Chung Kiu
Mr. and Mrs. Yaping Ou
Mr. and Mrs. Alberto & Elena Cortina
David Su
ART CARE Art Consultant Co., Ltd.
Shanghai International Culture Association
Shanghai Municipal 2018 Special Grant for "Expanding Chinese Culture"
Wendi Murdoch
Xin Li
Diego Strazzer
Morra Foundation
Golden Age Group
American Express
Ernst & Young Global Ltd.
Telstra
Qantas
Bank of America
The Kate Cassidy Foundation
YT Pictures
Eslite Gallery
Mingpo Cai
Cathay Capital

## Cai Studio

*Participating Former Staff*
Ting Ting Chen
Béatrice Grenier
Mariluz Hoyos
Lin King
Stephanie Lee
Essa Li
Chinyan Wong
Anqi Xu
Chiaying Yu
Xiao Yu
Xinran Yuan
Yvonne Zhao

*Participating Former Interns*
Juntian Dai
Clara Leverenz
Raymond Liu
Jing Ma
Cindy Peng
Alina Selivanova
Qisen Song
Dongpeng Wang
Kevin Wu
Joey Xia
Sijia Yang

## Collaborators

Hiro Ihara, Photographer
Lin Yi, Photographer
Kenji Ryuko
Liuyang Tang Hua Fireworks Co., Ltd.

# Copyright Notices

Unless otherwise noted, all works are by Cai Guo-Qiang. Used by permission: © 2021 Cai Guo-Qiang.

Photo credits accompany images in the sections other than Catalogue. Unless otherwise credited, all images are courtesy Cai Studio or photo courtesy Cai Studio.

## Catalogue Photo Credits

Ron Amstutz: 3 images of no. 8.1
© Amedeo Benestante: nos. 3.1, 3.13; figures 3.13–15, 3.17
Leonardo Bianchi: figure 2.9c
Blackbow: no. 10.3
Christopher Burke: nos. 1.26, 1.12a–c, 1.13a–b, 7.4
Cai Guo-Qiang: figures 1.6, 3.3, 6.3, 7.1, 7.4–5, 7.11, 8.11, 9.14, 10.8b, E7
Guosheng Cai: figures 10.3c–d
Wen-You Cai: nos. 1.2, 1.4–7, 1.13, 1.21–24, 1.27, 2.3, 2.7, 2.10–11, 2.18–19, 2.22–23, 3.2–3, 3.6–9, 3.12, 3.14, 4.6, 4.8–9, 4.10–12, 5.1–4, 6.10, 6.12, 7.1–3, 10.1, 10.4–5, 11.1–5; figures 1.2, 2.3, 2.9a, 2.9d, 2.9f, 3.2, 3.9, 3.12, 3.16, 5.3–4, 5.8, 8.2, 8.13, 9.1, 11.2
Zhijun Cai: figure 7.7
Ting Ting Chen: figure 9.11
Béatrice Grenier: figure 7.2
David Heald, © SRGF, NY: figures 5.6, 6.7
Harry Heuts, courtesy Bonnefanten Museum: figure 8.12
Biagio Ippolito: figures 3.6, 3.8
Wataru Kai: figure 6.2
Lin King: figures 2.5, 3.11a–b, 4.6
Hsiu-man Lin: figure E5
Lin Yi: nos. 7.5, 10.2; figures 2.9k, 2.10, 7.9, 7.10, 7.12, 10.4–5, 10.6a, 10.7c, 10.9b, 10.9d, E1, E4, E6, E9–10, E13–15, E16a–c, E17
Linhan Lu: figure E14
Sang Luo: no. 1.16; figures 2.1–2, 2.7–8, 3.4–5, 3.10, 5.2, 7.3, 7.8, 11.3a, 11.3d–g, 11.3k, 11.3m, 11.3p
Siqiao Lyu: figures 5.5, 6.1, 6.6–10, 10.1
Javier Molina, © Museo Nacional del Prado: figure 1.5
© Museo Nacional del Prado: figures 1.1, 1.3, 1.7, 1.11
Lydia Ohl: nos. 1.11–12, 1.14–15, 8.4
The Palace Museum, photo courtesy: no. 11.6
Pushkin State Museum of Fine Arts, photo courtesy: nos. 4.1, 4.3–5, 4.13; figures 4.5, 4.9–10, 4.12–13, 4.15–16
Scott Rudd, © SRGF, NY: figure 5.1
Nataliya Sidorova: figure 4.11
Bo-Ying Su and Hong-Gang Luo: 27 images of no. 8.1
Kristy Sun, courtesy HTC VIVE Arts: figure E11
Miao Sun: figure E2
Shanshan Sun: figure 3.7
Tang Hua Fireworks: figures 10.6b–d, 10.7a–b, 10.8a
Tatsumi Masatoshi: figure 4.8
Tobias Titz, courtesy National Gallery of Victoria, Melbourne: nos. 9.1–5; figures 9.2–10, 9.12–13, 9.15
Chinyan Wong: figure 1.8
Daxin Wu: figures 2.9h, 2.9m
Hong Hong Wu: figures 5.7, 7.6, 11.1
Anqi Xu: figure 1.4
Sijia Yang: figure E8
Yokohama Museum of Art: nos. 8.2–3
Yunqin Zhang: figure 10.3b
Mengjia Zhao: nos. 4.7, 6.2–6, 6.8–9, 56 images of no. 8.1; figures 4.1, 8.1, 10.2, 11.3b–c, 11.3n–o, 11.3q
Yvonne Zhao: nos. 1.1, 1.3. 1.8–10, 1.17–18, 1.19–20, 1.25, 1.28, 2.1–2, 2.4–6, 2.8–9, 2.12–17, 2.20–21, 3.4–5, 3.10–11, 4.2, 5.5, 6.11, 1 image of no. 8.1; figures 1.9, 3.1, 4.2, 4.7, 11.3h–j, 11.3l
Yi Zhou: figure E3
33 Studio: figures 2.4, 2.6a–d, 2.9b, 2.9e, 2.9g, 2.9i–j, 2.9l, 4.14, 4.17, 10.3a, 10.9a, 10.9c

*Heritage* (2013) on page 345: Commissioned with funds from the Josephine Ulrick and Win Schubert Diversity Foundation through and with the assistance of the Queensland Art Gallery | Gallery of Modern Art Foundation. Collection of Queensland Art Gallery | Gallery of Modern Art, Brisbane. Photo by Natasha Harth, courtesy Queensland Art Gallery | Gallery of Modern Art

Photo on page 372: Cai Guo-Qiang and the fireworks for *Sleepwalking in the Forbidden City* in Liuyang, China in 2020. Photo by 33 Studio